The Latinx Philosophy Reader

The Latinx Philosophy Reader showcases a wide range of significant philosophical works about Latinx people and their experiences, displaying the breadth, distinctiveness, originality, and diversity of Latinx philosophy. Readings include discussions of what it is like to be perceived as undocumented, ethical quagmires affecting those who interpret for their family members, the difficulty of pursuing career success without compromising one's cultural identity and values, the nature of citizenship, disputes about labels, the significance of language, and debates about the nature of Latinx identity.

The editors' detailed introduction orients readers with an overview of the origins of the field of Latinx philosophy, a guide to terminology, and a history of the idea of Latinx identity in the United States. The volume's 35 readings are made up of both widely read and cited articles from journals and books and newly commissioned contributions from the leading voices in the field. All of them are organized into seven thematic units in contemporary Latinx philosophy:

  I. Social Identity
 II. Mestizaje and Indigeneity
III. Cross-Cultural Challenges
 IV. Epistemology, Phenomenology, and Coloniality
  V. Language and Communication
 VI. Immigration and Citizenship
VII. Metaphilosophy

Each of these seven units includes its own introduction that connects each reading to the overarching themes of the unit and volume. Throughout, the readings provide an accessible entry point to readers who are new to philosophy. The texts generate opportunities for philosophical reflection without requiring readers to consult additional resources to grasp the major insights. They can be read in any order, allowing for ready adaptation to the particular interests of instructors and students.

Lori Gallegos is Associate Professor of Philosophy at Texas State University and the editor of *APA Studies on Hispanic/Latino Issues in Philosophy*. She works in the areas of Latinx philosophy and the philosophy of emotions, and her publications have appeared in edited volumes and in journals including *Hypatia*, *Philosophical Topics*, *Journal of Intercultural Studies*, *Critical Philosophy of Race*, *Topoi*, and the *Inter-American Journal of Philosophy*.

Manuel Vargas is Professor of Philosophy at the University of California San Diego and the author of *Building Better Beings: A Theory of Moral Responsibility* (2013); *Mexican Philosophy* (forthcoming), and a co-author of *Four Views on Free Will, 2nd Ed.* (2024). He has been the recipient of multiple prizes from the American Philosophical Association, including its Book Prize, Prize in Latin American Thoughts, and the Alvin Plantinga Prize.

Francisco Gallegos is Associate Professor of Philosophy at Wake Forest University. He works on the politics of emotion, Latin American philosophy, Latinx philosophy, and existential phenomenology. He is the co-author of *The Disintegration of Community: The Social and Political Philosophy of Jorge Portilla* (with Carlos Sánchez, 2020).

"*The Latinx Philosophy Reader* is a welcome resource for anyone interested in the recent development and current state of the field. This thoughtfully curated collection will provide students with important introductions to how thinkers have wrestled with concepts like identity, coloniality, culture, agency, and epistemology—with U.S. Latines in mind. Established scholars, on the other hand, will appreciate having these crucial defining texts compiled in a single volume. This book offers the already familiar and the newly curious an invitation to dive into some of the most generative and exciting scholarly conversations of recent decades."

—**Michael Hames-García,** *Professor of Mexican American and Latina/o Studies and Interim Director of the Latino Research Institute at the University of Texas at Austin, USA*

The Latinx Philosophy Reader

Edited by Lori Gallegos, Manuel Vargas, and Francisco Gallegos

Routledge
Taylor & Francis Group
NEW YORK AND LONDON

Designed cover image: Adobe Stock/Moe Shirani

First published 2025
by Routledge
605 Third Avenue, New York, NY 10158

and by Routledge
4 Park Square, Milton Park, Abingdon, Oxon, OX14 4RN

Routledge is an imprint of the Taylor & Francis Group, an informa business

© 2025 selection and editorial matter, Lori Gallegos, Manuel Vargas, and Francisco Gallegos; individual chapters, the contributors

The right of Lori Gallegos, Manuel Vargas, and Francisco Gallegos to be identified as the authors of the editorial material, and of the authors for their individual chapters, has been asserted in accordance with sections 77 and 78 of the Copyright, Designs and Patents Act 1988.

All rights reserved. No part of this book may be reprinted or reproduced or utilised in any form or by any electronic, mechanical, or other means, now known or hereafter invented, including photocopying and recording, or in any information storage or retrieval system, without permission in writing from the publishers.

Trademark notice: Product or corporate names may be trademarks or registered trademarks, and are used only for identification and explanation without intent to infringe.

Library of Congress Cataloging-in-Publication Data
Names: Gallegos, Lori, editor. | Vargas, Manuel, 1973– editor. |
 Gallegos, Francisco, 1983– editor.
Title: The Latinx philosophy reader / Lori Gallegos, Manuel Vargas, and
 Francisco Gallegos.
Description: New York, NY : Routledge, 2025. | Includes bibliographical
 references and index.
Identifiers: LCCN 2024054221 (print) | LCCN 2024054222 (ebook) |
 ISBN 9781032472881 (hbk) | ISBN 9781032472874 (pbk) |
 ISBN 9781003385417 (ebk)
Subjects: LCSH: Philosophy, Latin American.
Classification: LCC B1001 .L393 2025 (print) | LCC B1001 (ebook) |
 DDC 199/.8—dc23/eng/20250201
LC record available at https://lccn.loc.gov/2024054221
LC ebook record available at https://lccn.loc.gov/2024054222

ISBN: 978-1-032-47288-1 (hbk)
ISBN: 978-1-032-47287-4 (pbk)
ISBN: 978-1-003-38541-7 (ebk)

DOI: 10.4324/9781003385417

Typeset in Sabon LT Pro
by Apex CoVantage, LLC

Contents

List of Contributors	*xi*
Acknowledgments	*xvi*
Permissions	*xvii*
Introduction	1

PART 1
Social Identity — 9

Introduction — 11

1 Is Latina/o Identity a Racial Identity? — 14
   LINDA MARTÍN ALCOFF

2 Identities: General and Particular — 31
   JORGE J. E. GRACIA

3 "Being-in-the-World-*Hispanically*": A World on the "Border" of Many Worlds — 45
   ENRIQUE DUSSEL

4 From the Caribbean to the U.S.: Afro-Latinity in Changing Contexts — 59
   GERTRUDE GONZÁLEZ DE ALLEN

5 Open Questions in the Metaphysics of Habitable Categories — 72
   AXEL ARTURO BARCELÓ ASPEITIA

PART 2
Mestizaje and Indigeneity — 91

Introduction — 93

6 Mestizaje (Preface to *The Cosmic Race*) — 95
   JOSÉ VASCONCELOS

7 The Mestizo Concept: A Product of European Imperialism 109
JACK D. FORBES

8 *La Conciencia de la Mestiza*: Towards a New Consciousness 124
GLORIA ANZALDÚA

9 Geographies of Race and Ethnicity III: Settler Colonialism
and Nonnative People of Color 136
LAURA PULIDO

10 Mestizaje, Métissage, and Mixedblood: Tracing Some Political Terms
of Racial and Cultural Mixture Across the Americas 146
ANDREA J. PITTS

PART 3
Cross-Cultural Challenges 169

Introduction 171

11 Latina/o Identity Politics 173
LINDA MARTÍN ALCOFF

12 Playfulness, "World"-Traveling, and Loving Perception 185
MARÍA LUGONES

13 Mestiza Autonomy as Relational Autonomy: Ambivalence
and the Social Character of Free Will 199
EDWINA BARVOSA

14 Cultural Code-Switching: Straddling the Achievement Gap 216
JENNIFER M. MORTON

15 The Philosophy of Accidentality 235
MANUEL VARGAS

PART 4
Phenomenology, Hermeneutics, and Coloniality 253

Introduction 255

16 Heterosexualism and the Colonial/Modern Gender System 258
MARÍA LUGONES

17 Mujerista Discourse: A Platform for Latinas' Subjugated Knowledge 277
ADA MARÍA ISASI-DÍAZ

18 Hometactics: Everyday Practices of Multiplicitous Selves   295
    MARIANA ORTEGA

19 Between Hermeneutic Violence and Alphabets of Survival   310
    ELENA FLORES RUÍZ

20 Decolonial Feminist Movidas: A Caribeña (Re)thinks "Privilege,"
    the Wages of Gender, and Building Complex Coalitions   322
    XHERCIS MÉNDEZ

PART 5
Language and Communication   337

    Introduction   339

21 How to Tame a Wild Tongue   341
    GLORIA ANZALDÚA

22 The Interpreter's Dilemma: On the Moral Burden of Consensual
    Heteronomy   350
    LORI GALLEGOS

23 Cultural Alterity: Cross-Cultural Communication and Feminist Theory
    in North-South Contexts   365
    OFELIA SCHUTTE

24 Language, Power, and Philosophy: Some Comments on the Exclusion
    of Spanish from the Philosophical Canon   380
    ELIZABETH MILLÁN BRUSSLAN

PART 6
Immigration and Citizenship   391

    Introduction   393

25 Becoming Citizens, Becoming Latinos   395
    EDUARDO MENDIETA

26 Cesar Chavez and the Pluralist Foundations
    of U.S. Democracy   407
    JOSÉ-ANTONIO OROSCO

27 The Latinx Racial Disintegration Thesis: Whiteness, Democracy,
    and Latinx Identity   420
    JOSÉ JORGE MENDOZA

28 Socially, Not Legally, Undocumented 443
AMY REED-SANDOVAL

29 Jus Sanguinis vs. Jus Soli: On the Grounds of Justice 460
EDUARDO MENDIETA

30 The Gendered Nature of U.S. Immigration Policy 478
ALLISON B. WOLF

PART 7
Metaphilosophy 491

Introduction 493

31 Oro del Barrio in the Cyber Age: Leapfrogging the Industrial
Revolution 495
TOMÁS ATENCIO

32 The Philosophical Gift of Brown Folks: Mexican American
Philosophy in the United States 515
JOSÉ-ANTONIO OROSCO

33 Philosophy sin más?: Notes on the Value of Mexican Philosophy
for Latino/a Life 525
CARLOS ALBERTO SÁNCHEZ

34 Implicit Bias and Latinxs in Philosophy 536
ALEX MADVA

35 Notes on Decolonizing Philosophy: Against Epistemic Extractivism
and Toward the Abolition of the Canon 549
NELSON MALDONADO-TORRES

Index 557

Contributors

Linda Martín Alcoff "Is Latina/o Identity a Racial Identity?"; "Latina/o Identity Politics": Alcoff is Professor of Philosophy and Co-Director of the Mellon Public Humanities and Social Justice Program at Hunter College in New York, NY. She works on Latin American philosophy, feminist epistemology, and critical race theory among other areas, and is the author most recently of *Rape and Resistance* (2018), *The Future of Whiteness* (2015), and *Visible Identities: Race, Gender and the Self* (2006), which won the Frantz Fanon Award.

Gloria Anzaldúa "La Conciencia de la Mestiza/Towards a New Consciousness"; "How to Tame a Wild Tongue": Anzaldúa (1942–2004) was a scholar of Chicana feminism, cultural theory, and queer theory. Her book *Borderlands/La Frontera: The New Mestiza* (1987) reflects on her experiences living near the Mexico–Texas border. With Cherríe Moraga, she edited and contributed to *This Bridge Called My Back: Writings by Radical Women of Color* (1981). She was also an author of many fictional and poetic works, received multiple awards, and is considered an icon of queer history.

Axel Barceló Aspeitia "Open Questions in the Metaphysics of Habitable Categories": Barceló is a researcher at the Institute for Philosophical Research at the National Autonomous University of Mexico. He has wide-ranging research interests that include logic, the philosophy of mathematics, cognitive science, metaphysics, philosophy of science, and metaphilosophy. He is the author of *Sobre el análisis* [On Analysis] (2019) and *Falibilidad y normatividad* [Fallibility and Normativity] (2019).

Tomás Atencio "Oro del Barrio in the Cyber Age: Leapfrogging the Industrial Revolution": Atencio (1932–2014) was a scholar, community activist, and co-founder of La Academia de la Nueva Raza (The Academy of the New Humanity) in Dixon, New Mexico, who taught in the Department of Sociology at the University of New Mexico. He is author of *Resolana: A Chicano Pathway to Knowledge* (1988) and *Resolana: Emerging Chicano Dialogues on Community and Globalization* (with Miguel Montiel and E. A. Mares, 2009).

Edwina Barvosa "Mestizaje Autonomy as Relational Autonomy": Barvosa is a professor in applied social and political theory at the University of California Santa Barbara. She specializes in Chicana/Latina feminist thought, political philosophy, and gender studies. She is the author of *Wealth of Selves: Multiple Identities, Mestiza Consciousness, and the Subject of Politics* (2008), and *Deliberative Democracy Now* (2018).

Enrique Dussel "Being-in-the-World-Hispanically": Dussel (1934–2023) was a major figure in 20th-century Latin American philosophy, best known for his development of an influential version of the philosophy of liberation, which takes as its central task the liberation of peoples from all forms of oppression. Representative translations of his major works include *The Philosophy of Liberation* (1980); *The Invention of the Americas: Eclipse of "the Other" and the Myth of Modernity* (1995); *Twenty Theses on Politics* (2008); and *Ethics of Liberation in the Age of Globalization and Exclusion* (2013).

Jack D. Forbes "The Mestizo Concept as a Product of European Imperialism": Forbes (1934–2011) was a scholar and political activist who focused on Native American issues. He was a founder of the Native American studies programs at University of California Davis, as well as the Deganawidah-Quetzalcoatl University, a prominent Native American college in Davis, California. He is author of several books, including *Columbus and Other Cannibals* (1978) and *Africans and Native Americans: The Language of Race and the Evolution of Red- Black Peoples* (1993).

Lori Gallegos "The Interpreter's Dilemma: On the Moral Burden of Consensual Heteronomy": Gallegos is an associate professor of philosophy at Texas State University and the editor of *APA Studies on Hispanic/Latino Issues in Philosophy*. She works in the areas of Latinx philosophy and the philosophy of emotions, and her publications have appeared in edited volumes and in journals including *Hypatia*, *Philosophical Topics*, *Journal of Intercultural Studies*, *Critical Philosophy of Race*, *Topoi*, and the *Inter-American Journal of Philosophy*.

Gertrude González de Allen "From the Caribbean to the U.S.: Afro-Latinity in Changing Contexts": González de Allen is an associate professor of philosophy at Spelman College. She works on Africana philosophy, especially Afro-Caribbean and Afro-Latino philosophy, existential phenomenology, the history of philosophy, and colonialism and its aftermath.

Jorge J. E. Gracia "Identities: General and Particular" (excerpts): Gracia (1942–2021) was the SUNY Distinguished Professor and Samuel P. Capen Chair in Philosophy and Comparative Literature at the University of Buffalo. He was a significant contributor in a wide range of areas of philosophy, including philosophical historiography, medieval philosophy, metaphysics, and Latin American philosophy, and his work on race and ethnicity was particularly important in the development of what is now recognized as Latinx philosophy. Among his many monographs are *Philosophy and its History: Issues in Philosophical Historiography* (1991); *Hispanic/Latino Identity: A Philosophical Perspective* (2000); *Surviving Race, Ethnicity, and Nationality: A Challenge for the 21st Century* (2005); and *Latinos in America: Philosophy and Social Identity* (2008).

Ada María Isasi-Díaz "Mujerista Discourse: A Platform for Latinas' Subjugated Knowledge": Isasi-Díaz (1943–2012) was a Cuban American theologian. She was the founder and co-director of the Hispanic Institute of Theology at Drew University. Her books include *Mujerista Theology: A Theology for the 21st Century* (1996) and *La Lucha Continues: Mujerista Theology* (2004).

María Lugones "Playfulness, 'World'-Traveling, and Loving Perception"; "Heterosexualism and the Modern/Colonial Gender System": Lugones (1944–2020) was a major contributor to the development of Latina feminism, and her work focused on political identity, gender, and decolonial philosophy. Many of her early essays were collected in *Pilgrimages/Peregrinajes: Theorizing Coalition Against Multiple Oppressions* (2003).

List of Contributors xiii

Alex Madva "Implicit Bias and Latina/os in Philosophy": Madva is Associate Professor of Philosophy at Cal Poly Pomona and Director of the California Center for Ethics & Policy. He works on philosophy of mind, race, feminism, cognitive science, and social science. He edited *An Introduction to Implicit Bias: Knowledge, Justice, and the Social Mind* (with Erin Beeghly, 2020) and *The Movement for Black Lives: Philosophical Perspectives* (with Michael Cholbi, Brandon Hogan, and Benjamin Yost, 2021).

Nelson Maldonado-Torres "Notes on Decolonizing Philosophy: Against Epistemic Extractivism and toward the Abolition of the Canon": Maldonado-Torres is a professor of philosophy at the University of Connecticut-Storrs. His research focuses on decolonial thought and Caribbean philosophy. He is author of *Against War: Views from the Underside of Modernity* (2008) and editor of *Latino/as in the World-system: Decolonization Struggles in the 21st Century U.S. Empire* (2015).

Xhercis Méndez "Decolonial Feminist Movidas: A Caribeña (Re)thinks 'Privilege,' the Wages of Gender, and Building Complex Coalitions": Méndez is an associate professor in the Women and Gender Studies Department at California State University Fullerton. Her research focuses on race, gender, and sexuality at the intersection of science and religion.

Eduardo Mendieta "Becoming Citizens, Becoming Latinos"; "Jus sanguinis vs. Jus soli: On the Grounds of Justice": Mendieta is a professor of philosophy and Latina/o studies at Pennsylvania State University. His research interests include: Frankfurt School Critical Theory, Latin American philosophy, Liberation Philosophy, the work of Enrique Dussel, and Latino/a philosophy. His most recent book is *The Philosophical Animal: On Zoopetics and Interspecies Cosmopolitanism* (2024).

José Jorge Mendoza "The Latinx Racial Disintegration Thesis: Whiteness, Democracy, and Latinx Identity": Mendoza is an associate professor of philosophy at the University of Washington and an editor at *Radical Philosophy Review*. His research deals with topics concerning migration ethics, Latinx identity, and racial justice, and he is the author of *The Moral and Political Philosophy of Immigration: Liberty, Security, and Equality* (2017).

Elizabeth Millán Brusslan "Language, Power, and Philosophy: Some Comments on the Exclusion of Spanish from the Philosophical Canon": Millán Brusslan is a professor and chair of philosophy at DePaul University. She works on aesthetics, German idealism/romanticism, and Latin American philosophy, and her publications include: *Friedrich Schlegel and the Emergence of Romantic Philosophy* (2007); with Bärbel Frischmann, *Das neue Licht der Frühromantik/The New Light of German Romanticism* (2008); with Judith Norman, *Brill's Companion to German Romantic Philosophy* (2019), and most recently *The Palgrave Handbook of Germany Romantic Philosophy* (2020) and with Jimena Solé and *Fichte in the Americas*, a volume in the Fichte Studien Series (2023).

Jennifer M. Morton "Cultural Code-Switching: Straddling the Achievement Gap": Morton is Presidential Penn Compact Professor of Philosophy at the University of Pennsylvania. Her work focuses on how poverty and social class shape agency, and she is the author of *Moving Up Without Losing Your Way: The Ethical Costs of Upward Mobility*, which was recognized with several national awards.

José-Antonio Orosco "The Philosophical Gift of Brown Folks"; "Cesar Chavez and the Pluralist Foundations of U.S. Democracy": Orosco is a professor of philosophy at Oregon

xiv *List of Contributors*

State University, where he specializes in the areas of social and political philosophy, philosophy of the Americas, and issues in multiculturalism, immigration, and decolonization. He is the author of *Toppling the Melting Pot: Immigration and Multiculturalism in American Pragmatism* (2016) and *Cesar Chavez and the Common Sense of Nonviolence* (2008), and he is an associate editor for *Acorn: Philosophical Studies in Pacifism and Nonviolence*.

Mariana Ortega "Hometactics: Everyday Practices of Multiplicitous Selves": Ortega is associate professor of philosophy and women's, gender and sexuality studies at Pennsylvania State University. She works on feminism, phenomenology, philosophy of race, and aesthetics, and is the founder and director of the Latina/x Feminisms Roundtable. She is author of *In-Between: Latina Feminist Phenomenology, Multiplicity, and the Self* (2016) and co-editor of *Theories of the Flesh, Latinx and Latin American Feminisms, Transformation and Resistance* (2019) and *Constructing the Nation: A Race and Nationalism Reader* (2009).

Andrea J. Pitts "Mestizaje, Métissage, and Mixedblood: Tracing Some Political Terms of Racial and Cultural Mixture Across the Americas": Pitts is an associate professor in the Department of Comparative Literature at the University at Buffalo. They do interdisciplinary research on a variety of topics, including Latinx philosophy, Latina feminism, carceral medicine, and radical health activism. They are author of *Nos/Otras: Gloria E. Anzaldúa, Multiplicitous Agency, and Resistance* (2021), and co-editor of *Trans Philosophy* (2024), *Theories of the Flesh: Latinx and Latin American Feminisms, Transformation, and Resistance* (2020), and *Beyond Bergson: Examining Race and Colonialism through the Writings of Henri Bergson* (2019).

Laura Pulido "Settler Colonialism and Nonnative People of Color": Pulido is a professor in the Department of Indigenous, Race, and Ethnic Studies at the University of Oregon. She works on topics at the intersection of geography and critical ethnic studies and is the author of *Environmentalism and Economic Justice: Two Chicano Struggles in the Southwest* (1996) and *Black, Brown, Yellow and Left: Radical Activism in Los Angeles* (2006).

Amy Reed-Sandoval "Socially, Not Legally, Undocumented": Reed-Sandoval is an associate professor in the Department of Philosophy at the University of Nevada, Las Vegas, and founder of the Oaxaca Philosophy for Children Initiative and the Philosophy for Children in the Borderlands program. She is the author of *Socially Undocumented: Identity and Immigration Justice* (2020), and the co-editor of *Latin American Immigration Ethics* (2021) and *Ética, Política, y Migración* (2021).

Elena Flores Ruíz "Between Hermeneutic Violence and Alphabets of Survival": Ruiz is an assistant professor of philosophy and global studies at Michigan State University, where she also founded and directs the Research Institute for Structural Change (RISC). Her work focuses on structural justice, violence, and colonialism. She is the author of *Structural Violence* (2024).

Carlos Alberto Sánchez "Philosophy sin más?" (excerpts): Sánchez is a professor of philosophy at San José State University. He is author of several books, including *Mexican Philosophy for the 21st Century* (2023), *Emilio Uranga's Analysis of Mexican Being: Translation and Critical Introduction* (2021), *A Sense of Brutality: Philosophy and Narco Culture* (2020), and *The Suspension of Seriousness: On the Phenomenology of Jorge Portilla* (2012). He also edited *Mexican Philosophy in the 20th Century: Essential Readings* (with Robert E. Sanchez, 2017).

Ofelia Schutte "Cultural Alterity: Cross-Cultural Communication and Feminist Theory in North-South Contexts": Schutte is Professor Emerita of Philosophy at University of South Florida with research interests in feminism in Cuba and decolonial theory. She is the author of *Beyond Nihilism: Nietzsche without Masks* (1984), *Cultural Identity and Social Liberation in Latin American Thought* (1993), and numerous articles on feminist theory, Latin American thought, and continental philosophy.

Manuel Vargas "The Philosophy of Accidentality": Vargas is Professor of Philosophy at the University of California San Diego. He has written on free will, moral responsibility, topics in moral psychology, the philosophy of law, the history of philosophy in Latin America, and ethno-racial social identities. He is the author of *Building Better Beings: A Theory of Moral Responsibility* (OUP); *Mexican Philosophy* (OUP); co-author of *Four Views on Free Will*, 2nd Ed. (Wiley); and co-editor of several volumes on agency, sociality, and moral psychology.

José Vasconcelos "Mestizaje": Vasconcelos (1882–1959) was a Mexican writer, philosopher, and politician, as well as Mexico's first secretary of education between 1921–1924. He wrote a five-volume autobiography and was a prolific author of philosophical texts, including *La raza cósmica* (1925; "The Cosmic Race"), *Metafísica* (1929; "Metaphysics"), *Pesimismo alegre* (1931, "Cheerful Pessimism"), *Estética* (1936; "Aesthetics"), *Ética* (1939; "Ethics"), *Historia del pensamiento filosófico* (1937; "A History of Philosophical Thought") and *Lógica orgánica* (1945; "Organic Logic").

Allison B. Wolf "The Gendered Nature of U.S. Immigration Policy": Wolf is an associate professor of philosophy at Universidad de los Andes in Bogotá, Colombia, where she teaches political philosophy, philosophy of immigration, and feminist philosophy. She is author of *Just Immigration in the Americas: A Feminist Account* (2020) and co-editor of *Incarnating Feelings, Constructing Communities: Experiencing Emotions via Education, Violence, and Public Policy in the Americas* (2021).

Acknowledgments

Even when you have a team of editors, there is always a wider team of people who help bring any volume into existence. We'd like to thank Andy Beck, our editor at Routledge for his steadfast guidance in shepherding this volume into existence. Thanks also to Graham Clarke for his assistance in preparing the text, Karina Ortiz Villa for her research assistance, the various publishers for their permission to reprint the readings in this volume, and the financial support of the philosophy departments at Wake Forest University and Texas State University. Special thanks to our teachers and students, without whom this volume would not exist.

LG would like to thank Eduardo Mendieta for his extraordinary mentorship over the years, and her colleagues from the Society of Mexican American Philosophy, who first welcomed her into the field and have offered ongoing support and encouragement. Lori agradece a Rodrigo por su apoyo y paciencia.

MV would like to thank Jorge J. E. Gracia, Eduardo Mendieta, and Linda Martín Alcoff for teaching him how to think philosophically about these issues. Special thanks to Jess Nieto, whose foresight in taking these issues seriously was an inspiration throughout. Thanks to the referees of this volume, as well as the philosophers of the Society of Mexican American Philosophy and the UC San Diego Mexican Philosophy Lab, for their contributions throughout. The University of California San Diego provided crucial sabbatical support that enabled the completion of this volume. Most of all, many thanks to Stephanie for her unflagging support of tilting at windmills.

FG would like to thank his colleagues in the WFU Philosophy Department, whose support has made this volume possible. He also thanks Amy Oliver and Carlos Alberto Sánchez for their mentorship, and Petra and José for their support and guidance. His research for this volume was supported by a residency at the UCSD Mexican Philosophy Lab in 2023.

Permissions

The editors thank the presses and authors who gave us permission to use previously published material, including:

Alcoff, L. (1999) "Latina/o Identity Politics," in D. Batstone and E. Mendieta (eds.), *The Good Citizen*, 93–112, New York: Routledge.

Alcoff, L. (2000) "Is Latina/o Identity a Racial Identity?" in J. J. E. Gracia and P. De Greiff, (eds.), *Hispanics/Latinos in the United States: Ethnicity, Race, and Rights*, 23–44, New York: Routledge.

Anzaldúa, G. (1987) "How to Tame a Wild Tongue," in *Borderlands/La Frontera: The New Mestiza*, 53–64. San Francisco: Aunt Lute Books.

Anzaldúa, G. (1987) "La Conciencia de la Mestiza/Towards A New Consciousness," in *Borderlands/La Frontera: The New Mestiza*, 77–91. San Francisco: Aunt Lute Books.

Atencio, T. (2009) "Oro del Barrio in the Cyber Age: Leapfrogging the Industrial Revolution," in M. Montiel, T. Atencio and E. A. Mares (eds.), *Resolana: Emerging Chicano Dialogues on Community and Globalization*, 9–68, Tucson, AZ: University of Arizona Press.

Barceló Aspeitia, A. A. (2020) "Open Questions in the Metaphysics of Habitable Kinds," *EurAmerica* 50: 669–707.

Barvosa-Carter, E. (2007) "Mestiza Autonomy as Relational Autonomy: Ambivalence and the Social Character of Free Will," *The Journal of Political Philosophy* 15: 1–21.

Dussel, E. (2009) "Being-in-the-World Hispanically," *Comparative Literature* 61: 256–273.

Gracia, J. J. E. (2008) "Identities: General and Particular," in *Latinos in America: Philosophy and Social Identity*, 3–26, Malden, MA: Blackwell Pub.

Sánchez, C. A. (2016) "Filosofía *sin más*? Notes on the Value of Mexican Philosophy for Latino/a Life," in *Contingency and Commitment: Mexican Existentialism and the Place of Philosophy*, 113–140, Albany, NY: SUNY Press.

Vasconcelos, J. (2011) "Mestizaje [Prologue to *La raza cósmica*]," in I. Stavans (ed.), *José Vasconcelos: The Prophet of Race*, 45–90, New Brunswick, NJ: Rutgers University Press.

Forbes, J. D. (1973) "The Mestizo Concept: A Product of European Imperialism," in *Aztecas del Norte: The Chicanos of Aztlan*, 178–205, Connecticut: Fawcett, Greenwich.

Gallegos, L. (2021) "The Interpreter's Dilemma: On the Moral Burden of Consensual Heteronomy," in A. Reed-Sandoval and L. R. Díaz Cepeda (eds.), *Latin American Immigration Ethics*, 243–264, Tucson, AZ: University of Arizona Press.

González de Allen, G. (2012) "From the Caribbean to the US: Afro-Latinity in Changing Contexts," *Transmodernity* 1: 133–145.

Isasi-Díaz, A. M. (2012) "Mujerista Discourse: A Platform for Latinas' Subjugated Knowledge," in A. M. Isasi-Díaz and E. Mendieta (eds.), *Decolonizing Epistemologies: Latina/o Theology and Philosophy*, 43–67, New York: Fordham University Press.

Lugones, M. (1987) "Playfulness, 'World'-Travelling, and Loving Perception," *Hypatia* 2: 3–19.

Lugones, M. (2007) "Heterosexualism and the Colonial/Modern Gender System," *Hypatia* 22: 186–209.

Madva, A. (2016) "Implicit Bias and Latina/os in Philosophy," *APA Newsletter on Hispanic/Latino Issues in Philosophy* 16: 8–15.

Maldonado-Torres, N. (2021) "Notes on Decolonizing Philosophy: Against Epistemic Extractivism and Toward the Abolition of the Canon," *APA Newsletter on Hispanic/Latino Issues* 21: 11–15.

Méndez, X. (2020) "Decolonial Feminist *Movidas*: A Caribeña (Re)thinks 'Privilege,' the Wages of Gender, and Building Complex Coalitions," in A. J. Pitts, M. Ortega and J. Medina (eds.), *Theories of the Flesh*, 74–93, New York: Oxford University Press.

Mendieta, E. (1999) "Becoming Citizens, Becoming Hispanics," in D. Batstone and E. Mendieta (eds.), *The Good Citizen*, 113–132. New York: Routledge.

Millán Brusslan, E. (2012) "Language, Power, and Philosophy: Some Comments on the Exclusion of Spanish from the Philosophical Canon," in G. Yancy (ed.), *Reframing the Practice of Philosophy: Bodies of Color, Bodies of Knowledge*, 327–339, Albany: State University of New York Press.

Morton, J. (2014) "Cultural Code-Switching: Straddling the Achievement Gap," *The Journal of Political Philosophy* 22: 259–281.

Orosco, J.-A. (2016) "Cesar Chavez and the Pluralist Foundations of US American Democracy," In *Toppling the Melting Pot: Immigration and Multiculturalism in American Pragmatism*, 103–149, Bloomington: Indiana University Press.

Orosco, J.-A. (2016) "The Philosophical Gift of Brown Folks: Mexican American Philosophy in the United States," *APA Newsletter on Hispanic/Latino Issues in Philosophy* 15: 23–28.

Ortega, M. (2016) Hometactics. *In-Between: Latina Feminist Phenomenology, Multiplicity, and the Self*, 193–210, Albany, New York: State University of New York Press.

Pulido, L. (2017) "Geographies of Race and Ethnicity III: Settler Colonialism and Nonnative People of Color," *Progress in Human Geography* 42: 1–10.

Reed-Sandoval, A. (2020) "Socially, Not Legally, Undocumented," in *Socially Undocumented: Identity and Immigration Justice*, 35–61, New York: Oxford University Press.

Mendieta, E. (2021) "Jus Sanguinis vs. Jus Soli: On the Grounds of Justice," in A. Reed-Sandoval and L. R. Díaz Cepeda (eds.), *Latin American Immigration Ethics*, 265–290, Tucson, AZ: University of Arizona Press.

Ruíz, E. F. (2020) "Between Hermeneutic Violence and Alphabets of Survival," in A. J. Pitts, M. Ortega and J. Medina, *Theories of the Flesh*, 204–219, New York: Oxford University Press.

Schutte, O. (1998) "Cultural Alterity: Cross-Cultural Communication and Feminist Theory," *Hypatia* 13: 53–72.

Vargas, M. (2020) "The Philosophy of Accidentality," *The Journal of the American Philosophical Association* 6: 391–409.

Introduction

Let's get this out of the way: there is no single ideal label for the group whose name figures in the title of this volume. Some like 'Latinx'; others prefer the term 'Latino'; other people prefer 'Latine'; some like 'Latin@'; others like 'Latina/o'; and many people continue to prefer 'Hispanic'. And, of course, some people think we shouldn't use any of these terms. Debates about these issues are just one of the many things covered by this volume.

For our part, we're not particularly interested in policing language use. We think the preferable label varies by context. Among academics it will likely continue to shift in the years to come. Indeed, the very question of how best to identify the group is itself philosophically interesting. In the following, we say more about some of the terms and why there can sometimes be reasons to prefer one over the other. For the moment, though, we just want to acknowledge that any choice is fraught. (Take your pick: we can either use terms that are unfamiliar or even alienating to many who are thus labeled; or we can do violence to norms of the Spanish grammar and pronunciation; or we can ignore concerns about misgendering or the lack of gender neutrality in Spanish.) At the time this volume went to press, adoption of 'Latine' seemed to be accelerating in Latin America and among Spanish speakers, while 'Latinx' seems to be in greater use in academic circles in the United States. If it helps, feel free to substitute whatever term you @ prefer to pick out people of Latin American descent living in the United States.

So what's Latinx philosophy? What is it about? There is no single characterization that will satisfy everyone. Still, sometimes imperfect characterizations are useful. Here's a provisional first pass at one characterization that captures many of the kinds of things in this volume: Latinx philosophy is philosophy about Latinx people and communities. Somewhat more carefully, we can say that *Latinx philosophy is philosophical work substantively concerned with Latinxs, including the moral, social, political, epistemic, metaphysical, and linguistic significance of Latinxs. This can include the circumstances, concerns, or ways of being that are distinctive or characteristic of Latinxs.* In this way of putting things, Latinx philosophy doesn't have to be written by Latinxs, although most of it is. Instead, it is like many other fields in philosophy, including ethics, metaphysics, feminist philosophy, and philosophy of science, in that it is defined by its subject matter and not by who produced it.

That's just a provisional characterization, though. There are other ways one might wish to characterize the field, and we're not going to try to rule out those alternatives. As is the way of philosophy, most parts of our proposed definition are contestable. For example, we might argue over what counts as philosophy, or who falls into the category, or whether there are any shared experiences had by all Latinxs, and so on. Again, these are all topics that will come up in the readings that follow. Despite the fact that aspects of our proposed definition are contestable, we nevertheless think this does a good job of capturing most of the things

DOI: 10.4324/9781003385417-1

that people have in mind when they talk about Latinx philosophy. (There's a lesson in here about how to think about one thing we are doing when we do philosophy: we are trying to understand things that in some sense remain open questions, and we can make progress doing that, even if we don't have a perfect account that everyone agrees on.)

Why study Latinx philosophy? Why *this* volume? One basic reason is that it is interesting, and that a lot of the work discusses topics that aren't discussed in any other part of philosophy. Outside of Latinx philosophy, it is difficult to find discussions of, say, what it is like to be perceived as undocumented, or the challenges of navigating conflicting cultural norms, or the kinds of ethical quagmires that affect people who work as interpreters for family members.

A different kind of reason for studying Latinx philosophy is demographic: inasmuch as Latinxs are a growing percentage of the United States—in some cities and counties they are already majorities—we are talking about the philosophical interests, experiences, and significance of a *lot* of people. Philosophy everywhere has grown out of the reflections, puzzles, and experiences of people in particular times and places, but in doing so we sometimes learn things not just about particular times and places, but also about the human condition in a more general way. So, to the extent that academic philosophy has, at best, rarely paid attention to the thoughts and concerns of Latinxs in anything like a systematic way, there is reason to be interested.

For us, the editors, there's a more personal reason for focusing on these texts. In our schooling, we almost never encountered Latinx professors and authors. It wasn't that they didn't exist, but they were few and far between. For example, as undergraduates none of us was ever assigned a paper or book by a Latinx author in any of our philosophy classes. By and large, we had to teach ourselves about these things, hunting down the work of those who came before us, many of whom had the same disorienting and challenging experience of an education that seemed devoid of people of Latin American descent. We eventually found those texts, and we eventually found others who, like ourselves, had been interested in the very same things. We started teaching this material, and in doing so, we discovered that both we and our students tended to fall in love with this material in an unusual way. This wasn't just someone else's puzzles, these were topics and issues that mattered to us in a visceral, sometimes foundational way. Philosophy became something that belonged to us and our students in a different way. It has been our experience that when students see themselves reflected in their readings, it can be transformative.

It was this experience that led us to assemble this volume, in the hope that you and others wouldn't have to do all the hard work of tracking down these readings, ideas, and thinkers in the same slow and painful way as we and our forerunners did. In assembling this volume, we sought to include pieces that did several different things. First, we wanted pieces that read well as standalone pieces, where readers didn't have to read a whole book or a series of other articles before they could have any hope of following what was going on. Second, we wanted essays that made some important philosophical contribution, or that otherwise provided an especially valuable opportunity for philosophical reflection. In that spirit, most of our pieces are written by academic philosophers, but not all are. Nevertheless, all the writings are ones that we think philosophers and philosophy students should read precisely because of their usefulness for thinking about philosophical issues. Third, we sought to represent a diversity of *latinidades*, or ways of being Latinx. Latinxs are a famously diverse people, and as much as possible, we sought to portray a range of Latinx experiences and concerns.

In that same spirit, we acknowledge that a different group of editors would undoubtedly have made a different set of selections, or would have favored a different set of themes. Indeed, our own list of 'must-read' texts in Latinx philosophy would have looked different a decade ago, and we expect that in another decade our sense of what's important will have shifted again. Even so, many of these texts are undoubtedly central to how most people think about and teach Latinx philosophy today.

What we now think of as Latinx philosophy has a long history with diverse origin points. For example, there has been a long-standing tradition of philosophical reflections on what is unique or distinctive of the peoples who occupy what we now call Latin America. Some of these discussions are as old as 16th-century philosophical debates about the wars of conquest conducted by European powers. A different origin point might be located in those moments when some subsets of Latin America began to think of themselves as neither just European nor Indigenous, but instead, something new or different. As Independence movements began to gain traction in the early 19th century, there was an urgency to articulate what that difference consisted in, and to articulate whether and to what extent there were commonalities across the Americas. A different origin point can be located in U.S. civil rights movements, and in particular, in the Chicano movement. One dimension of the Chicano movement was an effort at self-conscious historical awareness, grounded in an understanding of the intellectual and cultural production of Latin America. In that context, texts like José Vasconcelos' *The Cosmic Race* (included in this volume) provided a vocabulary and patina of philosophical authority for the movement.

Perhaps the most significant genesis point for contemporary Latinx philosophy, though, arose from the work of Latina feminists in the 1990s, who drew from and critiqued the limits of both second-wave feminism and the Chicano movement of a generation before. Figures like Gloria Anzaldúa and María Lugones (readings from both are included in this volume) paved the way for philosophers inside and outside of the academic discipline of philosophy to take seriously the task of philosophical reflection on Latinxs, including their circumstances and experiences.

One of our goals with this volume is to equip readers to have a sense of the issues that have been most salient in Latinx philosophy over the past twenty years or so. This means that, apart from some classic texts, our focus is on relatively recent work. This isn't a judgment about the value of other, older texts, or texts that might otherwise more traditionally fit in a Latinx studies anthology. There are other places where people can find some of those things. Instead, our ambition here was to foreground the explosion of work on specifically Latinx philosophy, in hopes of adding to the resources of both teachers of philosophy and teachers of Chicanx/Latinx studies courses.

To be sure, many of the topics in this volume are already figure in Chicanx/Latinx studies courses. Even so, we think there is a value to adding the voices of philosophers to those discussions. Formal philosophical training tends to bring with it a distinctive set of skills, along with a particular conceptual toolkit, one that emphasizes nuance in how language, practices, and concepts relate to one another. The discipline of philosophy provides an institutional infrastructure and set of incentives for academic philosophers to be especially scrupulous about distinctions and arguments. We believe that philosophical voices have been insufficiently present in the academy and the wider culture, and our hope is to amplify some of those voices to those wider conversations.

Still, the proof is in the *postre*. We think you'll find that these readings offer a rich variety of resources for illuminating a wide range of phenomena connected to Latinxs and their experiences. For those who hold that the point of philosophy is not just to describe the world, but to change it, we add that one part of the power of many of these texts is that they orient us to different ways to go about doing that, sometimes illuminating obscured possibilities, other times identifying problems of which we might have been dimly aware but didn't know how to articulate. The payoffs of these readings are diverse.

This doesn't mean that the only way to approach these texts is with philosophical training or with specifically philosophical interests. Again, we chose these texts because, by and large, we think they are or can be accessible to a wide range of readers.

A Guide to Terminology

We use the term 'Latinx' (and other labels like 'Latinos' and 'Latines') to refer to people of Latin American descent who are in the United States. This category includes people born in the United States who have never been to any Latin American country, who may not speak any language other than English, or may not even be aware of the fact that they are descended from people from Latin America. It also includes people who were born in Latin America and now reside in the United States. In U.S. contexts, at least, these people are often treated as having a shared kind of identity. That identity might not be recognized or regarded as important outside of the United States. In Colombia, for example, a Mexican national and Mexican-American might not be regarded as having any notable identity in common. However, in the United States, those same two people—and, for that matter, a Cuban-American, a Chilean, and a Brazilian—will collectively be regarded by many people and institutions as Latinx.

Some people think of the category of Latinxs as broader than that, as a category that includes people who reside in Latin America, even if they are not and never have been in the United States. For this volume, we favor a more restricted notion, one that emphasizes some connection to the United States, in the same way that, say, 'Californian' or 'Midwesterner' are categories that ordinarily only apply to people from or in the United States. We think there is a good reason to have a category with this restriction: roughly, there is something distinctive about a life that is governed by the way this category works in the United States, something that is not characteristically shared by people from outside the United States. This narrower understanding of Latinxs needn't exclude Latin Americans, though. Latin Americans can become Latinxs by living in or residing in the United States in such a way that it makes sense to apply U.S. identity categories to them.

What about other terms like 'Chicano,' 'Boricua,' and so on? There are a variety of other labels for identities that cross-cut or are within the broader umbrella of *latinidad* ('Latinx-ness'). For example 'Chicano' and its cognates (e.g., 'Chicana,' 'Chicanx,' 'Xicanxs') tends to pick out people of Mexican descent who self-consciously resist cultural assimilation to the United States, whereas 'Mexican-American' doesn't imply anything one way or another about whether that person is committed to resisting assimilation to wider U.S. culture, and simply denotes that they are of Mexican descent. 'Boricua' refers to people who are Puerto Rican, or descendants of Puerto Ricans. And so on. There are lots of labels, and we won't try to capture them all.

Every nation of Latin America, and many regions in Latin America, have their own local set of categories by which they distinguish between groups of people, and these categories sometimes shift and push against other identity categories as populations meet, migrate, and mingle. Sometimes those categories are racial or quasi-racial categories, which inevitably have their own histories and tangles of local significance. Thus, there are Afro-Latinxs, Asian-Latinxs, White Latinxs, and really, as many other permutations of *latinidad* as local social identity categories permit.

One notable axis of complexity for the category as a whole concerns Indigeneity identities. Many Indigenous peoples in Latin America have long histories of resisting the identities imposed on them by the nation states that grew out of European colonization. In some cases, the land and peoples of these groups were artificially divided by nation state boundaries. This means that members of a tribe or nation on one side of the border have a very different international legal status than members on the other side of that border. There are, for example, the Pascua Yaqui tribe and the Tohono O'odham Nation, whose people and lands are split by the U.S./Mexico border. Thus, by some lights, members of the same tribe can count as, on one side, Native American, and on the other, as (Indigenous) Latin American. At the same time, there may be members of this group that would reject either of these characterizations.

There are two further complications. In some places (for example, the United States), there is a relatively strict legal framework surrounding federal and state-recognized Indigenous groups. In other places, there is little or no formal or legal control over these things, apart from mutual recognition by members of a group. A second complication intersects with this: the embrace of Indigeneneity in some Latin American communities has often come independent of real dialogue or engagements with existing Indigenous communities. Against a background of centuries of repression and resistance across the Americas, there is reason for caution in readily assimilating, or, alternatively, readily excluding Indigeneity from discussions of *latinidad* and Latinx identity.

Useful History

The history of the idea of Latinxs in the United States is complicated, with many local variations. The history of changing borders gives one piece of the story. For example, after European colonization, New Orleans was a city controlled by Spain (so, a part of Latin America?), then France, and then the United States; what is now the state of Texas was briefly a quasi-autonomous region, before that Mexican, before that Spanish, and before that the land of the Apache, Caddo, and other Indigenous peoples. When these places became a part of the United States, U.S. categories for distinguishing between kinds of peoples were always layered on top of prior categories. Sometimes these changes in categories and borders had legal implications, and in other cases they had less formal but nevertheless real implications for the rights and privileges of people subjected to those categories. In short, the identity of Latin American peoples in the United States has always been both complicated and consequential.

One indicator of the complexity and arbitrariness of social identity categories is given by the history of U.S. census categories. For example, despite the presence of Indigenous peoples in the Americas since long before the United States' existence, it wasn't until 1860 that the U.S. Census added to its racial categories the category of 'Indian.' In 1930, 82 years after the end of a war that added half of Mexico's territory to the United States, the U.S. Census added the category of Mexican to the 'color or race' category. It disappeared in the next census. In 1976, bowing to pressure from the Chicano Movement and others, Congress passed a law requiring the collection of data on people with family origins in Mexico, Puerto Rico, Cuba, Central and South America, and other Spanish-speaking countries. In response to this change, in 1980 the term 'Hispanic' was introduced into the census.

By the 1990s, academics and activists began to argue that 'Hispanic,' with its origins in *Hispania*, or the Iberian portion of the Roman Empire, was misguided because it properly designated those from Spain or the Iberian Peninsula. It seemed a poor name for people descended from the former Iberian colonies, as many of those descendants were descendants of those who fought, resisted, and died during Spanish and Portuguese colonization. Instead of 'Hispanic,' there were various proposals for alternative labels that included

'Latino', 'Latina/o', and 'Latin@'. In 1997, the U.S. Office of Management and Budget (the OMB), the group that runs the U.S. Census, decided to add 'Latino' to government documents, using it interchangeably with 'Hispanic'.

In 2000, 'Latino' was added to the census as an ethnic, and thus not racial designation. The animating thought was that Latinxs could be of any race, so that it didn't make sense to add it as a racial category, despite many people thinking of the category in racial terms. Recently, the OMB issued guidelines that indicate that the 2030 U.S. census will dispense with the distinction between ethnic and racial categories, instead asking a single question, 'What is your race and/or your ethnicity?' while permitting 'Hispanic or Latino' as the answer.

The history of U.S. census categories only tells one part of the story. Some of the most recent transformations in terminology never appeared in the government documents. For example, some people use 'Latin' to refer to people of Latin American descent, rather than the people of the Roman Empire or their language. More recently, a number of students, scholars, and activists have sought to move away from the traditionally gendered nature of the Spanish language, which requires either a masculine (and sometimes putatively gender neutral) *latino* or a specifically feminine *latina*. This effort gave birth to the idea of 'Latinx,' and more recently, 'Latine.' These innovations come at a cost; both require changing familiar ways of talking. Moreover, 'Latinx' doesn't work in spoken Spanish, and 'Latine' followed so swiftly after efforts to propagate the usage of 'Latinx' that it is unclear whether it will ever have widespread uptake.

Which term should you use? As we noted earlier, we're not going to try to police your choice of terms. Indeed, there is a broader issue here in linguistics and the philosophy of language, about whether definitions should aim to accurately describe use, or whether they should instead prescribe usage, for example, on grounds of conceptual clarity. These are debates we can't hope to settle here.

Moreover, there are strong generational differences in preferences. The longer a term has been around, the more comfortable people tend to be with describing themselves in those terms. (This may be a large part of why so many people are happy to describe themselves as Hispanic and resistant to newer terms like 'Latinx'). The only advice we have to offer is this: be flexible. This is one reason why, in this volume, we have chosen to preserve each author's choices about terminology, even at the expense of consistency.

Coming Attractions

This volume covers a lot of ground, and there are individual introductions to each "Part" of the volume that say a bit more about the themes that organize the volume. None of these groupings are intended to be the final word on the sequence or organization of these materials. There are lots of ways to mix and match these readings within and across the volume, and we encourage you to try out different pairings or sequences. Here, we'll restrict our remarks to some brief explanation of the book's structure.

Each Part or unit has some internal ordering we've tended to find useful in our own classes, but the basic structure is flexible by design. No unit presumes material from any other unit, and indeed, each of the readings stands alone. That said, we've organized the readings into seven topical parts units, and within each we've ordered readings in a way that provides some natural links from one reading to the next.

Part 1 concerns the nature of Latinx identity—if not always using that term—as a specific social identity. Readings span a wide range of philosophical approaches and proposals for how to understand what it is to be Latinx, but all the readings emphasize the complexity and contextual specificity of peoples of Latin American descent in the United States.

Part 2 explores the idea of mestizaje or 'mixedness' that has often been appealed to in characterizations of Latinx identity, and its complex relationship to the Indigenous peoples of the Americas.

Challenges that arise from cross-cultural contexts, where Latinx populations can find themselves at odds with aspects of dominant norms, meanings, and values, is the subject matter of Part 3. Many of the readings in this section explore strategies for dealing with those challenges.

Part 4 collects readings that emphasize broadly feminist, decolonial, and phenomenological approaches to knowledge, gender, and resistance.

The significance of language, both for self-identification, but also in terms of its facilitating or impairing shared cooperative life in the contexts where language and accents can have other associations, is the central theme of readings in Part 5.

Part 6 contains a variety of readings that center on the nature and experience of immigration and the significance of citizenship for Latinx peoples. Some readings focus on aspects of U.S. immigration policies and its costs, and others on the varied relationship Latinxs have had with the histories and ideals of citizenship in the United States.

Part 7 takes up an array of metaphilosophical issues, or questions having to do with how we think about philosophy, and Latinx philosophy in particular. Some readings appeal to the idea that philosophy can and perhaps should be found outside of the academy; others argue for transformations in academic philosophy, or a different understanding of the relationship of Latinxs to the discipline of philosophy.

As we noted earlier, there is no reason these readings have to be approached in the order we've given. Indeed, the same set of texts could be organized in a very different way with very different units providing the general structure. For those teaching with this volume, we recommend experimenting with different ways of organizing your own reading of these texts.

Part 1
Social Identity

Introduction

A sometimes-illuminating exercise for any group that includes several people who self-identify as Hispanic, Latina/o, or Latinx is to ask the group whether this category is a *racial* category (one having to do with biological descent), an *ethnic* category (having to do with learned cultural features like language and social practices), or some other thing. Typically, it doesn't tend to take long for vigorous disagreement and puzzlement to emerge.

Some people tend to think of this category or concept as primarily a matter of biological descent (so, roughly, a racial category); others tend to think it is more a matter of fluency in certain characteristic cultural practices (an ethnic category, that can be acquired without descent); others think it is both; and many are unclear on the difference between racial and ethnic categories. Indeed, the fact that it can be unclear, or that there is disagreement about how to understand the category, is for some itself a startling discovery. The answer, whatever it is, has consequences for how Latinxs can and should think of themselves. The stakes are not just a matter of labels. To the extent that our social identity is constructed by others, we typically want that identity to be accurate, and to be a reflection of how we think about ourself.

The readings in this section are about these questions. Collectively, they are an effort to get clear on several puzzles: the nature of the category; what it requires; what the function or use of the concept is for us; what the alternatives are to our existing concepts; and what kinds of facts (whether racial, cultural, historical, or other) provide constraints on how we think about identities. What makes these questions philosophical is that each involves contestable questions about the nature of concepts and how to organize our understanding of the lived experiences and varied interests in our use of the categories. These are the kinds of questions that cannot be settled by simply appealing to social science, because they are just as much questions about how we *ought* to think about things as they are questions about how we think and talk about the world. Similarly, these are questions that cannot be resolved by simply appealing to everyday usage, for it might be that everyday understandings about these things are inconsistent, confused, or fractured across several distinct but competing ideas.

The issues discussed in these readings are what we might think of as taxonomical or categorical, in that they are about how to understand or think about the identity category that is variously referred to as Hispanic, Latino, Latina/o, Latinx, or Latine. Although these authors sometimes take up other issues along the way, these readings are less centrally concerned with political or normative questions that follow from the identity. In later sections of this volume, other readings take up the urgent questions of whether this identity can serve as a basis for collective politics, whether the very idea of *latinidad* or Latinx-ness "bakes in" some political commitments or has untoward implications, and so on.

DOI: 10.4324/9781003385417-3

As we noted in the introduction of this volume, at least among academics, the preferred terminology for referring to the group of people that are the subject matter of these essays has changed a good deal over the past 30 years or so. We have not tried to impose any artificial uniformity, so the varied terminology in these essays reflects the varied contexts and sensibilities of the authors when these essays were written. In discussing those essays, we adhere to the terminology used in each essay.

The opening essay in this section is Linda Martín Alcoff's "Is Latina/o Identity a Racial Identity?" In it, Alcoff explores the sometimes deeply puzzling nature of how this identity category works. In some contexts, it seems to operate as a racial category, fitting into the wider U.S. practices of taking race to be a central social identity category, one that is tracked by legal and other social practices. In other contexts, it seems to function more like an ethnic category. Her overarching question is this: what is the best way to make sense of this lived but varied reality? Her answer is that we need a new kind of social identity category to capture the distinctiveness of Latina/o identity.

Jorge J. E. Gracia's "Identities: General and Particular" proposes what he calls the "Familial-Historical View of Latino identities." The idea is, roughly, that what unifies Latinos (his preferred terminology) is some suitable causal-historical connection to the events of 1492. In that sense, it is a historical account, but it is also a contextually specific account because which things are suitable traits or suitable connections varies by time and place. By Gracia's lights, the advantage of this picture is that it resolves a number of conceptual conundrums for thinking about Latino identity. In particular, his picture doesn't require us to be essentialists about what it is to be Latinx (so: there is no single trait that every Latinx has). And it shows how there is no problem with embracing a general identity (like Latino) while also embracing more specific identities (like Puerto Rican, Chicano, etc.).

The essay by Enrique Dussel, entitled "Being-in-the-World-Hispanically," offers a history of distinct social, economic, and cultural worlds that produce what he characterizes as a Hispanic or *hispano* identity. His interest is historical and phenomenological, in that it is focused on how history has produced a distinctive configuration of lived experience. In his account, the *hispano* identity is a complex identity with many overlapping histories. Because of that history, it requires an active and collective effort of construction and historical self-awareness, something that overcomes its erasure and suppression, and that affirms its own dignity.

An important complexity about how Latino identity works in the United States is that it is not exclusively a matter of how U.S. social identity categories operate. Latin American countries, including those in the Caribbean, have their own identity categories which operate according to local social norms and histories. That means that many Latinxs have a sense of identity that is at least partly structured by the way identity categories work in their countries of origin, or in the countries of origin of their families. The chapter by Gertrude González de Allen takes up the complicated status of Afro-Latinity, and its varied nature across contexts.

The final reading in this section concerns the general nature of social identity categories. Consider the difference between some identities, like being a fan of some musician or sports team on the one hand, and on the other, one's identity as a member of a racial group. To have an identity of the former sort seems like a matter of whether one self-identifies in that way and performs the identity in a suitable fashion. However, for many people, this seems like the wrong way of understanding racial identities. The very idea of "passing" (that is, performing a racial identity that society denies that one has) seems to require that some identities are not just matters of performance. What's going on in these cases? These are the sorts of questions that animate the last reading of this section of the volume. Axel Barceló offers a general framework for thinking about social identity categories, or what he calls "habitable categories." Barceló identifies several different approaches to social identity, each corresponding to different interests we can have in talk about identities. He argues that in many contexts, these interests converge. However, there are contexts where our interests in different notions of identity come apart, and these divergences are at the heart of different attempts to understand how identity categories work.

1 Is Latina/o Identity a Racial Identity?

Linda Martín Alcoff

Is Latina/o identity a racial identity? Given the social basis of racializing categories and the dynamic nature of identities, there is no decontextual, final, or essential answer to this question. However, I would describe my concern in this paper as being in the realm of social ontology in the sense that I seek the truth about how Latina/o identity is configured as well as lived in the context of North America today. The question then can be formulated in the following way: What is the best, or most apt, account of Latina/o identity that makes the most sense of the current political and social realities within which we must negotiate our social environment? Although I am interested here in the politics of identity, that is, the political effects of various accounts of identity in and on popular consciousness, both among Latinas/os and among Anglos, my principal concern is at the level of experience, ideology, and meaning rather than the attendant political rights that may be associated with identity.

As will be seen, much of the debates over Latinas/os and race weave together strategic considerations (a concern with political effects) and metaphysical considerations (a concern with the most apt description). It is not clear to me that these concerns can, in fact, be disentangled. There are two reasons for this. One is that strategic proposals for the way a community should represent itself cannot work if there is no connection whatsoever to lived experience or to the common meanings that are prominent in the relevant discourses and practices. Thus, the strategic efficacy of political proposals are dependent on correct assessments of metaphysical realities. But second, the question of what is the most apt description of those metaphysical realities is not as clear-cut as some philosophers might suppose. And this is because the concepts of "race," "Latina/o," and even "identity" admit of different meanings and have complicated histories, such that it is not possible to simply say, "This is the meaning." Thus, we must make a judgment about meaning, a judgment that will be underdetermined by usage, history, science, or phenomenological description of experience. And in making these judgments, we must look to the future and not just the past. In other words, given that we are participating in the construction of meanings in making such judgments, we must take responsibility for our actions, which will require carefully considering their likely real-world effects.

The question of Latina/o identity's relationship to the conventional categories of race that have been historically dominant in the United States is a particularly vexing one. To put it straightforwardly, we simply don't fit. Racialized identities in the United States have long connoted homogeneity, easily visible identifying features, and biological heredity, but none of these characteristics apply to Latinas/os in the United States, nor even to any one national subset, such as Cuban Americans or Puerto Ricans. We are not homogeneous by

DOI: 10.4324/9781003385417-4

"race": we are often not identifiable by visible features or even by names, and such issues as disease heredity that are often cited as the biologically relevant sign of race are inapplicable to such a heterogeneous group.

Moreover, the corresponding practices of racialization in the United States—such as racial border control, legal sanctions on cross-racial marriage, and the multitudinous demands for racial self-identification on nearly every application form from daycare to college admissions—are also relatively unfamiliar south of the border. Angel R. Oquendo recounts that before he could even take the SAT in Puerto Rico, he was asked to identify himself racially. "I was caught off-guard," he says. "I had never thought of myself in terms of race" (Oquendo 1998: 61). Fortunately, the SAT included "Puerto Rican" among the choices of "race," and Oquendo was spared what he called a "profound existential dilemma." Even while many Latinas/os consider color a relevant factor for marriage, and anti-black racism persists in Latin America along with a condescension toward indigenous peoples, the institutional and ideological forms that racism has taken in Latin America are generally not analogous to those in the North. And these differences are why many of us find our identity as well as our social status changing as we step off the plane or cross the river: race suddenly becomes an all-important aspect of our identity, and sometimes our racial identity dramatically changes in ways over which it feels as if we have no control.

In the face of this transcontinental experiential dissonance, there are at least three general options possible as a way of characterizing the relationship between Latina/o identity and race; one option is to refuse a racialized designation and use the concept of "ethnicity" instead. This would avoid the problem of racial diversity within Latina/o communities and yet recognize the cultural links among Latinas/os in the North. The concept of ethnicity builds on cultural practices, customs, language, sometimes religion, and so on. One might also be motivated toward this option as a way of resisting the imposition of a pan-Latina/o ethnicity, in order to insist that the only meaningful identities for Latinas/os are Cuban American, Puerto Rican, Mexican American, and so on.[1]

A second option would resist the ethnic paradigm on the grounds that, whatever the historical basis of Latina/o identity, living in the context of North America means that we have become a racialized population and need a self-understanding that will accurately assess our portrayal here. A third option, adopted by many neoconservatives, is to attempt to assimilate to the individualist ideology of the United States both in body and in mind, and reject the salience of group identities a priori.

None of these responses seems fully adequate, though some have more problems than others. It is hard to see how the diversity among Latinas/os could be fairly represented in any concept of race. And it is doubtful that many Latinas/os, especially those who are darker-skinned, will be able to succeed in presenting themselves as simply individuals: they will still be seen by many as instantiations of a group whose characteristics are considered both universally shared within the group and largely inferior, even if they do not see themselves this way. On the face of it, the first option—an account of Latina/o identity as an ethnic identity—seems to make the most sense, for a variety of reasons that I will explore in this paper. This option could recognize the salience of social identity, allow for more internal heterogeneity, and resist the racializing that so often mischaracterizes our own sense of self. However, I will ultimately argue that the "ethnic option" is not fully adequate to the contemporary social realities we face, and may inhibit the development of useful political strategies for our diverse communities. My argument in this paper primarily will take the form of a negative: that the ethnic option is not adequate. Developing a fully adequate alternative is beyond my scope or ambitions here, but the very failure of the ethnic option will establish some of the necessary criteria for such an alternative.

My argument will take the following steps. First, I will explain briefly the context of these debates over identity, which will go some way toward refuting the individualist option. Next, I will go over some of the relevant facts about our populations to provide the necessary cultural context. Then I will zero in on the ethnicity argument, assess its advantages and disadvantages, and conclude by posing the outline of an alternative.

Why Care About Identity?

If I may be permitted a gross overgeneralization, European Americans are afraid of strongly felt ethnic and racial identities. Not all, to be sure. The Irish and Italian communities, as well as some other European-American nationalities, have organized cultural events on the basis of their identities at least since the 1960s, with the cooperation of police and city councils across the country. The genealogy of this movement among the Irish and the Italians has been precisely motivated by their discrimination and vilification in U.S. history, a vilification that has sometimes taken racialized forms.

But there is a different attitude among whites in general toward "white ethnic" celebrations of identity and toward those of others, that is, those of nonwhites. And this is, I suspect, because it is one thing to say to the dominant culture, "You have been unfairly prejudiced against me," as southern European ethnicities might say, and quite another to say, "You have stolen my lands and enslaved my people and through these means created the wealth of your country," as African Americans, Latinas/os, and Native Americans might say. The latter message is harder to hear; it challenges the basic legitimizing narratives of this country's formation and global status, and it understandably elicits the worry, "What will be the full extent of their demands?" Of course, all of the cultural programs that celebrate African, indigenous, or Latina/o heritage do not make these explicit claims. But in a sense, the claims do not need to be explicit: any reference to slavery, indigenous peoples, or Chicano or Puerto Rican history implies challenges to the legitimizing narrative of the United States, and any expression of solidarity among such groups consciously or unconsciously elicits concern about the political and economic demands such groups may eventually make, even if they are not made now.

This is surely part of what is going on when European Americans express puzzlement about the importance attached to identity by non-European Americans, when young whites complain about African Americans sitting together in the cafeteria, or when both leftist and liberal political theorists, such as Todd Gitlin and Arthur Schlesinger, jump to the conclusion that a strong sense of group solidarity and its resultant "identity politics" among people of color in this country will fracture the body politic and disable our democracy (Gitlin 1995; Schlesinger Jr. 1992; Hochschild 1996; Elshtain 1997).

A prominent explanation given for these attachments to identity, attachments that are considered otherwise inexplicable, is that there is opportunism at work, among leaders if not among the rank and file, to secure government handouts and claim special rights. However, the demand for cultural recognition does not entail a demand for special political rights. The assumption in so much of contemporary political philosophy that a politics of recognition—or identity-based political movements—leads automatically to demands for special rights is grounded, I suspect, in the mystification some feel in regard to the politics of cultural identity in the first place. Given this mystification and feeling of amorphous threat, assumptions of opportunism and strategic reasoning become plausible.

Assumptions about the opportunism behind identity politics seem to work on the basis of the following understanding of the recent historical past; in the 1960s, some groups began to clamor for the recognition of their identities, began to resist and critique the cultural assimilationism of liberal politics, and argued that state institutions should give these identities public recognition. Thus, in this scenario, first we had identity politics asserting the political importance of these identities, and then we had (coerced) state recognition of them. But denigrated identity designations, particularly racial ones, have originated with and been enforced by the state in U.S. history, not vice versa. Obviously, it is the U.S. state and U.S. courts that initially insisted on the overwhelming salience of some racial and ethnic identities, to the exclusion of rights to suffrage, education, property, marrying whomever one wanted, and so on. Denigrated groups are trying to reverse this process; they are not the initiators of it. It seems to me that they have two aims: (1) to valorize previously derided identities, and (2) to have their own hand at constructing the representations of identities.

The U.S. pan-Latina/o identity is perhaps the newest and most important identity that has emerged in the recent period. The concept of a panLatina/o identity is not new in Latin America: Simón Bolívar called for it nearly two hundred years ago as a strategy for anticolonialism, but also because it provided a name for the "new peoples" that had emerged from the conquest. And influential leaders such as José Martí and Che Guevara also promoted Latin American solidarity. It is important to note that populations "on the ground" have not often resonated with these grand visions, and that national political and economic leaders continue to obstruct regional accords and trade agreements that might enhance solidarity. But the point remains that the invocation of a pan-Latina/o identity does not actually originate in the North.

Only much more recently is it the case that some Latina/o political groups in the North have organized on a pan-Latina/o basis, although most Latina/o politics here have been organized along national lines, for example, as Puerto Ricans or Chicanos. But what is especially new, and what is being largely foisted on us from the outside, is the representation of a pan-Latina/o identity in the dominant North American media, and it is this representation we want to have a hand in shaping. Marketing agencies have discovered/created a marketing niche for the "generic" Latina/o. And Latina/o-owned marketing agencies and advertising agencies are working on the construction of this identity as much as anyone, though of course in ways dominated by strategic interests, or what Habermas calls purposive rationality. There are also more and more cultural representations of Latinas/os in the dominant media and in government productions such as the census. Thus, the concern that U.S. Latinas/os have with our identity is not spontaneous or originating entirely or even mostly from within our communities; neither is the ongoing representation of our identity something we can easily just ignore (Mato 1997: 2–7; Flores and Yudice 1990).

What We Are Depends on Where We Are

Social identities, whether racial or ethnic, are dynamic. In Omi and Winant's study of what they call "racial formations" in the United States between the 1960s and the 1980s, they argued, "Racial categories and the meanings of race are given concrete expression by the specific social relations and historical context in which they are embedded" (Omi and Winant 1986: 60). Moreover, these categories are constantly facing forms of resistance and contestation that transform both their impact and their effective meaning. Clearly this is the case with ethnic as well as racial identities. As social constructions imposed on variable experiential facts, they exist with no stable referent or essential, non-negotiable core. And because such identities are often also the site of conflict over political power and economic resources, they are especially volatile. Any analysis of Latina/o identity, then, must chart historical trends and contextual influences, which themselves will vary across different parts of the country.

Since the passage of the 1965 immigration law that ended the quotas on immigration from South and Central America and the Caribbean, millions of Latinas/os have entered the United States from various countries, causing a great diversification of the previously dominant Chicano, Puerto Rican, and Cuban communities. Thus, today, Dominicans are vying with Puerto Ricans in New York City to be the largest Latina/o population, and even Cubans no longer outnumber other Latinas/os in Miami. As the immigrant communities settle in, younger generations develop different identities than their parents, adapting to their cultural surroundings. Young people also tend to experience similar problems across the national divisions, such as Dominican and Puerto Rican, and this promotes a sense of common identity. So in one sense diversity has increased as new immigrations continue and new generations of younger Latinos depart from some aspects of their parents' cultural identity, such as being Spanish-dominant or being practicing Catholics, while in another sense diversity has decreased as Latinas/os experience common forms of discrimination and chauvinism in the United States and an increasingly common cultural interpellation.

In the 1960s, U.S. state agencies began to disseminate the ethnic label "Hispanic" as the proper term for identifying all people of Latin American and even Spanish descent (Oboler 1995: xiii). So today we have a population of thirty million or so "Hispanics" in the United States. The mass media, entertainment, and advertising industries have increasingly addressed this large population as if it were a coherent community (Mato 19972). As Suzanne Oboler's study reveals, this generic identity category feels especially socially constructed to many of the people named by it, given that it is not how they self-identified previously (Oboler 1995). Oboler asks, somewhat rhetorically:

> Are marketers merely taking advantage of an existing "group" as a potentially lucrative target population? Or are their advertising strategies in fact helping to "design" the group, "invent" its traditions, and hence "create" this homogeneous ethnic group?
> (Oboler 1995: 13)

One might well be concerned that adapting to any such pan-Latina/o identity as constructed by dominant institutions—whether economic or political ones—represents a capitulation or is simply the inevitable effect of what Foucault might call governmentality.

However, much of the debate over this interpellation among those named by it does not so much critique the fact of its social construction or even the fact that its genesis lies in government and marketing agencies, but focuses instead on its political implications and its coherence with lived experience, for example, the way in which it disallows multiplicity or the way in which it erases national allegiance. In this way, the debate shifts to a more productive set of concerns, it seems to me. I witnessed an interesting exchange on some of these points at the "Hispanics: Cultural Locations" conference held at the University of San Francisco in 1997. Ofelia Schutte, a leading Latina philosopher, presented a paper arguing that a pan-U.S. Latina/o identity may be a means to disaffiliate us from our nations of birth or ancestry, nations that have been invaded or otherwise harmed by the U.S. government. Thus, thinking of ourselves primarily as U.S. Latinas/os rather than, say, Panamanians or Salvadorans may work to dislodge or weaken feelings of loyalty to countries outside the

U.S. borders. In the discussion period after her paper, one member of the audience argued strongly that as a half-Spanish, half-Puerto Rican woman who grew up among Chicanos in California, she had found the emergence of a pan-Latina/o identity a welcome relief. Although she recognized the dangers that Schutte was describing, identifying herself simply as Latina allowed her to avoid having to make complicated choices between the various aspects of her identity, and it helpfully named her experience of connection with a multiplicity of Latina/o communities.[2]

Another political concern I have heard voiced against overhomogenizing Latina/o identities is that it could allow those members of the group who are themselves less disadvantaged to reap the benefits of affirmative action and other forms of economic redress that have mainly been created for (and often mainly fought for by) Chicanos and Puerto Ricans, that is, the more disadvantaged members. We are already seeing this happen because of the label "Hispanic." It is unclear how to effectively police this problem other than to rely on people's own moral conscience (which is not terribly effective). In some cases, targeted groups are designated with specificity as Mexican Americans or Puerto Ricans in order to avoid, for example, giving scholarships to Argentinians of recent European extraction. However, the problem here is that one cannot assume that no Argentinians in the United States have suffered discrimination, given their particular racialized identity, skin tone, the way their accent may be mediated by their class background, and so forth. Given the racial heterogeneity of every Latin American and Caribbean country, one cannot exclude an entire country from measures aimed at redressing discrimination without excluding many who are racially marked as inferior north of the border.

The resistance to a pan-Latina/o identity is most likely a losing battle, moreover, as both government and marketing agencies are increasingly winning hegemony in their public interpellations. Moreover, as both Arlene Davila and Daniel Mato have argued in separate studies, the marketing and advertising agencies are not simply forcing us to use labels that have no real purchase on our lives, but participating in a new subject construction that affects how Latinas/os think about and experience our identity and our interrelatedness to other Latinas/os with whom we may have felt little kinship before (Davila 2001; Mato 1997). Mato points out that the television corporation Univisión, which is jointly owned by U.S. and Latin American companies, is exposing its viewers to a wide array of programming such that viewers are becoming familiar with a diversity of communities, in both the South and the North, and in this way "Univisión is participating in the social construction of an imagined community" (Mato 1997). To say that an identity is socially constructed is to say not that it does not refer to anything in reality, but that what it refers to is a contingent product of social negotiations rather than a natural kind. And the exchange I described above at the "Hispanics: Cultural Locations" conference indicates that the pan-Latina/o identity does in fact correspond at least to some contemporary Latina/os' lived experience.

Latin America itself is probably the most diverse area in the world, producing extreme racial and ethnic diversity within Latina/o communities. By U.S. categories, there are black, brown, white, Asian, and Native American Latinas/os. There are many Latinas/os from the Southern Cone whose families are of recent European origin, a large number of Latinas/os from the western coastal areas whose families came from Asia, and of course a large number of Latinas/os whose lineage is entirely indigenous to the Americas or entirely African. The majority of Latinas/os in North and South America are no doubt the product of a mix of two or more of these groups. And being mixed is true, as Jorge J. E. Gracia reminds us, even of the so-called Hispanics who are direct descendants of Spain and Portugal. And it is true as well of many or most of the people identified as black or *moreno*, as is the case in the United States. Latin Americans are thus generally categorized "racially" in the following way: white (which often involves a double deceit: a claim to pure Spanish descent, very rare, and a claim that pure Spanish descent is purely white or European, also very rare); black (meaning wholly or mostly of African descent, usually sub-Saharan); Indian (meaning being some or mostly of pre-Columbian or Amerindian descent); and mixed (which is sometimes divided into subcategories, mestizo, mulatto, *cholito*, and so on), with the mixed category always enjoying a majority. Asians are often entirely left off the list, even though their numbers in several countries are significant.

Different countries vary these main racial designations, however. During a recent weekend festival for Latino Heritage Month in Syracuse, Latinas/os of different nationalities provided information about their countries for passersby, information that included statistics, culled from government sources, on what in every case was called the country's "ethnic makeup." Racial categories of identity were given within this larger rubric of ethnic makeup, suggesting an equation between ethnicity and race. For example, in the Dominican Republic the ethnic makeup is said to consist of 73 percent "mixed people," 16 percent "white," 11 percent "black." In Ecuador the categories are listed as "mestizo," "Indian," "Spanish," and "black." In Chile there is a single category called "European and mestizo," which makes up 95 percent of the population. In Cuba we get categories of "mulatto," which is 51 percent of the population, and we also get categories of "white," "black," and "Chinese." In Bolivia the breakdown is between "Quechua," "Aymara," "mestizo," and "white."

One is reminded of the encyclopedia invented by Borges, which divides dogs into such categories as "(a) belonging to the Emperor . . . (b) tame . . . (c) drawn with a very fine camel hair brush . . . and (d) having just broken the water pitcher" (cited in Foucault 1970: xv). There is no internally consistent or coherent theory of ethnic or racial identity underlying the diversity of categorizations. Under the rubric of ethnicity are included a mix of cultural, national, and racial groups, from Spanish to Quechua to white. The sole point that seems to be consistent throughout is that the category "black" is the only one that is invariably racialized, that is, presented as black or mulatto and never presented as "West Indian" or "African." Interestingly, the category "white" is also often racialized, though it is sometimes replaced with "European" or "Spanish." I would suggest that there is a strong relationship between these two facts. That is, it becomes important to use the category "white," and to self-identify as "white," when the category "black" is present, in order to establish one's clear demarcation, and out of concern that a category such as "mestizo" might be allowed to include black people. "White" is also used to distinguish oneself from "Indian," a category that bears racialized meanings in Latin America and negative associations similar to the associations with African Americans in the United States.

Blackness does, of course, signify differently in Latin America; thus it is not likely that a typical white American landing in Santo Domingo would look around and think only 11 percent of the population is black. However, it seems clear that the striking use of the category "black" for all people of African descent, rather than cultural and national markers, is an indication of antiblack racism. The people so designated are reduced to skin color as if this were their primary characteristic rather than some self-created marker such as nationality, language, or culture. One may have been born into a culture and language not of one's own choosing, but these are still more indicative of human agency than is any classification by phenotype. From this, one might argue that replacing "black" with another ethnicity category, such as "West Indian" or "African," might help equalize and dignify the identities.

The category "Indian," however, even though it might initially look to be more of an ethnicity than a race (since it is not merely the name of a color), has primarily a racial meaning, given that the term does not say anything about language, mode of life, religion, or specific origin. Also, in nonindigenous communities of discourse, the term often carries associations as negative as "black" does. Here one might argue that disaggregating the category "Indian" would be helpful. If the main meaning of "Indian" is a kind of racial meaning, then the use of "Quechua," "Aymara," and so on reduces the significance of the racialized connotations of the identity, subordinating those to the specificity of linguistic and cultural markers.

Despite all this variety and heterogeneity, when Latinas/os enter the United States, we are often homogenized into one overarching "Hispanic" identity. This generic Hispanicity is not, as Jorge J. E. Gracia reminds us, actually homogeneous. That is, in European-American eyes, "Hispanic" identity does not carry the same connotations in every part of the United States. Gracia explains:

> In Miami it means Cuban; in New York City it means Puerto Rican; and in the southwest it means Mexican. So in California I am supposed to have as my native food tacos, in New York City, arroz con gandules, and in Miami, *arroz con frijoles negros*!
> (Gracia 1998)

I, too, cannot even count the times it has been assumed that I must naturally like hot and spicy food, even though the typical food in Panama is extremely mild.

Still, there is one feature at least that persists across this variety of "generic" Hispanic identities, and that is that our identity in the United States, whether or not it is homogenized, is quite often presented as a racial identity. In a recent report in the Chronicle of Higher Education, just to give one example, differences in average SAT scores were reported in the following way:

> The average verbal scores by race were: white, 526; black, 434; Asian-American, 498; American Indian, 480; Mexican-American, 453; Puerto Rican, 452; and other Hispanic students, 461.
> ("Disparities Grow in SAT Scores of Ethnic and Racial Groups" 1998)

So again, like Angel Oquendo, we find that "Puerto Rican" is a racial identity, and a different one at that from the "race" of Mexican Americans. Whereas in the categorizations I just analyzed from Latin America, racial categories are subsumed within an overall account of "ethnic makeup," in this example from the United States, ethnic categories are subsumed within an overall account of racial difference. But in both cases, race and ethnicity are all but equated.

The Ethnicity Paradigm

Latinas/os in the United States have responded to racialization in a variety of ways. One response, still ongoing, has been to deny vigorously any racial interpellation as other-than-white. Thus some Latinos have literally campaigned to be called white, apparently thinking that if they are going to have to be racialized, whiteness is the one they want. Anita Allen reported in 1994 that the largest petitioning group that had thus far requested changes to the year 2000 U.S. census was the Association of White Hispanics, who were agitating for that designation to be on the census form (Allen 1994). In the self-interested scramble for social status, this group perceived correctly where the advantages lay.

Another response, especially among groups of young people, has been to use the discourse of racialization as it exists in the United States to self-identify, but in positive rather than derogatory ways. Thus Chicanos in the August Twenty-Ninth Movement and in Mecha, as well as the primarily Puertorriqueno Young Lords in the Northeast, at times adopted and adapted the concept of a brown racial identity, such as the "Brown Berets," as if Latinas/os in these communities shared a visible phenotype. One relevant causal factor for this among Puerto Ricans may be their long experiential history of U.S. colonization, which imposed racialization even before they ever entered the United States. Latinas/os from countries without this experience of intensive colonization are more surprised by being racially designated when they come here (Grosfoguel and Georas 1996: 199).

But neither "white" nor "brown" works for a pan-Latina/o identity (or even for the specific nationalities they want to represent). What better unites Latinas/os both across and even within our specific national cultures is not race or phenotype but precisely those features associated with culture: language, religious traditions, cultural values, characteristics of comportment. Thus, another response to forced racialization that has existed for a long time among some Latina/o communities and which has enjoyed a recent resurgence is to deny that race applies in any way to Latinas/os and to argue for, and self-identify as, an ethnic group that encompasses different nationalities and races within it (See, for example, Jorge Klor de Alva 1996: 55–63). The U.S. census has adopted this approach at times, in having no Latina/o identity listed under possible racial categories and including it only under the list of ethnic categories. Let us look at the main arguments in favor of this approach, both the political as well as the metaphysical arguments.

1. There is powerful sentiment among Latinas/os toward resisting the imposition of U.S. racializations and U.S. categories of identity. It is not as if the system of racial classification here has benefited anyone except the white majority. As Jorge Klor de Alva provocatively put it to Cornel West in a conversation in Harper's, "What advantage has it been, Cornel, for blacks to identify as blacks?" (Klor de Alva 1996: 56). Oquendo argues against the use of such racial terms as "Black Hispanics" and "White Hispanics" on the grounds that these categories "project onto the Latino/a community a divisive racial dualism that, much as it may pervade U.S. society, is alien to that community" (Oquendo 1998: 60). Our identity is about culture and nationality, not race: for example, as Clara Rodriguez has shown, Puerto Ricans of all colors self-identify first as Puerto Rican (Rodriguez 1989).

   But in the United States, cultural, national, ethnic, religious and other forms of identification are constantly subordinated to race. So Afro-Cubans, English-speaking West Indians, and Afro-Brazilians are grouped as "black," in ways that often counter people's own felt sense of identity or primary group alliances. Race trumps culture, and culture is sometimes even seen as a simple outgrowth of race. Shouldn't this ridiculous biological essentialism be opposed and the use of race as an identity or as an all-important category of identity be diminished?

2. Within the United States itself, many African Americans have been opting out of racial categories ever since Jesse Jackson started pushing for the use of the term "African

American" in the late 1980s. This was a self-conscious strategy to encourage analogies between African Americans and other hyphenated ethnic groups to, in a sense, normalize African-American identity by no longer having it set apart from everyone else. Shouldn't Latinas/os unite with and support this trend?

3. The strategy of using ethnic terms rather than racial ones will have the effect of reducing racism or prejudice generally. This was clearly Jackson's thinking. A representation by ethnic terms rather than racial ones confers agency on a people; it invokes historical experience as well as cultural and linguistic practices, all of which are associations with human subjectivity, not objectivity. In contrast, race is often said to be something one has no control over, something one "can't help." This surely perpetuates the association between denigrated racial categories and victimhood, animal-driven natures, inherent inferiority and superiority, and so on. For whites, racial essentialism confers superiority whether or not they've done anything to deserve it; superior intelligence is just in their genes. These beliefs may be more unconscious than conscious, but given the historically sedimented and persistent layers of the ideology of race as an essential determinant, no matter what one intends by use of a word, its historical meanings will be brought into play when it is in use. Naomi Zack, Anthony Appiah, Klor de Alva, and many others today argue that any use of racial terms will be inevitably embedded with biological essentialism and historically persistent hierarchies of moral and cognitive competence (Appiah 1992; Zack 1993). Luis Angel Toro calls on us to "abandon the outdated racial ideology embodied in [the Office of Management and Budget's Statistical] Directive no. 15 and replace it with questions designed to determine an individual's membership in a socially constructed, cultural subgroup" (Toro 1998: 58). The goal here, of course, is not only to change whites' assumptions about racialized groups, but also to help alter the self-image of people in those groups themselves toward a more affirming identity, an identity in which one can take justifiable pride.

Some also point to the relative success of Jamaican immigrants in the United States as an example here. Grosfoguel and Georas write,

> The Jamaican's community's strategy was to emphasize ethnic over racial identity. The fact that Jamaicans were not subsumed under the categorization 'African American' avoided offsetting the positive impact of their skilled background. Thus Jamaicans were successfully incorporated into the host labor market in well-paid public and private service jobs . . . [and] are currently portrayed by the white establishment in New York as a model minority.
>
> (Grosfoguel and Georas 1996: 197)

These are strong arguments. To summarize them, the political arguments are that (1) the use of ethnicity will reduce racism because it refers to selfcreated features rather than merely physiological ones, and (2) this will also resist the imposition of U.S. forms of identifying people, thus disabusing North Americans of their tendency to naturalize and universalize the predominant categories used here in the United States. The metaphysical arguments are that (3) ethnicity more accurately identifies what really holds groups together and how they self-identify, and (4) ethnicity is simply closer to the truth of Latina/o identity, given its racial heterogeneity. All of these arguments are, in my view, good ones. But the problem is that there are other considerations, and once they are put on the table, the picture unfortunately becomes more complicated.

Racial Realities

Let us look at the case of Cuban Americans. By all measures, they have fared very well in this country in terms of both economic success and political power. They have largely run both politics and the press in Miami for some time, and presidential candidates neglect Cuban issues at their peril. Of course, one cannot argue, as some do in the case of Jamaicans, that Cubans' strong ethnic identification is the main reason for their success; most important has been their ability to play an ideological (and at times military) role for the United States in the cold war. The enormous government assistance provided to the Cubans who fled the Cuban revolution was simply unprecedented in U.S. immigration history: they received language training, educational and business loans, job placement assistance, and housing allocations, and their professional degrees from Cuban institutions were legally recognized to an extent other Third World immigrants still envy. In 1965, when President Johnson began his Great Society programs, the amount of assistance they received from the government actually increased (Grosfoguel and Georas 1996: 198).

But one may legitimately wonder whether the Cubans' status as refugees from Communism was all that was at work here, or even the overriding factor. The Cubans who came in the 1960s were overwhelmingly white or lightskinned. They were generally from the top strata of Cuban society. It is an interesting question whether Haitians would ever have been treated the same way. The Cubans who left Cuba after 1980, known as the Marielitos, were from the lower strata of Cuban society, and a large number were Afro-Cubans and mulattos. (Grosfoguel and Georas 1996: 199). These Cubans found a decidedly colder welcome. They were left penned in refugee camps for months on end, and those who were not sent back to Cuba were released into U.S. society with little or no assistance, joining the labor ranks at the level of Puerto Ricans and Dominicans.

There are no doubt many factors at work in these disparate experiences of Cuban immigration, having to do, for example, with the geopolitical climate. But surely one of these important factors is race, or racialized identity. Perceived racial identity often does trump ethnic or cultural identity.

Look again at the passage about Jamaicans quoted earlier from Grosfoguel and Georas, with certain words emphasized: "The Jamaican community's strategy was to emphasize *ethnic* over *racial* identity. The fact that *Jamaicans* were not subsumed under the categorization '*African American*' avoided offsetting the positive impact of their skilled background." Grosfoguel and Georas contrast the *ethnic* Jamaican identity with what they revealingly take to be a *racial* African American identity, even though the term "African American" was Jackson's attempt to replace race with ethnicity. This again suggests that the racialization of black Americans will overpower any ethnic or cultural marker. It may also be the case that the category "African" is overly inclusive, since under its umbrella huge cultural and linguistic differences would be subsumed, and thus it is incapable of signifying a unified ethnic identity. But that may be assuming more knowledge about Africa among white Americans or even among Latinas/os than one reasonably should. More likely is the fact that "African American" is still understood primarily as a racial designation, in a way that terms such as "German American" or "Irish American" never are. Thus it is questionable whether the strategy of using an ethnic term for a currently racialized group will have the effect of reducing racism if it continues to simply signify race.

And after all, the first meaning given for the word ethnic in Webster's Unabridged Dictionary is "heathen, pagan." The concept of ethnicity is closely associated with the concept of race, emerging at the same moment in global history, as this meaning indicates. The common usage of the category "white ethnic" indicates that unless otherwise identified, "ethnics" are assumed to be nonwhite and thus they are racialized. For many people in the United States, "ethnic" connotes not only nonwhite but also the typical negative associations of nonwhite racial identity. Meanings given for the word heathen in the same dictionary include "rude, illiterate, barbarous, and irreligious." In this list, it is striking that "irreligious" comes last.

Like "African American," the fact is that in the United States the category "Latina/o" often operates as a racialized category. Grosfoguel and Georas themselves argue that "no matter how 'blonde or blue-eyed' a person may be, and no matter how successfully he can 'pass' as white, the moment a person self-identifies as Puerto Rican, he enters the labyrinth of racial Otherness" (Grosfoguel and Georas 1996: 195). Virginia Dominguez even makes this case in regard not only to ethnicity but to cultural identity as well. She suggests that case studies from Canada to Brazil reveal that "people may speak culture but continue to think race. Whether in the form of cultural pluralism or of the current idiom of multiculturalism, the concept of culture is used in ways that naturalize and essentialize difference" (Dominguez 1998).

My suspicion is that this works for some Latina/o identities, such as Puerto Rican, Dominican, and Mexican, but not always for others, such as Chilean or Argentinian or perhaps South Americans in general, depending on their features. And as mentioned earlier, some of these groups, Puerto Ricans and Mexicans in particular, have a long history of seeing their identities interpellated through dominant U.S. schemas. In terms of the panLatina/o identity, this would mean that when Mexicans or Puerto Ricans are called "Latina/o," the latter category will connote racial meanings, whereas Argentinians who are called "Latina/o" in the North may escape these connotations. Identity terms, as Omi and Winant argue, gain their meaning from their context. Just as Gracia said "Latino" means tacos in California and *arroz con gandules* in New York, it will mean race in California, Texas, New York, and Florida, and perhaps ethnicity only in a few locations. Thus, moving from race to ethnicity is not necessarily moving away from race.

Surely, an optimist might want to interject here, the persistence of racial connotations evoked by ethnic categories is not insurmountable. After all, the Irish did transform in wide popular consciousness from a race to an ethnicity, and Jews are making the same transition, at least in the United States. Is it truly the case that only light-skinned people can enjoy this transformation, and that darker-skinned people will never be able to?

In order to answer this question, we need to ask another one: What are the obstacles to deracializing people of color in general?[3] Is it really the mere fact of skin tone?

I would make two suggestions. First, race, unlike ethnicity, has historically worked through visible markers on the body that trump dress, speech, and cultural practices. In Mississippi, a Jamaican is generally still a black person, no matter how skilled. Race demarcates groups visually, which is why racist institutions have been so upset about nonvisible members of "races" and why they have taken such trouble in these cases to enforce racial identifications. What I am suggesting is that in popular consciousness—in the implicit perceptual practices we use in everyday life to discern how to relate to each other—ethnicity does not "replace" race. When ethnic identities are used instead of racial ones, the perceptual practices of visual demarcation by which we slot people into racial categories continue to operate because ethnic categories offer no substituting perceptual practice. In other words, the fact that race and ethnicity do not map onto the same kinds of identifying practices will make race harder to dislodge. This was not the case for the Irish or for at least some Jewish people, who could blend into the European American melting pot without noticeable distinctiveness. For them, ethnicity could replace race, because their racial identity as Irish and Jewish did not operate exclusively or primarily through visible markers on the body so much as through contextual factors such as neighborhood and accent. So their identity could shift to white race plus Jewish or Irish ethnicity without troubling the dominant perceptual practices of racial identification. However, for those who are visibly identified by such dominant practices as nonwhite, as "raced," the shift to a primary ethnic identity would require eradicating these practices. It is unlikely that the use of new terms alone will have that effect. At best, for people of color, ethnic identities will operate alongside racial ones in everyday interactions. At worst, ethnic identities, perhaps like "African American," will operate simply as a racial identity.

Although this is a fact about the visible features of the body, it is not an immutable fact: the meanings of the visible are of course subject to change. However, the phenomenology of perception is such that change will be neither quick nor easy, and that word usage will be nowhere near sufficient to make this change (I make these arguments in more depth in Alcoff 1999: 15–26). The transformation of perceptual habits will require a more active and a more practical intervention.

The second obstacle to the deracialization of (at least most) people of color has nothing to do with perception or bodily features. This obstacle refers back to a claim I made at the beginning, that assertions of group solidarity among African Americans, Native Americans, and Latinas/os in the United States provoke resistance among many whites because they invoke the history of colonialism, slavery, and genocide. Thus, their acceptance as full players within U.S. society comes at much greater cost than the acceptance of previously vilified groups such as the Irish and Jews—groups that suffered terrible discrimination and violence including genocide but whose history is not a thorn in the side of "pilgrim's progress," "manifest destiny," "leader of the free world," and other such mythic narratives that legitimize U.S. world dominance and provide white Americans with a strong sense of pride. The Irish and Jews were (are) colonized peoples in Europe, and there they are reminders of colonization and genocide. But they do not play this role in the legitimizing narratives of the U.S. state. Thus, the line between European ethnicities and people of color is not merely or perhaps even primarily about skin tone but about history and power and the narratives by which currently existing power arrangements are justified.

So what are we to do? If the move from race to ethnicity is not as easy as some have thought, what is a more realistic strategy, one that will also resist being fatalistic about racialization? How can we avoid both fatalism and naivety? Are we to accept, then, that Latina/o identity is a racial identity, despite all the facts I have reviewed about our heterogeneity and different methods of self-identification, and all the pernicious effects of racialized identity? In conclusion, I can only sketch the outlines of an answer.

Although racial ideology and practices of racialization seem to always carry within them some commitment to biological essentialism, perhaps the meaning of race is transformable. If race is going to be with us for some time to come, it might still be the case that race itself will alter in meaning, even before the perceptual practices of racialization can be done away with. It seems to me that this change in meaning is exactly what Paul Gilroy is attempting to chart, as well as to promote, in The Black Atlantic, as well as what some other African-American theorists are doing, such as Robert Gooding-Williams, bell hooks, Lewis Gordon, and Patricia Williams (Gilroy 1993; Gooding-Williams 1998; Williams 1997; Gordon 1995). You will notice in their works an intentional use of the term black rather than African American; I think this is meant as a way to "be real" about the social reality we live in, and also as a way to suggest a linked fate between all black people across nationalities, at least in the diaspora. But in their works, blackness has been decidedly de-essentialized and given a meaning that consists of historical experience, collective memory, and forms of cultural expression. For Gilroy, there is a "blackness" that transcends and survives the differences of U.K., Caribbean, and U.S. nationalities, a blackness that can be seen in culture and narrative focus. Blackness is social location, shared history, and a shared perception about the world. For Gooding-Williams, black identity requires a certain self-consciousness about creating the meaning of blackness. It requires, in other words, not only that one is treated as a black person, or that one is "objectively" black, but that one is "subjectively" black as well, and thus that one exercises some agency in regard to their identity. His argument is not simply that this is how we should begin to use the term black, but it is how the term is actually used in common parlance, as in "Is Clarence Thomas really black?"

Whether such an approach can be used for Latinas/os, I am not sure. There is probably even greater diversity among Latinas/os in relation to history, social location, and forms of cultural expression than there is among black people across the diaspora. And the question of where black Latinas/os "fit" is still unresolved, even when we make racial identity a matter of selfcreation. This is a serious weakness in Gilroy's broad conceptualization of a "black Atlantic": Brazil, as large a country as it is, is nowhere to be found. But I believe that we can take an important lesson from this body of work because it suggests that, even while we must remember the persistent power of racialization and the inability of ethnicity to easily take its place, the meanings of race are subject to some movement. Only a semantic essentialist could argue that race can mean nothing but biological essentialism; in reality, this is not the way meaning works. Let me be clear about my position here: I don't believe, *a la* some postmodernists, that signifiers are slippery items whose meanings and associations can be easily transformed. Like Michelle Moody-Adams, I would argue that some can be (as in "black is beautiful") and some cannot be (as in "spic")[4] (Moody-Adams 1997: 13–14). Meaning works through iterability, that is, the invocation of prior meanings. When those prior meanings are centuries old and globally spread, they are going to be hard to dislodge. On the other hand, words do not simply pick out things that exist prior to their being picked out, and thus reference is mutable.

So the first point I am making is this: despite our hopes that the influx of Latinas/os on the North American continent, in all of our beautiful diversity, would transform and annihilate the binaries and purist racial ideologies prevalent in the United States, this is not likely, at least not very soon. Existing systems of meaning will absorb and transform our own self-identifying terms in ways that may not be immediately obvious but which we need to become aware of. However, although we may be stuck with racial categories for longer than some of us would wish, it may be easier to help "race" slowly evolve than to try to do away with it as a first step.

Latinas/os in the United States have without a doubt been racialized. And I would argue that the history, and even the contemporary socioeconomic situation, of Latinas/os in the United States simply cannot be understood using ethnicity categories alone; we have been shut out of the melting pot because we have been seen as racial and not merely cultural "others." However, this has not been true to the same degree for all of us. It has been true of Mexicans, Puerto Ricans, and Dominicans most of all, much less so of some others. So what are we to do in the face of this diversity of historical experience and social location? Is race perhaps a way to understand some Latina/o identities but not all? For a pan-Latina/o moniker, shouldn't we refer to ethnicity?

My argument has been that given the way in which our ethnicity has been racialized, this is a doubtful solution. Moreover, we are in almost all cases racially different from Anglos, in the commonly used sense of race. That is—even for Spaniards, as Jorge J. E. Gracia is arguing—we are not "purely European," claims of white Hispanicity notwithstanding. In the very name of antiracism and solidarity with other racialized people of color, shouldn't we acknowledge this, and not go the route of those who would seek to better their social status by differentiating themselves from the vilified racial others? Perhaps we can help lift the meaning of race out of its status as an insult by uniting with the efforts of those such as Gilroy and Gooding-Williams, who seek to give it a cultural meaning.

Of course, it does not make sense to say simply that Latinas/os constitute a "race," either by the common-sense meaning or by more nuanced references to historical narrative and cultural production. I (still) believe that if the concept of "mestizo" enters into U.S. culture, it can have some good effects against the presumption of purity as having an intrinsic value. Still, the concept of mestizo when applied to Latinas/os in general, as if all Latinas/os or the essence of being Latina/o is to be mestizo, has the effect of subordinating all Latinas/os, both North and South, whose descendants are entirely African, Indian, or Asian. Mestizos then become the cornerstone of the culture, with others pushed off to the side. This is clearly intolerable.

A concept that might be helpful here has been coined by David Theo Goldberg: ethnorace. Unlike race, ethnorace does not imply a common descent, which is precisely what tends to embroil race in notions of biological determinism and natural and heritable characteristics. Ethnorace might have the advantage of bringing into play the elements of both human agency and subjectivity involved in ethnicity—that is, an identity that is the product of self-creation—at the same time that it acknowledges the uncontrolled racializing aspects associated with the visible body. And the term would remind us that there are at least two concepts, rather than one, that are vitally necessary to the understanding of Latina/o identity in the United States: ethnicity and race. Using only ethnicity belies the reality of most Latinas/os' everyday experiences, as well as obscures our own awareness about how ethnic identifications often do the work of race while seeming to be theoretically correct and politically advanced. Race dogs our steps; let us not run from it lest we cause it to increase its determination.[5]

References

Alcoff, L. (1999) "The Phenomenology of Racial Embodiment," *Radical Philosophy* 95 (May/June): 15–26.

Allen, A. (1994) "Recent Racial Constructions in the U.S. Census," paper presented at the *Race: Its Meaning and Significance Conference*, Rutgers University, November.

Angel Toro, L. (1998) "Race, Identity, and 'Box Checking': The Hispanic Classification in OMB Directive No. 15," in R. Delgado and J. Stefancic (eds.), *The Latino/a Condition*, New York: New York University Press.

Appiah, A. (1992) *In My Father's House: Africa in the Philosophy of Culture*. New York: Oxford University Press.

Bethke Elshtain, J. (1997) *Democracy on Trial*, New York: HarperCollins.

Davila, A. (2001) "Advertising and Latino Cultural Fictions" in A. Davila and A. Lao-Montes (eds.), *Mambo Molltaje: The Latinization of New York*, New York: Columbia University Press.

"Disparities Grow in SAT Scores of Ethnic and Racial Groups" (1998) *Chronicle of Higher Education*, September 11, A42.

Dominguez, V. (1998) "Editor's Foreword: The Dialectics of Race and Culture," *Identities: Global Studies in Culture and Power* 1 (4): 297–300.

Flores, J., and Yudice, G. (1990) "Buscando América: Languages of Latino SelfFormation," *Social Text* 24: 57–84.
Foucault, M. (1970) *The Order of Things: An Archaeology of the Human Sciences*, New York: Random House.
Gilroy, P. (1993) *The Black Atlantic: Modernity and Double Consciousness*, Cambridge: Harvard University Press.
Gitlin, T. (1995) *The Twilight of Common Dreams: Why America Is Wracked by Culture Wars*, New York: Henry Holt.
Gooding-Williams, R. (1998) "Race, Multiculturalism, and Justice," *Constellations* 5 (1): 18–41.
Gordon, L. (1995) *Bad Faith and Antiblack Racism*, Atlantic Highlands, NJ: Humanities Press.
Gracia, J. (1998) *Personal communication*, December.
Grosfoguel, R., and Georas, C. S. (1996) "The Racialization of Latino Caribbean Migrants in the New York Metropolitan Area," *CENTRO Journal of the Center for Puerto Rican Studies* 8 (1–2): 199.
Hochschild, J. L. (1996) *Facing Up to the American Dream*, Princeton: Princeton University Press.
Klor de Alva, J. (1996) "Our Next Race Question: The Uneasiness between Blacks and Latinos," *Harper's* (April): 55–63.
Mato, D. (1997) "Problems in the Making of Representations of All-Encompassing U.S. Latina/o—'Latin' American Transitional Identities," *The Latino Review of Books* 3 (1–2): 2–7.
Moody-Adams, M. (1997) "Excitable Speech: A Politics of the Performative," *Women Review of Books* 15 (1): 13–14.
Oboler, S. (1995) *Ethnic Labels, Latino Lives: Identity and the Politics of (Re)Presentation in the United States*, Minneapolis: University of Minnesota Press.
Omi, M., and Winant, H. (1986) *Racial Formations in the United States: From the 1960s to the 1980s*, New York: Routledge.
Oquendo, A. R. (1998) "Re-imagining the Latino/a Race" in Richard Delgado and J. Stefancic (eds.), *The Latino/a Condition: A Critical Reader*, New York: New York University Press.
Rodriguez, C. E. (1989) *Puerto Ricans Born in the U.S.A.*, Boston: Unwin Hyman.
Schlesinger Jr., A. M. (1992) *The Disuniting of America: Reflections on a Multicultural Society*, New York: W. W. Norton.
Williams, P. (1997) *Seeing a Color Blind Future: The Paradox of Race*, New York: Farrar, Straus, and Giroux.
Zack, N. (1993) *Race and Mixed Race*, Philadelphia: Temple University Press.

Notes

1 I do not mean to imply here that the recent marketing construction of a panLatina/o U.S. identity is the first or only time such an identity has been imagined. I will discuss this further on.
2 As a Panamanian American who vividly remembers the 1989 U.S. invasion but who has lived most of my life in the United States, growing up especially around Cubans, I found both arguments persuasive.
3 I am very aware of the paradoxical way this question is raised (since in a project of deracialization one shouldn't refer to people by their color), and of other paradoxes with the categories I've used at times in this paper (e.g. the use of the category "black" when I have argued that it is oppressive). It is impossible to avoid all such paradoxes while maintaining clarity about which groups one is trying to pick out. All I can hope to have done is to problematize all such categories, and increase our self-reflectiveness about them.
4 And I would suggest that even John Leguizamo's brilliant comic use of terms like "Spic-o-rama" plays off the negative connotations of the term rather than transforming it into a positive term.
5 Jorge J. E. Gracia gave me substantive help with this paper at all stages, for which I am extremely grateful. I am also very grateful to Pablo De Greiff, Eduardo Mendieta, Paula Moya, Angelo Corlett, and an anonymous reviewer for their helpful comments.

Reading Questions

1. What does it mean to say that Latina/o identity is a social construction?
2. Why should we care about the identity category of Latina/o? Why not just reject any fixation on identity?

3. According to Alcoff, what criteria should determine how we construct Latina/o identity?
4. Describe the debate about whether group identities should be celebrated. In what ways have you seen this debate continue to play out?
5. Why does Alcoff conclude that Latina/o identity isn't merely a racial identity?
6. Why does Alcoff conclude that Latina/o identity isn't merely an ethnic identity?
7. Do you think Latina/o identity is racial, ethnic, ethnoracial, or something else? Why?

2 Identities

General and Particular

Jorge J. E. Gracia

The difficulties raised by social identities are many, complex, and confusing. They have at least two sources: first, the very notion that there are overall and general social identities for groups at all; second, the fact that this kind of identity seems to dissolve into many other, more particular, identities. We are Latinos, but some of us are also Puerto Ricans or Mexicans. Can we make sense of this? Can we talk meaningfully about a Latino identity and Latino identities? These questions take on added significance when the social and political implications of the use of social identity labels is considered.

Two difficulties are particularly vexing. The first is a version of the old problem of the one and the many: How is it possible for someone to have an overall, general identity, such as Latino, and at the same time have other, less general ones, such as Mexican and Tarahumara? Does it make sense for the same person to have several social identities, and if so, how is this to be understood?

The second problem has to do with the question of what social identities entail. Does having these identities entail common properties that constitute the ground for the identities and distinguish between those who have the identities and those who do not? At first our intuitions seem to justify this idea, but upon reflection serious difficulties come up. For it is far from clear that the members of a group that signals a social identity of the sort Latino is, share any properties.

In this chapter, I suggest that the issue of identity among Latinos presents us with at least two major dilemmas. One is a choice between what I label *generalism* and *particularism*, and the other between *essentialism* and *eliminativism*. I argue that there is a third alternative to the second dilemma that favors neither essentialism nor eliminativism, and that there should be no need to choose between generalism and particularism, for both positions have something valuable to offer in context. In short, I reject the dilemmas and propose a more nuanced solution to the problem of identity among Latinos which should open the way for dealing with the social and political significance of Latino identities. I call this the Familial-Historical View of Latino identities.

The issue I take up here and the solution I offer to the difficulties it poses are closely related to two other topics that have received some attention recently. The first concerns the number and kind of identities that persons can have. The examples I have provided are of ethnic identities because our topic here is Latino identity and this is an ethnic identity. But ethnic identities, although extraordinarily important, both personally and socially, are only one kind of social identity. Other social identities frequently mentioned these days include racial, gender, sexual, religious, and national, to name just a few.

The second topic that is receiving considerable attention today is the way these various identities are related to each other and how they are negotiated by both individual persons and particular groups. What difference does it make personally and socially if a person is both Latina and female, or if she is Angla and female? And what of a man who is Anglo but gay and one who is Anglo but heterosexual? Even a superficial perusal of these cases indicates that there are differences, sometimes significant, because ethnic identities often include behavioral patterns and views about gender orientation and sexuality. And matters become even more complex when we consider national identities, particularly because in some cases the same terms used to refer to them are also used to refer to ethnic ones. 'Mexican' is used to talk about Mexican nationals and ethnic Mexicans whether they are also nationals or not. So how do these different identities function within an individual person and within society? This topic is sometimes discussed under the label 'intersectionality.' Obviously, both the question concerning the number and kind of identities persons have, as well as the issue of intersectionality, are related to the questions I raise in this chapter, and whatever one concludes about them will affect the topic of the chapter. However, it would be impossible to give them the kind of treatment they deserve, and so I must put them aside for another time.[1]

I. Two Dilemmas

Let me begin by formulating the two dilemmas. Here is the first:

> Either there is one general Latino identity or many particular Latino identities. If there is one general identity, then there cannot be many particular ones, and if there are many particular ones, then there cannot be one general identity.

According to this dilemma, we cannot maintain that I am both Latino and Cuban, for example. I am one or the other, and to be one precludes that I am the other. Let me call this conundrum the *Generalism vs Particularism Dilemma*. The idea is that more general identities preclude more particular ones, and vice versa, because one can have one and only one group identity of the sort we are talking about. In our especial case, the general Latino identity precludes more particular identities, such as Cuban or Mexican, and each of these particular identities precludes a general one. We must, therefore, choose one identity and discard the talk about the others.

The problem is that no matter which horn of the dilemma we choose, we end up dissatisfied. The rejection of an overall Latino identity appears to be as unsatisfactory as the rejection of particular identities, because we both understand and feel right when we are described as, say, Latino and Cuban, Latino and Mexican, or Tarahumara and Mexican. The second dilemma runs as follows:

> Either there is an essential set of properties entailed by an ethnic identity or there is not. If there is such a set, all those persons who instantiate the properties in the set also share in the Latino identity. But if there is no such a set of properties, then there is no group of persons who share the identity.

According to this dilemma, I cannot maintain that I am Latino or Cuban, or have the Latino or Cuban identity, unless I can point to a set of necessary properties that I share with other Latinos or Cubans. Let me call this the *Essentialism vs Eliminativism Dilemma*. The thought here is that an essence is necessary for the concept of a group identity. Latino or Cuban identities require essences, otherwise they do not exist. But this dilemma, just as the first, leaves us dissatisfied because neither of its horns is acceptable. The facts seem to contradict it: we seem not to share an essential set of properties with the other members of the social groups to which we belong, and yet we seem to have these identities. [. . .]

Essentialism vs Eliminativism

Essentialism is the view according to which things have essences and essences consist of sets of properties that characterize the things that have those essences. In common philosophical jargon: sets of necessary and sufficient conditions. Thomas Aquinas was an essentialist with respect to human nature, for example, because according to him, human beings share a set of properties specified in a definition that expresses their essence: humans are rational animals. If one is an essentialist with respect to Latino identity or Mexican identity, one holds that there is a set of such properties that characterizes anyone who is Latino or Mexican.

At the opposite end of the spectrum we have the view that there are no essences. Jean-Paul Sartre was an eliminativist with respect to human essence. His position is known as existentialism rather than eliminativism, because he argued that humans exist (whence the term existentialism), but what they are (their essence) is the result of their individual free choice. I prefer to call it eliminativism in this context, rather than existentialism, for two reasons: its negative claim about essence and the fact that this term is used in the recent literature concerned with social identities.[2] According to Sartre, we are free to choose what we want to be, and there is no set of properties that we necessarily share. When this view is applied to our question, the answer is that there is no such a thing as a Latino, or even a Mexican identity, for there is no essence to them. There are only individual identities forged by individual humans. [. . .]

I claim that the alternatives from which to choose are not just essentialism and eliminativism, or generalism and particularism, but that there is a third alternative to essentialism and eliminativism, which if adopted also opens a third alternative to generalism and particularism. The notion of identity does not require that one subscribe to essentialism or that identities be exclusive of each other. It is possible for the same person or persons to share a variety of identities, some of which are more general and some less general. One can be Latino, Mexican, and Tarahumara. But how is this possible? By taking into account the relational, contextual, and historical nature of identity.

II. Four Basic Questions about Identity

One way to make this point clear is by asking four questions:

1. How do identities function?
2. How do identities arise?
3. How do identities endure?
4. What does having an identity entail?

The first question is intended to ask for the use we make of identities. Let's look at a concrete case, say, me. I am Cuban, but I am also considered to be Latin American and Latino. It would be difficult to contradict anyone who says that I am one of these, and in fact I feel quite comfortable when I am described in these ways. I was born in Cuba, of Cuban parents. When I hear Cuban music I have difficulty keeping my feet still. I love hot weather, the beach, the sweet/sour humor from the island, and the easygoing, friendly attitude of

Cubans. When I encounter a group of Cubans at a gathering, I tend to gravitate toward them because I feel comfortable in their company, never mind their political allegiance. And a few years ago, when I decided that I was going to collect art, I decided to do it with Cuban-American art. And what kind of pieces do I collect? All sorts, but some of them clearly have a connection to my particular Cuban experience. One example is Alberto Rey's painting of *El Morro*, one of the architectural icons of Havana. El Morro is a fortress that guards the port of Havana, and is the first and last thing one sees when arriving or departing by boat from the Havana harbor. Rey's painting is done mono-chromatically in shades of grey, which is exactly what I saw in 1961 when I was leaving the port at dusk on my way to West Palm Beach. Would I have acquired the painting if I were not Cuban and not had the experience of leaving? Perhaps, because it is a stunning rendition of an impressive structure. But the fact that I am Cuban and the painting arouses certain feelings and memories surely had something to do with it.

But I am also Latino, am I not? I feel that way in particular when I travel to Europe, or when I am in the company of Anglo Americans. I am not part of them in some significant ways—I am from another part of the world. And they agree. For some Spaniards, those with stereotypical ideas and prejudices against Latin Americans, who indiscriminately lump all of us together, I am a Sudaca (even if coming from Cuba), and for Anglo Americans I am a Hispanic. Moreover, I share a strong kinship with the places I have visited in Latin America. I have traveled almost everywhere in Mexico—indeed, I know Mexico better than most Mexicans. I can identify with the food, the music, the courtesy of the Mexicans. I am married to an Argentinian (yes, they are Latinos too, in spite of what many of them think). So I have learned to cook *bife a la plancha*, and *dulce'e leche* sends me to Olympus (it is almost as good as *dulce'e guayaba*).

And I feel Latino. I have strong ties to other Latinos in the United States and elsewhere, and with them I feel something different from what I feel when I am with Latinos who live in Latin America. And I also act Latino. Indeed, I was the founding member and first chair of the American Philosophical Association Committee for Hispanics in Philosophy, so I have been committed to a certain course of action, promoting the interests of Latinos for some time. Whenever possible I try to help Latino graduate students and young philosophers in their careers, and often I encourage them to learn something about their intellectual heritage.

These examples illustrate both feelings of solidarity and certain actions I take. I feel Cuban, Latin American, and Latino, but I also act in certain ways, gravitating toward Cubans at parties, collecting Cuban-American art, visiting Latin American countries, eating certain foods, and promoting the interests of other Latinos and of Latino cultures. Let me summarize the point by saying that I both *feel* and *act* in accordance with my Cuban, Latin American, and Latino identities. These are two major functions of identities: they generate feelings of solidarity with certain people and they give rise to certain actions that otherwise would probably not take place.[3]

Now for the second question: How do identities arise? Well, how did I become Cuban and Latino? Surely the factors involved are many and variegated. The tendency these days is to focus on one factor to the exclusion of others. I constantly hear the mantra that the United States government created Hispanic identity—this in spite of the fact that the term "Hispanic" was in use long before United States bureaucrats adopted it to refer to people like me and that it was picked by United States bureaucrats precisely because it was available. I also hear that United States international policies created Hispanic identity—and this in spite of the fact that Latinos were talking about themselves as a group long before there was a United States at all. The first distancing and contrast developed in Latin America was not between Latin America and the United States, but between *criollos* (descendants of Iberians born in Latin America) and *peninsulares* (born in Iberia), although the membership of these divisions fluctuates from place to place. I have not yet heard that Cuban identity was created by anybody, but perhaps some will argue that it is the United States again that is responsible for it. If this were true, then I really would be a rather curious artifact, created by the United States. Am I? Just tell the father of the Cuban nation, José Martí, that he was a United States created artifact! He talked about Hispanics and "our America" long before United States bureaucrats thought of putting all of us together under a label.

Do I want to deny that there is some truth to the claims concerning the influence of the United States on Latino identities? Of course not. American foreign policy, American bureaucrats, and the United States government have had to do with the creation of much that I am. But, contrary to what many believe, the United States is not as powerful as it thinks. Indeed, it has proven to be very ineffective insofar as it often fails to accomplish much that it tries to do in the world. And although it is true that the United States may have been responsible to some extent for the creation of some Latino countries and United States bureaucrats have helped consolidate a Hispanic identity in this country, it is just not the case that this extends to all countries of Latin America or makes the United States government and its bureaucrats solely responsible for Latino identities in the United States or elsewhere.

My identities are not the result of an act or acts of political or economic fiat, whether American or otherwise. There is more to their origin than this. Any one-sided attempt to analyze the origin of my identities, and for that matter of any other identities, is simply inaccurate. Identities are the result of complex historical processes that shape us individually and as groups. Isolation contributes to them, provided that there is also some other identity with which they can be contrasted. Being on an island is certainly a major factor in the development of a Cuban identity. Particular events tie people in certain ways and separate them in others. A war, a dispute, a treaty, a natural disaster, topography, an invasion, government actions, migrations, economic forces, the publication of a book, all these are important factors in the construction of identities. Some of these factors do not consist in conscious efforts to create identities, and indeed most of them do not. The formation of identities involves both conscious and unconscious factors. In the contemporary philosophical jargon, identities, including social ones, are the result of both "internal" (what we think) and "external" (causes other than our thought) factors. This is the answer to the second question concerning how identities arise.

And what are we to say to the third question: How do identities endure? Well, how is it that I personally endure as Jorge J. E. Gracia? We must acknowledge that the key to the answer is that I change and yet remain the same. Certainly I am not the baby that wet its diapers in the early forties. I might get to the stage of wetting diapers again, if I live long enough, but somehow that situation will not be the same as it was in the early forties. I remain the same while I also change. Change is of the essence when it comes to endurance, and this applies to social identities. Cuban identity has changed and has been affected by events during the past one hundred years, and the same could be said about Latino identity. This very discussion might affect Latino identity insofar as it might modify how some of us think about it and promote events—publications, discussions, and so on—that will influence not only our feelings, but also our actions.

Change is of the essence for certain identities; survival requires adaptation, and adaptation involves change. Consider the need for change in organisms. Evolution has demonstrated that change is necessary for the survival of species, and the same could be said when it comes to organic individuals. We survive because we adapt to new circumstances. How is it that some species have endured whereas others have been annihilated? How is it that I am still alive while many of my friends from high school are dead? Without change, most species and individuals would die out in time as a result of the challenges they have to face in their environment.

Now let me turn to the fourth and crucial question: What does having an identity entail? We know that an identity is a source of feelings and actions, it originates through conscious and unconscious historical processes, and it is subject to change. If this is so, then it would seem that the two dichotomies we considered earlier fail to explain what Latino identity, or for that matter any other group identity, is. Essentialism appears misguided insofar as it does not allow for change. If an identity entails a fixed number of unchanging properties, then endurance is doubtful. Yet, the fact that an identity is a source of feelings and actions points to its existence, so eliminativism cannot be right either. Indeed, the discussion of the various identities that have a claim on me, some more general (Latino) and some more particular (Cuban), indicate that the generalism vs particularism dichotomy also does not work. But, then, in what does an identity consist, and what does it entail?

Clearly, it cannot consist in a set of unchanging, essential properties. Identities need to be conceived as flexible, contextual, historical, and relational. The position I propose, the Familial-Historical View, satisfies these conditions. I have discussed it in greater detail elsewhere in the context of Hispanics in particular and ethnic groups in general, and therefore here I limit the presentation to its fundamental tenets in order to avoid duplication. Let me apply it to the case of Latinos.

III. The Familial-Historical View of Latino Identities

Alexander Crummell and W. E. B. Du Bois were the first to make use of the notion of a historical family to explain the unity of social groups, but they did it in the context of race. The former gives only a sketchy idea of what he has in mind, and therefore is of no help to us here. Du Bois is more specific. After rejecting the nineteenth-century biological view of race, he presents his sociological position in an often-quoted passage:

> the history of the world is the history, not of individuals, but of groups, not of nations, but of races. What then is a race? *It is a vast family of human beings*, generally common blood and language, *always common history, traditions and impulses*, who are both voluntarily and involuntarily striving together for the accomplishment of certain more or less vividly conceived ideals of life.[4]

A race is a family that always has a common history, traditions, and impulses, although other things, such as language and blood, also enter into the mix. Elsewhere Du Bois returns to the kinship provided by history:

> [O]ne thing is sure and that is the fact that since the fifteenth century *these ancestors of mine and their descendants have had a common history*; have suffered a common disaster and have one long memory. The actual ties of heritage between the individuals of this group vary with the ancestors that they have in common with many others. But the physical bond is least and the badge of color relatively unimportant save as a badge; *the real essence of this kinship is its social heritage* of slavery; the discrimination and insult;

and this heritage binds together not simply the children of Africa, but extends through yellow Asia and into the South Seas.[5]

This is still not enough for our purposes, because Du Bois does not sufficiently dwell on what he takes a racial family to be, or specify what he means by history and the pertinent aspects of it for his view. The vagueness of this position has led to a number of criticisms and interpretations. Is he an essentialist or a non-essentialist? He seems to waver.[6] If his view is essentialistic, then it would be of no help to us insofar as we need an alternative to essentialism. And if it is not essentialistic, then we need more than he has given us in order to apply the view to Latinos.

I propose, instead, to use the version of the Familial-Historical View I have defended elsewhere and apply it to Latinos.[7] It is more developed, containing some of the specific elements missing in Du Bois, and can effectively answer the objections based on the difficulties posed by the individuation of races and ethne.... Here is the formula:

> Latino identities are identities of Latino ethne, and Latino ethne are sub-groups of individual humans that satisfy the following conditions: (1) they belong to many generations; (2) they are organized as families and break down into extended families; and (3) they are united through historical relations that produce features which, in context, serve (i) to identify the members of the groups and (ii) to distinguish them from members of other groups.

The fundamental tenet of this formulation is that ethnic groups, such as Latinos, Mexicans, or Dominicans, are best conceived as constituting extended historical families whose members have no identifiable properties, or set of properties, that are shared by all the members throughout the existence of the familial groups, but that the historical connections that tie them give rise to properties which are common to some members of the groups and, in context, serve to distinguish them from other social groups. The lack of common properties accounts for the lack of agreement concerning any particular conditions, or even kinds of conditions, that are necessary and sufficient for Latino identity in general, or any Latino identities in particular. Even the most superficial consideration of available research points to difficulties in the identification of any such conditions. According to the Familial-Historical View of Latino identities, then, we must abandon the project of trying to develop essentialistic conceptions of those identities. And the relations that tie Latinos as well as the properties some of us share account for both our individuation and identification.

The common properties that this view rejects are significant first-order properties. I am not speaking about trivial properties such as the property of belonging to the group, or second-order properties such as identity. I mean primarily phenotypical or genotypical properties, such as skin color and capacities, or cultural properties, such as tastes and values, frequently associated with ethne. This means, in turn, that in order to be Latino or Puerto Rican it is not necessary that one share a first-order property (or set of properties) with other members of the group.[8] Latinos may lack Spanish fluency and be Latinos, just as Jews may be atheists and be Jews. Indeed, contrary to what some philosophers and sociologists think, it is not even necessary that Latinos name themselves in particular ways or have a conscious sense of belonging to the group of Latinos. Some of them may in fact consider themselves so and even have a consciousness, or sense, of themselves as a group, but it is not necessary that all of them do. After all, Latino children and people suffering from Alzheimer's disease cannot be expected to have a sense of Latino identity and yet their identity is not questioned for that reason, and the same applies to Latino groups, such as Puerto Ricans or Dominicans. . . .

Latinos and Latino groups are tied by the same kind of thing that ties the members of a family. We are related, as a mother is to a daughter, and grandparents to grandchildren. The notion of family does not require genetic ties. One does not need to be tied by descent to other members of a family to be a member of the family.[9] Indeed, perhaps the most important foundation of a family, namely marriage, takes place between persons who are not related by descent but by contract. In-laws become members of families indirectly, again not through genesis. And the same applies to Latinos: it is not necessary that one share a property or set of properties with others who also have Latino identity. Are all Latinos conscious of a Latino identity? Do all Mexicans have a sense of themselves as Mexican? How about the *campesino* lost in the ravines of the Copper Canyon? How about the descendants of the Maya living in isolation, somewhere in Yucatan? This extends to knowledge of the group's history. Being Latino or ethnically Mexican does not entail knowing anything about Latino or Mexican history, and even less having an accurate knowledge of those histories.

History generates relations that in turn generate properties among Latinos and serve to unite us among ourselves and to distinguish us from others in particular contexts. The use of the Spanish language is one of the properties that unites many Latinos and can serve to distinguish us from other ethnic groups in certain contexts. Some Latinos in the southwest are united by their knowledge of Spanish and this serves also to distinguish them from most Anglos who live in that part of the country. They speak Spanish as a result of certain historical events, such as the invasion and colonization of the southwest by Spaniards in the sixteenth century. Had these events not occurred, these Latinos would not know any Spanish, but they would still be Latinos if the southwest had been invaded and colonized by the Portuguese.

The same could be said about a Mexican identity. Do all Mexicans have to share something that characterizes them? Do they have to share values, a biological feature, a physical mark, or even a cultural trait? There seems to be nothing like that which ties all Mexicans, and this in spite of the strong efforts of the Mexican government at ethnic homogenization for the purpose of nation building. Mexicans share a history, a past, and certain relations that tie them in various ways. Factors such as territory, religion, political organization, and values need not be common to everyone who shares in the Mexican identity. But everyone who shares in this identity must be tied in some ways to other people who share in it. The ties, however, can be different, and they can also change throughout time and location. Identities are messy, just like reality. There are no Euclidean triangles in the world, the Euclidean triangle is an idealization. Yet, the notion of a triangle is of much use to us. Likewise, it is not necessary that there be neat, clear, and fixed boundaries between Latinos and non-Latinos, or between Cubans and Mexicans, just as there are no such boundaries between families.

Although historical events and relations tend to generate common properties in ethne, such properties are usually restricted to certain periods, regions, or subgroups within an ethnos. Latino identity entails both unity and distinction in a world of multiplicity such as ours, and unity and distinction are easily understandable when there are properties common to all the members of a group, but such properties are not necessary. The unity and distinction of Latinos can be explained as long as there are relations or properties that tie each member of the group with at least one other member without assuming that there are common properties to all members. Of course, in most cases the tie will not be with just one member, but with several, as happens with families. Indeed, the number of members involved is not as important as the various ties and whether these ties are significant for the ethnic group. Elsewhere I have argued that it is not possible to establish what these ties are for all ethnic groups, but that the particular group and its historical reality determine what they are in each case, and so they may vary substantially. The single most important factor for Jews to be Jewish is that their mothers be Jewish. But other ethnic groups emphasize the relationship with the father, and many do not have this kind of genetic requirement, but are more concerned with other human relations and with culture.[10]

The unity of Latinos, Cubans, Argentinians, Brazilians, and Tarahumara does not involve commonality; it is a familial-historical unity founded on historical relations and the properties they generate in context among members of the group. This is one reason why membership in the groups that share identities is neither permanent nor closed. Latino identities, like all identities, are fluid, open, and changing; those who share in them come and go, enter and leave, as they forge new relations, among themselves and with others, which depend on particular and contingent circumstances.[11] If we use the Familial-Historical View of Latino identities, we can understand how these identities do not require that we subscribe to essentialism. There is no essential core of properties required for an identity of the sort Latinos share. But the lack of an essence does not entail the lack of an identity; it does not entail eliminativism.

The view I propose recognizes that when the classification of particular persons comes up, there will be some cases in which classification is clear and some in which it is not. A Cuban American who came from Cuba last year, does not know English, and lives immersed in a Cuban-American environment is surely Cuban American. And I think I have shown above that I am obviously Latino: I act Latino, I feel Latino, both Latinos and Anglos think of me as Latino, and I was born in a country that is part of Latin America. On the other hand, Bill Clinton is not Latino. He does not think of himself as Latino, he does not act Latino, others do not think of him as Latino, and he was born in the United States and from non-Latino ancestry. So it seems that the cases of the Cuban American mentioned, of Bill Clinton, and of myself are clear and decidable. But not every case is like this. What do we make of my granddaughter Clarisa? Her mother is my daughter, but her father has pure English ancestry and was born in Canada, and she takes after her father's family in looks and temperament. Is she Latina? And what will we make of her children if she turns out to marry another Anglo, and they never have any contact with Latinos? These are cases in which Latino identity is up for negotiation, but this should not militate against the idea of a Latino identity. That the case of my great grandchild is difficult to decide, or perhaps even impossible, or that the decision needs to be made contextually and in terms of negotiation, does not alter the fact that I am Latino and Bill Clinton is not.

Elsewhere I made this point clear by noting that many of our concepts have members that clearly belong, some that clearly do not belong, and others that are unclear.[12] A mistaken assumption about ethnic categories is that they must have clear and strict boundaries so that their membership is never in doubt. This is quite out of step with the conditions under which we accept many of our most valued categories and concepts, so there is no reason why we should impose on ethnicity, conditions without which we are willing to do in other cases.

Consider, for example, as common a concept as "most of the Xs," as we use it when we say "Most of the students who are taking my course in ethnicity this semester will pass it." Everyone understands what this means, but when one looks at the situation more closely, it is clear that the membership of the category is clear in some instances but not in others. Say that the course has 20 students enrolled. In this case, it is clear that "most of the students" does not refer to 1, 2, 3, 4, 5, 6, 7, 8, 9, or 10 students, for these would not be most of the students. Nor is it 20, for that would be all of the students. It is also clear that most of the students would cover 19, 18, and 17. But once we get below 17 questions arise. Can one consider 11, 12, 13, 14, 15, and 16 to constitute most of the students? Interestingly enough, the total number of students affects also the numbers in doubt. If the course has an overall enrollment of 10, then clearly 1 through 6 and 10 are not most of the students; 9 and 8 do constitute most of the students; but what do we make of 7? Here it is only one number that seems to be in doubt, rather than the 6 numbers in the case of 20. Now, if we increase the number of students to 50, then we will find that the number in doubt is even larger than in the case of 20.

Two things are clear from this example. First, the category "most of the Xs" has members that are in doubt and members that are not. Second, the exact number of members that are in doubt depends very much on the particular number that constitutes the totality, which means that it results from contextual factors particular to the situation. None of this, however, stands in the way of our using the concept "most of the Xs," and certainly we do not think any less of the category to which this concept refers because of it. There is no reason, then, to assume that, because a particular category has an undetermined membership, it is useless or must be abandoned. And this applies obviously to the category of Latinos.

The Familial-Historical conception of Latinos serves to explain in particular how the same person can share in different identities, for the conditions of one identity need not preclude another. I can be Latino and Cuban. If there is no fixed necessary set of properties that I have to have for membership in each of these groups, the grounds for incompatibility between these identities diminishes considerably. There is always the possibility of accommodation and negotiation, particularly when change is essential for identity preservation.

Finally, the adoption of this position makes clear that the use of more general labels to describe more general identities does not entail rigid parameters of homogenization, nor does it exclude the use of less general labels to indicate more particular identities. This is important insofar as a great objection against all talk about general identities is precisely that they homogenize and preclude the use of more particular ones. If I have to choose between being Latino and being Mexican, someone says, I prefer being Mexican, for that is closer to me. But if we adopt the Familial-Historical View of Latino identities, this kind of conflict and choice is not inevitable. For each of these labels indicates something about me that is important, and this is not a set of properties that defines and confines me.

A Latino identity is a historical marker. It tells me that I am here and I am now a part of a group within which I fit in many ways. It does not tell me that I am like everyone else in the group and different from everyone else who does not belong to the group, or that I have been and will continue to be what I am. Rather, it tells me that I am part of the group because I am related in various ways to other members of the group and that I have properties that these relations generate in context with some members of the group, and that all these relations and properties set me and other members of the group apart from other groups. I am not part of those other groups because either I have no relations with their members or because the relations I share with them do not justify membership and thus identity, or even because I do not share with them certain properties that in context identify the groups that have them. Clearly I am not Jewish—I share no history with the Jews and there are no properties resulting from that history that I also have. And the citizenship relation I share with other Americans does not warrant Latino identity, because citizenship is not an ethnic marker for Latinos. This reference to nationality and its close relation to ethnicity requires that I say something about it in passing.[13]

IV. Ethnicity and Nationality

In the discussion of ethnic identities I have frequently used terms that can also refer to national identities and I have used examples of national identities to make a point about the relationship between different identities. But nationality and ethnicity should not be confused. A nation is a voluntary political organization of people based on a system of laws devised for the regulation of the relations and governance of the members of the group of people who accept it in a certain territory with the aim of ensuring justice and the good of all members. Belonging to a nation is ultimately a matter of political will, laws, territory, justice, and the well-being of its members, whereas this is not the case with ethnicity. Ethnicity has to do with historical relations of various sorts that contingently tie people.

The identification of nationality and ethnicity, however, is widespread.[14] Its origin goes back at least to the eighteenth century.[15] It has at least three sources. One is that nations require some foundation. The glue that binds nations together is the political will of a people to live under a system of laws that regulate the relations of the members of the nation, and this in turn involves a certain degree of self-identification of the members with the group. But this also requires that there be some common background to the members of the group. If they are going to self-identify with the group and accept certain laws, there must be some common values and shared assumptions. Moreover, self-identification requires symbols through which the members of the group can unite, such as flags, celebrations, anthems, and particularly traditions.[16] Naturally, these could also be part of the ethnicity of the members of the group, and can be easily considered ethnic elements because ethnicity tolerates all kinds of features, and particularly cultural ones. So this leads some to think that a nation is, after all, an ethnos. The mistake here is that the requirements for nationality are minimal if compared with the requirements for ethnicity. Agreement about living together under certain laws is not enough to constitute an ethnos. More is required. The foundational structure of nationality is too basic and skeletal to sustain an ethnos. This is in fact a substantial advantage, for it makes possible for nations to be constituted by many ethnic groups.

A second reason why ethnicity is frequently identified with nationality is that, just as in the case of race, nationality can give rise to ethnic features. If the key to ethnicity is the historical relations among members of a group, then a nation constitutes a powerful factor of ethnicity generation. Nations force their members to deal with each other, consign them to a territory helping develop their relations further, and bring them together in all sorts of ways. Moreover, isolation from other nations and groups helps the process. And, as is well known, nations often try to promote the ethnic (and even racial) homogenization of their members in order to create stronger national bonds and make governing easier.[17] Indeed, in some cases attempts have been made to make a certain ethnicity a condition of membership in certain nations.[18] And it is often the case that, even after the dissolution of a political group, an ethnic feeling remains in the group.[19] But, again, this does not mean that we need or should conflate the notions of ethnos and nation. It only means that one can contribute to the origin of the other in particular circumstances and that the categories can overlap or even coincide in certain contexts.

A third reason why nationality is often conceived in ethnic terms has to do with the legitimate complaints of ethnic groups in states in which they are oppressed. The Kurds in Iraq felt for a long time that their only way to terminate the oppression they have suffered in the Iraqi state because of their ethnicity was to liberate themselves and form a sovereign state themselves. Obviously, their experience of ethnic discrimination led them to think that the only way to avoid it is by forming an ethnic state of which they are the nation.[20] Oppression, however, is not a sufficient reason for the ethnic understanding of nations insofar as there are other ways of doing away with such oppression without incurring the problems that result from the creation of ethnic states.

We need, then, to keep in mind that, although closely related, the notions of nationality and ethnicity are not the same. Moreover . . . some pernicious consequences often follow in countries where ethnicity and nationality are not distinguished. In the present context the confusion does not rise with the Latino ethnos, for there is no such nation as the Latino or Latin American nation. But when we use terms such as Mexican or Cuban, we must be clear as to whether we are using the terms for ethne, nations, or a combination of the two.

V. Latino Identities

In conclusion, to reject essentialism does not force us to reject Latino identities, and to accept the value of particular identities does not, prima facie, preclude general identities. That Latinos share no essence does not mean that we do not share a general identity. And the same applies to more particular identities such as Mexican or Dominican. Moreover, that we are Latinos does not entail that we reject the Mexican identity some of us have, or vice versa. We do not need to choose between generalism and particularism. We can be Latinos and Mexicans or Quechua. General and particular identities can, and do, coexist. The Essentialism vs Eliminativism Dilemma and the Generalism vs Particularism Dilemma are based on a misguided conception of identity. If we adopt the Familial-Historical View of Latino identities, the dilemmas disappear. So, yes, I am Latino and Cuban, among many other things, and all these identities serve to describe me, give rise to particular feelings in me, and function as sources of action for me.

References

Alcoff, L. M. (2006) *Visible Identities: Race, Gender, and the Self*, Oxford: Oxford University Press.
Appiah, A. (1992) *In My Father's House: Africa in the Philosophy of Culture*. New York: Oxford University Press.
Appiah, A. (2007) "Does Truth Matter to Identity?" in J. J. E. Gracia (ed.), *Race or Ethnicity? On Black and Latino Identity*, 19–44, Ithaca, NY: Cornell University Press.
Buchanan, A. (1991) *Secession: The Morality of Political Divorce from Fort Summers to Lithuania and Quebec*, Boulder, CO: Westview.
Corlett, J. A. (2003) *Race, Racism and Reparations*, Ithaca, NY: Cornell University Press.
Du Bois, W. E. B. (1940) *Dusk of Dawn: An Essay Toward an Autobiography of a Race Concept*, New York: Harcourt, Brace and Co.
Du Bois, W. E. B. (2001) "The Conservation of Races," in R. Bernasconi (ed.), *Race*, 84–92, Oxford, UK: Blackwell.
Eriksen, T. H. (1997) "Ethnicity, Race, and Nation," in M. Guibernau and J. Rex (eds.), *The Ethnicity Reader, Nationalism, Multiculturalism and Migration*, 35, Cambridge: Polity Press.
Gracia, J. J. E. (2003) *Old Wine in New Skins: The Role of Tradition in Communication, Knowledge, and Group Identity*, 67th Marquette University Aquinas Lecture, Milwaukee, WI: Marquette University Press.
Gracia, J. J. E. (2005a), *Hispanic/Latino Identity* and *Surviving Race, Ethnicity, and Nationality: A Challenge for the Twenty-First Century*, New York: Rowman & Littlefield.
Gracia, J. J. E. (2005b) *Surviving Race, Ethnicity, and Nationality: A Challenge for the 21st Century*. Lanham, Maryland: Rowman & Littlefield.
Guibernau, M. (1996) *Nationalisms: The Nation-State and Nationalism in the Twentieth Century*, Cambridge: Polity Press.

Guibernau, M. (1997) "Nations without States: Catalonia, a Case Study," in M. Guibernau and J. Rex (eds.), *The Ethnicity Reader: Nationalism, Multiculturalism and Migration*, Cambridge: Polity Press.
Jenkins, R. (1999) "Ethnicity Etcetera: Social Anthropological Points of View," in M. Bulmer and J. Solomos (eds.), *Ethnic and Racial Studies Today*, London: Routledge.
Kymlicka, W. (1997) "Ethnicity in the USA," in M. Guibernau and J. Rex (eds.), *The Ethnicity Reader, Nationalism, Multiculturalism and Migration*, 240, Cambridge: Polity Press.
Llobera, J. (1994) *The God of Modernity: The Development of Nationalism in Western Europe*, Oxford: Berg.
McGary, H. (2007) "Racial Assimilation and the Dilemma of Racially Defined Institutions" in Jorge Gracia (ed.), *Race or Ethnicity?: On Black and Latino Identity*, Ithaca, NY: Cornell University Press, 155–169. https://doi.org/10.7591/9781501727245-010.
Medina, J. (2003) "Identity Trouble: Disidentification and the *Problem* of Difference," *Philosophy and Social Criticism* 29 (6): 655–680.
Smith, A. (1986) *The Ethnic Origins of Nations*, Oxford: Blackwell.
Smith, A. D. (1994) "The Problem of National Identity: Ancient, Medieval, and Modern," *Ethnic and Racial Studies* 17: 382.
Smith, D. (2000) "Ethical Uncertainties of Nationalism," *Journal of Peace Research* 37 (4): 494.
Smith, M. G. (1986) "Pluralism, Race and Ethnicity in Selected African Countries," in J. Rex and D. Mason (eds.), *Theories of Race and Ethnic Relations*, Cambridge: Cambridge University Press.
Symposia on Gender, Race, and Philosophy, May 2005, http://web.mit.edu/sgrp.
Thompson, E. P. (1963) *The Making of the English Working Class*, New York: Pantheon Books.
Vincent, J. (1974) "The Structuring of Ethnicity," *Human Organization* 33 (4): 375–379.
Weber, M. (1997), "What Is an Ethnic Group?" in M. Guibernau and J. Rex (eds.), *The Ethnicity Reader: Nationalism, Multiculturalism and Migration*, 15–26, 19, Cambridge: Polity Press.

Notes

1 For recent discussions of intersectionality, see Medina (2003) and (Alcoff 2006). For a discussion of Medina's article, see *Symposia on Gender, Race, and Philosophy* (2005).
2 See Howard McGary, "Racial Assimilation and the Dilemma of Racially Defined Institutions," in Gracia (ed.), *Race or Ethnicity?* pp. 155–169.
3 See Kwame Anthony Appiah, "Does Truth Matter to Identity?" in Gracia (ed.), *Race or Ethnicity?* pp. 19–44.
4 Du Bois, *The Conservation of Races*, p. 74. My emphasis.
5 W. E. B. Du Bois, *Dusk of Dawn: An Essay Toward an Autobiography of a Race Concept* (New York: Harcourt, Brace and Co., 1940), p. 117. My emphasis.
6 See Appiah's discussion in *In My Father's House*, ch. 2.
7 As developed in Jorge J. E. Gracia, *Hispanic/Latino Identity* and *Surviving Race, Ethnicity, and Nationality: A Challenge for the Twenty-First Century* (New York: Rowman & Littlefield Publishers, Inc., 2005).
8 This explains why, in his attempt to characterize ethnicity, Max Weber concluded that it is not feasible to go beyond vague generalizations. Max Weber, "What Is an Ethnic Group?" in M. Guibernau and J. Rex (eds.), *The Ethnicity Reader: Nationalism, Multiculturalism and Migration* (Cambridge: Polity Press, 1997), pp. 22, 24.
9 Some have argued for necessary genetic ties among members of ethnic groups, particularly Latinos. See J. Angelo Corlett, *Race, Racism and Reparations* (Ithaca, NY: Cornell University Press, 2003), chs. 2 and 3. For a criticism of this position, see Gracia, *Surviving Race, Ethnicity, and Nationality*, ch. 3.
10 Gracia, *Surviving Race, Ethnicity, and Nationality*, ch. 3.
11 The fluidity of ethnic groups has been frequently recognized. See, Joan Vincent, "The Structuring of Ethnicity," *Human Organization* 33, 4 (1974), 376; E. P. Thompson, *The Making of the English Working Class* (New York: Pantheon Books, 1963), p. 9; Richard Jenkins, "Ethnicity Etcetera: Social Anthropological Points of View," in Martin Bulmer and John Solomos (eds.), *Ethnic and Racial Studies Today* (London: Routledge, 1999), p. 90; and Corlett, *Race, Racism, and Reparations*, chs. 2 and 3.

12 Gracia, *Surviving Race, Ethnicity, and Nationality*, pp. 59–60.
13 I say much more in chapters 5 and 6 of *Surviving Race, Ethnicity, and Nationality*.
14 J. Llobera, *The God of Modernity: The Development of Nationalism in Western Europe* (Oxford: Berg, 1994), p. 214; M. G. Smith, "Pluralism, Race and Ethnicity in Selected African Countries," in J. Rex and D. Mason (eds.), *Theories of Race and Ethnic Relations* (Cambridge: Cambridge University Press, 1986), p. x.
15 Anthony D. Smith, "The Problem of National Identity: Ancient, Medieval, and Modern," *Ethnic and Racial Studies* 17 (1994), 382.
16 For the role of tradition in the identity of groups, including national ones, see Jorge J. E. Gracia, *Old Wine in New Skins: The Role of Tradition in Communication, Knowledge, and Group Identity*, 67th Marquette University Aquinas Lecture (Milwaukee, WI: Marquette University Press, 2003).
17 M. Guibernau, "Nations without States: Catalonia, a Case Study," in M. Guibernau and J. Rex (eds.), *The Ethnicity Reader: Nationalism, Multiculturalism and Migration* (Cambridge: Polity Press, 1997), p. 5 and *Nationalisms: The Nation-State and Nationalism in the Twentieth Century* (Cambridge: Polity Press, 1996), p. 11. Indeed, Thomas Hyland Eriksen, in "Ethnicity, Race, and Nation," in Guibernau and Rex (eds.), *The Ethnicity Reader*, p. 35, points out that the distinguishing mark of nationalism is the view that "political boundaries should be coterminus with cultural [i.e. ethnic, for him] boundaries."
18 Guibernau, "Nations without States," p. 6. See also Will Kymlicka, "Ethnicity in the USA," in Guibernau and Rex (eds.), *The Ethnicity Reader*, p. 240.
19 Weber, "What Is an Ethnic Group?" in Guibernau and Rex (eds.), *The Ethnicity Reader*, p. 19.
20 Many authors argue that this aim to create a state that represents the nation is essential to nations and a nationalist spirit. See, for example, Dan Smith, "Ethical Uncertainties of Nationalism," *Journal of Peace Research* 37, 4 (2000), 494. Allen Buchanan, *Secession: The Morality of Political Divorce from Fort Summers to Lithuania and Quebec* (Boulder, CO: Westview, 1991), pp. 152–153, has proposed a list of conditions in which ethnic groups seek secession from a state. See also Anthony Smith, *The Ethnic Origins of Nations* (Oxford: Blackwell, 1986).

Reading Questions

1. Why does Gracia reject the idea that a social identity cannot consist in a set of unchanging, essential properties?
2. Does Gracia succeed in avoiding the dilemma of eliminativism or essentialism about Latinos? Why or why not?
3. Gracia is surely right that we can have overlapping identities. But what might he say about worries that some identities erase or make it tough to recognize someone's particularity?
4. In disagreements about whether to favor more and less general/particular identities (e.g., Latinx vs. Salvadorean), is there a reason to reject an answer that emphasizes both?
5. Gracia thinks that Latinos share a "familial-historical" relationship. What exactly is the historical tie that unites all Latinos, according to his account? How does that tie avoid being an essential property?
6. Is Gracia committed to there being a unified or single best concept of Latino? Or could there be different concepts for different purposes? Why or why not?

3 "Being-in-the-World-*Hispanically*"
A World on the "Border" of Many Worlds

Enrique Dussel

Translated by Alexander Stehn[1]

I do not intend to propose a utopic "cosmic race" like that of José Vasconcelos, or the "hybridity" of Néstor García Canclini, or a history interpreted literally like that of Octavio Paz in *The Labyrinth of Solitude*, but rather a moving discovery of the *hispano* as "located" creatively "in-between" many worlds that continuously constitute a historical identity on the intercultural "border."[2] This identity is neither substantialist nor essentialist but instead creates its own elements dialectically through the continuous integration of new challenges in the very process of history. But this historical experience is also normative: it must be discovered and affirmed in its dignity, especially when the present state of the *hispanic* community sets out from a negative self-evaluation of its own existence. The cultural complexity of being-in-the-world-*hispanically* must be lived subjectively, by means of active and creative intersubjectivity, which accepts challenges and integrates them rather than living them merely as a dispersion or tear.

My strategy in this contribution, originally presented in a seminar at the University of Pittsburgh, is situated in a committed pedagogical horizon that attempts to be comprehensible to a *hispano* who is neither a college student nor an academic, but rather from the social base to which I have spoken many times, from California to North Carolina at Duke, from New York to Chicago, and in many other North American universities and cities. When the *hispano* discovers his/her complex, constitutive history, he/she reacts to the comments with a certain annoyance: "Why didn't they ever tell us this? Why have they hidden our history from us in the educational system and other North American institutions?" I have responded more or less as follows: "It would be difficult for an elementary school, high school, university, labor union, or religious group to demonstrate to the *hispano* an existence[3] so rich and ancient and with such present potential. The *anglo* zealously defends his/her cultural, political, and religious superiority." In this contribution, then, I wish to maintain a colloquial tone comprehensible to the average common sense of *hispanos* in the United States; I will treat this subject like an outline for a course, seminar, or lecture for *hispanos* interested in developing their own "historical-critical consciousness."

The *hispano*,[4] like every human being,[5] lives (exists) inevitably in a "world." His/her "being-in-the-world" (Heidegger § 12, 78ff) has a "world" that has subsumed "many" worlds whose histories are not chronologically simultaneous but have instead unfolded with different rhythms and in diverse places, developing distinct contents. We name the resulting horizon "being-in-the-*hispanic*-world" as a concrete, current, and complex facticity whose intercultural riches converge to form an identity. This identity is always in formation, interstitial, born in a "border land" with such a wide range that *hispanos* pass from one tonality to another continuously without ceasing to experience themselves within *hispanic* solidarity. The *hispano* can be an indigenous Guatemalan in Chicago, a Mexican *mestizo*

DOI: 10.4324/9781003385417-6

in San Diego, a white *criollo* Uruguayan in Washington, an Afro-Caribbean Puerto-Rican in New York or Cuban in Miami, a *mulato* from the Dominican Republic in Houston, to name a few. Many worlds in one world. A world that today in the hegemonic North American society is despised, dominated, impoverished, and excluded (beyond the horizon of the acceptable *anglo* world, beyond the "line" of Heideggerian ontology, on the border where non-being, the non-sense of Levinasian alterity commences). They are the last ones on the social, cultural, and epidemiological scale (a higher percentage of them have AIDS, for example). The "*hispanic* world" is like a phantom, a specter that roams around in "exteriority" but has recently begun showing itself with a new face, acquiring new rights thanks to its struggle for recognition of a distinct existence. I believe that this struggle could serve as a model of the narrative I will present after drawing a basic map of the history and territorialization of this "*hispanic* world." Teachers, leaders, and militants in communities might use this sketch to affirm their frequently underappreciated dignity. My narrative is intended to be an ethical-pedagogical one; I do not propose to denigrate the *anglo* but simply to demonstrate and affirm dialectically the historical values of the *hispano*. It may seem tendentious, but it is not altogether bad to be an apologist for those who are depreciated, persecuted, and marginalized. I imagine each one of the five "worlds" that I suggest as a circle that coincides with the others around the *hispano*, who nonetheless maintains a certain exteriority with reference to the hegemonic world. Every *hispano* lives in and through these worlds to a greater or lesser extent.

It may be worthwhile to begin by recounting an anecdote, an experience I had years ago at the University of Notre Dame. While filling out an administrative form for my position as a professor, I had to respond to a question about my "ethnicity," which disconcerted me as obviously racist. The form began with the questions: "Are you White (non-Hispanic)?" "Are you African-American (non-Hispanic)?" "Native-American (non-Hispanic)?" and finally, "Are you Hispanic?" I asked the secretary, "What do you think?" Hearing my "accent" in English, she asked me, "You're from Mexico? Put *Hispanic*."[6] Thus was I classified by (under) the possible "ethnicities." With this anecdote, I open the present historical-cultural reflection.

I. The "First of Worlds."[7] On the "Mother's" Side

The Eastern Extreme of the Far East

When one encounters a Mexican in Los Angeles or San Jose, even if one quickly realizes that the person is, for example, a Zapotec from Oaxaca who speaks his/her Amerindian language and perhaps will shortly express himself/herself more fluently in English than in Spanish, one discovers a *hispano* who differs from many others who identify with this same cultural, historical, and political community.

In effect, the *hispano* always has a certain constitutive, originary reference to the Amerindian cultures. For one who belongs by race, language, culture, religion, or history to an indigenous community, this belonging is obviously much stronger, but in any case, *hispanos* react spontaneously to an indigenous person from Latin America as a member of their own community. This can be observed in the murals that cover numerous walls in the *hispanic* neighborhoods of North American cities (the art simultaneously so Aztec and so Mexican, which inspired Rivera, Orozco, and O'Gorman at the beginning of the twentieth century). The indigenous person frequently appears as a symbolic moment in these historical representations, not as a depreciated "native" but as a foundation upon which a historical identity is built. It is as if the painters of these murals wanted to say: "We have *always* been here! We come from Aztlán!" This referential component is essential. The *hispano* (whether indigenous or *mestizo*) relates to America as his/her "own" ancestral, originary continent (geographic and cultural) through "Malinche," his/her "mother," who provides the link with "mother earth" ("Pacha Mama" of the Andes, "Coatlicue" of the Valley of Mexico, or "Tonantzín": our little mother). This American land was originally *hispanic* on the mother's side. It was not the "vacant" land of John Locke or Walt Whitman but instead full of historical-cultural significance. More than anyone else, the indigenous person merits the name "American" (*americano*).

As we have explained in other works concerning the movement of our native peoples,[8] humanity carried out a long process of civilization creation in the Afro-Asian continent, beginning with the Neolithic cultures in present-day Turkey, with cities as old as the seventh millennium BCE in Mesopotamia, passing through Egypt in the fourth millennium, and appearing in the civilizations of India and China. Contrary to the Eurocentric Hegelian opinion, this was the "long march" towards the East—from the West to the East. We want to insert the origin of the cultural history of *hispanos* into this movement. On their maternal side, they were born in the eastern extreme of the Far East on the Asian continent—the ultimate West for America, beyond the Pacific Ocean, the central reference for the Polynesian civilizations to which the Amerindian cultures owe so much. From there, after tens of thousands of years of traveling on foot by way of the Bering Strait, always moving towards the east, they began entering America from the north (Alaska), arriving twenty thousand years later in the south (Tierra del Fuego) by the most diverse migratory routes from eastern Asia and the western Pacific. Today we are sure that all of these originary American cultures were Asian, that they passed through Mongolia, Siberia, and the islands and coasts of the western Pacific, driven out by the fiercest of peoples and fleeing towards the north. The Eskimos were the last to arrive, and they remain in Siberia and Canada to this day, perhaps originally driven out by Turkish peoples. The racial similarity, down to facial features, of our indigenous peoples with the inhabitants of Mongolia, Indonesia, the Philippines, Polynesia, and Micronesia is widely recognized.

The important thing for a reconstruction of the "historical-critical consciousness" of *hispanos* is that their native ancestors not be situated as defeated people from "nowhere," as if they fell from heaven and were just here in America on the beaches of some Caribbean islands "awaiting" the arrival of Christopher Columbus, the "discoverer" who would invest them with a "place" in history. They were the first inhabitants of America and created great urban civilizations similar to those of the Egyptians, the Mesopotamians, the people of the Indus Valley, or the people of the Yellow River, chronologically continuing the journey towards the east. Arriving from maternal Asia, they had already "discovered" the entire continent when the European invasion began in 1492.[9]

The *hispano* must experience existentially (subjectively and intersubjectively) the reality of having been on the American continent, in its valleys, rivers, mountains, jungles, etc., from the furthest reaches of human history, from millennial antiquity, "before" all of the subsequent invasions. *Hispanos* should know the dignity of being "the first," "the oldest," with respect to all those who would arrive "later." This would neither demean them nor make them superior, but facilitate their experience of the free gift of receiving those who arrived from other "worlds." *Hispanos* offered food (the "turkey" is an American, an Amerindian animal) to the European souls who disembarked hungry, and who would later celebrate by remembering the food provided to them, but forget the assassination with which they repaid those who so generously gave them hospitality with their own scarce goods in their own land.

48 *The Latinx Philosophy Reader*

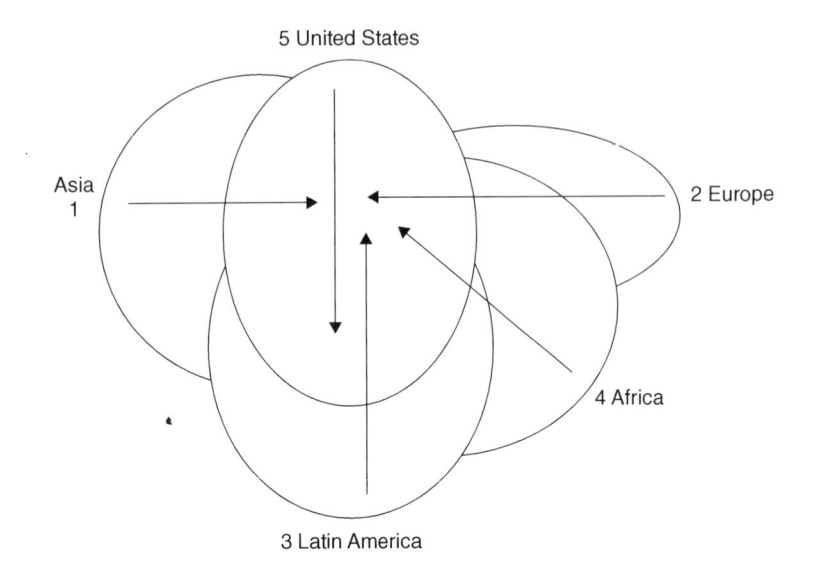

Figure 3.1 The *Hispano*: A "World" as "Border Land" Between (In-Between) Many "Worlds"

(1) From the eastern extreme of the Asian Far East; (2) From the western extreme of the European Far West; (3) The far north of the Latin American South; (4) From the west of Africa; (5) The far south of the Anglo-Saxon North.

Hispanos must know and appreciate the Amerindian world, not only the existence of nomadic communities (from the north of the United States down to the south of the Incan empire) or the planters of the Caribbean and Amazonian grasslands, but also the imposing urban cultures of "nuclear America": the Mayans, Aztecs, Chibchas, Incas, etc. The establishment of these civilizations, their historical feats, their foundational texts, their magnificent cultural, political, religious, esthetic, commercial, economic, and military structures must be recognized. *Hispanos* should study these cultures as a moment in the constitution of their own identity, which goes on changing, growing, and developing in their steps through space and time. In this case, memory is a fundamental moment in the creation of an identity of solidarity.

II. The "Second of Worlds." On the "Father's" Side: The Far West of the Western Extreme

In the fortieth century BCE, on the north of the Black Sea, there were peoples who smelted iron, domesticated the horse, and buried dead riders together with their horses.[10] This was the "Kurgan" culture (in southern Russia). Centuries later we observe an aggressive bronze statue of a rider with an iron sword in his hand, the figure of Francisco Pizarro in the main plaza of Lima, marking the arrival in America of the culture of the horse and iron. It is the history of a people that arrived in our continent by moving from east to west.

Spain and Portugal were the *finisterrae* (the end of the world) of this ancient system, which, beginning with Japan and China in the east, culminated in the west with Europe. Spain was colonized by Phoenicians in the second millennium BCE and was a province of the Roman Empire at the end of the first millennium BCE. (The Indo-European language called "Spanish" was born in the Middle Ages during the Spanish "reconquest" of the

Muslims, and it bears the closest resemblance to ancient Latin.) Spain would go on to shelter a Christianity whose plenitude (with Isidore of Seville) was replaced by the caliphate of Córdoba as cultural center (another Spanish glory that no other European country could boast), philosophical center (with Ibn-Rushd), and theological center (with Maimonides). At this time, the West obtained Latin versions of Greek works translated from Arabic or Greek itself, which in turn permitted the classical medieval thirteenth century in Paris. The "reconquest," which began in 718 in a skirmish that tradition calls the Battle of Covadonga, would last until January of 1492, when the kings of Castile and Aragon occupied Granada. This "reconquest" would be continued seamlessly as the "conquest" of America.

The Iberian countries had already begun the first Early Modernity in the fifteenth century. Spain, together with Portugal (which anticipated the Spanish undertaking by a century), would produce the opening to the Atlantic, thus constituting the "bridge" between the ancient world and Modernity. Spain and Portugal originated Modernity precisely with the "invasion" of the West Indies, the *Abbia Yala* of the Kuna Indians of Panama, inadequately called "America" in honor of the Renaissance figure Amerigo Vespucci.

The cultures of the far west (Europe) of the Afro-Asian continent were never "central" with respect to this gigantic civilized space. The connecting territory was the Persian empire (the Hellenists), then the Byzantine empire (the Sassanids), a region eventually occupied by the caliphate of Baghdad, the commercial "center" of the ancient system from the eighth to the thirteenth century, the five hundred years of classical Islamic culture. Europe was never hegemonic in this sphere. In fact, the north of Europe was submerged in the barbarism of the Germanic peoples until well into the Middle Ages. The fundamental pole of the entire continent, with the greatest population, culture, and commerce, was always China and Hindustan. They were connected to the Byzantine world by the Muslim commercial civilization, which stretched from the Philippines to Spain, passing through Málaga, the Mughal Empire, and the kingdoms of the Middle East, as far as Egypt and Morocco.

The hegemony of Genoa and Venice (both Byzantine) that had connected Latin-Germanic Europe with the "ancient system" passed to Spain and Portugal by virtue of their being situated between the Mediterranean and the Atlantic, and because they achieved unity before any other country of northern Europe (Portugal in the fourteenth century and Spain in 1476 with the uniting of Castile and Aragon). Spain and Portugal initiated Modernity, not northern Europe as has been previously taught (an interpretation promulgated by northern Europe itself). The Italian Renaissance was merely the Mediterranean awakening, brought about by the fall of the Greek Constantinople, whereas Spain and Portugal inherited the Renaissance and opened the wider world of the Atlantic (the geopolitical center of Modernity). Still under the commercial hegemony of China and Hindustan, and against the Muslim Ottoman world that connected these powers with Europe, Portugal discovered the Atlantic southeast with the nautical school of Henry the Navigator, who opened Europe to the "Arab Sea" (the Indian Ocean). Spain did the same with the tropical Atlantic, connecting the Caribbean with Europe thanks to the Genovese Christopher Columbus.

The cultural collision of the easternmost part of the East (Amerindia) with the westernmost part of the West (the Iberian countries) is the most formidable intercultural confrontation in all world history. The land had already been completely occupied, but now humanity united in an embrace (fatal for the Amerindians)—the entwining of Malinche and Cortés, "two worlds" of the many that constitute "the" *hispanic* world. Their meeting is incredible but nonetheless historical, and it was made flesh five hundred years ago. It is a cultural collision that the *hispano* carries in his/her culture, blood, and history, an embrace that the *anglo* cannot comprehend, experience, or appreciate. The *hispano* has an amazing

American historical complexity, a European Latino for a "father" with behaviors befitting the Islamic refinement of Cordoba, Seville, and Granada, so far from the barbarity of Medieval Europe.

The Spanish presence in America since 1492 and that of Portugal in Brazil since 1500 preceded the Dutch and English invasion of the northern coasts of America by a century. It is the beginning of the first Early Modernity, the original deployment of the "World-System" about which Immanuel Wallerstein has spoken so accurately (see *The Modern World System*). Latin America (Amerindia plus Iberian countries) is modern from its origin. It suffers the Modernity that always begins with armed violence (in Latin America, Africa, and Asia), whose first sign is the "conquest" that begins in the Caribbean in 1492 and arrives at the Maule River in Chile in approximately 1540. "Nuclear America," which contained the majority of the continent's population, was occupied within fifty years.

Whether *mestizo* or *criollo*, the *hispano* comes into relation with a part of himself/herself when thinking about modern Europe. On the "father's" side there is the chauvinist Cortés who dominates the delicate indigenous princess Malinche in the correct interpretation of Octavio Paz's *Labyrinth of Solitude*, but the *hispano* relates nonetheless to the Amerindian cultures through his/her "mother," and also with the Spaniard, but not in the disparaging sense of the Latin Americans (the "royalists," the "gachupines"). I think that the *hispano* has a geopolitical interest in reminding *anglos* of their descent from the Spain that made England tremble with the "Invincible Armada" at the end of the sixteenth century. In fact, when Carl Schmitt wanted to give an example of the meaning of "enemy," he cited one of Cromwell's texts about the Spanish.[11] The confrontation between *hispano* and *anglo-saxon* is many centuries old, beginning before the Roman Empire but becoming especially bitter in the sixteenth century with the Spanish hegemony in Europe. Unlike England in the Atlantic Europe of the North Sea, which was Germanic, medieval, never in contact with the great Phoenician, Egyptian, and Greek cultures, and only became a part of the Roman Empire very late, Spain was situated in the Mediterranean, and was one of the historical opponents of the *anglo-saxons* (in contrast to Portugal, which in many cases was subsequently allied with England against Spain). The *hispano*, then, on the "father's" side, awakens in the *anglo* many "bad memories" (Shakespeare knew that the "One-Armed Man of Lepanto"[12] initiated modern literature). The *anglo* cannot consider *hispanos* an inferior people but, on the contrary, must consider them a more ancient, more numerous, and more developed people (all this, of course, until the early seventeenth century, with the decline of Spain and the ascendency of England).

So the *hispano* should be conscious of the fact that his/her language, culture, and Baroque religion all have a European component that cannot be denied and must be integrated with his/her Amerindian past in order to constitute an inimitable historical personality. This "other" world, which the *hispano* lives as his/her own, creatively combines with and comes to enrich the "first."

III. The "Third of Worlds." Like a "Brother/Sister" of "*Mestizo/a*" Descent: The Far North of the South

The *mestizo*, the "pocho" in Los Angeles that Octavio Paz spoke about, is a racial and cultural mixture as old as Modernity. No other race or culture can take this dignity and this stigma away from the *mestizo*. Martín Cortés, the son of Malinche and the Spanish captain, would die in Spain, forgotten for reasons not attributable to war, thus demonstrating the destiny of a *mestizo*, a symbol of forgetting one's origin and the meaning of one's existence.

The *hispano* is a synthesis (the "third of worlds"), a brother/sister of the Latin Americans (who expanded into the "North"), a descendent of the first of worlds (Malinche), the second (Cortés), and the third, the *criollo* (a white European born in America and thus American). It was one of these young *criollos* who founded the Jesuit reductions (*reducciones*) (see Dussel, *A History*) after having rowed canoes through the immense and infinite rivers of *guaraní* Paraguay, having eaten, slept, and dressed like the indigenous people of the region since childhood. The Jesuits in the reductions respected the customs of the Amerindians by going without private property, speaking Amerindian languages, and adopting local practices. The Spaniards who came from Europe could no longer understand the spirit of the *hispanos* (*criollos*) born on this continent. *Hispanos* are, for this reason, older "Americans" than those who would come later (by way of their indigenous "mothers" and the people born in these lands, whether *mestizos* or *criollos*—inhabitants of this continent since the end of the fifteenth century). The other groups who would subsequently arrive in New England (not only Africans but also Europeans from non-Anglo-Saxon regions) were fully conscious of being in a strange and already colonized land.[13] On the other hand, *hispanos* were fully conscious of the fact that these American lands were inhabited by them before any other group, including *anglos*. *Hispanos* were stripped of these lands, which were declared "vacant"; they were thus excluded from their own lands as the Canaanites were excluded from theirs when Joshua occupied Jericho, coming from the desert and having been a slave in Egypt.

The history of the Latin American side of the *hispano* develops as a colonial history from the Caribbean to *terra firma*, from Panama to Venezuela and Florida, heading south by way of the viceroyalty of Nueva Granada (northern South America, largely what is now Panamá, Colombia, Venezuela, and Ecuador) along the Pacific coast of Ecuador, Peru, and Chile, an area united by the mining of silver, then joining the colonizing current of the southwest Atlantic in the viceroyalty of Río de la Plata—Asunción and Buenos Aires. With Huancavélica and Potosí, silver (discovered in the Potosí Mountains in 1546) inundated Spain, Holland, and all of Europe. And by way of Portuguese land routes and ships, the colonizing current eventually reached China, stretching from Acapulco to Manila. Towards the north, the Latin American colonial world expanded into Central America, continental Aztec Mexico, and the realm of the Yucatecan-Guatemalan Maya. Finally, the conquering current moved north, towards the mines of Durango and Saltillo, towards California.

By 1620,[14] all of the Latin American political organization, with its viceroys, *audiencias* (appellate courts), *capitanías generales* (colonial military and administrative jurisdictions not under the charge of a viceroy), town councils, etc., had been put in place. The ecclesiastical organization, with more than thirty-five dioceses (the diocese of Durango in the north and the diocese of Buenos Aires in the south were founded this year), remained practically unchanged until the end of the eighteenth century. The Latin American colonial civilization would come to organize great universities of the rank of Salamanca (in 1553) as well as tens of university colleges and theological seminaries.[15] The "lettered city" was Baroque in the seventeenth century and entered the Enlightenment in the eighteenth.

In 1610, when arrivals from the South were reaching the far north of Mexico (the far north of Latin America), the Mexican city of Santa Fe was founded in "New Mexico" (just as Mexico was "New Spain"). In considering the southern territory currently occupied by the United States, we contemplate what was the northern region of the Latin American world—a world already more than a century old by then, with all of its libraries (like Puebla's Palafoxiana), printing presses, artistically imposing cathedrals, grand urban palaces, splendid fortified ports (like those of Havana, San Juan de Ulúa, and Cartagena de Indias), roads, aqueducts, haciendas, sugar refineries, etc. All of these institutions are prior to the origin of the Anglo-Saxon world in the American continent with the arrival of the Pilgrims in 1620. The Jesuit reductions and Franciscan missions in Texas, for example, tell us of the presence of *hispanos* in the far north of a Latin America that, from Patagonia, kept expanding northward beyond the Rio Grande/Río Bravo.

The *hispano* is, then, a Latin American, a "Latino," who, like the tip of an iceberg, is supported by an immense cultural mass that lies hidden underwater in the shadow of history. They are a population of more than four-hundred million citizens who, like the Visigoths bound for the Byzantine Roman Empire, began crossing their own Danube (the Visigoths were also "wetbacks" moving towards the south, the *hispanos* towards the north). So these Northern Latin Americans are conscious of having been in these lands since before the occupation of the desert, before anyone would cross the Appalachians, spread out by way of the Mississippi River, or reach Texas or California from the east. *Hispanos/as* are the Latin American brothers/sisters of the north, a Latin American nation to be considered as such.

IV. The "Fourth of Worlds." The Afro-Caribbean, Another *Hispano*

In their "world," *hispanos* have yet another world of extreme vitality and antiquity. It originated in 1520 in Hispaniola when the conquistadors finished extracting gold from the rivers, finished off the indigenous Taínos in like fashion, and began the sugar cycle, for which they brought the first African slaves from Spain and later directly from West Africa (see Blackburn). Thus was born the "world" of the exiled Afro-Caribbeans, which spread throughout all the islands as well as the east coast of Central America, the north of Venezuela and Colombia, the coasts of the Pacific down to Guayaquil in Ecuador, and Portuguese Brazil, where sugar and other tropical products became the most prized of the Luso-Brazilian world.

The Afro-Latin American grew up creating culture, religion, myth, and rhythm while doing the interminable work that their inhuman owners demanded. They survived thanks to their music, their dance, their spirits (*orishas*), and their amazing fortitude. The Puerto Ricans were the first Afro-Caribbean population to arrive in New York at the start of the twentieth century after the United States annexed the three Spanish island colonies of the Philippines, Cuba, and Puerto Rico in 1898. All *hispanos* adopted the rhythms of the Afro-Caribbean as their own. *Hispanos* of indigenous background and white *criollos* learned the harmonious cadences of the African drum. For this reason, the racist questions posed at the North American university—"Are you African (not Hispanic)?"—makes little sense, because the Afro-Caribbean is African *and also hispano*. *Hispanicity* neither negates nor confuses *africanicity*. It is another "world" (the fourth) that contributes to *hispanic* consciousness in the United States. They are Latino-Caribbeans, Afro-Caribbeans from Puerto Rico and the Dominican Republic with their "salsa," Cubans with their ceremonies of *Santería*, Haitians with their *Voodoo* drumbeat, and Brazilians with their *Macumba* and *Candomblé*. The *hispano* is African as well, with beautiful eyes (often Eastern from his/her "mother") and sensual African lips, moving his/her hips in the dance as only a "Latino" could. This is the complexity created "in-between" the borders of many worlds, "in-between" the interstices of many cultures.

V. The "Fifth of Worlds." The Far South of the North

England, the British Isles, has a history different from that of Spain and Portugal. Antiquity and the European Middle Ages separate them. The Franciscans founded Oxford and

Cambridge. The contingent "will" of Duns Scotus and the empiricism of the Bacons tell us of a cultural tradition distinct from that of the Dominicans, a tradition more inclined to the continental "intelligence" of Paris or Salamanca. Baroque Catholicism had little to do with Anglicanism, democratic Presbyterianism, or utopic Puritanism. The absolute Spanish monarchy, fortified by American silver, defeated the nascent Spanish bourgeoisie in 1521 at the Battle of Villalar. Moreover, millions of Jews who should have been the internal financial class of the Spanish empire were thrown out and replaced by foreigners, Renaissance Genovese merchants. In contrast, the weakness of the English monarchy permitted the first triumphant bourgeois revolution in the seventeenth century, and it was this same bourgeoisie that took charge of organizing the parliamentary state, supporting commerce, and deploying the colonial structure of the growing English empire (which would slowly replace the Iberian powers beginning in the seventeenth century). The *anglo* projected the growing British splendor of the seventeenth and eighteenth centuries back into the past and carefully hid the sixteenth century in the shadows, whereas the *hispano* must begin with the sixteenth century in order to interpret himself/herself positively and resist humiliation and domination.

In America, the first *anglo-saxons* were preceded by the Dutch. "New England" had been "New Holland," and "New York" had been "New Amsterdam." Thus, the primitive utopian communities that de Tocqueville admired so much, which avoided an England under the model of Hobbes's *Leviathan* (the absolute State), were already modern in the spirit of the "second" Early Modernity (of Amsterdam, London, and Edinburgh). In the eighteenth century, the North Americans creatively assimilated the Enlightenment and carried out "their" Industrial Revolution, not in order to diminish the proportion of wages in the value of the product but rather to permit small, free owners better production. The colonies in New England thus participated in the origin of capitalist, liberal, and industrial Late Modernity, and had no other industrial or military power on the American continent that could compete with them at their level. Their expansion was a matter of time.

The communities of the thirteen colonies of the northeast Atlantic coast, emancipated from the English yoke in 1776, began to occupy the Mexican territory towards the west (the long journey towards the "far West," which commenced by way of Louisiana—also originally a part of New Spain—and continued towards the south with Texas and the west through Arizona, New Mexico, and California). They incorporated not just the territories but also the *hispanic* population, which, having come from before, remained trapped inside a new world unknown to them, a world that came from the northeast: the world of the United States of North America. This "inclusion"—which would be continued by a slow *hispanic* dispersion from the south towards the north during a long century—would have all the characteristics of an "expulsion" (like that of the people elected under Joshua, who defeated the Canaanites at Jericho, but now with Indian or Mexican faces: *hispanos*).[16] This expulsion was not on behalf of foreign Europeans but now rather on behalf of the Americans from the north, who would expand by occupying territories and managing the *hispanic* populations that remained in the south.

The included populations were defenseless, without protection. Consider the protagonist figure of priest Martínez (see Dussel, *Fronteras*), trained in the seminary of Durango in Mexico, parish priest of Santa Fe in New Mexico. He was elected as a delegate to represent his province in Mexico City on various occasions, then was part of the independent assembly of New Mexico as an autonomous state, and finally served as a representative of New Mexico in Washington. As a Mexican Catholic priest in rebellion against the management of the Church by "foreigners" (not *hispanos*), he would be excommunicated by Bishop

Lamy, who was of French nationality and did not understand the *hispanic* community, which made up the majority of the Catholic population there. Lamy was a bishop named by a Vatican that trusted the North American government more than the Mexican one. Thus, the *hispanos* remained a people "like sheep without a shepherd."

Over the course of a century, from 1848 until the end of World War II (1945), the *hispanic* people were ignored, oppressed, eliminated. Their language was prohibited. By their participation as soldiers in this war and in those that followed, by the growth of their population, by the massive Puerto Rican presence in the East, the Mexican presence in the Southwest, and the Cuban presence in Florida, the political importance of the *hispanic* community could no longer be silenced. The social and artistic Chicano movement, the syndicalism of people like César Chávez, the presence of "Fathers" and "Mothers" (priests and nuns) in the Catholic Church as well as the naming of many *hispanic* bishops, the appearance of political, commercial, intellectual, and artistic leaders has given the *hispanic* community the face of the largest minority in the United States. Mobilizations like those achieved against Proposition 187 in California have already demonstrated a community becoming conscious of its rights.

But the future is by no means guaranteed. The complex, rich, and "American" culture of *hispanos* needs to be creatively developed by acquiring greater political autonomy and refusing to jump on political bandwagons without first demanding conditions for the development of their communities. In fact, *hispanos* are now crucial to the election of the leaders of the United States because of their organized presence in Florida, New York, Chicago, Texas, and California. This is a historical opportunity to enrich the education of the members of the community, and these remarks might serve as a rough draft for a course, a seminar, a book of cultural history, or a sketch to teach the *hispano* to become conscious of his/her own millennial, centennial history.

Hispanos need Latin America because the nutritive "roots" of their world lie there. They need the vital reserve of millions of "brothers/sisters" who press north- ward out of a contagious hope to escape their poverty. And Latin America needs *hispanos*. We do not need *hispanos* who, upon making themselves present in the south (for example, in commercial, military, or diplomatic roles), speak the language of Latin American culture in order to impose the imperial Will to Power. We need them to make present an American culture, that of the south, in the great country of the north. This culture can show the North American citizen other continental horizons and impart an increased responsibility for the poverty of millions and for populations who are not just markets but dignified human beings. It has fallen to us to inhabit this American continent, that of the south and that of the north. We need *hispanos* in order to learn how to live with a diverse, hostile, aggressive *anglo-saxon* culture whose rationality is founded almost exclusively in the competition of *homo homini lupus*. But its rationality also has immense critical reserves with which we must organize a front in order to save the life of humanity today amidst the risk of collective suicide.

References

Bhabha, H. (1994) *The Location of Culture*, London: Routledge.
Blackburn, R. (1999) *The Making of New World Slavery: From the Baroque to the Modern 1492–1800*. London: Verso.
Dussel, E. (1966) *Hipótesis para el estudio de Latinoamérica en la Historia Universal*. Resistencia: Universidad del Nordeste.
Dussel, E. (1981) *A History of the Church in Latin America*. Grand Rapids: Eerdmans.

Dussel, E. (1983) *Fronteras: A History of the Latin American Church in the USA since 1513*. San Antonio: Mexican American Cultural Center.

Dussel, E. (1993) *El encubrimiento del Otro: Hacia el origen del mito de la modernidad*. Madrid: Nueva Uto- pia, 1993. (Trans. as *The Invention of the Americas*. New York: Continuum Publishing Group, 1995).

Dussel, E. (1998) *Ética de la Liberación en la edad de la globalización y la exclusion*. Madrid: Trotta. (Trans. as *Ethics of Liberation in the Age of Globalization and Exclusion*. Durham: Duke UP, forthcoming).

Elizondo, V. (1983) *Galilean Journey. The Mexican-American Promise*. New York: Orbis.

Heidegger, M. (1962) *Being and Time*. New York: Harper and Row.

Schmitt, C. (1966) *Der Begriff des Politischen*. Berlin: Dunker und Humblot.

Wallerstein, I. (1974) *The Modern World System*. New York: Academic Press.

Notes

1 *Translator's note*: . . . Instead of a modernity centered in Europe and imposed as a global design upon the rest of the world, Dussel argues for a multiplicity of decolonizing critical responses to Eurocentric modernity from heretofore peripheral cultures and peoples around the world. Dussel's transmodern project is thus neither a premodern attempt to provide a folkloric affirmation of an imagined common past nor a reckless postmodern project that affirms only incommensurable difference. In fact, one could argue that some version of Dussel's transmodern project is often assumed as an unstated premise or perhaps even as an ideal goal for the comparatist enterprise. What besides "transmodern worldhood" (Dussel's term) could better provide the hermeneutic horizon for the practice of comparing literatures and cultures across all manner of times and places? As Djelal Kadir has suggested while discussing Dussel, the discipline of comparative literature "emerges from and institutionalizes this 'step towards a transmodern worldhood.'"[1] In effect, Dussel—who is himself situated on the border of many linguistic, cultural, and disciplinary worlds—offers us an interesting model for approaching InterAmerican studies as a form of global studies, and something like his model seems to underlie this volume's call for papers that "contemplate the Americas as a plural and yet sometimes integral entity, that weigh vast differences against shared histories, and that manage to connect cultures and languages across borders and boundaries of all kinds." At the very least, Dussel's attempt to see the world, its history, and its various peoples (especially *hispanos*) as part of a single world-historical system (that nonetheless remains a pluriverse) is fundamentally comparative.[1]

. . . Dussel offers a Heideggerian analysis of "being-in-the-world" for a human being identified, or self-identifying, as *hispano*. I have chosen to leave each occurrence of the Spanish term *hispano* untranslated in order to forestall familiar classificatory systems of race and/or ethnicity. Dussel's use of the word does not coincide with the English noun "Hispanic," which, as Dussel suggests in a footnote, has its own ambiguous and problematic genealogy. Nor does his technical use of *hispano* coincide with conventional Spanish usage, because he aims at deconstructing the everyday understanding of the term in order to subject it to rigorous philosophical development. In other words, Dussel does not intend to provide yet another description of who the *hispano* is (as though the identity of *hispanos* was pre-determined by race, history, or culture) but rather to develop a description of how *hispanos* live creatively given a remarkably multifaceted history. For Dussel, existing as a *hispano* is a particular way of being human, and the *hispanic*-being (*ser-hispano*) is a particular mode of the human being (*ser humano*). Given Dussel's modal analysis, I translate *ser-hispano* in the essay's title as "being-in-the-world-*hispanically*." The italics are not for emphasis, but instead mark the technical sense of the adverbial and adjectival forms of *hispano*. For instance, in rendering "communidad *hispana*" as "*hispanic* community," I leave *hispanic* in italics and lower case so that the adjective will be read as a term whose meaning is under development, and I treat parallel terms like *anglo* in the same way.

. . . The task that Dussel sets for himself, then, is to describe in admittedly broad and sweeping strokes the world-historical context for the *hispano*'s particular way of being human. As Dussel notes, this is an attempt to move previous philosophical discussions of identity in America beyond idealism (José Vasconcelos), hybridity (García Canclini), and self-conflicted historicity (Octavio Paz). His analysis is comparative by virtue of the five historical-cultural "worlds" that overlap to form the "border" where the *hispano* dwells. By philosophically inflecting both Homi Bhabha's notion of the liminal spaces "in-between" standard categories of identity and the Cuban anthropologist Fernando Ortiz's analysis of the "transculturation" that results from cultural exchanges and displacements, Dussel describes the "world" and "existence" of *hispanos* in terms of the diverse cardinal and cultural directions and dynamics that have produced new ways of life, new patterns of localization, and ever-evolving identities. In sum, Dussel revises traditional philosophical notions of human universality by combining them with the recognition of irreducible difference in order to think of group identity as a *diversality*, thereby establishing the imperative of constituting a broader *hispanic* "we." As Dussel writes in this essay, translated here for the first time, such an identity is "neither substantialist nor essentialist but instead creates its own elements dialectically through the continuous integration of new challenges in the very process of history."

Nonetheless, some readers may find Dussel's discussion of the "worlds" from which *hispanos* have historically emerged to be problematic or even offensive. For instance, one might ask why the "fourth of worlds" constituted by the Afro-Caribbean receives such brief treatment in comparison with the others, especially since it relies so heavily on themes like sensuality and dancing, stereotypes associated with the white racism that Dussel attempts to undermine. Likewise, one may wonder about the strategic wisdom of Dussel's attempt to rid derogatory terms of their sting by historically re-contextualizing them. He does this, for instance, when he refers to the Visigoths bound for the Byzantine Empire as "wetbacks," since they crossed the Danube River. Finally, one might be troubled by the fact that the main agent in Dussel's story, the *hispano*, remains grammatically masculine until well into the essay. Obviously, Dussel does not think that being *hispanically* is an exclusively masculine way of being-in-the-world, but in his semi-mythical mode of presentation, the *hispano* does not appear as both grammatical genders (*hispano/a*) until the third section, which describes the "third of worlds" as a kind of synthesis between the "first of worlds" (Malinche the indigenous mother) and the "second of worlds" (Cortés the Spanish father). Unlike most essays, where the subject to be discussed is articulated at the outset in order to serve as the foundation upon which the rest of the inquiry is built, Dussel's essay uncovers the identity of its subject as it proceeds. The disagreements occasioned by this essay, no less than the agreements, will thus serve Dussel's ongoing project of surveying the polyphonic identity of the *ser-hispano*.

2 The "in-between" of Homi Bhabha; see *The Location of Culture*. This "border" is not a line but a dense territory in the sense of Gadamer's "fusion" of horizons. It is more a "space" than a limit, a "space" between many worlds that the (intersubjective) subjectivity of the actor inhabits simultaneously. The actor articulates all of them, each one being both "my world" and "our world," in the solidarity of the Hegelian "being-at-home" [*zu-Hause*] but "exterior" to the hegemonic world of the *anglos*, in (Levinasian) "alterity."

3 In this instance, in the title, and in this "paper" generally, the word "existence" will be a technical term with a Sartrean or Heideggerean meaning ("ex-": the point of origin; "-istence": transcendence or "being-thrown" in the "world").

4 Twenty years have passed since "Hispanics" were the white citizens of New Mexico who did not want to be confused with "Chicanos." Later, they were called "Latinos," but now I believe that the term "Hispanic" is being imposed. Of course, the question of the political opportunities offered by this cultural and political community denomination remains to be considered.

5 Heidegger names this mere ex-istence "Dasein." See *Being and Time* § 9ff, pp. 67ff.

6 At the time, I was an Argentine citizen and resident of Mexico, a fourth-generation Latin American whose origins are part German and part Italian.

7 I write "First of Worlds" and not "First World" for obvious reasons in order to avoid a geopolitical confusion. [Dussel reverses the normal Spanish order of noun and adjective, writing "mundo primero" ("world first") instead of "primero mundo" ("first world"). I have substituted "first of worlds" for the awkwardly literal "world first" and have done the same for the worlds that follow.—TRANS.]

8 See *Hipótesis*, *El encubrimiento del Otro*, and *Ética de la Liberación* 15–98. Full-text versions of these first two works (as well as many others in both English and Spanish) are available at www.enriquedussel.org.

9 This experience of "arriving" in Amerindia from the west should be lived by *hispanos* as an ontological experience of the first order.

10 These riders arrived from China and India (by way of Kabul), reaching the Medes, Persians, Greeks, and Latins. They were the first "cowboys," who, after crossing the Arabian deserts,

arrived in Andalusia as Muslim *vaqueros*. From there, they passed through Mexico towards the south of the continent as *llaneros* in the Colombian plains, and as gauchos in the Argentinean pampas. Finally, they moved north through Mexico to the south of what is now the United States. Their history is already the history of the "father" of *hispanos*.

11 On September 17, 1656, Cromwell wrote: "The first thing therefore . . . is that: . . . Being and Preservation . . . Why, truly, your great Enemy is the Spaniard. He is a natural enemy . . . by reason of that enmity that is in him against whatsoever is of God" (qtd. in Schmitt 67).

12 And it is not too much to recall that the battle of 1571, in which Miguel de Cervantes participated and where Spain defeated the Ottomans, is also the end of Spain's importance in the Mediterranean and the beginning of its uninterrupted hegemony over the Atlantic, the greatest geopolitical change of the last five hundred years, which Spain initiated. [Cervantes's left arm was permanently maimed while fighting in this famous battle, and he was especially proud of both his role in the battle and the resulting nickname mentioned by Dussel: *El manco de Lepanto*.—TRANS.]

13 It is interesting to remember, among so many histories, the Spanish Jewish communities that fled to Portugal after their unjust expulsion in 1492. From Portugal, some (like the family of Spinoza) set out in exile towards the United Provinces of Holland. From there, some went to the Dutch Caribbean colonies, for example, Curaçao. The wandering Jewish community ultimately moved to New Amsterdam in New Holland. This community would remain when New Amsterdam passed into England's hands, and it would transform itself into the Jewish community of New York long before the *anglos*.

14 Paradoxically, this is also the year that the Pilgrims arrived in the north.

15 At Harvard, there is a plaque in front of a statue of the founder that reads: "Since 1636, the first university of America." However, in 1536 the first American center of philosophical and theological studies, the Colegio de Santa Cruz in Tlatelolco (now part of Mexico City), was founded by the Dominicans. In 1540, in Tiripetío, Michoacán, Alfonso de la Vera Cruz founded the first Augustinian school. In the year 1553 just mentioned, the universities of Lima and Mexico were founded with prerogatives equal to those of Salamanca, Paris, Oxford, and Cambridge, in philosophy, theology, law, and medicine. *Hispanos* can claim, on behalf of their Latin American "brothers," to have inaugurated university studies on the continent. [Dussel is technically wrong about the inscription on the plaque at Harvard, which reads "John Harvard—Founder—1638." To further complicate matters, the plaque itself is factually incorrect and is even known on campus as "The Statue of the Three Lies," since 1) the figure depicted is not John Harvard but rather a student from the nineteenth century used as a model; 2) John Harvard was not the founder but rather an early financial contributor after whom the school was named; and 3) Harvard was not founded in 1638 but rather in 1636. Of course, while Dussel is technically wrong about the inscription and while the inscription itself is inaccurate, Dussel is certainly right to question Harvard's (or any other U.S. university's) claim to being the first institution of higher education in the Americas.—TRANS.]

16 The *hispanic* thinker from Texas, Vergilio Elizondo, shows how the discourse of liberation of Moses leaving Egypt with the former slaves (and by extension, the utopian-Christian communities that fled England or Ireland, poverty and persecution, in order to enter the "Promised Land" of the "God of slaves") is transformed into the contrasting discourse of appropriation. Joshua and the former slaves take up this discourse in order to justify the conquest of the "wilderness," that is, the land that they appropriated in the name of the "God of armies." See Elizondo. This discourse would remain permanently in the United States, from the occupation of the "far West" to George Bush's war against terrorism in the present, inspired by the "Western Design" of Cromwell, by "Manifest Destiny" and the Monroe Doctrine, and by the narratives of Fundamentalist Christian, North American expansionism.

Reading Questions

1. Dussel claims that the identity of US Latinxs—what he calls "hispanos"—are structured by a history of living on the border of five worlds. What does that mean? What are the five worlds?
2. Dussel claims that "the hispano always has a certain constitutive, originary reference to Amerindian cultures" (263). What does this mean?
3. Part of Dussel's argument for the distinctiveness of "hispanos" is that they have some form of continuity with Amerindian groups. Is that continuity cultural, linguistic, descent, or something else?

How does that continuity work in the case of hispanos who are descended of Europeans, Asians, or other groups outside the Americas?
4. Dussel claims that his account is "neither substantialist nor essentialist" (261) but something that is a matter of ongoing construction and integration of ongoing history. However, he also claims that certain historical and cultural conflicts are "a collision that the hispano carries in his/her culture, blood, and history, and embrace that the anglo cannot comprehend, experience, or appreciate" (267). Are these claims consistent? What is their relationship to one another?
5. Does a theory about membership in any social identity group always require some kind of essentialism? How can we characterize whether someone is a member of a group, and/or whether they could be wrong about it, without appealing to an essential characteristic had by members of the group?

4 From the Caribbean to the U.S.
Afro-Latinity in Changing Contexts

Gertrude González de Allen

This essay, which engages Afro-Latin identity as it shifts from the Caribbean to a mainland U.S. context, begins with an acknowledgement of its challenges. The first is race. This challenge lies in accounting for the changes in perception, understanding and use of racial categories as subjectivity shifts location. The second is culture. Since this essay addresses Afro-Latin identity as it moves through various national contexts, this analysis must necessarily have a trans-national dimension.[1] The challenge is to account for cultures within cultures, given that Caribbean and U.S. mainland cultural spaces are not monolithic. The third is migration. This challenge lies in identifying rhythms, movements, and their fragmentations, disruptions, and gatherings.

Despite the fact that there are similarities between race in the Caribbean and the United States, there are also differences. A dimension of U.S. race relations that can be seen as repeated in the Caribbean is the way in which racism exists to protect white privilege. However, in the Caribbean, one added dimension of race relations is an ever-present colonial power transformed: the transformation is either as an owner of the island(s), as is the case with the Virgin Islands (which the U.S. bought from Denmark), as an extension of the colonial government through commonwealth or an overseas department, or as a latent influence exercised by a former colonial power. This latent influence may manifest as economic, political, and/or cultural dominance; for example, England may still exercise influence over Jamaica, Barbados or Trinidad, although these islands are independent. Despite the fact that commonwealth status gives Puerto Ricans greater control over their internal political affairs and ethnic and cultural identity, these freedoms are limited by U.S. legal, constitutional, military, diplomatic, and economic sovereignty. The race hierarchy seen in the United States and whose residue is found in the Caribbean and in any former colonized region is splintered by the uniqueness of the Caribbean as a region, and even more so by the individual resonance of cultural, social and economic rhythms of the particular group of islands to which one may refer. This means that the Virgin Islands, Puerto Rico, Jamaica, and the Dominican Republic may have similar dimensions of race, but that there are "unique particulars" as well. This essay attempts to begin to address this notion of unique "particulars of race." What does the term "unique particulars" mean? Within this context, it means nuances such as history, economy, migratory patterns, ethnic diversity and culture.

Although race is a very important component of this essay, it is not the main focus or emphasis. This essay is also about showing how conversations about Afro-Latin descendants living in the Caribbean, Latin America and the United States must be seen as a valuable component of Diaspora studies, dialogues about identity, thinking through colonial, post-colonial and de-colonial problems and ideologies, as well as Africana philosophy. As such, this essay contributes to the de-colonial turn by advancing the constructive engagement with Afro-Latin thinkers and their conversations with Africana and Latin American philosophy. I will begin by summarizing elements of another essay, "Discourse of Memory," where I explore some key ideas related to the problems that I am engaging here. Second, I will elaborate on the question of what happens when Afro-Latinity as a concept enters U.S. discourse. Finally, I will show what this discourse has to offer Afro-Caribbean and Latin American philosophy.

1. Summary of "The Discourse of Memory"

In the essay "Discourse of Memory," I explore how the works of Afro-Latin American writers, Manuel Zapata Olivella (Colombia), Quince Duncan (Costa Rica) and Nelson Estupiñán Bass (Ecuador), converse with existing and pre-existing theoretical and philosophical discourses in Latin America, Europe and the African Diaspora. It argues that there exists a vibrant theoretical discourse within the Afro-Latin American intellectual tradition that has been ignored by contemporary African-American and Latin American philosophy. This work is necessary, because although Zapata Olivella, Duncan, and Estupiñán Bass are accomplished creative writers and essayists, to date much of the examination of their work has focused on their literary, cultural, and political production. The notion that these writers are also thinkers with philosophical import has been largely ignored.

This project is inspired by Paget Henry's *Caliban's Reason: Introducing Afro-Caribbean Philosophy*, which argues that a philosophical tradition exists in the Caribbean, among its creative writers, essayists, historians, and critical cultural theorists. "Discourse of Memory" arrives at a similar conclusion about the Afro-Latin American intellectual tradition. The conclusion is that there exists philosophical import in the work of Afro-Latin intellectuals, particularly its essayists, that is worth serious consideration. Manuel Zapata Olivella, Quince Duncan and Nelson Estupiñán Bass were chosen from among many Afro-Latin writers because they have produced a large body of essays, creative writing and interviews that are more easily accessible (from the U.S.) and clearly point to the ways in which each author converses with the Africana philosophical tradition.

Certainly, Zapata Olivella, Duncan, and Estupiñán Bass are not trained philosophers. This fact should not deter the reader from seeing the ways in which they are philosophical, since philosophy—particularly Afro-Diasporic philosophy—can be and is often rooted in discourses about daily life. About this issue, Paget Henry writes the following in his book, *Caliban's Reason*:

> From the Afro-Caribbean perspective, philosophy is an intertextually embedded discursive practice, and not an isolated or absolutely autonomous one. It is often implicitly referenced or engaged in the production of answers to everyday questions and problems that are being framed in nonphilosophical discourses.
>
> (2000: 2)

As Henry argues, one does not need to be a trained philosopher to be philosophical. In addition, philosophy is not always practiced as an independent self-sustained discourse; instead, it is often the opposite, i.e., set in discourses about daily life. After careful examination of these three writers, it becomes evident that Zapata Olivella's, Duncan's, and Estupiñán Bass's writings contained general philosophical themes and pre-occupations that address the same issues and questions found in Africana thought and more specifically shows influence and conversations with Africana and Latin American philosophical discourses.

Memory is a major thread that links Zapata Olivella, Duncan, and Estupiñán Bass to a broader diasporic and global conversation, as well as serving as the everyday life thematic from which other theoretical questions emerge. Some of the important questions tackled by Zapata Olivella, Duncan, and Estupiñán Bass include: Are Latin Americans, particularly Afro-Latin Americans free? Do God and/or the ancestors exist as sources of knowledge? What is truth for a colonized subject? Can truth be known through reason or intuition? Is memory able to provide the knowledge needed to survive and prosper? Does the individual have rights vis-à-vis the state? And, what is the function of punishment?

2. When Afro-Latinity Enters U.S. Discourse about Identity

When Afro-Latinity enters U.S. discourse, it dissipates into one of several tropes of identity and political discourses. First, Afro-Latinity engages the discourse of race. Out of this engagement comes the question: what does it mean to be Black in the U.S.? The question of Blackness and its implications in this context are crucial when moving from one cultural context to the next. Although Afro-descendants are disenfranchised all around the world, race distinctions and their meanings vary on different continents, and in different regions, national and political cultures. Understanding Blackness within the context of history and politics in the United States is necessary in this evaluation. More important than the U.S. context are the ways in which Blackness shifts and changes across regions as the Afro-Latin subject transforms her way of interpreting Blackness and the changing climate. Second, Afro-Latinity enters the discourse of ethnic and cultural identity. When it becomes evident that an Afro-Latin person is not an African-American, questions about ethnic and cultural identity arise. The citizenry insists on knowing the other elements of the subject's identity location. They ask: are you Hispanic, Latina, Chicana, Iberian? Third and finally, Afro-Latin subjects also dialogue with the discourse of national identity. This means that they engage the question: are you Puerto Rican, Virgin Islander, Dominican, Cuban, Costa Rican, American, etc.? In this exchange, national and cultural loyalties are investigated and even tested.

In addition to the aforementioned questions of identity location, Afro-subjects are forced into identity categories without choice. This means that in a new national community, there is an external over-determination. Among the first identity determinations is race, which in a U.S. context supersedes ethnicity; that is, it is given more importance as an identity marker than ethnicity.

In the book *Racist Culture Philosophy and the Politics of Meaning*, David Theo Goldberg argues that racialized discourse changes (as a discourse and as an expression) when a variety of new concerns are generated by and from modernity (1993: 43). To this idea, I add that racialized discourse also shifts for the subject when crossing psycho/social borders such as culture, class and migration history and when altering geography within and without a nation state. Evidence of this pervasiveness can be found in the situating of subjects based on notions of phenotype rather than on expressions of individual character. Of course, phenotype is also linked to what Goldberg calls pre-conceptual elements of racialized discourse: "classification, order, value, and hierarchy" (49). In practical terms, the "classification value and hierarchy" may have linked race to class. Ultimately, the body that is racialized becomes an abstract entity. For Goldberg, this means that in modernity "subjectless bodies were thus dramatically transformed into bodies of subjection" (50). This grammar or order in which "Black" bodies in particular were classified, remains an integral part of identity-construction and racialized discourse in the contemporary United States. In this grammar of racialized subjection, the body is nothing but an empty shell to which all others respond. It is absent of personhood—the second person—the "You." In the essay "Sociality and Community in Black: A Phenomenological Essay," Lewis Gordon argues that the "You" is "peculiarly absent in discussions of race and racism" (1997: 112). Part of this absence, he contends, is related to an "ontological suspension" where general perceptions and ideas about an object or subject ("thematization") rather than its being ("what something is") are conversed with and emphasized (112). In entering the racist culture of the United States, the transition may be very difficult, especially if the Afro-subject comes from a place where a sense of self has been strongly defined in a community where sociality predominates over excessive individualism.[2] Lack of awareness of this shift in perception of the "You" might mean that an Afro-Latin subject may have to live in "ontological suspension." This is a hazard of moving into the U.S.'s unique anti-black context.

In the U.S. context, difference has multiple categories such as class, age, sex, race, sexuality, etc. These categories can serve to mask the central role race has had in identifying distinction. These distinctions are subtle yet nefarious, labeled silly and no longer in existence, but nevertheless remain at the core of day-to-day social relations. This is the reason why in the Northern United States, I might be perceived mostly as a Black subject, but in the Southern United States I am clearly a "fair-skinned" Black subject. Despite the fact that many would insist that there is no difference—because to be "Black is to be Black"—some might argue, today shadism still matters in some Black communities, particularly in southern areas of the United States. It also matters in places like Cape Town, South Africa, where the so-called "coloureds" currently struggle to redefine themselves in a changing political, social, and economic climate, and where activists continue to work against racial hierarchies in a post-apartheid system.

According to Goldberg, "difference and identity inhere in the concept of race," adding that "domination of a particular race is established in respect to a series of differences from other individuals or groups and by virtue of a series of identities between those considered alike" (51). In contemporary U.S. racial politics, particularly in the South, to be "white" still has more relevance for day-to-day privileged relations than whether an individual is of German, English or French ancestry, because it is "whiteness" that garners the privilege rather than the ethnic identification. Similarly, to be perceived as "Black" has more consequence than to be known as African, Haitian, Costa Rican, or American. Police brutality against Black men is pervasive and does not discriminate on the basis of ethnicity. Senseless treatment of Black men by police officers in the late twentieth century continues. For this reason, racial over-determination from without is a first relational identity marker that Afro-Latin subjects must contend with when moving into a U.S. context. In practical terms, this means what Lewis Gordon indicates: "Blacks are forced to take extra-ordinary measures to live ordinary lives; an ordinary life, after all, should not involve expected encounters with the criminal justice system" (Gordon 1997: 118).

When entering into a U.S. context, an Afro-descendant is first identified as a "Black" entity (without question). This racial identification is both empty and filled with meaning. It is empty for the arrivant in the sense that she may not fully understand and/or relate to the situated connotations carried by the term. However, the term "Black" is always already designated with meaning within the host country. More sophisticated and informed evaluators of the Afro-subject may identify her ethnicity (Hispanic or Latina), but not before the presence of some other marker, such as language barriers, accent, dress, mannerism, cultural references, etc. For many Afro-Latinos who migrate to the U.S., there exists a tension between race and ethnicity. Racial identity not only denotes political and social class, but also has cultural undertones. In the U.S., race and culture are so closely linked that there are often used interchangeably. This can be seen in the phrases: "she does not act 'Black'" and "she acts white." The ambiguity created by the multiple functions and meaning of the term affects those who might be racially Black, but culturally some other nationality other than the U.S. mainland.

Given the ambiguities in understandings of the term race, an Afro-Latin subject, who has never taken part in an African-American culture, may be asked to reproduce it. This is the source of tension. When Afro-Latin subjects show confusion or assert ethnic and cultural difference, while also saying that they cannot reproduce desired elements of the African American culture or even understand what is meant by Blackness in a U.S. context, the accusations of racial prejudices begin.

It is easy for the average citizen of the United States to confuse race and ethnicity, because although race is a central identity category, it is an ambiguous term. This ambiguity comes from not only a long history of use, but also a wide range of theories about race in an equally wide variety of points of view with respect to how race is used, understood and classified. In the essay "Racial Formations," Michael Omi and Howard Winant articulate the idea that race is "largely a modern phenomenon" (13). They show how race has always been a subject of religious, scientific and social debates (1994: 13–16). Furthermore, Omi and Winant assert that for Christians the question is the following: if there are different kinds of people, then how does one reconcile the story of Adam and Eve? (14). Scientists, on the other hand, cannot agree on a scientific basis for difference based on biology (16). Finally, sociologists are more inclined to look at race as a social concept, since they believe that "race categories and the meaning of race are given concrete expression by the specific social relations and historical context in which they are embedded" (16).

Noted global social theorist Immanuel Wallerstein has a different point of view about race. Wallerstein conceptualizes race as a method of explaining or categorizing pastness, which can be seen as both a reflection of what actually happened or a construction of the prior based on contemporary interpretation (1987: 78). Wallerstein concludes that the latter characterization is the most common understanding and response to identity categories based on pastness. In the essay "The Construction of Peoplehood: Racism, Nationalism, Ethnicity," Wallerstein writes:

> This being the case, it makes little difference whether we define pastness in terms of genetically continuous groups (races), historical social-political groups (nations) or cultural groups (ethnic groups). They are all peoplehood constructs, all inventions of pastness, all contemporary political phenomena.
>
> (78–79)

For many Africana thinkers, race goes beyond peoplehood constructs. These thinkers see race not only as a category of identity, but even more so intimately linked to oppression of African descendants. Among the most noted of these are Africana intellectuals who have analyzed oppression of Afro-descendants from the point of view of Marxism. Among the first was Aimé Césaire, who in his earlier years as a radical Black intellectual identified himself as not only a Marxist, but also a communist. However, from a very early stage, Césaire became disillusioned with Marxism's narrow view of all oppression as exploitation of subjects based on a value placed on their labor, and thus class. For this reason, Césaire was among the first to point out that Marxism did not account for race; as such, Marxism faced difficulties for being an ideology that would liberate African descendants.[3]

Cornel West looks at race from what he calls a genealogical materialist analysis. In *Prophesy and Deliverance*, West shows how race is a phenomenon of meaning and practice of identity and power that is made possible by developments in Modern discourse, such as the scientific revolution, the Cartesian transformation of philosophy, and the classical revival (1982: 50). In *Keeping the Faith: Philosophy and Race in America*, West agrees with Césaire's earlier critique of the uncritical use of Marx for developing race theory. West articulates his disagreement with Marxist theory (as it relates to race theory) as double-edged (1993: 267). He writes:

> First, I hold that many social practices, such as racism, are best understood and explained not only or primarily by locating them within modes of production, but also by situating them within the cultural traditions of civilizations. . . . Second, I claim that the Marxist obsession with the economic sphere as the major explanation factor is itself a reflection of the emergence of Marxist discourse in the midst of an industrial capitalism pre-occupied with economic production; and, more important, this Marxist obsession is itself a symptom of a particular Western version of the will to truth and style of rationality which valorizes control, mastery and domination of nature and history.
>
> (267)

More recently, in *From Class to Race: Essays in White Marxism and Black Radicalism*, Charles Mills also moves from a class-based theory of oppression to one that is founded on an expansion of the material social "base" to include race (2003: 55). He holds this view in part because of the belief that "racial self-identification and group solidarity trump other identities and group belongings (170).

The ambiguity of race often confuses the arrivant, who attempts to understand where to fit in within the scheme of political, social, and economic relations. This might mean choosing to identify as an African-American, because there are no alternate discourses or categories in which they fit. It is into this category that those with few language barriers fall. Those who do not speak English are identified as Latin American, but fade into the background like in many Latin American communities where they already exist. Certainly, when asked to fill out job, college, and graduate school applications, an Afro-Latina is often asked to choose an identifying category, and even today the choices are limited: Black or Hispanic (non-Black). The question is the following: what happens in the translation from the Latin American and the Caribbean to the U.S.?

In *Black Skin, White Masks*, Frantz Fanon can be interpreted as answering this question. This answer is unmistakable: once Black, always Black, no matter where one goes in a colonial/post-colonial world. Similarly, in the "Introduction" to *Existence in Black*, Lewis Gordon would also argue the same, i.e., that Blackness travels and persists in what he calls an anti-Black world. It is true that in examining Black neighborhoods in Latin America, such as Colombia's "El Choco," one may see a similar thematic to that found in places where there exists racial oppression against Blacks, such as poverty, a poor educational system, high unemployment rates, etc. Yet there is still a difference: the choice of self-identification. For example, in St. Croix where I was born and raised, the majority of the population is Afro-descendant. In the mid-to late-twentieth century, the most important marker of social location could be characterized as family and migratory history—i.e., not a racial category but rather where your family came from. The privileging of family history is also driven by the fact that the U.S. Virgin Islands experienced a wave not only of varying national colonial occupations, but also of colonizers and subsequent immigrant communities for labor and other financial opportunities. For these reasons, race was not always a primary identity marker. Instead, migratory history, ethnicity, and national identity were essential descriptors of class, privilege, and social location.

Before being purchased by the United States in 1916, the Virgin Islands changed colonial hands six times. Among its colonial owners were Spain, France, the Knights of Malta, and Denmark. Cultural shifts were exacerbated by a wide variety of cultural groups passing through for economic opportunities. For example, during Danish colonial rule non-Danish Western European opportunists were invited to lease the plantations for a chance at turning a profit. This was because the Danish citizenry had little interest in plantation life; however, its government saw it necessary to participate in ownership of colonies as a demonstration of political and economic strength and competitiveness. Later, in the early twentieth century, during U.S. American rule, many immigrants were welcomed to the Virgin Islands, particularly St. Croix, to work the sugar cane plantations. When those plantations were shut down, immigrants from other islands continued to come for work in the tourist industry to fill the need for skilled labor for construction projects, and to gain U.S. citizenship or passage to the United States. This means that since its modern conception and perhaps even before during pre-Colombian native rule, these islands had witnessed waves of immigrant communities come and go, replenishing the population and creating growth in the local economy. In such a place—where Afro-descendant groups of various kinds control community social, cultural, and political interests—discourse about identity places less emphasis on race and more on family history and on commitment to community. Often this migratory history has class implications, and class, in this context, is also rather complex.

From the time of colonization, race and class have been intimately linked. Since European colonists have always been more privileged than any other groups, Afro-descendants of course were always treated as an inferior group. Nevertheless, in the twentieth century, Afro-descendants in the Virgin Islands directed the islands culturally, socially and politically. However, the economy is still controlled by foreign corporations and non-Afro descendants. At the same time that they control much of the economy, they live largely secluded from the majority of the population, choosing to seemingly fade into the background, particularly when it comes to cultural, social, and political dialogue. Given these dynamics, several Virgin Islands emerge. It is a place where foreign business interests can be cultivated, attracted, and protected, as long as there is an appearance of contribution to the local economy by way of jobs. These foreign interests, however, remain foreign. This means that there are varying degrees of investment by these companies and the U.S. expatriates who work in them into the local population. The investment has cultural and social implications to the degree that separate communities are formed and fostered. When the HOVENSA oil refinery in St. Croix was fully operational most of the foreign workers lived in the company's gated community. Many of those who live in this gated community lived maintained lives from the locals, and thus separate communities were formed and maintained.[4] Because there is a neo-colonial dimension in their relationship of to the island, the interests of these groups are protected despite the fact that their economic and social contribution to the community might be in question. In an island community, this migration history is noted in such a way that it means something about how the community responds to these separate communities in terms of social and cultural relations.

Because I grew up in a neighborhood that was predominantly Puerto Rican, my primary communal identity marker would not be Blackness (an understood category of being), but rather family history (or even ethnic identity), i.e., my Puerto Rican-ness. On the other hand, in the U.S. an essential identifying marker would be the color of my skin. Within a mostly African American community in the South, this light skin may symbolize privilege. This privilege, based on a special version of a racial category (light-skinned Black), is also prevalent in Cape Town, South Africa, where phenotype is still an important marker of privilege.[5] However, in St. Croix (among the majority population), family history would be the primary marker of class and social status, not the color of one's skin.[6] That is, to be identified and marked as a Puerto Rican in the 1950s, 1960s, 1970s and early 1980s meant, in many cases, to be on the lower end of the social scale.[7] This is because Puerto Ricans in St. Croix were migrant workers who came to cut sugar cane in the early twentieth century. Over time, this community established itself and gained greater status in the community. Early migrants to St. Croix from Vieques, Puerto Rico, represented the opposite of privilege. Any Puerto Rican-identified person had to contend with many negative stereotypes.

Also note that there is a further class complexity between "big island" and "small island" politics. Those migrating from Vieques, a small island, were considered uneducated and not cosmopolitan. Descendants of these groups suffered greater social alienation both from "big island" people (like the Puerto Rico mainland) and "small island" people (with U.S. English-speaking privilege). For these reasons, one must conclude that class categories in St. Croix were not exclusively racial or marked by skin color like in the U.S. Instead, I have argued for the view that a combination of economic resources, family history, and a long-standing relation to the community and the island mark class and social privilege. Note that this essay does not assert that race or phenotype is not relevant in the Virgin Islands; in fact, phenotype does play a role in the race dialogue. Instead, it contends that race was not the only or most important marker of identity in community and "island to island" relations (affecting class privilege and discrimination).[8]

Evidence of the other more relevant identity markers is found in the ways in which locals socialize with each other on a daily basis. In social circles, one of the primary questions does not relate to the color of your skin, but to which family you belong and where on the island you live. So, in answering the question, "who are you?" one might say, I am a Jones from Fredericksted or a Galiber from Christiansted. Sometimes, instead of being asked, "who are you?" one might hear the question, "to whom do you belong"? In Spanish, they will say, "¿de quién tú eres?" Again, here family in community is privileged, because it is usually an elder that attempts to situate you within the context of a history of familial relations.

When moving from the Virgin Islands to the U.S., the identity question changes. In the U.S., the question would be the following: "what are you"? A better-informed person might ask, "how do you identify"? or "what do you call yourself"? These questions come from the point of view of classification. Here again, the "you" is empty, because it is transformed into a framework. The question "who are you?" or "to whom do you belong?" speak more to a depth of history and requires the subject to identify herself in terms of family and community. The second set of questions requires that the subject identify herself through external markers, in many cases related to the categories resulting from a dialogue about personhood and difference during modernity. In the latter case, significant weight is given to race as a social, political, and economic category.

When moving from the Caribbean to the U.S., there is a shift in the use and function of Blackness. In changing contexts, an Afro-Latina moving from the U.S. Virgin Islands to the mainland U.S. has to shift from a space rich and layered with differences based on more than just phenotype and economic means to a condition summarized by one word, one meaning, one attitude: "Black." In the United States, the term "Black" often collapses race, class, ethnicity, culture, and national and familial history. In St. Croix, the term Black would not translate the migratory history of families (moving from Vieques, PR, to the

Virgin Islands or moving from Montserrat to the Virgin Islands and the Virgin Islands to Denmark and back again). Certainly, Blackness exists in the Virgin Islands. But Blackness is often invoked when referring to a colonial and post-colonial situatedness. Blackness arises when: 1) engaging colonial history; 2) relating to the colonial relationship with the U.S.; 3) articulating whiteness and white privilege manifesting on the island; 4) articulating a neo-colonial condition; and 5) engaging individuals in community from the point of view of knowledges and powers that disagree, subjugate, and suppress, i.e., "coloniality of power" (Quijano) and "an other thinking" (Mignolo). That is, the notion of Blackness emerges whenever one has to engage in discourse about colonized Afro-descendant subjects from the colonizing episteme, i.e., thinking with and within the "coloniality of power." In the latter case, Blackness emerges when Afro-subjects see themselves and similar other subjects primarily as subjects of imperial domination; an additional complexity results from an inability to function epistemologically, politically, and socially outside of the "coloniality of power." This means failure or inability to exist or think from the borders and/or practice "an other thinking." For example, in the twentieth- century Virgin Islands, white Americans were often viewed as experts, even though many arrive ignorant of local nuances and particulars. The concept of the "white" American person as expert and better-capable in almost any and all circumstance is a symptom of those who lack "an other thinking." From this vantage point, white Americans can come to the Virgin Islands, get jobs, and set up business more quickly and more successfully with little questioning of their abilities and qualifications. There is equally the stereotype of the local Black person who does not like to work and lacks basic skills to do minor or complex tasks efficiently.

In the U.S., Blackness is a fixed category denoting social (class), cultural, and political location. Blackness, a racial category, is the answer for all. In dialogues among Afro-Latinos, one of the most significant themes is that the complexities that speak about family and cultural history unique to the ways in which we call or understand each other is lost in Afro-U.S. racial discourse. First, there is no choice of self-identification. Second, the terms are so limited that they function mostly as a socio-political position from which one wages political, social, and economic battles. Third, Blackness has often symbolized the negation of one's humanity and dignity. Although Negritude, the Harlem Renaissance, and the Civil Rights and Black Power movements sought to redefine "Blackness," residues of its fundamental meaning remain.

3. Contributions of these discussions to Caribbean and Latin American philosophy

Contemporary U.S. dialogues about identity must continue to engage the complex ways in which identities are constructed and operate in Latin America and the Caribbean. The U.S. dialogue, with its unique particulars, often dominates and obfuscates other parallel dialogues about identity that are equally (if not more) intricate and valid, and which provide valuable information for understanding identity in changing contexts. For this reason, a greater and continued dialogue and exploration of identity, particularly its effects on Latin American and Caribbean migrations, is necessary. Second, race discourse is so central in the U.S. that its dominance re-inscribes the colonizing dynamics of power that put racial categories into place. Continued dialogue about the importance of race, when not viewed in tandem with other realities of existence and constructions of the self in the Americas re-affirms racial discourse in its most negative forms. Therefore, the discussions about identity in this essay and in works by Afro-Latin thinkers contribute to the de-colonization project through a decentralization of dominant U.S. epistemological identity frameworks.

In the essay, "The De-Colonial Option and the Meaning of Identity in Politics," Walter Mignolo makes a distinction between "identity politics" and "identity in politics," while advocating the latter (2007: 43). Race dialogue in the U.S. is often riddled with "identity politics," a discussion about how race is manifested. Afro-Latin dialogues about race and identity seek to engage in "identity in politics," that is, in discussions about how to change the political climate in such a manner that Blacks are empowered and accounted. These conversations pay particular attention to the ways that Afro-descendants exist and contribute to the communities and nations in which they live.

In the "Introduction" to *Teoría y práctica del racismo*, Quince Duncan and Lorein Powell point to a "new consciousness that arises from the specificity of the problem of Blacks" in Latin America (1988: 9). This "new consciousness" created a movement inspired by a conference Manuel Zapata Olivella organized in Colombia; out of this conference held in 1977 arose a series of other conferences around Latin America, the Caribbean, and Africa (Powell and Quince 1988: 9). This movement was global in scale and showed the ways in which discourse around identity, race, and racism can build bridges and spark political movements that link communities and continents, i.e., a practice of "identity in politics." This global perspective helps us not only to understand how Afro-Latinos understand race and racism in Latin America, the Caribbean, and Africa, but also helps to combat both U.S. intellectual hegemony and continued political and economic hegemony from other former colonial powerhouses. Borrowing from Moroccan philosopher Abdelkebir Khatibi's discourse about the marginality of Arabic languages, thinking and philosophies vis a vis those of the West, Mignolo has called this stance "pensamiento otro," "an other thinking" (Mignolo 2000: 71). Writing in this tradition also engages in "an other thinking."

In general, the question of Afro-Latin subjectivity in its changing contexts adds much-needed dialogue and complexity to the question of race, in particular to the concepts of "Blackness" and racism and the narrative of the geo-politics of the interstices. The question of "Blackness" highlights the need to revisit the term and disrupt its location. In attempting to complete the de-colonial project, one must then ask the following questions: Does the continued re-appropriation of the term Black still serve as a useful political and social category for identification? In what ways (if any) do dominant U.S. identity frameworks limit the ways in which those who reside or think on the borders may choose to be in the world? In what ways do Afro-descendant subjects define themselves? And how are these constructions of self and community relevant to the unique particulars of specific social, political, and economic conditions?

The dialogue about Afro-Latin subjectivity also addresses the question of the geo-politics of the interstice, and the ways in which it forces a continued discussion about race construction and highlights how identities are not exclusively determined from without. That is, there are other significant ways in which Afro-communities structure their identities. These conversations are not just about a colonial hegemonic presence, but also most importantly about how communities of Afro-descendants see themselves and their relationships with other African Diaspora subjects. This conversation is an interstitial one, because it does not always already work through the lens of dominant colonial discourse.

A key issue is how identity dialogues may place greater emphasis on different aspects of identity markers or realities according to different or changing historical circumstances. In Latin America, theorists of African descent like Quince Duncan reject both multi-cultural theories and theories regarding the obsolescence of race on the grounds that both of these theoretical points of view are ways in which the dominant discourse chooses to ignore the racism they have caused (Powell and Quince 1988: 28–36). According to Duncan, those who believe in the obsolescence of race fall into a trap set by hegemonic discourses that seek to end the struggles against racism. In the essay "El fenómeno del racismo," Duncan writes:

> A growing effort to deny the existence of races (also derived from Europe) is nothing but a mere manifestation of racism, . . . to negate the existence of these phenotypic differences among human beings, is to run away from the problem of racism, falling into a new and subtle trap of the West (Western culture).
> (Powell and Quince 1988: 36)

One must understand the importance of Duncan's point of view within the context of Latin American history and theories about culture and race. Earlier in his essay, Duncan calls attention to the Argentine thinker Domingo F. Sarmiento who, in the book *Facundo o civilización y barbarie* (1845), pointed to the products of race mixture as people who were "lazy and incapable of competing in the industrial movement" (Powell and Quince 1988: 28). Theories like those purported by Sarmiento in the nineteenth century are Duncan's evidence of a long history of racist bias against any subject who is even in part Afro-descended. Given this discourse, it is evident that theories about race mixture and multiculturalism have been used historically in Latin America to hide the long presence of African descendants and their significance throughout the region. In this socio-political context, for Afro-Latin theorists in the 1970s, 80s and 90s, asserting difference and resisting homogenization became an important political strategy to fight the unique particulars of racial discourse and racist discrimination in Latin America. Asserting existence and calling attention to differences, their meanings and consequences became important. Emphasis on this perspective was the main reason why, after much criticism from his Afro-Latin colleagues, Manuel Zapata Olivella re-thought his tri-ethnic view of identity theory outlined in his book *La rebelión de los genes*.

To understand the aforementioned view about race and racism held by Quince Duncan, it is important to take into account the dynamics of identity in changing contexts. In the U.S., African American activists of the twentieth century, like Martin Luther King, sought to lessen the emphasis on racial difference and highlight the importance of an ethical obligation to granting full human and citizenship rights as a political strategy for economic, political, and social freedoms and opportunities. This perspective can be seen in a speech delivered in 1957, in which Martin Luther King talks about the repealing of the *Plessy vs. Ferguson* decision as the coming of a "new age" in the U.S. About the reversal of *Plessy vs. Ferguson*, King said:

> It affirmed in no uncertain terms that separate facilities are inherently unequal and that to segregate a child because of his race is to deny him equal protection of law. With the coming of this great decision we could gradually see the old order of segregation and discrimination passing away, and the new order of freedom and justice coming into being.
> (King Jr. 1957: 27–28)

For King, this new age meant "to rise above the narrow confines of our individualistic concerns to the broader concerns of humanity" (27–28). Although Duncan is not calling for segregation, his theory does emphasize racial difference, whereas thinkers like Martin Luther King needed to call for a more integrative approach to social relations. Although in the 1960s other cultural and political movements were to attempt to influence Afro-political thought in the U.S. to think through the importance of racial difference and racial solidarity, social integration and class mobility would dominate the political agenda for many African-Americans, particularly the middle class in the mid- to late-twentieth century.

This essay does not seek to put values on the varying approaches to understanding the multiple epistemic locations of identity, particularly as they are viewed and defined by Afro-descendants in changing contexts. However, this essay emphasizes the importance of understanding the unique particulars about the dynamics of identity as Afro-subjects change contexts. Dialogues about race and identity, as one moves from the Caribbean to the U.S. to Latin American and Africa, show some interesting and different circumstances that relate to the same subject matter. The de-colonial turn must address in greater detail these unique particulars.

References

Césaire, A. (2000) *Discourse on Colonialism, Discourse on Colonialism*. New York: Monthly Review Press.
Fanon, F. (1967) *Black Skin, White Masks*, London: Pluto Press.
Goldberg, D. T. (1993) *Racist Culture: Philosophy and the Politics of Meaning*, Oxford: Wiley-Blackwell.
Gordon, L. R. (ed.) (1997) *Existence in Black: An Anthology of Black Existential Philosophy*, New York: Routledge.
Gordon, L. R. (2002) "Sociality and Community in Black: A Phenomenological Essay" in R. Birt (ed.), *The Quest for Community and Identity: Critical Essays in Africana Social Philosophy*, 105–123, Lanham, MD: Rowman & Littlefield.
Henry, P. (2000) *Caliban's Reason: Introducing Afro-Caribbean Philosophy*, New York: Routledge.
King, Jr., M. L. (1957) "Facing the Challenge of a New Age," *The Phylon Quarterly* 18 (1): 25–34.
Mignolo, W. D. (2000) *Local Histories/Global Designs*, Princeton: Princeton University Press.
Mignolo, W. D. (2007) "The De-Colonial Option and the Meaning of Identity in Politics" in H. Martins, D. J. Sadlier, Z. K. Montgomery and R. Alvim (eds.), *Studies in Honor of Heitor Martins*, 11–31, Indiana University, Department of Spanish and Portuguese.
Mills, C. (2003) *From Class to Race: Essays in White Marxism and Black Radicalism*, Lanham, MD: Rowman & Littlefield.
Omi, M., and Winant, H. (1994) *Racial Formation in the United States* (2nd ed.), New York: Routledge.
Powell, L., and Quince, D. (1988) *Teoría y práctica del racism*, San José: Editorial Departamento Ecuménico de Investigaciones.
Quijano, A. (2000) "Coloniality of Power, Eurocentrism, and Latin America," *Nepantla* 1: 533–580.
Wallerstein, I. (1987) "The Construction of Peoplehood: Racism, Nationalism, Ethnicity," *Sociological Forum* 2: 373–388.
West, C. (1982) *Prophesy Deliverance! An Afro-American Revolutionary Christianity*, Philadelphia: Westminster.
West, C. (1993) *Keeping the Faith: Philosophy and Race in America*, New York: Routledge.
Zapata Olivella, M. (1997) *La rebelión de los genes*. Bogotá, Colombia: Altamir.

Notes

1 In this essay, I use the term Afro-Latin instead of the term Afro-Hispanic. Part of the reason for this choice is that I wish to not only call attention to Afro-descendants who are Spanish speaking or derive from a Spanish speaking community (but do not speak Spanish) living in the United States, but also to address those who live in Latin America and the Caribbean. The term Hispanic is embedded in and reflective of U.S. discourse about identity. Part of the project here is to dislodge the dominance that U.S. dialogue often commands when confronted with perspectives outside of it.

2 The notion of sociality used here is also derived from Lewis Gordon. It means a relation bond in community that exists beyond a pragmatic end, such as a building project, or a political end, such as the election of a senator, governor, president. For more information about sociality as developed by Gordon, see the essay "Sociality and Community in Black: A Phenomenological Essay."
3 For more information, see Aimé Césaire's *Discourse on Colonialism*.
4 The St. Croix oil refinery was created, owned and operated by Hess Oil in 1966. HOVENSA represents the efforts of two companies Hess Oil Cooperation and Petroleos de Venezuela. The refinery closed its refinery capacity in February of 2012.
5 In summer of 2005, I taught at a Human Rights program in Cape Town, South Africa. During this time, I was able to witness and experience a racism that lingers in varying levels of the social, economic, and political culture.
6 An important note here is that color does indeed have important dimensions for social interactions; phenotype does have some implications for how beauty was conceptualized. However, note that not all women and men who had European features were considered attractive. For example, to be thin in the early twentieth-century Virgin Islands was not the most appealing feature. Women with well defined curves and with "meat on her bones" received much attention. Excessively thin women/girls were often teased. Phenotype values within racial dialogue does have complexity in this context.
7 Note that the Virgin Islands have seen waves of immigrants from other islands in the 1970s, 80s, 90s like Dominica, St. Lucia, Nevis, St. Kitts, Montserrat, Trinidad and Tobago, St. Bart's, the Dominican Republic, etc. Immigrants from these islands also suffered from prejudice and discrimination due to their immigration history.
8 Here the phrase "in community" is very important, since outside of communal relations with much class and ethnic conflict, there was a race dialogue. The race dialogue was in direct relation to neo-colonial dominance by the U.S.

Reading Questions

1. What is Afro-latinidad?
2. Why is Afro-latinidad often invisible? How do U.S. categories create problems for Afro-Latinxs who come to the United States?
3. Is there a difference between "invisibility" and mere lack of salience or familiarity with that thing? Why is Afro-Latinidad less familiar to some people?
4. Why does González de Allen think it is a problem to deny the existence of races, and does mestizaje help this problem or make it work, according to her account?
5. González de Allen uses Afro-Latinidad to show problems with U.S. ideas about blackness. Could you use ideas about U.S. blackness to show puzzles or problems about Afro-Latinidad? Why or why not?

5 Open Questions in the Metaphysics of Habitable Categories

Axel Arturo Barceló Aspeitia

It is a truism that we often think of ourselves and others not as individuals but as members of broader human kinds: races, generations, nationalities, genders, etc. Despite continuous efforts to eradicate these from our ultimate picture of reality, facts such as my being Mexican, brown, and able-bodied ought still to be accounted for in our philosophical ontology. Yet, there is not a widespread consensus of what sort of facts these are. What sort of fact is my being Mexican? What makes me able-bodied instead of disabled? Is it just my color of skin that makes me brown or is there more to it than that? And if so, what more? Did I have to do something to become all these things that I am? How much of a choice did I have? Such are the questions driving this essay. In particular, my goal is to bring into focus the main threads binding together the many debates on the metaphysics of human distinctions. My hope is that, presenting them at a more abstract level than usual might reveal interesting connections that might be easy to miss at ground level—in the very trenches of theoretical and political action, so to speak.

The paper is structured as follows. In the first section I motivate the critical and rigorous study of what I will call habitable categories, canvasing the important roles they play in our theoretical, normative and subjectivizing practices. I then focus on the question of what makes or what sort of fact it is for someone to belong to some category or another, presenting what I take to be the three major trends in the debate: common sense, socio-historical and performative, trying to fairly identify their achievements and challenges. In the final section, I present the reasons why I think I have shown (not argued for) the value of an abstract perspective as the one I adopt here. In particular, I argue that my abstract approach shows how interstitial cases like migration, passing, transition, etc. are especially problematic for unitary accounts of habitable categories and, therefore, that a pluralistic account is preferable. I also sketch my proposal of such a pluralistic view.

I. On Habitable Categories

Habitable categories, like those pertaining to our nationalities, gender, class, marital status, etc., play a key role in many of our most important theoretical, normative and subjectivizing practices. They figure centrally in the many ways we try to describe, explain and predict the human world in both everyday life and many of our scientific practices—in medicine, economics, anthropology, sociology, linguistics, etc. We usually say things like, "John skipped the flag salutation because he is a Jehovah's Witness," or, "The celebrations of the 25th of May were full because many Argentines live nearby." In other words, we expect people to behave in certain ways and we make sense of what they do in part by identifying them as

DOI: 10.4324/9781003385417-8

belonging to one category or another, just as we use other categories to generate expectations and explanations in other domains.

Besides these theoretical uses, habitable categories play a central role in all of our normative practices. How we evaluate someone's actions is deeply interwoven with what kind of person we think they are (Rudder 2014), just as how we evaluate our own actions is deeply interwoven with what kind of person we think we are. Inhabiting a kind usually entails duties as well as obligations, and there are duties and obligations that are conditional on whether we inhabit certain social kinds. Minors commonly have different rights than adults, aliens have different duties than citizens, etc. Even the most abstract theories of obligations recognize this (Demolombe and Louis 2006).

Finally, habitable kinds are key to a series of practices through which we recognize and develop our own and others' subjectivity. By inhabiting certain categories and not others, we identify with some people but not others; we make sense of our own existence and experience, and those of others. "I never spent anytime whatsoever contemplating the subject of femaleness"—wrote Elizabeth Gilbert in her 2009 autobiographical essay—"For that reason . . . I never became very familiar with myself" (Gilbert 2009: i). The question of identity is usually answered by a list of categories with which one identifies. Even on the negative side, we also assert our own subjectivity by resisting the pull of certain categories. Literary critic Stephanie Burt calls this aspect of subjectivization "the resistance to memoir, to narrative"—which echoes Paul De Man's deconstructive resistance to theory—that is, the resistance "to identifying your true self with one story" even while referring to such stories in the search for this elusive true self (Burt 2012). The categories we inhabit also shape our desires, thoughts, and actions. As Burt (2012) herself writes, the desire to look pretty has a different significance when one is a woman and when one is a man, or neither. Nevertheless, talk about the theoretical, normative and subjective domains of application of these categories must not lead us to believe that some categories are just normative, others just theoretical, and some simply subjective. For most habitable categories, their theoretical, normative and subjective uses are deeply interwoven. One would be mistaken to think that the subjectivizing functions are quite independent from the theoretical ones, for example. As Felwine Sarr (2016) has argued, it is possible that in order to heal the effects of colonisation, Third World subjects must also develop the sort of intellectual sovereignty that requires a decolonisation of the theoretical scholarship of the categories we inhabit. This means that for categories to play the role we want in building our subjectivity, we must also change how we theorize about them, thus bringing together their subjectivizing and theoretical roles. Precisely one of the reasons why it is such a pressing issue to be clear on the metaphysics of habitable kinds is because they are vehicles of cross-pollination between theoretical, normative and subjectivizing domains. Scientific theories, for example, have the sort of authority that makes them very attractive for ethical and political normative co-option (López Beltrán 2004). A satisfactory metaphysical account of habitable categories must recognise the heterogeneity of their theoretical and political uses, and the complexity of their interactions.

This work has been done in a variety of philosophical fields: of social science, feminism, race, critical philosophy, Marxism, liberal and communitarist political philosophy, etc. Nevertheless, common issues and arguments arise, and it is the purpose of this text to trace them. Yet, it is worth noticing that nothing I will say here requires that a single answer work for all habitable categories. Despite their all being habitable categories, it is often assumed that debates regarding the metaphysical nature of, say, race must be sharply distinguished from those of gender, class, disability, etc., and that metaphysical arguments relevant to one kind of habitable category might not apply to others (see, for example, Guerrero McManus 2019 or Díaz-León's remarks on Weinberg 2015). For example, there is relatively widespread agreement that material conditions are fundamental for determining who is or is not poor, but this might not generalize to other categories such as gender or race. Material conditions may also be fundamental to these other cases, or they may not, yet this is a question that must be resolved on a case-by-case basis. In the end, it is very likely that the metaphysics of race will substantially differ from those of gender, for example. The historical and political differences between these categories are so profound that accounts that might serve to build better racial relations could nevertheless reinforce gender injustices if applied in that domain. This is because the struggles and oppression experienced by racial and gender minorities are substantially different, and any good metaphysical account of race and gender must account for these differences.

One might be skeptical about the value of talking about habitable categories in such abstract, detached and general terms as I plan to do here. Unfortunately, I have little to say to convince anyone already skeptical of dealing with social problems as pressing as these at such a general level except to ask her to read my paper and see for herself whether something important emerges from changing the focus in these debates. I take it that even if it is true that different sorts of categories have different metaphysical profiles, it is precisely because they behave differently when considered under the same criteria. Thus, for example, if it is true that there is a stronger metaphysical link between gender and self-testimony than between, say, class and self-testimony, this must manifest itself as differences in the way we shall answer specific general questions about gender and class as habitable categories. Thus, it is fundamental to know the general issues and challenges that face any metaphysical account of a habitable category in order to even try to understand whether different sorts of categories are metaphysically different.

Finally, before getting fully into the question that drives this essay, I want to distinguish the question I am interested in, i.e., what sort of fact is it for someone to inhabit one category or another?—what I will call the *what-makes* question—from other important metaphysical questions regarding habitable categories: which questions, whether questions, systematization questions, and second order questions. *Which* questions are questions about which are the habitable categories and why. For example, is being blond a habitable category or not, and why? *Whether* questions concern whether or not these categories are empty. For example, are there really Hispanics, or is it just an empty moniker? Systematization questions look into the structure of the systems of categories to which categories belong, like what categories belong to the same system of classification? For example, is Jewishness a racial characteristic? Are races and ethnicities the same sort of categories? How many genders are there?, etc. Finally, second order questions concern the epistemological and methodological issues that should be taken in consideration when trying to answer the questions identified above. For example, what criteria should we apply when evaluating different metaphysical proposals, etc. how descriptive/prescriptive should our answers be (Alcoff 2005)? Are we looking for absolutely general, or should the answers be valid only in constrained historical circumstances?, etc.

As important as these questions are, I want to focus my attention here on the perhaps more fundamental question of what it is for someone to inhabit one category or another. What sort of fact makes it the case that I am a man, or that I am not disabled? In the next sections of the article I will present three broad ways of answering such questions, pondering both their strengths and challenges, before advancing my own pluralist proposal.

II. Common Sense Accounts

In broad strokes, we can classify the main positions in the what-makes debate into three major camps: common-sense accounts, socio-historical accounts and performative accounts. I call the first camp "common sense accounts" because they endorse common sense answers to the what-makes questions (or something as close to them as possible). So, for example, consider the follow common sense accounts of the distinctions underlying different cases of discrimination and oppression: that the main differences between men and women are biological, that poverty just is the scarcity of material resources (Cole 2019; Kingston 2000), that belonging to a given generation is just sharing the common experiences resulting from being of more or less the same age at the same time in the same place (Schuman and Scott 1989; Williams and Page 2011), that being Mestizo is just to have mixed Spanish and Indian ancestry (Chance 1979), that being of a certain race is just to have some biological (cladistic) profile (Andreasen 1998; Spencer 2014), that being ignorant is lacking much important knowledge, etc. Some social categories, however, lack a straightforward common sense definition. A common sense account of the category of *naco*, a largely socio-economic label used in Mexico, for example, has proven to be quite elusive (Báez-Jorge 2002; Bürki 2014).

Despite the fact that "common sense has no absolute authority in philosophy" (Lewis 1986: 134), respecting common sense is still usually accepted as an epistemic virtue in ontology (Daly and Liggins 2010). As Anil Gupta has quipped, "any theory that would wage war against common sense had better come loaded with some powerful ammunition" (Gupta 2006: 178), as they face the challenge of having to explain why, while mistaken, common sense theories are widely accepted. Yet, common sense ontological theses still need to be developed into full theories, and this can be done in different ways. A biological account of parenthood, for example, can be as crude or as sophisticated as the biological theory in which it is embedded. Thus, it is important not to fall prey to strawman fallacies and think that common sense conceptions are nothing but naive pre-theoretical intuitions that need to be overcome by rigorous and politically-informed theorization and action.

Regarding the subjectivizing function of habitable categories, common sense accounts have the relative advantage of making recognition easier. It is easier to be recognized as, say, *gyuru* or a Muslim if what we mean by "*gyuru*" or "Muslim" is widely shared by those around us. However, this relative advantage has the cost of privileging a third-person perspective on most habitable categories, insofar as our common sense conceptions of them are usually shaped by people who do not actually inhabit them. After all, for almost any habitable category there will usually be fewer people inhabiting it than people who do not, and in the case of most discriminated against categories, those who do not will usually have more power to shape common sense than those who do. This is especially pernicious in cases where common sense accounts are "confining or demeaning or contemptible" to those who inhabit them (Taylor 1994: 25).

For similar reasons, common sense theories are also favoured for their helpfulness in pushing eliminativist ontological agendas. Eliminativists, i.e., those who take discriminatory categories to be empty, usually (but not necessarily) endorse common sense accounts, and use them as arguments for their eliminativist arguments. For example, it has been argued that race is an empty category because our common sense conceptions of what a race is— i.e., substantial phenotypic differences between social groups of common ancestors—do not correspond to anything in biological reality (Mallon 2006). Similarly, some philosophers have argued recently that since it is constitutive of our common sense understanding of some social categories that people who belong to them are somehow inferior, and that this is patently false, nothing can fit inside them (I will not mention examples, because these categories are commonly expressed by the use of slurs and other derogatory terms, but see the work of philosophers of race like Appiah 1996 or Zack 2002).[1] In such cases, common sense classification involves a false presupposition that renders the category empty.

Yet, even though they have the obvious descriptive advantage of respecting common sense, few philosophers endorse common sense accounts nowadays (even though this varies largely depending on the category), for a variety of reasons. For starters, they usually embrace essentialism. There is ample empirical evidence that, from a very young age, people adopt a default form of essentialism, that is, "the common belief that natural and social categories are underlain by hidden, causally powerful essences" (Cimpian and Salomon 2014). That is why many common sense accounts of gender, race, sexual orientation, etc. identify these categories with essential or internal traits shared by all those that inhabit them. The resulting essentialist common sense accounts face the challenge of having to account for the historical development and heavily contingent nature of our common-sense beliefs. Given the enormous variation in what it means to be, say, a child (Heywood 2018), or a lesbian (Halperin 2002), or disabled (Tremain 2010), etc. in different historical and socio-cultural contexts, whoever wants to defend a current common sense conception as having finally captured the metaphysical underpinnings of such categories faces an enormous explanatory challenge. Given how much it has changed through history, how could we be justified in believing that we have finally got what it is to be a child, or to be disabled, for example?

From a political perspective, common-sense accounts tend to be criticised for having limited ameliorative political value insofar as they do not address (or, even worse, contribute to perpetuating) the oppressive and discriminatory nature of the distinctions they are supposed to characterise. Common sense might tell us that racial differences are biological, for example, yet a biological characterisation of racial differences would fail to account for the power asymmetries between those that inhabit them (Ludwig 2020; Mallon 2006). Common sense might tell us that in order to be Hispanic, one has to be of Spaniard descent, yet identifying Hispanics that way might hide "the fact that [they] suffer because they are Indian descended, not because they might have a distant European ancestor" (Hayes-Bautista 1980). Similarly, following common sense in characterising poverty as scarcity would suggest that the problem is economical, instead of political—one of resource distribution, instead of one of exclusion and discrimination, etc.

Furthermore, common sense accounts tend to present themselves as ideologically neutral when, in fact, they heavily reflect the prevailing ideology of those who hold them. In other words, what is, or is not, common sense depends heavily on the context and, in particular, to who holds power in such a context. Thus, giving ontological weight to so-called "common sense" ends up reifying the *Weltanschaung* of a privileged elite:

> This is an important methodological issue. We philosophers (especially analytic ones) rely quite a lot on folk intuitions and on what we take to be common-sense. But once we get into a politically charged discussion, we must recognise that these folk intuitions vary across cultures.
>
> Now what? Well, to settle on mainstream intuitions and common-sense is to make a political decision to further marginalize what Kristie Dotson called "diverse practitioners" in the field.
>
> (Bettcher 2018)

III. Socio-Historical Accounts

Efforts towards addressing these shortcomings of common sense theories have given rise to more sophisticated theories of habitable categories that stress their social, historical and ethnic aspects. According to these socio-historical accounts, what enlists someone in a given category are social, historic and cultural traits, facts and/or relations she has in common with others like her, or which bind her to them. These traits, facts and relations are not just there, impassive and inert, but are instead imposed through disciplinary practices, and even through the application of coercive force. Thus, feminists who consider the sex/gender distinction central to understanding womanhood typically adopt a socio-historical stance towards gender in this sense (Lecuona 2018; Oakley 1972). Similar stances lay behind ontological theses like identifying Mexican nationality with certain cultural practices, habits, signifiers, values, etc. shared by many, but not all, and certainly not only the people born or living in Mexico (Hobsbawm 1990). Social constructivist theories are another paradigmatic example of socio-historical accounts; for example, considering that what makes someone short, dirty or ignorant are standards of height, hygiene or knowledge that are not objective (like an average, for example) but depend on many social factors that deeply interweave them with other social categories, like class, race and gender (Knorr Cetina 1993; Mallon 2007); thus how clean a white American woman ought to be in order to be considered clean is substantially different from how clean an African American man must be in order to fit the same category (Berthold 2010). Philosophers who think that what makes a person an African American is a shared history or common experiences (Mallon 2006: 535; Piper 1992) are also embracing a socio-historical stance towards these categories. The social facts, relations and structures that are relevant to a category usually include those resulting from the very way we use it (Ásta 2018). For example, the fact that we use some categories to discriminate against and marginalize certain kinds of people is part of what makes those categories the sort of categories they are (I will not give examples to avoid the risk of legitimating such uses). The fact that we use certain external clues to apply our categories even if we know that such clues can mislead us is also a part of what makes those categories what they are (Knobe et al. 2013). This means that, for example, even if wearing some particular clothes or others does not make someone a lesbian, the social fact that young lesbians in Canada use certain brands of sportswear to signal their lesbianism is part of what it is for them to be lesbians (Anonymous 2011; Clarke and Turner 2007). The fact that we have institutionalised practices of conferral and classification, like census or civil registries, is part of the content of categories like race or marital status (Ásta 2018). In general, more often than not, social practices of classification contribute as much as they respond to the content of those very classifications. This circularity is not vicious, because our practices of categorisation are neither stable nor infallible, and thus still need to cohere with the rest of the relevant social and material facts pertinent to the given category. The aforementioned practice of using certain brands of sportswear to signal one's lesbianism, for example, has ontological significance in part because of how well it coheres with other aspects of lesbian identity. An officer of the civil registry has the power to confer marital status only insofar as this power coheres with other institutional, social and material facts and practices linked to marriage.

It is worth remarking that not all socio-historical accounts postulate common traits shared by all those that inhabit a category and only them (but some do, like Haslanger 2000). Some of them, like Parsons (1973) for "human" or Stoljar (1995) for "woman," conceive of them as family resemblance cluster concepts, where membership is grounded on "various resemblances between the members" of the category (Wittgenstein 1953: 67), so that "there is no single feature in common to all of them, though there are many common features overlapping" (Wittgenstein 1958: 20). Others conceive of inhabitable categories as social structures, i.e., complex systems of social relations, so that to inhabit a category is but to occupy a location or play a role in it (Wright 2000). Categories so understood bind those that inhabit them, not from an inner common nature, but from the outside—so to speak—so that people of radically different kinds, with different traits, goals, etc. can still partake in the same structure by fulfilling different roles within it. As Iris Marion Young has argued, "the search for . . . common characteristics . . . leads to normalizations and exclusion" (Young 1994: 713), and thus it is better to conceive of habitable categories as "material social facts that each individual must relate to and deal with" (Young 1994: 730–731). In a similar fashion, Marilyn Frye (1996) proposes that we conceive of (at least some) habitable categories as joint onto-political ventures, where persons of different kinds, with different traits, goals, etc. can collaborate in a collective project. Consequently, she argues, we should stop looking for what all women have (or lack) that makes them women, for example, and instead work on building together a positive category for women of all sorts to inhabit.

As I had mentioned, since common sense theories tend to favor essentialist accounts of habitable categories, socio-historical accounts can better account for the heterogeneous, contingent and dynamic nature of social categories, how practically every category we have devised to classify our fellow human beings has historically evolved and been contested, adapted to different circumstances and how, even at the same historical moment, different communities have understood and applied the same category with different criteria, criteria that many times is not even true about those it is applied to.

Nevertheless, it would be a mistake to think that socio-historical accounts completely abandon common sense. For example, many socio-historical accounts of class do not ignore the importance of economics in defining class differences, yet they do not think that that is all there is to them. Instead, they usually conceive of class as a social structure grounded in "both the material substance of social life (wealth, education, work) and the individual's construal of his or her class rank" (Kraus et al. 2012: 546). In this way, they incorporate the insights of common sense into a more sophisticated analysis. In a similar fashion, socio-historical accounts of parenthood do not just disregard matters of biological reproduction, but instead are conscious that these biological matters are also social, historical, economical and culturally constructed (Kenny and Müller 2018). In other words, they do not just take the common sense biological notion of parenthood, for example, and then throw some history, sociology, economics and anthropology on top. Instead, they aim to show how one cannot properly understand the biological dimension of parenthood independently from its social, historical, cultural and economical dimensions (and vice versa).

Unfortunately, many social, cultural, economic and historical processes and mechanisms tend to be too complex to play the theoretical and political roles that we want for our habitable categories (Kim 2020). For instance, attempts to define what it is for someone to belong to a certain habitable category, like a nationality or a race, by appealing to historical facts fail because they just move the demarcation question up a higher level. This is so, because they still need to determine what makes certain historical facts relevant and not others. Trying to define the Mexican identity by appealing to a historical process of cultural syncretism or *mestizaje*, for example, gives rise to the problem of trying to define what historical facts, process and effects are part of this so-called *mestizaje* and which are not; yet this problem is not actually simpler than the original one, and furthermore, it is not clear that we can solve it without appealing to some previous notion of Mexican identity. Thus, the proposed account fails to capture our national identity. Historical facts are just not sharp enough to serve as the kind of foundations that historicists' accounts want for their social categories.

Other socio-historical accounts face similar shortcomings: whatever mechanisms they appeal to end up being much messier than expected (Antony 2012). As a result, their attempts at providing an ontology well suited to the goals of redistributive justice face a series of problems that challenge their political and theoretical soundness (probably the best known of which is commonly known as the "nonidentity problem" [Roberts 2019]). For example, as aforementioned, many historico-social accounts aim to make constitutive of a habitable category at least some social injustices the members of such category have endured in such a way as to make them worthy of the benefits of restorative redistribution of resources (Hayes-Bautista 1980). For example, it has been argued that part of what makes someone Native-American is the historical fact that they have and still endure the negative effects of European colonialism in America, and that this is part of what makes some forms of affirmative action in their benefit just. However, filling the blanks of exactly how to link Native identity to colonization has not been easy, precisely because the current life and situations of American natives are so embedded in the overall effects of colonialism. We want to recognise that practically every aspect of current native American identity has been shaped by colonialism, and we want to say that the overall effect of colonialism on current native Americans has been harmful, yet we do not want to reach the seemingly unavoidable conclusions that being a native American or being born one is some kind of harm. Finding the right balance has proved to be quite difficult.

Some defenders of socio-historical accounts have embraced this complexity and, while recognising the possible theoretical advantages of univocal definitions of certain habitable categories, they reject the thesis that redistributive justice requires consistent and well-defined habitable categories. Instead, they have theorized that it is precisely because of their complex multiplicity that habitable categories contain the seed of their own emancipatory potential. For this sort of account, complexity, multiplicity, and even inconsistency are not liabilities, but assets of habitable categories (Solnit 2020). María Lugones (2003), for example, has argued that "the logic of purity is conceptually linked to a desire for control" (Bailey 2007: 83) and that well-defined categories belong within a logic of domination, so that in order to be truly liberating, we need to embrace equivocal categories. When resisting hegemonic systems of oppressions, the argument goes, it helps to inhabit slippery categories. Nazan Üstündağ (2019), for example, has shown how Kurdish mothers of the disappeared in Turkey have exploited the tensions in the category of motherhood in their socio-historical context to acquire political agency. According to Üstündağ,

> the mother [is] a limit figure who, on the one hand, because she dwells in the private of the everyday, 'knows' truths unassimilable by law and, on the other, . . . when she transgresses her assigned space and expresses such truths to larger publics, creates an exception that cannot be easily ignored.
>
> (2019: 120)

By identifying as mothers, they gained political access to the power of making demands of hegemonic power by assuming stereotypical ritualized domestic duties (associated with mourning) that entail contesting public political rights (associated to justice). It is as if they were telling the hegemonic patriarchal state: "I cannot fulfil the role you have assigned me (as grieving mother) if you do not recognise the death of my children (and thus insert their death into the public discourse from which you have excluded them)." As there seem to be both political and theoretical advantages to both well defined and elusive accounts of habitable categories, the debate continues.

Since socio-historical accounts place social categories outside the classified subject, they are alienating to the subjects that inhabit them. This alienation might be considered a precondition for emancipation and genuine agency (Hyppolite 1969); however, it has also been variously interpreted as not leaving enough room for genuine agency.[2] As Philippe Bourgois has written, "a focus on structures often obscures the fact that humans are active agents of their own history, rather than passive victims" (Bourgois 1995: 17). According to these criticisms, by defining social kinds by the social conditions under which the persons who belong to them live, including those that oppress them, it makes such oppression constitutive of the kind, and as such, they leave not enough room for liberation (without abandoning the category itself) (Mikkola 2011: 2016).

However, this criticism is grounded on a questionable division between individuals and society, as if individuals did not actively shape their social and material conditions. In actuality, most socio-historical accounts emphasize this constructive dimension of habitable categories. Charles Mills, for example, recognises that oppressive systems evolve over time, in part precisely because of marginalized groups' political struggles against them (Mills 1997: 101). María Lugones (2003) similarly stresses that oppressive systems are shaped by acts of resistance at least as much as by reinforcing ones. Thus, the criticism that socio-historical accounts are incompatible with emancipatory human agency is clearly unfounded.

Finally and unsurprisingly, socio-historical accounts have also been criticized for overemphasizing the social, historical and cultural aspects of habitable categories. From one direction, defenders of common sense theories argue that criticisms against them are question-begging insofar as they assume, instead of show, that the socio-political aspects in question lie within the ontological category itself, instead of belonging to the more complex material and social network in which it is situated. From a different direction, what I will call performance accounts have also argued that, even though socio-historical accounts are superior to essentialist accounts that postulate unchangeable and innate inner natures, they still stack the deck against individuals. Thus, even though it is true that many socio-historic accounts recognise the important role of individual action in constructing the material and social circumstances that ultimately bind individuals to the categories they inhabit, they still conceive of these social structures as ontologically fundamental and thus as mediating between individual action and category inhabitation. In socio-historical accounts, we do not inhabit our categories "from the inside"—to borrow a phrase from Kymlicka (1988: 184)—but from the outside, i.e., not primarily because of the features of our true inner selves, but from our external (even if internalized) circumstances, so that the only way we can change those categories is by changing our external circumstances—and only indirectly by changing ourselves. This is a complex issue indeed, and in order to properly assess it, it is necessary to understand what these performative accounts propose first, and only then evaluate whether they actually propose a better alternative.

IV. Performative Accounts

The aforementioned concern regarding social accounts has given rise to a new set of theories that I will call "performative accounts." According to performative accounts, to inhabit a category is to perform a kind of constrained act or similar, like a public avowal or a personal project (Bettcher 2009; Butler 1990). In the words of Appiah (2018), habitable categories are "an activity, not a thing . . . not a fate, but a project."

Performative accounts incorporate the insights from both socio-ethnic and common-sense accounts as constraints to the act, while also placing the agent at the center of her inhabiting one category or other (Baumeister and Muraven 1996). Thus, they hold categories like class, gender, disability, nationality, etc., not so much as things that one is, but more fundamentally, as things one does. To be a Mexican, for example, is to act in a certain way in given occasions—like partying the night of September the 15th while listening to ranchera music from the mid-20th century and eating certain foods (like tacos and pozole) and not others (like hamburgers)—constrained by the social and material factors affecting her in her context—such as those that would make it hard for her to find good tacos in downtown Reykjavik, but would make it hard to avoid if she lived in downtown Coyoacán in Mexico City. In this sense, whatever actions constitute one's inhabiting one category of another are always socially constrained. "Persons may not declare themselves teapots and thereby make it so," as Bettcher rightly states (Bettcher 2018: 98). The circumstances must be propitious, the action must adequately fit the circumstances and the agent must acknowledge proper ethical responsibility for her action (Bettcher 2018: 101; Jenkins 2018).

This performative aspect of inhabiting a category is very well illustrated by a key scene in Xaime Hernandez's *Wig Wam Bam* (1994) episode of his long-lasting Chicano series of graphic novels. After a couple of hipsters make racist commentaries to her at a party on the East Coast of the USA, one of the series' main characters, Margarita Luisa Chascarillo, relates the abuse she suffered to her friend and lover Esperanza Leticia Glass, telling her she is more than happy to leave town soon, which means going back to their Chicano neighborhood in southern California. Esperanza tries to make little of the event and to have Margarita drop the subject, raising the point that "It's the same shit all over." Margarita is angered by the lack of solidarity shown by Esperanza, who has Colombian ancestors but, unlike her, can pass for white American. "Ok, then don't go back to California!"—she screams at her friend—"Shit, just 'cause you can turn off your 'ethnic' half whenever it's goddamn convenient!" Now, I was born in Mexico, as were my parents. My skin is brown, my hair is thick and black and my mother tongue is Spanish. I have lived most of my life in Mexico City and currently live in the typical Mexican neighbourhood of Coyoacán, just a couple of blocks from historical monuments of early Colonial history. For me, it is very easy and natural to be—that is, to behave—Mexican, so much that it might seem more appropriate to say that I did not have to do much to be Mexican and that I was just born this way, i.e., that being born in the place where I was born, into the family and culture I was born made me Mexican. This is just what the socio-ethnic accounts hold. However, not everyone shares the same circumstances, as the aforementioned scene in Hernandez's novel illustrates very well. For Esperanza, her situation allows her to become white American or Colombian depending on what she does. She has reached a point where she has to make the decision as to whether to act in one way or another. This decision is both enabled and constrained by her circumstances—her skin color, her ancestry, her relation to California and to Margarita—but it is still hers to make. She has what Bettcher has called an "ethical first person authority" over her own ontological performance. Whatever way she acts will have not only an ontological effect, but also an ethical one. The way Xavier Hernandez sets the scene, it is clear that the ethical decision is to resist her whiteness and live up to her Colombianess.[3] Only then can she take proper responsibility for her ontological performance. As a matter of fact, I would contend that one of the most attractive aspects of performative accounts is how they bind the political, the ethical and the metaphysical.

For Performative accounts, if we look back at a case like mine, and compare it with an interstitial case like Esperanza's, we can see that action also plays a central, even if not salient, role in my being Mexican: that being born in Mexico, being brown, etc. are not what makes me Mexican, but only the material circumstances that enable and constrain my actions, and that it is ultimately these actions that ground my Mexican identity. Considering cases like these is very helpful in this respect, insofar as it allows us to disentangle the action from the circumstances that frame it (Jardina 2019; Vargas 2020). As a matter of fact, the experiences and reflections of immigrants and, in general, peoples who identify with categories that do not sit comfortable in their material circumstances have been fertile sources of performative theories of this sort.

Performative theories have been criticized for being either overtly individualistic or not genuine alternatives to socio-historical theories, and for drawing the boundaries between categories in the wrong place (where "wrong" here means both "inaccurate" and "unjust") by overestimating the importance of individual action and choice. Let's look at those criticisms in more detail.

First of all, performance accounts seem to fit better within a very individualistic view of politics, the kind of atomistic politics that is concerned mainly with "securing the conditions for individuals to exercise their powers of autonomous choice" (Bell 2020), and thus is at tension with an alternative view of politics where "we also need to sustain and promote the social attachments crucial to our sense of well-being and respect, many of which have been involuntarily picked up during the course of our upbringing" (2020). As important as it is to have the chance to become who we choose to become, it is also important to recognize that, on the one hand, we cannot be expected to choose everything we are and, on the other, some of the things we might end up being not by choice might still be as fundamental to who we are as those that we choose.

In other words, because we are not (and we must not be) just what we choose to be, our inhabitable categories cannot be grounded on personal choice (or at least not all of them, and not for everyone who inhabits them).

A further consequence of the individualistic stance of performance theories is that they can easily slip into dangerous relativism. Giving subjects ultimate authority over their self-identity might allow those who would otherwise be identified as members of privileged groups to identify as members of historically disenfranchised groups, giving them unfair access to resources aimed to restore historical injustices. In this way, unscrupulous members of privileged groups might abuse restorative measures to access resources and spaces reserved for members of discriminated groups (Hayes-Bautista 1980). American readers might be familiar with the controversial case of Rachel Dolezal (Krishnamurthy 2015), yet the phenomenon in question is more widespread. In recent years, for example, groups of otherwise white, French descendant settlers in Quebec, through suspect genealogical practices, have demanded an "Indigenous" identity that has allowed them to dispossess genuine indigenous people from their hunting and fishing territories (Leroux 2019).

However, as I had already mentioned, performance accounts like Bettcher (2009) and Jenkins (2018) contain an ethical clause, and insist on responsibility as a requisite condition for an avowal or action to have the desired ontological effect. In other words, according to Bettcher, it is not enough to just assert one's willingness to inhabit a category, one must also "stake her claim" by taking full responsibility for the avowed desire (Bettcher 2009: 101). This condition aims precisely to exclude this sort of abuse. Thus, the criticism misses its mark.

However, even after taking this ethical clause into consideration, it is still worth mentioning that making it too easy for anyone to inhabit a category or another, regardless of their material, cultural, social or historical circumstances, runs the risk of building categories that bring together people which, from the perspective both from the common sense and socio-historical perspective, are too diverse to serve in efforts to diversify sites of power like governing bodies or boardrooms. People who perform in accordance to their social and material conditions and people who do not might end up having such different bodies, social histories, structural power, access to resources, etc. that one could not properly represent the experiences and concerns of the other. Thus, there is no political use in bringing them together into a single category.

Within performative accounts, there is ample debate on whether it is the act itself that constitutes our inhabiting the category or something deeper that manifests itself in such acts, either something that we feel or perceive within ourselves (and thus, something for which we have privileged first person access) or the feeling itself. How the debate turns has important consequences to how performative accounts can avoid the sort of relativism just sketched (Ozturk 2017). On the one hand, if it is not the act itself, but something else within each person that makes them inhabit the categories they do, then the relevant performances can be appropriate only if they correctly manifest what the person actually is. This means that people's first-person authority over the categories they inhabit is purely epistemic and, therefore, fallible (Bettcher 2009; Lawlor 2003). On the other hand, if it is the act itself that is constitutive, then relativism can be avoided by recognising that ontological performances, just like any performative act, are subject to external normative conditions (Austin 1962). Either way, despite their ontological significance, our actions are not unbound but constrained and, as such, they are very unlikely to have the undesirable relativist consequences that their critics impute them.

As I have already mentioned, most socio-historical accounts give the subject relative power over what makes her inhabit one category or another. Yet, this power is not as direct as it is in performative accounts. Nevertheless, this difference must not be overstated. After all, performative accounts (mostly in response to the accusations of radical relativism just sketched) recognise that one cannot just will oneself into any habitable category. One must perform the right kind of actions in the right sort of circumstances. However, they have a hard time trying to specify what makes the circumstances be of the right kind without reiterating the central tenants of socio-historical accounts. Going back to Xavier Hernandez's example above, it is clear what aspects of Esperanza's context gave her decision its ontological significance: her skin color, her ancestry, her relation to California and its history, her personal relation to Margarita, etc. What makes these be the relevant aspects and not, say, her height or the time of the season (which, in turn, may be ontologically relevant for other ontological performances and other categories)? It is unclear how performance accounts could answer, without recognizing the ontological importance of, in this case, one's body, one's social and personal relations to others, one's place and its history, etc., that is, without incorporating the central insights of socio-historical accounts. Thus, performance accounts seem to become more of a variety, instead of a true alternative to socio-historical accounts.

Summarising, the main problem with performance accounts is that the notion of a constrained act of self-identification at their heart is still an ill-defined notion, unstable between two equally undesirable positions. On the one hand, if such a constrained act were just the mere act of freely asserting one's will of belonging to a certain social group, that would cheapen the social categories to the point of being too arbitrary for being of any use in the fight for social justice. Such an action would not be a constrained action. On the other hand, if we require the act to be socially recognised within the group as being the kind of act that constitutes the kind, then it seems that it is not the agent but the group who confers the relevant category, making it socially constructed (Ásta 2018). In other words, it would not be the act, but its enabling and constraining social, historical, cultural and material circumstances that would serve as ontological grounds for the inhabiting of the category. Thus, performative theories would not be an actual alternative to socio-historical theories, and would not have achieved the desired de-exteriorization of our social ontology. For performative theories to be a genuine alternative, there must be some third alternative, but it is not clear that there really is such a third way, as much as performative theorists have certainly made substantial efforts in building one.

From the opposite direction, performative theories can also be faulted for making it too hard for those who could and should benefit the most from being recognized as inhabiting a given marginalized category. By insisting on an active engagement with the category, performative theories seem to require from those who are already in a practically diminished status to make an extra effort to be recognised as such. According to this criticism, by belittling victimhood, performative theories have also belittled victims (Convery 2011). Consider again, the previous contrast I raised between me and the fictional Esperanza Glass. According to a performative theory of Latinx identity, it is much easier to me to identify as a Latinx than her, and the ethical stakes are also higher for her than for me. It can be argued that, for a proposal that tries to ameliorate the marginalization of groups like migrant Latinxs in the USA, it is strange that it makes higher ethical and ontological demands from migrants than from non-migrants. From this perspective, race (or class or gender, etc.) consciousness seems more of a burden that one would like to be liberated from than a mechanism of empowerment (Brody 1992).

V. Final Remarks

In this essay I have tackled the complex metaphysical question of what makes a person inhabit one category or another, i.e., what makes someone Latinx, poor, disabled, etc.? Common sense might tell us that different sorts of categories will require different sorts of answers. And even though this may be true about the details, I hope to have shown that much might be achieved by adopting a more abstract perspective. I hope to have shown that approaching the question at such a general level as I have done here allows us to detect general threads that weave through a vast range of philosophical theories of social categories and to compare and contrast them by identifying their central achievements and challenges. I hope to have shown the value of adopting an abstract point of view in condensing a wide variety of complex debates into a few simple questions and issues. This not something that can be argued for, but only shown, and that is just what I presume to have done here.

Thus, what is the picture of habitable categories that emerges from the abstract roadmap I have just laid out? I take that one major conclusion to draw is that who we are cannot be easily reduced nor detached from what we choose to do, what our circumstances are and how others perceive us; and that performative, socio-historical and common sense approaches tend to privilege each one of these dimensions. Performative accounts stress our personal choices and actions; socio-historical accounts stress our location in a material, social and historical world not entirely of our personal creation, while common sense accounts seem better suited to account for how we are seen from the third person perspective of everyday people. Yet, as I have tried to stress throughout the text, their overlap is at least as large as their discrepancies: Performance theories recognize, incorporate but also problematize the insight of socio-historical accounts as much as socio-historical accounts do the same with the insights of common sense theories. This should not be surprising insofar as the threads that each sort of accounts privilege are deeply interwoven within each category. And we understand this complexity precisely by seeing them as distinct threads and theoretical responses to different questions.

From a performative perspective, for example, I am a Mexican because of many actions and choices I have made throughout my life—including not just my everyday choices of what to eat, what language to speak, what festivities to celebrate, etc. but also more institutional choices related to my legal status as a Mexican citizen—even if many of those choices I have made by default. From a socio-historical perspective, in contrast, I am Mexican because of the complex system of material facts and social-relations that have constrained and given ontological significance to those very choices and acts. In the end, when I say I am Mexican, what most people will think, and what will ultimately determine their first expectations of me, will be the commonsensical belief that I am from Mexico. And notice that this expectation would still be attached to my being a Mexican even if I were not actually from Mexico. These expectations, although commonsensical, are still socially and historically conditioned and, therefore, do not present an insurmountable challenge to socio-historical accounts just as the existence of social and historical constraints to human action does not preclude the ontological significance of human choice and action asserted by performative accounts.

As long as we think of non-problematic examples like mine—i.e., someone who acts Mexican, looks Mexican, lives and was born in Mexico, etc.—the differences between the three approaches seem negligible: each one just seems to bring to the fore a particular aspect of a complex phenomenon. It is when we think of the clearly more complex interstitial cases like Hernandez's white Latina Esperanza Glass, or the Kurdish mothers mourning their sons, that the discrepancies acquire major significance. It is only then, when different perspectives deliver different answers, not only to our original question of what makes someone, say, white, or indigenous, or middle-class, but also whether someone is middle class, indigenous, or white. It is because of Latinas like Esperanza Glass, that it makes sense to ponder the relative ontological importance of self expression over social circumstance or appearance in determining whiteness, for example. Cases like these show that when addressing the question *who we are?*, the answer may be different if we take it to be asking about how we act and think of ourselves (as performative accounts do), than asking about our socio-historical position, or about what categories we fit in from the external perspective of common sense. Once we realize that the answers can be different, we ought to wonder why we ever thought they had to be similar.

Once we take a step back from the details of these debates and see the general pattern that emerges, we can advance the debate in a way that may be easily missed from a ground level perspective, so to speak. Having identified the different aspects of the phenomenon that each camp privileges immediately suggest the possibility of a pluralist account that reconciles the three perspectives in a straightforward way. It suffices to remember that the general structure of pluralist strategies in philosophy is to try to dissolve paradoxes and impasses by arguing that each of the positions in dispute deals with different, yet related questions. That way, they can all be right about their own topic, and they can all shed light on different aspects of the same complex phenomenon. Thus, where we thought we were dealing with a single question, we were actually confusing different ones (Barceló 2019). In the case at hand, we thought there was a single what-makes question behind every habitable category. Now we can see that there were three: the question of how one thinks and acts as inhabitant of a category, the question of how our socio-historical position binds us to (and separates us from) others, and the question of what categories we fit in from the external perspective of common sense. These aspects of our habitable categories all interact in complex ways, and that is why we had been confused into thinking they all responded to the same phenomenon. Yet, now that we can disentangle these threads, we can see the way out of the confusion. We can see the value of each perspective to shed light on one of the aspects of categories of this sort as well as its limitations when trying to make sense of them as a whole.[4] We can see, for example, the value of socio-historical approaches to make sense of how our habitable categories are linked to our social and material circumstances as well as their limitations when trying to account for what it is to inhabit a category from the first person perspective, when those social and material circumstances situate us at the border of those categories. In a similar fashion, common sense accounts can be very valuable when trying to make sense of how people categorize us from their third person perspective, but not when trying to account for the relation between these categories and our true inner selves, especially when our actions are at odds with what is expected from us from that third person perspective, etc. Hence, a complete account of habitable categories that reconciles these perspectives while recognizing that what we do, what happens to us and what is expected from us does not always result in a coherent and unified picture of who we are is indeed possible.[5]

References

Abrams, K. (1995) "Sex Wars Redux: Agency and Coercion in Feminist Legal Theory," *Columbia Law Review* 95 (2): 304–376. https://doi.org/10.2307/1123232.
Alcoff, L. M. (2005) "Latino vs. Hispanic: The Politics of Ethnic Names," *Philosophy & Social Criticism* 31 (4): 395–407. https://doi.org/10.1177/0191453705052972.
Andreasen, R. O. (1998) "A New Perspective on the Race Debate," *The British Journal for the Philosophy of Science*, 49 (2): 199–225. https://doi.org/10.1093/bjps/49.2.199.
Anonymous. (2011) *The New Lesbian Uniform: A Lesbian in Brighton*. Brighton Lesbian, http://brightonlesbian.blogspot.com/2011/08/new-lesbian-uniform.html.
Antony, L. (2012) "Different Voices or Perfect Storm: Why Are There So Few Women in Philosophy?" *Journal of Social Philosophy* 43 (3): 227–255. https://doi.org/10.1111/j.1467-9833.2012.01567.x.
Appiah, K. A. (1996) "Race, Culture, Identity: Misunderstood Connections," *The Tanner Lectures on Human Values* 17: 51–136. https://doi.org/10.1515/9781400822096-002.
Appiah, K. A. (2018) *The Lies that Bind: Rethinking Identity: Creed, Country, Color, Class, Culture*, New York: Liveright.
Ásta. (2018) *Categories We Live By: The Construction of Sex, Gender, Race, and Other Social Categories*, Oxford: Oxford University Press.
Austin, J. L. (1962) *How to Do Things with Words*, Oxford: Clarendon.
Báez-Jorge, F. (2002) "Los indios, los nacos, los otros . . . (apuntes sobre el prejuicio racial y la discriminación en México)," *La Palabra y el Hombre* 121: 21–40.
Bailey, A. (2007) "Strategic Ignorance," in S. Sullivan and N. Tuana (eds.), *Race and Epistemologies of Ignorance*, 77–94, Albany, NY: SUNY.
Barceló, A. (2019) *Falibilidad y normatividad: Un análisis filosófico de la suerte*, Madrid: Cátedra.
Baumeister, R. F., and Muraven, M. (1996) "Identity as Adaptation to Social, Cultural, and Historical Context," *Journal of Adolescence* 19 (5): 405–416. https://doi.org/10.1006/jado.1996.0039.
Bell, D. (2020) "Communitarianism" in E. N. Zalta (ed.), *The Stanford Encyclopedia of Philosophy* (Summer 2020 ed.), https://plato.stanford.edu/archives/sum2020/entries/communitarianism.
Berthold, D. (2010) "Tidy Whiteness: A Genealogy of Race, Purity, and Hygiene," *Ethics & The Environment* 15 (1): 1–26. https://doi.org/10.2979/ete.2010.15.1.1.
Bettcher, T. M. (2009) "Trans Identities and First-person Authority," in L. Shrage (ed.), *You've Changed: Sex Reassignment and Personal Identity*, 98–120, Oxford: Oxford University Press.
Bettcher, T. M. (2018) "When Tables Speak: On the Existence of Trans Philosophy," *Daily Nous*, May 30, http://dailynous.com/2018/05/30/tables-speak-existence-trans-philosophy-guest-talia-mae-bettcher.

Born, G., and Hesmondhalgh, D. (2000) "Introduction: On Difference, Representation, and Appropriation in Music," in G. Born and D. Hesmondhalgh (eds.), *Western Music and its Others: Difference, Representation, and Appropriation in Music*, 1–58, Berkeley: University of California Press.

Bourgois, P. (1995) *In Search of Respect: Selling Crack in El Barrio*, Cambridge: Cambridge University Press.

Brody, J. D. (1992) "Clare Kendry's 'True' Colors: Race and Class Conflict in Nella Larsen's Passing," *Callaloo* 15 (4): 1053–1065. https://doi.org/10.2307/2931920.

Bürki, Y. (2014) "Prácticas Discursivas y Estereotipos: La Figura del naco en la Sociedad Mexicana Actual," in M. Kunz, C. Mondragón and D. Phillips-López (eds.), *Nuevas narrativas mexicanas II*, 399–427. Linkgua.

Burt, S. (2012) "My Life as a Girl," *The Virginia Quarterly Review* 88 (4): 202–211.

Butler, J. (1990) *Gender Trouble: Feminism and the Subversion of Identity*. London: Routledge.

Carbonell, V. (2019) "Social Constraints on Moral Address," *Philosophy and Phenomenological Research* 98 (1): 167–189. https://doi.org/10.1111/phpr.12450.

Casey, C. (1995) *Work, Self and Society: After Industrialism*. London: Routledge.

Chance, J. K. (1979) "On the Mexican Mestizo," *Latin American Research Review* 14 (3): 153–168.

Cimpian, A., and Salomon, E. (2014) "The Inherence Heuristic: An Intuitive Means of Making Sense of the World, and a Potential Precursor to Psychological Essentialism," *Behavioral and Brain Sciences* 37 (5): 461–480. https://doi.org/10.1017/S0140525 X13002197.

Clarke, V. C., and Turner, K. (2007) "Clothes Maketh the Queer? Dress, Appearance and the Construction of Lesbian, Gay and Bisexual Identities," *Feminism & Psychology* 17 (2): 267–276. https://doi.org/10.1177/0959353507076561.

Cole, N. L. (2019) "What Is Social Class, and Why Does It Matter?" *ThoughtCo*. www.thoughtco.com/what-is-social-class-and-why-does-it-matter-3026375.

Convery, A. (2011) *Feminist Theory and Discursive Intersections: Activating the Code of "Political Correctness"*, Unpublished doctoral dissertation, University of Newcastle.

Daly, C., and Liggins, D. (2010) "In Defence of Error Theory," *Philosophical Studies* 149 (2): 209–230. https://doi.org/10.1007/s11098-009-9346-1.

Demolombe, R., and Louis, V. (2006) "Norms, Institutional Power and Roles: Towards a Logical Framework" in F. Esposito, Z. W. Raś, D. Malerba and G. Semeraro (eds.), *Foundations of Intelligent Systems. ISMIS 2006*, 514–523. New York: Springer. https://doi.org/10.1007/11875604_58.

Frye, M. (1996) "The Necessity of Differences: Constructing a Positive Category of Women," *Signs* 21 (4): 991–1010.

Gilbert, E. (2009) *Committed: A Skeptic Makes Peace with Marriage*, New York: Penguin.

Guerrero McManus, S. F. (2018) "Naturalezas, culturas y arquitecturas disciplinarias. La infrapolítica de un debate (necesariamente) interminable," *Metatheoria* 8 (2): 77–85.

Guerrero McManus, S. F. (2019) "Transgeneridad y transracialidad: Contrastes ontológicos entre género y raza," *Diánoia* 64 (82): 3–30. https://doi.org/10.22201/iifs.18704913e.2019.82.1633.

Gupta, A. (2006) *Empiricism and Experience*, Oxford: Oxford University Press. https://doi.org/10.1093/acprof:oso/9780195189582.001.0001.

Halperin, D. M. (2002) *How to Do the History of Homosexuality*, Chicago: University of Chicago Press.

Haslanger, S. (2000) "Gender and Race: (What) Are They? (What) Do We Want Them to Be?" *Noûs* 34 (1): 31–55. https://doi.org/10.1111/0029-4624.00201.

Hayes-Bautista, D. E. (1980) "Identifying 'Hispanic' Populations: The Influence of Research Methodology upon Public Policy," *American Journal of Public Health* 70 (4): 353–356. https://doi.org/10.2105/AJPH.70.4.353.

Hernandez, X. (1994) *Wig wam bam*, Seattle: Fantagraphics.

Heywood, C. (2018) *A History of Childhood*, New York: John Wiley & Sons.

Hobsbawm, E. J. (1990) *Nations and Nationalism Since 1780: Programme, Myth, Reality*, Cambridge: Cambridge University Press.

Hyppolite, J. (1969) *Studies on Marx and Hegel*, New York: Basic Books.

Jardina, A. (2019). *White Identity Politics*, Cambridge: Cambridge University Press. https://doi.org/10.1017/9781108645157.

Jenkins, K. (2018) "Toward an Account of Gender Identity," *Ergo* 5 (27): 1–25.

Kenny, M., and Müller, R. (2018) "Of Rats and Women: Narratives of Motherhood in Environmental Epigenetics" in M. Meloni, J. Cromby, D. Fitzgerald, and S. Lloyd (eds.), *The Palgrave Handbook* of Biology and Society, 799–830, London: Palgrave Macmillan. https://doi.org/10.1057/978-1-137/52879-7_34.

Kim, E. T. (2020) "The Perils of 'People of Color,'" The New Yorker, July 29, www.newyorker.com/news/annals-of-activism/the-perils-of-people-of-color.

Kingston, P. W. (2000) The Classless Society, Redwood City, CA: Stanford University Press.

Knobe, J., Prasada, S., and Newman, G. E. (2013) "Dual Character Concepts and the Normative Dimension of Conceptual Representation," Cognition 127 (2): 242–257. https://doi.org/10.1016/j.cognition.2013.01.005.

Knorr Cetina, K. (1993) "Strong Constructivism—From a Sociologist's Point of View: A Personal Addendum to Sismondo's Paper," Social Studies of Science 23 (3): 555–563. https://doi.org/10.1177/0306312793023003005.

Kraus, M. W., Piff, P. K., Mendoza-Denton, R., Rheinschmidt, M. L., and Keltner, D. (2012) "Social Class, Solipsism, and Contextualism: How the Rich Are Different from the Poor," Psychological Review 119 (3): 546–572. https://doi.org/10.1037/a0028756.

Krishnamurthy, M. (2015) "Philosophers on Rachel Dolezal," Daily Nous, June 15, http://dailynous.com/2015/06/15/philosophers-on-rachel-dolezal.

Kymlicka, W. (1988) "Liberalism and Communitarianism," Canadian Journal of Philosophy 18 (2): 181–203, https://doi.org/10.1080/00455091.1988.10717173.

Lawlor, K. (2003) "Elusive Reasons: A Problem for First-person Authority," Philosophical Psychology 16 (4): 549–564. https://doi.org/10.1080/0951508032000166969.

Lecuona, L. (2018) "El género y su tiro por la culata," Revista de la Universidad de México 840: 53–60.

Leroux, D. (2019) Distorted Descent: White Claims to Indigenous Identity, Winnipeg: University of Manitoba Press.

Lewis, D. (1986) On the Plurality of Worlds, Oxford: Wiley-Blackwell.

López Beltrán, C. (2004) El sesgo hereditario: Ámbitos históricos del concepto de herencia biológica, UNAM.

Ludwig, D. (2020) "Understanding Race: The Case for Political Constructionism in Public Discourse," Canadian Journal of Philosophy 50 (4): 492–504. https://doi.org/10.1017/can.2019.52.

Lugones, M. (2003) Pilgrimajes/peregrinajes: Theorizing Coalition Against Multiple Oppressions, Lanham, MD: Rowman & Littlefield.

Mallon, R. (2006) "'Race': Normative, Not Metaphysical or Semantic," Ethics 116: 525–551. https://doi.org/10.1086/500495.

Mallon, R. (2007) "A Field Guide to Social Construction," Philosophy Compass 2 (1): 93–108. https://doi.org/10.1111/j.1747-9991.2006.00051.x.

Mikkola, M. (2011) "Ontological Commitments, Sex and Gender," in C. Witt (ed.), Feminist Metaphysics: Explorations in the Ontology of Sex, Gender and the Self, 67–83. New York: Springer. https://doi.org/10.1007/978-90-481-3783-1_5.

Mikkola, M. (2016) The Wrong of Injustice: Dehumanization and Its Role in Feminist Philosophy, Oxford: Oxford University Press.

Mills, C. (1997) Blackness Visible: Essays on Philosophy and Race, Ithaca, NY: Cornell University Press.

Oakley, A. (1972) Sex, Gender, and Society, New York: Harper and Row.

Ozturk, B. (2017) "The Negotiative Theory of Gender Identity and the Limits of First-person Authority" in R. Halwani, A. Soble, S. Hoffman and J. M. Held (eds.), The Philosophy of Sex: Contemporary Readings, 139–159, Lanham, MD: Rowman & Littlefield.

Parsons, K. P. (1973) "Three Concepts of Clusters," Philosophy and Phenomenological Research 33 (4): 514–523. https://doi.org/10.2307/2106541.

Piper, A. (1992) "Passing for White, Passing for Black," Transition 58: 4–32. https://doi.org/10.2307/2934966.

Roberts, M. A. (2019) "The Nonidentity Problem" in E. N. Zalta (ed.), The Stanford Encyclopedia of Philosophy (Summer 2019 ed.), https://plato.stanford.edu/archives/sum2019/entries/nonidentity-problem.

Rudder, C. (2014) Dataclysm: Who We Are (When We Think No One's Looking), Crown.

Sarr, F. (2016) Afrotopia, Paris: Philippe Rey.

Schuman, H., and Scott, J. (1989) "Generations and Collective Memories," American Sociological Review 54 (3): 359–381, https://doi.org/10.2307/2095611.

Solnit, R. (2020) "Trans Women Pose No Threat to Cis Women, But We Pose a Threat To Them If We Make Them Outcasts," *The Guardian*, August 10, www.theguardian.com/commentisfree/2020/aug/10/trans-rights-feminist-letter-rebecca-solnit.
Spencer, Q. (2014) "A Radical Solution to the Race Problem," *Philosophy of Science* 81 (5): 1025–1038. https://doi.org/10.1086/677694.
Stoljar, N. (1995) "Essence, Identity, and the Concept of Woman," *Philosophical Topics* 23 (2): 261–293. https://doi.org/10.5840/philtopics19952328.
Taylor, C. (1994) "The Politics of Recognition," in A. Gutmann (ed.), *Multiculturalism: Examining the Politics of Recognition*, 25–73, Princeton: Princeton University Press. https://doi.org/10.2307/j.ctt7snkj.6.
Thompson, E. P. (1966) *The Making of the English Working Class*, New York: Vintage Books.
Tremain, S. L. (ed.) (2010) *Foucault and the Government of Disability*. Ann Arbor: University of Michigan Press.
Üstündağ, N. (2019) "Mother, Politician, and Guerilla: The Emergence of a New Political Imagination in Kurdistan Through Women's Bodies and Speech," *Differences: A Journal of Feminist Cultural Studies* 30 (2): 115–145. https://doi.org/10.1215/10407391-7736077.
Vargas, M. (2020) "The Philosophy of Accidentality," *Journal of the American Philosophical Association* 2020: 1–19. https://doi. org/10.1017/apa.2019.15.
Weinberg, J. (ed.) (2015) "Philosophers on Rachel Dolezal," *Daily Nous*, June 15, http://dailynous.com/2015/06/15/philosophers-on-rachel-dolezal.
Williams, K. C., and Page, R. A. (2011) "Marketing to the Generations," *Journal of Behavioral Studies in Business* 3 (1): 37–53.
Wittgenstein, L. (1953) *Philosophical Investigations*, Oxford: Blackwell.
Wittgenstein, L. (1958) *The Blue and Brown Books*, Oxford: Blackwell.
Wright, E. O. (2000). *Class Counts: Studies in Marxism and Social Theory*, Cambridge: Cambridge University Press. https://doi.org/10.1017/CBO9780511488917.
Young, I. M. (1994) "Gender as Seriality: Thinking About Women as a Social Collective," *Signs* 19 (3): 713–738. https://doi.org/10.1086/494918.
Zack, N. (2002) *Philosophy of Science and Race*, London: Routledge.

Notes

1 I find it interesting that this relation between eliminativism and common sense happens in other areas of metaphysics, for example, in the philosophy of mathematics, where nominalists (that is, eliminativists regarding mathematical entities) adopt a commonsense view of the ontological nature of mathematical objects—i.e., that they are abstract entities—and then use this common sense account as a premise for the conclusion that there are no mathematical objects.
2 See Thompson (1966) and Casey (1995) make this argument for class; Born and Hesmondhalgh (2000) and Jardina (2019) for ethnicity; Abrams (1995) and the works there discussed for gender; Guerrero McManus (2018) for humankind; Carbonell (2019) for a more general argument; etc.
3 This does not mean that all such choices have always such a clear ethical profile. Consider the case of Nicole Richie, who was adopted when she was three. Her African American parents, the successful singer and songwriter Lionel Richie and his then-wife Brenda Harvey, knew Nicole's biological parents, who were Mexican American. She went to live with and be cared for by the Richies in early childhood and was legally adopted at nine. Growing up in the spotlight, she was pressured into testifying to her ethnic identity and she could have chosen to identify as Mexican American or African American without much ethical fault.
4 Furthermore, this pluralism can also do justice to the presumption that transition, migration, *mestizaje* or even the very notion of a "middle class" are all constitutively linked both to the category one transits, passes or migrates from as much as the category one transits, passes or migrates to. Unfortunately, this is an idea I cannot fully develop here.
5 Special thanks to Sally Haslanger, Manuel Vargas, Daniel Drucker and this journal's referees for their very helpful comments. An earlier version of this paper was presented at *Seminario permanente de historia y filosofía de la ciencia racializada*, organized by Red Integra and the *Instituto de Investigaciones Filosóficas*; I am also very thankful to them.

Reading Questions

1. Suppose Barceló is right that we cannot easily detach questions about "what kind?" from what people choose, their circumstances, and how others perceive them. Does that fact mean that there is never a decisive/authoritative/correct answer about which kind of answer is central, definitive, or otherwise most important for the category? If there can be authoritative answers to kind questions, what settles that, i.e., what settles which answers are authoritative?
2. What might Barceló say in response to someone who objects that performative or common sense accounts are only secondary or frequently irrelevant senses?
3. Name some kinds where the performative is especially important or authoritative for what kind one belongs to?
4. What should a socio-historical account say about the demarcation worry (which socio-historical facts settle and why?) and the worry that if being an X is defined in terms of, say, a colonized subject position, to be X is always to be harmed?
5. Is there a way to escape this dilemma for performative accounts, i.e., that they either run the risk of being too flexible, and thus, insensitive to moral/political interests (compare: "One can be Indigenous simply by performing it!") or they have conditions about socio-historical ties that collapse into a socio-historical kind?

Part 2
Mestizaje and Indigeneity

Introduction

"Mestizaje," a Latin American term for "mixedness," is a central theme in the history of Latin America. Traditionally, the term "mestizo" ("mixed") refers to the people created by the genetic and cultural exchange between people of European and Indigenous descent. Being considered "too Indigenous" to enjoy the rights and privileges of Europeans, yet "too European" to belong to the Indigenous cultures of their ancestors, mestizos occupied a middle place in the colonial social hierarchy.

Latin American philosophers—including some of the region's most celebrated statesmen, artists, and intellectuals—made important contributions to the history of the region by advancing alternative frameworks celebrating the positive qualities of mestizos. This discourse provided key justifications for a wave of revolutionary independence movements that would remake the region by imposing new social and political systems that aspired to liberal ideals while privileging the interests of mestizos.

For over fifty years, Latinx philosophers have examined and debated the nature of mestizaje, taking the philosophical discussion of this topic into new and generative directions. What comes to light when we examine mestizaje from a Latinx perspective? As we will see, some Latinx writers argue that mestizaje is still vitally important in the contemporary US context. If it is true, can Latinx philosophers articulate a conception of mestizaje that affirms the positive value of "mixture," without thereby contributing to the oppression of Indigenous and other marginalized communities?

To set the stage for this discussion, this section begins with an excerpt from José Vasconcelos' book, *The Cosmic Race*. This text from 1925 is the oldest in the volume, and it is the only text included that is not a work of Latinx philosophy (even on relatively generous interpretations of that category). Our hope is that it will be useful for readers to have easy access to key excerpts of this text, which has been brilliantly rendered in a recent translation by John Polt. *The Cosmic Race* has long served as a common point of reference among Latinx philosophers, intellectuals, and activists, and it dramatically showcases the best and worst features of this branch of Latin American thought.

In "The Mestizo Concept as a Product of European Imperialism," Jack D. Forbes articulates one salient objection that has been raised against Vasconcelos and others. When we examine the historical origins of the concept, we find that the idea of the "mestizo" was introduced as a colonial legal fiction designed to divide and control Indigenous peoples by creating artificial castes and encouraging assimilation into European culture. In a historical context marked by centuries of coercive detribalization, there is good reason to worry that discourses aiming to valorize mestizaje ultimately promote the erasure of Indigenous communities and perspectives.

DOI: 10.4324/9781003385417-10

In "*La Conciencia de la Mestiza:* Towards a New Consciousness," we find Gloria Anzaldúa's famous response to this line of critique. This chapter, taken from her 1987 book *Borderlands/La Frontera*, offers an original and compelling philosophical analysis of mestizaje from her perspective as a lesbian, working-class, Mexican-American woman with deep ties to Latin American, Anglo-European, and Indigenous cultures. The text showcases Anzaldúa's now-iconic style of writing, which weaves philosophical argumentation and scholarship together with evocative snippets of poetry, autobiography, and history, while switching frequently between English and Spanish without explanation or apology—techniques allow the reader to experience firsthand some of the distress and delight that she says characterizes life in the "borderlands" between social binaries.

As generations of thinkers have been inspired to adapt Anzaldúa's concepts and methods to explore their own lives, *Borderlands/La Frontera* has arguably gained the status of a "Great Text" of world philosophy. Anzaldúa's work helps us to appreciate the ways that Latinx people can experience an additional layer of mixture and marginalization when compared with their Latin American counterparts—not only can they not properly identify as European or Indigenous; they also find that they are often seen as "too Latin American" to be included fully in mainstream US culture, yet nevertheless "too American" to belong in the Latin American cultures of their heritage. As a result, many Latinx people find themselves in social locations that are especially vague, complex, and even self-contradictory.

Nevertheless, Anzaldúa insists that these experiences of social dislocation can be the source of tremendous philosophical insights—and even spiritual and political power. Channeling Vasconcelos' utopian view of Latin Americans as the "cosmic race," Anzaldúa argues that Latinx communities are in an ideal position to build new coalitions across old social divisions. Using the methods of "autohistoria-teoría," a philosophically oriented style of auto-ethnography, Anzaldúa's work can teach us how to appreciate the wisdom Latinas and other overlooked groups may have to offer about how to resolve difficult social problems in ways that are creative, authentic, and life-affirming.

One salient line of objection to Anzaldúa's perspective that has emerged over the years can be found in Laura Pulido's 2017 essay, "Settler Colonialism and Nonnative People of Color." Pulido's essay makes the case that Latinx philosophers have failed to respond adequately to Indigenous challenges. In particular, Pulido points to advancements in the academic discipline of geography in understanding the mechanisms that drive "settler colonialism," colonization that seeks the elimination of native peoples for the purpose of appropriating their land. She argues that engaging with this research into settler colonialism will help to disrupt the tendency to overlook the role of Latinx communities in perpetuating coloniality.

The section concludes with a rejoinder to this line of objection in a commissioned essay from Andrea J. Pitts. This deeply researched work of scholarship reflects the author's expertise and respect for both the tradition of Latinx philosophy represented by Anzaldúa, one the one hand, and traditions and lineages of praxis outside academic philosophy centering perspectives and experiences of Indigenous, Africana, queer, and disabled communities, on the other. The essay, titled "Mestizaje, Métissage, and Mixedblood: Tracing Some Political Terms of Racial and Cultural Mixture Across the Americas," uses the method of genealogy to show that Indigenous and Afro-diasporic communities have both resisted and strategically utilized various conceptions of race and race mixture to advance their claims to land, rights, and belonging in the Americas. As a result of this history of contestation, "mestizaje" and other colonial concepts of race and race mixture are undoubtedly problematic. Nevertheless, it appears that, for better or worse, they are ideas we must continue to contend with. If so, then we would do well to approach these questions in ways that are both strategic and historically informed.

6 Mestizaje (Preface to *The Cosmic Race*)

José Vasconcelos

I

[. . .] Empirical history, afflicted with myopia, bogs down in details but fails to identify even one predecessor of historical times. It shuns general conclusions and sweeping hypotheses; but it falls into such puerilities as cranial indices and the description of utensils, along with many another merely external detail, trivial except when integrated in a sweeping, comprehensive theory.

Only a spiritual leap, sustained by facts, will bring us to a vision that transcends the micro-ideology of the specialist. From that position we can probe the mass of events to find in them a direction, a rhythm, and an aim. And precisely where the analyst finds nothing, the synthesis and the creator find light.

Let us therefore attempt to form explanations, and to do so not with the imagination of the novelist, but with intuition based on the facts of history and science.

The race we have agreed to call Atlantic rose and fell in America. After an extraordinary flowering, its cycle and particular mission completed, it sank into silence and progressive decay until it was reduced to the petty empires of the Aztecs and the Incas, wholly unworthy of the superior earlier culture. With the decline of the Atlantic race, the dynamic process of civilization shifted to other places and other breeds: it dazzled in Egypt; it gained breadth in India and in Greece as it took root in new races. The Aryan, mingling with the Dravidian, produced the people of Hindustan, while creating Hellenic culture through other mixtures. The foundations of Western or European civilization were laid in Greece, and this white civilization expanded until it reached the forgotten shores of America to consummate a labor of recivilization and repopulation. And so we have four periods and four human lineages: the black, the red, the yellow, and the white. The last of these, after a formative period in Europe, has invaded the whole world and come to believe in its mission of dominance, just as each earlier dominant race believed in turn. The supremacy of the whites will of course also be temporary, but their mission differs from that of their predecessors: their mission is to serve as a bridge. Throughout the world the white man has created the conditions for the fusing of all races and cultures. The civilization achieved by him and shaped by our age has established the material and spiritual bases for the union of all men in a fifth race, a universal race that is the fruit of all earlier races and surmounts all that is past.

White culture is expansive, but it was not Europe as a whole that was charged with initiating the reincorporation of the red world into the forms of that not yet universal culture represented during centuries of domination by the white race. This transcendental mission was reserved for the two boldest branches of the European family, the two strongest and most dissimilar human types: the Spaniard and the Englishman.

***

Ever since the beginning, from the time of the discovery and conquest, it was Spaniards and Englishmen—or Latins and Saxons if we wish to include the Portuguese and the Dutch, respectively—who accomplished the task of beginning a new period of History by conquering and peopling the new hemisphere. They may have thought of themselves merely as colonizers, as transplanters of culture, but they were in fact laying the bases of a period of general and definitive transformation. The so-called Latins, bold and brilliant, seized the best regions, those they thought richest, and the English had to settle for the leftovers of fitter peoples. Neither Spain nor Portugal allowed the Saxon to approach her dominions, certainly not with arms, and not even to participate in trade. Latin superiority was indisputable at the outset. No one could have suspected, in those times of the papal bull that divided the New World between Portugal and Spain, that a few centuries later the New World would no longer be Portuguese or Spanish, but English. No one could have imagined that the humble settlers along the Hudson and the Delaware, peaceful and hardworking, would step by step gain possession of the biggest and best stretches of land until they had established the republic that is today one of the greatest empires in History.

Our time has become, and continues to be, a struggle of Latin against Saxon, a struggle of institutions, aims, and ideals, a crisis in the centuries-old struggle that begins with the destruction of the Invincible Armada and intensifies with the defeat at Trafalgar. After that, however, the arena of combat begins to shift, to move to the new continent, where further disastrous incidents occurred. The defeats at Santiago de Cuba, Cavite Bay, and Manila are distant but logical echoes of the catastrophes that befell the Armada and the fleet at Trafalgar. And now the conflict is staged wholly in the New World. In history, a century is like a day; it is not surprising that we have not yet shaken off the impression of defeat. We go through periods of discouragement, we continue to lose not only territorial sovereignty but also moral authority. Far from feeling united in the face of disaster, our will is fragmented in pursuit of vain and petty goals. Defeat has brought us confusion of values and of concepts; the diplomacy of the winners deceives us after having defeated us; trade conquers us with its petty benefits. Stripped of our former greatness, we take pride in an exclusively national patriotism and do not even notice the dangers that threaten our race as a whole. We deny and reject each other. Defeat has degraded us to the point where we unwittingly collaborate in the enemy's policy of beating us piecemeal, of offering separate advantages to each of our brothers while sacrificing the vital interests of another. Not only in battle did they beat us; they continue to defeat us ideologically. The greatest battle was lost the day that each of the Hispanic republics set out to live on its own, detached from its sisters, negotiating treaties and receiving false benefits with no thought for the common interests of our race. Without knowing it, the creators of our nationalism were the best allies of the Saxon, our rival for the possession of the continent. The display of our twenty flags at the Pan-American Union in Washington is something we should see as mockery by astute enemies. Nonetheless, each of us takes pride in his humble rag, which represents an empty illusion, and our disunion in the face of the powerful North American Union does not bring forth even a blush. We do not notice the contrast between Saxon unity and the anarchy and isolation of Ibero-America's escutcheons. We maintain a jealous independence one of the other, but in one way or the other we submit to or ally ourselves with the Saxon Union. Even the unification of the five Central American peoples has remained unattainable, because an outsider has refused to sanction it and because we lack the true patriotism that is prepared to sacrifice the present to the future. A lack of creative thought and an excess of critical zeal, which, to be sure, we have borrowed from other cultures, draw us into fruitless arguments in which we no sooner affirm the oneness of our aspirations than we deny it; but we fail to notice that when the time for action comes, and in spite of all the doubts harbored by learned Englishmen, the Englishman seeks to ally himself with his brothers in America and Australia, and at that point the Yankee feels himself to be as English as is the Englishman in England. We shall never be great as long as the Spaniard in America does not feel himself to be as Spanish as are the sons of Spain. That does not prevent our being different whenever necessary, though never at the expense of our supreme joint mission. This is how we must proceed if Iberian culture is finally to yield all its fruits, if we are to keep Saxon culture from triumphing in America unopposed. It is useless to dream of any other solution. A civilization can be neither improvised nor cut off, nor can it be based on the paper of a constitution; it always grows in the course of centuries through a slow elaboration and distillation of elements transmitted and blended since the beginnings of History. That is why it is so foolish to date our patriotic sentiments from Father Hidalgo's call for independence, or from the Quito conspiracy, or from the great deeds of Bolívar.[1] If we do not root them in Cuauhtémoc and in Atahualpa, they will lack a solid foundation, though at the same time we must trace them back to their Hispanic source and shape them in keeping with what we should have learned from the defeats, which are also our defeats, of the Invincible Armada and Trafalgar.[2] If our patriotism is not linked to the different stages in the ancient struggle between Latins and Saxons, we shall never be able to bring it to the point at which it is more than a mere regionalism devoid of universal aims, and we shall see it inevitably degenerate into narrowness and parochial shortsightedness and the powerless inertia of the mollusk clinging to its rock. [. . .]

The present state of civilization still requires our patriotism as the guardian of our material and spiritual interests, but it is essential that this patriotism pursue great and transcendental aims. Its mission was, in a sense, cut short at the time of our independence, and now we must channel it once more toward its world-historical destiny. [. . .]

The Spaniards went to the New World with the plethora of vigor that their successful reconquest of the Iberian Peninsula had left idle. Those free men called Cortés and Pizarro and Alvarado and Belalcázar were neither lackeys nor Caesars, but great captains who combined a destructive impulse with creative genius.[3] On the morrow of victory they laid out new cities and drew up the laws that were to govern them. Later, when bitter disputes arose with the homeland, they knew how to repay tit for tat, as did one of the Pizarros during a famous trial. They all felt themselves to be the equals of the king, as El Cid had done, as did the great writers of the Golden Age, and as do all free men in great epochs of history.

But with the completion of the conquest, control over the entire new structure slipped into the hands of courtiers and royal favorites, men incapable, not only of conquering, but even of defending what others had conquered with their skill and daring. Degenerate sycophants capable of oppressing and humiliating the natives, but obsequious to royal power, they and their masters did nothing but degrade what the Spanish spirit had accomplished in America. The astonishing achievement begun by indomitable conquerors and consummated by wise and selfless missionaries sank toward collapse. [. . .]

The obsession with imitating the Roman Empire—which has brought such harm to Spain as well as to Italy and France—militarism, and absolutism brought about decadence at the very time when our rivals, strengthened by virtue, grew and expanded in liberty.

Their sense of the practical, their instinctively successful strategies, developed along with their material strength. The colonists in New England and Virginia broke with England, but only so as better to grow and become stronger. Their political separation has never kept them from being of one mind and acting in unison in what concerns their common ethnic mission. Emancipation, instead of weakening this great race, split it into two branches, increased it, and, starting from the impressive nucleus of one of the greatest empires of all time, extended its power over the whole world. And ever since then, whatever is not conquered by the Englishman of the Old World is seized and held by the Englishman of the New.

On the other hand, we Spaniards, whether Spanish by blood or by culture, began to reject our traditions as soon as we achieved emancipation; we broke with our past, and there were those who disowned their blood, saying it would have been better had the conquest of our part of the world been carried out by the English—treasonable words, which some would excuse as a reaction against tyranny and as blindness born of defeat. Yet for a race to allow its fate to strip it of its historical sense is absurd, is equivalent to our denying strong and wise parents when it is we, not they, who are to blame for our decadence. [. . .]

In spite of this solidarity in the face of an invading enemy, our struggle for independence was diminished by provincialism and by the lack of vast and visionary plans. The race that had dreamed of ruling the world, the supposed descendants of Roman glory, yielded to the puerile satisfaction of creating mini-nations and petty principalities inhabited by souls that in every mountain range saw not a peak but a wall. With the illustrious exception of Bolívar and Sucre and the Haitian Pétion, and at most half a dozen more, the founders of our independence dreamt of Balkan glories.[4] [. . .]

In Mexico, for example, almost no one except Mina thought of the interests of the whole continent; what is worse, for a whole century the prevailing patriotism taught that we triumphed over Spain thanks to the indomitable valor of our soldiers, with hardly a mention of the Cortes de Cádiz or the uprising against Napoleon, which electrified the whole race, or of the triumphs and sufferings of our Spanish American brothers.[5] This sin, which we share with all the other countries in America, is the product of a time when History is written to flatter despots, when jingoism, not content to depict its heroes as parts of a continentwide movement, presents them in isolation, without realizing that by so doing it diminishes them instead of aggrandizing them.

Another reason for these aberrations is that the native element had not, and still has not, wholly amalgamated with the Spanish blood; but this conflict is more apparent than real. Speak to the most exalted partisan of the Indians of the need to adapt ourselves to Latin culture, and he will not demur in the least; tell him that our culture is Spanish, and he will immediately raise objections. The stain of blood once shed remains, a cursed stain that centuries have not wiped away but that our common danger must remove. And there is no other way. Even the pure-blooded Indians are Hispanized, Latinized, just as our cultural environment is Latinized.

No race returns; each one defines its mission, fulfills it, and departs. [. . .]

The days of the pure white race, today's conquerors, are as numbered as were those of its predecessors. By fulfilling its destiny through the technological development of the world, it has unwittingly laid the foundations of a new age, the age of the fusion and amalgam of all peoples. The Indian has no door toward the future but the door of modern culture, no path but the already cleared path of Latin civilization. The white man, too, will have to surrender his pride, and he will seek progress and ultimate redemption in the souls of his brothers of other races, and he will be absorbed and perfected in each of the higher varieties of our species, in each of the manifestations through which revelation becomes manifold and spirit more powerful. [. . .]

This imperative of History first became manifest in the abundance of love that allowed the Spaniards to create a new race in combination with the Indian and the African, disseminating white stock by means of the soldier who engendered a native family, and Western culture by means of the teaching and example of the missionaries that made the Indian capable of entering the new stage, the stage of One World. Spanish colonization created a mixed race; this distinguishes its character, determines its responsibility, and defines its future. The Englishman continued to breed only with whites and exterminated the native, and he goes on exterminating him in the silent economic struggle that is more efficient than armed conquest. This proves how limited he is and indicates his decadence. On a large scale, it is the equivalent of the incestuous marriages of the Pharaohs, which undermined the vigor of that race; and it contradicts the ultimate aim of History, which is to achieve a fusion of all peoples and all cultures. Making the whole world English, wiping out the red man so that all of America may replicate a northern Europe made up of pure-blooded whites, is merely to repeat the victorious process followed by every conquering race. The red men did the same, and every strong and homogeneous race has done or tried to do the same; but this is no solution to the problem of humanity, and it was not for so petty a purpose that America was held in reserve for five thousand years. Our new-and-old continent is meant for something far more important: it is predestined to become the cradle of a fifth race that will combine all peoples to replace the other four that have independently been shaping History. It is on the soil of America that dispersion will come to an end; it is there that unity will be consummated by the triumph of fruitful love and that every separate lineage will be transcended. And in this fashion a synthesis will be engendered, a human type that shall combine all the treasures of History to give expression to the sum of the world's aspirations.

The Latin peoples, as we call them, having been faithful to their divine mission in America, are those destined to consummate this synthesis. And that faithfulness to the hidden design is the guarantee of our triumph.

Even in the chaotic period of the struggle for independence, which deserves so much rebuke, one can glimpse that passion for universality that heralds the desire to blend all humanity in a universal synthesis. In part because he realized the danger into which we were falling as we split into isolated nations, and thanks also to his gift of prophecy, Bolívar already had formulated a plan for an Ibero-American federation that some fools oppose even now. And if the other leaders in that struggle generally had no clear concept of the future, if it is true that under the sway of provincialism, which we now call patriotism, or of limitation, which is now termed national sovereignty, each of them concerned himself only with the immediate fate of his own people, it is also surprising to note that almost all of them felt stirred by a universal human sentiment that corresponds to the destiny that we assign to the Ibero-American continent today. Hidalgo, Morelos, Bolívar, the Haitian Pétion, the Argentineans at Tucumán, Sucre—all of them were concerned with freeing the slaves, declaring the equality of all men in natural law, the social and civic equality of whites, blacks, and Indians.[6] At a critical moment in History, they formulated the transcendental mission that is assigned to our portion of the globe, the mission of ethnically and spiritually fusing all peoples.

Something was thus done among the Latins that never entered anyone's mind on the Saxon continent. There the opposite thesis continued to prevail, the open or tacit aim of cleansing the earth of red, yellow, and black men for the greater glory and happiness of the white. In fact, the two systems that to this day place the two civilizations in opposite sociological camps became clearly defined at that time. One seeks the exclusive supremacy of the white man; the other is creating a new race, a race of synthesis, which aims to embrace and express all humanity through a process of constant elevation. If proof were needed, it would suffice to observe the accelerating spontaneous intermixture among all peoples on the Latin continent and, on the other hand, the rigid line that separates black from white in the United States and the ever-more rigorous laws that exclude the Japanese and Chinese from California.

The so-called Latins—perhaps because, to begin with, they are not, properly speaking, Latins but a conglomerate of types and races—persist in not paying much attention to the ethnic factor in their sexual relations. Whatever opinions may be voiced in this respect, and no matter what repugnance prejudice may evoke in us, the fact is that there has been and continues to be a mingling of blood lines; and it is in this fusion of blood lines that we must seek the most basic distinguishing trait of the Ibero-American character. [. . .]

The young ladies of San Francisco have refused to dance with officers of the Japanese navy, who are as well groomed, intelligent, and, in their way, as handsome as those of any other navy in the world. Nevertheless, these ladies will never understand that a Japanese can be handsome. Nor is it easy to convince the Saxon that if the yellow race and the black have their characteristic odor, so does the white man for others, even if we are unaware of it. In Latin America the revulsion felt by one blood on encountering another also exists, but in infinitely more attenuated form. There we find countless bridges toward the sincere and cordial fusion of all races. The contrast between the northerners' ethnic immurement and the southerners' far more relaxed openness is for us the most important as well as most favorable fact if one thinks, no matter how superficially, of the future, because it will then be immediately plain that we belong to tomorrow, while they are on the way to belonging to yesterday. The Yankees will create the last great empire of a single race, the final empire of white power, while we continue to suffer amid the vast chaos of an as yet inchoate breed. The germ of every human type will ferment within us, but we shall know that a better race is coming. Nature will not repeat one of its partial attempts in Spanish America: the race that will now issue from forgotten Atlantis will no longer be of a single color and particular features, will not be a fifth race or a sixth, destined to triumph over its predecessors; what will arise there is the definitive race, the integral race, the synthesis, made of the character and blood of all peoples and for that very reason better capable of true brotherhood and a truly universal vision.

To work toward fulfillment of this aim we must gradually create the cell tissue, as it were, which is to serve as the frame and flesh of the new biological entity; and in order to create this protean, malleable, profound, ethereal, and essential tissue, the Ibero-American race will have to comprehend its mission and embrace it as a form of mysticism. [. . .]

If Latin America were nothing but another Spain, to the same degree that the United States is another England, the old struggle between the two breeds would only be repeating its various phases on a larger stage, and one of the two rivals would eventually prove the stronger and would prevail. But this is not the natural law of opposites, neither in mechanics nor in life. Clash and struggle, especially when transported to the realm of the spirit, serve better to define the opponents, to impel each of them to the zenith of his destiny, and, in the end, to combine them in a common and victorious transcendence.

The Saxon's mission has been fulfilled earlier than has ours, because it was a more immediate mission and one already familiar to History; fulfilling it required nothing but following the example of other victorious peoples. The white man's values reached their peak, their bearers acting as a mere prolongation of Europe in that part of the American continent occupied by them. This is why the history of North America is like the uninterrupted and vigorous *allegro* of a triumphal march.

How different are the sounds that accompany the molding of Ibero-America! They resemble the profound *scherzo* of a deep and infinite symphony, voices that bear echoes of Atlantis, abysses dwelling within the eyes of the red man, who thousands of years ago knew so much and seems now to have forgotten everything. His soul is like a Mayan cistern in the middle of the forest, filled with deep, green, motionless water, so ancient that even the legend of its existence has been lost. And this stillness of the infinite is stirred up by the drop contributed to our blood by the black man, craving sensual delight, drunk with dancing and unbridled lusts. The yellow man appears, too, with the mystery of his slanted eye, which sees everything from a strange angle, which discovers who knows what new folds and dimensions. The mind of the white man, clear like his skin and his dreams, also plays its part. Hidden in the blood of Spain since the days of the cruel expulsion, strands of Jewish blood are revealed, and so are the melancholy moods of the Arab, the aftertaste of the morbid sensuality of the Muslim. Who does not hold some part of all this within himself, or does not want to hold it all? And then there is the Hindu, who will also come, who has already come in spirit; and though he is the last to come, he seems our closest kin. So many who have come, and others yet to come; and thus shall our heart grow sensitive and broad, reaching out to everything, holding everything, vibrating in sympathy with everything, but also bursting with vigor, laying down new laws for the world. And we sense that our head, too, will be different, making use of every perspective to achieve the marvel of transcending our globe.

II

[. . .] The world of the future will belong to whoever conquers Amazonia. Near the great river, Universopolis will rise, from which the evangelizers, the fleets and airplanes spreading the good news, will set out. If the Amazon became English, the capital of the world would not be called Universopolis but Anglotown, and fleets of warships would set out from there to impose on other continents the stern law of the supremacy of the blond-haired white man and the extermination of his dark rivals. On the other hand, if the fifth race gains control of the axis of the world of the future, airplanes and armies will spread out over the entire planet educating all peoples to achieve wisdom. Life based on love will come to express itself in forms of beauty.

Naturally, the fifth race will not attempt to exclude whites, any more than it intends to exclude any other people; it is constituted precisely on the principle of utilizing every potential to produce a more integrated power. Our aim is not war against the white man, but war against every sort of violent supremacy, whether of the white man or, conceivably, of the yellow man, if Japan should become an intercontinental threat. As for the white and his culture, the fifth race counts on them and still expects to benefit from their genius. Latin America owes what it is to the white European and will not disavow him; it owes a great part of its railways and bridges and business enterprises to the North American, and it similarly has need of every other race. Nevertheless, we accept the white man's higher ideals, not his arrogance; we wish to offer him, as to all peoples, a free fatherland in which he will find home and refuge, but not a prolongation of his conquests. The whites themselves, disturbed by the materialism and social injustice into which their race, the fourth race, has fallen, will come to us to aid in the conquest of liberty.

Perhaps the characteristics of the white man will predominate among those of the fifth race, but this supremacy must result from the free play of inclinations and not from violence or economic pressure. Superior cultural and natural traits will have to triumph, but this triumph will be solid only if based on its voluntary acceptance by the rational mind and on the unfettered choice of the imagination. Until now, life has been shaped by man's inferior faculties; the fifth race will be the fruit of his highest faculties. The fifth race is not exclusive: it garners life; hence the exclusion of the Yankee, like the exclusion of any other human type, would constitute an a priori mutilation, even more disastrous than a subsequent amputation. If we do not wish to exclude even those races that might be deemed inferior, it would be an even greater folly to banish from our enterprise a race possessed of energy and solid social virtues.

After explaining the theory of the formation of the future Ibero-American race and the way in which it will be able to utilize the environment in which it lives, we need consider only the third factor of the transformation that is taking place in the new continent, the spiritual factor that is to guide and consummate this extraordinary enterprise. Some may think that the fusion of today's different races into a new race completing and transcending all others will be a repulsive process of anarchic mongrelization, in comparison with which the English practice of marrying only within the same breed will appear as an ideal of refinement and purity. The first Aryans of India essayed precisely this English system to defend themselves against mixture with the colored races; but because the wisdom possessed by these dark races was the necessary complement to that of the blond invaders, the genuine culture of India only appeared after the centuries had consummated the mixture in spite of all written prohibitions. This predestined mixture, moreover, was useful not only for cultural reasons, but because man needs to draw physical renewal from the genetic pool of mankind. The North Americans hold very firmly to their resolution to maintain the purity of their breed; but this is because what faces them is the black man, the other extreme, as it were, the very opposite of a fungible element. In Ibero-America the problem does not arise in such stark terms; we have very few blacks, and most of them have already been turning into a population of mulattoes. The Indian is a good bridge toward fusion. Besides, the hot climate favors relations among all peoples and their unification. Furthermore—and this is essential—interbreeding among the races will not be owing to simple propinquity, as occurred at the beginning, when the white settler would take a native or black woman because no other was available. Eventually, as social conditions improve, crossbreeding will become ever more spontaneous, until it is no longer subject to necessity but to taste or even to curiosity.[7] Spiritual considerations will thus come to outweigh physical needs; and spiritual considerations should not be understood to mean thought, but rather the taste that is our guide in the mysterious choice of one person among so many.

III

This law of taste as the criterion for human relations is one that we have expounded more than once, calling it the law of the three stages of society, stages defined not in the manner of Comte but in a far more ample sense.[8] The three stages identified by this law are the material or military, the intellectual or political, and the spiritual or aesthetic. They constitute a process that is gradually liberating us from the rule of necessity and subjecting all of life to the higher criteria of feeling and imagination.

Material factors are the sole arbiters of the first stage; when peoples come into contact, they fight or combine in obedience only to violence and their relative strength. Sometimes one will exterminate the other, or they will form pacts in keeping with their needs and interests. The hordes or tribes of every race live like this. Under these conditions, physical force, the only cohesive element of the group, is also what causes one stock to mix with another. There can be no choice when the strong takes or rejects the conquered female as his whim may dictate.

Of course the instinctive affinities that attract or repel in keeping with the mystery we call taste, the secret foundation of all aesthetics, underlie human relations even in this period; but the promptings of taste do not dominate in the first period, nor do they in the second, which is subject to the rigid norms of reason. Reason is also present in the first period as the motive of human conduct and action, but it is a weak reason, comparable to the suppressed taste. It is not reason that decides, but force, usually a brutal force to which judgment, enslaved to primitive will, submits. When judgment is thus perverted to become astuteness, it degenerates in the service of injustice. In the first period it is impossible to work for the harmonious fusion of the races, both because the rule of violence to which it is subject makes spontaneous cohesion impossible, and because geographical conditions do not even permit constant communication among all the peoples of the planet.

Reason tends to prevail in the second period, artfully utilizing the conquests of force and rectifying its errors. Borders are defined by treaty, and mores are organized according to the laws of mutual benefit and logic. Roman society is the most perfect model of this rational social system, although it actually began before Rome and still lingers in our age of nationalities. Under such a regime, the mixture of races arises in part from the whims of free instinct operating beneath the constraints of social norms, but especially from concern for immediate ethical or political benefits. In the name of morality, for example, almost indissoluble matrimonial bonds are imposed on persons who do not love each other; in the name of politics, inner and outer liberty is curtailed; in the name of religion, which ought to function as sublime inspiration, dogma and tyranny are imposed; but each case is justified with the appeal to reason, recognized as supreme arbiter of human affairs. A superficial logic and a questionable science are also the guides of those who condemn miscegenation in the name of a eugenics based on incomplete and false scientific data and therefore unable to produce valid results. This second period is characterized by faith in the formula; therefore in every respect it merely establishes norms for intelligence, limits for action, borders for the fatherland, and curbs to feeling. The rule, the norm, and tyranny are the law of the second period, in which we are today trapped and from which we must escape.

In the third period, whose coming can already be discerned in countless ways, our behavior will be guided not by poor reason, which explains but does not discover, but by creative feelings and irresistible beauty. Norms will be derived from the supreme faculty, the imagination; that is, men will live without norms, in a state in which all that is born of feeling is right. Instead of rules, constant inspiration. The worth of an action will not be sought in its immediate tangible results, as occurs in the first period, or in its obedience to certain rules of pure reason; even the ethical imperative will be transcended, and beyond good and evil, in the world of aesthetic emotion, the only concern will be that an action produce happiness through its beauty. To follow our impulse, not our duty; to walk the path of taste, not that of appetite or syllogism; to experience joy founded on love—that is the third stage.

We are unfortunately so imperfect that in order to achieve so godlike a form of life we shall first have to travel every road: the road of duty, where the lower appetites are purified and overcome; the road of dreams, which stimulates the highest aspirations. Then passion will come, redeeming us from low sensuality. To live passionately, to feel so intense an emotion toward all things that their movement falls into the rhythms of happiness—this is one aspect of the third period. It is achieved by releasing our divine impulse, so that with a single agile bound, without bridges of morality or logic, it may reach the zone of revelation.

Unmediated intuition, which leaps over the chains of syllogistic reasoning and, being a passion, transcends duty from the outset and replaces it with exalted love, is an artistic gift. We know that both duty and logic are the scaffolding and mechanics of the building, but the soul of architecture is a rhythm that goes beyond the mechanical and obeys no law but the mystery of divine beauty.

What role is assigned in this process to that sinew of human destinies, the will, which the fourth race came to deify in the intoxicating moment of its triumph? The will is force, blind force that pursues confused ends. In the first period it is guided by the appetite, which uses it to satisfy all its whims; next the light of reason dawns, and the will is restrained by duty and shaped by logical thought. In the third period the will becomes free, transcends the finite, bursts and plunges into a kind of infinite reality, is filled with distant echoes and aims. No longer satisfied with logic, it puts on the wings of imagination, descends into the deepest depths and glimpses the highest heights, swells with harmony and ascends in the creative mystery of melody, finds satisfaction and release in emotion and is one with the joy of the universe: it becomes a passion for beauty.

If we recognize that humanity is gradually nearing the third period of its destiny, we shall understand that the task of racial fusion will be accomplished on the Ibero-American continent in keeping with a law derived from the exercise of our highest faculties. The laws of emotion, beauty, and joy will govern the choice of partners, with results infinitely superior to those of a eugenics based on scientific reason and attentive only to the least important aspect of the act of love. The mysterious eugenics of aesthetic taste will prevail over the eugenics of science. Where radiant passion rules, restraints are unnecessary. The very ugly will not procreate, will not want to procreate; what will it matter, then, that all races will blend into one, if ugliness will find no cradle? Poverty, deficient education, the scarcity of beautiful individuals, the wretchedness that makes people ugly—all these calamities will vanish in the future stage of society. Then it will seem repulsive and criminal for a mediocre couple to boast, as is now common, of having multiplied misery. Marriage will cease to be a consolation for misfortunes that there is no reason to perpetuate and will become a work of art.

With the spread of education and prosperity, the danger of mixing radically opposite types will vanish. Unions will take place in keeping with the unique law of the third period, the law of mutual attraction, refined by the sense of beauty—a genuine attraction and not the false one imposed on us now by necessity and ignorance. These unions, sincerely passionate and easily dissolved in case of error, will produce bright and beautiful offspring. The whole species will change its physical appearance and its temperament; the higher instincts will prevail, and the elements of beauty that are now scattered among the various peoples will be fixed in a happy synthesis.

At present, in part out of hypocrisy and in part because such unions are formed between wretched persons in unfortunate circumstances, we are profoundly horrified by the marriage of a black woman to a white man. We should feel no repugnance whatsoever at the union of a black Apollo with a blond Venus, which proves that beauty sanctifies everything. On the other hand, it is repulsive to see those couples that every day issue from the courthouse or the church, about 90 percent of them ugly. Thanks to our vices, our prejudices, and our misery, the world is thus filled with ugliness. Procreation motivated by love is a good harbinger of choice offspring; but love must itself be a work of art, and not the refuge of despair. If what is to be passed on is stupidity, then what links the parents is not love, but a low and disreputable instinct.

A mixture of races consummated in keeping with the laws of social benefit, mutual attraction, and beauty will lead to the formation of a human type infinitely superior to all previous ones. By the Mendelian law of heredity, the crossbreeding of opposites will produce widely diverse and extremely complex variants, just as the human elements to be crossed are manifold and diverse; but precisely this assures us of the boundless possibilities that a well-directed instinct opens for the gradual perfection of our species.[9] If heretofore it has not improved much, that is because it has lived in crowded and miserable conditions that have impeded the functioning of the free instinct of beauty; reproduction has occurred after the fashion of beasts, with no quantitative limit and no aspiration toward improvement. The spirit has taken no part in it, only the appetite, which seeks satisfaction as best it can, so that at this point we cannot even imagine the modalities and effects of a series of truly inspired crossings. [. . .]

Humanity's most illustrious epochs have been precisely those in which dissimilar people have come into contact and mixed. India, Greece, Alexandria, Rome, are so many examples of the fact that only geographical and ethnic universality can yield the fruits of civilization. [. . .]

Only a long-term experiment will be able to show the results of a mixture carried out not through violence or out of necessity, but through choices arising from bedazzlement with beauty and confirmed by the emotional power of love.

In the first and second periods we are living in, the human species, because of isolation and wars, is in a sense living in conformity with Darwinian laws. The English, who see nothing but the present of the external world, did not hesitate to apply zoological theories to the field of human sociology. If this incorrect application of a physiological law to the realm of the spirit were acceptable, then speaking of the ethnic absorption of the black would amount to a defense of retrogression. Implicitly or openly, the English theory presupposes that the black is a kind of link closer to the ape than to the blond man. There is consequently no option other than making him disappear. The white man, on the other hand, especially the English-speaking white man, is presented as the sublime culmination of human evolution; crossing him with another race would mean befouling his stock.

Such a view of things, however, is nothing but the illusion cherished by every successful people during the time of its hegemony. Each of the great peoples of history has deemed itself the last and the chosen. When we compare these childish instances of pride one with another, we see that the mission that each people assigns to itself is at bottom nothing but lust for booty and the desire to exterminate its rival. Even official science is, in each period, a reflection of the pride of the dominant race. [. . .]

Every imperialism has need of a philosophy to justify it. The Roman Empire preached order, that is, hierarchy: first the Roman, then his allies, and slavery for the barbarian. The British preach natural selection, with the implied conclusion that by natural and divine right the world belongs to the dolichocephalic inhabitants of their islands and to their descendants. This science that came to invade us along with the products of conquering commerce can, however, be fought in the same way that every imperialism is fought, by opposing to it a superior science, a broader and more vigorous civilization. The fact is that no race is sufficient unto itself and that Humanity would be—indeed, is—the loser every time that a race disappears by violent means. It is all very well for each race to evolve as it chooses, but always within its own vision of beauty and without interrupting the harmonic development of human elements.

Each thriving race needs to create its own philosophy, the wellspring of its success. We have been educated under the humiliating influence of a philosophy devised by our enemies, sincerely perhaps, but with the aim of exalting their own purposes and crushing ours. Thus we have ourselves come to believe in the inferiority of the *mestizo*, in the hopelessness of the Indian, in the condemnation of the black, in the irremediable decadence of the Oriental. The rebellion of our arms was not followed by the rebellion of consciousness. We rebelled against the political power of Spain and did not notice that, along with Spain, we fell under the economic and spiritual domination of the race that has been mistress of the world since Spain's greatness came to an end. We shook off one yoke only to fall under another. We became victims of a shift in the locus of power that would have been inevitable even had we understood it in time. There is an inevitability in the destiny of peoples, just as in that of individuals, but now that a new phase of History is beginning it becomes necessary to reconstruct our ideology and organize every aspect of the life of our continent in keeping with a new ethnic doctrine. Let us then begin to live our own lives and make our own science. If we do not first free the spirit, we shall never succeed in redeeming the flesh.

***

Our obligation is to formulate the bases of a new civilization, and for that very reason we must bear in mind that neither in form nor in substance do civilizations repeat themselves. The theory of ethnic superiority has merely been a weapon employed by every warlike people, but the combat that faces us is so important that it allows of no such specious ruse. We do not maintain that we are or will become the world's leading race, the most enlightened, the strongest and most beautiful. Our aim is even higher and more difficult to achieve than a transient superiority. Our values exist in potentiality, so much so that we are as yet nothing. Nonetheless, for the proud Egyptians the Hebrew race was nothing but a vile breed of slaves, and from it was born Jesus Christ, founder of the greatest movement in History, proclaiming love for all men. This love will be one of the fundamental dogmas of the fifth race that will arise in America. Christianity liberates and engenders life, because it contains a universal, not national, revelation, which is why the Jews, who could not bring themselves to join with Gentiles, had to reject it. America, however, is the homeland of the Gentiles, the true promised land of Christians. If our race proves unworthy of this sacred soil, if it comes to lack love, it will be replaced by peoples more qualified to carry out the predestined mission of these lands, the mission of serving as the home of a humanity made up of every nation and every breed. The form of life that the progress of the world forces on Hispanic America is not a rival creed that in the face of its adversary says, "I shall overcome you or do without you," but an infinite yearning for integration and wholeness that necessarily invokes the universe. [. . .]

The doctrine of sociological and biological formation that we expound here is not simply an ideological effort to lift the spirits of a depressed race by offering it a thesis that contradicts the doctrine with which its rivals have tried to hold it down. The truth is that as the falseness of the scientific premise on which the dominance of today's world powers rests becomes more evident, we also come to glimpse, in experimental science itself, indications of a road that leads not to the triumph of one single race but to the redemption of all men.[10] [. . .]

If we set about building the fifth race according to the law of the second period, a battle of wits would ensue in which the clever and unscrupulous would win out over the dreamers and the good-hearted. In that case the new humanity would probably be primarily Malay, as it is said that no one outdoes the Malays in wariness and astuteness and even, if necessary, in perfidiousness. The path of intelligence might even bring us, should we so desire, to a humanity of Stoics that accepted duty as the supreme norm. The world would become something like a vast Quaker village, where the plans of the spirit would eventually feel choked and deformed by rigid precept. For reason, pure reason, can recognize the benefits of the moral law but cannot endow action with the fighting zeal that makes it productive.

On the other hand, the true power to create joy is contained in the law of the third period, which is the emotion of beauty and a love so pure as to become indistinguishable from divine revelation. Since ancient times, for example in *Phaedrus*, love has been deemed to have the quality of pathos: its dynamism touches and moves our souls, transforms things and destiny itself. The race best able to sense this law and impose it on life and on things will be the matrix of the new era of civilization. Fortunately the *mestizos* of the Ibero-American continent, a people for whom beauty is the supreme justification of all things, possess this gift, necessary for the fifth race, to a high degree. Keen aesthetic sensibility and profoundly beautiful love, heedless of base self-interest and unfettered by formalism, are both necessary for the third period, impregnated with a Christian aestheticism that touches even ugliness itself with a redeeming pity that makes a halo to glow around all creation.

We have, thus, on our continent all the elements for the new humanity, a law that will select the factors for the creation of the predominant types and that will not be guided by national criteria, as a single conquering race would have to be, but by criteria of universality and beauty, and we also have the space and the natural resources. No European people, no matter how well endowed, could replace the people of Ibero-America in this mission, for each of those peoples has an already constituted culture and a tradition that is a hindrance in tasks of this kind. No conquering race could replace us, because it would necessarily impose its own characteristics, even if only out of the need to exercise violence to maintain its conquest. Neither can the peoples of Asia fulfill this universal mission; they are worn out, or at least lack the boldness for new undertakings. [. . .]

Many obstacles stand in the way of the plan of the spirit, but they are obstacles that progress always faces. An immediate objection might be to ask how the different races will join in harmony when not even the children of a single stock can live in peace and joy within the economic and social system that now oppresses mankind. But this state of mind will have to change quickly. All the trends of the future are currently interrelated: Mendelism in biology, socialism in government, a growing openness in souls, general progress, and the appearance of the fifth race that will fill the planet with the triumphs of the first truly universal, truly cosmic culture.[11]

Notes

1 Miguel Hidalgo y Costilla, aka Miguel Gregorio Antonio Ignacio Hidalgo y Costilla y Gallaga Mondarte Villaseñor (1753–1811), a priest and leader in Mexico's War of Independence from Spain. Simón José Antonio de la Santísima Trinidad Bolívar y Palacios, aka Simón Bolívar (1783–1830), Venezuelan military figure and the most important leader in South America's struggle for independence from Spain.
2 Cuauhtémoc, aka Cuauhtemotzin, Guatimozin, or Guatemoc (ca. 1502–1525), last Aztec ruler of Tenochtitlán, from 1520 to 1521. Atahualpa, aka Atahuallpa, Atabalipa, and Atawallpa (1497–1533), last ruler of the Inca Empire.
3 Hernán Cortés (1485–1547), Spanish conquistador, credited with bringing down the Aztec Empire. Francisco Pizarro y González (ca, 1471–1541), Spanish conquistador, instrumental in bringing down the Inca Empire. Pedro de Alvarado (ca. 1485–1541), Spanish conquistador and governor of Guatemala. Sebastián de Belalcázar (ca. 1479–1551), Spanish conquistador of present-day Ecuador.
4 Antonio José de Sucre y Alcalá (1795–1830), Venezuelan independence leader, one of Simón Bolívar's closest friends and collaborators. Alexandre Sabès Pétion (1770–1818), founding father of Haiti and its president from 1806 until his death.

5 Francisco Javier Mina (1789–1817), Spanish lawyer and army officer who fought in Mexico's War of Independence. The Cortes de Cádiz were a series of legislative sessions during the French occupation of Spain that served as an important step toward the nation's embrace of liberalism and democracy.
6 José María Morelos y Pavón (1765–1815), priest and revolutionary leader during Mexico's War of Independence.
7 Translator's note: Here and in subsequent passages, I render the Spanish word *gusto* as "taste." This, I believe, is its primary meaning in this context; but the reader should bear in mind that *gusto* can also mean "pleasure," a meaning that resonates to some degree in Vasconcelos's prose.
8 Referring to Auguste Comte (1798–1857), French philosopher and the founder of the doctrine of Positivism.
9 Mendelism, a series of genetic tenants derived from Austrian scientist and priest Gregor Johann Mendel (1822–1884), related to the transmission of hereditary characteristics from organisms to their offspring.
10 Jakob Johann von Uexküll (1864–1944), German biologist, a pioneer in the fields of muscular physiology, animal behavior studies, and cybernetics.
11 Translated from the Spanish by John H.R. Polt. First published as preface to *La raza cósmica* (Barcelona: Agencia Mundial de Librería, 1925); the essay was repositioned as chapter 1 in the revised edition (Mexico City: Espasa-Calpe, 1948), and a prologue was added to the book.

Reading Questions

1. How does Vasconcelos argue for the idea that mestizaje will contribute to political progress for humanity?
2. According to Vasconcelos, why are Latinos uniquely situated to carry out this project?
3. In what sense might Vasconcelos be described as an anti-racist?
4. Does endorsement of mestizaje necessarily or always imply the erasure of minority groups? Why or why not?
5. Can Vasconcelos' utopianism play the same kind of role as ideals of freedom (in liberal cosmopolitanism), a transcendent cosmic order (in religion), or the people (in ethno-racial states)? Why or why not?
6. Vasconcelos argues that aesthetic judgment is in some important sense foundational, the thing that integrates scientific knowledge, ethics, and emotion. Is this plausible? Why or why not?
7. How appealing is the idea that we could organize a society on aesthetic judgments and principles?

7   The Mestizo Concept
A Product of European Imperialism
Jack D. Forbes

The Mestizo Concept

The terms *mestizo* and *metis* (as well as such comparable words as *half-caste, half-breed, ladino, cholo, coyote*, and so on) have been and are now frequently used in Anishinabe-waki (the Americas) to refer to large numbers of people who are either of mixed European and Anishinabe (Native American) racial background or who possess a so-called mixed culture.

In Canada, people of mixed European and Anishinabe background are ordinarily referred to as *metis*, that is, "mixed." In the United States, terms such as *half-breed, half-blood* and *quarter-blood* are most commonly used but *mustee* (derived from *mestizo*) and even mulatto have been used in the South. From Mexico through Argentina *mestizo* ("mixed") is the standard term, but *cholo, ladino, coyote*, and other words are also commonly used. In Brazil, *caboclo, mameluco* and a variety of other terms are used, along with *mestizo*. The concept of *mestizo* has also been introduced into the United States scholarly literature and is becoming accepted among anthropologists and sociologists as a technical term replacing *half-breed* and similar words.

For the purposes of this article the word *mestizo* will be used as the equivalent of all such words. It should be kept in mind that there are several distinct ways in which the term *mestizo* is used:

(1) As a simple description—a person, or a group, who possesses a recent mixed background;
(2) As a kind of permanent ethnic or caste categorization—a person, or a group, who is not only of mixed background but whose ethnic nature, or social status, is also mixed;
(3) As a strictly biological concept, referring only to mixture through sexual reproduction;
(4) As a cultural concept, referring to a mixture of customs, ways of behaving, and so on.

The first usage does not concern us here to any great extent, but the other three are of critical importance to the current status of native peoples in Anishinabe-waki.

Mestizo Peoples Who Are Not Mestizo

Today, virtually all of the peoples who are categorized as half-caste or mestizo live in zones where European imperialism has been active during the past several centuries (the South Pacific, the Philippines, Hong Kong, Macao, Vietnam, India, Singapore, South Africa, and throughout Anishinabewaki).

Peoples categorized as "half-caste" or "mestizo" tend to have several characteristics in common: they reside in areas subjected to recent European colonialism and imperialism;

DOI: 10.4324/9781003385417-12

they seldom possess the power or resources to determine their own destiny (either political or intellectual-psychological); their existence is usually a direct byproduct of European imperialism and colonial policy; and they are primarily people with both European and non-European ancestry, almost never with mixed European national backgrounds.

To place this discussion in proper perspective, let us contrast the situations in Mexico and Spain. North American social scientists and intellectuals and the ruling elite of Mexico commonly seem to agree that Mexico is a mestizo nation, that not only are most of its people racially mixed but that its dominant culture is also mestizo. North American Anglo-Saxon scholars, in particular, delight in using the mestizo and Indo-Hispano concept when discussing Mexico and Chicanos (persons of Mexican background in the United States). It is very clear that Anglo scholars (and the Mexicans and Chicanos influenced by them) regard the very essence of the Mexican-Chicano people as mestizo (except for the perhaps ten percent of the Mexican people who are regarded as indio).

Now, is this mestization of the Mexican-Chicano people a concrete social reality or is it primarily the Europeans' imposition of alien descriptive categories upon the Mexican-Chicano masses? Let us look at the situation of Spain and Mexico with this question in mind.

Spain is, clearly, far more of a mestizo nation (if that term is ever properly to be used) than is Mexico. (1) The Spanish people speak a totally borrowed language, a dialect or branch of Italo-Latin mixed with many thousands of Arabic words. Very few words of the indigenous Hispano-Iberic language remain in use. (2) The culture of Spain is a complex mixture of Latin-Italic, North African, Middle Eastern, Greek, Gitano (Gypsy), and other characteristics, with very few indigenous (pre-Roman) traits remaining, except among the Basques and Gallegos. (3) Racially, the modern Spaniard probably carries relatively few indigenous genes, the latter having been greatly overwhelmed by Carthaginian, Celtic, Latin-Roman, Germanic, Arab, Moorish, Berber, Jewish, black African, and Gitano intermixture.

In both a racial and cultural sense, then, the Spaniard is profoundly a mestizo. In fact, it is safe to say that (except among the Basques) the Spanish culture of modern times is almost wholly non-Spanish in origin (in terms, at least, of specific traits) and is thoroughly mixed.

Surprisingly, however, one never finds Anglo-Saxon social scientists categorizing the Spaniards as a mestizo. One never finds scholars describing a Spanish subgroup as part Gitano or as a North African physical type. One never finds social scientists attempting to dissect the Spanish people and then to tell them who they are!

Why is this so? We know that during the fifteenth century, for example, there were many subgroups (such as maranos, mozarabes, moriscos, and so on) among the population. We know also that even today regional variations can probably be identified in Spain.

Why is the Castilian-speaking Spaniard allowed to have dignity and security of being simply a Spaniard, of possessing an ethnic identity, a nationality, while the Mexican and the Chicano are even now dissected and categorized, first, as mestizos and only second as Mexicans or Chicanos?

Indisputably the Spaniard is a mestizo in the sense that he is mixed and has a mixed culture. But he is never categorized as a mestizo, but always as a Spaniard (or an Andalucian, Malagueno, Catalan, and so on), because since 1491 the Castellano-Spaniard has not been subjected to political and intellectual colonization.

The Spanish people have been free to develop themselves without having any alien government officials classifying individuals as one-quarter Gitano, one-eighth Jewish, one-half Arab, and so on. They have not had foreign scholars investigating them (trying to "understand" them) and then developing conceptualizations which dominate the thinking of even native intellectuals. In short, the Spaniard has been free to define his own nationality and categories of existence.

It is true, of course, that Spain possesses minority ethnic groups, but neither the minorities nor the majority are classified as mestizo even though all are of mixed origin. It is also true that the Christian Spanish hierarchy did, for a time, keep records of converted Jews and Muslims and their descendants, but this was not to permanently categorize people, but instead to root out any secret Jewish or Islamic religious practices. The records concerned religion rather than race (in fact, many Hispanic Jews and especially Muslims were of Christian Spanish, not North African, descent).

The same kind of analysis can be made about England, Scotland, Russia, and a number of other nations. The English are clearly mestizos—a mixture of Celtic (and pre-Celtic), Anglo, Saxon, Danish, Norman-French, Flemish, and other descent. Likewise, English cultures is highly mixed (for example, half of the words in the so-called English language are of Latin origin, the English practice a "foreign" religion—Christianity—and the great bulk of contemporary English characteristics are of foreign origin—including even tea drinking). It is safe to say that the modern Englishman has very little in common with the Britons and pre-Roman times or even with the Anglo-Saxons before Christianity.

The Scots are, of course, a mixture of Pictish, Gaelic (Scottish), Norse, Norman-French, Flemish, English (Anglic), Saxon, and other stocks. Culturally, little remains (except for a few place names) from the indigenous Picts. Even the culture of the invading Scots (coming from Ireland) had been eroded to such an extent that the Scottish language is spoken only in a few remote regions and is officially ignored by the government. Except for some "colorful" Highland characteristics there is little left of purely Celtic origin, although many Celtic, Germanic, and Latin traits have mixed together to produce modern Scottish culture.

The Russians continue to speak their native Slavic language, but their culture is extremely mixed (showing Greek, Turkish, Mongol, and German influences). Racially the Russians have absorbed large quantities of Finish, Kahzar, Turkic, Mongol, Greek and other alien ancestry.

Interestingly, the English, Scots, and Russians (like the Spanish) are never categorized as mestizos. Seldom does one ever ask a Scotsman if he is part Norman-French, nor indeed, does anyone ever ask a Scotsman if he has even a drop of Celtic (Pictish-Scottish) blood. Such questions are seemingly only asked of knocked-down, conquered, colonized, and powerless peoples.

The same kind of analysis can be made of almost all major ethnic groups—Chinese, Japanese, East Indians, Arabs, Turks, and so on. Almost all such peoples possess a mixed racial heritage and a mixed culture. But they are not mestizos (even when their ancient "race" and culture have been almost totally erased or altered). Furthermore modern Mexican and Chicano people possess far greater connection with their ancient Mexican past than many European groups do with their respective past. For example:

(1) The Mexicans and Chicanos of today are perhaps eighty percent native Anishinabe descent, while only twenty percent of their ancestry is of European-North African, African, and Asian descent. In contrast, it is likely that Spaniards possess relatively little pre-Roman ancestry (native Iberian), certainly less than eighty percent.
(2) The Mexican and Chicano peoples' modern language, Spanish, possesses several thousand native Mexican words, while the Spanish is wholly non-Iberian in origin.

(3) The native religions of Spain have almost, if not completely, disappeared. In Mexico, however, the native religion has survived in many regions and has modified Christianity. Furthermore, Christianity is as foreign to Spain as it is to Mexico.
(4) The modern culture of Spain is almost entirely non-Iberian in origin. In contrast, the culture of Mexico, even among Spanish-speaking people, is, to a significant degree, of native Mexican origin.

In short, the Mexicans and Chicanos possess far greater continuity with their native past than do the Spaniards, and yet the Spanish are categorized as "unified" people (in spite of great regional variations), while the Mexicans and Chicanos must perpetually carry the burden of genuflecting before the idol of mestisaje.

Ethnicity and Integration

Many social scientists have written about Mexican villages as mestizo villages and Indian villages. In point of fact there is often no racial difference existing between such villages, but even if there were, I would challenge the idea that there are mestizo villages in Mexico.

It is true, of course, that one can find many pueblos in Mexico where the culture of the people can be traced to Spain, North Africa, and the Middle East, as well as to Native Mexico. But this historical fact of mixture does not in and of itself produce a mestizo village.

If we were to visit such a pueblo, we would find that the people possess an integrated culture perceived as being their very own. They have no conscious concept of being "mixed," but instead have a sense of unity and wholeness. To categorize them as living in a mestizo village is as nonsensical as it would be to say that Davis, California, is a mestizo town because of the people's diverse ethnic origins and historically mixed culture.

Most people possess a mixed culture and mixed ethnic background. To say, therefore, that a village is mixed when it is an integrated community, is either to lie or to add nothing new to our knowledge of that village.

It is true that there are cities, villages, and even entire regions where peoples of different ethnic loyalties and cultures are living in close juxtaposition (as the Greeks and Turks in Istanbul). Such a place can be regarded as being multiethnic or biethnic, but it is not truly mixed precisely because the different ethnic groups are separate, although geographically intermingled.

Mestizo and such comparable terms imply outcast (i.e., belonging to no ethnic group or caste). People who possess a national or ethnic identity, no matter how much they have mixed historically with other peoples, can never be mestizo.

A people who possess an integrated culture, especially a gradually changing, relatively stable one, are also not mestizo culturally. Since all known cultures are of diverse, mixed origin, it follows that the Mexican culture of today is precisely that, i.e., Mexican culture and not a mestizo culture. Change, with borrowing, no matter how much, does not by itself produce a mestizo culture.

The Bulgarian people, for example, have shifted their homeland, changed their language, changed their religion, changed their physical appearance (through interethnic marriage), and changed almost their total culture, but the Bulgarians are not mestizos, they are not outcasts, they are not a new nation, they are simply Bulgarians.

Why? Because as a people, as a collection of related village-groups together forming a nationality, they have a historical bond of continuity with their past. The ethnic continuity implied by Bulgarian-ness and the gradual nature of change have ensured that the

Bulgarians are not mestizos (although the Turks, and other former rulers, tried to erase that continuity).

The Mestizo as Outcast

Historically speaking, Europeans have often used such terms as *mestizo, half-breed, half-caste,* and so on, to refer to no-caste, out-caste, or groupless individuals—that is, to a person of mixed race having no clear ethnic affiliation.

A mestizo without a nationality or ethnic group to belong to is indeed an outcast. There is no doubt but what there are individuals or mixed race in Anishinabe-waki who are loners, without ethnic affiliation. But such individuals are relatively few in numbers in comparison with the broad masses of mixed-bloods who commonly possessed a group, an ethnic affiliation, or a community. For example, the mixed Cherokees of the nineteenth century were, for the greater part, Cherokee-speaking people who were citizens of, and emotionally a part of, the Cherokee Nation. In no sense could most racially mixed Cherokees be regarded as outcasts. Neither could they be regarded as mestizos, except in a purely descriptive sense.

In most regions of Anishinabe-waki there has been a gradual, imperceptible transition of a village (or tribe) from being composed of people of purely indigenous descent to being composed of people of mixed racial descent. In many cases the group has experienced no sharp change in ethnic identity. Thus, many North American Anishinabe groups have changed from being racially Indian to being racially mixed. However, they have retained their identity as Cherokees, Powhatans, Mohawks, and so on. Similarly, many Mexican, Central American, and South American villages have gradually acquired European or African admixture without any sharp transition, although in some instances the people have come to regard themselves as no longer being indios, because the government (and racist custom) regards the term *indio* as a derogatory one.

An example of the latter trend is the gradual "disappearance" of the Opata people of eastern Sonora. It is quite clear from the historical evidence that the Opatas imperceptibly changed as a result of missionization, serving in the Spanish army (against the Apaches), fighting in the many post-1821 civil wars and rebellions in Sonora, and perhaps to a lesser degree, intermarrying with Spanish-speaking Mexicans. In 1821 most Opata towns were still "Indian," although undoubtedly many residents were bilingual in Opata and Spanish, and virtually all were Catholics. By about 1900 the grandparents were still speaking Opata, but their grandchildren had shifted largely to Spanish and wanted to be thought of as Mexicans. The Opata towns had, in effect, ceased being Opata and had become simply Mexican (or mestizo, as the Anglo-Saxon researcher and Mexican census-taker might assert). In this area, as in many others throughout Anishinabe-waki, the change from tribal loyalty to a new national loyalty was not primarily a biological-racial change but simply a gradual, imperceptible change in self-definition by others.

Thus, we see that some native nationalities have become racially mixed while retaining their old identity, while other native nationalities have been absorbed into a larger nationality without significant race mixture. In neither case, however, did the bulk of the people become no-caste or out-caste or half-caste in the process. Whether changing because of acculturation, race mixture, or both, they always have retained a community, an identity, and a sense of peoplehood.

It is interesting, of course, to study such persons as Garcilaso de la Vega el Inca, the Inca-Spanish mestizo who was torn between native and Iberian loyalties, but it seems very unlikely that most persons of native descent in Anishinabe-waki ever went through such a process. And it is very unlikely that such a split identity, when it occurred, extended far beyond the first generation.

The mestizo as outcast is simply not a significant reality in Anishinabe-waki. Instead of inventing collections of no-caste individuals, we should concentrate our attention upon the history of real "peoples"—tribes, villages, bands, towns, regions, and nations.

The Mestizo Concept and the Strategy of Colonialism

One of the fundamental principles of the European invaders, and especially of the Spaniards, was to follow the policy of divide and conquer, or keep divided and control. This policy pitted native against native, and tribe against tribe, until Spanish control was established. Later this same policy prevented a common front of oppressed people from developing, by creating tensions and jealousies between the different sectors of the population.

The Spaniards were shrewd colonialists. They gave minor privileges (uniforms, batons of office, and the right to collect tribute) to caciques (chiefs), in order that the native leadership would prevent their people from rebelling. They also gave privileges (of a minor nature) to each different caste (indios living in villages sometimes were exempt from certain taxes, while mestizos, mulattos, and others were able to obtain minor positions in the army, move about freely, except in Indian villages and so on). People with some degree of European ancestry were ordinarily able to wear European-style clothing and obtain concessions not available to most Anishinabe (Indians).

A racist system was created by the Spaniards which favored light skin and European descent. Natives were regarded as inferior or childlike beings, and almost all who were ambitious sought to deny nonwhite ancestry or at least to be as white as possible.

This system, which saw each minor caste or class trying to curry favor from above at the expense of those below, served very well to keep the masses divided and distrustful of each other. It also resulted in many people of predominantly native descent pretending to be either mestizo or criollo (white or near-white) in order to be considered "una persona de razon" (a rational person). To the Spaniards, the native generally was *not* "de razon," but mixed-bloods could be!

The concepts of *mestizo, coyote, lobo, cholo, pardo, color quebrado*, and many others, were invented by the Spaniards, and Spanish policy kept these categories alive throughout the colonial epoch. *Were those concepts of any real objective value, apart from being useful to the ruling class?* It is extremely doubtful if the differences between a coyote (three-quarters Anishinabe), a mestizo (one-half Anishinabe), a lobo (Anishinabe-African), a pardo (Anishinabe-African-European), and so on were at all significant *except insofar as the Spanish rulers sought to make them significant*. It is true that there may have been cultural differences between natives and mixed-bloods speaking a native language and living in a native village, on the one hand, and Spanish-speaking person (of whatever ancestry) on the other hand. But those differences relate to political loyalty and culture and not directly to mestisaje as such.

The colonial documents mention several cases where *mestizos, mulattos*, and so on, took part in Indian rebellions on the native side. The documents (padrones or censuses in particular) also reveal that some Spanish soldiers of lower rank were "indios," at least when first recruited. Therefore, it is clear that the differences between indio and mestizo were not necessarily even of political significance.

On the other hand, if there were cultural differences and antagonisms existing between mestizos and indios, whose fault was it? Who created the conditions of exploitation which caused Anishinabeg to rebel? Who created a system wherein one could rise upward only by repudiating one's native blood and exploiting native people?

In short, the Spaniards created the system that created castes that were different one from another. They also created such rankings to accomplish their selfish purposes.

Let us dwell on this point for a moment by contrasting the development of Aberdeen, Scotland, with Santa Fe, New Mexico. The people of Aberdeen have a mixed origin, being of Scottish (Gaelic-speaking), Scandinavian, Norman-French, Flemish, and Anglo-Saxon descent. But this fact of biological mixture is of little ultimate significance in the history of Aberdeen. Of much greater importance is the fact that Aberdeen became a Broad Scotch and English language enclave in what have been a Gaelic-speaking region and that Aberdeen was a royal burg, a town loyal to the Scottish crown rather than to any Highland clan (tribal) chief. Of greater significance, also in the history of Aberdeen is the fact of socioeconomic and religious tensions within the city, totally unrelated (it would seem) to ethnic origins. In sum, whether an Aberdonian is one-fourth Gaelic or one-half Scandinavian or all Anglo-Saxon is of only passing interest. Loyalties to Aberdeen, to religion, to economic classes, to Scotland, are all of infinitely greater significance. Finally, all native-born Aberdonians are, and have been considered Scots, whether of Scottish or non-Scottish descent.

Similarly, Santa Fe was a Spanish royal settlement established in the far north of the Spanish Empire (Aberdeen was established to control and civilize the unruly Gaelic Scots, as Santa Fe was created to control and civilize the unruly Anishinabeg). The bulk of the initial settlers of Santa Fe, who lived in the barrio of Analco, were Mexicans, that is, Aztec-speaking people of Anishinabe blood. As time went by, the people became mixed, with Spanish, Anglo-Saxon, African, Pueblo Indian, Apache, Navajo, Plains Indian, and Paiute ancestry being absorbed into the community. Likewise, the Mexican language was gradually replaced by Spanish, religion changed, and so on. Whether or not a person of Santa Fe, by say 1848, was all-native, three-quarters native, one-half native or one-eighth native is utterly without intrinsic significance. What is important is whether he was rich or poor, ruler or ruled, Catholic or fold religion, Spanish-speaking or native-speaking, and soon.

Ah, but there is a difference between Aberdeen and Santa Fe. In Santa Fe, the racist colonialist, strategy of the Spaniard had implanted the notion of nonwhite inferiority. Therefore, whether one was dark or light or classed as mestizo, blanco, or indio did make a difference! *The difference is not, however, due to the intrinsic significance of mestisaje but only to a racist-colonialist stratification based upon racial descent.*

The French pursued a policy somewhat different from that of the Spanish (except in Louisiana where part-blacks were classified as quadroons, octoroons, and so forth). The French were never able to recruit many settlers to come to Anishinabe-waki, so the interests of the empire (and of the fur trade) demanded that the Metis, the mixed-blood, be incorporated into the French system wherever possible. It appears that prior to 1763 no distinct class of mixed-bloods developed, since the Metis was absorbed into French Canadian society (albeit initially as a fur trader, canoe man, or trapper) or into a particular native group. It seems highly likely that most French-Canadians have some degree of native descent, while many Anishinabeg in the northern United States and Canada are part-French.

During the nineteenth century, however, along the banks of the Red River, Lake Winnipeg, and the Saskatchewan River, there developed a group who came to be known as Metis, and most of their descendants (now spread all over western Canada) are still known by that term. These people, sometimes called Red River Metis fought against the Canadian government on several occasions between 1860 and 1890, in alliance with Cree, Assiniboin, and Chippewa groups.

Who are these Metis? Initially some were French-native hybrids, some were Scottish-native hybrids, and a few were English-native hybrids. Generally speaking, they were closely connected with Cree and other Anishinabeg both in terms of annual migrations, alliances, marriages, and language. (Modern studies have shown that a large majority of Metis people speak Cree in their homes, at least in certain provinces.) The culture of the Metis was (and often still is) basically of a native character modified by European influence. (For example, they observed an annual buffalo-hunting migration cycle similar to that of the Cree and Assiniboin, with whom they frequently lived).

My tentative analysis is as follows: *The so-called Metis were nothing more nor less than a partially Europeanized sector of the Cree-Chippewa-Assiniboin confederation (or alliance system).* (It may well be that having a European father or grandfather was of crucial importance in becoming Europeanized, but that is not at all surprising [intermarriage is often a key element in an acculturation process].)

If left alone, the so-called Metis would have been to the Cree people what the mixed-bloods were to the Cherokee Nation: an influential subgroup within the overall nationality. To some degree this undoubtedly occurred in Manitoba, Saskatchewan, and Alberta, since the line between Indian and Metis even today is ethnically obscure in many areas.

The Anishinabeg of the Canadian prairies were not left alone, however. British imperialism (in particular, the Hudson Bay Company) attempted to distinguish between Metis and Indian. The Metis, being somewhat more European in orientation and usually bilingual, were favored over Indians for certain purposes, but were never recognized as being the equal of whites. Later the British and white Canadians recognized "Indian tribal" land rights and rights to special federal services but denied these to Metis. In point of fact, however, many people whom the Canadian government chose to regard as Metis were indistinguishable from Indians. They simply were left out of treaty negotiations, were ignored, or were too mobile to live on a reserve.

Are the Metis truly mestizo, or is their present status a result of current British-Canadian policy? Some Metis call themselves non-status Indians, and perhaps that is a good description of some of them. Perhaps overall they represent simply a Europeanized, partly landless sector of the native population, confused about their identity by years of being denied Indian status. Or perhaps some of them are a distinct people for whom the name *Metis* does not mean mestizo but has become an ethnic (national) appellation.

In any case, the Red River Metis did not, and do not, exist as a no-caste collection of half-breeds. They seem to have always lived in communities or groups they considered home. Whenever they are to be known as Anishinabe is a matter for them to decide and not the Canadian government.

The United States and the Atlantic seaboard British colonies approached the Spanish system of caste categorization (mulattos, half-breeds, quarter-bloods, eight-bloods, mustees, high yellows, quadroons, sixteenth-bloods, and so on), but extreme racism somewhat altered the nature of colonialist policy.

Generally, the lighter the skin color the more acceptable a person was in colonial Atlantic seaboard society. Elaborate government records were not kept, but it would appear that visual inspection and local white opinion was utilized to determine whether or not a person was sufficiently white to vote, bear arms, hold office, or marry a white person (the laws varied from area to area, requiring anywhere from one-half to seven-eighths white blood to qualify as a white).

The Anglo-Americans very definitely adopted a system of giving different rewards to different castes and keeping nonwhite groups at odds with each other whenever possible. This was especially true in keeping Indians, free coloreds, and blacks (mostly slaves) from associating with each other (the fear of combined Indian-slave rebellions or raids was great in certain regions). After being militarily subdued, Indians generally became exempt from being enslaved (although many were enslaved before ca. 1750). They also were *sometimes* able to preserve a small tract of land in return for paying tribute. Free coloreds (mixed-bloods of all shades and free blacks) were able to move about more than tributary Indians and sometimes were able to vote and bear arms in the militia. Light-skinned mixed-bloods, who were able to prove they met the admission standards, could become white.

This system did several things: (1) it forced many mixed-bloods to identify as tributary Indians in order to live on a reservation and be safe from the possibility of enslavement; (2) it forced all visibly nonwhite people, no matter what the degree of blood, to become a part of a free-colored caste if they wished to live away from an Indian reservation; (3) it accentuated notions of white supremacy and encouraged people to try to be as white as possible (except for those who chose to be a tributary Indian and even the latter were affected psychologically); and (4) it made people caste conscious and encouraged disunity among the oppressed nonwhites.

It may well be that many of the free colored were initially mestizos, that is, in between, no-caste people. Soon, however, the free colored began to gather together (frequently clustering together with a remnant Indian group), and they developed a community of their own. The nature of this community is, however, too complicated a subject for us to pursue here.

The Bureau of Indian Affairs (the United States' colonial office for Indians) at a later date became (and still is) the government's most ancestry-oriented agency. The bureau keeps records on every Indian, recording the supposed exact degree of blood in detailed manner undreamed of even by the Spaniards. Furthermore, the bureau also decides who is an Indian and who is not an Indian and which Indians are eligible for Indian services.

One can well ask if there is any significant reason for keeping records of five-eighths Indians, one-quarter Indians, one-tenth Indians, "full-bloods," "half-bloods" and so on. What purpose does it serve? *The categorization of Anishinabeg by degree of blood serves to transform the Anishinabe people from a group of nationalities into a series of castes.*

The overall objective of United States native policy has been to liquidate the Anishinabe people entirely (a subject discussed below). One step in liquidation is to prevent Indians from assimilating (absorbing) outsiders and even to prevent them from retaining the loyalty of their own racially mixed children or grandchildren. A second step is to get the people of native descent to think of themselves as full-bloods, quarter-bloods, and so on, to keep them from thinking of themselves as Comanches, Cherokees, or other tribal groups, and to introduce jealousy and disunity.

This attempt to divide the Anishinabe into subcastes and to make much of the degree of blood may be useful to the bureau, but it does not really reflect the truly significant divisions within the native community. For example, from the 1820s through the 1860s the Cherokee people were at times divided into two major factions. One group was highly Indian in loyalty and was composed of full bloods, but it also included many mixed-bloods, and its official leader was John Ross (seven-eighths white, one-eighth Cherokee, by blood). The other group was oriented toward the slave-owning, plantation economy of the south and was composed primarily of mixed-bloods. However, its leaders included full-bloods such as Stand Watie.

The key difference between these two Cherokee groups was the degree to which they were oriented toward Anglo-American values. One was quite interested in Southern-style wealth acquisition while the other was more traditionally Cherokee in its values. Mixed-bloods and full-bloods were found in both groups. Therefore, we again see that being biologically mixed is less significant than other factors, such as ethnic loyalty and values.

White writers often make much of the fact that Sequoyah was part-white. But since Sequoyah was raised as conservative Cherokee, thinking and speaking in Cherokee rather than English, is his white blood of any actual significance? Clearly, Sequoyah was a complete Cherokee nationalist, and he died seeking out lost Cherokees in northern Mexico. Quite obviously he was not mestizo, confused or split in his ethnic-cultural loyalties. To the Bureau of Indian Affairs, however, he would be regarded as a half-blood or a half-Cherokee, whatever that means! The same can be said of such racially mixed native leaders as Cornplanter, Quanah Parker, and Alexander McGillivray.

No general class or caste of Anishinabe-white mestizos has actually developed in the United States for several reasons: (1) most of the mixed groups who have lost their specific native identity (such as these-called the so-called Mestizos of South Carolina or the Lumbees of North Carolina) have developed a new identity of their own (the "Lumbee" identity, for example, is a new invented identity—the name is a local pronunciation of "Lumbar River"); (2) white racism has usually forced recognizable mixed-bloods to remain in the nonwhite community, where they originated, or at least to remain loyal to it; (3) because native national (tribal) loyalties have remained strong.

It may be that there are Anishinabe-white-black mixed-bloods in the South and East who possess almost no group pride and who would choose to become white if they could. (Too dark to become white, many are being absorbed into the black population.) Such people perhaps come closest to the concept of being mestizo or out-caste.

The colonial policies of Spain, Britain, and the United States have invented the concept of mestizo and given reality to the concept through racist, caste-oriented policies that favor white persons over nonwhites while distinguishing grades of people within the nonwhite world. Isn't it time that this grading system is halted forever?

The Plan to Liquidate the Anishinabe Peoples

In Mexico an indio who puts on shoes, learns Spanish, and moves to a larger city becomes a non-Indian (he becomes mestizo or a Mexicano).

In Peru an Anishinabe woman who sets up a small shop becomes a chola. She is no longer an india.

In Guatemala a Cakchiquel who learns Spanish and moves to the city becomes a ladino. He is no longer indio.

In Peru, Bolivia, Mexico, and elsewhere, millions of people who were indios just a few years ago are now officially campesinos. Bolivia has no more Anishinabegs, only peasants.

In Brazil an Indian who takes up farming away from a tribal village becomes a caboclo or perhaps a mestizo or simply a Brazilian peasant.

In the United States an Indian whose reservation is terminated becomes officially a non-Indian.

In Canada an Indian whose group never signed a treaty or received a reservation is a metis.

In the United States many Chicanos of unmixed physical appearance are classified as whites with Spanish surnames.

In Mexico a man of complete Indian appearance who wears a suit, has a college education, and speaks Spanish has to be mestizo, since he could never be an indio.

Throughout the Americas a strange phenomenon exists. Almost every country in the hemisphere is doing away with Indians, either by genocide (as in Brazil, Colombia, and Ecuador) or by legislation and custom. The computers of the minds who dominate Anishinabe-waki have decided that the Anishinabe is programmed to disappear, *but, of course, this disappearance is completely imaginary and exists only in the minds of the European-oriented ruling class.*

The plan to liquidate the native people originated with the Spanish, English, and Portuguese imperialists. It involved several components: (1) killing Anishinabe in wars of conquest; (2) forcibly destroying native identity and culture in programs of missionization of or "civilizing"; (3) transforming economically independent native into serfs, slaves, or urban proletariat and thereby making them part of the imperial economy; (4) making native (indio) ways of life a bad thing and encouraging, via racism, everyone to try to become español, white, portuguesa or at least mestizo; (5) discouraging the association of mixed-bloods with people still identified as Indian and developing jealousy and shame on the part of the various castes; and (6) doing everything possible to be sure that all people, whether of European ancestry, mixed ancestry, or native ancestry, regard everything European as good (civilized) and everything Anishinabe as bad (uncivilized or, at best, rustic).

This European colonial policy, so vicious and one-sided, has had the effect of making it literally impossible, in most of Anishinabe-waki, for an Indian to be anything other than a rural peasant or inhabitant of some remote region. By definition, no Indian can be a professor, a doctor, an engineer, a statesman, or even an industrial worker, a sailor, a miner, a cowboy, or a truck driver. Since Indians are defined as rural peasants (or jungle dwellers), they cannot be a part of modern society. As soon as Indians become part of society they are given the "courtesy" of being regarded as cholos, ladinos, mestizos, caboclos, or Peruanos, Bolivianos, Brasilenos, Mexicanos, Chilenos, or Guatemaltecos, or campesinos, trabajadores, and so on. This is true to some degree even in the United States, where tourists and white children want to see "real" Indians in war bonnets and feathers and where anthropology has stereotyped Indian culture, such as the pre-white contact period.

European imperialists thinking has denied Anishinabeg the right to possess large (mass) nationalities. The anthropologists and colonialists generally have decided that Indians are tribal forever. Whereas other peoples have had the right to merge tribes together and form large nation-states, Anishinabe become something else whenever they leave their village.

For instance, the Paraguayans, Hondurans, Nicaraguans, and El Salvadoreans are not Indians. How could they be? They belong to nation-states! But why not? Have they magically changed their races merely because of intertribal mixture and the absorption of a few aliens? Are the Germans no longer Germans because they merged different tribes, changed their religion and social system? If Europeans can remain Europeans while going through processes of tremendous social change, Anishinabeg can remain Anishinabeg while doing the same thing (no matter what white social scientists want to tell us)!

Since 1492 the conscious European colonialist policy has been to transform Anishinabe into an urban or rural proletariat. To accomplish this, tribes and villages had to be destroyed or uprooted, millions had to be killed, ancient values had to be destroyed, and a whole new mass of landless, economically dependent people had to be created. In the United States this policy has determined much of the present circumstances of the urban Indian, the landless Chicano migrant, the urban Chicano worker, and of course, the landless black population. South of the United States the result of this policy has been the creation of the mestizo-ladino-cholo-caboclo population.

Basically and fundamentally, the so-called mestizos of Anishinabe-waki are nothing more nor less than proletarianized Anishinabe. They are simply the descendants of Indians forced off their land, forced to mix with divergent tribes and languages, forced to learn Spanish or Portuguese, forced to become Christians, and forced to become an impoverished mass of rural or urban wage laborers. Of course, in the process of being proletarianized, European, African, and even Asiatic genes have been absorbed. But the fact of race mixture is of no real significance—*whether the proletarianized, detribalized mass is of pure Anishinabe or mixed descent is inconsequential.* What real difference can be shown between the predominantly Indian, Spanish-speaking proletariat of Mexico and the somewhat more mixed proletariat of El Salvador, aside from the fact that one is Mexicano in its specific history and the other is Salvadorian?

The Spanish-speaking Peruano is every bit as Anishinabe as the Quechua-speaking Peruano. The differences between the two groups are due to specific cultural characteristics and not the race. (Essentially these differences derive from the way colonialism affected the two groups. Both are equally pawns and victims of white manipulation and white-oriented thinking.)

In this connection, it should be stressed that the colonial policies of Spain, Portugal, Britain, and the United States have never been assimilationist. It was not the intention of the white invaders to absorb nonwhites into their own superior race. On the other hand, it was, and is, the policy of the white ruling groups of Anishinabe-waki to proletarianize nonwhites!

Let us not confuse these two processes. Both assimilation and proletarianization would demand that the native Anishinabe (or African) cultures and tribes be destroyed. Both would demand that the conquered groups learn new skills, learn European language, and become part of the cash economy. But there the similarity ends. An assimilation policy would require the liquidation of racism, color consciousness, and resistance to intermarriage. Clearly, the white ruling groups of the Americas (even in the so-called relaxed Latin countries) have had no intention of doing that.

We might ask also, how is it that the white-oriented ruling groups stay in power in such overwhelmingly non white countries as Ecuador, Paraguay, Bolivia, Peru, Guatemala, and so on? Perhaps these rulers have learned to use the Spaniard's old trick of pitting cholo against indio, caste against caste, and city against countryside. Doesn't the policy of liquidating the Indian fit into this nicely? For example, an Inca-oriented Quechua revolution cannot probably occur in Peru as long as the cholos are led to believe that they are different and better than indios. No real revolution can take place in Guatemala as long as indios distrust ladinos and ladinos look down upon indios. It all seems so clever and (thus far) so successful.

Divide and conquer. Keep divided and control.

The Mestizo as a Cop Out

Before 1910 it was common for the Mexican intelligentsia to refer to themselves as blancos in contrast to los indios. Until very recently also it was common for Mexican-Americans to refer to themselves as whites, Latinos, Spanish-Americans, or Hispanos. More recently, first in Mexico and now in the United States, the mestizo concept has come to be used (along with the ambiguous la raza terminology and se habla español in the United States).

This movement from whiteism and Spanishism to mestizoism can be as a progressive step, in that apparently the presence of Anishinabe ancestry is being acknowledged. In that sense perhaps it should be encouraged.

On the other hand, to be a mestizo is to be a nothing in particular (as discussed above). All people are mestizos to one degree or another, so for the Mexicano or Chicano to say he is a mestizo is to say, in effect, "I am a human being." Moreover, in its usage it says, "I am an out-caste, a confused in between person." (It may well be that many Chicanos are confused about the clash between Mexican and Anglo-American values, but mestizo is not used to refer to that cultural conflict.) The traditional culture of most Chicanos is not mixed. It is a well-blended, fully integrated culture that has been evolving and changing for thousands of years.

More significantly, to be a mestizo is to cop-out. It is to accept the Spaniard's colonialist-racist ideology. It is to fall supine before the European's racial grading system instead of struggling for psychological liberation. It is to deny one's own people's history in order to have a masochistic, obscene relationship with the invaders and conquerors.

It is to be suspected that many Chicanos, Mexicans, and other nonwhite groups in Anishinabe-waki grasp at being called mestizo, not because of a desire to acknowledge Anishinabe descent, but quite the opposite reason, to affirm white descent. A mestizo (according to the racist caste system) is, after all, not a lowly indio. He is at least part-white and, therefore, part-civilized, una persona de razon.

The affirmation of being mestizo is, therefore, a counter-productive, neocolonialist stage of thinking. It is based upon a continued subjection to white categories of denigration and racism.

The mestizo-ladino-cholo-caboclo syndrome is also a major weapon in the arsenal of the white or near-white ruling cliques of many regions of Anishinabe-waki. It prevents the unification of the oppressed nonwhite masses in a common liberation struggle.

Who are the Mexicans? The Mexicans are what they always have been—Mexicans. Since (and before) 1520 they have absorbed many non-Mexicans (including other Anishinabeg as well as Asiatics, Africans, Spaniards, and so on); and their culture has changed (as do all cultures). Fundamentally, the Mexican people go back into history as far as we can see into the past. They have no need to explain their present status by denying their continuous past or by genuflecting before the shrine of mestisaje! The word *Mexican* historically means Aztec-Nahuan. Isn't that enough?

Basically, the peoples of Mexico, Guatemala, El Salvador, Honduras, Nicaragua, Ecuador, Peru, Bolivia, and Paraguay are, at one and the same time, both Mexicans, Guatemaltecos, Salvadoreans, et cetera, and Anishinabeg.

A clear distinction must be made between the use of the term *mestizo* as a purely descriptive statement of fact and the use of the term to categorize an entire community or people forever. For example, Winston Churchill could (I suppose) have been classed as a mestizo, that is, a person of mixed ethnic descent (since he was part-Indian). His identity was not that of a mestizo, however, since he was clearly and completely British.

It follows that when the term mestizo is merely used as a descriptive term, a person can be both mestizo and Indian, or both mestizo and French, or both mestizo and Filipino. For example, Cornplanter can be described as a mestizo (i.e., as an individual of known ethnic intermixture) and also as a Seneca. His nationality was, however, Seneca.

Similarly, individual Chicanos can be described as mestizo if they look part-European or know of a non-Indian ancestor. Their identity, however, is Chicano, and the Chicano group, by virtue of its cultural, racial, and historical continuity, cannot be categorized as mestizo.

Liberation from Colonialism

The oppressed peoples of the world are struggling to liberate themselves from both the material and the psychological forces of imperialism. Unfortunately, a "Brown is beautiful" movement has not yet penetrated many sections of Anishinabe-waki. Many people are still castrated by feelings of racial and cultural inferiority implanted by European colonialists and their neocolonialists successors.

The mestizo concept, as used by the Spaniards, by white ruling cliques, and by social scientists, is an anti-Indian, psychologically paralyzing tool of colonialism. It must be exposed and replaced by concepts rooted in the realities of American life.

Bibliography

Clark, V. S. (1908) "Mexican Labor in the United States," *Bulletin of the Department of Labor* 78, September.
Cordoza Orozco, E. (1966) "Mexica: An Identity for Mexican-Americans," mimeographed pamphlet.
Dana Jr., R. H. (n.d.) *Two Years Before the Mast*, New York: A. L. Burt Co.
Driver, H. (1961) *Indians of North America*, Chicago: University of Chicago Press.
"El Plan Espiritual de Aztlan" (1969) *El Grito del Norte* 2 (9).
Forbes, J. D. (n.d.) *The Mestizo Concept: A Product of European Imperialism*, Unpublished manuscript.
Gamio, M. (1930) *Mexican Immigration to the United States*, Chicago: University of Chicago Press.
Law Olmstead, F. (1857) *A Journey Through Texas*, Dix: Edwards and Co.
McWilliams, C. (1949) *North from Mexico: The Spanish-Speaking People of the United States*, New York: J. P. Lippincott Co.
Occidental College (1963) "Social and Educational Problems [of] Rural and Urban Mexican American Youth: Summary of Proceedings of the Southwest Conference," revised edition, 144 pages, *Occidental College*, April 6, https://books.google.com/books/about/Social_and_Educational_Problems_of_Rural.html?id=71cXAAAAIAAJ.
Raab, E. (ed.) (1962) *American Race Relations Today*, New York: Doubleday.
Silva Sloss, P. (1972) "One Spark Can Start a Prairie Fire," *La Palabra Alambre de MASH* 4 (5): 15–66.
"Staff Paper-Spanish-Speaking Peoples" (1964) United States Commission on Civil Rights, February 5 (draft).
Taylor, P. S. (1928) "Mexican Labor in the United States: Imperial Valley," *University of California Publications in Economics* 6 (1).
Taylor, P. S. (1929) "Mexican Labor in the United States: Valley of the South Platte, Colorado," *University of California Publications in Economics* 6 (2).
Taylor, P. S. (1931) "Mexican Labor in the United States: Dimmit County, Winter Garden District, South Texas," *University of California Publications in Economics* 6 (5).
Taylor, P. S. (1932) "Mexican Labor in the United States: Chicago and the Calumet Region," *University of California Publications in Economics* 7 (2).
Weinberg, A. K. (1963) *Manifest Destiny*, Chicago: Quadrangle Books.
Wilson Record, C. (1963) "Intergroup Conflict in the Bay Area," in *Public Affairs Report, Bulletin of the Institute of Governmental Studies*, 4, Berkeley: University of California Press.

Reading Questions

1. What does Forbes say is the function of mestizaje as an identity category? How does this category impact real-world social relations?
2. What is Forbes' vision for a more accurate, more just form of identification?
3. Forbes thinks the invention and use of the category of mestizo was massively destructive to Indigenous communities. Does that history mean we cannot or should not use it? Does it matter if people now think of themselves in that way? Can the term 'mestizo' be reconceived or reclaimed? Can it be transformed from community-destroying to community-building?
4. In this article, Forbes tends to discuss Native or Indigenous peoples as having relatively unified kinship practices, and tends to speak in terms that don't distinguish between, say, the Inka, the Maya, the Oneida, and the Apache. Would it matter for his argument if there were important differences

in the kinship practices of these groups, or if they were not inclined to understand themselves as sharing a unified history of the sort Forbes describes?
5. Suppose the mestizo peoples of Latin America began to identify themselves as Indigenous. Would it be a problem if existing Indigenous communities in Latin America did not recognize these newly self-identified Indigenous peoples as Indigenous? Why or why not?
6. Many identities claim some historical roots, or some special time period that anchors the origin of that group of people. Does it always need to be in the past? Is there some reason for making some past (or present or future) time period the special basis of the identity? Can't we always argue for another category?

8 *La Conciencia de la Mestiza*
Towards a New Consciousness

Gloria Anzaldúa

Por la mujer de mi raza hablará el espíritu[1]

Jose Vasconcelos, Mexican philosopher, envisaged *una raza mestiza, una mezcla de razas afines, una raza de color—la primera raza síntesis del globo*. He called it a cosmic race, *la raza cósmica*, a fifth race embracing the four major races of the world (Vasconcelos 1961). Opposite to the theory of the pure Aryan, and to the policy of racial purity that white America practices, his theory is one of inclusivity. At the confluence of two or more genetic streams, with chromosomes constantly "crossing over," this mixture of races, rather than resulting in an inferior being, provides hybrid progeny, a mutable, more malleable species with a rich gene pool. From this racial, ideological, cultural and biological cross pollinization, an "alien" consciousness is presently in the making—a new *mestiza* consciousness, *una conciencia de mujer*. It is a consciousness of the Borderlands.

Una Lucha De Fronteras/A Struggle of Borders

> Because I, a *mestiza*,
> continually walk out of one culture
> and into another,
> because I am in all cultures at the same time,
> *alma entre dos mundos, tres, cuatro,*
> *me zumba la cabeza con lo contradictorio.*
> *Estoy norteada por todas las voces que me hablan*
> *simultáneamente.*

The ambivalence from the clash of voices results in mental and emotional states of perplexity. Internal strife results in insecurity and indecisiveness. The *mestiza's* dual or multiple personality is plagued by psychic restlessness.

In a constant state of mental nepantilism, an Aztec word meaning torn between ways, *la mestiza* is a product of the transfer of the cultural and spiritual values of one group to another. Being tricultural, monolingual, bilingual, or multilingual, speaking a patois, and in a state of perpetual transition, the *mestiza* faces the dilemma of the mixed breed: which collectivity does the daughter of a darkskinned mother listen to?

El choque de un alma atrapado entre el mundo del espíritu y el mundo de la técnica a veces la deja entullada. Cradled in one culture, sandwiched between two cultures, straddling all three cultures and their value systems, *la mestiza* undergoes a struggle of flesh, a struggle of borders, an inner war. Like all people, we perceive the version of reality that our culture communicates. Like others having or living in more than one culture, we get multiple, often opposing messages. The coming together of two self-consistent but habitually incompatible frames of reference[2] causes *un choque*, a cultural collision.

Within us and within *la cultura chicana*, commonly held beliefs of the white culture attack commonly held beliefs of the Mexican culture, and both attack commonly held beliefs of the indigenous culture. Subconsciously, we see an attack on ourselves and our beliefs as a threat and we attempt to block with a counterstance.

But it is not enough to stand on the opposite river bank, shouting questions, challenging patriarchal, white conventions. A counterstance locks one into a duel of oppressor and oppressed; locked in mortal combat, like the cop and the criminal, both are reduced to a common denominator of violence. The counterstance refutes the dominant culture's views and beliefs, and, for this, it is proudly defiant. A reaction is limited by, and dependent on, what it is reacting against. Because the counterstance stems from a problem with authority—outer as well as inner—it's a step towards liberation from cultural domination. But it is not a way of life. At some point, on our way to a new consciousness, we will have to leave the opposite bank, the split between the two mortal combatants somehow healed so that we are on both shores at once and, at once, see through serpent and eagle eyes. Or perhaps we will decide to disengage from the dominant culture, write it off altogether as a lost cause, and cross the border into a wholly new and separate territory. Or we might go another route. The possibilities are numerous once we decide to act and not react.

A Tolerance for Ambiguity

These numerous possibilities leave *la mestiza* floundering in uncharted seas. In perceiving conflicting information and points of view, she is subjected to a swamping of her psychological borders. She has discovered that she can't hold concepts or ideas in rigid boundaries. The borders and walls that are supposed to keep the undesirable ideas out are entrenched habits and patterns of behavior; these habits and patterns are the enemy within. Rigidity means death. Only by remaining flexible is she able to stretch the psyche horizontally and vertically. *La mestiza* constantly has to shift out of habitual formations; from convergent thinking, analytical reasoning that tends to use rationality to move toward a single goal (a Western mode), to divergent thinking,[3] characterized by movement away from set patterns and goals and toward a more whole perspective, one that includes rather than excludes.

The new *mestiza* copes by developing a tolerance for contradictions, a tolerance for ambiguity. She learns to be an Indian in Mexican culture, to be Mexican from an Anglo point of view. She learns to juggle cultures. She has a plural personality, she operates in a pluralistic mode—nothing is thrust out, the good the bad and the ugly, nothing rejected, nothing abandoned. Not only does she sustain contradictions, she turns the ambivalence into something else.

She can be jarred out of ambivalence by an intense, and often painful, emotional event which inverts or resolves the ambivalence. I'm not sure exactly how. The work takes place underground—subconsciously. It is work that the soul performs. That focal point or fulcrum, that juncture where the *mestiza* stands, is where phenomena tend to collide. It is where the possibility of uniting all that is separate occurs. This assembly is not one where severed or separated pieces merely come together. Nor is it a balancing of opposing powers. In attempting to work out a synthesis, the self has added a third element which is greater than the sum of its severed parts. That third element is a new consciousness—a *mestiza* consciousness—and though it is a source of intense pain, its energy comes from continual creative motion that keeps breaking down the unitary aspect of each new paradigm.

En unas pocas centurias, the future will belong to the *mestiza*. Because the future depends on the breaking down of paradigms, it depends on the straddling of two or more cultures. By creating a new mythos—that is, a change in the way we perceive reality, the way we see ourselves, and the ways we behave—la *mestiza* creates a new consciousness.

The work of *mestiza* consciousness is to break down the subject-object duality that keeps her a prisoner and to show in the flesh and through the images in her work how duality is transcended. The answer to the problem between the white race and the colored, between males and females, lies in healing the split that originates in the very foundation of our lives, our culture, our languages, our thoughts. A massive uprooting of dualistic thinking in the individual and collective consciousness is the beginning of a long struggle, but one that could, in our best hopes, bring us to the end of rape, of violence, of war.

La encrucijada/The Crossroads

A chicken is being sacrificed
   at a crossroads, a simple mound of earth
a mud shrine for *Eshu*,
   Yoruba god of indeterminacy,
who blesses her choice of path.
   She begins her journey.

Su cuerpo es una bocacalle. La mestiza has gone from being the sacrificial goat to becoming the officiating priestess at the crossroads.

As a *mestiza* I have no country, my homeland cast me out; yet all countries are mine because I am every woman's sister or potential lover. (As a lesbian I have no race, my own people disclaim me; but I am all races because there is the queer of me in all races.) I am cultureless because, as a feminist, I challenge the collective cultural/religious male-derived beliefs of Indo-Hispanics and Anglos; yet I am cultured because I am participating in the creation of yet another culture, a new story to explain the world and our participation in it, a new value system with images and symbols that connect us to each other and to the planet. *Soy un amasamiento*, I am an act of kneading, of uniting and joining that not only has produced both a creature of darkness and a creature of light, but also a creature that questions the definitions of light and dark and gives them new meanings.

We are the people who leap in the dark, we are the people on the knees of the gods. In our very flesh, (r)evolution works out the clash of cultures. It makes us crazy constantly, but if the center holds, we've made some kind of evolutionary step forward. *Nuestra alma el trabajo*, the opus, the great alchemical work; spiritual *mestizaje*, a "morphogenesis,"[4] an inevitable unfolding. We have become the quickening serpent movement.

Indigenous like corn, the *mestiza* is a product of crossbreeding, designed for preservation under a variety of conditions. Like an ear of corn—a female seed-bearing organ—the *mestiza* is tenacious, tightly wrapped in the husks of her culture. Like kernels she clings to the cob; with thick stalks and strong brace roots, she holds tight to the earth—she will survive the crossroads.

La Conciencia de la Mestiza   127

Lavando y remojando el maíz en agua de cal, despojando el pellejo. Moliendo, mixteando, amasando, hacienda tortillas de masa.[5] She steeps the corn in lime, it swells, softens. With stone roller on *metate*, she grinds the corn, then grinds again. She kneads and moulds the dough, pats the round balls into *tortillas*.

> We are the porous rock in the stone *metate*
> squatting on the ground.
> We are the rolling pin, *el maíz y agua,*
> *la masa harina. Somos el amasijo.*
> *Somos lo molido en el metate.*
> We are the *comal* sizzling hot,
> the hot *tortilla*, the hungry mouth.
> We are the coarse rock.
> We are the grinding motion,
> the mixed potion, *somos el molcajete.*
> We are the pestle, the *comino, ajo, pimienta,*
> We are the *chile colorado,*
> the green shoot that cracks the rock.
> We will abide.

El camino de la mestiza/The Mestiza Way

Caught between the sudden contraction, the breath sucked in and the endless space, the brown woman stands still, looks at the sky. She decides to go down, digging her way along the roots of trees. Sifting through the bones, she shakes them to see if there is any marrow in them. Then, touching the dirt to her forehead, to her tongue, she takes a few bones, leaves the rest in their burial place.

She goes through her backpack, keeps her journal and address book, throws away the muni-bart metromaps. The coins are heavy and they go next, then the greenbacks flutter through the air. She keeps her knife, can opener and eyebrow pencil. She puts bones, pieces of bark, *hierbas*, eagle feather, snakeskin, tape recorder, the rattle and drum in her pack and she sets out to become the complete *tolteca*.

Her first step is to take inventory. *Despojando, desgranando, quitando paja.* Just what did she inherit from her ancestors? This weight on her back—which is the baggage from the Indian mother, which the baggage from the Spanish father, which the baggage from the Anglo?

Pero es difícil differentiating between *lo heredado, lo adquirido, lo impuesto.* She puts history through a sieve, winnows out the lies, looks at the forces that we as a race, as women, have been a part of. *Luego bota lo que no vale, los desmientos, los desencuentos, el embrutecimiento. Aguarda el juicio, hondo y enraízado, de la gente antigua.* This step is a conscious rupture with all oppressive traditions of all cultures and religions. She communicates that rupture, documents the struggle. She reinterprets history and, using new symbols, she shapes new myths. She adopts new perspectives toward the darkskinned, women and queers. She strengthens her tolerance (and intolerance) for ambiguity. She is willing to share, to make herself vulnerable to foreign ways of seeing and thinking. She surrenders all notions of safety, of the familiar. Deconstruct, construct. She becomes a *nahual*, able to transform herself into a tree, a coyote, into another person. She learns to transform the small "I" into the total Self. *Se hace moldeadora de su alma. Según la concepción que tiene de sí misma, así será.*

Que No Se Nos Olviden Los Hombres

> "*Tú no sirves pa' nada*—
> you're good for nothing.
> *Eres pura vieja.*"

"You're nothing but a woman" means you are defective. Its opposite is to be *un macho*. The modern meaning of the word "machismo," as well as the concept, is actually an Anglo invention. For men like my father, being "macho" meant being strong enough to protect and support my mother and us, yet being able to show love. Today's macho has doubts about his ability to feed and protect his family. His "machismo" is an adaptation to oppression and poverty and low self-esteem. It is the result of hierarchical male dominance. The Anglo, feeling inadequate and inferior and powerless, displaces or transfers these feelings to the Chicano by shaming him. In the Gringo world, the Chicano suffers from excessive humility and self-effacement, shame of self and self-deprecation. Around Latinos he suffers from a sense of language inadequacy and its accompanying discomfort; with Native Americans he suffers from a racial amnesia which ignores our common blood, and from guilt because the Spanish part of him took their land and oppressed them. He has an excessive compensatory hubris when around Mexicans from the other side. It overlays a deep sense of racial shame.

The loss of a sense of dignity and respect in the macho breeds a false machismo which leads him to put down women and even to brutalize them. Coexisting with his sexist behavior is a love for the mother which takes precedence over that of all others. Devoted son, macho pig. To wash down the shame of his acts, of his very being, and to handle the brute in the mirror, he takes to the bottle, the snort, the needle, and the fist.

Though we "understand" the root causes of male hatred and fear, and the subsequent wounding of women, we do not excuse, we do not condone, and we will no longer put up with it. From the men of our race, we demand the admission/acknowledgment/disclosure/testimony that they wound us, violate us, are afraid of us and of our power. We need them to say they will begin to eliminate their hurtful put-down ways. But more than the words, we demand acts. We say to them: We will develop equal power with you and those who have shamed us.

It is imperative that *mestizas* support each other in changing the sexist elements in the Mexican-Indian culture. As long as woman is put down, the Indian and the Black in all of us is put down. The struggle of the *mestiza* is above all a feminist one. As long as *los hombres* think they have to *chingar mujeres* and each other to be men, as long as men are taught that they are superior and therefore culturally favored over *la mujer*, as long as to be a *vieja* is a thing of derision, there can be no real healing of our psyches. We're halfway there—we have such love of the Mother, the good mother. The first step is to unlearn the *puta/virgen* dichotomy and to see *Coatlalopeuh-Coatlicue* in the Mother, *Guadalupe*.

Tenderness, a sign of vulnerability, is so feared that it is showered on women with verbal abuse and blows. Men, even more than women, are fettered to gender roles. Women at least have had the guts to break out of bondage. Only gay men have had the courage to expose themselves to the woman inside them and to challenge the current masculinity. I've encountered a few scattered and isolated gentle straight men, the beginnings of a new breed, but they are confused, and entangled with sexist behaviors that they have not been able to eradicate. We need a new masculinity and the new man needs a movement.

Lumping the males who deviate from the general norm with man, the oppressor, is a gross injustice. *Asombra pensar que nos hemos quedado en ese pozo oscuro donde el mundo encierra a las lesbianas. Asombra pensar que hemos, como femenistas y lesbianas, cerrado nuestros corazónes a los hombres, a nuestros hermanos los jotos, desheredados y marginales como nosotros.* Being the supreme crossers of cultures, homosexuals have strong bonds with the queer white, Black, Asian, Native American, Latino, and with the queer in Italy, Australia and the rest of the planet. We come from all colors, all classes, all races, all time periods. Our role is to link people with each other—the Blacks with Jews with Indians with Asians with whites with extraterrestrials. It is to transfer ideas and information from one culture to another. Colored homosexuals have more knowledge of other cultures; have always been at the forefront (although sometimes in the closet) of all liberation struggles in this country; have suffered more injustices and have survived them despite all odds. Chicanos need to acknowledge the political and artistic contributions of their queer. People, listen to what your *jotería* is saying.

The *mestizo* and the queer exist at this time and point on the evolutionary continuum for a purpose. We are a blending that proves that all blood is intricately woven together, and that we are spawned out of similar souls.

Somos Una Gente

> *Hay tantísimas fronteras*
> *que dividen a la gente,*
> *pero por cada frontera*
> *existe tambien un puente.*
> —Gina Valdés (1982: 2)

<u>Divided Loyalties</u>: Many women and men of color do not want to have any dealings with white people. It takes too much time and energy to explain to the downwardly mobile, white middle-class women that it's okay for us to want to own "possessions," never having had any nice furniture on our dirt floors or "luxuries" like washing machines. Many feel that whites should help their own people rid themselves of race hatred and fear first. I, for one, choose to use some of my energy to serve as mediator. I think we need to allow whites to be our allies. Through our literature, art, *corridos*, and folktales we must share our history with them so when they set up committees to help Big Mountain Navajos or the Chicano farmworkers or *los Nicaragüenses* they won't turn people away because of their racial fears and ignorances. They will come to see that they are not helping us but following our lead.

Individually, but also as a racial entity, we need to voice our needs. We need to say to white society: We need you to accept the fact that Chicanos are different, to acknowledge your rejection and negation of us. We need you to own the fact that you looked upon us as less than human, that you stole our lands, our personhood, our self-respect. We need you to make public restitution: to say that, to compensate for your own sense of defectiveness, you strive for power over us, you erase our history and our experience because it makes you feel guilty—you'd rather forget your brutish acts. To say you've split yourself from minority groups, that you disown us, that your dual consciousness splits off parts of yourself, transferring the "negative" parts onto us. (Where there is persecution of minorities, there is shadow projection. Where there is violence and war, there is repression of shadow.) To say that you are afraid of us, that to put distance between us, you wear the mask of contempt. Admit that Mexico is your double, that she exists in the shadow of this country, that we are irrevocably tied to her. Gringo, accept the doppelganger in your psyche. By taking back your collective shadow the intracultural split will heal. And finally, tell us what you need from us.

By Your True Faces We Will Know You

I am visible—see this Indian face—yet I am invisible. I both blind them with my beak nose and am their blind spot. But I exist, we exist. They'd like to think I have melted in the pot. But I haven't, we haven't.

The dominant white culture is killing us slowly with its ignorance. By taking away our self-determination, it has made us weak and empty. As a people we have resisted and we have taken expedient positions, but we have never been allowed to develop unencumbered—we have never been allowed to be fully ourselves. The whites in power want us people of color to barricade ourselves behind our separate tribal walls so they can pick us off one at a time with their hidden weapons; so they can whitewash and distort history. Ignorance splits people, creates prejudices. A misinformed people is a subjugated people.

Before the Chicano and the undocumented worker and the Mexican from the other side can come together, before the Chicano can have unity with Native Americans and other groups, we need to know the history of their struggle and they need to know ours. Our mothers, our sisters and brothers, the guys who hang out on street corners, the children in the playgrounds, each of us must know our Indian lineage, our afro-*mestizaje*, our history of resistance.

To the immigrant *mexicano* and the recent arrivals we must teach our history. The 80 million *mexicanos* and the Latinos from Central and South America must know of our struggles. Each one of us must know basic facts about Nicaragua, Chile and the rest of Latin America. The Latinoist movement (Chicanos, Puerto Ricans, Cubans and other Spanish-speaking people working together to combat racial discrimination in the marketplace) is good but it is not enough. Other than a common culture we will have nothing to hold us together. We need to meet on a broader communal ground.

The struggle is inner: Chicano, *indio*, American Indian, *mojado*, *mexicano*, immigrant Latino, Anglo in power, working class Anglo, Black, Asian—our psyches resemble the bordertowns and are populated by the same people. The struggle has always been inner, and is played out in the outer terrains. Awareness of our situation must come before inner changes, which in turn come before changes in society. Nothing happens in the "real" world unless it first happens in the images in our heads.

El día de la Chicana

> I will not be shamed again
> Nor will I shame myself.

I am possessed by a vision: that we Chicanas and Chicanos have taken back or uncovered our true faces, our dignity and selfrespect. It's a validation vision.

Seeing the Chicana anew in light of her history. I seek an exoneration, a seeing through the fictions of white supremacy, a seeing of ourselves in our true guises and not as the false racial personality that has been given to us and that we have given to ourselves. I seek our woman's face, our true features, the positive and the negative seen clearly, free of the tainted biases of male dominance. I seek new images of identity, new beliefs about ourselves, our humanity and worth no longer in question.

Estamos viviendo en la noche de la Raza, un tiempo cuando el trabajo se hace a lo quieto, en lo oscuro. El día cuando aceptamos tal y como somos y para donde vamos y porque—ese día será el día de la Raza. Yo tengo el conpromiso de expresar mi visión, mi sensibilidad, mi percepción de la revalidación de la gente mexicana, su mérito, estimación, honra, aprecio, y validez.

On December 2nd when my sun goes into my first house, I celebrate *el dia de la Chicana y el Chicano*. On that day I clean my altars, light my *Coatlalopeuh* candle, burn sage and copal, take *el baño para espantar basura*, sweep my house. On that day I bare my soul, make myself vulnerable to friends and family by expressing my feelings. On that day I affirm who we are.

On that day I look inside our conflicts and our basic introverted racial temperament. I identify our needs, voice them. I acknowledge that the self and the race have been wounded. I recognize the need to take care of our personhood, of our racial self. On that day I gather the splintered and disowned parts of *la gente mexicana* and hold them in my arms. *Todas las partes de nosotros valen.*

On that day I say, "Yes, all you people wound us when you reject us. Rejection strips us of self-worth; our vulnerability exposes us to shame. It is our innate identity you find wanting. We are ashamed that we need your good opinion, that we need your acceptance. We can no longer camouflage our needs, can no longer let defenses and fences sprout around us. We can no longer withdraw. To rage and look upon you with contempt is to rage and be contemptuous of ourselves. We can no longer blame you, nor disown the white parts, the male parts, the pathological parts, the queer parts, the vulnerable parts. Here we are weaponless with open arms, with only our magic. Let's try it our way, the *mestiza* way, the Chicana way, the woman way."

On that day, I search for our essential dignity as a people, a people with a sense of purpose—to belong and contribute to something greater than our *pueblo*. On that day I seek to recover and reshape my spiritual identity. *¡Anímate! Raza, a celebrar el día de la Chicana.*

El Retorno

> All movements are accomplished in six stages,
> and the seventh brings return.
> —I Ching (Wilhelm 1950: 98)

> *Tanto tiempo sin verte casa mía,
> mi cuna, mi hondo nido de la huerta.*
> —"Soledad"[6]

I stand at the river, watch the curving, twisting serpent, a serpent nailed to the fence where the mouth of the Rio Grande empties into the Gulf.

I have come back. *Tanto dolor me costó el alejamiento.* I shade my eyes and look up. The bone beak of a hawk slowly circling over me, checking me out as potential carrion. In its wake a little bird flickering its wings, swimming sporadically like a fish. In the distance the expressway and the slough of traffic like an irritated sow. The sudden pull in my gut, *la tierra, los aguaceros.* My land, *el viento soplando la arena, el lagartijo debajo de un nopalito. Me acuerdo como era antes. Una región desértica de vasta llanuras, costeras de baja altura, de escasa lluvia, de chaparrales formados por mesquites y huizaches.* If I look real hard I can almost see the Spanish fathers who were called "the cavalry of Christ" enter this valley riding their *burros*, see the clash of cultures commence.

Tierra natal. This is home, the small towns in the Valley, *los pueblitos* with chicken pens and goats picketed to mesquite shrubs. *En las colonias* on the other side of the tracks, junk cars line the front yards of hot pink and lavender-trimmed houses—Chicano architecture we call it, self-consciously. I have missed the TV shows where hosts speak in half and half, and where awards are given in the category of Tex-Mex music. I have missed the Mexican cemeteries blooming with artificial flowers, the fields of aloe vera and red pepper, rows of sugar cane, of corn hanging on the stalks, the cloud of *polvareda* in the dirt roads behind a speeding pickup truck, *el sabor de tamales de rez y venado.* I have missed *la yegua colorada* gnawing the wooden gate of her stall, the smell of horse flesh from Carito's corrals. *Hecho menos las noches calientes sin aire, noches de linternas y lechuzas* making holes in the night.

I still feel the old despair when I look at the unpainted, dilapidated, scrap lumber houses consisting mostly of corrugated aluminum. Some of the poorest people in the U.S. live in the Lower Rio Grande Valley, an arid and semi-arid land of irrigated farming, intense sunlight and heat, citrus groves next to chaparral and cactus. I walk through the elementary school I attended so long ago, that remained segregated until recently. I remember how the white teachers used to punish us for being Mexican.

How I love this tragic valley of South Texas, as Ricardo Sanchez calls it; this borderland between the Nueces and the Rio Grande. This land has survived possession and ill-use by five countries: Spain, Mexico, the Republic of Texas, the U.S., the Confederacy, and the U.S. again. It has survived Anglo Mexican blood feuds, lynchings, burnings, rapes, pillage.

Today I see the Valley still struggling to survive. Whether it does or not, it will never be as I remember it. The borderlands depression that was set off by the 1982 peso devaluation in Mexico resulted in the closure of hundreds of Valley businesses. Many people lost their homes, cars, land. Prior to 1982, U.S. store owners thrived on retail sales to Mexicans who came across the border for groceries and clothes and appliances. While goods on the U.S. side have become 10, 100, 1000 times more expensive for Mexican buyers, goods on the Mexican side have become 10, 100, 1000 times cheaper for Americans. Because the Valley is heavily dependent on agriculture and Mexican retail trade, it has the highest unemployment rates along the entire border region; it is the Valley that has been hardest hit.[7]

"It's been a bad year for corn," my brother, Nune, says. As he talks, I remember my father scanning the sky for a rain that would end the drought, looking up into the sky, day after day, while the corn withered on its stalk. My father has been dead for 29 years, having worked himself to death. The lifespan of a Mexican farm laborer is 56—he lived to be 38. It shocks me that I am older than he. I, too, search the sky for rain. Like the ancients, I worship the rain god and the maize goddess, but unlike my father I have recovered their names. Now for rain (irrigation) one offers not a sacrifice of blood, but of money.

"Farming is in a bad way," my brother says. "Two to three thousand small and big farmers went bankrupt in this country last year. Six years ago the price of corn was $8.00 per hundred pounds," he goes on. "This year it is $3.90 per hundred pounds." And, I think to myself, after taking inflation into account, not planting anything puts you ahead.

I walk out to the back yard, stare at *los rosales de mamá*. She wants me to help her prune the rose bushes, dig out the carpet grass that is choking them. *Mamagrande Ramona también tenía rosales.* Here every Mexican grows flowers. If they don't have a piece of dirt, they use car tires, jars, cans, shoe boxes. Roses are the Mexican's favorite flower. I think, how symbolic—thorns and all.

Yes, the Chicano and Chicana have always taken care of growing things and the land. Again I see the four of us kids getting off the school bus, changing into our work clothes, walking into the field with Papi and Marni, all six of us bending to the ground. Below our feet, under the earth lie the watermelon seeds. We cover them with paper plates, putting *terremotes* on top of the plates to keep them from being blown away by the wind. The paper plates keep the freeze away. Next day or the next, we remove the plates, bare the tiny green shoots to the elements. They survive and grow, give fruit hundreds of times the size of the seed. We water them and hoe them. We harvest them. The vines dry, rot, are plowed under. Growth, death, decay, birth. The soil prepared again and again, impregnated, worked on. A constant changing of forms, *renacimientos de la tierra madre*.

> This land was Mexican once
> was Indian always
> and is.
> And will be again.

To live in the Borderlands means you

> are neither *hispana india negra española*
> *ni gabacha, eres mestiza, mulata,* half-breed
> caught in the crossfire between camps
> while carrying all five races on your back
> not knowing which side to turn to, run from;

> To live in the Borderlands means knowing
> that the *india* in you, betrayed for 500 years,
> is no longer speaking to you,
> that *mexicanas* call you *rajetas*,
> that denying the Anglo inside you
> is as bad as having denied the Indian or Black;

> *Cuando vives en la frontera*
> people walk through you, the wind steals your voice,
> you're a *burra, buey,* scapegoat,
> forerunner of a new race,
> half and half—both woman and man, neither—
> a new gender;

> To live in the Borderlands means to
> put *chile* in the borscht,
> eat whole wheat *tortillas*,

Speak Tex-Mex with a Brooklyn accent;
be stopped by *la migra* at the border checkpoints;

Living in the Borderlands means you fight hard to
   resist the gold elixir beckoning from the bottle,
   the pull of the gun barrel,
   the rope crushing the hollow of your throat;

In the Borderlands
   you are the battleground
   where enemies are kin to each other;
   you are at home, a stranger,
   the border disputes have been settled
   the volley of shots have shattered the truce
   you are wounded, lost in action
   dead, fighting back;

To live in the Borderlands means
   the mill with the razor white teeth wants to shred off
   your olive-red skin, crush out the kernel, your heart
   pound you pinch you roll you out
   smelling like white bread but dead;

To survive the Borderlands
   you must live *sin fronteras*
   be a crossroads.

References

Gilliam, H. (1981) "Searching for a New World View," *This World*, January.
Rothenberg, A. (1979) *Creative Process in Art, Science, and Other Fields*, Chicago, IL: University of Chicago Press.
Valdes, G. (1982) *Puentes y Fronteras: Coplas Chicanas*, Los Angeles: Castle Lithograph.
Vasconcelos, J. (1961) *La Raza Cósmica: Misión de la Raza Ibero-Americana*, Mexico: Aguilar S.A. de Ediciones.
Wilhelm, R. (1950) *The I Ching or Book of Changes*, trans. Cary E. Baynes, Princeton, NJ: Princeton University Press.

Notes

1 This is my own "take off" on Jose Vasconcelos' (1961) idea.
2 Arthur Koestler termed this "bisociation" (Rothenberg 1979: 12).
3 In part, I derive my definitions for "convergent" and "divergent" thinking from Rothenberg (1979: 12–13).
4 To borrow chemist Ilya Prigogine's theory of "dissipative structures." Prigogine discovered that substances interact not in predictable ways as it was taught in science, but in different and fluctuating ways to produce new and more complex structures, a kind of birth he called "morphogenesis," which created unpredictable innovations (Gilliam 1981: 23).
5 *Tortillas de masa harina*: corn tortillas are of two types, the smooth uniform ones made in a tortilla press and usually bought at a tortilla factory or supermarket, and *gorditas*, made by mixing masa with lard or shortening or butter (my mother sometimes puts in bits of bacon or *chicharrones*).

6 "*Soledad*" is sung by the group *Haciendo Punto en Otro Son*.
7 Out of the twenty-two border counties in the four border states, Hidalgo County (named for Father Hidalgo who was shot in 1810 after instigating Mexico's revolt against Spanish rule under the banner of *la Virgen de Guadalupe*) is the most poverty-stricken county in the nation as well as the largest home base (along with Imperial in California) for migrant farmworkers. It was here that I was born and raised. I am amazed that both it and I have survived.

Reading Questions

1. In what way is the mestiza experience one of a "lucha de fronteras," according to Anzaldúa?
2. How does Anzaldúa argue for the claim that the mestiza experience gives rise to a distinctive form of consciousness?
3. Why does Anzaldúa affirm this form of consciousness?
4. In the section "El Camino de la Mestiza," Anzaldúa illustrates a process of a more authentic self-creation. If you were to take inventory of your own "baggage," what would you bring along with you? What would you leave behind?
5. What is the significance of the term "la mestiza"? Is this intended to exclude men or masculinity? Why or why not?
6. What is the relationship of the new mestiza consciousness to whiteness?
7. In what way does Anzaldúa affirm the spirit of Vasconcelos' work?
8. Vasconcelos' work has been criticized for relying on an objectionable set of assumptions and attitudes about the nature of race, the history of race, and racial "progress." How much of Anzaldúa's account presumes a racial story? To what extent is her work susceptible to similar lines of criticism?
9. What does Anzaldúa mean when she says "the struggle is inner"? How does this inner struggle relate to the need for Latinxs to know each other's history of struggle?
10. What is the significance of this chapter ending with the notion of "return"?

9 Geographies of Race and Ethnicity III

Settler Colonialism and Nonnative People of Color

Laura Pulido

I. Introduction

In this progress report I consider the politics of settler colonialism in relation to nonnative people of color. Over the past decade the concept of settler colonialism, a distinct form of colonization, has become increasingly prominent (Trask 2000; Wolfe 2006). Rather than seeking to control land, resources, and labor, settler colonization eliminated native peoples in order to appropriate their land. The US, Canada, Israel, and Australia are all examples of settler states. Early theorizations focused on white settlers, but questions soon arose from ethnic studies scholars regarding the role of nonwhite peoples. Though these are global conversations (Lawrence and Dua 2005; Wright and Sharma 2008/2009), I focus on US ethnic and native studies debates (Byrd 2011; Tuck and Yang 2012), as I am concerned with Chicana/o studies' response. While both Asian American and Black studies scholars have contributed to this discussion, Chicana/o studies, the study of ethnic-Mexicans in the US, has been relatively silent. And, for very different reasons, so has geography.

Chicana/o studies' ambivalence, I argue, is due to settler colonialism's potential to disrupt core elements of Chicana/o political subjectivity. Specifically, it unsettles Chicanas/os' conception of themselves as colonized people by highlighting their role as colonizers. Acknowledging such a role is difficult not only because it challenges key dimensions of Chicana/o identity, as seen in Aztlán, Chicanas/os' mythical homeland, but also because of the precarious nature of Chicana/o indigeneity.

Geography, with a few exceptions (Kobayashi and De Leeuw 2010; Bauder 2011), has only considered whites in relation to settler colonialism (Bonds and Inwood 2015; Radcliffe 2015). This reflects geography's larger anti-racist scholarship, which operates from a white/nonwhite binary which, in turn, reflects the overwhelming whiteness of the discipline. Geography simply lacks the racial diversity, scholarly expertise and comfort to explore such questions.

Despite being radically different, I wish to put these two disciplines in conversation. Besides being my two intellectual homes, geography must learn to wrestle with the complexities of racial and (de)colonial dynamics. Its contributions to the study of racism will always be limited if the fullness of the racial landscape is overlooked. Chicana/o studies' avoidance of settler colonialism illustrates how racial and political subjectivity is structured by colonization, contemporary nation-states, white supremacy, anti-racist struggle and decolonial projects. Deciphering the historical reasons why Chicana/o studies has failed to grapple with settler colonialism illuminates the deeply geographical nature of racial and political subjectivity. Ethnic-Mexicans, like all people of color, are diverse and multifaceted

DOI: 10.4324/9781003385417-14

(contrary to the tidiness implied by 'Latina/o'), and it is only through exploring the spatialities of their historical experiences that we can understand this avoidance.

In this progress report I first introduce settler colonialism and ethnic studies' response to it. Then, drawing primarily on cultural studies scholarship, I explore the precarious nature of Chicana/o indigeneity and the significance of Aztlán, both of which are deeply geographic. Chicana/o indigeneity is embedded in questions of scale, territory, boundaries, and empire, while Aztlán is an imagined place. Although I focus on US ethnic studies, these issues should resonate in all settler societies.

II. Settler Colonialism, Native Peoples and Nonwhite Others

What makes settler societies unique is their desire to *replace* indigenous peoples in order to take their land, rather than simply control resources and labor. While the US acknowledges that it is a settler country, it does so by evacuating the violence associated with this process. Huntington (2004), for instance, distinguishes settlers from immigrants. He states that settlers came to *build* a country, while immigrants come to *join* it. While settlers are routinely admired in US culture, their celebration requires imagining the process as nonviolent or, at best, involving justifiable violence (Blackhawk 2006). Key to erasing this violence are transition narratives—discourses that serve to make the past more palatable. Foregrounding settler colonialism, however, forces us to recognize the whitewashing associated with hegemonic representations of colonization (Dunbar-Ortiz 2014) and re-centers native peoples.

Settler colonialism demands that the experience of indigenous peoples be taken seriously, which has profound implications for white settlers, immigrants, and various minoritized populations, which in the US includes African Americans, Asian Americans, Latinas/os, Muslims, and other racially-subordinated groups. As Moreton-Robinson notes, "the question of how anyone came to be white or black in the United States is inextricably tied to the dispossession of the original owners" (2008: 84).

While many routinely collapse native and ethnic studies, there are important distinctions. First, many in native studies reject the category "minority" and the larger politics of multiculturalism (Byrd 2011; Kobayashi and De Leeuw 2010). This is because US minority status usually results from racism, but indigenous peoples have been colonized. And while the US has been somewhat willing to acknowledge a racist past, it has refused to grapple with the violence of settler colonialism. Though settler colonization is a racial project (Wolfe 2016), it cannot be reduced to racism. Indeed, the solution to racism is inclusion, but this does not address colonization (Coulthard 2014).

> When the remediation of the colonization of American Indians is framed through discourses of racialization that can be redressed by further inclusion into the nation-state, there is a significant failure to grapple with the fact that such discourses further reinscribe the original colonial injury.
>
> (Byrd 2011: xxiii)

Theorizing how minoritized groups participate in settler colonialism is challenging (Trask 2000; Kobayashi and De Leeuw 2010; Tuck and Yang 2012; Byrd 2011; Saranillo 2013; Wright and Sharma 2008/2009). Though some conceptualize all nonnatives as settlers (Lawrence and Dua 2005), ethnic studies generally rejects such simple equations. Terms like "arrivant" and "subordinate settler" describe various minoritized positions. Theorizing the roles of Black slaves, Asian immigrants, and Mexican settlers can be discomfiting, which, Tuck and Yang (2012) say, is entirely appropriate. They argue that since the US is both a settler colonial nation-state *and* an empire, it displaces native peoples and compels others onto indigenous lands through slavery, war, and economic dislocation (2012: 7). In an effort to overcome the seeming binary between colonization and racism, Wright and Sharma (2008/9) interpret colonization as the commons, which foregrounds capitalism rather than nationalism, and offers one way forward. Smith has sought to unify these processes under white supremacy, arguing that it is underlain by three logics: slaveability, genocide, and orientalism. Each logic in turn enables a particular social relation: capitalism, colonization, and war, respectively. These logics preclude easy solidarity.

> For example, all non-Native peoples are promised the ability to . . . settl[e] indigenous lands. All non-Black peoples are promised that . . . they will not be at the bottom of the racial hierarchy. And Black and Native peoples are promised that they will advance economically and politically if they join U.S. wars.
>
> (Smith 2012: 70).

Black studies scholars have responded in diverse ways to these debates. Miles (2005) explored how Black and indigenous peoples intersected through white supremacy, slavery, and settler colonization, while challenging conventional ideas of temporality. Instead of assuming native dispossession was first and slavery second, she shows how they informed each other simultaneously. Other African American studies scholars, often associated with "Afro-pessimism," have rejected relational interpretations and their concomitant politics (Wilderson 2010; see also Kauanui 2016).

Asian American studies has focused on immigrants' role in colonizing Hawai'i, especially how Asian "success" promotes multicultural harmony.

> In their focus on racism, discrimination, and the exclusion of Asians . . . such studies tell the story of Asians' civil rights as one of nation building in order to legitimate Asians' claims to a place for themselves in Hawai'i.
>
> (Fujikane and Okamura 2008: 2)

Saranillo (2013), among others, has argued that settler colonialism works *through* immigrants. Writing from a Canadian perspective, Day (2016) explores how the narrative of Asian labor's hyper-efficiency has become associated with a negative form of capital. While this review is in no way comprehensive, it should be apparent that vibrant debates exist in which scholars are struggling to understand how white supremacy and colonization intersect.

In contrast, Chicana/o studies has been peripheral to such discussions. Certainly Chicana/o studies is no stranger to colonization, given US conquest of Mexico (Acuña 1972; Barrera 1979; Almaguer 1994; Rivera 2006). Chicana studies scholars have challenged conventional historiography (Pérez 1999), often including native women in their analyses (Castañeda 1993; Chávez-Garcia 2004). Scholars have interrogated Chicana/o indigeneity (Saldaña-Portillo 2001, 2016; Contreras 2008; Hartley 2012), and more recently indigenous Latina/o migration (Castellanos et al. 2012; Fox and Rivera-Salgado 2004). Researchers have considered Chinese immigrants as settlers in the US southwest (Luna-Peña 2015), and compared Chicanas/os and Palestinians in terms of settler-colonialism (Lloyd and Pulido 2010). Sánchez and Pita (2014) have challenged claims of Chicanas/os as victims of US settler colonialism, insisting instead that American Indians are, while Cotera and Saldaña-Portillo (2015) have exposed the tensions underlying such claims.[1] In short, the discipline is dancing around settler colonization and its implications, but has not taken the plunge. Instead, Chicanas/os are still largely scripted as the colonized. Guidotti-Hernandez (2011) suggests that because Chicana/o studies is fixated on one conflict, the US conquest of Mexico, it has major blind spots. Indeed, the larger historiography of the US West is replete with Mexican violence towards indigenous peoples (Reséndez 2016; Smith 2013; González 2005; Guidotti-Hernandez 2011).

González, for example, documented Mexican dispossession of native peoples in Los Angeles. His analysis centers on an 1846 letter written by Mexicans to the Governor in which they complained about native people and requested that 'the Indians be placed under strict police surveillance or the persons for whom the Indians work give [them] quarter at the employer's rancho' (2005: 19). González argues that Mexican Angelenos embraced hegemonic Mexican culture, including eliminating *el indio barbaro* (the savage Indian) (Saldaña-Portillo 2016).

There is also evidence of Mexican complicity in US settler colonialism. Guidotti-Hernandez's (2011) study of Euro-American violence towards Mexicans and Mexico's genocide towards *indios barbaros* includes the Camp Grant Indian massacre of 1871. Both Mexico and the US fought the Apaches because they raided and refused a sedentary lifestyle. In 1871 the US promised a group of Apaches safety at Camp Grant, Arizona, but locals, including Mexican leadership, massacred 144, mostly women and children. In short, we have clear evidence of Mexicans and Chicanas/os participating in settler colonialism, but we are unable to frankly discuss it and consider its meanings.

III. Chicana/o Studies' Ambivalence Towards Settler Colonialism

An inability to acknowledge such violence and its corresponding subjectivities suggests deep anxieties. Indeed, there are parallels between the US's refusal to acknowledge settler colonialism (Dunbar-Ortiz 2014) and that of Chicana/o studies. Recognizing ethnic-Mexicans' role in settler colonization is threatening because it would force Chicana/o studies to recognize multiple subjectivities, which, in turn, would require rethinking the dominant narrative. This is similar to American Indian studies acknowledging, for example, that Cherokees owned slaves. But it's not just a desire to avoid uncomfortable work. There is significant confusion regarding Chicana/o indigeneity, which has been made almost illegible by colonization. Though both Indian and indigenous are constructed categories, Klopotek (2016) has argued that Indian functions as a racial term, while indigenous is a cultural and political one. While ethnic-Mexicans are overwhelmingly Indian, indigeneity is different. Exactly what are Chicanas/os indigenous to? When, if at all, does indigeneity cease? How does indigeneity function within multiple national formations? Not only do Mexico and the US have radically different conceptions of and approaches to indigeneity (Contreras 2008), but Chicanas/os, as transnational people, exist in the interstices of multiple national and regional racial formations (Saldaña-Portillo 2016).

IV. Chicanas/os: Indians or Indigenous?

Before examining Chicana/o indigeneity more closely, I must distinguish between two distinct threads. One thread stems from the centuries-long history of the peoples and lands of North America. A second strand has recently emerged through indigenous immigration from Latin America to the US (Castellanos et al. 2012; Fox and Rivera-Salgado 2004). While Chicana/o studies includes both, they embody different temporalities. Specifically, the second is usually *recognized* as indigenous, while the first is more contentious. I focus on the first, which is foundational to Chicana/o studies.

Chicana/o studies exists as both a scholarly enterprise and a nation-building project. And like any nation, it had to forge a new identity. Previous to "Chicana/o," which became widespread in the 1960s, ethnic-Mexicans living in the US identified as Mexican-American. Chicana/o is an explicitly oppositional term that drew upon counter-hegemonic histories, meanings, and experiences. Central to this was reclaiming an indigenous heritage, which had been undermined by Mexico's ideology of mestizaje as well as US racism. Mestizaje, the idea of cultural and biological mixing, was a nation-building strategy that both assimilated and erased *lo indio* (Cotera and Saldaña-Portillo 2015). Within Chicana/o studies, the idea of decolonial mestizaje has emerged (Anzaldúa 1987), which is an attempt to overcome the inherent racism of mestizaje (Hartley 2012; Morgensen 2011: 183–7; Saldaña-Portillo 2001).

Debates around Chicana/o indigeneity must be located in larger discussions of indigeneity itself (Teves et al. 2015; Castellanos et al. 2012). According to one definition, the communities, clans, nations, and tribes we call "indigenous peoples" are just that:

> Indigenous to the lands they inhabit, in contrast to and in contention with colonial societies that have spread out from Europe and other centers of empire. It is this oppositional and place-based existence, along with the consciousness of being in struggle against colonization by foreign peoples, that fundamentally distinguishes Indigenous peoples.
> (Alfred and Corntassel 2005: 597)

While seemingly straightforward, this definition hints at underlying complexities. For instance, locating indigeneity in relation to a specific place overlooks indigenous peoples' contemporary and historic mobility (Diaz 2015). When does tenure begin? Despite having lived in a place for hundreds, perhaps thousands of years, we know that native peoples were on the move. Moreover, US dispossession and the reservation system challenge any simple associations to land, boundary, or place.

Another key dimension suggested above is political awareness and struggle. But what about Indians who identify as assimilated and are not in struggle? Are they no longer indigenous? Perhaps not surprisingly, this requirement conflicts with the US government, which defines indigeneity by blood (see Simpson 2014). Still others emphasize cultural practices and connections. This might include those who are part of native communities, but not blood members (Simpson 2014). While American Indians have long debated these issues, they have been amplified by the growth in native studies, which has highlighted how indigeneity is rooted in colonization and nation-state processes.

Chicana/o indigeneity, like all other forms, must be grounded in the state (Hartley 2012). As noted earlier, Chicana/o subjectivities and identities have been forged in and through overlapping Mexican and US racial formations and nation-building projects (Saldaña-Portillo 2016). These formations are both sequential and spatially and temporally overlapping. Here, we must draw on our most sophisticated understandings of place—how to understand a region as a palimpsest, a border zone, and a boundary simultaneously? While Mexico incorporated indigeneity into its nation-building efforts, mestizaje has been highly contradictory. In contrast, the US sought to obliterate native people physically and forged a white racial and national identity *exclusive* of them. Consequently, in the US, native peoples are seen as distinct from the larger nation and insist they are sovereign. Though indigenous Mexicans may oppose the state, like the Zapatistas, they do not necessarily see themselves as distinct nations (Saldaña-Portillo 2001).

Chicana/o indigeneity is based on several claims (see Cotera and Saldaña-Portillo 2015). First, it is based on Mexicans' long tenure in North America. This, however, raises the question of scale: does North American indigenous count as US indigenous? Some American Indians say 'no'. In response, Chicanas/os charge that American Indians are reifying the colonizers' borders. A second pillar of Chicana/o indigeneity is the belief that their ancestors originated in what is now the US southwest and migrated south. This supposed homeland, Aztlán, actually appears on several maps.[2] As Chicana/o activists began reclaiming their indigeneity, they drew heavily on an Aztec heritage: Nahuatl, Aztec art, dancing, and Day of the Dead celebrations. Aztlán is even the name of Chicana/o studies' foremost journal. Ironically, activists were actually celebrating an imperial power, since the Aztecs conquered many Indian nations (Contreras 2008; Urrieta 2012). A third claim to Chicana/o indigeneity is colonization by Spain and US colonization of Mexico. Mexicans lost land, power, status, and rights through the Mexican-American War. The parallels between Indian and Mexican dispossession have long been noted (Horsman 1981). "That the Indian race of Mexico must recede before us, is quite as certain as . . . the destiny of our own Indians" (Thompson in Dunbar-Ortiz 2014: 117). Mexico, as an indigenous and colonized country, continues to be subject to US domination.

A fourth and final pillar of Chicana/o indigeneity is mixing between American Indians and Mexicans, which has occurred for centuries under diverse circumstances, including pre-Columbian migrations, conquest, slavery, refuge, adoption, and everything in-between. There are more than a few Chicanas/os who claim, for example, Pueblo heritage. And though Pueblos, understandably, may not wish to claim Mexican ancestry, it is apparent in their names, language, religious practices, and such. Despite this reality, the US insists on neat boundaries, however fictitious. Indeed, the Choctaw-Apache Tribe of Louisiana was initially denied federal recognition because they speak Spanish (Klopotek 2016).

While Chicanas/os identify as indigenous, they are not considered as such by the US, including many American Indians. This is due to the US's emphasis on blood, a specific relationship to land (Contreras 2008: 6), and continuous existence as a polity (Klopotek 2016). Moreover, as Miranda has noted, some American Indians refuse to recognize Chicana/o indigeneity because legitimating 'mestizos' could diminish their own status (in Hartley 2012: 61). Others see Chicanas/os as simply another ethnic group desiring indigeneity (Cotera and Saldaña-Portillo 2015). These denials of recognition make Chicana/o indigeneity precarious.

Complicating claims of indigeneity is the fact that Chicanas/os are categorized as white, although they have never been treated as such (Lopez 2003; Menchaca 2001). White status is the result of the Treaty of Guadalupe Hidalgo. Mexico insisted on classifying its people as white to shield them from US racism. The US conceded because of its unwillingness to tolerate racial ambiguity, which Mexicans epitomized, and because it sought to categorize all Indians in the newly acquired territory as 'savage', in order to justify continued dispossession and war, particularly against the Apache and Comanche (Saldaña-Portillo 2016: 179).[3] Chicanas/os' legal whiteness and the various attempts to erase their indigeneity illustrate the power of the state in shaping racial and political subjectivity.

It is because of such a tangled history that Chicanas/os desire to reclaim their past. Chicana/o indigeneity is rooted in a "longing for a pre-colonial past that can never be known. The allure of Indigenous myth is strong as it may seem to provide a new grammar with which to challenge European and Euro-American domination of Native America" (Contreras 2008: 165). But this reclaiming is not just about identity, it is also about grieving (Cotera and Saldaña-Portillo 2015; Saldaña-Portillo 2016; Contreras 2008). Much has been lost through colonizations and conquest, and Aztlán addresses that grief.

V. Aztlán: Colonization and Decolonization

Aztlán, as Chicanas/os' mythical homeland, embodies a binational spatiality (Saldaña-Portillo 2016). As a diasporic and transnational population, Chicanas/os must reconcile their relationship to two places. Their connection to Mexico (and indigeneity) is apparent in the Aztecs, while the need to fit somehow in the US is expressed through Aztlán.

As the ancient homeland of the Mexica, Aztlán is located in the US southwest. Chicana/o activists reappropriated the territory Mexico lost to the US and called it Aztlán. This was very strategic. First, activists were fashioning a homeland for themselves.

For Chicanos the concept of Aztlán signaled a unifying point of cohesion through which they could define the foundations of an identity. Aztlán brought together a culture that had been somewhat disjointed and dispersed, allowing it, for the first time, a framework within which to understand itself. (Anaya and Lomelí 1989: ii)

Aztlán not only performed internal work, but it also did important external work. Essentially, activists claimed land that had been "stolen" from Mexico through the war, as their ancient homeland. This not only foregrounded an imperialist war fueled by manifest destiny (Horsman 1981), but challenged their perceived status as foreigners and "illegal immigrants." Activists routinely reject imperialist boundaries with the refrain, "We didn't cross the border, the border crossed us."

While Aztlán is clearly a decolonial act, it is also true that other peoples were living on the territory when Chicanas/os claimed it—including the Navajo, Apache, Comanche, Pueblo, Tohono O'odham, Mojave, Paiute, the many native peoples of California, and binational tribes, such as the Yaqui. While many American Indians have engaged in political alliances with Chicanas/os, I see Aztlán as problematic. For over 45 years Chicana/o activists have imagined their homeland on the territories of dispossessed people. Certainly it is understandable why Chicanas/os would want to claim these lands, but at the very least such a decision must be handled with respect, honesty and in a spirit of solidarity. As far as I know, Chicanas/os never collaborated or consulted with American Indians on Aztlán. As such, Aztlán is simultaneously a decolonial and colonizing gesture.

American Indians are cognizant of this. While there have been moments of solidarity, and Chicanas/os have been granted membership in such organizations as the International Indian Treaty Council, some reject Chicanas/os as indigenous, as noted earlier (Cotera and Saldaña-Portillo 2015: 552). These tensions are readily apparent in New Mexico, which has the largest land-based Mexican population in the US. The land grant struggles of the 1960s were one of the rallying points of the Chicana/o movement and were emblematic of their colonized status. Hispanos have historically celebrated their long history in the region, but American Indian activists have begun challenging the dominant narrative of Spanish colonization. The Red Nation recently protested the historical re-enactment of La Entrada, which marks Spain's reconquest of Santa Fe in 1692. It was not well-received by Hispanos. One local responded, "This is our town. You had your chance and you lost" (Chacón 2016). Such sentiments cannot be dismissed. While it is understandable why Chicana/o studies is reluctant to acknowledge settler colonialism, both intellectual integrity and political commitment require recognizing Chicanas/os' multiple subjectivities.

VI. Conclusion

By analyzing Chicana/o studies' muted response to settler colonialism I hope to not only encourage the discipline to acknowledge the multiple subjectivities of Chicanas/os, but also show geographers the importance of studying relations between minoritized populations. It should be apparent that studying the political and racial subjectivity of any group is a deeply spatial exercise. Increasingly, scholars of indigeneity are drawing on geography, both theoretically (Saldaña-Portillo 2016; Goeman 2013) and through popular education projects, such as Mapping Indigenous LA (https://mila.ss.ucla.edu). The question of indigeneity raises issues of land, place, borders, migrations, human-environment relations, and empire—questions that are central to geography. But it also raises questions that geography is less steeped in. I tread carefully here. I refuse to issue the typical call, "geographers should be studying this." I do not think white geographers should rush to study the dynamics I have outlined. White people studying conflict between racially subordinated groups is ethically and politically loaded. This does not mean they should not do it, but it requires a particular set of experiences and commitments to do so in a way that does not negatively impact already marginalized groups. Rather, I simply wish to underscore how much geography is missing given our demographics and dominant approaches to studying race. Hopefully, one day when the discipline is more diverse, such a call could be made, but we are not there yet. Addressing settler colonialism is a long, painful, and difficult process, yet grasping its many manifestations is essential.

References

Acuña, R. (1972) *Occupied America*. New York: Harper Collins.
Alfred, T., and Corntassel, J. (2005) "Being Indigenous: Resurgences Against Contemporary Colonialism," *Government and Opposition* 40 (4): 597–614.
Almaguer, T. (1994) *Racial Faultlines*, Berkeley: University of California Press.
Anaya, R., and Lomelí, F. (1989) *Aztlan: Essays on the Chicano Homeland*, Albuquerque: Academia/El Norte Publications.
Anzaldúa, G. (1987) *Borderlands/La Frontera: The New Mestiza*, San Francisco: Aunt Lute Books.
Barrera, M. (1979) *Race and Class in the Southwest*, Notre Dame: University of Notre Dame Press.
Bauder, H. (2011) "Closing the Immigration-Aboriginal Parallax Gap," *Geoforum* 42 (5): 517–519.
Blackhawk, N. (2006) *Violence Over the Land: Indians and Empires in the Early American West*, Cambridge, MA: Harvard University Press.
Bonds, A., and Inwood, J. (2015) "Beyond White Privilege: Geographies of White Supremacy and Settler Colonialism," *Progress in Human Geography*. https://doi.org/0309132515613166.
Byrd, J. (2011) *Transit of Empire: Indigenous Critiques of Colonization*, Minneapolis: University of Minnesota Press.
Castañeda, A. (1993) "Sexual Violence in the Politics and Policies of Conquest," in A. De la Torre and B. Pesquera (eds.), *Building with Our Hands*, 15–33, Berkeley: University of California Press.
Castellanos, M. B., Najera, L. G., and Aldama, A. (eds.) (2012) *Comparative Indigeneities of the Americas*, Tucson: University of Arizona Press.
Chacón, D. (2016) "Protestors Turn Up Volume at Entrada," *Santa Fe New Mexican*, September 9, www.santafenewmexican.com/news/local_news/protesters-turn-up-volume-at-entrada/article_571ce07b-2a80-59eb-8590-23129975921b.html.
Chávez-Garcia, M. (2004) *Negotiating Conquest: Gender and Power in California, 1770s–1880s*, Tucson: University of Arizona Press.
Contreras, S. (2008) *Blood Lines*, Austin: University of Texas Press.
Cotera, M., and Saldaña-Portillo, J. (2015) "Indigenous but not Indian? Chicana/os and the politics of indigeneity," in R. Warrior (ed.), *The World of Indigenous North America*, 549–567, New York: Routledge.
Coulthard, G. (2014) *Red Skin, White Masks*, Minneapolis: University of Minnesota Press.

Day, I. (2016) *Alien Capital: Asian Racialization and the Logic of Settler Colonial Capitalism*, Durham, NC: Duke University Press.
Diaz, V. (2015) "No Island Is an Island" in S. N. Teves, A. Smith and M. Raheja (eds.), *Native Studies Keywords*, 90–108, Tucson: University of Arizona Press.
Dunbar-Ortiz, R. (2014) *An Indigenous Peoples' History of the United States*, New York: Basic Books.
Fox, J., and Rivera-Salgado, G. (2004) *Indigenous Mexican Migrants in the United States*, La Jolla: Center for U.S.-Mexican Studies, University of California, San Diego.
Fujikane, C., and Okamura, J. (2008) *Asian Settler Colonialism*, Honolulu: University of Hawai'i Press.
Goeman, M. (2013) *Mark My Words*, Minneapolis: University of Minnesota Press.
González, M. (2005) *This Small City Will Be a Mexican Paradise: Exploring the Origins of Mexican Culture in Los Angeles, 1821–1846*, Albuquerque: University of New Mexico Press.
Guidotti-Hernandez, N. (2011) *Unspeakable Violence: Remapping U.S. and Mexican National Imaginaries*, Durham, NC: Duke University Press.
Hartley, G. (2012) "Chican@ indigeneity, the nation-state, and colonialist identity formations" in M. B. Castellanos, L. G. Najera and A. Aldama (eds.), *Comparative Indigeneities of the Americas*, 53–66, Tucson: University of Arizona Press.
Horsman, R. (1981) *Race and Manifest Destiny*, Cambridge, MA: Harvard University Press.
Huntington, S. (2004) *Who Are We? The Challenges to America's National Identity*, New York: Simon & Schuster.
Kauanui, K. J. (2016) Paper presented at "Racializing the National Home," American Studies Association annual meeting, Denver, CO, November.
Klopotek, B. (2016) *Indian on Both Sides: Indigenous Identities, Race, and National Borders*, Unpublished manuscript, Ethnic Studies, University of Oregon.
Kobayashi, A., and De Leeuw, S. (2010) "Colonialism and the Tensioned Landscapes of Indigeneity," in S. Smith, R. Pain, S. Marston and J. Jones (eds.), *SAGE Handbook of Social Geographies*, 118–138, London: SAGE.
Lawrence, B., and Dua, E. (2005) "Decolonizing Antiracism," *Social Justice* 32 (4): 120–143.
Lloyd, D., and Pulido, L. (2010) "In the Long Shadow of the Settler: On Israeli and US Colonialisms," *American Quarterly* 62 (4): 795–809.
Lopez, I. H. (2003) *Racism on Trial: The Chicano Fight for Justice*, Cambridge, MA: Harvard University Press.
Luna-Peña, G. (2015) "Little More than Desert Wasteland: Race, Development and Settler Colonialism in the Mexicali Valley," *Critical Ethnic Studies* 1 (2): 81–101.
Menchaca, M. (2001) *Recovering History, Constructing Race: The Indian, Black, and White Roots of Mexican Americans*, Austin: University of Texas Press.
Miles, T. (2005) *Ties That Bind: The Story of an Afro-Cherokee Family in Slavery and Freedom*, Berkeley: University of California Press.
Moreton-Robinson, A., Casey, M., and Nicoll, F. (2008) *Transnational Whiteness Matters*, Lanham, MD: Lexington Books.
Morgensen, S. L. (2011) *Spaces Between US: Queer Settler Colonialism and Indigenous Decolonization*, Minneapolis: University of Minnesota Press.
Pérez, E. (1999) *The Decolonial Imaginary: Writing Chicanas into History*, Indianapolis: Indiana University Press.
Radcliffe, S. (2015) "Geography and Indigeneity I: Indigeneity, Coloniality and Knowledge," *Progress in Human Geography*. https://doi.org/0309132515612952.
Reséndez, A. (2016) *The Other Slavery*, New York: Houghton Mifflin Harcourt.
Rivera, J. M. (2006) *The Emergence of Mexican America*, New York: New York University Press.
Saldaña-Portillo, J. (2001) "Who's the Indian in Aztlan? Rewriting Mestizaje, Indianism, and Chicanismo from the Lacandon," in I. Rodriguez (ed.), *The Latin American Subaltern Studies Reader*, 402–423, Durham, NC: Duke University Press.
Saldaña-Portillo, J. (2016) *Indian Given: Racial Geographies across Mexico and the United States*, Durham, NC: Duke University Press.
Sánchez, R., and Pita, B. (2014) "Rethinking Settler Colonialism," *American Quarterly* 66 (4): 1039–1055.
Saranillo, D. (2013) "Why Asian Settler Colonialism Matters," *Settler Colonial Studies* 3 (3–4): 280–294.

Simpson, A. (2014) *Mohawk Interruptus: Political Life Across the Borders of Settler States*, Durham, NC: Duke University Press.
Smith, A. (2012) "Indigeneity, Settler Colonialism, White Supremacy" in D. HoSang, O. LaBennett and L. Pulido (eds.), *Racial Formation in the Twenty-First Century*, 66–90, Berkeley: University of California.
Smith, S. (2013) *Freedom's Frontier*, Chapel Hill: University of North Carolina Press.
Teves, S. N., Smith, A., and Rajeha, M. (2015) *Native Studies Keywords*, Tucson: University of Arizona Press.
Trask, H. K. (2000) "Settlers of Color and 'Immigrant' Hegemony: 'Locals' in Hawaii," *Amerasia Journal* 26 (2): 1–24.
Tuck, E., and Yang, W. (2012) "Decolonization Is Not a Metaphor," *Decolonization: Indigeneity, Education & Society* 1 (1): 1–40.
Urrieta, L. (2012) "Las identidades también lloran," in M. B. Castellanos, L. G. Najera and A. Aldama (eds.), *Comparative Indigeneities of the Americas*, 321–335, Tucson: University of Arizona Press.
Wilderson, F. (2010) *Red, White & Black: Cinema and the Structure of U.S. Antagonisms*, Durham, NC: Duke University Press.
Wolfe, P. (2006) "Settler Colonialism and the Elimination of the Native," *Journal of Genocide Research* 8 (4): 387–409.
Wolfe, P. (2016) *Traces of History: Elementary Structures of Race*, New York: Verso.
Wright, C., and Sharma, N. (2008/2009) "Decolonizing Resistance, Challenging Colonial States," *Social Justice* 35 (3): 120–138.

Notes

1 I use the term American Indian because, while problematic, it is legible.
2 The Gemelli map of 1704 traces this migration and Aztlán appears on the Disturnell Map of 1847.
3 The Pueblo were the exception because they were sedentary.

Reading Questions

1. What is settler colonialism, according to Pulido?
2. How does Pulido argue for the claim that settler colonialism disrupts core aspects of Chicanx identity? What aspects of Chicanx identity are disrupted, and why are these aspects said to be "core"?
3. Do the problems described by Pulido generalize to other identities, or to a general Latinx identity? Why or why not?
4. What does Pulido mean by political subjectivity?
5. Pulido maintains that "Aztlán is simultaneously a decolonial and colonizing gesture" (p. 138). What does she mean?
6. Can there be a non-colonizing version of Aztlán or Chicanx identity? Is it possible for a specifically Latinx identity to escape the colonizing dynamics described by Pulido, or is that unavoidable, too?
7. Pulido argues that Latinxs of both European and "mestizo" descent have played a role in perpetuating settler colonization on Indigenous communities. However, Forbes characterizes *mestizo* as itself a colonial category, one that functions to eradicate Indigenous identities. If Forbes and Pulido are both right, does this mean that Indigenous peoples played a role in perpetuating settler colonization?

10 Mestizaje, Métissage, and Mixedblood

Tracing Some Political Terms of Racial and Cultural Mixture Across the Americas

Andrea J. Pitts

The mixture of racial and cultural groups—referred to as *mestizaje* in Spanish-speaking contexts of Latin America—has been a contentious issue in the Americas since the earliest colonial projects of Europe. For example, while Spanish colonial administrators sought to prevent intermarriage and familial bonds among Indigenous and Spanish peoples in the 16th century, by the 20th century, Latin American intellectuals like Mexican philosopher José Vasconcelos would embrace the value of race mixture. In fact, Vasconcelos, along with other philosophers and social theorists of the 20th century, would consider racial mixture as an important historical feature of Latin America, which, according to these thinkers, heralded a unique moral and aesthetic future for the region (Vasconcelos 1997). Notably, there have also been long-held critiques of such ideals of racial mixture, including from Indigenous and Afro-descendent communities who express concerns that mestizaje is an attempt to "Europeanize," colonize, or otherwise *blanquear* ("whiten") the peoples of the Americas. Moreover, in English-speaking and French-speaking contexts of North America, the status of "mixed-blood" and *métis* peoples are likewise disputed categories, including concerns among Indigenous communities regarding their political futures and continued relations to their traditional homelands.

To explore this complex history of mixture in the Americas and its philosophical implications, this chapter first draws from historical sources to examine colonial-era conceptions of mixture, including religious and racial mixture. Then, the second section turns to 19th- and 20th-century literary discourses of *mestizaje, metissage,* and "mixedblood" relations, focusing primarily on origin myths and other colonial narratives that frame mixture in the Americas. The final section of the chapter seeks to show that while derogatory and/or otherwise harmful framings of mixture have been used as tools of conquest across the Americas, one key consideration for readers will be how Indigenous, Black, Latinx and Latin American authors have also reinterpreted and repurposed such categories to negotiate the political status and ongoing life of Indigenous and Afro-diasporic communities. This means that rather than deriving an ethical or political assessment of categories like *mestizaje, metissage,* and "mixedblood" from an abstracted "outside" of the communities that are most impacted by them, we should consider the stakes of racial and cultural mixture from within the contextual sites of those who utilize or contest such categories. What such an analysis demonstrates is that the questions raised by mestizaje and other forms of mixture—including questions of political autonomy, the possibility of political alliances between members of differing social groups, and the ongoing threats of subjugation impacting Indigenous and Black communities—continue to shape philosophical discussions of politics today in ways that often defy simplistic categorical binaries of race, nationhood, and culture.

Lastly, regarding method, this chapter does not seek to resolve the many political debates about conceptions of mixture across the Americas. Instead, I offer some genealogical pathways through historical and literary sources to examine the existence of questions of racial and cultural mixture as itself a product of settler colonialism. I also highlight reflections from Indigenous- and non-Indigenous-identified authors (including self-identified "mixed" authors who identify differently across both categories), regarding the stakes of racial, cultural, and political group membership in the context of ongoing forms of settler colonization and Indigenous self-governance in the Americas.

I. Pre-Conquest and Colonial Discourses of Mixture

To begin to illustrate the complexity of race categories of the Americas, it is important to analyze the precursors to modern conceptions of race. A contextual framing of the pre-colonial conceptual landscape helps foreground how discourses of mixture eventually take shape and influence across the Americas. Notably, European forms of rationalization and social group formation that pre-date the efforts of Iberian conquistadors give historical scope and breadth to the race categories that would become enforced and upheld across the Americas. For example, prior to European efforts to conquer the Americas, Spanish Catholic authorities sought to regulate the *limpieza de sangre* ("purity of blood") of Jews and Muslims on the Iberian Peninsula. The concept of "blood purity" in medieval Iberia was first developed, according to colonial historian María Elena Martínez, to describe "the absence of Jewish and heretical antecedents . . . and thus a 'pure [Christian] lineage,' was the critical sign of a person's loyalty to the faith" (Martínez 2008: 1). One such precursor to the development of racial hierarchies in the Americas occurred in the decades before Europeans made first contact with Indigenous peoples of the Americas. Martínez notes that "as of the middle of the fifteenth century, [Spanish Catholics] increasingly wielded the notion to deprive the conversos of access to certain institutions and public and ecclesiastical offices" (Martínez 2008: 1). One example of such pre- conquest forms of social exclusion and hierarchization occurred through the 1449 *Sentencia-Estatuto*. According to Gregory Kaplan, a scholar of medieval Spanish literature and culture, the *Sentencia-Estatuto* was one of the first official Spanish legislative orders to draw sharp distinctions that barred "new" converts to Christianity from access to social organizations, religious and military orders, and guilds (Aronson-Friedman and Kaplan 2012: 30). Moreover, by the 1480s, the law created segregated zones where *conversos* (Jewish converts to Christianity) could not live (Aronson-Friedman and Kaplan 2012: 30). While anti-*converso* and anti-Semitic discriminatory practices predate these official legal decrees in Iberian history, the adoption of widespread tribunals and the eventual establishment of the Spanish Inquisition in 1478 created new legal mechanisms through which Spanish officials could demand proof that *conversos* were not "heretics." Such tribunals required that *conversos* provide documentation regarding the number of generations by which their family's lineage had converted to Christianity, as well as testimony and proof of their participation in public Catholic festivals and social life (Aronson-Friedman and Kaplan 2012: 21–22). These forms of surveillance, control, and prohibition impacting *conversos* and other non-Christians (i.e., others considered by the Catholic Church to be "infidels," "pagans," and "heretics") provide an example of an ordering logic for relations of supremacy and inferiority that would later impact non-Christians in the New World. Such distinctions between Christians and non-Christians, and accompanying beliefs regarding rationality, order, and proximity to the divine, thereby served as justifications for land acquisition, governance, and forced labor in the colonies of the Americas. Such justifications thus supported and converged with processes of racialization impacting Indigenous, African, and Asian peoples for centuries thereafter.[1] In fact, the year 1492, commonly known as the year that Christopher Columbus makes haphazard landfall on an island in the Caribbean, also marks the very year that King Ferdinand II and Queen Isabella sign the Alhambra Decree that forces Jews and Muslims to convert to Catholicism or face exile from the Iberian Peninsula.

Additionally, before this trans-Atlantic colonial conquest and exploration, Spanish and Portuguese participation in the enslavement and genocide of peoples across the Canary Islands and coastal regions of West Africa throughout the 14th and 15th centuries demonstrate that Iberian conquistadors were deploying forms of geographic, religious, and sometimes physical distinctions between Christians and non-Christians to justify their exploits (Berquist Soule 2018). In these ways, regulations and scrutiny regarding the impurity or mixture of one group with another based on ancestry and visible features (in this case of the Iberian context, "Old" and "New" Christians, as they were called in Medieval Spain) pre-date and eventually co-exist alongside the racialized distinctions of the colonial projects in the Americas.

Within the colonial Americas, although building from Iberian logics of purity, social tensions and concerns regarding mixture took on a shape of their own. One early and clear example of how conceptions of religious, cultural, and racial mixture occurred throughout the early colonial period were efforts to distinguish forms of political order, on the one hand, for Spanish bureaucrats, missionaries, and conquistadors in the Americas, and on the other, Indigenous elites, administrators, and commoners. In this sense, part of the Spanish colonial project in what is today Mexico included distinguishing the Spanish hierarchy and political order from those among the Indigenous peoples they encountered. For example, Camilla Townsend, an historian of conquest-era Mexico, notes that the Mexica (otherwise referred to as the "Aztecs") practiced and lived under a complex and highly stratified political society prior to their first encounters with the Spanish, including systems of tribute impacting various townships across the region and with complicated political factions, debate, and conflict (Townsend 2019). As such, the Spanish initially granted relative autonomy to the Mexica political order in the early period of conquest. These "repúblicas de los indios" ["republics of the Indians"] were a variety of townships and city-states ruled by Indigenous officials and were understood as distinct from "la república de los españoles" ["the republic of the Spanish"], the political units of the Spanish Crown. Such distinctions embedded clear hierarchies and demands, with Spanish authorities requiring conversion among Indigenous communities and the payment of tribute to the Spanish Crown. Martínez writes:

> Construed as contractual and voluntary, this relationship required that native towns pay tribute and remain loyal to the Catholic faith and the Spanish crown in return for the right to maintain internal hierarchies, retain their lands, and enjoy relative political autonomy.
>
> (2008: 92)

In this way, the threat of militaristic violence from the Spanish was wielded to enforce forms of so-called "protection" for local Indigenous practices and politics.

However, Martínez also notes that efforts to maintain distinct political orders in the colonial world thoroughly failed, although such segregative efforts created lasting consequences for religious, racial, and cultural distinctions throughout the Americas.

One notable consequence was the proliferation of legal and social categories to interpret the generations of people who were of mixed parentage and ancestry. Namely, if political jurisdiction was demarcated based on Indigenous or Spanish belonging, how would people who were of *both* Indigenous and Spanish parentage, or African and Spanish parentage, or African and Indigenous parentage be subject to a given political order? Martínez notes on this point that

> the emergence of [mixed] population[s] made it increasingly difficult to establish institutional jurisdictions, tributary obligations, and the citizenship rights and privileges that were accorded to the members of each republic, a problem that led to the growing use of mechanisms to determine 'Indian purity.'
>
> (2008: 104)

Akin to the Spanish tribunals governing *conversos* in Iberia, the Spanish Holy Office would often be called upon to adjudicate whether someone was "un indio puro"/"a pure Indian," i.e., someone who descended only from pre-Hispanic Indigenous parentage. The status of "indio puro" came with the requirement to pay tribute to the Spanish Crown, but also with the possibility of being recognized as Indigenous nobility within *una república de los indios*. In this, the Spanish also controlled and reshaped many pre-Hispanic forms of inheritance, succession, gender roles, and political order. For example, Martínez states that the Spanish influenced social changes such as

> the simplification of native genealogies, the replacement of varied forms of transmitting inheritance and property with more of a patrilineal model, and a stress on the nuclear family and married couple as social and moral units at the expense of the multihousehold complex typical of the pre-Hispanic period.
>
> (2008: 112–113)

By the mid-17th century, colonial authorities began to distinguish the baptismal, marriage, and death records of the Spanish and "Indian" from those of the "castas" or mixed-status peoples, and Martinez states that "by the end of the [17th] century, main colonial categories of difference, including *mestizo* and *mulato* [people of mixed Afro-diasporic ancestry], started to appear in administrative records on a regular basis" (2008: 142). Accordingly, the categories of mixture that are more familiar to us today ("mestizo," "mulatto," "mixed") stem from a context in which colonial governments were attempting to control and manage Indigenous and Afro-diasporic populations. Such efforts to govern non-European populations of the Americas, as we will see in the sections below, continue to shape racial and Indigenous relations today.

II. Origin Myths of Mixture in the Americas

In the first section, we examined several historical precursors to discourses of mixture in the Americas, focusing on Spanish colonial contexts. In this section, we turn specifically to origin myths regarding mixture that begin to delve into some aspects of the desires, worries, and fears that shaped conceptions of mixture in the Americas.

Spanish colonial projects proliferated categories of mixture through legal and cultural projects to account for the wide variety of peoples who were forming kinship relations, including the pregnancy and birthing of children that occurred by force through sexual assault. In fact, the ubiquity and familiarity with such forms of sexual violence even shaped a longstanding cultural myth in Mexico, as noted by Chicana feminist scholar Alicia Gaspar de Alba, that all Mexicans are "hijos de la chingada"/"sons of the fucked one," which was described in detail centuries later by Octavio Paz (1981) (Gaspar de Alba 2014: 8).[2] In his famous essay, "Hijos de la Malinche," Paz writes of the figure of "La Malinche," which, according to accounts by Spanish conquistadors, was the Spanish name given to Malintzin, an Indigenous enslaved adolescent girl who was sold during military expeditions between warring Indigenous groups in what is Mexico today. According to such conquest-era accounts, Malintzin was born of noble status, although to ensure the inheritance of the family's land and title, the family wished to pass their wealth to her half-brother. As such, she was initially sold into slavery to avoid "disputes over inheritance" (Lyall et al. 2022: 2). Eventually, the group of Indigenous traders with whom she was being held fought and were defeated by the Spanish conquistador Hernán Cortés and his army in 1519. In response to this defeat, Malintzin was offered to Cortés as tribute and she was renamed and baptized by the Spanish as "Marina." Malintzin/Marina knew several languages, including Nahuatl, her mother tongue, as well as Mayan from living among the Mayan peoples to whom she had been sold (Ibid.). She also eventually learned Spanish and became an interpreter for Cortés, and, in this role, she is considered to have aided in the fall of the Aztec empire, including the death of Moctezuma II and the conquest of the imperial heart of the Aztec empire, the metropolis of Tenochtitlan. Her legend also considers her to have been the mother of "the first" mestizo child, and while this is likely false, historical records indicate that she did bear two children, one son whose father was Cortés and who was eventually sent to the royal court in Spain, and another, a daughter, whom she bore with her husband, another Spaniard.

While the historical records of Malintzin complicate her role as a mere accomplice to Spanish conquest, often noting her role in attempts to protect the lives of common people, including children and the elderly during conquest, her legend was revived in the 19th century, during Mexico's independence from Spain (Lyall et al. 2022: 3). In these figurations of Malintzin, 19th century artists either "celebrated Cortés and Malinche as the Mexican Adam and Eve, [or] vilified the union, casting the resultant mestizaje (the mixing of races) as the ultimate betrayal" (Lyall et al. 2022: 3). Such radically divergent narratives continue well into the 20th century, including through the work of Paz and others, and by the late 20th century, Mexican American women begin reclaiming her story, seeking to describe how cultural, sexual, gendered, and racial forms of social conflict and negotiations with colonial and oppressive power regimes are core features of Mexican American and other women of color's existence (Gaspar de Alba 2014).

While we will explore some further implications of these accounts below, it is important to mention here how mestizaje becomes directly implicated in national and political narratives of futurity and teleology. Most notably, the historical facts of Indigenous enslavement, the warfare and systems of tribute and Catholic conversion that characterize Spanish conquest, and the prominence of sexual violence and forced relations impacting Indigenous and African peoples during this period have transformed into various national and hemispheric myths regarding the metaphysical, moral, and existential features of peoples in the Americas and the meaning and significance of colonial violence. Notably, mixed status has been used as a form of denigration and as a justification for violence across the Americas. In contrast, in some contexts, mulataje and other forms of mixture have been revered as forms of kinship and intimacy between African, Indigenous, and European peoples. For example, the myth of "racial democracy," drawn from the writings of the world-renowned Brazilian anthropologist of the 20th century, Gilberto Freyre, assumes a form of social harmony prefaced on presumed intimacy and kinship relations formed through the living arrangements and social conditions between enslaved Black peoples and European slaveholding families in the plantation economy of Brazil (Bernardino-Costa 2023: 102).

Likewise, Mexican philosopher José Vasconcelos proposed a view of mixture that heralded a new aesthetic and ethical age forged through mixture, noting that beauty and intelligence would be the result of miscegenation across the Americas. However, as critics of such utopian framings of mixture often point out, for proponents of mixture like Freyre and Vasconcelos, these presumptions of social and political harmony often belie the entrenched forms of anti-Black and anti-Indigenous hierarchies that continue to shape the Americas. For example, as one commentator on the writings of Brazilian Black feminist Lélia González's critique of Freyre notes: the idea of the racial democracy is refuted not only by the violence and brutality of slavery in Brazil, but also by the inequalities and socioeconomic conditions of Black women in contemporary Brazilian society (Rios 2021).

Beyond Spanish and Portuguese colonial contexts, British and French colonialism is also characterized by foundational myths about racial mixture. For example, one such myth is the "Pocahontas perplex," which serves as a "controlling metaphor in the [U.S.] American experience" (Green 1975: 703). Indigenous feminists Maile Arvin (Kanaka Maoli), Eve Tuck (Unangax̂), and Angie Morrill (Klamath) describe the Pocahontas perplex in the following way:

> This perplex references the tendency of American Indian women to be constantly caught between images of a seductive though saintly Indian princess who helps white men (a representation with a history far preceding the actual life of Pocahontas) and the "Princess' darker twin, the Squaw"—a fat, beleaguered, and crude woman who is shamed for having sexual relationships with white men.
>
> (2013: 26)

In this sense, the myths of Pocahontas and Malinche each depict Indigenous women as caught between colonial Christian gender roles as a saint-like or Eve-like figure, or as morally and sexually corrupt betrayers of Indigenous peoples.

Against these double binds, Arvin, Tuck, and Morrill urge scholars and educators to challenge these myths by shifting from a focus simply on a pre-modern past, and instead to "take seriously the notion that settler colonialism is a structure, and not an event, that continues to shape the everyday lives of Indigenous and non-Indigenous peoples" (2013: 27).[3] Accordingly, the ongoing political lives and futures of Indigenous peoples should be foregrounded on this account, rather than merely fixating on foundational settler myths regarding miscegenation. One concern they note is that mythical figurations like Pocahontas, Malinche, and associated narratives regarding the fantastical emergence of "mixedblood" peoples can often erase or obfuscate the contemporary political projects of present-day Indigenous communities, including demands for land reclamation, self-governance, and intergenerational cultural continuity.

On this point, María Josefina Saldaña-Portillo (2016) explores differing, overlapping racial geographies of the U.S. Southwest, including both Spanish and English colonial histories and racial figurations of belonging and place that continue to influence the ongoing colonial projects of the U.S. and Mexico. For example, the title of her book, *Indian Given: Racial Geographies Across Mexico and the United States*, notes colonial tropes that shape both U.S. and Mexican narratives of settlers' presumed right to the traditional lands of Indigenous peoples (2016). She writes:

> An "Indian giver" is someone who takes back something they have willingly given or sold, and the slur derives its meaning from another popular myth of U.S. history, that the Indians gifted colonists their land, fair and square, and now they unjustly demand its return. By contrast, Mexican historiography openly recognizes the violence and injustice of indigenous dispossession at the hands of Spanish conquistadors. Indeed, public culture memorializes the injustice in Mexico City, whether in the Diego Rivera murals that adorn the walls of the National Palace or on the plaque outside Tlatelolco in the Plaza de las Tres Culturas commemorating the armed encounter of the Nahuas and Spanish as neither a victory nor a defeat ("No fue triunfo ni derrota"), but as the "doloroso nacimiento del pueblo mestizo" (the painful birth of the mestizo people). The violence and suffering of indigenous peoples in the conquest is constantly, iteratively affirmed and projected onto the landscape. . . . The slur from which this book takes its title reveals a deep historical anxiety on both sides of the border: the indigenous peoples rightfully demand their land back!
>
> (2016: 12)

Importantly, in Saldaña-Portillo's account, if the myth of "painful birth of the mestizo people" is conceived as a violent yet inevitable process that gave rise to the "mixture" that is Mexico today, then this means that the colonial violence of the conquistador is distributed across the Mexican population and likewise, the suffering of such violence is distributed as well. She notes on this point, referring to both perpetrator and victim statuses under conditions of colonial violence, that

> If all Mexicans are equally injured by/responsible for/born of colonialism, then all were equally defrauded and defrauder, and in a manner that is similar though not identical to Indian given [in the U.S.], hijo de la chingada deflects national culpability.
>
> (2016: 14)

In this way, mestizaje, as it has functioned historically and in concert with the rise of Mexican nationalism, dissipates or renders illegible the ongoing present-day claims of Indigenous communities for land and an end to the violations they endure.[4] As such, Saldaña-Portillo's central claim throughout the book is that in each racial framing of Euro-American settler claims to belonging (in Mexico and the U.S.), there are attempts to displace, ignore, or render meaningless the demands of Indigenous communities for self-governance and restored relations with the land.

In addition to discourses of mestizaje across the Americas, other categories of mixture such as "mixedblood" in British settler colonial contexts and *métis* in French settler colonial contexts have circulated and are often reshaped by the authors and communities to which they are intended to refer. For example, Native American Studies scholar Jace Weaver describes the "half-breed" as a dominant stereotype within English settler literary representations of Indigenous peoples that depicts a tragic figure who is of mixed Indigenous and non-Indigenous ancestry and is "the degenerate project of miscegenation . . . has no redeeming qualities whatsoever and is distrusted by both whites and Natives" (Weaver 1997: 184). Notably, as literary scholar Kristina Fagan Bidwell notes, the term "metis" or "Métis" in the Canadian colonial context has been used in a similar manner. The term has several differing functions among Indigenous and non-Indigenous communities, including "as a racial category, as a product of identity legislation, as the identity of a single and distinct community, or as an identity claimed by many communities" (Bidwell 2014: 118). In the northern hemispheric contexts of the Americas, métis can likewise refer to "people of mixed Indigenous and European descent," as mestizo functions in Hispanophone contexts of the Americas. However, in Canadian settler contexts,

> The Métis National Council (MNC), the dominant organization representing Metis people today, explains on their website that the Metis began in the seventeenth century as the children of Indian women and European fur traders. Although the MNC definition goes on to explain that those 'mixed offspring' eventually became a people with a distinct history and culture for most Canadians, it is racial mixedness that is the defining characteristic of the Metis.
>
> (Bidwell 2014: 119)

Importantly, however, "[t]his understanding of Metis identity fits into a view of Indigenous people as defined by race, a view that arguably has little to do with traditional Indigenous values" (Bidwell 2014: 119). Thus, this distinction points to differences between *race-based* views of Indigeneity and *community knowledge-based* views of Indigeneity.

Regarding this distinction, there are a variety of ways in which métis people have been characterized by others and characterize themselves. For example, Red River Métis author Gregory Scofield, in his memoir *Thunder Through My Veins* (1999), describes a scene from his childhood that exemplifies what Bidwell calls "dilution theory." An encounter between a loved one and himself in the memoir includes a description of his facial features that supposedly depict him as being a "half-breed," which frames Métis people through "a racializing logic that says that the Metis, being neither fully white nor fully 'Indian' are therefore less than either" (quoted in Bidwell 2014: 120). Akin to concerns with racial purity in the Spanish Americas, mixed peoples in the Canadian and U.S. contexts are also considered to "dilute" a racial bloodline. Moreover, Indigenous literary theorist Craig Womack (Muscogee Creek-Cherokee) writes that he wonders "if identifying as a mixedblood, rather than as part of a tribal nation diminishes [tribal] sovereignty" (1997: 32). In this case, Womack is concerned with how people identify themselves and the political implications of such self-ascriptions.

Additionally, Indigenous communities and scholars have challenged the claim that Indigeneity is a race category at all, opting instead for politically oriented community-based views. For example, Audra Simpson (Mohawks of Kahnawà:ke) states that Indigenous peoples are not a "racial group" or even a simple "cultural group," as some popular anthropological views might assume.[5] Rather, Indigeneity can and should be framed, in Simpson's view, as a political category involving claims to self-governance, binding treaties, relations to land, and systems of governance that pre-date the existence of the U.S. and Canada. In this manner, Simpson also critiques forms of racial or cultural purity among Indigenous peoples. For example, in the early 18th century, she notes:

> The Mohawks of Kahnawà:ke, as an Iroquoian people, had among their numbers assimilated outsiders—whites and other Indians who had been taken captive prior to the move to the North and who continued to impact Kahnawà:ke's politics. . . . Ascribed differences, such as race, did not figure into the Mohawk's potential equation for a captive; what mattered were situational factors: their nation in relation to current Iroquois

foreign policy of the time, their fortitude, their usefulness, and their commitment to Mohawk ideals.

(Simpson 2019: 47–48)

Moreover, she claims that this "heterogeneous" composition of the Mohawks of Kahnawà:ke is also the cause for contested claims regarding membership within the Indigenous political community today:

"Premodern" (and later modern) Mohawks were open to those who at this time might be considered outsiders, to people of different nations and races. The clan structure that was in place made it possible for all those people to become Mohawk. Thus identity was not . . . problematic, an ethical issue, a matter to be confused by. *It was not confused with political membership; it was political membership.* And this was so because the governmental authority within the community could choose to recognize (or not) those who had rights to residency and life in the community, who had clans and thus families and responsibilities to something much larger than themselves. However, that historic structure of admission and the resultant "racial mixing" of early [members of Kahnawà:ke] is today perceived to be a problem that Mohawks have inherited from the past and must guard against for the future.

(Simpson 2019: 48)

On this reading, for Simpson and other critical indigenous studies scholars, Indigeneity is not an identity category like race or culture that can be taken in a more general register. Rather, Indigenous identity is a political category that functions to demarcate jurisdictional governance and belonging. As such, unlike the origin myths of Pocahontas and La Malinche, or the differing republics of colonial New Spain, mixed racial parentage or lineages do not delineate or determine political allegiance, belonging, or futurity.

Moreover, Simpson's work and the political practice of theorizing Indigenous sovereignty, land reclamation, and Indigenous knowledges can be understood through the critical view mentioned above that colonization is an ongoing process that continues to shape settler and non-settler relations to land, governance, and social group formation. On this point, Brendan Hokowhitu (Ngāti Pūkenga), an editor of the *Routledge Handbook on Critical Indigenous Studies* notes:

as editors, we are completely disinterested in re-gazing at Indigenous peoples via the typical anthropological methods, which continue to plague Indigenous Studies. We are far more interested in scholarship that speaks to Indigenous sovereignty and the regeneration of Indigenous knowledges.

(Hokowhitu 2020: 3)

Accordingly, he and his fellow editors define "critical Indigenous studies" in the following manner:

In this handbook, Critical Indigenous Studies, first, emanates out of a genealogy of Indigenous, Black, and Brown scholarship that has sought to criticise the unsettler/white claims to possession over knowledge itself. Second, Critical Indigenous Studies refers to scholarship grounded in resistance to the multiple forms of violence and microaggressions that Indigenous peoples and communities face every day in their neo-colonial realities. Third, Critical Indigenous Studies refers to scholarship that upholds sovereign claims to Indigenous lands, languages, cultures, ecologies, ontologies, and existentiality.

(2021: 3)

As Hokowhitu points out here and as we will discuss in the final section, what exactly determines those political terms within ongoing contexts of settler colonialism remains highly contested. Accordingly, as I have hoped to show thus far, the terms of mixture across the Americas have always been a political process. Whether we are referring to attempts to demarcate belonging within *la república de los indios* or membership within the Mohawks of Kahnawà:ke, settler colonial efforts to control, contain, and erase Indigenous relations to land, governance, and the growth of their communities have been at play for centuries. Discourses of mestizaje, mixedblood status, and metissage, both then and now, bear relevance due to such contestations and critiques made by Indigenous and Afro-diasporic peoples for affirmation of their political rights to place and futurity across the Americas.

III. Critical Latinx Indigeneities and Discourses of Race Mixture Today

While the previous two sections trace colonial-era and 19th- and 20th-century discourses of mixture across Spanish, French, and English settler contexts, this final section builds from the concluding point in the section above regarding a political conception of mixture. For example, among authors who self-identify as of both Indigenous and non-Indigenous kinship relations, formulations of mixed status vary immensely and show the very complicated political negotiations that "mixed" people and communities continue to endure. In his preface to *Earthdivers: Tribal Narratives on Mixed Descent* (1977) Gerald Vizenor, an enrolled member of the White Earth Nation who describes himself as being of Anishinaabe and Swedish American parentage, writes that "The words Metis and mixedblood possess no social or scientific validation because blood mixture is not a measurement of consciousness, culture, or human experiences; but the word *Metis* is a source of notable and radical identification" (ix). Building from Anishinaabe and other Indigenous figurations of animals who plunge into deep waters to retrieve the material sources for building a new world, a figure found in a number of Indigenous creation stories, Vizenor states the following: "The Metis, or mixedblood, earthdivers in these stories dive into unknown urban places now, into the racial darkness in the cities, to create a new consciousness of coexistence" (ix). From this, as with other self-identified "mixedblood" authors and communities, the status of mixture does not eliminate Indigenous life or presence, as settler myths of the "vanishing Indian" might assume. Rather, mixture, as Vizenor and other writers conceive it, can be a place from which to reimagine and reassert political commitments to Indigenous knowledge, sovereignty, and futurity.

Writing within the overlapping contexts of Spanish and English settler colonialisms impacting the U.S. Southwest, Mexican American author, Gloria Anzaldúa, writes in her 1981 autobiographical piece titled "La Prieta" ["the dark girl"] that her mother was ashamed of their family's Indigenous ancestry. She writes:

"Don't go out in the sun," my mother would tell me when I wanted to play outside. "If you get any darker, they'll mistake you for an Indian. And don't get dirt on your clothes. You don't want people to say you're a dirty Mexican." It never dawned on her that, though sixth-generation American, we were still Mexican and that all Mexicans are part Indian.

(Anzaldúa 2009: 38)

Anzaldúa, raised in the Río Grande Valley of southern Texas, describes that being "part Indian" is viewed with disdain by those in her community, and she appears likewise to draw on the national myths that Saldaña-Portillo mentions that "all Mexicans are part Indian." Elsewhere in her writings, Anzaldúa describes what she calls "mestiza consciousness," which refers, in her work, to a politicized consciousness that defies dualistic thinking. She writes of this "new mestiza" figuration:

> The new mestiza copes by developing a tolerance for contradictions, a tolerance for ambiguity. She learns to be an Indian in Mexican culture, to be Mexican from an Anglo point of view. She learns to juggle cultures. She has a plural personality, she operates in a pluralistic mode—nothing is thrust out, the good the bad and the ugly, nothing rejected, nothing abandoned. Not only does she sustain contradictions, she turns the ambivalence into something else.
>
> (p. 121 of this volume)

By gesturing at the foundational myths of Mexican nationalism and José Vasconcelos, Anzaldúa seeks to describe mestizaje not as a future-oriented mode of moral and aesthetic unity that places Indigenous peoples in a mythic past. Rather, this "new mestizaje" is a way of asserting the non-dominant relations that one is in (e.g., facing anti-Mexican xenophobia in the U.S. and myths of primitivism impacting Indigenous peoples of Mexico) and recognizing the violence of settler colonization and processes of "mixture" in the Americas. To be "Indian in Mexican culture" or "Mexican from an Anglo point of view," she opts to reject patterns of white- and mestizo-dominance within both the U.S. and Mexico. Moreover, the future proposed is not composed of a form of racial harmony, but one that retains "the good, the bad and the ugly" of the political contestations over governance and social group formation:

> The work of mestiza consciousness is to break down the subject-object duality that keeps her a prisoner and to show in the flesh and through the images in her work how duality is transcended. The answer to the problem between the white race and the colored, between males and females, lies in healing the split that originates in the very foundation of our lives, our culture, our languages, our thoughts. A massive uprooting of dualistic thinking in the individual and collective consciousness is the beginning of a long struggle, but one that could, in our best hopes bring us to the end of rape, of violence, of war.
>
> (p. 122 of this volume)

Like her Mexican predecessors, Anzaldúa does express optimism for new forms of social relations and an end to violence that she hopes will emerge through breaking with dualisms implicit in racial and gender hierarchies. As such, her view has also been critiqued for the dangerous nationalistic and settler interpretations that this kind of proposal can pose for Indigenous and Afro-descendant populations in the Americas.

To elaborate one such critical interpretation of Anzaldúa's work, Two-Spirit author Deborah A. Miranda (Ohlone–Costanoan Esselen Nation of California) (Miranda and Keating 2002) discusses some significant issues that divide Indigenous and Chicanx communities in the U.S. Miranda writes that there are significant differences in how Indigenous communities and Chicanx communities are impacted by settler colonization in the United States. Miranda writes that in the settler United States, the reservation system, treaties, and paternalism impact Indigenous communities in ways that are specific to these communities:

> Chicana/os never had a reservation system. While this means they have not been legally restrained to certain patches of land, it also means Chicana/os do not "own" even a portion of their homeland as token recognition of indigenous rights. Being Indian means growing up on, or with the idea of, "the Rez." Even urban, non- or off-reservation Indians, like it or not, have this construction of being internally boundaried, or interned within our own homeland. The idea of the Rez has both restrained and connected U.S. Indians to the idea of homeland.
>
> (Miranda and Keating 2002: 205)

Such relations of containment and control impact Indigenous communities in ways distinct from mestizos/as in the United States. The forced disavowal of Indigenous ancestry by mestizos/as is not equivalent to the forcing of a reservation system and carceral control of Native movement and community associations to one another and to the land. Additionally, Miranda argues that "blood quantum," "ID cards," and the administrative violence that many Indigenous people suffer at the hands of the settler state for access to health care and educational resources do not impact Chicanx communities in the same manner. Lastly, she writes that there are deep differences in how Chicanx and Indigenous communities have been impacted by the anthropological sciences. That is, "Indians are a separate race to be studied, used, documented, and filed away. I have not seen many dissertations on the ceremonial uses of Chicana/o artifacts, or the differences between contemporary and traditional Chicana/os" (206). The result of this, she writes, is that "U.S. Indians learn to essentialize our Indianness because to do otherwise is to vanish completely, legally erased" (206). From this, she proposes that Native communities impacted by a U.S. settler logic fight against any denials of "Indianness" because the United States does not tolerate any "'official' category for mixedbloods" (206). Miranda is thus raising the question of why Indigenous peoples in the U.S., despite various forms of non-Indigenous kinship and parentage relationships, would not identify as "mixed" or "mestizo/a." The scarce resources and constraints on self-governance forced on tribal nations within the settler United States leads to "a heresy that would ensure the futility of any fight for justice or repatriation or reparation; and that, we will not allow" (206). Akin to the concerns expressed by Saldaña-Portillo and Simpson in the previous section, the "heresy" Miranda points to here is the risk imposed on Indigenous peoples of the U.S. to adopt any kind of "mixed" status, because such an identification could perpetuate racialized myths of the "vanishing Indian" that threaten Indigenous rights to land and self-governance.

Accordingly, Miranda points here to forms of state intervention that impact Indigenous communities in ways that are distinct from the mestizo/a populations of the U.S. Southwest, and she highlights that any proposal to embrace mestizaje risks erasing Indigenous solidarity and survival. Yet it is important to note that Miranda then shifts her analysis to the terms that divide Chicanx and Indigenous communities due to forms of colonial violence and forced scarcity.

Bringing in the question of Chicanx-Indigenous solidarity, she offers a framing of potential coalition building:

> By using the word Mestiza, I suddenly realize that it is much larger than simply blood or genetics: "Mestiza" is even larger than gender, despite its gendered origins. Mestiza

means that which does not obey or even see boundaries; that which blurs sharp distinctions in favor of what is best or most appropriate; that which thrives in ambiguity because ambiguity means survival, creation, movement. Mestiza is all that is transgressive to "the norm," all that breaks the rules of male/female, white/not-white, normal/abnormal. Mestiza is richly fluid, deeply strong.

(206)

This is an analysis that forces readers to examine the conditions that divide communities, like those of the settler U.S. and Mexican nation-states and the terms by which communities must identify in their effort to retain political governance and community survival. These include different demands for relations to place, including how identification with Indigeneity and land become a means for community stability and the continuation of Indigenous knowledge traditions. Moreover, challenging norms, boundaries, and conceptual binaries that attempt to erase and destabilize the futures of oppressed groups are central to both Miranda's and Anzaldúa's shared projects. Harkening to an account of such positionings, Miranda states:

Thus, all people who engage in breaking boundaries are engaged in what I would call "mestiza acts." Mestiza may have originated as a racial term to indicate mixed-race, but the ways that I am seeing that word and that way of being now are much more about self-directed identities, a personal, historically, psychically informed and aware construction of self that resists static definitions, craves the joy found in constant, organic, positive change. After all this time! I am finally beginning to understand what Gloria meant by the term "mestiza consciousness." We are just beginning to form the Mestiza Nation that she saw twenty years ago. That's got to be the ultimate in heresies.

(206–207)

Here, Miranda marks an interpretation of Anzaldúan mestizaje that is neither a harmonized vision of Mexican nationalism nor an erasure of Indigenous subjectivity under a U.S. settler racial logic. Rather, through this reading by Miranda, Anzaldúa's "new mestizaje" is described more like an attentive, contextual, and historically informed way of transgressing norms in the service of Indigenous sovereignty and other shared forms of political struggle. This is a position that she notes could be considered "heretical" within political contexts in the U.S. wherein Indigenous peoples face the risk of losing land and rights to the settler state. Such risks are imposed through the very systems of settler control over Indigenous peoples' bodies and territories (reservations, blood quantum, tribal enrollment cards, etc.), and settler conceptions of race and culture that determine "Indigenous" and "non-Indigenous" status for access to (or denial of) resources and rights within settler states.[6]

In light of similar concerns of risk and vulnerability to the settler state, especially concerns regarding the political violence of mestizaje used by settler states to dispossess Indigenous communities, a number of authors have likewise begun to rethink the relationship between Latinx and Indigenous politics, developing ways of affirming Indigenous presence, futurity, and forms of historical continuity and change among Native and non-Native communities. For example, Jennie Luna and Gabriel Estrada (2020), both from Caxcan family lineages, each seek to engage in what Luna describes as "building a Xicana Indígena philosophical base" (Luna 2012). This is a lifelong process, she notes, that encourages Chicanx and other Latinx peoples to turn to oral storytelling traditions within their own kinship relations, ancestral plant knowledges and medicinal teachings, Indigenous languages, and forms of knowledge like dance, art, and music to build connections with Indigenous communities that have otherwise been eroded through settler state-sponsored forms of detribalization and dispossession. However, rather than turning to a mythic past or anthropologically based form of knowledge that decenters and repackages Indigenous lifeways and politics toward an assumed inevitable settler future, Luna and Estrada seek to connect with and affirm contemporary Indigenous communities and their current political projects, including continued stewardship of the land, waterways, and lifeways on their traditional territories.

Moreover, as authors like Maylei Blackwell (Cherokee), Floridalma Boj Lopez (K'iche' Maya), and Luis Urrieta Jr. have proposed, there is also a need to examine "how indigeneity is defined and constructed across multiple countries and at times, across overlapping colonialities" (2017: 126). Responding to discourses of migration that can reproduce logics of Indigenous erasure, they reject the claim that "when Indigenous people migrate, they cease to be Indigenous" and they assert "that im/migrants [also] arrive on the homelands and nations of Indigenous peoples and that this awareness brings with it responsibilities and the possibility of new relationships of tension and solidarity" (127). They thus propose a new framework called "Critical Latinx Indigeneities" to interpret "the co-constitutive relationship of multiple contexts of power and multiple colonialities and begins the difficult conversation about the role of Indigenous people who are settlers in the homelands and nations of other Indigenous people" (127). Notably, authors like Saldaña-Portillo who likewise take up the framework of Critical Latinx Indigeneities as a method of analysis, respond to the question "When is an Indian not an Indian?" with the following analysis:

> To (begin to) answer the question, in the United States an Indian is not an Indian when s/he is also African American or Latinx. Even with all the permutations implied by the generic term 'Latino'—a term used to designate the descendants of Latin American nations whose racial identifications were forged in the wake of Spanish colonialism and through the ideology of mestizaje—a Latinx cannot be a proper Indian in the United States.
>
> (Cotera and Saldaña-Portillo 2015: 139)

However, she notes that responses to this question differ by historical context across the Americas. She continues:

> In contradistinction [to U.S. racial logics], following the logic of Spanish colonial governmentality, mestizos and afromestizos (predecessors of today's Latinxs and Afro-Latinxs) were forged and recognized as intimate, intermingled communities, who followed the strictures of church and crown with regard to marriage and procreation. Moreover, the fact of mixture did not alienate one from their Indigenous heritage. To the contrary, claiming Indigenous heritage enabled mestizos and afromestizos to access freedom, land, urban property, and other privileges afforded Indigenous populations in the viceroyalties of New Spain and Lima.
>
> (Cotera and Saldaña-Portillo 2015: 140)

In this, there are important differences in how Indigeneity and mixture, including cultural and racial relations with and among Afro-diasporic and Indigenous communities across the Americas, shapes relationships to Indigeneity, Blackness, land, labor, and rights. Critical Latinx Indigeneities contests how racialized logics of elimination and control seek to eradicate the continued existence of Indigeneity across the U.S., including among African American and Latinx populations. She writes:

> The rendering invisible of the Indigenous ancestry of African Americans and Latinxs, the banishment of Indigenous peoples from the modern scene of labor, has had a deleterious impact on the counter-hegemonic scholarly formations of Native American, African American and Latinx studies. The colonial calculus of "pure blooded" Indigenous authenticity and the "one-drop rule" of African American racial embodiment on the one hand, and the colonial requirement for importation of black and brown bodies to labor, on the other, has led to the compartmentalization of the study of race and ethnicity; one in which Native American studies tends to devote itself to the study of Indigenous genocide and reservation, African American studies to chattel slavery and its carceral afterlives, and Chicanx/Latinx studies to colonial annexation and labor migration.
>
> (Saldaña-Portillo 2017: 143)

Contesting such demands for purity and the scholarly trajectories that have consolidated around them, Saldana-Portillo and others seek to analyze how multiple racial geographies or "colonialities" can be at play within a given context across the Americas.

For example, Saldaña-Portillo examines the context of Garífuna migrants, Afro-Indigenous peoples from Honduras, who live in New York City, which is home to the largest enclave of Garífuna peoples outside of Central America. Garífuna peoples are "a UNESCO-recognized group of Afro-indigenous people who span the Atlantic coast from Belize to Nicaragua, descendants of sixteenth-century escaped African slaves who intermarried with Carib and Arawak Indians to form cimarrón (maroon) communities throughout the Caribbean" (Saldaña-Portillo 2017: 147). However, despite having protected rights, including land rights and distinct political representation in Honduras, Guatemala, and Nicaragua, as Saldaña-Portillo writes, these groups have been displaced from their homelands by tourism industries in Central America. Thus, as Afro-Indigenous migrants in the state of New York, Garífuna peoples come to exist within the racial logics of the U.S. Northeast whereby stark distinctions between African Americans, Latinxs, and Indigenous peoples shape access to resources and identity claims.

Given the distinctly Afro-Indigenous and migrant status of Garífuna peoples in New York, understanding the political and social organizing of these communities requires, Saldaña-Portillo proposes, a framework like that of Critical Latinx Indigeneities. Namely, Garífuna peoples, unlike many African Americans, are not descendants of enslaved Africans who endured racialized labor under a plantation economy or other forms of racialized exploitation in the U.S. The Garífuna are, instead, descendants of maroon communities who formed political alliances and communities with Native peoples and thereby developed, like other Afro-diasporic maroon communities across the Americas, longstanding cultural, linguistic, and land-based relations that afford them distinct political status. Thus, while the one-drop rule often divided Native and African peoples in the U.S., in places like Nicaragua, Honduras, Guatemala, Colombia, and Brazil, Afro-diasporic communities have made claims under the new multicultural models of governance in these nation-states to claim land-bases and state protections.

Yet, despite land titles for traditional territories in Honduras, corporate interests in the transnational tourism industries along the coastal regions of Central America have threatened the livelihoods and lands of Garífuna peoples. Saldaña-Portillo also notes that this process of dispossession bears similarities with settler colonization in the U.S.:

> The Garífuna have already lost land through corruption, fraud, and squatting, or through coerced transactions with [transnational corporations] mediated by corrupt government officials, despite the fact that the Honduran Constitution prohibits foreign ownership of coastal territory. These transactions are not terribly dissimilar from the fraudulent and coerced methods used by Anglo-American colonists to purchase lands from Native Americans in the seventeenth and eighteenth centuries.
>
> (2017: 147)

In this, the coerced and forced forms of migration impacting Garífuna peoples in Honduras also returns us to threats to Indigenous self-governance and relations to traditional territories, including, in this case, transnational corporate interests in securing settler demands to sites for pleasure and property, like the tourism industries seizing land across the Caribbean coasts of Central America.

Juliet Hooker (2005) elaborates a related point regarding rights for Afro-diasporic communities across the Americas:

> The need to assert an ethnic or culturally distinct group identity in order to successfully claim collective rights means that not only the majority of Afro-Latinos, but some indigenous groups as well, are unable to gain such rights. The problem is that . . . Afro-Latinos who are unable to assert an 'ethnic' identity lack a solid claim to collective rights even though they may also suffer from political exclusion and racial discrimination. Afro-Latinos have been able to gain group rights where they have been able to assert an indigenous-like position. But if the majority of black populations in Latin America are in fact urban, and do not possess an ethnic identity distinct from the larger mestizo culture, this means that they are less likely to be able to successfully claim group rights, at least so long as these are conceived in terms of cultural difference.
>
> (Hooker 2005: 306–307)

Notably, this problem of a distinct cultural and ethnic identity likewise impacts the claims to Indigenous ancestry across the Americas. This includes the U.S. where a number of Indigenous groups are denied land rights and federal status due to being unable to prove that their group has "maintained a continuous community from historical times to the present day" (U.S. Department of the Interior 1997: 44).

For example, the Lumbee Tribe of North Carolina in the southern U.S. has sought federal acknowledgment from the United States as a sovereign Indigenous nation, but, as of 2023, still has not gained full status. Malinda Maynor Lowery, a Lumbee historian and enrolled member of the tribe, writes on this matter:

> Strictly speaking, multi-racial ancestry was not a reason for denying acknowledgment; after all, it would be difficult to find an acknowledged tribe that did not have multiracial ancestry. But race has often played a role in outsiders' and insiders' discourse over another persistent fact of Lumbee life, that of political factions and tribal name changes. Our official tribal name has changed four times between 1885 and 1956; we were called Croatans, Cherokee Indians of Robeson County, Siouan Indians of the Lumber River,

and in 1956 a congressional act formally recognized us as Lumbee Indians. These name changes arose not because Indians did not know who they were or what constituted their identity but because federal and state officials kept changing their criteria for authenticity. Prior to the 1950s the Bureau of Indian Affairs believed in cultural, anthropological standards of identity, while Congress promoted a politically expedient vision of a racially Indian identity that mainly served to uphold segregation in the South or assimilation agendas in the West.

(2009: 502–503)

Lowery's historical work traces the shifting U.S. settler government policies and their demands for "anthropological categories that classify peoples as discrete (and preferably pure) groups, and personal, paternalistic categories that measure everyone with a yardstick of whiteness" (503), which have negatively impacted the Lumbee tribe's legal pathway to federal acknowledgment. Such volatile standards include members of the U.S. Congress refusing to grant federal acknowledgement based on the assumption that, as one South Dakota congressional member put it in the 1913 case for Lumbee federal recognition:

the Lumbee were not 'full-blooded'. . . . [The congressman] implied his suspicion that 'these Indians' were actually 'Negroes' or in any case did not have enough 'Indian blood' to justify federal interference with the South's race problem by recognizing them as a separate group with separate rights.

(504)

In this, the association (imagined or real) between Indigenous and Black populations in the U.S. South has repeatedly served as a means to disenfranchise both populations, including Afro-Indigenous populations, and constitute a sustained effort to maintain an imagined racial "purity" of whiteness (Colman 2013).

The legal terms across Latin America shift to the dominance of mestizo nationalism, as I mentioned, whereby Afro-diasporic and Indigenous communities must prove their distinction from the assumed majority "mixed" populations. Moreover, in places like Colombia where Afro-descendant communities have been granted land titles along the Pacific coastal regions, the logic of proving a distinct group status likewise occurs via the demonstration of a distinct collective ethnic group identification. This is particularly difficult for some Afro- diasporic groups in Colombia because they have had to prove that they are "Indigenous-like" in some ways to be granted land titles. What these contestations reveal, as Bettina Ng'weno (2012), has proposed, is that:

relations to land are essential to the present use of ethnicity, which is informed by past racial categories created during colonial times and which are fundamental to the idea of modernity. In this construction, deterritorialization is a process of removing culture whether through Diaspora or through urbanization. Put another way, it is a perceived relation to land that legitimates both claims to ethnic identity and to culture, and thus to a "different legal treatment" that in turn legitimates claims to land.

(2008: 418)

This circular logic reveals a co-constitutive relation between ethnicity and race, and one that can be strategically used toward Eurocentric and white supremacist ends to deny claims to land and self-governance among Indigenous and Afro-diasporic communities, and which requires such communities to negotiate within the terms of these organizing circular and often arbitrary settler logics.

Yet, as scholars of métis communities in Canada note, "ethnogenesis, the historical moments when mixed-race people collectively [develop] distinct identities" can be a very contested project for Indigenous-identified communities as well. For example, Red River Métis scholar Chris Andersen writes: "I'm Métis because I belong (and claim allegiance) to a set of Métis memories, territories, and leaders" (2011: 165). By this, Andersen is referring in part, to the Red River Métis's historical and political alliance with the armed rebellion led by Louis Riel against the Canadian government in 1869 and 1885 in the Red River Region near Winnipeg, Manitoba. This armed resistance is part of this group's historical claims to land, kinship, and political status, which traces back to 17th-century practices of intermarriage among French fur traders and Cree and other Indigenous communities in the region. In the present-day, the Red River Métis are represented by the Métis National Council (MNC) and are considered an Indigenous nation under Canadian constitutional law, which acknowledges the nation's self-governance rights and status accordingly. It is the MNC's definition of "Métis identity," however, that remains controversial within the political context of settler Canada. Notably, the definition of "Métis" according to the MNC is the following: "'Métis' means a person who self-identifies as Métis, is distinct from other Aboriginal peoples, is of historic Métis Nation Ancestry and who is accepted by the Métis Nation" (MNC 2023). Bidwell has noted, "The effort to pin down Metis identity is understandable from a political perspective but does not reflect the historic fluidity and internal diversity of the Metis [across settler Canada]" (2014: 126). Bidwell continues:

> The Red River Metis are not the only distinctive community of mixed European and Indigenous descent in Canada. They are the most well known, in part because their armed resistance has led to their presence in historical documents and to public and academic interest. But it is a controversial question whether the Red River Metis's nationalist resistance makes them qualitatively different from all other mixed Indigenous communities and should give them distinctive rights.
>
> (2014: 128)

Yet, similar to Miranda's concerns that an acceptance of a mixed identity like "mestiza" would pose an added vulnerability for Indigenous claims to rights and resources in the settler U.S., the Red River Métis have also sought to protect their status via the distinctiveness of their identity when faced with the threat of settler dispossession and disenfranchisement. Andersen, when presented with the question of what obligations Red River Métis owe to other mixed peoples writes:

> We are not a soup kitchen for those disenfranchised by past and present Canadian Indian policy and, as such, although we should sympathize with those who bear the brunt of this particular form of dispossession, we cannot do so at the expense of eviscerating our identity.
>
> (2011: 165)

The threats posed by settler governance include granting land title to groups of peoples who pose or present as Indigenous but who bear no historical relations to the land or kinship relations to Indigenous peoples, referred to in a derogatory manner as "pretendians." For example, Bidwell's own community, formerly known as the "Labrador Metis" and now known as "NunatuKavut," was issued a Memorandum of Understanding from the Canadian government in 2019, which they considered a step on the process toward federal recognition of their Indigenous right to self-governance (NunatuKavut 2023). However, this legal agreement has been contested by the Métis National Council (MNC 2023), the Inuit Tapiriit Kanatami (ITK 2023), and the Inuit Circumpolar Council (ICC 2023), with each organization claiming that the NunatuKavut Community Council are fraudulently seeking "to secure the lands and rights of legitimate Indigenous peoples and to further misappropriate the already limited resources that are intended to benefit Inuit, First Nations, and Métis" (ITK 2023). In this, the stakes of inclusion are extraordinarily high, as the traditional homelands of Indigenous peoples, the ITK proposes, are being fraudulently offered to non-Indigenous communities who are opportunistically posing as Indigenous.

As such, categories of mixture remain contested terms across the Americas, with land, rights, and self-governance as the ongoing stakes of the debate. In this, the politicized spaces of mixedblood, mestizo/a, and métis collective identities take shape in ways that often require complex navigations through settler colonial logics of appropriation and land possession, as well as ongoing Indigenous and Afro-diasporic dispossession and disenfranchisement. This chapter has not sought to resolve these issues, but instead to demonstrate the terms of the debate, both in the terms of those who identify with these categories, as well as the nationalistic and governmental terms through which these categories operate. What remains today are political questions regarding the affirmation of Indigenous claims to land and self-governance, and the ongoing intertwinement of categories of race, ethnicity, and political membership that complicate and thereby cast doubt on demands for Indigenous political governance. Among the tasks ahead are questions regarding political solidarity with Indigenous and Afro-diasporic peoples across the Americas, and given the disagreements among these communities, this also often includes a call to diminish and, for some, to eradicate the settler state's claims to authority over the adjudication of Indigenous and Afro-diasporic lives and futures.

References

Andersen, C. (2011) "'I'm Métis, What's Your Excuse?': On the Optics and the Ethics of the Misrecognition of Métis in Canada," *Aboriginal Policy Studies* 1 (2): 161–165.

Anzaldúa, G. (1999) *Borderlands/La Frontera: The New Mestiza* (2nd ed.), San Francisco: Aunt Lute Books.

Anzaldúa, G. (2009) "La Prieta" in A. Keating (ed.) *The Gloria Anzaldúa Reader*, 38–50, Durham: Duke University Press.

Aronson-Friedman, A., and Kaplan, G. (2012) *Marginal Voices: Studies in Converso Literature of Medieval and Golden Age Spain*, Leiden: Brill.

Arvin, M., Tuck, E., and Morrill, A. (2013) "Decolonizing Feminism: Challenging Connections between Settler Colonialism and Heteropatriarchy," *Feminist Formations* 25 (1): 8–34.

Bernardino-Costa, J. (2023) "Opening Pandora's Box: The Extreme Right and the Resurgence of Racism in Brazil," *Latin American Perspectives* 50 (1): 98–114. https://doi.org/10.1177/0094582X221147596.

Berquist Soule, E. (2018) "From Africa to the Ocean Sea: Atlantic Slavery in the Origins of the Spanish Empire," *Atlantic Studies* 15 (1): 16–39.

Blackwell, M, Lopez, F. B., and Urrieta Jr., L. (2017) "Critical Latinx Indigeneities," *Latino Studies* 15 (2): 126–137.

Bidwell, K. F. 2014. "Metis Identity and Literature" in J. H. Cox and D. H. Justice (eds.), *The Oxford Handbook of Indigenous American Literature*, 118–136, New York: Oxford University Press.

Byrd, J. A. (2011) *Transit of Empire: Indigenous Critiques of Colonialism*, Minneapolis: University of Minnesota Press.

Colman, A. L. (2013) *That the Blood Stay Pure: African Americans, Native Americans, and the Predicament of Race and Identity in Virginia*, Indianapolis: Indiana University Press.
Cotera, M. E., and Saldaña-Portillo, M. J. (2015) "Indigenous but Not Indian? Chicana/os and the Politics of Indigeneity," in E. Warrior (ed.), *The World of Indigenous North America*, 549–568, New York: Routledge.
Dussel, E. (2014) "Anti-Cartesian Meditations: On the Origin of the Philosophical Anti-discourse of Modernity," *Journal for Cultural and Religious Theory* 13 (1): 11–52.
Gaspar de Alba, A. (2014) *[Un]framing the "Bad Woman": Sor Juana, Malinche, Coyolxauhqui, and Other Rebels with a Cause*, Austin: University of Texas Press.
Green, R. (1975) "The *Pocahontas* Perplex: The Image of Indian Women in American Culture," *The Massachusetts Review* 16 (4): 698–714.
Hokowhitu, B., Moreton-Robinson, A., Tuhiwai-Smith, L., Andersen, C., and Larkin, S., eds. (2020) *Routledge Handbook of Critical Indigenous Studies*. Routledge.
Hooker, J. (2005) "Indigenous Inclusion/Black Exclusion: Race, Ethnicity and Multicultural Citizenship in Latin America," *Journal of Latin American Studies* 37 (2): 285–310.
Inuit Circumpolar Council (ICC) (2023) "Statement on the Nunatukavut Community Council (NCC)," Press Releases, *Inuitcircumpolar.com*, www.inuitcircumpolar.com/news/statement-on-the-nunatukavut-community-council-ncc.
Inuit Tapiriit Kanatami (ITK). (2023) "An Open Letter from Inuit Tapiriit Kanatami to Alert Canadians to False Claims to Inuit Identity," *ITK.ca*. www.itk.ca/wp-content/uploads/2023/11/20231103-open-letter-false-claims-to-inuit-identity-EN.pdf.
Kauanui, J. K. (2016) "'A Structure, Not an Event': Settler Colonialism and Enduring Indigeneity," Lateral, 5 (1), 2016. *JSTOR*. https://www.jstor.org/stable/48671433.
Lowery, M. M. (2009) "Telling Our Own Stories: Lumbee History and the Federal Acknowledgment Process," *American Indian Quarterly* 33 (4): 499–522.
Luna, J. M. (2012) "Building a Xicana Indígena Philosophical Base," *APA Newsletter on Hispanic/Latino Issues in Philosophy* 11 (2): 9–16.
Luna, J. M., and Estrada, G. S. (2020). "Translating the Genderqueer -x Through Caxcan, Nahua, and Xicanx Indígena Knowledge," in A. J. Aldama and F. L. Aldama (eds.) *Decolonizing Latinx Masculinities*, 251–274, Tucson: University of Arizona Press.
Lyall, V. I., Romo, T., and Robb, M. H. (2022) *Traitor, Survivor, Icon: The Legacy of La Malinche*, New Haven: Yale University Press.
Martínez, M. E. (2008) *Genealogical Fictions: Limpieza de sangre, Religion, and Gender in Colonial Mexico*, Stanford: Stanford University Press.
Métis National Council (MNC). (2023) "Métis National Council Supports Inuit Tapiriit Kanatami's Alert on False Identity," *Globe Newswire*. November 7, www.globenewswire.com/en/news-release/2023/11/07/2775350/0/en/M%C3%89TIS-NATIONAL-COUNCIL-SUPPORTS-INUIT-TAPIRIIT-KANATAMI-S-ALERT-ON-FALSE-IDENTITY.html.
Miranda, D. A., and Keating, A. (2002) "Footnoting Heresy: E-mail Dialogues," in G. E. Anzaldúa and A. Keating (eds.), *This Bridge We Call Home: Radical Visions for Transformation*, 202–208, New York: Routledge.
Ng'weno, B. (2012) "Beyond Citizenship as We Know It: Race and Ethnicity in Afro-Colombia Struggles for Citizenship Equality," in K. Dixon and J. Burdick (eds.), *Comparative Perspectives on Afro-Latin America*, 156–175, Gainesville: University of Florida Press.
NunatuKavut. (2023) "Our Rights Recognition," *Nunatukavut.ca*. https://nunatukavut.ca/about/rights-recognition.
Paz, O. (1981) *El laberinto de la soledad*, Mexico D. F.: Fondo de Cultura Económica.
Paz, O. (2022) "The Sons of La Malinche," in G. M. Joseph and T.J. Henderson (eds.) *The Mexico Reader: History, Culture, Politics* (2nd ed.), 22–29, Durham, NC: Duke University Press.
Rios, F. (2021) "Notes on the Essay 'Racism and Sexism in Brazilian Culture': Notas Sobre o Ensaio 'Racismo e Sexismo Na Cultura Brasileira'," *Women's Studies Quarterly* 49: 395–406.
Saldaña-Portillo, M. J. (2016) *Indian Given: Racial Geographies across Mexico and the United States*, Durham, NC: Duke University Press.
Saldaña-Portillo, M. J. (2017) "Critical Latinx Indigeneities: A Paradigm Drift," *Latino Studies* 15 (2): 138–155.
Simpson, A. (2018) "Why White People Love Franz Boas; or, The Grammar of Indigenous Dispossession," in N. Blackhawk and I. L. Wilner (eds.), *Indigenous Visions: Rediscovering the World of Franz Boas*, 166–182, New Haven: Yale University Press.

Simpson, A. (2019) *Mohawk Interruptus: Political Life Across the Borders of Settler States*, Durham, NC: Duke University Press.
Townsend, C. (2019) *Fifth Sun: A New History of the Aztecs*, New York: Oxford University Press.
U.S. Department of the Interior. (1997) "The Official Guidelines to the Federal Acknowledgment Regulations," *25 CFR 83*. Washington DC: Office of Federal Acknowledgment.
Vasconcelos, J. (1997) *The Cosmic Race: A Bilingual Edition*, D. T. Jaén (trans.), Baltimore: Johns Hopkins University Press.
Vizenor, G. (1977) *Earthdivers: Tribal Narratives on Mixed Descent*, Minneapolis: University of Minnesota Press.
Weaver, J. (1997) *That the People Might Live: Native American Literatures and Native American Community*. New York: Oxford UP.
Wolfe, P. (1999) *Settler Colonialism and the Transformation of Anthropology*, London: Cassell.
Womack, C. (1997) "Howling at the Moon: The Strange but True Story of My Life as a Hank Williams Song," in W. S. Penn (ed.) *As We Are Now: Mixedblood Essays on Race and Identity*, 28–49, Berkeley: University of California Press.
Wynter, S. (2003) "Unsettling the Coloniality of Being/Power/Truth/Freedom: Towards the Human, After Man, Its Overrepresentation—An Argument," *CR: The New Centennial Review* 3 (3): 257–337.

Notes

1 For more on this point see Wynter (2003) and Dussel (2014).
2 To emphasize the violence implicit in this phrase, note this passage from Paz's 1950 essay: "The idea of breaking, of ripping open, appears in a great many of these expressions [of "hijos de la chingada"]. The word has sexual connotations but it is not a synonym for the sexual act: one may chingar a woman without actually possessing her. And when it does allude to the sexual act, violation or deception gives it a particular shading. The man who commits it never does so with the consent of the chingada. Chingar, then, is to do violence to another. The verb is masculine, active, cruel: it stings, wounds, gashes, stains. And it provokes a bitter, resentful satisfaction. The person who suffers this action is passive, inert and open, in contrast to the active, aggressive and closed person who inflicts it. The chingon is the macho, the male; he rips open the chingada, the female, who is pure passivity, defenseless against the exterior world. The relationship between them is violent, and it is determined by the cynical power of the first and the impotence of the second. The idea of violence rules darkly over all the meanings of the word, and the dialectic of the 'closed' and the 'open' thus fulfills itself with an almost ferocious precision" (Paz 2022: 23).
3 The claim that "settler colonialism is a structure and not an event" is often attributed to Patrick Wolfe (2006). However, reflecting on the circulation of this view from Wolfe, American Studies scholar J. Kēhaulani Kauanui (Kanaka Maoli) notes, Wolfe himself attributed this claim to Indigenous scholars before him (2016: 1). For more on this point by Wolfe, see Wolfe (1999: 3).
4 To support this claim, Saldaña-Portillo "pairs historical and legal documents with literary, epistolary, or filmic texts that respond to these documents" (2016: 30). For example, she reads the 1848 Treaty of Guadalupe Hidalgo and 19th-century Mexican scalping laws with Américo Paredes's novel *George Washington Gómez* to foreground the practices of the Apache and Comanche who "refused to vanish into mestizaje or onto reservations in the newly annexed territory of the U.S. Southwest" (Saldaña-Portillo 2016: 30).
5 Simpson critiques anthropological views of "culture" based on the work of the influential anthropologist Franz Boas in Simpson (2019; 2018).
6 For more on how race and culture place constraints on Indigenous rights to land and self-governance, see Simpson (2019) and Byrd (2011).

Reading Questions

1. What is the idea of mestizaje?
2. What does Pitts mean by the claim that mestizaje is "implicated in national and political narratives of futurity and teleology"?

3. Pitts argues that we can better appreciate the social function or significance of concepts like mestizaje when we consider how such concepts work from the standpoint of people who sometimes had reason to resist or strategically utilize these concepts. What is one example in the text that illustrates how the same racial concept can be both oppressive and liberating, depending on the context?
4. Make the case for two or three other concepts that might be illuminated by considering how they apply to people who have reason to resist or strategically use the concept. What new questions or insights about Pitts' account arise when comparing these cases?
5. An important part of Pitts' account is that different groups have had different standards for membership. Importantly, not all groups in the Americas accepted a model according to which being Indigenous is to be understood as racial or descent-based. In those cases of disagreement, is there a satisfactory way of settling the disagreement? Why or why not?
6. Why does the history of a concept or term bear on whether we should use the term, here and now? Consider that, for example, some people have thought that not that long ago, marriage and medical interventions were, on balance, really harmful to the people who were subjected to them. Yet, awareness of these histories doesn't always make people think that marriage and cancer treatments are a bad idea. So, why would the history of mestizaje make a difference to whether we should now make use of the idea?
7. Pitts argues that states have had a tremendous amount of power over how people think about their identities. Should states have that power? Are there effective ways to limit or avoid states having that power?
8. What is one significant implication of Pitts' account for debates among Latinx and Indigenous scholars and activists today, according to the author? Do you agree? Why or why not?

Part 3
Cross-Cultural Challenges

Introduction

Some people think that within the United States, like it or not, Latinxs will continue to be regarded as "Other," alien, or otherwise not quite like some taken-for-granted notion of "us." If so, how should Latinxs navigate that environment? Is there a way to navigate cultural differences without being inauthentic? And anyway, what would it mean to be authentically oneself, or to act autonomously, in the face of conflicts in norms, meanings, and values of the different groups of which one is a member? These are the kinds of questions explored in this section's selection of readings.

Linda Martín Alcoff's "Latina/o Identity Politics" takes up several interrelated questions: (1) whether U.S. Latina/os should simply identify as "American" (or alternately, as some Latin American national identity in opposition to a U.S. identity), and (2) whether the idea of a pan-Latina/o identity is ultimately a threat to the integrity of things like national identities with more robust cultural overlaps. Alcoff holds that there is a way to navigate the dual challenges of assimilation and foreignness. On her account, the key is to see Latina/os as contributing to a transformation of U.S. identity, and to hold that a pan-Latina/o identity is compatible with diverse individual national identities.

In her landmark article, "Playfulness, 'World-Traveling', and Loving Perception," María Lugones focuses on the experiences of Latinas in the United States. She argues that many Latinas are forced to acquire a certain degree of flexibility in moving between cultural spaces, especially in the context of moving in and out of White-dominant spaces. This useful ability also can come at some significant costs to many of those who do this cultural shifting: as one moves across these contexts, one's modes of interaction can be governed by social norms that have the effect of changing or distorting one's identity. How one is expected to behave, and how one's behavior is interpreted can make inaccessible important and meaningful ways of being in the world for those who "world-travel." Where one's forms of being and self-expression are substantially influenced or controlled by alien norms and interests, it tends to screen off the possibility of genuine or authentic recognition of the subjectivity of those subject to the alien norms. Lugones goes on to propose an alternative, one where women can jointly explore and construct norms that allow for non-subordinating recognition of the subjectivity and agency of others.

Gloria Anzaldúa's influential work on "mestiza consciousness" (see the readings in Part 2 of this volume) championed the idea that people living in the overlap of conflicting cultural practices (including metaphorical and actual, physical, borderlands between nations) do well to tolerate or even embrace ambivalence in their identities and commitments. (Lugones recommends a related strategy for agency-affirming shifting of identities across contexts in her work on "world-traveling.") In contexts of cultural conflict and social subordination,

DOI: 10.4324/9781003385417-17

this facility with ambivalence can allow people to navigate particularly complex cultural worlds with an enhanced capacity to reason critically about those worlds.

But can people who embrace that ambivalence ever be autonomous? According to an important tradition of thinking about autonomy, autonomy necessarily involves a kind of structured, coherent hierarchy of attitudes, values, or commitments. So, one might think that the flexibility that Anzaldúa recommends is incompatible with autonomy. In "Mestizaje Autonomy as Relational Autonomy," Edwina Barvosa argues that this is not so. Instead, building on an idea in Lugones' work, one can have multiple identities that are nevertheless unified enough to prevent fragmentation. By actively making ambivalent endorsements and disavowals, agents can retain a kind of organized flexibility that is responsive to social circumstances that are familiar and common to many.

The multiplicity of commitments and ambivalent values that distinguishes many people living in cross-cultural contexts has sometimes been discussed under the idea of "cultural code-switching." Many people have thought that fluency at "cultural code-switching" is a key to upward mobility, and that it is important for enabling low-income populations to gain access to the goods of middle-class life in the United States. By being able to present oneself in ways that comply with dominant norms, socially disadvantaged populations can gain access and acceptance to spaces that would otherwise be more difficult for them to access. However, engaging in these practices comes at the risk of code-switchers becoming ethically unmoored, having multiple conflicting sets of values that can destabilize or undermine people's values. In Jennifer M. Morton's "Cultural Code-Switching: Straddling the Achievement Gap," Morton takes up the question of how educators can be sensitive to the ethical challenges involved, and how they can effectively teach their students to navigate those challenges in a way that does not ultimately undermine their agency over time. Her favored approach involves an effort at helping students form a comprehensive picture of values under which cultural code-switching is a licensed part, but in a way that is explicitly integrated with the student's other evaluative commitments and dispositions.

Children of immigrants sometimes report feeling some degree of estrangement from the norms, meanings, and values of their parents and from the dominant cultural norms of the society that their families have immigrated to. In "The Philosophy of Accidentality," Manuel Vargas approaches experiences like this through the lens of "accidentality," an idea developed by the 20th-century Mexican existentialist Emilio Uranga. Accidentality, in this sense, is a state characterized by the lack of a stable or unified package of commitments about norms, meanings, and values. People who are accidents contrast with people who are substances, in the sense that substances typically take for granted a set of relatively stable and unified commitments about norms, meanings, and values. Accidents are characterized by a distinctive psychology that arises because of this normative uncertainty. Although accidentality is typically experienced as a burden, at least in Uranga's presentation, accidentality is something that should be embraced as capturing an important feature of the human condition, namely, the contingency of any set of normative commitments. Vargas goes on to emphasize that accidentality is not limited to the experience of immigrants or their descendants, but that it plausibly applies to those whose social identities do not mesh with the identities valorized by society at large. He concludes by discussing the relationship of accidentality to other phenomena, including biculturality and W.E.B. Du Bois's idea of double-consciousness.

11 Latina/o Identity Politics

Linda Martín Alcoff

"OK by me in America!"
"For a small fee in America"
　　—*West Side Story*

In one of my classes some time back. during a group discussion of identity, a young Puerto Rican woman from New York City insisted against the disagreement of her classmates that she was an "American." She didn't want to be called Puerto Rican; she thought of herself simply as an "American." Knee-jerk leftist responses, mine included, have long treated such pronouncements as a species of false consciousness or ideological conditioning. Puertorriquenas in this country are never considered simply "Americans" by Anglos, and to identify as such has seemed a naive position that will make one less prepared for racism. Moreover, identifying as American might be an indication of one's own internalized racism or great nation chauvinism.

But after this particular class, for some reason, I left dissatisfied and troubled by our routine critique of the professed desire to be seen simply as an "American." I began to try to think about her claim differently, to see what must be presupposed in her ability to make the claim, and to consider its political possibilities. This paper is my attempt to work out what these possibilities might mean.

The question of citizenship for U.S. Latinos is fraught with tensions that are in some respects different than for any other ethnic group. We are persistently seen by Anglo America as perennial foreigners: unassimilated, inassimilable, even uninterested in assimilation. Unlike other immigrant groups, our countries of origin are too close, our numbers here too numerous and concentrated, to motivate the loss of Spanish language or cultural custom (Flores and Yudice 1990; see also Oboler 1995). Even though we may have lived in North America for generations, even if as Chicanos our families have never lived anywhere else, we are perceived as a foreign peoples squatting within the United States. This has prompted two sorts of responses. One is to reject those who have rejected us and to seek a life of dignity within a safe enclave, to turn the ghetto into a barrio where a communal life can flourish. The other response strives to make peace with the hegemonic Anglo society and learn to master its ways. This sometimes requires proving our loyalty by landing with the Marines in Panama City or infiltrating the parallel market in Los Angeles. But in both cases we have been pushed to choose one or the other, a Latino life on the margins, or an Anglicized participant in the life of the nation.

This is beginning to change. Latinas/os have just in this generation become visible in the mainstream media even without changing their name and hiding their accent, as symbolized by the father-son stars Martin Sheen and Emilio Estevez. We are holding public office, hosting national radio shows, appearing on the nightly news as reporters and commentators and not just victims or perpetrators, and getting tenure in research universities. Latinas/os have made it into public culture, albeit still in small, unproportional numbers. The emergence of a Latina/o middle class creates the conditions both for more class collaboration and treachery as well as a better negotiating position with dominant Anglo institutions. And thus new worries emerge: Will the new pan-Latin identity lead eventually to Anglo assimilation once again, as our substantive and specific national identities are subsumed in an identity that only makes sense from the perspective of the AngloLatino divide? Will the price of entry into public culture be a loss of cultural integrity? Or will it bring to realization the hope expressed by Guillermo Gomez-Pena that Latinos in the United States can someday "participate actively in a humanistic, pluralistic and politicized dialogue, continuous and not sporadic, and that this [will] occur between equals that enjoy the same power of negotiation" (Gómez-Peña 1988: 133)?

Before Gomez-Pena's hope can be realized, however, I believe that "public intellectuals" in the United States need to rethink their understanding of the politics of identity in their dominant discourses and conversations. Both liberals and leftists are squeamish about identity politics, precisely out of a fear that emphasizing and politicizing identity gets in the way of creating progressive models of citizenship in which political judgment and the possibility of coalition should be based on one's views and commitments rather than one's background. In this paper I hope to cast some doubt on this truism.

(Particular) Identities/(Universalist) Politics

Identity politics is today attacked by right, left, and center. Todd Gitlin, the well-known and widely published white leftist, provides a representative critique. In his view,

> . . . identity politics makes a fetish of the virtues of the minority, which, in the end, is not only intellectually stultifying but also politically suicidal. It creates a kind of parochialism in which one is justified in having every interest in difference and no interest in commonality. . . . As soon as I declare I am a Jew, a black, a Hispanic, a woman, a gay, I have no more need to define my point of view.
>
> (Gitlin 1992: 188)[1]

For Gitlin, identity politics distort, mislead, and generally thwart the development of a progressive political majority. The focus on identity directs us away from the class and economic issues by which we might build a unified, progressive agenda.

Interestingly, identity politics has also been rejected both by postmodernists and by liberals (which we should remember are not mutually exclusive categories) and is increasingly discredited within academic Anglo feminism. Postmodernism[2] has provided an influential critique of identities as dangerous fictions which efface difference and openendedness toward the aim of closure and absoluteness, and has also argued against reductionist or causal accounts of the relation between identity and politics (as if identities determine one's politics), which would obscure the socially constructed character of identities as well as the socially constructed nature of the experiences that identities are often thought to be based upon. Many feminists have believed that a postmodern deconstruction of identity is the best way to respond to criticisms of the false universalism and overgeneralizations of White-dominated feminism (for this argument see Fraser and Nicholson 1990; 19–38; for the counterargument see Strickland 1994: 265–274).

But another reason for rejecting identity politics is the general classical liberal ideology that understands the particularities of identity as less relevant to the political rights of persons than the universals of human *haecceity*. The great European revolutions of the modern period were articulated in universal terms for the rights of all, beyond differences of ancestry. This universalist language was a truly effective revolutionary stratagem against the feudal orders, in which identity determined one's life prospects without any chance for redress or alteration. The "rights of man" were counterposed to the rights of noblemen. By appealing to a universal human essence, revolutionaries could out trump feudal claims through the invocation of an underlying similarity between all men with more fundamental ethical and political importance than any differences of heritage or class identity.

This revolutionary discursive strategy of universalism has now become nearly hegemonic. Its use spread beyond class and heritage differences (i.e., nobility versus merchants) to other differences such as race and ethnicity. And thus the assumption that justice requires decreasing if not eliminating the social relevance of racial and ethnic particularity made its way into antiracist, integrationist movements in the United States. And the *political* value system of universalism over particularism was correlated with an *epistemological* value system where truth was defined as that which everyone can potentially know, as well as a *metaphysical* value system that derogated the particular to the universal. As Gary Peller has usefully pointed out:

> A commitment to a form of universalism, and an association of universalism with truth and particularism with ignorance, forms the infrastructure of American integrationist consciousness ... integrationist beliefs are organized around the familiar enlightenment story of progress consisting of the movement from mere belief and superstition to knowledge and reason, from the particular and therefore parochial to the universal and therefore enlightened.
>
> (Peller 1995: 74)

Where truth and justice are assumed to require universalism, cultural, racial, or ethnic identity cannot be accorded political significance without endangering progress.

It is in this ideological arena, which has heavily informed both the bourgeois mainstream thinking as well as the civil rights and social justice movements in the United States, which Latinos and Latinas are now entering as a recognized force. The apparently obvious need to make demands in the name of a universal is still a profound influence on both the left and the right, castigating specific demands to the derogatory realm of "special interests." Many are today concerned like Gitlin that U.S. multiculturalism is a form of tribalism that will produce a "homegrown Yugoslavia" if we continue to promote ethnic studies and divisive thinking on our college campuses (Gitlin 1995: 190). Citizenship requires an investment in shared political institutions that identity politics defines as collaboration. And as a young white Anglo women's studies major explained to me at a talk I gave in Binghamton, New York recently, identity politics keeps people apart, it keeps people from seeing our similarities, and thus it keeps us from being able to become an effective political force.

I politely disagreed with this young woman. The acknowledgment and understanding of existing differences strengthen the likelihood of effective alliances. And having the effective possibility of separation can improve the quality of a relationship. Consider the analogy with divorce, Marriages in which divorce is illegal or virtually impossible usually suffer: The weaker partner cannot negotiate effectively when they have no practical means to leave the marriage. The possibility of divorce, even if one never takes advantage of it, can improve the quality of a relationship by ensuring that people are there because they want to be, not because they have no recourse. The right of self-determination, as the African American communist Harry Haywood argued years ago, operates in the same way. If minorities in this country have no recourse to autonomy, their conditions within the majority white society are unlikely to improve. Thus, sometimes that which might seem to pull us apart, such as the right to separate or the insistence on differences. actually works to improve the quality and strength of our connection.

Moreover, I suspect that the anxiety about separate identities is also motivated by this denigration of the particular realm vis-a-vis the universal. The philosophical idea that only the universal realm has truth and that the realm of the particular and the specific has validity or importance only to the extent that it can be subsumed within a universal theory is an idea as old as Socrates and as wrong-headed as the idealization of the Greek polis. I would agree with Kierkegaard that actually the reverse is true: Any concept of the universal only has significance and truth to the extent that it is true for some particular "me." That is, to the extent that it can relate to my own, individual, particular existence, or to someone else's. Material reality is lived in the concreteness of particular lives, particular places, moments, and struggles. Universals are at times convenient but always inaccurate abstractions from concrete reality, and the criterion of their validity must always rest with the quality of their relation with the particular.

I would even agree with Judith Butler (and Hegel) that the *ontological* status of the universal subsists entirely in its particularist manifestation. As she explains:

> what one means by 'the universal' will vary, and the cultural articulation of that term in its various modalities will work against precisely the trans-cultural status of the claim. This is not to say that there ought to be no reference to the universal or that it has become, for us, an impossibility. On the contrary. All this means is that there are cultural conditions for articulation which are not always the same, and that the term gains its meaning for us precisely through the decidedly less-than-universal cultural conditions of its articulation.
>
> (Butler 1995)

But I don't really want to get into a philosophical argument here about the universal versus the particular. My point is that the evaluation of identity politics (and of multiculturalism and "special interests") has been stymied by assumptions that an emphasis on identity will fracture the body politic, this despite the fact that the critiques of identity politics are in some respects coming from opposite directions. Liberalism's aim is to achieve universality through emphasizing commonality, while postmodernism's goal is to acknowledge difference and avoid the totalitarian effects of closure by refusing identity. However, both sides unite in rejecting the political salience of *group identity* (on this latter point see Garcia 1995: 139–142; see also Wieseltier 1994: 24–32).

This has produced an impasse between those who demand that we only make claims in terms of some universal, minimal but common notion of personhood and others of us who react to these demands with understandable insistence on the necessity of recognizing and even validating our plentiful differences. I believe that there is a way to move beyond this impasse between universality and the reactive insistence on difference as it manifests itself among progressive thinkers and activists in the United States today, and I also believe that what Latinas/os can in particular bring to this debate may be key in forging a new position.

Before I sketch this out, it will be helpful to compare the position Coco Fusco develops in her collection of essays, *English Is Broken Here*. Fusco is an artist but often writes art criticism on Latina/o art, which sometimes puts her in the uncomfortable position of presenting and translating an exotic "Otherness" for Anglo consumption. In the face of this, Fusco has endeavored to reposition herself "from being a 'minority' critic dutifully explaining Otherness to one who addresses whites as agents in an ongoing dynamic of racialization" (Fusco 1995: 68). She wants to reposition the "Latina critic and Latina artist" from the margin to the center, from the observed to the observer, and through this reveal what is observable from this location, which is a process of racial identity construction that ranges over Latina/o art but that is not produced by Latina/o artists themselves. Thus Fusco makes two apparently contradictory points: The first is that Latino artists often include references to their particular historical experiences in their works, but the second is that the racialization of Latina/o art is produced not by Latinos themselves but by white Anglo consumers of "ethnic art." Her argument is that there is a disjuncture between what one might call the self-conscious particularity of a lot of Latino art—its overt reference to cultural history and experience—and the way in which this has been taken up and interpreted in many Anglo art contexts as marking and classifying the work as "ethnic art" and thus segregating it from most European art which is simply classified as "art." The classification of Latina/o art as ethnic art is not caused by features of the art so much as it is by classification processes in the mainstream art world, but Fusco develops this argument without it relying on an ability to prove that Latina/o art is mostly trans-ethnic. Thus she has successfully resisted framing the debate over Latina/o art in terms of "universality versus difference" and suggested instead that there is a clash of what we might think of as particular universals, that is, ways of thinking about what art is.

Following this, Fusco argues that what is fundamentally at stake for Latina/o artists is not so much "artistic freedom" (i.e., the freedom to make ethnic art or political art) but "power—the power to choose, the power to determine value" and the power to "change and redefine one's identity" (Fusco 1995: 68). In other words, the problem is not that Latina/o artists produce ethnic art that then must be championed by liberal Anglos under the banner of artistic freedom, but that the very definition and characterization of their art and of what art is and can be must be opened to contestation rather than blindly based on Eurocentric interpretive traditions. Using Fusco's argument, I want to claim that the aim of Latina/o identity politics is not simply greater visibility, a goal that so stated will most likely result in increasing the commodification of Latinas/os, but rather to make visible those processes that perpetuate our marginalization and disempowerment. The ultimate struggle is thus not simply to become visible (though this is a necessary part of the goal), but to have power over the interpretive schemas that structure mainstream social practices of perception.

In some ways this formulation shares elements of a postmodernist framework in emphasizing the processes by which representation occurs rather than simply attaining political rights for an already represented group, but I want to stress here that recognizing the political nature of processes of identity construction does not preclude the articulation of group identity or its political salience. Against those who would argue that any group categories oppress the individuals subsumed within them, I would argue that group-related differences and cultural and historical traditions are necessary to make sense of individual experience, to create narratives of the self that are vital for maximal agency and autonomy (in support of this point there are useful arguments in Mohanty (1997), Code (1995), and Tietjens Meyers [1997]). Sometimes what is shared most sharply are the very differences one has from the dominant cultural/political group, and those differences will be politically important in correlation to the extent the dominant group enjoys hegemony. The issue of noticing who has the power to represent is important not simply in order to resist any and all representations but in order to participate in the formulation of less reductive, less overly homogeneous, and more complex and adequate concepts of specific group identities.

Can We Learn from Latin America?

The political legacy of universalism is related to a particular European discourse of anti-aristocratic revolutionary struggle which, at the least, we should not automatically assume without argument is applicable to every political struggle. Moreover, as so many have shown, that universalist legacy was a false universalism exclusive of many constituencies, and thus the very pretension to universality made it difficult for these constituencies to reveal the exclusivist and particularist reality that the universalist discourses concealed. As a result, we have experienced a cultural period in which it was crucial to reveal specific differences and the particularities of identity. I want to turn now to the question of how we can move beyond this impasse between universalism and the insistence on difference.

To begin with, it is instructive to note that the great Latin American revolutions and liberation movements of the nineteenth and twentieth centuries were by and large not couched in universalist terms. The figure known as "The Liberator" of Latin America, Venezuelan Simón Bolivar, originally raised the demand for political self-determination as a right based on a specific identity. Europeans had justified their colonization of Latin America on the basis of claims about the Native peoples, as well as their mestizo offspring, claims in which indigenous peoples were characterized as sub-human and uncivilized and therefore incapable and unworthy of political autonomy. European intellectuals considered Latin America a bastard culture. without coherent traditions, and thus doomed to cultural impotence. They believed that racial hybridity led to decreased fertility and diminished health, and that race-mixing would degrade the "superior" race without comparably uplifting the "inferior" race (see e.g. Mignolo 1995; Leon-Portilla 1992; Harding 1993; Young 1995; Eze 1997; Greenblatt 1993; Rabasa 1993).

In response to this, the anticolonial discourse in Latin Americans made counterclaims concerning the character of Latin American identity and the fruitfulness precisely of our heterogeny. José Carlos Mariátegui, the Peruvian Marxist, created an original vision of a new society that would be based not only on socialist principles but also on "an Indo-Hispanic cultural legacy" (see Mariátegui 1971; Schutte 1993, especially chapter two). Like Mao Zedong, Mariátegui freely transformed European-based socialist thought to a Peruvian context with its own, agrarian-based, culturally specific form of indigenous communitarianism. Jose Vasconcelos, Mexican politician and author of *The Cosmic Race*, created a vision of intercontinental liberation that would be based on a newly emerging mestizo identity, claiming mestizos as the new vanguard population that could usher in political liberation for all. And the Mexican revolution itself, arguably the most important revolution of this hemisphere, articulated its mandate in racial and ethnic identity terms, not as an alliance of peasants and workers, but an alliance of Indians and mestizos. Some of these invocations of identity, of course, involved anti-black and anti-indigenous racisms. Vasconcelos' in particular had strong elements of anti-black racism and his valorization of mestizos was made in comparative terms as against black identity. But this fact does not prove that **any** discourse of identity will be racist or that it will exclude persons who should not be excluded. Before we peremptorily reject this different tradition of political discourse, there are important lessons to be drawn from it.

First, this tradition more readily recognizes that identities are developed historically and often in connection with political discourses and political claims. Linguistic conceptualizations of identity can directly affect the material reality of people's lives, their self-understanding and social practices, and the distribution of political and economic power. Revolutions that invoked mestizo peoples as central representatives of the nation, which valorized mestizo peoples against slavish European mimicry, but also put mestizo peoples above Afro-Latin and indigenous people as more central to the nation, had material, political effects and were self-conscious political strategies. In this discursive tradition, recognizing that identities were being socially constructed and that they were operating within historical contexts to advance strategic aims did not mean that identities were viewed as simple opportunist strategies or total illusions having no purchase on lived experience. In order to be taken up and have real effect, identity discourses must resonate with at least some of the contradictory truths of everyday reality. But Latin American theorists were concerned not merely to make identities visible, but to help form and shape identities as part of a decolonizing psychological process and political movement (one of the clearest examples of this approach is in Ramos (1962); see also Fanon (1965)).

Secondly, we can note that within Latin America, the developing discourse of identity, and in particular, the discourse of mestizo identity, has been from its inception intrinsically connected to a discourse of nationalism and of the right to national sovereignty and self-determination. In the face of a European aggressor who espoused universalist rhetoric, the most effective opposing rhetoric would not be one that replicated universalist pretensions, but one that asserted rights from within a specified identity. The result was that in much of Latin America what Lyotard calls legitimation narratives, or narratives that legitimated the current political institutions that made up the state, were grounded on identity narratives. Thus, an attentiveness to the specificity of Latin American identity, as against universal abstractions like "man," were not viewed as leading to Balkanization or a breakdown of the state or the society, but precisely as necessary for the consolidation of the society and its ability and right to demand sovereignty. Thus, identity narratives were necessary conditions *before* citizenship could be practiced or even contemplated.

Third, the history of identity discourse in Latin America used against universalist discourses from Europe reveals the often-unacknowledged interdependence of identity concepts. The construction of a concept of Latin American identity did not develop in isolation, based entirely on "internal" features. It was constructed in an oppositional relationship to Spain, Portugal, and other forces of colonization. The very arguments that Vasconcelos made to champion mestizo identity were made in comparative terms, that the internal heterogeneity of the mestizo peoples was superior to the homogeneity of the Europeans and Anglo-Americans.

Interestingly, this also meant that the argument for mestizo value became dependent on a suppression or deemphasis of Anglo-European heterogeneity. After all, it was only through the experience of conquest, through the mediation of the "New World," that Europe started thinking of itself as Europe rather than a collection of warring monarchies with different languages and different cultural traditions. And of course, it was also the case that the Anglo-European self-understanding as the highest civilization depended on its reflected contrast in cultures it labeled backward and barbarian. How could Europe portray its own history of constant internal warfare, its violent enforcement of social hierarchies, and the persistence of its monarchies as the paradigm of enlightenment? Only through its claims to a comparative superiority vis-a-vis the societies in the rest of the world. In this light, Winston Churchill's often-quoted remark that democracy, though terrible, is better than any of its alternatives, can be reread as an implicit claim about the European polis that would go something like this: "Though often chaotic and violent, still thank God we are Europeans and not Africans, Asians, or Latin Americans!" Most importantly, the interdependence of identity reveals the real source of resistance to demands for Latin American rights and sovereignty: if the colonized countries can claim to be great and progressive civilizations, the status of Europe's own civilization must come into question.

Identity Discourses in the United States

Although U.S. political discourse espoused universalism, there has also existed alongside this a strategy of exclusion and discrimination based on an identity discourse of Nativism, which based economic and political rights on claims of longevity and stories of origin. Nativist claims base a concept of U.S. identity (commonly understood in North America as being "American") on long-established tenure, on being here before the Revolution, and on contributing to the formation of the culture. These are the criteria of demarcation between "real Americans" and "foreigners." On this basis, it is argued that recent Latina/o immigrants, whether legal or illegal, have less claim than others to political and economic rights. One commonly hears statements of resentment toward Latinas/os getting jobs who "don't even speak English," as Derrick Bell has his figure Jesse B. Semple put it (Bell 1992: 24). Increasingly, all Latina/os, whether U.S. citizen or not, are being subjected to searches and interrogations at the border, demands for proof of citizenship not requested from others, and in some cases refused employment (Marmon Silko 1994).

Nativist discourse targets not only those who are considered unassimilated but also those considered inassimilable. White European immigrants such as Poles and Russians may have come more recently than others, but many people in the United States view them as more readily assimilable than immigrants from the Caribbean or Central and South America. Part of the reasoning here is racial, but language and cultural differences are also considered crucial. European immigrants are far from home and less likely to retain their language after the first generation. The similarities between their cultural traditions and dominant U.S. traditions are also thought to lead to easy assimilation. Asians, on the other hand, are considered "too different," and the proximity of a Spanish-speaking homeland reduces the motivation for U.S. Latina/os to adopt English as one's primary or even unique language. This criteria—involving the ability and motivation to assimilate—explains why even Chicanos are considered beyond the pale of interpellated "Americanness." If anyone could claim "Nativism," Mexicans who live north of the U.S.-Mexico border could claim it, of course. But by the criterion of assimilability, even Chicanos are treated as non-Native; they live here in spirit only, but are not part of the U.S. cultural identity.

Nuestra America

All of these concepts (Nativism, assimilability, racism) are strategies of exclusion based on sometimes implicit, sometimes explicit invocations of an American (meaning U.S.) *identity*, which has specific, particular attributes (White, or "Native," or Europeanized). Thus, what is interesting to notice about these various anti-immigrant arguments is that they amount to an identity discourse, a narrative of the polis fully dependent on and integrated with a specific cultural character and ethnic combination (sometimes including only whiteness and sometimes extending somewhat beyond whiteness). The paradox for Newt Gingrich and William Bennett is that what makes "Western values" superior is their (supposed) transcendent universal applicability, but what makes Western values possible is, as Peter Brimelow, Allan Bloom, and Pat Buchanan candidly argue, the maintenance of racial exclusiveness and cultural hierarchies. In other words, this country is superior to all others because it promotes tolerance and freedom for all, but it can only continue to promote these if we keep European-Americans in the majority and in political and cultural dominance over all others. This point of view reveals that, despite the opening of the Declaration of Independence and the pretensions of universalism, this country (like so many others) is founded on a substantive cultural and racial conception of what a specific U.S. identity is.

If this is right, and discrimination in the United States is justified ultimately not on a claim about American universalism but a claim about American specificity, then it may seem as if only a universal discourse about human rights and individuality can be an effective counter. On this view, multiculturalism and identity politics are in the long run, regardless of the intentions of their proponents, an obstacle to the true expansion of democracy, because they highlight the ways in which some U.S. constituencies are different from the paradigm of Americanness and therefore less capable of the investments required of citizenship. Moreover, it might be argued that identity discourses exacerbate those differences by promoting the maintenance rather than the withering away of difference. On this view, rather than promoting specific identities, we should be striving to lessen the political importance of identity through universalism.

I want to suggest that it might be more fruitful to think about this in a different way. The point of noticing that identity discourses are central to U.S. political discourse is that the United States is not, therefore, so unlike Latin America as it assumes. Its dominant legitimation narratives are about cultural identity, not anonymous individuality. Moreover, I would suggest that the particular conception of U.S. identity that has been dominant (not that there is a single, internally coherent one but more like a cluster) is also in some respects more like those in Latin America than in Europe. Latin American nations were founded out of a colonial history, initially in an anticolonial revolt, as was the U.S. Latin American nations were also from the beginning conglomerations of cultural, ethnic, and racial differences, as was the United States. An honest appraisal of U.S. identity would come to realize the way in which the similarity between the United States and the rest of the hemisphere has been suppressed. The United States is not a mono-racial, essentially European nation. Less and less is it an economic superpower, and thus less and less can it afford to maintain its status as a military superpower. Rather, the United States, like Canada, Mexico, and Brazil, must worry about attracting capital, must give non-U.S. based multinationals tax breaks to lure them here, and must be wary of having more capital-rich countries like Germany and Japan take advantage of it. This lesson in humility is of course, from my point of view, all to the good.

I am not suggesting that the United States of America will quietly and happily slip into more egalitarian relations with its hemispheric neighbors and through this come to accept its own internal Latina/o populations as full political players and cultural insiders. I agree with Richard Rodriguez's claim that the so-called celebration of hispano culture going on in the United States is in actuality, as he puts it, because "America wants to eat Mexico." But I do believe that the economic decline could motivate some moves in this direction, and that toward promoting this it is in our interest to encourage a new debate over U.S. identity, what it consists of, and what it means.

Given the similarities that actually exist throughout this hemisphere, and given the implicit identity narratives already at play in the United States, my suggestion, in short, is that rather than attempting to salvage an anonymous universalism, we need a new debate over the terms and constitution of a substantive U.S. cultural identity. What is needed is a national debate over the *specificity* of U.S. identity, one that will be able to explicitly address covert claims to Nativism and assimilability as well as racism. Such a project does not require us to de-emphasize identity and difference but to formulate a heterogeneous and inclusive cultural identity that incorporates our specific ethnic traditions. The choice is not between Latina/o identity versus a generic Americanness with no substantive content other than political platitudes, but rather to understand how we can choose both Latina/o identity and a larger substantive identity for all who live in the United States. To be an "American," or, as I would prefer, an *estadounidense*, is to be located in a country with a specific history, a history of paradoxical political valence and continuous negotiations between diverse cultural practices and values, a country that was capable of producing but incapable of embracing a James Baldwin, a country in which a world-inspiring movement for civil rights was both made necessary and made possible. To be an estadounidense is to be a person whose tastes in food, clothing, favorite slang words, and preferred music has been profoundly affected by Latino, European and African, Asian and indigenous traditions, even when we are unaware of the influence. I don't have the time or space here to provide more conjecture on what a newly configured American identity might contain, but it seems clear that its racial associations, historical teleologies, and global allegiances need to be radically transformed.

In the United States today, 73.6 percent of Latina/os identify as Latina/o first, American second (*Harper's Magazine* 1996: 60). Strengthening our participation in U.S. political culture does not require changing this identification. However, it does require a revised understanding of how Latinas/os relate to an "American" identity. We who are Latina/os need to begin to think of ourselves—and understand ourselves—as cultural insiders rather than cultural outsiders, as longstanding contributors to the essence of "Americanness," and as full players in formulating a new national consciousness rather than restricted to defending our embattled communities.

Thus, what I am suggesting is that Latina/o identity politics should be raised to the national level and understood as central to an ongoing discourse over national identity. It is a mistake to assume that Latina/o identity politics is sequestered to the realm of the particular. By suggesting it move to the national realm, I am not suggesting it aspire to universalism, but that it can contribute to the development of a new *concrete* (and thus particular formulation of the) universal. Such a concept does not simply side with difference against universality or vice versa, but attempts a reconfiguration.

As Baldwin argued many years ago, the struggle for citizenship requires teaching minority children to feel an ownership toward this country, a sense, not that they belong to it, but that it, in all its beauty and terror, belongs to them (Baldwin 1988). This will prove to be, perhaps, the most powerful resistance strategy of all. Ann Laura Stoler has explored such a resistance strategy that was used against French and Dutch colonial powers by women in Indochina, Madagascar, and the Indies in the late nineteenth century, in which

> children of "mixed-blood" or even of "purely native origin" were acknowledged by European men who were supposedly not their natural fathers. These claims to paternity, in which a European man of modest or impoverished means would allegedly be paid a fee by a native woman to recognize her child, could redefine who "by descent" was

European and who was not. . . . [Thus] these were racial reorderings outside the state's control.

(Stoler 1995: 48–9; see also Stoler 1992)

Colonial authorities were very threatened by what they called these "fraudulent recognitions," worrying that they would be "submerged by a flood of naturalized natives" by this introduction into their midst of a "questionable population" (Abor 1917: 41, cited in Stoler 1995: 49). My suggestion is that a similar effect of resistance may be produced when there is a cultural appropriation of "American" identity by young Puertorriquenos in New York. They are claiming rights to a patrimony most consider beyond their reach. Perhaps they will help us to refashion an American identity beyond no one's reach.[3]

References

Abor, R. (1917) *Des Reconnaissance Frauduleuses d'Enfants Naturels en Indo-chine*, Hanoi: Imprimerie Tonkinoise.
Baldwin, J. (1988) "A Talk to Teachers," in R. Simonson and S. Walker (eds.), *The Graywolf Annual Five: Multicultural Literacy*, 3–12, Saint Paul, MN: Graywolf Press.
Bell, D. (1992) *Faces at the Bottom of the Well: The Permanence of Racism*, New York: Basic Books.
Butler, J. (1995) "For a Careful Reading," in S. Benhabib et al. (eds.), *Feminist Contentions*, New York: Routledge.
Code, L. (1995) *Rhetorical Spaces: Essays on Gendered locations*, New York: Routledge.
Eze, E. (ed.) (1997) *Race and the Enlightenment*, Cambridge, MA: Blackwell.
Fanon, F. (1965) *Black Skin/White Masks*, C. Lam Markman (trans.), New York: Grove Press.
Flores, J., and Yudice, G. (1990) "Living Borders/Buscando America: Languages of Latino Self-Formation," *Social Text* 24 (1990): 57–84.
Fraser, N., and Nicholson, L. (1990) "Social Criticism without Philosophy: An Encounter between Feminism and Postmodernism," in L. Nicholson (ed.), *Feminism/Postmodernism*, 19–38, New York: Routledge.
Fusco, C. (1995) *English is Broken Here: Notes on Cultural Fusion in the Americas*, New York: The New Press.
Garcia, J. L. A. (1995) "Affirmative Action and Hispanic Americans," *APA Proceedings* 68 (5): 139–142.
Gitlin, T. (1992) "On the Virtues of a Loose Cannon," in P. Aufderheide (ed.), *Beyond PC: Towards a Politics of Understanding*, 188, Saint Paul, MN: Graywolf Press.
Gitlin, T. (1995) *The Twilight of Common Dreams: Why America is Wracked by Culture Wars*, New York: Henry Holt and Co.
Gómez-Peña, G. (1988) "Documented/Undocumented," in R. Simonson and S. Walker (eds.), *The Graywolf Annual Five: Multicultural Literacy*, 133, Saint Paul, MN: Graywolf Press.
Greenblatt, S. (ed.). (1993) *New World Encounters*, Berkeley: University of California Press.
Harding, S. (ed.). (1993) *The "Racial" Economy of Science*, Bloomington, IN: Indiana University Press.
Leon-Portilla, M. (ed.). (1992) *The Broken Spears: The Aztec Account of the Conquest of Mexico*, Boston: Beacon Press.
Mariaregui, J. C. (1971) *Seven Interpretative Essays on Peruvian Reality*, M. Urguidi (trans.), Austin, TX: University of Texas Press.
Marmon Silko, L. (1994) "Fences Against Freedom," *Hungry Mind Review* 31: 9–59.
Mignolo, W. (1995) *The Darker Side of the Renaissance: Literacy. Territoriality, and Colonization*, Ann Arbor, MI: University of Michigan Press.
Mohanty, S. (1997) *Literary Theory and the Claims of History: Postmodernism, Objectivity, Multicultural Politics*, Ithaca, NY: Cornell University Press.
Oboler, S. (1995) *Ethnic: Labels, Latino Lives: Identity and the Politics of (Re)Presentation in the United States*, Minneapolis: University of Minnesota Press.
"Our Next Race Question," *Harper's Magazine* (1996) April, 55–60.

Peller, G. (1995) "Race Consciousness," in D. Danielson and K. Engle (eds.), *After Identity: A Reader in Law and Culture*, 74, New York: Routledge.

Rabasa, J. (1993) *Inventing A-M-E-R-1-C-A: Spanish Historiography and the Formation of Eurocentrism*, Norman, OK: University of Oklahoma Press.

Ramos, S. (1962) *Profile of Man and Culture in Mexico*, P. G. Earle (trans.), Austin. TX: University of Texas Press.

Schutte, O. (1993) *Cultural Identity and Social liberation in Latin American Thought*, Albany, NY: SUNY Press.

Stoler, A. L. (1992) "Sexual Affronts and Racial Frontiers: European Identities and the Cultural Politics of Exclusion in Colonial Southeast Asia," *Comparative Studies in Society and History* 34 (2): 514–551.

Stoler, A. L. (1995) *Race and the Education of Desire: Foucault's History of Sexuality and the Colonial Order of Things*, Durham, NC: Duke University Press.

Strickland, S. (1994) "Feminism, Postmodernism, and Difference," in K. Lennon and M. Whitford (eds.), *Knowing the Difference: Feminist Perspectives in Epistemology*, 265–274, London: Routledge.

Tietjens Meyers, D. (1997) *Feminists Rethink the Seif*, Boulder, CO: Westview Press.

Wieseltier, L. (1994) "Against Identity," *New Republic* 28: 24–32.

Young, R. (1995) *Colonial Desire: Hybridity in Theory, Culture, and Race*, New York: Routledge.

Notes

1 See also Gitlin's (1995) full-scale attack on identity politics.
2 I recognize that this term tends to simplify and homogenize a very complex field of texts. All of what goes by the name "postmodernism" will not be subject to the descriptions I give in what follows. Nonetheless, it remains a useful shorthand.
3 I would like to thank the following people for extremely helpful comments and criticisms of an earlier draft of this paper: Paula Moya, Arlene Davila, Karin Rosemblatt, Eduardo Mendieta, and Caroline Tauxe.

Reading Questions

1. What does Alcoff mean by "identity politics"?
2. What are the reasons why some people reject identity politics?
3. According to Alcoff, what's the dominant narrative about the nature of U.S. identity? Has this changed since she wrote the essay?
4. Alcoff's argues that the possibility of separate identities strengthens the relationships between social groups within a country. What's her argument? Could there be cases where separate identities undermine the relationships between social groups?
5. Alcoff claims that the aim of Latina/o identity politics is "to make visible those processes that perpetuate our marginalization and disempowerment" and to "have power over the interpretive schemas that structure mainstream social practices of perception." What would it take to achieve that? Does it matter for Latina/o identity politics if those goals are difficult to achieve?
6. Why does Alcoff think that identity narratives are "necessary conditions *before* citizenship [can] be practiced or even contemplated"? Do you agree? Why or why not?
7. Alcoff concludes with the idea that Latina/os should assert a U.S. American identity, and that doing so might change that identity. What's her argument? Is there contemporary evidence that supports or undermines the claim that Latina/os asserting a U.S. American identity will change that identity?

12 Playfulness, "World"-Traveling, and Loving Perception

María Lugones

This chapter weaves two aspects of life together. My coming to consciousness as a daughter and my coming to consciousness as a woman of color have made this weaving possible. This weaving reveals the possibility and complexity of a pluralistic feminism, a feminism that affirms the plurality in each of us and among us as richness and as central to feminist ontology and epistemology.

The chapter describes the experience of "outsiders" to the mainstream of, for example, white/Anglo organization of life in the United States and stresses a particular feature of the out sider's existence: the outsider has necessarily acquired flexibility in shifting from the mainstream construction of life where she is constructed as an outsider to other constructions of life where she is more or less "at home." This flexibility is necessary for the outsider. It is required by the logic of oppression. But it can also be exercised resistantly by the outsider or by those who are at ease in the mainstream. I recommend this resistant exercise that I call "world"-traveling and I also recommend that the exercise be animated by an attitude that I describe as playful.

As outsiders to the mainstream, women of color in the United States practice "world"-traveling, mostly out of necessity. I affirm this practice as a skillful, creative, rich, enriching, and, given certain circumstances, loving way of being and living. I recognize that much of our traveling is done unwillingly to "worlds" and the compulsory nature of the "traveling" have obscured for us the enormous value of this aspect of our living and its connection to loving. Racism has a vested interest in obscuring and devaluing the complex skills involved in it. I recommend that we affirm this traveling across "worlds" as partly constitutive of cross-cultural and cross-racial loving. Thus, I recommend to women of color in the United States that we learn to love each other by learning to travel to each other's "worlds." In making this recommendation, I have in mind giving a new meaning to coalition and propose "Women of Color" as a term for a coalition of deep understanding fashioned through "world"-traveling.

According to Marilyn Frye, to perceive arrogantly is to perceive that others are for oneself and to proceed to arrogate their substance to oneself (Frye 1983: 66). Here, I make a connection between "arrogant perception" and the failure to identify with persons that one views arrogantly or has come to see as the products of arrogant perception. A further connection is made between this failure of identification and a failure of love, and thus between loving and identifying with another person. The sense of love is not the one Frye has identified as both consistent with arrogant perception and as promoting unconditional servitude. "We can be taken in by this equation of servitude with love," Frye says, "because we make two mistakes at once: we think of both servitude and love that they are selfless or unselfish" (Frye 1983: 73). The identification of which I speak is constituted by what

I come to characterize as playful "world"-traveling. To the extent that we learn to perceive others arrogantly or come to see them only as products of arrogant perception and continue to perceive them that way, we fail to identify with them—fail to love them—in this particular way.

Identification and Love

As a child, I was taught to perceive arrogantly. I have also been the object of arrogant perception. Though I am not a white/Anglo woman, it is clear to me that I can understand both my childhood training as an arrogant perceiver and my having been the object of arrogant perception without any reference to white/Anglo men. This gives some indication that the concept of arrogant perception can be used cross-culturally and that white/Anglo men are not the only arrogant perceivers.

I was brought up in Argentina watching men and women of moderate and of considerable means graft the substance of their servants to themselves. I also learned to graft my mother's substance to my own. It was clear to me that both men and women were the victims of arrogant perception and that arrogant perception was systematically organized to break the spirit of all women and of most men. I valued my rural gaucho ancestry because its ethos has always been one of independence, courage, and self-reliance in the midst of poverty and enormous loneliness. I found inspiration in this ethos and committed myself never to be broken by arrogant perception. I can say all of this in this way only because of what I have learned from Frye's "In and Out of Harm's Way: Arrogance and Love" (1983). She has given me a way of understanding and articulating something important in my own life.

Frye is not particularly concerned with women as arrogant perceivers but as the objects of arrogant perception. Her concern is, in part, to enhance our understanding of women "un touched by phallocratic machinations" (Frye 1983: 53), by understanding the harm done to women through such machinations. In this case, she proposes that we could understand women untouched by arrogant perception through an understanding of what arrogant perception does to women. Frye also proposes an understanding of what it is to love women that is inspired by a vision of women unharmed by arrogant perception. To love women is, at least in part, to perceive them with loving eyes. "The loving eye is a contrary of the arrogant eye" (Frye 1983: 75).

I am concerned with women as arrogant perceivers because I want to explore further what it is to love women. I want to begin by exploring two failures of love: my failure to love my mother and white/Anglo women's failure to love women across racial and cultural boundaries in the United States. As a consequence of exploring these failures I will offer a loving solution to them. My solution modifies Frye's account of loving perception by adding what I call playful "world"-travel. Then I want to take up the practice as a horizontal practice of resistance to two related injunctions: the injunction for the oppressed to have our gazes fixed on the oppressor, and the concomitant injunction not to look to and connect with each other in resistance to those injunctions through traveling to each other's "worlds" of sense. Thus, the first move is one that explores top down failures of love and their logic; the second move explores horizontal failures.

It is clear to me, that at least in the United States and Argentina, women are taught to perceive many other women arrogantly. Being taught to perceive arrogantly is part of being taught to be a woman of a certain class in both the United States and Argentina; it is part of being taught to be a white/Anglo woman in the United States; and it is part of being taught to be a woman in both places: to be both the agent and the object of arrogant perception. My love for my mother seemed to me thoroughly imperfect as I was growing up because I was unwilling to become what I had been taught to see my mother as being. I thought that to love her was consistent with my abusing her: using, taking her for granted and demanding her services in a far-reaching way that, since four other people engaged in the same grafting of her substance onto themselves, left her little of herself to herself. I also thought that loving her was to be in part constituted by my identifying with her, my seeing myself in her. Thus, to love her was supposed to be of a piece with both my abusing her and with my being open to being abused. It is clear to me that I was not supposed to love servants: I could abuse them without identifying with them, without seeing myself in them.

When I came to the United States I learned that part of racism is the internalization of the propriety of abuse without identification. I learned that I could be seen as a being to be used by white/Anglo men and women without the possibility of identification (i.e., without their act of attempting to graft my substance onto theirs rubbing off on them at all). They could remain untouched, without any sense of loss.

So, women who are perceived arrogantly can, in turn, perceive other women arrogantly. To what extent those women are responsible for their arrogant perceptions of other women is certainly open to question, but I do not have any doubt that many of them have been taught to abuse women in this particular way. I am not interested in assigning responsibility. I am interested in understanding the phenomenon so as to understand a loving way out of it. I am offering a way of taking responsibility, of exercising oneself as not doomed to oppress others.

There is something obviously wrong with the love that I was taught and something right with my failure to love my mother in this way. But I do not think that what is wrong is my profound desire to identify with her, to see myself in her; what is wrong is that I was taught to identify with a victim of servitude. What is wrong is that I was taught to practice servitude of my mother and to learn to become a servant through this practice. There is something obviously wrong with my having been taught that love is consistent with abuse, consistent with arrogant perception.

Notice that the love I was taught is the love that Frye (1983: 73) speaks of when she says "We can be taken in by this equation of servitude with love." Even though I could both abuse and love my mother, I was not supposed to love servants. This is because in the case of servants one is supposed to be clear about their servitude and the "equation of servitude with love" is never to be thought clearly in those terms. So, I was not supposed to love and could not love servants. But I could love my mother because deception (in particular, self-deception) is part of this "loving."

In the equation of love with servitude, servitude is called abnegation and abnegation is not analyzed any further. Abnegation is not instilled in us through an analysis of its nature but rather through a heralding of it as beautiful and noble. We are coaxed, seduced into abnegation not through analysis but through emotive persuasion. Frye makes the connection between deception and this sense of loving clear. When I say that there is something obviously wrong with the loving that I was taught, I do not mean to say that the connection between this loving and abuse is obvious. Rather, I mean that once the connection between this loving and abuse has been unveiled, there is something obviously wrong with the loving given that it is obvious that it is wrong to abuse others.

I am glad that I did not learn my lessons well, but it is clear that part of the mechanism that permitted my not learning well involved a separation from my mother: I saw us as beings of quite a different sort. It involved abandoning my mother even while I longed not to abandon her. I wanted to love my mother, though, given what I was taught, "love" could not be the right word for what I longed for. I was disturbed by my not wanting to be what she was. I had a sense of not being quite integrated, myself was missing because I could not identify with her, I could not see myself in her, I could not welcome her "world." I saw myself as separate from her, a different sort of being, not quite of the same species. This separation, this lack of love, I saw, and I think that I saw correctly, as a lack in myself (not a fault, but a lack). I also see that if this was a lack of love, love cannot be what I was taught. It has to be rethought, made anew.

There is something in common between the relation between me and my mother as someone I did not used to be able to love and the relation between women of color in the United States like me and white/Angla women: there is a failure of love. As I eluded identification with my mother, white/Angla women elude identification with women of color, identifications with beings whose substance they arrogate without a sense of loss. Frye helped me understand one of the aspects of this failure—the directly abusive aspect. But I also think that there is a complex failure of love in the failure to identify with another woman, the failure to see oneself in other women who are quite different from oneself. I want to begin to analyze this complex failure.

Notice that Frye's emphasis on independence in her analysis of loving perception is not particularly helpful in explaining these failures. She says that in loving perception, "the object of the seeing is another being whose existence and character are logically independent of the seer and who may be practically or empirically independent in any particular respect at any particular time" (Frye 1983: 77). But this does not help me understand how my failure of love toward my mother (when I ceased to be her parasite) left me not quite whole. It is not helpful since I saw her as logically independent from me. And it also does not help me understand why the racist or ethnocentric failure of love of white/Angla women—in particular of those white/Angla women who are not pained by their failure—should leave me not quite substantive among them.

I am not particularly interested here in cases of white women's parasitism onto women of color but more pointedly in cases where the relation is characterized by failure of identification. I am interested here in those many cases in which white/Angla women do one or more of the following to women of color: they ignore us, ostracize us, render us invisible, stereotype us, leave us completely alone, interpret us as crazy. All of this *while we are in their midst*. The more independent I am, the more independent I am left to be. Their "world" and their integrity do not require me at all. There is no sense of self-loss in them for my own lack of solidity. But they rob me of my solidity through indifference, an indifference they can afford and that seems sometimes studied. But many of us have to work among white/Anglo folk and our best shot at recognition has seemed to be among white/Angla women because many of them have expressed a *general* sense of being pained at their failure of love.

Many times white/Angla women want us out of their field of vision. Their lack of concern is a harmful failure of love that leaves me independent from them in a way similar to the way in which, once I ceased to be my mother's parasite, she became, though not independent from all others, certainly independent from me. But, of course, because my mother and I wanted to love each other well, we were not whole in this independence. White/Angla women are independent from me, I am independent from them; I am independent from my mother, she is independent from me; and none of us loves each other in this independence. I am incomplete and unreal without other women. I am profoundly dependent on others without having to be their subordinate, their slave, their servant.

Identification and Women of Color

The relations among "Women of Color" can neither be homogenized nor merely wished into being as relations of solidarity. To the extent that Women of Color names a coalition, it is a coalition in formation against significant and complex odds that, though familiar, keep standing in our way. The coalition or interconnecting coalitions need to be conceptualized against the grain of these odds. To a significant extent that is the point of this book. Audre Lorde is attentive to the problem of homogenization in coalition formation when she tells us to explore our relations in terms of "non-dominant differences." This epistemological shift to non-dominant differences is crucial to our possibilities. To the extent that we are "created different" by the logic of domination, the techniques of producing difference include divide and conquer, segregation, fragmentation, instilling mistrust toward each other for having been pitted against each other by economies of domination, instilling in us the distinction between the real and the fake. Here I will not address each one of these techniques of keeping us focused on dominant differences among each other, that is differences concocted by the dominant imagination.[1] Rather, I will emphasize the epistemological shift to nondominant differences.

To the extent that in resistance to oppressions, both men and women have historically fashioned resistant "communities," resistant socialities that have made meanings that have enabled us to endure as resistant subjects in the oppressing <=> resisting relation, we have created alternate historical lines that are in connection with each other—they do not exist in isolation—lines that we do not understand, as nothing requires that we understand the spatio-temporal differences among us. Systems of domination construct women of color as subordinate, inferior, servile. We can see each other enacting these dominant constructions, even when we do it against our own desire, will, and energy. We can see and understand these animations of the dominant imaginary, but we are not sufficiently familiar with each other's "worlds" of resistance to either cross, or travel to them, nor to avoid what keeps us from seeing the need to travel, the enriching of our possibilities through "world"-travel.

There is an important sense in which we do not understand each other as interdependent and we do not identify with each other since we lack insight into each other's resistant understandings. To put the point sharply, the resistant understandings do not travel through social fragmentation. Separatism in communities where our substance is seen and celebrated, where we become substantive through this celebration, combines with social fragmentation to keep our lines of resistance away from each other. Thus, it is difficult for women of color to see, know each other, as resistant rather than as constructed by domination. To the extent that we face each other as oppressed, we do not want to identify with each other, we repel each other as we are seeing each other in the same mirror.[2] As resistant, we are kept apart by social fragmentation. To identify with each other, we need to engage in resistant practices that appear dangerous. We have not realized the potential lying in our becoming interdependently resistant. As resistant, we appear independent from each other to each other. The coalition sense of "Women of Color" necessitates this identification that comes from seeing ourselves and each other interrelating "worlds" of resistant meaning. To the extent that identification requires sameness, this coalition is impossible. So, the coalition requires that we conceive identification anew. The independence of women of color from each other performed by social fragmentation leaves us unwittingly colluding with the logic of oppression.

"Worlds" and "World"-Traveling

Frye (1983: 75) says that the loving eye is "the eye of one who knows that to know the seen, one must consult something other than one's own will and interests and fears and imagination." This is much more helpful to me so long as I do not understand her to mean that I should not consult my own interests nor that I should exclude the possibility that my self and the self of the one I love may be importantly tied to each other in many complicated ways. Since I am emphasizing here that the failure of love lies in part in the failure to identify, and since I agree with Frye that one "must consult something other than one's own will and interests and fears and imagination," I will explain what I think needs to be consulted. It was not possible for me to love my mother while I retained a sense that it was fine for me and others to see her arrogantly. Loving my mother also required that I see with her eyes, that I go into my mother's "world," that I see both of us as we are constructed in her "world," that I witness her own sense of herself from within her "world." Only through this traveling to her "world" could I identify with her because only then could I cease to ignore her and to be excluded and separate from her. Only then could I see her as a subject, even if one subjected, and only then could I see at all how meaning could arise fully between us. We are fully dependent on each other for the possibility of being understood and without this understanding we are not intelligible, we do not make sense, we are not solid, visible, integrated; we are lacking. So traveling to each other's "worlds" would enable us to *be* through loving each other.

I hope the sense of identification I have in mind is becoming clear. But to become clearer, I need to explain what I mean by a "world" and by "traveling" to another "world." In explaining what I mean by a "world," I will not appeal to traveling to other women's "worlds." Instead, I will lead you to see what I mean by a "world" the way I came to propose the concept to myself: through the kind of ontological confusion about myself that we, women of color, refer to half-jokingly as "schizophrenia" (we feel schizophrenic in our goings back and forth between different "communities") and through my effort to make some sense of this ontological confusion.

Some time ago, I came to be in a state of profound confusion as I experienced myself as both having and not having a particular attribute. I was sure I had the attribute in question and, on the other hand, I was sure that I did not have it. I remain convinced that I both have and do not have this attribute. The attribute is playfulness. I am sure that I am a playful person. On the other hand, I can say, painfully, that I am not a playful person. I am not a playful person in certain "worlds." One of the things I did as I became confused was to call my friends, faraway people who knew me well, to see whether or not I was playful. Maybe they could help me out of my confusion. They said to me, "Of course you are playful," and they said it with the same conviction that I had about it. Of course I am playful. Those people who were around me said to me, "No, you are not playful. You are a serious woman. You just take everything seriously."[3] They were just as sure about what they said to me and could offer me every bit of evidence that one could need to conclude that they were right. So I said to myself, "Okay, maybe what's happening here is that there is an attribute that I do have but there are certain 'worlds' in which I am not at ease, and it is because I'm not at ease in those 'worlds' that I don't have that attribute in those 'worlds.' But what does that mean?" I was worried both about what I meant by "worlds" when I said "in some 'worlds' I do not have the attribute" and what I meant by saying that lack of ease was what led me not to be playful in those "worlds." Because, you see, if it was just a matter of lack of ease, I could work on it.

I can explain some of what I mean by a "world." I do not want the fixity of a definition at this point, because I think the term is suggestive and I do not want to close the suggestiveness of it too soon. I can offer some characteristics that serve to distinguish between a "world," a utopia, a possible "world" in the philosophical sense, and a "world" view. By a "world" I do not mean a utopia at all. A utopia does not count as a "world," in my sense. The "worlds" that I am talking about are possible. But a possible "world" is not what I mean by a "world" and I do not mean a "world"-view, though something like a "world"-view is involved here.

For something to be a "world" in my sense, it has to be inhabited at present by some flesh and blood people. That is why it cannot be a utopia. It may also be inhabited by some imaginary people. It may be inhabited by people who are dead or people that the inhabitants of this "world" met in some other "world" and now have in this "world" in imagination.

A "world" in my sense may be an actual society, given its dominant culture's description and construction of life, including a construction of the relationships of production, of gender, race, etc. But a "world" can also be such a society given a nondominant, a resistant construction, or it can be such a society or a society given an idiosyncratic construction. As we will see, it is problematic to say that these are all constructions of the same society. But they are different "worlds." A "world" need not be a construction of a whole society. It may be a construction of a tiny portion of a particular society. It may be inhabited by just a few people. Some "worlds" are bigger than others.

A "world" may be incomplete. Things in it may not be altogether constructed or some things may be constructed negatively (they are not what "they" are in some other "world"). Or the "world" may be incomplete because it may have references to things that do not quite exist in it, references to things like Brazil, where Brazil is not quite part of that "world." Given lesbian feminism, the construction of "lesbian" is purposefully and healthily still up in the air, in the process of becoming. What it is to be a Hispanic in this country is, in a dominant Anglo construction, purposefully incomplete. Thus, one cannot really answer questions like "What is a Hispanic?" "Who counts as a Hispanic?" "Are Latinos, Chicanos, Hispanos, black Dominicans, white Cubans, Korean Colombians, Italian Argentinians, Hispanic?" What it is to be a "Hispanic" in the varied so-called Hispanic communities in the United States is also yet up in the air. "We"[4] have not yet decided whether there is something like a Hispanic in our varied "worlds." So, a "world" may be an incomplete visionary nonutopian construction of life, or it may be a traditional construction of life. A traditional Hispano construction of northern New Mexican life is a "world." Such a traditional construction, in the face of a racist, ethnocentric, money-centered Anglo construction of northern New Mexican life, is highly unstable because Anglos have the means for imperialist destruction of traditional Hispano "worlds."

In a "world," some of the inhabitants may not understand or hold the particular construction of them that constructs them in that "world." So, there may be "worlds" that con struct me in ways that I do not even understand. Or, it may be that I understand the construction, but do not hold it of myself. I may not accept it as an account of myself, a construction of myself. And yet, I may be *animating* such a construction.[5]

One can travel between these "worlds" and one can inhabit more than one of these "worlds" at the same time. I think that most of us who are outside the mainstream of, for example, the United States dominant construction or organization of life are "world" travelers as a matter of necessity and of survival. It seems to me that inhabiting more than one "world" at the same time and traveling between "worlds" is part and parcel of our experience and our situation. One can be at the same time in a "world" that constructs one as stereotypically Latina, for example, and in a "world" that constructs one as simply Latina. Being stereotypically Latina and being simply Latina are different simultaneous constructions of persons who are part of different "worlds." One animates one or the other or both at the same time without necessarily confusing them, though simultaneous enactment can be confusing if one is not on one's guard.

In describing my sense of a "world," I am offering a description of experience, something that is true to experience even if it is ontologically problematic. Though I would think that any account of identity that could not be true to this experience of outsiders to the mainstream would be faulty, even if ontologically unproblematic. Its ease would constrain, erase, or deem aberrant experience that has within it significant insights into non-imperialistic understanding between people.

Those of us who are "world"-travelers have the distinct experience of being different in different "worlds" and of having the capacity to remember other "worlds" and ourselves in them. We can say "That is me there, and I am happy in that 'world.'" So, the experience is of being a different person in different "worlds" and yet of having memory of oneself as different without quite having the sense of there being any underlying "I." When I can say "that is me there and I am so playful in that 'world,'" I am saying "That is *me* in that 'world'" not because I recognize myself in that person; rather, the first-person statement is noninferential. I may well recognize that that person has abilities I do not have and yet the having or not having of the abilities is always an "I have" and "I do not have" . . . (i.e., it is always experienced in the first person).

The shift from being one person to being a different person is what I call traveling. This shift may not be willful or even conscious, and one may be completely unaware of being different in a different "world," and may not recognize that one is in a different "world." Even though the shift can be done willfully, it is not a matter of acting. One does not pose as someone else; one does not pretend to be, for example, someone of a different personality or character or someone who uses space or language differently from the other person. Rather, one is someone who has that personality or character or uses space and language in that particular way. The "one" here does not refer to some underlying "I." One does not *experience* any underlying I.

Being at Ease in a "World"

In investigating what I mean by "being at ease in a 'world,'" I will describe different ways of being at ease. One may be at ease in one or in all of these ways. There is a maximal way of being at ease, viz., being at ease in all of these ways. I take this maximal way of being at ease to be somewhat dangerous because it tends to produce people who have no inclination to travel across "worlds" or no experience of "world"-traveling.

The first way of being at ease in a particular "world" is by being a fluent speaker in that "world." I know all the norms that there are to be followed. I know all the words that there are to be spoken. I know all the moves. I am confident.

Another way of being at ease is by being normatively happy. I agree with all the norms, I could not love any norms better. I am asked to do just what I want to do or what I think I should do. I am at ease.

Another way of being at ease in a "world" is by being humanly bonded. I am with those I love and they love me, too. It should be noticed that I may be with those I love and be at ease because of them in a "world" that is otherwise as hostile to me as "worlds" get.

Finally, one may be at ease because one has a history with others that is shared, especially daily history, the kind of shared history that one sees exemplified by the response to the "Do you remember poodle skirts?" question. There you are, with people you do not know at all and who do not know each other. The question is posed and then everyone begins talking about their poodle skirt stories. I have been in such situations without knowing what poodle skirts, for example, were, and I felt ill at ease because it was not *my* history. The other people did not know each other. It is not that they were humanly bonded. Probably they did not have much politically in common either. But poodle skirts were in their shared history.

One may be at ease in one of these ways or in all of them. Notice that when one says meaningfully "This is my 'world,'" one may not be at ease in it. Or one may be at ease in it only in some of these respects and not in others. To say of some "world" that it is "*my* world" is to make an evaluation. One may privilege one or more "worlds" in this way for a variety of reasons: for example, because one experiences oneself as an agent in a fuller sense than one experiences oneself in other "worlds." One may disown a "world" because one has firstperson memories of a person who is so thoroughly dominated that she has no sense of exercising her own will or has a sense of having serious difficulties in performing actions that are willed by herself and no difficulty in performing actions willed by others. One may say of a "world" that it is "my world" because one is at ease in it (i.e., being at ease in a "world" may be the basis for the evaluation).

Given the clarification of what I mean by a "world," "world"-travel, and being at ease in a "world," we are in a position to return to my problematic attribute, playfulness. It may be that in this "world" in which I am so unplayful, I am a different person than in the "world" in which I am playful. Or it may be that the "world" in which I am unplayful is constructed in such a way that I could be playful in it. I could practice, even though that "world" is constructed in such a way that my being playful in it is kind of hard. In describing what I take a "world" to be, I emphasized the first possibility as both the one that is truest to the experience of "outsiders" to the mainstream and as ontologically problematic because the "I" is identified in some sense as one and in some sense as a plurality. I identify myself as myself through memory and I retain myself as different in memory. When I travel from one "world" to another, I have this image, this memory of myself as playful in this other "world." I can then be in a particular "world" and have a double image of myself as, for example, playful and as not playful. This is a very familiar and recognizable phenomenon to the outsider to the mainstream in some central cases: when in one "world" I animate, for example, that "world"'s caricature of the person I am in the other "world." I can have both images of myself, and, to the extent that I can materialize or animate both images at the same time, I become an ambiguous being. This is very much a part of trickery and foolery. It is worth remembering that the trickster and the fool are significant characters in many nondominant or outsider cultures. One then sees any particular "world" with these double edges and sees absurdity in them and so inhabits oneself differently.

Given that Latinas are constructed in Anglo "worlds" as stereotypically intense—intensity being a central characteristic of at least one of the Anglo stereotypes of Latinas—and given that many Latinas, myself included, are genuinely intense, I can say to myself "I am intense" and take a hold of the double meaning. Furthermore, I can be stereotypically intense or be the real thing, and, if you are Anglo, you do not know when I am which *because* I am Latin American. As a Latin American I am an ambiguous being, a two-imaged self: I can see that gringos see me as stereotypically intense because I am, as a Latin American, constructed that way but I may or may not *intentionally* animate the stereotype or the real thing knowing that you may not see it in anything other than in the stereotypical construction. This ambiguity is funny and not just funny; it is survival-rich. We can also make the picture of those who dominate us funny precisely because we can see the double edge, we can see them doubly constructed, we can see the plurality in them. So we know truths that only the fool can speak and only the trickster can play out without harm. We inhabit "worlds" and travel across them and keep all the memories.

Sometimes, the "world"-traveler has a double image of herself and each self includes as important ingredients of itself one or more attributes that are *incompatible* with one or more of the attributes of the other self: for example being playful and being unplayful. To the extent that the attribute is an important ingredient of the self she is in that "world" (i.e., to the extent that there is a particularly good fit between that "world" and her having that attribute in it, and to the extent that the attribute is personality or character central, that "world," would have to be changed if she is to be playful in it). It is not the case that if she could come to be at ease in it, she would be her own playful self. Because the attribute is personality or character central and there is such a good fit between that "world" and her being constructed with that attribute as central, *she* cannot become playful, she is unplayful. To become playful would be, for her, to become a contradictory being.

I suggest, then, that my problematic case, the being and not being playful, cannot be solved through lack of ease. I suggest that I can understand my confusion about whether I am or am not playful by saying that I am both and that I am different persons in different "worlds" and can remember myself in both as I am in the other. I am a plurality of selves. This explains my confusion because *it is to come to see it as of a piece* with much of the rest of my experience as an outsider in some of the "worlds" that I inhabit and of a piece with significant aspects of the experience of nondominant people in the "worlds" of their dominators.

So, though I may not be at ease in the "worlds" in which I am not constructed playful, it is not that I am not playful *because* I am not at ease. The two are compatible. But lack of playfulness is not caused by lack of ease. Lack of playfulness is not symptomatic of lack of ease but of lack of health. I am not a healthy being in the "worlds" that construct me unplayful.

Playfulness

I had a very personal stake in investigating this topic. Playfulness is not only the attribute that was the source of my confusion and the attitude that I recommend as the loving attitude in traveling across "worlds." I am also scared of ending up as a serious human being, someone with no multidimensionality, with no fun in life, someone who is just someone who has had the fun constructed out of her. I am seriously scared of getting stuck in a "world" that constructs me that way, a "world" that I have no escape from and in which I cannot be playful.

I thought about what it is to be playful and what it is to play and I did this thinking in a "world" in which I only remember myself as playful and in which all of those who know me as playful are imaginary beings. It is a "world" in which I am scared of losing my memories of myself as playful or have them erased from me. Because I live in such a "world," after I formulated my own sense of what it is to be playful and to play, I decided that I needed to look to the literature. I read two classics on the subject: Johan Huizinga's *Homo Ludens* (1968) and Hans-Georg Gadamer's chapter on the concept of play in his *Truth and Method*

(1975). I discovered, to my amazement, that what I thought about play and playfulness, if they were right, was absolutely wrong. Though I will not provide the arguments for this interpretation of Gadamer and Huizinga here, I understood that both of them have an agonistic sense of play. Play and playfulness have—in their use—ultimately, to do with contest, with winning, losing, battling. The sense of playfulness that I have in mind has nothing to do with agon. So, I tried to elucidate both senses of play and playfulness by contrasting them to each other. The contrast helped me see the attitude that I have in mind as the loving attitude in traveling across "worlds" more clearly.

An agonistic sense of playfulness is one in which *competence* is central. You'd better know the rules of the game. In agonistic play, there is risk, there is *uncertainty*, but the uncertainty is about who is going to win and who is going to lose. There are rules that inspire hostility. The attitude of *playfulness is conceived as secondary to or derivative from play*. Since play is agon, then the only conceivable playful attitude is an agonistic one: the attitude does not turn an activity into play, but rather presupposes an activity that is play. One of the paradigmatic ways of playing for both Gadarner and Huizinga is role-playing. In role-playing, the person who is a participant in the game has a *fixed conception of him- or herself*. I also think that the players are imbued with *self-importance* in agonistic play since they are so keen on winning given their own merits, their very own competence.

When considering the value of "world"-traveling and whether playfulness is the loving attitude to have while traveling, I recognized the agonistic attitude as inimical to traveling across "worlds." The agonistic traveler is a conqueror, an imperialist. Huizinga, in his classic book on play, interprets Western civilization as play. That is an interesting thing for Third World people to think about. Western civilization has been interpreted by a white Western man as play in the agonistic sense of play. Huizinga reviews Western law, art, and any other aspects of Western culture and sees agon in all of them. Agonistic playfulness leads those who attempt to travel to another "world" with this attitude to failure. Agonistic travelers cannot attempt to travel in this sense. Their traveling is always a trying that is tied to conquest, domination, reduction of what they meet to their own sense of order, and erasure of the other "world." That is what assimilation is all about. Assimilation is an agonistic project of destruction of other people's "worlds." So, the agonistic attitude, the playful attitude given Western man's construction of playfulness, is not a healthy, loving attitude to have in traveling across "worlds." Given the agonistic attitude, one *cannot* travel across "worlds," though one can kill other "worlds" with it.[6] So, for people who are interested in crossing racial and ethnic boundaries, an arrogant Western man's construction of playfulness is deadly. One cannot cross the boundaries with it. One needs to give up such an attitude if one wants to travel.

What, then, is the loving playfulness that I have in mind? Let me begin with one example: We are by the riverbank. The river is very low. Almost dry. Bits of water here and there. Little pools with a few trout hiding under the rocks. But it is mostly wet stones, gray on the outside. We walk on the stones for awhile. You pick up a stone and crash it onto the others. As it breaks, it is quite wet inside and it is very colorful, very pretty. I pick up a stone and break it and run toward the pieces to see the colors. They are beautiful. I laugh and bring the pieces back to you and you are doing the same with your pieces. We keep on crashing stones for hours, anxious to see the beautiful new colors. We are playing. The playfulness of our activity does not presuppose that there is something like "crashing stones" that is a particular form of play with its own rules. Instead, *the attitude that carries us through the activity, a playful attitude, turns the activity into play*. Our activity has no rules, though it is certainly intentional activity and we both understand what we are doing. The playfulness that gives meaning to our activity includes uncertainty, but in this case the uncertainty is an *openness to surprise*. This is a particular metaphysical attitude that does not expect the "world" to be neatly packaged, truly. Rules may fail to explain what we are doing. We are not self-important, we are not fixed in particular constructions of ourselves, which is part of saying that we are *open to self-construction*. We may not have rules, and when we do have them, *there are no rules that are to us sacred*. We are not worried about competence. We are not wedded to a particular way of doing things. While playful, we have not abandoned ourselves to, nor are we stuck in, any particular "world." We *are there creatively*. We are not passive.[7]

Playfulness is, in part, an openness to being a fool, which is a combination of not worrying about competence, not being self-important, not taking norms as sacred, and finding ambiguity and double edges a source of wisdom and delight.

So, positively, the playful attitude involves openness to surprise, openness to being a fool, openness to self-construction or reconstruction and to construction or reconstruction of the "worlds" we inhabit playfully, and thus openness to risk the ground that constructs us as oppressors or as oppressed or as collaborating or colluding with oppression. Negatively, playfulness is characterized by uncertainty, lack of self-importance, absence of rules or not taking rules as sacred, not worrying about competence, and lack of abandonment to a particular construction of oneself, others, and one's relation to them. In attempting to take a hold of oneself and of one's relation to others in a particular "world," one may study, examine, and come to understand oneself. One may then see what the possibilities for play are for the being one is in that "world." One may even decide to inhabit that self fully to understand it better and find its creative possibilities.

Conclusion

There are "worlds" we enter at our own risk, "worlds" that have agon, conquest, and arrogance as the main ingredients in their ethos. These are "worlds" that we enter out of necessity and that would be foolish to enter playfully in either the agonistic sense or in my sense. In such "worlds," *we* are not playful. To be in those "worlds" in resistance to their construction of ourselves as passive, servile, and inferior is to inhabit those selves ambiguously, through our first-person memories of lively subjectivity.

But there are "worlds" that we can travel to lovingly, and traveling to them is part of loving at least some of their inhabitants. The reason I think that traveling to someone's "world" is a way of identifying with them is that by traveling to their "world" we can understand *what it is to be them and what it is to be ourselves in their eyes*. Only when we have traveled to each other's "worlds" are we fully subjects to each other. (I agree with Hegel that self-recognition requires other subjects, but I disagree with his claim that it requires tension or hostility.)

Knowing other women's "worlds" is part of knowing them and knowing them is part of loving them. Notice that the knowing can be done in greater or lesser depth, as can the loving. Traveling to another's "world" is not the same as becoming intimate with them. Intimacy is constituted in part by a very deep knowledge of the other self. "World"-traveling is only part of the process of coming to have this knowledge. Also, notice that some people, in particular those who are outsiders to the mainstream, can be known only to the extent that they are known in several "worlds" and as "world"-travelers. Without knowing the other's "world," one does not know the other, and without knowing the other, one is really alone in the other's presence because the other is only dimly present to one.

By traveling to other people's "worlds," we discover that there are "worlds" in which those who are the victims of arrogant perception are really subjects, lively beings, resisters, constructors of visions even though in the mainstream construction they are animated only by the arrogant perceiver and are pliable, foldable, file-awayable, classifiable. I always imagine the Aristotelian slave as pliable and foldable at night or after he or she cannot work anymore (when he or she dies as a tool).[8] Aristotle tells us nothing about the slave *apart from the master.* We know the slave only through the master. The slave is a tool of the master. After working hours, he or she is folded and placed in a drawer until the next morning.

My mother was apparent to me mostly as a victim of arrogant perception. I was loyal to the arrogant perceiver's construction of her and thus disloyal to her in assuming that she was exhausted by that construction. I was unwilling to be like her and thought that identifying with her, seeing myself in her, necessitated that I become like her. I was wrong both in assuming that she was exhausted by the arrogant perceiver's construction of her and in my understanding of identification. I do not think I was wrong in thinking that identification was part of loving and that it involved in part my seeing myself in her. I came to realize through traveling to her "world" that she is not foldable and pliable, that she is not exhausted by the mainstream Argentinian patriarchal construction of her. I came to realize that there are "worlds" in which she shines as a creative being. Seeing myself in her through traveling to her "world" has meant seeing how different from her I am in her "world."[9]

So, in recommending "world"-traveling and identification through "world"-traveling as part of loving other women, I am suggesting disloyalty to arrogant perceivers, including the arrogant perceiver in ourselves, and to their constructions of women and to their constructions of powerful barriers between women. As Women of Color, we cannot stand on any ground that is not also a crossing. To enter playfully into each other's "worlds" of subjective affirmation also risks those aspects of resistance that have kept us riveted on constructions of ourselves that have kept us from seeing multiply, from understanding the interconnections in our historico-spatialities. Playful "world"-travel is thus not assimilable to the middleclass leisurely journey nor the colonial or imperialist journeys. None of these involve risking one's ground. These forms of displacement may well be compatible with agonistic playfulness, but they are incompatible with the attitude of play that is an openness to surprise and that inclines us to "world"-travel in the direction of deep coalition.

References

Frye, M. (1983) *The Politics of Reality: Essays in Feminist Theory*, Trumansburg, NY: Crossing Press.
Gadamer, H.-G. (1975) *Truth and Method*, New York: Seabury Press.
Huizinga, J. (1968) *Homo Ludens*, Buenos Aires, Argentina: Emece Editores.
Lorde, A. (1984) "Eye to Eye: Black Women, Hatred, and Anger," in A. Lorde (ed.), *Sister Outsider*, Trumansburg, NY: Crossing Press.
Lugones, M. (2003) *Pilgrimages/Peregrinajes: Theorizing Coalition Against Multiple Oppressions*. Lanham, MD: Rowman & Littlefield.
Wolff, J. (1992) "On the Road Again: Metaphors of Travel in Cultural Criticism," *Cultural Studies* 7 (2): 224–239.

Notes

1 [In this footnote, Lugones is discussing the connection of this essay to other essays in her volume of collected essays. Those essays are not in the present volume. —Eds.] It is an important aim of [*Pilgrimages/Peregrinajes* (Lugones 2003)] to come to understand these barriers to the possibility of coalitions of understanding. Most chapters in the book are relevant to this question, but I call your

attention in particular to the treatment of these difficulties in Chapter 7 ("Boomerang Perception and the Colonizing Gaze"). I consider the failure of nationalisms and separatisms to escape these difficulties. The distinction between split-separation and curdling-separation that I introduce in Chapter 6 ("Purity, Impurity, and Separation") is also relevant. The distinction between intermeshing oppressions and the interlocking of oppressions that I develop in the Introduction and in "Tactical Strategics of the Streetwalker" (Chapter 10) address the complexities of these barriers.
2 See Audre Lorde's treatment of horizontal anger in "Eye to Eye: Black Women, Hatred, and Anger" (1984). Lorde understands black women seeing the servile construction of themselves in each other with anger, hatred.
3 It is important that I have been thought a person without humor by whites/Anglos inside the U.S. academy, a space where struggles against race/gender and sexual oppression require an articulation of the issues. I have been found playful by my companions in struggles against white/Anglo control of land and water in the U.S. Southwest. Those struggles have occurred in the space-time of Chicano communities. Being playful or not playful becomes in those two contexts deep traits, symptomatic of larger incongruities.
4 This "we" embraces the *very* many strands of Latinos in the United States. But this "we" is unusually spoken with ease. The tension in the "we" includes those who do not reject "Hispanic" as a term of identification.
5 Indeed, people inhabit constructions of themselves in "worlds" they refuse to enter. This is true particularly of those who oppress those whose resistant "worlds" they refuse to enter. But they are indeed inhabitants of those "worlds." And indeed, those who are oppressed animate oppressive constructions of themselves in the "worlds" of their oppressors.
6 Consider the congruities between the middle-class leisurely journey that Wolff describes and the agonistic sense of play (Wolff 1992). Consider also the discussion of travel in the Introduction.
7 One can understand why this sense of playfulness is one that one may exercise in resistance to oppression when resistance is not reducible to reaction. Nonreactive resistance is creative; it exceeds that which is being resisted. The creation of new meaning lies outside of rules, particularly the rules of the "world" being resisted.
8 But I can also imagine the Aristotelian slave after hours as an animal without the capacity to reason. In that case, roaming in the fields, eating, and copulating would be distinctly passionate activities where passion and reason are dichotomized. Imagining people who are taken into servility in this manner is what leads oppressors to think of those they attempt to dominate both as dangerous and as nonpersons.
9 The traveling also permitted me *to* see her resistances in plain view in my daily life. She did not hide resistance.

Reading Questions

1. There are several ways in which one might be at ease in a world: (1) as a speaker of the language; (2) sharing the social norms; (3) having bonds with other people in the world; and (4) sharing a history with the other people in the world. Can you think of your own examples of each of these?
2. Lugones explains that some people have to world-travel out of necessity, but also suggests that it can be done willfully. Give examples of some practical ways in which a person might try to do so.
3. Why do you think Lugones picks these particular examples (her not loving her mom, white women not loving women of color?)
4. Lugones writes that, "I am not a healthy being in the 'worlds' that construct me unplayful?" Why do you think this is the case?
5. Lugones is explicit about her focus on women of color. Does the picture generalize to other groups? Why or why not? Why do you think Lugones focuses on this group?
6. Is there any reason non-"outsiders" or non-oppressed peoples can't world-travel? If loving perception requires traveling to worlds, does love of everyone require, for example, traveling to racist or sexist worlds of oppressors?
7. Why can't we say what Hispanicity/Latino-ness consists in, according to Lugones? Do you agree? Why or why not?

13 Mestiza Autonomy as Relational Autonomy

Ambivalence and the Social Character of Free Will

Edwina Barvosa

In years past numerous philosophers roundly criticized traditional conceptions of autonomy for ignoring the role that socialization and social relationships can play in autonomous thought and action. Often introduced by feminist thinkers, such critiques frequently objected to the use of atomistic conceptions of the self in accounts of autonomy and to the commonplace privileging of instrumental rationalism. The latter objection, in particular, emphasized the important contributions made to critical reasoning and autonomy by affect, intimate attachments, intuition, aesthetic judgment, relationships of dependence or interdependence, communal and familial identifications and the dynamics of the physical body (see e.g. Nedelsky 1989; Grovier 1993; Meyers 1989; Grimshaw 1988; Benhabib 1992). As Marilyn Friedman has noted however, recent decades have brought a significant response to such critiques. Mainstream conceptions of autonomy have come to recognize the socially embedded character of the self and to assume that the critical reflection that confers autonomy will necessarily involve language, desires, norms and emotions that are the legacy of a person's socialization. As Friedman has put it, such revised accounts of autonomy reflect the "widely shared intuition that autonomy is not antithetical to other social values and virtues that concern us all, such as love, friendship, care, loyalty, and devotion" (Friedman 2000: 41).[1]

The influences that socialization and social relationships have upon autonomy are complex however, and they can include both enabling and limiting effects. Tracing those complex relational influences requires looking not only at various formative dynamics, but also at the array of identifications and social relations that a particular agent has and to the interconnections and conflicts that potentially exist among them. Feminist theories of "relational autonomy" are among the most recent philosophical efforts to incorporate such complexities and to investigate their relevance for women and to struggles for social justice (Mackenzie and Stoljar 2000; Meyers 2004). While exploring the relational dimensions of autonomy, a number of feminist thinkers have identified the conception of *mestiza consciousness* as useful for theorizing the wide variety of intersecting and sometimes conflicting identifications and social relationships that agents can have (see e.g. Hoagland and Frye 1997; Meyers 2000: 155; Mullin 1995: 25–26). First formulated by influential Chicana thinker Gloria Anzaldúa (1943–2004) and widely discussed among other Latina philosophers, mestiza consciousness is a conception of the self that outlines how subjectivity is shaped and decentered by multiple and crosscutting forms of socialization, including relations of group conflict and social subordination.

In the pages that follow, I further explore the relevance of mestiza consciousness for relational autonomy. I focus in particular on the potential role of ambivalence in enabling autonomous thought and action. In her conception of mestiza consciousness, Anzaldúa argues that

DOI: 10.4324/9781003385417-20

ambivalence can enhance an agent's capacity for critical reasoning, especially when she has been socialized within interrelated sets of social group relationships. This possible effect—i.e. that ambivalence can aid critical reasoning—raises a further question related specifically to autonomy. Can an agent be ambivalent toward her endorsements and still be autonomous in reference to those endorsements? To investigate this question, I formulate in this essay an alternative procedural account of relational autonomy that I refer to as "mestiza autonomy." In mestiza autonomy, autonomous agents act in keeping with syncretic endorsements that they formulate through their critical reflection on the array of values and norms that are given to them socially as part of their different social and personal identities.

Applying this account of autonomy to several example cases, I contend that for agents socialized in and still living in the midst of social relations of group conflict, those conflicting social relationships can shape the practice of autonomy in ways that make two particular kinds of ambivalence useful to agents in their everyday attempts to achieve autonomy.[2] The first of these is ambivalence toward the principles that they have disavowed as those not among their guiding endorsements. The second is ambivalence toward the rank order of their endorsements. While attention to the significance of ambivalence for realizing relational autonomy in the context of social subordination is growing, its potential utility still remains underappreciated in prevailing accounts of procedural autonomy.

I. Ambivalence and Relational Autonomy

As philosophers have given increasingly greater attention to the relational aspects of autonomy, as discussed below, some philosophers have given increasing attention to the role of ambivalence in facilitating autonomy. This is a relatively new outlook, however, as many procedural approaches to autonomy, such as Harry Frankfurt's influential account, have considered ambivalence to be destructive of autonomy. In Frankfurt's account of autonomy, for example, the desire and principles that a subject acts upon autonomously may originate beyond him as desires that just "happen . . . to occur" in him like an "involuntary spasm" arising from the dynamics of social life.[3] Frankfurt (1987: 38) argues, however, that through critical self-reflection an agent can make such happenstance desires and aims his own by adopting as his guiding principles and endorsements elements that were only socially given before. When the agent acts upon his chosen endorsements consistently in everyday life, his actions may be considered autonomous.

On Frankfurt's procedural account of autonomy ambivalence is not simply unimportant, it is ruled out as detrimental to autonomy by the need for "wholeheartedness." Frankfurt contends that for us to arrive at our own set of endorsements, it is necessary for us to resolve any inner conflicts that we may have regarding whether a particular desire should be our own and how important that desire is to us. Resolving such conflicts and becoming wholehearted in our endorsements requires two things: (1) that our chosen desires are assigned a "single ordering" that ranks them in importance, i.e. *integration*, and (2) the full rejection as "outlaw" to oneself of all desires and principles that the agent does not endorse, i.e. *separation*. These acts of ranking and firm disavowal are for Frankfurt how we "create a self out of the raw materials of inner life." An agent is autonomous only when he is wholehearted in the choice and practice of his endorsements. That is, to be autonomous a person must identify entirely with his chosen hierarchy of principles and desires and observe them *without ambivalence* to the exclusion of his outlawed desires.[4]

This general procedural account of autonomy centered in critical reflection on socially given materials and the agent's choice of guiding principles is widely accepted. Yet, Frankfurt's additional standard of wholeheartedness may be hard to reach for individuals who must strive to achieve autonomy within complex and contentious sets of social relations. For example, discussing her competencies-based account of autonomy, Diana Tietjens Meyers (2000: 153)[5] has argued against Frankfurt that individuals socialized within relations of social subordination may find the ambivalence sometimes associated with their diversity of identities to be an asset for achieving autonomy. To develop this point, Meyers underscores how in complex societies people are socialized in multiple ways that "interact—sometimes compounding one another's effects and sometimes creating inner divisions and conflicts." She writes, "whether they know it or not, people have intersectional identities, and these [diverse] identities influence what they believe, how they deliberate, and how they conduct their lives" (2000: 157). Meyers states for example, (drawing on María Lugones's work on the advantages of mestiza consciousness) that those "border dwellers" who identify with a range of different social groups will often have a superior compound vantage point from which to critically assess different communities (2000: 155).[6]

While Meyers thus recognizes that having multiple social identifications can be important in autonomy, she also notes that the complexities generated by having significant inner diversity can engender useful forms of ambivalence. Members of subordinated groups who wholeheartedly *dis*identify with their victimization, for example, run the risk of denying their social circumstances and thereby compounding their vulnerability. Conversely, wholeheartedly identifying with one's victimization as part of a system of endorsements may lead to self-pity or to a self-denigrating attitude. Given the undesirability of both of these options, Meyers writes that "[i]ndeed, ambivalence toward one's victimization seems a better attitude to strike. Neither wholeheartedly embracing [one's victimization . . .] nor eschewing it, . . . seems more likely to preserve one's balance *and* one's autonomy" (2000: 170; emphasis in original).

While Meyers sees a positive role for ambivalence and for recognizing the multiplicity of our social identities in her competencies-based model of autonomy, she also contends that ambivalence may undermine autonomy. Specifically, Meyers suggests that having conflicting identifications can present the self with difficult "political conundrums," as when a Black woman with diverse racial, ethnic and gendered identities finds that her identity-based "commitment to antiracist politics may entail tolerating sexism, and commitment to feminist politics may entail tolerating racism" (2000: 157). As I will argue below, however, it is important to draw a distinction between perceptions of inconsistency that arise from the ascriptive elements of group identities and an agent's active and demonstrable betrayal of her own endorsements. The latter failure is not a necessary consequence of identifying with diverse or conflicting groups. Nor is that particular kind of inconsistency toward one's endorsements characteristic of the specific kinds of ambivalence that are most useful for achieving autonomy.

Setting this distinction aside for the moment, however, Meyers offers clearly persuasive reasons why autonomy is potentially compatible with ambivalence and why ambivalence may play a useful—though also complicating—role in autonomy for those who are embroiled in relations of social conflict. However, Meyers draws these connections in relation to her own competencies-based account of autonomy rather than to the procedural accounts that she rejects such as Frankfurt's (Meyers 1989: 76, 2004: 173). The question thus remains open whether or not a procedural account of autonomy can accommodate the kind of ambivalence that complex social relations can occasion. While contemporary accounts of procedural autonomy, such as Frankfurt's, often demand that ambivalence be replaced with wholeheartedness, it may nevertheless be possible for a person to be ambivalent toward her endorsements and still be autonomous toward them. To explore this possibility, it is useful to look more closely at the concept of mestiza consciousness and how its approach to ambivalence relates to established procedural accounts of autonomy.

II. Mestiza Consciousness and Mestiza Autonomy

The ability to take a critical and flexible approach to one's own beliefs and to tolerate significant levels of ambiguity and ambivalence in everyday life are highly valued capabilities in Chicana conceptions of mestiza consciousness. Gloria Anzaldúa first articulated the conception of mestiza consciousness in her influential 1987 book, *Borderlands/la Frontera: The New Mestiza*, a mixed-genre meditation on the complexity of identity in contemporary social life.[7] In the book, Anzaldúa defines *mestiza consciousness* as a subjectivity that contains an array of diverse and sometimes contradictory identities that were formed in and through various and often intersecting social dynamics. Those formative social dynamics may be part of different lifeworlds and cultural milieu, or aspects of different social groups or interpersonal relationships. They may include, for example, specific relations of class, ethnicity, race, gender, sexuality, nationality, religion, region, language community and subculture.

For Anzaldúa, therefore, a woman with mestiza consciousness has a multiple or "dual identity" in which she lives in and through multiple life worlds, often living in a manner that straddles divided social groups and domains. With reference to Chicanas/os, for example, Anzaldúa points out that Mexican Americans identify partly, but not completely, with both Mexican and Anglo-American cultural values. These multiple dimensions of social embeddedness and construction leave the individual with a composite identity that is a "synergy of two cultures with various degrees of Mexicanness or Angloness" (1987: 63).[8] Thus, *la mestiza* is any subject who, like the borderlands itself, has a subjectivity characterized by a diversity of different identities and worldviews that mingle and collide within the self in both conflict and mutual influence.[9]

As such, the mestiza must grapple with the variations and contradictions among her identities. In Anzaldúa's words, "[c]radled in one culture, sandwiched between two cultures, straddling all three cultures and their value systems, *la mestiza* undergoes a struggle of flesh, a struggle of borders" (1987: 78). That struggle is one of negotiating competing value systems and sets of meaning and practice to generate everyday thoughts and actions. The mestiza performs this negotiation of her diverse identities in at least two ways. The first is to engage in what María Lugones (1987, 1992) calls "world-traveling" in which the agent shifts among her different identifications from one social setting to another. This method of negotiating the plurality of one's identities involves different identity-related meanings, values and practices being utilized in different contexts as the mestiza crosses the borders from one lifeworld to the next. For example, a bicultural Korean American man might speak Korean and engage in Korean cultural practices at home with Korean-speaking family members, but speak English and engage in Euroamerican cultural practices while at work. His particular set of cultural identities enable him to function capably in a variety of different social contexts and sets of social relations, shifting back and forth between Korean and mainstream Anglo-American social worlds.

A second method of negotiating one's diversity of social identities and relationships involves the process of choosing and syncretically creating one's own set of outlooks from the variety of elements within one's array of social relations and identities.[10] The result of these creative acts is a hybrid set of outlooks that include an array of elements adopted whole from socially given materials and others created syncretically by the subject from elements extracted from different social sources. This second method is particularly emphasized by Anzaldúa, who contends that as the mestiza continually engages with the conflicting worldviews that comprise her subjectivity in a syncretizing way, she ceases to "hold concepts or ideas in rigid boundaries" between outlawed and admissible meaning and practice. Instead, in the course of living a diversity of identities, the mestiza can learn to continually fold diverse perspectives into positions greater than the parts from which they were forged (Anzaldúa 1987: 79).

As a consequence of the need to frequently engage with the complexities and contradictions of identity diversity in everyday life, ambiguity and ambivalence assume a central place in critical reasoning within Anzaldúa's account of mestiza consciousness (Anzaldúa 1987: 79). On this point Anzaldúa's conception of critical reasoning veers sharply away from the view that consistency and wholeheartedness in thought and action are *always* the necessary basis for sound moral and political thought and free will. Her argument bears quoting at length:

> These numerous possibilities leave *la mestiza* floundering in uncharted seas. The *borders and walls that are supposed to keep the undesirable ideas out are entrenched habits and patterns of behavior; these habitual patterns are the enemy within.* Only by remaining flexible is she able to stretch the psyche horizontally and vertically. *La mestiza constantly has to shift out of habitual formations*; from convergent thinking, analytical reasoning that tends to use rationality to move toward a single goal (a Western mode), to divergent thinking, characterized by movement *away from set patterns and goals and toward a more whole perspective, one that includes rather than excludes.*
>
> (Anzaldúa 1987: 79–80)

By defining critical reasoning in terms of divergence rather than convergence, Anzaldúa defines mestiza consciousness as a conscious state of cognitive struggle. Yet that struggle is fruitful in that it can generate an ongoing creative process that provides the self with a critical distance from which to assess, reject, adopt and/or transform the outlooks and paradigms that come to it by way of diverse forms of socialization.

Exploring and extending Anzaldúa's concepts of mestiza consciousness, María Lugones has stressed—more so than Anzaldúa—that the multiple identities that make up mestiza consciousness are not a fragmented but an interconnected multiplicity. Therefore, Lugones (1994: 475) argues that while the multiple identities that make up mestiza consciousness are different and distinct, they nonetheless may often be linked through common memories and meanings, and/or through the interconnections among the different social groups that are the referents for those identities. For example, the dynamics of ethnic identity in a given subject's life are inseparable from and mutually influenced by other identities including his gender, class, sexuality, physical ability, nationality and so on. For Lugones, this co-mingling of distinct identities within the self places the mestiza at the edge of different lifeworlds—a position that is a source of critiques and creativity, as well as a potential resource for social change and political resistance that can be born out of the "unsettling quality of being a stranger in our [own] society" (1994: 477).[11] Lugones thus contends that mestizas should embrace the potentially open, fluid and varied character of their perspectives and identities and the possibility for self-making that they present.

While neither Anzaldúa nor Lugones specifically discuss in detail the relationship between mestiza consciousness and procedural autonomy, it is possible to create from their accounts of mestiza consciousness a conception of what I call here *mestiza autonomy*. Mestiza autonomy, as I define it, is a procedural account of autonomy in which an agent who has a diversity of social relations and group memberships critically reflects upon the contents of her particular social and personal identities to forge a set of guiding endorsements.[12] Because each socially derived identity can be thought of as a scheme of meanings, values and practices, once it is internalized as a part of an agent's subjectivity each identity scheme can serve as a frame of reference for thought and action in specific contexts.[13] The mestiza/o develops a set of guiding endorsements by reflecting critically upon the elements of his or her various identity frames of reference. That set of endorsements can be developed in two ways.

First, endorsements can be picked and chosen "as is" from among the materials social given as aspects of her different internalized identifications and relationships. Second, other endorsements can be self-generated endorsements that the agent forges syncretically from elements of different identities and lifeworlds. The agent who creates syncretic endorsements or who chooses endorsements drawn from various lifeworlds may be said to have a *hybrid set of endorsements*. The mestiza renders her endorsements her own by way of the process of critical reflection that she uses to produce them. To the extent that the mestiza/o lives by those endorsements in her everyday activities, she is autonomous in her actions.

In complex societies, virtually everyone has some diversity of "social identities" and "personal identities" from which they can forge hybrid sets of endorsements.[14] Those different identities might include various social role identities, such as professional identities, or group identities such as ethnic, religious, national or regional identities. They are also likely to contain a range of personal identities with specific individuals such as family members, friends, lovers, neighbors and so on. However, while everyone may have some diversity of identifications, the degree of that diversity may vary considerably from one person to the next. Consequently, while mestiza autonomy faces every individual with the task of deriving a set of endorsements from the materials socially given to them, the complexity of that task will vary from one person to the next depending on the degree of difference between their various identifications and relationships.

In practice then, many people have an array of social identities that are but modestly diverse. Their identity frames of reference are constructed such that they include norms and values that are similar, or at least considered socially compatible. Consider as an example a 40-year-old man from Oregon who is married with two children. He attends a Unitarian church, works as an environmental activist in Portland, and identifies himself as a political progressive. He self-identifies as racially white, although also recognizes his Native American ancestry which he has through his maternal grandmother. While he is not significantly identified with his native cultural heritage, he attributes some of his environmentalist ethics to childhood teachings regarding the primacy of nature. For a man such as this, it is relatively straightforward to create and live by a set of hybrid endorsements that are drawn from his particular set of social and personal identities. His professional, political, religious and personal identities are socially constructed as generally compatible or nested. He raises his children with respect for the earth, lives in a home built from green materials and so on. In general, such acts of autonomy raise little notice among those with whom he is socially related or identified.

For others, however, their sets of social identifications and relations are more diverse and include identities that are socially constructed as generally incompatible, either because they encompass contradictory meanings, values and practices, or because they involve social relations of group conflict and social division. For example, given the social conflicts that link these groups, Gloria Anzaldúa (1987: 78) described the challenge of creating her own perspectives from her internalized social identities as a Chicana, an American woman, a lesbian and a Native American. She writes that, "like others having or living in more than one culture," she gets "multiple, often opposing messages" from living within different social groups, and "[t]he coming together of two self-consistent but habitually incompatible frames of reference cause *un choque*, a cultural collision" of conflicting social meanings and relationships. For the mestiza that collision can complicate the process of forging her endorsements.

Even so, social group identities that are constructed as socially incompatible or in conflict nevertheless often share overlapping or related norms and values that can be hybridized by an agent into a coherent set of endorsements. For instance, while Latina/o cultures do vary in significant ways from mainstream Euroamerican culture, there are also many points of overlap and convergence. Both Latina/o and Euroamerican cultures contain normative commitments to family, although those norms are given different priority and are practiced differently in each culture. From these generally overlapping norms, however, agents with these particular cultural identities can choose and/or syncretize endorsements from socially given materials that are in keeping, in some way or another, with each of their different identities and social relations.

In more rare instances, however, a person's social identities and relations will include mutually exclusive norms or values that further complicate the formation of endorsements from those particular social identities. For example, a woman who identifies as a Catholic, a Latina and as a lesbian will find that her various social relations and identifications involve deep conflicts regarding sexual norms. Nonetheless, an agent need not endorse *all* aspects of each of her internalized identity frames. Through critical reflection, she can, for example, disavow the homophobic aspects of Latina/o cultures and Catholic doctrine while also retaining other aspects of those ways of life as part of her hybrid set of endorsements.[15]

The diverse relational factors that add complexity to the creation of one's endorsements also add complexity to the observance and *practice* of those endorsements in everyday life. As mentioned above, when the man from Oregon acts autonomously toward his endorsements, those with whom he is identified will generally receive his acts positively or neutrally. In contrast, those with more highly diverse identities may sometimes forge syncretic endorsements that depart significantly from the norms and practices that prevail in some or all of the social groups in which they are strongly related and identified. When such agents act upon their endorsements, their autonomous acts are more likely to excite questioning, challenges and even overt conflict from others with whom they are socially related or otherwise identified.

The added challenge of contentiousness associated with observing some hybrid sets of endorsements can, I contend, make wholeheartedness less obtainable, but also less necessary, for achieving autonomy for those agents whose syncretic endorsements depart significantly from the norms prevailing in their social group relationships. In their cases, the ambivalence and flexibility ruled out in Frankfurt's procedural autonomy could become useful assets for agents, assets that can help them to observe their syncretic endorsements consistently in contexts of social or interpersonal conflict. That is, in some cases, contentious relational influences on autonomy can link the achievement of autonomy to the ability to maintain certain types of ambivalence and to maintaining flexibility in the priority of one's endorsements.

To examine more closely how ambivalence can play a facilitating role in observing one's syncretic endorsements, consider the case of a student who I'll call Patricia. Patricia was enrolled in a course that I offered recently. During every class meeting, Patricia sat by the door silently eating her lunch as she took notes, and ten minutes before the end of the class period, she would slip quietly out of the classroom. What seemed on its face to be inappropriate student conduct, upon greater knowledge of Patricia instead revealed her significant strength of purpose and commitment to her education. Patricia ate a late sack lunch in class because she spent her own lunch hour working as a server in an on-campus eatery. She left class early to catch the vanpool that would take her forty-five miles to her home in Oxnard where she lived with her husband in the home of her in-laws.

At 22, Patricia was the first in her Mexican American family to attend college. Her husband encouraged her studies and worked hard to support the couple and to contribute to Patricia's tuition while she studied full-time. While Patricia's husband looked upon her education as an investment in Patricia and in their shared future, Patricia's mother-in-law was opposed to and vocally critical of her daughter-in-law's efforts to obtain a college degree. She objected in particular because Patricia's studies infringed upon her homemaking in such a way that various household tasks were left undone, or requiring her son's assistance. To her mind, Patricia's choices were a departure from the core elements of what being a Chicana—i.e. what having a Chicana identity—really means. From her perspective, prolonged schooling is an Anglo-American self-indulgence, an elite, self-interested act that leaves Patricia shirking her responsibilities to her family.

In contrast, Patricia's own educational endorsement is a syncretic one that draws elements from both Chicana/o and Anglo-American cultures, but which also departs from both in various ways. Historically, neither Chicana/o nor Anglo-American cultures have valued or created opportunities for Chicanas to obtain a higher education. Within Chicana/o culture, traditional Chicana gender roles (although complex and historically varied in practice) have generally constructed higher education as insignificant to a Chicana's life. That life was to be largely devoted to family and to community life, typically in the form of caring for children, for family and by extension for one's ethnic community.[16] Within the liberal individualism of Anglo-American culture, however, higher education generally has been regarded as an important step toward personal development and independence, and considered a means to prepare oneself for the pursuit of individual goals, including personal wealth. At the same time, for much of American history, mainstream American culture situated higher education as the birthright of the privileged from which women, the poor and people of color, including Chicanas, could be excluded. The means of exclusion have included school segregation, a lack of access to college preparatory classes and college counseling in poor communities, ethnic and racial disparities in high school tracking systems and so on.

Departing from norms that have prevailed in both Euroamerican and Chicana/o cultures, Patricia values her education as a central aspect of her ethnic identity *as a Chicana*. Her syncretic educational endorsement adopts from Anglo-American culture an emphasis on education, but unites it with a Chicana specific commitment to familial needs and to *collective* community goals. Syncretized in this way, her endorsement departs from traditional stereotypical gender norms within Chicana/o culture by regarding education as important to her *as a woman*, and not as something from which she should be excluded based on her gender, her marital or familial commitments, or her working-class status. In addition, her syncretic endorsement departs from the individualist norms of the mainstream Euroamerican culture in that Patricia does not regard her education as something that serves primarily her personal needs or ambitions. Rather, she values her education as part of the work she must do in order to better support her family and to potentially benefit her Chicana/o communities as a whole.

While Patricia may fairly easily create such a syncretic endorsement from her various social relations to be autonomous she must also *practice* that syncretic endorsement within the context of her various social relationships. In some of those relations her educational endorsement is welcomed and affirmed. In others, it is regarded as suspect or denigrated. Thus, while many of Patricia's friends and professors support Patricia in her educational endorsement, others, such as her mother-in-law, do not. Such variations are not random. Rather, they mark the convergence of varying sets of cultural subgroups and divergent forms of socialization—the borderlands—*within* (as well as outside of) Chicano/a culture. That diversity involves many elements, including cultural divisions between those who subscribe to traditional and new female gender roles, and the complexities of balancing what is borrowed from the dominant Anglo culture with resistance to its subordinating, homogenizing and assimilating aspects.[17]

Given this cultural complexity, Patricia certainly could dismiss her mother-in-law's dissenting voice. Yet, her vociferous criticism gives Patricia pause. After all, Patricia has been socialized in and strongly identifies with a culture in which many women that she loves and respects have acted as her mother-in-law expects. Those beloved Chicanas have eschewed (sometimes reluctantly) the very choices that Patricia now embraces. Given such formative socialization, while Patricia does not endorse her mother-in-law's values and practices, to *totally* disavow them as outlaw to herself would be to turn away from the norms that have been, and which remain, central to one of her cultures and to some of her most important social relationships. Moreover, Patricia's "rejected" endorsements are still embraced by many Chicanas, many of whom have few practical alternatives available to them.

At the same time, Patricia's "turning away" from those long-prevailing Chicana norms may be vitally important both for Patricia's autonomous self-making and for fostering the incremental social changes that can benefit Patricia's family, her community and her cultures. As such, her syncretic educational endorsement is at once potentially denying *and* affirming of the Chicana lifeworld. Given these crosscutting relational factors, *the manner* in which Patricia turns away from some socialized principles is important for maintaining the social identifications and relationships that are the source, the ongoing context and the partial justification for her endorsements as a whole. In other words, if Patricia's rejection of unwanted cultural principles is done in a manner that "outlaws"—i.e. fully rejects—her social group's views, Patricia risks denying or alienating the social relationships she cares about most. To avoid this outcome while retaining her own endorsements, Patricia may opt to retain feelings of ambivalence in which she continues to feel an equivocating connection to selected principles that she ultimately does not endorse and will not act upon. By maintaining ambivalence toward some disavowed principles in this way, she can clear social space for acting autonomously upon her own syncretic endorsements without simultaneously devaluing "abandoned" ways of life that are still meaningful and socially important to others with whom she is closely socially related.

In addition to helping her to preserve her syncretic educational endorsements, feelings of ambivalence can also help Patricia to observe her other various endorsements when those endorsements have crosscutting implications for each other, and for her social relationships and commitments. For example, if Patricia endorses the value of showing respect for her family (a value widely endorsed among Chicanas), then adopting a posture of outright rejection and defiance toward her mother-in-law is not as consistent with that familial endorsement as would be a posture of ambivalent non-compliance that would acknowledge her oppositional views but not capitulate to them. By thus tempering her refusal with ambiguity and ambivalence, Patricia can mitigate the negative impact of her autonomous actions on specific familial relationships. In this way, ambivalence helps her to observe her educational endorsement while also maintaining in some fashion the conflicting familial priorities she also endorses.

In addition to enabling the exercise of autonomy within important but constraining social relationships, ambivalence can also be an important aid in achieving autonomy under conditions of social subordination and group conflict. Chicana gender norms have been the product of systematic ethnic and racial subordination, but they have also been constructed through various forms of Chicana agency and political resistance to that subordination (Ruiz 1998). Given that history, an outright or rigid rejection by Patricia of long-prevailing group norms in favor of norms hybridized from the dominant Euroamerican culture might imply a denigration of any Chicana who does not struggle to pursue higher education as Patricia does. In other words, unless Patricia's expression of her syncretic endorsement is tempered with ambivalence, her rejection of educational norms that are still endorsed by many Chicanas could reiterate existing relationships of group subordination and inequality.[18]

Paradoxically therefore Patricia's actions, while self-emancipatory and autonomous, could nonetheless be seen to have the *relational* consequence of compounding generations of ethnic and racial group subordination by dishonoring the life choices of Chicanas. Sensitivity to such relational contexts and the possible interpretations of one's syncretic endorsements is thus particularly important when one's "outlawed" principles invoke longstanding systems of group privilege and subordination. In Patricia's case, the historical lack of educational opportunities for Chicanas—which she resists and potentially escapes—nonetheless gives significance to her own endorsements. It also adds additional layered meanings to the dissenting voices of others such as her mother-in-law. Adopting an attitude of ambivalence toward outlawed endorsements is one way of holding such contradictory and crosscutting meanings and relationships together in a holistic understanding that appreciates the crosscutting implications of one's autonomous actions within intersecting sets of social relations. It is this kind of expanded and flexible approach to incorporating contradiction and ambiguity into one's outlooks that Anzaldúa regarded as most conducive to critical reasoning in the midst of social complexity.

In short, caught in the crosscurrents of diverse and changing cultural norms Patricia remains committed to her educational endorsements, yet remains ambivalent about them. She cannot unequivocally declare the endorsements of her mother-in-law as outlaw to herself without also denying aspects of her other endorsements and the social relationships and identifications that she values and endorses retaining. Some such "outlaw" principles are as much, or more, a part of the relational systems of meaning that constitute her Chicana social identity as her own (relatively novel) endorsements. Consequently, while Patricia does not choose to privilege homemaking over education in her endorsements, she must still continually regard her endorsements *in relation* to the social locations of others and to those group-defining principles that she does not embrace. Adopting postures of ambivalence can help her to observe all of her endorsements, while also maintaining a range of conflicting relational ties with others who subscribe to principles that are in tension with her own.

In addition to ambivalence, flexibility in the priority of endorsements can also help those with syncretic endorsements to exercise autonomy in conflictual social contexts. For example, in her work María Lugones describes how she identifies as a lesbian and a Latina and how she resists forms of racial/ethnic and sexual subordination as a member of both Latina and lesbian communities (Lugones 1990). At this period in U.S. history, however, the Latina and lesbian identities that Lugones claims are still largely socially constructed as mutually exclusive. Homosexuality is still largely regarded as anathema within Latina/o cultures.

Latina/o cultures and values are at best marginal, if not outright denigrated, within lesbian communities and cultures. Braving social marginalization and conflict within both groups, therefore, Lugones has chosen a hybrid set of endorsements in which she draws values from her social identities as both a Latina and as a lesbian to strongly endorse *both* anti-racist and anti-heterosexist principles.

When Lugones acts in keeping with these two endorsements her actions are considered autonomous. Yet, given the widespread hostility within Latina/o and lesbian social groups toward members of the other social group, Lugones's exercise of her anti-racist endorsement is often localized in lesbian settings. Likewise, her anti-heterosexist activities are often localized in Latino/a social settings. Consequently, for Lugones to observe her two endorsements across two particular social contexts she may need to privilege different moral priorities in different communities, i.e. acting primarily through her anti-racist endorsements in some contexts and primarily through her anti-heterosexist endorsements in others. In addition, practicing her endorsements well across these social domains may require Lugones to be sometimes inconsistent in how she identifies herself from one context to the next. That is, Lugones's hybrid set of endorsements and her social relations and commitments are such that she may find it useful to counter-identify as a lesbian in some Latina settings, and to counter-identify as a Latina in some lesbian dominated social contexts.

Given the crosscutting relational factors that influence her acts of autonomy, Lugones has strong reason *not* to establish a strict rank-ordered priority among her higher-order desires as Frankfurt's account of procedural autonomy requires. Rather, as a woman with a hybrid set of endorsements, Lugones's achievement of autonomy depends on her endorsements *not* being rigidly set in a single hierarchical order, but instead flexibly ordered and applied as may best fit different contexts. In certain times and places, struggles against racism will be most important and take priority over struggle against heterosexism and *vice versa*.[19] Yet, in no context would Lugones deny the importance of either of these endorsements. She remains committed and observant of both endorsements even while she attends to them to varying degrees in different situations.

Lugones's autonomous choices also introduce a kind of collateral ambivalence, unlike that described above. This ambivalence is the equivocation that seems to be implied when an agent maintains her identification with two or more mutually intolerant social groups. This ambivalence, in turn, can give a false impression that the agent is being inconsistent toward her most important endorsements. This impression is created because the social construction of group identities is such that those who claim a given social group membership must do two things: 1) to accept *at least some* of the meaning, values and practices that are used to define that particular social group, and 2) to be willing to be judged by the prevailing moral values of the social group.[20] When norms are stereotypically perceived as key aspects of a group identity that an agent wishes to retain, the latter of these two requirements can lead to the assumption that an agent is acting with complicity toward norms that they have actually outlawed to themselves.

In Lugones's case, for example, other Latinos/as will assume that because Lugones identifies as a Latina she accepts (and should be judged by) the homophobic values widespread in Latino/a communities. In fact, however, Lugones wholeheartedly refuses to accept homophobic values as part of her endorsements and since acceptance of only *some* values and norms of a social group are necessary to construct a social identity, she is free to reject various elements of Latina/o culture such as its heterosexism. Despite her rejection of particular Latina/o group values, however, Lugones does not reject her social identity as a Latina. Retaining her Latina identity is something that she strongly endorses and from it she is in a better social position to combat homophobia *within* Latina/o culture itself. By continuing to embrace her Latina identity, however, Lugones also associates herself with a still largely heterosexist culture, and in so doing she appears to be inconsistent toward her endorsements. Lugones is not inconsistent, however, but has placed herself in the ambivalent position of being "willing to be judged" by others according to a value systems that she vocally criticizes and rejects.

On the whole, then, Lugones's ambivalence is ambivalence *toward aspects of her social identity group* and is not the same as, and does not require, ambivalence *toward her own self chosen endorsements*. This distinction is not always drawn, however. As described above, for example, Diana Meyers suggests that those with multiple identities may experience "political conundrums" arising from identification with conflicting groups in which their group memberships force them to sometimes tolerate and sometimes resist the same forms of subordination in different contexts. Yet, as the Lugones example indicates, when an agent's syncretic endorsements require maintaining ties to conflicting groups, the endorsements stereotypically attributed to those groups will not necessarily reflect the agent's endorsements. Lugones's observance of her anti-homophobic and anti-racist endorsements in contexts hostile to them, demonstrates that it is possible to balance morally conflicting social identities through a consistent set of syncretic endorsements. This is possible, however, only *if* the order of those endorsements is flexible enough to accommodate prioritizing endorsements contextually in response to the varying demands of different social setting and relationships.

III. Conclusion

If ambivalence and flexibility can become tools for observing syncretic endorsements, then the answer to the question of whether an agent can be ambivalent in his endorsements and still be autonomous toward them is yes, at least in part. All autonomous agents must develop their own endorsements from whatever materials happen to be given to them socially. In some cases, the syncretic or hybrid sets of endorsements that they create will conflict significantly with the social relations in which they must act. In such cases, an agent may maintain an ambivalent posture toward the values and principles that they disavow as a way of observing their endorsements while simultaneously retaining a set of social relations that are inhospitable to their particular autonomous choices.

However, the forms of ambivalence that enable this delicate balancing act can erode wholeheartedness even as it serves as a tool with which to preserve autonomy. Any agent with a hybrid set of endorsements may utilize such ambivalence in the ways described above. Yet, it may be particularly useful to those with a highly diverse array of social identities whose syncretic endorsements conflict significantly with the various social groups with which they are highly identified. This may be so especially when those various groups are hierarchically ordered or linked through social relations of subordination and conflict.

If wholeheartedness is not always possible for autonomous agents, this is not to say that it is obsolete as an aspect of procedural autonomy. Wholeheartedness can be considered a sometimes-achievable aspect of mestiza autonomy, one that is especially possible when an agent's endorsements are generally unquestioned by others. When such wholeheartedness is lacking, however, its absence does not necessarily denote a lack of firm commitment to one's endorsements. Rather it is likely to be the cost of the struggle to exercise those commitments in the midst of complex social relations and hostile group conflicts. After all, for Patricia and for Lugones, the ultimate source of their ambivalence is the set of patriarchal, heterosexist, ethnocentric norms that are part of the longstanding social conflicts in which they have been socialized and continue to live. As long as Patricia and Lugones must cope with such intersecting sets of subordinating social relations, ambivalence and flexibility—more than wholeheartedness—will be the tools that they need to live autonomously in accordance with their endorsements. It is the process of coping *autonomously* with intolerance that ultimately erodes their wholeheartedness and snatches away the possibility of a simpler, less embattled manifestation of their autonomy.

Thus the wholeheartedness that Frankfurt describes may be regarded as an ideal that is best achieved by removing agents from social conflict. I contend that when wholeheartedness is not readily obtainable given particular relational contexts, the formation of syncretic endorsements through critical reflection can stand in for wholeheartedness as a clear indication that autonomy-conferring critical reflection has taken place. When agents forge syncretic endorsements from different social sources it is clear from the analysis that such a critical creative act involves that the agent has critically reflected on the material socially given to her. Consequently, the syncretic creation of endorsements is evidence of critical reflection in virtue of which we can call an agent's self-principled acts autonomous, regardless of any feelings of ambivalence that may accompany them. Moreover, the extra effort and creativity that it takes to utilize ambivalence and flexibility to observe syncretic endorsements can be regarded also as a sign of tenacious commitment to one's endorsements and to exercising autonomy in spite of social obstacles.[21] While such tenacity is not the same as Frankfurt's wholeheartedness, it does demonstrate the kind of principled purposefulness and thoroughgoing effort that we often associate with wholeheartedness in vernacular terms.

Finally, mestiza autonomy may cast light on other relational aspects of autonomy that have not yet been fully explored. For example, as described above, Anzaldúa argued that the complexity of contemporary social relations calls on us to develop inclusive modes of critical thinking in which we continually integrate new insights into our approaches to everyday life. Can taking such a syncretic approach to critical reasoning lead to new avenues for resisting and circumventing subordinating forms of socialization? Perhaps. Like historical procedural accounts of autonomy that emphasize the formative role of subordinating social relations, mestiza autonomy acknowledges that subordinating forms of socialization can impede autonomy. Yet, the examples of mestiza autonomy outlined above also suggest that the obstacle of subordinating socialization can be overcome when agents syncretize their endorsements from a deeply diverse set of different identifications and ways of life.

In Patricia's case, for example, her syncretic educational endorsement is, I would argue, emancipatory both for herself and for other Chicanas. Notably, however, her emancipatory syncretic educational endorsement is drawn from two lifeworlds, *both of* which have central norms and values that still largely subordinate Chicanas as women of color. Nevertheless, by hybridizing her set of endorsements from these divergent social domains and being willing to live with high levels of ambiguity and ambivalence, Patricia could achieve a degree of autonomy with emancipatory potential despite having suffered forms of subordinating socialization.

Consequently, emancipatory acts of autonomy based in syncretic endorsements may also have socially transformative potential. This is because an agent's relational autonomous actions are both informed by *and* formative of the social relations in which they are embedded. Because Patricia's educational endorsement is a syncretic fusion that transgresses prevailing social and political norms in her cultural communities, Patricia's autonomous action can, over time, contribute to the normalization of new social norms within both Chicano and mainstream culture. Moreover, because her autonomous actions are relational, they have an impact not only on her own social relationships but also on those of others like her husband, who in his relation to her is likewise drawn into the struggles over contested gender roles. Because Patricia's autonomous acts have implications for his gendered actions, he too will be faced with the opportunity to critically reflect upon and make choices regarding his endorsements of specific gender norms.

Critical reflection and the formation of syncretic endorsements alone are not sufficient for the achievement of autonomy, of course. The relational and socially embedded character of mestiza autonomy situates an individual's daily struggles to achieve autonomy within the local social conditions in which the agent lives, and also within broader social and political struggles. For Patricia, keeping her everyday desires and actions in line with her chosen guiding principles depends to a large extent on the degree of support and resistance that she encounters.

Structural elements such as affirmative action and financial aid policies can play a facilitating role in her achievement of autonomy. When the balance of social support (or neutrality) gives way to prevailing conditions of resistance, the material possibility of exercising autonomy is greatly reduced.[22]

Ongoing discussions as to the shape and significance of the relational aspects of autonomy will no doubt continue. As Marilyn Friedman has argued, social relations are so complex that the relational aspects of autonomy are likely to require philosophers to further explore how social relations can both foster *and* inhibit autonomy (Friedman 1997). Mestiza autonomy may provide one possible way of conceptualizing autonomy when a subject observes endorsements that are forged from a varying array of social group identifications and relationships.[23]

References

Alarcón, N. (1990) "The Theoretical Subject(s) of *This Bridge Called My Back* and Anglo-American Feminism," in G. Anzaldúa (ed.) *Making Face, Making Soul: Creative and Critical Perspectives by Feminists of Color*, 356–369, San Francisco: Aunt Lute Books.

Alarcón, N. (1994) "Conjugating Subjects: The Heteroglossia of Essence and Resistance," in A. Arteaga (ed.), *An Other Tongue: Nation and Ethnicity in the Linguistic Borderlands*, 26–27, Durham, NC: Duke University Press.

Anzaldúa, G. (1987) *Borderlands/La Frontera: The New Mestiza*, San Francisco: Aunt Lute Books.

Anzaldúa, G. (2000) *Interviews/Entrevistas*, New York: Routledge.

Barth, F. (1969) *Ethnic Groups and Boundaries: The Social Organization of Culture Difference*, Boston, MA: Little, Brown.

Baynes, K. (1996) "Public Reason and Personal Autonomy," in D. M. Rasmussen (ed.), *The Handbook of Critical Theory*, 243–254, Cambridge, MA: Blackwell.

bell hooks. (1990) *Yearning: Race Gender, and Cultural Politics*, Boston, MA: South End Press.

Benhabib, S. (1992) *Situating the Self: Gender, Community and Postmodernism in Contemporary Ethics*, New York: Routledge.

Benn, S. I. (1982) "Individuality, Autonomy, and Community," in E. Kamenka (ed.), *Community as a Social Ideal*, 191–197, New York: St. Martin's Press.

Benson, P. (1994) "Free Agency and Self-worth," *Journal of Philosophy* 91: 650–668.

Calhoun, C. (1995) "Standing for Something," *Journal of Philosophy* 92: 235–260.

Christman, J. (1993) "Autonomy and Personal History," *Canadian Journal of Philosophy* 21: 1–24.

Cohen, A. (1985) *The Symbolic Construction of Community*, London: Ellis Horwood/Tavistock.

Dworkin, G. (1988) *The Theory and Practice of Autonomy*, New York: Cambridge University Press.

Feinberg, J. (1989) "Autonomy," in John Christman (ed.), *The Inner Citadel: Essays on Individual Autonomy*, 27–53, Oxford: Oxford University Press.

Frankfurt, H. (1987) "Identification and Wholeheartedness," in F. Schoeman (ed.), *Responsibility, Character, and the Emotions*, 27–45, New York: Cambridge University Press.

Friedman, M. (1986) "Autonomy and the Split-level Self," *Southern Journal of Philosophy* 24: 19–35.
Friedman, M. (1997) "Autonomy and Social Relationships," in D. Meyers (ed.), *Feminists Rethink the Self*, 40–61, Boulder, CO: Westview Press.
Friedman, M. (2000) "Autonomy, Social Disruption, and Women," in C. Mackenzie and N. Stoljar (eds.), *Relational Autonomy*, 35–51, New York: Oxford University Press.
Grimshaw, J. (1988) "Autonomy and Identity in Feminist Thinking," in M. Griffiths and M. Witford (eds.), *Feminist Perspectives in Philosophy*, 90–108, London: Macmillian.
Grovier, T. (1993) "Self-trust, Autonomy, and Self Esteem," *Hypatia*, 8: 99–120.
Hoagland, S., and Frye, M. (1997) "Feminist Philosophy," in J. V. Canfield (ed.), *Philosophy of Meaning, Knowledge and Value in the Twentieth Century*, 320–325, New York: Routledge.
Hurtado, A. (2003) *Voicing Chicana Feminisms: Young Women Speak Out on Sexuality and Identity*, New York: New York University Press.
Lugones, M. (1987) "Playfulness, 'World-traveling', and Loving Perception," *Hypatia* 2: 3–19.
Lugones, M. (1990) "Hispaneando y lesbiando: On Sarah Hoagland's *Lesbian Ethics*," *Hypatia* 5: 139–146.
Lugones, M. (1991) "On the Logic of Pluralist Feminism," in C. Card (ed.), *Feminist Ethics*, 35–44, Lawrence: University of Kansas Press.
Lugones, M. (1992) "*On Borderlands/La Frontera: An Interpretive Essay*," *Hypatia* 7: 31–37.
Lugones, M. (1994) "Purity, Impurity, and Separation," *Signs* 19: 458–479.
Markus, H., et al., (1982) "Self-schemas and Gender," *Journal of Personality and Social Psychology* 42: 38–50.
Mackenzie, C., and Stoljar, N., eds. (2000) *Relational Autonomy: Feminist Perspectives on Autonomy, Agency, and the Social Self*. Oxford University Press.
Meyers, D. T. (1989) *Self, Society, and Personal Choice*, New York: Columbia University Press.
Meyers, D. T. (2000) "Intersectional Identity and the authentic self?" in C. Mackenzie and N. Stoljar (eds.), *Relational Autonomy*, 151–180, New York: Oxford University Press.
Meyers, D. T. (2004) *Being Yourself: Essays on Identity, Action, and Social Life*, New York: Rowman and Littlefield.
Mullin, A. (1995) "Selves, Diverse and Divided: Can Feminists Have Diversity Without Multiplicity?" *Hypatia* 10: 1–31.
Nancy, J.-L. (1994) "Cut Throat Sun," in A. Arteaga (ed.), *An Other Tongue: Nation and Ethnicity in the Linguistic Borderlands*, 113–123, Durham, NC: Duke University Press.
Nedelsky, J. (1989) "Reconceiving Autonomy: Sources, Thoughts, and Possibilities," *Yale Journal of Law and Feminism* 1: 7–36.
Ruiz, V. (1998) *From Out of the Shadows*, Oxford: Oxford University Press.
Turner, J. C. (1999) "Some Current Issues in Research on Social Identity and Self-categorization Theories," in N. Ellemers, R. Spears and B. Doosje (eds.), *Social Identity*, 6–34, New York: Blackwell.
Watson, G. (1982) *Free Will*, Oxford: Oxford University Press.

Notes

1 For examples of this shift see Dworkin (1988); Baynes (1996); Feinberg (1989); Benn (1982); Christman (1993). For an overview of the convergence between feminist and mainstream accounts of autonomy see Friedman (1997).

2 I assume throughout this essay that autonomy is an achievement that agents realize to varying degrees in different social contexts. Gary Watson put this point succinctly with his statement that "[f]ree will involves the capacity to reflect critically upon one's values according to relevant criteria of practical thought and to change one's values and action in the process. So viewed, free will is not something we simply have or lack, but is an achievement, that admits of degrees" (1982: 8). Because the "relevant criteria" of practical thought can vary widely, I also assume that systematic critical thought may incorporate a full range of socially given standards and components beyond instrumental rationality. These may include affect, intuition, aesthetic judgments and different systems of value from Native American spirituality to feminist norms to Kantian moral imperatives.

3 As some feminist philosophers have pointed out, however, Frankfurt (1987) does not theorize the role of socialization in his framework of autonomy, and thereby potentially perpetuates the gender bias common to earlier accounts of autonomy (see Friedman 2000: 39 and n. 29). While I acknowledge this point, as I read Frankfurt's framework, he does not rule out or deny the

influence of social construction on the subject. Desires that just "happen to occur" as part of our internalized worldviews may come to be there in many ways, including by the constructivist routes that Frankfurt himself does not specify or explore.

4 While identification and wholeheartedness are necessary to autonomy for Frankfurt, he does not argue that they will necessarily eliminate core conflicts between competing desires (or that some conflicts may not be reconsidered at a later time). Those conflicts may persist, but when they erupt they are already resolved for the subject who has already decided on his position, identified with one side of a conflict and disidentified with the other (1987: 40, 43). On this account, it is because no ambivalence remains toward his choice that the agent can be thought to be wholehearted.

5 Meyers (2000: 154–156) also draws on the work of various other thinkers who have written on intersectionality, including María Lugones, Kimberlé Crenshaw, Kirstie McClure and Chantal Mouffe.

6 Consequently, Meyers considers, "ignorance of one's intersectional identity . . . is a major threat to nuanced social critique" and "leads to self-deception . . . corruption of principles . . . and to moral heteronomy" (2000: 161).

7 Anzaldúa's work can also be seen as part of a broad body of work by feminists of color that emphasizes the intersection of different identities and identity group-related forms of subordination within the self. Much of this work also draws a connection between those intersections and struggles for social justice. For reference to this see Alarcón (1990) and Lugones (1991).

8 The terms Anglo and Anglo-American are used in Anzaldúa's work and in Chicana/o Studies generally as inclusive terms that refer to mainstream Euroamerican culture as the majority culture in United States. I employ it here in that manner and use it interchangeably with the term Euroamerican.

9 The term *mestiza* is sometimes controversial due to its origins as a referent for "mixed-blood" biological heritage and essentialist understandings of race. While Anzaldúa does refer to "mixed-blood" frequently in *Borderlands*, I take her to be referring (as she later clarified) to a *cultural mestizaje*—a mixture of socially constructed identities formed through a confluence of lifeworlds and social relations (see, for example, 1987: 55–61, 74, and also Anzaldúa's clarification (2000: 133, 238–241)). In addition, while I consider most people to have some greater or lesser diversity of social identities, I do not consider *mestizaje* to be a general state of being as does Jean-Luc Nancy (1994: 113–123). Instead, like Norma Alarcón, Anzaldúa and María Lugones, I use the terms *mestiza* and *mestizaje* to refer to the quality of empirical selves in which they exhibit specific forms of cultural mixture *mestizaje*. For Alarcón's response to Nancy, see (1994: 26–27).

10 The 8th edition of the *Oxford English Dictionary* defines to "syncretize" as "the attempt, esp. inconsistently, to unify or reconcile different schools of thought." This seems to me to be what Anzaldúa had in mind as the method by which the mestiza lives through her multiple identities.

11 bell hooks (1990: 145–153), among others, has made a similar argument regarding the creative potential of being at the margin of a social group.

12 Social identities are those identities associated with one's group memberships or social roles, such as professional, ethnic or national identities. Personal identities, in contrast, are identifications that are unique to us as part of the relationships that we have to particular individuals, e.g. "daughter to Alexander" or "sister to Eileen." This distinction is commonly drawn in various areas of social psychology and particularly emphasized in social identity theory. See Turner (1999: 6–34).

13 I borrow the term identity schema from experimental psychologist Hazel Markus, who has used it to refer to socially constructed social group identities such as gender identity. She defines an identity schema as a "structure of knowledge or systematic framework that participates in ongoing interpretive activity during information processing," or in what philosophers generally refer to as thought or cognitive reason. See Markus et al. (1982).

14 For the distinction between social and personal identities, see Note 13 above. The case of Patricia analyzed below indicates how social and personal identities can become intertwined.

15 I derive this point from Fredrik Barth's (1969: 14) account of ethnic group formation produced through ongoing processes of claiming social boundaries and membership in social contexts. For an extension of this approach to other types of social groups, see Cohen (1985).

16 Of course, female gender roles within Chicana/o culture are more diverse in practice than they are stereotypically drawn. While patriarchal norms have long structured Chicana gender role as home-centered, in practice poverty has often required Chicanas to engage in paid labor outside of the home as part of their care giving responsibilities. The double workday among Chicanas thus

further displaced opportunities for formal education throughout the twentieth century. While these patriarchal and economic pressures still remain, Chicana gender roles have been transforming for decades to include higher education, skilled or professional labor outside the home, sexual independence and political participation. See Ruiz (1998). As might be expected, during such social transformation the acceptance and practice of new norms remains uneven; see Hurtado (2003).

17 Anzaldúa (1987: 77–87) discusses the importance of such borrowings.
18 In an essay on integrity in which she analyzes María Lugones's work on resistance to ethnocentrism and heterosexism, Cheshire Calhoun makes a related point. She states, "[a]nyone who regards herself as an equal in autonomous judgment to others cannot be indifferent to what others think. When one's own and others' judgments come into serious conflict, ambivalence may be a way of acknowledging that equality" (1995: 241).
19 Others have also suggested that the rank order of endorsements should be more flexible in structural procedural accounts of autonomy. Marilyn Friedman (1986) argued that there should be an ongoing assessment in which everyday thoughts and actions and endorsements are considered in reference to each other on an ongoing basis. Diana Meyers makes a related suggestion that different endorsement should be considered as equally important rather than in a rank order (2000: 170–172).
20 This point is also drawn from the work of Fredrik Barth and Anthony Cohen on the social construction of social groups and group membership; see Note 14 above.
21 Diana Meyers (2000: 152) has made a related claim observing that those who experience multiple forms of social oppression are in some ways better positioned than those who are multiply privileged to exercise autonomy.
22 While I propose mestiza autonomy as a procedural, content neutral account of autonomy, it might be compatible with weak substantive accounts of autonomy in which self-esteem is an enabling factor in autonomous thought and action such as that presented by Paul Benson (1994). It is difficult to imagine that Patricia could have persisted in her educational endorsements against so many obstacles without a significant degree of self-worth and self-trust, assets that she may have drawn from her relationships with her own parents and/or her husband.
23 I'd like to thank Jane Flax, Drucilla Cornell and Jennifer Nedelsky for their comments on an early draft of this essay during an annual meeting of the American Political Science Association. My thanks go also to two anonymous reviewers for *The Journal of Political Philosophy* and to Peter Digeser, who commented on a later draft of this piece. I'd also like to extend my special thanks to Robert Goodin for his generous support and encouragement after an unexpected delay in completing the final revisions.

Reading Questions

1. What is mestiza consciousness, as Barvosa understands it?
2. What is autonomy, according to Barvosa? What is specifically *mestiza* autonomy?
3. Barvosa writes that "while mestiza autonomy faces every individual with the task of deriving a set of endorsements from the materials socially given to them, the complexity of that task will vary from one person to the next depending on the degree of difference between their various identifications and relationships." So is mestiza autonomy a different kind of autonomy, or is it an account of what autonomy, properly speaking, is or some other thing?
4. How is ambivalence liberatory? Can ambivalence be a problem?
5. What's the relationship between syncretic outlook construction, in Barvosa's sense, and subsumption in Morton's sense? What is the difference between biculturality (Vargas), world-traveling (as in Lugones), and compartmentalization?
6. What's the heart of autonomy? Why is it valuable? Barvosa says "the syncretic creation of endorsements is evidence of critical reflection in virtue of which we can call an agent's self-principled acts autonomous, regardless of any feelings of ambivalence that may accompany them" (19). However, that makes it sound like syncretic endorsement and action from it isn't autonomy but evidence of some further thing (maybe action coherent with critical reflection?) that is the root of autonomy. What do you think?

14 Cultural Code-Switching

Straddling the Achievement Gap

Jennifer M. Morton

When Barack Obama became the first African-American president of the United States he bolstered America's claim to be a nation of equal opportunity. Obama exemplifies an archetype of upward mobility for minorities, bridging the socio-economic achievement gap while remaining engaged with his African-American community; he appears as comfortable among his mostly white and affluent colleagues as among the mostly black and socio-economically diverse members of the congregation he attended. Obama's success appeared to be partially dependent on his ability to engage in cultural code-switching. Code-switching could be characterized as the ability to adapt one's behavior as a response to a change in social context much like bilingual speakers switch languages in response to a change in linguistic context. However, this statement of the ability is too general—every agent has to adapt her behavior in response to the different norms governing the various dimensions of her work, home, and social life. The case of upwardly mobile minorities is interesting because they exhibit an ability to switch between comprehensive and potentially conflicting value systems. Code-switchers appear able to navigate two (or more) distinct communities and reap the benefits of belonging to both.[1]

Consequently, this kind of code-switching has become a topic of interest to scholars examining the achievement gap because it appears to be a way for low-income minorities to remain authentically engaged with the values of their communities, while taking advantage of opportunities for further education and higher incomes available to those that participate in the middle-class. Sociologists,[2] psychologists (LaFromboise et al. 1993), and educators (Carter 2005) have made important contributions towards understanding code-switching. Yet, surprisingly little has been said about the ethical and normative dimensions of this phenomenon in the philosophical literature, even though it involves a normatively distinctive relationship between the agent and what she values. Though thoroughly completing that task is beyond the scope of this article, I take an initial step toward doing so by developing a moral psychological model of code-switching. The analysis I offer can be extended to think about the moral psychology of code-switching more generally; however, my concern here is with code-switching as a response to market pressures by members of disadvantaged minority communities. On the basis of my analysis, I argue that those who code-switch for the sake of better educational and career opportunities must subsume code-switching under a comprehensive normative perspective from which they confront and resolve value conflicts, if they are to avoid becoming ethically unmoored.

In Section I, I discuss recent empirical findings on the role that "non-cognitive skills"[3] play in achievement and why the potential conflict between two central commitments of a liberal egalitarian education—equal opportunity and respect for diverse conceptions of the good—lead us to code-switching as a strategy for bridging the achievement gap. In

DOI: 10.4324/9781003385417-21

Section II, I argue that agents who rely on code-switching to achieve socio-economic success take on a perilous strategy, risking a loss of their moral bearings steered by the demands of the labor market. After identifying three models through which to understand cultural code-switching—pretense, compartmentalization, and subsumption—I argue that the only viable model subsumes code-switching under a comprehensive normative perspective. Such a strategy can allow members of minority communities to curb the potentially corrosive effect of the labor market on their communities. In the final section, I argue that code-switching is a response to non-ideal conditions, which affect different communities in different ways. The account I offer requires a justification that stresses, rather than obscures, the nature of the non-ideal conditions for which code-switching is a remedy. This distinguishes it from citizenship accounts of education that aim for universal justification.

I. The Non-Cognitive Challenge

A. *Equal Opportunity and the Non-cognitive Gap*

Though there has been considerable discussion in the literature about whether an "equal" opportunity requires making sure everyone has exactly the same educational resources or meets a fair minimum threshold (Jencks 1988), there is general agreement that the systematic intergenerational disadvantage and lack of access to a college education and well-paying jobs confronting children born into disadvantaged communities is problematic.[4] Undeniably, part of the explanation for the socio-economic gap between Blacks and Hispanics in the United States can be attributed to structural factors (Spalter-Roth and Lowenthal 2005; Wilson 1996). However, the American educational system shares some of the blame insofar as it fails to provide students with the reading and math skills they need to be adequately prepared for the competitive job market, which currently places a premium on higher education (Jencks and Phillips 1998). Recent data shows that only 17% of Hispanic and 14% of Black 4th graders scored at or above proficiency level in reading skills, compared to 43% of White, and 46% of Asian/Pacific Islander 4th graders. The statistics in mathematics achievement are similar (Aud et al. 2010: 54). Recently, some economists, psychologists, and other social scientists have posited a different kind of educational gap that stresses the important role that non-cognitive dispositions, or "soft skills," play in socio-economic achievement (Borghans et al. 2008; Heckman and Krueger 2002; Heckman and Rubenstein 2001; Duckworth et al. 2012).

The term "non-cognitive disposition" is used as an umbrella term for the behavioral, social, and emotional dispositions, such as extroversion, aggression, assertiveness, and grit, that are distinguished from cognitive skills, such as those measured by IQ, reading, and mathematical ability tests. The data here is complex because it varies in methodology (quantitative to qualitative), demographic focus (race, gender, ethnicity, and socio-economic class), measured variables (personality measures, parenting skills, cultural capital), and measured outcomes (school achievement, graduation rates, income, and job performance). Furthermore, some oversimplification inevitably occurs when we are discussing a "labor market advantage" since labor markets are complex and diverse.[5]

Though these complexities are important and significant, research suggests that non-cognitive dispositions, or "soft skills," have a significant effect on future earnings potential. Research also suggests that parenting styles and neighborhood effects play a role in the transmission and entrenchment of the non-cognitive skills that advantage children born to middle and upper class families (Wilson 1996; Osborne-Graves 2005). Annette

Lareau's influential research shows that middle-class parents teach many of the dispositions valued by the labor market to their children that poor and working-class parents often do not (Lareau 2003). Finally, research into preschool intervention programs that have a significant focus on the development of non-cognitive skills, shows that participants have diminished rates of incarceration, lower unemployment, and better health than control groups, as adults (Heckman 2010; Campbell et al. 2002).

If the research is right in showing the importance that non-cognitive skills play in achievement, and the role that parents and schools can play in shaping them, then educational institutions must do their part to mitigate these effects by teaching children the dispositions rewarded by the labor market, if they are not learning them at home.

B. Liberal Respect for Conceptions of the Good

It is the other central commitment at the heart of liberal egalitarianism—respecting those who hold the diverse conceptions of the good that a multicultural society fosters—that leads to a challenge to the straightforward solution suggested above to the relationship between labor market rewards, equal opportunity, and education. Rawls characterizes a conception of the good as a person's "conception of what is valuable in human life," as well as her relationships and attachments to particular groups and associations (Rawls 2005: 19). A liberal egalitarian society's institutions show respect for its citizenry, in part, by respecting their various conceptions of the good. They do so by setting limits to the conceptions of the good they accommodate—wide enough to allow for a flourishing of diverse conceptions of the good—and, most importantly, by offering a liberal justification when they do curtail those limits. Those limits are contested in the literature (Brighouse 1998; Callan 1996; Galston 1995). Nonetheless, it's clear that a liberal society need not respect every cultural practice or conception of the good. It can offer a cogent justification, based on liberal tenets, for failing to accommodate those who hold views that are unjust, racist, or intolerant. However, if it is to show respect for those who belong to minority cultures that are not unjust or intolerant, it must be able to offer a suitable justification when it uses its institutions to undermine those ways of life.

The difficulty in applying this liberal ethos to the case of education is that children do not, yet, have fully formed mature conceptions of the good. Children generally do value particular persons (usually, family, and peers) and some groups and associations (for example, sports teams or classmates), but they haven't yet autonomously committed themselves to a particular set of ideals. The literature has framed the liberal dilemma for education as one about who has authority to shape the child's developing conception of the good, pitting the parents' conception of the good against the state's interest in its future citizens. However, even if a liberal society is only committed to fostering those conceptions of the good that are within the domain of reasonable conceptions of the good compatible with the core tenets of liberalism, and we grant that parents have a limited right to inculcate children with their own conception of the good, most liberal theorists would agree that a *liberal* educational system should not intend to educate students towards one single set of values or cultural practices (Brighouse 2000: Ch. 1). A liberal state is legitimate, in part, because citizens who have diverse and reasonable conceptions of the good would consent to it; inculcating future citizens with a comprehensive conception of the good would threaten to undermine its legitimacy (Brighouse 1998).

An account of liberal education need not endorse a value-free education but, in order to retain its liberal credentials, the values it encourages ought to be *normatively* justified on the basis of *liberal* tenets, in a way that shows respect for its citizenry and their diverse conceptions of the good. Educational institutions are not exempt from justification because they are serving children who do not yet have fully worked out conceptions of the good.

C. The Challenge

The dilemma regarding liberal neutrality and opportunity in the school system is often couched as a conflict between the school's authority in educating future citizens, and the parents' authority over educating their own children (Brighouse and Swift 2009). But thinking of the tension between liberalism and equal opportunity in this way obscures the role that the market plays in structuring the choices facing educators, whether parents or institutions. The non-cognitive challenge arises because the value of non-cognitive dispositions is not limited to educational or labor markets; social and emotional dispositions are also part of how human beings engage with their conceptions of the good.

I propose that a useful way to understand an agent's conception of the good is to use a notion of *valuing* drawn from the philosophy of action. This notion of valuing allows us to make sense of agents as valuing particular people, relationships, and groups as well as abstract ideals, thereby capturing more of what Rawls meant by a conception of the good.[6] Valuing has both cognitive elements (associated beliefs) and non-cognitive elements (behavioral, social, and emotional dispositions). These latter elements are central to the present topic. For example, if a person values sharing, at least part of what that entails is that she has the disposition to act in particular ways when she is in abundant possession of a good that others need or want. She will not be disposed to take as much as she can get, without regard for what others need. Similarly, if an agent values a particular person, she will be disposed to take the well-being of that person into account. Teaching values to children involves encouraging the patterns of behavior constitutive of engaging with those values, and discouraging incompatible patterns of behavior. The father who encourages his daughter to allow others to play with her toys is teaching her the value of sharing. The father who encourages his daughter to take her brother's feelings into account is teaching her to value her brother's well-being.[7]

Consider a family that has a reasonable conception of the good that de-emphasizes individuality and individual accomplishments, in favor of a collectivist orientation that values seeing oneself as a member of a community, taking very seriously one's commitments and relationships to extended family, and putting the interests of the group over those of the individual. There is extensive evidence that cultures do divide themselves between collectivist and individualist orientations in this way, and that these orientations have an effect on personality, cognition, and motivation (Markus and Kitayama 1991; Triandis and Suh 2002). The American labor market rewards assertiveness, competitiveness, and other dispositions, which are in tension with this family's focus on community. If a child raised in such a family is to have as many educational and career opportunities as those for which her talents make her eligible, she would benefit from learning these dispositions. However, learning the dispositions in question will undermine this child's engagement with her family's values.[8] For example, evidence from studies of Latino immigrants' children shows that as these children become more assimilated into mainstream American culture, parent-child conflict increases and the children's attitude towards family cohesion decreases (Rumbaut 2005). Ideally, the market would not make such a demand of this family, but this particular child is growing up in these particular circumstances. Parents and educational institutions have to confront how to weigh these competing considerations. Furthermore, educational institutions must justify making this trade-off in ways that are sensitive to their coercive power in shaping future citizens.

To be more precise, we need to remember that teaching a value to a child involves encouraging the dispositions constitutive of engaging with that value, and discouraging the dispositions that are contrary to it. Consider some value V, which is one of the values that is part of a way of life that a liberal society wants to allow to flourish, and a disposition to D1 that is partially constitutive of valuing V. And now consider a disposition to D2, valued by the labor market, but contrary to a disposition to D1, such that if the agent exhibits behavior D2, she is not exhibiting behavior D1. The challenge is that, in teaching her D2, we risk undermining her engagement with V. Return to our example, this child's family values their tight knit connection to their extended family (V), which requires being disposed to often place greater weight on the interests of one's extended family and community over one's individual accomplishments (D1). However, teaching this child the dispositions that will enable her to succeed in the labor market involves teaching her to be disposed to prioritize her individual accomplishments and long-term goals (D2) and learning this disposition would undermine her ability to engage with V (Morton 2011). Depending on how this trade-off is negotiated, the child would confront situations in which she has to prioritize competing commitments differently.

To be clear, the possibility that learning a disposition can potentially undermine a student's relationships or her commitment to her family's cultural practices is not sufficient to constitute an unanswerable challenge for a liberal egalitarian education. Cultures and related conceptions of the good are not static; it is unavoidable that as the child develops and goes through the public school system, she will develop different ideals, relationships, and associations that will alter her conception of the good. A liberal egalitarian educational system is not committed to preserving cultural practices, but it is committed to respecting those who hold reasonable conceptions of the good. Therefore, what the non-cognitive challenge raises is a burden of *justification*. For example, comprehensive liberal accounts of education offer a normative justification for the dispositions they seek to inculcate by arguing that some conceptions of the good, those that are illiberal, are justifiably undermined by liberalism's own lights. In the case we are considering, appealing to the market value of a particular disposition does not constitute an appropriate justification, because it threatens to allow the state to use educational institutions as a vehicle through which economic and labor markets shape the diversity of conceptions of the good, in our society. The problem isn't that there are fewer conceptions of the good for individuals to choose from; conceptions of the good might fall out of favor because adult individuals exercise their freedom to reject conceptions of the good they grew up with that they no longer find fulfilling.[9] The problem arises if reasonable conceptions of the good are eroded through educational institutions that are educating children towards those rewarded by the labor market, because they are so rewarded. Given that those labor market pressures already benefit groups in positions of economic and political power, using educational institutions to entrench their conceptions of the good—at the expense of the conceptions of the good of those who lack economic and political power—is manifestly disrespectful.

II. Code-Switching

Code-switching can be seen as a strategy that could potentially allow liberal egalitarians to bypass the uncomfortable position of promoting equal opportunity only at the cost of failing to respect reasonable conceptions of the good. In "No Citizen Left Behind,"

Meira Levinson advances a theory of civic education according to which students should be explicitly taught to code-switch as a tool to effectively engage with and change the dominant power structures that oppress them (Levinson 2012).[10] Just as bilingual children switch between languages, children could be taught to switch between the dispositions valued by the labor market and those valued at home, thereby allowing students to stem the effect of the market on their engagement with other values, while retaining the economic benefits of learning the dispositions valuable in the labor market. A child might be instilled with the disposition to D2 in one context, without undermining her ability to be disposed to D1 in a different context, thus preserving her ability to engage with value V and allowing the way of life of which that value is a part to flourish. This alternative would appear to allow liberal egalitarian educational institutions to bypass the need for further justification, since they would no longer be instrumental in allowing the market to undermine reasonable conceptions of the good.

Code-switching also allows us to understand how successful minority students navigate the tension between mainstream and minority cultural values and styles. This tension has been used to explain the achievement gap for some minority groups. John Ogbu and Signithia Fordham have famously argued that African-American students underachieve because of a fear of "acting white" (Fordham and Ogbu 1986), and, though this research has been called into question (Tyson et al. 2005), the kernel of truth in this theory is that minority children who do succeed appear particularly adept at negotiating mainstream ways of behaving. Prudence Carter's (2005) study of minority students in New York City public schools finds that many of the academically successful students are cultural-straddlers—minority students who "negotiate schooling in a way that enables them not only to hold on to their native cultural styles but also to embrace dominant cultural codes and resources." However, Carter also documents the tension students feel between adopting mainstream ways of behaving and negotiating peer relationships. The best way to understand the tension, for some of these students, might not be as a clash of values—thought of as abstract ideals—but rather as a tension between the behavior required by the mainstream for academic and socio-economic success, and that required by students' relationships, associations, and groups.

Though emerging empirical research will give us a clearer picture of the various factors at play in biculturalism,[11] the existing research is suggestive enough, and the implications for political and ethical theory important enough, that we need a clearer picture of the ethical and normative dimensions of code-switching as a strategy for minority students, who aspire to the educational and labor market opportunities open to the middle-class. My analysis will focus on elucidating code-switching from a normative perspective, in order to show how it could be used as a strategy to deal with the Non-cognitive Challenge, as it applies to the education of minority children. However, given that code-switching is often used by adults, parents, teachers, or members of minority communities who need to be successful in the mainstream labor market, what I say here can also help us start to get a better picture of the normative dimensions of code-switching in the case of adults. I start by describing the Integration model, which serves as a foil for the other three models of code-switching: Pretense, Compartmentalization, and Subsumption. I analyze each model in general terms and discuss its application to the case of education.

A. Integration

The example I use here, while hypothetical, is based on empirical data concerning the status of Latinos in the United States.[12] Consider Julia who grew up in a Latino family, with a collectivist cultural orientation in which relationships and obligations to family, and extended family are primary. Her childhood neighborhood was composed of mostly poor Black and Latino families with lack of access to good schools, public transportation, and other community resources. Julia is one of the very few who manages to succeed in her dismal school, win a scholarship to her state's university, attend law school, and become a lawyer at a prestigious law firm. Throughout this process, Julia increasingly develops an individualist mindset, placing more and more importance on her career and individual achievements, at the expense of honoring commitments to her extended family. During high school, she reluctantly prioritized studying over family commitments.[13] She makes these trade-offs with more ease as an adult, for example, by choosing to attend the firm's luncheon over tending to her sick cousin's children. She moves to a neighborhood that is closer to work and develops relationships with college friends and colleagues. Julia seeks to maintain relationships with her extended family, but finds it increasingly difficult to do so. I do not mean to suggest here that a collectivist orientation explains why Julia's community is poor or why most of the other members of her community will fail to be upwardly mobile. There is ample evidence from some Asian immigrant communities that a collectivist orientation does not necessarily have economically deleterious consequences. The challenges for minority groups participating in the mainstream vary depending on the ethnic group, socio-economic background, parental educational background expectations, gender dynamics, and so on. A large part of the explanation here is structural. The segregation of disadvantaged communities certainly plays a role since individuals in those communities rarely have relationships that extend into the mainstream (Wilson 1996; Anderson2010). Furthermore, some of these effects are magnified by the influence of stereotyping in the labor market; for example, evidence suggests that employers perceive black women as underperforming due to conflicting loyalties between the demands of their families and those of their jobs (Browne and Kennelly 1999). At the foreground of these larger structural factors are individuals, like Julia, who seek a path out of poverty and into the American middle-class, and find that they must adapt their behavior in order to do so.

Two ideas can help us make sense of Julia's case. The first is assimilation, according to which a member of a minority group adopts the culture, habits, language, and ways of interacting of the majority group so as to fully integrate into the mainstream. This does not adequately characterize Julia; her childhood values and relationships haven't been completely replaced, but rather rearranged as new values, relationships, and cultural practices have come to be integrated into her normative perspective. Julia has assessed the importance of helping with her nieces and nephews relative to the importance of advancing in her career and has decided that the latter matters more to her. This is not to say that Julia no longer feels the tension between them; though she still recognizes the importance of her relationships with her extended family, her commitment to invest time in them has weakened. Integration, which is a better characterization of Julia's case, is distinguished from assimilation in so far as more of the minority culture's values, habits, and ways of interacting are maintained. Nonetheless, both assimilation and integration take the agent to have arrived at an assessment of the relative importance of many of the potentially conflicting values, relationships, and cultural commitments at play, to develop a *unified* and full-fledged normative perspective that she brings to bear to particular situations.

According to this model, one cannot acquire a new disposition that is contrary to a value one holds, without thereby altering one's normative commitments or, at least, undermining one's engagement with the values with which that disposition is in tension. Of course, particular cases are much more complex. First, working through this confrontation of values can be more or less difficult depending on the communities involved, and the individual undertaking it. Second, this model assumes, for the sake of simplicity, that there are two sets of static values which are, after reflection, integrated into a coherent whole.[14] In reality, people often have various sets of values and commitments because they see themselves as members of various ethnic, geographical, or national groups, as being of a particular gender, and/ or as subscribing to certain political and ethical ideals. Furthermore, the values of particular groups are themselves dynamic; some minority communities are themselves undergoing profound transformations due to demographic, geographic, and socio-economic changes. Finally, the process of acquiring or rejecting many of these values is often not the outcome of reflection. Nonetheless, a philosophical analysis of this normative process requires some abstraction, and the model I present here is not inimical to the complexities presented by the particular situations confronted by individuals.

Applying this model to the case of education presents two difficulties. The first is that integration, in this case, would be a response to market pressures by minorities who are excluded from the mainstream, rather than genuine engagement with a different comprehensive conception of the good with which the agent also identifies, as might be the case for other bi-cultural individuals. The second is that we are dealing with children. An adult, when confronted with a situation that calls for such normative reevaluation, can meet this challenge and emerge with a more refined understanding of her own normative perspective. Children do not have a full-fledged normative perspective; they have not resolved which values are central to their lives, how to adjudicate conflicts between them, or weigh the interests of their families and communities against their own. In her wonderfully nuanced discussion of the moral status of children, Tamar Schapiro (1999) argues that the child's task is to develop such a normative perspective. She concludes that adults have an obligation to assist children in this task by allowing them to try out different perspectives, encouraging them to exercise their autonomy, and refraining from hindering them. According to the integration model, the trade-off between conflicting values and economic opportunities cannot be avoided, and if children are not up to the task, someone, the family or an educational institution, must undertake this process for the child.

B. Code-Switching as Pretense

In order to resist facing this conflict of values, an agent might choose to engage in code-switching as a kind of pretense. According to this model, undertaking a new non-cognitive disposition is compatible with withholding one's endorsement of an accompanying value. Returning to Julia, she might reject the values upheld in the competitive, individual achievement-oriented environment she works in, while recognizing that the accompanying behavior is required to succeed in her career path. She might see herself as truly being committed to the community-oriented values she grew up with, but feel forced to act as if she weren't when she is working.

The limitations of this approach are evident; acting in the context of a pretense cannot completely shield our behavior from normative evaluation. Julia might refuse to help her cousin take care of her sick children when it conflicts with her work commitments on the grounds that she has to act as if she values her career over her familial commitments. However, if Julia continues to act this way, her family might rightly object that her actions are inconsistent with highly valuing family relationships. An agent might have good reasons to engage in pretense for the sake of a job, but those reasons will not override competing reasons stemming from her other commitments in any situation she confronts within the context of her job, even if she doesn't identify with her behavior in a professional context. Valuing her family relationships requires that Julia feel the force of the demands they make on her and act accordingly in most contexts. In order to avoid becoming ethically unmoored while pretending, an agent must be sensitive to how the values she endorses impinge on the situation at hand; she cannot simply cordon them off. I return to a modified version of pretense that is meant to deal with this worry when discussing code-switching as subsumption.

Pretense as a strategy for students straddling the achievement gap is even more problematic than for adults. We would have to presume not only that children can adequately distinguish pretense from genuine engagement with a value, even when they are performing for many hours a day, but we also have to assume they will be able to adequately assess the limits when the performance comes into serious conflict with other values that they might not yet have a firm hold on. It is an open question whether, for example, a child could be assertive and competitive in the school system, while being community- and consensus-driven at home, and not have this switching back and forth affect which values he espouses. This is not to deny that children cannot benefit from pretense in developing a normative perspective—Schapiro suggests that it is an important part of their development. However, engaging in pretense in order to develop a normative perspective, under the guidance of a parent or educator, is different than being taught to engage in pretense in order to avoid resolving the conflicts between the values governing their school, and those governing their home. The latter is a risky and ethically problematic strategy.

C. Compartmentalized Code-Switching

A second alternative model is for the agent to undertake code-switching as compartmentalization. According to this model, an agent can learn a new non-cognitive disposition and even accept the accompanying value, but only within a certain context. The analysis this model offers of Julia's situation is that she truly values the relationships she cultivates at home and, in that context, she prioritizes the interests of her community over her individual success, but at work she values her individual success and, in professional contexts, she authentically prioritizes her career objectives over her community's interests. She is not merely pretending to do so. But how are we to understand this model as different from integration or pretense? One way of doing so is to suggest that Julia has two normative perspectives. From her normative perspective at work, succeeding at her job trumps many other values, including the interests of her community and developing deep relationships with her extended family. From her normative perspective at home, family obligations and relationships play a central role, often trumping her career. In this way, the two perspectives are shielded from one another so as not to be mutually undermining. Though this kind of splitting raises questions of integrity and alienation that deserve more careful attention, it is not unfamiliar. Sometimes, we find ourselves forced to adopt two perspectives, both of which we endorse even if they might be in tension with one another. For example, Cheshire Calhoun argues, drawing on an example from Lugones' (2009) work about being both a Latina and a Lesbian, that integrity need not require resolving inconsistencies in one's values, since agents sometimes have good reason not to resolve value conflicts (Calhoun 1995). In such cases, the agent is committed to two potentially conflicting normative perspectives, and she has to negotiate conflicts between them as they arise.

It is important to reiterate here the scope of my article. Cultures are dynamic and bicultural individuals are uniquely positioned to be a part of the changes that cultures undergo, as they come into contact with each other. However, the challenge here is not that educational institutions are failing to preserve cultures as intact artifacts, but rather that they are being used to corrode minority cultural values on the basis of market forces. The compartmentalization model, in this case, would have an agent adopt a set of dispositions, not because she endorses and identifies with those values, but *for the sake of labor market success*. Some bicultural individuals might be fortunate enough to endorse a set of values that happen to be rewarded by the labor market. However, for agents who come from minority cultures and feel alienated from mainstream culture, code-switching would require adopting a whole new set of cultural repertoires, habits, and associated values in order to have better economic opportunities, not because those values genuinely come to be seen as valuable. Compartmentalizing as a mode of code-switching, in this case, requires that one of the agent's perspectives be guided by the labor market and shielded from critical evaluation from her other comprehensive ethical perspective.

The danger of this proposal is magnified when we consider compartmentalization as a strategy for children to bridge the gap between the dispositions constitutive of engaging with their home values, and the dispositions that open up socio-economic opportunities. Cultural code-switching for the sake of equal opportunity would involve encouraging a child, in particular contexts, to behave in ways that allow her to succeed socio-economically, while putting aside the values she engages with at home. For example, the Latino child we have been discussing would be taught to prioritize her individual interests at school and do whatever is required to succeed, but to prioritize her family's interests, her role in the community, and empathizing with her extended family's needs when she is at home. Though I will not elaborate on this point here, it is important to note that such code-switching makes it increasingly difficult for the child to develop a unified and integrated normative perspective, which many have thought is an important part of a good life.[15] The main challenge, however, is that in asking children to adopt a normative perspective guided by labor market pressures in a way that shields that perspective from the values they are learning at home, we run the risk of leading them to lose their moral bearings before these are even fully developed.

It is helpful to contrast the case of instilling non-cognitive dispositions for the sake of giving children an equal opportunity at competing for the positions rewarded by the labor market with instilling non-cognitive dispositions for the sake of a liberal education that aims to inculcate core liberal values. If we adopt the integration model, the student who learns about the value of autonomy and tolerance at school has to eventually come to terms with how those values square with her values at home. It might well be that she finds a conflict there that she will have to resolve, eventually. But according to non-neutral accounts of liberal education, the possibility that values contrary to those of autonomy and tolerance might lose out is justifiable, rather than regrettable. Since such accounts of liberal education promote the full-blown adoption of core liberal values, they do not need to appeal to pretense or compartmentalization. In contrast, the reason to appeal to compartmentalization and pretense in the case of the non-cognitive dispositions associated with labor market success is to reap the opportunity benefit of adopting such non-cognitive dispositions without incurring the normative cost of allowing the labor market to erode cultural values that we have reason to respect. This strategy, however, either leads to a potentially alienating pretense that is not adequately anchored in one's normative perspective, or to a splitting of one's normative perspective that dangerously shields the agent's behavior from critical evaluation in light of her other values.

D. Code-Switching as Subsumption

The final model to consider is one that attempts to navigate the demands of the labor market by engaging in some kind of performance, while remaining firmly subsumed under the agent's normative perspective.[16] As in pretense, an adult agent adopts a disposition in one context, because it is valued in that context, without fully adopting the accompanying value. However, in so doing, the agent adopts an overarching narrative or project that justifies code-switching from her full-fledged normative perspective, and subjects her behavior within the performance to normative scrutiny.[17] This narrative or project can take many forms, but what is important is that it is not dictated by the whims of the market—it is anchored in a comprehensive conception of the good. Return to Julia's case. She could see her competitive and individualist behavior as a kind of performance that will help her secure a position with enough power to help her community. Suppose, for example, that budget cuts are being disproportionately apportioned on the already poor schools in the district in which she grew up. Julia wants to be in a position of economic and political power to stop this process, and sees her advancement in the legal world as part of that larger project.[18] Levinson (2012: Ch. 2) appears to have something like this model in mind when she suggests that students be taught to code-switch in the language and culture of those in power, in order to seek avenues to reform the system that oppresses them from the inside.[19]

However, before we turn to consider the difficulties of applying this model to children, four important aspects of the subsumption model must be noted. The first is that it requires a justification internal to the values espoused by the agent—the performance is subsumed under a comprehensive conception of the good. Unlike the two other kinds of code-switching, which seek to shield one's behavior from a conflicting and comprehensive conception of the good, this model requires that the agent locate and justify her behavior in light of such a conception. In some cases, this might not be possible. If the behavior demanded of an agent in a particular context is too antagonistic to her conception of the good, and the benefit accrued from engaging in it is not valuable enough, code-switching might not be justified. Even if she has a justification, the agent has to remain attuned to the balance of reasons favoring code-switching because the balance might change. For example, the agent could come to believe that she might not be successful at achieving her goals through code-switching and, consequently, she would no longer have a reason to code-switch.

The second related point is that subsuming code-switching in a comprehensive conception of the good allows the agent to monitor and limit how far to take her performance. Even if there is a justification to engage in code-switching, such a justification does not give the agent *carte blanche*. For example, Julia might decide that she cannot provide counsel to a political candidate whose record shows a disregard for the needs of her childhood community. There are delicate issues here about how far to take the performance within a particular context and where to draw the boundaries. However, in order for code-switching to be subsumed, the agent's behavior has to continue to be guided at some level by her comprehensive conception of the good.

This leads us to the third point. This mode of code-switching is a careful and delicate balancing act that can easily turn into assimilation, pretense, or compartmentalization. As noted, the agent must be regularly attuned to the overall narrative or project in negotiating the different situations she confronts. In addition, she must be careful not to let herself unwittingly buy into conflicting values. We should not underestimate how repeated performances of behavior that is in tension with our values can affect our normative perspective in the long run. Julia might come to forget what her ultimate goal was when she started and to lose sight of the values that initially motivated her. The final point to consider is that the agent might be misunderstood by others in her community, at school, or at her job, and risk undermining some of those relationships. In particular, agents who see code-switching as a path to subverting power structures might encounter resistance from fellow students or coworkers who authentically value those mainstream values.

Let's turn now to apply the code-switching model outlined to the case of students. Subsumption requires a comprehensive conception of the good that generates a narrative, project, or goal that justifies code-switching. For the remainder of this section I will focus on considering two conceptions that could play this role. But, first, there are two additional points we need to note. If we are to recommend code-switching to minority students as the most normatively viable strategy, then they should have a reasonable chance of success. Code-switching can only be justified internally if it does, in fact, help students achieve their goals. Even if students from impoverished backgrounds master code-switching, they have little chance of success if schools are too overcrowded for effective instruction, unemployment is so high that even those with a college education cannot find jobs, and if students cannot afford to attend college. Second, the cost that code-switching has on the students' relationships must be taken into account. This is an extremely important point that I will not be able to fully explore here, but which deserves further consideration.

There are two viable alternatives that could play the role of being the conception of the good under which code-switching is subsumed: the student's home culture or a non-neutral account of liberal education that espouses education for citizenship or autonomy. Let's consider the second of these alternatives first.

The appeal of code-switching is that it appears to be a way to limit the corrosive effect that market pressures can have on various reasonable conceptions of the good, which ought to be able to flourish in a liberal society. Subsumption allows an agent to code-switch, while relying on an underlying conception of the good that limits and controls the effect the market has on that conception of the good. The problem with non-neutral liberal accounts is that they are not comprehensive enough to limit and control the corrosive effect of the market. This is due to the nature of liberal accounts of education.[20] As Eamonn Callan notes, non-neutral accounts of education face the challenge of "conceiving the ends and means of civic education in a way that does not wrongly impair diversity" (Callan 2004: 12). Accounts that are able to meet that challenge and call themselves liberal are those that are limited enough to allow for the flourishing of a variety of conceptions of the good. But, precisely because of that feature, those accounts cannot guide an agent in navigating conflicts between the demands of the labor market and those of her home culture, unless the market or her home culture is making blatantly illiberal demands. What a liberal account of education can do is offer a filter on illiberal demands made by a student's home culture or the labor market. By including liberal principles of education into the curriculum, a school can be sure that the conceptions of the good it aims to respect are compatible with liberalism. For example, conceptions of the good that demean women would not pass this test. However, when two reasonable comprehensive conceptions of the good compatible with liberalism clash, liberal accounts cannot choose between them. Therefore, a liberal conception of the good that is limited enough to be called liberal cannot serve as the sole ground in which to anchor code-switching, because it does not have the resources to resist the threat of the market in undermining the diverse conceptions of the good we want to protect, though it can filter out some illiberal conceptions of the good.[21]

The alternative is to rely on the family's conception of the good. The educational approach that tailors teaching practices to a student's home culture is known as "cultural congruent education" and its premise is that education is more effective if children do not feel alienated from the school's culture (Levinson 2009).[22] Children do not arrive at school empty vessels. As Dewey (2008: 5) noted, the child's world is one of "personal contacts. Things hardly come within his experience unless they touch, intimately and obviously, his own well-being, or that of his family and friends." Dewey warns against developing a curriculum that is not sensitive to this fact; the more foreign an educational program is to the student's experience, the less likely it is to be effective in engaging the student. On other hand, Levinson makes a forceful argument for why minority children are not served by ethno-centric education that doesn't equip students to participate in the mainstream (Levinson 2012). Students do not have an equal opportunity if they are not also taught the dispositions rewarded by the middle-class.[23] Code-switching as subsumption attempts to combine an approach that respects the elements of a conception of the good that students bring to school, since this conception of the good serves to justify code-switching, while teaching them the dispositions that give them a better opportunity at socio-economic success. This justification will have to acknowledge the unjust conditions that necessitate code-switching—code-switching is a matter of necessity because mainstream economic opportunities cannot easily accommodate the student's burgeoning conception of the good.

Some theorists have stressed that code-switching should not be limited to minority students (Levinson 2009; Anderson 2007). The elites and those in dominant positions of power must also bear some responsibility for closing the achievement gap. Lareau suggests that teachers should be taught to code-switch in order to understand and adapt to those students who come from disadvantaged backgrounds (Lareau 2003: 255). It could be argued that elite students should be taught to code-switch as a way of enriching their understanding of themselves and others. Notice, however, that these justifications are of a markedly different kind than that offered to socio-economically disadvantaged minority students. Disadvantaged students are taught to code-switch as a way of opening socio-economic opportunities for themselves that are otherwise closed because socio-economically dominant institutions are not accommodating of their home culture. The difference in justification reveals the power asymmetries obscured by a naive appeal to code-switching. Therefore, one benefit of this last model of code-switching is that it does not hide the nature of the conflict it is attempting to remedy.

III. Conclusion

Many political, institutional, and structural factors lead to the concentration and segregation of poverty in predominantly minority communities, with little access to educational and health services, reliable public transportation, or jobs. Giving the members of these communities a better chance at a decent life will require radical changes in economic and political policy that extend far beyond changes in educational policy. Nonetheless, education is often a primary site in which these battles are played out; many see education as a way in which a new generation could be given the skills and knowledge they need to be on a more equal footing with their middle-class peers in attaining the educational and career opportunities that will enable them to lead a decent life. Against this background, individuals are caught between being members of disadvantaged communities and aspiring to access the opportunities for better employment available to the middle-class.

All agents, in navigating changing contexts, adapt to differences in normative expectations. Children are taught early on that what is appropriate at home might not be appropriate in other contexts. For some, adapting involves making minor adjustments, being attuned to differences in ways of address, dress codes, or norms governing the office or school. For large segments of the economically disadvantaged minority population, the distance between the world in which they grow up and that of educational institutions and well-paying careers is vast.[24] As we have seen, not only do they have to navigate differences in modes of address, language, and dress codes, but switch dispositions to ones that are often foreign, and in conflict with the dispositions and values central to their homes. In order to straddle the achievement gap, they have to learn to switch between considerably different and often conflicting *ways of being*. This is not, in itself, a problem. There are benefits to code-switching. Multicultural societies are characterized by the vibrant intermingling of cultural communities; individuals who belong to different communities are in a unique position to foster new relationships between them. However, when educational institutions are being used to shape students to adopt dispositions that potentially alienate them from their communities' values and relationships as a response to labor market pressures that unfairly favor the dispositions and habits of those who already hold positions of economic and political power, such institutions have become a site of further injustice.

Whether educational institutions are justified in undertaking the task of rectifying this injustice by shaping a student's non-cognitive dispositions, depends on the socio-economic conditions of the community at stake. For example, the potential disadvantage imparted by an orientation towards collectivism depends on the socio-economic position of the relevant community. In our current non-ideal situation, the harm to some minority groups in the form of entrenched poverty, poor health, and loss of dignity is alarming. The potential prevention of this harm might be enough to lead us to take considerations arising from equal opportunity to outweigh considerations of liberal respect. However, in doing so we are failing to respect these populations twice—by failing to provide them with a minimum standard of decent living and, because of it, by failing to respect their conception of the good in our educational institutions. In cases in which the harm is not of such a magnitude—as in the case of wealthier Asian-Americans, who are not adequately represented in positions of economic and political power, but whose average income is above that of white Americans—considerations of liberal respect are not clearly outweighed by considerations stemming from equal opportunity.[25] To put the problem bluntly, under non-ideal conditions, educational institutions appear more justified in rectifying problematic inequalities, by fostering the non-cognitive dispositions rewarded by the market among children of impoverished disadvantaged minority communities, even if, in doing so, they are potentially undermining reasonable conceptions of the good, because the socio-economic prospects of those children are so dire.[26] It should not come as a surprise that considerations stemming from equal opportunity in education will be weightier, and more likely to undermine our other liberal commitments, against a background of a non-ideal distribution of political and economic power.

This brings me to an additional reason to be wary of citizenship or autonomy accounts of education as a foundation for code-switching. These accounts support an educational vision composed of a core set of dispositions, values, and practices that are necessary for any good citizen, but non-ideal socio-economic conditions do not affect the opportunity prospects of different groups of citizens equally. An account that argues that we should all learn to code-switch to be better citizens, might have a point to make about what is required for good citizenship, but it obscures the fact that, for some students, code-switching is a necessity born of unjust socio-economic conditions. However, if we propose to respond to the achievement gap, we should not obscure this fact.

Cultural code-switching strikes many as an appealing model for fostering upward mobility, because it would appear to allow agents to inhabit both worlds without paying the price of resolving conflicts between them. However, cultural code-switching as a means to remedy the achievement gap is essentially a response to non-ideal conditions. Furthermore, as I have argued, once we analyze what it requires from a normative perspective, code-switching is a sensitive endeavor, even in the case of adults. An agent can engage in pretense or compartmentalization, but, thereby, shields her behavior from normative scrutiny and is easily swayed by the demands of the labor market, even if they run counter to her home values. Subsumed code-switching offers a delicate balance between integration and pretense, but it does not allow us to bypass confronting the conflict of value that motivated the adoption of code-switching in the first place.

Educational institutions play a powerful role in shaping future citizens and must exercise that power carefully. If the harms done to certain communities necessitate that we teach children the dispositions rewarded by the labor and educational market, the damage to disadvantaged communities should be minimized. The first element in doing so is to adopt code-switching as subsumption. The second is to offer a justification that acknowledges the non-ideal conditions that put certain communities and their way of life in a vulnerable position. If the state is going to take it upon itself to teach children how to behave in ways that will open up economic opportunities for them, but which will potentially undermine their engagement with ways of life we have reason to respect, we must be willing to engage in the normative work of confronting the value conflicts that arise in that process, and offer the appropriate kind of justification to those vulnerable communities.[27]

References

Anderson, E. (2007) "Fair Opportunity in Education: A Democratic Perspective," *Ethics* 117: 595–622.
Anderson, E. (2010) *The Imperative of Integration*, Princeton, NJ: Princeton University Press.
Aronowitz, M. (1984) "The Social and Emotional Adjustment of Immigrant Children: A Review of the Literature," *International Migration Review* 18: 237–257.
Aud, S., Fox, M. A., and Ramani, A. K. (2010) *Status and Trends in the Education of Racial and Ethnic Groups*, Washington, DC: U.S. Department of Education, National Center for Education Statistics.
Barry, B. (2001) *Culture and Equality*, Cambridge, MA: Harvard University Press.
Berry, J. W. (1997) "Immigration, Acculturation, and Adaptation," *Applied Psychology* 46: 5–34.
Borghans, L., et al. (2008) "The Economics and Psychology of Personality Traits," *Journal of Human Resources* 43: 972–1059
Borghans, L., Weel, B. T., and Weinberg, B. A. (2008) "Interpersonal Styles and Labor Market Outcomes," *Journal of Human Resources* 43: 815–858.
Bratman, M. E. (2000) "Valuing and the Will," *Philosophical Perspectives* 14: 249–265.
Brighouse, H. (1998) "Civic Education and Liberal Legitimacy," *Ethics* 108: 719–745.
Brighouse, H. (2000) *School Choice and Social Justice*, Oxford: Oxford University Press.
Brighouse, H., and Swift, A. (2009) "Legitimate Parental Partiality," *Philosophy & Public Affairs* 37: 43–80.
Browne, I., and Kennelly, I. (1999) "Stereotypes and Realities: Images of Black Women in the Labor Market," in I. Browne (ed.), *Latinas and African American Women at Work: Race, Gender, and Economic Inequality*, 302–326, New York: Russell Sage Foundation.
Calhoun, C. (1995) "Standing for Something," *Journal of Philosophy* 92: 238–240.
Callan, E. (1996) "Political Liberalism and Political Education," *Review of Politics* 58: 5–33.
Callan, E. (2004) *Creating Citizens: Political Education and Liberal Democracy*, New York: Oxford University Press.
Campbell, F. A., et al. (2002) "Early Childhood Education: Young Adult Outcomes from the Abecedarian Project," *Applied Developmental Science* 6: 42–57.
Carter, P. (2005) *Keepin' It Real: School Success Beyond Black and White*, Oxford: Oxford University Press.

Delpit, L. (1995) *Other People's Children: Cultural Conflict in the Classroom*, New York: The New Press.
Dewey, J. (2008) *The Child and the Curriculum*, New York: Cosimo Books.
Du Bois, W. E. B. (1897) "Strivings of the Negro People," *Atlantic Monthly* 80: 194–198.
Duckworth, A. L., Quinn, P. D., and Tsukayama, E. (2012) "What No Child Left Behind Leaves Behind: The Roles of IQ and Self-control in Predicting Standardized Achievement Test Scores and Report Card Grades," *Journal of Educational Psychology* 104: 439–451.
Fairlie, R. W., and Robb, A. M. (2008) *Race and Entrepreneurial Success: Black-, Asian-, and White-Owned Businesses in the United States*, Cambridge, MA: The MIT Press.
Fordham, S., and Ogbu, J. U. (1986) "Black Students' School Success: Coping with the 'Burden of "Acting White,"'" *The Urban Review* 18: 176–206.
Frankfurt, H. G. (1999) *Necessity, Volition, and Love*, Cambridge: Cambridge University Press.
Galston, W. A. (1995) "Two Concepts of Liberalism," *Ethics* 105: 516–534.
Heckman, J. J., et al. (2010) "The Rate of Return to the HighScope Perry Preschool Program," *Journal of Public Economics* 94: 114–128.
Heckman, J. J., and Krueger, A. B. (2002) *Inequality in America: What Role for Human Capital Policies?* Cambridge, MA: MIT Press.
Heckman, J. J., and Rubenstein, Y. (2001) "The Importance of Noncognitive Skills: Lessons from the GED Testing Program," *American Economic Review* 91: 145–149.
Hyun, J. (2005) *Breaking the Bamboo Ceiling: Career Strategies for Asians*, New York: Harper Business.
Jaworska, A. (2007) "Caring and Internality," *Philosophy and Phenomenological Research* 74: 529–568.
Jencks, C. (1988) "Whom Must We Treat Equally for Educational Opportunity to Be Equal?" *Ethics* 98: 518–533.
Jencks, C., and Phillips, M. (1998) "America's Next Achievement Test: Closing the Black-white Test Score Gap," *The American Prospect* 40: 44–53.
LaFromboise, T., Coleman, H. L. K., and Gerton, J. (1993) "Psychological Impact of Biculturalism: Evidence and Theory," *Psychological Bulletin* 114: 395–412.
Lareau, A. (2003) *Unequal Childhoods: Class, Race, and Family Life*, Berkeley: University of California Press.
Levinson, M. (2009) "Mapping Multicultural Education," in H. Siegel (ed.), *Oxford Handbook of Philosophy of Education*, 428–450, Oxford: Oxford University Press.
Levinson, M. (2012) *No Citizen Left Behind*, Oxford: Oxford University Press.
Lugones, M. (2009) "Hispaneando y lesbiando: on Sarah Hoagland's Lesbian Ethics," *Hypatia* 5: 138–146.
MacIntyre, A. (1984) *After Virtue*, Notre Dame, IN: University of Notre Dame Press.
Markus, H. R., and Kitayama, S. (1991) "Culture and the Self: Implications for Cognition, Emotion, and Motivation," *Psychological Review* 98: 224–253.
Morton, J. (2011) "The Non-cognitive Challenge to a Liberal Egalitarian Education," *Theory and Research in Education* 9: 233–250.
Osborne-Graves, M. (2005) "Personality and Intergenerational Transmission of Economic Status," in S. Bowles, H. Gintis, and M. Osborne-Graves (eds.), *Unequal Chances: Family Background and Economic Success*, 208–231, Princeton, NJ: Princeton University Press.
Rawls, J. (2005) *Political Liberalism*, New York: Columbia University Press.
Reich, R. (2002) *Bridging Liberalism and Multiculturalism in American Education*, Chicago: University of Chicago Press.
Rumbaut, R. G. (2005) "Children of Immigrants and Their Achievement: The Roles of Family, Acculturation, Social Class, Gender, Ethnicity, and School Context," in R. D. Taylor (ed.), *Addressing the Achievement Gap: Theory Informing Practice*, 23–59, Charlotte, NC: Information Age Publishing.
Schapiro, T. (1999) "What Is a Child?" *Ethics* 109: 715–738.
Scheffler, S. (2011) "Valuing," in R. Jay Wallace, R. Kumar, and S. Freeman (eds.), *Reasons and Recognition*, 23–42, New York: Oxford University Press.
Spalter-Roth, R., and Lowenthal, T. A. (2005) "Race, Ethnicity, and the American Labor Market: What's at Work?" *American Sociological Association Series on How Race and Ethnicity* Matter, ASA's Sydney S. Spivack Program in Applied Social Research and Social Policy.

Triandis, H. C., and Suh E. M. (2002) "Cultural Influences on Personality," *Annual Review of Psychology* 53: 133–160.

Tough, P. (2012) *How Children Succeed: Grit, Curiosity, and the Hidden Power of Character*, New York: Houghton Mifflin Harcourt.

Tyson, K., Darity, W., and Castellino, D. R. (2005) "It's Not 'A Black Thing': Understanding the Burden of Acting White and Other Dilemmas of High Achievement," *American Sociological Review* 70: 582–605.

Williams, B. (1984) "Persons, Character, and Morality," in A. Oksenberg Rorty (ed.), *The Identities of Persons*, 197–216, Berkeley: University of California Berkeley.

Wilson, W. J. (1996) *When Work Disappears*, New York: Vintage.

Notes

1. For the rest of the article, I assume that code-switchers are switching between the norms governing two communities, though in reality, agents might be switching between many more.
2. One of the most evocative early descriptions of the phenomenon is by sociologist W. E. Du Bois (1897), when he describes "double-consciousness."
3. "Non-cognitive skills" is the term used in the economics and psychological literature. In this article, I use the term "dispositions" instead of "skills" because I think their value is more complicated than the term "skills" suggests. Thanks to Randall Curren for asking me to clarify this point. I discuss the distinction between cognitive and non-cognitive in more detail in (2011) and (2014).
4. For an argument that inequalities among cultural groups are not unjust if they reflect a cultural group's preferences, see Barry (2001: 98).
5. I am grateful to Debra Satz for raising this point. The diversity of labor markets means that some markets reward dispositions that others do not. For example, interpersonal skills are more valuable in service professions. Consequently, these markets end up with a higher proportion of employees from groups that exhibit more highly developed interpersonal skills. See Borghans, Weel and Weinberg (2008). However, this does not fully address equality concerns; we need to consider how well represented minority groups are in markets with positions of economic and political power. Data suggests that minority groups are under-represented in having ownership stakes in the market. See Fairlie and Robb (2008).
6. The concepts of *caring* and *valuing*, in the philosophy of action literature, both capture what I have in mind here. Though there are important differences between the two, they are not relevant to the discussion here. See Bratman (2000) and Scheffler (2011).
7. For a particularly thoughtful discussion of how caring figures in our understanding of marginal agents, including children, see Jaworska (2007).
8. It might still be reasonable for such parents to decide that they want their child to forego this advantage. However, this trade-off would only appear reasonable if this family has enough resources to give the parents confidence that their child will do well regardless. I return to this point in the final section.
9. Thanks to Eamonn Callan for raising this challenge and asking me to clarify this point.
10. Lareau (2003: ch. 12) also recommends code-switching as a way of mitigating the effects of disadvantage.
11. Code-switching is a strategy employed by many bicultural individuals, and there is an extensive body of empirical research on biculturalism and acculturation, detailing its psychological costs and benefits. See Berry (1997); LaFromboise, Coleman and Gerton (1993); Aronowitz (1984).
12. The example is meant to be illustrative of the larger issues at stake for members of disadvantaged groups. Though there are important differences between the two ethnicities that are most in danger of being disadvantaged educationally, Latinos and African-Americans, many of the points I make apply to suitably modified examples of African-Americans.
13. Lisa Delpit notes that the educational system often ignores "the significance of human connectedness in many communities of color," which can conflict with the solitary pursuits required by the mainstream educational system (1995: 95).
14. I am grateful to Eamonn Callan for asking me to acknowledge the dynamic nature of this phenomenon.

15 Harry Frankfurt's notion of *wholeheartedness* and Alasdair MacIntyre's notion of *narrative unity* would seem to conflict with this kind of compartmentalization. See Frankfurt (1999) and MacIntyre (1984).
16 Thanks to Meira Levinson for suggesting I pursue this model.
17 I will not take a stance here on whether ground projects or narratives are necessary to have a comprehensive normative perspective; both could serve the role I have in mind. For a discussion of the importance of ground projects, see Williams (1984).
18 I am grateful to Eamonn Callan for inspiring this version of the example.
19 Another example of this kind of code-switching is that of some immigrants who see their work as part of a project to financially assist their families back home.
20 There is a lot to be said in favor of non-neutral liberal accounts of education serving as a foundation for code-switching. For example, it could be argued that code-switching is autonomy enhancing, since it allows students to try on different possible values without adopting them. It might also be argued that code-switching is necessary for citizenship, because it allows students to learn to talk to fellow citizens from different cultural backgrounds. Finally, it could be argued that code-switching allows students to find out what it is like being a member of a different community, and become more tolerant and empathetic. Versions of this argument can be seen in Reich (2002) and Levinson (2012). Note, however, all of these justifications for code-switching are not justifications to code-switch in order to open socio-economic opportunities, but rather to cultivate the dispositions that promote autonomy, make one a better citizen, or promote tolerance.
21 Thanks to Eamonn Callan for bringing up this point and to Debra Satz for helping me clarify it.
22 For a defense of this view see Delpit (1995).
23 Some schools, notably Knowledge Is Power Programs (KIPP), have been taking this lesson to heart by explicitly teaching poor, largely minority, students middle-class behavior, from how and when to make eye contact to full-blown character education. For a take on KIPP's success, see Tough (2012).
24 This is also probably true for poor whites and their complaint, though slightly different in character, would not be different in kind.
25 However, it has been suggested that it is a difference in social and emotional dispositions that leads Asian-Americans to confront a "bamboo ceiling"—that is, not occupying proportionally as many positions of power and authority as their white counterparts, despite outperforming them on measures of educational achievement. See Hyun (2005).
26 Complicated issues arise here about how finely to carve out the relevant groups. I do not deny that the weighing might come out differently for impoverished Asian-Americans.
27 I am grateful for invaluable feedback on this chapter to Jaime Ahlberg, Elizabeth Anderson, Harry Brighouse, Eamonn Callan, Meira Levinson, Debra Satz, and participants at the Race, Opportunity, and Education Conference at the Harvard School of Education, the New York Society for Women in Philosophy Workshop, the Stanford University Spencer Workshop, as well as audiences at Vassar College's Philosopher's Holiday, the Summer Institute for Diversity in Philosophy at Rutgers University, and the Equality of Opportunity and Education Symposium at the 2013 American Educational Research Association Annual Meeting. Research for this article was supported by a generous grant from the Spencer Foundation.

Reading Questions

1. What is "cultural code-switching"?
2. What are the costs or risks of what Morton characterizes as "integration," "pretense," and "compartmentalization," respectively?
3. Morton suggests that "subsumption" is the best option available for public schools. What does this mean, and how does it work? What are the risks to compartmentalization?
4. Why might Morton say to a critic who argued that public education that favors subsumption is just another way for states to use state power to accelerate the adoption of market-conducive dispositions by minority groups?
5. Why does (or why should) an education institution have that burden to remedy the injustice? Why not just think that people should be free to make choices about how to raise their kids that may

make them more and less competitive in the labor market, but also more and less competitive in other markets (including their own local cultural markets)? If we are concerned to protect value formation and autonomy, why is inculcation by the education system the right place to do that? Why not prefer information campaigns or incentives directed to parents and even students outside of educational contexts?

6. Besides ethnic minority groups, are there other groups or identities that face a similar set of problems with cultural code-switching? How are these cases similar or different?

15 The Philosophy of Accidentality

Manuel Vargas

> We must always know what we can count on, but the belief that we can never know what we can count on constitutes restlessness, or zozobra.
> —Emilio Uranga, "Essay on the Ontology of the Mexican"

Introduction

Consider two different experiences of moving to a new place. In one, things are different but good. You adapt to the local conditions of life. Things make sense relatively quickly. You connect with people, you engage in shared activities, and you form relationships you value. Although there are the inevitable adjustments and surprises, by and large your life takes on a shape you accept and maybe even like. In an alternative scenario, those happy alignments do not come to be. Maybe the local conditions of life seem alien. The habits of daily life never come to feel natural. Relationships seem structured around activities and values you do not quite share, or maybe even values you repudiate. How people relate is, for lack of a better word, off.

A precise characterization of these misalignments can be elusive. In relatively mild cases, the misalignment is localized to features of a job, or a group, or some particular practice. More encompassing cases of misalignment leave one feeling more radically at unease with wider or more comprehensive swaths of one's milieu. In these more extreme instances, we might characterize the situation as producing a sense that one is 'ungrounded', perhaps normatively unmoored, in that it is unclear how one is to proceed, what the significance of one's choices will be, and what results will follow if one acts on the old principles in the new context. A paradigmatic case of this more encompassing unease is sometimes expressed by children of immigrants. They sometimes experience a feeling of disconnect with both the culture of their parents and with the majority culture in which they find themselves. *Ni de aquí ni de allá*—from neither here nor there—is how it is said in Spanish, although the thought has at least as many expressions as there are languages. These stories of ungrounded lives, or ungrounded parts of lives, are familiar themes in immigrant narratives and the memoirs of members of marginalized social groups.

This is not just an immigrant story or the story of their children. Similar stories have sometimes been told by people with social identities that did not mesh with the valorized identities of a community and by people who feel pulled to reject the valuational structures in which they were raised. These stories can convey a sense of profound unease or ungroundedness of a special sort that I characterize as *accidentality*.

My aspiration in this essay is to chart some dimensions of accidentality and to gesture at some ways in which it figures in the lives of many people. Many of the ideas in

DOI: 10.4324/9781003385417-22

this account draw from a now mostly forgotten—or if remembered, then repudiated—mid-twentieth-century version of existentialism in Mexico. The central idea in what follows is that we can usefully explain what is going on in these cases of ungroundedness by appreciating some important roles that social patterns of meaningfulness and value play (or fail to play) in an individual life.

Culture and Contingency

I start with a discussion about culture and cultures. My interest is in what we might call *normative culture*, the part of culture that includes packages of social meanings, values, and practical norms that, in the ordinary case, tend to be relied upon to address various challenges in a form of life. We need tools, skills, and knowledge for navigation in complex, communal life. Normative culture provides an accumulated body of these navigational resources—linked patterns of meaning, symbols, practical norms, practical values, and the like, which can include things like rituals and frequently tacit decision procedures. On the present way of characterizing it, though, normative culture is a linked set of practical (as opposed to theoretical) norms, social meanings, and values that tend to travel together, often in mutually reinforcing ways.

The foregoing picture of practical culture is also compatible with the idea that cultural packages admit of some underdetermination about practical norms, social meanings, and values; that cultures can overlap and diverge; and that within a given culture normative conflict can come in degrees. It is also compatible with holding that a way for a normative culture to succeed is for it to provide its bearers with tools for moving successfully through social life, for it to provide answers to practical questions about what is worth doing, how it is to be done, and what follows when the wrong things are done. Nothing in what follows relies on this further thought, though.

The present way of thinking about an entangled package of practical norms, meanings, and values, is not meant to be tendentious. It is compatible with a range of traditional and oftentimes more expansive ways of thinking about culture. Characterizations of culture have been famously diverse in content and aim. (See Kwame Anthony Appiah (2018: 189–199) for an overview.) On one capacious notion, culture is 'any kind of information that is acquired from other members of one's species through social learning that is capable of affecting an individual's behaviors' (Heine 2016: 5). For comparison, culture has been characterized as the 'man-made part of the environment' (Herskovits 1948: 17); 'the total shared, learned behavior of a society or a subgroup' (Mead 1953: 22); 'an historically transmitted pattern of meanings embodied in symbols' (Geertz 1973: 89); 'information capable of affecting individuals' behavior that they acquire from other members of their species through teaching, imitation, and other forms of social transmission' (Richerson and Boyd 2008: 5); and 'the large body of practices, techniques, heuristics, tools, motivations, values, and beliefs that we all acquire while growing up' (Henrich 2016: 3). Given our more restricted concern for normative culture, to speak of different cultures—or better, practical cultures—is to speak of different communities that internally share a substantial overlapping cluster of practical norms, values, and social meanings.

Whatever one's more general account of culture, the point that matters for present purposes is just this: in a given time and place, the social world tends to present us with packages of practical norms, values, and social meanings that shape our sense of the world and ourselves, our valuations of the options that are before us, and our expectations about what kinds of social responses our choices are likely to produce.

The significance of a particular package of normative culture is most readily visible in cases where differences from one's own local practices stand out. For example, in the European Middle Ages, the practice of charging interest—usury, as it was called—was viewed negatively. The negative valence of charging interest was bound up in a web of cultural meanings—a commitment to the precepts of Christianity, anti-Semitism, and historically contingent rules about who could own property. The wrongfulness of charging interest was a contingent valuational feature, enmeshed in wider patterns of meaning that we tend not to share here and now. A more culturally proximal case might be recent shifts in how we think about addiction. The rise of the disease model, and the subsequent undercutting of the conviction that addiction is a culpable failure of volition, has altered many people's sense of the wrongfulness of addiction. The issue remains unsettled in popular attitudes.

Social identities, both in the nature of the category and the kinds of explicit and connotational meanings of those categories, is also a matter of local packages of norms. Being a Protestant means one thing in sixteenth-century Spain. It means something different in twenty-first-century Southern California. Even for categories ostensibly connected to relatively stable biological features of humans, the import of those identities is culturally loaded. As the slogan goes, *gender is the social meaning of sex*; the social significance—the meaning of gender, and the number of genders—has admitted of variation across time and place.

In noting the contingency of given configurations of normative culture, we need not be committed to more sweeping claims that all meanings are contingent in these ways, or that values and moral truths are always relative to a time and a place. (Litigating disputes about historicism and relativism is a task for another day.) For my purposes it is enough to recognize that many of our social identities, the significance of our behavioral dispositions, and the import of particular actions and practices is invariably experienced by individuals as saturated with a local meaning that is historically contingent.

Substance and Accident

For reasons that will become clear to the reader, in the discussion that follows, I do something that is otherwise ill-advised: I use relatively familiar technical philosophical vocabulary in a nonstandard, potentially obscure way.

Let *substances* be agents who experience themselves as having a relatively stable and unified package (or packages) of commitments about norms, values, and meanings. Characteristically, substances take their configuration of normative culture for granted. The particular commitments that constitute their normative culture tend to do an adequate or better job of guiding deliberations about what to do, identifying meaningful courses of action, and in general, helping people navigate practical challenges within their forms of life.

Let *accidents* be agents who are not substances. They do not experience themselves as having relatively stable or unified packages of commitments about norms, values, and meanings. The packages of normative culture that are seemingly available—perhaps culturally afforded in some circumscribed way—are not experienced by these agents as providing satisfying guidance on what to do, about what is valuable, and how one should think of the significance of one's choices.

(It is an interesting question, although one I do not pursue here, how to characterize precisely the agent's sense of difficulty and what availability of normative alternatives might come to. On the one hand, one could think features of contemporary life, including the fragmentation of narratives about what is valuable, might induce accidentality more readily than traditional forms of life. On the other hand, it may seem that ready access to information—books, the internet, travel—can make accidentality more avoidable by providing more compelling normative packages. Something to keep in mind, in either case, is that many norms, social meanings, and values require social cooperation. A culture that aspires to generate honor by dueling will do badly with a population of one.)

To put some of these ideas together: Recall the phenomenon noted at the outset, regarding the unease one can have with various practices, organizations, or roles one encounters in life. Relatively local misalignments between one's sense of being and the values and meanings of some practice do not constitute accidentality. Local, limited, or relatively narrow misalignments do not ordinarily threaten one's sense that one's overall package of norms, values, and meanings help one navigate the practical and normative challenges one faces.

In contrast, cases of ungroundedness—those more profound instances of alienation from available packages of normative culture—*do* constitute accidentality. That is, someone is an accident—in the sense at hand—if the culturally available packages of meaning and value (including the packages one has internalized) fail to provide ready and adequate answers to questions of meaning and value in some widespread and seemingly pervasive sense relative to one's own life.

On this picture, accidentality is not about whether one occupies a position of social marginality. One might be a member of a marginalized community but still a substance (that is, being able to take for granted in one's deliberations a stable network of norms, values, and meaning-making commitments). One might also be a member of a dominant social group and be an accident. Accidentality is about the absence of a stable, taken-for-granted relationship to normative culture.

The Psychology of Accidentality

Accidentality is a kind of relationship between an agent and normative culture. It is a state of an agent who pervasively experiences the available patterns of norms, values, and cultural meanings as unable to be taken for granted, as inapt for practical reasoning. If accidentality is a recognizable phenomenon, and it is characteristic of an identifiable kind of relationship of agents to norms and meanings, might it have a characteristic profile in affect and dispositions for action?

Here is one reason for thinking it could: If one is not relatively secure in some system of value and meaning, at least in a sufficiently wide range of contexts, then who one is, one's sense of one's self and the value of one's actions, is chronically threatened. One still has to make decisions about what to do, one may still have some sense of self, but the basis of these things is suspect. For an accident, the integrity of one's judgments about value is pervasively vulnerable to internal doubt and external condemnation.

The pervasiveness of an individual's sense of ungroundedness matters. Again, minimal or relatively isolated discomfort about some set of practices is very different from ungroundedness of the sort at stake here. The accident's more global sense of skepticism about the truth of systems of local meanings and values may be prone to inducing the thought that it is all contingent, that it is all potentially meaningless and without value.

So, we might think, ungroundedness produces a kind of internal fragility about one's sense of self and one's normative assessments that plausibly may give rise to a characteristic psychological syndrome. Consider the position of someone unhappy with the operative gender norms in her culture but also unsure about what an adequate alternative would look like. (This is therefore different from a case where one is clear and confident about one's gender identity, despite society's failure to recognize that identity or failure to provide ready ways for enacting it.) For the sort of person under consideration, to participate in various social practices implicated in the objectionable gender norms may strike her as repellent. Norms of dating and marriage may seem polluted by those problematic features of the operative gender norms. Nevertheless, to opt out of those gendered practices entirely would also be costly. She would have to forego various goods that are enabled by participation in those practices. For example, to opt out of dating and marriage practices might be to opt out of otherwise good access to companionship, financial security, certain valuable shared experiences, and so on.

Our gender-norm objector could, of course, take a principled and public stance against the existing gender norms, and their enactment in practices of dating and marriage. This stance would raise its own troubles. It would seem to signal a set of commitments to a different set of values, values about which she may also be wary. She may think to herself that she does not want to be seen as strident or ideological, especially about a matter about which she is not entirely sure. She faces an unhappy dilemma: for *any* action or *any* position, either she will face criticism from without, or she will run the risk of acting in a way that does not accord with her values—values that may, as yet, be partial, unformed, provisional, or in ongoing negotiation.

She might sit around imagining that the world regards her actions in different ways, or that she could create an entirely new practice not complicit in the difficulties of existing gender norms. Unless she is also motivated, these may remain mere fantasy. Even were she to act on those fantasies, it might commit her to acting on and advocating values about which she remains unsure.

There is a lot to say about this sort of case, but I want to focus on three psychological elements in the case as it has been described: (1) a reluctance to engage in action in the world that might be meaning-bearing in a way one rejects, what we might characterize as *unwillingness*; (2) a standing concern with avoiding having one's social standing impugned—that is, a concern for preserving one's sense of *dignity*; and (3) a disposition for turning inward—a kind of *introversion*—in the face of unhappiness about unappealing actional possibilities. In what follows, I say a bit more about each element.

On the present picture, people experience the world as structured by a system of meanings, norms, and values. For the accident, however, the available packages of meanings, norms, values are not compelling ways to understand the world. Indeed, the ungrounded person may find the world structured in these ways as repellent. Action that participates in, or that is complicit in these patterns of meaning may even strike the ungrounded person as disgusting precisely because it suggests a commitment to those frameworks of meaning about which one is skeptical (Uranga 2017: 168). The result is a disposition of *unwillingness* or aversion to action. The unwilling agent remains unmoved, preferring inactivity rather than taking up actions that are immediately bound up in systems of meaning and value that one does not accept.

On the present proposal, accidents tend to be preoccupied with preserving their sense of dignity. The gender norms case suggests one reason why. When an accident encounters an obstacle—a place where the world puts up an impediment to the attainment of her goals (say, of achieving a less problematic relation to gender norms), the accident is likely to be gripped by some unwillingness to engage. She may still condemn, of course. At least while in a position of normative uncertainty, she is unlikely to redouble her efforts at combating the effects of the gender norms. She will not get engaged (perhaps in the literal sense, especially) in the fight for a different set of gender norms. Instead, the pressure on her is not to expose her vulnerability and uncertainty about what is normatively authoritative. The accident has reason to avoid getting dirty. So the impulse to withdraw from engagement is perhaps especially prone to a bit of self-serving self-deception: unwillingness is recast as a commitment to preserving one's dignity, one's unimpugned social standing. The accident's preoccupation with dignity may come to manifest a dual concern for, on the one hand, a kind of conventional rectitude, and on the other, a kind of detachment from advocating for a real, concrete set of alternative commitments.

It is worth acknowledging that although this account has framed the accident's moral rectitude in terms of a preoccupation with dignity, there are other values around which one's moral rectitude might be organized. We might expect some culturally specific loading for what value organizes one's moral rectitude, whether it is in terms of dignity, honor, or generosity (Uranga 2017: 170). Honor might be a particularly common value in a range of cultures (Sommers 2018: 1–44). In a given instance, it might also be the case that there is no single value around which one's rectitude is fixated. So the value or values around which the accident's rectitude may be organized might sometimes be other than dignity, even if dignity is perhaps the most common present configuration.

The third aspect of the characteristic psychological syndrome of accidentality is a turn inward, something we can think of as an impulse to *introversion* and introspection. If one is averse to meaningful action in the world, and one is uncertain about whether any norms, values, and meanings are genuinely authoritative, one will seek to avoid attention or notice. I have already shown that this position tends to create a pressure to avoid external engagements. Any impulse to activity need not be entirely eradicated. On the present proposal, it is just turned inward. So the person in a position of accidentality tends toward rumination, perhaps sentimentality, and as was suggested above, considerable reflection on alternatives that might have been.

As noted above, accidents are plausibly prone to awareness of what we might think of as the existential condition. That is, there is an awareness that systems of meaning and value have an enormous amount of contingency built into them. Indeed, the old skeptical worry about whether *all* systems of meanings and value are at root fictions obscuring the meaningless nature of existence may be especially prone to emerging in those suffering from accidentality. (Perhaps accidents are epistemically privileged about this?) The turn to introversion and rumination may contribute to this sense of normativity being fictional. Preoccupation with constructing fantasy worlds, and reimagining one's actions within them, may provide the accident with a new sense of the possible values of one's acts and omissions. It may also serve to emphasize that the particular values and meanings of one's acts may all be fictional.

On this permutation of accidentality, the person thinks that what she *is* is a being that is *essentially* normatively ungrounded. No available norms, meanings, and values provide a satisfying ground for thinking about herself and the meaning of her actions. Melancholy may set in.

To sum up, accidents are agents who experience themselves as normatively unmoored. They are disposed to have a distinctive psychological profile, characterized by unwillingness, a concern for a sense of dignity, and introversion. That profile is a product of an unresolved effort to embrace and deploy satisfying systems of meaning and value, and that existential situation tends to give these folks what we might think of as a melancholic demeanor. Strictly speaking, this picture is neutral about how, all things considered, we ought to think about a range of questions concerning value. Perhaps some antirealists about value could go on to hold that accidentality is the price one pays for an accurate understanding of the nature of values.

Emilio Uranga

The preceding two sections are a partial reconstruction of Emilio Uranga's account of accidentality, first proposed in 'Essay on the Ontology of the Mexican' (originally published in 1951) and subsequently revisited and extended in his *Análisis del ser del mexicano* [Analysis of Mexican Being], published in 1952. My account draws from 'Essay on the Ontology of the Mexican' although the *Análisis del ser del mexicano* introduces some notable differences that, for present purposes, I mostly relegate to parenthetical remarks.

Uranga was trained in the phenomenological tradition, a student of José Gaos (Heidegger's first translator), and he was part of a group of philosophers that took seriously the idea that philosophy was to proceed by first reflecting on one's social context and that philosophical contributions were to be found in a detailed understanding of a particular, concrete, historical circumstance. The fact of Uranga's Mexicanness requires highlighting, but not just to gesture at where in the history of philosophy we might locate the origin of these ideas, and not to exoticize the ideas. It requires mention because these ideas were explicitly developed in the service of an effort to characterize Mexicanness. These ideas developed in the cause of a broadly existentialist, historicist, nationalist philosophical movement that was known as *la filosofía de lo mexicano*, or the philosophy of Mexicanness. According to its proponents, the nature of Mexicanness, and in particular, Mexican being, was taken as a philosophical subject matter, as a spur to philosophical reflection, and as the best hope for a world-historically significant contribution to philosophy from Mexico.

The project was undertaken roughly thirty years after the end of the Mexican revolution and the formation of the modern Mexican state. It was pursued by a number of Mexican philosophers in the wake of an intense national project to construct or discover a national identity. By the 1950s, there was a lurking sense among the Mexican intellectual class that the payoffs of all those nationalist cultural and political efforts were uncertain. Modern, postrevolutionary Mexico, and the nature of Mexicanness were felt to be something, but what that something was—the essence of Mexicanness—required reflection and articulation. A group of philosophers in Mexico City set out to do just that (see Hurtado 2007: 108–123; Sánchez 2016: 15–42).

According to the proponents of this project, what it was to be Mexican, to partake of Mexican being, was always indexed to a time and place (Sánchez 2018), although individuals had different views about how wide and narrow the scope of that time and place were. It is this contextualized notion of Mexicanness that provoked a good deal of fighting about whether this was a worthy philosophical project. That fight took the form of a debate about putatively universalist and historicist philosophy, and this disagreement in some way, shape, or form gripped large swaths of twentieth-century Latin American philosophy. (I am inclined to think that the focus of many disputes about historicism and universalism were ill-placed. No one denies the possibility of contextual, intersubjective, or conventional truths. The social significance of the issue was a fight over what kinds of truths, what kinds of questions and answers, deserved the honorific of *philosophy*, and what that meant for the various research programs throughout twentieth-century Latin American philosophy.)

There was already a tradition of 'psychological profiles' that purported to offer characterizations of widespread dispositions characteristic of the Mexican people. Indeed, this sort of psychological, cultural, and social profile of a nation or people was not an uncommon genre in Latin American writing at the end of the nineteenth century and the start of the twentieth (Stabb 1967: 12–33). What was different about the Mexican existentialists, of whom Uranga tended to be regarded as one of the most original and promising of that group, was that they took the purported prevalence of a Mexican psychological profile to be indicative of a particular mode of being—a distinctive configuration of historically situated experiences, meanings, and values.

My account of accidentality and the associated psychological syndrome left out some important elements that distinguish Uranga's picture. Those elements are worth highlighting because they raise interesting questions of their own about the extent to which a more general project can be extracted from Uranga's particular commitments.

According to Uranga, the Mexican circumstance—the forms of life, the system of meanings, the conceptual framework of people in those historical and national circumstances—is particularly distinctive. It is a historical accident in a very literal sense. It is the result of a collision between two kinds of substances—Spanish and Indigenous. But the ensuing society never generated its own distinctive substantiality. Instead, it produced a people who experience themselves and their form of life as an unstable, uncertain amalgam of norms, values, and meanings that do not cohere well in the actual conditions of Mexico and its history.

For Uranga, this situation of ungroundedness was experienced by (at least mid-twentieth century) Mexicans as a kind of constitutive or ontological *insufficiency* or *inadequacy* in their form of being, in the way they inhabit the world, and the way that their norms, values, and systems of meanings structure that world. To be sure, Uranga's account does not speak directly about many of the identity categories that had been historically important in Mexico—for example, the Indigenous, the mestiza/o, and so on. Nor does he recognize the diversity internal to these identity categories. His analysis seems to accept a picture of the Mexican Revolution as having revealed, created, or made possible a new kind of historical being that was the Mexican of his analysis. Partial or limit cases, including those might reject the social and political order that made possible the sort of being that was his interest, is mostly passed over in silence, apart from some brief remarks on indigenism and Europeanism.

As Uranga saw it, ungroundedness tends to seek its erasure, i.e., it tries to resolve itself into something else because, at bottom, accidentality involves some awareness of the looming threat of nothingness, of nonbeing. The melancholy life of the accident is lived in a condition he calls *zozobra*. Zozobra is a kind of oscillation between being and nonbeing, what we might think of as a state teetering between, on one side, the impulse to accept a problematic framework of meanings, norms, and values and, on the other side, the urge to abandon that framework in light of its inadequacy at providing answers the person experiences as ready, reliable, and unreflectively apt.

The most common reaction to accidentality, Uranga claims, is something he calls *subordination*. Subordination is an appeal to someone else's substantiality as a normative ground. Their package of norms, values, and meanings are treated as justifying one's own being. This can happen directly and indirectly. The direct form involves an embrace of a proximal substantiality—oftentimes a dominant cultural framework. The immigrant who aspires not only to assimilate, but to assimilate in the most jingoist way possible, may be an example. The indirect form of subordination does not attempt to wear another's substantiality as one's own, but instead seeks approval by those who enjoy substantiality. One can aspire to be a 'nice girl' or 'the bright, articulate, and clean' minority. Whether direct or indirect, the net effect is the same: the typical response to accidentality reinscribes the normative inadequacy of one's accidentality, doubling down on the subordination of oneself to another's substance.

(It is worth noting that normativity is a difficult problem for Uranga. In the later *Analysis of Mexican Being* (2013), Uranga holds that human agency is a relational thing, but the normativity that arises from the intersubjectivity of agents is elusive. Absent a fit between culture and circumstances, agents in zozobra cannot readily avoid recognizing the elusiveness of a compelling ground for normativity. How this compares to other existentialist notions—ennui, nausea, angst, anxiety, alienation, and so on, are interesting questions I do not try to pursue here. Also worth noting here is that the role of poetry plays an interesting and complicated role in the *Analysis*, and on one reading, its function is insight and expression of the present constitution of being. Might art have more resources than present-directed insight? Might it build community, afford shared experiences, or shape a possible ideal? Uranga never says.)

In the specifically Mexican context that was Uranga's interest, subordination paradigmatically took the forms of *malinchismo*—a glorification of the European, and especially Spanish culture—and *indigenismo*—indigenism, or a valorization of (an historic and Mexica, as opposed to an actual and typically not Mexica) indigenous culture above all else.

Beyond subordination, two options suggest themselves: value creation and nihilism. The value creation idea is as follows. One could attempt to resolve one's accidentality not by grounding it in someone else's substantiality. Instead, one could seek to construct a new substantiality, a 'new tablet of values', as Nietzsche would have put it (1995, Prologue § 9). Uranga says little about this possibility, except to highlight a deep problem for it. He writes that

> Individuals who have projected a world, and who have realized it, eventually turn their gaze toward the foundations or grounds of those constructions, and upon finding them in the imagination are thrown into an incurable uneasiness, into an inevitable restlessness of finding the human edifice built on contemptible grounds.
>
> (2017: 172)

To construct a new substantiality does not erase the crisis for the person who creates that substantiality. A socially effective fantasy of normative realism is unlikely to persuade the person who engineers the fantasy.

The second possibility is a (perhaps attenuated) nihilism. One could respond to the possibility of accidentality with abandonment of the aspiration for guiding one's life by non-contingent, nonsubjective, absolute grounds for value and action. Uranga says very little about this, at least in any direct way. At the same time, it is not hard to imagine that this is the looming possibility that animates the rest of the enterprise. The project of characterizing accidentality might be read as an account of what it is to live with the ongoing possibility of nihilism.

'Essay on an Ontology of the Mexican' concludes with only the slightest of answers to how one might respond to the fact of accidentality. He briefly gestures at the possibility of a life that accepts accidentality, a 'neutral state of being', but the idea is underdeveloped (2017: 173). He gestures at the possibility of living within zozobra in a manner that involves something like the constant re-opening of a scab, of living with the uncertainty of pervasive contingency. Rather than aspiring to the stable, permanent repair of one's normative wound, one might get by with temporary knittings of a functional (if irregular and impermanent) normative whole. The metaphor is meant to be uncomfortable. And, true to the spirit of the enterprise, Uranga gestures at this 'solution' but makes no commitment to it. He only notes that providing an account of how one ought to respond to accidentality is a matter for morality, and thus outside of his ontology of Mexicanness (2017: 177).

Here, we would be remiss if we failed to note an important twist that is present in the 'Essay on an Ontology of the Mexican' but most clearly emerges in the later *Analysis*: Uranga thinks that the accidentality of Mexicanness is not a problem to be solved, but something to be embraced and even valorized. The historical conditions that produce Mexicanness also produce a human type that is especially proximal to the actual nature of human beings more generally, or perhaps a kind of human experience that is especially well suited to reveal the actual nature of the human being. *All* humans are accidents, Uranga seems to want to say; most simply find a way to deflect awareness or attention to it by immersion into some form of substantiality. In the Mexican, the contingencies of history have created a type for whom the illusion is harder to sustain.

Perhaps the most promising interpretation reads Uranga as hinting at the possibility that splits the difference between nihilism and value creation of the sort one finds in substantiality. He notes that a concern for dignity grounds a kind of freedom, because the disconnection from the moral fray urged by dignity opens up a potential space for freedom and value-origination. He thinks that this possibility has been left inert by accidents precisely because of the correlative pathology of the accident's disposition of unwillingness. Read this way, Uranga's aspiration is not to replace accidentality with a new substantiality. Instead, he aspires to live with an ongoing acceptance of accidentality.

If this is something like a kind of living with nihilism, it cannot be total in its rejection of norms and normative force. There is a cautious normativity in his recommendation that the Mexican should seek to live in zozobra. In the later *Analysis*, Uranga suggests that cynicism may be one way to live in zozobra (2013: 75–78). It is an intriguing suggestion that exceeds the remarks he offers in the 'Essay on an Ontology of the Mexican'. It is unclear whether this is put forward as a solution or a strategy for living (in a truthful way) under zozobra. Perhaps cynicism is one way forward. This approach does suggest a way to try to vindicate the normative ambitions that underpin his analysis of Mexican being, as he claims that, 'what brings us to these types of studies is the project of performing moral, social, and religious transformations with that being' (2013: 34; my translation). Even so, it remains frustratingly elusive what the grounds could be for any recommendation that we persist in zozobra.

There is another puzzle here about how we are to understand Uranga and how we wish to make use of Uranga. Uranga is writing within a phenomenological tradition according to which accidentality is a kind of experience of relationship to meaning and value. This makes it difficult to see how anyone can be a substance if everyone qua human being must experience accidentality. However, if one is not wedded to a phenomenological framework, it may be more tempting to think that accidentality is about one's relationship to value (perceived or otherwise), and that certain cultural conditions make one more and less aware of that relationship. Whether and how this alternative reading of Uranga might be sustained is a matter we will return to in the next section.

Deeper into Accidentality

Let us now consider whether the reconstruction I offered at the outset might cast light on a range of cases beyond those that figure in Uranga's account. I will briefly consider four cases: double-consciousness, subversive substitution, transplanted substantiality, and biculturality.

Among the most important philosophical accounts of the difficulty of navigating a social world structured by norms, values, and meanings that one rejects, is W. E. B. Du Bois's 1903

Souls of Black Folk. A crucial idea in that account is *double consciousness*. Here is what he says about it:

> It is a peculiar sensation, this double-consciousness, this sense of always looking at one's self through the eyes of others, of measuring one's soul by the tape of a world that looks on in amused contempt and pity. One ever feels his two-ness,—an American, a Negro; two souls, two thoughts, two unreconciled strivings; two warring ideals in one dark body, whose dogged strength alone keeps it from being torn asunder.
>
> The history of the American Negro is the history of this strife—this longing to attain self-conscious manhood, to merge his double self into a better and truer self. In this merging he wishes neither of the older selves to be lost.
>
> (2017: 7)

The parallels with Urangan accidentality are striking. On one way of reading Du Bois's idea, blacks in the United States face a difficult project of reconciling two conflicting frameworks of meaning and value, without abandoning either, and without either being fully adequate to that person's cultural and historical circumstances. The worry is that the conflict cannot be resolved, and if so, then the souls of black folk seem vulnerable to a condition of accidentality structurally similar to the one examined by Uranga.

A different reading of double consciousness suggests another possibility. On this alternative reading, the essential feature of double consciousness is that one must always view one's actions under a dual lens of cultural significance. Even when a person feels no temptation to integrate the values, norms, and meanings of the dominant cultural framework, that person must nevertheless be conscious of the significance of her actions relative to the dominant practical cultural framework. The same act might have one significance under the cultural package one accepts, and another under the dominant cultural package. Moreover, oftentimes one might have little or no control over the wider social meaning of one's acts (Bierria 2014: 130–132).

On this picture, the doubly conscious person need not experience estrangement from all or any framework of meaning and values, as one must in the case of Urangan accidentality. The doubly conscious person might well be a substance, but she need not be. Still, there seems a greater potential for accidentality in people who, of practical necessity, operate with this form of double consciousness. Doubly conscious people may be especially likely to be aware of a certain amount of contingency about their condition. In particular, they may be especially aware of how vulnerable they are to being unable to live out the norms and values that they take as satisfying. Whether or not they are accidents, doubly conscious people are plausibly often proximal to accidentality.

A case that may manifest double-consciousness, but that has its own distinctive profile is something we might categorize as *subversive substitution*. A story helps to bring out the shape of this sort of case. A friend and neighbor of mine—call him Jerry—was born in Korea but raised from an early age in the United States by his Korean father. He related that as a kid growing up in Southern California, he strongly identified with US black culture. He has a ready explanation for why: it was the best available alternative to his particular situation. Traditional Korean life was not an option for him in Southern California at that time. Relatedly, there was not enough social scaffolding for him to grow up in a more broadly hybridized Korean-American cultural context. Nor did he feel like he could fully inhabit mainstream US culture, both because he was racialized as non-white and because too much of his home life was structured by distinct norms and social meanings. What was available, though, in music, media, and proximal community, was US black culture. It was something he identified with not as a kind of cultural tourism, or as an identity to be strategically exploited, and not as a form of subordination in the Urangan sense of deferral to the dominant identity group. Instead, for him it was about its being sufficiently rich to sustain a network of values, symbols, and social meanings that could be enacted and shared, without simply subordinating himself to the substantiality of the dominant US American culture. (I use *US American* to acknowledge that there is some dispute about the propriety of US citizens claiming the continental moniker *Americans*.) It was a sense of identification that manifested a subversion of, or a resistance to two different forms of substantiality, Korean and US American, although perhaps not without its own complicated relationship to the substantiality of US black culture.

This case suggests an alternative strategy to the dueling temptations of assimilation and nihilism. In it, the effort is animated by something like a liberatory strategy of recruiting existing counternormative packages. It is not Uranga's subordination precisely because it is not an effort to seek approval from various proximal forms of substantiality that enjoy cultural dominance. However, for it to succeed, the alternative cultural framework has to be culturally available, and sufficiently rich in social opportunities to tide one over. Its enactment or performance may require some uptake or reception by others. Even if it is not a permanent solution, the function of this sort of subversion is to resist the omnipresent alienation one can feel with respect to a dominant culture, against which one feels socially subordinate in some relevant way.

Finally, I return to some of the cases described at the outset: immigrants and their descendants. Some immigrant populations experience themselves as having a subordinate social identity. Of course, not all foreign nationals experience themselves as alien, as other, as having a subordinate identity in a cultural milieu. Whether these experiences obtain is, presumably, partly a function of whether those identities are externally marked or identified in those ways. What is of interest here is an interesting difference that can emerge between immigrants and their descendants in how they experience their practical agency.

Consider that some immigrants do not experience themselves as socially subordinate in their new home, even when they are aware of the fact that they may be marked as having subordinate social identities. The now-present cultural milieu may not afford them all the familiar ways of living out the norms, values, and meanings that they bring with them from the old country, but this need not affect their selves in a way that produces Urangan fragility, or a sense of normative ungroundedness.

Substantiality can survive transplantation. Immigrants can bring with them an ongoing, taken-for-granted, package of norms, values, and presumptions about social meaning. The local context does not always overturn that sense. The new cultural milieu can provide distinct, diminished but adequate, or even better affordances for enacting and expressing those norms, values, and social meanings. When this happens, the immigrant's sense of normative confidence may remain intact. An adult immigrant to the United States—call him Rogelio—once told me that he never felt like a minority here, despite his apparent membership in a US minority group. His explanation was that where he came from, he was a member of the majority group, so how could he feel like a minority? Taking him at his word, he lacked a sense of being socially and culturally subordinate. On the present account, we might say Rogelio's prior sense of identity, and the new local cultural circumstances, jointly afforded him adequate opportunities for living out the package of norms, values, and meanings he brought with him. His substantiality survived transplantation. For him, the persistence of a nonsubordinate identity may have been facilitated by the presence of a sufficiently robust community of people who shared an overlapping cultural framework. His sense of nonsubordinate identity was not disabused by experiences in the United States. Had either of those things been different, so might have his experience of his identity in the United States.

Even when substantiality survives transplantation, the immigrant may experience an increased sense of the contingency of one's relationship to her operative norms, values, and social meanings. Moving to a culturally distinct context just is the kind of thing that casts in relief the possibility of different arrangements of practical norms, values, and social meanings. Correspondingly, it raises the specter of a distinct social identity, a distinct fit between one's sense of self and the possibilities afforded by the social world. In at least some cases, though, it does not necessarily threaten the immigrant's sense of her default normative presumptions.

The situation tends to be somewhat different for the children of immigrants—and their proximal descendants—at least when they are readily marked out as members of some or another subordinate identity group. Under these conditions, it is harder to enjoy the presumption of substantiality, a sense of a relatively stable and unified package of norms, values, and meanings that reliably guide action in one's social world. Why? At home, the package is structured by the legacy of the old country; at school, in public, and much of the media, the affordances are structured by a different set of presumptions. A sense of normative ungroundedness is harder to avoid if one is forming one's social identity under these conditions, and that ungroundedness can come to be experienced as an *essential* feature of oneself. In contrast, her immigrant parents may experience any ungroundedness as fleeting, as a contingent thing that can come and go. For some immigrant children, though, Urangan accidentality may be more live for them than it ever will be for their parents. Other accidental or near-accidental configurations are possible. Consider various forms of bi- or polyculturality, where this is to be understood as the condition of persons who have a sense of comfort with multiple packages of practical norms, values, and social meanings. In this context, one is Armenian; in that context one is Californian; over there one is a ruthless capitalist; over here, a dedicated Christian. This situation is loosely similar to double consciousness. In this case, one identifies with all the various normative packages, or with a life that smoothly shifts between these packages. The worry here, of course, is that the result is a kind of fragmentation of self.

Philosophers have tended to valorize cross-situationally stable, normatively unified agents, and the Kantian and Aristotelian traditions have tended to defend this sort of view in different ways (for example, Korsgaard 2009: xi–xii, 18–27). (For dissent, see Doris 2002: 28–61; 2015: 157–158. See also Anzaldúa 2012: 99–113; Lugones 2003: 77–102; Alcoff 2006: 195–204, 264–284, for explorations and developments of the idea that there are distinctive psychic costs and opportunities for identities developed under conditions of cultural differences, social subordination, and the experience of cultural fragmentation.) Nevertheless, if one can withstand the psychic or rational demands of maintaining cultural silos in one's practical life, the pathologies—if that is what they are—of Urangan accidentality may not emerge. To be sure—oscillation between normative frameworks, or a living under an amalgam of distinctive normative packages can produce the requisite sense of normative unmooring characteristic of accidentality. The point here is that the mere fact that an agent experiences life as structured by discrete, even incompatible normative packages may not always produce the sense that there is no adequate normative basis for practical life.

This is one place where an analytic reconstruction of Uranga might come apart from the historical and phenomenological Uranga. If we think of accidentality as turning on the absence of a coherent and stable package of norms, or the absence of being rightly related to such norms, then we might want to insist that an agent with sufficiently unstable, unintegrated, and inconsistent normative commitments is an accident, even if that person does not experience life as normatively unmoored. Something like this sort of view makes it easier to see how accidentality just is the human condition, such that everyone is really an accident. In contrast, it seems the historical Uranga has to treat instances of bi- and polyculturality as cases of substantiality (or multiple substantiality, perhaps) whenever they were not accompanied by a sense of dissatisfaction or zozobra.

To take stock: The examples I have been considering—double consciousness, subversive substitution, transplanted substantiality, and biculturality—are less a taxonomy than a catalog of some of the phenomena that Uranga's framework can help illuminate. There are presumably other cases out there—including cases where people persist in the face of forms of cultural extinction—where Urangan tools might help illuminate the subtle relationship between lived experience, practical norms, and cultural situatedness.

It is not entirely clear whether we do better to think of the cases discussed in this section as *akin* to accidentality, or instead, as distinct *species* of accidentality. (I suspect we have to allow for the possibility that subversion may sometimes slide into subordination, or alternatively, into substantiality. I am going to put this possibility aside, though.) I am mostly inclined to think of these as species of accidentality, in part because the cases considered above—at least in paradigmatic forms—are marked by two interrelated features: (1) their bearers having a vivid sense of the contingency of their relationship to normative culture(s); and (2) in their practical reasoning, these agents do *not* take for granted a cross-situationally stable package of norms, values, and social meanings.

Thus, on the present proposal, Urangan accidentality—with its characteristic psychological syndrome—is only one species of accidentality. Psychological fragility might characterize a particular form of accidentality—perhaps it is essential to Urangan accidentality—but other forms of accidentality, with distinct moods and actional dispositions, can have divergent profiles.

Lingering Theoretical Estrangements?

The foregoing has mostly proceeded on the presumption that we can usefully extract a more general picture of accidentality from the distinctive particulars of Uranga's own account. Whether that project succeeds or fails is a matter of whether the account accurately describes its target phenomena, and the fruitfulness of that description. In that light, fidelity to Uranga's particulars is beside the point. However, the account is also intended as a reconstruction of ideas in Uranga. So it is worth considering whether, as an interpretation of key ideas in Uranga's account, things go wrong when notions like *accidentality* are disentangled from the project of developing an ontology of Mexicanness.

There is, of course, some sense in which a more general project of a philosophy of accidentality is at odds with some of the particulars of Uranga's account. For example, the particular psychological picture Uranga offers is intended not as a picture of accidentality in any and every historical circumstance. Instead, it is a characterization of the psychology that accompanies accidentality as he found it in the particular historical and cultural configuration of mid-twentieth-century Mexico. Accidentality elsewhere might differ in some of its particulars. For Uranga, a preoccupation with dignity is something specific to the distinctively Mexican psychological profile. He thought that different national contexts produce different characteristic virtues used to shield the accident from a commitment to action and a wider valuational framework (2017: 169–170). Among Uranga scholars, there is little disagreement that Uranga's project belonged to a distinctive moment in a cultural history, part of a shared project that took Mexicanness as a problem worthy of study, one that proceeded from a commitment to philosophical historicism, and one that took many of its key terms and philosophical inspirations from the work of Heidegger and Sartre (Hurtado 1994: 280–281; Villegas 1960: 181–187; Sánchez 2016: 22, 95–98). However, within philosophical circles in Mexico, there has been an important political and interpersonal dimension to the subsequent reception and evaluation of Uranga and his work (Valero Pie 2014: 155–156; Cuéllar Moreno 2018: 15–17). The present reconstruction has largely elided these elements, treating them as peripheral, at best.

The elision may seem less than fully innocent. Uranga has, until very recently, been abandoned by philosophers in Mexico. At the same time, it is not, shall we say, an accident that philosophers in Mexico were preoccupied with these questions, as opposed to philosophers in, say, England or the United States. Even a superficial familiarity with the history of the region suggests that centuries of colonialism, its aftermath, and the still-recent memory of the Mexican Revolution meant that there were widespread doubts within Mexico about whether various imported political, economic, and valuational systems (such as Catholicism, liberalism, and positivism) were genuinely responsive to the real-world conditions in Mexico. If philosophy was going to pull its weight, it needed to be responsive to, and perhaps originating in, features of what was distinctive in Mexico.

Today, though, the wider project of a philosophy of Mexicanness tends to be viewed as a philosophical dead-end. Not long after the project of a philosophy of Mexicanness was undertaken, philosophers began to raise serious doubts about whether there was anything philosophically interesting or puzzling about Mexicanness, whether the picture was committed to an implausible nationalist essentialism (Revueltas 2017: 216–221; Hurtado 1994: 283–288); and whether the metaphilosophical presumptions of the project were tenable (Villegas 1960: 211–228). So, to extract a standalone philosophy of accidentality may seem like a double mistake: it both separates out a project from its essential historical contexts, and it does so in a way that obscures the reason why the project was abandoned.

Yet, Uranga acknowledged that the core features of his account need not be limited to Mexicans and Mexicanness. As he put in the *Analysis*, 'any other character allows for the same operation, but my character is ready to hand, so it would be absurd to appeal to something alien' (2013: 56; my translation). So, while it is true that the extraction and generalization of a philosophy of accidentality from Uranga's wider project involves distortion, it is also faithful to a possibility he foresaw, but did not pursue. It is also faithful to a possibility his critics have thus far missed.

The theoretical insights produced by pursuing a broader picture of accidentality are worth the departures from Uranga's own concerns. We need not think, as Uranga did, that Mexicans are the 'most human of humans'. The question of who is the *most* human—in the sense of being best positioned to recognize the contingency of the normative, and of our systems of social meaning—is mostly idle. Perhaps it is a question that admits of an answer, but that answer would not tell us much. Whether Mexicans, Moldovans, or Mesopotamians might prove to be the most proximal to whatever one thinks is the truth about the normative foundations of socially enabled agency, one payoff of Uranga is that he provides us with tools for understanding features of culturally scaffolded agency that have otherwise been mostly invisible to philosophers. That so interesting and fecund a research program grew out of an effort at a regional ontology may suggest that we still have things to learn from a *filosofía de lo mexicano*, and potentially, other regional efforts at a philosophy of culture.[1]

References

Alcoff, L. (2006) *Visible Identities: Race, Gender, and the Self*, New York: Oxford University Press.
Anzaldúa, G. (2012) *Borderlands/La Frontera: The New Mestiza* (4th ed.), San Francisco: Aunt Lute Books.
Appiah, K. A. (2018) *The Lies That Bind: Rethinking Identity*, New York: Liveright Publishing.
Bierria, A. (2014) "Missing in Action: Violence, Power, and Discerning Agency," *Hypatia* 29: 129–145.
Cuéllar Moreno, J. M. (2018) *La revolución inconclusa: La filosofía de Emilio Uranga, artífice oculto del PRI*, Mexico City: Ariel.
Doris, J. M. (2002) *Lack of Character: Personality and Moral Behavior*, New York: Cambridge University Press.
Doris, J. M. (2015) *Talking to Our Selves: Reflection, Ignorance, and Agency*, Oxford: Oxford University Press.
Du Bois, W. E. B. [1903] (2017) *The Souls of Black Folk*, New York: Penguin Books.
Geertz, C. (1973) *Interpretation of Cultures*, New York: Basic Books.
Heine, S. J. (2016) *Cultural Psychology* (3rd ed.), New York: W. W. Norton & Company.
Henrich, J. (2016) *The Secret of Our Success: How Culture Is Driving Human Evolution, Domesticating Our Species, and Making us Smarter*, Princeton, NJ: Princeton University Press.
Herskovits, M. J. (1948) *Man and his Works: The Science of Cultural Anthropology*, New York: Knopf.
Hurtado, G. (1994) "Dos Mitos de la Mexicanidad," *Diánoia: Revista de filosofía* 40: 263–293.
Hurtado, G. (2007) *El Búho y la Serpiente*, Mexico City: National Autonomous University of Mexico.
Korsgaard, C. M. (2009) *Self-Constitution: Agency, Identity, and Integrity*, Oxford: Oxford University Press.
Lugones, M. (2003) *Pilgrimages/Peregrinajes: Theorizing Coalition against Multiple Oppressions*, Lanham, MD: Rowman & Littlefield.
Mead, M. (1953) "The Study of Culture at a Distance," in M. Mead and R. Métraux (eds.), *The Study of Culture at a Distance*, 57–82, Chicago: University of Chicago Press.
Nietzsche, F. (1995) *Thus Spoke Zarathustra*, W. Kaufmann (trans.), New York: Random House.
Revueltas, J. [1958] (2017) "Possibility and Limitations of the Mexican," in C. A. Sánchez and R. E. Sanchez (eds.), *Mexican Philosophy in the 20th Century: Essential Readings*, 216–232, New York: Oxford University Press.
Richerson, P. J., and Boyd, R. (2008) *Not by Genes Alone: How Culture Transformed Human Evolution*, Chicago: University of Chicago Press.
Sánchez, C. A. (2016) *Contingency and Commitment: Mexican Existentialism and the Place of Philosophy*, Albany: State University of New York Press.
Sánchez, C. A. (2018) "The Gift of Mexican Historicism," *Continental Philosophy Review* 51: 439–457.
Sommers, T. (2018) *Why Honor Matters*, New York: Basic Books.
Stabb, M. S. (1967) *In Quest of Identity: Patterns in the Spanish American Essay of Ideas, 1890–1960*, Chapel Hill: University of North Carolina Press.
Uranga, E. [1951] (2017) "Essay on an Ontology of the Mexican," in C. A. Sánchez and R. E. Sanchez, Jr. (eds.), *Mexican Philosophy in the 20th Century: Essential Readings*, 165–177, New York: Oxford University Press.
Uranga, E. [1952] (2013) *Análisis del ser del mexicano: y otros escritos sobre la filosofía de lo mexicano (1949–1952)*, in Guillermo Hurtado (eds.), México, DF: Bonilla Artigas Editores.
Valero Pie, A. (2014) "Review of Emilio Uranga, Análisis del ser del mexicano y otros escritos sobre la filosofía de lo mexicano (1949–1952)," *Diánoia: Revista de filosofía* 59: 155–161.
Villegas, A. (1960) *La filosofía de lo mexicano*, Mexico City: Fondo de Cultura Económica.

Note

1 Thanks to my students at the University of San Francisco and the University of California, San Diego, whose enthusiasm for Urangan themes provided impetus for this project, especially Crystal Vega, whose 'He's talking about us!' reaction made me think there was an article to be written about this aspect of Emilio Uranga's work. Thanks also to audiences where predecessors of this

article were presented, including the following places: University of California, San Diego; Washington University, California State Polytechnic University, Pomona; the University of Puget Sound; the University of Washington; the University of Vermont; Georgetown University; the National Autonomous University of Mexico; and Texas Christian University. Special thanks to Helen Beebee, Michael Cholbi, Jonathan Cohen, John Doris, Miranda Fricker, Sarah Goering, Randall Harp, Alan Hazlett, Guillermo Hurtado, Shen-yi Liao, Katherine Lindeman, Casey O'Callaghan, Carlos Alberto Sánchez, Dan Speak, Clinton Tolley, and Natalia Washington for notable questions, discussion, and feedback.

Reading Questions

1. What is it to be an accident? How is it different than being a substance?
2. Is accidentality a way we *feel* in relation to norms, or is accidentality a metaphysical *way* we are related we have to some norms? (To see the difference, think about someone who has internalized her oppression. Such a person might feel connected to the norms that oppress her (no psychological alienation), without those norms really in fact being proper or appropriate for her (metaphysical alienation).)
3. According to Vargas, does Uranga think people *should* live in accidentality? If so, what is supposed to be appealing about it?
4. What is the idea of double consciousness? How does it relate to being an accident?
5. What other groups today might be characterized as living in accidentality? Should those groups seek to stay in accidentality? Why or why not?
6. Is everyone an accident? Why or why not?

Part 4
Phenomenology, Hermeneutics, and Coloniality

Introduction

This section showcases some of the creative ways that Latinx philosophers have engaged with two important European philosophical traditions, phenomenology and hermeneutics. Phenomenology is a branch of philosophy focused on understanding structures of experience. Hermeneutics is an offshoot of phenomenology that explores how our experience is structured by language. A third element in what follows is the idea that Latin Americans, and the people descended from them, continue to be subject to the effects of centuries of European colonization. The texts included in this section represent one strand of those conversations. They focus on how phenomenology and hermeneutics can help us to understand and resist oppression in the Latinx context. In a variety of ways, these essays explore the provocative idea that the deepest roots of injustice are located in the most intimate domain of how we see, think, feel, speak, and relate to ourselves and others. That is, they are accounts of the deep-seated patterns that define how modern people have learned to perceive and experience the world.

The section begins with María Lugones' influential critique of Aníbal Quijano's account of the "coloniality of power." According to Quijano, the European colonization of the Americas established the basic operating system of the modern global order. This order divides humanity into races and divides the earth into geographic zones, such that resources extracted from the racialized global "periphery" flow toward Anglo-European "centers." In this way, the theory offers a lens to see through the chaotic churn of events, so that we can perceive the underlying logic of history, the hidden system that has prevented transformative change for centuries, despite the resilience of oppressed communities.

In "Heterosexualism and the Modern/Colonial Gender System," Lugones begins by crediting Quijano's research for its insight. However, she goes on to argue that the theoretical lens he offers has a serious defect. Quijano fails to give modern conceptions of gender the same critical scrutiny he gives to modern conceptions of race. As a result, his account is seriously compromised by its reliance on false and oppressive assumptions about sex and gender. Building on research in anthropology, Lugones makes the case that modern gender relations were a violent colonial imposition, and that in this system, gender is constructed in dramatically different ways for people on the "light" and "dark" side of the colonial racial divide.

Lugones' analysis of light-and dark-side gender arrangements has been recognized for illuminating a range of social and political issues. In addition, her critique of Quijano has served as a sobering reminder of the ways that unchecked assumptions can undermine our ability to theorize injustice, even among those who are sincerely dedicated to rooting out oppressive patterns of thought in their research practices.

DOI: 10.4324/9781003385417-24

These concerns about research methods are central to the work of Ada María Isasi-Díaz. In "Mujerista Discourse: A Platform for Latinas' Subjugated Knowledge," Isasi-Díaz explores the overlooked philosophical, political, and theological insights that can be gained by centering the everyday lives of grassroots Latinas. In sharp contrast to classical European phenomenologists, who viewed everyday life as a space of mindless routine, Isasi-Díaz argues that for many Latinas, "lo cotidiano" (the quotidian) is a dramatic stage in which they must make difficult choices that put their values and identities at stake.

Illustrated by poignant and memorable examples, Isasi-Días offers "mujerista" (or womanist) discourse as a framework to appreciate the extraordinary epistemic and moral richness of everyday life for the Latinas in her community. Isasi-Díaz describes mujerista discourse as an outgrowth of liberation theology, a Latin American tradition of Christian ethics that centers the liberation and flourishing of the world's oppressed. Moreover, she argues that mujerista discourse is "decolonial," in the sense that it recognizes oppressed Latinas as having expertise and strives to ensure that they receive the benefits of that expertise, thereby disrupting the extraction-oriented relationships that have characterized academic research within the modern/colonial order.

In "Hometactics," taken from Mariana Ortega's 2016 book, *In-Between: Latina Feminist Phenomenology, Multiplicity, and the Self*, we find a similar methodological orientation. Writing about her own experience, and centering the work of Latinas, such as Anzaldúa's account of "mestiza consciousness" and Lugones' account of "world-traveling" (included in Sections 2 and 3, respectively), Ortega challenges prevailing narratives of belonging and identity and traditional notions of home as a fixed, safe place. Although there is a sense in which we all experience the self as being multiple—as, for example, when we switch between our "work self" and the person we are at home—Ortega argues that there is a much more profound form of multiplicity that emerges for people who must navigate conflicting social identities. On this basis, she constructs a systematic analysis of the distinctive structures of experience that characterize existence for Latinas who are located "between" worlds.

Adapting Michel de Certeau's analysis of "tactics," Ortega describes hometactics as the "micropractices" that multiplicitous selves use to create pockets of comfort and belonging in their everyday lives, and especially in spaces where they cannot fully belong due to their diverse identities. Although these practices might put Latinas at risk of becoming complacent or complicit with unjust systems, Ortega ultimately celebrates hometactics as essential for navigating the "in-between" spaces of identity.

The next essay, "Between Hermeneutic Violence and Alphabets of Survival," by Elena Flores Ruíz, explores the ways that oppressive power relations are encoded in our language. Ruiz develops the concept of hermeneutic violence, defined as the unjust destruction of meaning-making systems and practices, and focuses on the existential impact of hermeneutic violence on women of color. When women of color seek to make sense of violence they have experienced, and make their struggles understandable and meaningful to others, they face pressure to speak, think, and relate in ways that are intelligible to those in positions of power. However, dominant sense-making frameworks are shaped by deep, structural inequities, and for this reason, these dominant frameworks often ignore and distort the lives of women of color and even render their struggles unintelligible. Ruíz concludes by offering a set of reflections on what theory can and cannot do to bring about meaningful change under such nonideal conditions.

In "Decolonial Feminist *Movidas*: A *Caribeña* (Re)thinks 'Privilege,' the Wages of Gender, and Building Complex Coalitions," Xhercis Méndez gathers some of the threads of this conversation and offers some principles for action. Building on the work of Lugones and others, Méndez recasts the "benefits" awarded to women who comply with the modern/colonial gender system in terms of "wages," and she uses this economic metaphor to shed new light on the difficulties of building liberatory coalitions among groups competing for scarce resource on the marketplace of social advantage.

However, rather than try to find a single theory to explain oppression and provide the foundation for a transformative change of the global order, Méndez suggests that decolonial approaches will be pluralistic, provisional, and responsive to emergence. In this spirit, Méndez discusses some of the basic "movidas" (moves) that decolonial feminists have learned to make when thinking and speaking about matters of justice—historicizing gender, mapping relational power dynamics, developing new social imaginaries, and ritualizing new embodied practices that disrupt colonial power structures.

Stepping back, the texts in this section show Latinx philosophers adapting existing philosophical traditions to take up novel questions and distinctive theses and create space in the academy where Latinx academics can speak and think together about their own experiences. Phenomenology and hermeneutics have always insisted that experience matters, that the ways we feel and speak is a matter worthy of serious investigation, and that the most important truths about experience and communication are irreducible to the facts described by scientific methods of objective quantification. Perhaps for this reason, Latinx philosophers have found these traditions to be amenable to alternative approaches to knowledge production that aim to provide better footholds for advancing new and ambitious philosophical projects.

16 Heterosexualism and the Colonial/Modern Gender System

María Lugones

In a theoretico-praxical vein, I am offering a framework to begin thinking about heterosexism as a key part of how gender fuses with race in the operations of colonial power. Colonialism did not impose precolonial, European gender arrangements on the colonized. It imposed a new gender system that created very different arrangements for colonized males and females than for white bourgeois colonizers. Thus, it introduced many genders and gender itself as a colonial concept and mode of organization of relations of production, property relations, of cosmologies and ways of knowing. But we cannot understand this gender system without understanding what Anibal Quijano calls "the coloniality of power" (2000a, 2000b, 2001–2002). The reason to historicize gender formation is that without this history, we keep on centering our analysis on the patriarchy; that is, on a binary, hierarchical, oppressive gender formation that rests on male supremacy without any clear understanding of the mechanisms by which heterosexuality, capitalism, and racial classification are impossible to understand apart from each other. The heterosexualist patriarchy has been an ahistorical framework of analysis. To understand the relation of the birth of the colonial/modern gender system to the birth of global colonial capitalism—with the centrality of the coloniality of power to that system of global power—is to understand our present organization of life anew.

This attempt at historicizing gender and heterosexualism is thus an attempt to move, dislodge, complicate what has faced me and others engaged in liberatory/decolonial projects as hard barriers that are both conceptual and political. These are barriers to the conceptualization and enactment of liberatory possibilities as de-colonial possibilities. Liberatory possibilities that emphasize the light side of the colonial/modern gender system affirm rather than reject an oppressive organization of life. There has been a persistent absence of a deep imbrication of race into the analysis that takes gender and sexuality as central in much white feminist theory and practice, particularly feminist philosophy. I am cautious when I call it "white" feminist theory and practice. One can suspect a redundancy involved in the claim: it is white because it seems unavoidably enmeshed in a sense of gender and of gendered sexuality that issues from what I call the light side of the modern/colonial gender system. But that is, of course, a conclusion from within an understanding of gender that sees it as a colonial concept. Yet, I arrive at this conclusion by walking a political/praxical/theoretical path that has yet to become central in gender work: the path marked by taking seriously the coloniality of power. As I make clear later in this essay, it is also politically important that many who have taken the coloniality of power seriously have tended to naturalize gender. That position is also one that entrenches oppressive colonial gender arrangements, oppressive organizations of life.

So, on the one hand, I am interested in investigating the intersection of race, class, gender, and sexuality in a way that enables me to understand the indifference that persists in much

DOI: 10.4324/9781003385417-25

feminist analysis. Women of color and Third World feminisms have consistently shown the way to a critique of this indifference to this deep imbrication of race, gender, class, and sexuality. The framework I introduce is wholly grounded in the feminisms of women of color and women of the Third World and arises from within them. This framework enables us to ask harsh but hopefully inspiring questions. The questions attempt to inspire resistance to oppression understood in this degree of complexity. Two crucial questions that we can ask about heterosexualism from within it are: How do we understand heterosexuality not merely as normative but as consistently perverse when violently exercised across the colonial/modern gender system so as to construct a worldwide system of power? How do we come to understand the very meaning of heterosexualism as tied to a persistently violent domination that marks the flesh multiply by accessing the bodies of the unfree in differential patterns devised to constitute them as the tortured materiality of power? In the work I begin here, I offer the first ingredients to begin to answer these questions. I do not believe any solidarity or homoerotic loving is possible among females who affirm the colonial/modern gender system and the coloniality of power. I also think that transnational intellectual and practical work that ignores the imbrication of the coloniality of power and the colonial/modern gender system also affirms this global system of power. But I have seen over and over, often in disbelief, how politically minded white theorists have simplified gender in terms of the patriarchy. I am thus attempting to move the discussion of heterosexualism, by changing its very terms.

I am also interested in investigating the intersection of race, class, gender and sexuality in a way that enables me to understand the indifference that men, but, more important to our struggles, men who have been racialized as inferior, exhibit to the systematic violences inflicted upon women of color.[1] I want to understand the construction of this indifference so as to make it unavoidably recognizable by those claiming to be involved in liberatory struggles. This indifference is insidious since it places tremendous barriers in the path of the struggles of women of color for our own freedom, integrity, and well-being and in the path of the correlative struggles toward communal integrity. The latter is crucial for communal struggles toward liberation, since it is their backbone. The indifference is found both at the level of everyday living and at the level of theorizing of both oppression and liberation. The indifference seems to me not just one of not seeing the violence because of the categorial[2] separation of race, gender, class, and sexuality. That is, it does not seem to be only a question of epistemological blinding through categorial separation.

Feminists of color have made clear what is revealed in terms of violent domination and exploitation once the epistemological perspective focuses on the intersection of these categories.[3] But that has not seemed sufficient to arouse in those men who have themselves been targets of violent domination and exploitation any recognition of their complicity or collaboration with the violent domination of women of color. In particular, theorizing global domination continues to proceed as if no betrayals or collaborations of this sort need to be acknowledged and resisted.

Here, I pursue this investigation by placing together two frameworks of analysis that I have not seen sufficiently jointly explored. I am referring, on the one hand, to the important work on gender, race and colonization done, not exclusively, but significantly by Third World and women of color feminists, including critical race theorists. This work has emphasized the concept of intersectionality and has exposed the historical and the theoretico-practical exclusion of nonwhite women from liberatory struggles in the name of women.[4] The other framework is the one Quijano introduced and which is at the center of his work, that of the coloniality of power (2000a, 2000b, 2001–2002).[5] Placing both of these strands of analysis together permits me to arrive at what I am tentatively calling "the modern/colonial gender system." I think this understanding of gender is implied in both frameworks in large terms, but it is not explicitly articulated, or not articulated in the direction I think necessary to unveil the reach and consequences of complicity with this gender system. I think that articulating this colonial/modern gender system, both in large strokes, and in all its detailed and lived concreteness will enable us to see what was imposed on us. It will also enable us to see its fundamental destructiveness in both a long and wide sense. The intent of this writing is to make visible the instrumentality of the colonial/modern gender system in subjecting us—both women and men of color—in all domains of existence. But it is also the project's intent to make visible the crucial disruption of bonds of practical solidarity. My intent is to provide a way of understanding, of reading, of perceiving our allegiance to this gender system. We need to place ourselves in a position to call each other to reject this gender system as we perform a transformation of communal relations.[6] In this initial essay, I present Quijano's model that I will complicate, but one that gives us—in the logic of structural axes—a good ground from within which to understand the processes of intertwining the production of race and gender.

The Coloniality of Power

Quijano thinks of the intersection of race and gender in large structural terms. So, to understand that intersection in his terms, it is necessary to understand his model of global, Eurocentered capitalist power. Both race[7] and gender find their meanings in this model (pattern).[8] Quijano understands that all power is structured in relations of domination, exploitation, and conflict as social actors fight over control of "the four basic areas of human existence: sex, labor, collective authority and subjectivity/intersubjectivity, their resources and products" (2001–2002: 1). Global, Eurocentered, capitalist power is organized characteristically around two axes: the coloniality of power and modernity (2000b: 342). The axes order the disputes over control of each area of existence in such a way that the coloniality of power and modernity thoroughly infuse the meaning and forms of domination in each area. So, for Quijano, the disputes/struggles over control of "sexual access, its resources and products" define the domain of sex/gender and the disputes, in turn, can be understood as organized around the axes of coloniality and modernity.

This is too narrow an understanding of the oppressive modern/colonial constructions of the scope of gender. Quijano also assumes patriarchal and heterosexual understandings of the disputes over control of sex, its resources, and products. Quijano accepts the global, Eurocentered, capitalist understanding of what gender is about. These features of the framework serve to veil the ways in which nonwhite colonized women have been subjected and disempowered. The heterosexual and patriarchal character of the arrangements can themselves be appreciated as oppressive by unveiling the presuppositions of the framework. Gender does not need to organize social arrangements, including social sexual arrangements. But gender arrangements need not be either heterosexual or patriarchal. They need not be, that is, as a matter of history. Understanding these features of the organization of gender in the modern/colonial gender system—the biological dimorphism, the patriarchal and heterosexual organizations of relations—is crucial to an understanding of the differential gender arrangements along "racial" lines. Biological dimorphism, heterosexualism, and patriarchy are all characteristic of what I call the light side of the colonial/modern organization of gender. Hegemonically, these are written large over the meaning of gender. Quijano seems unaware of his accepting this hegemonic meaning of gender. In making these claims I aim to expand and complicate Quijano's approach, while preserving his understanding of the coloniality of power, which is at the center of what I am calling the modern/colonial gender system.

The coloniality of power introduces the basic and universal social classification of the population of the planet in terms of the idea of 'race' (Quijano 2001–2002: 1). The invention of race is a pivotal turn as it replaces the relations of superiority and inferiority established through domination. It reconceives humanity and human relations fictionally, in biological terms. It is important that what Quijano provides is a historical theory of social classification to replace what he terms the "Eurocentric theories of social classes" (2000b: 367). This move makes conceptual room for the coloniality of power. It makes conceptual room for the centrality of the classification of the world's population in terms of races in the understanding of global capitalism. It also makes conceptual room for understanding historical disputes over control of labor, sex, collective authority, and intersubjectivity as developing in processes of long duration, rather than understanding each of the elements as predating the relations of power. The elements that constitute the global, Eurocentered, capitalist model of power do not stand separately from each other and none is prior to the processes that constitute the patterns. Indeed, the mythical presentation of these elements as metaphysically prior is an important aspect of the cognitive model of Eurocentered, global capitalism.

In constituting this social classification, coloniality permeates all aspects of social existence and gives rise to new social and geocultural identities (Quijano 2000b: 342). "America" and "Europe" are among the new geocultural identities. "European," "Indian," "African" are among the "racial" identities. This classification is "the deepest and most enduring expression of colonial domination" (2001–2002: 1). With expansion of European colonialism, the classification was imposed on the population of the planet. Since then, it has permeated every area of social existence, constituting the most effective form of material and intersubjective social domination. Thus, *coloniality* does not just refer to racial classification. It is an encompassing phenomenon, since it is one of the axes of the system of power and as such it permeates all control of sexual access, collective authority, labor, subjectivity/intersubjectivity and the production of knowledge from within these intersubjective relations. Or, alternatively, all control over sex, subjectivity, authority, and labor are articulated around it. As I understand the logic of "structural axis" in Quijano's usage, the element that serves as an axis becomes constitutive of and constituted by all the forms that relations of power take with respect to control over that particular domain of human existence. Finally, Quijano also makes clear that, though coloniality is related to colonialism, these are distinct as the latter does not necessarily include racist relations of power. Coloniality's birth and its prolonged and deep extension throughout the planet is tightly related to colonialism (2000b: 381).

In Quijano's model of global, Eurocentered, capitalist power, *capitalism* refers to "the structural articulation of all historically known forms of control of labor or exploitation, slavery, servitude, small independent mercantile production, wage labor, and reciprocity under the hegemony of the capital-wage labor relation" (2000b: 349). In this sense, the structuring of the disputes over control of labor is discontinuous: not all labor relations under global, Eurocentered capitalism fall under the capital/wage relation model, though this is the hegemonic model. It is important in beginning to see the reach of the coloniality of power that wage labor has been reserved almost exclusively for white Europeans. The division of labor is thoroughly racialized as well as geographically differentiated. Here, we see the coloniality of labor as a thorough meshing of labor and race.

Quijano understands modernity, the other axis of global, Eurocentered capitalism, as "the fusing of the experiences of colonialism and coloniality with the necessities of capitalism, creating a specific universe of intersubjective relations of domination under a Eurocentered hegemony" (2000b: 343). In characterizing modernity, Quijano focuses on the production of a way of knowing, labeled rational, arising from within this subjective universe since the seventeenth century in the main hegemonic centers of this world system of power (Holland and England). This way of knowing is Eurocentered. By *Eurocentrism* Quijano understands the cognitive perspective not of Europeans only, but of the Eurocentered world, of those educated under the hegemony of world capitalism. "Eurocentrism naturalizes the experience of people within this model of power" (2000b: 343).

The cognitive needs of capitalism and the naturalizing of the identities and relations of coloniality and of the geocultural distribution of world capitalist power have guided the production of this way of knowing. The cognitive needs of capitalism include "measurement, quantification, externalization (or objectification) of what is knowable with respect to the knower so as to control the relations among people and nature and among them with respect to it, in particular the property in means of production" (Quijano 2000b: 343). This way of knowing was imposed on the whole of the capitalist world as the only valid rationality and as emblematic of modernity.

Europe was mythologically understood to predate this pattern of power as a world capitalist center that colonized the rest of the world and, as such, the most advanced moment in the linear, unidirectional, continuous path of the species. A conception of humanity was consolidated according to which the world's population was differentiated in two groups: superior and inferior, rational and irrational, primitive and civilized, traditional and modern. *Primitive* referred to a prior time in the history of the species, in terms of evolutionary time. Europe came to be mythically conceived as preexisting colonial, global, capitalism and as having achieved a very advanced level in the continuous, linear, unidirectional path. Thus, from within this mythical starting point, other human inhabitants of the planet came to be mythically conceived not as dominated through conquest, nor as inferior in terms of wealth or political power, but as an anterior stage in the history of the species, in this unidirectional path. That is the meaning of the qualification "primitive" (Quijano 2000b: 343–344). We can see then the structural fit of the elements constituting global, Eurocentered capitalism in Quijano's model (pattern). Modernity and coloniality afford a complex understanding of the organization of labor. They enable us to see the fit between the thorough racialization of the division of labor and the production of knowledge. The pattern allows for heterogeneity and discontinuity. Quijano argues that the structure is not a closed totality (2000b: 355).

We are now in a position to approach the question of the intersectionality of race and gender[9] in Quijano's terms. I think the logic of "structural axes" does more and less than intersectionality. Intersectionality reveals what is not seen when categories such as gender and race are conceptualized as separate from each other. The move to intersect the categories has been motivated by the difficulties in making visible those who are dominated and victimized in terms of both categories. Though everyone in capitalist Eurocentered modernity is both raced and gendered, not everyone is dominated or victimized in terms of their race or gender. Kimberlé Crenshaw and other women of color feminists have argued that the categories have been understood as homogenous and as picking out the dominant in the group as the norm; thus *women* picks out white bourgeois women, *men* picks out white bourgeois men, *black* picks out black heterosexual men, and so on. It becomes logically clear then that the logic of categorial separation distorts what exists at the intersection, such as violence against women of color. Given the construction of the categories, the intersection misconstrues women of color. So, once intersectionality shows us what is missing, we have ahead of us the task of reconceptualizing the logic of the intersection so as to avoid separability.[10] It is only when we perceive gender and race as intermeshed or fused that we actually see women of color.

The logic of structural axes shows gender as constituted by and constituting the coloniality of power. In that sense, there is no gender/race separability in Quijano's model. I think he has the logic of it right. But the axis of coloniality is not sufficient to pick out all aspects of gender. What aspects of gender are shown depends on how gender is actually conceptualized in the model. In Quijano's model (pattern) gender seems to be contained within the organization of that "basic area of existence" that Quijano calls "sex, its resources, and products" (2000b: 378). That is, there is an account of gender within the framework that is not itself placed under scrutiny and that is too narrow and overly biologized as it presupposes sexual dimorphism, heterosexuality, patriarchal distribution of power, and so on.

Though I have not found a characterization of gender in what I have read of his work, Quijano seems to me to imply that gender difference is constituted in the disputes over control of sex, its resources, and products. Differences are shaped through the manner in which this control is organized. Quijano understands sex as biological attributes[11] that become elaborated as social categories. He contrasts the biological quality of sex with phenotype, which does not include differential biological attributes. On the one hand, "the color of one's skin, the shape of one's eyes and hair do not have any relation to the biological structure" (2000b, 373). Sex, on the other hand, seems unproblematically biological to Quijano. He characterizes the "coloniality of *gender* relations,"[12] that is, the ordering of gender relations around the axis of the coloniality of power, as follows:

(1) In the whole of the colonial world, the norms and formal-ideal patterns of sexual behavior of the genders and consequently the patterns of familial organization of "Europeans" were directly founded on the "racial" classification: the sexual freedom of males and the fidelity of women were, in the whole of the Eurocentered world, the counterpart of the free—that is, not paid as in prostitution—access of white men to "black" women and "indians" in America, "black" women in Africa, and other "colors" in the rest of the subjected world.
(2) In Europe, instead, it was the prostitution of women that was the counterpart of the bourgeois family pattern.
(3) Familial unity and integration, imposed as the axes of the model of the bourgeois family in the Eurocentered world, were the counterpart of the continued disintegration of the parent-children units in the "nonwhite" "races," which could be held and distributed as property, not just as merchandise but as "animals." This was particularly the case among "black" slaves, since this form of domination over them was more explicit, immediate, and prolonged.
(4) The hypocrisy characteristically underlying the norms and formal-ideal values of the bourgeois family are not, since then, alien to the coloniality of power. (Quijano 2000b: 378, my translation)

As we see in this complex and important quote, Quijano's framework restricts gender to the organization of sex, its resources, and products, and he seems to make a presupposition as to who controls access and who become constituted as resources. Quijano appears to take for granted that the dispute over control of sex is a dispute among men, about men's control of resources which are thought to be female. Men do not seem understood as the resources in sexual encounters. Women are not thought to be disputing for control over sexual access. The differences are thought of in terms of how society reads reproductive biology.

Intersexuality

In "Definitional Dilemmas," Julie Greenberg tells us that legal institutions have the power to assign individuals to a particular racial or sexual category:[13] "Sex is still presumed to be binary and easily determinable by an analysis of biological factors. Despite anthropological and medical studies to the contrary, society presumes an unambiguous binary sex paradigm in which all individuals can be classified neatly as male or female" (2002: 112). Greenberg argues that throughout U.S. history the law has failed to recognize intersexuals, in spite of the fact that 1 to 4 percent of the world's population is intersexed. That is, they do not fit neatly into unambiguous sex categories:

> they have some biological indicators that are *traditionally* associated with males and some biological indicators that are *traditionally* associated with females. The manner in which the law defines the terms *male, female*, and *sex* will have a profound impact on these individuals.
>
> (112, emphases added)

The assignations reveal that what is understood to be biological sex is socially constructed. From the late nineteenth century until World War I, reproductive function was considered a woman's essential characteristic. The presence or absence of ovaries was the ultimate criterion of sex (Greenberg 2002: 113). But there are a large number of factors that can enter into "establishing someone's 'official' sex": chromosomes, gonads, external morphology, internal morphology, hormonal patterns, phenotype, assigned sex, and self-identified sex (Greenberg 2002: 112). At present, chromosomes and genitalia enter into the assignment, but in a manner that reveals biology is thoroughly interpreted and itself surgically constructed.

> XY infants with "inadequate" penises must be turned into girls because society believes the essence of manhood is the ability to penetrate a vagina and urinate while standing. XX infants with "adequate" penises, however, are assigned the female sex because society and many in the medical community believe that the essence of womanhood is the ability to bear children rather than the ability to engage in satisfactory sexual intercourse.
>
> (Greenberg 2002: 114)

Intersexed individuals are frequently surgically and hormonally turned into males or females. These factors are taken into account in legal cases involving the right to change the sex designation on official documents, the ability to state a claim for employment discrimination based upon sex, the right to marry (Greenberg 2002: 115). Greenberg reports the complexities and variety of decisions on sexual assignation in each case. The law does not recognize intersexual status. Though the law permits self-identification of one's sex in certain documents, "for the most part, legal institutions continue to base sex assignment on the traditional assumptions that sex is binary and can be easily determined by analyzing biological factors" (Greenberg 2002: 119).

Greenberg's work enables me to point out an important assumption in the model that Quijano offers us. This is important because sexual dimorphism has been an important characteristic of what I call "the light side" of the colonial/modern gender system. Those in the "dark side" were not necessarily understood dimorphically. Sexual fears of colonizers led them to imagine the indigenous people of the Americas as hermaphrodites or intersexed, with large penises and breasts with flowing milk (see McClintock 1995). But as Paula Gunn Allen (1986/1992) and others have made clear, intersexed individuals were recognized in many tribal societies prior to colonization without assimilation to the sexual binary. It is important to consider the changes that colonization brought to understand the scope of the organization of sex and gender under colonialism and in Eurocentered global capitalism. If the latter did only recognize sexual dimorphism for white bourgeois males and females, it certainly does not follow that the sexual division is based on biology. The cosmetic and substantive corrections to biology make very clear that "gender" is antecedent to the "biological" traits and gives them meaning. The naturalizing of sexual differences is another product of the modern use of science that Quijano points out in the case of "race." Not all different traditions correct and normalize intersexed people. So, as with other assumptions, it is important to ask how sexual dimorphism served and continues to serve global, Eurocentered, capitalist domination/exploitation.

Nongendered and Gynecratic Egalitarianism

As global, Eurocentered capitalism was constituted through colonization, gender differentials were introduced where there were none. Oyéronké Oyewùmí (1997) has shown us that the oppressive gender system that was imposed on Yoruba society did a lot more than transform the organization of reproduction. Her argument shows us that the scope of the gender system colonialism imposed encompasses the subordination of females in every aspect of life. Thus Quijano's understanding of the scope of gendering in global, Eurocentered capitalism is much too narrow. Allen argued that many Native American tribes were matriarchal, recognized more than two genders, recognized "third" gendering and homosexuality positively, and understood gender in egalitarian terms rather than in the terms of subordination that Eurocentered capitalism imposed on them. Allen's work has enabled us to see that the scope of the gender differentials was much more encompassing and it did not rest on biology. Allen also showed us a gynecentric construction of knowledge and approach to understanding "reality" that counters the knowledge production of modernity. Thus she has pointed us in the direction of recognizing the gendered construction of knowledge in modernity, another aspect of the hidden scope of "gender" in Quijano's account of the processes constituting the coloniality of gender.

Nongendered Egalitarianism

In *The Invention of Women*, Oyéronké Oyewùmí raises questions about the validity of patriarchy as a valid transcultural category (1997: 20). She does so, not by contrasting patriarchy and matriarchy, but by arguing that "gender was not an organizing principle in Yoruba society prior to colonization by the West" (31). No gender system was in place. Indeed, she tells us that gender has "become important in Yoruba studies not as an artifact of Yoruba life but because Yoruba life, past and present, has been translated into English to fit the Western pattern of body-reasoning" (30). The assumption that Yoruba society included gender as an organizing principle is another case "of Western dominance in the documentation and interpretation of the world, one that is facilitated by the West's global material dominance" (32). She tells us that "researchers always find gender when they look for it" (31). "The usual gloss of the Yoruba categories *obinrin* and *okunrin* as 'female/woman' and 'male/man,' respectively, is a mistranslation. These categories are neither binarily opposed nor hierarchical" (32–33). The prefixes *obin* and *okun* specify a variety of anatomy. Oyewùmí translates the prefixes as referring to the anatomic male and the anatomic female, shortened as *anamale* and *anafemale*. It is important to note that she does not understand these categories as binarily opposed.

Oyewùmí understands gender as introduced by the West as a tool of domination that designates two binarily opposed and hierarchical social categories. 'Women' (the gender term) is not defined through biology, though it is assigned to anafemales. Women are defined in relation to men, the norm. Women are those who do not have a penis; those who do not have power; those who cannot participate in the public arena (Oyewùmí 1997: 34). None of this was true of Yoruba anafemales prior to colonization.

> The imposition of the European state system, with its attendant legal and bureaucratic machinery, is the most enduring legacy of European colonial rule in Africa. One tradition that was exported to Africa during this period was the exclusion of women from the newly created colonial public sphere.... The very process by which females were categorized and reduced to "women" made them ineligible for leadership roles.... The emergence of women as an identifiable category, defined by their anatomy and subordinated to men in all situations, resulted, in part, from the imposition of a patriarchal colonial state. For females, colonization was a twofold process of racial inferiorization and gender subordination. The creation of "women" as a category was one of the very first accomplishments of the colonial state. It is not surprising, therefore, that it was unthinkable for the colonial government to recognize female leaders among the peoples they colonized, such as the Yoruba.... The transformation of state power to male-gender power was accomplished at one level by the exclusion of women from state structures. This was in sharp contrast to Yoruba state organization, in which power was not gender-determined.
>
> (123–125)

Oyewùmí recognizes two crucial processes in colonization, the imposition of races with the accompanying inferiorization of Africans, and the inferiorization of anafemales. The inferiorization of anafemales extended very widely from exclusion from leadership roles to loss of control over property and other important economic domains. Oyewùmí notes that the introduction of the Western gender system was accepted by Yoruba males, who thus colluded with the inferiorization of anafemales. So, when we think of the indifference of nonwhite men to the violences exercised against nonwhite women, we can begin to have some sense of the collaboration between anamales and Western colonials against anafemales. Oyewùmí makes clear that both men and women resisted cultural changes at different levels. Thus, while

> in the West the challenge of feminism is how to proceed from the gender-saturated category of "women" to the fullness of an unsexed humanity. For Yoruba obinrin, the challenge is obviously different because at certain levels in the society and in some spheres, the notion of an "unsexed humanity" is neither a dream to aspire to nor a memory to

be realized. It exists, albeit in concatenation with the reality of separate and hierarchical sexes imposed during the colonial period.

(156)

We can see, then, that the scope of the coloniality of gender is much too narrow. Quijano assumes much of the terms of the modern/colonial gender system's hegemonic light side in defining the scope of gender. I have gone outside the coloniality of gender in order to examine what it hides, or disallows from consideration, about the very scope of the gender system of Eurocentered global capitalism. So, though I think that the coloniality of gender, as Quijano pointedly describes it, shows us very important aspects of the intersection of race and gender, it follows rather than discloses the erasure of colonized women from most areas of social life. It accommodates rather than disrupt the narrowing of gender domination. Oyewùmí's rejection of the gender lens in characterizing the inferiorization of anafemales in modern colonization makes clear the extent and scope of the inferiorization. Her understanding of gender, the colonial, Eurocentered capitalist construction is much more encompassing than Quijano's. She enables us to see the economic, political, and cognitive inferiorization as well as the inferiorization of anafemales regarding reproductive control.

Gynecratic Egalitarianism

> To assign to this great being the position of "fertility goddess" is exceedingly demeaning: it trivializes the tribes and it trivializes the power of woman.
>
> —Paula Gunn Allen

As she characterizes many Native American tribes as gynecratic, Paula Gunn Allen emphasizes the centrality of the spiritual in all aspects of Indian life and thus a very different intersubjectivity from within which knowledge is produced than that of the coloniality of knowledge in modernity. Many American Indian tribes "thought that the primary potency in the universe was female, and that understanding authorizes all tribal activities" (Allen 1986/1992: 26). Old Spider Woman, Corn Woman, Serpent Woman, Thought Woman are some of the names of powerful creators. For the gynecratic tribes, Woman is at the center and "no thing is sacred without her blessing, her thinking" (Allen 1986/1992: 13).

Replacing this gynecratic spiritual plurality with one supreme male being as Christianity did, was crucial in subduing the tribes. Allen proposes that transforming Indian tribes from egalitarian and gynecratic to hierarchical and patriarchal "requires meeting four objectives":

(1) The primacy of female as creator is displaced and replaced by male-gendered creators (generally generic) (1986/1992: 41).
(2) Tribal governing institutions and the philosophies that are their foundation are destroyed, as they were among the Iroquois and the Cherokee (41).
(3) The people "are pushed off their lands, deprived of their economic livelihood, and forced to curtail or end altogether pursuits on which their ritual system, philosophy, and subsistence depend. Now dependent on white institutions for their survival, tribal systems can ill afford gynocracy when patriarchy—that is, survival—requires male dominance" (42).

(4) The clan structure "must be replaced in fact if not in theory, by the nuclear family. By this ploy, the women clan heads are replaced by elected male officials and the psychic net that is formed and maintained by the nature of nonauthoritarian gynecentricity grounded in respect for diversity of gods and people is thoroughly rent" (42).

Thus, for Allen, the inferiorization of Indian females is thoroughly tied to the domination and transformation of tribal life. The destruction of the gynocracies is crucial to the "decimation of populations through starvation, disease, and disruption of all social, spiritual, and economic structures" (42). The program of degynocratization requires impressive "image and information control." Thus

> recasting archaic tribal versions of tribal history, customs, institutions and the oral tradition increases the likelihood that the patriarchal revisionist versions of tribal life, skewed or simply made up by patriarchal non-Indians and patriarchalized Indians, will be incorporated into the spiritual and popular traditions of the tribes.
>
> (42)

Among the features of the Indian society targeted for destruction were the two-sided complementary social structure; the understanding of gender; and the economic distribution that often followed the system of reciprocity. The two sides of the complementary social structure included an internal female chief and an external male chief. The internal chief presided over the band, village, or tribe, maintaining harmony and administering domestic affairs. The red, male, chief presided over mediations between the tribe and outsiders (Allen 1986/1992: 18). Gender was not understood primarily in biological terms. Most individuals fit into tribal gender roles "on the basis of proclivity, inclination, and temperament. The Yuma had a tradition of gender designation based on dreams; a female who dreamed of weapons became a male for all practical purposes" (196).

Like Oyewùmí, Allen is interested in the collaboration between some Indian men and whites in undermining the power of women. It is important for us to think about these collaborations as we think of the question of indifference to the struggles of women in racialized communities against multiple forms of violence against them and the communities. The white colonizer constructed a powerful inside force as colonized men were co-opted into patriarchal roles. Allen details the transformations of the Iroquois and Cherokee gynecracies and the role of Indian men in the passage to patriarchy. The British took Cherokee men to England and gave them an education in the ways of the English. These men participated during the time of the Removal Act.

> In an effort to stave off removal, the Cherokee in the early 1800s under the leadership of men such as Elias Boudinot, Major Ridge, and John Ross, and others, drafted a constitution that disenfranchised women and blacks. Modeled after the Constitution of the United States, whose favor they were attempting to curry, and in conjunction with Christian sympathizers to the Cherokee cause, the new Cherokee constitution relegated women to the position of chattel.
>
> (Allen 1986/1992: 37)

Cherokee women had had the power to wage war, to decide the fate of captives, to speak to the men's council, they had the right to inclusion in public policy decisions, the right to choose whom and whether to marry, the right to bear arms. The Women's Council was politically and spiritually powerful (36–37). Cherokee women lost all these powers and rights, as the Cherokee were removed and patriarchal arrangements were introduced. The Iroquois shifted from a Mother-centered, Mother-right people organized politically under the authority of the Matrons, to a patriarchal society when the Iroquois became a subject people. The feat was accomplished with the collaboration of Handsome Lake and his followers.

According to Allen, many of the tribes were gynecratic, among them the Susquehanna, Hurons, Iroquois, Cherokee, Pueblo, Navajo, Narragansett, Coastal Algonkians, Montagnais. She also tells us that among the eighty-eight tribes that recognized homosexuality, those who recognized homosexuals in positive terms included the Apache, Navajo, Winnebago, Cheyenne, Pima, Crow, Shoshoni, Paiute, Osage, Acoma, Zuñi, Sioux, Pawnee, Choctaw, Creek, Seminole, Illinois, Mohave, Shasta, Aleut, Sac and Fox, Iowa, Kansas, Yuma, Aztec, Tlingit, Maya, Naskapi, Ponca, Maricopa, Lamath, Quinault, Yuki, Chilula, and Kamia. Twenty of these tribes included specific references to lesbianism.

Michael Horswell (2003) comments usefully on the use of the term *third gender*. He tells that third gender does not mean that there are three genders. It is rather a way of breaking with sex and gender bipolarities. The "third" is emblematic of other possible combinations than the dimorphic. The term *berdache* is sometimes used for "third gender." Horswell tells us that male berdache have been documented in nearly 150 North American societies and female berdache in half as many groups (2003: 27). He also comments that sodomy, including ritual sodomy, was recorded in Andean societies and many other native societies in the Americas (27). The Nahuas and Mayas also reserved a role for ritualized sodomy (Sigal 2003: 104). Interestingly, Pete Sigal tells us that the Spanish saw sodomy as sinful, but Spanish law condemned the active not the passive partner in sodomy to criminal punishment. In Spanish popular culture, sodomy was racialized by connecting the practice to the Moors and the passive partner was condemned and seen as equal to a Moor. Spanish soldiers were seen as the active partners to the passive Moors (102–104).

Allen has not only enabled us to see how narrow Quijano's conception of gender is in terms of the organization of the economy and of collective authority, but she has also revealed that the production of knowledge is gendered, as is the very conception of reality at every level. Allen supported the questioning of biology in the construction of gender differences and introduces the important idea of gender roles being chosen and dreamt. Allen also showed us that the heterosexuality characteristic of the modern/colonial construction of gender relations is produced, mythically constructed. But heterosexuality is not just biologized in a fictional way; it is compulsory and permeates the whole of the coloniality of gender in the renewed, large sense. In this sense, global, Eurocentered capitalism is heterosexualist. I think it is important to see, as we understand the depth and force of violence in the production of both the light and the dark sides of the colonial/modern gender system, that this heterosexuality has been consistently perverse, violent, and demeaning, turning people into animals and turning white women into reproducers of "the (white) race" and "the (middle or upper) class." Horswell's and Sigal's work complements Allen's, particularly in understanding the presence of sodomy and male homosexuality in colonial and precolonial America.

The Colonial/Modern Gender System

Understanding the place of gender in precolonial societies is pivotal to understanding the nature and scope of changes in the social structure that the processes constituting colonial/modern Eurocentered capitalism imposed. Those changes were introduced through slow, discontinuous, and heterogeneous processes that violently inferiorized colonized women. The gender system introduced was one thoroughly informed through the coloniality of power. Understanding the place of gender in precolonial societies is also essential to understanding the extent and importance of the gender system in disintegrating communal relations, egalitarian relations, ritual thinking, collective decision making and authority, and economies. Thus, it is important to understand the extent to which the imposition of this gender system was as constitutive of the coloniality of power as the coloniality of power was constitutive of it. The logic of the relation between them is of mutual constitution.[14] But it should be clear by now that the colonial, modern, gender system cannot exist without the coloniality of power, since the classification of the population in terms of race is a necessary condition of its possibility.

To think of the scope of the gender system of global, Eurocentered capitalism it is necessary to understand the extent to which the very process of narrowing of the concept of gender to the control of sex, its resources, and products constitutes gender domination. To understand this narrowing and to understand the intermeshing of racialization and gendering, we must consider whether the social arrangements prior to colonization regarding the sexes gave differential meaning to them across all areas of existence. This will enable us to see whether control over labor, subjectivity/intersubjectivity, collective authority, sex—Quijano's "areas of existence"—was itself gendered. Given the coloniality of power, I think we can also say that having a dark and a light side is characteristic of the co-construction of the coloniality of power and the colonial/modern gender system. Considering critically both biological dimorphism and the position that gender socially constructs biological sex helps us understand the scope, depth, and characteristics of the colonial/modern gender system. The sense is that the reduction of gender to the private, to control over sex and its resources and products, is a matter of ideology, of the cognitive production of modernity that has understood race as gendered and gender as raced in particularly differential ways for Europeans/whites and colonized/nonwhite peoples. Race is no more mythical and fictional than gender—both are powerful fictions.

In the development of twentieth-century feminism, the connections among gender, class, and heterosexuality as racialized were not made explicit. That feminism centered its struggle and its ways of knowing and theorizing against a characterization of women as fragile, weak in both body and mind, secluded in the private, and sexually passive. But it did not bring to consciousness that those characteristics only constructed white bourgeois womanhood. Indeed, beginning from that characterization, white bourgeois feminists theorized white womanhood as if all women were white.

It is part of their history that only white bourgeois women have consistently counted as women so described in the West. Females excluded from that description were not just their subordinates. They were also understood to be animals in a sense that went further than the identification of white women with nature, infants, and small animals. They were understood as animals in the deep sense of "without gender,"[15] sexually marked as female, but without the characteristics of femininity.[16] Women racialized as inferior were turned from animals into various modified versions of "women" as it fit the processes of global, Eurocentered capitalism. Thus, heterosexual rape of Indian or African slave women coexisted with concubinage, as well as with the imposition of the heterosexual understanding of gender relations among the colonized—when and as it suited global, Eurocentered capitalism, and heterosexual domination of white women. But the work of Oyewùmí and Allen has made clear that there was no extension of the status of white women to colonized women even when they were turned into similes of bourgeois white women. Colonized females got the inferior status of gendering as women, without any of the privileges accompanying that status for white bourgeois women, although the histories Oyewùmí and Allen have presented should make clear to white bourgeois women that their status is much inferior to that of Native American or Yoruba women before colonization. Oyewùmí and Allen have also explained that the egalitarian understanding of the relation between anafemales, anamales, and "third gender" people has left neither the imagination nor the practices of Native Americans and Yoruba. But these are matters of resistance to domination.

Erasing any history, including oral history, of the relation of white to nonwhite women, white feminism wrote white women large. Even though historically and contemporarily white bourgeois women knew perfectly well how to orient themselves in an organization of life that pitted them for very different treatment than nonwhite or working-class women.[17] White feminist struggle became one against the positions, roles, stereotypes, traits, and desires imposed on white bourgeois women's subordination. They countenanced no one else's gender oppression. They understood women as inhabiting white bodies but did not bring that racial qualification to articulation or clear awareness. That is, they did not understand themselves in intersectional terms, at the intersection of race, gender, and other forceful marks of subjection or domination. Because they did not perceive these deep differences they saw no need to create coalitions. They presumed a sisterhood, a bond given with the subjection of gender.

Historically, the characterization of white European women as fragile and sexually passive opposed them to nonwhite, colonized women, including female slaves, who were characterized along a gamut of sexual aggression and perversion, and as strong enough to do any sort of labor. For example, slave women performing backbreaking work in the U.S. South were not considered fragile or weak.

First came, led by an old driver carrying a whip, forty of the largest and strongest women I ever saw together; they were all in a simple uniform dress of a bluish check stuff, the skirts reaching little below the knee; their legs and feet were bare; they carried themselves loftily, each having a hoe over the shoulder, and walking with a free, powerful swing, like *chasseurs* on the march. Behind came the cavalry, thirty strong, mostly men, but a few of them women, two of whom rode astride on the plow mules. A lean and vigilant white overseer, on a brisk pony, brought up the rear.... The hands are required to be in the cotton field as soon as it is light in the morning, and, with the exception of ten or fifteen minutes, which is given to them at noon to swallow their allowance of cold bacon, they are not permitted to be a moment idle until it is too dark to see, and when the moon is full, they often times labor till the middle of the night.

(Takaki 1993: 111)

Patricia Hill Collins has provided a clear sense of the dominant understanding of black women as sexually aggressive and the genesis of that stereotype in slavery:

The image of Jezebel originated under slavery when Black women were portrayed as being, to use Jewelle Gomez' words, "sexually aggressive wet nurses." Jezebel's function was to relegate all Black women to the category of sexually aggressive women, thus providing a powerful rationale for the widespread sexual assaults by White men typically reported by Black slave women. Jezebel served yet another function. If Black slave women could be portrayed as having excessive sexual appetites, then increased fertility should be the expected outcome. By suppressing the nurturing that African-American women might give their own children which would strengthen Black family networks, and by forcing Black women to work in the field, "wet nurse" White children, and emotionally nurture their White owners, slave owners effectively tied the controlling images of jezebel and mammy to the economic exploitation inherent in the institution of slavery.

(Collins 2000: 82)

But it is not just black slave women who were placed outside the scope of white bourgeois femininity. In *Imperial Leather*, as she tells us of Columbus's depiction of the earth as a woman's breast, Anne McClintock evokes the "long tradition of male travel as an erotics of ravishment."

For centuries, the uncertain continents—Africa, the Americas, Asia—were figured in European lore as libidinously eroticized. Travelers' tales abounded with visions of the monstrous sexuality of far-off lands, where, as legend had it, men sported gigantic penises and women consorted with apes, feminized men's breasts flowed with milk and militarized women lopped theirs off. . . . Within this porno tropic tradition, women figured as the epitome of sexual aberration and excess. Folklore saw them, even more than the men, as given to a lascivious venery so promiscuous as to border on the bestial.

(1995: 22)

McClintock described the colonial scene depicted in a sixteenth-century drawing in which Jan van der Straet "portrays the 'discovery' of America as an eroticized encounter between a man and a woman."

Roused from her sensual languor by the epic newcomer, the indigenous woman extends an inviting hand, insinuating sex and submission. Vespucci, the godlike arrival, is destined to inseminate her with his male seeds of civilization, fructify the wilderness and quell the riotous scenes of cannibalism in the background. The cannibals appear to be female and are spit roasting a human leg.

(25–26)

In the nineteenth century, McClintock tells us, "sexual purity emerged as a controlling metaphor for racial, economic and political power" (47). With the development of evolutionary theory "anatomical criteria were sought for determining the relative position of races in the human series" (50) and "the English middle-class male was placed at the pinnacle of evolutionary hierarchy. White English middle class women followed. Domestic workers, female miners and working class prostitutes were stationed on the threshold between the white and black races" (56). Along the same lines, Yen Le Espiritu tells us that

representations of gender and sexuality figure strongly in the articulation of racism. Gender norms in the United States are premised upon the experiences of middle-class men and women of European origin. These Eurocentric-constructed gender norms form a backdrop of expectations for American men and women of color—expectations which racism often precludes meeting. In general, men of color are viewed not as the protector, but rather the aggressor—a threat to white women. And women of color are seen as over-sexualized and thus undeserving of the social and sexual protection accorded to white middle-class women. For Asian American men and women, their exclusion from whitebased cultural notions of the masculine and the feminine has taken seemingly contrasting forms: Asian men have been cast as both hypermasculine (the "Yellow

Peril") and effeminate (the "model minority"); and Asian women have been rendered both superfeminine (the "China Doll") and castrating (the "Dragon Lady").

(1997: 135)

This gender system congealed as Europe advanced the colonial project(s). It took shape during the Spanish and Portuguese colonial adventures and became full-blown in late modernity. The gender system has a light and a dark side. The light side constructs gender and gender relations hegemonically, ordering only the lives of white bourgeois men and women and constituting the modern/colonial meaning of men and women. Sexual purity and passivity are crucial characteristics of the white bourgeois females who reproduce the class and the colonial and racial standing of bourgeois, white men. But equally important is the banning of white bourgeois women from the sphere of collective authority, from the production of knowledge, from most control over the means of production. Weakness of mind and body are important in the reduction and seclusion of white bourgeois women from most domains of life, most areas of human existence. The gender system is heterosexualist, as heterosexuality permeates racialized patriarchal control over production, including knowledge production, and over collective authority. Heterosexuality is both compulsory and perverse among white bourgeois men and women since the arrangement does significant violence to the powers and rights of white bourgeois women and serves to reproduce control over production and white bourgeois women are inducted into this reduction through bounded sexual access.

The dark side of the gender system was and is thoroughly violent. We have begun to see the deep reductions of anamales, anafemales, and "third gender" people from their ubiquitous participation in rituals, decision making, and economics; their reduction to animality, to forced sex with white colonizers, to such deep labor exploitation that often people died working. Quijano tells us that

the vast Indian genocide of the first decades of colonization was not caused, in the main, by the violence of the conquest, nor by the diseases that the conquerors carried. Rather it was due to the fact that the Indians were used as throwaway labor, forced to work till death.

(2000a, my translation)

I want to mark the connection between the work that I am citing here as I introduce the modern/colonial gender system's dark side and Quijano's coloniality of power. Unlike white feminists who have not focused on colonialism, these theorists very much see the differential construction of gender along racial lines. To some extent, they understand gender in a wider sense than Quijano; thus they think not only of control over sex, its resources and products, but also of labor as both racialized and gendered. That is, they see an articulation between labor, sex, and the coloniality of power. Oyewùmí and Allen, for example, have helped us realize the full extent of the reach of the colonial/modern gender system into the construction of collective authority, all aspects of the relation between capital and labor, and the construction of knowledge.

Important work has been and has yet to be done in detailing the dark and light sides of what I am calling the modern colonial gender system.[18] In introducing this arrangement in very large strokes, I mean to begin a conversation and a project of collaborative, participatory, research and popular education wherein we may begin to see in its details the long sense of the processes of the colonial/gender system enmeshed in the coloniality of power into the present, to uncover collaboration, and to call each other to reject it in its various guises as we recommit to communal integrity in a liberatory direction. We need to understand the organization of the social so as to make visible our collaboration with systematic racialized gender violence, so as to come to an inevitable recognition of it in our maps of reality.

References

Alexander, M. J., and Mohanty, C. (eds.). (1997) *Feminist Genealogies, Colonial Legacies, Democratic Futures*, New York: Routledge.
Allen, P. G. (1986/1992) *The Sacred Hoop: Recovering the Feminine in American Indian Traditions*, Boston: Beacon Press.
Amos, V., and Parmar, P. (1984) "Challenging Imperial Feminism" in K.-K. Bhavnani (ed.), *Feminism and "Race"*, Oxford: Oxford University Press.
Anzaldúa, G. (1987) *Borderlands/la Frontera: The New Mestiza*, San Francisco: Aunt Lute.
Brown, E. B. (1991) "Polyrhythms and Improvisations," *History Workshop* 31: 85–90.
Collins, P. H. (2000) *Black Feminist Thought*, New York: Routledge.
Crenshaw, K. (1995) "Mapping the Margins: Intersectionality, Identity Politics, and Violence Against Women of Color," in K. Crenshaw, N. Gotanda, G. Peller and K. Thomas (eds.), *Critical Race Theory*, New York: The New Press.
Espiritu, Y. L. (1997) "Race, Class, and Gender in Asian America," in E. H. Kim, L. V. Villanueva and Asian Women United of California (eds.), *Making More Waves*, Boston: Beacon Press.
Greenberg, J. A. (2002) "Definitional Dilemmas: Male or Female? Black or White? The Law's Failure to Recognize Intersexuals and Multiracials," in T. Lester (ed.), *Gender Nonconformity, Race, and Sexuality: Charting the Connections*, Madison: University of Wisconsin Press.
Horswell, M. (2003) "Toward an Andean Theory of Ritual Same-Sex Sexuality and Third-Gender Subjectivity," in P. Sigal (ed.), *Infamous Desire: Male Homosexuality in Colonial Latin America*, Chicago: University of Chicago Press.
Lorde, A. (1984) "The Master's Tools Will Never Dismantle the Master's House," in *Sister Outsider*, Trumansburg, NY: The Crossing Press.
Lugones, M. (2003) *Pilgrimages/Peregrinajes: Theorizing Coalitions Against Multiple Oppressions*, Lanham: Rowman & Littlefield.
Lugones, M. (2014) "Radical Multiculturalism and Women of Color Feminisms," *Journal for Cultural & Religious Theory* 13 (1).
McClintock, A. (1995) *Imperial Leather: Race, Gender, and Sexuality in the Colonial Contest*, New York: Routledge.
Oyewùmí, O. (1997) *The Invention of Women: Making an African Sense of Western Gender Discourses*, Minneapolis: University of Minnesota Press.
Quijano, A. (1991) "Colonialidad, Modernidad/Racionalidad," *Perú Indígena* 13 (29): 11–29.
Quijano, A. (2000a) "Colonialidad del Poder, Eurocentrismo y América Latina," in *Colonialidad del Saber, Eurocentrismo y Ciencias Sociales*, CLACSO-UNESCO 2000, Buenos Aires, Argentina.
Quijano, A. (2000b) "Colonialidad del Poder y Clasificación Social," *Festschrift for Immanuel Wallerstein. Special issue, Journal of World Systems Research* 5 (2) (Summer/Fall).
Quijano, A. (2001–2002) "Colonialidad del Poder, Globalización y Democracia," *Revista de Ciencias Sociales de la Universidad Autónoma de Nuevo León* 4 (7–8): 1–23.
Sigal, P. (2003) "Gendered Power, the Hybrid Self, and Homosexual Desire in Late Colonial Yucatan," in P. Sigal (ed.), *Infamous Desire: Male Homosexuality in Colonial Latin America*, Chicago: University of Chicago Press.
Spelman, E. (1988) *Inessential Woman*, Boston: Beacon.
Takaki, R. (1993) *A Different Mirror*, Boston: Little, Brown, and Company.

Notes

1 I use the U.S.-originated *women of color* throughout this piece as a coalitional term against multiple oppressions. It is a problematic term and not necessarily one of self-identification for many of the women who had the modern/colonial gender system imposed on them. Those women were

and continue to be the target of systematic and extensive state and interpersonal violence under global, Eurocentered capitalism.
2 I use *categorial* to mark arrangements in accordance with categories. I certainly do not mean *categorical*.
3 There is a very large and significant literature on this question of intersectionality. Here I refer only to a few pieces: Spelman (1988); Barkley Brown (1991); Crenshaw (1995); Espiritu (1997); Collins (2000); and Lugones (2003).
4 To the work mentioned already, I want to add Amos and Parmar (1984); Lorde (1984); Allen (1986); Anzaldúa (1987); McClintock (1995); Oyewùmí (1997); and Alexander and Mohanty (1997).
5 Anibal Quijano has written extensively and influentially on this topic. The interpretation I offer is gathered from (1991), (2000a), (2000b), and (2001–2002).
6 Popular education can be a method of collective critical exploration of this gender system both in the large stroke, and most importantly, in its detailed space/time concreteness toward a transformation of communal relations.
7 Quijano understands race to be a fiction. He always places quotation marks around the term to signify this fictional quality. When terms "European," "Indian," are in quotation marks, they signify a racial classification.
8 Quijano prefers *pattern* to *model* as a translation for *patron*. His reason is that model suggests something to follow or copy. Because this use of *pattern* is often awkward, I use *model*.
9 In dropping the quotation marks around race here, I do not mean to disagree with Quijano about the fictive quality of race. Rather, I want to begin to emphasize the fictive quality of gender, including the biological "nature" of sex and heterosexuality.
10 See my *Pilgrimages/Peregrinajes* (2003) and "Radical Multiculturalism and Women of Color Feminisms" (n. d.) for an unpacking of this logic.
11 I have not seen these attributes summarized by Quijano. So, I do not know whether he is thinking of chromosomal combinations or of genitalia and breasts.
12 I want to mark that Quijano calls this section of his "Colonialidad del Poder y Clasificación Social" (2000b), not the coloniality of sex but of gender.
13 The relevance of contemporary legal disputes over the assignation of gender to intersexed individuals should be clear since Quijano's model includes the contemporary period.
14 I am sure that those who read this piece will recognize much of what I am saying and some may think that it has already been said. That is quite fine with me, so long as it is accompanied by a theoretico-practical recognition of this mutual constitution, one that shows throughout the theoretical, the practical, and the theoretico-practical work. But I think something that may well be new here is my approach to the logic of intersectionality and my understanding of the mutuality of construction of the coloniality of power and the colonial/modern gender system. I think they are both necessary, but it is only the logic mutuality of construction that yields the inseparability of race and gender.
15 Spelman's interpretation (1988) of Aristotle's distinction between free men and women in the Greek polis and slave males and slave females suggested this claim to me. It is important to note that reducing women to nature or the natural is to collude with this racist reduction of colonized women. More than one Latin American thinker who decries Eurocentrism relates women to the sexual and the reproductive.
16 It is important to distinguish between being thought of as without gender because an animal, and not having, even conceptually, any gender distinctions. That is, having gender is not a characteristic of being human for all people.
17 The deep distinction between white working-class and nonwhite women can be glimpsed from the very different places they occupied in the evolutionary series referred to by McClintock (1995: 4).
18 I am clear now that there is an ambiguous in-between zone between the light and the dark side that conceives/imagines/constructs white women servants, miners, washerwomen, prostitutes as not necessarily caught through the lens of the sexual or gender binary and as racialized ambiguously, but not as white. See McClintock (1995). I am working on the inclusion of this crucial complexity into the framework.

Reading Questions

1. What does Lugones appreciate about Aníbal Quijano's analysis of the "coloniality of power"? What does she argue is missing?

2. Lugones claims that gender itself is a colonial introduction. What does this mean? What evidence does Lugones provide to support this claim?
3. How does Lugones describe the "light" and "dark" sides of the gender system with regard to power relations and violence?
4. Thinking about the way gender shows up in your own life, what new insights or questions arise when you consider the idea that the "light" and "dark" sides of the gender system operate in different ways?
5. Suppose it was discovered that gynecratic social arrangements often had their own oppressive features, just not along the lines of gender categories. Would this be a problem for Lugones' view? Why or why not?
6. What challenges does Lugones pose to traditional Western feminist perspectives through her critique of the modern/colonial gender system?
7. What does Lugones say about resistance to gender-based oppression? What implications does her analysis have for understanding social movements and activism today?

17 Mujerista Discourse

A Platform for Latinas' Subjugated Knowledge

Ada María Isasi-Díaz

One of the main goals of mujerista discourse has been to provide a platform for the voices of Latinas living in the United States. Mujerista discourse, particularly focused on Christian ethics and theology, has as its goal the liberation/flourishing of Latinas. It uses as its source the understandings and practices of Latinas, in particular the religious understandings and practices of grassroots Latinas who struggle against oppression in their everyday lives. Mujerista discourse, originally a liberationist one, highlights the voices of Latinas, which as a group are ignored by U.S. society.[1] Often considered intellectually inferior, Latinas' understandings are indeed one of the many subjugated knowledges that are ignored to the detriment not only of our own community but also of the whole of society.[2]

Mujerista thought is a "thinking-with" grassroots Latinas rather than a "thinking-about" them (Freire 1972: 24). Mujerista discourse is a "we" discourse that embraces commitment to being community while not ignoring specificity and particularity. Elaborated by academic Latinas, mujerista discourse takes very seriously what Paulo Freire noted long ago: At the heart of all liberation thinking there has to be a commitment to the people, what he calls a "communion with the people" (Freire 1972: 24). This communion, or solidarity, with the people has to find expression in an ongoing dialogue that profoundly respects the people's ability to reason and to participate reflectively in their own struggles against oppression (Freire 1972: 52).

In order to remain true to the struggle for liberation, one needs to continuously find ways of creating knowledge from the underside of history. This is why mujerista thought attempts to be beyond the controlling rationality of dominant discourses. To do this, we use the experience of Latinas as the source for knowledge: This is a nonnegotiable understanding in the struggle for our liberation. Our work is not to elaborate and explain our understandings against the background of "regular" knowledge, using the dominant discourse to validate our insights. As a decolonial discourse, mujerista thought seeks adequacy and validation from its usefulness in Latinas' struggles. This does not mean, however, that we can claim to be free of "dominant thinking" or that we can always evade its categories, or that we always find it necessary to do so. As a matter of fact, the goal of mujerista discourse, the liberation/flourishing of Latinas, obliges us to use in our methods, in our categories, and in our strategies whatever we find valuable to achieve our goal.

This makes clear that though mujerista theology and ethics have used the language of liberation discourse, they certainly understand liberation not as a project possible within Western civilization but rather one that has as its goal radical structural changes. Our attempt has always been to enable and further Latinas' thinking, that is, to shed light on the epistemological richness that emerges from our lived experiences and to value what we know and how we know it as our contribution to building a different world. Undoubtedly, we find many similarities between mujerista discourse and decolonial thinking—postcolonial philosophy—which we began to explore at the beginning of the twenty-first century. Though we agree with Walter Mignolo that liberation theology, one of the "parenting" discourses of mujerista thinking, was conceived within the Western episteme, mujerista thinking, as one of the instances of Latina/o thought, has taken liberation thought beyond its initial articulations (see Mignolo 2012). Perhaps because of our condition as an ethno-racial, minoritized, and marginalized group within the United States, mujerista theology, though indebted to Latin American liberation theology, also drinks from many of the same fountains as does decolonial thinking. It is not a matter of merely "changing dresses" but rather a welcoming of decolonial thinking as an addition to liberation thought and as a way of creating "coalitions" among scholars and schools of thought that are committed to local communities and that seek to contribute to the articulation of shared meanings.

That said, I turn to the themes of this essay that indeed fall within the paradigms of both decoloniality and liberation. This essay is about two elements at the heart of our communion with grassroots Latinas: an ongoing option for the oppressed, which, as mujeristas, is an option for Latinas, and a commitment to value lo cotidiano—the everyday of Latinas. Without these two commitments, one cannot contribute to unveiling subjugated knowledges. In this essay I first explain what I mean by the oppressed, of which Latinas are but one group. I then clarify the meaning of lo cotidiano in an attempt to discover and highlight its richness. In the third section of the essay, I analyze the option for the oppressed and why it has to be at the heart of all liberative and decolonial discourses. I conclude the essay with some important theological considerations.

The Oppressed

Injustice, which from the perspective of those suffering is called oppression, has different causes that need to be made explicit in order to struggle for justice in a more effective way than we have done since the 1960s. Different causes lead to different modes of oppression, which are interrelated but do not operate in the same way. There are five different modes of oppression: exploitation, marginalization, ethnoracism, powerlessness, and structural violence.[3] None of these different forms of oppression is more unjust or causes more destruction than the others. All of them are interconnected, creating institutions, organizations, laws, and customs that reinforce one another and create structural oppression. The dominant group, the group that has power, considers oppressed people as having no value or significance. Those who are oppressed—Latinas and Latinos, the impoverished, lesbians, gays, transsexuals, and transgender people, among many others—are not taken into consideration in determining what is normative for society.

Often when referring to the oppressed, I specify "the impoverished" because I am a middle-class Latina and though I have suffered economic exploitation, i.e., my salary in comparable situations has not been the same as that of my male colleagues,[4] being middle-class can easily lead me to ignore poverty. Consciously mentioning the impoverished is a way of reminding myself that I have to struggle for societal changes even if such changes will "cost me" some of the economic advantages and privileges I have being a middle-class Latina.

When I refer to the oppressed and the impoverished, I am referring to those who are conscious of their oppression and who struggle for their liberation, taking into consideration their communities. In this category I include those who know that liberation is about a radical change of structures and not about participation in oppressive structures. The oppressed and the impoverished are those who are conscious of being historical agents, though they would most probably not talk about it using this phrase. They are those who can and do explain to themselves what happens to them and in doing so take responsibility for their experience of being oppressed, for who they are as oppressed people and how they face the situation in which they find themselves.[5] I do not include, however, the impoverished whose struggle to survive makes it impossible for them to reflect on their circumstances. In no way does this mean that I devalue them or ignore them. A commitment to the impoverished and the oppressed is precisely a commitment to create spaces that will allow them the opportunity to become more conscious of the reasons for the injustices they suffer. Though one cannot "conscienticize" anyone else, we can facilitate opportunities for the oppressed and impoverished to reflect on their own reality.[6]

Not part of this category are those who consider themselves oppressed but whose situations are due to personal circumstances and not to structural ones. One needs to keep in mind, at least in the United States, that it has become somewhat fashionable to claim to be oppressed in order to benefit from government programs such as scholarships for minority children and youth. Therefore, in conclusion, the oppressed and impoverished are conscious of their oppression, and they know that their reality is not due solely or mainly to personal shortcomings; they neither seek an individualistic way out of their situation nor attempt to simply "move ahead" within oppressive structures.[7]

Lo Cotidiano

I start this section with a quotation from Martin Buber's work, for it situates me and my interest in lo cotidiano, and indicates the reason for my commitment to value it. "I possess nothing but the everyday out of which I am never taken. I know no full but each mortal hour's fullness of claim and responsibility. Though far from been equal to it, yet I know that in the claim I am claimed and may respond in responsibility, and know who speaks and demands a response" (Buber 1965: 14).

My interest in lo cotidiano is intrinsically linked to the principal axis of my ethical-theological work: an option for the impoverished and the oppressed. Therefore, lo cotidiano that interests me and to which I refer is that of the impoverished and the oppressed, particularly that of my community of accountability, Latinas living in the United States. I struggle to describe lo cotidiano in order to be able to make it concrete, for if not, I will not be able to affect it, that is, to change it.

The description of lo cotidiano that follows, which I propose not as a definition but as a heuristic device that has as its goal a better—deeper—understanding of both the oppression of Latinas and our liberative praxis, has hermeneutical and epistemological implications.

Lo cotidiano refers to the immediate space—time and place—of daily life, the first horizon of our experiences, in which our experiences take place. It is where we first meet and relate to the material world—by which I mean not just physical reality but also the way in which we relate to that reality (culture) and how we understand and evaluate our relationships with reality (our memories of what we have lived, which we refer to as "history").

The materiality of lo cotidiano brings into focus the fact that it always refers to embodied experiences; the embodied quality of lo cotidiano is consciously important to the oppressed and the impoverished.

Lo cotidiano has to do with the practices and beliefs that we have inherited, and with those habitual judgments that are part of our "facing life," of how we face and what we do with our reality (Geertz 1983: 74–76).

Lo cotidiano does not refer to the acritical reproduction or repetition of all that we have learned or to which we have become accustomed. Instead it refers to what is reproduced or repeated in a conscious manner, that which is part of the struggle for life and for liberation. Lo cotidiano, therefore, refers to the problematized daily reality—that is, to the limitations imposed by the material-historical reality one faces every day, and to the personal situations in which we find ourselves as we try to deal with such problematized reality. Lo cotidiano, then, refers to the space—time and place—which we face daily, but it also refers to how we face it and to our way of dealing with it. Realizing that lo cotidiano has hermeneutical value, that is, that it is not only what is but also the interpretative framework we use to understand what is, lo cotidiano is a powerful point of reference from where to begin to imagine a different world, a different societal structure, a different way of relating to the divine (or to what we consider transcendental/radical immanence), as well as a different way of relating to ourselves: to who we are and what we do. Lo cotidiano, therefore, has an extremely important role in our attempt to create an alternative symbolic order.

It is precisely because lo cotidiano refers to a problematized reality, that one can find in it subversive and creative elements that enable questioning oppression and resisting it.

Lo cotidiano is what makes specific—concrete—the reality of each person and, therefore, it is *in view of* it and *in* it that one lives the multiple relationships that constitute each one as a specific person, as me and not someone else.

Lo cotidiano has to do with our emotional and physical strengths and weaknesses, with the work we do, with the frustrations and hopes we have. Lo cotidiano refers to our family relationships and to our friendships; to the way we relate to our neighbors and to our different communities; to our experience of power and powerlessness—that is, how we relate to those who have power over us and to those over whom we have power; and to the role religious beliefs or other beliefs have in our lives (Levine 1992: 317).

The specificity of lo cotidiano makes focusing on the particular possible while it helps to question abstract universals that often ignore or falsify lo cotidiano.[8]

Lo cotidiano does not relate only to what is specific, but it also enters into contact with and is part of social systems. Lo cotidiano impacts structures and its mechanisms and is, in turn, affected by them. It is in lo cotidiano that the oppressed live, socially marginalized, economically exploited, and struggling against sexism and ethnoracism.[9]

Lo cotidiano is closely related to what is referred to as "common sense," which is why it is considered "natural." Natural here refers to the sense given to "of course," and not to the philosophical naturalism that limits reality to what the human mind can conceptualize. I use "natural" to insist on how lo cotidiano is enmeshed with the concrete and specific (Geertz 1983: 85–86).

Because lo cotidiano refers to what is specific about each of us, it is the main locus for considering diversity in a positive way. Now in the second decade of the twenty-first century we are certain that homogeneity turns people into masses easy to control and to manipulate. It is the diversity made present by and in lo cotidiano and the particularity and specificity of lo cotidiano that makes it possible to highlight differences and generate shared meanings as the basis for creating liberating societal structures. It is out of this diversity present in lo cotidiano of many different communities that subjugated knowledge emerges, helping the oppressed survive in the present-day suffocating globalization that ignores them.

Lo cotidiano refers to the simple reality of our world, which is not a simplistic reality. By simple reality I mean the one that we have to urgently tend to, that is dispersed throughout each day, and that we run into whether we want to or not. Without forgetting to deal with the reasons behind the reality, the urgency of surviving for the oppressed makes it necessary at times to leave for later the "whys," a later that often does not arrive because we do not conquer the urgency. Of course, that some have no time, energy, and/or resources to deal with the reasons for oppression does not mean that they are not conscious of them. In short, then, lo cotidiano is the reality strung along the hours in a day; it has to do with the food we eat *today*, with the subway or bus fare we have to pay *today*, with how to pay *today* for the medicine for a sick child or an elderly parent. Claiming that lo cotidiano has to do with the simple reality of our lives refers to the obviousness and the immediacy of lo cotidiano, to the many crises that grassroots people face with a wisdom and creativity made obvious by the fact that somehow they survive today and are ready to face tomorrow.

It is in lo cotidiano that we have and exercise power, appropriating information that we filter and shape according to our needs, our hopes, and our goals. This is why the powers that be might kill us but cannot conquer us, as Hemingway said.

Lo cotidiano is an ethical space—time and place—for in it we can move with a certain autonomy, take decisions and put them into play—decisions that might seem unimportant but which woven together constitute our ethical and moral horizon (de Certeau 1984: 254–255).

There are, of course, different cotidianos. Lo cotidiano that I refer to is that of the base/grassroots/Latino communities, mainly to lo cotidiano of Latinas. It refers to how Latinas understand and use the elements of our culture in common, ordinary, everyday realities, to how we appropriate traditions, language, symbols, and art. This cotidiano is very different from that of the dominant group. An example might be useful here. When using a public bus in New York City, many times I see two Latinas approach the bus but only one gets in. The other one waits outside until the first one uses the fare card and then quickly turns around and gives it to the woman who has stayed on the sidewalk. That they have to pay a $2.25 fare to ride the bus powerfully impacts their lives. They have to coordinate their efforts to face this reality of their cotidiano. They have to give it much thought: coordinate schedules, decide who pays for the card, how they are going to keep track of its use, and so forth. On the other hand, for those of us who do not have to worry about how we are going to pay for local transportation, lo cotidiano is less demanding, and we hardly pay attention to it. Often we stand on the sidewalk and signal a taxi, or those who are upper middle class or rich simply wait inside until the doorman of the building gets them one. When one gets in a taxi, how much it is going to cost is something one does not know until the end, but having more than a minimal amount of money means one does not worry. The taxis in the area where I live, an area of middle-class and working-class people, are different. Here you negotiate with the driver how much the taxi ride is going to cost before you get in.

This example reveals the aspect of lo cotidiano that Certeau called the tactics of lo cotidiano: the "what" and the "how" at the level of the particular situation. Grassroots people, of course, would like to have a general strategy to deal with their transportation expenses, an established way of paying for them, but they simply do not have the resources to do this. Their cotidiano is full of struggles to make ends meet. It is an *a pie cotidiano*—an on-foot cotidiano—in the sense that they have to deal with it with little resources other than their wit and popular wisdom. Their cotidiano deals with a reality that for the dominant group is a matter of routine. The dominant group does not have to decide whether to take the bus and pay $2.25 or walk fifteen blocks in order to have that money to buy food or soap to do the laundry. Those of us with resources often go through the day without having to think much about how to feed and dress ourselves, how to pay for transportation to get where we are going, or to pay for doing the laundry. It is at this level of facing the particularity and specificity of everyday life that grassroots people—Latinas—embrace lo cotidiano and in doing so, lo cotidiano becomes the space—time and place—where they exercise their moral agency and determine who they are, who they become, and how they live their lives. Why is it that lo cotidiano of the grassroots is not valued, is not taken into consideration when one analyzes reality and elaborates strategies for dealing with it? In philosophy there is both a valuing of lo cotidiano but also a disvaluing of it because it is seen often as a "place for inauthentic living" (Fornet-Betancourt 2010: 29). When lo cotidiano enters the academic discourse it is often dislodged from the actual living of the vast majority of people. It becomes abstract; and this is not the abstraction needed to talk about any and all themes and issues. Instead it is an abstraction that loses its footing in the historical reality of peoples. This is because most of us in the academy often have no contact with lo cotidiano of the people, and ours is too different from theirs, so it does not help us to be mindful of what constitutes the reality of most people. Again, an example here might prove useful in establishing the poignancy and urgency of the grassroots people's cotidiano and its difference from that of those of us in the academy.

I was at a bus stop last Sunday on my way to church, when I noticed a woman crossing the street. She seemed to be in her mid-fifties and had a little boy with her who was about six years old. The little boy was dressed in a pair of shorts and a T-shirt, a white one clean and pressed. He happily skipped across the street and came to sit on the bench next to me. He looked healthy and rested, for he did not have a sleepy face even though it was early. The woman, in contrast, was wearing a faded dress that was not ironed. She was very thin and looked distraught. She was munching on a donut and was drinking coffee from a paper cup that indicated she had bought her breakfast at a convenience store. The little boy sat next to me, and the woman sat next to him. After a few minutes the little boy, who in order not to bother me was crowded against the woman, said to her, "Mom, you stink." He repeated it a couple of times in a soft voice. Previously the woman had talked rather sharply to him telling him he needed to behave. Now she mumbled softly to him, "Yes, I know."

Their bus came before mine, and I was left to ponder on what I had just seen and heard. First of all I was surprised that the woman was the mother of the boy—he called her Mom—for she looked too old to have such a young child. I realized that most probably she was not in her mid-fifties but in her forties. She indeed looked older, her body wasted beyond her actual age. Then I thought about how smartly dressed the little boy was in contrast to how disheveled she looked. Most probably she had poured all her attention on the little boy and had little time, energy, or money left to get herself clean, to wash and iron her dress. She could have saved money by making coffee in her house instead of buying it at a convenience store. Well, that is, if she had a house and had paid for the gas or the electricity to run the stove, and owned a coffeemaker, and had the money to buy a can of coffee plus the filters needed to brew it, which all together would cost over $5. She might not have had $5; she might only have had $2.00 to buy one cup of coffee and a donut.

I thought long and hard about all the decisions she had made by 9 am that Sunday morning. She had to think about breakfast. She had fed the little boy, for if not, I thought, he would have been asking her for some of her donut, and she had fed him at home or his face might have smudges of powdered sugar or the glaze that covers the donuts. Her breakfast came second, given the fact that she was quickly eating before boarding the bus. She, perhaps, had to start thinking about breakfast the night before. Perhaps she had to decide not to buy a can of coffee. She needed the money for the bus fare.

In contrast, I had made no decisions about breakfast: I have all I need to make coffee at home and I have oatmeal to cook, or bread to toast. I did not have to choose between having money for the bus fare and eating a good breakfast. I have a fare-card that automatically gets recharged by debiting my bank card. I knew that if the bus did not come in time for me to make it to the church before the service started, I could and would take a taxi. I had been preoccupied with other things than the routine of surviving since I had gotten out of bed. The decisions I had taken on that Sunday morning were so trivial that I do not remember a single one of them. It was different for this woman. This woman probably had made half a dozen decisions that impacted her values, her commitments, her responsibilities, and her obligations. How important the child was for her was obvious by the contrast between his appearance and hers. And the fact that he felt he could tell her that she was smelly meant that, though she had spoken roughly to him at first, he was not afraid of her. Her soft reply to the child, I thought, was one of embarrassment, embarrassment that I too might have noticed her condition. However, even if she paid no attention to me, how embarrassing for your own child to tell you that you stink!

From the perspective of liberation, socio-political-economic liberation, I also had many questions. I wondered if she is alone or has a family or community that helps her in her daily struggle to make ends meet. I doubt she is paid a just wage that would make it possible for her to care for herself and her child. Maybe she does not even have a job, a reality today in the United States for almost 10 percent of the population. The terrible economic situation of the world today is a consequence of a neoliberal economics that does not take seriously the lives of the majority of people around the globe, people like this woman and this little boy. Neoliberal economics considers this woman and this child surplus people, and they are not taken into consideration by present-day systems. She is, if anything, blamed for her situation, for the myth that in the United States anyone who is willing to work hard can "make it" continues to influence the way in which many in this country look upon this woman. Her cotidiano is not factored into the "reality" of this society, of this nation; it is never taken into consideration by the economic mechanisms at work on Wall Street. How she understands her life and how she deals with it every day are given no attention or importance by those of us whose work is to explain, in order to influence, the world in which we live, be it from a political, economic, social, philosophical, or religious perspective. Much less is the academic discourse willing to engage this woman and the millions like her in order to understand lo cotidiano of the majority of the human race. Why?

I think there are three reasons why the reality of this woman is not considered in our discourse about lo cotidiano. First, we are not in touch with our own cotidiano, maybe because we consider it trite, but I think it is because it would make us question it. Yet, one of the first considerations we need to pay attention to when dealing with lo cotidiano is that "we exist in the everyday in a permanent presence that makes all attempts to escape it useless" (Fornet-Betancourt 2010: 45). Our cotidiano is related to that of the woman and the little boy who sat next to me at the bus stop, for the privileges and economic resources that make it possible for me not to worry about getting coffee in the morning have to do with her not having enough money for a decent breakfast and for washing her clothes. Until we understand the connection between what some of us have and what this woman does not have, we will not be able to understand her cotidiano, much less will we be able to factor it into our considerations. We do not look at her cotidiano, for we do not want our way of life to be challenged.[10]

If we claim to be about unveiling and enabling subjugated knowledges, definitely a liberation and decolonial move, then we have to enter into the world where that knowledge is produced, for there is no knowledge without "encountering" the reality we claim to know. As a Latina living in the United States, I indeed have experienced oppression. I also have some understanding of other forms of oppression—poverty and homophobia, for example—of which I have no personal experience. However, without the constant commitment to "encounter" the reality of impoverished Latinas, as a middle-class woman, I cannot claim to value Latinas' subjugated knowledges.[11]

Second, lo cotidiano is seen as trite. We consider the decisions that deal with structural issues, the ones that we believe impact society at large, and tend to not think about *lo de todos los días*—what happens in the dailiness of our lives and of the whole human race. We fail to value lo cotidiano of grassroots Latinas because we see it as belonging to the private sphere, not having political consequences. Yet it is the struggle about lo cotidiano that often sparks the great movements for justice, showing the political implication of everyday reality. Consider the fact that the spark for the Civil Rights movement in the United States was one trite, tiny event: Rosa Parks's refusal to move to the back of the bus, where the "people of color" where supposed to be (Brinkley 2000). Or think about the impact of Mexican American farmworker Cesar Chavez's fast in bringing powerful companies and rich landowners to the table ready to make concessions (Dalton 2003). Or, to make it really contemporary, think what set in motion the tumultuous struggles of people in Africa and the Arabian Peninsula to rid themselves of dictators and exploiters, even as this essay is being written. It was Mohamed Bouazizi, a street vendor in the town of Sidi Bouzid, Tunisia, who on December 17 fought to defend himself from abusive power. A policewoman had confiscated his scale. Without it he could not make a living to sustain his family. When he protested, she slapped him, spat on him, and tossed aside his cart and the produce he was selling. He went to the governor's office to complain, but the governor refused to see him. Humiliated and weighed down by his situation, less than an hour after the altercation with the policewoman, he poured gasoline over himself and set himself on fire. Protests against what had been done to Bouazizi started within hours of his self-immolation and continued to grow, moving into affluent areas and eventually into the capital. Bouazizi died on January 4 and on January 14, 2011, President Ben Ali, after twenty-three years of authoritarian rule, fled Tunisia with his family (Worth 2011).

Third, I think that the lack of attention to lo cotidiano of grassroots people is because they are not valued as intellectuals; they are not thought of as having and producing knowledge. In my experience the contrary is true. I have found grassroots Latinas admirably capable of explaining what they do and the reason for doing it. Their lives are not unreflected. On the contrary; the urgency of their situation makes them think and choose constantly. Their lives are indeed a constant action-reflection-action that keeps them alive and searching for ways to flourish. They might not be able to explain their lives in terminology that we in the academy find acceptable, or even understand. But they deal with their lives intelligently, that is, in ways that illumine the structures that they face and in which they have to find ways of fitting in in order to survive.

The lack of value given to Latinas' cotidiano goes hand in hand with the lack of appreciation for the epistemology of all oppressed people. Ignorance about the value of subjugated knowledges contributes to the oppression of the vast majority of the people in the world. The recognition and valuing of their subjugated knowledge are intrinsic to their liberation, which indeed is part and partial of the flourishing of all life.[12]

The Option for the Oppressed and the Impoverished

For a while, for a couple of decades, at least among those calling themselves liberals in the academic and church world in which I move, it was fashionable or politically correct to talk about an option for the oppressed and impoverished. However, for the last ten years approximately, we have been watering down such an option and, I propose, in doing so we have rejected it. We do this in great measure for the same three reasons given for not valuing lo cotidiano of the oppressed. We attempt to assuage our consciences by talking about a "preferential" option, an understanding that allows those of us who have some privileges in the dominant world, to keep them. A preferential option is not an option for the oppressed. It is merely a way of straddling the fence that shows as not true what we claim to do and invalidates much of our discourse, for it falsifies the ethical implications of opting. I believe we soften the option in order not to antagonize the liberals that we think are willing to struggle for justice, but who in fact are against any radical structural change.

A preferential option is an oxymoron, for to prefer is not the same as to opt: the two are mutually exclusive. Preferences are operative before one opts, but once an option is made, other possible preferences one might have considered cease to exist. You can prefer more than one thing among many others. As a matter of fact, the process of opting goes through a process of clarifying preferences and evaluating them. But when the moment of opting comes, one opts *for this*, and in doing so, one opts *not for that*. The option for the oppressed, as is true of all options, cannot be qualified. It can be changed, but once this happens it is not any longer an option for the oppressed. To claim to have a preferential option is a way of rejecting the demands of what it really means to opt for the oppressed and impoverished.

There are three reasons given for claiming that to opt for the poor is not correct. The first one has to do with the claim that such an option limits one's freedom; the second reason talks about fairness and impartiality as central elements of ethics; and the third one proposes that one cannot opt against the powerful and the rich, who constitute about one third of the human race. The discussion about these three points follows somewhat abstract arguments of the kind generally used in analytical thinking, the kind that yield "knowledge that." However, as in the first section of this essay, I also use narratives about experiences that yield "knowledge about," that is, knowledge "in which the qualia of the experience are among the salient part of the knowledge" (Stump 201056). I point this out because apart from the coherent analytical explanations I give—at least I think they are coherent and, therefore, convincing—the option for the poor is a commitment to a praxis (the intertwining of reflection and doing) that requires the nourishing of knowledge that knowledge about can provide much better than knowledge that.[13]

Personal Freedom and Moral Subjectivity or Agency—Self-Determination

One of the reasons given for modifying the option for the oppressed (I will refer to it simply as "the option") with the word "preferential" is that the option coerces, that it limits one's freedom and self-determination. This might be true from the liberal perspective that understands freedom in an individualistic way. However, there is a difference between an individual and a person. A person knows herself and thinks about herself as a social being. An individual, in contrast, thinks himself to be unrestrained by social ties and believes that to be fully himself he does not need to take anyone else into consideration.[14] The individual has a sense of totally unrestrained freedom. For the person, on the contrary, being herself carries a social mortgage; she knows her freedom is related to that of others.

The problem with the liberal way of thinking about freedom is that personal freedom is not without limits precisely because, even if they do not recognize it, as human beings we need others and others need us. As human beings we owe ourselves to others; we are accountable to others for who we are and what we do. As social beings, our personal freedom is restricted, and we are not free to opt without taking others into consideration. Taking others into consideration when opting does not limit one's freedom but rather helps us understand freedom in a realistic way, in a way that recognizes the sociality of human beings (Iyengar n.d.). To recognize that we have to take others into consideration when we choose is to accept the finitude of human beings, a finitude that is ever present to the oppressed in their cotidiano.

Besides the social-relational ontology behind the claim that our personal freedom has a social mortgage and, therefore, has to take others into consideration, our freedom to be self-determining also is limited by the historical reality in which we live. The circumstances in our lives, some of our own choosing but many of them not necessarily so, also limit our freedom. Some claim that circumstances not only limit our choices but determine our choices. I believe the possible options that we have are often given to us, thus determining partially what we will choose. An example helps clarify this point.

For seven years, 1997–2004, I stayed in my birth-country, Cuba, to teach at the Seminario Evangélico de Teología in Matanzas, to work with women's groups, and to work in a Catholic parish in Santiago de Cuba. While I was there some of the options I made were different from the ones I would have made were I in New York, where I live, because the choices I had were different. I was still free to opt, but the choices I had were different; the options I would have made in New York were not possible to make when I was in Cuba. However, I did not consider myself less free to opt while I was in Cuba, but the fact is that my choices were restricted by the limited possibilities among which I had to choose. The same is true when thinking of the inverse situation. In Cuba I had choices I do not have in New York.

Not individual but personal self-determination, responsibility, and the exercise of moral subjectivity happen socially, that is, they happen in and through the communities of which we are part.

> Human existence is a participatory and evaluative process, that is, a communitarian ordering by means of which a human conceives her or himself as a "self" who, precisely because of knowing that her or his own subjectivity or self-consciousness is in relation to an "other," or is a consciousness among others, conscious of others, and that, therefore, her or his subjectivity is an involved-with-others subjectivity.[15]
> (Fornet-Betancourt 2003: 56)

Human subjectivity—self-definition—therefore, which is part of the process of ethical formation, is a coming to know that to be human involves a being-with-others subjectivity. Such self-definition or affirmation of one's subjectivity is "concrete and alive, nourished by the memory of the liberation of all those who have struggled against their humanity being denied, [and is] based on a communitarian existence in resistance" (Fornet-Betancourt 2003: 56). This resistance is not negative but refers to establishing for oneself what is right and good as we stand in solidarity with others. Resistance speaks to being human among others, particularly when one protests against oppression and struggles for liberation. The process of self-definition, or of becoming one-self/oneself is, therefore, relational-communitarian, and it happens in the process of being in solidarity with an-other. Liberal individual freedom is simply impossible.

Fairness and Impartiality

Impartiality has to do with giving the same consideration to all, without prejudice, and without being influenced by one's self-interest. Deciding what is fair takes into consideration merit and the importance of the person involved. These two moral values, fairness and impartiality, seem to be ignored or violated by the option for the oppressed and impoverished. The fact is, however, that these values, as is true of all values, cannot be considered abstractly. What we have mentioned above regarding the materiality-historicity of reality and the sociality of human beings is the basis for insisting on the need to take into consideration the situations of those involved in order to be fair.

The situation of the oppressed and impoverished is different from that of the dominant group. It is not only different. It is worse. It is extremely bad. It is precisely this difference that demands partiality. The option is not unfair because its goal is to create circumstances in which there can be fairness for the oppressed and impoverished. To be unfair because one is partial to the oppressed is the result of an undistorted and full appreciation of their situation needed for the sake of applying moral norms fairly. Partiality, which is considered unfair and is used in arguments against the option for the oppressed, does not "violate cognitive impartiality" (Pope 1993: 246) if it is based on a reasonable gathering of relevant facts that uses a critical selectivity, aimed at presenting a picture that takes into consideration the situation at hand within the context of its societal reality and the reality of those involved. Neither is partiality in the case of the option for the oppressed intellectually dishonest; it is not "a bias that distorts experience, obstructs understanding, and undermines judgment" (Pope 1993: 246). On the contrary, partiality in favor of the oppressed urges profound honesty in examining the implications of the circumstances that are being assessed and the values used in evaluating them. Honesty requires a hermeneutics of suspicion when analyzing any situation that involves the oppressed.

The fact that the poor and impoverished constitute over two-thirds of humankind has to make one suspicious about the reason for their predicament (Segundo 1979: 231 ff). Honesty entails a critical assessment of the persons doing the so-called impartial evaluation as well as a serious consideration of who benefits from the actions resulting from the analysis they present. Partiality in favor of the oppressed, therefore, does not undermine judgment but rather enriches it by highlighting previously ignored elements that must be taken into consideration when making decisions. The option for the oppressed does not distort but rather takes into consideration experiences that have been ignored or discounted, for example, women's experience of gender bias, Latinas/os' experience of ethnoracism, gays' and lesbians' experience of heterosexism. Consequences of what is decided or chosen, that is, of how the decision or option will affect the oppressed also must play a key role in decision-making by those in charge of present structures and organizations.

Partiality in the case of the option is not only justifiable but desirable because it contributes to inclusiveness.[16] An understanding of impartiality has to include fair inclusion of the oppressed in all spheres of society and in the processes that set or influence what is normative for society (O'Neill 1994: 648). The partiality of the option for the oppressed contributes to inclusiveness by insisting on the human dignity of the oppressed, remembering that lack of recognition of their dignity also diminishes that of the oppressor. It is important to note in this regard the contribution that has been made to the argument for partiality by affirmative action, a significant outcome of the U.S. Civil Rights movement in the 1960s. Affirmative action is indeed partial; it is in favor of those in society who have been systemically excluded from opportunities—economic, social, educational. It has been a way of leveling the field so that those who are members of minoritized and marginalized communities can have an opportunity to contribute to society. The inclusiveness made possible by the partiality of affirmative action contributes not only to a particular person. Its goal is the enriching of society at large, making it possible for those who have been discriminated against to participate in creating the world in which we all live. Affirmative action is not about opening doors for those who are not qualified, as those who oppose such a program often claim. It is about making possible consideration of those who have been excluded, so that their talents can be used for the good of all. Those who benefit from affirmative action merit the jobs they are hired for, being accepted into an educational institution, and being economically successful. Partiality does not dispense with merit but rather provides opportunity for the merit of all persons regardless of their ethnicity, ethnorace, race, gender, sexual orientation, age, and so forth to be taken into consideration.

To be able to fairly concentrate on merit requires equality of opportunities and capabilities, which do not exist in our world today. Merit always has to be contextualized. And given what we have indicated about the need for partiality for the oppressed, the analysis of the context when it comes to judge merit has to pay particular attention to the oppressed. Merit as an abstract measure for judgment does not lead to fairness. Fairness is not possible if impartiality is taken to mean identical treatment for all.[17] Material and nonmaterial dissimilar needs and capabilities require a discriminate respond—a partial response (O'Neill 1994: 647). Insistence on privileging the oppressed is a denunciation of "apolitical neutrality," which in reality yields not impartiality but partiality or bias in favor of the oppressors (Pope 1993: 265).

The arguments against the option for the oppressed based on impartiality and fairness are part of the tendency to privilege the fixed, formulaic, and blandly categorical, instead of being, as is often claimed, an attempt to be theoretically rigorous (Urban Walker 1991: 773). Since the meaning of fairness is not static but is influenced by historical human claims, today there is an urgent need to consider those who suffer oppression, allowing them to exercise their moral agency by participating in deciding what is fair, taking into account their demands, their rights, and their human dignity. Therefore, partiality toward the oppressed emphasizes adequacy, which corrects the invalid attempts at "categorical uniformity" by

> a vigorous emphasis on facing up to the particular reality of each person [the majority of whom are oppressed] . . . and on refinement of perception, acuity of communication, flexibility of perspectives, and use of a range of moral categories.
> (Urban Walker 1991: 773)

Such as the needs and the rights of two-thirds of humanity. Without this emphasis on the needs and rights of the oppressed the understanding of impartiality is inadequate.

In conclusion, the option not only indicates the need to reinterpret the traditional way of understanding fairness and impartiality, freedom and self-definition, but it also shows the need to highlight other values, like the value of all life, of the dignity of all human beings, the importance of needs and desires, and the importance of human beings as persons and not as individuals, and the requirements to stand for and privilege the most vulnerable.

Not an Option Against the Oppressor as Person

The option for the impoverished and the oppressed is a fundamental option, one that makes clear not only what one is opting for but also what one is *not* opting for. Options always put aside other preferences because opting has consequences that cannot be ignored and that oblige until the option is rejected. No matter how much one insists that the option for the oppressed is not against the oppressor, the fact is that one cannot opt for both: to opt for one is not to opt for the other. Faced with the reality of how prevalent injustice is in our world today, one has to choose; one is forced to choose. One cannot decide not to opt, not to choose. Options must be made: One cannot escape (Shinn 1991: 3). The option for the oppressed cannot be put off; it is an urgent matter—a matter of life and death for two-thirds of humankind. Indecision and delay when it comes to the option for the oppressed and the impoverished are "as criminal as resolutely evil acts" (Shinn 1991: 4). Indecision and delay bring enormous suffering and even death to the oppressed.

Is the option for the oppressed and impoverished an option *against* the oppressor? For sure, the option for the oppressed questions and negates the perspective and rationality of the oppressor. It is an option to struggle against the structures that benefit the oppressor at the expense of the oppressed. It is an option not to be on the side of the oppressor: not to think, imagine, plan, and act the way the oppressor does. The option is to struggle to bring about radical change, change that the oppressors oppose at all costs.

However, the option is *not* an option to destroy the oppressor. It is *not* wishing the oppressor evil. On the contrary, the option for the oppressed and impoverished is also an option *for* the oppressors even if they do not understand this or accept it. The option to change the present death-dealing world order benefits not only the oppressed and impoverished but also the oppressors. The economic downfall being experienced all around the world makes this obvious: The present world order—a death-dealing world order—is prejudicial to all.

Theological Considerations

Lo cotidiano and the option for the poor are of such importance for mujerista discourse that they function as intrinsic elements of a mujerista worldview, that is, mujerista assertions, values, and praxis. This is why they are part of the *locus theologicus*—the source and context—we use to do mujerista theology. In saying that they are the source of mujerista theology, we reject the traditional division of the sources of Christianity into primary sources—scripture for all Christians, to which Catholics add tradition—and secondary sources—church teaching, theology, liturgy—adding to these latter ones others such as history and context. Mujerista theology makes explicit the prima facie consideration that for some of us scripture and tradition are always mediated through those interpreting them, who are in a given context and respond to certain interests (Segundo 1979: 116–120). Mujerista theology insists that the context and interests that should be at play in the reading of scripture and tradition are those of the oppressed and impoverished: their reality, how they come to know such reality, and how they interpret it. The option, which carries with it a valuing of lo cotidiano of the oppressed, operates, therefore, at this very fundamental level of doing theology.

In mujerista theology, we understand God's grace—God's free and efficacious self-disclosure and self-giving—to be present mainly among the oppressed and through the oppressed.[18] Such an affirmation is not a metaphysical claim, that is, we do not claim to be talking about God's nature per se. This is what we understand and believe based on our reading of the Christian Bible, using a mujerista hermeneutical lens shaped by the struggle for justice for Latinas. One can indeed point to passages in the Bible that, though the authors of the Gospels most probably were not making metaphysical claims—in the present-day understanding of metaphysical claims—they may be read as such. For example, our belief that God is in the midst of the oppressed and impoverished is based, among other passages, on Matthew 25:31–46 where the Son of Man, a title used in the Gospels to refer to Jesus, welcomes those who have favored the impoverished and oppressed and rejects those who have not helped them. Also relevant here is the first beatitude found in Luke 6:20, "Blessed are you who are poor, for yours is the kingdom of God." We believe that Jesus made clear that God is with the oppressed and impoverished, and because we value immensely what Jesus proclaimed, we make what Jesus proclaimed a matter of belief. We find further reason to believe in God's option for the poor in the argument presented by the author of the first letter to the Corinthians 1:26–31: God chooses the unimportant and those the world judges to be fools, to shame the wise, to bring the important people to naught so that no one will be able to be presumptuous in the face of God.

We do not choose the impoverished and oppressed as a categorical good among others; one does not opt for an austere style of life in order to be coherent with the growing poverty and oppression in the world. We respond to the teachings of the Bible by believing that God makes the reality of the poor divine reality.

> If it is so, the preferential option for the poor in our times, becomes stronger, because it does not depend on empirical verifications. . . . Today the poor are more oppressed, suffering more daily dyings, and yet, the commitment to justice, the option, and hope continue to be anchored in the faithfulness and the saving workings of God.
>
> If this is so, the option for the poor is a condition for the possibility of all knowledge. Furthermore, one's personal position in view of the poor, connotes and configures the moral personality of the agent.
>
> (Viñoles 2003: 109)

A second theological consideration is extremely important to our argument of using the option without "preferential" as a modifier. It is important because the argument for modifying the option has emerged as an explanation of the belief in the unlimited love of God. Therefore, those who want to soften the option say that love for the oppressed and impoverished cannot limit God's love for the oppressor and the rich. The option for the poor is seen as excluding the rich and the oppressor from God's love. God's option for the oppressed and impoverished, it is claimed, leaves no room for God to love the oppressors and the rich.

Together with a few others I argue that there is no need to soften or deradicalize God's option for the oppressed in order to assert God's love of the oppressors. However, that God loves the oppressor and the rich does not mean that God loves them because they are rich and because they are oppressors. On the contrary, God rejects the rich as rich and the oppressor as oppressor. That God loves them means precisely that God demands them to denounce unconditionally their benefits, privileges, and riches for their own sake. God's love for them comes in the guise of a demand to abjure their richness and privileges.

In God, we claim, there are no contradictions. Then God cannot love both, the oppressed and the oppressor, the impoverished and the rich. God cannot opt just a little—preferentially—

for the impoverished and the oppressed. There is no possibility of "a little" when it comes to options and much less is there a possibility of "a little" when it comes to God. In opting for the oppressed and impoverished, God questions the rich and the oppressor about their richness and privileges—a questioning that cannot be ignored, to which they must respond (Luke 9: 109).

> The option of the poor, which will never exclude that person of the rich—since salvation is offered to all and the ministry of the church is due to all—does exclude the way of life of the rich . . . and its system of accumulation and privileges, which necessarily plunders and marginalizes the immense majority of the human family, whole peoples and continents.
>
> (Casaldáliga 1992: 70–71)

Because God's grace is extended to all, and God's grace is precisely what makes possible human acceptance of God's commands, the rich and the oppressor are constantly being given the opportunity and strength to repent and radically change their ways. Just as the oppressed and the impoverished are being given constantly the opportunity and strength not to covet what the oppressor and the rich have.

Finally, there is an important ecclesiological consideration when it comes to the option for the oppressed and the impoverished. I believe the opposition to the option is not because it is theologically questionable but because it requires a radical change of ecclesiology. The option for the oppressed and the impoverished means that the church is *not for* the oppressed and the impoverished; the church must be *from them* and must be *their* church. The option requires a radical change in church structures, structures that privilege the church's hierarchies, its ministers, and those theologians recognized by church authorities. To radically affirm the option requires from the church a willingness to consider radically changing how it understands itself and its relationship to the kin-dom of God.[19]

The church has to be a church *of* the impoverished and oppressed, not a church *for* them, which is a church where they have no say in creating its meaning. The church has to privilege the oppressed and the impoverished epistemologically, hermeneutically, and in its ongoing praxis—both how it operates within as well as its pastoral activity. This is an extreme demand, but it is a Gospel commandment. The flesh is weak, but as Christians we are called to heed the Gospel and not to change its central visions and stipulations so we can continue to sustain structures that do not privilege the oppressed and impoverished.

References

Alcoff, L. (2012) "Anti-Latino Racism," in A. M. Isasi-Díaz and E. Mendieta (eds.), *Decolonizing Epistemologies: Latina/o Theology and Philosophy*, 107–126, New York: Fordham University Press.

Anzaldúa, G. (1987) *Borderlands/La Frontera: The New Mestiza*, San Francisco: Spinsters/Aunt Lute.

Ascuy, V. (2003) "Pobreza y Hermeneúticas. Senderos para una Resurrección de las Relaciones Sociales," in V. Ascuy and O. Groppa (eds.), *Suena la "Campana de Palo"*, Buenos Aires: Centro de Estudios Salesianos de Buenos Aires.

Brinkley, D. (2000) *Rosa Parks: A Life*, New York: Penguin.

Buber, M. (1965) *Between Man and Man*, New York: Macmillan.

Casaldáliga, P. (1992) *Cartas a mis amigos*, Madrid: Editorial Nueva Utopía.

Dalton, F. J. (2003) *The Moral Vision of Cesar Chavez*, Maryknoll, NY: Orbis.

de Certeau, M. (1984) *The Practice of Everyday Life*, S. Rendall (trans.), Berkeley: University of California Press.

Fornet-Betancourt, R. (2003) "Para una crítica filosófica de la globalización," in R. Fornet-Betancourt (ed.), *Resistencia y Solidaridad—Globalización Capitalista y Liberación*, Madrid, SA: Editorial Trotta.
Fornet-Betancourt, R. (2010) "Everyday Life: Space for Interchange or A Space for New Colonization between North and South," in Raúl Fornet-Betancourt (ed.), *Dokumentation des XIV Internationalen Seminars des Dialogprogramms Nord-Süd*, Mainz: Wissenschaftsverlag.
Freire, P. (1972) *Pedagogy of the Oppressed*, New York: Continuum.
Geertz, C. (1983) *Local Knowledge*, New York: Basic Books.
Isasi-Díaz, A. M. (1996) *Mujerista Theology—A Theology for the Twenty-first Century*, Maryknoll, NY: Orbis.
Isasi-Díaz, A. M. (2004) *En La Lucha—In the Struggle: Elaborating A Mujerista Theology* (2nd ed.), Minneapolis: Fortress Press.
Isasi-Díaz, A. M. (2010) "Kin-dom of God: A *Mujerista* Proposal," in V. Benjamín (ed.), *In Our Own Voices: Latino/a Renditions of Theology*, Maryknoll, NY: Orbis.
Iyengar, S. (n.d.) "On the Art of Choosing," *TED*, https://ed.ted.com/lessons/sheena-iyengar-on-the-art-of-choosing.
Levine, D. H. (1992) *Popular Voices in Latin America Catholicism*, Princeton: Princeton University Press.
Mignolo, W. D. (2000) *Local Histories/Global Designs—Coloniality, Subaltern Knowledges, and Border Thinking*, Princeton: Princeton University Press.
Mignolo, W. D. (2012) "Decolonizing Western Epistemology/Building Decolonial Epistemologies," in A. M. Isasi-Díaz and E. Mendieta (eds.), *Decolonizing Epistemologies: Latina/o Theology and Philosophy*, 19–43, New York: Fordham University Press.
Moya, P. M. L. (2002) *Learning from Experience: Minority Identities, Multicultural Struggles*, Berkeley: University of California Press.
Nussbaum, M. C. (2000) *Women and Human Development: The Capabilities Approach*, Cambridge: Cambridge University Press.
O'Neill, W. (1994) "No Amnesty for Sorrow: The Privilege of the Poor in Christian Social Ethics," *Theological Studies* 55 (4).
Pope, S. J. (1993) "Proper and Improper Impartiality and The Preferential Option for the Poor," *Theological Studies* 54 (2).
Rahner, K., and Vorgrimler, H. (1990) *Dictionary of Theology* (New Rev. ed.), New York: Crossroad.
Segundo, J. L. (1979) *The Liberation of Theology*, Maryknoll, NY: Orbis.
Shinn, R. (1991) *Forced Options: Social Decisions for the Twenty-First Century* (3rd ed.), Cleveland: Pilgrim Press.
Stump, E. (2010) *Wandering in Darkness: Narrative and the Problem of Suffering*, Oxford: Oxford University Press.
Urban Walker, M. (1991) "Partial Consideration," *Ethics* 101: 773.
Vasilachis de Gialdino, I. (2000) "Del sujeto cognoscente al sujeto conocido: una propuesta epistemológica para el estudio de los pobres y de la pobreza," in *Pobres, pobreza y exclusión social*, Buenos Aires: Ceil-Conicet.
Viñoles, D. (2003) "Opción Fundamental y Opción Preferencial por los Pobres—Diálogo entre Ambos Paradigmas," in V. Ascuy and O. Groppa (eds.), *Suena la "Campana de Palo"*, Buenos Aires: Centro de Estudios Salesianos de Buenos Aires.
Worth, R. F. (2011) "How A Single Match Can Ignite A Revolution," *New York Times*, January 21, www.nytimes.com/2011/01/23/weekinreview/23worth.html?src=twrhp.
Young, I. M. (1990) *Justice and the Politics of Difference*, Princeton: Princeton University Press.

Notes

1 For a fuller description of mujerista theology and ethics see Isasi-Díaz (2004).
2 I am greatly influenced by Gloria Anzaldúa's *Borderlands/La Frontera: The New Mestiza* (1987). Also see Mignolo (2000), particularly chapter one and afterword.
3 This is based on, but does not replicate exactly, the schema elaborated in Young (1990: 39–65). In this chapter, I do not have the space to explain each of these modes of oppression from the perspective of Latinas. For such an explanation, see Isasi-Díaz (1996: 105–127).

4. I use "impoverished" instead of "the poor" to indicate that poverty is not an inherent condition but rather is the result of how certain sectors of society are exploited. I thank Dr. Peter Kanyandago from Uganda for this insight in his presentation "Everyday Life: Site of Interchange or of New Colonization between the North and the South" at the Program of Dialogue North-South, San Leopoldo, Porto Alegre, Brazil, May 2010. See also Casaldáliga (1992: 112): "We in Latin America want to avoid the poor being thought of as spontaneously poor, isolated, outside the structures that exploit and marginalize them; that is why we speak about the 'impoverished.'"
5. In valuing the experience of the oppressed, I want to highlight their epistemological contribution. I make a difference between "raw data," what happens, which I am quick to admit we never know except through the lens that we use to see it, and experience, which has two elements: what happens and how we explain it. For a theoretical framework to understand the point I am making, see Moya (2002: 38–39).
6. For a fuller explanation of "conscientization" see Freire (1973).
7. I believe that those who seek an individualistic way out or who simply want to get ahead within oppressive structures exclude themselves from those who struggle for liberation, for at the heart of all liberative praxis lies the conviction that no one will be fully liberated unless everyone is liberated, and that the struggle for liberation is about radical structural change.
8. I am not following the postmodern trend of denouncing universals. I do believe that universals are possible, as long as they start from the specific, the historical, and proceed to point out shared understandings and practices. For a thorough discussion of this see Martha C. Nussbaum, *Women and Human Development: The Capabilities Approach* (Cambridge: Cambridge University Press, 2000), particularly chap. 1.
9. See the essay Alcoff (2012) for the meaning of and reason for the term "ethnoracism."
10. It is important to notice how the negative view of the Palestinians, the Iraq war, and the war in Afghanistan are understood and talked about as "defending the American way of life."
11. For a much more elaborated explanation of this point see Ascuy (2003: 11–32).
12. The interconnection between the one who knows and the one who is known, the relations between the epistemologies of both, is an important argument for insisting that academics need to be in touch with the cotidiano of the oppressed and impoverished. See Vasilachis de Gialdino (2000: 21–45).
13. For a rich discussion on these two types of knowledge, see, particularly part 1 of Stump (2010: part 1).
14. There is an expression that is difficult to translate into English that is for me the best way of describing an individual: "*dueño y señor de sí mismo*," owner and lord of himself. It is an expression used often in everyday Spanish to refer to someone who does not take anyone else into consideration.
15. All translations from the Spanish are my own.
16. I follow the arguments presented by Pope (1993: 264–67).
17. This understanding of fairness and impartiality has some faint resemblance to the liberal understandings of John Rawls and others. However, it radically disagrees with the priority given by liberalism to individual negative liberty (liberty from absence of interference) over social positive goods, and to negative rights or immunities over social and economic rights. In this discussion I follow the arguments of O'Neill (1994: 642–646).
18. For a concise theological explanation of grace see Rahner and Vorgrimler (1990: 196–200). Though this explanation is from a Catholic perspective, much of what it says is acceptable to other Christian denominations.
19. For the differences in meaning between kingdom of God and kin-dom of God see Isasi-Díaz (2010).

Reading Question

1. How does Isasi-Díaz define lo cotidiano, and why is it significant in mujerista discourse?
2. How do the everyday struggles that characterize lo cotidiano enable Latinas to exercise moral agency and construct their identities, according to Isasi-Díaz? Provide specific examples from the text.

3. According to Isasi-Díaz, how does ignoring the subjugated knowledges of Latinas affect not only *their* community, but also society as a whole? Discuss the broader societal implications.
4. How does centering lo cotidiano challenge dominant Western ideas about knowledge?
5. In what ways does mujerista theology draw from traditional liberation theology, according to Isasi-Díaz?
6. What comes to mind when you hear the term "mujerista" ("womanist")? How is mujerista discourse said to compare with "feminist" discourse? What is a possible advantage and disadvantage of using this terminology?
7. How does Isasi-Diaz argue against the notion of a "preferential" option? Why is this distinction important for mujerista discourse?
8. Explain the concept of "thinking-with" versus "thinking-about" in mujerista thought. How does this communal approach affect the discourse on liberation and justice?
9. How can the principles of mujerista discourse be applied in contemporary social justice movements? Discuss potential challenges and benefits of adopting this framework.

18 Hometactics

Everyday Practices of Multiplicitous Selves

Mariana Ortega

City ordinances that prohibit red doors and colorful houses. Rows and rows of white, gray, light brown houses—sad looking, needing joy. I need more colors, more plants. I want to feel warmth, when beautiful trees lose their every leaf, when whiteness blankets all there is to see, when I shiver and my skin cracks—a nurturing if fleeting sense—I am here.

To start, I have a confession to make: this writing is an exercise in self-mapping, an attempt to deal with a certain nostalgia, a painful fixation on loss and a desire to return to a place called home, a persistent desire that keeps returning as the snow of February in Cleveland, the city I sometimes call home. In self-mapping, one locates oneself in life and space and recognizes locations imbued with histories, power relations, cultural and economic forces, and personal dreams and imagination.[1] Home, says bell hooks, is "the safe place . . . the place where the me of me mattered" (2009: 215). Quoting Michael Seidel, Kaplan says that home is the exile's "'belated romance' with a past, through memory heightened by distance" (Kaplan 1996: 39). I am that exile that unwittingly falls for this romance yet is perfectly aware of its traps. Perhaps it is exile that brings forth the will to belong in a more insistent and gripping way—I am not sure. I think of Ana Mendieta, the Cuban artist who imprinted her silhouette on so many places—grass, sand, earth—only to see it disappear, until she returns to Cuba and carves figures on rock—so as to mark her return "home," the end of her exile—except, of course, she would always be an exile (Ortega 2004). I am writing my way home by leaving it, by stripping it away of its magic and its strong conjuration.

The notion of home calls forth the personal, the affective, such as "home is where the heart is," where I can feel comfortable and safe, where I can scratch my itches, where I can be who I am. "Home" is, as Dickens reminds us, a truly magical word, offering a most-needed relief from the world of the weird, the unsafe, the *unheimlich*. Yet, as personal as this notion is, Chandra Mohanty reminds us that it is also profoundly political. She asks, "What is home? The place I was born? Where I grew up? Where my parents live? Where I live and work as an adult? Where I locate my community, my people? Who are my 'people'?" (Mohanty 2003: 126). Answers to these questions are complex and call forth a nexus of histories and experiences, playful and painful, chosen and inherited. Home is where the personal sometimes unexpectedly, sometimes inextricably, meets the political. The home question can thus lead us from the confines of our own skin to the open spaces of worlds inhabited by others like and unlike me, to a politics of location.

In this chapter I discuss the notion of home in connection to the ideas of location, and belonging in light of the experience of multiplicitous selves. In the first section, I point out that the notion of home may be connected to a politics of location that reaffirms so-called authentic identities and serves to exalt those identities by negating those who are deemed as not belonging. Home may become the "barred room" that Bernice Johnson Reagon warned

DOI: 10.4324/9781003385417-27

us about in her now-famous speech on coalitional politics (1983: 356–368). I illustrate some difficulties that arise when considering the meaning of belonging given the multiplicity of the self. We will see that given this multiplicity we cannot adhere to a notion of belonging that privileges so-called authentic or primary characteristics of identity.

Informed by Michel de Certeau's analysis of tactics, in the second section, I introduce the notion of hometactics, practices that allow for a sense of familiarity with and a particular sense of "belonging" to a place, space, group, or world while avoiding the restrictive, exclusive elements that a notion of belonging might carry with it. Given my analysis of coalitional politics in chapter 5, which takes into consideration both location and relations with others, being and becoming-with, here I would like to reveal another part of the story of home, location, and belonging—the lived experience of multiplicitous selves, the small yet important everyday practices of those selves as they negotiate their multiple and complex identities and attempt to get a sense of connection to those worlds, what we may call micropractices of lived experience.

Belonging, Location, and Multiplicitous Selfhood

Following Aimee Carrillo Rowe, I see the notion of belonging as a point of departure for understanding, naming, and imagining location (2008: 29). In other words, the notion of belonging is intimately tied to a politics of location, location here meaning not just spatial but also social location.[2] Carrillo Rowe asks that a feminist politics of location theorize the conditions for the possibility of belonging rather than assume an individual subject as already belonging to a location (2008: 25–46). While Carrillo Rowe ultimately moves away from a politics of location to what she terms a "politics of relation," in which locations are formed by a series of affective and political ties with others, her insistence that we understand conditions for the possibility of belonging is key to an analysis of the relationships among home, belonging, and location.

A politics of location that merely assumes individual subjects as already belonging to a location is indeed problematic because belonging is quickly interpreted by way of specific identity markers. Rather than understanding the complex ways in which an individual is said to belong to a social location—the ways personal identity markers as well as relational aspects are linked and negotiated—such a politics of location might quickly turn into a "home" for some members but also a "barred room" for those who are deemed not to belong. In other words, when belonging is a matter of satisfying particular conditions of identity, which in turn become homogenizing conditions, home serves to block out those who are not like us or whom we deem are not like us. Our bodies, our selves, are thus blocked from the entrance of that special room that is home for some but not others, the barred room that Bernice Johnson Reagon warns us about.

As Mohanty notes, Johnson Reagon's concern lies with the problematic spaces created by oppositional political movements that provide a "nurturing space" for a while but ultimately provide only the illusion of community and a freezing of difference (Mohanty 2003: 117). Johnson Reagon is concerned with the idea that a coalition should be as safe as a home, when in reality it is not safe or comfortable. The barred room of those who believe in narrow identity politics and who are seduced by overly nationalistic tendencies might serve as a nurturing space, but not for long. Questions arise as to why I don't belong in that room, or why doesn't he or she belong? Why have others been let in and not me? Don't I satisfy the conditions of belonging? Am I not one of you? And, soon enough, the walls of that room become too thick. That nurturing space reminiscent of the mythic, safe home is transformed into an illusive community in the attempt to reify our difference as Latinos, as Asians, as African Americans, as lesbians, and so on.[3] Yet, as Johnson Reagon says, "The room don't feel like the room no more. And it ain't home no more" (1983: 359).

According to Johnson Reagon, community doesn't mean those that are or look like me. Spaces that have been created to reify certain characteristics can be modified when we take into consideration the heterogeneity within our group. I will then have to open the doors for others to get in or for me to get out of my zone of comfort. In the same way, we all have to leave the safety of the home at some point so as to not hide from the rest of the world and others in that world—not to mention those for whom home has never been safe or comfortable and those who have known better.

In order to problematize further the notion of home as connected to a particular kind of belonging, what we might call "authentic belonging," let us consider the experience of multiplicitous selves. As noted in chapter 2, all of us are multiplicitous selves, but there is a crucial difference between those who are comfortable and at ease in various worlds and those whose experience is marginalized, oppressed, or alienated in some way and who have to world-travel constantly. So, it is key to remember that multiplicity is more at issue for some selves than others, depending on the different ways in which their positionalities are perceived or negotiated given specific social, economic, and cultural contexts as well as power relations. For example, recall the way in which economic, social, and cultural issues related to the North-South border affect the new *mestiza* self and lead her to feel the contradictory aspects of herself and to be in-between worlds. Consider the way in which such power relations and social and cultural issues affect a newly arrived immigrant to this country who does not speak the language and who is marginalized, as opposed to the way in which these factors affect the life of someone who is part of the mainstream and whose experience is for the most part one of being-at-ease.

Multiplicitous selves are constantly negotiating their multiple social locations. They are also constantly world-traveling. As noted earlier, I, as a Nicaraguan-born, bilingual, lesbian, academic Latina living in the United States, have to constantly negotiate the multiple aspects of myself and travel to the different worlds associated with my various social positions. Yet, despite my status as a multiplicitous self, I also find myself asking the home question—a home question that comes in terms of geography—is Managua, Nicaragua, really my home, or is it Los Angeles, or Cleveland? And also in terms of associations with others—do I belong with US Latinos, Chicanos, Latin American exiles, or women of color?

The home question is particularly difficult for the multiplicitous self whose life and context are such that she has to continually world-travel, and thus the home question becomes a question of *homes*. Reflection on such a question paradoxically shatters any illusion of there being a definite place of belonging, while it also shatters the very multiplicity of our selves by way of a feeling and a questioning—that feeling of wanting to come home and that question of whether there is a home (or even homes) for me—as if there were a will to belong in the same way that Nietzsche claims there is a will to truth that inspires us to many a venture.[4] It cannot be denied that even for those multiplicitous selves who are border-crossers and world-travelers, the home question is still a question. Perhaps it is even a more painful question precisely because that home seems harder to find or cannot be found given one's multiplicity. Yet, despite the determination of this will to belong that might provide a feeling of security and comfort, we cannot avoid recognizing the limits and pitfalls of such security, namely, the reification of certain identity categories as opposed to others and thus the expulsion of those who do not fit a version of authentic belonging.

Let us look at María Lugones's early essay "Hispaneando y Lesbiando: On Sarah Hoagland's Lesbian Ethics," in which Lugones replies to the call of lesbian separatism (1990). In this essay, Lugones describes the contradictory nature of her lived experience as she asserts her identity as both a Latina and a lesbian in the context of Nuevomejicano culture. While she finds it empowering to participate in keeping the Nuevomejicano culture alive by being part of its community, she realizes that she cannot be openly lesbian there, and thus she feels that her self is diminished in that environment. As she says, "These communities do not recognize us as fully their own if lesbian. The culture is heterosexualist. It does not recognize the possibility of women loving women unmediated by male domination" (1990: 142). Yet Lugones still cannot follow Sarah Hoagland's advice to render the homophobic culture meaningless and agree to lesbian separatism, because this would entail her becoming an "obsolete being" or assimilating into another culture that disregards the needs of lesbians who are not white. Lugones concludes,

> Such a lesbian must, for her own survival and flourishing, acknowledge herself as needing more than "one world." Her ability to inhabit both a world where radical criticism of her culture is meaningful and to inhabit the world of her culture constitute part of the possibility of her future as a creative being.
>
> (1990: 144)

Lugones then inhabits both the Latina and the lesbian worlds. In each world she is lacking, and, as a border-dweller, she is not completely in either world. Inspired by Anzaldúa, she continues to have the perspective of the crossroads or the borderlands, a position that allows her a critical edge from which to interpret the multiple worlds she inhabits. She asserts her Latina and lesbian identities without accepting the homophobia present in the context of Nuevomejicano culture and the ethnocentrism present in the Anglo lesbian community.

Like Lugones, I have also found myself wanting to belong in the Latino community and yet being hurt as I experienced the Latino community's homophobia as well as alienation in the Anglo lesbian community. My identities as lesbian and Latina cannot be easily reconciled. In many cases these two identities appear as mutually exclusive. Consequently, I might experience a thick feeling of not-being-at-ease or an existential crisis about my selfhood given that in dominant Latino culture lesbianism is generally not accepted. I will not be accepted within the Latino community unless I hide an important aspect of myself or I confine myself to a smaller Latino community, that of Latina lesbians, yet another barred room. As Lugones so aptly puts it, "Pluralism also requires the transformation of those 'home' cultures so that lesbians can be rid of 'homophobia' in Anzaldúa's sense: 'the fear of going home'" (Lugones 1990: 143). Yet, like Anzaldúa and Lugones, I still want to be part of the Latino community. This example and countless others (consider Anzaldúa's own example about the difficulties of being Chicana and American, Chicana and lesbian; W. E. B. Du Bois's example of being an African American and an American; Audre Lorde's example of being lesbian and African American) illustrate why the experience of the multiplicitous self might be complicated and fraught with painful moments of what Anzaldúa describes as "intimate terrorism." It also illustrates the need that even the multiplicitous self has of belonging and the drawbacks that such a need generates. As we have seen, ambiguity and contradiction are part and parcel of a life of in-betweenness and being-in-worlds. The difficulties and pain encountered can, as Anzaldúa and Lugones have taught us, lead to creative ventures and critical resistance. While many women of color agree with Anzaldúa's claim that the ambiguities and contradictions of the self of the borderlands can open up constructive possibilities, others wonder whether all that the multiplicitous self can do is be tormented by the contradictions and ambiguities brought about by its multiplicity. What can multiplicitous selves do except feel the cactus needles embedded in their skin?

In *Wealth of Selves: Multiple Identities, Mestiza Consciousness, and the Subject of Politics*, Edwina Barvosa tackles critics of what she calls the multiple self and attempts to show that it is in fact this multiple self with its ambiguities and contradictions that can become an agent capable of political critique and social transformation (2008). Barvosa's strategy is to explain the ways in which a multiple, socially constructed self constitutes a cohesive whole that is capable of shifting its social identities in different contexts and of using ambiguity and contradiction to form a critical stance capable of being deployed for political activism. While Barvosa provides an interdisciplinary, complex explanation of the multiple systems at work in what she calls the multiple self, I would like to concentrate on the way she explains Lugones's experience of being a Latina and a lesbian. This example turns out to be as informative as Lugones's example of being playful and unplayful in different worlds.

According to Barvosa, Lugones integrates her mutually exclusive identities as a result of a conscious "self-integrative life project" rather than the usual rank-ordering of identities, as some philosophers suggest multiple selves should do. A self-integrative life project is one in which "self-chosen endorsements are loosely interwoven into broad self-guiding projects that serve as the basis for integrating the self" (Barvosa 2008: 141). For Barvosa, it is precisely the experience of contradiction, ambiguity, and ambivalence that plays an important role in the project of self-integration. Thus she sees Lugones as being able to integrate her different identities of Latina and lesbian because she has a life project of anti-racism, anti-ethnocentrism, and anti-heterosexism. Because of this life project, Lugones remains highly identified as a Latina and a lesbian while at the same time using different identity markers at different times to claim a group identity ("selective identification/differential self-presentation"), for example, not including the issue of her sexuality in the Latino context. Thus Lugones's own ambivalence about belonging to the Latino group given its homophobia represents a strategy to hold her multiple identities together (Barvosa 2008: 151). Through having a life project, Lugones, according to Barvosa, can form intersections between her mutually exclusive identities and can claim a space in both communities.

Like Moya, Barvosa calls for integration of the self's various aspects or identities, although her conception of integration is more open to instances of ambiguities and contradiction. As we have seen, the experience of contradiction is key in Barvosa's account because it allows not only for the formation of a critical stance but also for the possibility of integration. As she states,

> I argue that while self-chosen rank-ordered endorsements, narrative unity, and self-fulfilling authenticity may have roles to play for some individuals in their particular processes of self-integration, these three elements alone are inadequate to contain the complexity of self-integration of multiple identities. This inadequacy is especially acute under those circumstances of conflict or contradiction in which a person's multiple identities are socially constructed as mutually exclusive, or when their life projects have become contradictory due to social, political, or interpersonal conflicts beyond their control. Under these circumstances, enduring contradiction, ambivalence, and ambiguity can play important roles in the self-integration of multiple identities.
>
> (141–142)

While appealing to integration, Barvosa recognizes that not all multiple selves can achieve integration and thus states that in her view "the self permits degrees of cohesion from a bare and highly fragmented minimum to highly self-integrated identities" (20). I see the value of Barvosa's appeal to a strategic, self-integrating life project as it is something that might be helpful as multiplicitous selves carry on with their lives. Yet it should not be understood as the preferred or necessary practice guiding multiplicitous selves as they negotiate their multiple positionalities. Despite the advantages associated with practicing a strategic, self-integrating life project, not all multiplicitous selves have such a project or desire it. Many prefer to give up the illusion of integration and be willing to live with the ambiguities and contradictions that their multiplicitous selfhood entails; many will be in circumstances in which integration is not possible. Moreover, given Lugones's own characterization of her experience, her appeal to ontological pluralism, as well as the experience of world-traveling in general, it is unclear that she would call for integration, even in Barvosa's sense. Nevertheless, Barvosa's explanation of a multiple self's negotiation of its various and sometimes mutually exclusive identities by way of a self-integrating life project is illustrative of the complexity of the notion of belonging. What we learn from examples such as Lugones's and from Barvosa's attempt to deal with the contradictions inherent in multiplicitous selfhood is that, given the complexity of the selves as well as the complexity of spaces of belonging (in terms of their members as well as criteria for membership), there is no sense in which one can be said to *fully* belong. There are only different senses of belonging depending on which markers of identity are chosen. Full membership and belonging—the safe, comfortable home—is indeed an imaginary space in need of demystification.

In both its personal as well as political instantiations, "home" can easily become a space of exclusion despite its many possibilities of providing nurture and inclusiveness. The childhood home might awaken not only our sense of comfort and love, if there was love and comfort within its walls, but also the sense of insecurity and bitterness at being merely a child who does not know better and a sense of alienation from the outside world. The political "home," the space to nurture our identities, not only affirms us and empowers us as group members but can also deny entrance to others not deemed as belonging unless they silence themselves. When thinking of the case of Lugones strategically choosing different identity markers in different situations, I see how, despite being able to claim both identities as Latina and lesbian, when she joins the Nuevomejicano communities she has to follow their rules/practices/norms and is making herself vulnerable to them. She embeds herself within a regularized location, and silence about her sexual identity is probably the best approach if she is going to participate and build community in such a location. While she may have the possibility to negotiate her identities by way of a self-integrative self-project or by way of differential or *mestiza* consciousness, she remains between worlds and various aspects or identities are actively (or passively—due to outside circumstances) highlighted or covered over. I cannot speak for Lugones here. Yet there are times when I would like to be with Latinos as a Latina lesbian. Clearly, reconsiderations, reframings, remappings of the notions of home, of location, of belonging are necessary.

Hometactics

As we have seen, despite the problems associated with the notions of home, belonging, and location, there is no denying the power that the notion of home has in producing sentiments of safety, comfort, and belonging. But there is also no forgetting its mythical, "unreal" qualities. The reality of the notion of home is many times quite different from our imagined home, both in its personal and political instantiations. I wonder, though, whether we can go beyond the myth of home and move toward a decentered praxis of home-making and belonging, one that gives up the possibility of full belonging and allows for the possibility of not longing to be on one side or site of belonging.[5]

Here I would like to introduce such a praxis as "hometactics." Importantly, I am not suggesting that we should give up all notions of belonging connected to a politics of location, as in Mohanty's work, or to a politics of relation, as in Carrillo Rowe's work. My own position, coalitional politics, is a practice mindful of both location and relation. I am also not suggesting that we should give up all attempts at projects of self-integration, as in Barvosa's account. There is room and necessity for larger political projects of co-belonging as well as moments when it might be necessary to integrate certain aspects of our multiplicitous selves. Yet I would like to add another layer to our attempt to understanding home, location, and belonging, a layer that is many times overlooked as we emphasize the grander project of forging a politics capable of generating resistance to oppression or projects that emphasize unity or integration. This layer is that of the lived experience of multiplicitous selves that are being-between-worlds and being-in-worlds and that find themselves constantly negotiating their multiple identities in light of both ambiguities and contradictions but also in light of what I have referred to here as a will to belong. Thus my introduction of the notion of hometactics is an uncovering of what multiplicitous selves are already practicing in their everydayness, a disclosure of that which is *already* happening in our lived experience.

As opposed to strategies, which de Certeau sees as bound up with regulations or set ways (norms/practices/laws) upheld by a dominant order, de Certeau sees a tactic as "a calculated action determined by the absence of a proper locus" and as the "art of the weak" (1984: 37). Tactics are creative, inventive, combining different elements of a system (or a set of strategies) "blow by blow," and cannot be easily traced or mapped. In terms of their relation to specific spaces, unlike strategies that impose and place limits on spaces, tactics divert spaces. According to de Certeau, tactics use time in a clever way, produce alternative opportunities, and introduce play into the foundations of power (1984: 38). In short, tactics are temporal interventions aimed at producing favorable situations but not necessarily at abolishing a system of power.

De Certeau's classic example of practicing tactics is walking in the city (he also considers reading, storytelling, and cooking)—the different ways in which we improvise when we walk—walking in the city without a set map, getting a sense of the city despite its largeness and foreignness (the pedestrian reading the city but also writing it through her walking). For example, de Certeau discusses the example of a migrant of North African descent now living in Paris and walking this city's streets, the way he dwells in his housing development and uses his environment with plurality and creativity, and thus "by an art of being in between, he draws unexpected results from his situation" (1984: 30). According to de Certeau, he develops modes of use or "re-use" as he acculturates in his new environment.

Although I realize the difference of the context within which de Certeau introduces the distinction between strategies and tactics, an analysis of capitalist modes of production and consumption, it is possible to apply it to the context of an examination of the notion of belonging in light of the experience of multiplicitous selfhood. As we shall see later, Lugones has already engaged de Certeau's distinction to analyze the possibility of resistance on the part of those who are marginalized, although my discussion and hers have some significant differences. Hometactics share some of the characteristics described earlier by de Certeau, but not all. For example, while I doubt de Certeau would want to circumscribe tactics in this manner, I see hometactics as a decentered praxis that is at the same time capable of having a general aim or result. The aim of hometactics can be understood as the production of a sense of familiarity in the midst of an environment or world in which one cannot fully belong due to one's multiple positions and instances of thin and thick not being-at-ease. Such a sense of familiarity is, of course, not to be associated with the problematic idea of belonging that leads to barred rooms generally associated with so-called authentic markers of identity. And while hometactics can be said to have this general aim, no specific, set formulation of what these practices look like is possible, since one of the main features of tactics are precisely their unmappability and their working "blow by blow," taking advantages of opportunities as they present themselves.

In "Tactical Strategies of the Streetwalker/Estrategias Tácticas de la Callejera," Lugones problematizes de Certeau's dichotomous distinction between tactics and strategies (Lugones 2003: ch. 10). Lugones believes that de Certeau's view cannot offer the possibility of theorizing resistance from the point of view of the oppressed and from what she terms a concrete body-to-body engagement, because the strategist is not able to understand the logic of the tactical, and the tactical is seen as "haphazard, happenstance, disjointed intrusions on dominant sense, a troubled sort of passivity" (2003: 216). Lugones thus proposes "tactical strategies" in order to disrupt the dichotomy between strategy and tactic and to offer a position in which a liberatory project is not guided by a mastermind or strategist. Instead, the liberatory project is intersubjective and based on concrete, embodied subjects at the street level (tactical strategists, "streetwalkers," or "active subjects") who perform acts that go beyond merely "making do" (2003: 207–209, 216). As Lugones states, "As we move from tactics to tactical strategies we move from ephemeral contestatory negotiations of sense to more sustained engagements" (2003: 218).

For Lugones, such sustained engagement is connected to the resistant practice of hanging out, which, as we have seen, allows the tactical strategist to develop a sense of the spatial context so as to see new possibilities in it. This sense of the spatial context available to the streetwalker or tactical strategist, is, according to Lugones, neither the "nowhere" of de Certeau's tactician nor the "proper" space of the strategist. It is constituted by hang-outs, which are fluid spaces that allow for multivocal sense and critical interventions against structures of domination (2003: 221). In effect, then, while problematizing de Certeau's distinction between strategies and practices, Lugones provides a "spatial politics" (2003: 220).

Lugones's emphasis on spatiality is one aspect of her analysis that I find particularly important and helpful. I agree that de Certeau's analysis misses the significance of spatiality as it is connected to tactics. While de Certeau's own characterization of tactics as opposed to strategies prioritizes the importance of time to that of place, in my view it is possible to understand tactics as giving meaning to both time and space without necessarily reifying them. De Certeau notes,

> Tactics are procedures that gain validity in relation to the pertinence they lend to time—to the circumstances which the precise instant of an intervention transforms into a favorable situation, to the rapidity of the movements that change the organization of a space, to the relations among successive moments in an action, to the possible intersections of durations and heterogeneous rhythms, etc.
>
> (1984: 38)

According to de Certeau, tactics prioritize time because of the way in which our actions create possibilities that might be favorable to our lives. Yet it is possible to think how creating such possibilities might allow us to get a sense of connection to a particular location while we traverse the complicated world of multiplicitous selfhood without necessarily having a particular location designated as our home.

Lugones is right on the mark to expose the weaknesses of de Certeau's characterizations of strategies and tactics in light of the possibility of a more sustained liberatory project, or a "spatial politics." I welcome her proposal for a more intersubjective, fluid, spatial politics attentive to difference and leery of clearly marked dichotomies. My account of hometactics, however, does not emphasize a larger spatial politics, not because of lack of interest but because here I wish to bring to light the more personal day-to-day practices of multiplicitous selves as they struggle with the home question. While I realize the connection between the personal and the political, here I am pointing to daily practices connected to the home question that are not necessarily aligned to an explicit political project.

Importantly, Lugones does not have any affinity to the notion of "home." Consider a footnote in her tactical strategies chapter:

> Streetwalkers include women who are at odds with "home." The home-shelter-street-police station/jail/insane asylum-cemetery circle, in ever so many permutations, is their larger understanding of home. Home is lived as a place inseparable from other places of violence, including the street. One could punctuate any other place in this circle. I count myself more skillful at dodging violence in the street.
>
> (2003: 209)

For her, home is more reminiscent of violence. There are no magical conjurations in this concept, no appeal to comfort and ease. It is another chapter in yet another unfortunate dichotomy of public/private that Lugones also wishes to dismantle in her analysis of tactical strategies. For me, however, the question of home and the will to belong associated with it are still issues, deeply personal issues, despite my clear understanding of the dangers of the myth of home and my understanding of the larger political questions associated with the home question. It is precisely this paradoxical position that motivates this discussion. My account of hometactics is my response to the paradoxical will to belong while understanding the mythical, magical, and thus unreal, aspects of home. It is also my disclosure of what multiplicitous selves are already doing in their everyday experience. I clearly do not oppose grander and more sustained political projects, but I do not wish to overlook or forget those moments when multiplicitous selves struggle with everydayness and find ways, yes, to "make do," to feel comfortable in spite of a clear understanding of the ways in which power relations are bound to undermine, to hurt, to alienate.

In my view, hometactics can be deployed at a personal or relational level. They are everyday practices that multiplicitous selves can perform in order to have a sense of familiarity, ease, or sense of belonging in a space or location, even though that space is a new or foreign one, or in a social gathering or community, despite the fact that a community might be made up of members claiming different identities. Hometactics are practices that we might suddenly recognize as granting us new possibilities of belonging in a location and a sense of identification with others with whom we may or may not share social identities, all without the appeal to a fixed home location, an intentional self-integrating life-project, or a set of so-called authentic identity markers.

Since hometactics are everyday practices in which we literally "make do" with what we have, they do not form a robust sense of belonging or familiarity, whether it is associated with a location or a group, and thus they might not be capable of forging strong political coalitions that can establish practices of resistance. Yet, what can be viewed as a lack of political functionality or strength does not undermine their importance in terms of the lived experience of multiplicitous selves. The sense of individual or group "belonging" that they might provide is a great source of comfort in the midst of the complex, sometimes ambiguous, sometimes contradictory lives of multiplicitous selves. Such a comfort is not based on a great myth or conjuration, such as the traditional notion of home, or on a grand self-integrating life project, but on particular everyday practices of "making do" with the incredibly complex and thorny yet creative and resourceful lived experience of the multiplicitous self.

How multiplicitous selves "make do" in their everydayness, how they engage in hometactics, is an important issue that we need to consider if we are to understand the phenomenology of multiplicitous selfhood. What I am calling hometactics, microtechniques of lived experience, is already being put in practice by these selves and might prove to be useful for those who are not already doing it. Important questions as to the extent to which such hometactics might be found to be too opportunistic within dominant schemas, might be representative of not just making do but of "selling out," might be too passive, might be too complicit in dominant schemes, or might or might not preclude the possibility of more sustained political projects need to be examined. That is, some could claim that hometactics could create a certain comfort or a being-at-ease while we are in worlds that might take away our critical attitude or possibilities of resistance to dominant norms, thus minimizing the desire or need to world-travel. This is an important concern that needs to be taken into consideration when thinking about hometactics. Yet my point here is to emphasize the fact that, given the complexity and difficulty of the lives a multiplicitous selves, these selves are *already* engaging in practices that allow them to have a sense of comfort within worlds in which they are not welcomed. Engagement in these practices does not preclude the possibility of critical world-traveling or a more sustained, resistant political engagement.

Hometactics are practices that we develop as we travel our various worlds and that we can later repeat or maintain. Such practices are varied and depend on the specific experiences and locations of the selves that deploy them. They might range from painting the walls of your apartment with bright colors, such as the ones that remind you of a childhood home or your country origin; "reusing" your environment in various ways so as to make it more welcoming; making and sharing foods you used to eat in your past by improvising with ingredients that are available (here I pause to reflect on how satisfying it was to eat a *nacatamal*, a Nicaraguan tamale, in Cleveland); to rethinking, refeeling the meaning of family by developing new relationships with a neighbor, getting so close that he becomes family, too. Hometactics also include finding ways of relating to members of other groups with whom one was not associated before. There are linguistic hometactics as well, switching languages in different contexts or integrating words from familiar languages to feel more at ease.

An example of this latter case regarding linguistic practices is the way in which I immediately switch to speaking Spanish as soon as I find out that someone I have been introduced to speaks the language, or the way in which I add Spanish words while I am speaking in English. I still feel tremendous pleasure when speaking Spanish, and it gives me an incredible sense of comfort. As I live in an area where there are few Latinos, and I work at a university with very few Latinos, speaking Spanish becomes a treat, a joy. However, critics concerned with the deployment of hometactics that might lead to a "selling out" or to a too comfortable position within a dominant schema would have a different concern regarding linguistic hometactics. They might point out the way in which some immigrants might adopt the new language and prioritize it in order not just to feel more at ease but also to assimilate to the dominant culture. This might be a concern, although language assimilation is a lengthy process and might go well beyond "making do." Yet, as noted, an important aspect of hometactics is that they are micropractices used in different ways by different people. My view is that they do not necessarily have to be used in such a way to become complicit with dominant norms (e.g., passing, acting white, etc.). Although they may be used in this manner, what I find most interesting and meaningful about hometactics is the manner in which we deploy them in order to feel comfortable in strange or unwelcoming worlds, while at the same time being deeply aware of the oppressive nature of dominant norms in those worlds. Ultimately, I am appealing to the existential dimension of hometactics, to the manner in which they can facilitate my everyday being-in-worlds despite the ambiguity connected to my ability to find a sense of belonging while being aware that such belonging is not possible.[6]

There are many hometactics that we can practice and are already practicing in order to make our lives more comfortable, to alleviate the stress, pain, anxiety that can arise from a life of in-betweenness and world-traveling. As noted, these practices might be connected to remaking "home" within a new environment or performing activities reminiscent of the place/space/culture/people we once associated or currently associate with "home." Such practices make my new context easier to navigate. They are connected to our particular histories, desires, contexts, and abilities to make a better life in spaces in which we do not quite fit. These practices are varied and are usually not planned in advance. They are developed in the midst of, as Heidegger would say, our "thrownness" in our various worlds and borders. While some of these practices might provide being-at-ease, comfort, and a sense of belonging, they do not necessarily preclude a critical, resistant attitude in the worlds we traverse.

As noted in earlier chapters, the multiplicitous self's creative as well as resistant potential is tied to her very liminality. While multiplicitous selves at the margins may deploy a number of hometactics to gain a sense of comfort in their lives, I suspect that given their condition as multiplicitous, as marginalized, as not being part of dominant groups, they will also encounter many instances of what I have referred to as thin and thick not being-at-ease. That is, they will experience every day the breaking down of equipment or norms as well as more existential crises related to their identities that will continue to make them more aware of their liminal condition. Even when performing the dominant norms expected of dominant culture, we will be somehow reminded that we do not belong. It is not possible, then, to say with certainty how and whether hometactics are going to make us too complicit with dominant norms and practices as they will be deployed in various ways. Here my aim is not to provide a theory of hometactics that fully explains how they work and the specific roles that they play in the lives of multiplicitous selves. I am trying to bring to light practices that I already employ in my everyday existence in order to have some comfort in my life, practices that I suspect many multiplicitous selves are also engaging in as they negotiate their complex lives in worlds where they might not be wanted, respected, or even seen.

While I was inspired to think about hometactics as I examined my own lived experience and how I tried to find more comfort in unwelcoming worlds, I realize that my discussion has been limited to their use by multiplicitous selves who are alienated or marginalized. What about those multiplicitous selves that find themselves in more dominant positions? Given my view that all of us are multiplicitous selves, there arises the possibility that members of dominant groups or those occupying positions of power can engage in hometactics due to their not feeling comfortable in certain contexts. Given our multiplicity, it is very possible that members of dominant groups don't experience being-at-ease in all aspects of their lives, and so it is very likely that they also have to deploy hometactics in different contexts and worlds. As we have learned from Lugones, the simple dichotomy of dominant/marginalized, oppressor/oppressed is not enough to explain our lived experience. Recall that all multiplicitous selves are oppressing/being-oppressed ⇔ resisting. That is to say, given our multiplicity and the various worlds we inhabit, we may gain a great deal of advantage by virtue of some of our social identities but not others. In some worlds we are more marginalized than in others, and in some worlds we fall on the side of the dominant. For example, as a light-skinned, educated Latina, I have many more privileges than many other Latinas who have not had the opportunities that I have had. Yet this does not erase the fact that for many multiplicitous selves, for many *atravesados*, life continues to be difficult in many areas. It is understandable, then, how even multiplicitous selves that can be seen as being part of dominant groups, or that have a privileged position, might make use of hometactics under certain conditions.

Nevertheless, the worrisome issue is the possibility of these selves in dominant positions using hometactics to satisfy and carry forth colonialist and imperialist desires. Another way to make the point is by asking whether the colonizer can engage in hometactics if he does not feel at ease in specific contexts of the colonized society, and whether he can engage in those practices as a way of imposing his home in the new territory.[7] Here many images come to mind, including images of the British, Spanish, and other colonizing countries bringing their home with them to the new places of conquest, transforming these new territories so as to fit their customs and desires rather than adapting to their new land and customs. While initially some of the practices might be in fact a matter of being more comfortable in unfamiliar environments, one can easily see how these practices become impositions. In these cases, I would say that those practices the colonizers used in order to bring their homes with them cannot be seen as hometactics in the sense described here. They do not represent ways of "making do" in unfriendly, unwelcoming environments for the purposes of creating comfort in a life filled with difficulties due to one's in-betweenness, marginalization, and oppression. They are sustained, intentional practices with the specific purpose of imposing one's way of life on a world that one considers inferior and inhabited by inferior beings. These practices become strategies intentionally deployed to undermine, demoralize, and chip away at the fabric of a society that is not regarded as worthy of respect.

Hometactics, understood as practices deployed by multiplicitous selves in order to gain comfort and ease in a life of liminality and in-betweenness, a life that is not a stranger to oppression and marginalization, remain an important aspect of the lived experience of these selves. Yet given the open-ended and unmappable character of these practices, it is not possible to know what they always ought to be doing when they deploy these hometactics. For me, hometactics have been a way of not just surviving in my travels across worlds but of feeling a sense of much-needed familiarity and relief in the midst of an existence filled with contradictions and ambiguities that led both to moments of intimate terrorism—cactus needles embedded in the skin—and to exciting moments of creativity and resistance.

I would like to conclude with another confession. I am a philosopher working in an academic environment that continues to privilege maleness and whiteness and writing by maleness and whiteness, the two attributes still considered by many as the bearers of philosophical excellence. Recall how Hegel wrote that women are like plants and that Africans could not arrive at *Geist*—Hegel's views of women and people of color being just two of the many reminders of the narrow, restricting, and alienating intellectual space of philosophy, a space that I precariously inhabit. There have been changes; there has been growth. Talk of inclusiveness, talk of justice. But the writing that comes from the white female hand is still more important even within feminism, the movement pushing philosophy and others to see farther, to understand more. So what can I do? I take what is given to me and make it my own ... with words, with ink, with my lived experience. I offer you these words, these thoughts. I carve out a space for me in this philosophy that was never meant to be a home for me—this is one of my hometactics.

> When I write it feels like I'm carving bone. It feels like I'm creating my own face, my own heart.
>
> —Gloria Anzaldúa

It must be noted, however, that each woman of color cited here, even in her positing of a "plurality of self," is already privileged enough to reach the moment of cognition of a situation for herself. This should suggest that to privilege the subject, even if multiple-voiced, is not enough.

—Norma Alarcón

References

Barvosa, E. (2008) *Wealth of Selves: Multiple Identities, Mestiza Consciousness, and the Subject of Politics*, College Station: Texas A&M Press.
Carillo Rowe, A. (2008) *Power Lines: On the Subject of Feminist Alliances*, Durham, NC: Duke University Press.
de Certeau, M. (1984) *The Practice of Everyday Life*, Berkeley: University of California Press.
hooks, b. (2009) *Belonging: A Culture of Place*, New York: Routledge.
Johnson Reagon, B. (1983) "Coalitional Politics: Turning the Century," in B. Smith (ed.), *Home Girls: A Black Feminist Anthology*, 356–368, New York: Kitchen Table/Women of Color Press.
Kaplan, C. (1996) *Questions of Travel: Postmodern Discourses of Displacement*, Durham, NC: Duke University Press.
Lugones, M. (1990) "Hispaneando y Lesbiando: On Sarah Hoagland's Lesbian Ethics," *Hypatia* 5 (3): 138–147.
Lugones, M. (2003) *Pilgrimages/Peregrinajes: Theorizing Coalition against Multiple Oppressions*, New York: Rowman & Littlefield.
Mohanty, C. T. (2003) *Feminism without Borders: Decolonizing Theory, Practicing Solidarity*, Durham, NC: Duke University Press.
Ortega, M. (2004) "Exiled Space, In-Between Space: Existential Spatiality in Ana Mendieta's Siluetas Series," *Philosophy and Geography* 7 (1): 25–41.
Ortega, M. (2008) "Wounds of Self: Experience, Word, Image, and Identity," *Journal of Speculative Philosophy* 22 (4): 235–247.
Rich, A. (1986) *Blood, Bread, and Poetry: Selected Prose, 1979–1985*, New York: Norton.
Sartre, J.-P. (1966) *Being and Nothingness: An Essay on Phenomenological Ontology*, H. E. Barnes (trans.), New York: Philosophical Library.

Notes

1 My notion of self-mapping pertains the way in which one attempts to understand one's position in different worlds. Such a position is not to be understood as merely spatial—as related to establishing borders and engaging in an exercise that leads to fixity, as a cartographer might wish to do. Rather, I use self mapping as indicative of a process of being attuned to who one is and where one fits and does not fit, how one fares in the different worlds traveled, and why one feels the way one does while being in different worlds. Self-mapping, then, is not about naming one's country and differentiating its borders but about being attuned to feelings of be-longing, of being and longing, in the different worlds we traverse.
2 Adrienne Rich coined the notion "politics of location" in her analysis of her own positionality as a white, Jewish, lesbian, privileged woman (1986, 210–231). It has become a crucial idea in

feminism, as feminists carry out investigations about their own spatial and social positionality and how this positionality informs their political responsibilities.
3 Such "nurturing" spaces might not always become unsafe for those inhabiting them. However, given the heterogeneity of groups, it is likely that questions about who really belongs in them might arise.
4 I must be clear here and add that by appealing to a "will to belong" I am not appealing to some metaphysical or psychological aspect or drive that we all must have by virtue of being human. It would be incredibly pretentious for me to make such a claim. Perhaps Schopenhauer and Nietzsche knew more when they made their appeals to the "will to live" and the "will to truth" and "the will to power," respectively. I am simply naming a feeling, perhaps an attitude that I find in myself as well as many other people, whether they are immigrants or exiles or not, although many exiles certainly discuss it more. I am making explicit something that is already there in my lived experience as well as in the experience of others. It is not my wish to reify, naturalize, or generalize from such an experience, but I do wish to engage this feeling in light of questions of home, location, and multiplicitous selfhood.
5 I thank Kyoo Lee for her comments regarding the possibility of being without longing, or as she puts it, "without being forced to choose sites/sides of be-longing." I realize that I am still invested in being "with longing" even when the sites of belonging and belonging itself are being problematized.
6 Sometimes I wonder whether my use of hometactics can become, as Sartre would say, a project of "bad faith," what he describes as a certain lying to oneself, another way of denying one's transcendence or freedom to make choices in order to become a facticity—in this instance, a sense of having a "home" when in fact we have the freedom to move, to be nomads, if we so desire (Sartre 1966: I, ch. 2).
7 I thank Ada Demaj for pressing me to think more about this question regarding the use of hometactics in the context of the colonizer. It is important to remember that even practices such as world-traveling and hometactics can be used by those in dominant positions inappropriately, thus undermining their positive elements and the practices themselves.

Reading Questions

1. What is a "multiplicitous self," according to Ortega? How might this analysis challenge traditional notions of a singular, cohesive identity?
2. Based on your understanding of this text, describe how you might approach the task of "self-mapping." How might self-mapping be helpful for understanding the "politics of location," from Ortega's perspective?
3. How does Mariana Ortega define "hometactics," and what are some examples she provides?
4. Do you use hometactics in your own life? Describe how practices might help individuals with multiple identities navigate their environments and avoid the dilemmas presented by narrow demands for assimilation.
5. Hometactics is obviously important as a psychological matter. Can it have a political dimension? What's Ortega's view? Do you agree? Why or why not?
6. According to Ortega, how are hometactics different from what a colonizer does when recreating a world so that everyday life feels familiar and "homey"?
7. How might Ortega's analysis of hometactics be applied in other contexts in which feelings belonging are important? Imagine you are a consultant for your school, church, or a different client you care about. After thinking about Ortega's argument, what advice would you give? Create a fictional consultant's report describing who your client is, why they hired you, and how an understanding of hometactics would help them (and don't forget to attach a fictional invoice for your valuable services).
8. Ortega critiques the traditional notion of home as a fixed, safe place. Why, then, does she also challenge the view that home is entirely detachable from place? What do you think Ortega would say about the phrase, "home is where the heart is"?
9. Ortega notes that "Important questions as to the extent to which such hometactics might be found to be too opportunistic within dominant schemas, might be representative of not just making do

but of 'selling out,' might be too passive, might be too complicit in dominant schemes, or might or might not preclude the possibility of more sustained political projects need to be examined. That is, some could claim that hometactics could create a certain comfort or a being-at-ease while we are in worlds that might take away our critical attitude or possibilities of resistance to dominant norms, thus minimizing the desire or need to world-travel." Is this a serious worry? Why or why not? What might Ortega say in response?

19 Between Hermeneutic Violence and Alphabets of Survival

Elena Flores Ruíz

Te alejas de los nombres/que hilan el silencio de las cosas

—Alejandra Pizarnik (1990)

I know what will happen. You tell the story, and then it's retold as they wish, written in words you do not understand, in a language that is theirs, and not yours.

—Edwidge Danticat (2014)

It is difficult to grasp the existential impact of living amid systems of interpretation that are legitimized by what they exclude, the limbic terror of maneuvering through life with discursive tools designed to deflect awareness of their own impoverishment and complicity in systems of domination. Every step betrays when bodying through terrains that exclude the synchronous appearance of women, melanoid bodies and unregulated sexualities outside the colonial ordering of everyday life. Every step caves in ways philosophical feminisms have yet to account for, steps women of color and Indigenous feminisms have long been taking to remedy the lived impact of having to take them in the first place. What tools, what hard-won strides and self-authoring skills have arisen to defy the colonial will toward epistemicides and the Western dialectic of erasure? What strategies have formed to name the silence colonized languages inhabit—this alien god gone astray in the flesh of those risen from the wretched of the earth? The answer, if the language of interpretive horizons is decolonized enough to hear it, is many.

Many grammars, vast and plural, have formed to protest the sense of loss that is knowing you speak ten languages yet only have words for one. Anzaldúa speaks. Paredes speaks. Menchú speaks. Yet this epistemic resilience comes at a cost, one that cannot be altogether forgone in an age of intensifying neocolonial violence, but which can be partly mitigated by laying bare some of the mechanisms operative in the continued resilience and systematicity of neocolonial oppression against women of color. Ours is a history of visible and hidden harms, of violence by another name that requires a different archaeology of knowledge than previously supposed by European political philosophies. Too often, the conceptions of injury and harm they espouse are based on a metaphysics of presence that excludes the bodies of the oppressed (so that both visible and invisible harms coexist in our lives to confound us, to shroud the normalized coexistence of democratic antislavery with institutional racism and sexism). Too often, the parameters for freedom they beget are based on colonial subjugation of alternative political formations and acquiescence to the forms of power that maintain the modern colonial gender system intact, so that deeper diachronic forms

DOI: 10.4324/9781003385417-28

of violence against women remain sidelined, elided in our experience of our social worlds. Ours is a history of hidden harms taking place in open air, of histories buried by History. This demands an accounting.

This essay is one small step in that direction. I am interested in what keeps violence a productive phenomenon in the lives of women of color: what maintains and sustains the logical universe necessary to keep "resistance" a structural feature of our existence. We are undoubtedly resistant. Strong. We gather the slaughter and steward our pain towards survival: a beyond the beyond yet known. Yet this struggle is not an accidental feature of existence, but the outcome of deep, structural inequities and foundational fictions at the heart of modern liberalism and democratic civil society.

Disclosing these inequities and fictions alone will not yield their demise, as the rationalistic ideal behind such logical inference founders on the same epistemic foundationalisms that motivated European colonialism and imperialism. Tracing harms to their origins—even to unknown or undertheorized ontological levels of origins—dwells too much on the philosophical satisfaction reached by establishing more precise correspondences between self and world, or in grounding knowledge claims on yet more "primordial," transcendental conditions for human understanding. This alone is not the world. It's an explanatory framework for making sense of a world that will never be the world that most matters to those excluded by those frameworks: the lived-world(s) of marginalized beings often caught in the crags between disclosure and disappearance, between bones bent by pain that falls into medical metrics (and thus addressed as "real") and pain excluded by the unacknowledged sexist whiteness of those metrics. We acknowledge. And we're here to account. But this accounting, as a methodological pivot for our work, can never fully capture and remedy the harm itself. It can never be the thing that sutures closed the slaughter in the city square, that gives us back our missing loved ones, restores the water access route to our psyches, or frees our detained friends. It can never shake a tree limb with enough force to both dig up its roots and loosen the blood on its leaves. There is no blood on the ontological tree.

What philosophical investigations of structural oppressions in our lives can do, however, is in a very limited (but very important) way be theoretically responsive to the affective, phenomenological, and political consequences that emanate from the tacit continuity and unquestioned operationalization of structural oppressions in our daily lives.[1] It may even help catalyze our individual dismantling of the powerful asymmetries they produce—asymmetries once experienced as mystified factors in our interpretive lives. Revealing the productive violences sustaining the structural systematicity of oppressions can also help ground our voices in different kinds of self-confirming spaces that expand the possible modes of epistemic disobedience we can express. It is just one step, but one that can help us stand our ground when history, language, and philosophical systems gaslight us in the fight for our existence.

Looking at what keeps violence a productive phenomenon in the lives of women of color touches on a vision of liberation that I think is crucial for tackling the resiliency of colonial domination throughout its various historical iterations in neocolonialism, imperialism, and neoliberalism. It is a vision Graciela Hierro illustrated through her claim that, to date, strategies focused on empowerment and integrating women into existing hierarchies of social power have helped to "construct power to oppose power, but done little in the way of promoting a deeper, ontological vision of displacing the very centrality of gender subordination coursing through the many interlocking levels of culture" (Hierro 1994: 173).[2] Presently, the theoretical toolkit for thinking about such a move is very limited. Harms at the ontological level are almost unthinkable given that the analytic tools we have to grasp such a concept inflect (even to a minimal degree) predicative stability by virtue of their very use. In addition, the prevailing analytic paradigms in the social sciences and humanities have a difficult time identifying cultural formations prior to their appearance in social structures and socially legible interpretations of those structures. Our conceptions of violence are also hermeneutically compromised, leading to a situation where to talk about intersectional harms against women of color, and Indigenous women in particular, is to do so with frameworks that cannot acknowledge the fulsome complexity, depth, and systematicity of those harms. We are missing tools to talk readily and robustly about what's missing. One way to illustrate this is through what I call "hermeneutic violence."

Hermeneutic Violence

Defined as violence done to structures of meaning and intelligibility, hermeneutic violence has played an important role in the persistence of European colonialism through its various historical iterations in neocolonialism, imperialism, and neoliberalism. The idea of hermeneutic violence begins with a particular picture of how human beings understand and make sense of things that differs from the standard view in the social and natural sciences, where making sense of things is based on subject-dependent interpretations of a mind-independent reality. The understanding that arises from this naturalized framework is based on an objective knowledge that is reflective instead of prereflective, and is often reducible to cognitive procedures. This account does not foreclose social dimensions of knowledge, but it does bind them to doxastic attitudes and the epistemic effects they have on rational agents; at bottom, what does not drop out is a founding framework of an inner mind driven by neurophysiological processes and an outer world accessible through mental representations, even when talking about our shared intentions or "collective" forms of intentionality. On the hermeneutic view, the knowledge generated through this picture certainly counts as a kind of knowledge, but one that is limited to the history of social practices concerned with causal explanation and explanatory understanding, one that is very useful for distinguishing between things like knowledge attribution and possession. It is typically accompanied by a view of linguistic practice based on natural languages as tools or "mediums" of expression for the inner mental acts of knowing agents, thus making possible the manifestation of human understanding in propositional statements like "S knows that P." Under this framework the mind comes first, language second.

Hermeneutical understanding, by contrast, seeks to describe how human understanding is something we always already do prereflectively and cannot otherwise disengage ourselves from if we are to make basic sense of our world as we move about it.[3] The goal is not explanatory understanding but close, phenomenological description that gets at the contours of what it means to make sense of things, to hold them in a certain kind of intelligibility that is characteristic of human beings situated in particular historical contexts. This kind of basic, prereflective understanding serves to ground our various epistemic compartments (like self-reflexivity and intentionality) in a prior background of cultural interpretive familiarity that allows those compartments to emerge as meaningful possibilities for expression. Interpretive familiarity is in turn achieved by growing into a specific sociohistorical context that is held together by the shared reference points enacted in cultural acts and practices—a kind of referential background of meaning that prefigures ordinary language expression. Under this framework language (as an interpretive backdrop) comes first, the mind second.

The hermeneutic account of what makes intelligibility possible in the first place and the critique of representational language it upholds help frame hermeneutic violence as a unique kind of prereflective cultural violence that arose in the modern era in conjunction with the imperial and colonial projects of Western European powers. Bolstered by new linguistic strategies of subjugation in the Spanish war of unification and Reconquista of the Iberian Peninsula, European colonizers pursued a new kind of tactical occupation of Meso-America that differs from the standard historical account of colonialism as a war of cultural invasion driven by the state-building and religious projects of early modern European nation states. On the usual view, European colonizers "imposed" their worldview onto native Amerindians as either an intentional act of domination consistent with Western political paradigms of intercultural warfare (the most common view) or as an unintended byproduct of encountering a radically different culture, causing colonizers to revert to their default cultural understandings without critical self-awareness of their epistemic myopias. Because the benefit of keeping to the latter, uncritical perspective resulted in the self-serving accumulation or concentration of social power, the myopia that yielded the cultural imposition is typically seen as quasi-intentional and therefore subject to ethical claims of unjust epistemic practices.

Hermeneutic violence can thus be understood as violence done to structures of meaning and intelligibility that allow for the meaning of everyday cultural acts and practices definitive of a cultural tradition to emerge, as in Nahua, Olmec, Ojibwe, and other Amerindian worldviews. Hermeneutic violence can't be done directly, like behavioral and interpersonal violence. *Nor can it take the shape of structural violence* since the structures of intelligibility are prereflective, and have not assumed readily visible (as in socially articulated) shape through patterned use in culture. They have not assumed the position of (material, social, cultural) objects within settings of interrelated practices that can then be linked up to one another in structural form. It is a more primordial, tacit violence that prevents oppressed peoples from achieving prereflective interpretive familiarity with one's world along the same lines as their historical oppressors. This does not relegate oppressed peoples to positions of muteness or agential underdetermination; on the contrary, oppressed peoples who have suffered trauma to their interpretive resources and referential contexts of meaning are often hypervocal in their resistance and creative responses to their sense of displacement. There is certainly a worldly know-how and an experiential reality of significant epistemic standing: the long quillwork of communal alphabets of survival attest to this. The problem lies in the existing structures of power that permit the audibility of those resistant voices to rise in the official narratives of culture. Hermeneutic violence further suggests that one consequence of violence done to interpretive systems is a subordinated speaking position in culture.[4]

As an analytic tool, hermeneutic violence can help us think through precursors to the cultural epistemicides that dominated the modern imperial political projects of Western European powers (e.g., through strategies of religious, cultural, political, military, and especially racial and gendered violence). Its existence suggests that violence—deep violence, the kind that sustains and nurtures the limens of worlds where the savagery of power takes on cultural form, is not solely a destructive force. Quite the opposite. The disorders of socially visible oppressions are ordered ahead of their appearance in historical languages—what makes that mechanism hold, persist, sustain its own preservation throughout various permutations in culture is key to understanding the resilience of social oppressions throughout history. We can illustrate this by tracking the impact of hermeneutic violence on women in Latin America, particularly through the harms done to Native Amerindian discursive practices and the cultural structures erected to maintain them in the long term.

In Meso-America, the introduction of the Western alphabet and subject-predicate grammar (as well as the assumptions of exclusionary logic, interiorization, and narrative linearity that support it) have resulted in a unique kind of violence to the discursive practices of Native Meso-American communities that very often goes unacknowledged and continues to harm Indigenous women through their subordinated speaking position in culture. Colonization of pre-Columbian resources of expression with subject-object representational views of language covered over deep, metaphysical ambiguity laden in the interpretive backgrounds of Amerindian worldviews, and which could not be disclosed through the dominant conceptions of Western linguistics (where the mind comes first, language second). By weakening the relationship between Native Amerindians and the interpretive resources required to effectively participate in cultural processes, one powerful consequence of hermeneutic violence has been the degree of difficulty contemporary Indigenous women face in having claims of violence heard and recognized in their own language. Consider the double bind this creates: To cope with the fallout, contemporary campesina movements like El Movimiento de Mujeres de Cuscatlán constructed power to oppose power, identifying literacy as a primary community need and mobilizing alfabetizadoras (literacy teachers) throughout rural and Indigenous communities (Purcell-Gates 2000: 221). It would be difficult to critique this move as wrongheaded or ineffective since barring access to literacy has been a tool of gender-based violence since the start of colonial administrative bureaucracies. Foreign nongovernmental organizations operating in Latin America (often in conjunction with structural adjustment programs or Millennium Development Goals) have likewise focused on women's empowerment through alphabetic literacy, at times even recognizing the role Romanized alphabetic literacy played in colonial administration and domination of Indigenous communities. The structural oppressions created through colonial administrator's selective dissemination of cultural instruments of power have had palpable harms in the lives of modern Latin American women, especially racialized women in rural zones, yet the solutions are often bound to colonialism in such a way that they unwittingly help maintain the centrality of its organizing concepts in the negotiation of cultural processes. This speaks to Hierro's concern regarding the organizing fulcrum that sustains systems of subordination at the deepest, prepredicative levels of culture. But it also points to another double bind that goes unacknowledged as a kind of harm, whereby women are put in the impossible position, generation after generation, of defending a nonaccidental epistemic and interpretive scarcity in order to have claims of violence heard, recognized, or assert rights that were unnecessary to assert before rights-based discourses imposed the need to assert them as part of the social recognition of their agency. The liberal framework of women's empowerment is able to coexist almost seamlessly with the continued nonaccidental suppression of Native Amerindian languages and communities that create the need for access to literacy in the first place: when bill (PL) 5.954-C was introduced in in Brazil in 2013 to allow Indigenous communities to use their Native languages at school as well as develop processes of learning and assessment that best reflect the epistemic practices of Indigenous cultures, President Dilma Rousseff quickly vetoed it as "contrary to public interest" (Humanitarian News 2016). The long arc between 1513 and 2013 is shorter than it appears when we stop to consider the mechanisms behind the resilience of social oppressions.

Hermeneutic violence points to the ways the appearance of visible harms to marginalized communities is very often preceded by conditions of hermeneutic precarity and traumas to systems of interpretation. As a critical tool of analysis, hermeneutic violence can help us think through some of these deeply layered and complex predicaments as we move along the dual tracks of context-specific social justice work and collective reflection on our varied practices of liberation.[5] In the next section I turn to Latina feminist theory to highlight the creativity and epistemic resilience behind some of these varied practices, as they often take a significant physical and existential toll in women of color's lives. In particular, I point to the self-authoring skills and autohistorical practices Latina feminists have developed in response to the persistence of coloniality in women of color's lives. Drawing on Nelly Richard's work on cultural memory in postdictatorial Chile, I call these practices "alphabets of survival" and specifically turn to the work of Gloria Anzaldúa as illustrative of resistant practices to hermeneutic violence in a US-borderland context.

Alphabets of Survival

One of the lasting legacies of Latina feminist theory in the United States is the creation of a nonbinary "third critical space," as Norma Alarcón describes, that is generative of multiple points of subaltern resistance to the complex legacy of colonial domination on women of color's lives (2013: 205).

One way to think about such a space is as a relational epistemic resource hermeneutically marginalized communities produce in response to hegemonic interpretive spaces, one that illuminates alternative cartographies of reason for long enough to validate the sense, despite all evidence of reality to the contrary, of corporeally knowing otherwise. At times this can be a life-saving affirmation and an important praxis of self-healing from cultural trauma. At others it is an in-between state that facilitates critical transformations by expanding the limits of philosophical imagination to account for lives that are intricately affected by colonial domination, and which often do not have the ontological security afforded to those in settler epistemic communities. Generating descriptions, names, identities, artforms, narratives, and languages for lived experience (what together, I'm calling alphabets of survival) is therefore a critical aspect of this third space. Take, for example, Alarcón's account of the identic term Chicana:

> The name Chicana, in the present, is the name of resistance that enables cultural and political points of departure and thinking through the multiple migrations and dislocations of women of "Mexican" descent. The name Chicana is not a name that women (or men) are born to or with, as is often the case with "Mexican," but rather is consciously and critically assumed and serves as a point of redeparture for dismantling historical conjunctures of crisis, confusion, political and ideological conflict and contradictions of the simultaneous effects of having "no names," having "many names," "not know[ing] her names" and being someone else's dreamwork.
>
> (1990: 249–250)[6]

Drawing on Anzaldúa, Alarcón describes how identity and narrative practices are inherently creative in this context, since they rest on a prior rejection of the established hermeneutical power over discursive domains and where no prior authorization for self-legitimation of such autoethnographic moments exists.[7] On the philosophical hermeneutic view, self-authoring would be logically impossible, yet Latina feminists like Anzaldúa challenge the epistemic imperialism of that impossibility by drawing on the corporeal intuitions of subaltern knowledges—which are social and relational—in the multiple interpretive traditions she inhabits. In this vein, Anzaldúa builds theories that perform what she calls "interventions that subvert cultural genocide" by allowing for the possibility of self-making and self-mapping in the wake of hermeneutic violence (2015: 89).[8] One strategy she typically deploys is taking aspects of the devalued side of an Anglo-European binary (black/white, literal/nonliteral) and redeploying it in a way that subverts the stability of the binary, or in a way, "thirds" it. If "literal" is the dominant norm through which history is written, she takes the devalued side (nonliteral, fictive) and uses it to license personal and collective history that has been preemptively curated out of official (socially legible) history. Autohistoria is a prime example. "Autohistoria," she writes, "is a term I use to describe the genre of writing about one's personal and collective history using fictive elements, a sort of fictionalized autobiography or memoir; and *autohistoria-teoría* is a personal essay that *theorizes*" (Anzaldúa 2013: 15 and 518, my emphasis). It is a relational theory that can produce alternative understandings (as *conocimiento*) of reality for marginalized peoples negotiating the imprint of cultural and personal trauma on their narrative lives: "You turn the established narrative on its head, seeing through, resisting, and subverting its assumptions. Again, it's not enough to denounce the culture's old account—you must provide new narratives embodying alternative potentials" (560). As Andrea J. Pitts explains,

> Anzaldúa proposes autohistoria-teoría as a way to refer to the explicit task of developing theoretical resources out of descriptions of oneself and one's experiences. In this sense, speaking for oneself can extend toward others in ways that can be positive and conducive of further actions and forms of meaning-making.
>
> (Pitts 2016: 358)

One of the many things Anzaldúa's work teaches us is that memory-work is hard when meaning-making must also be fashioned to support it. Yes, it is hard when the social, cultural, and interpretive resources one relies on to confront the representation of the past in our daily lives are tacitly one's own, yet much harder when they're not. Indeed, it is much harder to contest social exclusions in our shared discourses—to address the social situation of Latinas in the United States and women of color in the global South, for instance—without recourse to the interpretive stability that comes with having a privileged subject-position in culture. Having privileged access to the cultural instruments for writing Official History—a voice that can be publicly heard, a pen with ink that can be published and read, a formal lexicon one is pre-predicatively at home with—certainly makes for a more facile contestation of History from within, but it is no easy task, for anyone.

I pause here, parsing and meting out ways to help us remember the general difficulty involved in bouldering history and language (to name a wound, redress a grievance, or heal a cultural harm) so as to not minimize the weight of human suffering on the scales of any life. Yet there are lives that bear weights that cannot be counted by the metrics given the most weight in public life; in the municipal hall, in the courtroom, in the day-to-day negotiations that hang precariously over marginal lives. The worry is that there are those who cannot combat social injustices and epistemic inequities without first having to see oneself as another—to do the epistemic equivalent of a double-shift workday of interpretive bridge-building and crossing-over so as to gain access to dominant cultural codes and established narrative modalities for contesting social roles in public life . . . to tools historically dispossessed from the very subjects most in need of cultural redress. On this view, K'iche women must learn Spanish or rely on translators, work with notions of narrative time discontinuous with their own, and so on, to get (for instance) legal redress on matters ranging from land title tenure and regularization to sexual assault and domestic abuse. One must often use another's voice to speak for oneself. And this is no small point. After all, herein lies the pain acts of attestation can bring when one is historically excluded from full and legitimate participation in the interpretive processes of culture: when to object, contest, or textualize dissent is to risk the experience of a fractured self, an enunciative standpoint that is torn between the twin crags of meaning/publicity and speechlessness/silence in the communal paradigms of history, politics, medicine, law . . . the places where our bodily experience of our "feminisms" is most often at stake.

Consider, for instance, Nelly Richard's poignant claim about the risk to our experience of selfhood when memory-work first requires a "disremembering" (*una desmemoria*) of the imprint of cultural and social trauma on our lives, of the gendered politics of negotiating the imprint of violence and trauma with (often asymmetrical/inequitable access to) cultural tools and resources of expression that are themselves often conceptually impoverished and unaccommodating of the intersectionally complex experiential realities of Latin American women and women of color. The question is—to use her phrasing—how to acknowledge the epistemic vulnerability, the "rupture that grew out of the challenge of having to name fragments of experience that were no longer speakable in the language that survived the catastrophe of meaning" (2004: 4). Richard's response, in part, is through producing an aesthetic "alphabet of survival" that points to corporeal intuitions, to subaltern truths that dominant side of binaries suppress to maintain both the binary and the dominance it supports in culture; they are "linguistic elements composing a new language based on, and necessitated by, *survival*" so that we don't, physically and metaphorically, *die of the truth*, to use Nietzsche's phrase (Richard 2004: 104).[9]

On this account, feminist anticolonial memory-work and autoethnography means more than the taxing psychic strain of—to use Otto Neurath's classic hermeneutic example—remaking a boat at sea. This is because it often requires a prior *undoing, uncoding, unbraiding, and dismantling of interpretive frameworks* that allow one to prereflectively handle, maneuver, and work with the materials the boat and the sea disclose *as available* to the oarswoman to survive and bridge-build while adrift—to remake culture with only the tools and language of her culture. It's a lot easier to rebuild when the things around you show up as things you can rebuild with, as tools ready to hand that can be used in the creative deployment of a new narrative. So the trick here is to appreciate the incredible difficulty one might face when one's position as a legitimate interpreter of culture is prematurely dismissed (at the interpretive level) when, owing to hermeneutic violence, one is not seen as having the right be out at sea in the first place—to appreciate the kinds of hurdles and double binds feminist anticolonial and decolonial work involves when one lacks access to privileged speaking positions at the same time that one is put in the material position to urgently communicate one's experiences as a matter of personal and communal survival.

Too often, whether reeling from state-sponsored lexicons of terror or traversing the epistemic land mines of sexist racism in daily life, we are forced to reconfigure survival. To coordinate our bodies across disjunctive times and opaque spaces in ways unsupported by the dominant cultural resources of meaning-making and interpretation. This is not an accidental harm. The relation between self and world, language and disclosure *is not symmetrically given to all in the postcolonial world*, so that our deepest social epistemologies are metaphilosophically compromised.

And yet. The thing about the lived body, the blood-soaked limen of our experience as gendered and raced beings bodying forth cloaked in the intricately woven language of culture, is that, existentially, the urgency is never without. We always begin where we are, in the grips of webbed circumstances and culturally proscribed meanings that lift our voices one way where we perhaps wanted to go another, even without knowing it. In that context, memory-work and making sense of experience is hard enough, for anyone. Much more for some, yes, and that is what motivates so much of this project—to give weight to the idea that hermeneutic happenings, disclosures, and disappearances *remain rooted in deeply value-laden colonialist frameworks that are based on deep violence, and that our conceptions of violence are tied to these hermeneutic limitations.* Violence never emerges as a solitary phenomenon, but is held up by a wider system of interpretive disarmaments and armaments that prefigure its emergence in culture. The first step, one of many, is to then pierce cracks in the Western dialectic of erasure that now resides under the banner of philosophy and legitimate knowledge, which exercise control over what counts as harms and violence.

We are living in a time when the burden of proof for demonstrating the existence of complex and intersectional harms against women of color is laid upon our own ability to give an account of those harms in a language those in power can always already understand. Not only is this a harmful epistemic situation, it is structured by the fact that the interpretive resources required to do justice to that task are also hermeneutically compromised, I repeat, in a nonaccidental way. In turn, our experience must conform somehow to interpretive systems that pre-predicatively discount many features of our experiences, yielding a kind of existential self-harm by design. We sense that the ability to bear witness and testify to lived experience in a language capable of capturing this background violence is at the epicenter of claiming knowledge over our own lives: it's not me, you sense. This language thing is rigged. And yet, this is nothing new. The struggle is real because so much of it is not acknowledged as being so, because it's a hard-won self-authoring lexical skill to combat the pain that comes with living through experiences that are not acknowledgeable in official discourses. We develop alphabets of survival not only to look forward, but to reimagine a past that was not imaginable to begin with. Our lives survive on parallel tracks. This is because if we've tracked the concept correctly, hermeneutic violence makes sense of violence through the sense-making instituted by hermeneutic violence. Such realization can act as a paralytic to our liberation, hooking its epistemic dependencies on cultural recursion itself. It is, at day's end, the classical argumentative strategy of orthodox hermeneutists to trap one in a hermeneutic circle of interpretive production, a kind of performative contradiction that highlights the explanatory power of the human hermeneutic situation and the conditions for worldly meaning it discloses. It seems like an impossible bind to escape. That is, until you have to live it.

Making sense of our lives in more just ways requires interpretive frameworks that re-envision the relationship between self and culture through a different archaeology of know-how.

Women of color and Indigenous women face complex webs of intersectional harms and injuries that are difficult to pinpoint and remedy given the limitations of Western political theories of harm and injury. Often, women's experiences of violence are disaggregated to fit a disciplinary typology of violence that, while critical to the eradication of one (possibly mortal) harm, helps perpetuate the continuation of generations of gender-based violences as culturally acceptable phenomena. On the long view, the mortality is the same. We can do better. We must do better. And theory alone cannot get us there. While hermeneutic violence can help diagnose the existence of deep harms and traumas to our interpretive systems (and thus partly mitigate the effects of structural gaslighting in, for example, cross-cultural negotiations and human rights instruments), it can't help one actually live, breathe air that isn't toxic, or enact the daily creative continuance of oppressed peoples and communities. For this, we need an ontology that can be lived, articulated in the flesh without fear of slippage, breaks or contradiction, yet without promoting a metaphysics based on fixity and essences (see Ortega 2001; Lugones 2003). We need a third critical space, an in-between to violence and survival, and we cannot be dogmatic in our methodologies to achieve this. Between disclosure and disappearance, the struggle demands an open stance. As the Guatemalan poet Alenka Bermudez (2003) writes:

> I reserve the right of the precisely exact
> Spanish word
> to name death and to name life
> as long as the blood holds itself suspended
> in our trees.

References

Alarcón, N. (1990) "Chicana Feminism: In the Tracks of 'the' Native Woman," *Cultural Studies* 4 (3): 248–257.
Alarcón, N. (2013) "Anzaldúan Textualities: A Hermeneutic of the Self and the Coyolxauhqui Imperative," in A. Castañeda, L. Mercado-López and S. Saldívar-Hull (eds.), *El Mundo Zurdo 3*, 189–206, San Francisco: Aunt Lute.
Anzaldúa, G. ([1987] 2012) *Borderlands/La Frontera: The New Mestiza* (4th ed.), San Francisco: Aunt Lute Books.
Anzaldúa, G. (2013) "Now Let Us Shift . . . the Path of Conocimiento . . . Inner Work, Public Acts," in A. Keating (ed.), *This Bridge We Call Home: Radical Visions for Transformation*, 540–576, New York: Routledge.
Anzaldúa, G. (2015) *Light in the Dark/Luz En Lo Oscuro: Rewriting Identity, Spirituality, Reality*, Durham, NC: Duke University Press.
Bermudez, A. (2003) "Guatemala, Your Blood," in D. Gioseffi (ed.), *Women on War: An International Anthology of Women's Writings from Antiquity to the Present*, 263, New York: Feminist Press at the City University of New York.
Danticat, E. (2014) *The Farming of Bones*, New York: Soho Press.
Dotson, K. (2011) "Tracking Epistemic Violence, Tracking Practices of Silencing," *Hypatia* 26 (2): 236–257.
Dotson, K. (2012) "A Cautionary Tale: On Limiting Epistemic Oppression." *Frontiers: A Journal of Women Studies* 33 (1): 24–47.
Dotson, K. (2014) "Conceptualizing Epistemic Oppression," *Social Epistemology* 28 (2): 115–138.
Fricker, M. (2007) *Epistemic Injustice: Power and the Ethics of Knowing*, Oxford: Oxford University Press.
Hierro, G. (1985) *Ética y feminismo, México*, Mexico City: Universidad Nacional Autónoma de México.
Hierro, G. (1994) "Gender and Power," *Hypatia* 9 (1): 173–183.
Humanitarian News. (2016) "Brazil's Rousseff Vetoes Indigenous Education Project," February 17, http://humanitariannews.org/20160217/brazil-s-rousseff-vetoes-indigenous-education-project.
Lugones, M. (2003) *Pilgrimages/Peregrinajes: Theorizing Coalition Against Multiple Oppressions*. Lanham, MD: Rowman & Littlefield.
Medina, J. (2012) "Hermeneutical Injustice and Polyphonic Contextualism: Social Silences and Shared Hermeneutical Responsibilities," *Social Epistemology* 26 (2): 201–220.
Medina, J. (2013) *The Epistemology of Resistance: Gender and Racial Oppression, Epistemic Injustice, and Resistant Imaginations*, New York: Oxford University Press.
Ortega, M. (2001) "'New Mestizas,' '"World"-Travelers,' and 'Dasein': Phenomenology and the Multi-voiced, Multi-cultural Self," *Hypatia* 16 (3): 1–29.
Ortega, M. (2006) "Being Lovingly, Knowingly Ignorant: White Feminism and Women of Color," *Hypatia* 21 (3): 56–74.
Pitts, A. J. (2016) "Gloria E. Anzaldúa's Autohistoria-teoría as an Epistemology of Self-Knowledge/Ignorance," *Hypatia* 31 (2): 352–369.
Pizarnik, A., and Lozano, O. (ed.) (1990) *Alejandra Pizarnik, 1936–1972: Antología poética*, Cali, Colombia: Fundación para la Investigación y la Cultura.
Pohlhaus, G. (2011) "Wrongful Requests and Strategic Refusals to Understand," in H. Grasswick (ed.), *Feminist Epistemology and Philosophy of Science: Power in Knowledge*, 223–240, New York: Springer.

Pohlhaus, G. (2012) "Relational Knowing and Epistemic Injustice: Toward a Theory of Willful Hermeneutical Ignorance," *Hypatia* 27 (4): 715–735.
Purcell-Gates, V. (2000) *Now We Read, We See, We Speak: Portrait of Literacy Development in an Adult Freirean-Based Class*, New York: Routledge.
Richard, N. (2004) *The Insubordination of Signs: Political Change, Cultural Transformation, and Poetics of the Crisis*, Durham, NC: Duke University Press.
Ruíz, E. (2006) "How to Hear the Unspoken: Engaging Cross-Cultural Communication through the Latin American Testimonial Narrative," M.L.S. thesis, University of South Florida.
Ruíz, E. (2018) "The Hermeneutics of Mexican-American Political Philosophy," *Inter-American Journal of Philosophy* 9 (2): 45057.
Schutte, O. (1998) "Cultural Alterity: Cross-Cultural Communication and Feminist Theory in North-South Contexts," *Hypatia* 13 (2): 53–72.
Schutte, O. (2002) "Indigenous Issues and the Ethics of Dialogue in LatCrit Theory," *Rutgers Law Review* 54: 1021–1029.
Spivak, G. C. (1988) "Can the Subaltern Speak?" in C. Nelson and L. Grossberg (eds.), *Marxism and the Interpretation of Culture*, 271–313, Urbana: University of Illinois Press.
Spivak, G. C. (1998) "The Politics of Translation," in G. Rajan and J. Munns, *Cultural Studies Reader: History, Theory, Practice*, 95–118, London: Longman.

Notes

1 For influential sources and contemporary work that address the issue of epistemic violence in women-of-color feminist philosophy see Spivak (1988; 1998), Anzaldúa (2012), Schutte (1998), Ortega (2006), Dotson (2011; 2014); for work in feminist social epistemology that also engages epistemic violence with a more direct focus on the epistemic injustice literature see Pohlhaus (2011, 2012), Medina (2012, 2013), Dotson (2012).

2 Hierro herself did not propose a framework for an ontological foundation of feminist liberation in Latina America. As a thinker, Hierro rejected large-scale theorizing that moved ethics away from the embodied situation of women in Latin American (and Mexican women in particular). Her work did, however, pose important questions for developing what she saw as deeper, long-term structural solutions to women's persistent ideological domestication in education, to the "mala educación" used to perpetuate women's subservience to patriarchal domination, in part, by erasing powerful feminist genealogies from history. She sought to prepare the groundwork for the "conditions necessary for feminist revolutions," especially in sexuality and erotic life (1985: 113, my translation). It is this structural aspect of her work that has been influential in this project.

3 This view is typically traced back to post-Kantian philosophical traditions that critique the account of meaning and subjectivity generated by transcendental consciousness and the paradigm of pure reason (especially through the work of German thinkers like Wilhelm Dilthey, Martin Heidegger, and Hans-Georg Gadamer, but is also present in the works of Friedrich Nietzsche, Michel Foucault, Merleau-Ponty, Paul Ricoeur, Georgia Warnke, and Charles Taylor). While each thinker places a different emphasis on hermeneutical understanding (for example, on textual interpretation and translation, on the lived experience of the hermeneutical subject, the politics of the production of knowing subjects in hermeneutical contexts, or the ontological foundation for the interpretation of meaning), the account generated by Heidegger, Gadamer, and Taylor is unfortunately centered in contemporary philosophical discussions of hermeneutics (Ruíz 2018). While I strongly favor the accounts of meaning formation and interpretation found in Nietzsche's early works, Indigenous social theory, and in Gloria Anzaldúa's ([1987] 2012) *Borderlands/La Frontera*, I make critical, provisional, and strategic use of the traditional paradigm here.

4 I am indebted to the work of Ofelia Schutte for the guiding contours of the ideas presented here. In particular, she has produced powerful accounts of the ways women of color and Indigenous women bear out the consequences of their hermeneutically subordinated speaking positions through culturally produced asymmetries and positions of what she calls "cultural alterity" (Schutte 1998). See also Schutte (2002). To be clear, the idea of hermeneutic violence was developed self-consciously outside the rising "epistemic injustice" literature in the early 2000s, turning instead to feminist interpretations of the testimonio and cultural imperialism in interpretation debate in Latin American literature (see Ruíz 2006). Fricker's (2007) work was available, but needed extensive decolonization to prove useful to my interests.

5 The picture of hermeneutic violence would not be complete without a self-conscious nod to its own conceptual captivity in systems of domination. In fact, the idea is conceptually indebted to many of the interpretive dilemmas that arose in the Western philosophical tradition following German Romanticism and its rejection of the objective, naturalistic outlook of the so-called hard sciences (naturwissenschaften), limiting its normative reach in anticolonial thinking. This is why it is a strategic concept, meant to be deployed where useful and retired thereafter.
6 Emphasis added. She is referencing Anzaldúa.
7 See especially Medina 2013 for an expansive account of epistemic resistance.
8 She is specifically referencing aesthetic interventions in this section, and Chicanx art in particular.
9 It should be noted that Richard points to art and aesthetic narratives of resistance.

Reading Questions

1. How does Ruíz define hermeneutic violence? What is one example of hermeneutic violence discussed in the text?
2. How does hermeneutic violence compare and contrast to other kinds of violence, such as physical violence and emotional violence? In what sense does hermeneutic violence give rise to harms that are "invisible"?
3. What is an epistemicide, according to Ruíz? How does this concept link hermeneutic violence to colonial and neocolonial histories? Provide examples from the text that illustrate this connection.
4. How have women of color developed "alphabets of survival" in response to hermeneutic violence? Provide examples of these survival strategies and discuss their significance.
5. Ruíz claims that violence has been "a productive phenomenon in the lives of women of color," for example by producing a self-understanding as strong and resilient. From this perspective, how might this self-understanding sustain oppressive hermeneutical frameworks? Why or why not?
6. Ruíz critiques the metaphysics of presence in Western political philosophies. In light of her analysis, what might be some problems with making sense of reality primarily in terms of what is present, rather than focusing on what is absent?
7. What does Ruíz mean by a decolonized hermeneutic approach? How does this approach differ from traditional Western hermeneutics?
8. What are the limitations of theorizing about oppression, according to Ruíz? With these limitations in mind, what are some concrete, positive contributions this analysis of hermeneutical violence might make to the struggle for transformative justice?

20 Decolonial Feminist Movidas

A Caribeña (Re)thinks "Privilege," the Wages of Gender, and Building Complex Coalitions

Xhercis Méndez

A Brief Genealogy and Grounding

This essay is titled "A *Caribeña* (Re)thinks 'Privilege,' etc." because I wanted to engage what it means to be a light-skinned Latina who seeks to work against the erasure of my own Afro-descendancy without claiming a history of oppression I did not live. I also wanted to mark my particular location as a queer-identified cisgender Boricua, whose identity has been forged and grounded in Afro-Latinx/Caribbean ways of being and knowing and in relation to black folks (primarily African Americans and Afro-Caribbeans) in the United States. My intention is to work against a pan-Latinidad that bypasses and/or obscures the question of race and the pervasiveness of antiblackness in Latinx communities. Instead I want to be attentive to the assimilationist projects that offer benefits for disidentifying[1] with and from black communities. Indeed, the color-coded arrangement of the United States, where the ability to "pass" can significantly improve access to benefits, more often than not informs the degree to which Latinx communities identify with and/or even associate themselves with black communities. Such assimilationist projects rely on the circulation of narratives that make distancing from and counteridentifying[2] with black communities particularly attractive, thus working against black and brown coalitions.

In my own community the disidentification with and counteridentification from "blackness" is deeply entangled with the efforts to distance themselves/ourselves from narratives that pathologize black folks as "lazy," "ignorant," and "inherently criminal" and which are then (re)deployed in relation to Puerto Rican communities both on the island and on the mainland. These are not excuses for the ways in which antiblackness appears within Latinx communities, but rather an effort to consider how disidentification and counteridentification from the narratives and practices tied to antiblack colonial logics create obstacles to our building complex coalitions, one of the primary motivations behind this essay.

In addition to being attentive to race and antiblackness, my political/coalitional orientation has been deeply informed by my experiences as a cultural broker for my mother, who does not speak English and needed these contributions in order to ensure our survival on the mainland. It has been informed by being an Ame/Rican "citizen" who became aware at an early age of our second-class access to the resources tied to citizenship.[3] My mother and family were often the subject and target of investigation by social service and welfare officials, while Child Protective Services operated like the bogeyman, lurking in corners, always ready to tear our family apart. Police surveilled our community not in order to "protect and serve" but to criminalize. These are the experiences that have made me attentive to particular connections with and to other marginalized communities of color,[4] and that inform my particular brand of women of color[5]/decolonial feminism-in-the-making.

This essay is ambitious in that it seeks to articulate a decolonial feminist methodology that holds all of these complexities in the frame. It is ambitious because it seeks to mobilize gender as a political category of analysis that is inextricable from race, and which works to *identify, denounce,* and *transform* oppressive and (neo)colonial arrangements of bodies and power. Rather than reduce gender to a cross-cultural category of analysis that primarily focuses on the relationship between "Men" and "Women," this essay explores how gender works to entice a series of complicities from racialized folks to and with colonial logics as well as undermine our efforts to organize coalitionally across deep differences.

Decolonial Feminism: A Specific and Local/ized Political Project

This specific thread of decolonial feminism is invested in making more of the *contributions* made by women of color feminists,[6] in particular, the powerful work on and efforts to build complex coalitions across multiple differences (Brown 1992; Crenshaw 1991; Lorde 2007; Anzaldúa 2007). It also seeks to engage the contributions made by *indígena*/indigenous and Afro-Latinx/diasporic feminists resisting (neo)colonial "development" projects and Eurocentric and heterosexist patriarchies within their own local and transnational contexts. Finally, it strategically builds on the politically productive concepts and orientations within the decolonial school of thought primarily coming from Latin American and Caribbean philosophers/thinkers.[7]

For example, the concept of *coloniality* is politically productive for orienting us toward the intergenerational consequences and violences resulting from a history of colonialism (Quijano 2000; Wynter 2003). For our purposes, coloniality can be broadly understood as referring to the colonial arrangements of bodies and power, the logics and practices, ways of being and knowing, and racialized capitalism that were born out of formal colonialism and continue to persist long after formal colonialism has ended. In other words, the coloniality of power, gender, being, and so on, outlives formal colonialism and persists in the structures and institutions that organize the nation states that emerge after "decolonization" regardless of which bodies actually operate those structures and institutions. To decolonize in this formulation refers to the active disrupting of coloniality in its many manifestations, including the ways in which racialized capitalism, and ongoing settler colonialism in the United States, continues to violently impact even the most intimate parts of our lives and relations.

In addition to the concept of coloniality, other orientations from this decolonial school of thought that are productive are the commitment to substantively engaging "non-Western" ways of being and knowing, and an attentiveness to the Eurocentric and universalizing assumptions that travel with many of the mainstream categories researchers and academics use to understand power, oppression, and by extension "liberation and decolonization" in local and transnational contexts. It is with this (re)orientation in mind that the brand of decolonial feminism I am proposing is a self-consciously *local/ized* political project. I am thinking from and with a US context and about women of color in that context, with an eye to the *transnational*.

My resistance to claiming a universal and/or universalizable approach comes from a recognition that the deployment of "gender" as a cross-cultural category of analysis has more often than not distorted and obscured alternative conceptions of being and local modalities of empowerment in transnational contexts (Allen 1986; Oyěwùmí 1997; Mohanty 2003; Wekker 1999, 2006; Méndez 2014a, 2014b). This historical and contemporary tendency has led me to ask, in what ways do racialized folks have to shift how they understand gender in order to identify and activate a communally oriented liberatory politic that does not mimic Western (neo)colonial and settler colonial arrangements of bodies and power?

In response to these questions, I first engage what is useful, suggestive, and politically productive about María Lugones's framing of the "coloniality of gender" and the "modern/colonial gender system" (2007). Second, I expand and further flesh out what I refer to as the *wages of gender*, a concept I developed in an effort to make explicit "gender's" grounding in colonial relations of power and the impact that has on the racialized communities produced as the constitutive outside of gender. Finally, I conclude with five preliminary methodological ingredients[8] and orientations[9] that work to identify and disrupt the coloniality of gender and move us toward complex coalitions. The methodological approach I am proposing proceeds as follows: (1) historicize gender, (2) map out relational power dynamics, (3) track the conditions produced by racialized capitalism that undergird and bolster complicities with the coloniality of gender, (4) produce new social and decolonial visions and imaginaries, and (5) develop and ritualize new lived and embodied practices.

Why We Need to Historicize Gender

In her 2007 article entitled "Heterosexualism and the Modern/Colonial Gender System," Lugones makes the claim that "gender" as we know it was and continues to be a colonial imposition. More intriguing than this particular claim is the relational system of gender she describes. As I have argued elsewhere, Lugones's relational approach to gender remains suggestive precisely because it draws our attention to the ways in which gender and "Women" were (re)defined in relation to enslaved physiognomically distinct laboring bodies, at least within the Americas and the Caribbean (Méndez 2015). As a result, Lugones's effort to begin from a historicized sense of "gender" functions to emphasize the relational process through which gender becomes racialized and a marker of humanity for colonizers. In other words, what you get from Lugones's effort to historicize gender is an attentiveness to the sets of colonial institutions and practices that produce a constitutive outside to gender. Without an understanding of how gender comes to be racialized through such colonial relationships of power we end up with a category of analysis that obscures as much as it claims to reveal.

In order to identify this relational process of racializing gender, Lugones introduces what she refers to as the "modern/colonial gender system," which is organized into "light" and "dark" sides. Within this framework the only bodies with gender are those on the light side. As a result, the gender categories of "Man" and "Woman" not only refer to specific body types, males versus females, but also to the hierarchical, incommensurate, and mutually exclusive arrangement of bodies and power that white bourgeois heterosexual males and females idealized for themselves, as the self-selected representatives of "humanity" (Wynter 2003). We can think of the cult of domesticity as a nineteenth-century American manifestation of this logic at work (Welter 1966; Santiago-Valles 2003). Within this version of a light-side gender arrangement, the category "Woman" exists as "Man's" negation. Thus, if he is of the "mind," she is of the "body"; if he is of the "public," she is relegated to the "private"; if he represents authority, she is banned from having authority, and so on and so forth.

On the "dark side" are the laboring bodies of those enslaved, whose bodies are sexed but not gendered. The reason their bodies are not gendered is because they are legally produced as chattel and because the "sex" of their bodies only matters to the extent to which they serve breeding practices and the purposes of capital accumulation. These are the colonial designs on their bodies, which is what the modern/colonial gender system framework is attempting to track. This framework then highlights how gender is intimately tied to those who are *structurally produced* and recognized as human over and against those structurally produced as a degeneration of humanity, a subhumanity with various degrees of nonhumanness. As a result, the characterizations of those on the dark side as "hypersexual" and "perverse" "animals" whose natures need to be transformed from the inside out should be understood as a racialized vision of the world that serves the purposes and practices of colonialism, settler colonialism, and (neo)colonialism.

In other words, Lugones's modern/colonial gender system delineates a *colonial cosmovision*, in that it centers how colonial actors perceived those they enslaved and colonized. Her description of the modern/colonial gender system does not center what those enslaved and colonized thought of themselves because she is attempting to track the colonial logics being produced. It is with this in mind that I would argue her description of this gender system as organized around a light and dark side should be understood as part of the critique. In my mind it is an indictment, and not a reifying, of a Western (provincial) cosmovision organized around an either/or, binary, and mutually exclusive logic that violently sought to reorganize other cosmosenses and cosmologies along these same lines.

My usage of her framework is with an eye toward tracking some of the intergenerational consequences of gender being racialized through specific colonial institutions and practices and in relation to specific geopolitics. It is not my aim to name and describe a single unified modern/colonial gender system but rather to provide a method for tracking the racialized gender arrangements produced under colonial conditions in a given context.[10] It is for this reason that I also do not understand Lugones as describing a system of gender that we want to identify with and/or be incorporated into. My goal is not to become or transform myself into someone that is recognized as a light-side "Woman" but rather to underscore the violence of that imposition.

In order to get a sense of why this matters for coalitional possibilities, it becomes necessary to highlight some of the colonial trappings of light-side gender and gender arrangements. Within the settler colonies that occupy the geographical space now known as the United States, for instance, there was a relational reduction of white women's worth, in that she mattered to the extent to which she participated in the imperial/colonial project through the contribution of her reproductive capacities. Depending on the location of the colony, anxieties about being outnumbered by racialized others was part of the heightened policing of sexuality and surveilling of white women's wombs. Indeed, the imperial/colonial project demanded that white women's bodies be transformed into instrumental vehicles for the reproduction of "pure" white babies that would later serve to inherit the capital that was violently being accumulated through the extracted land and labor of physiognomically distinct others.

I am aware that her participation in the imperial/colonial project was not always a question of willingness. At times her contributions to the settler colonial project were partially extracted through, for example, the ever-looming threat of impoverishment and/or being indefinitely confined to a lunatic asylum. And yet her profound reduction was also simultaneously ameliorated by the sets of "privileges/benefits"[11] (enticements) that came with being construed as desirable, feminine, passive, and delicate by white bourgeois heterosexual men and relative to racialized females. These forces were simultaneously operative and resulted in these "women" having contradictory desires, at times instrumentally motivated, but significantly acting as both oppressed and oppressor.

As I will illustrate below, the sets of privileges/benefits bestowed upon these white, heterosexual, bourgeois "women" are primarily considered privileges/benefits in relation to those on the dark side, who by comparison are subjected to exponential degrees of violence and abuse. For instance, being considered "too delicate" to work in the field was a privilege, in that it constituted *a special right* and/or *advantage* afforded light-side women in relation to racialized females since it kept them "safe" and their bodies protected and intact from the hard labor of the fields. However, this skewed system functions in a way that makes accessing the benefits tied to light-side gender desirable, such as the protections only available to those deemed recognizably "delicate." It is this exchange rate that I would like to attend to when discussing privilege among differently racialized "women." Indeed, it is this exchange rate, or rather the privileges/benefits that have as part of them colonial designs on our bodies, that I refer to as the *wages of gender* (Méndez 2015). As I will argue, identifying the colonial logics and concomitant practices of relation and arrangements of bodies and power contained in these "privileges" becomes necessary for opening our imaginations to more communally oriented arrangements of bodies and power for women and communities of color.

Identifying the Wages of Gender

The wages of gender track how gender is shaped by colonial relations of power and how it continues to operate as a (neo)colonizing force. Lugones's conception of light-side gender and gender arrangements is useful here because it draws our attention to the relation of power specifically between white bourgeois heterosexual males and females. In other words, gender in her formulation does not claim to be about the relationship of power between all males and all females. Tracking how the wages of gender operate allows us to see how light-side gender and gender arrangements become the model of relation to which we are all expected to aspire, regardless of what we desire and whether or not we have the material conditions to "successfully" inhabit such gender and gender arrangements.

The *wages of gender* can be understood as the *economic, social, political, legal, psychological and affective privileges/benefits one gets for being systematically recognized as an individual who fits into light-side gender and gender arrangements*. It is important to reiterate here that light-side gender does not include all people, but rather emphasizes those who are structurally recognized as "Men" and/or "Women," and for whom this acknowledgment includes a recognition of humanity and a systemically supported freedom. It is not just the privileges we need to track but also *the processes through which one is given benefits for identifying with, aspiring to, and successfully manifesting light-side gender and gender arrangements, regardless of where you fall in the modern/colonial gender system*. For example, contemporary versions of light-side gender and gender arrangements encourage racialized folks to aspire to patriarchal arrangements of power in order to be recognized as proper "Men" and "Women," which include a presumption of heterosexuality and heteronormativity, a nuclear family structure, and a policing of sexuality grounded in an antimiscegenist logic. And yet what constitutes the actual material wages of gender shifts dramatically according to one's location in the modern/colonial gender system.

Indeed, there are differential exchange rates for complicity with light-side gender and gender arrangements. This becomes critical for identifying what is at stake for differently situated women. For instance, the wages of gender for women on the light side have included, but are not limited to, privileges such as patriarchal "protection" from work in the fields, and patriarchal "protection" from the wild dangers of the public sphere as well as a partial empowerment, an often violent exercise of power, over those enslaved/colonized, both male and female (Glymph 2008). The wages of light-side gender have also been produced through antimiscegenation laws. Antimiscegenation laws are part of the structural conditions that made bourgeois heterosexual white "Women" become the "most" sought after and desirable females (sexually as well as for marriage partnerships) within the system, because they were the only females whose wombs were capable of reproducing legally recognized "humans." However, in order to access these privileges white bourgeois heterosexual "Women" had to become passive, submissive, and participate in/be complicit with the colonial/imperial project as well as the conceptions of beauty and the feminine that kept their bodies hostage to white bourgeois heterosexual "Men." Notably, many of these arrangements continue to be produced as desirable. By contrast the wages of gender for females on the dark side have included an altogether different exchange rate. For example, enslaved black "women's" insistence on being identified as "woman" (think: Sojourner Truth's infamous speech) encompasses the hope of being recognized as human and of being freed from the violence of slavery (White 1985). Tied to being identified as "woman" is the possibility of keeping and raising her own children and of being entitled to partial protection under the law, particularly as it relates to systematic sexual assault. These are fundamentally different stakes and wages tied to a colonial process of racializing gender. Juxtaposing the wages of gender in this way makes explicit what is materially at stake when black "women" have named and called out their exclusion from the category "Women" in the effort to access some of the privileges that white, middle-class, heterosexual females have been conditionally afforded. What also becomes clear is how the wages of gender have been racialized through colonial processes, in that white bourgeois heterosexual females have not had to worry about their children being sold or forcibly removed to boarding schools, as has been the case for indigenous communities. It is not just that the stakes for racialized women are materially different but that their claims to "womanhood," even when on light-side terms, are also bound up with their efforts to end profound degrees of violence and its intergenerational impact. However, I want to suggest that the critique that racialized females have been excluded from being recognized as "Women" is not necessarily an expression of a desire to enter into what it is yet another violent system of relations, namely light-side gender arrangements.

The Problem with Deploying Gender "As Is"

We are now in a position to identify some of the conceptual problems with applying "gender" retroactively to racialized bodies in "postcolonial" spaces. The "gender" categories of "Men" and "Women," as are most often deployed, tend to center a descriptive biology (the sexual difference) grounded in a Western, scientific, dual-sexed notion of the body (Laqueur 1990; Butler 1993, 2004; Fausto-Sterling 2000). This matters because within a Western, scientific, dual-sexed model of the human it is possible to conflate sex and gender as synonymous and/or interchangeable categories. However, as illustrated by the preceding historical examples, sex and gender were not structurally synonymous. Gender was a category reserved for those on the light side and the "gender" categories of "Men" and "Women" carried with them an acknowledgment of one's humanity and a systemically supported freedom that was not historically available to those on the dark side—and which continues to be in many ways inaccessible to racialized communities contemporarily.[12] The problem with this approach to gender as a category of cross-cultural analysis is that it has a difficult time accounting for the intergenerational impact of this history (Spelman 1988; Wynter 1990; Scott 1986, 2010). At least within "postcolonial" contexts, gender has to contend with the colonial history that produced alternatively sexed and racialized conceptions of the body.

Another way in which gender as the sexual difference becomes problematic is that it does the work of obscuring non-Western conceptions of the body, such as sacred (re)arrangements of the social (Voeks 1997; Strongman 2002; Wekker 1999, 2006). For instance, a secularized conception of gender built upon a dual-sexed notion of the body makes it difficult to contemplate *the sacred part* of two-spirit folks without unwittingly (mis)translating them into and subsuming them under a *secularized* queer and/or trans categorization (Driskill 2010). This is not to dismiss the power of identifying same-sex loving people across different spaces and times and/or the political significance of forging identities that resist mainstream and normative gender arrangements. However, these categories carry with them a history and sets of assumptions about bodies that politically matter. The problem for racialized folks is that mainstream approaches to gender obscure coeval logics with potentially greater or different liberatory possibilities.[13]

I do not want to do away with the category of gender altogether, but instead want to use it differently. Rather than using it as a way to primarily read sexual difference (think men versus women; queer versus heterosexual), the goal here is to use it as a category that works to *identify, denounce, and transform* light-side gender and gender arrangements that have been violently universalized through colonial institutions and practices, such as slavery, forced migration, and the "re-education"/cultural assaults through boarding schools (Lomawaima 1993; McClintock 1995; Stoler 1995, 2002). Retroactive inclusions into gender only obscure the violence of these histories and their intergenerational consequences. Here the *decolonial feminist movida*[14] would be to instead recognize how the gender terms "Men" and "Women" have been used to primarily refer to those males and females structurally recognized as of value to the settler state, those whose bodies and lives are protected by laws and whole armies are mobilized in their defense. The decolonial feminist *movida* I am suggesting is to use gender, particularly in "postcolonial" contexts, to track the multiplicity of oppressive relations that light-side gender and gender arrangements have produced and to attend to the sets of bodies (the enslaved, or unfree, the globally impoverished) that continue to be sacrificed on its behalf.

For communities of color this means (re)considering how we talk about the light-side gender and the gender arrangements that have been violently universalized so that we do not unwittingly make access and inclusion—particularly to the skewed modern/colonial system of "benefits" (wages of gender) it produces—desirable or even aspirational (Rowley 2010). It also means exploring the extent to which ahistorical incorporations into light-side gender and gender arrangements have moved us toward oppositional sexual politics (versus coalitional) and other oppressive manifestations of light-side gender (think: politics of respectability). These are political concerns because of the ways in which light-side gender and gender arrangements get framed as the only legitimate and legible way of relating and communities of color get pressured *to desire, aspire to, and mimic* those arrangements in order to actualize or give meaning to our struggles, sense of selves, bodies, sexualities, and freedom. This is the coloniality of gender in action.

For example, consider the modern/colonial narratives that claim black males have been denied their rightful place as heads and patriarchs of families by slavery and "emasculating" and/or "castrating" black women. These narratives often result in racialized males calling for a "manning up" over and against their racialized female counterparts as part of a "liberatory," "anticolonial," and "decolonial" agenda. Or consider the modern/colonial narratives framing racialized communities as "hypersexual" and as manifesting deviant sexualities (see Terry and Urla 1995; Findlay 1999; Briggs 2003; Hill Collins 2004). These have often had the effect of producing a politics of respectability that seeks to prove the untruthfulness of the narratives. What I am suggesting is that the counteridentification and strategic distancing from these narratives then forecloses the more liberatory possibility of decentering the colonial gaze and celebrating the sexual diversity that exists in all of our communities and strengthens our collective potential.

The question for me is, how can women of color and decolonial feminists begin to develop narratives and methods that actively denounce, disrupt, and transform the coloniality of gender in its many manifestations? In what ways have we constrained our liberatory possibilities by disidentifying with and counteridentifying from the survival-rich capacities of those relegated to the dark side because they have been framed as pathological in relation to the light side?

Developing a Decolonial Feminist Critique of Gender

To respond to these political concerns, I consider the following ingredients/orientations to be productive for denouncing and transforming the coloniality of gender and for our efforts to *decolonize* our social relationships and coalitional possibilities. Given my account, identifying the coloniality of gender in action demands that we first historicize "gender" from within multiple local histories and bodies. This theoretical shift can keep us from reducing gender to a descriptive biology (i.e., the sexual difference) that obscures the violence of the colonial project and the ways in which those legacies continue to bind us.

Historicizing gender can also open us up to identifying and recognizing coeval and coexisting arrangements of bodies and power that are simultaneously operative in "postcolonial" spaces. For example, in her book entitled *The Invention of Women: Making and African Sense of Western Gender Discourse* (1997), Oyèrónké Oyěwùmí argues that seniority played a significant role in the (re)arranging of bodies and power from within a Yoruban cosmosense in Nigeria. Seniority as a coexisting and simultaneously operative arrangement of the social becomes difficult to contemplate, let alone recognize, under a conception of gender that foregrounds sexual difference. However, historicizing gender can help us identify and mobilize to greater effect some of the more egalitarian social arrangements that have historically existed and that continue to exist within the cosmosenses and cosmologies of those relegated to the dark side.

Second, as demonstrated through the wages of gender, I propose a practice of mapping out relational power dynamics. Mapping out relational power dynamics can trouble facile accounts of power organized around reductive understandings of sexual difference. In so doing, we are able to acknowledge and denounce the oppressive relationship white bourgeois heterosexual "Men" had and continue to have in relation to white bourgeois heterosexual "Women," while also exploring how those oppressive modes of relating were undergirded by the material conditions of those enslaved and colonized. This methodological shift nuances how we approach the feminist goal of undoing "Patriarchy," by calling us to attend to all of the bodies that were sacrificed in order to make the oppressive set of relations on the light side seem relatively more attractive and even "liberatory" by comparison.

One critical result of this decolonial feminist *movida* is that we can use these relational power mappings to get beyond the Oppression Olympics[15] that continue to undermine our efforts to build complex coalitions across our differences. By mapping out the relational power dynamics we are able to see that white bourgeois heterosexual women's complicity and participation in oppressing those on the dark side is what partially sustains the oppressive relationship between those on the light side. What I am suggesting here is that "Women" who disidentify with, counteridentify with, and/or distance themselves from those on the dark side in exchange for the wages of gender are paradoxically in some sense collaborating in maintaining their own oppression. Thus, a myopic focus on individual access to the wages of gender afforded white heterosexual bourgeois "Men" can indeed work to undermine larger goals such as undoing institutionally supported heterosexist racialized patriarchy and decolonizing all of our relationships, including those to the sacred world and to the land.

Third, particularly for communities of color, it becomes necessary to track the conditions produced by racialized capitalism that undergird and bolster complicities with the coloniality of gender. A useful example of this is the 1965 Moynihan Report, which encouraged black males to be complicit in the oppression of black females in exchange for the promise of employment and integration into the mainstream economy. Concerned with the social movements of the time demanding civil rights and racial equality and the anticolonial movements taking place globally, Daniel P. Moynihan, the political scientist and senator, argued that the solution to racial unrest lay in providing black men with the material conditions to return to their "rightful place" as breadwinners, patriarchs, and heads of nuclear families. Moynihan's "assessment" of the black family argued that racial unrest could only be mitigated by providing black men with much-needed employment, in this case by enlisting them in the army, in order to help them correct the "dysfunctional matriarchy" (Spillers 1987) that had taken hold of the black community and had constrained the community's successful assimilation into American society. Moynihan claimed that as long as black women were "doing better" than their male counterparts, racial equality would never be achieved.

Moynihan's pathological framing of the black community was grounded in light-side gender and gender arrangements. His reading of the black community foregrounded an oppositional sexual politics (the "women" are "doing better" than the "men") by arguing that the key to racial equality was mimicking light-side gender and familial arrangements. Moynihan in many ways derailed the conversation on substantive racial equality by sparking debates around black women's "pathological tendency" to undermine black men by refusing to succumb to a patriarchal order and outperforming them in school and employment. In so doing, Moynihan framed black women, and not racialized capitalism, as both the "perpetrator" of harm and the subsequent target.

Rather than move toward an oppositional sexual politics, the decolonial feminist *movida* here would be to seek out economic solutions that foreground the well-being of all those impacted by the conditions of racialized capitalism. How does this oppositional sexual politic actually bolster capitalist exploitation at the expense of the black community? It does so by getting racialized males to focus on *outdoing* women of color (earning more money, getting more jobs, and even actively working to undermine their economic well-being) rather than identifying economic solutions and/or alternatives in which all community members' material needs are met. Ensuring that community members have what they need, and not doubling down on the recuperation of masculinity through a wage battle with and against your racialized female counterpart, is key for any version of collective racial justice. A decolonial feminist approach to "gender" provides a space for us to examine how such economic enticements and complicities both serve capitalist exploitation and undermine collective liberation.

(Re)imagining Decolonial Feminist Futures

Fourth, decolonial feminist futures are not possible for communities of color unless we seek out alternative systems and practices for (re)evaluating our worth. This decolonial feminist turn toward the "future" includes developing new social imaginaries and visions (Paredes 2008). Aspiring to and mimicking light-side gender and gender arrangements will not get us there. This is not a decolonial move, even when it is framed as such. Instead a decolonial feminist asks, what other liberatory possibilities and alternative modes of being and relating are available to us from within the communities relegated to the dark side? And perhaps these too will require creative transformations (Paredes 2008). Rather than primarily critiquing the world we don't want to live in, the (re)orientation I am suggesting includes allocating more time and energy toward imagining and activating the world we do want to live in.

In my own research on Afro-Cuban Santería, this has meant exploring how ritual enactments introduce explicitly non-Western formulations of the body that include *nongendered/ nonracialized* logics, culturally specific modalities of empowerment, and an alternative system of valuation for what it means to be human (Méndez 2014b).[16] Afro-Cuban Santería *in practice* introduces its own formation and brand of power through alternative categories, such as spiritual seniority. Spiritual seniority demands that those who have invested more time in the religion have accumulated greater degrees of spiritual knowledge, and have been recognized as knowledgeable spiritual advisors be given deference as sacred elders. These elders are to be given deference *regardless of body type, sexual preferences, and/or actual age*. Notably, spiritual seniority as a coexisting organizing logic has provided significant avenues for Afro-Cuban women and "queer"-identified folks in the Caribbean to become well-respected and valued leaders both within and beyond spiritual and communal networks.

Methodologically, the sustained engagement with Afro-Cuban Santería has provided me with powerful examples of why we need to be attentive to the assumptions that travel with the categories of analysis we deploy in our feminist research. It has also provided me with tools to decenter the colonial representations and narratives repeatedly mapped onto racialized communities and identify an alternative ground from which to produce possibly decolonial readings of the past in ways that move us toward transformative visions for the future.

Practices such as these can be powerfully suggestive in terms of reimagining systemically devalued beings and bodies, beyond the coloniality of gender. For instance, if we were to reimagine Sojourner Truth through a ritual practice like Santería, a practice that presupposes the full humanity of all its practitioners, what we are empowered to see is that her being included or incorporated into the category "Woman" requires that we (mis)translate her body and experience into the terms of the light side. This incorporation not only distorts the historical violence of gender but can function in ways that are (neo)colonizing. An Afro-diasporic/Latinx conception of the human is suggestive in that Truth's liberatory possibilities are more likely to be found in understandings of humanity and gender that do not depart from or require her relative dehumanization in order to exist.

Finally, transforming the coloniality of gender and decolonizing gender and feminism requires more than critique. Rather, it calls us to create and "ritualize" new everyday lived practices. The engagement with Santería is my effort to engage the very practices that have sustained those who have been systematically targeted for demise. Even though I do not believe that Santería is decolonial or resistant unto itself, it does have something to tell us about alternative systems of valuation that are not reducible to merely surviving in the face of extreme violence. Beyond survival, there are lessons within these practices that remind us that being the target of violence is not synonymous with successfully being transformed into a lesser human being. These ritual practices often include a process of "rebirth," and tend to focus on making bodies sacred and cultivating a sense of one's value, even in the face of systemic violence and violent histories. As a result, Afro-Cuban Santería can habituate the body to refuse a dehumanized conception of self.

If we agree that *El camino se hace al andar*,[17] then decolonizing gender calls us to develop practices that habituate and reorient us toward "moving differently" in the world and in so doing transform what we even think is possible. For those of us who find ourselves suffocated by light-side gender and gender arrangements, producing more critical analysis is not enough. We must also seek to develop practices that actively engage our bodies in the decolonizing process. The call to develop and "ritualize" new everyday lived practices that can rehearse, embody, and habituate us to new forms of socializing, being, and relating acknowledges the extent to which we can be transformed by our embodied experiences of freedom (Abod 2016). Indeed, how can we take back our bodies, and what can and do embodied experiences of freedom look like?

Conclusion: A Call for Theory/Practice That Centers Collective Wellbeings

This approach to gender is about doing theory that is attached to practice and about rethinking gender toward transformative ends. I have argued that colonialism and processes of racialization tied to capitalist accumulation are inextricably linked to how we contemporarily understand gender, sexed bodies, and sexuality. Given how I understand the gender categories to be tied to colonial relations of power and logics, this particular brand and localized version of decolonial feminism-in-the-making is not invested in women of color being retroactively included in the category "Woman" nor being assessed through light-gender or gender arrangements. If we understand gender in this way, then accessing light-side wages of gender means simultaneously being integrated into an arrangement of bodies and power that is equally oppressive and which has little to no decolonial liberatory potential for women of color. Indeed, how we understand gender makes a difference not only for how we frame our contemporary relations, but also for what we will consider to be the necessary ingredients for reimagining our various socials in liberatory ways.

In order to address these political concerns, I have proposed these ingredients (a decolonial feminist research practice/approach) as a way to perform different gender analyses and make it more difficult to bypass the concerns of women of color and/or produce these concerns as something additive. At stake in the troubling of privilege is the impact the battle to access the wages of (light-side) gender has on foreclosing our liberatory imaginations, visions, and coalitional goals. It is for these reasons that it becomes important to historicize gender and map out the relational power dynamics; to identify the colonial value system that undergirds capitalist expansion, extraction, imperialism, and exploitation and naturalizes a multiplicity of oppressive relations; to produce new decolonial social imaginaries and visions while also creating and ritualizing new everyday lived practices. I offer these methodological ingredients as a way to disrupt the weight and space Eurocentric frames of reference have occupied in shaping how we come to understand ourselves, our bodies, and the worlds around us. My hope is to carve out a space from which to radically (re)imagine and embody decolonial modes of being, knowing, and relating that center our collective and communal well-beings.[18]

References

Abod, J. (2016) *The Passionate Pursuits of Angela Bowen*. Documentary film, Women Make Movies.
Alexander, M. J. (2005) *Pedagogies of Crossing: Meditations on Feminism, Sexual Politics, Memory, and the Sacred*, Durham, NC: Duke University Press.

Alexander, M. (2011) *The New Jim Crow: Mass Incarceration in the Age of Colorblindness*, New York: New Press.
Allen, P. G. (1986) *The Sacred Hoop: Recovering the Feminine in American Indian Traditions*, Boston: Beacon Press.
Anzaldúa, G. (2007) *Borderlands/La Frontera: The New Mestiza* (3rd ed.), San Francisco: Aunt Lute Books.
Briggs, L. (2003) *Reproducing Empire: Race, Sex, Science, and US Imperialism in Puerto Rico*, Berkeley: University of California Press.
Brown, E. B. (1992) "'What Has Happened Here': The Politics of Difference in Women's History and Feminist Politics," *Feminist Studies* 18 (2): 295–312.
Butler, J. (1993) *Bodies That Matter: On the Discursive Limits of "Sex"*, New York: Routledge.
Butler, J. (2004) *Undoing Gender*, New York: Routledge.
Collins, P. H. (2004) *Black Sexual Politics: African Americans, Gender, and the New Racism*, New York: Routledge.
Crenshaw, K. W. (1991) "Mapping the Margins: Intersectionality, Identity Politics, and Violence against Women of Color," *Stanford Law Review* 43 (6): 1241–1299.
Crenshaw, K. W. (2014) "The Girls Obama Forgot: My Brother's Keeper Ignores Young Black Women," *New York Times*, July 29.
Crenshaw, K. et al. (2015) *Say Her Name: Resisting Police Brutality against Black Women*, New York: African American Policy Forum.
Driskill, Q.-L. (2010) "Doubleweaving Two-Spirit Critiques: Building Alliances between Native and Queer Studies," *GLQ: A Journal of Lesbian and Gay Studies* 16 (1–2): 69–92.
Fausto-Sterling, A. (2000) *Sexing the Body: Gender Politics and the Construction of Sexuality*, (1st ed.), New York: Basic Books.
Findlay, E. (1999) *Imposing Decency: The Politics of Sexuality and Race in Puerto Rico, 1870–1920*, Durham, NC: Duke University Press.
Garza, A. (2014) "A Herstory of the #blacklivesmatter Movement," *Feminist Wire*, October 7, www.thefeministwire.com/2014/10/blacklivesmatter-2.
Glymph, T. (2008) *Out of the House of Bondage: The Transformation of the Plantation Household*, New York: Cambridge University Press.
Imarisha, W., and Brown, A. M. (2015) *Octavia's Brood: Science Fiction Stories from Social Justice Movements*, Oakland: AK Press.
Laqueur, T. W. (1990) *Making Sex: Body and Gender from the Greeks to Freud*, Cambridge, MA: Harvard University Press.
Lomawaima, K. T. (1993) "Domesticity in the Federal Indian Schools: The Power of Authority over Mind and Body," *American Ethnologist* 20 (2): 227–240.
Lorde, A. (2007) *Sister Outsider: Essays and Speeches*, Berkeley, CA: Crossing Press.
Lugones, M. (2007) "Heterosexualism and the Colonial/Modern Gender System," *Hypatia* 22 (1): 186–209.
Martinez, E. (1993) "Beyond Black/White: The Racisms of Our Time," *Social Justice* 20 (1–2): 22–34.
McClintock, A. (1995) *Imperial Leather: Race, Gender and Sexuality in the Colonial Contest*, New York: Routledge.
Medina, J. (2003) "Identity Trouble: Disidentification and the Problem of Difference," *Philosophy & Social Criticism* 29 (6): 655–680.
Méndez, X. (2014a) "An Other Humanity: (Re)constituting Gender, Bodies, and the Social from within Afro-Cuban Santería," PhD dissertation, Binghamton University.
Méndez, X. (2014b) "Transcending Dimorphism: Afro-Cuban Ritual Praxis and the Rematerialization of the Body," *Journal for Cultural and Religious Theory* 13 (1): 101–121.
Méndez, X. (2015) "Notes toward a Decolonial Feminist Methodology: The Race/Gender Matrix Revisited," *Trans-Scripts* 5: 41–59.
Mohanty, C. T. (2003) *Feminism without Borders: Decolonizing Theory, Practicing Solidarity*, Durham, NC: Duke University Press.
Moynihan, D. P. (1965) "The Negro Family: The Case for National Action," *United States Department of Labor*, March, www.dol.gov/oasam/programs/history/webid-meynihan.htm.
Muñoz, J. E. (1999) *Disidentifications: Queers of Color and the Performance of Politics*, Minneapolis: University of Minnesota Press.
Oyěwùmí, O. (1997) *The Invention of Women: Making an African Sense of Western Gender Discourses*, Minneapolis: University of Minnesota Press.

Paredes, J. (2008) *Hilando Fino: Desde el feminismo comunitario*, La Paz, Bolivia: Comunidad Mujeres Creando Comunidad.
Quijano, A. (2000) "Coloniality of Power, Eurocentrism, and Latin America," *Nepantla: Views From South* 1 (3): 533–580.
Rowley, M. V. (2010) "Whose Time Is It? Gender and Humanism in Contemporary Caribbean Feminist Advocacy," *Small Axe* 14 (1): 1–15.
Santiago-Valles, K. A. (2003) "'Race,' Labor, 'Women's Proper Place,' and the Birth of Nations: Notes on Historicizing the Coloniality of Power," *CR: The New Centennial Review* 3 (3): 47–69.
Scott, J. W. (1986) "Gender: A Useful Category of Historical Analysis," *American Historical Review* 91 (5): 1053–1075.
Scott, J. W. (2010) "Gender: Still a Useful Category of Analysis?" *Diogenes* 57 (1): 7–14.
Spelman, E. V. (1988) *Inessential Woman: Problems of Exclusion in Feminist Thought*, Boston: Beacon Press.
Spillers, H. J. (1987) "Mama's Baby, Papa's Maybe: An American Grammar Book," *Diacritics* 17: 64–81.
Stoler, A. L. (1995) *Race and the Education of Desire: Foucault's History of Sexuality and the Colonial Order of Things*, Durham, NC: Duke University Press.
Stoler, A. L. (2002) *Carnal Knowledge and Imperial Power: Race and the Intimate in Colonial Rule*, Berkeley: University of California Press.
Strongman, R. (2002) "Syncretic Religion and Dissident Sexualities," in A. Cruz-Malav and M. F. Manalansan IV (eds.), *Queer Globalizations: Citizenship and the Afterlife of Colonialism*, 176–195, New York: New York University Press.
Terry, J., and Urla, J. L. (eds.) (1995) *Deviant Bodies: Critical Perspectives on Difference in Science and Popular Culture*, Bloomington: Indiana University Press.
Tuck, E. (2016) "Urban Education and Indigenous Social Thought," Presentation: Michigan State University.
Tuck, E., and Wayne Yang, K. (2012) "Decolonization Is Not a Metaphor," *Decolonization: Indigeneity, Education & Society* 1 (1): 1–40.
Voeks, R. A. (1997) *Sacred Leaves of Candomblé: African Magic, Medicine, and Religion in Brazil* (1st ed.), Austin: University of Texas Press.
Wekker, G. (1999) "'What's Identity Got to Do with It?': Rethinking Identity in Light of the Mati Work in Suriname," in E. Blackwood and S. E. Wieringa (eds.), *Female Desires: Same-Sex Relations and Transgender Practices across Cultures*, 119–38, New York: Columbia University Press.
Wekker, G. (2006) *The Politics of Passion: Women's Sexual Culture in the Afro-Surinamese Diaspora*, New York: Columbia University Press.
Welter, B. (1966) "The Cult of True Womanhood: 1820–1860," *American Quarterly* 18 (2): 151–174.
White, D. G. (1985) *Ar'n't I a Woman? Female Slaves in the Plantation South*. New York: Norton.
Wynter, S. (1990) "Afterword: Beyond Miranda's Meanings: Un/silencing the 'Demonic Ground' of Caliban's 'Woman'," in C. Boyce Davies and E. Savory Fido (eds.), *Out of the Kumbla: Caribbean Women and Literature*, 355–373, Trenton, NJ: Africa World Press.
Wynter, S. (2003) "Unsettling the Coloniality of Being/Power/Truth/Freedom: Towards the Human, after Man, Its Overrepresentation—an Argument," *CR: New Centennial Review* 3 (3): 257–337.

Notes

1 One of the differences between my usage and Jose Esteban Muñoz's conception of disidentification in this example is the directionality of the disidentifications we are concerned with. I am concerned with the political consequences of "white" folks as well as communities of color distancing themselves from racialized, impoverished, and marginalized communities in their moves to aspire to and mimic a white heterosexual upper-middle-class ideal. Muñoz is focused on the political possibilities of "minoritarian" communities, i.e., communities of color, finding ways to dissociate themselves from that very ideal of white heterosexual normativity. When mobilized in this direction, away from the ideal, Muñoz argues, and I agree, that this form of disidentification becomes a powerful resistant strategy. See Muñoz (1999).

2 Counteridentifying here refers to a process that foregrounds difference in a way that is oppositional. See Medina 2003. Such counteridentifications can include not only an impulse to dissociate from a given group but also how perceived differences can be construed as mutually exclusive, thus motivating actions that can work to undermine and devalue the group from which one is counteridentifying with and from.

3 "Citizenship" as a "liberatory" project is undermined by, for instance, the lack of federal assistance to Puerto Rico after Hurricane Maria and by the ways in which it is grounded in the settler colonial logic and organization of space, land, etc. Efforts to access the "benefits" tied to "citizenship" is incommensurate with the claims from indigenous communities regarding the "constant state of land theft that is consistently disavowed" in the United States. See Tuck and Yang (2012) and Tuck (2016).

4 These are some of the affinities I have with and to Latinx immigrant populations and their second-generation children and to African American, Pacific Islander, and Chicano populations in the United States that have been subjected to parallel racialized circumstances.

5 "Women of color" does not simply refer to any and all racialized women. While in its mainstream usage it tends to refer to cisgender women who have been racialized through colonial processes, as both non-"white" and non-"European," I am using it as a reference to racialized females who also explicitly seek to build complex coalitions to and with one another. This includes a commitment to learning each other's histories and contending with our differences both within and outside of the groups with whom we identify (Alexander 2005; Lorde 2007).

6 I am creatively building with multiple genealogies of decolonial feminist thought, methods, and politics.

7 Noting this particular genealogy does not make my usage of the terminology associated with it mutually exclusive with how others have previously used the term "decolonial" and/or how others are working to build "decolonial/ized" futures.

8 I use the word "ingredients" here purposefully. Different from "component," "ingredient" carries with it other layers of meaning that are important for this work. Ingredient conjures up the idea of cooking, an activity that is often correlated to female bodies and includes creatively bringing very different things together in order to create something new (a meal) that both contributes to life and is life-sustaining. The correlation to female bodies is historically produced, and my bringing it to bear here is about refusing to ignore the labor and contributions that females make to social reproduction. Moreover, the ingredients of any recipe are open and creatively tweaked to suit different needs, e.g., allergies, food restrictions, etc. I propose these steps as ingredients because they will be adjusted depending on the specificity of local and historical contexts. Finally, different from the word component, "ingredient" also carries with it the idea of "walking into" or "entering" something, perhaps a journey, together. The term functions as an invitation to create a new path and world together.

9 I am also using the word "orientation" here to explicitly conjure up another set of intentions. This methodology seeks to foreground relation, including how we position ourselves in relation to each other, the work, our communities and/or the folks with whom we want to think with. Orientation marks a position and location. It can also refer to the process of getting familiar with something new, for instance, as in an introduction into a different way of approaching and deploying gender as a category of analysis.

10 For example, the Spanish modern/colonial gender system, in terms of who counts as "Man," "Woman," and ultimately "Human," may have differed from that of the Portuguese. Understanding that this is not a unified system makes evident that different colonial practices produce different types of relations. However, I would argue that whatever the modern/colonial gender system is in a given context, there are colonial arrangements of bodies and power that continue to negatively impact racialized males and females.

11 Because I am troubling how we think privilege, for the remainder of the text the term "privilege" is to be considered bracketed.

12 See Alexander's (2011) *The New Jim Crow: Mass Incarceration in the Age of Colorblindness*. Her book illustrates in detail how racial discrimination in the American legal system is allowed to operate openly and freely as long as race-neutral language is used to bypass accountability. The Black Lives Matter movement (Garza 2014) and projects like Say Her Name (Crenshaw et al. 2015) are also organized efforts to illustrate the extent to which black communities in the United States continue to be targeted for demise with impunity. Other examples include the pattern of criminalizing Latinx communities through immigration and gang policies and Muslim communities through the war on terror.

13 For other accounts of non-western arrangements of the social see also Wekker (1999; 2006) and Allen (1986).

14 The term movida has multiple valences in Spanish that I want to bring to bear. It can refer to movement, not just in terms of a specified action (moves) but also in terms of a movement that

can be organized (a protest, series of protests) that has larger social cultural implications. Thinking ahead, we can ask, what would a decolonial feminist movement look like? What constitutes its politics? Movida can also carry with it the idea of un revolú, a Puerto Rican term used to refer to a situation that can be confusing and difficult to resolve, in the sense that there is a messy situation that we must deal with. The coalitions I am interested in are messy in that sense. On a more creative and productive note, it can also refer to spaces where things are "happening," and where potentially intimate shifts can happen, as in the space of nightlife. I am specifically thinking about the kinds of happenings that take place in queer nightlife, in that it is both happening (as in "this is the place to be") and happening as in there are cultural/political shifts and openings that take place through participation in and with these spaces.

15 Oppression Olympics refers to the practice of determining who is the "most oppressed" by creating hierarchies of disadvantages between and among differently marginalized communities, thus making it difficult to collectively organize. My approach explores some of the complicated ways in which we are simultaneously oppressed and oppressing. See Martinez (1993).

16 This is not the only site from which decolonial possibilities can be imagined. Science fiction and Afro-futurism are other sites where decolonial imaginaries have been and continue to be made possible. *Octavia's Brood: Science Fiction Stories from Social Justice Movements* (2015) is an example of how activists are using Octavia Butler's work to think about social movements and developing liberatory imaginations. Others who have been productively inspired by the move to take up a feminist Afrofuturism can be found at https://nolawildseeds.org/manifesta/ and http://octaviabutlerlegacy.com.

17 This saying, commonly heard in hispanophone contexts, literally translates into "The path is made by walking." The refrain serves as a reminder that the path toward something different will not be "ready-made" or even clear. It instead suggests that the path becomes a path because we choose to move in a direction. Moreover, it is a reminder that there will be emergent conditions and concerns that arise as we "walk," conditions and concerns that we cannot know at the outset. It useful for thinking about how a decolonial feminist politics will have to be open to creatively adjusting and responding to emergent conditions and concerns as they arise and as we move toward something new.

18 I would like to extend my sincerest gratitude to the following people whose critical questions and engaged dialogue made these reflections possible: Ganessa James, Mia Mingus, Kristie Dotson, Nikolay Karkov, Mariana Ortega, José Medina, and Andrea J. Pitts.

Reading Questions

1. What are the "wages of gender," according to the text?
2. What is illuminated when we think about the benefits of participating in dominant conceptions of sex/gender in terms of the economic metaphor of "wages," rather than as "privileges"? What is one possible limitation of this metaphor, in your view?
3. How do assimilationist projects impact solidarity between Latinx and Black communities, according to Méndez?
4. Why does Méndez describe her proposed methods as "movidas" or "moves" (as in the moves a player can make in a game)? How does her approach to politics relate to the common Latin American saying, "*El camino se hace al andar*"?
5. Méndez describes her decolonial methodology as follows: "(1) historicize gender, (2) map out relational power dynamics, (3) track the conditions produced by racialized capitalism that undergird and bolster complicities with the coloniality of gender, (4) produce new social and decolonial visions and imaginaries, and (5) develop and ritualize new lived and embodied practices." Choose an example of gender-based oppression, and describe how you would approach implementing each of these steps.
6. How might ritual be useful for decolonial projects, according to Méndez? Illustrate your view with an example from the text, or from your own life.
7. Méndez calls for theorists to allocate "more time and energy to imagining and activating the world we do want to live in," rather than focusing primarily on critique. With this essay in mind, how might you imagine a better world?

Part 5
Language and Communication

Introduction

It's not uncommon for Latinx people to have a fraught relationship with language. Those who do not speak English well are cut off from most segments of society in the U.S. For example, they are unable to access many jobs, connect with neighbors, or utilize a wide variety of services available to English speakers. They may also be the target of resentment and hostility from those who believe that they ought to assimilate and speak English. Meanwhile, the family members of non-English speaking immigrants—usually their children—are often charged with the heavy responsibility of interpreting for their loved ones. Latinx people who speak English, but do so with a foreign accent or diminished fluency, may find themselves being dismissed, silenced, or taken less seriously. Some Latinx people might be able to speak totally comprehensible English, but because of their community's dialect or accent, they are assumed to be uneducated, unintelligent, or low-class. For some native English speaking Latinx people, the inability to speak fluent Spanish is a marker of their distance from their Latin American heritage and family members and can be a source of shame or grief.

The texts in this section of the book view these experiences with language as a fruitful point of entry into an inquiry about injustices facing the Latinx community. These texts pose questions such as: How should we decide what is the "proper" way of speaking in each context? Is it just for a society to expect all of its members to learn English? What philosophical positions have informed public discourse about issues related to language and belonging? Has this discourse contributed to harms experienced by Latinx people? In what ways does social inequality manifest in our communicative practices? How do institutions perpetuate the silencing of Latinx voices—and how might such institutions be replaced or reformed?

The texts in this section investigate the sources of the denigration Latinx people have experienced regarding the ways they speak. They explore the idea that this denigration is part of the legacy of colonialist ideologies. From this perspective, privileging certain ways of speaking the English language is an extension of colonialist attitudes about the supposed superiority of Europeans and their right to "civilize" peoples deemed to be inferior. The authors of the next four chapters also identify specific attitudes, practices, and institutions that perpetuate language based oppression, and they propose ways of addressing the problems they identify.

In "How to Tame a Wild Tongue," Gloria Anzaldúa reveals how widespread beliefs and attitudes about language contribute to the oppression of Latinx communities. She argues that a person's language is a central part of their ethnic identity. When linguistic norms imposed by dominant cultures denigrate Chicanos' ways of speaking, they also assert the inferiority of Chicano cultural identities. Anzaldúa draws from her experiences in school, as well as experiences with her mother, with media, and with dominant language speakers,

DOI: 10.4324/9781003385417-31

to illustrate how oppressive norms are conveyed and enforced. Her work has been used to help identify, make sense of, and communicate about the profound impacts of linguistic oppression on speakers of minority languages and dialects.

In response to this form of oppression, Anzaldúa advocates for resistance to linguistic assimilation. After an evocative ode to her own "wild tongue's" inability to be tamed, she celebrates Chicano languages through a discussion of their innovativeness, adaptiveness, and variegation. Finally, Anzaldúa discusses the important role that teachers and producers of media play in supporting Chicanos' ability to experience pride in their linguistic and cultural identities.

Lori Gallegos' essay "The Interpreter's Dilemma" also explores some ways that attitudes about language have impacted Latinx communities. The essay focuses on the experiences of people who have the responsibility of interpreting for their non-English speaking family members. She argues that people belonging to this group are susceptible to a particular type of dilemma. Namely, they must decide whether to act in accordance with their own personal desires, or to acquiesce to their dependent loved one's request to act in a way that the interpreter does not endorse. At stake in this dilemma is the autonomy of the interpreter. To interpret successfully, they must fully invest in the project, even when they do not endorse the behavior they are carrying out. Complicating this picture is the fact that the non-English speaking family member is dependent upon their loved one. As a result, the interpreter may feel pressure to amplify their family member's agency, which is already threatened within a prejudiced society.

Gallegos argues that one reason that the interpreter's dilemma is unjust is that it is part of a larger context of systemic disadvantages that Latinx people face. She argues that the widespread lack of Spanish-language accessibility services in the U.S. contributes to linguistic oppression, not only for immigrants, but also for the family members and loved ones who interpret on their behalf.

The next essay is "Cultural Alterity: Cross-Cultural Communication and Feminist Theory in North-South Contexts." Here, Ofelia Schutte addresses the way prejudices towards Latinxs generate barriers to understanding and make people less likely to recognize Latinas as legitimate producers of knowledge and culture. Part of the problem, Schutte points out, is that culturally different perspectives often resist easy translation into the dominant language. What cannot be perfectly translated is all-too-often dismissed by those in the dominant cultural position as unimportant or as not making sense. Yet, that very content could be transformative of dominant cultural frameworks precisely because it is not already fully represented within it. Schutte's worry is that even well-intentioned feminists from globally dominant regions will harm feminist efforts in the Global South through their inability to see past their own perspectives.

In "Language, Power, and Philosophy," Elizabeth Millán Brusslan turns her attention to the way in which prejudice against the Spanish language generate barriers to appreciating philosophy that is produced in Latin America. Millán Brusslan points out that French, German, and English are taken to be the only significant languages in U.S. academic philosophy. The practice of privileging these languages is based on the oft-repeated narrative that philosophy began in Ancient Greece, progressed in Europe, and has reached its culmination in the United States. A result of this view of philosophy is that the canon excludes many philosophical works, such as those that are written in the Spanish language. The assumption that Spanish is not a philosophical language deprives us of the opportunity to learn from important philosophical voices.

21 How to Tame a Wild Tongue

Gloria Anzaldúa

"We're going to have to control your tongue," the dentist says, pulling out all the metal from my mouth. Silver bits plop and tinkle into the basin. My mouth is a motherlode.

The dentist is cleaning out my roots. I get a whiff of the stench when I gasp. "I can't cap that tooth yet, you're still draining," he says.

"We're going to have to do something about your tongue," I hear the anger rising in his voice. My tongue keeps pushing out the wads of cotton, pushing back the drills, the long thin needles. "I've never seen anything as strong or as stubborn," he says. And I think, how do you tame a wild tongue, train it to be quiet, how do you bridle and saddle it? How do you make it lie down?

"Who is to say that robbing a people of its language is less violent than war?"
—Ray Gwyn Smith

I remember being caught speaking Spanish at recess—that was good for three licks on the knuckles with a sharp ruler. I remember being sent to the corner of the classroom for "talking back" to the Anglo teacher when all I was trying to do was tell her how to pronounce my name. If you want to be American, speak 'American.' If you don't like it, go back to Mexico where you belong.

"I want you to speak English. *Pa' hallar buen trabajo tienes que saber hablar el inglés bien. Qué vale toda tu educación si todavía hablas inglés con un* 'accent,'" my mother would say, mortified that I spoke English like a Mexican. At Pan American University, I, and all Chicano students were required to take two speech classes. Their purpose: to get rid of our accents.

Attacks on one's form of expression with the intent to censor are a violation of the First Amendment. *El Anglo con cara de inocente nos arrancó la lengua.* Wild tongues can't be tamed, they can only be cut out.

Overcoming the Tradition of Silence

Ahogadas, escupimos el oscuro.
Peleando con nuestra propia sombra
el silencio nos sepulta.

En boca cerrada no entran moscas. "Flies don't enter a closed mouth" is a saying I kept hearing when I was a child. *Ser habladora* was to be a gossip and a liar, to talk too much. *Muchachitas bien criadas*, well-bred girls don't answer back. *Es una falta de respeto* to talk back to one's mother or father. I remember one of the sins I'd recite to the priest in the confession box the few times I went to confession: talking back to my mother, *hablar pa' 'tras, repelar. Hocicona, repelona, chismosa*, having a big mouth, questioning, carrying tales are all signs of being *mal criada*. In my culture they are all words that are derogatory if applied to women—I've never heard them applied to men.

The first time I heard two women, a Puerto Rican and a Cuban, say the word "*nosotras*," I was shocked. I had not known the word existed. Chicanas use *nosotros* whether we're male or female. We are robbed of our female being by the masculine plural. Language is a male discourse.

> And our tongues have become dry
> the wilderness has dried out our tongues
> and we have forgotten speech.
>
> —Irena Klepfisz (1986a: 49)

Even our own people, other Spanish speakers *nos quieren poner candados en la boca.* They would hold us back with their bag of *reglas de academia*.

Oyé Como Ladra: El Lenguaje De La Frontera

Quien tiene boca se equivoca.

—Mexican saying

"*Pocho*, cultural traitor, you're speaking the oppressor's language by speaking English, you're ruining the Spanish language," I have been accused by various Latinos and Latinas. Chicano Spanish is considered by the purist and by most Latinos deficient, a mutilation of Spanish.

But Chicano Spanish is a border tongue which developed naturally. Change, *evolución, enriquecimiento de palabras nuevas por invención o adopción* have created variants of Chicano Spanish, *un nuevo lenguaje. Un lenguaje que corresponde a un modo de vivir.* Chicano Spanish is not incorrect, it is a living language.

For a people who are neither Spanish nor live in a country in which Spanish is the first language; for a people who live in a country in which English is the reigning tongue but who are not Anglo; for a people who cannot entirely identify with either standard (formal, Castillian) Spanish nor standard English, what recourse is left to them but to create their own language? A language which they can connect their identity to, one capable of communicating the realities and values true to themselves—a language with terms that are neither *español ni inglés*, but both. We speak a patois, a forked tongue, a variation of two languages.

Chicano Spanish sprang out of the Chicanos' need to identify ourselves as a distinct people. We needed a language with which we could communicate with ourselves, a secret language. For some of us, language is a homeland closer than the Southwest—for many Chicanos today live in the Midwest and the East. And because we are a complex, heterogeneous people, we speak many languages. Some of the languages we speak are:

1. Standard English
2. Working class and slang English
3. Standard Spanish
4. Standard Mexican Spanish
5. North Mexican Spanish dialect
6. Chicano Spanish (Texas, New Mexico, Arizona and California have regional variations)

7. Tex-Mex
8. *Pachuco* (called *caló*)

My "home" tongues are the languages I speak with my sister and brothers, with my friends. They are the last five listed, with 6 and 7 being closest to my heart. From school, the media and job situations, I've picked up standard and working class English. From Mamagrande Locha and from reading Spanish and Mexican literature, I've picked up Standard Spanish and Standard Mexican Spanish. From *los recién llegados*, Mexican immigrants, and *braceros*, I learned the North Mexican dialect. With Mexicans I'll try to speak either Standard Mexican Spanish or the North Mexican dialect. From my parents and Chicanos living in the Valley, I picked up Chicano Texas Spanish, and I speak it with my mom, younger brother (who married a Mexican and who rarely mixes Spanish with English), aunts and older relatives.

With Chicanas from *Nuevo México* or *Arizona* I will speak Chicano Spanish a little, but often they don't understand what I'm saying. With most California Chicanas I speak entirely in English (unless I forget). When I first moved to San Francisco, I'd rattle off something in Spanish, unintentionally embarrassing them. Often it is only with another Chicana *tejana* that I can talk freely.

Words distorted by English are known as anglicisms or *pochismos*. The *pocho* is an anglicized Mexican or American of Mexican origin who speaks Spanish with an accent characteristic of North Americans and who distorts and reconstructs the language according to the influence of English (Ortega 1977: 132). Tex-Mex, or Spanglish, comes most naturally to me. I may switch back and forth from English to Spanish in the same sentence or in the same word. With my sister and my brother Nune and with Chicano *tejano* contemporaries I speak in Tex-Mex.

From kids and people my own age I picked up *Pachuco*. *Pachuco* (the language of the zoot suiters) is a language of rebellion, both against Standard Spanish and Standard English. It is a secret language. Adults of the culture and outsiders cannot understand it. It is made up of slang words from both English and Spanish. *Ruca* means girl or woman, *vato* means guy or dude, *chale* means no, *simón* means yes, *churro* is sure, talk is *periquiar*, *pigionear* means petting, *que gacho* means how nerdy, *ponte águila* means watch out, death is called *la pelona*. Through lack of practice and not having others who can speak it, I've lost most of the *Pachuco* tongue.

Chicano Spanish

Chicanos, after 250 years of Spanish/Anglo colonization have developed significant differences in the Spanish we speak. We collapse two adjacent vowels into a single syllable and sometimes shift the stress in certain words such as *maíz/maiz, cohete/cuete*. We leave our certain consonants when they appear between vowels: *lado/lao, mojado/mojao*. Chicanos from South Texas pronounce *f* as *j* as in *jue (fue)*. Chicanos use "archaisms," words that are no longer in the Spanish language, words that have been evolved out. We say *semos, truje, haiga, ansina*, and *naiden*. We retain the "archaic" *j*, as in *jalar*, that derives from an earlier *h*, (the French *halar* or the Germanic *halon* which was lost to standard Spanish in the 16th century), but which is still found in several regional dialects such as the one spoken in South Texas. (Due to geography, Chicanos from the Valley of South Texas were cut off linguistically from other Spanish speakers. We tend to use words that the Spaniards brought over from Medieval Spain. The majority of the Spanish colonizers in Mexico and the Southwest came from Extremadura—Hernán Cortés was one of them—and Andalucía. Andalucians pronounce *ll* like a *y*, and their *d*'s tend to be absorbed by adjacent vowels: *tirado* becomes *tirao*. They brought *el lenguaje popular, dialectos y regionalismos* [Hernández-Chávez et al. 1975: vii, xvii, 39].)

Chicanos and other Spanish speakers also shift *ll* to *y* and *z* to *s* (Hernández-Chávez et al. 1975: vii, xvii). We leave out initial syllables, saying *tar* for *estar, toy* for *estoy, hora* for *ahora* (*cubanos* and *puertorriqueños* also leave out initial letters of some words). We also leave out the final syllable such as *pa* for *para*. The intervocalic *y*, the *ll* as in tortilla, *ella, botella*, gets replaced by *tortia* or *tortiya, ea, botea*. We add an additional syllable at the beginning of certain words: *atocar* for *tocar, agastar* for *gastar*. Sometimes we'll say *lavaste las vacijas*, other times *lavates* (substituting the *ates* verb endings for the *aste*).

We use anglicisms, words borrowed from English: *bola* from ball, *carpeta* from carpet, *máchina de lavar* (instead of *lavadora*) from washing machine. Tex-Mex argot, created by adding a Spanish sound at the beginning or end of an English word such as *cookiar* for cook, *watchar* for watch, *parkiar* for park, and *rapiar* for rape, is the result of the pressures on Spanish speakers to adapt to English.

We don't use the word *vosotros/as* or its accompanying verb form. We don't say *claro* (to mean yes), *imagínate*, or *me emociona*, unless we picked up Spanish from Latinas, out of a book, or in a classroom. Other Spanish-speaking groups are going through the same, or similar, development in their Spanish.

Linguistic Terrorism

> *Deslenguadas. Somos los del español deficiente.* We are your linguistic nightmare, your linguistic aberration, your linguistic *mestisaje*, the subject of your *burla*. Because we speak with tongues of fire we are culturally crucified. Racially, culturally, and linguistically *somos huérfanos*—we speak an orphan tongue.

Chicanas who grew up speaking Chicano Spanish have internalized the belief that we speak poor Spanish. It is illegitimate, a bastard language. And because we internalize how our language has been used against us by the dominant culture, we use our language differences against each other.

Chicana feminists often skirt around each other with suspicion and hesitation. For the longest time I couldn't figure it out. Then it dawned on me. To be close to another Chicana is like looking into the mirror. We are afraid of what we'll see there. *Pena*, Shame. Low estimation of self. In childhood we are told that our language is wrong. Repeated attacks on our native tongue diminish our sense of self. The attacks continue throughout our lives.

Chicanas feel uncomfortable talking in Spanish to Latinas, afraid of their censure. Their language was not outlawed in their countries. They had a whole lifetime of being immersed in their native tongue; generations, centuries in which Spanish was a first language, taught in school, heard on radio and TV, and read in the newspaper.

If a person, Chicana or Latina, has a low estimation of my native tongue, she also has a low estimation of me. Often with *mexicanas y latinas* we'll speak English as a neutral language. Even among Chicanas we tend to speak English at parties or conferences. Yet, at the same time, we're afraid the other will think we're *agringadas* because we don't speak Chicano Spanish. We oppress each other trying to out-Chicano each other, vying to be the "real" Chicanas, to speak like Chicanos. There is no one Chicano language just as there is no one Chicano experience. A monolingual Chicana whose first language is English or Spanish is just as much a Chicana as one who speaks several variants of Spanish. A Chicana from Michigan or Chicago or Detroit is just as much a Chicana as one from the Southwest. Chicano Spanish is as diverse linguistically as it is regionally.

By the end of this century, Spanish speakers will comprise the biggest minority group in the U.S., a country where students in high schools and colleges are encouraged to take French classes because French is considered more "cultured." But for a language to remain alive it must be used (Klepfisz 1986b: 43). By the end of this century English, and not Spanish, will be the mother tongue of most Chicanos and Latinos.

So, if you want to really hurt me, talk badly about my language. Ethnic identity is twin skin to linguistic identity—I am my language. Until I can take pride in my language, I cannot take pride in myself. Until I can accept as legitimate Chicano Texas Spanish, Tex-Mex and all the other languages I speak, I cannot accept the legitimacy of myself. Until I am free to write bilingually and to switch codes without having always to translate, while I still have to speak English or Spanish when I would rather speak Spanglish, and as long as I have to accommodate the English speakers rather than having them accommodate me, my tongue will be illegitimate.

I will no longer be made to feel ashamed of existing. I will have my voice: Indian, Spanish, white. I will have my serpent's tongue—my woman's voice, my sexual voice, my poet's voice. I will overcome the tradition of silence.

My fingers
move sly against your palm
Like women everywhere, we speak in code

—Melanie Kaye/Kantrowitz (1980: 85)

"Vistas," corridos, y comida: My Native Tongue

In the 1960s, I read my first Chicano novel. It was *City of Night* by John Rechy, a gay Texan, son of a Scottish father and a Mexican mother. For days I walked around in stunned amazement that a Chicano could write and could get published. When I read *I Am Joaquin* (Gonzales 1972) I was surprised to see a bilingual book by a Chicano in print. When I saw poetry written in Tex-Mex for the first time, a feeling of pure joy flashed through me. I felt like we really existed as a people. In 1971, when I started teaching High School English to Chicano students, I tried to supplement the required texts with works by Chicanos, only to be reprimanded and forbidden to do so by the principal. He claimed that I was supposed to teach "American" and English literature. At the risk of being fired, I swore my students to secrecy and slipped in Chicano short stories, poems, a play. In graduate school, while working toward a Ph.D., I had to "argue" with one advisor after the other, semester after semester, before I was allowed to make Chicano literature an area of focus.

Even before I read books by Chicanos or Mexicans, it was the Mexican movies I saw at the drive-in—the Thursday night special of $1.00 a carload—that gave me a sense of belonging. "*Vámonos a las vistas*," my mother would call out and we'd all—grandmother, brothers, sister and cousins—squeeze into the car. We'd wolf down cheese and bologna white bread sandwiches while watching Pedro Infante in melodramatic tear-jerkers like *Nosotros los pobres,* the first "real" Mexican movie (that was not an imitation of European movies). I remember seeing *Cuando los hijos se van* and surmising that all Mexican movies played up the love a mother has for her children and what ungrateful sons and daughters suffer when they are not devoted to their mothers. I remember the singing-type "westerns" of Jorge Negrete and Miquel Aceves Mejía. When watching Mexican movies, I felt a sense of homecoming as well as alienation. People who were to amount to something didn't go to Mexican movies, or *bailes* or tune their radios to *bolero, rancherita,* and *corrido* music.

The whole time I was growing up, there was *norteño* music sometimes called North Mexican border music, or Tex-Mex music, or Chicano music, or *cantina* (bar) music. I grew up listening to *conjuntos,* three- or four-piece bands made up of folk musicians playing guitar, *bajo sexto,* drums and button accordion, which Chicanos had borrowed from the German immigrants who had come to Central Texas and Mexico to farm and build breweries. In the Rio Grande Valley, Steve Jordan and Little Joe Hernández were popular, and Flaco Jiménez was the accordion king. The rhythms of Tex-Mex music are those of the polka, also adapted from the Germans, who in turn had borrowed the polka from the Czechs and Bohemians.

I remember the hot, sultry evenings when *corridos*—songs of love and death on the Texas-Mexican borderlands—reverberated out of cheap amplifiers from the local cantinas and wafted in through my bedroom window.

Corridos first became widely used along the South Texas/Mexican border during the early conflict between Chicanos and Anglos. The *corridos* are usually about Mexican heroes who do valiant deeds against the Anglo oppressors. Pancho Villa's song, "*La cucaracha,*" is the most famous one. *Corridos* of John F. Kennedy and his death are still very popular in the Valley. Older Chicanos remember Lydia Mendoza, one of the great border corrido singers who was called *la Gloria de Tejas*. Her "*El tango negro,*" sung during the Great Depression, made her a singer of the people. The everpresent *corridos* narrated one hundred years of border history, bringing news of events as well as entertaining. These folk musicians and folk songs are our chief cultural myth-makers, and they made our hard lives seem bearable.

I grew up feeling ambivalent about our music. Country-western and rock-and-roll had more status. In the 50s and 60s, for the slightly educated and *agringado* Chicanos, there existed a sense of shame at being caught listening to our music. Yet I couldn't stop my feet from thumping to the music, could not stop humming the words, nor hide from myself the exhilaration I felt when I heard it.

There are more subtle ways that we internalize identification, especially in the forms of images and emotions. For me food and certain smells are tied to my identity, to my homeland. Woodsmoke curling up to an immense blue sky; woodsmoke perfuming my grandmother's clothes, her skin. The stench of cow manure and the yellow patches on the ground; the crack of a .22 rifle and the reek of cordite. Homemade white cheese sizzling in a pan, melting inside a folded *tortilla*. My sister Hilda's hot, spicy *menudo, chile colorado* making it deep red, pieces of *panza* and hominy floating on top. My brother Carito barbequing *fajitas* in the backyard. Even now and 3,000 miles away, I can see my mother spicing the ground beef, pork and venison with *chile*. My mouth salivates at the thought of the hot steaming tamales I would be eating if I were home.

Si Le Preguntas A Mi Mamá, "¿Qué eres?"

"Identity is the essential core of who we are as individuals, the conscious experience of the self inside."
—Kaufman (1984: 68)

Nosotros los Chicanos straddle the borderlands. On one side of us, we are constantly exposed to the Spanish of the Mexicans, on the other side we hear the Anglos' incessant clamoring so that we forget our language. Among ourselves we don't say *nosotros los americanos, o nosotros los españoles, o nosotros los hispanos.* We say *nosotros los mexicanos* (by *mexicanos* we do not mean citizens of Mexico; we do not mean a national identity, but a racial one). We distinguish between *mexicanos del otro lado* and *mexicanos de este lado.* Deep in our hearts we believe that being Mexican has nothing to do with which country one lives in. Being Mexican is a state of soul—not one of mind, not one of citizenship. Neither eagle nor serpent, but both. And like the ocean, neither animal respects borders.

Dime con quien andas y te diré quien eres.
(Tell me who your friends are and I'll tell you who you are.)
—Mexican saying

Si le preguntas a mi mamá, "¿Qué eres?" te dirá, "Soy mexicana." My brothers and sister say the same. I sometimes will answer *"soy mexicana"* and at others will say *"soy Chicana" o "soy tejana."* But I identified as *"Raza"* before I ever identified as *"mexicana"* or *"Chicana."*

As a culture, we call ourselves Spanish when referring to ourselves as a linguistic group and when copping out. It is then that we forget our predominant Indian genes. We are 70–80% Indian (Chávez 1984: 88–90). We call ourselves Hispanic[1] or Spanish-American or Latin American or Latin when linking ourselves to other Spanish-speaking peoples of the Western hemisphere and when copping out. We call ourselves Mexican-American[2] to signify we are neither Mexican nor American, but more the noun "American" than the adjective "Mexican" (and when copping out).

Chicanos and other people of color suffer economically for not acculturating. This voluntary (yet forced) alienation makes for psychological conflict, a kind of dual identity—we don't identify with the Anglo-American cultural values and we don't totally identify with the Mexican cultural values. We are a synergy of two cultures with various degrees of Mexicanness or Angloness. I have so internalized the borderland conflict that sometimes I feel like one cancels out the other and we are zero, nothing, no one. *A veces no soy nada ni nadie. Pero hasta cuando no lo soy, lo soy.*

When not copping out, when we know we are more than nothing, we call ourselves Mexican, referring to race and ancestry; *mestizo* when affirming both our Indian and Spanish (but we hardly ever own our Black ancestry); Chicano when referring to a politically aware people born and/or raised in the U.S.; *Raza* when referring to Chicanos; *tejanos* when we are Chicanos from Texas.

Chicanos did not know we were a people until 1965 when Cesar Chavez and the farmworkers united and *I Am Joaquín* was published and *la Raza Unida* party was formed in Texas. With that recognition, we became a distinct people. Something momentous happened to the Chicano soul—we became aware of our reality and acquired a name and a language (Chicano Spanish) that reflected that reality. Now that we had a name, some of the fragmented pieces began to fall together—who we were, what we were, how we had evolved. We began to get glimpses of what we might eventually become.

Yet the struggle of identities continues, the struggle of borders is our reality still. One day the inner struggle will cease and a true integration take place. In the meantime, *tenémos que hacer la lucha. ¿Quién está protegiendo los ranchos de mi gente? ¿Quién está tratando de cerrar la fisura entre la india y el blanco en nuestra sangre? El Chicano, si, el Chicano que anda como un ladrón en su propia casa.*

Los Chicanos, how patient we seem, how very patient. There is the quiet of the Indian about us.[3] We know how to survive. When other races have given up their tongue, we've kept ours. We know what it is to live under the hammer blow of the dominant *norteamericano* culture. But more than we count the blows, we count the days the weeks the years the centuries the eons until the white laws and commerce and customs will rot in the deserts they've created, lie bleached. *Humildes* yet proud, *quietos* yet wild, *nosotros los mexicanos*—Chicanos will walk by the crumbling ashes as we go about our business. Stubborn, persevering, impenetrable as stone, yet possessing a malleability that renders us unbreakable, we, the *mestizas* and *mestizos*, will remain.

References

Chávez, J. R. (1984) *The Lost Land: The Chicano Images of the Southwest*, Albuquerque, NM: University of New Mexico Press.
Gonzales, R. (1972) *I Am Joaquín/Yo soy Joaquín*, New York: Bantam Books.
Gwyn Smith, R. (n.d.) *Moorland Is Cold Country*, Unpublished book.
Hernández-Chávez, E., Cohen, A. D., and Beltramo, A. F. (1975) *El lenguaje de los chicanos: Regional and Social Characteristics of Language Used by Mexican Americans*, Arlington, VA: Center for Applied Linguistics.
Kaufman, G. (1984) *Shame: The Power of Caring* (2e.), Cambridge, MA: Schenkman Books.
Kaye/Kantrowitz, M. (1980) "Sign," in *We Speak in Code: Poems and Other Writings*, Pittsburgh, PA: Motheroot Publications.
Klepfisz, I. (1986a) "*Di rayze aheym/The Journey Home*," in M. Kaye/Kantrowitz and I. Klepfisz (eds.), *The Tribe of Dina: A Jewish Women's Anthology*, Special Issue no. 29/30. Sinister Wisdom.
Klepfisz, I. (1986b) "Secular Jewish Identity: Yidishkayt in America," in M. Kaye/Kantrowitz and I. Klepfisz (eds.), *The Tribe of Dina: A Jewish Women's Anthology*, *Sinister Wisdom* special issue, no. 29/30.
Ortega, R. C. (1977) *Dialectología del barrio*, H. S. Alwan (trans.), Los Angeles, CA: R. C. Ortega Publisher & Bookseller.

Notes

1 "Hispanic" is derived from *Hispanis* (*España*, a name given to the Iberian Peninsula in ancient times when it was a part of the Roman Empire) and is a term designated by the U.S. government to make it easier to handle us on paper.
2 The Treaty of Guadalupe Hidalgo created the Mexican-American in 1848.
3 Anglos, in order to alleviate their guilt for dispossessing the Chicano, stressed the Spanish part of us and perpetrated the myth of the Spanish Southwest. We have accepted the fiction that we are Hispanic, that is Spanish, in order to accommodate ourselves to the dominant culture and its abhorrence of Indians (Chávez 1984: 88–91).

Reading Questions

1. Why does Anzaldúa catalogue the different varieties of Chicano Spanish?
2. Why would it matter if an idea is expressed in English or Spanish? What's at stake for individuals, communities, or nations?
3. Consider this passage: "Often with mexicanas y latinas we'll speak English as a neutral language. Even among Chicanas we tend to speak English at parties or conferences. Yet, at the same time, we're afraid the other will think we're agringadas because we don't speak Chicano Spanish. We oppress each other trying to out-Chicano each other, vying to be the "real" Chicanas, to speak like

Chicanos. There is no one Chicano language just as there is no one Chicano experience." Does this resonate with you? Why or why not?
4. Re-read the passage in the above question. What is oppressive about the activity of trying to "out-Chicano" someone, according to Anzaldúa?
5. Anzaldúa wants to get people to take Chicano Spanish seriously as a language, and to change societal attitudes about that language and the people who speak it. The way she writes is part of that aim. What else would it take to bring about this sort of revaluation of the language, in your view? Draw on the text to discuss how that might be done.
6. Anzaldúa says that by mexicanos "we do not mean a national identity, but a racial one" (84); and she says she identified as raza before ever identifying as mexicana or Chicana. What does she mean, and how does she explain and justify this view? Why is it race, rather than culture or ethnicity, that plays this role for her?

22 The Interpreter's Dilemma
On the Moral Burden of Consensual Heteronomy

Lori Gallegos

Imagine the following scenario: Jorge wants to get out of a long-term contract that costs more than he can currently comfortably pay. Although the terms of the contract specify that he cannot terminate the contract early, Jorge believes that if one were to argue long enough and with enough people, eventually someone would be willing to cancel it. Jorge does not speak English. His contract is in Ignacia's name, since Ignacia speaks English and is therefore in a better position to handle things like billing and communication. *She* would have to argue for the cancellation of the contract. However, she does not want to, because she finds that behavior to be contemptible. At the same time, Ignacia sympathizes with Jorge and knows that he cannot better his own situation without her help.

In this chapter, I want to focus on dilemmas like the one Ignacia faces and on the ethical costs to interpreters in such cases.[1] Many families in the United States have members who do not speak the dominant language, so situations like the one described above are likely far more common than people realize. The U.S. Census Bureau's 2016 American Community Survey finds that over one-fifth of the U.S. population speaks a language other than English at home, with Spanish being the most common language (40.5 million people). The survey also finds that 8.6 percent of people in the United States—about 27.8 million—are classified as LEP, or "limited English proficient," which means that they read, write, speak, and understand English "less than very well," that is, at a level that does not allow them to communicate effectively with English speakers in a variety of situations (LanguageLine Solutions Team 2017). We might wonder how these millions of non-English speakers manage to get by.

The United States does not have a federally recognized official language, and Title VI of the Civil Rights Act of 1964 requires federal and state government agencies, as well as private companies that receive a certain amount of federal funding, to provide certain services to people in languages other than English (United States Department of Justice 2016). The legislation aims to prohibit discrimination against people based on language or country of origin. Unfortunately, the ideal of equal opportunity expressed in this legislation is far from the reality for most non-English speakers. While it may be possible to obtain service and official documents in Spanish at the DMV, medical centers, schools, and some social service agencies, the process of doing so is often complicated. A notice published in 2000 by the Office of Civil Rights for the U.S. Department of Health and Human Services (OCR) documents its findings about some of the barriers facing non-English speakers:

> LEP persons are often excluded from programs, experience delays or denials of services, or receive care and services based on inaccurate or incomplete information . . . OCR has found that persons who lack proficiency in English frequently are unable to obtain basic

knowledge of how to access various benefits and services for which they are eligible. . . . For example, many intake interviewers and other front line employees who interact with LEP individuals are neither bilingual nor trained in how to properly serve an LEP person. As a result, the LEP applicant all too often is either turned away, forced to wait for substantial periods of time, forced to find his/her own interpreter who often is not qualified to interpret, or forced to make repeated visits to the provider's office until an interpreter is available to assist in conducting the interview.

(Health and Human Services Department 2000)

In effect, these health and social services are not available or accessible at the time that non-English speakers need them—and these are services that are required to be available by federal law. Many more services, businesses, and organizations do not make any effort to be accessible. As a result, many non-English speakers rely on family members for translation and interpretation in a range of settings, including the doctor's office, banks, stores, legal situations, and parent-teacher conferences (Hall and Sham 2007). Without this support, they are effectively excluded from the communities in which they live.

Despite the fact that there is federal legislation prohibiting language-based discrimination, there seems to be a widely held belief that the burden of facilitating communication in the United States should fall on non-English speakers—that *they* should learn English if they hope to participate fully in society. Making English the official language was even part of several Republican presidential candidates' platforms leading up to the 2016 U.S. presidential election (see e.g. Kaplan 2015; Goldmacher 2016; Feeny 2015; "The 2016 Presidential Candidates . . ." 2017). But even those who do not support the United States having an official language often seem to take it for granted that non-English speakers have the responsibility of learning English and should not expect to be accommodated. While this view may be reasonable in some contexts, I aim to show in this chapter that the widespread lack of Spanish-language accessibility services in the United States comes at a *moral cost* for members of the Latinx community.

Specifically, I contend that it is not only non-English speakers who are the target of this oppression. Those who interpret for their non-English-speaking loved ones are also affected, because they suffer from a moral burden as a result of their role as interpreter. As I will show, this moral burden can only be fully appreciated in light of a conception of relational autonomy, which has been a central theme in the moral theoretical work known as care ethics. This body of (primarily feminist) work centers on the moral significance of human relationships and dependencies, such as those relationships where practices of caregiving are involved. In addition, the moral burden is better understood through conceptions of the pragmatics of language and the notion of emotional agency.

I also make the case that this moral burden is an *unjust* moral burden, rather than a *merely circumstantial* burden, which is not a matter of justice. An examination of this burden reveals one way that the marginalization of non-English speakers affects more than just the non-English speakers themselves, rippling throughout the broader Latinx community. Calling upon Marilyn Frye's theory of oppression, I argue that this encumbrance can be seen as a facet of the oppression of the Latinx community.

In the first section of this chapter, I examine several aspects of what I call the *interpreter's dilemma*, which arises when those who interpret for family members face the decision of whether to act in accordance with their own ethical values, principles, and commitments, or to act on behalf of their dependent loved one, whose requests may be inconsistent with the interpreter's values, principles, and commitments. In the second section, I argue that the interpreter's dilemma harms the interpreter because it demands heteronomy—that is, roughly, that the interpreter's will is subject to another's authority. Furthermore, the interpreter must personally invest in their own instrumentalized role in order to carry out their responsibilities effectively. I also discuss the ways in which racism contributes to this dynamic. Lastly, in section three, I show why this moral burden is unjust and can be seen as a facet of the oppression of the Latinx community.

I. The Interpreter's Dilemma

Much of the research on language and culture brokering, or the day-to-day mediation between parties who speak different languages, focuses on assessing the impacts of the practice on children, and falls broadly into two camps. In developmental psychology, one finds an emphasis on the harms suffered by children who are given the role of interpreter. Authors of one study find that "children . . . often feel overburdened in complicated and serious situations, such as when they are required to translate documentation" (Hall and Sham 2007). Another negative outcome is that it can lead to role reversal, where "parents express dependent behaviors and children, in an attempt to meet their parent's needs, acquire nurturing, supportive, and care-giving behaviors" (Ponizovsky et al. 2013). One study obtained data from 182 first- and second-generation Chinese fifteen-year-olds and found that "the children who more frequently acted as interpreters for their parents had poorer psychological health. Frequency of translation was also associated with parent-child conflict, particularly for those who held strong family values" (Hua and Costigan 2012).

Researchers in the field of education, however, have cast language brokering in a more positive light. Marjorie Faulstich Orellana conducted ethnographic fieldwork in three immigrant communities where, she says, most children simply see language brokering as a not-so-burdensome part of everyday life, similar to other ways in which kids are often expected to help their families out (Faulstich Orellana 2009b). Faulstich Orellana also highlights the skills children who interpret and translate develop as a result of the practice.[2] In particular, she argues that the accumulation of experiences of interpreting leads to the cultivation of "an orientation toward and ability to understand the perspectives of people from backgrounds different from one's own, and to adapt behaviors, communicative practices and epistemological stances flexibly in interactions with others" (Faulstich Orellana 2009b). As an educator of children, Faulstich Orellana has designed curricula to help all students cultivate the skills and versatility that interpreters tend to develop.

Faulstich Orellana also considers the relation between language brokers and society, and she emphasizes that language and culture brokers are not simply interpreting *for family members*—they are providing a vital service *to society*. This analysis counters narratives that immigrant children are merely a burden to society, taking from educational and health systems without giving back.[3] Faulstich Orellana makes a case for the value of this largely invisible labor, noting that there is a shocking absence of attention to it in historical accounts of child migrants, memoirs, and fiction about immigrant youth. She also notes that children are often represented as lacking agency in immigration narratives—they are the baggage that is "brought along," "sent for," or "left behind" when parents migrate (Faulstich Orellana 2009a: 15). In sum, Faulstich Orellana challenges the representation of language brokers in the developmental psychology literature and in society as mere victims of immigrant parents who will not learn the language.

In this chapter, I assess the impacts of language brokering in a way that differs from both these approaches. Like Faulstich Orellana, I am interested in acknowledging the agency of this often-ignored group of people, and I also analyze the labor they carry out in terms of a broader social context. However, contrary to Faulstich Orellana's efforts to emphasize the everydayness and innocuousness of interpreting for family members, I argue that the role of interpreter often comes with a moral burden. I do not deny that language brokers often acquire valuable skills as a result of their role. It is important to recognize, however, that people may cultivate skills under conditions that also generate costs to their well-being. For example, a farmworker might harvest turnips with astonishing speed and precision, but it is precisely because they work for a low piece rate that they develop such speed, and it is because the work is dangerous that they learn to work with great precision. At the same time, my goal is not to place blame on non-English-speaking immigrants who depend heavily on family members; it is, rather, to think about the moral burden that interpreters face in terms of how it fits into broader, structural inequalities that affect Latinx people. Further, my hope is that identifying this moral burden will give us an opportunity to think in new ways about the responsibilities that our society has toward immigrant communities.

My analysis of the moral burden faced by interpreters is rooted in the following moral dilemma: On the one hand, the interpreter has a duty to support a dependent family member who wishes for the interpreter to engage in an action on their behalf; on the other hand, the interpreter does not personally endorse the action that they are being asked to engage in.

I call this particular type of conflict the *interpreter's dilemma*. I am not suggesting that it arises in all acts of interpreting, or that all interpreters experience it. Instead, I mean to identify an experience that occurs frequently enough for those who interpret heavily for family members that it is a widely shared and often distinguishing feature of that role. Let's turn to two illustrative examples. You'll remember the first from the beginning of the chapter:

Example 1—Contract: Jorge wants to get out of a long-term contract that costs more than he currently can comfortably pay. Although the terms specify that he cannot terminate the contract early, Jorge believes that if one were to argue long enough and with enough people, eventually someone would be willing to cancel it. Jorge does not speak English. His contract is in Ignacia's name, since Ignacia speaks English and is therefore in a better position to handle things like billing and communication. *She* would have to argue for the cancellation of the contract. However, she does not want to, because she believes that the behavior would be contemptible. At the same time, Ignacia sympathizes with Jorge and knows that he cannot better his own situation without her help.

Example 2—Loan: Jorge wants to start a business and would like to apply for a small-business loan. The local banks do not offer extensive foreign-language services. Jorge turns to Ignacia for help with the process. Ignacia would like to support Jorge's dream of owning a business, but the process of applying for a small-business loan is frustrating and time consuming. It requires detailed and extensive paperwork, evidence collection, as well as interviews and ongoing phone-call negotiations with a loan officer. Jorge may be rejected at one or more banks, and each has its own procedures and documentation requirements, so the process could be lengthy.

In cases like these, the interpreter's autonomy is challenged when we understand autonomy as involving "a person's capacity to act in a way that reveals her sense of what matters to her." As Serene Khader puts it, a person with autonomy "identifies with her chosen courses of action rather than regarding them as instances of mere subjection. . . . She has a sense of what matters to her and attempts to act in a way that reveals this" (2011: 113).

In the contract example, Ignacia's belief that arguing to get out of a contract is morally contemptible reflects the moral standards she has for herself. To carry out this act would be to act contrary to her own values. The act undermines Ignacia's autonomy in the sense that it is inconsistent with what she would choose for herself. It is possible that Ignacia might yet find some way to autonomously reconcile herself to the cost if, for example, she decided that her commitment to considerations of family support would, upon further reflection, have her choose for herself to render assistance to Jorge. My point is that, absent some further reconciliation of this sort, there is a pro tanto cost to autonomy in this sort of case.

Now consider the loan example. In addition to being frustrating and emotionally depleting, going through the loan application process will no doubt compete for time with Ignacia's other commitments. Consider, too, that Jorge may be making requests of Ignacia that may be more or less demanding every week.[4] If Ignacia's own projects, goals, and other commitments make significant demands on her time, it's not difficult to see how acting on Jorge's behalf in this situation could contribute to the long-term undermining of her well-being. Ignacia's desire not to help with the loan application can be understood as a desire to act in ways that are consistent with her own flourishing, and this, too, is an important value.

At the same time, interpreters' responsibilities to their family members also have weight. In relationships of dependency, the person depended upon may experience an obligation to facilitate the dependent's expression of their agency. Both dependency and the distribution of labor among several people are features of many family relationships. Even when these expectations require some self-sacrifice, they may be for the most part fair within the context of a particular relationship (or at least not obviously exploitative). For the interpreter to transgress against those responsibilities might both harm the dependent loved one and the relationship that the interpreter shares with the loved one. Furthermore, insofar as the well-being of the interpreter is dependent on the well-being of the family member, the interpreter, too, will be harmed by their decision not to aid their family member. Love, loyalty, self-interest, and expectations that have emerged within particular relationships all generate compelling reasons to comply with the desires of the family member.

What an interpreter personally endorses can have moral weight when it is a reflection of their moral autonomy. The interpreter's dilemma is not merely that the interpreter is being called to do something they do not want to do. Rather, the dilemma is a potentially weighty *moral* dilemma, because it is a matter of having to choose to act contrary to a significant value or commitment in order to act in accordance with another.

The interpreter's dilemma has similarities to other sorts of dilemmas faced by those in relationships that have a significant element of dependency, such as caregivers and those they care for. People in positions of dependency rely on others for a fuller expression of their agency, but facilitating this agency may come at a significant cost to the person depended upon. The ambiguous moral nature of self-sacrifice has been a central theme in care ethics, a body of theoretical work that centers on the moral significance of human relationships and dependencies. As one philosopher puts it, self-sacrifice in the context of caregiving is "neither mere stupidity nor mere heroism" (van Nistelrooij 2017: 271). Self-sacrifice is an essential moral activity, but also one that can harm the caregiver.

In the case of interpreters, the question of self-sacrifice is likewise ambiguous and cannot be disentangled from power dynamics within the relationship. One thing that makes the case of interpreters distinctive is the intersection of the social identities of the people involved in these situations. This intersectionality gives rise to distinctive challenges that merit attention on their own terms, particularly since these challenges can be invisible to mono-dominant-language speakers. For instance, language brokering is typically a gendered activity (Buriel et al. 1998). Girls and women tend to occupy the role of interpreter within their families and thus bear the moral responsibility—and burdens—of this role. The responsibility for interpreting cannot always be separated from the tendency of many families to exploit women's and girls' labor. These factors often add to the messiness of the situation, making it even more difficult for the interpreter to determine the "right" way to respond to the dilemma. In addition, the job of interpreting often falls to children, and this is significant because of the children's often-total dependence on their parents, their need for their parents' love, their own love and dedication to their parents, and their sense of obligation to meet their parents' demands. Power dynamics outside of the relationship can also exacerbate the interpreter's dilemma. Interpreters may find themselves combating widespread prejudices in order to support their family members' well-being. Racism and its day-to-day manifestations form an important backdrop here. The dependent loved one is regularly at risk of being marginalized, exploited, ignored, mistreated, and having the worst assumed about them because of their ethnic and racial identity. These barriers to the flourishing and agency of the family member add weight to the interpreter's obligation to facilitate the latter's agency. The interpreter might recognize that their advocacy is a kind of resistance to the effects of racism on their loved one.

Illustrating this situation in her ethnographic work, Faulstich Orellana interviewed a fifteen-year-old boy named Josh, who describes helping his father buy a car and realizes that his father was the target of a salesman's prejudice. Josh explains:

> I don't think he really wanted someone to, I don't know, translate or whatever. Maybe like, 'Oh, this person doesn't know English, catch him right here with these different prices,' you know. 'By the end of the day, I'll have a sale,' you know. 'This guy doesn't know what he's doing,' you know. We were there, and then my sister said that she heard that guy talking about how us Mexicans can't buy a car.
>
> (Faulstich Orellana 2020)

The pervasive sense that one's family member is subject to prejudice may generate a desire to represent their agency more robustly. It also explains the frequency with which the interpreter may face the interpreter's dilemma. Interpreters may regularly find themselves in situations in which they function as an intermediary in the context of a family member being mistreated. The family member may have their own way of wanting to respond to this abuse—perhaps they want to return an insult, demand certain treatment, or just stay quiet—and this may differ from the way in which the interpreter would react to the abuse. It is not difficult to imagine why such discrepancies could generate significant tension and discomfort for both parties.

Given these various social dynamics, I hope it is clear why those who interpret for family members may find themselves facing a real dilemma time and time again. On the one hand, the interpreter has a duty to support a dependent family member by acting on their behalf. On the other hand, the interpreter does not personally endorse the action that they are being asked to engage in.

Note on an Initial Objection

One might object that the interpreter's dilemma is not a real dilemma because of what seems to be an obvious resolution to it: the dependency of a non-English-speaking family member could be addressed if the family member would simply learn English. One might argue that because the non-English speaker is responsible for making themselves dependent upon the interpreter—and because the interpreter may be enabling their family member by allowing them to remain dependent—the dilemma is resolvable by the interpreter simply refusing to interpret, no longer enabling the dependency of the family member. This argument, however, fails to take several factors into consideration. For one, language acquisition for adults may be difficult for a variety of reasons. At the very least, research on language acquisition indicates that while children preserve the ability to learn new grammars, this ability declines rapidly in late adolescence. Indeed, studies show that even full-immersion language learners experience a sharp drop in the learning rate at around seventeen to eighteen years of age (Hartshorne et al. 2018). Another reason the assumption that all immigrants should be able to pick up the English language is flawed is that they may not actually be immersed in the English language because their lives may take places largely within foreign-language communities. They may also have other priorities—such as working or caring for children—that outweigh their ability to focus on their own education. In addition, many towns do not offer classes to help those who are unable to learn on their own, or who have learning challenges. Furthermore, the objection that non-English speakers and their enabling family members are responsible for the dependency fails to account for the urgent quality of the needs of family members. It would be unfair to demand that interpreters refuse to help a family member communicate at the doctor's office, with the police, with the IRS, or with the landlord out of a tough-love attitude that would pressure the family member to learn English or suffer the consequences. And most importantly, even if there is a correct way to resolve the interpreter's dilemma in most cases, it's really the *experience* of the dilemma—the feeling that one is either failing to meet their responsibility to their family member or undermining their own autonomy—that is sufficient to constitute a pervasive sense of the weight of moral responsibilities that one cannot adequately meet.

II. The Moral Burden of Consensual Heteronomy

The interpreter's dilemma adversely affects the interpreter when it becomes a moral burden, that is, a kind of responsibility that weighs so heavily that it threatens to damage the moral self. Nancy Sherman's notion of "moral injuries," which she elucidates in her work on military veterans, conveys what is meant by harm to one's moral self. In *Afterwar*, Sherman explains that moral injuries "arise from (real or apparent) transgressive commissions and omissions perpetuated by oneself or others." Sherman notes that moral injury has to do with "a generalized sense of falling short of normative standards befitting good persons" (Sherman 2015: 8). While on duty, military members often witness or participate in acts that violate their own moral standards. Sherman argues that in order to help veterans heal from their experiences, it is important to understand this harm as a *moral* injury rather than merely in terms of mental-health diagnoses such as post-traumatic stress disorder.

Likewise, I contend that the interpreter's dilemma produces a moral burden that cannot be merely understood in terms of the psychology of children's role reversal with their parents or in terms of the stress of heavy responsibility. Instead, the weight of sorting through frequent moral dilemmas causes harm to the moral self because it involves potential transgressions against one's own autonomy. As a result, interpreters may face anxiety, emotional exhaustion, strained relationships, and self-alienation.

The interpreter's dilemma causes harm to the moral self because it demands that the interpreter engage in *heteronomous* action, that is, action that an agent does not identify with, experiencing it instead as subjection to the will of another person or influence. I argue that a central reason the interpreter's dilemma constitutes a moral burden is that complying with the family member's request to act on their behalf often requires not only that the interpreter act in a way that they do not want to but also that they *invest* themselves in this heteronomous action in a way that alienates the individual from herself. In other words, I claim that part of the burden of the interpreter's dilemma is that it requires a person to consent to that which undermines their own autonomy. Interpretation requires a high degree of personal investment, in part because one is interpreting for a loved one. Whereas a professional interpreter's responsibility for their client is temporary, the well-being of the person who is interpreting for a family member can depend to a greater or lesser degree on the outcome of a communicative exchange. Imagine, for example, that the non-English-speaking parent or spouse or sibling is desperately looking for work, and the interpreter is the intermediary in an exchange with a potential employer. The interpreter must not only live the joy, hope, shame, disappointment, or financial anxiety of their family member;[5] they may feel that they are to some extent responsible for whether their family member gets the job.[6] We can also imagine the burden of being personally invested during very high-stakes medical encounters, such as when the subject matter is very intimate or potentially devastating. In situations like pandemics, interpreters are especially vulnerable, as they are the public-facing voice of their family members. When non-English speakers are required to risk their health in order to carry out some errand, their interpreters will also be required to take the same risks.

Interpreting is also a complex activity that demands quite a bit of skill. Most obviously, the words in one language need to correspond accurately to the words spoken in another language. In addition to this, the interpreter also interprets culture. They must grasp and navigate the cultural context that forms the background to the communication. An interpreter may be more aware than their family member of the two differing sets of cultural norms and attempt to navigate those norms in their communication. For example, the question of whether a potential employee should be "we" focused or "I" focused, or the degree of formality or deference one should show to an employer, may be culturally specific, as are nonverbal communications such as personal space, eye contact, and appearance.[7]

Beyond exercising this specialized knowledge, the interpreter must, in a crucial sense, also wield their own emotional agency on behalf of others. That is, language brokers cannot merely translate words. They must also operationalize targeted emotional expression to be effective. This is because the expression of emotion is part of the pragmatic context of effective speech acts. As Trip Glazer argues, emotions are only expressed when they are perceptually manifested—through the body, face, tone, pace, and energy of an expression. He explains,

> Whether a speech act counts as an expression of emotion or not depends in every case on how the words are spoken. . . . To be an expression of emotion, a speech act must be spoken with a tone of voice, facial expression, or gesture that makes an emotion perceptually manifest.
>
> (Glazer 2017: 26)

For example, consider having to communicate the following idea: "She says this has been an unusually hard month. She promises she will have the rent check for you next week." In such cases, the manner in which this content is conveyed will greatly influence how the message is taken up by the listener—whether the listener is likely to respond with compassion or skepticism or something else. In other words, in order to accurately render emotional meaning, interpreters must *perform* those meanings.

In this way, emotional expression is not only important to accuracy but also serves various crucial social functions. In particular, "emotions serve as incentives or deterrents for other individuals' social behavior" and "emotional communication evokes complementary and reciprocal emotions in others" (Keltner and Haidt 1995). In other words, we utilize emotional expression to get other people to feel and do certain things. Therefore, an interpreter hoping to advance the interests of a dependent family member must utilize their emotional agency when navigating social situations on their loved one's behalf.

Sociologist Arlie Hochschild captures this aspect of emotional expression in her discussion of what she calls *emotion work*, which "requires one to induce or suppress feeling in order to sustain the outward countenance that produces the proper state of mind in others" (Russel Hochschild 2012: 7). Any high-stakes communicative interaction requires attunement and responsiveness to the subtleties of tone, body language, word choice, mood, and so on. The interpreter is concerned to intervene in a myriad of ways and to an appropriate degree in order to advance the interests of their loved one, given the complexity of a communicative interaction. In managing their own feeling in order to manage others' feeling well, interpreters must emotionally gear up to complain, to negotiate, to plead, to impress, or to defend.

While all people manage feeling in themselves and others, and many jobs require this kind of labor specifically, Hochschild's concern is about the possible cost of the work to those who do it often: "The worker can become estranged or alienated from an aspect of self . . . that is used to do the work" (Russel Hochschild 2012: 7). Specifically, Hochschild worries that by engaging in frequent emotional management, one loses touch with the part of the self that feels authentically.

A final point is that in language brokering, the interpreter is often concerned to mitigate racial stereotypes or prejudices that others might have about them and their family member. This aspect of emotion management has some resonance with Amia Srinivasan's notion of affective injustice: "the injustice of having to negotiate between one's apt emotional response to the injustice of one's situation and one's desire to better one's situation" (Srinivasan 2018: 135). Srinivasan is particularly interested in the ways in which targets of racism must decide whether to allow themselves to experience justified rage or whether to bury their apt anger in order to better their situation. Perhaps they are concerned about countering the way in which they are already stereotyped as rageful, violent, or shrill (136). The wrongness of this injustice, Srinivasan argues, lies "in the fact that it forces people, through no fault of their own, into profoundly difficult normative conflicts" (136). Interpreters must be concerned about the impact of their emotional presentation on the way in which they and their loved ones are being perceived by people whose perception of them may be shaped by racial stereotypes. Managing these perceptions may require setting aside more apt or authentic emotional engagement.

For all these reasons, acting on behalf of a loved one in ways one does not personally endorse can be morally burdensome. One cannot simply translate words and divest themselves from their emotional labor. In several ways, this type of work requires an investment, or commitment, of the self. The embodiment of emotional expression demands that, to some extent, the expression becomes one's own. One cannot merely go through the motions; one must care deeply enough to deliver a successful performance. In order to muster the intellectual and emotional energy to perform interpretation in a difficult situation when one does not want to for reasons of moral significance, one must consent to their heteronomy, to the betrayal of their own autonomy. The problem is not merely that the interpreter is experiencing coercion; rather, the interpreter is acting against their own will and must do so in a wholehearted kind of way.

III. The Interpreter's Moral Burden in Social Context

Up to this point, I've been making the case that the widespread lack of Spanish-language translation services generates a moral burden for members of the Latinx community. In this section, I make the case that this moral burden is also an injustice. That is, it contributes to the oppression of Latinxs. Many people face moral burdens, but not all are unjust. Some people may bear burdens that are greater than those that others have to bear, but they are circumstantial rather than the result of an unjust society. For example, being a parent can be morally burdensome. It typically involves a tremendous amount of emotional labor, the sense that one is never doing enough, that one is always failing a little bit, that one never has enough hours in the day to both provide for and nurture their children. People are parents at the expense of other commitments that they value. But we probably wouldn't want to describe all parents as victims of injustice. We can see, however, that *circumstantial* moral burdens can become *unjust* moral burdens. For instance, one might argue that a lack of affordable childcare in the United States unjustly burdens single parents—usually single mothers—and particularly those who struggle to make ends meet. In this case, the structure of society renders these women as a group more vulnerable to certain moral burdens.

We can distinguish unjust moral burdens from circumstantial ones by asking how much of a remainder would be left if the underlying social structure were to change. If affordable childcare were available, the unjust burden for low-income women would be alleviated to a significant degree. However, many of the moral burdens associated with parenting in general would remain. In a society where there is race-based oppression, it is plausible that the interpreter's dilemma will be a facet of that oppression precisely because the nature and frequency of the dilemma is likely to be produced by an interlocking set of social practices. Marilyn Frye's classic analogy between oppression and a birdcage is useful for illustrating why. According to Frye, oppression is like the birdcage in that it must be understood as a network of systematically related barriers. Focusing on a single wire of the cage without seeing the other wires and the ways in which they connect will lead to confusion about why the bird doesn't simply fly away. Similarly, oppression is hard to see if one focuses on a single situation. The situation must be looked at in terms of its relation to larger schemes in order to be properly understood. Frye thus demonstrates how situations that are seemingly innocuous may actually be facets of oppression. At the same time, she is concerned that the term "oppression" not be overused or applied inappropriately to any encounter with an unpleasant or frustrating force, lest the concept lose its critical thrust. She gives us a set of questions that we can ask ourselves in order to test whether something should be thought of as oppressive. She writes,

> One must look to the barrier or force and answer certain questions about it. Who constructs and maintains it? Whose interests are served by its existence? Is it part of a structure which tends to confine, reduce, and immobilize some group? Is the individual a member of the confined group?

(Frye 1983: 14)

If one believes the United States has structures of race-based oppression, then the interpreter's dilemma will itself likely be a facet of wider oppression for the Latinx community.

Applying the analogy to the Latinx community, we might start by looking at the big picture—the birdcage as a whole. Latinxs fare worse than white Americans across many measures, including income, health, political leadership, incarceration, and education (Stebbins and Comen 2018). Nationwide, Latinxs are up to five times more likely to experience four or more factors of what is known as compound poverty—a series of unstable circumstances that build upon each other, making it difficult to create stability or escape intergenerational poverty. These circumstances include things like low income, lack of education, no health insurance, living in a poor area, and living within a jobless family (White 2016). These economic disparities are built upon a brutal history of anti-Latinx discrimination in the United States—a history that began with white settler colonialism and later included school segregation, nation-wide assimilation programs in schools (which included humiliating, frequently corporal, punishment for speaking Spanish), lynchings, mob violence, mass deportations of people regardless of their immigration status, and other kinds of systematic brutality (Blakemore 2017).

Language has been an important part of this history. It is a wire in the birdcage. Gloria Anzaldúa suggests that language manifests the legacy of colonialism. She describes the deep shame that she and other people of the Borderlands come to feel around the way they speak, the various subtle and direct ways in which they are punished for the languages they do and do not speak, and whether they speak in the "right way." Language is one of the sites where social hierarchies manifest and are reinforced. It is a site where cultures undergo marginalization or erasure. As I have shown in this chapter, it also becomes a site through which interpreters are morally burdened.

One reason that language is so heavily policed is because of its links to ethno-racial identity. Anzaldúa writes,

> If you really want to hurt me, talk badly about my language. Ethnic identity is twin skin to linguistic identity—I am my language . . . and as long as I have to accommodate English speakers rather than having them accommodate me, my tongue will be illegitimate.
> (Anzaldúa 1987: 59)

Insofar as language is deeply linked to social identity, it is subject to the same forces that oppress people on the basis of social identity: racism, ethnocentrism, and xenophobia.

My account of the moral burden that interpreters face shows how linguistic marginalization ripples beyond just noncitizens, beyond just the non-English-speaking population, and throughout the Latinx community. Interpreters occupy the crossroads between mainstream society and the communities of cultural outsiders that make up the margins of that society. Insofar as immigrant communities suffer, so do these liminal members. They are an unseen part of the collateral damage of a white supremacist society. Their hardships, when isolated, may seem like the unfortunate price to pay for having family members who do not speak English. Interpreters themselves may even place significant blame on their non-English-speaking family members. I suggest that this blame is sometimes misdirected. When we put the hardship that interpreters undergo within the context of the many other ways in which Latinx people face barriers to full moral, legal, and social inclusion and recognition, we can see how the interpreter's moral burden constitutes a wire of the cage that surrounds Latinx communities.

What does this mean with respect to the responsibilities of societies in which this oppression occurs? Providing an adequate response to this question is beyond the scope of this chapter, but I would like to conclude by gesturing at what I believe is one of the implications of my account of the interpreter's dilemma. Some might say that although it is unfortunate that Latinx people face some disadvantages, they still have the biggest responsibility when it comes to learning the language. David Miller, for instance, argues that for the sake of social harmony and trust it is reasonable that societies require people to speak a dominant language in order to attain full membership (Miller 2016). He acknowledges that societies that make this demand may have reciprocal responsibilities to facilitate people's ability to meet the requirement, perhaps by offering English as a Second Language classes. But rarely is the argument made in the United States that anything beyond this and basic compliance with federal law is warranted.

It strikes me that this intuition—that it is Spanish-speaking immigrants who must adjust to English-speaking society—highlights the invisible privilege of Anglo-American society that allows the bearers of this privilege to assume that the unequal distribution of comforts, access, resources, and opportunities is morally acceptable. The assumption behind this lack of attention to the situation seems to be as follows: *Of course* people who don't speak the dominant language must live segregated lives, devoid of access to the services and community resources that the rest of us enjoy!

I argue, to the contrary, that if we are concerned with social trust and social harmony, and if we are concerned to address the structures that marginalize immigrant communities, we should work toward a future in which interpreting services are widely available in public spaces, particularly in cities and towns with large immigrant populations. To meet this responsibility, schools must strengthen their foreign-language offerings and requirements in order to promote multilingualism among U.S. Americans. In addition, technology might play a role in alleviating some of the costs of meeting this responsibility. It is not so difficult to imagine walking into a local bank and having the opportunity to video chat with an associate who speaks your language, or trying a restaurant or coffee shop that you would have otherwise been too embarrassed to patronize because they now have digital menus that allow you to make requests of your server or explore the ingredients of a dish in your language. These social changes wouldn't only help to address the exclusion of immigrant communities. They would also help to alleviate the burden on the family-member interpreters who currently bear the weight of this labor.[89]

References

Anzaldúa, G. (1987) *Borderlands/La Frontera: The New Mestiza*, San Francisco: Aunt Lute Books.
Blakemore, E. (2017) "The Brutal History of Anti-Latino Discrimination in America," *History.com*, September 27, www.history.com/news/the-brutal-history-of-anti-latino-discrimination-in-america.
Buriel, R., et al. (1998) "The Relationship of Language Brokering to Academic Performance, Biculturalism, and Self-Efficacy among Latino Adolescents," *Hispanic Journal of Behavioral Sciences* 20 (3): 283–297.
Corona, R., et al. (2012) "A Qualitative Analysis of What Latino Parents and Adolescents Think and Feel about Language Brokering," *Journal of Child and Family Studies* 21 (5): 788–798.
Faulstich Orellana, M. (2003) "Responsibilities of Children in Latino Immigrant Homes," "Understanding the Social Worlds of Immigrant Youth," special issue of *New Directions for Student Leadership* 100: 25–39.
Faulstich Orellana, M. (2009a) *Translating Childhoods: Immigrant Youth, Language, and Culture*, Piscataway, NJ: Rutgers University Press.

Faulstich Orellana, M. (2009b) "Immigrant Youth's Contributions to Families and Society as Language and Culture Brokers," *Lecture given at Fairhaven College, Western Washington University*, December 8, https://vimeo.com/8059479.

Faulstich Orellana, M. (2020) "Language Brokering," *MarjorieFaulstichOrellana.com*, www.marjoriefaulstichorellana.com/archive/language-brokering.

Feeny, N. (2015) "Sarah Palin Tells Immigrants 'Speak American' in Inter- view," *Time*, September 7, http://time.com/4024396/sarah-palin-speak-american-energy-department.

Frye, M. (1983) "Oppression," in *The Politics of Reality: Essays in Feminist Theory*, Freedom, CA: The Crossing Press.

Glazer, T. (2017) "Looking Angry and Sounding Sad: The Perceptual Analysis of Emotional Expression," *Synthese* 194: 26.

Goldmacher, S. (2016) "Trump's English-only Campaign," *Politico*, September 23, www.politico.com/story/2016/09/donald-trumps-english-only-campaign-228559.

Hartshorne, J. K., Tenenbaum, J. B., and Pinker, S. (2018) "A Critical Period for Second Language Acquisition: Evidence from 2/3 Million English Speakers," *Cognition* 177: 263–277.

Hall, N., and Sham, S. (2007) "Language Brokering as Young People's Work: Evidence from Chinese Adolescents in England," *Language and Education* 21 (1): 16–30.

Health and Human Services Department. (2000) "Title VI of the Civil Rights Act of 1964; Policy Guidance on the Prohibition against National Origin Discrimination as It Affects Persons with Limited English Proficiency," *Federal Register*, October 30, www.federalregister.gov/documents/2000/08/30/00-22140/title-vi-of-the-civil-rights-act-of-1964-policy-guidance-on-the-prohibition-against-national-origin.

Hua, J. M., and Costigan, C. L. (2012) "The Familial Context of Adolescent Language Brokering within Immigrant Chinese Families in Canada," *Journal of Youth and Adolescence* 41 (7): 894–906.

Kaplan, R. (2015) "Bobby Jindal: 'Immigration without Assimilation Is Invasion,'" *CBSNews.com*, August 30, www.cbsnews.com/news/bobby-jindal-immigration-without-assimilation-is-invasion.

Keltner, D., and Haidt, J. (1995) "Social Functions of Emotions at Four Levels of Analysis," *Cognition and Emotion* 13 (5): 505–521.

Khader, S. (2011) *Adaptive Preferences and Women's Empowerment*, New York: Oxford University Press.

LanguageLine Solutions Team. (2017) "Census Report: More Than 20 Percent of U.S. Residents Speak a Language Other Than English at Home," *Language- Line.com*, September 20, http://blog.languageline.com/limited-english-proficient-census.

Lor, M. (2012) "Effects of Client Trauma on Interpreters: An Exploratory Study of Vicarious Trauma," *St. Catherine University, Sophia*, https://sophia.stkate.edu/cgi/viewcontent.cgi?article=1053&context=msw_papers.

Miller, D. (2016) *Strangers in Our Midst: The Political Philosophy of Immigration*, Cambridge, MA: Harvard University Press.

Palm, K. M., Polusny, M. A., and Follette, V. M. (2004) "Vicarious Traumatization: Potential Hazards and Interventions for Disaster and Trauma Workers," *Prehospital and Disaster Medicine* 19 (1).

Ponizovsky, Y., et al. (2013) "The Satisfaction with Life Scale: Measurement Invariance across Immigrant Groups," *European Journal of Developmental Psychology* 10 (4): 526–532.

ProEnglish. (2017) "The 2016 Presidential Candidates on Official English," https://proenglish.org/the-2016-presidential-candidates-on-official-english.

Russel Hochschild, A. (2012) *The Managed Heart: Commercialization of Human Feeling*, Berkeley: University of California Press.

Sherman, N. (2015) *Afterwar: Healing the Moral Wounds of Our Soldiers*, New York: Oxford University Press.

Srinivasan, A. (2018) "The Aptness of Anger," *Journal of Political Philosophy* 26 (2).

Stebbins, S., and Comen, E. (2018) "Economic Inequality: The Worst States for Hispanics and Latinos," *USAToday.com*, January 19, www.usatoday.com/story/money/economy/2018/01/19/economic-inequality-worst-states-hispanics-and-latinos/1035606001.

Tse, L. (1996) "Language Brokering in Linguistic Minority Communities: The Case of Chinese- and Vietnamese-American Students," *Bilingual Research Journal* 20 (3–4): 485.

u/AsianSecretary. (2014) "My Parents Are Becoming Too Dependent On Us. Please Advise," *Reddit.com*, June 10, www.reddit.com/r/AsianParentStories/comments/27t3to/my_parents_are_becoming_too_dependent_on_us.

United States Department of Justice. (2016) "Title VI of the Civil Rights Act of 1964 42 U.S.C. § 2000D ET SEQ," *Justice.gov*, January 22, www.justice.gov/crt/fcs/TitleVI-Overview.

van Nistelrooij, I. (2017) "Self Sacrifice and Care Ethics," in J. Duyndam, A.-M. Korte and M. Poorthuis (eds.), *Sacrifice in Modernity: Community, Ritual, Identity, Studies in Theology and Religion*, 22, Leiden: Brill.

White, G. B. (2016) "Poverty, Compounded," *Atlantic*, April 16, www.theatlantic.com/business/archive/2016/04/how-poverty-compounds/478539.

Notes

1 The term "translation" typically refers to written language, "interpretation" refers to spoken or real-time language communication, and "language brokering" refers more generally to the facilitation of communication between linguistically and/or culturally different parties. The literature emphasizes that "brokers mediate, rather than merely transmit information." See Tse (1996): 485. In this chapter, I use the three terms loosely and sometimes interchangeably. I tend to use the terms "interpreting" and "brokering" rather than "translating," because I primarily have spoken exchanges in mind, but the translation of written documents is also a part of the labor that I'm describing here.

2 Research has shown that "children who translate for parents acquire enhanced cognitive, social, emotional and interpersonal skills" due to being exposed to adultlike experiences on a regular basis. See Buriel et al. (1998). A survey based on 280 sixth-grade (aged around eleven to twelve) Latino family translators at a Chicago school found they performed significantly better on standardized tests of reading and math than their non-translating peers. See Faulstich Orellana (2003). In addition to these enhanced skills, interpreting may also contribute to self-esteem. In one study, "researchers interviewed 25 Latino children of around 12 years who were translating for their parents. These children said their responsibilities made them feel proud, helpful and useful." See Corona et al. (2012).

3 Indeed, language brokers make it possible for their family members to sustain themselves as workers and consumers in a host country—a fact that should be considered when we contemplate the ways in which economies in the Global North rely on immigrant labor. See Faulstich Orellana (2009a: 124).

4 On a Reddit forum about interpreters' experiences, one woman's post captures this frustration:
    Ever since I turned 14, I was always ordered/asked to take care of billing issues, inquiries, etc. At first I didn't mind it as much. After all, it wasn't a frequent thing, and my parents couldn't speak English. What else could they do? As I grew older they lumped more translation responsibilities onto me but this time with verbal abuse. This would happen nearly every week. If I didn't take care of it immediately, I was a worthless daughter . . . Health insurance set-ups, phone bill errors, water bill is too high, mom got her name wrong on the dentist insurance. Would you call to see why [sic] got two cards instead of one? What does this stock letter say? Why can't you understand what this technical bank term means, you grew up in America! (See u/AsianSecretary 2014)

5 As the expression "don't kill the messenger" implies, the intermediary often bears the weight of their loved one's response to difficult news.

6 Although a professional translator is not as personally invested as someone who brokers for a family member, research indicates that those working empathetically with survivors of trauma—such as therapists, social workers, nurses, and lawyers—can still experience vicarious trauma. See Palm, Polusny and Follette (2004: 74). Vicarious trauma can produce PTSD-like symptoms. Interpreters sometimes act as intermediaries between victims of trauma and these professionals, but not much work has been done on the ways in which they take on this trauma. Some studies indicate that interpreters' shared experiences with those for whom they are interpreting creates heightened sensitivity to others. See Lor (2012). We might surmise that these effects are even more pronounced for those interpreting for family members.

7 Faulstich Orellana gives us an example of this cultural shifting in her research. She refers to a fifteen-year-old boy named Sammy, who describes his experience language brokering between an English-speaking woman and fieldworkers on a golf course. Sammy remembers that when he was talking to the woman, he would use the word "nice," but when talking to the workers, he would use the word "*chido*," or "cool." Sammy was concerned about adapting his level of formality for the comfort of each of the speakers (2009b).

8 An aspect of my claim regarding the responsibility to accommodate non-English speakers is that this responsibility extends to Spanish-language speakers, in particular. There are several reasons for this, including the simple fact that it is the most spoken second language in the United States, so there are more people with the need; Spanish speakers lived in what is now considered the United States prior to the existence of the nation, so that Spanish cannot be called a "foreign" language; and, as I am arguing here, because of the history and ongoing oppression of this particular demographic.
9 I thank Bob Fischer, Manuel Vargas, and Francisco Gallegos for their helpful comments on this project.

Reading Questions

1. What is the interpreter's dilemma? How does the dilemma threaten the autonomy of the interpreter, according to the text?
2. In your view, do the conditions that give rise to the interpreter's dilemma generalize to other ways of being peripheral to a mainstream culture? Why or why not?
3. What does Gallegos recommend as a strategy to improve the problems she identifies?
4. Would it be reasonable to expect societies to be more inclusive towards non-English speakers? Draw on the text to discuss your view.
5. Interpretation is a significant burden on family members. Yet family members are also uniquely attuned to the needs of their loved ones, and for this reason, we might worry about state-sponsored or private technological solutions to the interpreter's dilemma. Drawing on the text, develop in more detail one possible way to address the interpreter's dilemma in a particular context (education, healthcare, law, and so on), and discuss the trade-offs involved.
6. How should we describe the badness of the interpreter's dilemma, according to Gallegos? Is it that interpreters in this context are forced to be heteronomous, subsuming their own autonomy and being used like a tool by another person? Or is the frequency with which they must be heteronomous under unjust conditions? Discuss how the answer to this question might point towards the kinds of responses that are called for.
7. Gallegos argues that U.S. society ought to be more inclusionary towards Spanish-speakers in particular. What reasons does she give to support this claim? Are we not equally responsible for accommodating speakers of other minority languages?

23 Cultural Alterity

Cross-Cultural Communication and Feminist Theory in North-South Contexts

Ofelia Schutte

This essay will address the issue of understanding cultural differences in the context of cross-cultural communication and dialogue, particularly those cases in which such communication or attempted communication takes place between members of a dominant culture and a subaltern culture. From an examination of these issues we can perhaps draw some ideas that will permit us to reach a fuller understanding of cross-cultural feminist exchanges and dialogues. The reason for focusing on the topic of cross-cultural communication is that recently, I have become increasingly aware of the levels of prejudice affecting the basic processes of communication between Anglo-American and Latina speakers, as well as the difficulties experienced by many Latin American immigrants to the United States. It seems to me that in these times of massive prejudices against immigrants and of extraordinary displacements of people from their communities of origin, the question of how to communicate with "the other" who is culturally different from oneself is one of the greatest challenges facing North-South relations and interaction. If the question before us is how to frame the conditions for the possibility of a global feminist ethics—or whether such an ethics is indeed possible—I see no better place to start than to examine the conditions of possibility for cross-cultural communication as such.

My methodology for understanding what is at stake in cross-cultural and intersubjective communication will depend largely on an existential-phenomenological concept of alterity. In this tradition, the breakthrough in constructing the concept of the other occurs when one combines the notion of the other as different from the self with the acknowledgment of the self's decentering that results from the experience of such differences.[1] Moreover, the breakthrough involves acknowledging the positive, potentially ethical dimensions of such a decentering for interpersonal relations (as in Levinas 1979; Irigaray 1993; Kristeva 1991), in contrast to simply taking the decentering one might experience in the light of the other's differences as a deficit in the individual's control over the environment. According to this understanding, interpersonal and social interactions marked by cultural difference (as well as sexual, racial, and other kinds of difference) allow us to reach new ethical, aesthetic, and political ground.

In other words, the other is not the one who passively confirms what I am predisposed to think about her; she is not the one who acts as the mirror to myself or the one whose image justifies my existing ego boundaries. If this were the case, the other would only be a stand-in for the self's narcissism. Just the contrary; the other is that person or experience which makes it possible for the self to recognize its own limited horizons in the light of asymmetrically given relations marked by sexual, social, cultural, or other differences. The other, the foreigner, the stranger, is that person occupying the space of the subaltern in the culturally asymmetrical power relation, but also those elements or dimensions of the self that unsettle or decenter the ego's dominant, self-enclosed, territorialized identity.

In addition to these presuppositions regarding otherness and difference derived from the phenomenological-existential and poststructuralist tradition, I will take into account recent methodological developments regarding the concept of cultural difference as represented in postcolonial feminist theory. Working against the background of the West's history of colonial enterprises and its exploitation of other societies and cultures, postcolonial theory, in its various manifestations, pays special attention to issues of language, class, racial, ethnic, sexual, and gender differences, and to the justification of narratives about the nation-state.[2] Postcolonial feminist theory, in turn, directs its attention to the lives of women and to the tensions affecting women whose voices appear in national narratives and accounts of diasporic migrations. At stake in these "post" theories is a certain loss of innocence with regard to narratives of identity because of a more critical awareness of the regulative power such narratives have in defining who we are, who we aren't, and who others are and aren't.[3] The regulative power of narratives of identity is something with respect to which we are, to some extent, complicit, but we are also able to examine these narratives from some distance. Postcolonial and feminist critics have therefore used psychoanalytic theory to investigate further and to elaborate aspects of the relation between self and other in the light of accepted narratives of cultural identity and difference. In particular, Kristeva has studied symbolic analogies between the foreign other and the Freudian concept of the uncanny in the self—what she has called the stranger within the self (Kristeva 1991). Postcolonial feminisms, problematizing the Western concept of self, question the regulative use of gender in national and postnational narratives, but also the Enlightenment concept of individualism that fails to notice the complex, multilayered, fragmented, contradictory aspects of the self.

Finally, and on a different note regarding issues of alterity and identity, one more presupposition guiding these reflections is the belief that what we hold to be the nature of knowledge is not culture-free but is determined by the methodologies and data legitimated by dominant cultures. In other words, the scientific practices of a dominant culture are what determine not only the limits of knowledge but who may legitimately participate in the language of science. In everyday practices, outside of university environments, women are seen as particularly illiterate when it comes to having scientific knowledge or being able to discuss scientific issues with experts in the field. One does not need to have read Foucault to realize how very interconnected is the relation of knowledge to power. My point is that cultural (not just scientific) knowledge involves a highly constraining form of power. This power involves constraints over oneself and constraints over others. The type of constraints I shall try to examine and deconstruct to some extent are those dealing with a dominant culture's understanding of cultural differences. In addition, my analysis tries to understand sociocultural differences without subjecting them to masculine-dominant, gender-normative categories and maxims.

There is a need to develop a model of ethical and philosophical understanding in which the meaning of sexual difference is not limited by a gender-normative bias regarding what constitutes "the female body" or the proper function of a woman's mental abilities. Similarly, there is a need to develop a model for the understanding of subaltern cultural differences. In other words, both the critique of gender-normative biases and the critique of cultural imperialism need to be taken into account. Nevertheless, given that quite a number of critiques of cultural imperialism are themselves based on masculinist (often highly authoritarian) models of liberation from imperialism, which in turn presuppose and reinforce the domination of men over women in liberation struggles, the critique of cultural imperialism should be tempered by some kind of pluricultural feminist perspective. All these considerations lead to a feminist postcolonial perspective that can balance the struggle against the legacy of colonial-imperial domination with the struggle for the creation of feminist and feminist-compatible societies.

The Disparity in Speaking Positions

These reflections begin with some of my personal impressions regarding the difficulties of cross-cultural communication when one culture circumstantially holds the upper hand over another. The culture with the upper hand will generate resistance in the group that fails to enjoy a similar cultural status, while the culture of the subaltern group will hardly be understood in its importance or complexity by those belonging to the culturally dominant group unless exceptional measures are taken to promote a good dialogue. Even so, it is my view that no two cultures or languages can be perfectly transparent to each other. There is always a residue of meaning that will not be reached in cross-cultural endeavors, a residue sufficiently important to point to what I shall refer to more abstractly as a principle of (cross-cultural) incommensurability.[4]

The most common way to point to this excess of meaning is to refer to the untranslatable aspects of a language vis-a-vis another language. In this case, one might think of incommensurability arithmetically as a kind of minus effect to cross-cultural communication—what I get from the differently situated speaker is the conveyable message minus the specific cultural difference that does not come across. Theorized in this manner, the way to maximize intercultural dialogue would be to devise a way to put as much meaning as possible into the plus side of the exchange, so that as little as possible remains on the minus side of it. But although creating more effective means of communication between disparate groups can help reduce social conflict and tension, I don't believe much is understood about cultural difference if incommensurability is thought of in this predominantly quantitative manner.

Another way to think of incommensurability, and one that is much more relevant and fruitful for our discussion, is to look at nodes in a linguistic interchange or a conversation in which the other's speech, or some aspect of it, resonates in me as a kind of strangeness, as a kind of displacement of the usual expectation. Cultural alterity requires that one not bypass these experiences or subsume them under an already familiar category. Even the category of cultural diversity is called into question when diversity is institutionalized so as to mask a more radical view of differences. Postmodern postcolonial discourse looks for the possibilities of using nontotalizing concepts of difference rather than "the consensual, ethnocentric notion of the pluralistic existence of cultural diversity" (Bhabha 1994: 177). In the establishment's view of diversity, the rules controlling the representation of diversity usually reflect the will of the winners in political and military struggles. As Lyotard's debate with Habermas makes clear, the rationality of consensus is only a few steps from the desire for one system, one truth—in sum, one rationality—to dominate human civilization. In its extreme, the will to one truth has yielded the totalitarian Reign of Terror.[5] The representation of the one system as "pluralist" and favorable to cultural diversity must be called into question because of the sweeping power exercised by the system to harness the many into the yoke of the one (cf. Bhabha 1994: 152–155, 162–164). Even when the system is formulated as pluralist, the drawback is that only those differences are likely to enter the plural stage as are able to fit within the overall rationality that approves and controls the many as one.

Perhaps partly, though not exclusively, on account of this reason—because the new paradigm is born specifically out of the life experiences of many migrant and postcolonial peoples—some postcolonial critics have started to theorize the question of cultural difference in terms of what Homi Bhabha has called a "disjunctive temporality" (Bhabha 1994: 177) and Néstor García Canclini has labelled a "multitemporal heterogeneity."[6] These categories refer, in the first case, to the splitting, and in the second case to the superimposition of temporalities marking off cultural differences, speaking positions, and narrative timeframes. In Latin American societies, as García Canclini's work demonstrates, African, indigenous, Spanish colonial, modern, and global narrative timeframes may intersect, simultaneously or disjunctively, a speaker's discourse. Taking this thought further, I would note that when such culturally situated speakers enter diasporic locations—as happens when they migrate from their original societies to the United States—they will bring with them these forms of cultural difference and hybridity. It is not exceptional for many Latin Americans to become acculturated as a result of sociocultural influences crisscrossed by two or more incommensurable cultures, sometimes in literal juxtaposition. For example, in the Caribbean, because of the effects of colonization, some of the Yoruba deities gained counterparts in the Spanish Catholic roster of saints. We could say the Catholic and the Yoruba figures inhabit two very different kinds of temporalities. From the standpoint of the worshipers' experiences, in some cases one of the temporalities would be superimposed on the other, while in other cases the two would become distinct.

In *Borderlands/La Frontera*, Gloria Anzaldúa, speaking as a Chicana-Tejana-lesbian-feminist writer, juxtaposes the temporality of ancient indigenous myths with her postcolonial North American existence. The shifts from English to Spanish to Nahuatl in Anzaldúa are not just shifts in languages or "codes," as she calls them, but in temporalities of perception and consciousness (Anzaldúa 1987: viii). These pluricultural temporalities create a disjunctive tension with the linear temporality of modernity governing the identities of producers and consumers in advanced capitalist societies. These multiple and disjunctive temporalities create a displacement in the relation between self and other, allowing the recognition of alterity both inside and outside the self. Their premise of selfhood begins with the acknowledging and appreciation of the nonidentical self. Anzaldúa's multihyphenated *mestiza* self reminds us of Kristeva's stranger within. More broadly, it exemplifies feminism's notion of the differences not only among but within women. These multiple layers within the self, responding to different perceptive fields and different, not necessarily commensurable temporalities, can predispose us psychologically to appreciate both the richness and the incommensurability of cultural differences. They lay the groundwork for cognitive, perceptual, and linguistically constituted relations between ourselves and others where the other's differences, even if not fully translatable into the terms of our own cultural horizons, can be acknowledged as sites of appreciation, desire, recognition, caring, and respect. I am speaking here of a psychological state in which the stranger is not abjected, derided, persecuted, shut out of view, or legalized out of existence, but—departing from the premise that the other is also human—neither is she subjected to the demand that she be the double, or reflected mirror image, of ourselves.

The question arises of how the principle of incommensurability applies to feminist ethics when feminist ethics is engaged in making and executing normative judgments cross-culturally. Will the feminist ethical claim or the normative judgment be impaired by the principle of incommensurability, and if so, to what extent? How are feminist ethical terms negotiated cross-culturally? Should they be negotiated at all? My first task is to try to explain how the principle of incommensurability works at the concrete level of everyday experience. I will address this issue from an existential standpoint based in part on my personal experience.

The Culturally Different Other

What does it mean to be culturally different and to speak, at the level of culture, in a different voice? This question is generally answered by those with the power to mark others (or "the other") as different, rather than by those whose difference is in question in relation to the majority, or main members, of a given group. To be culturally different is not the same as being individually different or different by virtue of one's age or sex. If I am in a group among other women with roughly the same kind of education and occupational interests as myself and if we are roughly of the same age, what will mark me as culturally different is that I am, in today's terms, a Latina—a name that, while pointing to some aspects of my background, also erases important aspects of my individuality and the actual specificities of my cultural genealogy, which includes Caribbean, Latin American, and Western European background.

"Latina" casts me in a recognizable category, through which the meaning of my difference is delimited according to whatever set of associations this term may evoke. "Latina" is not simply a descriptive term referring to someone with a Latin American or Iberian ancestry currently residing in the United States. It is a signifier that both masks and evokes a range of associations—hot-blooded, temperamental, submissive, defiant, illegal or illicit, sexually repressed or sexually overactive, oppressed, exploited, and so on. But the thread that draws together all the stereotypical associations is one of invisibility as a producer of culture. One reason for this is that women in masculine-dominant societies, including Anglo-American society, are viewed primarily as transmitters rather than producers of culture. They are viewed principally as caregivers whose function in culture is to transmit and conserve, not question and create, cultural values.

Latinas in the United States are also invisible as producers of culture because the term "Latina" lacks a specific national reference and, in the mind of Western modernity, nation and culture are still tightly interrelated. (For example, the great national museums of art and science exhibit those works that illustrate the cultural standards and the aesthetic and scientific power of various nations.) As a concept, Latina exceeds the category of the national. Because as Latinas we are not tied to a specifiable national culture (in contrast to members of a culturally dominant group), to be culturally visible in the dominant culture we have to show that we know how to incorporate two or more cultures into our way of being. Furthermore, we must demonstrate that the way we bring such cultures together can benefit the Anglo-American public. In order to receive recognition as a cultural agent, I must show that I can be both a Latina and a North American; that I can alternate between these identities, so much so that in extremely "tight" cultural situations, I can perform, in my North American voice, a public erasure of my Latina voice, if need be. My white, Anglo-American counterpart is not called on to perform such a feat with respect to her own cultural background. She does not have to erase her Anglo-American cultural background to be legitimated as a member of North American society. If she comes from a working-class background, she may have to erase her class background to be fully accepted in some strata of society; and if she is a lesbian, she may have to erase her sexual orientation (keep it closeted) to be acceptable in some groups. But to gain recognition as a cultural agent she does not have to erase or dilute her Anglo-American background as such. Moreover, she does not need to combine her cultural background with, say, that of Middle Eastern, Asian, African, or Latin American people before being accepted as an important contributor to society and culture. If she is Jewish, she will face special problems the farther she is removed from assimilating fully into the Protestant, Anglo-American, Western European tradition.

Returning to the problem of the culturally successful Latina woman, an interesting phenomenon can be observed. Once I am able to perform the feat of representing my culture in some distinctive way in the context of the dominant Anglo-American culture, I am no longer considered only a culturally marked "other." To my favor, I am now recognized as an accomplished handler and knower of cultures. In this capacity, I earn a special place in the group. I have stepped out of the "immanent" place of the other. I have, to some extent, transcended the "Latina" object-position and claimed my position as a cultural agent in terms recognized by the dominant cultural group. But in order to do this, I need to be knowledgeable in the language and epistemic maneuvers of the dominant culture, the same culture that in its everyday practice marks me as culturally "other" than itself. From a cultural standpoint as well as a psychoanalytical one, I have become a split subject. When I act as "myself" (in my reflexive sense of self, the "me" that includes and grows out of my early Cuban upbringing), my Anglo-American sociocultural environment will often mark me as "other." When, alternatively, I discursively perform the speaking position expected of a subject of the dominant culture, I am recognized as a real agent in the real world.

Still, something fundamentally important is missing in this latter recognition (a misrecognition, actually). What my interlocutor fails to recognize is that delimiting my capacity to speak in my culturally differentiated voice will have an effect on what I say in response. When one feels rejected, one switches tracks, as it were, and enters the dominant discourse, not without realizing what is lost. What my interlocutor recognizes is not what I would have liked—an encouragement to communicate insights I offer from a standpoint of cultural difference—but only my ability to enter a standard Anglo-American speaking position, a position that exists in negotiated tension with my culturally differentiated, reflexive sense of self. In other words, the local master narrative exists in tension with what the Latina knows and experiences, and the former shuts out the latter. This is why sometimes, when some interlocutor responds to me (say, at the office) in reference to the self I perform there as a speaking subject, I get the sense that this colleague is not speaking to me at all; that my interlocutor is missing something, because the "me" that is culturally different is ignored, shut off, or bypassed.

There is a sense of frustration but also of missed opportunity in these mishaps in cross-cultural communication. What remains to be understood in the statements of the culturally differentiated other—that is, the incommensurable something not subject to perfect cultural translation—may actually be the most important part of the message my Anglophone interlocutor needs to receive. As I perceive it, my interlocutor takes in a fragment of the message and discards the rest. But one suspects it is precisely because the discarded part of the message would require the radical decentering of the dominant Anglophone speaking subject that it fails to reach such a subject's ears. Who or what is the other for the dominant, enlightened subject?[7] It is the one he would like to speak with occasionally, preferably in a foreign or distant location; it is the one he defends abstractly in arguments for democracy or against oppression. But let not the other (as other) make any demands in his everyday world, for in this case he might have to change his way of being. He might have to acknowledge his own split subjectivity, change his fixed way of life, welcome the stranger within, and perhaps alter his views and relations with others in ways he had not foreseen.

Cultural alterity therefore points to an ethics and to ways of knowing far deeper than the type of thinking wherein dominant cultural speakers perceive themselves to be at the epistemic and moral center of the universe, spreading their influence outward toward other rational speakers. Cultural alterity demands that the other be heard in her difference and that the self give itself the time, the space, and the opportunity to appreciate the stranger without and within. As Kristeva poignantly observes, "How could one tolerate a foreigner if one did not know one was a stranger to oneself?" (Kristeva 1991: 182).

If I may extrapolate from the kind of personal experience mentioned above to the situation of communication and dialogue among women North and South of the border, one sees how difficult it is for groups that are deeply entrenched in their own values, and that have the power to ignore the values of other groups, to attain any adequate understanding of cultural alterity. The reason for this is that people of different cultures do not speak the same (cultural) language and do not share the same cultural imaginary order. The science of anthropology has had to deal with the issue of cultural incommensurability for a long time. Why is this sense of incommensurability so hard to grasp for philosophy? Philosophers are often taught that philosophical claims can be stated in a language that is essentially outside of culture. This move essentializes philosophy, requiring an arsenal of conceptual weapons to police its boundaries, much as governments hire border patrols to keep illegal aliens outside the border. But isn't the language used to put forward philosophical claims—even the most formal and abstract language—already part of a culture? Aren't our conceptions of ethics, reason, and philosophy part of culture? Perhaps the issue should be put another way. Philosophers may acknowledge that incommensurability exists among various cultural formations and that it will impede the mapping of various cultural discourses exactly so that all of them match perfectly. The debate lies in whether such incommensurable elements should be assigned to what is irrelevant to philosophical meaning and knowledge, and thus irrelevant to the operations of reason; or whether, as I suggest, the incommensurable elements should be seen as inherent to the processes of reasoning itself.

In my view, cross-cultural (rational) discourse should be seen as limited by those elements of cultural difference that I have called incommensurable. That these elements of cultural difference cannot be fully apprehended in their "internal" intracultural meaning by outsiders, however, should not be taken as a sign that they are irrelevant to an understanding of cultural difference. Nor does it mean that acknowledging incommensurability will weaken the possibility of cross-cultural dialogue. Quite the contrary. Communication, including cross-cultural communication, involves two aspects, the second of which is often neglected. First, one must understand what is being said. Second, one must relate what is being said to a complex set of signifiers, denoting or somehow pointing to what remains unsaid. It is because of this very important (open-ended) dialectic between the said and the unsaid that the principle of incommensurability in cross-cultural communication assumes considerable importance.

In cross-cultural communication, each speaker may "say" something that falls on the side of the "unsaid" for a culturally differentiated interlocutor. Such gaps in communication may cause one speaker's discourse to appear incoherent or insufficiently organized. To the culturally dominant speaker, the subaltern speaker's discourse may appear to be a string of fragmented observations rather than a unified whole. The actual problem may not be incoherence but the lack of cultural translatability of the signifiers for coherence from one set of cultural presuppositions to the other.[8] Alternatively, the dominant speaker, relating only to fragments in the other's narrative, may believe that the whole message was transmitted, when only part of it was. This asymmetrical, nonreciprocal gap in communication can be tested, for example, if a third party interrupts the conversation and the subaltern speaker tries to resume it after the interval. The dominant speaker, lacking the sense that some element in the communication was still missing and believing that s/he has already heard the whole statement, does not perceive that the interlocutor should have the space to complete what was left unsaid. The subaltern speaker, in turn, is at a loss to explain that she had saved the most important part of the message for the end. Now she realizes that the interlocutor wants to move away from the subject of cultural difference, not toward it.

The speaker from the dominant culture is basically saying: communicate with me entirely on the terms I expect; beyond this, I am not interested. The ethical principle of cultural alterity must point to the inadequacy of such a speaker to engage in cross-cultural as well as interpersonal dialogue and conversation. Yet by the conventional norms of his own culture, the dominant speaker may never understand that he is silencing the culturally differentiated other because it never occurred to him to think that cross-cultural communication contains important, yet incommensurable, elements. Alternatively, he may be conscious of such incommensurable elements, but pay special attention to them only when the contrast between cultures involves a strong polarity, as in the cases of Asian or African cultures in contrast to Anglo-American culture. In this case, too, the Latina's subaltern message will not be heard, because her closer proximity to the West will disqualify her from the neoromanticized picture of the more culturally distant other.

It is incumbent on those speakers of the dominant cultural language not to foreclose the meaning of statements to only those meanings that are readily available to them. Assuming that one could map the statements of the culturally differentiated other according to three categories—readily understandable, difficult to understand, and truly incommensurable—one should never close the communication at the level of the first category, but should make the effort to let understanding reach into the other two domains. For example, if a Latina speaker alters the usual syntactical order normally used by English speakers, and if she also speaks with a heavy accent, these factors may make it harder for the native English speaker to understand what she is saying. With some effort, however, it is possible to figure out what is being said, if one is intent on paying attention and in engaging in follow-up questioning. Unfortunately, I have seen repeated cases of a Latina treated as if she were speaking nonsense, only because her accent, her sentence structure, and perhaps her vocabulary differ from that of ordinary English usage. Rather than taking the effort to listen to what the other is saying, the native speaker will treat the non-native speaker as if she were linguistically or intellectually incompetent. From the perception "I don't immediately understand what the other is saying," the dominant speaker will draw the invalid conclusion, "the other is speaking nonsense," "the other is incompetent," "the other does not belong here," and so on. The relegation of the culturally different "other" to a subordinate position, as this exemplary exercise shows, may itself be diagnosed as a lack of culture. Cultural prejudice of this sort is indeed a sign of a cultural deficit on the part of the dominant culture.

Furthermore, and with respect to the third category or level, placing a high stake on the incommensurable as that which requires recognition (rather than erasure or denigration in relation to a dominant culture) is fundamental to acquiring an understanding, even if only a partial understanding, of the culturally differentiated "other." If we hypothesize that incommensurability is largely manifested not only linguistically but in terms of disjunctive or heterogeneous temporalities, given the centrality of the concept of time in human existence, the very fabric of all social relationships will be affected by it. For example, intergenerational issues, productivity, leisure, and aging will not carry the same overall meaning for people of different cultural backgrounds.[9] Recognizing how culturally incommensurable clusters of meaning affect basic everyday interactions will bring culturally differentiated speakers one step closer to improved communication and understanding.

Woman as "Other" of Another Woman

Although in some of my examples I have been using the masculine pronoun to designate the culturally dominant speaker and the feminine to designate the subaltern, the relations of cultural dominance and subalternity can also obtain among speakers of the same gender or in the reverse combination. Basically, in coupled dualisms or binaries, the normative term "others" the nonnormative one (that is, the normative term subjects the nonnormative term to the subordinate position of "other"). This is one of the reasons why deconstructive feminist theory is so intent on moving beyond oppositional binaries and their corresponding forms of exclusion. For example, as Beauvoir and others have shown, in the man-woman binary, man is taken as normative for the human species, while woman is cast in the position of "other" of the normative. But take other examples: if the lady of the house is considered normative with respect to domestic authority and values, the female domestic worker will be seen as "other"; if the white woman is considered normative with respect to social status, the mulata will be other, and so on. Conversely, in popular culture, if the barrio is considered normative, high culture will be considered "other." In North-South and West-East binaries, if North and West are considered normative in terms of cultural standards, then South and East will be considered "other."

In antiimperialist politics, the terms are reversed. The Northern and the Western aggressors take on a lower cultural status while the Southern and Eastern cultures are hailed. When Western feminist theory fails to take into account the issues of colonialism and imperialism, the dangerous outcome will be that women from Eastern and Southern cultures will see in feminism the mark of Western colonization. Feminism in this instance will be tied symbolically to Western (capitalist) modernity and will not be dissociated from its values. In contrast, if feminism is seen as a movement of women in different parts of the world getting together and joining forces to overcome social, political, economic, and gender oppression, then this movement of emancipation becomes normative and the "other" becomes the outsider to, or obstructor of, this movement.

Herein lies the point of vulnerability for Western feminism, for if feminism is defined too narrowly, it will make an "other" of women whose path to emancipation it may fail to understand or recognize. In particular, it may relegate to the status of "other" many women in Eastern and Southern countries whose views do not fit squarely into Western feminist categories. Moreover, if Western feminism defines itself too narrowly or in terms that women in Eastern and Southern countries may not quite understand or appreciate—given the factor of cultural incommensurability—women in these countries may reject Western feminists as "other." This potential type of mutual exclusion takes us back to the impasse between feminism North and South, East and West. As Trinh Minh-ha notes in *Woman, Native, Other*, it is easy for conservative males in Third World countries to denounce feminism as a foreign, Western influence. When Western feminists try to denounce the conditions of women's oppression in Third World countries in "terms made to reflect or fit into Euro-American women's criteria of equality," this indirectly "serves the cause of tradition upholders and provides them with a pretext for muddling all issues of oppression raised by Third World women" (Minh-ha 1989: 106).

Fortunately, thanks to the insistent voices of women from developing countries and ethnic minorities and to the growing sensitivities of Western feminists when it comes to conveying feminist messages in the light of cross-cultural differences, these difficulties are better handled now by feminists engaged in worldwide activism and politics.[10] What is less clear to me is whether Western feminists (as they pursue philosophy, for example) view themselves as one of many voices in the struggle for women's social, political, economic, and gender emancipation on a worldwide scale. It seems to me that Western feminism still harbors the hope that its own views of emancipation are universally valid for all the world's women, if only because Western thought generally does not mark itself as culturally specific. Instead, it engages in the discursive mode of a universal logos, which it takes to be applicable to all rational speakers. Here the issue of colonialism must be brought up, even if it is unpleasant and even if it interrupts the discussion about the criteria for recognizing rationally competent speakers across cultures. Without reference to the historic conditions of colonialism, it is impossible to understand fully the Western mind's presumption of speaking from the privileged position of universality.

The Western colonial enterprise and its impact on the Americas were such that there was no way to understand the disparity of Western and non-Western cultures in an ethically responsible, reciprocal way. The conquest of America offered no reciprocal way of accounting for the differences among Western and non-Western cultures and peoples. To those people who were judged "less developed" in Western European terms it brought the forces that colonized and enslaved them. While the racial composition of the Americas has changed since the conquest and colonization, the problem persists that the people who have not reached the West's level of material development are often considered inferior. The impoverished Mexican migrant to California and the Haitian migrant to South Florida become, more than five hundred years after the conquest, the targets of the combined historical effects of colonialist, racial, linguistic, class, and, where applicable, gender prejudices.

Is it possible for contemporary Western feminism to disentangle itself from the historical forces of Western colonialism and from the erasure of otherness that such forces entail? What are the points of contact today between feminists from developing countries and Western feminism? Is there reason to place hope in a new way of looking at things, the recently developed approach of postcolonial feminisms?

Postcolonial Feminisms

Postcolonial feminisms are those feminisms that take the experience of Western colonialism and its contemporary effects as a high priority in the process of setting up a speaking position from which to articulate a standpoint of cultural, national, regional, or social identity. With postcolonial feminisms, the process of critique is turned against the domination and exploitation of culturally differentiated others. Postcolonial feminisms differ from the classic critique of imperialism in that they try to stay away from rigid self-other binaries.[11] In addition, an intense criticism is directed at the gender stereotypes and symbolic constructs of the woman's body used to reinforce outdated masculinist notions of national identity.[12] Postcolonial feminisms call attention to the process of splitting the culturally dominant subject in terms of the demands placed on the dominant subject by culturally disadvantaged others. These feminisms hypothesize, at the psychosubjective level, that the unity of self or mind felt by the dominant subject is a totally artificial one, and that the oneness of his or her subjectivity (covering the fragments that make up his or her personality) is made possible only by adherence to a philosophy of colonialism, whether the adherence is owned up to or only enacted indirectly. In other words, postcolonial feminisms propose the view that we are not born a unified self, that the sense of being "one," of being a self, is something derived from language (becoming a competent speaker in a language), and that language itself is part of culture and reflects certain arrangements of cultural constructs with respect to how to understand cultural differences.

When a child is given a name, for example, Caroline, she is not told that the culture giving her this name is one that had a history of colonizing other people and of imposing its values on them. The psychological process of decolonization involves the attempt to unhinge the genealogy of one's name, of one's identity, from the inherited colonial culture. One must learn that one could not be oneself without a relationship to the other and that such a relationship ideally must not be wrought with injustices. While one cannot make time go backward, annulling Western culture's colonialist legacy, it is possible partially to deactivate this legacy by establishing alternative practices and values with the intent of reversing the effects of colonialism. A coordination of heterogeneous elements with a special emphasis on undermining colonialism's understanding of cultural difference becomes the alternative route to the construction of identity in what we would like to call a postcolonial perspective or context.

If the postcolonial perspective entails acknowledging the reality of colonialism (or the fight against it) in the construction of cultural values and personal identities, what does a postcolonial feminism entail regarding the problem of cross-cultural communication? Postcolonial identities put in question the belief in the neutrality of the sign and the separation of the subject and object of knowledge, as accepted by the Enlightenment. They point out that these semiotic and epistemic assumptions will ultimately have repercussions on women's bodies and on women's affective well-being. As literary critic Nelly Richard observes from Chile, feminist (postcolonial) criticism should be able to uncover the concerted interests of the dominant culture hidden behind "the supposed neutral transparency of signs and the model of mimetic reproduction propitiated by the market through a passive consumption" (Richard 1996: 744).

Moreover, as Gayatri Spivak aptly illustrates by allusion to the status of indebted families in India, the interests of transnational global capital hiding behind the purported neutrality of global consumption are not gender-neutral.

> In modern "India," there is a "society" of bonded labor, where the only means of repaying a loan at extortionate rates of interest is hereditary bond-slavery [Below family life at the level of survival] there is bonded prostitution, where the girls and women abducted from bonded labor or kamiya households are thrust together as bodies for absolute sexual and economic exploitation.
>
> (Spivak 1993: 82)

The deceptive transparency of signs, the growing expansion of passive consumption, the recourse to loans as the concrete mechanism for maintaining consumption, the exorbitant rates of interest imposed on already subaltern populations, and the woman's body as "the last instance in a [global] system whose general regulator is still the loan" (Spivak 1993: 82) are interconnected forms of exploitation that only postcolonial feminisms can fully address at this time. Whether in Chile, in India, or much closer to home, postcolonial feminisms alert us to the voices of split subjects deconstructing the logic of the totality in the light of cultural alterity.

Feminist Agency and the Restructuring of the Imaginary-Symbolic Order

These comments on bonded labor illustrate a final and nevertheless familiar point for feminists; namely, that the ultimate oppression a human being can experience is to be bereft of any meaningful agency. African American feminist bell hooks has described oppression as the lack of choices.[13] I take this to mean that oppression involves conditions in which persons are deprived of agency, or that their options are limited to those that effectively fail to promote their own good.

If we look at the conditions that would empower women around the world to promote their own good, we see powerful interests set against women. There are powerful religious fundamentalisms all over the world and in various cultures that seek to define for women in categorical and absolutist terms what their own good is and to constrain women to act accordingly. These fundamentalisms also define the meaning of "nation" and "family" in categorical terms, promoting self-sacrifice and often war, while impeding those who are influenced by these ideologies from acting on their own desires for personal fulfillment and happiness. Some government and private institutions, moreover, derive enormous material benefits from women's cheap labor and from women's traditional family caregiving roles. There are forces in society that benefit from women ending up in prostitution, remaining illiterate, or being confined to economic and social conditions which, from girlhood on, subject them to recurrent violence and abuse. It seems that nothing could be more ethical than a universal feminist ethics designed to identify and correct such problems. How this is done, however, requires careful rethinking of how to employ the concepts of gender, identity, and oppression.

In my view, feminist ethical thinking needs to be "negotiated" cross-culturally. Such negotiation can be conducted on a case-by-case basis by individuals, or collectively by groups. The presence of so many mixed unions among people of different cultures offers some hope that effective cross-cultural communication in matters that pertain to intimate details of peoples' lives is not some sort of utopian fantasy. But people in mixed unions that are based on parity, as compared to the practices of dominant cultures with regard to subaltern cultures, are very strongly motivated to understand each other, as well as to communicate with each other so as to deepen and strengthen their understanding. Such individuals commit themselves to lifestyles in which giving of one's time to reach out to the other, as well as making space for the other's differences, are part of the very fabric of daily existence, neither a forced nor an occasional happening. People in mixed unions have also presumably experienced the positive benefits of their association to the extent that they would rather affirm what remains incommensurable in their distinct cultural horizons than shut the other out of their intimate life and feelings. No doubt, individuals who either work or live successfully with culturally differentiated others are highly skilled communicators, making optimum use of opportunities for cross-cultural, interactive engagements. The postcolonial feminist perspective highlights these interactive realities, deconstructing the traditional binarism of self-other paradigms, in which each side lays claim to either mutually exclusive or equal but separate realities.

Collectively, feminists can do much to promote cross-cultural understanding. Whether these groups are all-women groups or whether they include female and male feminists, perhaps their basic contribution is building and strengthening networks of solidarity. Although solidarity is an old term, long familiar to activists, the present circumstances at the turn of the century demand that we rethink and reawaken its meanings. Feminists from dominant global cultures and better-off economic sectors need to connect more closely with projects involving women and feminists from the periphery. We need to lobby actively for the inclusion of voices from the periphery so as to shake off the weight of colonialism and other oppressions that still mark the center's discourses. This is not to say that the voices from the periphery are not marked by the effects of colonialism, racism, and other oppressions, but that when such voices attempt to address these oppressions or engage in avant-garde cultural criticism, there is a common bond between us, despite our differences. It is up to us to recognize the centrality that this (other) bond represents and to help it assume its long overdue and legitimate place in the West's symbolic order and cultural imaginary. There is no other recourse but to destabilize and displace the subject of modernity from its conceptual throne and to sponsor alternative ways of relating and knowing that no longer shut out from "home" the realities of Latino, Asian, African, and other culturally marginalized peoples.

I believe that Western feminism cannot reach a point of maturity in this age of global, transnational, and diasporic ventures unless it openly adopts a postcolonial perspective. If it does, we will switch our identities away from subjects of a totalized notion of culture and will come to view ourselves as subjects of cultural difference. The West needs to learn how to step out of its colonial boots and start experiencing the reality of its subaltern environment and the cultures of the peoples it has disenfranchised and continues to disenfranchise. A challenging but not impossible task lies ahead. This is why the struggle continues.

References

Anzaldúa, G. (1987) *Borderlands/La Frontera: The New Mestiza*, San Francisco: Aunt Lute Books.
Beverley, J., Oviedo, J., and Aronna, M. (eds.) (1995) *The Postmodernism Debate in Latin America*, Durham: Duke University Press.
Bhabha, H. K. (1994) *The Location of Culture*, London: Routledge.
Fanon, F. (1963) *Black Skins, White Masks*, New York: Grove Press.
Fernández Retamar, R. (1989) *Caliban and Other Essays*, Minneapolis: University of Minnesota Press.
Garcia Canclini, N. (1995) *Hybrid Cultures: Strategies Farentering and Leaving Modernity*, Minneapolis: University of Minnesota Press.
Grewal, I., and Kaplan, C. (eds.) (1994) *Scattered Hegemonies: Postmodernity and Transnational Feminist Practices*, Minneapolis: University of Minnesota Press.
hooks, b. (1984) *Feminist Theory: From Margin to Center*, Boston: South End Press.
Irigaray, L. (1993) *An Ethics of Sexual Difference*, Ithaca, NY: Cornell University Press.
Kristeva, J. (1981) "Women's Time," *Signs* 7 (1): 13–35.
Kristeva, J. (1991) *Strangers to Ourselves*, L. S. Roudiez (trans.), New York: Columbia University Press.
Levinas, E. (1979) *Totality and Infinity*, Boston: Martinus Nijhoff.
Lyotard, J. F. (1984) *The Postmodern Condition: A Report on Knowledge*, G. Bennington and B. Massumi (trans.). Minneapolis: University of Minnesota Press.
Minh-ha, T. T. (1989) *Woman, Native, Other: Writing Postcoloniality and Feminism*, Bloomington: Indiana University Press.
Olea, R. (1995) "Feminism: Modern or Postmodern?" in J. Beverley, J. Oviedo and M. Aronna (eds.), *The Postmodernism Debate in Latin America The Postmodern Debate in Latin America*, Durham: Duke University Press.
Richard, N. (1993) "The Latin American Problematic of Theoretical-cultural Transference: Postmodern Appropriations and Counterappropriations," *South Atlantic Quarterly* 92 (3): 453–559.
Richard, N. (1996) "Feminismo, experiencia y representación," *Revista Iberoamericana: Special Issue on Latin American Cultural Criticism and Literary Theory* 62 (176–177): 733–744.
Sagar, A. (1996) "Postcolonial Studies," in M. Payne (ed.), *A Dictionary of Cultural and Critical Theory*, Cambridge, MA: Blackwell.
Spivak, G. C. (1990) *The Post-colonial Critic*, New York: Routledge.
Spivak, G. C. (1993) *Outside the Teaching Machine*, New York: Routledge.

Notes

1 Although Sartre, Merleau-Ponty, Beauvoir, Heidegger, and Lacan function as key background figures for the concepts of the other and alterity, it is Levinas who is remembered primarily for formulating an ethics of alterity. With the advent of poststructuralism, important new perspectives have been offered by Irigaray's feminist ethics of sexual difference and Kristeva's (1981) psychoanalytic-semiotic studies.
2 For a concise overview of postcolonial theory see Sagar (1996). For classics from the Caribbean region see Fanon (1963) and Fernández Retamar (1989). For contemporary poststructuralist postcolonial criticism see Spivak (1990, 1993) and Bhabha (1994). For postcolonialism and Latin American literary criticism (in Spanish) see the special issue on Latin American cultural criticism and literary theory of *Revista Iberoamericana* (1996); for postmodern studies in Latin America

see Beverley et al. (1995) and the special issue on "Postmodernism: Center and Periphery" of *South Atlantic Quarterly* (1993).
3 This point is made by Sagar (1996, 427) with specific reference to the work of Spivak, but it applies generally to deconstructive and poststructuralist feminisms.
4 I will not be using the term *incommensurability* in the Kuhnian sense of two incommensurable scientific theories that explain the same phenomena. By this term I try to designate the lack of complete translatability of various expressions or blocks of meaning between two or more linguistic-cultural symbolic systems. It may also refer to incommensurable ways of thinking insofar as the differences are culturally determined.
5 "We have paid a high enough price for the nostalgia of the whole and the one, for the reconciliation . . . of the transparent and the communicable experience" (Lyotard 1984: 81–82).
6 Garcia Canclini (1995: 46–47). Using Latin America's elites as a reference point, Garcia Canclini describes "multitemporal heterogeneity" as a feature of modern culture resulting from modernity's inability to superimpose itself completely on Latin America's indigenous and colonial heritages. I am using the term somewhat differently because my primary references are neither to the perspective of modernity nor to that of the elites. My primary reference point is the existential-phenomenological sense of two or more experienced temporalities as manifested in the lived experiences of members of the population, including the economically disadvantaged, the popular sectors, the racial minorities, and, yes, extending to the middle and upper classes, where relevant.
7 I refer to the dominant enlightened subject in the masculine gender here because this account is based primarily on my concrete experience; in a later section, I address women's assumption of this voice.
8 It would help to be acquainted with the underrepresented culture in order to appreciate this point. For example, feminists know that all too often, the patterns of gender socialization and the power one gender (the masculine) holds in the overall legal-ethical system of thought over the feminine will make it appear that a woman's reasoning is fragmentary or insufficiently coherent comparison to the reasoning of successfully socialized males. Asymmetrically given cultural differences can have a similar effect. A Latina feminist must communicate with her Anglo audience not only as a feminist but as a Latina, because she is already marked as such by the dominant culture. If she draws too heavily on her own cultural imaginary to explain her views, an account that is perfectly coherent to her may simply not carry over as such to her audience. The audience might complain that at times it could not follow the speaker or that the speaker was not sufficiently organized. This is not a matter of agreeing or disagreeing with the content of the speaker's message but of failing to connect the various aspects of the message into a fully coherent account. In my view, this could mean (though it does not necessarily have to mean) that the grounds for the speaker's reasoning are not readily available to speakers located in the dominant culture. Again, this could show how asymmetrical relations of power are reinforced between culturally differentiated speakers when one of the cultures is fully dominant over the other. Many different examples could be given of this phenomenon, not all of them similar. For especially racist dimensions of such asymmetry, consider Frantz Fanon's charge that a characteristic of the racism he encountered in France was the expectation that as a black person from the Caribbean, he could not speak French coherently (Fanon 1963: 35–36). Compare also Homi Bhabha's example of the Turk in Germany who feels he is being looked down on as an animal when he tries to use the first few words he has learned in the German language (Bhabha 1994: 165).
9 Obviously, there may be some overlap among people of different cultures regarding certain values, just as there may be differences in values among people of roughly the same cultural background. For example, political values can vary significantly among people of similar cultural backgrounds. Strong variations and disagreements can occur even among members of the same family just as, where such opportunities exist, a person can develop an affinity with the values of people from distant cultures. Agreement or disagreement on such *values* is a separate issue from the argument I am making about the principle of incommensurability as a factor to be reckoned with in cross-cultural communication between speakers from dominant and subaltern cultures.
10 Since the opening conference in Mexico City sponsored by the United Nations' Decade on Women (1975-1985), Western feminists have learned that women from other parts of the world, including the West's own minority populations, have views of their own that require specific attention. These views cannot be assimilated into those of the Western feminisms, because the way a woman

looks at her condition in the world will depend on many factors, including her cultural and economic location. Theoretically, a helpful orientation toward greater acknowledgment of diversity came with the wave of "feminisms of difference" in the 1980s. Compare Olea (1995).

11 I offer a broad characterization of postcolonial feminisms to include different kinds of feminist critiques and my own voice in these debates. Racial, ethnic, class, and other differences are often incorporated, along with cultural and gender differences, into postcolonial feminist work. For some differences of opinion on the use of "postcolonial" as a category, see Sagar (1996). I read Anzaldúa's *Borderlands/La Frontera* as postcolonial, though it is not clear she would accept this term, given the Chicana practice of not subsuming this identification under others. But the fit is quite clear: she talks about the land of ancestors that has been taken over by several different countries, as well as the different cultural formations emerging there over time. Moreover, she states, "I grew up between two cultures, the Mexican (with a heavy Indian influence) and the Anglo (as a member of a colonized people in our own territory)" (Anzaldúa 1987: vii).
12 Grewal and Kaplan's *Scattered Hegemonies* (1994) addresses this point, as do Anzaldúa (1987) and Spivak (1993: 77–95).
13 "Being oppressed is the absence of choices" (hooks 1984: 5).

Reading Questions

1. What is cross-cultural incommensurability, according to the text, and how does it manifest? What are the sorts of things that might not be translatable across cultures?
2. How do people from the dominant culture tend to experience cross-cultural incommensurability, according to Schutte? What about those belonging to the cultural minority group?
3. How do members of a dominant group often react to communication that they only partially understand, according to Schutte? How does she think people ought to act in these situations?
4. What are some of the possible benefits of engaging in cross-cultural communication and confronting that which cannot be fully translated, according to the text?
5. Schutte writes that "to be culturally different is not the same as being individually different or different by virtue of one's age or sex." Why is cultural difference a unique sort of difference when it comes to sharing ideas?
6. What are some of the hurdles that Latinas in the United States must confront in order to be recognized as producers of culture, according to Schutte?
7. Schutte writes, "The local master narrative exists in tension with what the Latina knows and experiences, and the former shuts out the latter." What is lost when a cultural outsider enters into the dominant discourse, in her view?
8. Cross-cultural communication requires a great deal of work. Why does Schutte think this task is vital? Do you agree? Why or why not?

24 Language, Power, and Philosophy
Some Comments on the Exclusion of Spanish from the Philosophical Canon

Elizabeth Millán Brusslan

It is no secret that philosophy in the United States is far from inclusive. The reasons are many, yet the rigorous assessment of some of those reasons is beyond the grasp of the philosopher's analysis. However, there are some rather obvious limitations concerning the ways in which philosophy is conducted in the United States, which any philosopher interested in truth and justice should comment on and critique. The exclusionary practice that I discuss is one that results when an entire tradition is silenced. This silencing is rooted in a glaring limitation of philosophical practice in the United States: the problem of language. We come to this problem via a narrative that excludes far too many voices from the canon of philosophy. Certain philosophers are quite fond of claims that philosophy was born with the Greeks and reached its culmination in Europe and then in the United States. I take my work in Latin American philosophy to be part of the process of rectifying what we might call philosophy's "mendacious cultural autobiography."[1]

Philosophy's mendacious tale of its birth in ancient Greece to its culmination in western Europe not only oversimplifies a more complex state of affairs, it also is perniciously exclusionary. The exclusion is far-reaching and contaminated at every level with falsehoods. The "Ancient Greece to western Europe" story of philosophy is filled with lofty claims regarding the "authentic" roots of philosophy, and a sudden shrinking of Europe to a collection of just three countries and their languages: France, Germany, and England. So, French, German, and English receive special status as "philosophical" languages, a status honored in graduate programs where the study of such languages is part of the serious training students undergo to become masters or doctors of philosophy. Spain and Spanish disappear from the map of philosophy, and, of course, so does all of Latin America. This slighting of Spanish as a philosophical language is just one of many acts of exclusion that have led important philosophical voices to be silenced and our path to truth to be truncated. Moreover, those of us who want to include this language and these voices are looked upon as confused nomads who have lost our way, unaware of what "true" philosophy really is and of where the boundaries of the sacred territory lie.

The silencing of the Spanish-language tradition can be corrected, or so I argue. We need to accomplish the following:

(1) Cure ourselves of the historical amnesia under which we suffer.
(2) Remove the pugnacious philosophical minutemen who patrol the borders of our field and open those borders to include more voices.
(3) Strive for a true cosmopolitanism in philosophy, one that would liberate us from the exclusionary (and often downright racist) gaze that has infected philosophy.

These are just three of the steps that will make an important voice of philosophy audible; a voice that speaks in Spanish, but is no less philosophical than any English, French, or German philosophical musings.

The Problem of Historical Amnesia

I begin with a focus on a problem that is a serious hindrance to the very recognition of Spanish-language intellectual traditions: the problem of historical amnesia. Cuban essayist, Roberto Fernández Retamar, in *Caliban*, which he describes, not without a certain tone of understatement, as "a simple essay on Latin American culture" (as if anything about Latin American culture could possibly be simple) (1989: 29; 2003: 71), complains of the "relative oblivion into which the work of the Cuban hero [Jose Martí] fell after his death" (1989: 17; 2003: 49). In particular, he is shocked that so careful a scholar as the Dominican, Henríquez Ureña, had made observations about Martí's positions that were "completely erroneous." He writes:

> Given the exemplary honesty of Henríquez Ureña, [the mistakes] led me, first to suspect and later, to verify that it was due simply to the fact that during this period the great Dominican had not read, *had not been able to read*, Martí adequately. Martí was hardly published at the time. "Our America" is a good example of this fate. Readers of the Mexican newspaper *El Partido Liberal* could have read it on 30 January 1891. It is possible that some other local newspaper republished it, although the most recent edition of Martí's *Complete Works* does not indicate anything in this regard. But it is most likely that those who did not have the good fortune to obtain that newspaper knew nothing about the article—the most important document published in America from the end of the past century until the appearance in 1962 of the Second Declaration of Havana.
> (1989: 17–18, 2003: 49–50)

Fernández Retamar draws attention to what has been a serious problem for the reception of much Spanish-language philosophy, namely, the absence of authoritative editions, seriously hindering scholarship in the field. Until a given tradition is deemed worthy of attention, critical editions remain scarce. Fernández Retamar also remarks that even the names evoked by Martí, as he makes claims that the inhabitants of "our America" are descended from "Valencian fathers and Canary Island mothers and feel the inflamed blood of Tamanaco and Paramaconi coursing through our veins" will be unfamiliar references to most readers in Latin America (1989: 19; 2003: 53). Fernández Retamar claims that this lack of familiarity "is but another proof of our subjection to the colonialist perspective of history that has been imposed on us, causing names, dates, circumstances, and truths to vanish from our consciousness" (2003: 53).

Fernández Retamar diagnoses a serious malady, something that, in another article, I dubbed "a great vanishing act" (Millán-Zaibert 2008). This vanishing act has nothing to do with spells or magic, but rather with something far less enchanting: exclusion and the invisibility born of such exclusion. The historical vanishing act of people, places, and events of Spanish America has had a deleterious effect on attempts to build a canon, to assemble a history of philosophy for the region. This vanishing act has given rise to a host of enduring problems, the most salient of which is the invisibility of an entire philosophical tradition. This invisibility is one reason why the question: Does a Latin American philosophy exist? endures. The question, as Fernández Retamar points out, is related to the "irremediable colonial condition," of those countries emerging from colonialism, which have been "ineptly and successively termed *barbarians, peoples of color, underdeveloped countries, Third World*," a condition that has led to the view that intellectual activity carried out beyond the borders of the "civilized" world is "but a distorted echo of what occurs elsewhere" [*un eco desfigurado de lo que sucede en otra parte*] (Fernández Retamar 1989: 3–4, 2003: 21–22). The upshot of such a dismissive view of the intellectual products of the "Third World": If Latin American philosophy exists at all (and the same would hold true of all philosophies of the Third World), it deserves no serious attention from the First-World philosophers, because it is merely derivative, and contributes nothing original to the philosophical discussions that shape "real" philosophy of the First World.

Alas, vestiges of this sort of dismissive treatment are all too prevalent in the academic world today. For example, Latin American philosophy and Spanish-speaking philosophers remain ghettoized. We have special committees to oversee the treatment of Hispanics in philosophy, in part because inclusiveness of this group cannot be taken for granted. We have to market sessions at the American Philosophical Association so that they will appeal to mainstream philosophers: Logic in Brazil is a crowd pleaser, whereas the topic of Indigenous thought in America draws only a few eccentrics. The theme of German philosophy in the Americas is seen as more valuable than addressing the problem of modernity in Latin America, for the stentorian philosophical voice of the German tradition inevitably overpowers the muffled voice of the Latin American tradition. Paying serious attention to something like the problem of modernity in Latin America would surely be a sign of progress, of an overcoming of the "colonial condition" in which Latin American philosophy has been placed, for it would present Latin American thought in an autonomous way, a way that frees it of the ghetto where it remains silent and isolated.[2]

Spain as the Other of Europe: Latin America as the Other of Spain

Another force fueling the invisibility of the Spanish-language philosophical tradition is a perception of Spain as non-European, not part of the Europe that exists in the wake of the philosophical map drawn to keep out the barbarous elements from west of the Pyrenees. In his essay, "Against the Black Legend," Fernández Retamar addresses the common link of exclusion that exists between Spain and Latin America:

> It is not surprising, given its origin, that the Black Legend should find a place among the diverse and permanently unacceptable forms of racism. We need only mention the sad case of the United States, where the words, "Hispanic" or "Latino" as applied to Latin Americans—to Puerto Ricans and Chicanos in particular—carry a strong connotation of the disdain with which the apparently transparent citizens of that unhappy country habitually deal with persons "of color." It may be useful, as well, to recall a statement attributed in its classical form to Alexandre Dumas: "Africa begins at the Pyrenees." The sacrosanct West thus shows its repugnance toward *the other*, which is not itself, and finds the embodiment par excellence of this *other* in Africa, whose tortured present was *caused* by Western capitalism, which "undeveloped" it in order to make its own growth possible.
> (Fernández Retamar 1989: 63)

The Black Legend was sparked by Bartolomé de las Casas' account (1992) of the devastation the Spaniards wreaked on the Indigenous cultures of Latin America, and it served to demonize Spain. Fernández Retamar attempts to clear Spain's name in order to reclaim Latin America's Iberian heritage. To be sure, the relation of Latin American philosophy to the European tradition is a complicated one. Simón Bolívar addressed the difficulty early in the region's period of nation-building. In the famous *Carta de Jamaica* we find the following description of an identity crisis that continues to plague the citizens of Latin America:

> [W]e scarcely retain a vestige of once was; we are moreover, neither Indian nor European, but a species midway between the legitimate proprietors of this country and the Spanish usurpers. In short, though Americans by birth we derive our rights from Europe.
> (Bolívar 2004: 65–66)

Just as the people of the newly liberated territories of Spanish America struggled to define themselves in terms of their position between two distinct cultural legacies, Latin American philosophy also struggles with the tensions born of its hybrid identity. Within the peculiar map of philosophy, this hybrid identity becomes even more complicated. Even today, philosophy in Latin America has a notable Franco-German tone.[3] The value of the Latin American philosophical tradition still is not fully recognized, either in the United States or in Latin America, and if one wants to do work in this area, there must be a justification for it. In contrast, the value of Anglo-American, French, and German philosophy is taken to be self-evident. Part of what it means to be a good philosopher, even in Latin America, is to be acquainted with figures such as Kant, Hegel, Nietzsche, Derrida, even Davidson or Searle—Zea and Martí just don't have the same currency. In part, this is because Zea and Martí don't speak the "right" language. As Gloria Anzaldúa points out: "By the end of [the 20th century], Spanish speakers will comprise the biggest minority group in the U.S., a country where students in high schools and colleges are encouraged to take French classes because French is considered more 'cultured'" (Anzaldúa 2007). Anzaldúa is concerned with what she calls "linguistic terrorism" and the slighting of those who speak "español deficiente" or the Spanish of America. If Spain's geographical location places it on the margins of Europe, Latin America's colonial location places it at the margins of "civilized" culture. What Anzaldúa observes about the status of the French language as "cultured" and the Spanish language (and the Spanish of America in particular) as beneath that level of culture, could be said of the perception of philosophy with those adjectives. For example, French-language philosophy is considered more "philosophical" than Spanish-language philosophy, which is why the inclusion of Spanish-language philosophy requires justification in graduate programs and philosophy curricula, whereas, as I have emphasized, the value of the Anglo-American, French, and German traditions is taken as self-evident.

Part of the reason that the French and German philosophical traditions found a welcome reception in Latin America is because those traditions were seen to come "with no strings attached," that is, to represent intellectual traditions not sullied by the colonial baggage that a relation to Spain would carry. Yet, Latin American philosophy is a philosophy carried out in Spanish (and Portuguese), and so it remains bound to Spain (and the Iberian peninsula) and is victimized by the same Eurocentrism that excludes Spain (and by association, Latin America) from entrance to the archons of philosophy.

What we need, if we really want to rid the field of philosophy from the ghettos that isolate and silence important voices is a more critical approach to philosophy itself. The work of Jacques Derrida offered important tools in this direction. As he indicates in the last interview he did before his death: "Deconstruction in general is an undertaking that many have considered, and rightly so, to be a gesture of suspicion with regard to all Eurocentrism"

(Derrida 2007: 40).[4] Derrida carefully unpacks the relation between deconstruction and Europe. He writes:

> What I call "deconstruction" even when it is directed toward something from Europe, is European; it is a product of Europe, a relation of Europe to itself as an experience of radical alterity. Since the time of the Enlightenment, Europe has undertaken a perpetual self-critique, and in this perfectible heritage there is a chance for a future. At least I would like to hope so, and that is what feeds my indignation when I hear people definitively condemning Europe as if it were but the scene of its crimes.
>
> (Derrida 2007: 44–45)

So, although deconstruction attacks Eurocentrism, it acknowledges itself as part of the European tradition, but as that part of the tradition engaged in a constant state of self-critique. Latin American philosophy is European too, but just as Bolívar so trenchantly captured with his reference to Latin Americans as "Americans by birth and Europeans by right," Latin American philosophy is of mixed Euro-American lineage and so in questioning Europe, it questions itself. Its hybrid identity and its failure to fit on the traditional map of philosophy have led to a crisis of identity which has generated what might be called an excessive cycle of self-criticism and self-questioning within its philosophical tradition.

Aspects of this self-criticism are healthy, but some aspects are the result of certain pathologies that plague the field of philosophy. Philosophers are obsessed with boundaries and borders—the tighter the better. And it is not just voices that speak in other languages that are silenced or dismissed when the map of philosophy is drawn too narrowly. Plenty of German-speaking philosophers have sought to exclude other German-speaking philosophers. We can think of Kant's critical project and the leading role that borders play in the drama of his critiques. For Kant, boundaries are linked to progress and security in philosophy: Only with the proper boundaries in place can philosophy retain its place as the queen of the sciences. Philosophers who play with these boundaries are immediately looked on with suspicion. An obsession with strict boundaries is one of the reasons why philosophers have tended to be uncomfortable with moves to bring other disciplines into close company with philosophy. This explains the unhappy fate of the early German Romantics. Their call for the unification of poetry and philosophy led, until quite recently, to their banishment from the field of philosophy. The task of those who we may call the philosophical border police reached its pinnacle with the development of analytic philosophy.[5] Carnap tried to run Heidegger out of the territory of philosophy. Some strands of analytic philosophy involved such a reductionist view of the tasks of philosophy (linguistic analysis, conditions of verifiability, etc.) that the borders of philosophy became drawn so narrowly that many important voices were cast aside as nefariously nonsensical or irrational.[6] Of course, we need some limits to guide our philosophical investigations—the right borders can help to keep the field healthy and progressive, but when the boundaries are drawn too rigidly, then philosophy risks becoming a most barren, desolate field. The philosophical minutemen of our tradition do great harm to the field of philosophy as they proliferate hierarchies based on power rather than philosophical quality. We do need some borders in place to define the field of philosophy, and surely also criteria to distinguish the value of various contributions to the field. This is not the place to discuss the details of how to erect the borders of philosophy or how to generate a list of criteria for assessing the value of a given contribution, but one thing is clear: Blanket condemnations of all foreign contributions (or those that don't come in the languages of English, French, or German) should have no place in shaping our field.

Toward a New Internationalism for Philosophy

The presence of voices that speak languages other than English, French, and German to the field of philosophy will help us move to a new, enriching level of internationalism. In his foreword to *Caliban*, Frederic Jameson emphasizes, referencing Goethe's sense of world literature, that world literature

> has nothing to do with eternal invariants and timeless forms, but very specifically with literary and cultural journals read across national boundaries and with the emergence of critical networks by which the intellectuals of one country inform themselves about the specific intellectual problems and debates of another.
> (Fernández Retamar 1989: xi)

From this observation he concludes:

> We, therefore, need a new literary and cultural internationalism which involves risks and dangers, which calls us into question fully, as much as it acknowledges the Other, thereby also serving as a more adequate and chastening form of self-knowledge. This "internationalism of the national situations" neither reduces the "Third World" to some homogenous Other of the West, nor does it vacuously celebrate the "astonishing" pluralism of human cultures.
> (xii)

We can apply Jameson's insights to the field of philosophy. Part of the reason for the exclusion of Spanish-language philosophy from the professional canon in the United States is the result of a rather provincial notion of philosophical internationalism, a provincialism that reduces the so-called Third World to a group of second- or even third-rate copies of French, German, or Anglo philosophical currents. One balm against this sort of myopic view of the philosophical world is to take a closer look at intellectual history and to make a commitment to including more voices in philosophy. We can take our cue from Martí, who was well aware of the importance of intellectual history:

> To know one's country and govern it with that knowledge is the only way to free it from tyranny. The European university must bow to the American university. The history of America, from the Incas to the present, must be taught in clear detail and to the letter, even if the archons of Greece are overlooked. Our Greece must take priority over the Greece which is not ours. We need it more. Nationalist statesmen must replace foreign statesmen. Let the world be grafted onto our republics, but the trunk must be our own.[7]
> (Martí 1977: 88)

In the spirit of Martí's claim, I call for a move to integrate more languages into our canon of philosophy. I have been arguing for one excluded language and its tradition: the Spanish-language philosophical tradition. The attention to Spanish as a philosophical language and to the traditions of the nations of the Spanish-speaking world is no move toward making philosophy nationalistic. Quite the contrary, the move toward inclusion of more voices is part of a project of creating a world philosophy.

Although he is deeply committed to the Latin American cause (and to the Cuban Revolution), Fernández Retamar is clear that dedication to a true intellectual internationalism should trump merely national interests:

> My wish is not, and never was, to present Latin America and the Caribbean as a region cut off from the rest of the world but rather to view it precisely as a part of the world—a part that should be looked at with the same attention and respect as the rest, not as a merely paraphrastic expression of the West.
>
> (Fernández Retamar 1989: 55, 2003: 129)

The internationalism that Fernández Retamar returns to is just the call that I think we need to take up if we want our field to be engaged in the sort of internationalism that will breed an inclusive canon in which no tradition is made to vanish.

Concluding Remarks

Paul Gilroy (1993) notes that specialist and nationalist gazes are obstacles in the way of developing a truly international intellectual dialogue. When philosophers erect boundaries that replicate what the nation-states put into place, the philosophical lens becomes myopic. Long before Gilroy voiced his concerns regarding overspecialization, José Enrique Rodó warned us of this danger. In his essay, *Ariel*, written in 1900 to alert Latin Americans of the perils that the United States (symbolized as plodding, monstrous Caliban) posed to their culture (symbolized as the pure creature of spirit, Ariel), we find this impassioned statement on the price of progress:

> Unhappily, it is in civilizations that have achieved a whole and refined culture that the danger of spiritual limitation is most real and leads to the most dreaded consequences. In fact, to the degree that culture advances, the law of evolution, manifesting itself in society as in nature to be a growing tendency toward heterogeneity, seems to require a corresponding limitation in individual aptitudes and the inclination to restrict more severely each individual's field of action. While it is a necessary condition to progress, the development of specialization brings with it visible disadvantages, which are not limited to narrowing the horizon of individual intelligence and which inevitably falsify our concept of the world. Specialization, because of the great diversity of individual preferences and habits, is also damaging to a sense of solidarity. Auguste Comte has tellingly noted this danger in advanced civilizations. In his view, the most serious flaw in a state of high social perfection lies in the frequency with which it produces deformed spirits, spirits extremely adept in one aspect of life but monstrously inept in all others.[8]
>
> (Rodó 1988: 42–43)

Rodó's insight is an important one, and although he was concerned with Latin American culture, his insight helps us identify a problem facing philosophy in the United States and the sort of limitation that threatens to make of our field an impoverished, overspecialized area that will produce deformed spirits, extremely adept in one area of philosophy and monstrously inept in all others. The monsters born of the overspecialization of philosophy are many: The ones I have tried to battle in this chapter include a historical myopia, an exclusionary gaze, and rigidly prohibitive borders for a field that should be ever striving to expand and grow. Taking the tradition that speaks in the Spanish language seriously would be one small step in helping to correct a tendency toward just the sort of spirit squeezing overspecialization against which Rodó warned. Opening the field of philosophy to more voices will diversify the canon of philosophy and lead us to question some of the criteria that have been used to justify the exclusion of entire traditions from that canon.[9]

References

Anzaldúa, G. (2007) *Borderlands/La Frontera: The New Mestiza*, San Francisco: Aunt Lute Books.
Arthur Pap (trans.). (1959) "The Elimination of Metaphysics through Logical Analysis," in A. J. Ayer (ed.), *Logical Positivism*, 60–81, New York: The Free Press.
Bolívar, S. (2004) "Jamaica Letter," in J. Gracia and E. Millán-Zaibert (eds.), *Latin American Philosophy for the 21st Century*, 63–66, Amherst, NY: Prometheus Books.
Carnap, R. (1931) "Die Überwin-dung der Metaphysik durch die logische Analyse der Sprache," *Erkenntnis* 2: 219–241.
de Las Casa, B. (1992) *The Devastation of the Indies: A Brief Account*, H. Briffault (trans.), foreword by B. Donovan, Baltimore: The Johns Hopkins University Press.
Derrida, J. (2007) *Learning to Live Finally: The Last Interview*, P.-A. Brault and M. Naas (trans.), Hoboken, NJ: Melville Publishing House.
Edwards, J. (1991) *Persona Non Grata: A Memoir of Disenchantment with the Cuban Revolution*, A. Hurley (trans.), preface by O. Paz, New York: Nation Books.
Fernández Retamar, R. (1989) *Caliban and Other Essays*, E. Baker (trans.), foreword by F. Jameson, Minneapolis: University of Minnesota Press.
Fernández Retamar, R. (2003) *Todo Caliban, prólogo de Frederic Jameson*, San Juan: Ediciones Callejón.
Gilroy, P. (1993) *The Black Atlantic: Modernity and Double Consciousness*, Cambridge: Harvard University Press.
Hörisch, J. (2005) *Theorie-Apotheke: Eine Hand-reichung zu den humanwissenschaftlichen Theorien der letzten fünfzig Jahre, ein-schließlich ihrer Risiken und Nebenwirkungen*, Frankfurt am Main: Eichborn Verlag.
Martí, J. (1964) *Obras Completas*, Volume III, J. Quintana (ed.), Caracas: Litho Tip.
Martí, J. (1977) "Our America," in E. Randall et al. (trans.), *Our America: Writings on Latin America and the Struggle for Cuban Independence*, New York: Monthly Review Press.
Millán-Zaibert, E. (2008) "A Great Vanishing Act? The Latin American Philosophical Tradition and How Ariel and Caliban Helped Save It from Oblivion," *CR: The New Centennial Review* 7 (3): 149–169.
Ramos, J. ([1989] 2003) *Desencuentros de la modernidad en América Latina. Literatura y política en el siglo xix*, México: Fondo de la cultura económica. In English as (2001) *Divergent Modernities: Culture and Politics in Nineteenth-Century Latin America*, J. D. Blanco (trans.), Durham: Duke University Press.
Rodó, J. E. (1988) *Ariel*, M. S. Peden (trans.), foreword by J. W. Symington, prologue by C. Fuentes, Austin: University of Texas Press.
Rodó, J. E. (2004) *Ariel, edición de Belén Castro*, Madrid: Catedra.

Notes

1 I borrow this phrase from Cuban essayist Roberto Fernández Retamar, who brings it up within the context of dismantling the myth "according to which Reason was revealed to Greece, became an Empire in Rome, and assimilated a Religion that was destined after several centuries in hibernation, to reappear like an armed prophet in the works of the (post-barbarian) Westerners, who were to spend the next several centuries fulfilling the onerous mission of bringing the light of 'civilization' to the rest of the planet. If any country permits us to unmask the genial fraud implicit in this 'history' appropriated by the developed Western bourgeoisie, it is Spain—a fact that no doubt has contributed in no small measure to the denigration it has suffered at Western hands. I do not pretend to

be an expert on the matter, but common knowledge is sufficient to begin to rectify this mendacious cultural autobiography" (Fernández Retamar 1989: 63). I refer to Fernández Retamar throughout this chapter, not without awareness of his dubious standing in the eyes of some thinkers. Jorge Edwards, for example, describes him as a "fierce bureaucrat of literature," a standing that freed him of any suspicion by the Castro regime and essentially made him untouchable (Edwards 1991: 139). There are moments in his work when Fernández Retamar obviously allows his enthusiasm for the Cuban Revolution to lead him into making quite biased claims, but I think that many of his points do stand up to strong critique and his insights can serve as tools to help us deal with the unjust position in which the Latin American intellectual tradition finds itself.
2 Some thinkers have done this, yet the philosophical world is slow to catch on to their work. See, for example, Ramos (2003; 2001). Of course, a focus on the problem of modernity is not the only way to liberate Latin American philosophy from its colonial condition. Recent work by thinkers such as Linda Martín Alcoff and Jorge J. E. Gracia on the problem of race has done much to highlight the unique philosophical contributions of the Latin American philosophical tradition.
3 When I taught in Venezuela at the Universidad Simón Bolívar in 1998, I gave seminars on Kant and the early German Romantics, and even a course on Bertrand Russell. The students were not interested in anything on Leopoldo Zea, José Enrique Rodó, José Martí, Domingo Faustino Sarmiento, or Andrés Bello, to name just a few of the central figures of the Latin American tradition.
4 I am grateful to Michael Naas for bringing this text to my attention.
5 For more on this, see Hörisch (2005: 35–44).
6 An excellent example of such a view is Rudolph Carnap's "Die Überwin-dung der Metaphysik durch die logische Analyse der Sprache" (1931).
7 See also Martí (1964: 108): "Conocer el país, y gobernarlo conforme al conocimiento, es el único modo de librarlo de tiranías. La Universidad europea ha de ceder a la Universidad Americana. La historia de América, de los incas a acá, ha de enseñarse al dedillo, aunque no se enseñe la de los arcontes de Grecia. Nuestra Grecia es preferible a la Grecia que no es nuestra. Nos es más necesaria. Los políticos nacionales han de reemplazar a los políticos exóticos. Injértese en nuestras Repúblicas el mundo; pero el tronco ha de ser el de nuestras Repúblicas."
8 Disregarding Carlos Fuentes' aesthetic assessment of Rodó's style (in the prologue of the aforementioned volume, Fuentes calls Ariel "a supremely irritating book" whose "rhetoric is insufferable"), I would like to give the citation in Rodó's beautiful Spanish:

Por desdicha, es en los tiempos y las civilizaciones que han alcanzado una completa y refinada cultura donde el peligro de esta limitación de los espíritus tiene una importancia más real y conduce a resultados más terribles. Quiere, en efecto, la ley de evolución, manifestándose en la sociedad come en la Naturaleza por una creciente tendencia a la heterogeneidad, que, a medida que la cultura general de las sociedades avanza, se limite correlativamente la extension de las aptitudes individuales y haya de ceñirse el campo de acción de cada uno a una especialidad más restringida. Sin dejar de constituir una condición necesaria de progreso, ese desenvolvimiento del espíritu de especialización trae consigo desventajas visibles, que no se limitan a estrechar el horizonte de cada inteligencia, falseando necesariamente su concepto del mundo, sino que alcanzan y perjudican, por la dispersión de las afecciones y los hábitos individuales, al sentimiento de la solidaridad. Augusto Comte ha señalado bien este peligro de las civilizaciones avanzadas. Un alto estado de perfeccionamiento social tiene para él un grave inconveniente en la facilidad con que suscita la aparición de espíritus deformados y estrechos; de espíritus 'muy capaces bajo un aspecto único y monstruosamente ineptos bajo todos los otros' (Rodó 2004: 155).

9 I have had the good fortune to consider these issues in a wide array of forums over the past few years. I would like to thank my fellow participants at a roundtable held in Chicago in April 2006 on "Inclusiveness Issues in the Profession" sponsored by the American Philosophical Association's Committee on Inclusiveness and the Committee on the Statue of Women and from the session on *The Writer as a Philosopher in Latin America* at the American Philosophical Association Eastern Division Meeting, held in Washington, DC in December 2006. Thanks also to the students at the University of Oregon who attended my talk "Towards a New Philosophical Internationalism," and to John Lysaker for inviting me to participate in his seminar on Latin American philosophy. I also thank my undergraduate and graduate students at DePaul, who have been wonderful interlocutors as I developed my thoughts on these matters.

Reading Questions

1. Have you been taught that philosophy emerged in Ancient Greece, progressed in Europe, and has reached its current state of development in the U.S.? Where does this narrative come from, according to Millán Brusslan? How does it influence the way in which we think about philosophy? How does it influence the way we think about the places that are not a part of this narrative?
2. How has colonialism contributed to historical amnesia about Latin American philosophy, according to the text?
3. What incentivizes philosophers to police the borders of the discipline? Draw from the text to discuss what is to be gained by this border-policing, and what is sacrificed.
4. In what ways is the supposed nonexistence of Latin American philosophy reinforced by academic institutions, according to Millán Brusslan? What could be done to change this set of circumstances?
5. Millán Brusslan quotes the Cuban philosopher José Martí, who writes, "The history of America, from the Incas to the present, must be taught in clear detail and to the letter, even if the archons of Greece are overlooked. Our Greece must take priority over the Greece which is not ours." Is this call to prioritize Latin American history in tension with Millán Brusslan's project of creating a more integrated world philosophy? Why or why not?
6. Drawing on the text, summarize Rodó's critique of specialization, then discuss: What does the worry about specialization have to do with the Eurocentrism of academic philosophy?

Part 6
Immigration and Citizenship

Introduction

Some of the questions about immigration and citizenship that philosophers have explored are: Can a nation have an unjust conception of citizenship? On what basis can people be justly excluded from political membership? How should immigration laws be enforced? Do nations have any moral obligations to people outside of their borders? On what basis can a state rightly separate people from their families? For many Latinx people, philosophical questions about immigration and citizenship are more than theoretical. The ways in which we answer questions about who gets to be a citizen and why, and about how non-citizens should be treated, often have profound and personal consequences. Latinx people who are not themselves immigrants are likely to have immediate or extended family members who are. And even those Latinx people whose families have resided for centuries in what is now the U.S. are sometimes treated as though their citizenship is suspect.

The essays in this section of the volume explore the ideas of citizenship, democracy, and ethno-racial identity in ways that are attuned to the histories, cultures, social positionalities, and experiences of Latinx communities. This work is invaluable not only because it centers the concerns of those who are most frequently harmed by U.S. immigration policy. The essays also offer innovative ways of seeing central theoretical and practical problems related to immigration and citizenship. They are deeply informed by political histories, the history of ideas, and interviews and news stories, so they provide us with the opportunity to view these philosophical issues from both the widest and narrowest lenses.

In the first essay, "Becoming Citizens, Becoming Latinos," Eduardo Mendieta opens with the idea that the development of democracy within the U.S. has been the result of struggles for citizenship by those who had been hitherto viewed as unworthy of it. Social movements begin with the experiences of privation and suffering of particular groups, which they seek to translate into generalizable rights claims. This process ultimately changes the political landscape for all members of a political body. From this perspective, Mendieta argues, American imperial politics has constituted Latinxs as an underclass. Despite their heterogeneity, what Latinx immigrants have in common is that processes associated with the geopolitics of the United States generated the conditions that led to their immigration and marginalized social and political status. Mendieta calls for Latinxs to assume a new political consciousness in pursuit of the necessary rights of citizenship.

One implication of this conclusion is that through their pursuit of citizenship rights, Latinxs, too, will contribute to the evolution of democracy in the U.S. This argument is the explicit focus of José-Antonio Orosco's essay, "Cesar Chavez and the Pluralist Foundations of U.S. Democracy." Chavez maintains that the presence of Mexican immigrants in the United States is a resource for creating conditions of peace, preserving social justice, and reinvigorating democratic commitments. For Chavez, a growing Latinx community

DOI: 10.4324/9781003385417-37

represents an opportunity to reexamine, through an intercultural dialogue, the public political values of an American society dedicated to military strength and corporate dominance. Orosco demonstrates how Chavez worked to develop a broad-based social movement grounded in Mexican folk culture and history to initiate this reexamination of values. Chavez hoped that American democracy could ultimately accommodate, rather than assimilate, Latinx immigrants.

Chavez's vision for a genuinely multicultural nation is followed, in the next essay, by a more pessimistic picture of the future of Latinxs and U.S. democracy. In "The Latinx Racial Disintegration Thesis: Whiteness, Democracy, and Latinx Identity," José Jorge Mendoza envisions the disintegration of Latinx as a racial category. Mendoza observes a strong correlation between Whiteness and the composition of the electorate, such that Whites must constitute the majority-of-the-majority to preserve their political dominance. Historically, this correlation has been challenged by demographic changes, but each time this challenge has been met through an expansion of U.S. Whiteness, whereby previously racialized groups culturally assimilate and come to be seen as White. This history provides reasons for believing that demographic changes driven by the growth of the Latinx population will not turn the U.S. into a "minority-majority" country. Instead, these changes will lead to some Latinx people being co-opted into Whiteness, while others will continue to be racialized as non-White.

In "Socially, Not Legally, Undocumented," Amy Reed-Sandoval discusses the situation of Latinxs who are presumed to be undocumented on the mere basis of their appearance. Being "socially undocumented" often entails being taken to "look like" someone who is from Mexico and working class. This group of people is subjected to demeaning immigration-related constraints based on their social identities, regardless of their legal status. Conversely, there are people who, despite being undocumented, are rarely subject to legal and informal constraints on how they live their lives. Reed-Sandoval's chapter illuminates the ways in which how people are treated is often disconnected from their legal status and instead a function of stereotypes and expectations

The next essay offers a defense of the Fourteenth Amendment, which protects birthright citizenship, against efforts to weaken or overturn it. In "Jus sanguinis vs. Jus soli: On the Grounds of Justice," Eduardo Mendieta describes the disgraceful racial supremacy that has marked U.S. politics through an analysis of the work of Samuel Huntington, a proponent of the "Latino Threat" narrative—the notion that Latinxs are a threat to the culture, security, and prosperity of the U.S. Mendieta traces the historical development of the idea of citizenship. He argues that the Fourteenth Amendment deracializes citizenship, making it a revolutionary principle that takes the conception of citizenship to new moral and legal heights.

The concluding essay focuses on the gendered dimensions of immigration. Allison B. Wolf's "The Gendered Nature of U.S. Immigration Policy" proposes that U.S. immigration policy differentially affects members of different genders, and it both reflects and perpetuates gender oppression. For example, according to John Lafferty, the former Asylum Chief for the U.S. Citizenship and Immigration Service, the Trump administration's family separation policy was developed to deter *mothers* from migrating to the United States with their children. The policy thus put many migrant women in a double bind—either risk their lives by remaining in their home country or risk having their children taken from them while pursuing safety in the U.S.

Wolf notes that her methodology, which includes drawing from anecdotes, news stories, and the testimonies of migrants and their loved ones, is consistent with what distinguishes discussions of immigration in Latinx philosophy generally. Namely, whether theorizing about citizenship, democracy, race, or justice, these discussions tend to focus on concrete policies that affect the lives of Latin American migrants and their loved ones, and they position Latinx experiences at their core.

25 Becoming Citizens, Becoming Latinos

Eduardo Mendieta

There is no more central institution to democracy than that of citizenship. A government of the people, by the people, for the people is meaningless without this mechanism that empowers and enables human beings to assume the charge, responsibility, and right to rule themselves as a community. Without citizens, there is no democracy. But just as democracy has been the accomplishment of social and political movements, citizenship has also been redefined by some of these same movements. In fact, many of the sociopolitical movements that through their struggles brought about greater democracy in American society were social movements that sought redefinitions of American citizenship. American citizenship has evolved by having been made more inclusive and more expansive. In other words, citizenship has been made to apply to and subsume members of the community who were up to that point not recognized as civic partners and equals. Or, citizenship has been transformed, making it more expansive, and thus more inclusive and welcoming to persons who were not members of the civic community but participated, or could participate, in the national project in some fashion. In short, just as American democracy has a history, American citizenship also has a history. At times their histories have run parallel, but at other times they have been at odds. It is known, for instance, that while American democracy was born proclaiming the equality of all human beings, its citizenship was inaugurated with the exclusion not only of African slaves and women, but also of white males who owned no property. American citizenship, which was supposed to ensure the integrity of American democracy, has been racialized and sexualized since its inception, thus contradicting the fundamental tenet of American democracy that all human beings are born equal. This racialization and sexualization became so entrenched in American democratic thought and practice that it was only until the first half of the twentieth century that American citizenship began to be commensurate with the universal, liberal, and civic ideals proclaimed in the American Constitution and its amendments. In many ways one can even say that American democracy has been realized through the acquisition of citizenship by groups, peoples, races, and ethnicities that had previously been seen as both not worthy and not capable of participating in the self-legislation of the American body politic. American democracy has been the result of the struggles for citizenship by purported unworthy or problematic selves and subjects.

Today, as in the nineteenth century and the early part of the twentieth, American citizenship faces serious challenges. These challenges come both from without and within. From without, the challenges stem from the processes of globalization that are making us all citizens of one world. Globalization ought to be understood not solely in terms of greater economic integration and interdependence, but also as the cultural, political, and social creolization and hybridization of the planet. Globalization, thus, means that we have become vulnerable to risks assumed by others, and vice versa, but also that we have become co-producers of a world culture. One of the most important aspects of globalization, however, is the challenge to the hegemony and autonomy of the nation state, the means through which communities and nations affirm their right to self-legislation. This aspect of globalization, onerous to some but appealing to others, requires that we, as nominal citizens of one world, reach decisions together about matters that affect us all. Indeed, in our contemporary context we may even speak of a "global citizen." This topic, however, is the other half of this essay that cannot be presented.

From within, the challenges to American citizenship come from voter apathy, the disintegration of a common civic culture, the resurgence of nativism movements, and from the growing resentment and even hate of immigrants and foreigners who are seen as both threats and social leeches. The Reaganite neo-liberal economic revolution of deregulation and Bush's attack on big government, coupled with close to two decades of recisionist economy, created a general feeling of fear and anxiety in the United States. Fear and anxiety are always fertile ground for xenophobia, jingoism, and nativism. And the attack on the welfare state, the reluctance to seriously consider a national healthcare program, the general skepticism and backlash against feminist ideals and goals, as well as the attack on affirmative action programs, as manifestation of this fear and anxiety, have corroded any notion of a common national ethos or calling. The fact is that while feminist, racial, ethnic and identity politics are faulted for the "disuniting of America," the real culprits are neo-liberal policies, the restructuring of the American economy, and the increasing ostracism and exclusion of greater numbers of American citizens. As we squat in the squalor of a public square, private affluence reaches unthought and unscalable heights. In such times, the "foreigner," whether real or imagined, becomes the target of our social intolerance and atavism.

Although it might seem otherwise, these two challenges to American citizenship are related. Globalization does not proceed one way. America is not the only agent of globalization; it is also globalized by other agents. One of the main ways in which American citizenship is challenged by these processes and pressures can be found in the claims for social justice made by immigrants and ethnic minorities within the United States. These immigrants are part and parcel of United States' history of colonial/imperial intervention, occupation, economic neo-colonization, and military vigilantism. Today, the United States has the largest immigrant population of any nation in the world. Immigrants amount to almost 10 percent of the total population. Of this percentage, the greatest number are Latinos. In fact, it has been forecasted by many demographers and by the U.S. Census Bureau that by the turn of the next millennium, Latinos will constitute the largest ethnic minority in the country, surpassing African Americans.

In the following, I hope to illuminate the issue of an evolving American citizenship and the immediate challenges it faces vis-a-vis immigrants and ethnic minorities in the United States. At the same time, I will look at Latinos and explore the interconnected questions of cultural identity and political participation. But this investigation is no mere academic exercise. I hope that my analysis will result in making clear a dual challenge: one to American citizenship and another to Latinos. At stake, it seems to me, is the future of American democracy in an age of greater ethnic diversity and global codependence.

Becoming Citizens

Citizenship first evolved, as T. H. Marshall noted almost fifty years ago, through a dual process of geographical fusion and functional separation (Marshall 1963). Citizenship developed with the creation of nations, and later expanded with the transformation of nations into nation states (Habermas 1992). It is for these reasons that citizenship is both a cultural status and a legal capacity. The contemporary nation state is often plagued by the inner paradox of including as members of the community only those individuals who form part of the imaginary community that constitutes the nation while at the same time declaring in its Constitution that it, as a legal state, counts as equals all its members, regardless of their social, cultural, racial, gender status. Analogously, citizenship is plagued by the internal contradiction that it must be seen simultaneously as both a cultural and social status and a legal capacity, a capacity which allows citizens to stand above any kind of social inequality (Schulze 1996). We will see how this internal tension is compounded by conflicts in contemporary society. For the moment, let us note that this tension refers to the two modalities in which citizenship can be enacted or participated in by social agents: as an ascribed cultural and social status or as an inalienable legal capacity and entitlement.

One may speak of the elements or parts of citizenship, but also of ideal citizenship, of the way in which social agents can best live out their citizenship. The cogency and feasibility of ideal citizenship, or of model citizenship, is, however, predicated on both the differentiation and interconnection of the elements that constitute citizenship. Following Marshall and Macpherson, we can say that citizenship has as its central elements civil, political, and social rights (Marshall 1985; Macpherson 1985). Civil rights can be thought of as the neural column upon which the whole organic system of rights is predicated. Political rights are the muscles of the organism. And social rights are its nourishment and sheltering flesh, so to speak.

Civil rights are personal and individual. Sometimes they are said to be inalienable and thus to appear as part of natural law. They provide the rationale for the following: freedom of speech and publication, freedom of conscience and religion, freedom of association and movement, freedom from the arbitrary use of state force and from the impartial use of justice, freedom from invasion of one's privacy by either the state or other persons, and freedom to own private property, and thus, freedom to enter and execute valid contracts. In general, these are rights protecting against the state and against the illegitimate use of coercion whether political, legal, or physical.

Political rights are also personal rights, but they only acquire meaning or significance in the context of social relations. In other words, these rights acquire meaning only when used in concert with other citizens striving for similar political goals. Political rights include the right to participate in the development, acquisition, and delegation of political power. It is through political rights that civil rights become a power or force that can be enacted against the state, through the state. Finally, social rights, which are of a more recent vintage in the unfolding of citizenship rights, are less rights of individuals than of groups. These rights, in other words, are not assumed to be equally valid for all, but only for some. In contrast to civil rights and political rights, furthermore, they are not rights against the state, but are rights granted, or enabled, by the state. They are thus dependent on the kinds of institutions that constitute the modern welfare nation state. Social rights constitute the following rights: to work, to a minimum wage, to education, to social security against involuntary unemployment and the social consequences of old age, illness, even the death of the head of a household. These rights even include rights to leisure and rest (paid vacations and holidays, for instance), to maternal and paternal leave, and even to bereavement. In short, social rights are rights to social services. Social rights consist of rights to a level of existence consistent with human dignity, and respect for the well-being of the whole person. Through these rights, a citizen is empowered to participate in the cultural, political, social, and institutional heritage of a nation (Walzer [1992], esp. last the chapter "Constitutional Rights and the Shape of Civil Society").

Citizenship, then, is made up of a neural system constituted by individual rights against the state; rights to participate in the state that constitutes a system of muscles that allows individuals to act in concert with others; and rights that are conditional upon the state, but that attend to the integral dignity of the person, and thus can be thought of as the flesh that shelters the neural and muscular systems. While each element may have evolved at different stages, more or less, in tandem with the evolution of the state, they nonetheless constitute a systematic and coherent whole. Many political theoreticians have noted that the unfolding of these elements that constitute citizenship corresponded to the English, American, and French revolutions, each more or less having inaugurated the next level of internal differentiation of rights pertaining to citizenship. This historical parallelism, however, must be accepted with great reservations. For, in the last instance, regardless of whether the English, the American, or French revolutions had taken place, civil rights inevitably would have demanded for political rights, which in turn would have required social rights. In Habermas's view, in fact, the unfolding of rights corresponds to an internal normative dynamic of both nation states and their concomitant citizenship. The point to be established here is that today we can see that while citizenship has evolved, its contemporary integrity and meaning hinges on the interconnection of all three sets of rights (Habermas 1996).

It was already noted that citizenship is transformed by being made either more inclusive or more expansive. Existing rights are either extended to hitherto disenfranchised members of the community, or new rights are articulated and claimed that will address needs or conditions not covered by already existing rights. This distinction might turn out to be merely heuristic and analytic, for in practice, and as history has amply demonstrated, when members of a community are made civic equals, new rights are necessitated that will make possible their equal participation in all the other rights of the civic union.

Similarly, when new rights are "discovered" for both new and old members of the community, these require that all pre-existing rights be equally accessible to the new citizens. A case in point is the Fourteenth Amendment, from which the whole fabric of rights against discrimination and equal participation in the benefits and duties of society stem. More concretely, from the Fourteenth Amendment there unfolded logically the rights not only against sexual discrimination, but also against discrimination because of a physical handicap, and discrimination based on sexual orientation. The important point to be foregrounded about this heuristic distinction is that the rights of citizens are contingent upon social movements. Whether citizenship rights are made to apply to new citizens, or new rights are discovered or pronounced, this all depends upon the efforts of groups that claim inclusion and argue for their own equal participation in the community. Now, social movements ought to be broadly understood to mean not just political and economic movements, but also cultural and even spiritual movements. It is because there have been social movements that have put pressure on the state, and the ruling opinion of the day, that citizenship has expanded and has been made more inclusive. Constitutional amendments have been the result as much of major changes in the structure of the nation, such as the Civil War, as of movements like the Woman Suffrage movement and the Civil Rights movement. Social movements, most importantly, have brought about a transformation of citizenship through the transformation of citizens themselves. Indeed, it is in the context of the new social movements that more expansive notions of citizenship were first forged. Social movements have been the crucible in which new citizens were created. It is later that these notions of a new citizen solidified, so to say, into the constitutional and legal codes of the body politic. If the law is a relay mechanism between the constitution of a nation and its moral character, as Habermas notes, social movements are the place where the moral insights of a political community are lived out, nurtured, and transformed into feasible citizenship rights.

Social movements, interestingly, are agents of transformation insofar as they raise, if not universalizable, at least generalizable claims within a society out of their own particular and unique experiences of deprivation, exclusion, and disenfranchisement. In other words, social movements translate their particular and unique experiences of privation and suffering into either universalizable or generalizable rights claims. Thus, for instance, the first social movement of all, the workers movement, transformed their social status of privation into a critique of the political status quo, thus bringing about the expansion of citizenship through the expansion of political rights. The worker, living in a situation of inequality, claimed political rights to associate, to enter into contract, to a fair trial, etc., so that his/her situation of inequality could be matched by a situation of civil and political equality. Yet the rights that workers claimed for themselves were rights that ought to have been extended to every member of the community. Conversely, subjects of the civic community that did not receive these rights would be thereby deprived of a full standing in this community and thus denied complete access to its benefits, rights, and duties. In short, a worker without rights came to be seen as no less than an indentured servant, and the individuals with complete access to the rights of the nation as no more than another aristocracy.

In her Tanner Lectures Judith Shklar brilliantly illustrated how the struggle for inclusion has been a struggle for rights that ought to be generalizable to all. She demonstrated how the shadow of slavery has darkened the history of American citizenship precisely insofar as those who have sought inclusion in the body politic by means of a transformation of its citizenship have always used the condition of the slave as the negation of the dignity of the person (Shklar 1991). Thus, social movements within the United States have always referred to the slave as the negative condition that would result from either privation of the right to vote or the right to earn one's own living. Slavery is the absolute negation of all humanity, thus any movement that sought to depart from, or keep in abeyance, any social structure that might lead to this condition made universalizable rights claims. In other words, no one ought to be treated as a slave and no one should submit to any situation in which she would be treated as though she were a slave. Women argued thus, although equivocally. At first, by suggesting that women would be no less than slaves if they were not enfranchised. Later, by suggesting that they could not be slaves because of their high moral standing and education, and thus their not being enfranchised was an affront to them. The condition of the slave was what no one should have been made to descend to and what everyone should have been protected from.

To this day, American citizenship has yet to disavow its deeply entrenched racism, which takes shape in its racialization of citizenship. It remains bewitched by the dark gaze of slavery. It should not be forgotten that "Asians" could not become citizens until the second half of this century, and that many a Mexican American, despite the Guadalupe Hidalgo Treaty of 1848, continued to be treated as second-class citizens until after World War II. Many other similar cases can be brought forth (Smith 1997). Nonetheless, the point I am trying to illustrate and establish is that social movements always begin from situations and conditions of political, economic, social, and cultural privation, isolation, exclusion, and suffering. These experiences are then translated into claims that are applicable to all. For, in short, an injustice to one is an injustice to all, and conversely, a right that only some have is but a privilege and thus not a real right. Rights are powers and entitlements that we all should be able to claim and have access to. It is, however, only individuals in social contexts who have insight into the rights that they both possess and might lack. As Linda Martín Alcoff noted with respect to her defense of identity politics, "any concept of the universal has significance and truth to the extent that it is true for some particular 'me,' that is, to the extent that it can relate to my own individual, particular existence, or to someone else's" (Alcoff 1997). Rights, in short, only have meaning if they have significance for a particular person or group. For they alone can test their validity and reach. This, in turn, has as its other side, or complement, the fact that social movements are made possible by citizenship rights even though they are contributing to the elucidation of such rights. As J. M. Barbalet put it: "Social movements contribute to and are facilitated by citizenship" (Barbalet 1988: 98). In other words, citizenship rights need and call forth social movements. A social movement is witness to an inchoate right or a right yet to be made explicit. A lack of social movements reveals the absence of citizenship rights. Social movements, in fact, are the lifeline of citizenship rights. On the other hand, a complete absence of citizenship rights can result in the birthing of social, political, and cultural movements for the right to have rights. In such cases, social movements become struggles for the social space in which citizens can be citizens.

It is this interdependence between social movements and citizenship rights, their mutuality in short, that is at issue when questions of cultural identity and political participation are raised. Social movements are ways of claiming cultural identity; that is, cultural identity is affirmed and forged through social movements. In contrast, political participation has often been construed as a process by means of which one disavows one's cultural uniqueness and social locality. This at least has been the way political participation and cultural identity have been related within the liberal tradition that has guided American political thought. Yet, as was noted above, political participation is an extension of one's cultural identity. Indeed, with Renato Rosaldo, we must speak of a "cultural citizenship," or a culture of citizenship (Flores and Benmayor 1997). Culture, the ways in which social agents construct their social space, determines their citizenship, while the enactment of citizenship in turn transforms and conditions one's culture. Social movements are a place where this codetermination is catalyzed.

Becoming Latino

Social labels, ethnic markers, and racial categories are no less arbitrary and no less fraught with power differentials than the lines that mark a map circumscribing a geopolitical unit. Like the boundaries that determine the limits of nations, ethnic and racial labels include as well as exclude. They are the result of the enactment of power by some over others. Yet there is a dynamic between being labeled and identifying oneself. One resists a label by naming oneself. By naming oneself, one might circumvent or disable and neutralize a label. Frontiers and borders are contested, and not just from the side of the colonizer. They remain ever porous sites of negotiation and even compromise. At times, similarly ethnic and racial labels become the testimony of a compromise. The ethnic label "Hispanic" was one such compromise.[1] In contrast to African Americans, Hispanics were not an ethnic minority, they became one. The label was imposed, but today it is taken on as the result of a compromise between entrenched racist values and Latino resistance (Acosta-Belen and Santiago 1995). Still, the Latino condition is not a point of departure, but a point of arrival. To this extent, one can say that in inverse relationship to African Americans who are born as such, Latinos are made, or rather, they become Latino. The Latino condition is particularly important, not only for personal and existential reasons—given that I am a so-called Latino—but also because, as I argue in the following, a series of challenges is presented by it to both American citizenship and to the peoples who are agglutinated under the label "Latino."

Many social scientists have rightly pointed to the problems with the ethnic label of "Hispanic" (Oboler 1995; see also Rumbaut 1992). Hispanics are said to be all persons of Latin American descent, who have been in the United States for several generations, or who might have arrived yesterday. They are said to speak Spanish, although many do not. Some are immigrants, while others are political refugees. Some could come from Latin American countries, although it is not clear whether Spaniards and Brazilians could be considered Hispanic. It is also not clear whether Blacks, descendants of slaves from the Caribbean and many Latin American countries with sizable black populations, are either Hispanics or Blacks. In short, the peoples that the label "Hispanic" hopes to embrace are too heterogeneous and diverse to be done justice to by this rather homogenizing label. Furthermore, as Mary Romero has pointed out, the term "Hispanic" has contributed to the depoliticization of the history of each group subsumed under the label and it has deleteriously and even disrespectfully placed too much weight on the European elements of the traditions that inform the cultures of peoples of Latin American descent (Romero et al. 1996: xv). Indeed, the label "Hispanic" was introduced into the census under President Nixon, precisely at the height of political mobilization and radicalization of Chicanos and Puerto Ricans (Klor de Alva 1989), and as such it may be interpreted as an attempt to undermine the politicization and radicalization of Latinos. Today, I prefer the term "Latino" to "Hispanic," although it shares some of the same problems.

It is required that we take a closer look at the groups subsumed under the label "Latino." Latinos are made up of peoples of Mexican, Puerto Rican, Cuban, Central and South American, and other Latin American descent. Each group has a very different history, and each one constitutes a different percentage of the more than twenty million Latinos in the United States. Before proceeding beyond the issue of who gets counted, we must highlight a problem. Should this total number of Latinos include or exclude Puerto Ricans on the island? If we include the latter, then we accrue another three and a half million so-called Latinos. Nevertheless, if we proceed, we will note that each group constitutes a different percentage of the total number: Mexicans constitute 62.6 percent, Puerto Ricans 11.6 percent, Cubans 7.8 percent, Central and South Americans 12.7 percent, and other Latinos constitute 5.3 percent of the total number of Latinos (Romero et al. 1996: xvii, 106 ff). Now, let us consider the three major groups of Latinos. This will allow us to have a more precise understanding of the problems and challenges that Latinos have faced and how they pose these problems and challenges to American citizenship.

Mexicans are people that have formed part of the country since the early part of the nineteenth century when the United States colonized the West and Southwest. Through the 1840s, these lands were part of Mexico. After the Mexican-American War, the United States went on to acquire almost half of its present territory by annexing half of Mexico's territory. But Mexicans are also the immigrants that might have just crossed the border. They are a large migrant labor force that cross the border seasonally, in many cases under amnesty. It has been pointed out that sometimes citizenship is extended to new citizens through either immigration or by the result of war. Mexicans became citizens, if only nominally and not in practice, through the effects of imperialistic war (Takaki 1993: 166 ff; see also Zinn 1980: ch. 8). Still, this does not explain the waves of immigration that began to flow with regularity since the turn of the century. With the expansion of the American economy through the first part of this century, and later with the two world wars, the United States actively recruited cheap farm labor in Mexico. This was not just an informal arrangement, but also a national policy. The Bracero Program, begun in 1943, is a case in point. To this day, despite nativism and xenophobic outbursts against "immigrants," Mexicans continue to be courted by the labor markets of the United States. NAFTA, in fact, must be put in the context of this history of labor assimilation from across the border.

Puerto Ricans have a similar history. They were incorporated into the American body politic in 1898 after the Spanish-American War, when the island of Puerto Rico became a territorial protectorate of the United States. In July of 1898, Guam, Puerto Rico, and the Philippines were turned over by Spain to the United States for a payment of $20 million. Interestingly, however, it was only until the Jones Act of 1917 that American citizenship was effectively imposed upon Puerto Ricans, even though they were deprived of the right to participate in the election of the president that would send them to wars, which was one of the primary reasons for incorporating them as citizens. Nonetheless, like Mexicans, Puerto Ricans have also been actively recruited by the Eastern industrial labor markets. Combined with a policy of industrialization and financial investment that has turned the island into a plantation of U.S economic lords, plus incentives to migrate to the mainland, Puerto Ricans have been left without a homeland, and have yet to be fully accepted in their adoptive country. Puerto Ricans, Mexicans, Native Americans, Hawaiians, and Alaskan Indians, constitute national minorities who have been forcefully brought into the Union only to be made second class citizens. Puerto Ricans, like Native Americans and African Americans, suffer the most severe forms of social privation and stagnation: They have the largest rate of unemployment and the lowest standard of living. Perhaps analogously to Native Americans, most Puerto Ricans are concentrated in their urban reservation: Fort New York.

Cubans, in contrast to Mexicans and Puerto Ricans, came to the United States, partly as a consequence of long-term American policies, but also due to political exile. It is not to be forgotten that Cuba has been under the sphere of American influence since 1898, when the United States challenged the colonial hold of Spain over the Caribbean.

Since the Cuban War of Independence, essentially aborted by the Platt Amendment, up through its revolution in 1959, Cuba was an economic colony of the United States. From the revolution, exiles coming from the upper economic classes of Cuban society landed in the United States receiving all kinds of economic aid and sympathy from Americans. At the beginning of the Cold War, Cubans had the "fortune" of being categorized as refugees from a communist regime. Later groups of Cubans coming to the states have not come under such auspicious conditions, yet they have also come as political refugees from a communist dictatorship. Curiously, the imperialism and anticommunism of American history could be said to be summarized and embodied in the history of Cuban immigrants.

Now if we compare these groups, we will note the following similarities and contrasts. While Mexicans have mostly immigrated toward the West and Southwest, Puerto Ricans have concentrated in the tristate area of Connecticut, New York, and Boston, with New York being the primary area of concentration for Puerto Ricans. While a substantive number of Mexicans migrate toward the major metropolises of the West, significant numbers of them gravitate toward the rural labor markets of the West and Southwest. Puerto Ricans, in contrast, remain a mostly urban immigrant population. Cubans, similarly, have remained an urban exile community, concentrating in Miami. In contrast to Mexicans, Cubans show the largest and fastest rates of naturalization among Hispanics. Colombians alone show, in absolute numbers, the largest number of naturalizations. Mexicans take the longest to naturalize, when they do. In this they are similar only to Canadians.

Latinos from Central America and South America have become part of more recent waves of immigrants to the United States in this second half of the twentieth century for reasons similar to those that brought Mexicans, Puerto Ricans, and Cubans to the United States. Thus, if we look at the Nicaraguans, Guatemalans, Salvadoreans, and Costa Ricans, we will notice that they were integrated into the sphere of U.S. influence through either military intervention or economic colonization. The case of Nicaraguans and Guatemalans, however, is a particularly sad chapter in the history of American immigration. Most Nicaraguans and Guatemalans immigrated to the United States aided by relief, peace, and religious organizations. These immigrants were escaping political repression, war, and in many cases violent military persecution and extermination. As is well known today, these conditions were brought about by U.S. policies in Central America, such as direct support of paramilitary organizations in order to destabilize the Sandinista government in Nicaragua. Yet, when most of these political refugees arrived in the United States, they were labeled "illegal aliens" thus not qualifying either for refugee visas or government relief programs such as those that Vietnamese, Cambodians, and now Russians, are receiving.

What should have become patently clear by now is that in all cases, Latinos have become immigrants due to bidirectional processes having to do with the geopolitics of the United States. In other words, Latin Americans have formed part of the American sphere of influence not only because of foreign policies like the Monroe Doctrine and national self-understanding like the mythology of Manifest Destiny, but also because of more immediate economic and political policies like the Bracero and Bootstrap programs that have actively recruited workers from Mexico and Puerto Rico respectively. In many ways, as Alejandro Portes has aptly put it, many Latin Americans were already Americanized even before they became immigrants (Portes 1990: 162). Or, more accurately, they were Latinized even before they had become immigrants.

Despite their differences, Latinos possess the following statistical characteristics. They are younger than the general population. They tend to have lower levels of educational attainment. Over one third of Latinos tend to be immigrants, which means they tend to be politically isolated. They also have lower levels of employment and experience the worst working conditions, whether in rural or urban settings. They also tend to earn less than the national average by the large margin of ten thousand dollars. Cubans alone tend to depart from this demographic sketch. From the standpoint of immigration politics and citizenship, Latinos constitute too heterogeneous a group to make quick generalizations. Some, as we noted, became citizens by being colonized, others by being granted political asylum, and others by immigrating and receiving amnesty. Further, the rates of naturalization vary tremendously between groups. Mexicans are the least likely to naturalize, just as the Colombians are the quickest and most numerous to become citizens. Furthermore, as Portes and Rumbaut note in *Immigrant America*, while turn of the century immigrants came from countries without nationhood, or countries that were in the process of obtaining nationhood, most recent immigrants, especially Latin Americans, arrive in the United States with a strong sense of nationality and of belonging to another national ethos (Portes and Rumbaut 1996: 107). This has made the process of their acculturation all the more difficult. Most importantly, however, it has hindered the development of a common Latino civic culture, or a culture of political participation.

This is the point I want to make: American imperial politics has constituted a veritable underclass that is taking over the role that Blacks occupied in the United States throughout the eighteenth and nineteenth centuries. At the same time, Latinos have participated in the development, growth, and enrichment of this nation. Latinos have fought in the wars that this country undertook. Through their labor, enfranchisement, political, and economic struggles, they have also contributed substantively to the transformation and expansion of American democracy. Recognition of this substantive contribution is still forthcoming, even as we approach a new millennium in which Latinos will constitute more than 15 percent of the U.S. population.

American citizenship, as I hope it has become apparent, faces a serious challenge for Latinos. Latinos fit all the categories of a typology of immigrants. They also constitute both "national" and "ethnic" minorities. Some have been citizens since birth, others have yet to become citizens, and some may never do so, although their families might have been American citizens for generations. These different modalities of the Latino condition present challenges because as national minorities, Latinos require particular rights: As ethnic minorities they require special policies to address their entrenched exclusion and marginalization, and as immigrants they also require particular policies that address their unique relationships to the United States. And as citizens-to-be, they call for a policy of civic education and mobilization. American voter participation has been particularly low in the last decades. This apathy will, in effect, become political disenfranchisement if the new Americans are not included, politicized, and conscienticized—to "Anglicize" using Paulo Freire's term—into and through their civic empowerment.

Latinos, on the other hand, face the challenge of having to disavow obsolete forms of nationalism, to assume a new political consciousness, and even to learn a new form of patriotism, constitutional patriotism, to use Habermas's suggestive expression (Habermas 1992: 465–467, 499–500).[2] Constitutional patriotism not for a nation that was their place of birth, but for the homeland that is their future and the future of their children. They also face the challenge of having to recognize their unity and commonalities, despite their diverse nationalities and local differences. "Latino" (and, for that matter, "Hispanic") is an imposed label. It is certainly not historically conscious or generous. Yet it is one that may allow Latinos to develop a pan-Latin consciousness and a Latino American citizenship.[3]

References

Acosta-Belen, E., and Santiago, C. E. (1995) "Merging Borders: The Remapping of America," *The Latino Review of Books* 1 (1): 2–12.
Alcoff, L. M. (1997) "Latina/o Identity Politics" in D. Batstone and E. Mendieta (eds.), *The Good Citizen*, New York: Routledge.
Barbalet, J. M. (1988) *Citizenship*, Minneapolis: University of Minnesota Press.
Flores, W. V., and Benmayor, R. (eds.) (1997) *Latino Cultural Citizenship*, Boston: Beacon Press.
Habermas, J. (1992) "Citizenship and National Identity: Some Reflections on the Future of Europe," *Praxis International* 12 (1): 1–19.
Habermas, J. (1996) *Between Facts and Norms: Contributions to a Discourse Theory of Law and Democracy*, W. Rehg (trans.), Cambridge: MIT Press.
Klor de Alva, J. J. (1989) "Aztlán, Borinquen and Hispanic Nationalism in the United States," in R. A. Anaya and F. Lomeli (eds.), *Aztlán: Essays on the Chicano Homeland*, Albuquerque: University of Mexico Press.
Macpherson, C. B. (1985) "Problems of Human Rights in the Late Twentieth Century," in C. B. Macpherson (ed.), *The Rise and Fall of Economic Justice and Other Papers*, Oxford: Oxford University Press.
Marshall, T. H. (1963) "Citizenship and Social Class (1949)," *Sociology at the Crossroads and Other Essays*, London: Heinemann.
Marshall, T. H. (1985) "Citizenship and Social Class," in C. B. Macpherson (ed.), *The Rise and Fall of Economic Justice and Other Papers*, Oxford: Oxford University Press.
Oboler, S. (1995) *Ethnic Labels, Latino Lives: Identity and the Politics of (Re)Presentation in the United States*, Minneapolis: University of Minnesota Press.

Portes, A. (1990) "From South of the Border: Hispanic Minorities in the United States," in V. Yans-Mclaughlin (ed.), *Immigration Reconsidered: History, Sociology and Politics*, New York: Oxford University Press.
Portes, A., and Rumbaut, R. G. (1996) *Immigrant America: A Portrait* (2nd ed.), Berkeley: University of California Press.
Romero, M., Hondagneu-Sotelo, P., and Ortiz, V. (eds.) (1996) *Challenging Fronteras: Structuring Latina and Latino Lives in the U.S.*, New York: Routledge.
Rumbaut, R. G. (1992) "The Americas: Latin American and Caribbean Peoples in the United States," in A. Stepan (ed.), *Americas: New Interpretative Essays*, Oxford: Oxford University Press.
Schulze, H. (1996) *States, Nations and Nationalism: From the Middle Ages to the Present*, Oxford: Blackwell.
Shklar, J. N. (1991) *American Citizenship: The Quest for Inclusion*, Cambridge, MA: Harvard University Press.
Smith, R. M. (1997) *Civic Ideals: Conflicting Visions of Citizenship in U.S. History*, New Haven: Yale University Press.
Takaki, R. (1993) *A Different Mirror: A History of Multicultural America*, Boston: Little, Brown and Company.
Walzer, M. (1992) *What it Means to be an American*, New York: Marsilio.
Zinn, H. (1980) *A People's History of the United States*, New York: Harper & Row.

Notes

1 [This chapter was originally published with the title "Becoming Citizens, Becoming Hispanics," but the terminology in the title and throughout has been updated for this volume to reflect the author's current preferences. Note that "Hispanic" and "Latino" have often been taken to be synonyms, but in some usages the former includes people from Spain and Portugal, and in the latter it does not, and this has sometimes been taken to have important political significance.—Eds.]
2 I think that Walzer defined just as well this very same concept when he wrote: "Citizens learn to ask, in addition to their private questions, what the common good really is. In the course of sustained political activity enemies become familiar antagonists, known to be asking the same (contradictory) questions. Men and women who merely tolerated one another's differences recognize that they share a commitment—to *this* arena and to the people in it. Even a divisive election, then, is a ritual of unity, not only because it has a single outcome, but also because it reaffirms the existence of the arena itself, the public thing, and the sovereign people. Politics is a school of loyalty, through which we make the republic our moral possession and come to regard it with a kind of reverence, And election day is the republic's most important celebration" (1992: 100).
3 I would like to thank Pedro Lange-Churión, who has been my most important thought partner and critic; Raymond Dennehy, who offered many important suggestions and corrections; and Julio Moreno, who raised questions that I hope to answer in a sequel to this chapter.

Reading Questions

1. What is the difference between citizenship as a legal capacity, on the one hand, and citizenship as a cultural and social status, on the other? Why might there be a tension between these forms of citizenship, according to the text?
2. How does Mendieta describe the three kinds of rights that make up citizenship? How are they said to be interrelated?
3. What is meant by the familiar principle, "an injustice to one is an injustice to all"? Drawing on the text, discuss the relationship between a particular group's pursuit of justice for themselves, and the rights that can be claimed universally.
4. According to Mendieta, in what sense is it the case that "African Americans are born as such," but Latinos *become* Latinos?
5. Mendieta claims that American imperial politics has constituted Latinos an underclass. What evidence is offered to support this claim?

6. Mendieta argues that social movements are "the lifeline of citizenship rights." If Latinos lack the citizenship rights enjoyed by other U.S. Americans, what sorts of social movements might be needed for the expansion of these rights? Drawing on the text, discuss some of the possible barriers to Latinos attaining full citizenship, given their distinguishing characteristics?
7. Do you agree with Mendieta that Latinos must learn U.S. patriotism in order to secure full citizenship? Why or why not?
8. Do you agree that, in spite of their significant differences, adopting the imposed label of "Latino" is necessary to the project of equal citizenship? Draw on the text to support your answer.

26 Cesar Chavez and the Pluralist Foundations of U.S. Democracy

José-Antonio Orosco

In early 2011, a Washington State man experienced a big surprise when he tried to get an enhanced driver's license to visit his relatives in Canada. It turned out that Leland Davidson did not have the documentation to prove he was a U.S. citizen, despite living here for ninety-five years and fighting for the United States during World War II. He had been born in Canada to U.S. American parents and had lived there until he was five years old, but his parents had failed to register his birth with the U.S. government. Proof of his parents' birth in the United States was lost, too. Davidson had never traveled outside of the country, other than to Canada, so he did not have a passport. Many commentators who noticed this case felt that strict rules about the need for papers to prove his citizenship were ludicrous: Had Leland Davidson not done more than enough to merit the privilege of citizenship, they asked, by being a productive member of this society for almost one hundred years and serving in the armed forces in defense of the nation?

Mexican American civil rights leader Cesar Chavez would have been one to answer this question affirmatively. Chavez shares the intuition that long-time service and participation in society ought to matter as proof of citizenship, perhaps even more so than official documentation issued by the state. It is for this reason that Chavez eventually came to support the inclusion of undocumented immigrants in U.S. American society. Like Addams, he develops a certain interpretation of democracy from our public political culture which holds that restrictive immigration measures are contrary to the radical democratic traditions of U.S. American society. He believes these traditions enshrine equality, civic participation, and respect for cultural diversity. In this chapter, I analyze Chavez's interpretation and how he thinks it supports the "right to stay" for undocumented immigrants.

I begin by examining claims that Chavez was actually opposed to open borders and undocumented immigrants. I argue that at certain points in his career Chavez did advocate for restrictions, but his eventual considered opinion was that irregular migrants deserve amnesty because of the civic and moral obligations of U.S. American democracy. More importantly, I maintain that Chavez holds that Mexican immigration, in particular, can actually impact the United States positively. The cultural contributions of this group of immigrants in particular, Chavez believes, can infuse the U.S. habits of the heart with certain values that can create the foundation for a more just and peaceful nation.

Cesar Chavez: Labor Leader, Not Civil Rights Hero

Ruben Navarette Jr. makes the case that Chavez ought not to be thought of as a Chicano activist or civil rights hero, but primarily as a labor leader. Navarette means that Chavez's major concerns were not with racial or social justice broadly conceived, but instead with

DOI: 10.4324/9781003385417-39

more narrow concerns, such as the wages and working conditions of farmworkers. In that sense, it is inappropriate to invoke Chavez's name in support of major national public policy outside of union matters. For instance, on March 31, 2010—Chavez's birthday—the National Council de La Raza issued a statement that urged Congress to pass comprehensive immigration reform legislation. Navarette objects to his invocation, saying that the historical record proves Chavez to be hostile to guest worker programs, any form of amnesty, and indeed, to undocumented workers themselves: "It's a safe bet that Chavez would be an opponent of any legislation that gave illegal immigrants even a chance at legal status" (Navarette Jr. 2010).

To support his position, Navarette lists the efforts that Chavez took during the 1960s and 1970s to staunch the flow of undocumented workers into the United States. Many of these events are well known today. For instance, during the Delano grape strike from 1965 to 1970, Chavez lobbied the federal government to step up its efforts to patrol the border and to prevent undocumented workers from being used as strikebreakers in the fields. In May 1968, he organized hundreds of activists to picket a speech by then U.S. Attorney General Ramsey Clark in San Francisco in order to protest a lack of immigration enforcement along the United States–Mexico border. At the same time, Chavez ordered his cousin Manuel Chavez to set up a union medical clinic in Mexicali, Baja California, to track down and discourage Mexican immigrants from crossing over into the United States. Sometimes these efforts led to violent confrontations between United Farm Workers union organizers and immigrants.[1]

Richard Griswold del Castillo and Richard Garcia emphasize that this stance on immigration often put Chavez at odds with leadership within the Chicano civil rights movement (del Castillo and Garcia 1995: 167). Burt Corona, for example, vehemently criticized Chavez's backing of deportation measures, suggesting the better approach would be to organize the immigrants, as he himself was doing with his organization, La Hermandad Mexicana Nacional, and get them to support the strike (la Botz 2006: 84; Ortega 2001: 26–27). Chavez felt he had to make some hard choices that affected the very livelihood of farmworkers in the United States. He continually claimed that their chance for a better life was severely undermined by the presence of undocumented workers as strikebreakers in the labor chain of California agribusiness (Pawel 2009: 140–141). Indeed, Chavez distinguished his approach this way early on; in 1970, he called on President Nixon to enforce border restrictions, but, at the same time, underscored that such restrictions were necessary primarily because government and agribusiness were exploiting Mexican workers, treating them as objects: "Our poor Mexican brothers who are allowed to come across the border for the harvest are tools in the Government's and the grower's attempts to break our strike" (Chavez 2008: 77).

Randy Shaw argues that Chavez's decision to limit the undocumenteds' ability to enter and to stay in the country was nonetheless still qualitatively different, in a moral perspective, from those who attack undocumented immigrants today based on racist or nativist foundations (Shaw 2008: 197). In other words, Chavez should be labeled, more appropriately, as antiscab rather than antiimmigrant, according to Shaw. Yet, there is also evidence that during this period in the 1970s, Chavez felt strong antipathy toward undocumented immigrants as a whole. He is reported to claim that they took jobs away from U.S. American citizens and should be stopped for that reason. His attitudes at the time seemed to verge on a kind of neonativism (Bardacke 2012: 491–493).

However, by the 1980s, Chavez changed his stance and became a vocal supporter of legalization of the undocumented. Many saw his endorsement of the 1986 federal amnesty law as a pragmatic realization about the changing needs of farmworker organizing. Undocumented immigrants had become a major component of the agricultural workforce in California. If the United Farm Workers union was going to survive, then it needed to find a way to help them emerge from their positions of subordination and exploitation and into the ranks of union membership. Chavez also came to understand the farmworker struggle as more than just a labor movement focused on wages and working conditions. In his Exposition Park speech, delivered in 1971 as a public statement against the Vietnam War, Chavez explicitly described *La Causa*, the farmworker struggle, as a nonviolent social movement designed to counter the influence of militarism and corporate greed that he believed were undermining democratic community in the United States. He had decided to speak out against the conflict in Vietnam because it highlighted to him how deeply American culture associated violence with power, strength, and moral authority. Chavez pointed out the numerous ways in which violence is portrayed as an acceptable way to settle disputes and implement decisions: everywhere police and security forces use guns to enforce their wills, television glorifies violence and war, and men and women batter their children and one another in the home: "Most of us honor violence in one way or another. . . . We insist on our own way, grab for security and trample on other people in the process" (Chavez 2008a: 120).

In addition to the practical reasons about organizing conditions, Chavez had ethical-political justifications for coming to reject his previous immigration restriction position. They are justifications that are rooted in Chavez's continuing reflections on the meaning of U.S. American democracy and the role of *La Causa* as a social justice movement. For Chavez, part of *La Causa*'s role is to become a social movement with the purpose of cultivating a culture of peace in the United States. By "a culture of peace," I mean a "set of values, attitudes, modes of behavior, and ways of life that reject violence and prevent conflicts by tackling their root causes and solving problems through dialogue and negotiation among individuals, groups, and nations" (UN General Assembly 1999). Building a culture of peace, for Chavez, means building a social movement that can inject new values into U.S. American society, ones that he hopes will set the United States on firmer democratic foundations and remove institutional obstacles that perpetuate authoritarian and discriminatory tendencies. Federal immigration policy became a focus for Chavez in this endeavor for two reasons: (1) immigration policy, traditionally grounded in assumptions from the melting pot ideal, reinforces values that undermine U.S. American democracy and the culture of peace, and (2) Latino/Latina immigrants might be best positioned to be the carriers of the cultural resources that catalyze the deepening of a culture of peace within the United States.

Chavez and the Foundations of U.S. American Democracy

In a speech from 1982, Chavez interprets U.S. American democracy as a political system built around two interrelated values: equality and participation. In this sense, the idea of democracy is less about specific institutional arrangements, such as separation of powers, or free and fair elections, and more about a society with certain ethical commitments on the distribution of power. By equality, Chavez means the right of each person to be treated with equal moral respect by the state. A democratic society enshrines this fundamental respect for the dignity of each and every human being by entrusting them, Chavez suggests, with "the power to control [their] own future," the capacity for self-determination (2008d: 169). Each person should be recognized as an equal, then, in the sense of everyone being an autonomous agent entitled to participate in the decision-making processes of the major institutions that affect his or her life. As Chavez puts it, "If you don't participate in the planning, you just don't count" (2008c: 82). When it comes to evaluating actually existing U.S. American democracy, Chavez believes these values have been frequently ignored in the design of immigration and naturalization policies, in at least two ways.

First, throughout most of its history, the United States has relied heavily on the cheap labor of immigrants for many of its industries, especially in the garment and agricultural industries (Ngai 2003). However, the United States has not been particularly interested in allowing these immigrants "to stake a claim to the promise this country offers to people here and around the world" (2008c: 170). Chavez refers not only to the exploitation of undocumented workers, who labor for low wages under the constant threat of incarceration and deportation, but also to laborers imported through guest worker programs, such as the Bracero Program, which brought several millions of Mexicans to the country between 1943 and 1962. Such guest worker programs, according to Chavez, create nothing better than "a new class of slave laborers imported from outside the U.S.," since they usually subject people to miserable living situations, with poor working conditions that do not allow for unionization, and do not give workers the chance to become citizens after their service (2008c: 171). Undocumented labor and guest workers, in other words, are two groups not regarded as civic equals; they are not treated with same kind of respect given to other members of society since they are not allowed to participate in the political decision-making processes of the society to which they contribute so much of their labor power. They are not social peers, but subordinates to the will of the citizenry. This situation creates a "democratic legitimacy gap"; no democratic society which holds that the equal recognition of rights is an expression of equal human dignity can ethically permit the existence of large numbers of second-class members who must simply obey whatever treatment is ordained by its political class (Rubio Marin 2000: 236–237). On this point, Chavez's intuitions match up with those of political theorist Michael Walzer: immigration and guest worker programs that supply significant amounts of foreign laborers to prop up the prosperity of a nation, but do not leave open an opportunity for them to participate eventually in major political institutions, are ones that create hierarchal relationships of masters to subjects that is simply incompatible with the modern democratic ideal of equality (Walzer 1984: 60–61).

The second way in which actually existing U.S. American democracy has disregarded its democratic norms has to do with the kinds of national origin stories and myths that developed about immigrants. Here, Chavez agrees with the pragmatist lines of inquiry that we have considered so far. He thinks the popular national narratives about the cultural and civic roles of immigrants in the United States have fueled nativist sentiment and actually created hostility toward the idea of the United States as a deeply democratic and genuinely pluralistic society. Chavez finds all the talk of the United States being a melting pot as racially charged ideology that deflects from the truth. Despite references to the fusion model, or to the Americanization model, in which all immigrant groups somehow come together to form a completely new identity that encompasses and yet transcends all ethnicities, the United States has, in reality, tended more toward being a nationalist state based on the Anglo-Saxon conformity model. Carol Gould labels a "nationalist state" as one which makes

> a particular ethnicity or nationality a condition for citizenship and thus for full political rights. Such a state is exclusively national in that it makes no provision for the equal treatment of minority ethnic, national, or cultural groups and regards members of them at best as resident aliens or denies them rights to reside there altogether.
>
> (Gould 2004: 133)

Indeed, from 1790 until 1952, being a "white person" was a formal prerequisite for naturalization in the United States—a legal standard that was upheld at least twice by the U.S. Supreme Court in the twentieth century (Lopez 2006: 31; Roediger 2005: 59). Chavez holds that the melting pot models of assimilation may have accurately described U.S. immigration:

> when the bulk of immigrants were white Europeans. But with the large numbers of Third World people, particularly Asians, Latin Americans, and Africans, coming to our shores, it is no longer possible or desirable to Anglicize the waves of new immigrants. . . . They would like all of us to be melted, poured, and cast . . . and cloned into the all-American boy and girl.
>
> (2008d: 172)

In this passage, Chavez underscores the tension between democracy and the melting pot narrative, and how those stories operate as a kind of nativist ideology. Like Kallen, Adamic, Bourne, and Dewey, Chavez thinks the melting pot myth is not only a historical fiction that does not accurately describe how immigrants were received into the United States, but it is also normatively problematic. The melting pot, in Chavez's estimation, really means conformity to an Anglo-Saxon cultural standard in exchange for the standing of citizenship. That is, participation in the major decision-making processes that affect each person's life is dependent on whether a person can demonstrate possession or embodiment of morally arbitrary characteristics, such as "whiteness." For Chavez, this expectation creates undue hardship on new immigrant groups, particularly Latinos/Latinas, to fit in and succeed. More importantly, it directly violates the democratic value of equal moral respect for each person.[2] The melting pot model tells us that only those people who have been fused, or "Americanized," that is, who look and act in very culturally specific ways, should be allowed the privilege to participate in the exercise of power. The more compelling idea of deep democracy that Chavez is trying to build falls in the tradition of Du Bois's account of the African American contribution to U.S. American democracy: participation in power is the right of every human being. It is an institutional way of organizing power to respect their capacity for self-determination, that is, their right to know and to choose what is good and appropriate for themselves, including how they wish to embody or partake in culture and ethnicity.[3] The melting pot ideal is a cultural artifact that undermines those normative commitments.

Chavez and the American Radical Democratic Tradition

Thus, in regard to the way the United States has drafted programs dealing with immigrant workers, especially the undocumented, as well as the way in which those policies have been influenced by nativist social narratives, such as the melting pot story, Chavez finds the United States wanting as a modern democratic society. Fortunately, he thinks, like Addams, that there *are* cultural resources in the U.S. American tradition that are available for confronting these democratic deficits. Evidence of this tradition, he writes, is embedded in "our Bill of Rights and especially for the First Amendment" (2008d: 172–173). For Chavez, these legal foundations—the right to free speech, the right to assembly, and the establishment clause—imply a commitment to civic participation and cultural pluralism by guaranteeing a civic space for the expression of different worldviews, different religious perspectives, and the right to confront the political authority over disagreements about the legitimate exercise of power.

Chavez frames this alternative democratic tradition as operating according to a principle he calls *juntos pero no revueltos*—we can be united without having to be blended together (2008d: 173). In other words, solidarity is possible without some kind of enforced cultural assimilation. Chavez writes,

> For this country to continue to be great we need to include people but not strip them of their cultural values in the process. I can eat tortillas and still be an American. Our country needs to understand that. Groups of people will tolerate many things—but don't tamper with their language; don't threaten their religion. And don't meddle with their food or there's going to be a lot of problems. The greatest contribution our government and society can make is to recognize that we are all Americans, yet we are all different.
> (2008d: 173)

Here, Chavez seems to rely on the same distinctions implicit in Kallen's work among a societal culture, common national culture, and public political culture. Through such disjunctures, it is possible to imagine individuals participating fully in the processes of U.S. American democratic political life, as well as in civil society, without having to Anglicize their cultural or linguistic traditions. As the Principle of Cultural Group Flourishing indicates, participating in political life ought not mean the same thing as participating in the cultural mores of the dominant majority.

However, Chavez's understanding of democratic requirements is more radical than most of the cultural pluralist pragmatists. Whereas Kallen and others see participation in the political process as a right of citizens, Chavez suggests a picture of democratic society in which even some undocumented foreigners ought to have the opportunity to participate or, at least, ought to be given easier access to become full participants. He writes, "We must replace policies that exclude people from participation in our economic and political life because of their race, language, or immigration status with politics that encourage people to participate in society. We need to get people involved" (2008d: 173).

I argue in chapter 6 that Addams's work encourages us to think about the participation of undocumented immigrants in U.S. American civic life more expansively. Some scholars suggest that the participation of undocumented immigrants in political life is already virtually indistinguishable from that of citizens, with the exception of voting and sitting on juries. But Chavez is encouraging radical political participation even for noncitizens. The notion that noncitizens ought have some rights to participate in political decision-making processes that affect their lives is not necessarily unheard of in some modern democratic nations (Benhabib 2004: 129–169). Indeed, it is not an idea that is foreign to the United States at all. Throughout most of the history of the United States, even into the twentieth century, noncitizens have been able to vote in local, state, and federal elections and run for office (Hayduk 2006). Today, there are several local municipalities, Takoma Park, Maryland, being the best known, that even allow undocumented immigrants the right to vote in local elections (Bedolla 2004: 55–70). Other states have experimented with allowing undocumented immigrants the right to vote in school board elections, on the justification that immigrant parents have a stakeholder interest in how districts affect the well-being of their families through educational practices.

Chavez's point here is not that citizenship should have no special meaning or value whatsoever. He does not believe that any individual should be able to enter into the United States and have full rights of membership immediately. Nor is he claiming that the state has no right to police its borders or enforce any kind of immigration or naturalization law.

What he is saying is that the right of the state to enforce immigration and naturalization restrictions on who can be a member of society is not absolute. There are ethical considerations that emanate from the idea of democracy itself that limit the state's power over some undocumented individuals to participate in major decision-making processes that affect them. As Dewey puts it: "The very fact of exclusion from participation is a subtle form of suppression. It gives individuals no opportunity to reflect and decide upon what is good for them" (Dewey 2008: 218).

One of those considerations that limits the state's policing power in regard to immigrants is an undocumented individual's social and economic integration into civic life. Instead of merely demonstrated cultural competency or legal documentation as proof of standing as a citizen, Chavez thinks we also can look to see how deeply involved the person is as a member of society. Chavez's intuition here is the same one that underlies the support for Leland Davidson's bid to be recognized as a U.S. American citizen. What should matter more, Davidson's proponents argue, is not merely the existence of legal documentation of his birth to U.S. American citizens, but the evidence of his consent to the public authority for many decades, his involvement in social and economic life, and his willingness to make a supreme sacrifice for that authority through military service (Carens 2013). Chavez would agree with these conditions:

> What should count is the fact that he or she has lived here and is paying taxes and is making a contribution to the country. And of course, the person would have to say 'Yes, I want to live under this system.'
>
> (2008d: 173)

Thus, for Chavez, many, but not necessarily all, undocumented immigrants should be eligible for inclusion into the most extensive rights to participate because of the range and density of their actually existing social and economic ties. To ignore these bonds—connections of family, friends, and community, especially if they are long-lasting—in the name of enforcing immigration rules seems out of proportion to the wrong of their violation.

Latino/Latina Immigrants and Intercultural Democracy

Chavez's idea of *juntos pero no revueltos* also differs from Kallen in terms of how it frames the interconnectivity of different immigrant or ethnic groups with the public political culture of U.S. American democracy. Chavez does not want the ethnic diversity of immigrant communities to be reduced to a single white standard in order to qualify for political participation, but that does not mean that the public political culture must be neutral or remain contact-free from influences that flow from the cultural experiences of immigrant communities. Indeed, a completely culturally neutral public political sphere is impossible since there will always be official languages, school curricula, or national holidays that will tend to reflect the common national culture and history of a dominant majority and, therefore, not resonate with the cultural backgrounds of all members of society (McCarthy 2002: 255). Kallen expects immigrant communities to at least learn how to be conversant in the terms of the U.S. American political sphere, and this means assimilating some of this cultural knowledge. Yet, Chavez, like Dewey and Du Bois, values the Principle of Cultural Contribution. In other words, he hopes that the cultural transmission can be more than one-sided and that Latino/Latina immigrants can offer ideas, traditions, and habits of the heart to deepen democracy. He seems to point to U.S. American democratic political culture and, eventually, its institutions, being transformed by the influence of different immigrant cultures as they participate in the processes of economic and political life:

> What I am really talking about . . . is making it possible for more people to participate in the democratic process. If these changes come to pass we will witness a radical reordering—for the better—in our country. For whenever new blood is transfused into our national social and political life our nation is enriched and strengthened.
>
> (2008d: 174–175)

Chavez considered Mexican immigration to the United States important for precisely this reason. Despite the many theorists, such as Huntington and Victor Davis Hanson, and political pundits, such as Patrick Buchanan, who contribute to what Leo R. Chavez (2008) calls the "Latino Threat Narrative"—the view that the large-scale presence of Latinos/Latinas in the United States fundamentally destabilizes U.S. American political, economic, and social institutions—Chavez believes that Mexican immigrants, in particular, might infuse U.S. American society with traditions that could help further the development of a deeply democratic culture of peace. One of the ways Chavez tried to contribute to this process was to infuse the farmworker social movement with Mexican cultural and religious traditions that emphasize nonviolence. The farmworker struggle thus became part of the U.S. American Civil Rights Movement, drawing on its history of protest and civil disobedience, but it did so with moral foundations drawn from Mexican and Mexican American history and practices, thereby creating a unique tradition that did not simply copy the work of Gandhi, Martin Luther King Jr., or the American labor movement.

For instance, Chavez always emphasized that his formative understanding of nonviolence, though honed by the study of Thoreau, Gandhi, and Martin Luther King Jr., actually stemmed from Mexican folk traditions, particularly those that he learned from his mother. He explains how Juana Estrada Chavez instructed him in nonviolence through the use of *dichos*, or Mexican folk sayings, that encapsulated wisdom concerning conflict resolution:

> She taught her children to reject that part of a culture which too often tells its young men that you're not a man if you don't fight back. She would say 'No, it's best to turn the other cheek. God gave you senses like eyes and mind and tongue and you can get out of anything. It takes two to fight and one can't do it alone.'
>
> (2008b: 223)

Chavez's childhood was suffused with Mexican cultural and spiritual ideals that careful consideration, reason, and dialogue are alternatives to violence, and that a good life is one devoted to serving the needs of the poor and unfortunate. These lessons came to frame his understanding of the ethical limits to direct action and civil disobedience. Moreover, in some of the earliest documents of the farmworker movement, Chavez explained how these Mexican cultural values were to be institutionalized as essential parts of *La Causa*'s nonviolent direct action practices. In the "Sacramento March Letter," issued before the 250-mile march from Delano, California to Sacramento in 1966, Chavez laid out what I term elsewhere as a "logic of nonviolence," that is, a theory about how certain direct action practices are to express nonviolent values in such a way as to generate support and solidarity with different sectors of society (Orosco 2008). The Sacramento march was the first major attempt to fashion the Mexican cultural practices of pilgrimage, penitential procession, and revolutionary action into a framework to guide the future activism of the farmworker movement as it sought to create a culture of peace and become a model for other social justice movements in the United States.

So instead of being a Kallenian cultural pluralist, then, Chavez is, along the lines of Dewey, an "interculturalist." Interculturalism is a contemporary intellectual movement among Indigenous activists in Latin America, particularly Colombia, Ecuador, and Peru, that involves "achieving interethnic dialogue based on relations of equivalence" between mainstream and minority cultures (Rappaport 2005: 7). Thus, instead of a liberal group pluralism, in which minority ethnic groups and their ways of life live side by side in isolated silos, and are tolerated by the state as long as they can acculturate to the public political culture, or even a Kallenian cultural pluralism, in which minority ethnic groups and their ways of life live side by side and influence the development of the common national culture, but do not alter the public political culture of the United States, interculturalism calls for an examination of the ways in which those minority groups can intermingle with one another, and with dominant society, exchanging perspectives, experiences, and values. More importantly, those minority ethnic groups can challenge how the state itself, and its public political culture, is organized, so as to reconsider the principles "grounding politics, economy, and ethics" from the standpoint of alternative principles embedded within the minority ethnic culture (Mignolo 2005: 118).

Chavez is not calling for Latino/Latina immigrants simply to "Hispanicize" the common national culture and replace its language, history, traditions, and folkways with Latino/Latina alternatives. Instead, the idea is for Latino/Latina activists to engage within the public political sphere and begin Roycean deliberative dialogues about the meaning and sustainability of U.S. American social, political, and economic arrangements, especially the dedication to military dominance and corporate control. The crucial aspect of this kind of deliberative dialogue is using the standpoint of Latino/Latina culture and history as critical standards, in much the same way that Du Bois recommended using the history of the African American freedom struggle as a way to think about the ethical dimensions of U.S. American democracy.[4]

An example of such intercultural effort from Latin America is the movement in Bolivia that arose out of grassroots Indigenous activism to endow nature, or "Mother Earth," with certain rights and legal immunities that must be respected by public agencies when considering certain forms of economic development ("Act of the Rights of Mother Earth" n.d.). This is an example in which the culture and spirituality of the Andean Indigenous community has been enshrined within the legal and political processes of the Bolivian nation-state, an institution imported from Europe, in order to impact the future of economic and social development in the country. Other examples, which I have discussed elsewhere, include the attempts of the Zapatista rebels of southern Mexico to build alternative systems of local government existing underneath the Mexican nation-state. These systems are founded in Indigenous principles of democracy that emphasize consensus decision making and economic distribution based on ideas of gifting and reciprocity rather than individual competition. Finally, in the United States, activists within the Chicano civil rights movement, who were contemporaries of Chavez, often theorized about building alternative social, economic, and political institutions that would embody Latino/Latina cultural attitudes about public space, leisure time, family, and communal living (Orosco 2011: 242–243). One particular example involves the struggle of young Mexican American activists in the town of Mt. Angel, Oregon, who in the early 1970s established a small college, the Colegio Cesar Chavez (May 2011). Inspired by the example of Chavez, the college organizers worked for over ten years to maintain the institution dedicated to a multicultural curriculum and experimental learning. The hope was to provide a social center for the growing Mexican American community of Oregon, but also to provide a forum for people to encounter new traditions, practices, and ways of life drawn from the Latino/Latina immigrant experience.

Chavez's Deep Democratic Legacy

Chavez hopes that *La Causa* can instigate a revolutionary cultural change in the United States. In this way, he revives the aspirations of Louis Adamic, who believed that the labor movement could engender a widespread analysis of the intersection between political economy and racial/ethnic inequality that would dislodge the chokehold the melting pot has over U.S. American society's vision of democracy. Chavez believes that training in nonviolent resistance and direct action can transform the growing populations of Latino/Latina workers and immigrants into democratic agents who have the skills and abilities to participate, deliberate, and make U.S. American democracy more responsive to the needs and interests of ordinary people and not just wealthy, corporate interests.

More importantly, however, Chavez hoped that the militant nonviolence of the farmworkers, built on a foundation of Mexican values and traditions, could model alternatives for a U.S. American society saturated with images of violence and of greed. In the way that Addams looked to the immigrants in urban, industrial areas to provide glimpses of different ways of organizing living space, land use, and religious observance, Chavez imagines that immigrant farmworkers can occasion an intercultural dialogue that will catalyze a reconsideration of U.S. American public policy and remind us of the importance of equality and participation as foundational U.S. American values. For Chavez, the grandest legacy of *La Causa* would be to gift elements of the Latino/Latina culture of peace to the United States that would solidify social justice in its deep democratic traditions.

Chavez knew this kind of social change would be difficult work. It would require the development of talented leaders to dedicate their lives as community organizers. Ronald Mize and Grace Pena Delgado suggest that one of *La Causa*'s strongest legacies is the fact that so many of Chavez's protégés went on to become effective leaders in politics and a variety of social justice struggles, including the Justice for Janitors campaign in California, and the nationwide Immigrant Worker Freedom rides in 2003 (Mize and Delgado 2012: 94–107). These campaigns mobilized thousands of immigrant workers, many of whom were unfamiliar with the history of *La Causa*, and through new direct action techniques, street theater, and bilingual/bicultural awareness were able to link labor struggles to immigration and binational citizenship issues in ways that have not been seen before in the United States.

Overcoming the stereotypes of Latinos/Latinas as irrational and prone to violence would also be an arduous task. Chavez knew that most U.S. Americans associate Mexico, particularly the border regions, with crime, random violence, drug trafficking, political corruption, and sexual vice—not with a commitment to peace and justice. Moreover, Chavez was not naïve to think that Mexican culture is completely nonviolent. He knew it also contained noxious traditions, such as racism and machismo, that are obstacles in the formation of a culture of peace (Orosco 2008: 71–96). However, he did think that there were rich enough resources within the Mexican traditions of pilgrimage, penitence, and revolutionary organizing that could be distilled into unique organizing guidelines for building a richer multicultural society. In this way, Chavez's work and legacy is about sustaining the pragmatist conversation on cultural pluralism and represents a widespread movement to embody the principles of Cultural Group Flourishing, Cultural Contribution, and Harm Prevention through the daily activism of thousands of new immigrants who can introduce a new vocabulary into our national conversation about the requirements of deep and creative democracy in the twenty-first century.

References

"Act of the Rights of Mother Earth," (n.d.) http://f.cl.ly/items /212y0r1R0W2k2F1M021G/Mother_Earth_Law.pdf.

Almaguer, T. (1994) *Racial Fault Lines: The Historical Origins of White Supremacy in California*, Berkeley: University of California Press.

Bardacke, F. (2012) *Trampling Out the Vintage: Cesar Chavez and the Two Souls of the United Farm Workers*, London: Verso.

Bedolla, L. G. (2004) "Rethinking Citizenship: Noncitizen Voting and Immigrant Political Engagement in the United States," in T. Lee, S. Karthick Ramakrishnan, and R. Ramirez (eds.), *Transforming Politics, Transforming America: The Political and Civic Incorporation of Immigrants in the United States*, 55–57, Charlottesville: University of Virginia Press.

Benhabib, S. (2004) *The Rights of Others: Aliens, Residents, and Citizens*, Cambridge: Cambridge University Press.

Bourne, R. (1977) "Transnational America," in O. Hansen (ed.), *Randolph Bourne: The Radical Will*, 248–264, Berkeley: University of California Press.

Buchanan, P. J. (2006) *State of Emergency: The Third World Invasion and Conquest of America*, New York: Thomas Dunne.

Carens, J. (2013) *The Ethics of Immigration*, New York: Oxford University Press.

Chavez, C. (2008a) "At Exposition Park," in I. Stavans (ed.), *An Organizer's Tale: Speeches*, 119–121, New York: Penguin.

Chavez, C. (2008b) "Juana Estrada Chavez," in I. Stavans (ed.), *An Organizer's Tale: Speeches*, 220–224, New York: Penguin.

Chavez, C. (2008c) "Sharing the Wealth," in I. Stavans (ed.), *An Organizer's Tale: Speeches*, 77–83, New York: Penguin.

Chavez, C. (2008d) "What Is Democracy?" in I. Stavans (ed.), *An Organizer's Tale: Speeches*, 169–174, New York: Penguin.

Chavez, L. R. (2008) *The Latino Threat: Constructing Immigrants, Citizens, and the Nation*, Stanford: Stanford University Press.

del Castillo, R. G., and Garcia, R. (1995) *Cesar Chavez: A Triumph of Spirit*, Norman: University of Oklahoma Press.

Dewey, J. (2008) "Democracy and Educational Administration," in J. A. Boydston (ed.), *Later Works of John Dewey, Vol. 11*, 217–225, Carbondale: Southern Illinois Press.

Garcia, M. (2012) *From the Jaws of Victory: The Triumph and Tragedy of Cesar Chavez and the Farm Worker Movement*, Berkley: University of California.

Gould, C. (2004) *Globalizing Democracy and Human Rights*, Cambridge: Cambridge University Press.

Habermas, J. (2000) *The Inclusion of the Other*, Cambridge, MA: MIT Press.

Hayduk, R. (2006) *Democracy for All: Restoring Immigrant Voting Rights in the U.S.*, New York: Routledge.

Kallen, H. (1997) *Culture and Democracy in the United States*, New Brunswick, CT: Transaction Publishers.

Kant, I. (1939) *Perpetual Peace*, N. M. Butler (ed.), New York: Columbia University Press.

King Jr, M. L. (1991) "A Testament of Hope," in J. M. Washington (ed.), *A Testament of Hope: The Essential Writings and Speeches of Martin Luther King, Jr.*, 313–328, New York: Harper Collins.

La Botz, D. (2006) *Cesar Chavez and La Causa*, New York: Pearson Longman.

Lopez, I. H. (2006) *White by Law: The Legal Construction of Race*, New York: New York University Press.

Marin, R. R. (2000) *Immigration as a Democratic Challenge: Citizenship and Inclusion in Germany and the United States*, Cambridge: Cambridge University Press.

May, G. A. (2011) *Sonny Montes and Mexican American Activism in Oregon*, Corvallis: Oregon State University Press.
McCarthy, T. (2002) "On Reconciling Cosmopolitan United and National Diversity," in Pablo de Greiff and C. Cronin (eds.), *Global Justice and Transnational Politics: Essays on the Moral and Political Challenges of Globalization*, Cambridge, MA: MIT Press.
Menchaca, M. (2001) *Recovering History, Constructing Race: The Indian, Black, and White Roots of Mexican Americans*, Austin: University of Texas Press.
Mendoza, J. J. (2009) "Introduction to the Ethics of Illegality," *Oregon Review of International Law* 11 (1): 123–128.
Mignolo, W. (2005) *The Idea of Latin America*, London: Blackwell.
Mize, R. L., and Pena Delgado, G. (2012) *Latino Immigrants in the United States*, Malden, MA: Polity Press.
Navarette Jr, R. (2010) "Cesar Chavez Would Not Have Supported Amnesty for Illegals," *PJ Media.com*, April 8, http://pajamasmedia.com/blog/cesar-chavez-would-not-have-supported-amnesty-for-illegals/?singlepage=true.
Ngai, M. (2003) *Impossible Subjects: Illegal Aliens and the Making of Modern America*, Princeton: Princeton University Press.
Orosco, J.-A. (2008) *Cesar Chavez and the Common Sense of Nonviolence*, Albuquerque: University of New Mexico Press.
Orosco, J.-A. (2011) "Pragmatism, Latino Intercultural Citizenship, and the Transformation of American Democracy," in G. F. Pappas (ed.), *Pragmatism in the Americas*, 227–244, New York: Fordham University Press.
Ortega, C. (2001) "The Legacy of Burt Corona," *The Progressive*, August, 26–27.
Pawel, M. (2014) *The Crusades of Cesar Chavez*, New York: Bloomsbury Press.
Pawel, M. (2009) *The Union of Their Dreams: Power, Hope, and Struggle in Cesar Chavez's Farm Worker Movement*, New York: Bloomsbury Press.
Rappaport, J. (2005) *Intercultural Utopias: Public Intellectuals, Cultural Experimentation, and Cultural Pluralism in Colombia*, Durham, NC: Duke University Press.
Roediger, D. R. (2005) *Working toward Whiteness: How America's Immigrants Became White*, New York: Basic Books.
Silva, G. (2010) "Towards a Latin American Political Philosophy of/for the United States: From the Discovery of the Americas to Immigrant Encounters," *APA Newsletter of Hispanic/Latino Issues in Philosophy* 9 (2): 2–6.
UN General Assembly (1999) "Declaration on a Culture of Peace," *General Assembly Official Records*, 53rd sess., Suppl. no. 49. https://digitallibrary.un.org/record/299381?ln=en&v=pdf.
Walzer, M. (1984) *Spheres of Justice*, New York: Basic.
West, C. (1994) *Race Matters*, New York: Vintage.

Notes

1 For assessments of Chavez's attitude toward undocumented immigration see Bardacke (2012), Garcia (2012) and Pawel (2014: 288–295).
2 For instance, several studies highlight the manner in which Mexicans were racialized in such a way as to bar them from citizenship and political participation in the United States. See Almaguer (1994) and Menchaca (2001).
3 See Appiah (2005) for a discussion of the importance of this kind of self-determination.
4 For the development of this kind of Latino/Latina political philosophy, see Silva (2010: 2–6).

Reading Questions

1. What is the significance of the "melting pot" as a metaphor for U.S. culture, according to the text? What is Cesar Chavez's criticism of this metaphor?
2. What vision of multiculturalism does Chavez offer in contrast to the "melting pot"? Do you think this conception of democracy is feasible? Why or why not?
3. What are some of the ways in which Mexican culture can contribute to U.S. democracy, according to the text? How does Orosco respond to the claim that Chavez is really just aiming to Hispanicize the U.S.?

4. What rights does Chavez want to extend to undocumented immigrants? What argument does he offer in support of this view?
5. On what basis do you think a person should have the right to political participation? Draw on the text to discuss your answer.
6. If U.S. democracy were to transform in the way that Chavez proposes, how do you think specific policies might change as a result?

27 The Latinx Racial Disintegration Thesis
Whiteness, Democracy, and Latinx Identity

José Jorge Mendoza

Introduction

Latinx are the fastest growing minority group in the United States. So much so that by 2050 they are projected to comprise almost a quarter of the U.S. population. This will not only make Latinx the largest minority group in the U.S., but their growth is thought to be the driving force behind the U.S. becoming a racial "minority-majority" country. In other words, if demographic trends continue as they have been, by the year 2050 more than 50% of the U.S. population will be non-White (Colby and Ortman 2014).

According to most political pundits, this oncoming demographic change has the potential to dramatically alter the U.S. political landscape. This is because, at least since the 1950s, Republican candidates have rarely gotten more than 30% of the collective non-White vote (Bump 2015). Republican politicians have therefore become adept at winning elections, especially national elections, by securing a sizeable majority of the White vote i.e., winning 55% or more of the White vote (Abramovitz 2023). In a country where Whites have historically comprised an overwhelming majority of the electorate, this has proven to be a successful strategy. However, given the oncoming demographic changes, it would stand to reason that this electoral strategy—a strategy built on conceding the non-White vote, while focusing almost exclusively on the White vote—should soon become obsolete.

If demographic trends continue as predicted, there are four scenarios that could possibly play out. The first, and perhaps most intuitive, is that the oncoming demographic changes spell the end for the Republican party. Republicans have sowed the wind with their electoral strategy and now must reap the political whirlwind. Much like the nineteenth century Whig Party before them, the Republican party is running the risk of going extinct. This scenario would be welcome news to the Democratic party.

A second possibility is that the Republican party pivots and begins to show concern for the interests of non-Whites. This would mean eschewing the racist elements many in their party, through their unscrupulous attempts to attract anxious White voters, have flirted with if not endorsed. This second option is less good for the Democratic party, as it would mean more competition for votes they have come to take for granted. But it would be welcome news for non-Whites, who would suddenly find two political parties heavily vying for their vote.

A third option is for Republicans to embrace what Ramón Grosfoguel has called the "neo-apartheid" approach. On this approach, even if non-Whites come to collectively constitute a majority of the U.S. population, there are ways in which they could be politically excluded or disempowered—either through voter suppression, gerrymandering, disenfranchisement laws, changes in citizenship laws, or by pitting non-Whites against each other—so that they do not come to form a unified majority of the electorate. These neo-apartheid

DOI: 10.4324/9781003385417-40

measures would be an addition to, but would not substantially change, the current Republican strategy of winning elections by securing a sizeable majority of the White vote.

These three options garner the most attention in current political discussions. In this essay, however, I want to take seriously a fourth alternative. I want to suggest that in 2050 non-Whites might not actually comprise a collective majority of the U.S. population. This is not because the projected demographic changes will not occur as predicted. Those demographic trends seem set in stone and unlikely to change at this point. The reason non-Whites might not come to comprise a collective majority of the U.S. population is that certain segments of the Latinx community will be coopted into U.S. Whiteness. We can call this the Latinx racial disintegration thesis. If this thesis turns out to be correct, it has the potential of keeping the majority of the electorate White and, with the aid of neo-apartheid tactics, giving a new lease on life to the Republican strategy of winning elections by having to capture only a sizeable majority of the White vote.

Beyond helping us make short-term electoral predictions, if the Latinx racial disintegration thesis is correct it will tell us something deeper about the nature of Whiteness. First, it will confirm that Whiteness is neither fixed nor natural; that it is a social construction and as with any social construction, it can and will change in response to powerful social pressures. Second, Whiteness is a racial identity, but it is unlike any other racial identity. If the Latinx racial disintegration thesis is correct, we will see that Whiteness occupies both a position of domination—much like a "master" occupies a position of domination with respect to the "slave"—and a position of presumed universality—much like "mankind" has been used as a stand-in for all of humanity. These positions of domination and presumed universality grants the bearer of Whiteness the freedom of having their race—and sometimes even their ethnicity and nationality—constantly in the background, while nonetheless relegating non-Whites to a position of subordination.

The argument in support of the Latinx racial disintegration thesis will proceed in four parts. In the first section we will briefly look at the history of Whiteness in the U.S. and the role it has played in determining the electorate or who gets to count as a "real American." We will look at demographic changes that occurred between 1850–1950 and see that—despite worries to the contrary at the time—those changes did not lead to the U.S. becoming a "minority-majority" country. Instead, those changes led to an expansion of U.S. Whiteness (i.e., an expansion of who got to count as a "real American"). This expansion of U.S. Whiteness is often distorted by the myth of the U.S. as a "nation of immigrants." In section two we will look at how the expansion of U.S. Whiteness came to affect U.S. democratic politics. We will see that this expansion went hand in hand with the rise of what has come to be known as "dog whistle politics."

In section three we will consider the case against the optimistic view. The optimistic view holds that demographic changes will lead to the end of "dog whistle politics" and thereby usher in a new golden era of progressive politics. After dispensing with the optimistic view, we will consider one of the more likely pessimistic alternatives, the neo-apartheid approach. We will see that, even though neo-apartheid tactics can explain a lot, they do not explain enough. In order to make sense of what has happened in recent U.S. elections (and perhaps what will happen in future elections) we have to get even more pessimistic. We have to come to grips with the idea that the Latinx community is racially disintegrating. In other words, in much the same way as the Irish and non-Northern Europeans eventually were welcomed into U.S. Whiteness, there is now good reason to think that some Latinx—those who we will call racially "in-between"—will be brought into U.S. Whiteness as a way to keep the U.S. electorate majority White.

In the final section of this essay, I consider and respond to three objections found in the work of Linda Martín Alcoff. These objections express skepticism that Latinx can be incorporated into U.S. Whiteness and, at the same time, they hold out hope for recasting Whiteness in non-oppressive ways. This concluding section will therefore outline two distinct ways to think about the nature of White identity: as either inherently oppressive (i.e., the *Whiteness-as-domination* model) or as merely in need of correction (i.e., the *distorted identity* model). The latter model undergirds hopeful accounts like Alcoff's. It recognizes that U.S. Whiteness has and will continue to undergo changes, but it holds that these changes need not always be in support of White supremacy. It believes that White identity can be reconstructed in a positive sense. The former model undergirds pessimistic accounts, like the Latinx racial disintegration thesis. It also maintains that U.S. Whiteness has and will continue to undergo changes, but it sees these changes as reactions aimed at keeping White supremacy in place. This essay will make the case for pessimism; that the future development of U.S. Whiteness is something we should be worried, not hopeful, about.

1. U.S. Whiteness

The following claim might come off as a gross oversimplification, but it has the virtue of being true. The story of democracy in the U.S. is a story about non-Whites being consistently denied the vote. The denial of the franchise was originally part of an even larger form of exclusion, an exclusion from citizenship. Three examples from U.S. history suffice to make this clear. The first is the Naturalization Act, which from 1790 until 1952 restricted naturalized U.S. citizenship to only members of the White race (1952 Immigration and Nationality Act). The second is the case of Black Americans who were ineligible for U.S. birthright citizenship—a denial codified into law by the 1857 *Dred Scott v. Sandford* Supreme Court case—and remained ineligible until the conclusion of the U.S. Civil War and the adoption of the 1865–70 Civil War Amendments. The third example is the case of Native Americans, who were also denied birthright citizenship, but for whom the Fourteenth Amendment's birthright citizenship clause did not apply—at least not according to the 1884 *Elk v. Wilkins* Supreme Court case. It was not until the passing of the Indian Citizenship Act in 1924 that all Native Americans born in the territorial U.S., and specifically those born on Indian reservations, were automatically granted U.S. citizenship at birth.

As this brief recap shows, for more than half of U.S. history those eligible to vote in U.S. elections were, due to racist restrictions on citizenship, rarely of Asian, Black, or Native American descent. Yet the worry that U.S. elections might be decided contrary to the will of its White majority first arose sometime in the mid-1800s—well before Asians, Blacks, or Native Americans were eligible for naturalized, and in most cases birthright, citizenship. The worry about the U.S. becoming a "minority-majority" country and of foreigners taking "democratic" control of the U.S. was motivated by the threat of an oncoming demographic change. This change threatened the majority status of White Anglo-Saxon Protestants and led to a rise in xenophobia and the creation of nativist organizations such as the infamous Know-Nothing Party.

One of the primary targets of folks who joined these nativist organizations were Catholics. These folks in particular thought Catholic immigrants were coming to the U.S. in droves and that they were bringing with them a subversive ideology. They feared Catholics were having too many children and doing so on purpose, as part of an effort to increase their numbers and eventually "democratically" install a government more loyal to the Vatican than to the U.S. constitution. For these reasons, the Know-Nothing Party and similar organizations employed what we will come to call "neo-apartheid" measures. They tried to prevent Catholic U.S. citizens (who at that time came to be strongly correlated with being of Irish and non-Northern European descent) from obtaining positions in government or any other jobs, arguing that U.S. business owners had a patriotic duty to employ only "real Americans." Know-Nothing activists would stand watch at polling stations during elections to make sure there were no voting irregularities, but in practice their "poll watching" functioned more as a form of voter intimidation and suppression.[1]

By the end of the nineteenth century and the beginning of the twentieth, the worry about an oncoming demographic change went from fringe conspiracy theory to a perceived mainstream crisis. This concern was exemplified in the writings of nativist-racists like Madison Grant, who in 1916 wrote the widely influential *The Passing of the Great Race*. In that book, Grant argued that the founding race of the U.S., the Nordic race, was heading towards extinction. This was the result of various factors, but the most pressing was the continued immigration of inferior races, especially what he termed the "Alpine" and "Mediterranean" races, which roughly correlated with people of Eastern and Southern Europe (Grant 1936).

The kneejerk policy response to this perceived crisis was a more expansive set of immigration restrictions. The hope was that if enough Irish and non-Northern European immigrants could be kept out, perhaps this would slow or even stop the oncoming demographic change. Legislators passed various forms of immigration restrictions during this period, but these policies did nothing to slow the oncoming demographic change. The wave of migration from 1890–1920 of Southern and Eastern Europeans was just too big. By 1950, the demographic changes that so terrified proponents of White U.S. purity, such as Madison Grant, had come to fruition. Those who would have been considered "real Americans" in 1850 (i.e., White Anglo-Saxon Protestants) no longer constituted the majority of U.S. citizens by 1950. Yet something strange happened (or failed to happen). The U.S. did not become a "minority-majority" country as the nativist-racists had feared. Instead, what happened was that the notion of U.S. Whiteness (i.e., who got to count as a "real American") had expanded and, to the chagrin of folks like Madison Grant, it had come to include folks like the Irish and other non-Northern Europeans.

The conventional story of how and why the Irish and other non-Northern Europeans became White in the U.S. is often told as the "melting pot" story. According to this narrative, the U.S. had always been a "nation of immigrants," despite the fact that most immigrant groups first had to endure a period of xenophobia. Following the historian Erika Lee, we can trace the roots of U.S. xenophobia to the early 1700s, well before the U.S., as a nation-state, existed. At that time, xenophobes like Benjamin Franklin were primarily concerned with increases in German immigration. Franklin was even quoted as saying that German immigrants were one of the biggest problems that American colonists had to deal with. This was because German immigrants were "herding together [and] establish[ing] their languages and manners to the exclusion of ours." Not to mention that, according to Franklin, Germany was clearly not sending us their best and brightest, only their "most ignorant stupid . . . [those not] used to Liberty . . . [and who would soon] outnumber us."[2] Despite the initial vitriol they received, Germans eventually came to be accepted as "real Americans," and this transformation took less than a hundred years.

The "melting pot" story tends to downplay these periods of U.S. xenophobia and instead rests on the idea that U.S. nationalism is a unique brand of nationalism. It is unlike that of other nations because the U.S. is fundamentally a "nation of immigrants." José-Antonio Orosco has termed this view the "Americanization" model. On this account:

> Immigrants become U.S. Americans by pledging allegiance to its constitutional principles or acculturating themselves to values and traditions associated with US American popular culture . . . [U.S. nationalism is therefore] a kind of nonsectarian faith, a 'civil

religion,' which is accessible to any newcomer, regardless of national or ethnic origin, as long as he or she sincerely believes.

(Orosco 2016: 20)

This "melting pot" story is now an essential part of the U.S. national narrative, but it is based on two controversial premises. The first is that the U.S. has always embraced the idea of being a nation of immigrants. The second is that there has always been a clean distinction between race and ethnicity. This is not an accurate historical representation of the U.S. To better understand this, it is helpful to consult Donna Gabaccia's "Nations of Immigrants: Do Words Matter?" In that essay, Gabaccia traces the history of the phrase "nation of immigrants" and looks specifically at how that phrase was historically used to describe the U.S. What she finds might surprise a lot of us today. It turns out that for most of U.S. history:

it was no compliment to label newcomers as immigrants. Given the negative associations of the term "immigrant," it is scarcely surprising that few Americans adopted the phrase "nation of immigrants" when it was first used. In fact, many who first used the phrase actually did so in order to justify the exclusion of immigrants.

(Gabaccia 2010: 7)

Gabaccia's findings also show that it was not until around 1950 that the phrase "nation of immigrants" was used overwhelmingly in a positive sense to describe the national character of the U.S. The inclusion of the Irish and other non-Northern Europeans into U.S. Whiteness therefore not only changed the identity of the individuals belonging to those groups (i.e., making them fully White) but it also changed the definition of "real American."

The inclusion of the Irish and other non-Northern Europeans into the U.S. national narrative and making them White in the social imaginary required a change in how Whiteness was conceived of in the U.S. For the "melting pot" story to work it needed to assume that there was always a strict separation between race and ethnicity. The concept of "race" was supposed to denote those essential biological differences between people—specifically inherent and immutable differences in morality, intelligence, aesthetic sensibilities, or athletic abilities. These differences were closely correlated with particular regions of the world and often identifiable by the presence of certain phenotypic (i.e., bodily) markers. Today we know that this story of "race" is false, but this is what "race" was supposed to refer to. The concept of ethnicity, on the other hand, was supposed to be tied to culture, customs, or the shared history of a particular group. This made ethnicity something subject to change and required effort and commitment on the part of the individual to renew or maintain.

So, on this account it was possible that members of different races could share a similar ethnicity. But more importantly, it meant members of the same race could have different ethnicities. This second point is key if the story of the "melting pot" was going to work. According to the "melting pot" story, the Irish and other non-Northern Europeans initially experienced a kind of xenophobia that excluded them from "real American" status. With time, however, the individuals who comprised these groups came to shed the unassimilable parts of their identity—parts that were connected to their ethnicity—and in doing so allowed their White race to shine through. As ethnicities melted into the pot of U.S. Whiteness, the Irish and other non-Northern Europeans—unlike those who were racially different (e.g., Asians, Blacks and Native Americans)—came to be seen as having the right kind of racial stock (i.e., Whiteness) out of which "real Americans" are made.

This version of the "melting pot," however, requires that we read a concept like "ethnicity" back into this period of U.S. history, which is something historians like David Roediger have warned against. According to Roediger, the term "ethnicity" rarely shows up during this period of U.S. history, and the few times that it does it is not used in the way that we use the term today. The racialized language of that period was far messier, and it often conflated the nice, neat distinction we make today between "ethnicity" and "race." As Roediger explains:

This loose, state-endorsed linkage of biology to culture, history, and class can mislead modern historians of race who characteristically attempt to disentangle the biological from other rationales for oppression, regarding the former as underpinning racism and the later as underpinning [ethnic discrimination]. But what was so striking about restrictionist and racist thought at the beginning (and indeed, at the end) of the twentieth century was its very entanglement of the biological and the cultural.

(Roediger 2006: 66)

So instead of there being a clear distinction in the U.S. between racial Whiteness and non-Whiteness, Roediger proposes that there is a space of racial "in-betweenness." In allowing for this space, Roediger claims we can come to better understand the place "new immigrants" (e.g., non-WASP Europeans) occupied at the turn of the twentieth century and how it is they became fully White by the middle of that same century.

The takeaway is that with enough time and pressure, those occupying an "in-between" racial space in the U.S. can potentially become "real Americans" and thereby be fully White. The same offer, however, does not extend to those clearly on the non-White side of the racial divide. No matter the changes in law or the degree to which they assimilate to U.S. customs, culture, and values, those clearly on the non-White side (e.g., Asians, Blacks, and Native Americans) have been and will continue to be perpetually excluded from U.S. Whiteness. They can be U.S. nationals, but in name only. So, what impact did this change in U.S. Whiteness have on the nature of U.S. democracy? It created the conditions under which "dog-whistle politics" were not only possible but became an attractive strategy for winning elections in a "post-racial" U.S. (i.e., a U.S. where race technically no longer disqualified one from citizenship nor disenfranchised them).

2. Dog-Whistle Politics

The phrase "dog-whistle politics" was popularized by Ian Haney López to refer to a strategy for winning democratic elections in societies in which naked appeals to racism, nativism, and xenophobia are considered politically out-of-bounds, but where nonetheless the majority of the electorate remains White and willing to vote against their economic interests if candidates affirm (even if only indirectly) their fears, anxieties, and prejudices about non-Whites. López believes that the U.S. represents such a democracy, and in *Dog Whistle Politics* he lays out a convincing case for why this is so.[3]

He points out that at least from the 1930s until the 1970s, the majority of U.S. voters strongly supported progressive economic policies. For López, this means support for the basic idea that government has an obligation to protect the least powerful from the excesses of free-market capitalism. On this view, the government, not the market, ought to decide on things such as minimum wage and what constitutes safe or acceptable working conditions. It also means support for a progressive scheme of taxation that aims both to prevent the rise of gross economic inequality and that funds social programs that benefit the whole of society, such as welfare, social security, unemployment, public education, healthcare, etc.

Under the banner of progressive politics, Franklin Roosevelt built a juggernaut coalition, the New Deal coalition, that came to dominate national politics from his election in 1932 until the election of Richard Nixon in 1968. During this 36-year reign of progressive politics, the U.S. experienced a Civil Rights Movement, the end of Jim Crow segregation, and the dismantling of overt racist immigration policies. This meant that for a brief moment in time, the idea of unregulated capitalism (an ideology that, at the turn of the twentieth century, came to define the Republican party) was unappealing to the vast majority of poor and working-class voters of any race. During this time, as racist restrictions on U.S. citizenship were withering away, the racist ideology of the southern "Dixiecrat" gave way to the contemporary multi-racial Democratic party.

Always lurking underneath the New Deal coalition, however, was a deep sense of racial animosity. Republican candidates such as Barry Goldwater and even Democratic candidates like Strom Thurmond and George Wallace suspected the existence of White anxiety and animosity toward non-Whites, and tried to exploit this for their own political advantage. They hypothesized that if they could tap into this White anxiety and animosity, they could win a sizable majority of the (post-1950s) White electorate, and thereby win national elections—even if the means they used to attract White voters alienated non-White voters. This strategy did not pan out for their particular campaigns, but their hunch turned out to be correct. The strategy, which came to be known as the "Southern Strategy," yielded fruit for Nixon's 1968 presidential campaign. In an anonymous interview in 1981, Republican Party strategist Lee Atwater infamously outlined how the Nixon campaign's coded racist message was delivered to a receptive White audience that otherwise would have been turned off by Nixon's anti-progressive politics. As Atwater recounts:

> You start in 1954 by saying 'Nigger, nigger, nigger.' By 1968 you can't say 'Nigger.' That hurts you. It backfires. So you say stuff like forced busing, states' rights and all that stuff and you get so abstract. Now you talk about cutting taxes and these things you're talking about are totally economic things and a byproduct of them is, blacks get hurt worse than whites. And subconsciously maybe that's part of it. I'm not saying that. But I'm saying that if it is getting that abstract and that coded, we are doing away with the racial problem one way or the other. Obviously sitting around saying we want to cut taxes and we want this, is a lot more abstract than even the busing thing and a hell of a lot more abstract than nigger, nigger.
>
> (Quoted in Haney López 2014: 57)

Kevin Phillips, a political commentator who was part of Nixon's campaign, wrote the following reflection on the Southern Strategy and the future of the Republican party:

> From now on, the Republicans are never going to get more than 10 to 20 percent of the Negro vote and they don't need any more than that . . . but Republicans would be shortsighted if they weakened enforcement of the Voting Rights Act. The more Negroes who register as Democrats in the South, the sooner the Negrophobe whites will quit the Democrats and become Republicans. That's where the votes are. Without that prodding from the blacks, the whites will backslide into their old comfortable arrangement with the local Democrats.
>
> (Quoted in Boyd 1970)

Nixon's election was therefore a watershed moment in U.S. politics. A generation before Nixon's embrace of "dog-whistle politics," the Republican party (i.e., the party of Lincoln) had been the party under which most Black voters registered and to whom they felt a certain sense of loyalty (Bump 2015). Roosevelt's New Deal coalition began the exodus of Black voters away from the Republican party and toward the Democratic party. Nixon's campaign greatly accelerated this shift in party affiliation, while subsequent Republican campaigns have locked it in.

Taking their lead from Nixon, Republican candidates Ronald Reagan and George H.W. Bush continued to employ the Southern Strategy. Reagan famously decried food stamps and welfare programs by telling stories on the campaign trail about how "real Americans" should be fed up with "strapping young bucks" using food stamps to buy T-bone steaks while they had to settle for hamburger, and how "welfare queens" could be seen driving around in new Cadillacs while "real Americans" continued to struggle economically. On the surface, Reagan appeared to merely be advancing an anti-progressive agenda, but his style and rhetoric (i.e., his dog whistle) made it clear he was attacking the Black community.

Bush took a similar approach when chastising his Democratic opponent, Michael Dukakis, for not being tough on crime by using racially charged commercials. These coded racist appeals had the veneer of neutrality, but their racist message resonated in the ears of a key demographic that began to break away from the New Deal coalition and move toward the Republican party: blue-collar White workers in the U.S. rustbelt.

According to Lopez, it did not take long for Democrats to also get into the game. By 1992, the progressive champions of the Democratic party, such as Jimmy Carter, Walter Mondale, and Michael Dukakis, were out of favor and in their place came the "New" Democrats. The "New" Democrats, epitomized by Bill Clinton and Al Gore, employed a political tactic dubbed triangulation, which was a mixture of pro-free-trade, anti-welfare, and tough-on-crime policies. This strategy of triangulation brought some of the rust-belt White working class back to the Democratic party. Non-White voters had no other political party to turn to, so despite Democrats taking up the dog whistle, non-White voters doubled down on their support of the Democratic party. In this way, Democrats rebuilt their coalition, except this time under new terms (i.e., triangulation), and they experienced wins in both the 1992 and 1996 presidential elections.

The 2000 and 2004 U.S. elections were excruciatingly close but both went to Republicans, in large part due to neo-apartheid tactics that we will consider in more detail in the next section. But with the election of Barack Obama in 2008, and his subsequent reelection in 2012, the thought was that the era of "dog-whistle politics" was coming to an end. Demographic changes (i.e., the increase in non-White voters) had made it so that there were not going to be enough Whites willing to sacrifice their economic interests (or sense of racial justice) in exchange for politicians willing to assuage their racial fears and anxieties.

This is how things stood until 2016, when Donald Trump blew the racist dog whistle louder than any candidate before him had ever dared. The whistle was so loud that its racist message was audible to even the most racially tone-deaf Republicans, such as Mitt Romney (Schleifer 2016). In an era of heightened racial and xenophobic fear and anxiety, Trump captured almost 58% of the White vote. At the same time, however, he lost nearly 75% of the non-White vote, but the pummeling he took among non-White voters didn't matter. Trump was able to win the presidential election in an electoral landslide. This lopsided result was largely due to the quirks in the electoral college system, where the candidate who wins the popular vote (in 2016 it was Hillary Clinton) is not guaranteed to end up with the most electoral college votes. But the results of the electoral college were due to the fact that non-Whites comprised only about 25% of the overall electorate in 2016. In other words, Trump could afford to lose a super-majority of the non-White vote, but could still win the election if he captured a substantial majority of the White vote. He, unlike Mitt Romney in 2012, accomplished this feat by leaning even harder into "dog-whistle politics."

Leaning into "dog-whistle politics" was something the Republican party's 2012 post-election autopsy report had warned against (Franke-Ruta 2013). Many Republicans thought it might be time to pivot and begin appealing to non-White voters and actively eschewing the racist elements in their party. There was a minority within the party, however, who argued the opposite. This far-right group openly implored Republican candidates to double down on "dog-whistle politics" and follow a course of action like the one outlined by Ann Coulter:

> The way that Republicans win is by driving up the White vote. . . . It's not by appealing to women or Hispanics or Blacks. In fact, those groups are going to start fighting among one another. . . . If [Mitt] Romney had won 71 percent of the Hispanic vote, he still loses. . . . If he had gotten four points more of the white vote [in 2012], he would have won. What should Republicans be going for?
>
> (Quoted in Hains 2015)

Trump's election seemed to prove folks like Coulter right, which was terrible news for progressives. The one potential silver lining of the 2016 and subsequent 2020 election was that as successful as "dog-whistle politics" had proven to be, the impact of the increased Latinx electorate was beginning to make its mark. The increase in Latinx voters gave Joseph Biden's 2020 campaign victories in states like Nevada and Virginia. It turned Republican strongholds, such as Arizona, Georgia, and (to some degree) Texas, into much more competitive states. Progressives might therefore be tempted to take comfort in this and to think that this doubling down on "dog-whistle politics" was shortsighted and foolhardy. As dark as things seemed in 2016, optimistic progressives can tell themselves that this was White supremacy's last electoral gasp. With the oncoming demographic changes, the future looks bright for progressive politics.

This is the view put forth by Steve Phillips in his *New York Times* bestselling *Brown Is the New White: How the Demographic Revolution Has Created a New American Majority*. As the title of the book suggests, the oncoming demographic changes combined with a continued embrace of "dog-whistle politics" by Republican candidates will produce an environment favorable to progressive politicians. It will make them almost unbeatable in national elections because the logic of "dog-whistle politics" will be turned on its head. Now politicians who capture the majority of the non-White vote (i.e., the "Brown" vote) will be the ones who win elections, even if capturing the majority of the non-White vote comes at the expense of losing the majority of the White vote (Phillips 2016).

Phillips's reasoning makes a lot of sense. As already mentioned in the introduction, it is estimated that by around 2050 non-Whites (or at least those currently considered non-White in the U.S.) will collectively account for the majority of the U.S. citizenry. If this is the case, then a strategy built on securing a sizeable majority of the White vote while conceding the majority of the non-White vote should no longer be effective. Yet there are at least two reasons to be pessimistic: neo-apartheid tactics and the racial disintegration of the Latinx community. I want to consider both of these pessimistic alternatives in the next section and suggest that we have historical reasons for thinking that not only are neo-apartheid tactics effective, but that the racial disintegration of the Latinx community is a real possibility. And if this takes place, then it is unlikely that, at least with respect to U.S. national elections, "Brown" will be the new electoral majority.

3. The Case for Pessimism

Despite not being one of the staple race groups (e.g., Asian, Black, Native American, or White), Latinx, on the whole, have been considered a non-White group in the U.S. This is in part due to the conflation of race and ethnicity mentioned earlier, but it is also because historically the U.S. has adhered to a "one-drop rule" approach to racial classification. This approach is based on an idea, infamously propagated by race theorists like Arthur de Gobineau (2000) that racial miscegenation always produces inferior offspring, and therefore "mixed-race" peoples must either be racialized as members of the lesser race group or be considered members of a "mongrel" race. Despite the high degree of racial admixture that has taken place in the U.S., the "one-drop rule" has informally continued to be the way race in the U.S. is assigned. It is the reason why, for example, people like Barack Obama are classified as racially Black, even though Obama's mother is racially White (Sundstrom 2008).

This is in stark contrast to the way race is assigned in many Latin American countries. For example, in Mexico those who would be considered "mixed-race" in the U.S. have historically (or at least before the Mexican Revolution of 1910) had their own specific racial category. So even though the primary races in Latin America are also Asian, Black, Native American, and White, the *casta* system of New Spain allowed for over a hundred possible race (or at least race-like) combinations, each with its own unique social identity. Even after the *casta* system was done away with and even after the Mexican Revolution was supposed to have ushered in a post-racial society in Mexico, theorists like José Vasconcelos advanced racial theories that inverted the "one-drop rule" paradigm.

According to theorists like Vasconcelos, racial miscegenation could improve the racial stock of a country because, more often than not, mixed-race offspring received the best (not the worst) traits of the combined races. Such racial admixture, he believed, would eventually lead to a fifth (i.e., cosmic) race. Vasconcelos therefore argued that it was the national race projects of *mestizo* (i.e., mixed-race) countries like Mexico, and not the national race projects of White purity, as pursued in North American and Northern European countries, that ought to be emulated (Vasconcelos 2004).

There are serious problems with Vasconcelos's view,[4] but the point here is not to defend his view but to show that there have always been different and competing national race projects. North American and Northern European countries overwhelmingly have subscribed to race projects in which racial miscegenation is seen as automatically leading to racial degeneration. This, however, was not always the type of national race project pursued in Latin American—or even Latin European—countries.[5] Because of these different national race projects, North Americans and Northern Europeans have always harbored racial suspicions about nationals from Latin American—and even Latin European—countries. Latin Americans were seen as comprising an inferior "mongrel" race within the U.S.—even if the Latin Americans in question would have been considered White in their own country. To take just one example, see the following passage from Madison Grant's *Passing of the Great Race*:

> What the Melting Pot actually does in practice can be seen in Mexico, where the absorption of the blood of the original Spanish conquerors by the native Indian population has produced the racial mixture which we call Mexican, and which is now engaged in

demonstrating its incapacity for self-government. The world has seen many such mixtures of races, and the character of a mongrel race is only just beginning to be understood at its true value.

(Grant 1936: 17)

This passage shows us two things. First, it highlights how nativist-racists at the turn of the twentieth century loathed to think of the U.S. as a "nation of immigrants" and considered the "melting pot" ideology a threat to U.S. White purity. Relatedly, this is also proof that the antipathy and inferiorization experienced in the U.S. by Latinx peoples has a history of being race based. In other words, Latinx have been denied "real American" status on the basis of perceived racial differences and not just differences in customs, culture, or values.

Returning now to the present and the looming demographic changes that threaten (yet again) the majority status of Whites in the U.S., the question before us is which way do things go? Does this demographic change signal the end of "dog whistle politics" and perhaps with it the end of the Republican party? Does it signal a change in the Republican party's electoral strategy? Answering either of these questions in the affirmative is optimistic, at least optimistic for proponents of progressive politics and racial justice in the U.S.

There are, however, two pessimistic alternatives. The first is the "neo-apartheid" alternative. On this pessimistic alternative, the projected demographic changes occur as they are expected to occur, and Latinx remain squarely on the non-White side of the national race divide. Under these conditions, "dog-whistle politics" are largely at a disadvantage, but they can be supplemented by tactics that exclude or disempower non-White voters. The second pessimistic alternative is the racial disintegration of the Latinx community. On this view, the projected demographic changes occur as they are expected to occur, but not all Latinx remain squarely on the non-White side of the national race divide. Instead, enough Latinx (i.e., those racially "in-between") move to the White side of the national race divide and in doing so allow "dog-whistle politics" to remain an effective electoral strategy.

Let us begin with the first pessimistic alternative by considering an argument put forth by Ramón Grosfoguel in "Latin@s and the Decolonization of the US empire in the 21st Century." In that essay, Grosfoguel argues that the projected demographic changes will turn the U.S. into a "neo-apartheid" democracy. Drawing a parallel with Apartheid South Africa, Grosfoguel postulates that Whites could maintain political dominance in the U.S., even if they were no longer the majority. They could do this by politically excluding or disempowering non-Whites, which would then allow the new demographic minority (in this case Whites) to continue to be the segment of the electorate that ultimately determines the outcome of elections.

In this regard, Grosfoguel believes we should look to states like California as test cases for neo-apartheid democracy. Grosfoguel reminds the reader that for a long time California was a Republican bastion, producing the likes of Richard Nixon and Ronald Reagan, but as Whites became a minority the state became increasingly progressive. Because of this, Grosfoguel contends, California has become an experimental lab for political conservatives. Since the mid-1990s, California has seen many proposed policies on the state's ballot that have little chance of succeeding. This has been done not as political "Hail Marys," but as a means to divide and pit non-White groups against each other. For example, the 1994 anti-immigrant Proposition 187 had little chance to survive a court challenge, but it was put on the ballot anyway. This was done in large part to sow seeds of discontent between the Black community and the Asian and Latinx communities. The state has also seen various attempts to try to contain the political power of non-Whites—who now constitute a majority in California—through practices like gerrymandering and voter suppression. In short, Grosfoguel's argument is that even if the U.S. does become a "minority-majority" country, there are neo-apartheid tactics, which are already being tested, that can ensure "dog-whistle politics" remains a viable electoral strategy (Grosfoguel 2008).

Now, regardless of whether one takes an optimistic view or adopts the pessimistic neo-apartheid view, the political evolution of the state of Florida seems to raise some difficulties. For some time now, dating as far back as at least the infamous 2000 presidential election, Florida has been a closely contested state. Back in 2000, when the state of Florida was decided by only a few hundred votes, Latinx made up less than a fifth (16.8%) of the state's population (Census 2000). Sixteen years (i.e., four presidential cycles) later, Latinx came to comprise almost 25% of the state's population (Pew Research Center 2016). Given an optimistic account like that of Steve Phillips, the state of Florida should have—like California before it—become an easy win for Democrats. Instead, Donald Trump carried the state in the 2016 election by a little more than a percentage point (Krogstad and Flores 2016). Four years later, with the Latinx population now closing in on 27% (Census 2020), Trump again won Florida, except this time he won it by more than three percentage points (Florida Election Results 2020). These results should give pause to proponents of the optimistic account, especially those proponents who assume Latinx to be a cohesive non-White racial group. It seems that in order to explain what happened in Florida we will need a more nuanced and, I believe, pessimistic account.

The pessimistic neo-apartheid account goes a long way in providing such an explanation. It is true, for example, that the 2016 election was the first presidential election in almost 50 years that lacked the full protections of the 1965 Voting Rights Act. This is because in 2013 the Supreme Court shot down section 4 of the Voting Rights Act in the *Shelby County v. Holder* case. Section 4 of the Voting Rights Act had required that state and local governments, especially those with a history of racial discrimination, get preclearance by the federal government before making any changes to their voting laws or practices. The ruling in the *Shelby County v. Holder* case has opened the door for states with Republican governors and Republican controlled state legislatures, like Florida, to pass and enforce laws restricting how, where, and when people in those states could vote. These laws, while facially neutral and universally applicable, disproportionately target non-White voters. To add insult to injury, proponents of these laws made no secret of what they were trying to accomplish. They acknowledged that their aim was to suppress votes for the Democratic party, but it turns out that suppressing a political party's vote is not technically illegal (Eckholm and Fausset 2014).

Along with finding ways to get around the spirit of the Voting Rights Act, Florida also had one of the most draconian disenfranchisement policies in the country. The state permanently barred anyone from voting if they had a felony conviction, and in Florida this has been responsible for removing close to 20% of the Black population from its voter rolls.[6] The neo-apartheid account can therefore explain a lot, but does it account for everything that happened in Florida? I submit that it does not, and that to get a better explanation we need to look at the divisions within the Latinx community in Florida.

When we look at the voting results, we find that in 2016 Clinton lost the state to Trump by a little more than 1%. In that election, non-Latinx Whites constituted 62% of the electorate and Trump received 64% of that group's vote. Non-Latinx Blacks constituted 14% of the electorate and Clinton got 84% of that group's vote (2016: Exit Polls). So far, we have results consistent with "dog-whistle politics." We see that even if Clinton would have gotten 100% of the Black vote, it would not have been enough to overtake Trump. But there is still almost 25% of the state vote that needs to be accounted for.

This is where the Latinx vote comes in. Latinx constituted about 18% of the Florida electorate and as a group they voted 62% for Clinton and 35% for Trump (ibid). This is still a bad showing for Trump, but not as bad of a showing as he had with Black voters. In fact, if Clinton would have done as well with Latinx voters as she did with Black voters, she would have easily won Florida. But one of the problems with this line of thinking is that it only works under the assumption that Latinx are a monolithic group. We start to see the problem with this assumption when we separate out Cuban Americans from the rest of the Latinx electorate. When we do that, we see that the non-Cuban Latinx vote broke for Clinton 71% to 26% (ibid). Even here Clinton does not do as well with Latinx voters as she did with Black voters. Still, if this is how the Latinx vote as a whole had broken down, it likely would have been enough for Clinton to pull out a narrow victory. But as we know, this is not how the Latinx vote went down. The overall Latinx vote was more favorable to Trump because of Cuban-Americans, who in Florida made up 31% of the Latinx electorate (Krogstad and Flores 2016), and as a group broke for Trump 54% to 41% (CNN 2016).

If we then move to the 2020 election, we find that the vast differences in the Black and White vote remain largely the same. Despite demographic changes that have lowered their overall percentage of the state's population, Whites still continue to constitute 62% of the state's electorate. This discrepancy between share of population and share of the electorate can largely be explained by the aforementioned neo-apartheid tactics. Whites continued to overwhelmingly support Trump, breaking for him 62% to 37%. Black voters again constituted 14% of the electorate and they supported Biden even more strongly than they supported Clinton, breaking for him 89% to 10%. Latinx, on the other hand, increased their percentage of the electorate to 19%, but were much less supportive of Biden then they had been of Clinton. Latinx still broke for Biden, but only by a 53% to 46% margin (CNN 2020). This meant that even though a smaller percentage of both Black and White voters went to Trump in 2020, Trump was still able to increase his overall margin of victory in Florida. This increase was due to an 11% improvement in the Latinx vote.

What neo-apartheid tactics might explain is how, despite demographic changes that are shrinking their overall percentage in the state's population, Whites continue to represent a significant majority of Florida's electorate. What neither an optimistic nor neo-apartheid account can explain is why the ramping up of "dog-whistle politics" did not lead to a decrease, but instead led to an increase in Latinx votes for a Republican candidate like Trump. One response is to try to evade the problem by suggesting that Cuban Americans simply have a different history and relationship to U.S. politics than other Latin Americans. This is true, and I will have more to say about this in Section 4.2. But if one thinks of Cuban Americans as not racially White, this is where the problem comes in. How do we explain an increase in support for a dog-whistling Republican candidate like Trump over another equally anti-communist, but less dog-whistling, Republican candidate such as Mitt Romney?[7] My suggestion is that what is happening in the state of Florida is better accounted for by a pessimistic outlook, but one that goes beyond neo-apartheid tactics and begins to challenge the assumption that Latinx are and will remain a monolithic non-White race group. When we begin to challenge this assumption, we not only see the case of Florida in a different light; we also start to see how, and in what direction, Whiteness is transforming in the U.S.

As we saw in Section One, Whiteness in the U.S. has already undergone at least one major expansion. This happened at a particular moment in U.S. history, when Whites feared they would stop constituting the majority of the U.S. electorate and have their political will subject to the overrule of the collective non-White vote. It is at this point in time when certain non-White groups—those whom Roediger termed racially "in-between"—underwent a process of racial disintegration. The "Alpine" and "Mediterranean" races that so terrified Madison Grant in 1916 were out of existence by the 1950s. This is not because members of these races all disappeared or completely lost racial designations. Instead, those who composed the Alpine and Mediterranean races were re-racialized as White, and the prior differences between these race groups came to be thought of in "ethnic" rather than "racial" terms.[8]

I want to suggest that something similar is happening with Latinx folks today. There is no doubt that nativists today view Latinx as an existential threat to the U.S. nation. These nativists hold many of the same negative views about Latinx as xenophobes like Benjamin Franklin held about German immigrants in the 1750s and nativist Know-Nothings held about Catholics in the 1850s. But much the same way that the Germans, the Irish, and other non-Northern Europeans were able to gain entry into U.S. Whiteness by the middle of the twentieth century (and some of them even before that), there is reason to think that the Whiter segments of the Latinx population—those who can be said to be racially "in-between"—will (if they have not already) join the melting pot of U.S. Whiteness. I call this the Latinx racial disintegration thesis.

I want to stress that unlike the cases of the Alpine and Mediterranean races, the offer of U.S. Whiteness will not be there for all Latinx. A number of Latinx will likely be re-racialized into one of the other non-White or mixed-race groups. Ironically, what has helped to prevent the racial disintegration of Latinx in the U.S.—keeping them firmly on the non-White side of the U.S. racial divide and preventing them from becoming an "ethnic" group in the full and proper sense of the term—has been the way nativists weaponize xenophobia against the Latinx community. So, if the xenophobia directed at Latinx ever dies down—big "if"—and if the demographic changes continue as predicted, then it's very likely we will see a dramatic acceleration of Latinx racial disintegration. Given the oncoming demographic changes, this disintegration is the key to Whites continuing to constitute a majority of the U.S. electorate. In this regard, a state like Florida is not so much an outlier—as it so often and quickly gets dismissed—but a harbinger of where Latinx identity, U.S. Whiteness, and U.S. democratic elections are all heading.

4. Whiteness and Latinx Identity

The Latinx racial disintegration thesis rests on the assumption that U.S. Whiteness can expand to include a significant segment of the Latinx population—or at least enough Latinx that Whites will continue to constitute a majority of the U.S. electorate. There are, however, reasons to be skeptical of this possibility. In *The Future of Whiteness*, Linda Martín Alcoff provides three such reasons. The first is that the Latinx racial disintegration thesis is working with an incorrect understanding of Whiteness. The thesis understands Whiteness as being coterminous with White supremacy and in so doing suggests there is nothing redeemable in a White identity. Alcoff believes this is wrong and counterproductive to the larger struggle for racial justice. Second, she is skeptical that Whiteness can expand to the degree needed for the Latinx racial disintegration thesis to work. Finally, she notes that even when Whiteness has expanded in the past and has come to include "in-between" groups, the inclusion of the racially "in-between" has not always been what we or they imagined it to be. Specifically, it has not always been a good thing for those who gain admission into

Whiteness (Alcoff 2015). In this section, I will expand on and respond to each of these three objections. The overall objective of this section is to articulate and distinguish these two competing conceptions of Whiteness and to provide some reasons for favoring the conception of Whiteness that undergirds the Latinx racial disintegration thesis.

4.1 White Identity, White Supremacy

What worries folks like Alcoff is that even if the demographic changes occur as they are expected to occur, and even if Whites no longer constitute a majority of the U.S. electorate, they will still constitute a significant part of it. For her this means that in order to achieve racial justice, some Whites will need to be brought into the racial justice fold. Bringing White allies onboard will be hard, but she thinks it will be even harder if we are working with an account of Whiteness that suggests there is nothing positive to Whites' racial identity—that their racial identity is at best empty, or at worst is defined exclusively by its domination over non-Whites.

This understanding of Whiteness—as an identity of both presumed universality and domination—is what undergirds the notion of "white privilege." A notion famously described by Peggy McIntosh as "an invisible weightless knapsack of special provisions, maps, passports, codebooks, visas, clothes, tools, and blank checks" (McIntosh 1989: 10). On this account, Whiteness is the dominant racial identity within a particular racial system, which at the same time manages to pass itself off as a race-neutral position. George Yancy refers to this positionality as the transcendental norm of Whiteness, which he explains in the following way:

> To say that whiteness is deemed the transcendental norm is to say that whiteness takes itself to be that which remains the same across a field of difference. Indeed, it determines what is deemed different without itself being defined by that system of difference. Whiteness is that according to which what is nonwhite is rendered other, marginal, ersatz, strange, native, inferior, uncivilized, and ugly.
>
> (Yancy 2008: 3)

For Alcoff, accounts like those of McIntosh and Yancy are unhelpful because they seem to suggest that Whites can only join the struggle against White supremacy if they were to renounce their White identity (i.e., become non-White). But this seems like a strange, if not impossible, request. Furthermore, she sees these accounts as leading to racial eliminativism. Racial eliminativism is the view that race is not real and, furthermore, given all the damage it has wrought, we would be better off without it (Appiah 1996; Zack 2002). Racial eliminativists believe that the way to achieve racial justice is to stop giving so much weight to racial identities. We should instead strive for the ideal of a "post-racial" society.

Most race theorists today, including Alcoff, think of the eliminativists' recommendations as naïve. They believe that race is real, not merely an illusion, but it is a social construction rather than a natural kind. They think of race as something more akin to money; where the entity itself might not exist in nature, but it nonetheless has real effects and is ignored at one's peril. As a social construct, Whiteness has historically undergone various changes, which we have noted, and is open to undergoing even more. On this point, not only are Alcoff and proponents of the Latinx racial disintegration thesis in agreement, but recent changes to the U.S. census—changes that will recognize "Latino" and Middle Eastern and North African ("MENA") as non-White groups for the first time beginning in 2030—seems to suggest that there is broad agreement on Whiteness being an evolving, and not fixed, racial category (Wang 2024).

The difference between Alcoff and proponents of the Latinx racial disintegration thesis is in how they conceive the potential changes to (i.e., the future of) U.S. Whiteness. Proponents of the Latinx racial disintegration thesis think of Whiteness as inherently a position of domination. They work with the understanding that White supremacy is a relationship of domination encapsulated in the notion of Whiteness itself. In this way, one could draw an analogy between White supremacy and feudalism. Under feudalism, one cannot define lords or serfs in isolation from each other. A feudal lord is master precisely because of the kind relationship they have with the serfs and vice versa. This relationship can be altered to some degree, the relationship could become a little more or a little less oppressive, but there are limits to the changes this relationship can undergo before it (and the groups that comprise it) become something else entirely.

For example, the relationship between lord and serf cannot become a relationship between and among equals without in turn undermining the feudal order and destroying the classes of "lord" and "serf." Proponents of the Latinx racial disintegration thesis understand Whiteness and non-Whiteness to be in this sort of relationship. It sees the overcoming of White supremacy as requiring the destruction of the positions of "White" and "non-White." It is committed to the view that the social construct of race exists to oppress one or more groups for the benefit of another, and that absent this relationship of domination the concept of "Whiteness" becomes vacuous. We can call this the *Whiteness-as-domination* model.

As already mentioned, Alcoff finds the *Whiteness-as-domination* model unhelpful for projects of racial justice. She is convinced that racial justice cannot be achieved without some Whites getting onboard, and this will not be possible (or at least less likely) if Whites cannot cultivate a positive White identity. This positive White identity is not one that can easily be ignored, as the eliminativists recommend, nor defined exclusively by or through the subordination of other races, as the *Whiteness-as-domination* model holds. Whiteness, Alcoff believes, has to have "a place in the rainbow . . . as one among others, neither more nor less, without state-enforced advantage or border control" (Alcoff 2015: 188–189). On the view Alcoff is proposing, the relationship between Whites and non-Whites can be understood as more analogous to the relationship between men and women or cisgender and transgender peoples. We can call this the *distorted identity* model because it sees the dominant identity (in our case a White identity) as not inherently oppressive, but as having obtained an outsized and unbalanced status with respect to the other identities, which requires correction, not elimination.

On the *distorted identity* model, ending oppression would not necessarily require the abolition of sex and gender identities. Theoretically at least, sex and gender identities could survive the end of patriarchy and transphobia, but dominant identities that have passed themselves off as universal identities (e.g., maleness or masculinity) will need to be positively reconstructed. In this way, sex and gender identities do not necessarily have to be eliminated, but all sex and gender identities should come to be regarded as equally valid (i.e., the imbalance between them should be corrected) and the boundaries separating these identities should be more fluid and less rigid.

Alcoff believes that if we conceive of Whiteness as a *distorted identity* that has the potential for positive redemption, we are more likely to achieve racial justice than if we were to conceive of Whiteness as always and forever oppressive. One point in her favor is that, unlike the *Whiteness-as-domination* model, her account clearly rejects racial eliminativism, which is often seen as recommending a naïve path to racial justice. By suggesting that the end of White supremacy will require the elimination of White positionality—in much the same way that getting rid of feudalism means eliminating the position of "lord"—it does seem that the *Whiteness-as-domination* model (and with it the Latinx racial disintegration thesis) is committed to some brand of racial eliminativism.

One thing that can be said in response to this objection is that the *Whiteness-as-domination* model does not necessarily endorse the simplistic recommendations of racial eliminativism. Alcoff rightly admonishes the simplistic recommendations of racial eliminativism because they assume that if we just stop giving weight to race, race will simply wither away. Alcoff is right that race will not magically go out of existence. For race to disappear we need to make serious material changes to our world, and even then, race might come to enjoy a kind of afterlife. It might continue to haunt us before the identities that comprise it finally settle into something more akin to class or ethnic identities. But the real objective, which we should not lose sight of, is creating a world that is no longer divided along racial lines. It's true that individuals simply divesting themselves of their White identity will not bring this world into fruition. But the takeaway from here should not be that the way forward is to increase or better allocate one's investment in Whiteness. In short, the simplistic recommendations of the eliminativists are wrong, but achieving racial justice will require more than bringing White identity into proper alignment with other racial identities. This recommendation seems equally simplistic and naïve. Ending White supremacy must mean ending White positionality.

In summary, we have considered two competing conceptions of Whiteness. The conception that undergirds the Latinx racial disintegration thesis is the *Whiteness-as-domination* model, and it is controversial. Reasonable people can and do prefer the *distorted identity* model of Whiteness, but I have tried to suggest that this model offers recommendations that are as viable and efficacious as the simplistic racial eliminativist approach. I concede that a proper defense of this claim will require more argumentation than I have so far provided. Due to space constraints, I will leave it to the reader to take stock for themselves and decide. If you are convinced that "Whiteness" is not necessarily an identity of domination but one that has been distorted (like "man" or "maleness"), then you might find Alcoff's view more attractive and her criticism more compelling. If, however, you think of "Whiteness" as inherently an identity of domination (like "lord" or "master"), then the *Whiteness-as-domination* model, which undergirds the Latinx racial disintegration thesis, should be more appealing to you and make you suspicious of the sorts of changes Whiteness will be undergoing in the future—changes primarily aimed at its continued existence.

4.2 How Elastic Can Whiteness Be?

A second objection to the Latinx racial disintegration thesis bears on the elasticity of Whiteness. Again, we can look to Alcoff as someone who raises such an objection. Alcoff is deeply skeptical that Whiteness can expand to the degree required for the Latinx racial disintegration thesis to work. In her view, Whiteness "has a very particular and unique relationship to historical atrocities such as slavery and the genocide of native peoples" (2015: 7). If this is true, then it is unlikely that "those whose family were Indigenous and subject to genocide or to slavery or to imperial wars in which the U.S. played a leading part" (2015: 8) would either accept admission or be allowed into Whiteness, especially U.S. Whiteness.

The elasticity objection, however, rests on a shaky assumption. It assumes both that there is a common denominator among all Latinx peoples and that this common denominator makes them all equally unassimilable to U.S. Whiteness. In other words, there is a common denominator among Latinx that would make their case more akin to that of Asians, Blacks, and Native Americans than to cases like those of the Irish and non-Northern Europeans. For Alcoff, this common denominator is the fact that all Latinx people were (or have family that was) subjected to genocide, slavery, or imperial wars where the U.S. played a leading part. This is the reason that, on Alcoff's account, U.S. Whiteness can expand, but never expand wide enough to include Latinx.

Alcoff's view is historically accurate, but it overlooks the fact that the individuals who comprise the Latinx group in the U.S. have not had the same experiences with these atrocities. There are Latinx who have, or come from families that have, benefited greatly from the genocide, slavery, and imperial wars that ravaged Asian, Black, and Native American peoples. In fact, this is why some have argued that the case of Cuban Americans in Florida is an outlier case. They argue that the historical relationship Cuban Americans have with the U.S. is different from that of other Latin American groups, and it is this difference that explains why they favor conservative (i.e., anti-communist) candidates at a higher rate than other Latin American groups. The Cuban American case shows us that there are Latinx who have benefited, not as "race traders" or simply by "passing" as White, but by being authentically White—and White specifically per Alcoff's definition.

At first blush this might seem paradoxical, but recall from our earlier discussion that Whiteness in Latin America is not the same as Whiteness in the U.S. So, there is no contradiction in saying that some Latinx have both historically benefitted from White supremacy as Whites in Latin America, even though they might currently be victims of White supremacy in the U.S. The main takeaway is that from a historical point of view, not all Latinx fall on the same side of the genocides, slavery, and imperial wars that have ravaged the Americas. So, either this is not a common denominator shared by all Latinx peoples, or not everyone we currently think of as Latinx falls on the same side of the non-White racial divide.

Here it might be helpful to take a slight detour and consider the debate over the *common bundle* view of Latinx identity. In this debate, Jorge J. E. Gracia (1999) criticized the view, while Ernesto Rosen Velásquez (2011) defended it. As the name suggests, the view holds that there is no one thing, no necessary and sufficient condition, that comprises a Latinx identity in the U.S. Instead, the view suggests that there are multiple potential properties that can comprise an authentic Latinx identity, and one need only secure enough of them. According to Velásquez, these properties are mostly lower-order ones such as: "Speaking Spanish, being named Juan, using sazón or dancing salsa or tango, eating menudo, and having cuchifritos" (2011: 328). On this view, there is a common denominator among Latinx people, there is something that holds a Latinx identity together, but it is a shared ethnicity, not a race.

On the *common bundle* view, Latinx identity is never more real than when confronting xenophobic attacks, which target the group's language (e.g., Spanish), culture (e.g., music, food, and names) or in some other way portray Latinx ways of life as somehow antithetical to being "real American." Therefore, you rarely find a stronger sense of Latinx identity than when something like the Latinx *common bundle* comes under attack. But where a Latinx identity starts to fall apart is when it is forced to deal with issues of race and racism. Here we see how White supremacy has been a continent-wide (as opposed to merely national) project. White Cubans in Florida do not suddenly stop being White because they also happen to be victims of xenophobia. They do not suddenly forget what Whiteness is or the privileges that come with it. Similarly, Black Latinx in Georgia do not stop being Black because they have a Hispanic surname or because they are also targets of xenophobia. Nor are Latinx (especially Indigenous Latinx) in the American Southwest—where historically they have been the victims of both U.S. Manifest Destiny and Spanish conquest—confused about the difference between settler colonialists and non-White migrants fleeing violence and starvation.

In short, Alcoff is perhaps right that there is both a common denominator among all Latinx peoples and a limit to the elasticity of U.S. Whiteness. But as we have seen, this common denominator might apply only to something like ethnicity and not to race. Furthermore, while it is true that U.S. Whiteness cannot possibly come to include all Latinx, it might nonetheless expand wide enough to include many Latinx. To be more specific, it might be able to expand wide enough (as the Cuban American case in Florida shows) to include enough Latinx to keep Whites as the majority of the U.S. electorate.

4.3 The Double-Play of Whiteness

A final objection to consider is that even when Whiteness expands, historically this expansion has not always been a blessing to those who have had Whiteness bestowed upon them. As Alcoff correctly notes, the times that Latinx have legally been recognized as White in states such as Texas and California, these folks continued to experience social prejudice and discrimination. In fact, official White status has often been used to cover over anti-Latinx discrimination or to hamper attempts at redressing these injustices. So even if U.S. Whiteness can expand to include some Latinx, this might not necessarily be a good thing and may be more of a trick than an authentic welcome.

The famous example that buttresses this third objection is the 1954 *Hernandez v. Texas* Supreme Court case. That case involved the murder conviction of Peter Hernandez. Hernandez's lawyers appealed his murder conviction because Hernandez was of Mexican descent and Mexicans had been systematically excluded from Texas juries, including Hernandez's jury. His lawyers therefore argued that his constitutional rights had being denied—specifically his right to a jury of his peers. The State of Texas countered that Mexicans—not being Asian, Black, or Native American—were members of the White race and so Hernandez's all-White jury was in fact a jury of his racial peers. This is exemplary of the double-play of Whiteness: non-Whites are legally granted Whiteness, but only as a means to occlude their subordinate status and at the same time making it even harder to fight against their subordination.

This concern is well-founded and is perhaps the driving force behind the aforementioned changes to the U.S. census that will recognize "Latino" and "MENA" as non-White groups beginning in 2030 (Wang 2024). We should note, however, that as it stands the objection is conflating "legal" Whiteness with "social" Whiteness. We would do well to keep these two things separate because as we are seeing, one can be legally recognized as White, while nonetheless being socially treated as non-White. Being White by law matters but sometimes only to the extent that it also comes to be reflected in the social imaginary. It is the social imaginary, after all, that motivates things like "dog-whistle politics," and so it is with "social" Whiteness that we should be primarily concerned. For Latinx to be actually accepted into Whiteness, they need to not only be "legally" White, but also "socially" White. The double play of Whiteness is only a problem for those who get "legal" Whiteness without the accompanying "social" Whiteness. Those Latinx who get socially left behind are left behind precisely because they are seen as being too Asian, Black, or Native American.

Ultimately, however, what motivates the double play objection is a worry about solidarity. As a seasoned activist, Alcoff knows that in order to defeat White supremacy we will need a united front. This is why neo-apartheid tactics are so disconcerting. Those sorts of tactics deploy a "divide and conquer" strategy, which is effective in undermining solidarity among non-White folks. The potential for Latinx racial disintegration therefore raises more than a problem of identity; it raises a moral and political quandary: do racially "in-between" Latinx have a duty that goes beyond self-interest, to resist their assimilation into U.S. Whiteness?

This third objection therefore begins to shift the terrain a bit. Instead of questioning the expansion of Whiteness, it asks about the responsibility Latinx have to resist being incorporated into Whiteness. In "Why the Struggle Against Coloniality Is Paramount to Latin American Philosophy," Grant Silva offers a hardline response to this quandary. He suggests that instead of thinking about Latinx as either a racial or ethnic identity, we should think of it as a political project, as a group that understands itself from the beginning to be pluri-racial, not monoracial or multicultural. Following Alcoff, he suggests that those who embrace a Latinx identity should understand themselves as the product of—and as those who struggle against—colonialism and imperialism in the Western hemisphere. He suggests that those Latinx who have benefitted the most from this history (e.g., the "in-between" Latinx) have an even stronger duty to fight against assimilation into U.S. Whiteness. Again, the reason is not because admission into U.S. Whiteness will necessarily hurt them—some Latinx might benefit from this—but they should resist out of a sense of justice and political solidarity—a solidarity that does not merely coopt Latin Americans' Indigenous history, erase its African heritage, or deny its Asian and Polynesian ancestry (Silva 2015).

What this will look like or how it will work on the ground is another question that is beyond the scope of this essay. However, thinking of a Latinx identity as a political project to which one has an obligation to remain faithful to is not without some risk or potential pitfalls.[9] These dangers have been thoroughly outlined by folks like Elizabeth Millán Brusslan (2015) and Gregory Pappas (2017). They worry that defining a Latinx identity in a narrow and sectarian way, as they see Silva doing, might disqualify some Latinx who are not personally onboard with a project of decolonization and might even be opposed to it, but nonetheless ought to be understood as having a Latinx identity.

Fortunately, we do not have to resolve this debate in order to respond to the objection. What is important to see is that in all these cases, the concern over the double-play of Whiteness does not necessarily conflict with the Latinx racial disintegration thesis. Instead of challenging the thesis, the various competing accounts offer different prescriptions for what Latinx should or should not do when (and if) U.S. Whiteness is on offer. We can all agree that solidarity is crucial to the struggle against White supremacy, but simply because something (e.g., Latinx solidarity) is crucial to achieve a shared end (e.g., racial justice), it does not mean that there is nothing (e.g., Latinx racial disintegration) that is threatening to undermine this crucial response.

Conclusion

Even if their citizenship status today is legally recognized, Latinx's claim to U.S. citizenship is socially suspect. Latinx, as a group, are not considered part of the fabric of "real America," at least not in the U.S. social imaginary. Today, nativists hold the same level of contempt for Latinx as British colonists held for Germans in the 1750s and the Know-Nothing party did for Catholics in the 1850s. But just as "in-between" race groups in the early twentieth century came to gain full Whiteness (i.e., full entry into "real America"), racially "in-between" Latinx today are candidates for full admission into U.S. Whiteness. This expansion is the price U.S. Whiteness is going to have to pay if, in the face of the oncoming demographic changes, it wants to keep its hold on the U.S. electorate. So, as unlikely as it seems to some of us now—especially those of us who constantly experience anti-Latinx discrimination—with enough time and pressure U.S. Whiteness will expand once more. This time the expansion will grant Whiteness to just enough of those racially "in-between" Latinx to keep Whites as the electorate majority and at the same time vindicate the "melting pot" myth—a myth that celebrates the inclusiveness of U.S. nationalism while blaming non-Whites for their subordinate status. This, in short, is how you keep America White, again.[10]

References

Abramovitz, A. (2023) "The Transformation of the American Electorate," *The Center for Politics*, March 23, https://centerforpolitics.org/crystalball/the-transformation-of-the-american-electorate/.
Alcoff, L. (2015) *The Future of Whiteness*, Malden, MA: Polity.
Appiah, K. (1996) "Race, Culture, Identity: Misunderstood Connections," *The Tanner Lectures on Human Values* 17: 51–136.
Beltrán, C. (2010) *The Trouble with Unity: Latino Politics and The Creation of Identity*, New York: Oxford University Press.
Boyd, J. (1970) "Nixon's Southern Strategy," *New York Times*, May 17, www.nytimes.com/1970/05/17/archives/nixons-southern-strategy-its-all-in-the-charts.html.
Bump, P. (2015) "When Did Black Americans Start Voting So Heavily Democratic?" *The Washington Post*, July 7, www.washingtonpost.com/news/the-fix/wp/2015/07/07/when-did-black-americans-start-voting-so-heavily-democratic.
Census Profiles Florida. (2000) *Florida Profile*, https://www2.census.gov/geo/maps/special/profile2k/FL_2K_Profile.pdf.
Census Profiles Florida. (2020) *Florida Profile*, https://naleo.org/wp-content/uploads/2021/12/2020-Census-Profiles-FL.pdf.
CNN. (2016) "2016: Exit Polls," November 9, www.cnn.com/election/2016/results/exit-polls/florida/president.
CNN. (2020) "2020: Exit Polls," www.cnn.com/election/2020/exit-polls/president/florida.
Colby, S. L., and Ortman, J. M. (2014) "Projections of the Size and Composition of the U.S. Population: 2014 to 2060," in *Current Population Reports, P25-1143*, Washington, DC: Census Bureau. www.census.gov/content/dam/Census/library/publications/2015/demo/p25-1143.pdf.
De Gobineau, A. (2000) "The Inequality of Human Races," in R. Bernasconi and T. L. Lott (eds.), *The Idea of Race*, 45–53, Indianapolis, IN: Hackett Publishing Company.
Eckholm, E., and Fausset, R. (2014) "As New Rules Take Effect, Voters Report Problems in Some States," *New York Times*, November 4, www.nytimes.com/2014/11/05/us/election-tests-new-rules-on-voting.html.
"Florida Election Results," (2020) *New York Times*, www.nytimes.com/interactive/2020/11/03/us/elections/results-florida.html.
Franke-Ruta, G. (2013) "What You Need to Read in the RNC Election-Autopsy Report," *The Atlantic*, March 18, www.theatlantic.com/politics/archive/2013/03/what-you-need-to-read-in-the-rnc-election-autopsy-report/274112.
Gabaccia, D. (2010) "Nations of Immigrants: Do Words Matter?" *The Pluralist* 5 (3): 5–31.
Gracia, J. (1999) *Hispanic/Latino Identity: A Philosophical Perspective*, Hoboken, NJ: Wiley-Blackwell.
Grant, M. (1936) *The Passing of the Great Race or the Racial Basis of European History*, New York: Charles Scribner's Sons.
Grosfoguel, R. (2008) "Latin@s and the Decolonization of the US Empire in the 21st Century," *Social Science Information* 47 (4): 605–622.
Hains, T. (2015) "Coulter: 'Republicans Win by Driving Up the White Vote; How About for Once Appealing to Your Base?'" *Real Clear Politics*, June 9, www.realclearpolitics.com/video/2015/06/09/ann_coulter_republicans_win_by_driving_up_the_white_vote_how_about_for_once_appealing_to_your_base.html.
Haney López, I. (2014) *Dog Whistle Politics: How Coded Racial Appeals Have Reinvented Racism and Wrecked the Middle Class*, New York: Oxford University Press.

Krogstad, J. M., and Flores, A. (2016) "Unlike Other Latinos, About Half of Cuban Voters in Florida Backed Trump," *Pew Research Center*, November 15, www.pewresearch.org/short-reads/2016/11/15/unlike-other-latinos-about-half-of-cuban-voters-in-florida-backed-trump.

Lee, E. (2019) *America for Americans: A History of Xenophobia in the United States*, New York: Basic Books.

Lopez, A. (2023) "Advocates in Florida Clamor for a Fix for the Formerly Incarcerated Who Want to Vote," *NPR*, May 4, www.npr.org/2023/05/04/1173786694/felon-voting-database-florida-registration-card-disclaimer.

McIntosh, P. (1989) "White Privilege: Unpacking the Invisible Knapsack," *Peace and Freedom Magazine* (July/August): 10–12.

Mendoza, J. J. (2023) "Go Back to Where You Came From! Racism, Xenophobia, and White Nationalism," *American Philosophical Quarterly* 60 (4): 397–410.

Millán Brusslan, E. (2015) "Philosophy Born of Colonial Struggle: One Theme or the Whole Story of the Latin American Philosophical Tradition?" *APA Newsletter on Hispanic/Latino Issues in Philosophy* 18 (1): 13–20.

Orosco, J. A. (2016) *Toppling the Melting Pot: Immigration and Multiculturalism in American Pragmatism*, Bloomington: Indiana University Press.

Pappas, G. F. (2017) "The Limitations and Dangers of Decolonial Philosophies Lessons from Zapatista Luis Villoro," *Radical Philosophy Review* 20 (2): 265–295.

Pew Research Center. (2016) "Latinos in the 2016 Election: Florida," *Pew Research Center*, January 19, www.pewresearch.org/hispanic/fact-sheet/latinos-in-the-2016-election-florida/#:~:text=The%20Hispanic%20population%20in%20Florida,Hispanic%20statewide%20population%20share%20nationally.

Phillips, S. (2016) *Brown Is the New White: How the Demographic Revolution Has Created a New American Majority*, New York: The New Press.

Reilly, K. (2016) "Here Are All the Times Donald Trump Insulted Mexico," *TIME*, August 31, https://time.com/4473972/donald-trump-mexico-meeting-insult.

Roediger, D. R. (2006) *Working Toward Whiteness: How America's Immigrants Became White: The Strange Journey from Ellis Island to the Suburbs*, New York: Basic Books.

Schleifer, T. (2016) "Mitt Romney Says Donald Trump Will Change America with 'Trickle-Down Racism'," *CNN*, June 11, www.cnn.com/2016/06/10/politics/mitt-romney-donald-trump-racism/index.html.

Silva, G. J. (2015) "Why the Struggle Against Coloniality is Paramount to Latin American Philosophy," *APA Newsletter on Hispanic/Latino Issues in Philosophy* 18 (1): 8–12.

Stepan, N. L. (1996) *The Hour of Eugenics: Race, Gender, and Nation in Latin America*, Ithaca, NY: Cornell University Press.

Sundstrom, R. (2008) *The Browning of America and the Evasion of Social Justice*, Albany, NY: SUNY Press.

Vasconcelos, J. (2004) "The Cosmic Race," in J. J. E. Gracia and E. Millan-Zaibert (eds.), *Latin American Philosophy for the 21st Century: The Human Condition, Values, and the Search for Identity*, 269–278, Amherst, NY: Prometheus Books.

Velásquez, E. R. (2011) "Is the 'Common-Bundle View' of Ethnicity Problematic?" *Philosophy & Social Criticism* 37 (3): 325–344.

Wang, H. L. (2024) "Next U.S. Census Will Have New Boxes for 'Middle Eastern or North African,' 'Latino'," *NPR*, March 28, www.npr.org/2024/03/28/1237218459/census-race-categories-ethnicity-middle-east-north-africa.

Yancy, G. (2008) *Black Bodies, White Gazes: The Continuing Significance of Race*, Lanham, MD: Rowman & Littlefield.

Zack, N. (2002) *Philosophy of Science and Race*, New York: Routledge.

Notes

1 For a more in-depth history of xenophobia during this period see Lee (2019).
2 Quoted in Lee (2019: 1–2).
3 What follows is largely a summary of the view put forth by Ian Haney López in *Dog Whistle Politics* see Haney López (2014).

4 See Sundstrom (2008) for some of these criticisms.
5 For a fascinating historical account of these different national race projects see Stepan (1996).
6 A 2018 ballot measure was supposed to fix this problem in Florida, but legislators continue to drag their feet. See Lopez (2023).
7 Recall that Donald Trump began his presidential campaign by stating that Mexico was no friend to the U.S. and that Mexican immigrants were nothing more than rapists and criminals. Add to this that for Trump "Mexico" is a stand in for all Latin American countries. See Reilly (2016).
8 For a more in-depth account of "racial disintegration," "racialization," and "racial formation," see Mendoza (2023).
9 For example, Cristina Beltrán has also argued that Latinx is more of a political project than a racial or ethnic group. On her account, however, this is the reason Latinx will disintegrate rather than continue as a group. See Beltrán (2010).
10 A special thank you to Manuel Vargas, Lori Gallegos, Francisco Gallegos, and the Society for Mexican American Philosophy for all their helpful comments, encouragement, and continued support of this work.

Reading Questions

1. How does Mendoza suggest we think about the claim that the U.S. is "a nation of immigrants"? In his view, how might this claim distort the ways in which the U.S. has been a nation of White dominance?
2. The author describes two ways to think about the nature of White identity—the *Whiteness-as-domination* model and the *distorted identity* model. What assumptions about Whiteness do these two models share? Where do they diverge?
3. The Latinx racial disintegration thesis holds that segments of the Latinx community will be co-opted into Whiteness. If this is true, why does Mendoza think it is something we should be worried about? If Whiteness is a condition for being considered a "real American," why wouldn't it be a good thing for more Latinxs to be considered White?
4. Mendoza recounts the history of the incorporation of non-Northern European immigrants into the country to illustrate how it could be possible for a group once considered non-White to *become* White. What was it about these groups that made it possible for them to become White, according to the text? What does this imply about what could determine whether Latinx people come to be considered White?
5. The text discusses recent political history, describing how overtly racist laws were gradually overturned, while indirect methods of preserving white supremacy have been advanced in the guise of voting restrictions and "dog whistle politics." Based on this history, Mendoza concludes that his version of pessimism—the Latinx racial disintegration thesis—is more plausible than both the neo-apartheid view and Alcoff's optimistic view. Can you think of any evidence that might challenge Mendoza's hypothesis, or lend support to one of the alternatives?
6. What does it mean to understand Latinx as a political project, rather than as a racial or ethnic identity? Do Latinx people have an obligation to resist assimilation to Whiteness? Draw on the text to support your answer.

28 Socially, Not Legally, Undocumented

Amy Reed-Sandoval

Political philosophers working on immigration have too often considered only the justice of hypothetical people crossing hypothetical borders. As a result, questions of immigrant identity are frequently absent from philosophical debate about immigration justice and the ethics of borders. Fortunately, however, there are now some important exceptions to this: those philosophers who take as their philosophical starting point the interests and lived experiences of actual migrants in our actual social world.

An important example of this approach comes from José Jorge Mendoza. He argues that immigration enforcement mechanisms in the United States interior—including surveying, identifying, interrogating, and apprehending—are unjust inasmuch as they (further) marginalize Latina/o/x citizens and legal residents of the U.S. (Mendoza 2014).[1] Given that approximately 80% of undocumented migrants in the United States are from Latin America, "aggressive internal enforcement strategies . . . disproportionately target citizens who are (or appear to be) of Latin American descent" (Mendoza 2014: 75). Mendoza argues that it violates the political equality of Latina/o/x citizens that they should bear this immense burden when other social groups, particularly whites, are largely exempt from it. He concludes by arguing that internal immigration enforcement strategies cannot be performed justly and should be stopped altogether.

Mendoza's conclusion is, I believe, correct but incomplete. Immigration policies in the United States that marginalize Latina/o/x citizens are, indeed, anti-egalitarian and impermissible.

However, his assessment of the moral wrong of internal immigration enforcement strategies is limited. This is because Mendoza's argument—as it stands—depicts the "rights" of undocumented migrants strictly *in terms of* the rights of Latina/o/x citizens and legal residents of the United States. In other words, these immigration enforcement mechanisms are cast as unjust not because they wrong the undocumented migrants in question but because they contribute to or are the source of disproportional harassment of Latina/o/x citizens and legal residents.

Mendoza's argument, while powerful, thus circumvents a fundamental question of immigration justice: what rights and protections are owed to undocumented migrants *themselves*? Clearly, Mendoza is striving to develop a firm basis for articulating the rights of the undocumented. But he has encountered a conceptual barrier—one that is attributable, I believe, to a widespread tendency in immigration philosophy and politics to understand the term "undocumented migrant" as referring strictly to legal status as opposed to a social group membership. While many immigration philosophers think of "Latina/o/xs" or "women" as social groups whose moral equality can be undermined by unjust immigration policies (Narayan 1995; Jaggar 2014; Wilcox 2008), "undocumented migrants" are generally regarded *legalistically*—as a collection of idiosyncratic individuals who happen to lack legal authorization to be in the state they currently inhabit. Working within this framework, Mendoza only has the means to argue that the oppression of undocumented migrants is wrong because it contributes to unjust treatment of "legal" Latina/o/x citizens and legal residents.

In response to this conceptual barrier, I argue in this chapter that the term "undocumented migrant" should be taken by political philosophers and policymakers to refer not primarily, or even necessarily, to the *legal status* of being undocumented but to an oppressed social group. I call the social group of people who are oppressed as undocumented migrants the "socially undocumented." The socially undocumented, I shall argue, *endure a common set of unjust, immigration-related constraints on the basis of being perceived to be undocumented*. Crucially, these are not constraints that necessarily stem from being legally undocumented.

The understanding of "social group" that I employ is—to borrow from Rawls's old slogan—political, not metaphysical. Importantly, the groups of socially and legally undocumented people are not comprised of exactly the same sets of individuals. As we shall see, one can endure unjust constraints on the basis of being perceived to be undocumented without being legally undocumented. Similarly, one can be legally but not socially undocumented. How will thinking of what it means to "be undocumented" in terms of social group status help us to understand the rights of undocumented migrants *themselves*—and not strictly in terms of the rights of citizen and legal resident Latina/o/xs? As we shall see, when we are restricted to understanding the term "undocumented migrant" as a legal status, it is conceptually very difficult, if not impossible, to identify the injustice of undocumented migrant oppression. Oppression is something that happens to people not as individuals but as members of social groups (Clatterbaugh 1996). Thus, in the absence of a satisfactory account of the social group of undocumented migrants, we can neither explain the injustice of undocumented migrant oppression nor develop adequate solutions for alleviating that injustice. In addition, there are political consequences to understanding "undocumented migrant" solely in terms of legal status. I shall argue over the course of this book that it often serves as a red herring, distracting policymakers from fully uncovering what is owed to the undocumented at the bar of justice.

My argument proceeds as follows. I begin by motivating my claim that we should distinguish between the legally and the socially undocumented. Second, I develop and defend a political understanding of a social group. Third, I provide an account what it means to be socially undocumented. And finally, I show how this account enables us to understand the injustice of undocumented migrant oppression.

Before I begin, let me review two important guiding assumptions that I make in this chapter and throughout this book—both of which were discussed in greater detail in the introduction. First, recall that I assume that national borders are, in at least some respects, morally and politically justified. It follows from this assumption that undocumented migrants break just laws in crossing borders without legal authorization. I recognize that this is a contentious claim, and I shall explore in detail arguments for open borders and their implications for ongoing socially undocumented oppression in chapter 6. For now, note that operating within such a framework need not entail a defense of the *status quo* in immigration policy. One can consistently hold that borders are, in at least some respects, just but also maintain that unduly physically harming undocumented migrants at the border and elsewhere—or denying them access to health care or other vital social services—unjustly oppresses them.

Second, allow me to review briefly my understanding of justice in this chapter and throughout this book. Justice, as I understand it, entails respect for the moral equality of all people across the globe. Just states are duty-bound to uphold universal moral equality; they cannot regard their own citizens as possessing more moral worth than citizens of other countries (even those who currently reside in other countries). In accordance with the aforementioned tenets of relational egalitarianism, I assume that respect for universal moral equality requires dismantling oppressive structural social relations affecting not only individuals but also social groups. Thus, dismantling injustice will require, among other things, a thorough understanding of the deep social structures and the patterns of relationship that perpetuate inequality.

I. "Undocumented Migrant": Legal or Social Group Status?

In both philosophy and contemporary politics, the term "undocumented migrant" has often been used to denote a person who lacks legal permission to be in the state the individual currently inhabits. The most prominent example of this understanding of what it means to be an undocumented migrant comes from Joseph Carens (2010). He argues that those *legally* undocumented migrants who have resided in their new society for over six years are entitled to a right to remain due to the de facto social membership that they have developed over time. Carens discusses the infamous case of Marguerite Grimmond, who was born in the United States but moved to Scotland with her family as a young girl. Grimmond remained in Scotland until the age of 80, at which time she took a vacation to Australia. She was told upon her return to the U.K. that she was, in fact, a legally undocumented migrant who needed to return to her "home" in the United States.[2]

Carens uses Grimmond's story to highlight an intuition shared by many. After a certain amount of time, legally undocumented migrants develop a moral right to stay in the country to which they have migrated—making it "cruel and inhumane" to deport them.

There is much to admire in Carens's social membership argument, and it is not my intention to argue against it. However, I do wish to convey that Carens's influential position regards "undocumented" status primarily as a *legal one*. That is, for Carens, an undocumented migrant is someone who lacks *legal* permission to reside in the country in which she now resides. While this may seem like a minor observation, it has very important consequences for the manner in which we view the scope of immigration justice. To illustrate this, allow me to introduce the "cases" of Gary and Alicia, both of whom are *legally* undocumented migrants in the U.S. (These cases are hypothetical but inspired by commonplace "real world" narratives.)

(1) Gary is a white, middle-class citizen of the United Kingdom who plays in a punk rock band. While he enjoys a moderate level of success as a punk rocker in London, he has trouble distinguishing himself from the competition. He decides to try his luck in Washington, DC—a city with a thriving punk scene. Gary is convinced that the fact that he is British will give him the artistic "edge" in DC that he had been striving for in London. However, Gary is quite unsuccessful in his efforts, and he spends the next six years performing what he considers to be uninspired children's music at birthday parties (all the while lacking legal permission to be present in the United States). Gary feels that his lack of legal permission to be in the United States is thwarting his artistic progress, as he once had to turn down a well-paying gig because of his "lack of papers." Furthermore, he misses the U.K. and laments that he cannot travel there on a quick vacation without

being "found out" as undocumented. In addition, U.S. politics angers Gary and he is annoyed that he cannot vote in U.S. elections. He eventually considers returning to the U.K. permanently.

(2) Alicia, a citizen of Mexico, has been an undocumented migrant in Los Angeles, California, for a year. Her husband died while attempting to cross the U.S.-Mexico border without authorization, after losing his livelihood as a small farmer. Since that time, Alicia found herself unable to make ends meet for herself and her children, so she decided to undertake the perilous journey on foot to the United States. She is now a domestic worker for a number of wealthy white families in Los Angeles.

She spends approximately four hours per day on public transportation to and from her employers' homes, and she lives in a small room that she shares with several other families (all of whom are undocumented migrants from Mexico and Central America). Alicia's employers frequently force her to work with dangerous chemicals and deduct from her wages if they are not completely satisfied with her work. Despite the fact that she moves around Los Angeles with great caution, after a year in the U.S. Alicia's legally undocumented status is found out and she is threatened with deportation back to Mexico.

Most people will acknowledge that Alicia has been wronged in ways that Gary has not.

However, some may be reluctant to conclude that Alicia has been *oppressed* and *treated unjustly*. After all, Alicia lacks legal permission to be in the country where her wrongful treatment is taking place. Thus, one might argue that while Alicia is indeed being treated in a morally problematic manner, this treatment is simply not the stuff of oppression and injustice. She is "free to leave," one might say, and so she cannot be oppressed. Furthermore, she lacks any *legitimate* legal recourse to a minimum wage and other workplace protections, so in denying her these things her employers cannot be said to act oppressively toward her.

The problem here, I contend, is that we are conceiving of what it means to be an "undocumented migrant" solely in terms of legal status. I will now argue that while both Gary and Alicia are undocumented migrants in legal terms, Alicia—but not Gary—is socially undocumented. Clarifying what this means will enable us to articulate the injustice endured by Alicia *as an undocumented person*.

II. Social Groups—Political, Not Metaphysical

Before I describe what it means to be socially undocumented I must provide a satisfactory conception of a social group. In this section I turn to this task. Following Ann Cudd and Iris Marion Young, I submit that *politically*, we should try to understand our social world in terms of social groups because doing so is explanatorily useful for understanding and alleviating oppression.[3] Recall that, as argued by Young, "evaluating inequality in terms of social groups enables us to claim that some inequalities are unjust . . . because such group-based comparison helps reveal important aspects of institutional relations and processes" (Young 2001: 2)

Similarly, Cudd argues that thinking in terms of social groups can enable us to understand "unjust group-based hierarchies" (Cudd 2006: 28). A "group-conscious practice of assessing inequality" (29) can enable us to uncover why women lack social equality with men all over the world, Latina/o/xs with whites in the United States and elsewhere, persons with disabilities with the able-bodied, etc. In sum, in a *political* conception of a social group we posit social groups inasmuch as doing so enables us to uncover oppression, injustice, and inequality.

But what is a social group? I employ Ann Cudd's externalist account. Cudd argues that "what makes a person a member of a social group is not determined by any internal states of that person but rather by objective facts about the world, including how others perceive and behave toward that person" (36). She calls these objective facts about the world "constraints." These constraints include "legal rights, obligations, burdens, stereotypical expectations, wealth, income, conventions, norms and practices" (50).

Thus, just as the formal denial of equal rights is a constraint, so is the expectation that people dress and talk in a particular way in professional settings. Importantly, the constraints of which Cudd speaks also include incentives and rewards for certain behaviors. They are "facts that one does or ought to rationally consider in deciding how to act or plan one's life, or facts that shape attitudes about other persons" (1). For example, the expectation that men not cry in public is a constraint that the social group of men rather uniquely face. But this constraint also brings with it social rewards—namely, those that are associated with being perceived as masculine (Frye 1983). In sum, I follow Cudd in understanding a social group to be "a collection of persons who share (or who would share under similar circumstances) a set of constraints on action" (Cudd 2006: 44).

The constraints themselves are put in place by social institutions. Social institutions exist in a variety of forms. They can include "government, legal systems, schools, banks, gender rules and norms, rules of etiquette, media outlets, stereotypical beliefs, class, caste systems, and racial declassification systems" (Cudd 2006: 44). As Peter Higgins summarizes it, social institutions "create social groups by conditioning the lives of some people in one way, other people in another way" (2013: 112).

They often serve to privilege some groups while marginalizing others. Importantly, "these social institutions and constraints can, but need not, give rise to thoughts and feelings on the part of the group member which serve to reinforce her membership in the social group" (Higgins 2013: 112). In other words, while some people will wholeheartedly identify as being members of particular social groups, others will resist membership or be largely unaware of it. For instance, one can be identified by others as female and be subjected to constraints on that basis, even if one rejects that label and self-identifies as male. Similarly, one can enter into the social group of Latina/o/xs if one is taken to be Latina/o/x by one's fellow society members—even if one strives to distance oneself from that ethno-racial label and identity.

With this conception of social grouphood in mind, we are now in a position to understand what an *oppressed* social group is. Cudd defines an *oppressed* social group as a collection of persons who share (or who would share under similar circumstances) a set of *unjust* constraints on action (Cudd 2006: 36–37). How do we know whether the constraints that are placed on one's action are, in fact, unjust? To answer this question, Cudd first notes how sets of constraints can fall disproportionately, or unequally, on some groups more than on others. She provides the example of segregated public restrooms. If, on average, the restrooms assigned to one group are of lesser quality (in terms of general wait time and cleanliness, for instance), then a certain set of constraints are being borne unequally by that group. Cudd then suggests—a bit too quickly, I believe—that the unequal constraints are unjust if the inequality in question is itself *unjustifiable* (2006: 51).

While Cudd does not spend very much time establishing what it means for an unequally distributed constraint to be unjustifiable, I believe we can extract from her account the following guiding principles. First, some group-based constraints on action are uncontroversially *justifiable*. For example, the social group of people who study philosophy rather than medicine are *justifiably constrained* by the fact that their local hospital denies them permission to perform open heart surgeries on its patients.

Alternatively, unjust or unjustifiable constraints on action are those that stem from the ways that one's social group identity leads to one's interests being systematically thwarted by unjust group-based hierarchies. In other words, an *unjustifiable* shared constraint on action for a social group is one that undermines the moral equality of members of that group (or that reinforces their extant inequality). It is a constraint that is imposed upon them as a result of morally arbitrary features that they possess—i.e. in terms of race/ethnicity, gender, ability, etc.[4]

For instance, the expectation that women regularly wear uncomfortable clothing and shoes to "look attractive" is an unjustifiable constraint because it stems from the belief that women should devote themselves to their exterior beauty for the pleasure and acceptance of men. This systematically undermines and reinforces women's inequality in relation to men. However, the expectation that medical doctors regularly read important medical journals to "stay on top of their fields" is not an unjust or unjustifiable constraint, as it does not respond to or reinforce any unjust group-based hierarchies.

I want to make clear, at this stage, that the distinction I have drawn, following Cudd, between "justifiable" and "unjustifiable" constraints on action does not mirror the distinction between "option luck" and "brute luck" that has motivated a great deal of luck in egalitarian literature, and which Elizabeth Anderson has called into question in her arguments for relational egalitarianism. It is not the case that "unjustifiable" constraints are strictly those for which the individuals upon whom they are imposed can be held morally responsible. For example, on this view, the poor are an oppressed social group on the grounds that they endure a variety of unjust constraints. These include, but are not limited to, lack of opportunities to earn wages that support their capabilities; social attitudes that regard them as inferior; social attitudes that regard their work as unimportant, etc. On my reading of Cudd's account, these constraints are unjust even if some of the poor can be held morally accountable or "liable" for their social position as poor/economically disadvantaged. All that matters is that the poor/economically disadvantaged are socially positioned as moral inferiors. In this sense, I perceive Cudd's account of an oppressed social group as complementary to relational egalitarianism.

Allow me to summarize the account of social groups—and oppressed social groups—that I employ. Social groups are collections of people who share, or who would share under similar circumstances, a set of constraints on action. These constraints are generated by a variety of social institutions. People can be members of social groups without knowing it or claiming it. An *oppressed* social group is "a collection of persons who share (or who would share under similar circumstances) a set of *unjust* constraints on action" (Cudd 2006: 44). Unjust constraints on action are those that undermine one's moral equality in relation to others, or that reinforce one's extant inequality in relation to others, on the basis of one's social group membership.

III. The Socially Undocumented

I now turn to the question of what it means to be socially undocumented. I will argue that (1) there is a social group of people facing similar constraints that stem from being *perceived to be undocumented*; and (2) these constraints are *unjust*. Let me begin, however, by arguing that being *legally* undocumented is neither necessary nor sufficient for being oppressed as an undocumented migrant. As we shall see, being legally undocumented does not, in and of itself, lead to unjust constraints. Thus, if the legally undocumented can be said to comprise a social group on the basis of a shared set of constraints, it is not necessarily an *oppressed* social group.

To see why this is the case, let us consider some of the constraints on action that both Alicia and Gary share strictly as a result of being legally undocumented. Neither of them can vote in U.S. elections. They cannot serve on U.S. juries. They both lack a legal right to work in the United States. However, recall that only those constraints that are *unjust* entail membership in an oppressed social group. I have assumed national borders to be morally and politically legitimate. Thus, these are not (prima facie) unjust constraints. Alicia and Gary are not necessarily oppressed on the basis of the constraints that stem from being legally undocumented.

This point is further illustrated by an example from Michael Blake. The fact that I, as a citizen of the United States, cannot vote in French elections is not unjust. That is, the French government, in denying me permission to vote in French elections, does not regard me as *morally inferior* to the citizens of France. Blake explains:

> The restriction recognizes ... the distinct institutional contexts in which French and American citizens are situated. French citizens, being coercively ruled by a set of French legal and political institutions, are entitled to guarantees of political equality simply inapplicable to the set of both French and American citizens. Nothing here is a denial of moral equality. The different set of political entitlements reflects the distinct implications of moral equality in distinct institutional circumstances; it respects, rather than abandons, the notion of moral egalitarianism.
>
> (2008: 967)

In denying me the right to vote in French elections, the French government simply recognizes that I am a member of a distinct institutional context. I am treated as neither superior nor inferior to the citizens of France. My inability to vote in French elections is thus not an *unjust* constraint on my action, for it does not undermine my moral equality to the French in any way.

In the very same way, the constraints that Alicia and Gary face strictly on the basis of not being U.S. citizens—i.e., lacking legal permission to vote and to serve on U.S. juries, and to reside and work legally in the United States—are not necessarily unjust and unjustifiable constraints. I conclude, then, that the social group of those who are oppressed as undocumented migrants (if it exists) is not the same as the group of legally undocumented migrants. Furthermore, the constraints stemming from being legally undocumented are not necessarily oppressive.

I will now argue that Alicia is socially undocumented not on the basis of her legal status but because of how she is perceived on the basis of how she looks. I argue for this in terms of the following. First, Alicia faces a host of constraints (associated with immigration status) that Gary does not.[5] Second, Alicia endures these constraints because she is *perceived* to be undocumented—not because she is legally undocumented. Third, these constraints are *unjustifiable* and therefore *unjust* because they are imposed on the basis of morally arbitrary features such as race/ethnicity and socioeconomic class, thereby undermining her moral equality with others. They are therefore different from legitimate constraints that are imposed because Alicia (and Gary) are legally undocumented—i.e., being able to vote in United States elections. Because of this, Alicia—and those similarly positioned—share a set of unjust constraints. They therefore comprise an oppressed social group, the socially undocumented.

I turn, then, to my first point. Alicia faces a host of constraints associated with undocumented status that Gary does not. For instance, she lives in greater fear than Gary does of being pulled over or otherwise targeted by the police in an encounter that could lead to her deportation. She thus moves around Los Angeles timidly, with a sense of limitation and caution. Gary, on the other hand, navigates Washington, DC, with general ease. He does not fear that his immigration status will be called into question if he gets pulled over at a traffic light, and he happily goes to boisterous parties and punk rock concerts on a regular basis.

In addition, Alicia is subjected to a range of offensive stereotypes and assumptions in her interactions with many U.S. citizens and institutions because people assume that she does not belong in the United States. Indeed, people assume that she cannot speak English and even tell her to go back to her country. This may have a disparaging impact on the way Alicia views herself. Gary, however, can interact with the Americans around him with far greater ease. People do not doubt his intelligence or English language ability when they come across him. Indeed, his English accent often leads people to assume that he is remarkably intelligent.

Alicia is also compelled to engage in underpaid and sometimes degrading labor that most U.S. citizens and legal residents would be reluctant to perform. When she seeks employment as a domestic worker or a farmworker, her employers will not think twice about paying her less than minimum wage and denying her basic workplace safety protections. On the other hand, when Gary applies for work as a musician at children's birthday parties he gets paid more than the minimum wage. While he may not thoroughly enjoy this work, he is treated roughly the same way—in terms of respect and workplace safely—as a U.S. citizen in a similar position would be treated. Were Gary to apply for work in places traditionally associated with exploitable undocumented migrant labor (like a meat-packing plant) he may even struggle to get hired because he does not seem to them to be undocumented.

In sum, we have seen that Alicia faces a host of constraints that Gary does not. People assume that Alicia is an immigrant who does not belong in the United States and cannot speak English. They both underpay and under-protect her in jobs that undocumented migrants usually perform because they assume that she will not complain for fear of deportation. Alicia constantly fears that she will be targeted by the police in an encounter that will eventually lead to her deportation.

I now turn to my second claim. Alicia does not face these constraints because she is legally undocumented. When Alicia is harassed, demeaned, and exploited to by a range of U.S. citizens and institutions it is not because authorities have confirmed that she lacks legal permission to live and work in the United States. Rather, it is because of *how she is perceived* on the basis of how she looks, which includes how she comports herself.

It will be easier to illustrate this by turning to "real world" examples of people who face the same constraints as Alicia. I will explore the grounds on which many people who are positioned in a way that is similar to Alicia are demeaned, harassed by the police and immigration enforcement, and exploited in worksites that are traditionally associated with undocumented migrant labor. As I explore these narratives, I will argue that this treatment is not in response to the fact that the people in question are legally undocumented. Rather, it is in response to how they are perceived on the basis of how they look. I end this section with a brief discussion of what it means to "look undocumented."

I have argued that Alicia is demeaned by U.S. citizens and legal residents in ways that are associated with immigration status. The following statement from Alma, a Latina child, illustrates even more clearly what this often entails:

> Just last year I went into a store and I was paying for my groceries and the clerk didn't think I spoke English. She was out of plastic bags so she said to the bagger, "Just go ahead and put it in paper bags, they don't care," as if I didn't know what she was saying.

But I said, "But I do care. I like it in plastic better." I think because we're Hispanic and they know we do field work, and we're new in the area, they think less of us. We're human and we work hard. Maybe we don't work in a store, but we're picking apples for them to sell in the store.

(Miles and Sonneville 2001)

In this statement we see that Alma was demeaned by a U.S. citizen or legal resident. The clerk at the grocery store automatically assumed that Alma was a foreigner who could not speak English, and that she did not care about the quality of her grocery bags like a U.S. citizen would.

Importantly, this demeaning treatment did not occur because the clerk somehow knew that Alma was legally undocumented. In fact, Alma is a citizen of the United States and speaks English as one of her first languages. Instead, this treatment occurred on the basis of how Alma was perceived by the clerk. On the basis of being taken to look like a Mexican farmworker, Alma was perceived as someone who does not belong in the United States. She then was demeaned and constrained on that basis.

Similarly, when people assume that Alicia does not speak English, and when they tell her to go back to her country, this occurs because of judgments people make on the basis of how Alicia looks. This does not transpire because Alicia is legally undocumented.

I have also claimed that the sense of trepidation with which Alicia navigates the city on the way to and from work is attributable not to her legally undocumented status, but rather to the way that Alicia is perceived. To further argue for this, let me begin by noting that Alicia's experiences are shared by many others in the United States.

In their chapter "Deportation in the U.S.-Mexico Borderlands: Anticipation, Experience, and Memory," anthropologists Victor Talavera, Guillermina Nuñez-Mchiri, and Josiah Heyman discuss the ways that "deportability" is experienced profoundly by a subset of the population in the United States—including people who have never been physically deported (Talavera et al. 2010). The authors argue that many people feel "branded" as undocumented and deportable on the basis of how they look. This produces tremendous anxiety and trauma for those who feel thus branded. It constrains their movement and often forces them into a state of social isolation.

To illustrate this, the authors discuss a series of 2005 raids that took place in El Paso, Texas, in which police officers used routine traffic stops to locate and apprehend undocumented migrants (eventually turning them over to Immigration and Customs Enforcement [ICE] agents). The El Paso County Sheriff's Department purposefully targeted neighborhoods that are heavily populated by Mexican farmworkers by putting a disproportionate amount of checkpoints in those areas (Talavera et al. 2010: 169). Talavera, Nuñez-Mchiri, and Heyman interviewed an undocumented Mexican woman in El Paso who reported that people like her "move around the city like rats, quickly, hoping not to get caught" (Talavera et al. 2010: 175). Once again, this treatment is not a response to the fact that the targeted people in question are legally undocumented. To see why, note that Gary does not face similar constraints. While Gary's case is hypothetical it nevertheless has argumentative force. It seems truly absurd—at least, in the context of our current, xenophobic social world—to imagine a white, middle-class, legally undocumented U.K. citizen would move around Washington, DC, with trepidation, hoping that his immigration status will not be called into question if and when he gets pulled over at a traffic light.

There is further evidence that the trepidation with which Alicia, and those similarly positioned, move about the cities and towns where they live does not stem from their legally undocumented status. Indeed, many *U.S. citizens and legal residents* endure this very same constraint. To illustrate this point, let us consider a passage from Gloria Anzaldúa in her *Borderlands/La Frontera: The New Mestiza*:

> In the fields, *la migra*. My aunt saying, "*No corran*, don't run. They'll think you're *del otro lao*." In the confusion, Pedro ran, terrified of being caught. He couldn't speak English, couldn't tell them he was a fifth generation American. *Sin papeles*—he did not carry his birth certificate to work in the fields. *La migra* took him away while we watched. *Se lo llevaron*. He tried to smile when he looked back at us, to raise his fist. But I saw the shame pushing his head down, I saw the terrible weight of shame hunch his shoulders. They deported him to Guadalajara by plane. The furthest he'd ever been to Mexico was Reynosa, a small border town opposite Hidalgo, Texas, not far from McAllen. Pedro walked all the way to the Valley. *Se lo llevaron sin un centavo al pobre. Se vino andando desde Guadalajara.*
>
> (Anzaldúa 1987)

As Anzaldúa's passage demonstrates, one can be constrained to move about with trepidation even if one is a U.S. citizen or legal resident. Pedro's deportation is in response to the way that he is *perceived* on the basis of how he looks (and, in turn, to the way that he has internalized himself as being perceived). Pedro was not legally undocumented, but he was certainly socially undocumented.

Talavera, Nuñez-Mchiri, and Heyman provide yet another powerful example of how U.S. citizens and legal residents can face this very constraint. They interviewed Gloria, a woman who had previously been undocumented but is now a legal resident of the United States. Gloria said:

> It has been twelve years since I have not been to Mexico. I lived many years in the United States as an illegal. Today I am a legal resident, but I feel the same. My mind-set has not changed; I continue living in fear. I do not feel important. I live my life in hiding. I still do not go out in public much. I have no self-confidence, and I continue to live my life as if I was still illegal. I want to live my life differently, but I just can't.
>
> (2010: 184)

Like Pedro in Anzaldúa's passage, Gloria has a legal right to be present in the United States. However, just like Alicia, who happens to be legally undocumented, Gloria is subjected to constraints on her movement as a result of the ways that her "deportability" was internalized.

In sum, given that Gary does not navigate DC with a sense of trepidation, and given that many U.S. citizens and legal residents experience this constraint, I submit that the (constraining) fear with which Alicia moves around Los Angeles stems not from her status as legally undocumented but because of how she looks. Finally, I have also claimed that when Alicia is asked to do degrading work that U.S. citizens are not inclined to do (and, in many cases, should not be expected to do), and when she is paid less for that work than a U.S. citizen would be, this is not in response to the fact that she is legally undocumented. On what grounds can I make such a claim? Are Alicia's employers not exploiting her *explicitly* in response to her *legally* undocumented status?

It is important to note that many exploited legally undocumented migrants do, in fact, possess "working papers"—they just happen to be false. Thus, it cannot be said that the exploitation is a direct response to their *legally* undocumented status, for they have presented paperwork that asserts that they have legal permission to work.

I acknowledge that many employers willingly "accept" falsified documents from workers, all the while knowing very well that the documents were, in fact, falsified. This process "lets employers off the hook," so to speak, because they do not get penalized for hiring legally undocumented workers if they can demonstrate that they were presented with "papers" that looked legitimate—even if those papers turn out to be fake. Even though many employers are aware that they are being presented with false documents, however, the fact that so many employers choose simply to accept the documents presented to them rather than running them through a system like E-verify (which uses databases to track documents) shows that employers are not purposefully seeking out legally undocumented workers in their efforts to obtain highly exploitable labor. On a related note, it is clear that Alicia could easily get hired for a position that is traditionally associated with undocumented migrant labor (i.e., field work, employment in a factory) without ever having to "prove" that she is legally undocumented. She would swiftly be hired for such positions on the basis of how she looks.

Further evidence that exploitation that Alicia, and those similarly positioned, is not in response to their legal status comes from the fact that one can have legal authorization to work in the United States and still be exploited as an undocumented migrant. Mary Romero argues in her ethnography of the working conditions of domestic workers, *Maid in the USA*, that many Latina legal residents of the United States who are employed as household workers often labor under the same conditions as legally undocumented household workers who are also Latina.[6] They are in this respect "grouped in" with those who are oppressed as undocumented migrants.

Alternatively, Seth Holmes, a white American anthropologist who worked alongside Oaxacan Triqui migrant workers in the state of Washington as part of his anthropological fieldwork, reports that he was paid more and treated better by his overseers on the basis of being perceived as educated and white. This occurred even though he had deliberately sought out the experience of working and being treated like a legally undocumented farmworker for ethnographic purposes (Holmes 2013).[7]

I have suggested that these constraints faced by Alicia, and others similarly positioned, are imposed not because they are legally undocumented but because of how they are perceived on the basis of how they look. José Jorge Mendoza has argued that immigration enforcement and expulsion strategies in the U.S. interior are imposed disproportionately on those who "look Latina/o/x" or possess "Mexican appearance" (Mendoza 2014: 74; see also *United States vs. Brignoni-Ponce*, 422 U.S. 873, 1975). Note, in addition, that all of the examples of mistreated undocumented migrants I have explored are themselves Latina/o/x. With this in mind, one might raise the following objection. Why have I opted to develop an account of a social group called the "socially undocumented" as opposed to referring to the social group of Latina/o/xs?

I argue that just as the respective social groups of legally and socially undocumented people are not comprised of exactly the same groups of individuals, the respective social groups of Latina/o/xs and the socially undocumented are not coextensive. First, it is possible to be Latina/o/x without "looking undocumented"—or even "looking Latino/a/x" in accordance with problematic and widespread stereotypes about how a Latina/o/x "looks." Jorge J. E. Gracia argues in his paper "The Nature of Ethnicity with Special Reference to Hispanic/Latino Identity" (1999: see also 2000) that many Latina/o/xs lack genetic linkages to most other Latina/o/xs. He explains that "for instance, some children of Welsh immigrants to

Argentina are as Hispanic/Latino as any other Hispanic/Latino—indeed, when they visit Wales they feel they do not belong there" (1999: 33).

However, these children of Welsh immigrants to Argentina are unlikely to be "read" as Latina/o/x in the context of the United States. I submit that just as one can be Latina/o/x without being taken to "look Latina/o/x," one can be Latina/o/x without being taken to "look undocumented."

Furthermore, considerations of economic class also trouble the suggestion that these social groups are precisely coextensive. Take, for instance, this exchange in an ethnographic interview that Josiah Heyman conducted with an Immigration and Naturalization Service (INS) inspector:

Q: How do you pick one Hispanic out of a crowd of Hispanics in downtown Nogales?

A: That's something I can't tell you but after a year, in a crowd of ten, I can pick out the one illegal. Clothes are real important, their demeanor, how they present themselves, the way they walk around. Dirty clothes, ill-fitted clothes. But the only way to really know was to ask, and we had that right, so we asked.

(Heyman 1998: 166)

As this example demonstrates, the socially undocumented are perceived to be undocumented not only on the basis of race and ethnicity but also on that of socioeconomic class.

In sum, I acknowledge that there is great overlap between the social group of Latina/o/xs and the socially undocumented. And I certainly agree with Mendoza that U.S. and legal resident Latina/o/xs in the United States disproportionately bear the burden of U.S. internal enforcement and expulsion strategies. However, I submit that the term "socially undocumented" refers not simply to or necessarily to being Latina/o/x but to a more complex interplay of racial/ethnic and class identity. I return to this point in the ensuing chapters, in which I argue that "being socially undocumented" entails having a "real" identity that embodies ethnoracial, class, and gendered lines.

We have seen, then, that there is a social group that faces a common set of constraints associated with immigration status—the socially undocumented. Alicia, but not Gary, belongs to this group. This brings me to my final question. Is this an *oppressed* social group? That is, are these constraints—restricted movement; workplace exploitation in worksites that are associated with undocumented migrant labor; and the general, demeaning presumption that the socially undocumented do not belong—*unjustifiable* and *unjust*? Now that we have carefully distinguished between the (prima facie) justifiable constraints that one faces on the basis of being *legally* undocumented (i.e., lacking a legal right to work in the United States, to vote in U.S. elections, and to own property), it becomes clearer that the constraints that the socially undocumented face are, indeed, unjust.

Indeed, unlike justifiable constraints that respond strictly to one's legal status (and, as we have seen, do not undermine moral equality—just as my moral equality to the French is not undermined when I am barred from voting in French elections), the socially undocumented face unique constraints on the basis of morally arbitrary features such as race/ethnicity and class. As such, these constraints are unjustifiable, for they reinforce unjust group-based hierarchies. These constraints are inconsistent with the requirement of just states to uphold universal moral equality. The socially undocumented are therefore an (unjustly) oppressed social group consisting of many, but not all, legally undocumented migrants, as well as many "legal" U.S. citizens and residents.

IV. Objections

In the final chapters of this book, I explore what this means for immigration justice—arguing for a new vision for immigrant rights in the United States and potentially on a global scale. For now, allow me to address a series of possible objections to my claim that Alicia—and, more broadly, the socially undocumented—is unjustly oppressed.

(1) I have argued that it is *not* unjust that Alicia lacks a right to be present in the United States (at least at first, as I discuss in more detail below), but that it *is* unjust that she is oppressed while in the United States. One might insist that if Alicia lacks a right to be in the United States, then the oppression she endures simply cannot be unjust.

In response to this objection, let me clarify that one's moral equality cannot permissibly be violated even in response to one's having engaged in an unauthorized activity. I will illustrate this point with a comparatively trivial example. If a police officer catches me running a red light, he may permissibly force me to pay a fine or endure some other just penalty. This responds to the fact that I have broken a just law. It respects me as a moral equal to the officer himself, and to other U.S. citizens. It would be impermissible, however, for the police officer to respond to my running a red light by loudly proclaiming to me and others that women (myself included) are incompetent drivers. This undermines, rather than respects, my moral equality with men. Clearly, the fact that I broke a just law does not give the police officer a right to undermine me this way. It is equally absurd to suggest that Alicia can be oppressed because she crossed the US-Mexico border without legal authorization.

(2) The objector might respond that Alicia's unauthorized border crossing should be likened not to the act of running a stop sign but to the act of breaking into someone's house without permission. Imagine that Jane breaks into Bill's home and he finds her sitting in his living room, calmly drinking what remains of his orange juice. He repeatedly asks her to leave, and she refuses. Bill could use a reasonable amount of force to extract Jane from his home, but instead he decides to act oppressively toward her. He tells her that as long as she remains in his home, Jane will have to cook and clean for Bill while reflecting upon what it means to be properly feminine.

Here, the objector may make two different arguments: (a) Bill is allowed to treat Jane this way while she is on his property; and (b) since Jane is free to leave whenever she wishes, Bill's demands do not constitute an "unjust constraint" on her action. Similarly, Alicia has "broken into the United States" and can, like Jane, justifiably be oppressed. Given that she is free to leave the United States whenever she wishes, her disagreeable experiences do not constitute "unjust constraints" on her action.

The first strand of objection relies on a false analogy. The relationship between individuals and their property is not the same as the relationship between states and their territories. States do not "own" the land in the same way that a homeowner owns her property—nor do the citizens of the United States collectively "own" the U.S. national parks and other public spaces (for further discussion see Cole 2000). The relationship between states and their territory is not one of ownership but of sovereignty; this is a crucial distinction. Just states are required to uphold universal moral equality in ways that individual citizens are not (at least not in their homes). While parents can favor their sons over their daughters (legally, not morally)—perhaps by paying for their sons, but not their daughters, to go to college—legitimate, just states are not allowed to discriminate in this fashion.[8]

I now turn to the second strand of objection. The fact that one is "free to leave" an undesirable context does not make the constraints one faces in that context unjust. A person suffering the constraints associated with racism in his place of work, or in his neighborhood, is "free to leave" in hopes of finding a kinder neighborhood or office. But this does not mean that the constraints he faces in his place of work and neighborhood can be justified. The test of whether someone faces unjust constraints is not whether they are free to leave but whether those constraints *violate one's moral equality*. Thus, though Alicia entered the United States without authorization and is "free to leave," the oppressive constraints she faces are still unjust.

(3) One might object that my account neglects difficult (and even unjust) experiences that some people have on the basis of being legally, rather than socially, undocumented. For example, I previously explored Carens's discussion of Marguerite Grimmond, who, upon taking a vacation in Australia, was not permitted to reenter Scotland after living there for 80 years. Marguerite Grimmond did not, presumably, have a socially undocumented identity, and yet it seems extraordinarily unjust for Scotland to have denied her permission to reenter.

Furthermore, in the U.S. context, many argue that "Dreamers"—or those who were previously protected under President Obama's Deferred Action for Childhood Arrivals (DACA) program, having been brought by adult relatives to the United States as children without legal authorization to be in the United States—should be given a right to remain in the United States. While many different types of arguments have been made in support of granting a right to remain to Dreamers (see e.g. Blake 2018), a commonplace argument is that the Dreamers grew up and built lives for themselves in the United States. To invoke Carens's arguments, it seems wrong that their de facto social membership in U.S. society is not recognized in the form of amnesty and the right to remain. Once again, such arguments do not hinge on socially undocumented oppression. Rather, they focus on the perceived injustices associated with living as a *legally* undocumented migrant for an extended period of time.

I have two responses to this objection. First, let me once again clarify that I am not arguing against Carens's argument that long-term legally undocumented migrants deserve a right to remain in the society in which they live. Socially undocumented oppression is not the only form of immigrant oppression, and my account is certainly not intended to detract from the importance of arguments that focus on other elements of immigration injustice. I am arguing that we should substantially *broaden* our understanding of what it means to be "undocumented" or "illegal" in the United States—not that we should cease to focus on legally undocumented status entirely. Furthermore, I think that Carens's argument provides valuable resources for articulating why Dreamers, for instance, should be granted a right to remain in the United States.

Second, I believe that an attentiveness to socially undocumented oppression could, in fact, *strengthen* arguments for legalization for long-term (legally) undocumented migrants. This is because living as a long-term, legally undocumented migrant can certainly exacerbate the effects of socially undocumented oppression, which connects Carens's arguments to the present analysis. As I noted in the introduction, it is no accident that Carens initiates his argument for amnesty for long-term legally undocumented migrants with the story of Miguel Sanchez—who is, in my view, not only a long-term legally undocumented migrant but also socially undocumented. I believe—and I think it is quite feasible to assert—that Sanchez's story brings up, for readers, complicated moral intuitions that are not simply connected to the wrongness of residing in a country as a long-term undocumented migrant.

Carens (2010) writes that Miguel Sanchez and his wife live "under constant threat of deportation," as "a traffic stop or an accident could lead to Miguel's removal from the country." Something certainly seems wrong here—but the "wrong" is not exclusively or even necessarily about long-term legally undocumented status. Miguel Sanchez's story is (in part) morally compelling, I submit, because Miguel is *socially undocumented*. After all, we have seen that Gary—a white, middle-class citizen of the U.K.—does not live with a constant threat of deportation and does not move around his city with trepidation. Thus, Carens's argument would lose some of its force were he to substitute Miguel's story with that of Gary.

But it seems right to say, once again, that long-term legally undocumented status can exacerbate one's socially undocumented oppression over time. Furthermore, this may help to ground a case for amnesty for the long-term socially undocumented who lack legal authorization to be in the United States (including most Dreamers). In this sense, I present these arguments as an extension of and engagement with those of Carens. Furthermore, I believe that those who, like Carens, argue for amnesty for long-term legally undocumented migrants should consider whether socially undocumented people, like Miguel Sanchez, have somewhat stronger claims to amnesty than their non-socially undocumented counterparts, like Gary.

To conclude, I have argued in this chapter that understanding the injustice of undocumented migrant oppression requires us to distinguish between being *socially* and *legally undocumented*. The socially undocumented, I have maintained, are those who are presumed to be undocumented on the mere basis of their appearance and subjected to demeaning, immigration-related constraints on that basis. Legally undocumented status is not necessarily unjust (though long-term legally undocumented migrants may be owed a right to remain, among other things), but socially undocumented oppression *always is*. We have also seen that "being socially undocumented" often overlaps with "being Latina/o/x" and working class. However, more work needs to be done to establish the precise nature of socially undocumented identity (which is not the same thing as Latina/o/x or working-class identity), as well as the importance of understanding socially undocumented identity in the pursuit of immigration justice. In the ensuing four chapters, I offer a descriptive, phenomenological account of socially undocumented identity with the ultimate goal of articulating a forward-looking framework for dismantling socially undocumented oppression. To begin, in Chapter 2, I address the question of what socially identities actually *are*.

References

Anzaldúa, G. (1987) *Borderlands/La Frontera: The New Mestiza* (25th Anniversary ed.), San Francisco: Aunt Lute Books.
Blake, M. (2008) "Immigration and Political Equality," *San Diego Law Review* 45 (4).
Blake, M. (2014) "Immigration, Association, and Anti-Discrimination," *Ethics* 122 (4): 748–762.
Blake, M. (2018) "Why Deporting Dreamers Is Immoral," *Salon*, March 1, www.salon.com/2018/03/01/why-deporting-the-dreamers-is-immoral_partner.
Carens, J. (2010) "Immigrants and the Right to Stay," *Boston Review*, September 13, www.bostonreview.net/articles/immigrants-and-right-stay.
Clatterbaugh, K. (1996) "Are Men Oppressed?" in *Rethinking Masculinity: Philosophical Explorations in Light of Feminism*, 289–305, Lanham, MD: Rowman & Littlefield.
Cohen, E. F. (2018) *The Political Value of Time: Citizenship, Duration, and Democratic Justice*, Cambridge: Cambridge University Press.
Cole, P. (2000) *Philosophies of Exclusion: Liberal Political Theory and Immigration*, Edinburgh: Edinburgh University Press.

Cudd, A. (2006) *Analyzing Oppression*, Oxford: Oxford University Press.
Frye, M. (1983) *The Politics of Reality*, Berkeley, CA: Crossing Press.
Gracia, J. J. E. (1999) "The Nature of Ethnicity with Special Reference to Latino/Hispanic Identity," *Public Affairs Quarterly* 13 (1): 25–43.
Haslanger, S. (2012) "What Are We Talking About? The Semantics and Politics of Social Kinds," in *Resisting Reality*, Oxford: Oxford University Press.
Heyman, J. (1998) "State Effects on Labor Exploitation: The INS and Undocumented Migrants at the Mexico United States Border," *Critique of Anthropology* 18 (157): 166.
Higgins, P. (2013) *Immigration Justice*, Edinburgh: Edinburgh University Press.
Holmes, S. (2013) *Fresh Fruit, Broken Bodies: Migrant Farmworkers in the United States*, Berkeley: University of California Press.
Jaggar, A. (2014) "Transnational Cycles of Gendered Vulnerability: Rethinking Some Basic Assumptions of Western Political Philosophy," in Alison Jaggar (ed.), *Gender and Global Justice*, 18–19, Cambridge: Polity Press.
Mendoza, J. J. (2014) "Discrimination and the Presumptive Rights of Immigrants," *Critical Philosophy of Race* 2 (1): 68–82.
Miles, A., and Sonneville, C. (2001) "The Cultural Construction of Poverty," in Bruce Morrison and Roderick Wilson (eds.), *Ethnographic Essays in Cultural Anthropology: A Problem-Based Approach*, Boston: Wadsworth Cengage Learning.
Narayan, U. (1995) "Male-Order Brides: Immigrant Women, Domestic Violence and Immigration Law," *Hypatia* 10 (1): 104–119.
Okin, S. (1999) *Is Multiculturalism Bad for Women?* Princeton, NJ: Princeton University Press.
Romero, M. (2002) *Maid in the U.S.A.*, New York: Routledge.
Talavera, V., Núñez-Mchiri, G., and Heyman, J. (2010) "Deportation in the US Borderlands: Anticipation, Experience and Memory," in Nicholas De Genova and Nathalie Peutz (eds.), *The Deportation Regime: Sovereignty, Space, and the Freedom of Movement*, Durham, NC: Duke University Press.
Wilcox, S. (2008) "Who Pays for Gender Institutionalization?" in Ana González (ed.), *Gender Identities in a Globalized World*, 53–74, Amherst: Humanity Books.
Young, I. M. (2001) "Equality of Whom? Social Groups and Judgments of Injustice," *Journal of Political Philosophy* 9 (1): 2.

Notes

1 For further exploration of the type of argument Mendoza is making, see Michael Blake (2014).
2 For an interesting and somewhat related discussion see Cohen (2018).
3 Also, following Cudd, I bracket interesting metaphysical questions about the nature of groups. For further exploration of these interesting questions, see Haslanger (2012).
4 While I acknowledge that there will be debate about whether some features are indeed "morally arbitrary" in the relevant sense, the distinction nevertheless seems clear in paradigm cases such gender, race/ethnicity, ability, economic class, etc.
5 I add the qualifier "associated with undocumented status" to distinguish the sorts of constraints that are relevant to undocumented migrant oppression, broadly conceived, from other unevenly distributed constraints that are imposed on the basis of other features of Alicia's identity, such as gender. My aim is to uncover what is unique about undocumented migrant oppression in particular.
6 For further discussion see Romero (2002: 101–126).
7 Holmes (2013) develops this theme over the course of the ethnography.
8 Susan Okin (1999) has argued that just states cannot permissibly permit gender-based discrimination even in the private realm.

Reading Questions

1. What's the difference between Gary and Alicia, according to the text?
2. What does it mean to be "socially undocumented?" How does this differ from being legally undocumented?

3. Gary doesn't face the same kinds of constraints as Alicia. Would it be unjust if he did? For example, if Gary were excluded from certain jobs because he *doesn't* appear to an employer as undocumented, would this count as an instance of oppression? Why or why not?
4. How does Reed-Sandoval critique traditional views of justice and moral equality in the context of immigration? What new perspective does she introduce?
5. Reed-Sandoval claims that being socially undocumented is a distinctive status. Is it something above and beyond the combination of race and class associated with a legal status? Or, does it just reduce to a particular combination of these things? If the latter, is that a problem for Reed-Sandoval's account of the importance of the status?
6. What sorts of treatment constitute violations of moral equality, as opposed to justifiable differential treatment? Draw from the text to support your answer.

29 Jus Sanguinis vs. Jus Soli
On the Grounds of Justice

Eduardo Mendieta

Introduction

Section 3 of Article III of the Constitution of the United States explicitly defines a special type of crime:

> Treason against the United States shall consist only in levying war against them, or in adhering to their enemies, giving them aid and comfort. No person shall be convicted of treason unless on the testimony of two witnesses to the same overt act, or on confession in open Court. The Congress shall have power to declare the punishment of treason, but no Attainder of Treason shall work Corruption of Blood, or Forfeiture except during the Life of the Person attainted.[1]

Three years after the aforementioned was signed and approved as part of the Constitution of the United States, Congress enacted what has been called the "Crimes Act of 1790" and "Federal Criminal Code of 1790." This Act states that

> If any person or persons, owing allegiance to the United States of America, shall levy war against them, or shall adhere to their enemies, giving them aid and comfort within the United States, or elsewhere, and shall be thereof convicted on confession in open Court, or on the testimony of two witnesses to the same overt act of the treason whereof he or they shall stand indicted, such person or persons shall be adjudged guilty of treason against the United States, and *shall suffer death*; and that if any person or persons, having knowledge of the commission of any of the treasons aforesaid, shall conceal, and not, as soon as may be, disclose and make known the same to the President of the United States, or some one of the Judges thereof, or to the President or Governor of a particular State, or some one of the Judges or Justices thereof, such person or persons, on conviction, shall be adjudged guilty of misprision of treason, and shall be imprisoned not exceeding seven years, and fined not exceeding one thousand dollars (emphasis added).[2]

Treason is thus defined as a crime against the United States that is punishable by death, although in contrast to European nations, acts of treason are limited to the perpetrator and not the entire family and descendants of the person judged a traitor. But what do we call it when the nation commits acts of war against some of its citizens, and sides with enemies, avowed adversaries, and despisers, of some of its citizens? What do we call it when the nation breaks faith and betrays its citizens by treating them as enemy combatants, as resident aliens, in fact, as suspect citizens, as unworthy citizens, as dispensable and contemptible citizens? These are important questions to ask, particularly when we consider that in 1791 the Constitution would be amended with the "Bill of Rights," which can be understood as a compendium of "rights against the state," or rights that limit the power of the state. When we think about the fact that already in the original Constitution, and in one of the first Acts of the first Congress, the question of punishment by death for "treason" is explicitly addressed, but not that of the betrayal by the state of its people, we are confronted with a unique prism through which to see the evolution of U.S. conceptions and practices of citizenship. In fact, the power to put to death for treason is a very striking feature of the U.S. constitutional jurisgenetic corpus, which is made more notable by the fact that the articles of the Constitution are then followed by the amendments from 1791—that is, the Bill of Rights. It is in this Bill of Rights that something like a counterpart to the punishment for treason could have been articulated in terms of betrayal and treason by the state. What should strike us is that citizens can be held criminally liable for "betraying" the state, but the "state" itself can't be held liable for violating the rights of persons, and after 1868, the rights of citizens. It is only more recently that citizens have been empowered to "sue" the state for violating their rights or for failing to protect them. The state is now held liable for violating the rights of citizens, and while it cannot be called treason, you can say that when the state abridges, disregards, neglects, or fails to protect the rights of citizens, it is itself engaging in treason, a crime made all the more heinous by the fact that it is committed by the putative protector of the liberty and equality of citizens. After World War II, the legal categories of "crimes against the peace" and "crimes against humanity" were introduced at the Nuremberg Trial of Nazi criminals—in this case, the assumption was that the German state was acting treasonously not only against other states but also against its own citizens, by denationalizing them and denaturalizing them, thus rendering Jews, Gypsies, and others stateless (Roland 2012). Perhaps by the same token, we ought to be developing a notion of our own state's crimes against its citizens.

Foremost German legal philosopher and constitutional scholar Ernst-Wolfgang Böckenförde, who was also a German federal court judge, addressed the betrayal and treason by the German state of its citizens in an important essay dating from 1997. The title of the essay says it all: "The Persecution of the German Jews as a Civic Betrayal." Let me elaborate further. Böckenförde writes, beautifully and powerfully,

> What happened to the German Jews between 1933 and 1945, their disenfranchisement and persecution rising to systematic annihilation, was organized by the state towards its own citizens, particularly loyal ones; and to that extent that it became known, it was carried out without any broad opposition or at least revulsion and outrage among the population, the very compatriots of the Jewish citizens. That constitutes the betrayal and breach of trust, the disgrace of the disgrace of the Jewish persecution in Germany, apart from its criminal nature. . . . Civic Courage—civic bravery, acting as *citoyen*—is what sustains civic society and creates it in the first place. If everyone withdraws upon himself to live only his own life, if fellow citizens and what happens to them cease to matter, civic society is betrayed from within and dissolves.
>
> (Böckenförde 2017: 312, 313)

We can be outraged that someone would betray our state, but why not be more outraged when the state betrays its citizens? What happened under Jim Crow, and then in the aftermath of the partly successful civil rights movements, was a civic betrayal of black Americans—and we continue to betray them. This is what we are witnessing when so-called "anchor babies" are demonized, vilified, criminalized. So much is failing here: our civic imagination is failing, our sense of civic outrage, our sense of civic loyalty and solidarity. We do not have a sense of civic courage and sense of civic hope. I can't tell you how it makes me shudder with outrage and disgust and disappointment and dread to see what is happening at the border, but also what happens when police profile Latino/as, or when people yell at some of us when we speak Spanish, spitting in our faces, telling us to go back to where we came from. The border has become the ground of our civic betrayal and the failure of our civic imagination and courage. This border has moved to the center of our civic life.

Indeed, the United States has a long history of betraying its citizens: African American, Japanese, Native Americans, Hawai'ians, Puerto Ricans, Jews, and more recently Mexican Americans, in particular, and Latino/as in general. Donald Trump launched his presidential candidacy with an attack on the character and worthiness of Mexicans to be in the United States, thus denigrating the citizenship of Mexican Americans and other Latino/as. To recall, Trump questioned the ability of Judge Gonzalo Curiel to be impartial in a class-action suit by students who charged that they had been defrauded by Trump University; his basis for doing so was that Curiel was "Mexican," although he was born in the United States. Trump's presidency was defined not solely by the relentless challenge of the Constitution and the separation of powers but most specifically by his racial animus directed at African Americans and Mexicans and Mexican Americans most consistently and relentlessly. The hysterical chanting of "build the Wall," the longest shutdown in the history of the U.S. government in the winter of 2019 over the funding of the Wall, the assault by ICE (Immigration and Customs Enforcement) on immigrant families, the moves in Congress to repeal or qualify the Fourteenth Amendment to the Constitution to disenfranchise so-called anchor babies—all this, and more, projected the nauseous shadow of deep dislike and has fueled hatred of Mexicans and Mexican Americans. The attempt to revoke DACA, the separation of immigrant children from their parents, and the extradition of all kinds of both legal and irregular immigrants also reflects the treason and betrayal by the government of the United States of one of its largest minorities, Latino/as in general and Mexican Americans in particular.

Trump and Trumpism, however, are the culmination of by now nearly four decades of assault on the worthiness and legitimacy of Latinx citizenship. More emphatically, Trumpism should be read as exemplary of what political philosopher Amy Reed-Sandoval calls the "illegalization" of *socially undocumented* citizens and noncitizens of Mexican and Latinx backgrounds (Reed-Sandoval 2020). The process of rendering someone illegal comes on the heels of decades of socially undocumented oppression. Leo R. Chavez, in his brief but powerful *Anchor Babies and the Challenge of Birthright Citizenship*, which expands and updates his earlier *The Latino Threat: Constructing Immigrants, Citizens, and the Nation*, chronicles these four decades of the fabrication of Latino/as as a threat, beginning with the discourse of their inability to assimilate in the eighties and culminating with the recent attempt to either revoke or amend the Fourteenth Amendment (Chavez 2017; 2013). As Reed-Sandoval shows, however, the fabrication of the "Latino Threat" extends further back into the middle of the twentieth century, with the infamous "Operation Wetback" of 1954 that deported as many as 1.3 million Mexicans and Mexican Americans, many of whom were U.S. citizens (Blakemore 2018).[3]

Trumpism, as a political phenomenon, however, raises a series of important questions about the nature of citizenship in the United States in the twenty-first century. It puts in relief what I will call "the unfinished work of building citizenship" in the United States, not as an aberration but as the culmination of a political and social dynamic. Trumpism, additionally, is the distillation of a particular type of attempt to roll back the accomplishments in the task of building citizenship in the United States. This attempt has taken the form of frontal attack on the Fourteenth Amendment, the constitutional pillar of equal citizenship, guaranteed by law and under the equal protection of the law, which furthermore and most distinctly is granted on the basis of birthright and not descent. The Fourteenth Amendment enshrined into the Constitution, and thus into the law of the land, the principle of "Birthright Citizenship" (Jones 2018; Foner 2019). Birthright citizenship constitutionalizes the principle of citizenship by jus soli and rejects the principle of citizenship by jus sanguinis. In this chapter, I want to consider why the juridification of jus soli into the vault of U.S. citizenship is a revolutionary principle that takes the conception of citizenship to new moral and legal heights. Jus soli, as a foundational principle of equal citizenship under the protection of the law, is the complement, the other face, of the Universal Declaration of Human Rights. Jus soli is the ground of the justice promised by both human rights and the rights of citizens declared by the French in 1789.

In order to arrive at this conclusion, I want to, first, focus on what I call the hysterical ethno-racial animus against Mexicans, Mexican Americans, and Latinos through a brief revisiting of an important moment in the attempt to reconfigure the U.S. political imaginary by Samuel P. Huntington, who singled out Mexican Americans not only as a problem but also as a threat to the very core "identity" and geographical integrity of the United States. Huntington's thesis, however, is not the most egregious chapter in the history of the "fabrication" of Latino/as as a threat.

Second, I want to visit some key moments in the history of citizenship so as to build up the idea that jus soli as the key principle of U.S. citizenship is a unique and unparalleled expansion and accomplishment of a very important, today perhaps the most important, political institution of political membership. Indeed, what I hope will become explicit is that "citizenship" remains an "unfinished" project. Third, and finally, I conclude that unless we abolish all forms of jus sanguinis, the revolutions begun with the American, French, and Haitian revolutions in the eighteenth century remain also "unfinished."

I. The Fabrication of the Latino Threat

In late fall 2000, Harvard political scientist and public intellectual Samuel P. Huntington published two articles, one on the website of the conservative Center for Immigration Studies (Huntington 2000a) and the second in the *American Enterprise* magazine (2000b), laying out his analysis that Mexican Americans presented a distinct challenge, nay a "problem," to the United States. The arguments first sketched in these two articles were further elaborated and articulated in a lengthy and pugilist feature article published during the spring of 2004 in *Foreign Policy*. The long polemical essay is titled "The Hispanic Challenge" and begins as follows:

> The persistent inflow of Hispanic immigrants threatens to divide the United States into two peoples, two cultures, and two languages. Unlike past immigrant groups, Mexicans and Latinos have not assimilated into mainstream U.S. culture, forming instead their own political and linguistic enclaves—from Los Angeles to Miami—and rejecting the Anglo-Protestant values that built the American dream. The United States ignores this challenge at its peril.
>
> (2004a: 30)

This is without question quite an alarmist proclamation. I need not note that this was in 2004, barely three years after 9/11. The United States had just launched the so-called Second Gulf War, and while the occupation of Iraq was just shy of a year old, U.S. soldiers were already coming under attack. The rumblings of Iraqi resistance were loudly audible. In this context, in which U.S. soldiers were already fighting in Afghanistan in the midst of a "global war on terror," the publication of this incendiary article was shocking. Indeed, Huntington published in a very notable and highly respected journal, which he helped found, what in fact was a call to arms, so much so that I want to suggest that this piece was instrumental in giving voice to the "white nativism" that would later elect Donald Trump.

However, before I turn to Huntington's piece, I want to exegete the cover of the issue of *FP* (as the journal *Foreign Policy* is known) in which it appeared. On the cover we see a young adult, mestizo male, perhaps of Mexican, but in general of Latin American background. His hand is over his heart holding, tenuously, with extended fingers, a small U.S. flag. He appears to be at a swearing-in ceremony, perhaps at his naturalization ceremony, when he finally becomes a U.S. citizen. I remember very clearly this cover, for I bought it when it first came out. If you look closely, the man's fingernails are long and dirty. The young adult looks awkward in his tie—and he is not clutching the flag but just barely pressing it down with the tips of his fingers. The title of the cover reads, "José, Can You See?" Now, I doubt that *FP* was literally addressing "José"—and it is noteworthy that the editors used the diacritic on José's name, as if to underscore a point. What is it that José is supposed to see? If José had turned to page thirty, where Huntington begins with his ominous three-sentence paragraph, he would have realized, he would have seen that he was a peril, a threat, someone who is a clear and present danger to the United States. Given that the editors of *FP* undoubtedly know who their readership is, the question really should read, "Can't you see what José is doing to our nation?"

Huntington begins his piece by regurgitating the myths about the origins of the United States: that it was "created" in the seventeenth and eighteenth centuries by settlers who were "overwhelmingly" white, British, and Protestant. In the eighteenth century, after defining the colonies on this continent along racial, ethnic, cultural, and religious lines, they, the founding fathers, began to define it along "ideological lines." These white, Protestant males created a "creed" that would both justify and legitimate their independence from the "Mother" country, England. The creed, however, was "the product of a distinct Anglo-Protestant culture." The basic tenets of this creed were framed by "key elements" of that Anglo-Protestant culture: the English language, Christianity, religious commitment, reverence to the English concept of the "rule of law," and the "dissenting Protestant values of individualism, the work ethic, and the belief that humans have the ability and duty to try to create a heaven on earth, a 'city on a hill'" (2004a: 32). The creed, then, has at its core the following: English monolingualism, an unwavering commitment to Christianity, a reverence for the "English" respect for the law, and, of course, individualism, deference to the work ethic, and, above all, a religiously fueled sociopolitical utopianism. All these values, norms, principles, and hopes, according to Huntington, are rooted in, they originate, they emanate, and thus belong to a particular racial, cultural, religious profile: the Anglo-Protestant male. Perhaps we should shake our heads in incredulity and disbelief. Perhaps Huntington had drunk for too long at the well of racist imaginaries.

It is this creed, this Rosetta stone, this set core of political, economic, religious, and racial values and profile that Hispanics threaten. Why and how? Huntington is not an uninformed scholar, as is evidenced by the fact that he taught at Harvard for many years. He had teams of researchers at his disposal (as we learn later), and thus, he has an analytics that demonstrates, or aims to persuade his readers, why Hispanics are an immediate, real, and present danger. Although begrudgingly, for there were waves and waves of immigrants who came to join the project of building the glorious "city on the hill," Huntington must frame his invective against Hispanics in terms of how their pattern of immigration differs from those earlier ones. The linchpin of his argument hinges precisely on a selective and distorting reading of the ways in which the United States was a nation of immigrants, who, however, were assimilated into the creed, who cast off their prior identities by becoming members of the Anglo-Protestant project. In fact, the reason why Hispanics are a threat is because

> contemporary Mexican and, more broadly, Latin American immigration is without precedent in U.S. history. . . . [Then, an interesting slippage in the narrative takes place, barely a sentence later, when Huntington continues] Mexican immigration [note Mexican and not simply Latin American] differs from past immigration and most other contemporary immigration due to a combination of six factors: contiguity, scale, illegality, regional concentration, persistence, and historical presence.
>
> (2004a: 33)

The slippage is not unintentional. It is deliberate, as it aims to conflate Hispanic with Mexican and, at the same time, cover over the intricacies but also glaring facts about the convoluted intimacy of Hispanics with the United States.

Let me briefly gloss these six factors. Contiguity: the United States shares a very long border with Mexico, one that was traced, made, and now militarized and fortified by the United States. This border grew with the Mexican-American War (1846–1848), which resulted in the United States taking half of Mexico's territory. The United States also took possession of Puerto Rico, after the Spanish-American War, and then gave special immigrant status to Cubans, who because of the Cuban Revolution in 1959 became exemplars and geopolitical pawns in the Cold War. It can be argued that the United States has labored to increase that contiguity for over two hundred years. Scale: in absolute numbers—that is, in numbers relative to the actual population of the United States—during the late nineteenth and early twentieth centuries, the United States received more immigrants than it is presently receiving from Mexico and Latin America. The number of undocumented Mexicans has waxed and waned in accordance with the needs of U.S. labor markets, but it is also a legal irregularity that is rooted in centuries of labor, economic, cultural, and familiar relations that reach across generations. It is important to note that the construct "illegal" to refer to Mexican migrants is a relatively recent invention, belonging to the last quarter of the twentieth century. Regional concentration is also a rhetorical mirror, as demographers very well know that not all "Hispanic" regional concentrations are the same. "Hispanics" in Connecticut are very different from those in Miami, from those in San Antonio, from those in Los Angeles. The only thing that needs to be said about persistence is that this persistence was inaugurated with the Monroe Doctrine and continued relentlessly until very recently, when, because of the Gulf Wars, the United States diverted its attention away from Latin America. By historical presence, Huntington means, in an oxymoronic or performative self-contradictory way, that "Mexicans" have actually been present since the birth of the United States, since he has to acknowledge that almost a quarter of the United States was taken from Mexico. It is a performative contradiction because they can't be aliens and yet have been already present. Of course, Huntington does not deal with NAFTA, which in 2004 had been in effect for a decade, having thus further settled that "historical presence."

I am not doing justice to Huntington's piece, surely. The *FP* article was a long but also highly condensed version of an entire book, which was published later in 2004, with the title *Who Are We? The Challenges to America's National Identity* (2004b). In fact, "The Hispanic Challenge" was a salvo, an intellectual Molotov cocktail, hurled at the U.S. public sphere at a moment when we were facing several actual war fronts abroad. I want to enter here an important parenthesis. Huntington was the U.S. political philosopher of the armed forces. His career began in 1957, when he published *The Soldier and the State: The Theory and Politics of Civil-Military Relations*, a book that, along with Michael Walzer's *Just and Unjust Wars* (1977), has become canonical text for the U.S. Armed Forces. In 2004, among the first casualties of the second Gulf War was a Hispanic American soldier. As journalist Gabriel Lerner documents in his *Huffington Post* essay, "The Iraq Conflict: The War That Changed Latinos" (2012), Latino/as—that is Huntington's Hispanics—made up 11 percent of the total casualties, comparable to their enrollment in the armed forces. This parenthesis is about the many lives of Hispanics that were lost in that war and many others. And it is, above all, about the American dream. Among the first casualties in the second Gulf War was Jose Gutierrez (he was either the first or second fallen, along with Therell Shane Childer), a kid who had come from Guatemala, was undocumented, and joined the army as a way to get his citizenship. He was twenty-two. He had a dream, and he was willing to put his life on the line. He earned his citizenship posthumously. Now, close parenthesis.

Huntington concludes "The Hispanic Challenge" with a gloss on Lionel Sosa's book *The Americano Dream* (1997), an inspirational book for entrepreneurs. Here one must wonder why a Harvard scholar would want to quote from a book that can only be found in bookshops in airports in the business section; was it because of the perversion of American dream by that contaminating "o", that Spanglish version of the "American," as an adjective, dream? In any event, this is how the essay ends on page forty-five, after fifteen pages of a minute font: "There is only the American dream created by an Anglo- Protestant society. Mexican Americans will share [I want to underscore this word 'share'] in that dream and in that society if they dream in English" (Huntington 2004a: 45). Those are two breathtaking sentences. America only has one dream, which was created by one race and one religion, and it can only be dreamt in English! I wonder what Jose Gutierrez would have said had he read that sentence.

Samuel P. Huntington has been shaping the lexicon of our public vocabulary, if not since 1957, at the very least since 1996, when he published the also highly polemical and debated *Clash of Civilizations and the Remaking of the World Order* (1996), which many in Washington took to be a prophetic text that presaged 9/11. In fact, this text pitted Islam as the great new enemy of civilization. It is not difficult to see that *Who Are We?* is a rhetorical reply of *The Clash of Civilization*, but now brought home. The next *Clash of Civilizations* is not on the world stage but on the home territory, the heartland. It is beyond the present context to elaborate how these two books work on the same semantics and syntax of the American "social imaginary," but I do want to focus, briefly, on three distinct linkages and continuities, which, however, allows me to deepen my argument about the interdependence between a religious imaginary and a racial imaginary that distorts our democratic imaginary.

First, and as I already noted above, Huntington is preoccupied with the way in which the Anglo-Protestant culture that created "America" is being threatened by Hispanics in general and Mexicans in particular. At the core of his racial-ethnic-monolingual culture is what he calls the distinct Protestant character of U.S. Protestantism, which, quoting Edmund Burke, he identifies as the "dissidence of dissent." Burke, referring to Americans, writes,

> [They] are Protestants, and of that kind which is most averse to all implicit submission of mind and opinion. All Protestantism, even the most cold and passive, is a sort of dissent. But the religion most prevalent in our northern colonies is a refinement on the principle of resistance: it is the dissidence of dissent, and the Protestantism of the Protestant religion.
>
> (2004b: 64)[4]

Implicit in the so-called Latino threat is the challenge to and potential dissolution of the "dissidence of dissent" of all those Catholics who would bring their submissive and deferential religious attitudes to the United States. It is difficult to square this claim with the long history of social activism, dissent, protest, and radical transformation in the history of the United States that was inspired not just by illiterate slaves, subordinated women, poor farmers from Ireland, Italy, and Mexico, without even mentioning the long history of Jewish and Catholic-inspired dissent.

The second linkage has to do with Huntington's discussion of "white nativism." As in the *FP* piece, where a whole page was devoted to it, in *Who Are We?* there are nearly seven pages on this topic. In the book, Huntington refers to "white nativism" as a "rebellion" in quotes, but according to him, it is "not difficult to see" why white people, whether poor or not, might be motivated to "rebel." Among some of their reasons are the emergence of exclusivist sociopolitical movements to challenge their socioeconomic status; the loss of their jobs to immigrants and foreign countries; and—now I am directly quoting—"the perversion of their culture, the displacement of their language, and the erosion or even evaporation of the historical identity of their country" (2004b: 310). Huntington closes his apologetics for "white nativism" thusly: "The most powerful stimulus to white nativism, however, is likely to be the threat to their language, culture, and power that whites see coming from the expanding demographic, social, economic, and political role of Hispanics in American society" (2004b: 315–316). This is nothing but an apologia for the militaristic and vitriolic racial supremacy that we saw culminate in the Unite the Right rally, turned white supremacy riot, which took place in Charlottesville, on August 11–12, 2017, as well as the riot that led to the storming of the United States Capitol on January 6, 2021, during which Trump supporters carried Confederate flags.[5]

Third, and finally, Huntington closes his book with a section titled "America in the World: Cosmopolitan, Imperial and/or National?" There are three possible paths that the United States can pursue as it faces the *Clash of Civilizations*. It can opt to become cosmopolitan—that is, aim to assimilate all cultures—but in the process give up its core Anglo-Protestant culture and identity. It can opt to become an empire, and thus force everyone to be like it, but in the process, its core Anglo-Protestant culture would be compromised and diluted. Or, thirdly, it can hold on to its core identity, pursue the path of nations that are faithful to their identity, and be neither cosmopolitan nor imperial. This is how Huntington articulates the difference among the options:

> Cosmopolitanism and imperialism attempt to reduce or to eliminate the social, political, and cultural differences between America and other societies. A national approach would recognize and accept what distinguishes America from those societies. America cannot become the world and still be America. Other people cannot become America and still be themselves. America is different and that difference is defined in large part by its Anglo-Protestant culture and religiosity. The alternative to cosmopolitanism and

imperialism is nationalism devoted to the preservation and enhancement of those qualities that have defined America since its founding.

(2004b: 365)

This is the rhetoric of "America First" and "Make America Great Again." This is the rhetoric of white nativism that demeans, defaces, criminalizes, and rejects the cultural, sociopolitical, economic contributions of African Americans, Native Americans, Jews, women, gays, and, of course, Latino/as. I concur with what José Casanova claimed at a conference at which we were both speakers, namely that Trump was the first candidate to bring together two great civilizational enemies: Muslims and Mexicans/Latinos. I want to close this section by underscoring two things. First, note the power of religious identities in Huntington's image and imaginary of "America." Here race and religion are one. We thus ought to speak of Huntington's racialization of religion, which can evidently cut many ways: Muslims, for instance, in this racial/religious imaginary are terrorists, while Mexicans are lazy, criminal, and uncouth, and so on. Second, notice the biologistic-organicist reduction of the identity of America. America's identity, vitality, future hinges on the purity and inviolability of its racial-religious body: the Anglo-Protestant body (Bottici and Challand 2010; Haynes 2019).

II. The Unfinished Project of Citizenship

The concept of citizenship that informs, at the very least, Western culture is one that harkens back to the Greeks. The word "citizen" is rooted in the Latin *civitas*, the latter being a translation of *politeia*, from which we get the terms "politics," "political," "police," but also "polite" and thus "impolite." In Greek, politeia refers to not simply the polis but to the web of relations that being a member of the polis entails. Politeia means "on government," or "on ruling," or on the matters of the polis. When Cicero wrote his own version of Plato's *Politeia*, he titled it *De Republica* (On the Republic), which interestingly is the way now we know Plato's *Politeia*, namely as the *Republic*. In Greek, however, "citizenship" is synonymous with politeia. The polis creates the condition of citizenship, and this in turn defines what it means to be a member of a polis. We could say then that politeia by definition includes its performance in terms of citizenship. No polis without citizen, and no citizenship without politics within the polis.

Following a bit in the tracks left by historian Peter Riesenberg's synoptic *Citizenship in the Western Tradition: Plato to Rousseau* (1992), I would note that the Greek notion of citizenship begins to accrue meaning, and be defined, by Cleisthenes's reforms of Greek democracy in 506 BC (see also Heater 2004). Key in Cleisthenes's reforms was the shift from membership in a *gene* or clan to membership in the polis as the condition for claiming membership and thus rights and privileges within the growing cities in the Greek world. While Greek citizenship did retain an element of descent, Cleisthene's reforms unleashed an important dynamic that saw membership in terms of an office that calls for duties and responsibilities rather than something that was granted only by way of blood descent (Riesenberg 1992: 20). Pericles, half a century later, as one of the greatest orators and rulers of Athens, presided over the Athenian Enlightenment, expanded Greek notions about citizenship by expanding the rights and privileges of what in Greek were known as *metics* (i.e., resident aliens). Among the famous *metics* whom Pericles invited to Athens is Cephalus, of Plato's *Politeia* fame. What is noteworthy is that while Plato's *Republic*, to use the now standardized translation of *Politeia*, is the fountainhead of Western political philosophy, this book is not the source for any significant contributions to our understanding of citizenship. That honor goes to Aristotle, who was not native to Athens, was considered a *metic*, and in fact had to leave Athens after Plato's death because he was seen as a possible spy from Macedonia.

Aristotle's *Politics*, which incidentally is presented as an explicit critique of Plato's *Republic*, actually takes up the question of who is a citizen, or what makes a citizen, a definition that Plato seems to have failed to provide. In Book 3, Chapter 2, we find what I take to be a remarkable definition of citizenship. In this book, Aristotle acknowledges that there are many types of citizens depending on the polis and after the rules of the polis have changed, as was the case after a revolution, and Aristotle refers specifically to Cleisthenes's reforms. Thus, we have citizens who are so decreed by political-legal fiat, those who were naturalized, those who are descendants of old members of the polis, and so on. Aristotle specifically highlights that there are many different types of citizens. He is interested in what defines the citizen as such and concludes that, as he writes, "the citizen was defined by the fact of his holding some kind of rule or office—he who holds a certain sort of office fulfills our definition of a citizen" (1984: *Politics*, 1276a 2–5). The citizen is he who governs. As Riesenberg put it, "Not origin but action is what makes a man a citizen, at least in a philosophical, analytical sense" (Riesenberg 1992: 44). What one does, rather than what one is, is what determines one's citizenship. In Aristotle, citizenship is a way of dwelling within a polis; it is not a biological or ontological condition. It is from this definition that civic republican conceptions of citizenship descend to our day.

As was already noted, our notions of citizen and citizenship revert to Cicero's translation of Plato and Aristotle's usage of *Politeia* into *De Republica* or, alternatively, and perhaps more accurately, *res publica*, on the matters and concerns of the polis or republic. Cicero is surely perhaps one of the most important sources for our contemporary conceptions of citizenship. For him, as it is clear from his numerous works on what today we call political philosophy, citizenship is not simply the institution of entitlements and rights but above all a vocation, the exercise of the moral and political excellence of the human being. Citizenship is the vocation of the social animal, his calling, so to speak. For Cicero, and the stoics in general, citizenship is the exercise of man's cosmopolitan dwelling, and it is thus exemplary of our social existence. Like for Aristotle, citizenship is not a *potentia* but a *dunamis*, not a passive state but a kinetic form of existence, civic existence at its height. In fact, in Cicero there is a linkage between citizenship and what we could call civic poetics. This is clearly evident in one of Cicero's most famous speeches, his *Pro Archia Poeta*, given in defense of Archias the poet, who was threatened with disenfranchisement. Cicero rose to his defense and produced one of the most celebrated panegyrics to a poet as well as to the role poetry plays in the civic life of a people, a republic. Cicero challenged the charges to disenfranchise Archias, demonstrating their falsity. Yet he spends most of the speech arguing why, even if Archias had not already been a Roman citizen, due to all the reasons why non-natives of Rome could and would have been made citizens, he should be made one on the grounds of his contributions to poetry. By bestowing on such an exemplary poet the protection of its citizenship, he would do honor to Rome in the annals of human memory by the tribute it paid to the muse of poetry. Cicero added something to Aristotle's notion of citizenship that remains important to our day, and that is that citizenship is the means for the celebration of the creative aspect of our social existence. Citizenship is both an expression and means for the exaltation of our poetic capacities.

During the Middle Ages, after the collapse of the Holy Roman Empire in the West, there was a hiatus in the philosophical contributions to our conception of citizenship. It can be argued that during this period there occurred a redirection of the aims of civil loyalty away from polis and community toward the spiritual self and the *civitate dei*. In fact, Augustine in his famous and momentous *City of God* juxtaposes the city of man against the city of God—the former with its narcissistic and hedonistic love of the material self, and the latter with its selfless love of God. Christian spiritual citizenship in a city "to come" advocated withdrawal from the mundane, materialistic, and corrupt affairs of the city of man, albeit while postulating that we were de jure, if not de facto, citizens of this divine and saintly city. In fact, Christian political thinking, at least as it is expressed in Augustine, synthesized Ciceronian and Aristotelian notions of citizenship into a universalistic creed: We are all citizens of an invisible city—the city of God. To the active and poetic dimension of citizenship is added a spiritual dimension: citizenship becomes a type of sacrament, a sacramental duty.

Still, as we proceed along the Middle Ages, we see the revival of the cities through commerce, and citizenship becomes decisive for the merchant class, which in the works of Medieval historians such as Henri Pirenne became the pivotal agent of social transformation. Citizenship, after its partial eclipse during the Middle Ages, reemerges with a new impetus and importance. Now, however, citizenship is not simply about the privileges of political participation but perhaps principally, if not exclusively, about the economic privileges and rights that citizenship in a given city entitles and bestows upon the rising merchant class. During the Middle Ages, then, citizenship acquires a material dimension that it did not have before, even if economic rights were implicit in the holding of political office in the polis.

During the late Middle Ages and the early Renaissance, however, a unique convergence between the economic and spiritual dimension of citizenship takes place, giving us the phenomenon of the citizen as a benefactor of both the city and the poor. As Michel Mollat has shown in his *The Poor in the Middle Ages: An Essay in Social History* (from 1978 but translated into English in 1986) (1996), toward the end of the Middle Ages, as cities became more populous and wealthier, thus becoming destinations for the itinerant poor of the time, it became both a practice and an expectation that the wealthy would endow houses of the poor and would in fact leave a large portion, if not all, of their wealth to such houses.

The Renaissance period gave us humanism, sometimes called Renaissance humanism, which rejected the bleak and negative image of the human being that had crystallized during the Middle Ages. Renaissance humanism instead celebrated the goodness and, above all, the potentiality of the human being. No one gave better expression of this new vision than Pico della Mirandolla in his *Oratio on the Dignity of the Human Being* (1996), which elaborates a humanistic reading of the Christian doctrine of *imago dei*, the doctrine that humans are created in the image of God. Against Augustine and his Neoplatonic political philosophy, which turns the human away from the city of man toward the heavenly city, civic humanists reaffirm the political and communal character of human beings: humans only become properly human within human communities dedicated to the exaltation of each human being. If Pico della Mirandola claimed that there is no greater example of the fact that we are created in the image of God than that we create ourselves through our own will and acts of innovation and imagination, then, by same token, there is no greater creation than the *civitas*. If we are our greatest creation, then, next to it is the creation of the city as the accompaniment to our creative excellence. Cities as such became exemplars of our creative powers and the exaltation of our civic nature.

When we get to the Revolutionary period, which builds on the insights of the Enlightenment, there are some momentous shifts in the conception of citizenship. I think two figures exemplify these: Diderot and Kant. Let me briefly discuss Diderot, who wrote the entry on "Citizen" for the *Encyclopédie* that he co-edited with d'Alembert. In this entry, in fact, Diderot articulated the spirit of both the French and American Revolutions. There is one passage that is noteworthy and merits citation. Diderot (2005), criticizing Pufendorf's restriction of citizenship to the founders of a city and to their descendants, thus advocating citizenship as lineage or as being based on descent, writes the following:

> The *citizens* in their capacity as *citizens*, that is to say in their societies, are all equally noble; the nobility comes not from ancestry but from the common right that honors the primary principles of the magistrate. The moral, sovereign being is to the *citizen* what the physical despot is to the subject, *and* the most perfect slave does not give all of this being to his sovereign.

Diderot expressed here the idea that citizenship, which is understood as the performance of the "principle of the magistrate"—that is, the performance of the duties of the citizen—is the democratization of the spirit of nobility to all citizens. Citizenship is a noble calling, if you will. Second, Diderot juxtaposes the moral sovereign to the despot: to the former corresponds the citizen, to the latter the subject. And furthermore, only in citizenship is the full moral calling of the human being exercised, which not even the condition of being a slave to a despot can hope to extinguish. In this definition of "citizen," then, Diderot links morality as an imperative to the vocation of the citizen.

Diderot eloquently gives expression to the core ideas that will animate the 1789 "Declaration of the Rights of Man and Citizen," which begins in article 1 with the proclamation of the universal equality and freedom of all human beings. This is followed, in article 2, with the affirmation that the "aim of all political association is the preservation of the natural and *imprescriptible* rights of man."

With these two articles, the Declaration of the Rights of Man and Citizen provided us with two ideas that revolutionized our conception of citizenship. First, that citizenship is subordinate—that is, at the service, of the rights of man, above all which are the rights of equality and liberty; and second, that these rights are imprescriptible—that is to say, inalienable. Citizenship thus is universalized as the means for the promotion of the fundamental rights of humans, while at the same time being given as its supreme goal the preservation of these rights. This revolution in the Western conception of citizenship will be brought to higher revolutionary heights with the Fourteenth Amendment to the U.S. Constitution. What are generally known as the Reconstruction Amendments, or the Civil War Amendments, the Thirteenth, Fourteenth, and Fifteenth Amendments that were ratified between 1865 and 1870 abolished slavery while radically transforming U.S. citizenship. These amendments accomplished a foundation of the republic by, on the one hand, making birthright a constitutional principle, while denying states (specifically Southern states) the power of curtailing or suspending citizens' right to participate in government through the denial of the right to vote on the basis of race, gender, class, or past state of servitude.

Let us recall the language of the Fourteenth Amendment, specifically section 1, which is the one that concerns me crucially. It reads,

> All persons born or naturalized in the United States, and subject to the jurisdiction thereof, are citizens of the United States and of the state wherein they reside. No state shall make or enforce any law which shall abridge the privileges or immunities of citizens of the United States; nor shall any state deprive any person of life, liberty, or property, without due process of law; nor deny to any person within its jurisdiction the equal protection of the laws.

I want to call your attention to the "born or naturalized" in the first sentence, for in the same breath those born in the United States, or in territories under the jurisdiction of the United States, and those "naturalized"—that is, those who through some legal procedure have become members of the U.S. nation—are "citizens," and no state shall make or enforce any law that may abridge in any way whatsoever the privileges of said citizenship.

The Fourteenth Amendment was meant to make constitutional what had already been enacted with the Civil Rights Act of 1866, which reads as follows:

> That all persons born in the United States and not subject to any foreign power, excluding Indians not taxed, are hereby declared to be citizens of the United States; and such citizens, of every race and color, without regard to any previous condition of slavery or involuntary servitude, except as a punishment for crime whereof the party shall have been duly convicted, shall have the same right, in every State and Territory in the United States, to make and enforce contracts, to sue, be parties, and give evidence, inherit, purchase, lease, sell, hold, and convey real and personal property, and to full and equal benefit of all laws and proceedings for the security of person and property, as is enjoyed by white citizens, and shall be subject to like punishment, pains, and penalties, and to none other, any law, statute, ordinance, regulation, or custom, to the contrary notwithstanding.

In the summer of 1865, after Abraham Lincoln had been assassinated and succeeded by Andrew Johnson, a political fight between the newly inaugurated president and the Republican-controlled Congress ensued. Johnson announced his plan for reconciliation with the South. Although Johnson was an unwavering defender of the Union, he was an "inveterate" racist and strong defender of states' rights. Johnson's plan was to allow southern states to establish their governments in exchange for "abolishing slavery, repudiating secession, and abrogating the Confederate debt, but otherwise letting southerners retain control over local affairs" (Foner 2001: 178). These new state governments, expectedly, then proceeded to enact the infamous "Black Codes" that for all intents and purposes reinstated slavery by legal means, rather than through property claims. Meanwhile, violence against black freemen was rampant throughout the South (Foner 2002: 119–123). White southerners were as determined to hold on to their antebellum form of life as they were determined to deny black freemen their freedom and newly acquired political rights. The Thirty-Ninth Congress, elected in November 1864 but assembled for the first time in December 1865, called for the abrogation of the new state governments allowed by President Johnson, and the establishment of new ones based on equality before the law and universal "manhood suffrage." This is why Congress quickly enacted the Civil Rights Act of 1866 and set to work on the Fourteenth Amendment (Foner 2019: 93 ff).

The Fourteenth Amendment, however, was also meant to resolve ambiguities and tensions within the constitution. The original U.S. Constitution of 1787 recognized both state and U.S. citizenship, but it did not specify how one became a citizen of either states or the nation. This meant that citizenship was left to the discretion of states. The *Dred Scott* decision of 1857, which denied slaves and their descendants claims to citizenship, was exemplary of this constitutional ambiguity. The Black Codes made it clear that former slave states would move to deny former slaves access to the protection of the law by denying or severely curtailing their claims to citizenship. Thus, as Professor of Jurisprudence George P. Fletcher put it in his book *Our Secret Constitution: How Lincoln Redefined American Democracy* (2001),

The first item of business in the Fourteenth Amendment was to establish who, as a formal matter, belonged to the American Polity. To find a simple definition, the Constitution adapted the English rule that it is not blood but place of birth that matters.... Applying the traditional rule of Jus soli to everyone born on American soil ... had the radical effect of eliminating family and racial history from the definition of the bond between citizens and government in the United States.

(Foner 2001: 125)

The antebellum United States was a racial polity that allowed states to determine the citizenship status of its members on the basis of race: black people could not be citizens, nor their children, as the Dred Scott decision made it clear. Membership was thus defined as white citizenship. The Fourteenth Amendment de jure if not de facto deracialized membership in the U.S. polity.

The Fourteenth Amendment also transformed the relationship between states and federal government. Constitutional theorist Bruce Ackerman in his monumental three volume *We the People* (1994–2014) writes that the Fourteenth Amendment "nationalized" the polity both in substance and procedure. What Ackerman means by this is that by producing a unified conception of citizenship, flowing from the Constitution and not the states, the amendment produced a unified nation; and the way this was enacted, first through the 1866 Civil Rights Act of Congress, and then through the states' ratification of the Fourteenth Amendment, meant that states, in concert, assented and approved the modification of the law of the land that would in essence subordinate states to the federal government's protection of the rights of citizens. With its 1866 Act, as well as with the drafting of all the Reconstruction amendments, Congress acted as a "constitutional convention," not unlike that which drafted the constitution of 1787. Ackerman again: "By a remarkable bootstrapping operation, the Convention/Congress was proposing to redefine We the People of the United *States* as We the People of the *United* States" (199). And, as he put it more pointedly in volume 1 of *We the People*,

The Republican Reconstruction of the Union was an Act of *constitutional creation* no less profound than the Founding itself: Not only did the Republicans introduce new substantive principles into our higher law, but they reworked the very process of higher lawmaking itself.

(46; my emphasis)

With this second act of "constitutional creation," the Republican congress had redefined not only membership but also the role of the federal government. Now, the latter would not be conceived as an enemy or threat to individual freedom—which Jefferson believed it to be; instead, the federal government had become "the custodian of freedom," as the abolitionist senator Charles Sumner from Massachusetts declared (Foner 2001: 178). The rewriting and reestablishing of the Constitution on the basis of nationalized citizenship and equality before and under the law meant that "the rights of individual citizens were intimately connected to federal power" (Foner 2001: 178–179).[6]

The Fourteenth Amendment was made up of five sections, three of which no longer have any or little significance (those that barred Confederates from office, those dealing with Confederate debt, and those that reduced a state's representation in Congress if men are denied the right to vote—although this last provision was never enforced even as Southern states continued to blatantly disenfranchise former slaves with disastrous consequences for the re-founded Republic). But as Eric Foner put it succinctly and powerfully, "the Fourteenth Amendment has since become, after the Bill of Rights, the most important constitutional change in the nation's history" (2001: 176).

The Unfinished Revolution

Eric Foner's indispensable history of the reconstruction has the subtitle "America's Unfinished Revolution 1863–1877." In a sense, Foner is right to have thought that the period of reconstruction after the Civil War constituted the unleashing of a sociopolitical revolution that would transform the very nature of the polity. But Reconstruction was followed by what was called Redemption, the reassertion of White Southern power. The rollback of the gains of the Reconstruction period would open the floodgates to decades of violence against black freemen, decades of lynching and white race riots against black people, and the legalization of Jim Crow. We have to be sanguine about what the Reconstruction Amendments did, for they were followed by what can justifiably be called a "white supremacy counter-revolution," the effects of which we are still living through, from Jim Crow to the rise of the ghettos, from Reagan to Trump. As Henry Louis Gates Jr. shows in *Stony the Road: Reconstruction, White Supremacy, and the Rise of Jim Crow* (2019), the dismantling of the many gains made during the Reconstruction period by Southern intransigency and anti-black activism and Northern passivity and acquiescence led to the fracturing of the polity, once again, along racial lines (46). The *Plessy v. Ferguson* Supreme Court decision of 1896 neutralized both the Civil Rights act of 1866 and the Fourteenth Amendment, sundering racially what had been deracialized in 1868 (Luxenberg 2019). Just as importantly, the period after Reconstruction gave birth to a new racial imaginary that assaulted the worthiness and desirability of black people to be citizens. This imaginary has continued to evolve, expand, resemanticize, and semiotically metastasize into more sophisticated and subtle racial and ethnic stereotypes, even as some of its basic premises have been challenged on scientific, political, and legal basis. Political philosopher Michael Walzer has written that "the primary good that we distribute to one another is membership in some human community" (1983: 31). After the French and American Revolutions, we have a new credo that affirms that political membership is a fundamental good and right that is distributed to members of a polity through the rights of citizens. The constitutionalization of jus soli into national citizenship through the Fourteenth Amendment, however, has elevated those nineteenth century revolutionary ideals to a new level: membership on the basis of descent and racial origin are delegitimated and delegalized—just as equality before the law and the right to membership on the basis of birthright and naturalization are asserted. Birthright citizenship is the utmost form of the rejection of jus sanguinis—the deracialization of both membership and citizenship.[7]

References

"14th Amendment," (n.d.) *Cornell Law School Legal Information Institute*, www.law.cornell.edu/constitution/amendmentxiv.
Ackerman, B. (1994–2014) *We the People*, 3 vols, Cambridge, MA: Belknap.
Aristotle. (1984), *The Complete Works of Aristotle. The Revised Oxford Translation*, J. Barnes (ed.), Vol. 2, Princeton, NJ: Princeton University Press.
Blakemore, E. (2018) "The Largest Deportation in American History," *History*, March 23, www.history.com/news/operation-wetback-eisen hower-1954-deportation.

Böckenförde, E. W. (2017) *Constitutional and Political Theory: Selected Writings*, Vol. 1, Oxford: Oxford University Press.
Bottici, C., and Challand, B. (2010) *The Myth of the Clash of Civilizations*, New York: Routledge.
Caldwell, C. (2019) *Deported Americans: Life After Deportation to Mexico*, Durham, NC: Duke University Press.
Chavez, L. R. (2013) *The Latino Threat: Constructing Immigrants, Citizens and the Nation* (2nd ed.), Stanford, CA: Stanford University Press.
Chavez, L. R. (2017) *Anchor Babies and the Challenge of Birthright Citizenship*, Stanford, CA: Stanford University Press.
"Civil Rights Act of 1866," (n.d.) *Wikisource*, https://en.wikisource.org/wiki
"Declaration of the Rights of Man—1789," (n.d.) *Yale Law School*, http://avalon.law.yale.edu/18th_century/rightsof.asp.
Diderot, D. (2005) "Citizen," in *The Encyclopedia of Diderot and d'Alembert Collaborative Translation Project*, S. Dhanvantari (trans.), Ann Arbor: University of Michigan Press.
Fletcher, G. P. (2001) *Our Secret Constitution: How Lincoln Redefined American Democracy*, New York: Oxford University Press.
Foner, E. ([1988] 2002) *Reconstruction: America's Unfinished Revolution 1863–1877* (updated ed.), New York: Harper and Row.
Foner, E. (2001) "June 13, 1866: Equality Before the Law," in James M. McPherson (ed.), *Days of Destiny: Cross Roads in American History*, London: Dorling Kimberly Publishing.
Foner, E. (2019) *The Second Founding: How the Civil War and Reconstruction Remade the Constitution*, New York: W. W. Norton Company.
Gates Jr., H. L. (2019) *Stony the Road: Reconstruction, White Supremacy, and the Rise of Jim Crow*, New York: Penguin Press.
Haynes, J. (2019) *From Huntington to Trump: Thirty Years of the Clash of Civilizations*, Lanham, MD: Lexington Books.
Heater, D. (2004) *Citizenship: The Civic Ideal in World History, Politics and Education* (3rd ed.), Manchester: Manchester University Press.
Huntington, S. P. (1957) *The Soldier and the State: The Theory and Politics of Civil-Military, Relations*, Cambridge, MA: Belknap.
Huntington, S. P. (1996) *The Clash of Civilizations and the Remaking of the World Order*, New York: Simon and Schuster.
Huntington, S. P. (2000a) "Reconsidering Immigration: Is Mexico a Special Case?" *Center for Immigration Studies*, November 1, https://cis.org/Report/Reconsidering-Immigration-Mexico-Special-Case.
Huntington, S. P. (2000b) "The Special Case of Mexican Immigration," *The American Enterprise* 11 (8).
Huntington, S. P. (2004a) "The Hispanic Challenge," *Foreign Policy* 141: 30.
Huntington, S. P. (2004b) *Who Are We? The Challenges to America's National Identity*, New York: Simon and Schuster.
Jones, M. S. (2018) *Birthright Citizens: A History of Race and Rights in Antebellum America*, Cambridge: Cambridge University Press.
Lerner, G. (2012) "The Iraq Conflict: The War That Changed Latinos," December 20, www.huffingtonpost.com/2011/12/19/iraq-war-changed-latinos_n_1158488.html.
Luxenberg, S. (2019) *Separate: The Story of Plessy vs. Ferguson and America's Journey from Slavery to Segregation*, New York: W. W. Norton.
Mollat, M. (1986) *The Poor in the Middle Ages: An Essay in Social History*, A. Goldhammer (trans.), New Haven: Yale University Press.
Pico della Mirandola. (1996) *Oratio on the Dignity of the Human Being*, A. Robert Campogrini (trans.), Washington, DC: Gateway Editions.
Reed-Sandoval, A. (2020) *Socially Undocumented: Identity and Immigration Justice*, New York: Oxford University Press.
Riesenberg, P. (1992) *Citizenship in the Western Tradition: Plato to Rousseau*, Chapel Hill: University of North Carolina.
Roland, P. (2012) *The Nuremberg Trials: The Nazis and Their Crimes Against Humanity*, London: Arcturus.
Sosa, L. (1997) *The Americano Dream: How Latinos Can Achieve Success in Business and Life*, New York: Dutton.

"Unite the Right Rally," (n.d.) *Wikipedia*, https://en.wikipedia.org/wiki/Civil_Rights_Act_of_1866/Unite_the_Right_rally.
Walzer, M. (1977) *Just and Unjust Wars*, New York: Basic Books.
Walzer, M. (1983) *Spheres of Justice: A Defense of Pluralism and Equality*, New York: Basic Books.
White, R. (2017) *The Republic for Which It Stands: The United States During Reconstruction and the Gilded Age, 1865–1896*, New York: Oxford University Press.

Notes

1 The text of the Constitution can be found at: www.archives.gov/founding-docs/constitution-transcript#toc-article-iii-.
2 This is part of statute 2, chapter 9, sections 1 and 2, which can be found online at http://memory.loc.gov/cgi-bin/ampage?collId=llsl&fileName=001/llsl001.db&recNum=235.
3 This story is unfinished and has more sordid chapters. See Caldwell (2019).
4 Huntington is quoting from Burke's Reflections on the Revolution in France.
5 On this rally, see the informative Wikepedia entry: https://en.wikipedia.org/wiki/Unite_the_Right_rally.
6 Stanford professor of American history Richard White summarized the accomplishments and goals of the Fourteenth Amendment in the following way: "The broad principles of the Fourteenth Amendment were clear. The Republicans sought to abrogate judicial interpretations of the Constitution that, in the name of federalism, had limited the extension of a uniform set of rights applicable to all citizens everywhere in the Union. Congress intended the new amendment to extend the guarantees of the Bill of Rights so that they protected citizens against actions by the states as well as by the federal government. The equal protection clause was supposed to ensure that no state discriminated among its own citizens or against the citizens of another state. The amendment would protect both new black citizens and white Unionists in the South. The Republicans desired a national citizenship with uniform rights. Ultimately the amendment was Lincolnian: it sought, as had Lincoln, to make the sentiments of the Declaration of Independence the guiding light of the republic. It enshrined in the Constitution broad principles of equality, the rights of citizens, and principles of natural rights prominent in the Declaration of Independence and in Republican ideals of free labor and contract freedom" (2017: 74).
7 There are many questions that the abolition of jus sanguinis raises, many of which I cannot take up in the present context. However, making jus soli the primary form of granting and securing citizenship solves more problems than jus sanguinis is able to solve or even begin to address. For instance, what of children born out of wedlock to a parent of one nationality and another of a different one? This child would not live in limbo, as they would be granted citizenship in the country where they were born under jus soli. My argument for the moment is that the jus soli is the culmination of the project of deracialized citizenship that began with the Universal Declaration of the Rights of Man and the Citizens, and which was advanced by the Civil War amendments to the U.S. Constitution. Another interesting example is that of German Jews who were stripped of their citizenship because they were not Aryans, who most likely no longer have descendants in Germany or blood descendants who could advocate for their jus sanguinis German citizenship. Under the primacy of jus solis, in my estimation, they could. At the very least, I can see a combination of both developing over the next decades as increasing numbers of constitutional democracies aim to "deracialize" their citizenship laws.

Reading Questions

1. According to the text, what reasons does Samuel Huntington give to support his claim that Latinxs pose a problem for the U.S., distinctive from the problems posed by ethno-racial minority groups in the past? How does Mendieta attempt to refute Huntington's argument?
2. What is at the core of the U.S.'s identity, according to Huntington? What are the assumptions that underpin this view?
3. Mendieta draws a connection between Huntington's defense of "white nativism," Donald Trump's rhetoric of "Make America Great Again," and the storming of the U.S. Capitol on January 6, 2021. What is this connection? What does it indicate about the nature of racist supremacy?

4. Huntington argues that nationalism—not cosmopolitan or imperialism—is the path forward if the U.S. hopes to avoid the loss of its cultural identity. In this sense, Huntington is concerned about preserving international diversity. Do you find this concern to be compelling? Why or why not?
5. What does Mendieta mean when he describes the "unfinished work of building citizenship"? How does the Fourteenth Amendment elevate the nineteenth-century ideals of political membership to a new level, in his view?
6. Mendieta argues that citizenship has historically been understood as being more than a mere legal category or bureaucratic label. According to the Aristotelian conception, citizenship is what one *does* rather than what one *is*. From Cicero, we get the idea that "citizenship is . . . the exercise of the moral and political excellence of the human being." Then, Augustine portrays citizenship as a type of "sacramental duty." Given this set of ideals, what sorts of citizens does Mendieta expect us to be in response to the state's betrayal of Latinxs? What is he calling for when he writes, "So much is failing here: our civic imagination is failing, our sense of civic outrage, our sense of civil loyalty and solidarity"?
7. Why should we be worried about the Latino threat narrative, according to Mendieta? What is the possibility he wants to warn us about?

30 The Gendered Nature of U.S. Immigration Policy

Allison B. Wolf

> "*Desgraciada, ¿porque tienes tantos niños si no los puedes cuidar? Puta, prostituta.*" ("Disgraced woman, why do you have so many kids if you can't take care of them? Slut.")
> —Comments from CBP (U.S. Customs and Border Protection) Officers (Issacson and Martens 2023: 21)

Border Patrol expelled a young Guatemalan woman to Nogales, Mexico after she had been repeatedly raped by the guides who brought her across the border into the United States. She showed paperwork from the hospital examination to a Border Patrol agent as proof of the attack, and the agent confiscated it and the woman was expelled back to Mexico without the documentation. The Guatemalan consulate later attempted to help her apply for a U-Visa (for victims of criminal activity) since she had experienced the crime in the United States, but she no longer had any of the medical documentation to substantiate it.

(Issacson and Martens 2023: 21)

In January 2023, Border Patrol agents apprehended and transported a pregnant woman who was having contractions to a San Diego hospital. While at the hospital, they tried to separate the pregnant woman from her school-aged daughter. The agents communicated that they would be returning the daughter to the Border Patrol station without her mother. It was only because the treating physician and advocates with Jewish Family Service of San Diego intervened that the separation and return to the Border Patrol station were prevented.

(American Civil Liberties Union 2023)

These are just some of the incidents that illustrate how U.S. immigration policy towards Latinx migrants and asylum-seekers is both gendered and oppressive (and, by extension, unjust).[1] In particular, such policies and practices target people differently according to gender, are motivated by desires to maintain oppressive gender roles, affect members of different genders distinctly, and reflect, perpetuate, and create gender oppression. The aim of this essay is to explain and defend these claims.

I employ a methodology that reflects Latinx and feminist philosophical approaches. I first listen to testimonies, narratives, and anecdotes from migrants and their loved ones throughout the Americas. Based on these accounts, I ask myself what the most germane theoretical lens is to understand them. Repeatedly, I conclude that the feminist approach—specifically, its focus on oppression (gender and otherwise)—is the most apt to comprehend, explain, and address the migration experiences of Latinx people in the Americas and the injustices they endure.

DOI: 10.4324/9781003385417-43

This choice of methodology is intentional. First, consistent with many Latinx methodologies (Isasi-Díaz 2011), I do this to emphasize that migrants deserve epistemic authority and should be seen as epistemic sources and agents. Second, I find it hard (if not impossible) to understand, assess, or make recommendations about migration in the Americas without the voices of migrants. Third, what distinguishes discussions of immigration in Latinx philosophy (as opposed to the more traditional Western philosophical discussions, such as those conducted by folks like Joseph Carens, David Miller, Michael Walzer, Phillip Cole, and Christopher Heath Wellman, who barely mention the experiences of migrants) is precisely how they position Latinx migrant experiences at their core and/or concrete policies affecting them and other Latin American migrants. Amy Reed-Sandoval, for example, starts with ethnography and interviews with migrants from Mexico and then theorizes based on those interactions (Reed-Sandoval 2021). Carlos Alberto Sánchez (2014), Grant Silva (2015), and José Jorge Mendoza (2016) center concrete motivations, experiences, and consequences of referring to unauthorized Latinx migrants as "illegal" immigrants to make larger claims about the racist, nativist, and dehumanizing nature both of this term and U.S. immigration policy (past and present) more broadly. And Lori Gallegos starts with the experiences of migrants' family members who speak English having to serve as interpreters for their Spanish-speaking relatives to explore what she terms "the interpreter's dilemma" and the injustices that linguistic marginalization generates (Gallegos 2021). This essay aligns with these approaches. It is substantively concerned with the experiences of Latinx migrants in particular (rather than being about migration in general or migration that takes place in other regions of the world).

What Does It Mean to Analyze U.S. Immigration Policy Through a Gendered Lens?

While I am interested in immigration justice for all Latinx people in the Americas, I am especially interested in how immigration policy is entwined with gender. Migration policy is often motivated by gender ideologies, disproportionately affects women, non-binary, and trans migrants, and places women, non-binary, and trans migrants in uniquely dangerous situations. To show this, however, we need to conduct a gendered analysis of U.S. immigration policy. So, allow me to briefly explain what that entails.

At its most basic level, a gendered analysis simply explains how policies are motivated by ideas about gender roles, target members of certain genders, or have distinct consequences for members of different gender categories. These types of analyses may focus on a specific gender group (by asking, for example, how the family separation policy specifically targets Central American women) or they might involve comparative analyses (for example, by exploring how border enforcement affects cis and trans men versus cis and trans women). In these cases, a gendered analysis need not be a feminist analysis (though it certainly could be).

A gendered analysis may also be synonymous with a feminist one, however. While there are many definitions of feminism, the simplest one is that feminism maintains that:

1. Gender oppression exists.
2. Gender oppression is not natural; there is nothing in the nature of men, women, or non-binary people (not genes, not biology, not hormones, not muscle mass or brain size) that explains or justifies oppression.
3. We can resist and overcome gender oppression.[2]

In this type of gendered analysis, one interrogates the degree to which a policy or practice reflects, creates, or perpetuates gender oppression. Put differently, as I will now explain, one investigates the degree to which said policy or practice is (un)just.

A Brief Overview of Immigration (In)Justice

Before showing how U.S. immigration policy is gendered in the two ways just described, we need to define immigration justice. While some define immigration justice as being about protecting immigrants' human rights or being about a nation's border and admissions policies (so that immigration justice is achieved with more open or closed borders, depending on one's perspective), I employ a feminist approach to immigration justice. On this view, immigration justice is fundamentally about identifying and resisting the oppression of immigrants, asylum seekers, refugees, and displaced persons (Wolf 2021). In this way, if a policy or practice creates, perpetrates, and/or reflects oppression of any sort in relation to migration, it is unjust.

But how do we know if something is oppressive? According to Marilyn Frye, oppression is a structural phenomenon that places social groups and their members into double binds simply because of their membership in those groups. Oppression catches social groups and their members "between or among forces and barriers which are so related to each other that jointly they restrain, restrict, or prevent the thing's motion or mobility" (Frye 1983) in ways that are neither random, accidental, occasional, or avoidable, nor the result of bad luck or the actions of a few bad apples. Under oppression, structures "work *together* to reduce, immobilize, and mold the oppressed" (Frye 1983: 2) by placing them in double binds, or situations where their "options are reduced to a very few and all of them expose one to penalty, censure, or deprivation" (Frye 1983: 3). A common example of a double bind is young women's sexual expression. If young women have sex, then they are chastised as "whores," but if they abstain, they are deemed "prudes," "teases," and "frigid." If they masturbate (if that can even be conceived), they are called "crazy," "gross," or "hyper-sexed." Regardless of their choice, young women are vulnerable to censure and rebuke; they are caught in a double bind principally due to their membership in the particular social group, WOMEN.

Of course, we have multiple social group memberships, which means that oppression is perpetuated and experienced in various ways, which Iris Marion Young refers to as the *faces* of oppression. According to Young, there are at least five faces of oppression: exploitation, marginalization, powerlessness, cultural imperialism, and systemic violence (Young 1990). When one or more of these phenomena are present, then so is oppression.

Now that we have defined the types of gendered analyses and the concepts of immigration justice and oppression being employed in this essay, we can explore how U.S. immigration policy is gendered and oppressive and thus unjust. I will begin by conducting a gendered analysis in the first sense, e.g., by detailing various ways that U.S. immigration policy and practice distinctly affects members of different genders. Then, I will conduct a gendered analysis in the second sense to show how some U.S. immigration policies, practices, and enforcement mechanisms are motivated by traditional gender ideologies and how they reflect and create gender oppression.

U.S. Immigration Policy, Practice, and Enforcement as They Relate to Women

U.S. immigration policy and enforcement affects women and men differently. This is most prominently seen in relation to how they place women in danger of sexual and other types of gender-based violence. On top of the perils all immigrants endure (being vulnerable to crime, hunger, sickness, etc.), women face unique risks of rape, sexual assault, kidnapping, abandonment, and death. One study found that 90% of migrant women experience sexual violence (De León 2015), with border patrol agents being both its frequent perpetrators and key enablers (Vera 2013). In fact, as Sylvanna Falcón reports, for many women, "being raped was the price exacted of them to cross the border without being apprehended or deported, or to receive their confiscated documents" (Falcón 2001).

U.S. enforcement policies enable gender-based violence. For example, Falcon found that "despite claiming that they follow protocol and do not deport women at night, agents often ignore this policy in order to deter migrants from crossing again" (Steinberg 2020). Sara Duvisac and Irene Sullivan confirmed this finding, reporting that "CBP will expel women at 3 a.m. in one of the most dangerous cities in the world. So, they are completely unprotected" (Duvisac and Sullivan 2022: 14).

Gender-based violence also combines with violence that targets people's sexual identities to make LGBTQI+ migrants especially vulnerable. These migrants face physical assault, significant harassment by police in Mexican border towns, housing discrimination, and violence in camps and shelters (Duvisac and Sullivan 2022: 16). This occurs in detention facilities as well since

> detention centers don't have any specific area for trans folks, and they're not very willing to house trans folks with men or with women. And so, they'll just put them in solitary for the whole time that they're in detention—[for] months at a time—not to mention [lack of] access to hormones [and other] medication
>
> (Duvisac and Sullivan 2022: 17)

And for those who wonder if this is not just something that happens to all migrants, Almudena Cortés Maisonave found that attackers often make comments during the assaults like, " 'I'll teach you how to be a real woman' when they know that the person identifies as lesbian or queer," indicating that sexual identity is a central motivation for the attacks (Cortés Maisonave 2022).

In addition to these more explicit violent attacks, gender violence manifests itself in the treatment of pregnant migrants and asylum seekers. In 2018 the Trump Administration began detaining pregnant migrants, leading to miscarriages (Garcia Lawler 2019). The American Civil Liberties Union (ACLU) reports numerous pregnant migrants in immigration custody who endured distinct kinds of mistreatment, including: being repeatedly slammed against a chain link fence by a Border Patrol agent; miscarrying in a Border Patrol facility for 12 days without receiving any hygienic products or medical care; being denied abortion access and other medical attention; and at least four reported forced hysterectomies (Amiri 2020). In one instance, a pregnant Guatemalan asylum seeker—despite her repeated requests for medical attention—was taken to the Chula Vista Border Patrol Station, rather than a doctor. Within 30 minutes, the woman's pain became excruciating, and she soon gave birth into her pants while standing up and bracing herself against the edge of a garbage can (American Friends Service Committee 2020).[3] These are some ways that pregnant migrants are uniquely affected by immigration and detention policies.

Specific policies, like "prevention through deterrence," also have specific consequences for women. The prevention through deterrence strategy, initially implemented in the mid- to late 1990s, created measures that intentionally redirect hundreds of thousands of migrants away from busy crossing points in California and Texas into Arizona's perilous desert (Rubio-Goldsmith et al. 2006). The idea behind this approach is that if migrants cannot enter the U.S. through easier-to-access crossing points, then they will choose not to come to the United States at all since the risks would be too great. However, the evidence conclusively shows that this does not occur; to the contrary, these policies create what is known as the "funnel effect," such that migrants face more treacherous conditions as they attempt to enter the U.S. (Rubio-Goldsmith et al. 2006).

Prevention through deterrence strategies disproportionately put women at risk by making them more vulnerable to the kinds of violence already highlighted and exposing them to more dangerous conditions. The Binational Migration Institute

> found that women were nearly three times more likely to die of exposure than men. Some researchers have linked this imbalance to the tendency of smugglers to perceive women as liabilities while *en route*, which increases the likelihood of abandonment, exposing them to mortal danger in the desert.
>
> (Steinberg 2020)

These policies also make women even more vulnerable to smugglers and abuse, as happened to Maria Salinas, who recently tried crossing with her 18-year-old daughter. When Salinas couldn't keep up, one coyote said he'd help on the condition that she let him have sex with her daughter. She refused and he abandoned them. "It's awful," Salinas said about making this trip as a woman. "I wouldn't wish it on anyone" (Joffe-Block 2014).

While many policies target and uniquely affect women, some also single out men, such as the 1986 Immigration Reform and Control Act and the 1996 Illegal Immigration Reform and Immigrant Responsibility Act. When the former was passed, it introduced a criminal alien program designed to deport convicted felons (Macías-Rojas 2016). Originally, the program was created to expel undocumented immigrants who had committed serious and violent crimes, including gang members (Cantor et al. 2015). However, in 1996, when the Illegal Immigration Reform and Immigrant Responsibility Act was passed, it expanded the list of aggravated felonies for which one could be deported to include petty theft, minor drug offenses, and DUIs, while also requiring mandatory detention of noncitizens who had completed their prison sentences (Cantor et al. 2015: 61 and 63). A major target of this policy was those who belonged to the gang MS-13, whose members began negotiating with the Mexican mafia for protection in jails and prisons from other Latino gangs (Lajka 2019). And so, with the expanded list of deportable crimes, U.S. deportations included members of MS-13 and others (Lajka 2019).

Aside from the gendered effects of detention and deterrence policies, Reed-Sandoval notes that the experience of being a migrant itself is distinct for pregnant migrants and migrant women (Reed-Sandoval 2020). For one, racism and sexism intersect on their bodies, for example, via campaigns to eliminate birthright citizenship and calling migrants' children "anchor babies" (Reed-Sandoval 2020: 2). Reed-Sandoval also notes that migrants seeking reproductive care, such as abortions, are often denied it despite the legality of such requests. In fact, we saw such a case in the United States during the Trump Administration when, in 2017, the Office of Refugee Resettlement (ORR) instituted a policy of blocking pregnant young people from accessing abortion, including a then-17-year-old Central American immigrant. Federal officials responded to her request for an abortion by refusing it and forcing her to receive counseling at a religiously affiliated crisis pregnancy center. Only after the Supreme Court ruled in her favor was the girl able to access the care she needed (Amiri 2020).

Reed-Sandoval also highlights how migrant mothers and their children endure distinct burdens and challenges, such as mothers being separated from their children via deportation (when the mothers are not U.S. citizens, but their children are, for example) or migration (when mothers must migrate to provide for their children). This is supported by Monisha Das Gupta's work, which finds that migrant mothers suffer unique consequences in (1) being left to navigate the economic burdens when male migrant fathers are deported; (2) experiencing miscarriages due to the stress of their partner's deportation; and (3) enduring disproportionate burdens of transnational parenting (Das Gupta 2013). Moreover, Reed-Sandoval notes, mothers who migrate and "leave their children behind" in their countries of origin are frequently criticized for the choice, especially by their children and other family members, whereas fathers who migrate are not (Reed-Sandoval 2020: 4).

All these points illustrate how U.S. immigration policies and enforcement mechanisms are gendered in the first sense that I discussed. In other words, policies affect women and men differently. As we will now see, this is not accidental or random, but rather is a structural part of border policies and their enforcement in the United States in ways that are oppressive and, by extension, unjust.

U.S. Immigration Policy, Practice, and Enforcement and Gender Oppression

In addition to affecting women disproportionately, U.S. immigration policy is oppressive. First, immigration policies and border enforcement strategies are motivated by a desire to maintain oppressive gender norms and ideologies. As Almudena Cortés Maisonave observes:

> The gender order is key in understanding the mechanisms that organize migration, but especially in the development of policies that govern human mobility and that generally legitimize gender mandates. . . . While male migration is rewarded and socially legitimized, female migration suffers social sanction for not complying with gender, sexual, emotional and care mandates.
>
> (Cortés Maisonave 2022: 4–5)

In other words, some immigration policies are meant to maintain women's traditional societal roles, keep them "in their place," and punish those who challenge these ideas. And this is at play in U.S. immigration policy. For example, the family separation policy was, in part, motivated by a desire to both utilize traditional gender norms to achieve the Trump Administration's immigration goals and to maintain gender roles.[4] In fact, this was made explicit by then Asylum Chief for the U.S. Citizenship and Immigration Service, John Lafferty, who said that the Department of Homeland Security was developing a plan for separating women and children crossing into the United States "to deter *mothers* from migrating to the United States with their children" (Edwards Ainsley 2017). In particular, the idea was that women (upholding their traditional gender roles) would never allow themselves to be separated from their children and therefore would choose not to come.

Policies like family separation and prevention through deterrence also exemplify a second way that U.S. immigration policies connect to gender oppression. Namely, they create, reflect, and perpetuate gender oppression (as opposed to these effects being unintended consequences or the results of a few bad actors). For one, the effects of these policies and their oppressive roots are neither random nor accidental; they result from a deliberate set of actions and policies by the United States government to place Central American migrants into double binds because of their gender and nationality. These policies force Central American women to decide whether they ought to stay in their home country under dangerous, if not life-threatening, conditions or go to the U.S. and face terrible conditions along the way and when they arrive. Worse, women are portrayed as bad mothers for either decision; they are bad mothers for exposing their children to a treacherous journey to the States, bad mothers for not getting their kids out of danger in their home nations, and bad mothers if they leave the children in their home nation with relatives so that they can migrate to the U.S. and provide for themselves and their families. No matter what these women do, they face negative consequences. So, these policies perpetuate and reflect oppression at a general level.

Beyond the broader ways that U.S. immigration policies are oppressive, U.S. immigration policies create, reflect, and promote gender oppression in particular ways. This is most evident in another recent policy, namely the Migrant Protection Protocols (MPP; aka the Remain in Mexico Policy). This policy reversed previous U.S. asylum law, which followed the principle of refoulment that allowed most asylum seekers to pass their initial screening and enter the U.S. while they waited for their asylum hearing (O'Toole 2019). Instead, these protocols require migrants trying to enter the United States on its Southern border to wait in Mexico until their court date, unless they explicitly state that they fear for their safety *in Mexico* (as opposed to the usual protocol of explaining why they fear for their safety in their home countries).

The Remain in Mexico Policy has created, reflected, or perpetuated various forms of oppression (powerless, exploitation, marginalization, and derivatization to name a few), but I will focus on how it creates and perpetuates gender oppression in the form of systemic violence. Systemic violence occurs when "members of some groups live with the knowledge that they must fear random, unprovoked attacks on their persons or property, which have no motive but to damage, humiliate, or destroy the person" (Young 1990: 61). As Young explains, "What makes violence a face of oppression is less the particular acts themselves, though these are often utterly horrible, than the social context surrounding them, which makes them possible and even acceptable" (Young 1990: 61–62).

The context and normalization of these acts of violence toward migrants show that these are not random, but rather systemic attacks. Moreover, this violence is normalized and seen as inevitable (Women's Refugee Commission 2021). In fact, it is so prevalent that one woman asked a nurse, Helen Perry, who works in a makeshift refugee camp on the Mexican side of the U.S.-Mexico border if they would give out condoms so she could ask her rapist to wear one the *next* time she is raped (Glass 2019). Tragically, her perception seems supported by individual experiences and studies on these matters. For example, Jessica, a Honduran asylum-seeker, and her friend were detained by the National Guard in Ciudad Juárez after being expelled from the U.S., and then both were sexually abused by the agents. Another Honduran woman who had been returned to Ciudad Juárez under the MPP was kidnapped and raped in mid-June (Human Rights Watch 2019). Delfina, a 20-year-old asylum seeker who fled Guatemala with her four-year-old son, was also grabbed and sexually assaulted by two men on the street in Ciudad Juárez after she was returned to Mexico as part of the MPP. They told her not to scream and threatened to kill her son. "I can still feel the dirtiness of what they did in my body," she told Human Rights Watch (Human Rights Watch 2019). And Laura, a trans woman fleeing Honduras due to death threats and her house being burned down, told the Women's Refugee Commission (WRC) that she was threatened at gunpoint by Mexican authorities during her journey to Tijuana (Women's Refugee Committee 2021).

These are not exceptions to the rule. In fact, 68 percent of immigration lawyers surveyed stated that their clients have been raped and/or sexually assaulted frequently at the border (Duvisac and Sullivan 2022). And the United Nations High Commissioner for Refugees said that "two thirds of the LBGTI refugees from Central America they spoke to in 2016 and 2017 had suffered sexual and gender-based violence in Mexico" (Amnesty International 2017). All this systemic sexual violence is part and parcel of the Remain in Mexico Policy and the general U.S. plan to make life so miserable for migrants and asylum seekers that they will stop coming.

It is so clear that the Remain in Mexico policy creates and promotes gender oppression via systemic violence that large numbers of asylum officers resigned in protest (O'Toole 2019). One asylum officer said:

> It's the first time that we have been asked to affirmatively do harm to people. You're not just saying, 'I don't think you're eligible.' You're literally saying, 'I believe what you're saying, I believe you're in danger. Go back to that danger.'
>
> (O'Toole 2019)

Another asylum officer, Ursela, echoed these sentiments, saying that she interviewed a woman who told her she was afraid that if she was sent back to Mexico, she would be raped. But Ursela was obligated to send her back (despite evidence supporting her claim and the fact that Ursela believed her) because the policy requires that the woman could only not be sent back if she could identify the specific individual who might rape her in Mexico, not point to a general fear (O'Toole 2019). As one asylum officer said: "You're literally sending people back to be raped and killed. . . . That's what this is" (O'Toole 2019).

The United States has yet to remedy the situation. In August 2022, the Biden Administration tried to end the policy (Associated Press 2022), only to be thwarted by a Texas judge in December 2022 (Ables 2022). Recently, the Biden Administration has also tried to implement other policies restricting the ability to seek asylum, such as the colloquially known "asylum ban," prohibiting anyone who enters the U.S. in an unauthorized way from seeking asylum (though the Supreme Court rejected this move) (International Rescue Commission 2023). And while the Biden Administration is proposing to allow up to 50,000 refugees to come to the United States from Latin America in 2024, they must first apply in third countries to be considered (Montoya-Galvez 2023). These actions suggest that they are leaving women, non-binary, and trans migrants vulnerable to these and other dangers, just under a different policy guise, thus continuing to implement policies that create, reflect, and promote gender oppression.

These examples are just some ways that U.S. immigration policies and practices not only affect people differently according to their gender but also are oppressive in their own right. Sometimes these policies further or reflect gender oppression in the reasons they were created or defended. Other times, the policies create or promote specific forms of gender oppression, like systemic violence. In each case, however, U.S. immigration policy is deeply connected to gender (and other) oppressions, and fighting it requires noting that this is the case.

Gender Oppression in U.S. Immigration Policy and Latinx Philosophy

Before concluding these reflections, I want to suggest how Latina feminist thought—specifically (but not exclusively) the work of Gloria Anzaldúa and María Lugones—can help us understand the connections between Latinx migrations and gender oppression I have identified. I will start with Anzaldúa.

In her groundbreaking book, *Borderlands/La Frontera*, Anzaldúa describes the real-life consequences of living on various sides of the *herida abierta*, while demonstrating how the experience of living in the borderlands—the third nation that is neither Mexico nor the United States—is distinct for members of different genders. In one sense, Anzaldúa shows how the borderlands (and the political and cultural wars to define and enforce them) have unique oppressive consequences for women. She explains how Mexican women are especially at risk from *coyotes* (smugglers) because he "doesn't feed her or sells her into prostitution," but she does not feel she can do anything since she does not know English and fears deportation (Anzaldúa 2012: 34). On top of that, Latinas face sexism from their own culture. Anzaldúa explains: "The culture expects women to show greater acceptance of, and commitment to, the value system than men. The culture and the Church insist that women are subservient to males. If a woman rebels she is a *mujer mala*" (Anzaldúa 2012: 39). "But worse, there is no safe place for her because her own culture, and white culture, are critical of her . . . the males of all races see her as prey" (Anzaldúa 2012: 42). In these statements, and throughout her work, Anzaldúa shows the unique expression of gender oppression women face from both *gringos* and Latino men on both sides of the border.

Anzaldúa also explicitly ties the world of Latinx feminism to the struggles around migration and borders via her discussion of the *mestiza* consciousness and identity. For example, she says that "*la mestiza* undergoes a struggle of flesh, a *struggle of borders*, an inner war" (Anzaldúa 2012: 100). But this should not be interpreted as negative. To the contrary:

[i]n attempting to work out a synthesis, the self has added a third element which is greater than the sum of its severed parts. That third element is a new consciousness—a *mestiza* consciousness—and though it is a source of intense pain, its energy comes from a continual creative motion that keeps breaking down the unitary aspects of each new paradigm.
(Anzaldúa 2012: 100–101)

In other words, this *mestiza* consciousness also gives those who have it tools of resistance against the oppression they undergo. For example, these experiences in the borderlands can help one develop *la facultad*, or "the capacity to see in surface phenomena the meaning of deeper realities, to see the deep structure below the surface . . . the one possessing this sensitivity is excruciatingly alive to the world" (Anzaldúa 2012: 60). In this way, *mestiza consciousness* is a source of power and knowledge to resist oppression(s). Through her writings, Anzaldúa not only reveals connections between migrations and oppressions but also suggests how these connections provide paths for resisting oppression, and she gives us a model for connecting Latinx philosophy and immigration studies.

Years later, and in a different way, María Lugones also revealed potential important connections between Latinx philosophy and immigration. Utilizing the work of other Latino thinkers, like Juan Ricardo Aparicio and Aníbal Quijano, Lugones reveals the logic of the modern colonial gender system. Briefly, Lugones notes that part of the conquest of Latin America entailed imposing various binary hierarchies delineating, first, pre-modern/primitive and modern/civilized, and then human and non-human, all of which were racialized and gendered categories (Lugones 2010: 743). According to this logic, not only was human synonymous with being white, but only humans had genders (whereas other beings were simply biologically male and female). Since only white people were human, only white people could rightly be called men and women. In this way, if sexism or gender oppression is waged against women, and only white women are women, then sexism is only aimed at white women. What happened(s) to Latina women, Indigenous women, and other women of color constitutes a distinct form of oppression.

Considering this, I think it could be argued that what is happening now in terms of the gendered nature of immigration policy is deeply connected to the modern colonial gender system. More specifically, at the core of U.S. immigration policy is precisely the negation of Latina (Latinx) humanity. As such, we should not worry about its gendered effects precisely because Latinx women are not women at all (since they are not fully human). Or the policies are intended to erase Latina migrants' humanity altogether. In either case, this framing helps us connect specific intersections of colonialism, racism, and sexism underlying U.S. immigration policy and how it uniquely affects Latina migrants.

Beyond their specific contributions (which I have presented in very simplified form), Anzaldúa and Lugones's works both demonstrate the core relationship between immigration justice and Latinx philosophy. When we question why, for example, U.S. immigration policy favors those from Canada and Europe (or why Latin American immigration policies favor those from the so-called Global North), the answer is connected to longstanding racist, sexist, and colonial histories, not just the current moment. Similarly, when we explore the history of border policy and enforcement, it is evident that they were born out of (and continue to be motivated by) racist and colonial histories and the desire of Western nations to prevent brown people from getting to their shores.[5] As such, Latinx feminist philosophy can help us answer not just *how* these immigration policies reflect and contribute to gender (and other forms of) oppression, but also *why* they are aimed at Latinx bodies and how they manifest uniquely on those bodies and cultures.

Of course, there are many more instances of gendered U.S. immigration policies and practices than I can detail here and, given this, the analysis presented here is just a beginning; what I have said here invites further inquiry (as all good philosophy does). What is important, for now, however, is identifying the ways in which these policies are gendered in both senses I introduced earlier—they both target and affect women distinctly and generate or reproduce gender oppression in various ways that make them unjust. Knowing this, I hope you will join me in contributing to the larger project of Latinx philosophy, Latinx feminism, and most importantly, getting us closer to achieving immigration justice for Latinx migrants.

Bibliography

Ables, K. (2022) "U.S. Judge in Amarillo Halts Biden Administration's Attempt to End 'Remain in Mexico' Policy," *The Washington Post*.

American Civil Liberties Union. (2023) "New Evidence of Horrific Treatment of Pregnant People in CBP Custody Reignites Demands for Change," https://www.aclu.org/press-releases/new-evidence-of-horrific-treatment-of-pregnant-people-in-cbp-custody-reignites-demands-for-change.

American Friends Service Committee. (2020) "Report Shows Pervasive Abuse of Pregnant Immigrants and Asylum Seekers," www.afsc.org/newsroom/report-shows-pervasive-abuse-pregnant-immigrants-and-asylum-seekers.

Amiri, B. (2020) "Reproductive Abuse is Rampant in the Immigration Detention System," *American Civil Liberties Union*, www.aclu.org/news/immigrants-rights/reproductive-abuse-is-rampant-in-the-immigration-detention-system.

Amnesty International. (2017) "Mexico/Central America: Authorities Turning the Backs on LGBTI Refugees," *Amnesty.org*, https://www.amnesty.org/en/latest/press-release/2017/11/mexico-central-america-authorities-turning-their-backs-on-lgbti-refugees/.

Anzaldúa, G. (2012) *Borderlands/La Frontera: The New Mestiza* (25th Anniversary 4th ed.), San Francisco: Aunt Lute.

Associated Press. (2022) "Biden Administration ends Trump-Era 'Remain in Mexico' Policy," *NPR*. www.pbs.org/newshour/politics/biden-administration-ends-trump-era-remain-in-mexico-policy.

Cantor, G., Noferi, M., and Martínez, D. (2015) "Special Report: Enforcement Overdrive: A Comprehensive Assessment of ICE's Criminal Alien Program," *American Immigration Council*, www.americanimmigrationcouncil.org/research/enforcement-overdrive-comprehensive-assessment-ice%E2%80%99s-criminal-alien-program.

Cortés Maisonave, A. (2022) "Crossing Political and Gender Borders: A Feminist Analysis of Migration," *Frontera Norte: International Journal of Borders, Territories, and Regions* 34.

Das Gupta, M. (2013) "Don't Deport our Daddies: Gendering State Deportation Practices and Immigrant Organizing," *Gender and Society* 28 (1): 83–109.

De León, J. (2015) *The Land of Open Graves: Living and Dying on the Migrant Trail*, Berkeley and Los Angeles: University of California Press.

Duvisac, S., and Sullivan, I. (2022) *Surviving Deterrence: How US Asylum Deterrence Policies Normalize Gender-Based Violence*, OXFAM and the Tahirih Justice Center.

Edwards Ainsley, J. (2017) "Exclusive: Trump Administration Considering Separating Women, Children at Mexican Border," *Reuters*, www.reuters.com/article/us-usa-immigration-children-idUSKBN16A2ES.

Falcón, S. (2001) "Rape as a Weapon of War: Advancing Human Rights for Women at the U.S.-Mexico Border," *Social Justice* 28 (2).

Frye, M. (1983) *The Politics of Reality*, California: The Crossing Press.

Gallegos, L. (2021) "'The Interpreter's Dilemma': Latin American Immigration Ethics," in A. Reed-Sandoval and L. R. Díaz Cepeda (eds.), *Latin American Immigration Ethics*, Tucson, AZ: University of Arizona Press.

Garcia Lawler, O. (2019) "Nearly 30 Women Have Miscarried While Detained by ICE Since 2017," *The Cut*, www.thecut.com/2019/03/nearly-30-women-miscarried-while-detained-by-ice-since-2017.html.

Glass, I. (2019) "Prologue: The Out Crowd," *This American Life, National Public Radio*, www.thisamericanlife.org/688/the-out-crowd.

HumanRights Watch Report. (2019) "We Can't Help You Here: US Returns Asylum Seekers to Mexico," www.hrw.org/report/2019/07/02/we-cant-help-you-here/us-returns-asylum-seekers-mexico.

International Rescue Committee. (2023) "What Is President Biden's 'Asylum Ban' and What Does It Mean for People Seeking Safety?" www.rescue.org/article/what-president-bidens-asylum-ban-and-what-does-it-mean-people-seeking-safety.

Isasi-Díaz, A. M. (2011) "Mujerista Discourse: A Platform for Latinas' Subjugated Knowledge," in A. M. Isasi-Díaz and E. Mendieta (eds.), *Decolonizing Epistemologies: Latina/o Theology and Philosophy*, New York: Fordham.

Issacson, A., and Martens, Z. (2023) *Abuses at the U.S.-Mexico Border: How to Address Failures and Protect Rights*, Washington Office for Latin America (WOLA).

Joffe-Block, J. (2014) "Women Crossing the U.S. Border Face Sexual Assault with Little Protection," *PBS Newshour*, www.pbs.org/newshour/nation/facing-risk-rape-migrant-women-prepare-birth-control.

Lajka, A. (2019) "MS-13 and the Violence Driving Illegal Immigration from Central America," *CBS News*, www.cbsnews.com/news/ms-13-illegal-immigration-families-in-crisis-cbsn-originals.

Lugones, M. (2010) "Toward a Decolonial Feminism," *Hypatia* 25 (4).

Luiselli, V. (2017) *Tell Me How It Ends: An Essay in Forty Questions*, Minneapolis: Coffee House Press.

Luiselli, V. (2019) *Lost Children Archive*, New York: Vintage Books.

Macías-Rojas, P. (2016). *From Deportation to Prison: The Politics of Immigration Enforcement in Post-Civil Rights America*, New York: New York University Press.

Mendoza, J. J. (2016) "Illegal: White Supremacy and Immigration Status," in A. Sager (ed.), *The Ethics and Politics of Immigration: Core Issues and Emerging Trends*, London: Rowman & Littlefield.

Montoya-Galvez, C. (2023) "U.S. Aims to Resettle up to 50, 5000 Refugees from Latin America in 2024 Under Biden Plan," *CBS News*, www.cbsnews.com/news/us-refugee-cap-2024-biden-latin-america.

O'Toole, M. (2019) "Goodbye Stranger: The Out Crowd," *This American Life, National Public Radio*, www.thisamericanlife.org/688/the-out-crowd.

Parekh, S. (2020) *No Refuge*, London and New York: Oxford.

Reed-Sandoval, A. (2020) "Maternity and Migration," *Philosophy Compass* 15 (3).

Reed-Sandoval, A. (2021) "Oaxacan Transborder Communities and the Political Philosophy of Immigration," in A. Reed-Sandoval and L. R. Díaz Cepeda (eds.), *Latin American Immigration Ethics*, Tucson, AZ: University of Arizona Press.

Rubio-Goldsmith, R, McCormick, M. M., Martinez, D., and Duarte, I. M. (2006) "The 'Funnel Effect' & Recovered Bodies of Unauthorized Migrants Processed by the Pima County Office of the Medical Examiner, 1990–2005," *Binational Migration Institute*.

Sánchez, C.A. (2014) "'Illegal' Immigrants: Law, Fantasy, and Guts," *Philosophy in the Contemporary World* 21 (1): 99–109.

Silva, G. (2015) "Embodying a 'New' Color Line: Racism, Anti-Immigrant Sentiment and Racial Identities in the 'Postracial' Era," *Knowledge Cultures* 3 (1): 65–90.

Steinberg, A. (2020) "The Gendered Impact of US Border Militarization," *Gender and Intersectional Analysis*, https://sites.tufts.edu/gender/the-gendered-impact-of-us-border-militarization/#_edn4.

Vera, V. (2013) "Border Patrol's Not-So-Secret: The Normalized Abuse of Migrant Women on the U.S.-Mexico Border," *International Affairs Review* (Fall): 1–11.

Wolf, A. (2021) "Immigration Injustice in Colombia: Beyond the Question of Borders," *Border Criminologies Blog*, Oxford, www.law.ox.ac.uk/research-subject-groups/centre-criminology/centreborder-criminologies/blog/2021/04/immigration.

Women's Refugee Commission. (2022) *Stuck in Uncertainty and Exposed to Violence: The Impact of US and Mexican Migration Policies on Women Seeking Protection in 2021*, Women´s Refugee Commission and Instituto para las Mujeres en la Migración.

Young, I. M. (1990) *Justice and the Politics of Difference*, Princeton: Princeton University Press.

Notes

1 For further discussion of the connection between oppression and injustice, see Young (1990).
2 Of course, as I indicated, there are many schools of feminism—liberal feminism, radical feminism, socialist feminism, transnational feminism, just to name a few. Still, they all agree on these three general points. Where they disagree is on the source/cause of gender oppression and, by extension, what is needed to resist and overcome it.
3 For excellent fiction and nonfiction accounts of this, see Luiselli (2019; 2017) and de León (2015).
4 Created on April 6, 2018, the policy directs the arrest and detention of all who enter the United States "illegally" on the Southern Border. This means that adults suspected of crossing the U.S. border without documents are sent to federal prison or detention centers while they wait for their cases to be heard. This leads the government to separate children from their parents because the law mandates that children be taken away from/not housed with those who are criminally detained. In other words, criminalizing unlawful entry triggers the legal mandate to take children into separate custody facilities, thus separating thousands of children from their families.
5 The same is true for refugee policy, as Serena Parekh explains in her book, *No Refuge* (2020).

Reading Questions

1. What methodology does Wolf employ in her work? In what way is such a methodology specifically reflective of Latinx philosophy and thought?
2. What are the two kinds of gender analysis that Wolf conducts in this essay? Are they both feminist?
3. In what ways is U.S. immigration policy gendered in the first sense that Wolf describes?
4. In what ways is U.S. immigration policy gendered in the second sense that Wolf describes?
5. Do you agree with Wolf that U.S. immigration policy is not only gendered, but also unjust? Why or why not?
6. At the conclusion of her essay, Wolf suggests some other areas related to immigration justice that could be explored. What additional aspects of immigration policy in the U.S. or in the Americas more broadly do you think should be investigated further in light of her essay?
7. Wolf's focus in this essay is immigration. Describe another issue facing Latinx populations and discuss how Wolf's theoretical framework might be useful. What are possible limitations of this approach?

Part 7
Metaphilosophy

Introduction

Latinx philosophy has made innovative and significant contributions to numerous areas of inquiry. Yet although the field continues to grow, Latinxs and Latinx philosophy remain underrepresented in philosophy. These circumstances have led Latinx philosophers to examine a variety of questions about the nature and purpose of philosophy itself. These topics are metaphilosophical; that is, they are philosophical questions about philosophy itself: What is the ultimate goal of engaging in philosophy? How does philosophy differ from and relate to other fields like science, theology, or literature? What is the value of doing philosophy? How can the practice or discipline of philosophy be improved? Accordingly, the essays in this section examine, for example, whether Latinx philosophy has anything distinctively valuable to offer the world; whether there are distinctive barriers to the further development of Latinx philosophy; what relationship Latinx philosophy has to existing topics and traditions in philosophy; and how theorizing the experiences of Latinx peoples can make positive contributions outside of the academy.

The section begins with a text that recounts some of the historical roots of this metaphilosophical conversation. In "Oro del Barrio in the Cyber Age: Leapfrogging the Industrial Revolution," Tomás Atencio provides a semi-autobiographical account of the Chicano movement in northern New Mexico during the mid-20th century. This movement recognized the importance of reclaiming historical knowledge and ancestral wisdom—referred to as "el oro del barrio"—for revitalizing communities in the wake of industrialization. Atencio argues that this wisdom, which ensured both meaning and survival for Mexican Americans within a dominant U.S. industrial society, is best transmitted through intergenerational dialogue and storytelling. He envisions a future "cyber age" where advanced communication technologies are democratized, yet the wisdom and values of traditional lifeways are retained and celebrated. Atencio's work offers conceptual resources that appreciate the ways in which everyday people are engaged in practices of generating and sharing philosophical knowledge.

In "The Philosophical Gift of Brown Folks," José-Antonio Orosco takes up a related question: What is to be gained when the concerns and intuitions of Latinx communities inform philosophical investigation? The framework for this essay is an adaptation of W.E.B. Du Bois' description of the contributions of African American thought. In a similar vein, Orosco examines the contributions that Mexican American philosophy has made and can make, not only to philosophy but also to public life in the U.S. Orosco sketches a preliminary canon of Mexican American authors who provide theoretical lenses for understanding Mexican Americans' relationships to the dominant society and correcting distortions in philosophy resulting from a lack of diversity.

Carlos Alberto Sánchez, in excerpts from the 2016 essay, "Philosophy sin más?", argues for the value of reading Mexican philosophy, particularly for U.S. Latinxs who often feel alienated from the idea of "America." Although this lack of belonging may lead Latinx to experience "zozobra" or anxiety, Sánchez encourages Latinxs to confront and embrace this otherness. Drawing on the existentialist work of mid-20th-century Mexican philosophers, especially the Hyperion group, he argues that the value of Mexican philosophy lies in its distinctiveness from traditional Western philosophy and its potential to provide a blueprint for a future Latinx philosophy.

One question philosophers interested in Latinx issues have raised is: How can we transform our institutions to counteract the underrepresentation of Latinxs in professional philosophy? Alex Madva's chapter, "Implicit Bias and Latinxs in Philosophy," explores this question through the lens of social scientific research on implicit bias in education. Madva provides resources for philosophers to counteract this bias in the profession and in classrooms, and he offers some reasons to think that teaching and learning about Latinx philosophy can play an important role in directly counteracting the conditions that contribute to anti-Latinx bias.

The section ends with a warning that making progress toward these liberatory goals will require more than increasing Latinx representation in the field. In "Notes on Decolonizing Philosophy: Against Epistemic Extractivism and toward the Abolition of the Canon," Nelson Maldonado-Torres calls for a fundamental transformation in the teaching and practice of philosophy. He critiques the practice of epistemic extractivism, where social movements are theorized about in ways that do little to challenge the existing liberal order of knowledge production. Instead, he calls us to continue searching for a philosophy that is not confined by traditional academic boundaries, and which represents a return and recommitment to truly transformative philosophical thinking.

31 Oro del Barrio in the Cyber Age
Leapfrogging the Industrial Revolution

Tomás Atencio

El oro del barrio is not a product of academic philosophers. It is a name given in the 1960s to the values, wisdom, and applied knowledge that assured both meaning and survival to the Mexican American community within the dominant U.S. industrial society. El oro del barrio is both actual and imagined. It is known through the stories people tell. When people tell a story, either from their own experience or one that has been passed on to them, they often add their own reflections and interpretations. Moreover, the story unveils both memories of real activities as well as activities and images of the psyche. Psychic creations, or imagination, such as *cuentos* (stories), *mentiras* (tall tales), *chistes* (jokes), images, symbols, ceremony, and rituals, are integral parts of a community's knowledge foundations (Pacheco 1991). El oro del barrio is not, therefore, uncovered with social scientific methods; it is disclosed and understood through dialogue. The best way I can illustrate el oro del barrio and its importance to the subordinated Indohispanic society is through my own story.

I left my hometown in 1951. In my sporadic short, return visits, I noticed creeping changes in the village: roads were being paved; people with jobs in Los Alamos were building cinder-block houses; domestic water associations were bringing running water to homes; more people had automobiles. I thought nothing of these trends. In 1962 I returned permanently, settled in my ancestral village, and took a job as a child welfare worker with the New Mexico Department of Public Welfare in Rio Arriba County. Now the changes appeared ominous: the region was in the painful stages of profound transformation. Thus started my search to understand my changing homeland.

I began by ruminating on the texts and lectures I had read and heard as a student of social work, recalling episodes of the transition from an agricultural to an industrial society in eighteenth- and nineteenth-century Britain, and the ensuing social and cultural disarray. The conditions in the growing industrial cities fed by thousands of immigrants to the United States after the Civil War and the rise of social work in response to the social upheaval and suffering inflicted by industrialization lingered in my memory. I reflected on the birth of the American welfare state as a response to the Great Depression of 1929. I had lived through that in my childhood and remembered the PWA (Public Works Administration) workers who had dug latrines and built outhouses for rural villagers. As a public welfare worker, I carried out vestiges of these earlier policies.

Interestingly, I found myself in villages that had not fully made the transition to the industrial age. Yet some of them were less than twenty miles from Los Alamos, the birthplace of the nuclear age and the cradle of postindustrial society. In the 1960s, Los Alamos and the ancient pueblos and villages were at the center of this paradoxical transition. Los Alamos had grown out of the industrial age and was rapidly leading the world toward the cyber age; meanwhile, Indohispanic villagers and most Pueblo Indians had their minds and

DOI: 10.4324/9781003385417-46

souls in an agrarian society and were barely touched by industrialization. This contradiction stirred thoughts that the Indohispanic and Indian villagers had skipped industrial society and suddenly found themselves in the midst of a rapidly advancing postindustrial age. Remarkably, these preindustrial societies and their traditions had endured to the middle of the twentieth century and had given meaning and social cohesion to their communities.

The jump over the industrial epoch had deprived the natives of the era's bounties and opportunities, yet had saved them from its perils. Villagers had missed the education and training necessary to develop the skills to succeed in an industrial society, but they had kept their culture intact. Ironically, for some villagers Los Alamos provided an employment substitute in the absence of an industrial economy. Welfare afforded a marginal but stable economic prop yet eroded the moral fiber of the community; it became industrial society's predominant legacy to New Mexico's villagers.

One villager and itinerant laborer often repeated to me his analysis of welfare, reasoning that it had introduced canned foods and dried milk to its recipients, which had caused homemakers to abandon homegrown foods and vegetables. Homemakers not receiving public assistance, he complained, were lured to this lifestyle as well, which placed an economic burden on the breadwinner who was still farming. Operating as he was from a male and subsistence agricultural perspective, my friend might not have had all the facts, but his analysis made sense. Women, too, had their say. Taxed to the limits of their time and energy in running households from the products of the land and doing farm chores when their husbands left the village for itinerant labor, homemakers sought relief wherever they could find it. In reality, families gained very few financial resources through wage labor. For some, welfare was the only source of cash in the village itself. As time passed, subsistence agriculture declined; concurrently, Indohispanic villagers were drawn into consumption and debt; many sold their homes and land because they needed the money, or just abandoned their inheritance and moved to the cities.

The modernization trend introduced by the railroad in the 1880s and accelerated by itinerant labor away from home and welfare at home made money a necessity but did not provide it through market avenues in the villages themselves. The New Mexico *manito* cultural enclave entered the modern age in the 1930s as an impoverished region,[1] a description the natives found unacceptable. It was a putdown. They did not see themselves as poor: they were living according to their traditions, which were threatened by a modernizing society. Within this changing society, the native wisdom and applied knowledge prevailed and the culture endured. This body of knowledge was not written down, it was not systematic; it lived in the people's memories and everyday life activities. As I was privileged to learn this knowledge by listening to people's stories, I pondered whether and how this wisdom could be applied in a society that was just emerging, a society that would otherwise have nothing to guide it but industrial-age values and institutions controlled by its dominant actors. Village culture had endured because industrial institutions and values had skipped over the northern New Mexican cultural enclave.

The homeland I found upon my return home was indeed a different place. My personal and professional vocation was forged by this awareness; my work, as I saw it, was to try and soften the blow to those caught in the vortex of change, and at the same time to rescue the subjugated knowledge that had sustained the community and had given meaning to its people living in an "agri-cultural" settlement within a predominantly industrial society.

In 1968, the counterculture movement discovered the villages. A wise Hispano elder observed that this was the "last invasion of the Anglo. After this," he cautioned, "we will no longer have claim over New Mexico as our homeland." He was right. People sold their land as if they were selling to a relative or village neighbor: below market value. Our inheritance was in fact placed on the marketplace, and soon its value as real estate escalated beyond most natives' reach.[2]

By the 1990s, money channeled into the villages from Los Alamos employment had raised the income levels of many families, transforming a subsistence economy to a wage-earning consumer economy based on a different set of values and thus creating personal and cultural tensions.[3] The postindustrial cultural fallout of Los Alamos onto the manito homeland had triggered a deadly social cancer: drugs. Other postindustrial phenomena, such as Indian gaming, have also entered the region, inflicting both direct and collateral social and cultural damage on Indohispanics and Native Americans while bringing income to the impoverished Pueblo community. Landownership among Indohispanic villagers has drastically decreased during the past two decades, changing the appearance and complexion of the historic settlements.

In launching my vocation, I unconsciously drew from all my experiences and formal education. In my training as a caseworker, I had completed part of my practicum at the Reiss-Davis Child Guidance Clinic in Los Angeles, California, under the tutelage of a psychoanalyst trained in Europe before World War.II.[4] After working as a child-welfare caseworker for a year and a half in northern New Mexico, I became a community mental health consultant. Gradually, I turned away from casework to community organization, then known also as community development.

I worked in community organizing for many years but never identified my work or its theoretical underpinnings with any school. Undoubtedly, my social work training influenced my direction. I recall saying very early in my career that community development was not physical development; rather, it was an undertaking to bring people together around shared concerns, values, and visions to enhance one another's lives and to reach toward meaning and plenitude. Community, in other words, provides individuals with meaningful and authentic social security, builds the foundations for a more democratic and humane physical environment, and allows its members to take on a larger and more effective role in public service and social and political action.

In searching for that sense of community in northern New Mexico villages, I found that the social linkages that had kept the community alive were rapidly disintegrating. The extended family had collapsed along with correlated values of solidarity and reciprocity. The only apparently viable social institution left was the *acequia* and its decision-making body, *la comisión*. An acequia is a gravity-flow irrigation canal whose origins are in the Middle East. I focused on the acequia as creating a "community of interest"—a group with common interests and shared needs—which I used as a strategy for organizing.[5] The acequia worked well as an example of a community of interest because active participants in the organization were driven by the shared need for irrigation water to sustain family subsistence farming. On the sociopolitical side of the equation, the *comisión de acequia*, in fact, was a living example of village democracy that made possible peaceful negotiations over the distribution of water, a precious resource in an arid region. From then on, I looked for visions, needs, concerns, grievances, or interests that people shared with one another, all social characteristics of the acequia, in order to identify other communities of interest. Then I assessed what external forces and personal motives might prompt individuals to come together to affirm themselves and protest impediments to their quality of life. The "community of interest" is the first stage in this process. The second stage uses dialogue to deepen the community of interest's understanding of its shared concerns and visions and to discern possible pathways toward common goals and strategies for resisting obstacles to freedom and fulfillment. This process I initially called the "community of solution"; I now call it the "community in dialogue." In "community in action," the third stage, the "community of interest" acts on the knowledge, understanding, and elevated consciousness attained through dialogue.

In addition to the community of interest's legacy as an organizing tool, it also inspired a spiral of thought and action through dialogue and reflection on the action embedded in the individual and community stories. In short, this process leads to a new awareness and respond-ability. The ability to respond implies that action and reflection also foster the commitment, courage, and fortitude to respond to the revelations that occur in this new awareness.

I propose this logic for confronting the challenges of the cyber age. Its conclusion or goal is the revitalization of our community; the path toward that end is reclaiming el oro del barrio, the knowledge of our historical experience as well as the values and wisdom of our ancestors.

La Resolana and el Oro del Barrio

Here is a little history of la resolana and el oro del barrio, the context in which they were thought up and thought out, and their place within the emerging cyber age: In the late fifties, while a college student absorbed in the Socratic dialogues, I wondered whether other cultures and societies used dialogue to find meaning in their lived experience and understanding of their ultimate commitments. I was especially interested in my own heritage as an Indohispanic villager from northern New Mexico. Did our men come together as Socrates and the Sophists had done at the agora, to talk with one another and artfully spar to unmask rhetoric, unveil truth, and reflect on the meaning of their everyday lives? I found no parallels. There was, however, one place where men gathered to talk on sunny fall, winter, and spring days. It was known as la resolana. La resolana is the space defined by the south wall of a building that is shielded from the east and west winds, where the sun reflecting off the wall creates a place of warmth, light, and tranquility. In that place, men have gathered across the years to pass the time of day, exchange good and bad news, gossip, share jokes, and also talk about everyday life, about birth, and about death; they have told stories and shared memories of the past and have pondered the future. In la resolana there was no Socrates, a master at asking questions and fostering dialogue; instead, whoever was most knowledgeable on the subject at hand illuminated and guided the discussion. The counterparts to the Sophists were not the trained teachers in the village who promoted progressive cultural trends; rather, they were tradition-bound *pícaros* (men who survived by their wits), who were moored in agrarian society and lamented the changes that eventually would do away with la resolana and their lifeways.[6] While la resolana obviously originated as an activity of men in a patriarchal society, the process of resolana need not be restricted to males and in fact has not been in its subsequent development.

I did not mention my insight, or fantasy, to anyone for fear I would be charged with intellectual blasphemy for comparing a peasant gathering place in northern New Mexico to the enlightened Athenian agora or Plato's Academy. Yet, from time to time I reflected on the idea. Upon my return from schooling in social work, the vision of la resolana as a possible Indohispanic village parallel to the Athenian models resurfaced.

The possibilities for developing a reinterpreted and formalized resolana rested on an understanding of the culture, its values, and its ways of transmitting knowledge, information, and wisdom. I used my social work position to gain this understanding. As a social worker in a traditional Indohispanic rural area, I listened to the people's stories of the changes in the region and how these were affecting the intimate and spiritual relationship they had with the place where they were born and had lived all their lives. Most of these elderly folks had already reared their children, a good number of whom had left and settled somewhere else, mainly in California, Utah, Colorado, or Albuquerque. A few offspring remained in the villages and commuted anywhere from twenty to a hundred miles to jobs in Los Alamos. Among people I visited I found storytellers, *cuentistas*, who not only told of their immediate experiences but shared stories from the past, folktales, and folk songs. Almost everyone used *refranes* or *dichos*, proverbs or aphorisms, to make a point with a phrase of distilled wisdom. Often they coined their own sayings to express their most profound and meaningful beliefs. *Querencia*, the "meaning of place," for example, would be expressed, "De aquí no me salgo porque tengo que tener un lugar donde caer muerto" (I will not leave because I need a place to die). This was an elderly couple's response to my naive question whether they would ever move from the village to live with one of their children. In essence this phrase speaks of the people's tie to the earth in life and in death. It reveals their profound attachment to the earth, which in turn, disclosed its mysteries to them. Land and people were mutually ensouled, a phenomenon Theodore Abt calls "participation mystique" (Abt 1989: 255–267).[7]

Listening to stories helped me understand individual perceptions about life, but I also detected a collective undercurrent, a collective consciousness or perhaps collective unconscious, that told of a people's shared beliefs and views about life. These conversations also revealed the knowledge and skills they used in everyday life to survive.

Life was *entre verde y seco*: it had its hills and valleys. Significantly, these stories highlighted the contradictions in northern New Mexico as well as the tensions and the quest for balance in everyday life; these stories fueled the development of la resolana and el oro del barrio.

The more I listened to people's life histories, the more I connected with my father's tales, which had lulled me to sleep when I was a child. I remembered some of them, but I felt the need for details. I had grown up with a father who was born in 1876, twenty-four years before the turn of the twentieth century; his father had been born in 1838, when New Mexico was part of present-day Mexico. My father's stories about his own life and about his father's and his father's father's connected with a lineage that stretched 150 years into the past and beyond. My father's only surviving brother, Eliseo, was in his late sixties. He had never married, lived alone, and refused to connect electricity to his modest home; he had no running water and had never owned an automobile. He preferred the preindustrial age. He had been a subsistence farmer and itinerant farmworker all his life. He was truly a peasant. One day I walked over to his place and sat on a bench in his room, which served as receiving room, kitchen, and library; he sat on the edge of his bed. I asked him about my grandfather's stories that my father had shared with me; he begged off, saying he had been born twenty-some years after my father and had missed most of those cuentos. Then he reached under his bed, pulled out a leather pouch, and drew from it a neat collection of old documents, stacked and folded in half. "But I have these," he said. They were the "Atencio papers" from the Atencio ancestral home.

I leafed through the fragile papers. The oldest was dated 1776, one hundred years before my father was born and as old as the United States. They were last wills and testaments, deeds of property transfer, and receipts dating up until the 1920s. Apparently, after my grandfather Noberto died, the addition of new documents had ceased. My uncle gave them to me with the understanding that they belonged to the Atencio heirs.

It was a sunny, unusually calm March day. I left my uncle's place and walked back to my home about a mile away. I had to pass by *la plaza*, the site of the main resolana in the village. Some *resolaneros* were chatting there,[8] and I was invited to join them. One asked what I had in the paper sack—my uncle had not given me the satchel. I pulled out the papers. "No me han de creer lo que me dio mi tío Eliseo" (You won't believe what my uncle gave me). The men gathered around while we tried to decipher the ancient classic Spanish script. That activity spun off conversations that lasted until the sun sank behind the black mesa to the west and what was left of the day turned chilly, causing the men to disperse.

In la resolana that day the resolaneros told stories of their families and reminisced about similar papers stored somewhere in the attics of their parents' homes. Others told how documents had been lost or trashed. Most significant for my journey, the papers spurred conversations beyond the relaxed chatter, bringing other themes to the fore, as other activities in the village sometimes did as well. La resolana in my native village that day confirmed the possibilities of resolana, the concept I had envisioned a decade before. Plato's Academy had found its counterpart in la resolana Chicana, with modifications, of course.[9]

A few years later the Chicano movement exploded in the streets of Denver, Los Angeles, and other urban centers, in land grant activism in New Mexico, in farmworkers organizing from Texas and California to Ohio. There were school walkouts in major cities. These events gave rise to Chicano studies as a university discipline. I was then at the University of Colorado, directing a program for migrant workers. Although there is much to say about that experience in relation to the application of the community of interest model, my concern here is with the idea of Chicano studies in universities. Here we are, I mused, missed by an educational system that equipped people for industrial society, and when we are at the threshold of a postindustrial world, the university offers us the ideological drippings of its industrial legacy (Atencio 1971: 262–265).

Fortuitously, the rise of the Chicano movement coincided with a growth in writings about the future and the impact of technology on society and culture. I found the writings on technological progress relevant to the future of Chicanos. Lewis Mumford wrote in *The Myth of the Machine* that technological progress would directly affect traditional societies by destroying or burying the knowledge derived from those peoples' life experiences. Robert Theobald warned in "The Cybernation Revolution" that automation would affect the distribution of income through employment, recommending that we must develop a new "human and constitutional right—the right to an income." He also called for a new social ethic generated from within the community rather than one imposed from above. This suggested to me that we must develop values and institutions appropriate to the coming cyber age rather than embracing remnants from industrial society. In *The Technological Society* (1967), Jacques Ellul warned, "Man has lost all contact with his natural framework. He cannot pierce the shell of technology to find again the ancient milieu to which he was adapted for hundreds of thousands of years" (Mumford 1970: 10; Theobald 1964: 5; Ellul 1967: 428).

If these futurists were right, why should we Chicanos want access to the waning industrial society? Why should we not prepare ourselves for a direct transition from a preindustrial to a postindustrial age? Why not offer our traditional, preindustrial institutions, values, and ways of knowing and learning as guides and models for the postindustrial age?[10] I saw the emerging field of Chicano studies in the context of these questions, but I could not envision the university system responding to them and empowering Chicano studies to address them. At that point in my life I saw the establishment of Chicano studies as condescending and, from the Indohispanic vantage point, as a maneuver, the co-optation of a valuable resource. The university was not giving us much, but through Chicano studies it was introducing its students to another civilization: the mestizo, with its legacy anchored in Arabic Spain and pre-Columbian America. Why not bring along its long-subjugated body of knowledge?

It seemed the right time to launch a process corresponding to Plato's Academy, to build a knowledge base from the Chicano experience, paralleling at a different level of conceptualization and action what the Athenians had done in their golden era. I returned to my hometown of Dixon (La Plaza del Embudo), New Mexico, and with others interpreted and created a "new resolana."[11] The collaborators came together under an organization known as La Academia de Aztlán, later renamed La Academia de la Nueva Raza, a name that claimed the Western intellectual legacy (in the adoption of "Academia") and incorporated the idea of a new humanity. The quest for a new humanity was both a vision and a vocation. In naive arrogance and ignorance of the enormous and uncertain task ahead, we proposed to build a body of knowledge from the stories and folklore of the Mexican American—Chicano—people in the Southwest. We would create an alternative educational process that would uncover and compile knowledge as well as raise and expand consciousness. This process would validate our own experience as a basis for knowledge and prepare us for the challenges of the postindustrial age.

As La Academia was evolving I also was an occasional consultant on Chicano-related programs to the National Institute of Mental Health (NIMH). With the same theme in mind of building an autochthonous body of knowledge, I proposed that Chicano mental health programs create a body of knowledge from the culture's history and the everyday life experiences of Chicanos. This knowledge could inform strategies for reaching out to the community with preventive services and also contribute to the development of culturally appropriate therapeutic models.

The name el oro del barrio had not yet become part of my vocabulary. But because of my occasional work with the NIMH, I was recommended as a consultant to a barrio mental health program in San Antonio, Texas, then under the San Antonio Unity Council. In that role I was a learner as well as a teacher. The project introduced me to the idea of el oro de barrio. *Barrio*, which means neighborhood, had often been talked of by some observers with derision and seen as the source of the social problems in the Mexican American community. The young activists in San Antonio turned this attitude around and offered the hidden gems of knowledge, wisdom, rituals, and beliefs in the barrio and its culture as the healing source for their social and psychological ills. Their idea that the healing could come from the community and culture—that *la cultura cura* (culture heals)—was a perfect fit with the goals and ongoing work of La Academia.

With the project's staff approval, I appropriated the term el oro del barrio for La Academia. At the same time, Academia efforts, which had been focused on northern New Mexico, expanded to San Antonio. Under the leadership of Tito Villalobos Moreno, a musician-composer-arranger, and Jesús "Chista" Cantú, an artist, who were collaborating with barrio mental health worker José María "Chema" Saenz and several artists, La Academia de la Nueva Raza en San Antonio was organized.

The concepts of la resolana and el oro del barrio came together. The gold of the neighborhood, reflected in the bright sun of our dialogues, became the currency of knowledge building and consciousness raising. The body of knowledge uncovered in and by la resolana was the people's story, their wisdom, beliefs, values, reflections, joys, sorrows, ceremony and ritual, as well as practical and applied knowledge. The stories and their content became el oro del barrio, and the process keeps evolving as it is applied to diverse experiences.

The Chicano Movement and La Academia de la Nueva Raza

My initial concern that Chicano studies would not respond to the need for an autochthonous body of knowledge did not prove universally true. Chicanos studies programs at UCLA, Berkeley, and California State University at Northridge, as well as the Chicano Fellows at Stanford University moved rapidly in this direction. Chicano colleges built on the existing university model yet committed to alternative learning and indigenous knowledge sprouted throughout the country. The alternative education movement spread among Chicano activists, who challenged the theory and practice as well as the social arrangements of the mainstream learning experience. Moreover, the Chicano movement developed a strong cultural front. The most visible and effective groups were, in some cases still are, El Teatro Campesino, Centro Cultural de la Raza in San Diego, Con-Safos in Los Angeles and San Antonio, the Royal Chicano Air Force (RCAF) in Sacramento, and Octavio Romano's Tonatiuh International and Quinto Sol Publications. Within this cultural movement, La Academia de la Nueva Raza carved out the role and task of recovering and refining el oro del barrio as the basis for cultivating a Chicano consciousness and creating a relevant body of knowledge.[12]

Although there are other approaches to understanding the Chicano movement, I suggest the movement was both driven by and drawn by an emerging ethnic and class consciousness. The origin of the term *Chicano* tells of its relationship to ethnicity and class. Diego Vigil wrote in "Marx and Chicano Anthropology" that the word Chicano originated with the Spanish conquerors' pronunciation of the *x* in *Mexica* as *ch*—hence, Mechica or Mechicano. *Mexica* was used in the colonial period as a descriptor for all Aztec lower classes (Vigil 1978: 21). Ernesto Galarza, a scholar and activist, used to say that Mexican Indian peasants immigrating to this country during the Mexican Revolution were referred to as Chicanos, a term of derision. In the movement, Chicano identity emphasized for mestizos the Indian part of their Indohispanic mixed heritage.[13]

Chicanos found their indigenous roots in Aztlán, a mythical place in the region of the Four Corners, where New Mexico, Arizona, Utah, and Colorado come together and whence supposedly originated the Aztecs, who ended up in Tenochtitlán, now Mexico City. The road to Aztlán was the Chicanos' pathway to a homeland—a place both mythic and real to which they could anchor their identity as Indios. The term had political implications as well, for the region of Aztlán also constituted the central part of the southwestern United States, which was annexed from Mexico in the settlement of the Mexican War in 1848. Chicanos were, in theory, reclaiming a captured homeland that also happened to be the cradle of their Indian ethnicity (Mares 1973).

La Academia de la Nueva Raza interfaced with the Chicano movement's quest to recover what had been lost to Mexican Americans. Its vision was to create a new humanity out of the pathos that we and our ancestors have endured as strangers in our own land, and out of the faith that sustained our culture and us. In the face of uncertainty in a world bent on unfettered competition in the marketplace, global political conflict between the haves and the have-nots, the clash of cultures, and gross environmental degradation in the name of progress and technological advancement, we accepted the distant dream of La Nueva Raza.

In forging this new humanity, Academia cofounder Luis Jaramillo declared a

> belief in the mystery of man because we refuse to accept a destiny that is not ours to forge.... La Nueva Raza is both a vocation and a dream.... The vocation to bring about that which is beyond the ethnic and beyond poor and rich. For now we are ethnic,

mestizos, mulattos, and like others with a similar legacy, we must become the 'new cornerstone for democracy.'

(Jaramillo 1971b)[14]

Reaching for La Nueva Raza, Jaramillo argues, is a cultural evolutionary process. Robert Wright, a science writer, and Luis Jaramillo tread parallel paths. Both perceive evolution as a branch of science, but they also see it as a process with purpose, with direction. For Jaramillo the direction is toward La Nueva Raza. Wright is interested in the idea that evolution can be directed by consciousness in living bodies, laying a burden as well as a challenge on the human species to guarantee its own survival (Wright 2000). Both reflect the thinking of Pierre Teilhard de Chardin.

Pierre Teilhard de Chardin (1881–1955), a French Jesuit priest and paleontologist, believed in biological evolution and also that there is an evolution of a collective body of thought. In his introduction to Teilhard de Chardin's *The Phenomenon of Man*, Sir Julian Huxley summarizes this idea as follows: "The incipient development of mankind into a single psychosocial unit, with a single noosystem, or common pool of thought, is providing the evolutionary process with the rudiments of a head." He adds, "It remains for our descendants to organize this global noosystem more adequately, so as to enable mankind to understand the process of evolution on earth more fully and to direct it more adequately" (Huxley 1965). Evolution at its next level will lead toward the unity of humankind.

Teilhard de Chardin and Jaramillo offer optimistic outlooks, but neither the noosphere—that is, the development of a common pool of thought—nor La Nueva Raza is assured. These are visions of what the world can be and where it is logically headed. As Wright says, "it is the logic of human destiny" (Wright 2000). It is up to the "head"—humans—to direct the evolution to the next sphere. This should be our vocation, our commitment to ensuring the survival of the human species (Huxley 1965).

Wright's work distills Teilhard de Chardin's vision to the notion that societies and cultures have endured, as has nature, because there are no absolute winners or absolute losers among the contenders for survival. Everybody, every cell, every living thing, wins and also loses in a nonzero-sum game. The opposite would be a zero-sum environment where some win while the others lose; there evolution would stop and life would eventually cease.

Those of us involved in La Academia recognized that the cyber revolution would create both opportunities and perils that could either advance the noosystem and guide evolution toward La Nueva Raza or destroy the global ecological and political balance. The most terrifying possibility is a human maladaptation to the cyber age in which some win and others lose, as occurs in the global free market. Community as the source of authentic and meaningful social security is an example of a nonzero-sum approach. Such a way allows for sharing of resources, of meaning; it entails embracing the values of cooperation, sharing, and respect for others.

Turning to philosophy has been logical and natural for La Academia and its legacy, for the biggest challenges of this transformation impelled by technological advances are moral and spiritual. Asociados of La Academia recognized this, as did many Chicano cultural activists. Among them were those who followed the teachings of Maestro Andrés Segura. Maestro Andrés, a Nahuatl spiritual leader, came to the United States from Mexico to assist Chicanos in their journey back to Aztlán. The vision and logic of La Nueva Raza, although derived from Western thought, had a parallel, we realized, in the ideas of this Mexican spiritual leader.[15]

The wisdom of the ancients, as exemplified by Segura, may be invoked as we struggle toward a nonzero-sum world. It teaches that we must look at the other person as our other self. In Mayan this is expressed *in lah kech: tu eres mi otro yo*. A similar belief in Judeo-Christian doctrine is "love thy neighbor as thyself." La resolana and el oro del barrio are pathways toward La Nueva Raza, the dreams, visions, and aspirations of a common pool of thought, a nonzero-sum society.

El Oro del Barrio and the Future

Although Chicanos generally missed industrial society's opportunities and benefits, that loss strengthened the Mexican American community's resolve to survive. El oro del barrio was in part responsible for that strength of mind and will. It is in family solidarity, reciprocity, respect, courage, honor, and *vergüenza* (moral sensibility); in *la vida buena y sana* (a life of health, wholeness, and well-being) and *herbolarios/as* and *curanderas/os* (traditional healers); in spirituality, ceremony, ritual, faith, and belief in mystery; in querencia (sense of place); in the viability of the economics of frugality, a commitment to self-reliance, and a work ethic that was not tied to employment; in fiesta; in humor; in the virtue of working the land; and in the value of harmony with nature. Most important, el oro del barrio carries the consciousness and meaning of sharing and of community; it encompasses the nonzero-sum idea and its practice.

My challenge has been to interpret these cultural vestiges and to demonstrate their value and utility in a postindustrial age, while heeding Alvin Toffler's warning not to invent "a fake romantic past in our rush to judge the present" (Toffler 1980: 137). I arrived at my interpretation by going back to my early days as a social worker and by reflecting on my conversations with my uncle.

That spring when I got the Atencio documents I had another significant conversation with Tío Eliseo.[16] I sought advice on planting chile and corn. His response was a question: "¿Y 'onde vas agarrar la semilla?" Where was I going to get the seed? I told him, "from an old lard bucket in la despensa [the storeroom], left there by my father at least eight years ago, five years before he died."

"You are fortunate," he said, "because those are native seeds. Son del maíz concho y el chile nativo." He advised me never to use Las Cruces seeds; they are made in laboratories and are not attuned to the seasons. (Las Cruces is the home of New Mexico State University and a center of agricultural research.) "Only the native seeds can adapt to climatic changes," he explained.

He went on to say that the seasons would change in New Mexico around the turn of the coming century, and we would be better prepared if we had native seeds. I was startled by his explanation! Forty years later I am amazed by the accuracy of his predictions.

I listened intently and pondered whether some things of the past would be well suited to deal with a world of climatic changes and uncertainty. As he explained the old ways, Tío Eliseo lamented the changes, pointing out that we were losing our language; that farming—people raising their own food—was also declining. He also talked about the loss of respect and trust in family and community relations. This loss has weakened the core of community. "Ya no hay respeto, ni tampoco hay palabra de hombre" (There is neither respect nor honor in man's word). "In the future," he said,

> We are going to have to live as we lived in the past, when food went from the earth to the kitchen without going through a store. This was possible because the family members

worked and lived together. We will return to those ways—when we have to trust each other, work together, and help each other—because "science" will destroy itself and send us to the past. It is destroying nature, the way things are intended to be. We have to save what we can. Start with the seeds.

This made sense: everything starts with a seed of one kind or another. Seeds sustain and ensure the cycle of life.

Tío Eliseo's perspective was not without theoretical or academic support. Lewis Mumford wrote,

Western man not merely blighted in some degree every culture that he touched, whether 'primitive' or advanced, but he also robbed his own descendants of countless gifts of art and craftsmanship, as well as precious knowledge passed on only by word of mouth that disappeared with the dying languages of dying peoples.

Referring to Westerners' colonization and technological progress, Mumford adds, "Western man . . . would have been far more successful had he paid closer attention to the cultures he disrupted and destroyed; for in wrecking them he was reducing his own intellectual working capital" (Mumford 1970: 10, 19).

Writing about the end of the industrial era, Robert Theobald has called for new values and institutions for the postindustrial age:

The goals of the industrial era are obsolete. We can no longer afford to strive for maximum economic growth. To do so will worsen water, land, and environmental problems; increase unemployment because of the job-replacement effects of computers and robots; and make the rich countries even more dependent on Third World countries for energy and raw materials.

(Theobald 1981: xvii)

Theobald was not touting preindustrial modes of life; he was saying we must build institutions appropriate for this coming age because we cannot rely on the institutions and values of the industrial age. Unfortunately, the cyber age is driven by industrial-age values and organized around its institutions. A real concern is that, with America's triumph in the Cold War and its military might, industrial-age capitalism is being adapted to the cyber age, and thus interconnecting the globe but ignoring the need for regulation and contributing to the destruction of traditional societies. Western, or U.S.–style, globalism is zero-sum: one party wins while the other loses.

In its absence of regulation and zero-sum posturing, postindustrial capitalism mimics nineteenth-century unregulated industrial phenomena. The challenge we face is enormous. The peasant reaction to unregulated capitalism in the nineteenth century turned into fascism; in the industrial working class it resulted in Marxism or communism. Out of that also emerged the more benign welfare state, which came to an end with the rise of the cyber age. For years futurists have predicted that the "third wave," in Alvin Toffler's terms, will bring a rise of tribalism and retribalization, terrorism, and other modes of defense by the defenseless in the face of the unlimited power of an unbridled global free-market economy and the exploitation of natural resources—oil and other energy sources—in "underdeveloped" countries.[17] The next encounter on this global economic freeway is certain to be the clash of civilizations. For rather than tempering its global free-market posture, the United

States has embarked on a course that would remake the rest of the world into its image of human progress.[18]

In the United States, the middle class is vanishing. This is evident in the displacement of traditional industrial workers, who must seek new employment in the knowledge and service sectors. The former requires additional training and education; the latter generally offers lower-paying, unstable jobs without benefits. Immigrants, both legal and illegal, hold many of these latter jobs. More poignant is the great number of single mothers holding two jobs to support their children and provide the basics and still unable to afford child care or health insurance (Ehrenreich 2001). We must heed the wisdom of sages like my Tío Eliseo and futurists such as Mumford and Theobald.

Technology and el Oro del Barrio

An important emblem of the cyber age is the computer and its impact on society and culture. Information technology is rapidly changing the occupational patterns that had become institutionalized in industrial society. The blue-collar industrial worker is disappearing in the face of technological advances. Instead of factory workers, society now calls for knowledge workers who must be adequately prepared to hold new occupations. And the word is that preparation is not a one-time effort. Learning must continue in order for the worker to keep up with the changes in the world. There is no class distinction among the knowledge workers; rather, they are "uniclass," even if some make more money than others (Drucker 1994: 25). Knowledge professionals are generally defined by key components of postindustrial society: information and media technology, globalization, and medical and biotechnology. These knowledge-related professions range from traditional ones such as medicine and law, to the sciences and engineering, software, business, banking, finance and management, higher education, media management, and transportation. Eventually the uniclass will develop into the dominant social class, but it will not be the large middle class of the industrial age; it will be a smaller upper class. The lower classes will probably start where the middle class used to be and scale downward to the service workers, the working poor, the poorly educated, and the single parents formerly supported by the welfare state. The unemployable will be the destitute, homeless, ill, or disabled.

. . . The assertion that codified theoretical knowledge is central to postindustrial society does not invalidate traditional and everyday life knowledge. We must assert the value of indigenous and traditional knowledge in everyday life. We must also be vigilant about who or what controls and defines knowledge and wary of attempts to subjugate particular types of knowledge and their keepers.[19] These brief narratives demonstrate the urgency to develop the appropriate institutions and values that will make the transition to the cyber age more peaceful, just, and civil. We are at the threshold of a dark new age.

How can el oro del barrio play a role in this gargantuan task? If Tío Eliseo were alive today, I would sit on the same old bench and thank him for teaching me about the nurturance of life expressed in the logic of nature and in the ability of the old seeds to adapt to climatic changes. I would also discuss present realities.

"Yes, Tío, you are right," I would say, "We must not lose our language; we must reclaim our ways, in which people had vergüenza; children respected their elders; and people respected life and each other, and valued cooperation, trust, and a strong community. We should restore the faith of our ancestors, their ways of health and wholeness, and work with the natural balance in nature to live una vida buena y sana y alegre. We need to question the use of genetically altered seeds. We must preserve water for agriculture and oppose making it a commodity. And we need to be aware of the limitations of modern science and be cognizant that technology cannot solve all our problems, including the ones it might create. Yet, we must also honor the fact that science has contributed immensely to our understanding of nature and to human well-being."

What we need is a way of looking at life, a philosophy, that gives ultimate value to the sanctity of life and protects it so that it can continue. Some years back, my wife, Consuelo, and I were searching our memories for a phrase that describes a state of total well-being, where one feels content, healthy, and whole. Consuelo came up with the descriptive phrase and concept that our people use: bueno y sano.

The concept of una vida buena y sana has undergone considerable reflection and dialogue since I first suggested it as an ethic for the postindustrial society. Since then we have discovered in the folklore the concept of *alegría* (happiness) as part of la vida buena y sana. We now say "la vida buena y sana y alegre," a life of health, wholeness, well-being, and happiness (Atencio 1991).

One of the greatest social impacts of industrialization on agricultural communities has been the division of labor and the creation of individual employment outside the home, which has had the effect of severing production from consumption. People no longer farm and consume their own food; today they are only consumers. This has altered the family in many ways. The nuclear family has replaced the extended family, and numerous institutions have assumed the roles of community. The values of reciprocity and the consciousness of sharing and community solidarity have been distorted or replaced by individualism and competition. The practice of helping one another has been institutionalized through tax codes and organized charities. The values of honor, trust, and vergüenza have been replaced by contracts and legal agreements. Natural ways of health and healing have been largely ignored or belittled by modern medicine. Community as the source of meaningful and authentic social security has begun to crumble. The game has been changing from a nonzero-sum to a zero-sum approach in which some are absolute winners while others are absolute losers.

From a strictly pragmatic viewpoint, the primary reason for seeking guidance from preindustrial values, institutions, and ways of living—the major thrust of this essay—is that industrialization has disabled or distorted many traditional values and their corresponding institutions. I suggest using el oro del barrio and adopting the concept, vision, and practice of una vida buena y sana y alegre—a life of health, wholeness, well-being, and happiness—to reclaim the values of human dignity, justice, sharing, and respect for nature and to foster a balance between human values and science and technology. El oro del barrio holds vestiges of wisdom that are still vital in many cultures around the world, a treasure that needs to be recognized. It is time to uncover those life-sustaining cultural beliefs and practices and apply them in reenergizing our communities: the future may be yesterday.

La Resolana: A Pathway Toward a Learning Society for the Cyber Age

As we open our minds and hearts to spiritual and moral ideals, we also must seek practical avenues to confront the challenges of the cyber age. The vision of a learning society made up of learning communities can be used as an overarching concept for responding to the requirements of the cyber age. The learning society is a strategy for making learning and the uncovering and building of knowledge ubiquitous in everyday life; its two fundamental goals are cognitive learning and consciousness raising. The first entails learning how to use our minds critically to acquire knowledge and practical human skills appropriate for everyday life and especially to meet the technological requirements of the cyber age. The principal skill demanded by the cyber age is a literacy that extends beyond traditional literacy to include technology, information, health, legal, economic, media, ecological, and global literacy (Kist 2004, especially chapter six). It takes into account not only the cognitive aspects of learning, but also the total field and experience within which the individual lives and moves. Consciousness raising, on the other hand, provides a new awareness of the challenges of the cyber age. These two components of the learning society bear the fruit of a "new awareness with respond-ability" (Atencio 1988).

In La Academia de la Nueva Raza the idea of a learning society grew out of our examination of and reflection on everyday life in traditional New Mexican villages.[20]

From the stories of traditional people, ideas of a new literacy and of consciousness raising emerge. We discovered that individuals learned by doing daily tasks. Young men learned how to butcher animals under the supervision of experienced men. Young men and women learned anatomy as they prepared the animal parts. As the young were carrying out their tasks, they were instructed on the meaning and importance of certain procedures: "Mucho cuidado con la hiel, si quebras la vejiga se contamina la carne. Córtale el nervio en la pierna pa' que se ablande la carne." (Be very careful with the bile, if you puncture the gallbladder, you'll spoil the meat. Cut the nerve in the thigh so that the muscles relax and the meat softens.) And so went the instruction.

Young women learned to deliver babies by apprenticing under experienced midwives. They learned to plaster with mud, make *hornos* (adobe ovens), and weave cloth through observation and practice.

Beliefs, ceremony, and rituals were passed on to young men through the Penitente society, a lay religious brotherhood (Chavez 1981: 45).[21] They learned the doctrine and ethical commitments by actively participating in prayers, hymns, rituals, and service to the Penitente brotherhood and their families. Young women learned the rites, rituals, prayers, and hymns through participation in female religious societies. They got their practical knowledge about the use of herbs for health and well-being as well as cooking from parents and mentors.

Storytelling was the primary way of passing on life lessons, knowledge, values, norms, and moral guideposts. We believe there is a strong parallel between this traditional educational model and the new model arising out of the needs of a postindustrial society.

So the young learned to understand their everyday life experiences and their culture while incorporating a body of knowledge and traditional values and norms. It occurred to me that if one were to place a canopy over a traditional New Mexican village, one would have a school, a learning community where the skills and knowledge necessary to sustain and give meaning to life in that particular society were taught experientially. Learning and doing were inseparable: one did and thereby one learned. Conversation and reflection usually took place between activities, and the next time the same task was performed an opportunity to apply compounded knowledge from the first experience was created. A growing body of knowledge emerged from such experiences.

This insight brought to mind Paulo Freire's praxis learning.[22] In the educational institutions of industrial society, learning has become separated from practice. And once knowledge has been severed from practice, learning becomes the mere transference of information from those who have it to those who do not. Learning and knowledge have thus become isolated from each other and from action, yet they mesh with each other, like cogs in the industrial wheel.

The idea of a learning society took a leap into the policy arena as I began to ponder the fate of the welfare state—an industrial-epoch institution that some were beginning to call learnfare because of its emphasis on training for jobs—in postindustrial society. Most compassionate individuals would agree that some form of the welfare state, or at least its safety-net aspects, must endure for those who fall through the cracks in a market economy. Theobald's idea of the right to an income accompanied by a comprehensive health-care system would be a perfect fit. It seemed to me that as social policy was turning away from the welfare state, the prudent response would be to implement a guaranteed income and a single-payer health-care program and move toward a learning society. The government would make a full commitment to ensure its citizenry would have the opportunity to become technologically literate, especially in media technology. It would also prepare the populace in the use of appropriate (low-tech) and affordable technology that sustains a healthy environment. Such a learning society would also emphasize the arts and humanities. Learning processes such as dialogue would be used to uncover and reclaim subjugated autochthonous and historical knowledge. In addition, the arts and humanities would inspire the psyche, sharpen the mind, and open the pathway to creativity and innovation, the driving forces in a knowledge-based society. Ultimately, this would contribute toward a new awareness and an expanded consciousness. Such a policy, if implemented, would make the general population fully literate.

Recognizing that political economy is not part of the market equation, I realize the idea of a state-supported learning society is utopian. Nonetheless, the idea of a learning society driven by experiential learning seemed like a logical approach for reclaiming the self-reliance of preindustrial society, thus filling the gap left by the welfare state. La Academia de la Nueva Raza encouraged experiential learning by way of storytelling. Its members conducted dialogues with people, asking them to talk about their childhood experiences and their lives as adults and recording these stories on audiotape. These conversations were framed by the participants' perceptions and interpretations of changes they had witnessed from their childhood to the present. The dialogues proceeded through imagined spirals of thought and action as we probed for meaning.

. . .When I first saw the term *phenomenology* in a journal of existential philosophy many years ago, I was intimidated. For decades I ignored the word. Then, in the mid-seventies, Pedro David, a sociologist and phenomenologist, heard a presentation on our project, after which he exclaimed: "This is social phenomenology." He went on to explain that he was referring to an application of Martin Heidegger's phenomenology to the social world, an unlikely development because of Heidegger's individualistic orientation. The connection to Heidegger was that we were uncovering "meaning" from the community's experience through conversations with people.[23] I took David's comments seriously, along with his invitation to enroll in the University of New Mexico's doctoral program in sociology which, incidentally, did not promote or endorse phenomenology.

There are several ways of explaining phenomenology. Martin Heidegger, for example, proposed a process of dialogue that uncovers what is hidden as a means of understanding the meaning of being. He wrote that "phenomenon" is what is uncovered "in-itself," and "logos" is the process by which it is uncovered.[24] Resolana could be another word for phenomenology, as it is a process of disclosing experience and its meaning through dialogue and reflection, bringing to light in a place of light what is covered up. Reflexive and reflective learning are phenomenology also. Their principal tasks are to disclose the themes of the narrative and reach consensual understanding, or validation, of the meaning of individual yet similar experiences.[25]

In summary, la resolana as reflexive and reflective learning is based on the following assumptions: (1) life stories are history and sources of knowledge; (2) imagination, visions, and other psychic productions are foundations for knowledge; (3) traditional cultures have indigenous knowledge by which they interpret themselves to themselves; (4) stories consist of themes that are universal while remaining specific to time and place; themes are essential to democratizing knowledge, allowing for dialogue within as well as across cultures, by crossing cultural boundaries and linking cultures through the universal thematic bridge...

Traditional Knowledge in the Cyber Age

Traditional knowledge was subjugated but not totally blotted out from people's memories. La resolana and el oro del barrio provide an approach for recovering this knowledge and validating everyday life experience as a basis for knowledge. They also offer ways to democratize knowledge, which guarantees its perpetuation and continuous development and thwarts its subjugation.

I turn now to a cursory view of other voices calling on traditional knowledge and wisdom for revitalizing our communities in the cyber age. In describing the impact of Los Alamos on northern New Mexico's villages, Arellano quotes Wendell Berry, who lives in Kentucky:

> I am convinced that the death of my community is not necessary and not inevitable. I believe that such remnant communities as my own, fallen to the ground as they are, might still become the seeds of a better civilization than we now have.
>
> (Arellano 1997: 31)

From the Piedmont in Europe we hear from Carlo Petrini and Enzo Bianchi, lamenting the weakening of the "long established traditions, lifestyles, and ties between people and the land." They acknowledge that these traditions reflect the people's shared humanitarian values, which are embedded in a way of life that is rapidly changing. These communities and their culture cannot survive or be re-created, but in fact, they "have a lot to give and teach our urbanized society," asserts Petrini. Bianchi adds,

> What we have to do is somehow recover a form of social life that is typical of our towns and villages. . . . We have to think how we can reinject life into these communities, looking back to the past and providing a means for communicating with others, understanding what living together really means.
>
> (Petrini 2004)

Peter Van Dresser, a Depression-era decentralist and an early activist for sustainable communities, conducted a successful experiment in sustainability on a three-acre plot in El Rito, New Mexico, in the 1960s. After removing himself from the New Mexico State Planning Office, he produced a "counter-industrial" plan for the highland region of northern New Mexico that built on its natural ecology and its traditional culture (Van Dresser 1972). Theodore Abt, an engineer and Jungian analyst, has outlined the threats of industrialization to land-based people in the Swiss Alps in his book *Progress without Loss of Soul*. These acts and ideas represent el oro del barrio from other cultures. They stand for traditional wisdom, indigenous and local knowledge that must be validated and reclaimed as legitimate local and popular knowledge that can guide us as we rebuild institutions and reclaim values for the cyber age.

But honoring the power of local knowledge to revitalize our communities has not been without its challenges. The central concept of democratizing knowledge means uncovering the knowledge from everyday life experience, objectifying it, connecting it with other intellectual achievements, and ensuring it is never alienated from those from whom it came. But we ran into a troublesome paradox as we were developing la resolana as a learning and consciousness-raising process in the 1970s. What happens to everyday life knowledge once it is reflected on and objectified? Is it decolonized knowledge? Is it in the marketplace of ideas to be exploited and recolonized? Despite these concerns, we proceeded, convinced we were doing the right and ethical thing.

La resolana shows that knowledge from everyday life experience can be reflected upon, and that a body of knowledge can link with universal knowledge and as such is transmissible to others. Ortega y Gasset has written that knowledge acquired from life experiences is part of life itself, and that it forms automatically: "It is the kind of knowing which is at once, and of itself, living. At the same time it has the inconvenience that it cannot be transmitted to anyone" (Ortega y Gasset 1973: 28). The basic assumptions of la resolana that themes in the stories of life are both specific to time and place and universal leads logically to the conclusion that empirical knowledge can be communicated and transmitted, not only within but across cultures. This is what is meant by the democratization of knowledge. The few examples given earlier of shared understanding of traditional values among people of different cultures and in different parts of the world attest that knowledge from everyday experience can be transmitted and exchanged, thus preparing the ground for the creation of a learning society. We need both a learning society and the ethic of una vida buena y sana y alegre.

La vida buena y sana y alegre is a philosophy of life, an ethical belief that defies Western philosophical discourse about the nature of good. Well-being and a wholesome life are about plenitude, justice, happiness, and being at peace with oneself and others. It honors, respects, and seeks harmony with nature and is rooted in a faith and a belief in a power beyond us. It is an ideal that can guide and sustain us as we face the challenges of the cyber age.

References

Abt, T. (1989) *Progress Without Loss of Soul: Towards a Wholistic Approach to Modernization Planning*, Wilmette, UL Chiron Publications.
Arellano, J. E. (1992) *Inocencio: Ni pica ni escarda, pero siempre st come ti major elote*, Mexico, DF: Grijalbo.
Arellano, J. E. (1997) "La Querencia: La Raza: Bioregionalisrn," *New Mexico Historical Review* 72 (1): 31–38.
Atencio, T. (1971) "The Survival of la Raza Despite Social Services," *Social Casework* 52 (5): 262–265.
Atencio, T. (1973a) "La Academia de la Nueva Raza: El Oro del Barrio," *El Cuadertto (de Vez en Cuando)* 3 (1): 4–14.
Atencio, T. (1973b) *A Journey in Self-Reliance: A Report on the Status of the Papago Health Programs*, Sells, AZ: Papago Tribe.
Atencio, T. (1980) *Ghost Ranch: The First 15 Years*, [Commemorative pamphlet.] Abiquiu, NM: Ghost Ranch Conference Center.
Atencio, T. (1988) "Resolana: A Chicano Pathway to Knowledge," *Third Annual Ernesto Galarza Commemorative Lecture*, Stanford Center for Chicano Research, Stanford University.
Atencio, T. (1991) "Una vida buena y sana: A Philosophy of Life," in *Thought and Action Papers*, 1–16, Albuquerque: Rio Grande Institute.
Atencio, T. (1996) "Crypto-Jewish Remnants in New Mexico Manito Society and Culture," *Jewish Folklore and Ethnology Review* 18 (1–2): 59–67.

Atencio, T. (2001) "El Oro del Barrio in the Cyber Age: Revitalizing the Mexican American Community," *Paper presented for Motorola Community Revitalization Project, Department of Chicana and Chicano Studies*, Arizona State University, Tempe, November 17.
Buchanan, S. (ed.), (1971) *The Portable Plato*, B. Jowett (trans.), New York: Viking Press.
Chavez, A. (1981) *But Time and Chance: The Story of Padre Martrnez of Taos, 1793–1867*, Santa Fe: The Sunstone Press.
Drucker, P. F. (1994) *The New Realities: In Government and Politics*, New York: HarperBusiness.
Ehrenreich, B. (2001) *Nickel and Dimed: On (Not) Getting by in America*, New York: Henry Holt and Co.
Ellul, J. (1967) *The Technological Society*, New York: Vintage.
Foucault, M. (1980) *Power/Knowledge: Selected Interviews and Other Writings, 1972–1977*, edited by Colin Gordon, New York: Pantheon Books.
Freire, P. (1971) *Pedagogy of the Oppressed*, New York: Herder and Herder.
Freire, P. (1985) *The Politics of Education: Culture, Power, and Liberation*, South Hadley, MA: Bergin & Garvey.
Friedman, T. L. (2000) *The Lexus and the Olive Tree*, New York: Anchor Books.
Gomez-Quinones, J. (1974) *Study Commission on Undergraduate Education and the Education of Teachers, Southwest Network. Parameters of Institutional Change: Chicano Experiences in Education*, Hayward, CA: La Causa Pub.
Harrison, L., and Huntington, S. P. (eds.), (2000) *Culture Matters: How Values Shape Human Progress*, New York: Basic Books.
Heidegger, M. (1962) *Being and Time*, New York: Harper and Row.
Huntington, S. P. (1996) *The Clash of Civilizations and the Remaking of World Order*, New York: Simon and Schuster.
Huxley, J. (1965) *Introduction to The Phenomenon of Man, by Pierre Teilhard de Chardin*, New York: Harper and Row.
Jaramillo, L. (1971b) "La Nueva Raza: An Introduction to the New Humanity," in *The Centro LNR Bulletin*, San Anselmo, CA: El Centro de Comunicación.
Kist, W. (2004) *New Literacies in Action: Teaching and Learning its Multiple Media*, New York: Teachers College Press.
Mares, E. A. (1973) "Myth and Reality: Observations on American Myths and the Myth of Aztlán," *El Cuaderno (de Vet en Cuando)* 3 (1): 33–50.
Masuda, Y. (1985) "Computopia," in T. Forester (ed.), *The Information Technology Revolution*, Cambridge, MA: MIT Press.
Mumford, L. (1970) *The Myth of the Machine: The Pentagon of Power*, New York: Harcourt Brace Jovanovich.
National Commission of Community Health Services. (1966) *Health Is a Community Affair: Report*, Cambridge, MA: Harvard University Press.
Ortega y Gasset, J. (1973) *An Interpretation of Universal History*, M. Adams (trans.), New York: Norton.
Pacheco, C. (1991) "The Archetypal Image and the New Mexican lndo-hispano," in *Thought and Action Papers*, 1–29, Albuquerque: Rio Grande Institute. https://www.commoncrowbooks.com/pages/books/K26/consuelo-pacheco/the-archetypal-image-and-the-new-mexican-indo-hispano-sana-sana-colita-de-rana-si-no-sanas-hoy.
Petrini, C. (2004) "Carlo Petrini talks with Enzo Bianchi, Part One," *La Stampa* [Italy], March 2, www.slowfood.com/sloweb/eng/archivo/lasso?pagina=8&cod/=007–31-k.
Theobald, R. (1964) "The Cybernation Revolution," address by Robert Theobald; Email Theobald on healing in 21st century, 1964, 1998, Box: 12, Folder: 33. UNM Center for Southwest Research & Special Collections.
Theobald, R. (1981) *Beyond Despair: A Policy Guide to the Communications Era*, Washington, DC: Seven Locks Press.
Toffler, A. (1980) *The Third Wave*, New York: William Morrow and Co.
Van Dresser, P. (1972) *Landscape for Humans: A Case Study of the Potentials for Ecologically Guided Development in an Uplands Region*, Albuquerque Biotechnic Press.
Van Manen, M. (1990) *Researching Lived Experience: Human Science for an Action Sensitive Pedagogy*, New York: State University of New York Press.
Vigil, D. (1978) "Marx and Chicano Anthropology," *Grito del Sol: A Chicano Quarterly* 3 (1): 19–34.
Wright, R. (2000) *Nonzero: The Logic of Human Destiny*, New York: Pantheon Books.

Notes

1 Manito/as refers to New Mexican Indohispanics whose historical threads extend back to the colonial period. *Manito* is the shortened diminutive *of hermano*, brother. *Spanish American* is another self-designation of northern New Mexican Indohispanics. *Mexican American* is used for people whose roots are in Mexico but who settled in the United States around the time of the Mexican Revolution in 1910–1920. *Chicano* is a street term derived from colonial-period Aztec usage and adopted by Mexican Americans as well as manito youth.

2 This was drawn from informal conversations with Arturo Martinez y Salazar from Taos, New Mexico, between 1966 and the early 1980s.

3 Los Alamos employment was a boon to the subsistence farmer since he had his plot where he could build his home and continue farming while enjoying a relatively well-paying job. This created an illusion that one could succeed and become affluent without much education; unfortunately, this attitude has spread among young people, and education has been a low priority in many families.

4 The analyst Rudolf Ekstein (1912–2005) conducted weekly seminars for psychiatric residents, psychology interns and social workers.

5 The community of interest model is discussed in National Commission of Community Health Services, *Health Is a Community Affair*.

6 *Pícaro* is usually translated as "rogue." In Spanish, he is an antihero who survives by his wits. He has been immortalized in Spanish literature from the anonymous publication in 1554 of *Lazarillo de Tormes* to Juan Estevan Arellano's 1992 novel of northern New Mexico, *Inocencio*.

7 Abt's (1989) study of the effects of industrialization and government policy on Swiss mountain villages offers intriguing parallels with the situation in northern New Mexico.

8 *Resolaneros* are the men who gather in la resolana.

9 "His mind is always on the story, the narrative account of things done . . . It is not an accident that the highest philosophic teaching that Plato offers is not doctrine, but dialectic, a conversation in which ideas animate persons in search of wisdom" (Buchanan 1971: 6).

10 From 1972 to 1977, La Academia de la Nueva Raza conducted seminars on lifestyles in a postindustrial society at the Ghost Ranch Conference Center in Abiquiu, New Mexico.

11 The village's original name was El Puesto del Embudo de San Antonio, commonly known as La Plaza del Embudo. In 1904, a post office was established in the village, and the name of the postal agency became Dixon, named after Collins Dixon, a Civil War veteran who stayed in New Mexico and was honored for having taught children English.

12 The Stanford Chicano Fellows developed a special relationship with the Academia. A group of students initiated "el oro de la universidad," and an undergraduate student, José Padilla, conducted an oral history project in his home region. The Royal Chicano Air Force (RCAF) also had a very dose relationship with the Academia. Among the "established university" *colegios* were Jacinto Treviño in Mercedes, Texas; La Universidad de Aztlán in Fresno, California; Colegio Cesar Chávez, Mount Angel, Oregon; DeganawidahQuetzalcoatl, (DQ-U) at Davis, California; and Escuela y Colegio Tlatelolco in Denver, Colorado. See Gómez-Quiñones (1974: 153–166).

13 In the 1940s, the *pachucos*, Mexican American zoot-suiters appropriated the term *Chicano*. Most adults, in contrast, shunned the term as it signified lower-class status and Indian identity. Some Chicanos became activists in the Mexican American civil rights movement.

14 Luis Jaramillo, a Roman Catholic priest from New Mexico, distinguished himself as a religious thinker and committed advocate for social justice.

15 In 1973, Segura Granados published a summary of his work as "La continuidad de la tradición filosófica Nahuatl en las danzas de concheros" in *El Cuaderno (de Vez en Cuando)*, an Academia publication. In 1995, Segura Granados and Gonzalez edited "La continuidad de la sabiduría y la tradición Nahuatl en las danzas de concheros," which corrected material in the earlier Academia publication.

16 Based on my recollections of conversations with Eliseo Atencio in Dixon, New Mexico, in 1963.

17 "The problems of the information society will be future shocks . . . the inability of people to respond smoothly to rapid societal transformation" (Masuda 1985: 625).

18 Huntington (1996) gives a detailed examination of the "clash of civilizations"; Friedman (2000) is an apologist for globalization. See also Harrison and Huntington (2000).

19 Foucault (1980: 78–108) discusses this theme.

514   *The Latinx Philosophy Reader*

20 In forging the idea of a learning society, La Academia presaged Masuda's assertion that "the past developmental patterns of human society can be used as a historical analogical model for future society" (1985: 620).
21 The Penitentes are men belonging to a brotherhood known as La Cofradía de Nuestro Padre Jesús Nazareno. In 1833, Bishop Zubiría of the Diocese of Durango, Mexico, banned them from the Catholic Church for their excessive "corporal penances."
22 A connection was made between Paulo Freire and La Academia de la Nueva Raza in a resolana in the Dixon Learning and Documentation Center and at the Ghost Ranch Conference Center in Abiquiú, New Mexico, in 1973.
23 Pedro David, a native of Argentina, is a well-known criminologist and is active in the International Phenomenological Society.
24 Heidegger (1962: 54–59). I use Heidegger's definition of phenomenology because he breaks this word into *phenomenon* and *logos*. *Phenomenon*, "the showing-itself-in-itself, signifies a distinctive way in which something can be encountered" (54). Logos is the Greek root of the process of disclosure "a definite mode of letting something be seen" (57). This understanding of phenomenology more accurately describes the resolana process of uncovering the themes in a story and discerning their meaning.
25 Van Manen (1990: 1–46) explains phenomenology and hermeneutics in relation to the pedagogy of experiential learning.

Reading Questions

1. What does Atencio mean by "el oro del barrio"? How is it understood and transmitted, according to the author?
2. How does Atencio describe the transformation of his ancestral village in northern New Mexico from an agricultural to a postindustrial society? What are some of the advantages and disadvantages of "leapfrogging the industrial revolution," according to the text?
3. Atencio describes the notion of "la vida buena y sana y alegre" as "an ideal of well-being and a wholesome life that emphasizes plenitude, justice, happiness, and being at peace with oneself and others." Is this ideal out of date? Why or why not?
4. How does Atencio emphasize the importance of storytelling and intergenerational dialogue in preserving community knowledge and values? Can you think of an example from your own life that illustrates or challenges Atencio's argument?
5. What is Atencio's vision for combining advanced communication technology with traditional ways of life? How does he propose achieving this balance?
6. How does Atencio develop the concept of "la resolana" as a place of philosophical dialogue? What role does it play in community learning and knowledge sharing?
7. How might Atencio's analysis of "el oro del barrio" and "la resolana" be used to design a place of learning? Support your discussion with examples from the text.

32 The Philosophical Gift of Brown Folks
Mexican American Philosophy in the United States

José-Antonio Orosco

In his 1924 book *The Gift of Black Folk*, W. E. B. Du Bois examined the ways in which the traditions of the African American community have benefited, enriched, and gifted the culture, politics, and economic life of the United States. The book was written at a time in which great waves of immigration from Europe were inundating U.S. American shores.[1] Scholars, politicians, and the public were all involved in debating the value of ethnic and cultural diversity for the melting pot. *The Gift of Black Folk* details the ways in which Negro spirituals changed U.S. American folk music, explains how Black laborers contributed to the economic infrastructure of the nation, and analyzes the moral perspective which the African American community injected into political debates about the nature of U.S. American democracy.

In a similar spirit, I want to present the idea of Mexican American philosophy as a new field of study that can enrich the conception of philosophy, and of public life, in the United States. I begin by examining the conditions for the possibility of such a specialization as Mexican American philosophy, drawing on debates in Latin America about the aims and nature of philosophy, for comparison. I then identify several authors who might serve as the beginning of a canon for Mexican American philosophy. I maintain that Du Bois's early examination of African American intellectual work offers suggestions for the way in which this new area of specialization might develop. Mexican American philosophy can provide a theoretical lens for the Mexican American community to understand its relationship to dominant society in the United States. It may also offer philosophical insights that can help to correct any systematic epistemic distortion in U.S. American social and political philosophy that results from the lack of diversity within the profession. Finally, it may add a new voice to political discussions about the role of Latinos/as in the United States and to public policy decisions surrounding multiculturalism, immigration, and racial justice.

The Possibility of Mexican-American Philosophy

What exactly is Mexican American philosophy, and what makes such a thing as Mexican American philosophy possible? Students of Latin American philosophy will immediately recognize these kinds of questions. For decades, Latin American thought has been almost entirely defined as a debate about the identity of Latin American culture and of the possibility of producing philosophical knowledge that somehow reflects this reality. If there is such a thing as a distinctly Latin American philosophy, then it will be something intimately connected to features of a broader Latin American society and its cultural makeup. This debate has coalesced around several positions. I want to concentrate on four of these here to help understand how Mexican American philosophy, as a subgroup within Latin American thought, might be possible as a field of study.

The first position, universalism, denies that there is any kind of philosophy that might be called distinctively Latin American. Philosophy, under this conception, is a field of inquiry that is more like mathematics, or a hard science such as physics. That is, it utilizes logical methods of analysis to arrive at objectively true statements about the world and of human experience within it. Whatever conclusions philosophy reaches, say universalists, will not depend on any specific cultural formations or historical developments. The truth value of statements about the world are grounded in logic and reason and are not affected by the traditions and practices of any particular human society, in the same way that a physical or chemical reaction is the same, under the appropriate conditions, in any place in the world. According to universalists such as Risieri Frondizi or Carlos Pereda, we can talk about philosophy being done *in* Latin America, in the sense of there being philosophy departments and institutes in Latin America that are teaching students and are conducting research on philosophical problems, but it makes little sense to talk about Latin American, Mexican American, or any kind of distinct national philosophy. The truths produced by philosophical inquiry are universal and apply to all human beings regardless of national origin (Frondizi 1949; Pereda 2006).

Culturalists, such as Mexican scholars Leopoldo Zea or Samuel Ramos, take philosophy to be a humanistic discipline that is concerned to articulate and formalize a culture's worldview or perspective from within. As Zea puts it, the task of philosophy is to consider the issues of "man—not man the abstract, but man the concrete, of flesh and bone, with his own particular problems, yet not particular that they do not cease being proper to man" (Zea 2004: 378). Under this conception, the philosopher's responsibility is to reflect on the cultural traditions and practices of her own circumstances, elaborating what is often taken for granted, and then to look for any human universals by comparing them to the worldviews of other cultures that have been worked up similarly by other philosophers. Zea writes: "Through these particular problems, and precisely because they are particular, other men can be acknowledged as peer, an acknowledgment and respect for what is acknowledged in a search for a horizontal relation of solidarity of peers among peers" (2004: 378). Examples of this sort of effort are found in Samuel Ramos's attempt to describe Mexican national culture through the lens of neurosis provided by psychoanalysis or Jorge Portilla's attempt to articulate what it means to be authentically Mexican using Heideggerian existentialism (Ramos 1972; Sánchez 2012). To the culturalist, all philosophy is essentially a situated effort by a philosopher to explore and explain his or her cultural surroundings. Therefore, it makes complete sense to talk about the existence of a Latin American, German, Chinese, or even Mexican American philosophy, if by that we mean an attempt to describe the particular problems and issues that attend to Mexican American culture.

A third perspective, criticism, responds to this debate between universalists and culturalists by arguing that the kind of project which culturalists describe has been essentially impossible in Latin America throughout most of the modern era. According to Augusto Salazar Bondy, Latin America has, since the European Conquest in 1492, lived under a "culture of domination" (Salazar Bondy 2004: 395). In large part, the traditions, ways of life, practices, and cultural ideals of the region have been those that were imposed first by European colonial powers and then by the military and economic power of the United States in the nineteenth and twentieth centuries. Latin American philosophy, as the elaboration of a unique cultural perspective, is impossible since Latin American societies have not had an opportunity to develop a genuine or authentic culture. Speaking of attempts at producing Latin American philosophy, Salazar Bondy writes:

> Because of its imitative nature across the centuries, until today it has been an alienated and alienating conscience that has given a superficial image of the world and life to man in our national communities. It has not truly been responsive to motivations felt by this man, but rather has responded to the goals and vital interests of other men. It has been a plagiarized novel and not the truthful chronicle of our human adventure.
>
> (2004: 392)

To the extent that Mexican Americans have been discriminated and oppressed within the United States, they have not lived under conditions in which they are free to develop their own authentic culture. For the criticalists, any potential Mexican American philosophy will be a dominated, inauthentic, and unoriginal perspective that borrows on ideas imported from other people's culture and intellectual efforts. Mexican Americans have not had philosophy, in other words, but might be able to produce it given different social, economic, and political circumstances.

A fourth approach, developed by Jorge J. E. Gracia, attempts to move the question of Latin American philosophy and identity away from rigid notions of philosophy and culture assumed by the previous positions. Gracia's view is that we ought to understand Latin American philosophy as ethnic philosophy, that is, the philosophy of the ethnos of Latin Americans. An ethnos, Gracia explains, is a group of people who have been brought together by history. The model of the family is used as a metaphor to understand how an ethnic group can have unity without having all the members of the group necessarily share some first order properties at any particular time in the history or throughout that history. Not all of them need have the same height, weight, eye color, degree of intelligence, customs or even ancestry. Ethne are like families in that they originate and continue to exist as a result of historical events, such as marriage, but their members need not share common properties, although they may in certain circumstances do so (Gracia 2010: 260).

Under this conception, Latin Americans are a group of people formed by the encounter of Europeans and indigenous peoples of the Americas starting in 1492 and who are connected together still through this historical continuity even though they do not all share the same properties today. Latin American philosophy, then, will be the working up or the elaboration of the perspective of the Latin American ethnos. Since this ethnos is historical and contextual, the criteria for what counts as Latin American philosophy will be open, changing, and nonessentialist, as is the makeup of the ethos itself. For instance, Mexican and Argentinian intellectual work might be Latin American philosophy, as these societies are part of the Latin American ethnos—tied to the same historical origins of the Conquest—even though they are today different nations and very culturally distinct. And pre-Columbian indigenous thought, such as that of the Aztecs or the Mayas, might be Latin American philosophy, depending on how we understand the historical relations of Europeans and indigenous people in the context of Mexico.

Using Gracia's framework, I claim that Mexican American philosophy is best understood as an ethnic philosophy; that is, it is the philosophical work produced by the Mexican American ethnos. That Mexican Americans form an ethnos is not particularly difficult to establish. Mexican Americans are a distinct group of people who, like Latin Americans in general, were brought into existence by a particular set of historical circumstances. In 1848, the Treaty of Guadalupe-Hidalgo put an end to the Mexican-American War, and the United

States took over the northern half of Mexico, or what is now most of the U.S. Southwest. The treaty specified that those thousands of Mexicans who lived in the territory occupied by the United States had a choice: they could leave to Mexican jurisdiction, or they could stay and within one year be recognized as U.S. American citizens. Those Mexicans who elected to stay came to be known as the first U.S. American citizens of Mexican descent, or Mexican Americans. Thus, as historian Juan Gomez-Quiñones (1977) argues, the Treaty of Guadalupe Hidalgo had the effect of constituting the community of Mexican Americans as a unique population within U.S. American society. Moreover, because of the U.S. Supreme Court case of *Hernandez v. Texas* in 1954, the U.S. government continues to recognize Mexican Americans as a distinct national group within the United States, deserving of special protected status under the Fourteenth Amendment. Thus, Mexican Americans appear to fit Gracia's description of an ethnos; they are a group of people brought into existence by specific historical circumstances. Even though they do not all share the same properties, such as race, language, or phenotype, they are connected through family relations to the historical origins of 1848. Mexican American philosophy is, then, the philosophical work produced by members of this ethnos.

Obviously, some of the themes of Mexican American philosophy will overlap with those within Latin American philosophy, as the Mexican American ethnos has historical ties with the Latin American ethnos in general. Yet, we can also expect Mexican American philosophy to be unique and distinct since the Mexican American ethnos is also distinct from the Latin American, and from other Latino/a ethne, in particular. For example, the second largest Latino community in the United States, Puerto Ricans, might also be thought of as an ethnos. Puerto Ricans were constituted as U.S. American citizens of Puerto Rican descent much in the same way as Mexican Americans were—by a specific act of Congress, the Jones Act, in 1917. It makes sense to speak of the possibility of Puerto Rican philosophy as a field of study as well. That is, we can speak of the philosophical work produced by the Puerto Rican ethnos. Puerto Rican philosophy would be similar to Mexican American philosophy in some ways and very different in others. Both ethne share an experience of being tied to the Latin American ethnos through complex historical-family ties. Both were formed by U.S. American imperialism and have had their cultures and traditions repressed by U.S. American dominant society. Yet, there is at least one important difference: the Puerto Rican experience of being able to travel between the island and the U.S. mainland gives Puerto Ricans an experience of a homeland that is not quite the same as the Mexican American experience of being situated in-between Mexico and the United States nor the same kind of immigrant experience of Mexicans coming to the United States. Indeed, much of Gloria Anzaldúa's groundbreaking phenomenology in *Borderlands/La Frontera* is an explication of this sense of Mexican American *nepantla*—being stuck between different worlds and not being able to feel at home except in the interstices or borders (Keating 2006). These different transnational dynamics would provide rich material for phenomenological accounts of Mexican American and Puerto Rican identity that could complement the extensive historical and cultural studies about the relationships of these two Latino communities.

Features of Mexican American Philosophy

There is indeed a large body of artistic, literary, and scholarly work produced by Mexican Americans, but does any of it count as philosophical? To respond to this concern, it is instructive to turn to the work of Alejandro Santana and his attempt to solve the impasse in the debate about whether or not the pre-Columbian Aztec people of Mexico did philosophy.

Mexican scholar Miguel León-Portillo argues that certain Aztec writings display a skepticism toward the religious worldview of their society and seem to ask certain kinds of questions about metaphysical reality that suggest a philosophical attitude (León-Portilla 1963). On the other hand, Susana Nuccetelli finds that while some Aztec texts seem to exhibit inquiries into reality beyond the official religious myths of Aztec culture, this is not enough to justify saying that the Aztecs engaged in philosophy properly speaking (Nuccetelli 2002). To count as philosophical work, she maintains, the Aztec texts would have to offer alternative theoretical accounts to explain the world, and this is simply not something they do.

Santana (2008: 4) responds to this debate by reflecting on the variety of activities that philosophers often take to constitute philosophical work. These are often divided in terms of the subject matter, origins, aims, and methods of philosophy. He catalogs them as such:

Regarding *subject matter*, we might note that (1) philosophy addresses, but is not limited to, the various problems or questions that make up the generally recognized areas of philosophical investigation: metaphysics, epistemology, ethics, etc. Alternatively, we might note that philosophy is primarily concerned with (2) living a worthwhile, meaningful life or living in the right way.

Regarding *origins*, we might say that philosophy begins with (3) wonder, (4) reflection, or (5) the clash between traditional beliefs and the need for justification.

Regarding *aims*, we might mention that philosophy seeks (6) wisdom, (7) knowledge, (8) a clear, comprehensive, and plausible worldview, (9) the elimination of doubt, confusion, or nonsense, (10) intellectual liberation and autonomy.

Regarding *methods*, we might note that philosophy proceeds by (11) formulating and answering fundamental questions, (12) critically examining and evaluating fundamental assumptions, (13) giving justification, (14) raising and addressing objections, (15) analysis, (16) clarifying concepts, or (17) synthesizing ideas.

Santana (2008: 5) then asks whether we find these characteristics of philosophy in Aztec writings. His answer is that we do find some of them, but not all. Yet, rather than try to determine the necessary and sufficient criteria among these points for a work to count as philosophy, Santana utilizes a Wittgensteinian family resemblance approach and looks to "the complicated network of similarities overlapping and criss-crossing; sometimes overall similarities, sometimes similarities in detail" that bridge many different philosophical works. Just as Wittgenstein did not believe there were neat conceptual boundaries on language, Santana holds we ought to not think of any on philosophy. There is no one characteristic or set of characteristics that distinguish philosophical work from non-philosophical work: "Instead what we see is a family of various ways of doing philosophy that bear similarities to each other in various ways, with nothing common to them all." As such, some Aztec texts can be considered philosophy proper since they exhibit *some* of the aims and subject matter of other philosophy texts, even though they do not contain *all* of the methods found in other philosophical works.

Similarly, I would claim that if we look at a variety of Mexican American intellectual works, we can find authors engaging in a variety of intellectual tasks that overlap and crisscross with the kind of inquiries we find in other philosophical texts. Many texts from the era of the Chicano Civil Rights movement ought to count as Mexican American philosophy, and with them we can imagine building a kind of philosophical canon for this area of specialization. I have argued previously that the work of Cesar Chavez, co-founder of the United Farm Worker union, ought to be considered as philosophical meditations on nonviolence and social change (Orosco 2008). Armando Rendon's *Chicano Manifesto* (1971) examines Mexican American cultural identity and argues that its terms provide the possibility of expanding U.S. national identity in a cosmopolitan direction that recognizes the ethical obligation of the United States to other peoples. Elihu Carranza's *Chicanismo: Philosophical Fragments* (1977) uses Kierkegaardian existentialism to examine the hybridity of Mexican American identity and proposes that the resolution of the Mexican American identity problematic could offer a new concept for conceiving of race in the United States. Gloria Anzaldúa's *Borderlands/La Frontera* (1981) is perhaps one of the most well-known and influential Chicana texts, widely regarded in literary, ethnic, and women's studies, as well as philosophy, primarily for what might be called a phenomenological investigation of Mexican American life and culture along the U.S./Mexico border. In numerous essays, Elizabeth "Betita" Martinez attempts to provide new vocabulary to interrogate white supremacy beyond a black/white binary. She also raises questions about the discourses of diversity and multiculturalism that still privilege a white dominant-colonial perspective. Tomás Atencio's decades-long work draws parallels between Socratic dialogue and the conversations among Northern New Mexico villagers in an attempt to develop a model of grassroots knowledge production grounded in Heideggerian phenomenology, Habermasian discourse ethics, and Freirean pedagogy (Montiel et al. 2009). Finally, the recent work of Carlos Alberto Sánchez attempts to bridge U.S. American philosophers such as Ralph Waldo Emerson and Stanley Clavell with Mexican American thought and, most notably, attempts to articulate a phenomenology of the Mexican immigrant experience and its continuing impact on the Mexican American ethnos (Sánchez 2011: 31–32).

The Philosophical Gift of Brown Folks

So far I have argued that Mexican American philosophy is a possible field of specialization and that there are works now that deserve study as examples of Mexican American philosophy. But why *should* we study Mexican American philosophy? Why should we think it is an important field of study? W. E. B. Du Bois can offer some guidance here.

In 1897, Du Bois addressed the second gathering of the American Negro Academy in Washington, D.C. In his speech, he laid out a mission statement for the organization of politically committed African American men that would guide his insights as a scholar and activist for many decades (Lewis 1993: 174). Du Bois argued that the American Negro Academy ought to devote itself, in general, to the task of "racial uplift," that is, to improving the situation of Black Americans in the United States through two main strategies (DuBois 2015). First, the members of the academy ought to delve into engaged scholarship in history, philosophy, and law in order to help reveal the "ideals of life" buried in the traditions and practices of African American life. Here, Du Bois relied on a framework that he inherited from German Romanticism that held different races or cultures shared certain common ideals or purposes, implicit in their folkways, tying all the members of that race or culture together (Appiah 2014). Knowing these ideals of life could help a people to understand themselves better and appreciate their strengths and abilities more robustly. The second task of the academy was to be more outward focused. Du Bois recommended investigating the ideals of life of the Black community and learning how they could make a contribution to the "culture of the common country" and towards humanity as a whole. This second task was the focus of Du Bois's *The Gift of Black Folk*, in which he tried to make explicit the numerous cultural contributions of African Americans to U.S. American society and politics.

The importance of Mexican American philosophy might be justified along the two lines identified by Du Bois. First, the task of Mexican American philosophy might be to examine and articulate the experience of the Mexican American ethnos for the purpose of developing theories and strategies of resistance against discrimination and oppression from dominant U.S. society. In this regard, Mexican American philosophy would be akin to the approach of liberation philosophy in Latin America (Marquez 2010: 301). Its purposes would be, first, to decolonize, that is, to reduce or eliminate its reliance on ideas, methods, and aims from European and North American philosophy, or to elaborate new ways of philosophizing that are more consonant with the experiences of Mexican Americans. Along these lines, Mexican American philosophy would also endeavor to develop ways of better understanding systems of political, social, and economic oppression, largely controlled by North American and European power, that confront Mexican American people today. Some of the classic works of Chicano/a thought, such as those of Cesar Chavez, Rodolfo "Corky" Gonzales, or Reies Lopez Tijerina, attempt to outline cultural features of Mexican American life that can serve as alternatives to the materialist values of dominant U.S. American society. A more recent example of this kind of effort is the work of Jacqueline M. Martinez. She uses Merleau-Ponty as a starting point to recognize a unique form of Chicana lesbian phenomenology in the work of Cherie Moraga and Gloria Anzaldúa that contains important insights into intersectional collective liberation (Martinez 2000). In such a mode, Mexican American philosophy would be like a theoretical toolbox that would allow the Mexican American ethnos to better understand its situation in the United States and work toward more effective liberation from arbitrary institutional and cultural constraints. This mission has long been part of Chicano and Chicana studies in the United States, but philosophers have rarely, if at all, been involved in this discourse, which has long been dominated by historians, social scientists, and literary scholars.

The second task of Mexican American philosophy would then be oriented outward, focused on identifying ideals, concepts, or what Manuel Vargas calls "cultural resources" that might be offered as "gifts" to the broader society (Vargas 2010). In particular, developing Mexican American philosophy as an area of specialization is one way of addressing what is being called a problem of "arrogant whiteness" in U.S. American philosophy (LaSusa 2014). According to the American Philosophical Association (APA), almost 80 percent of employed philosophers in the United States are men, and almost all of them are white. The APA also finds that only about 2 percent of philosophers in Ph.D.-granting institutions are Latino/a—one of the lowest of all ethnic groups in the United States—despite the fact that Latinos, and particularly those of Mexican heritage, are the fastest growing ethnic group in the United States and expected to be about 20 percent of the U.S. population in just a few years (Sanchez 2013: 2). These numbers indicate that philosophy in general is not a particularly attractive area of study for students of color to pursue. A specialization in Mexican American philosophy could create a space, alongside the field of Latino/a and Latin American philosophy, for underrepresented students and faculty to enter in the profession, build networks, and create mentorship pipelines that are crucial to encouraging students to pursue academic work.

There is a related epistemic aspect to this part of the gift. Manuel Vargas indicates that the lack of diversity in certain fields of philosophy, such as moral, social, and political thought, makes them subject to possible epistemic error and distortion. If some perspectives are left out of critical discussions in these areas, then the basic background assumptions can come to reflect the experiences and understandings of some groups of people rather than others. What, then, is taken as "reasonable" interpretation of our moral, social, or political life might actually be very partial or limited. For instance, Charles Mills has demonstrated that social contract theory tends to rely on conjectures and beliefs that reflect the outlooks of the propertied male philosophers who first set out the theory (Mills 1999). If Mexican American philosophy can create a home for more voices in the profession, then it not only helps in terms of demographic representation, but also in terms of improving the kind of truth that can be produced by our philosophical theories. As Vargas points out,

> [U]ntil our discipline has had substantial engagement with the beliefs, intuitions, convictions, concerns, and standpoints of those in non-male, non-white social positions, it should, on the present account, be extraordinarily difficult for us to make out the precise ways in which we are subject to distortion.
>
> (in Sanchez 2013: 2)

Mexican American philosophy may also be able to contribute a variety of gifts toward the study of U.S. American political and social life. The first gathering of Mexican American philosophers at the Pacific Division meeting of the APA in Vancouver, Canada, in spring 2015 yielded a collection of papers over a wide range of issues about contemporary U.S. American society including immigration, the nature of the nation state, the relationship of Mexican American thought to North American pragmatism, the legacy of U.S. American colonialism, and the place of indigeneity in Mexican and North American culture. Clearly, Mexican American philosophers are now contributing to an ongoing investigation that seeks to explore and define new diverse concepts of democracy, citizenship, human rights, and cultural production from the perspective of particular historical subjects on the "silenced, subalternized, and dominated side of the colonial difference" (Grosfoguel 2008).

The growth of Latino/a philosophy in general represents an opportunity to discuss issues about the discipline of philosophy and about the culture and intercultural possibilities within the Americas in new and exciting ways. In less than a year after the first gathering of Mexican American philosophers in Vancouver, a new group, the Society for Mexican American Philosophy (SMAP), has developed, which hopes to maintain and broaden these discussions as part of philosophical scholarship. In a short time, SMAP has been able to organize group meetings at two divisional meetings of the APA and has been invited to offer a special guest panel at the annual gathering of the Society for the Advancement of American Philosophy in 2016. Mexican American philosophy, then, represents another theoretical lens with which to continue examining questions about identity, power, and citizenship in the United States. With an added level of granularity and attention to Latino/a historical development, Mexican American philosophy can hopefully yield results for improving the lives of Mexican Americans and for refining the conceptual resources of U.S. American philosophy, and of public policy discussions, in general.

References

Appiah, K. A. (2014) *Lines of Descent: W. E. B. Du Bois and the Emergence of Identity*, Cambridge and London: Harvard University Press.

DuBois, W. E. B. (2015) "The Conservation of the Races," in N. D. Chandler (ed.), *The Problem of the Color Line at the Turn of the Twentieth Century*, New York: Fordham University Press.

Frondizi, R. (1949) "Is There an Ibero-American Philosophy?" *Philosophy and Phenomenological Research* 9: 345–355.

Gracia, J. J. E. (2010) "Identity and Latin American Philosophy," in S. Nuccetelli, O. Schutte, and O. Bueno (eds.), *A Companion to Latin American Philosophy*, Malden, MA: Wiley-Blackwell.

Gomez-Quiñones, J. (1977) "On Culture," *Chicano-Riqueña* 5 (2) (Spring 1977): 29–47.
Grosfoguel, R. (2008) "Latin@s and the Decolonization of the U.S. Empire in the 21st Century," *Social Science Information* 47 (4): 618.
Keating, A. (2006) "From Borderlands and New Mestizas to Nepantlas and Nepantleras: Anzaldúan Theories for Social Change," *Human Architecture: Journal of Sociology of Self-Knowledge* IV: 5–16.
LaSusa, D. M. (2014) "In a Profession Plagued by Homogeneity, a Philosophy Conference Offers Diversity," *Truthout.org*, August 16, http://www.truth-out.org/news/item/25589-in-a-profession-plagued-by-homogeneity-a-philosophy-conference-delivers-diversity.
Leon-Portilla, M. (1963) *Aztec Thought and Culture*, Norman: University of Oklahoma Press.
Lewis, D. L. (1993) *W. E. B. Du Bois: A Biography of A Race: 1868–1919*, New York: Henry Holt.
Marquez, I. (2010) "Liberation in Theology, Philosophy, and Pedagogy," in S. Nuccetelli, O. Schutte, and O. Bueno (eds.), *A Companion to Latin American Philosophy*, Malden, MA: Wiley-Blackwell.
Martinez, E. (2003) "Don't Call This Country 'America': How the Name Was Hijacked and Why It Matters Today More Than Ever," *Z Magazine* (July-August): 69–72.
Martinez, J. M. (2000) *Phenomenology of Chicana Experience and Identity: Communication and Transformation in Praxis*, Lanham: Rowman & Littlefield.
Mills, C. (1999) *The Racial Contract*, Ithaca, NY: Cornell University Press.
Montiel, M., Atencio, T., and Mares, E. A. "T." (2009) *Resolana: Emerging Chicano Dialogues on Community and Globalization*, Tucson: University of Arizona Press.
Nuccetelli, S. (2002) *Latin American Thought: Philosophical Problems and Arguments*, Boulder: Westview Press.
Orosco, J.-A. (2008) *Cesar Chavez and the Common Sense of Nonviolence*, Albuquerque: University of New Mexico Press.
Pereda, C. (2006) "Latin American Philosophy: Some Vices," *Journal of Speculative Philosophy* 3: 192–203.
Ramos, S. (1972) *Profile of Man and Culture in Mexico*, P. B. Earle (trans.), Austin: University of Texas Press.
Sálazar Bondy, A. (2004) "The Meaning and Problem of Hispanic American Philosophic Thought," in Jorge J. E. Gracia and Elizabeth Millan-Zaibert (eds.), *Latin American Philosophy for the 21st Century*, New York: Prometheus.
Sánchez, C. A. (2011) "Philosophy and the Post-Immigrant Fear," *Philosophy in the Contemporary World* 18 (1): 31–32.
Sánchez, C. A. (2012) *The Suspension of Seriousness: On the Phenomenology of Jorge Portilla*, Albany: State University of New York Press.
Sánchez, R. E. (2013) "The Process of Defining Latino/a Philosophy," *APA Newsletter on Hispanic Latino Issues in Philosophy* 13 (1): 2.
Sántana, A. (2008) "Did the Aztecs Do Philosophy?" *APA Newsletter on Hispanic/Latino Issues in Philosophy* 8 (1): 4.
Vargas, M. (2010) "On the Value of Philosophy: The Latin American Case," *Comparative Philosophy* 1 (1): 33–52.
Zea, L. (2004) "Identity: A Latin American Philosophical Problem," in Jorge J. E. Gracia and Elizabeth Millan-Zaibert (eds.), *Latin American Philosophy for the 21st Century*, New York: Prometheus.

Note

1 I follow Elizabeth Martinez (2003) in using the term "U.S. American" to refer to citizens and residents of the United States in order to distinguish them from other communities in North and Latin America that also consider themselves as "American."

Reading Questions

1. What are some of the key philosophical contributions that Mexican American philosophy can make to U.S. American social and political thought? Provide specific examples from the text.
2. What is a "philosophical gift"? What new connections or questions come to mind when thinking about philosophy in this way?

3. What does Orosco mean by the term "brown folks"? What parallels does Orosco draw with W.E.B. Du Bois's examination of African American intellectual contributions?
4. What historical circumstances led to the formation of the Mexican American "ethnos," according to Orosco? How do these circumstances shape the potential for Mexican American philosophy?
5. Summarize the four positions in the debate about the nature and possibility of Latin American philosophy as presented by Orosco. Compare and contrast two of these positions, and then explain which is strongest, in Orosco's view and in yours.
6. What does Orosco mean when he refers to "arrogant whiteness" in U.S. American philosophy? Explain how Mexican American philosophy could contribute to a more inclusive philosophical discourse in this context.

33 Philosophy sin más?

Notes on the Value of Mexican Philosophy for Latino/a Life

Carlos Alberto Sánchez

And now I say to this jury of international thinkers before me: recognize the right to world citizenship that we have achieved. We have come of age. Very soon you will have to get used to dealing with us.

—Alfonso Reyes (1950: 41)

We have reached that historical and cultural age in which we commit ourselves to live in accordance with our own being, and from there arises the imperative to clearly reveal [*sacar en limpio*] the morphology and dynamics of our being.

—Emilio Uranga (1952: 10)

Philosophy exists wherever thought brings men to an awareness of their existence.

—Karl Jaspers (1963: 3)

Toward a Phenomenology of the Latino/a Experience

In analyzing what he calls "the spiritual crisis of the United States," Jorge Portilla notes that for Mexicans (in Mexico), "the United States always appears under the aspect of a radical 'otherness' ['*otredad*']" (1952: 69). This observation, made in 1952, could still be made today, not only by mexicanos but by anyone who is enchanted by the very *idea* of the United States as a place of freedom, opportunity, and all that comes with that way of life that is singularly "American." The implication here is that for those living within the boundaries of the nation, particularly for its citizens, the United States is what is most familiar; moreover, we who are internal to the idea can see ourselves reflected in it. For us, in other words, the idea of the United States is not an otherness but a sameness.

The reality, however, is quite different. Latinos in the United States, for example, do not always see themselves reflected in the idea of the United States or "America"; this idea—and its implicit promises—gives itself as an alterity that is *always already*, or *siempre*, beyond our reach. As an ideal, it is always fleeing, abstract, impossible to situate. Its apparent refusal to be instantiated correlates to a refusal by Latino/as to accept it as a mere ideal. There is thus an element of zozobra in the Latino/a identity, an existing in the vertigo and in-betweenness of attraction and rejection.

Because Latino/as do not see themselves reflected in the idea, or ideal, of the United States, because they do not see themselves in harmony with the whole, with its past, present, and future, Latinos (and I count myself as one), generally speaking, are other to that idea; there is no relationship of sameness between us and it, as Portilla's comment would suggest.

Yes, we are constitutive of the idea of the United States in the sense that with every generation we help structure its contours and possibilities, but we do this mostly negatively. Thus, for instance, our modern "America" is partly shaped by its incessant *rejection* of Latino culture(s), the denial of the Spanish language, and an unfounded hatred of "Mexican" immigrants, all of which contribute to the "devaluation of American citizenship" (Huntington 2005: 137, quoting Schuck 1989).[1] So we are part of the idea, but only as its limit, and then, only marginally; in the nativist discourse, we take part in the story of its destruction.

In these and many other ways, Latinos as *other* constitute the boundary limits of the very notion of "American" citizenship and American identity—it stops where we begin, so to speak. So the "United States," as an idea and a reality, is not only *other* to Mexicans in Mexico but also to Latinos *in* the United States. That this is the case can readily be seen in the way in which Latinos interact and are interacted with in American politics, as if Latinos are a "sleeping giant" that once awakened will guard the gates to political office (Jackson 2011). Latinos are a political otherness that is quietly emerging, and whose difference must be nurtured (for instance, by the liberal rhetoric of the Democratic Party) or seduced (for instance, by the self-reliance narratives of the Republican Party). But the otherness of Latinos is most apparent in the public sphere, where Latinos are a threat to the national culture and the death of its future (as we find in the nativist writings of Brimelow 1995, Huntington 2005, and Buchanan 2007). They are "illegals," "aliens," immigrants, whether they are *in fact* any of those things. As Jorge J. E. Gracia put it over a decade ago, "in one sense we [Latinos] are part of the country, but in another we are perceived as not belonging to it. And even when we are tolerated, we are never completely accepted" (2000: 188).

The alienation and marginalization of Latinos before the idea of "America" will naturally affect, for instance, political participation, social activism, and educational success. I could list a myriad of examples that lend support to how our otherness to the idea impacts us in these different areas, but I will stick to one—a very personal one, namely, the lack of Latinos in academic philosophy. The fact is that Latinos in philosophy are *other* to the philosophical profession, just as Latinos in the United States are *other* to that way of life that is particularly American. The realization of our otherness can be a heavy cross to bear. It might frighten us into avoiding questions that are pertinent to our lives *as* Latinos; and it certainly forces many of us, in philosophy, into avoiding, through denial or through ideological commitments assumed for the sake of professional survival, philosophy from south of the border all together.

In what remains, I propose that Latino/as must confront and embrace their otherness to the idea of "America" if Latino/a identity itself is to be preserved and, also, for the sake of a Latino/a philosophy that might emerge. More important, our identity as Latino/as will be positively defined in the narratives we weave as we struggle to describe and redescribe our role as citizens and intellectuals before the oppressions and marginalizations of inherited metanarratives. Those narratives we weave will be the prolegomena to our philosophy.

A model to emulate has been sketched out in the previous four chapters by philosophers that we have, perhaps unwillingly, sought to avoid in the history of our philosophical education. I believe that the attempt by Mexican philosophers to philosophically reveal their own being and identity through a rigorous examination of self and circumstance is a blueprint for a Latino/a liberatory consciousness and a Latino/a philosophy. And hence the title of this chapter is part of the question I aim to answer here: what is the value, for Latinos, of reading Mexican philosophy? This question might not be relevant to *all* Latinos/Hispanics in the United States, but it is relevant, at the very least, to Latinos in American academic philosophy.

I proceed with a brief overview of the Latino condition/circumstance/situation, focusing on the way in which Latino/as have been *altered*, or othered, in America's public imaginary. I next propose the view that the value of reading Mexican philosophy resides precisely in its otherness to an ideal; this will involve a consideration of two exemplary members of the philosophical group Hyperion already discussed, namely, Emilio Uranga and Jorge Portilla. In way of conclusion, I reconsider the question regarding the value of reading Mexican philosophy for Latino life as well as the value of this reading for a future Latino/a philosophy.

The Circumstance: Latino/as as "Other"

There is, according to the sociologist Leo Chavez, a "Latino threat narrative" that filters perceptions of Latinos in the United States (2008). This narrative reproduces the fear that Latino/as, as Buchanan and other nativists propose, undermine "American" culture. It claims that Latinos are a threat to "mainstream" American society because of their relation and allegiance to other cultures or other *streams*. The narrative effectively *alters* Latino/as before the idea. The narrative has a dramatic structure:

> According to assumptions and taken-for-granted 'truths' inherent in this narrative, Latinos are unwilling or incapable of integrating, of becoming part of the national community. Rather, they are part of an invading force from south of the border that is bent on reconquering land that was formally theirs (the U.S. Southwest) and destroying the American way of life.
>
> (Chavez 2008: 2)

Of course, it is imperative, if this narrative is to have any social or cultural force, to forget that a great number of "Latinos" are US-born citizens, many of whom have never been south of the US-Mexico border—or who do not recall ever being there (as is the case with the present author/reader). Another way to say this is that this narrative assumes a strict, or essentialist, conception of Latino identity itself. Latino philosophers such as Corlett (1999), Gracia (2000), Schutte (2004), and Alcoff (2006) have labored intensively in recent years to deconstruct, and dismantle, such essentialist notions of Latino identity. Corlett, for instance, says that "Latino" is an ethnic category that picks out individuals who are "in some way descendants of (and including) Iberians" (1999: 275). This "in some way," he says, is a "matter of degrees."

Corlett goes on to propose a "moderate conception of Latino identity" where one can be "more or less" Latino, so long as one can tie one's identity "genealogically" to a Latino ancestry (288). Gracia disagrees with Corlett, suggesting the latter's genealogical view to be a form of essentialism, where genealogical ties serve as either a necessary or sufficient condition for Latinoness. Gracia instead proposes that Latino identity is more about "family relationships" between members of historical communities that change over time than it is about lines of descent (2000). Alcoff, like Gracia, avoids traces of essentialism by conceiving Latino identity as historically situated and circumstantially informed, as changing and malleable. Alcoff, however, and like Zea and Uranga, places much more emphasis on what the recognition of one's identity can accomplish—politically and existentially. Alcoff defines identities as "embodied horizons from which we must confront and negotiate our shared world and specific life condition" (2006: 288). As a horizon "from which" one engages and confronts the world, moreover, Latino identity is not just one, but a set of sites of resistance and overcoming. And, for Latinos, all of these sites of resistance can be differently situated, or differently grounded. Against Corlett, there is not *one* grounding for this horizon, but many.

Latino/a philosophers, like the Mexican existentialists of el Grupo Hiperión, recognize the value of a clear consciousness of identity. While Mexican philosophers could not escape the traps of an essentialist conception of "lo mexicano," they nonetheless found it necessary to attempt its philosophical clarification, if only for the sake of *saving the circumstances*. While trafficking in a different conceptual field, Latino/a philosophers seek the same. Ofelia Schutte, for instance, proposes that consciousness of our multifaceted identities allows us to better negotiate "[our] way through the different pressures, conflicts, and tensions that bear on [our] concept of self as well as on [our] ongoing understanding of [our] social and political identity" (2004: 380). For his part, Corlett writes that for an ethnic group, "being able to name and define itself is empowering" (1999: 278).

The negation of Corlett's insight, however, is that allowing someone else to name and define a group, no matter how complex or multifaceted that group may be, is *disempowering*. The "embodied horizon" that can negotiate a shared world is closed off by the "symbolic systems" (Alcoff 2006: 228) of the narrative that defines and names. The Latino threat narrative is a manifestation of such a symbolic system.

Ultimately, the pervasiveness of the Latino threat narrative, in media and popular culture, justifies a belief that the picture that it paints is right, that it is a factual account of American reality. Under such scrutiny, Latinos, Chavez notes, are seen as "alien-citizens" and "perpetual foreigners despite their birthright" (2008: 6).

As perpetual foreigners, Latinos perpetually pose the threat of trespass and violation. Latinos trespass when they "cross over" into mainstream "American" music, when they break records in sports, when they star in their own, primetime television shows, when they make a career in philosophy, or when they write a best-selling book *in English*. When Latinos succeed in those endeavors into which they trespass, they are heralded for their courage, their uniqueness, and their pioneering spirit; when they fail, they are exposed, at best, not as exceptions to the rule but as *the* rule, and at worst, as frauds, cheats, or criminals. I do not think examples are necessary, but a quick look at the sports and entertainment industries and the trespassers and violators are easy to spot. The perpetual otherness of Latinos thus has a commercial appeal, since any accomplishment or any crime can be plugged into the capitalist apparatus and sold to a culture hungry for novelty or scandal. More important, it also has political and social value, since against the foreignness and otherness of Latinos, Anglo-American culture defines its purity and its right to sovereignty.[2]

The Threat Narrative thus serves two functions: first, it alters Latinos; and second, it produces this alteration for the benefit of Anglo-American culture's desire to define itself. Again, while "Mexico, Mexican immigrants, and U.S.-born of Mexican origin are the core foci of the Latino Threat Narrative" (Chavez 2008: 22), the narrative ultimately essentializes Latinos, clumping them together despite factual group differences, and on these generalizations proposes the mythology that Latinos are "people who will not and cannot become part of U.S. society" (41).

This narrative, imbued as it is with fear and suspicion, is not explicit in the everyday lives of twenty-first-century Latinos. But it is at work, sometimes in subtle yet impactful ways. For instance, one could argue that the views the narrative espouses are responsible for the lack of Latinos in the US philosophical establishment.[3] Jorge J. E. Gracia's decades-old observation that even within the philosophical community "we are perceived as alien" still rings true (2000: 181). The sense of being *other* to the US philosophical establishment (a sense one gets merely from the lack of recognizably Hispanic surnames among college or university philosophy faculty) leads many of us to refrain from pursuing philosophy as a profession, or even from pursuing it as a pastime, as philosophy is not the kind of thing one does when there are other more urgent tasks at hand, such as undermining the narrative by assimilating into the consumerist-capitalist culture and living in accordance with the demands of the American dream—which sometimes means, for instance, majoring in business or engineering, or anywhere else but in majors that promote the unproductive, *lazy*, life of thought. Those of us who do pursue it as a profession find that success is tied to our capacity to cleanse ourselves of our differences, to embrace a manner of thinking that eschews particular, circumstantially driven, passion-fueled, vital concerns.[4] Gracia suggests that perhaps "if we abandon our cultural heritage and become 'Americanized' can we have a significant place in the American philosophical community" (2000: 181). And, indeed, this seems like the only, and more attractive, option. After all, the success-narrative (at least in philosophy) states that it is best to stick to the issues preordained by the "tradition," on figures the tradition has vetted and cleared, to shy from passion projects and write without hinting at our culture, race, history, gender, or desires. If we choose to dwell on issues pertinent to the existence as Latinos in the United States, we will feel the oppressive weight of our alterity—our papers will not be published, our books will go unread, and our philosophy will always be defending itself from the charge that it is something other than philosophy. After all, as we saw in chapter 3, if it does not transcend contingency, the tradition states, it is something like poetry, but not philosophy. Gracia, for one, recognizes the danger and warns: "These are the two ways of disenfranchising philosophers: locating them in a non-European or non-American tradition, or classifying what they do as non-philosophical" (2000: 182).

It is this marginalization and disenfranchising to which Mexican philosophy can speak; it is here where we can locate the value of Mexican philosophy for Latino life. As a US-born Latino of Mexican origin, that is, Mexican-American, who is also a philosopher by profession, my experience of reading Mexican philosophy brings with it a certain sense of camaraderie and familiarity to what Wittgenstein would call a "family resemblance" or what my father would call *familiaridad*. This familiaridad might be due to my experiences within a common history, one passed down through memories and communal narratives. Or the sense of familiaridad might be due to a consciousness of a shared struggle, of the knowledge that Mexican philosophers have themselves been disenfranchised by "philosophy."

As we have seen, philosophy from Plato to Descartes to Kant and Husserl is supported by a metanarrative of purity and universality that demands rigor, or the rigorous discipline to ignore passion and desire, a metanarrative that fiercely guards against the invasion of contingency and difference in all of its forms. This means, again, that an anthology of twentieth-century existentialism, published in the United States, will not include Uranga, Portilla, Villoro, or Zea, who clearly engaged in existential analyses in the 1940s and 1950s, when existentialism was less an academic curiosity and more of a way of life or intellectual commitment. It will not include these hiperiones because of the concern over culture that they brought into their readings and reflections. The same could be said of important Mexican Marxists, Neo-Kantians, or analytic philosophers. The claim could be made that adequate translations are at fault. But the fact is that professional philosophers in the United States will be more disposed to translate an obscure German or French text rather than *any* text in Spanish, or risk marginalization themselves. Sixty years ago, the American academic Arthur Berndston (1953) complained that the main difficulty in teaching a course in Latin American philosophy was a lack of available resources in his campus library. How surprised would he be to face the same difficulty today? Of course, this is due to a culture of privileging European philosophers over thinkers from the Global South (a culture that exists both in the universities and in the world of academic publishing). Or, it could be said, it is due to a thwarted understanding of what philosophy from that space-time is *like*. Berndston himself says that part of the reason for this absence is that Latin American philosophy lacks "original ideas . . . logical and thorough development" and is "closely related to feeling and to action" (1953: 263). As we have seen, the latter of these sentiments is not far off base—Mexican philosophy is a philosophy of action, rooted in concrete situations, that does not shy away from passion and commitment. The former reason, that Mexican philosophy lacks originality and logic, is a hasty generalization that privileges the Eurocentric standard. Nevertheless, even supporters like Berndston, who want to include this manner and style of doing Latin American/Mexican philosophy in the *teachable* narrative, cannot help but marginalize it, if simply for lack of self-representation.

Consequently, so long as Mexican philosophers (and Mexican philosophy) are disenfranchised, so will be those of us writing and thinking about them (and it). But instead of dissuading us, these facts should empower us to push through, especially if by doing so we gain something valuable and vital to our lives as Latino/as in the United States and in the US philosophical establishment, namely, a model to emulate in our struggle to overcome the weight of our otherness while retaining and protecting our difference. More than a simple sense of familiaridad that appears when confronting Mexican existential philosophers, the shared experience of disenfranchisement also offers an experience of *familia*.

Toward a Liberatory Latino/a Consciousness

For us, Latino/as, what is it that we must face, or confront, and thus transcend? What must be confronted is the image of ourselves as other to what presents itself as absolute or substantial, in other words, that which is fundamentally "American"—this includes but is not limited to whiteness, Protestantism, and "legality." In the essay quoted at the beginning of the present chapter, Portilla gives us an untimely observation. Speaking of how media spectacle (particularly, American cinema of the time) represents its heroes, he writes:

> The North American hero appears always already [*siempre ya*] justified; he is the center that determines the world that surrounds him, and in determining this sense, transforms himself as the lord of the world. The "others" cannot have an opinion about him that cannot be easily overcome by the most elemental moral judgment. [This is because] the others are *evil*.
>
> (1952: 74)

This insight into American film's portrayal of its heroes can be easily extended into the present-day North American ethos, where some persons are considered *always already justified* while others are "evil." We do not have to look far: anti-immigrant sentiment works under this assumption. Nativists believe that the very fact that they are "American" justifies their existence, while immigrants are bent on destroying the sanctity of American life by either breaking the sacred laws of the land in the act of crossing borders or by polluting American culture with their own. The "illegal" immigrant is *always already* evil and villainous.

The same could be said about the philosophy profession. The metanarratives in which philosophers traffic allow no dissent, thus philosophers who speak from their own circumstance and speak from a unique historical and existential experience will not be heard—even when they proclaim that although not universal, their philosophy *aspires* to universality, that although their pronouncements are not timeless, these *can* apply to the existential predicaments of at least one absent other now or in the future. In the United States, the Latino philosopher is "other" to the always already justified image of what philosophers look and sound like. The problem (because it is a problem) is not so much that we understand this to be the case; the problem is that we accept it as such.

Internal to Mexican philosophy, particularly in the readings of the Mexican existentialists, is that this need not be the case. We need not accept our condition as it is. But before we challenge it, we must see it, understand it, and appropriate it. But to do this, we must see ourselves; we must see the different ways in which we have contributed to our own marginalization, for example, through acts of self-sabotage (something like relajo) or through acts of avoidance (something akin to desgana or waiting to be saved by others). Whatever we find in our auscultation, or autognosis, we must confront, and if necessary, transcend. What we find might not be a unique mode of being specific to us; it might be generic and familiar to universalizing perspectives, but the point is that it will come from us. In suggesting how Mexican philosophy can come about, Guillermo Hurtado writes that "we must rethink what we have read in light of our circumstance, that is, we must do philosophy as Mexicans" (2007: 43). The same can be said about a possible Latino philosophy; and it can certainly be said about the more general possibility of unraveling our being as Latinos in the United States. We must understand ourselves in light of our circumstance, but we must do this as Latinos—in other words, while preserving our historical, cultural, and existential difference.

What this shows is that the value of Mexican philosophy for Latino life does not lie in Uranga's and Portilla's analyses of insufficiency, desgana, or relajo but in the *accomplishment* of these analyses themselves. What these accomplishments reveal is a thinking that recovers the bases of Western philosophical ideology in the being of situated, concrete, historical persons. The analyses carried out by the Mexican existentialists, once encountered, motivate and instruct. Whether they failed or triumphed as motivating and instructional tools for Mexicans of the mid-twentieth century is not important for our purposes; it is the work itself that is. It gives us an opportunity to engage in a similar project, which Hurtado tells us was "committed, therapeutic, and liberating" (2006: xx). Like the hiperiones, we must likewise be activists for our cause, and find ourselves, warts and all, in the immense and troubled spectacle that is the United States, a material ground that challenges our identities by marginalizing, assimilating, or refusing our difference.

I began this chapter by suggesting that Latinos are other to the idea of "America." In several instances, for example, in the realm of higher education, this otherness can be harmful or, at least, not conducive to a good life. The realization that we are simultaneously in and outside the idea might lead us to hesitate or refrain from its pursuit. The Mexican philosophical project of Hyperion serves as a model, not to imitate verbatim but to assume and make our own—that is, appropriate. We begin with the consciousness of our difference, and go from there, asking ourselves the three fundamental questions that Hurtado suggests Mexicans themselves should ask, namely, "who were we? who are we? and who do we want to be?" (2007: 51).

Finally, Latino history reflects a continual struggle to find our bearings, and the philosophical project of Hiperión can at least encourage us to go at it more rigorously and, perhaps for the first time, *philosophically*. Not that I cannot be encouraged by Sartre or Rorty or even Ortega, but what can they possibly say about my father's struggles to find himself in his world as a Mexican in a foreign land, an immigrant, and, strangely still, an "illegal" other? Or about mine in mine? Those are questions with which I struggle as a Latino in philosophy. But these are the same questions that bring me to Mexican philosophy, especially of the Hiperión flavor, time and again.

Sketch of a Latino/a Philosophy: Philosophy *Sin Más*? No. Philosophy *Y Más*!

Common questions asked of us who teach and write on "Latin American" philosophy (or, in my case, "Mexican" philosophy) include the following (always asked in a somewhat passive-aggressive tone): *What is that? What makes Latin American philosophy "Latin American"? Isn't philosophy just philosophy?* These questions are always followed by one or more statements of belief that are supposed to settle, once and for all, the questions just asked: *We don't ask what makes German philosophy German . . . it's just philosophy! Philosophy is universal and calling it "Mexican" or "Greek" doesn't add anything to it!* When we reply that, by virtue of its historical or cultural emergence, we can locate certain differences between Latin American philosophy and the rest of (at least) the Western philosophical tradition, or that the questions asked by Latin American philosophers express a difference that we find philosophically interesting, the interrogation usually stops (at least that has been my experience), but not before a version of "Okay! Well, you'll have to tell me about it sometime" is condescendingly expressed or uttered with feigned curiosity.

I am not suggesting that the question is not legitimate, especially when we have been taught that something is philosophy if and only if its pronouncements are universalizable, impersonal, absolutely detached from passion, and applicable to all for all time. And that something is philosophy if it has *all* of these things and more, and not just one of them, so that if a pronouncement has universal validity it *cannot* be attached to some specific human worry. Naturally, the person who asks the question about the Latin Americanness of our philosophy will find it strange that we seem to want to localize it in a specific geopolitical space, and that is why they ask it. They will, naturally, think that such localizations will introduce impurities into the mix, that the philosophical well can only be polluted by such introductions.

These concerns or worries over the purity of philosophy are not new, and anyone with any decency will surely respect philosophy's history and traditions and affirm that philosophy does not allow for the impurities of history, culture, or concrete life. For this reason, that of faithfulness to the dogma of tradition or the force of Eurocentric authority, Mexican philosophers would like nothing more than to be recognized for simply *being* philosophers without the added burden of being "Mexican" philosophers. The adjective seems to dilute their chosen task, as it suggests that this philosophizing and this philosophy is of a particular kind, that it is different, and thus somehow not pure, unbiased philosophy. "Mexican" and "Latin American" are derogatory terms when paired with "philosophy," and as such, an affront to those who practice philosophy in Mexico or Latin America (I touched on this in Sánchez 2016: Ch. 3).

I would like to suggest the opposite: that the addition of the adjective adds value to that philosophizing and, moreover, to its readers, present and future; that the quest for purity in philosophy excludes and marginalizes voices and thinking; that, in our time, all that we can hope for from "universality" is the possibility of sharing an insight that survives its transit in space and time—this insight need not be atemporal, as the insight might flame out, lose its material justification, or change in value in a generation or two, realities that depend on our historical circumstance. Moreover, the desire for purity can only lead to conflict and anxiety (Sánchez 2016: Ch. 3). Emilio Uranga himself indirectly alludes to the value of this particular determination: "Of course, it would be preferable not to philosophize like Mexicans," he says in passing, suggesting that instead it would be preferable to philosophize from a broader perspective. "But," he laments, "that is not possible. Such expansion [of perspective] evokes nothing, it tells us nothing" (2013: 189). What *does* evoke, what tells us something, is a philosophizing *as we are*, from where we stand.

In his *La filosofía americana como filosofía sin más* of 1969, the unimpeachable Leopoldo Zea famously argued that Mexican, or Latin American, philosophy should be understood as "filosofía sin más," in other words, as simply philosophy and nothing more. By "nothing more" he meant, of course, that Mexican philosophy should be thought of in the same way that we think of Greek, Roman, or German philosophy. And this is how Latin American philosophers, and most North American philosophers, would like to think of philosophy that emerges from, concerns itself with, or speaks to the Latin American world, namely, as a philosophy that deals with universals and transcendentals. But, as I have shown, this is not entirely the case; this is not all that philosophy in Latin America concerns itself with, nor what gives it its character *as* philosophy or as valuable. Philosophy sin más can only be an ideal, for Zea, for Western philosophers, or for us. And indeed, this is how Zea, in his "Dialéctica," understands "sin más." Speaking of the picture of humanity that he and the members of Hyperion are painting for their people, Zea writes: "We do not tell [the Mexican] what he is, certainly, we tell him what he must be. In drawing the profile of man in Mexico we are also drawing the profile of man *sin más*" (1952: 214). This is a pragmatic "sin más," one that sketches a possibility and a trajectory. In the same way, a philosophy without apology, without history or culture, is an ideal but not a reality. In its reality, Mexican philosophy can only be thought as being philosophy *y más*, that is, as philosophy *and then some*. It is this "y más" that defines it; it is this that makes it valuable for Latino life.

Latino philosophy is likewise a philosophy y más—it is committed and emerges from the concrete situation of the Latino experience. Strictly speaking, Latino philosophy is structured as a response to competing inheritances—traditions, languages, spiritualities, orientations. And so it is pluralistic and dynamic—in other words, a *philosophy of contingency*.

As such, it is pragmatic in its framework and existential in its content. The phenomenology of the Latino experience, like the ontology of Mexican being, reveals Latinonness as zozobrante; unlike Mexicanness, however, Latinonness appears as hyper-zozobrante, as perpetually swinging between multiple in-betweens: metaphysico-epistemological in-betweens where Latinos swing to-and-fro the allure of the idea of "America" and the reality of our marginalization; politico-ethical in-betweens, in-between the demands for self-sufficiency inherent to Anglo-protestant culture and those values placed on togetherness and intersufficiency written into our historical communities; and a myriad of other in-betweens that manifest themselves in the struggle with anti-Latino, nativist, or other threat narratives that inhabit contemporary culture.

As committed, Latino philosophy calls for, and sketches out, the possibility of self-empowerment through critical appropriations of both the authoritatively given standard philosophical narrative and those narratives (threat, nativist, and so on) that scaffold Latino life in its concreteness. These emerge together in the interpretation of life and world. Militancy and activism may politically affect the material circumstances underlying vital oppressions, and might indeed be required for the possibility of overcoming and flourishing, but what must change are the standard narratives that inform our inner selves. To challenge those narratives what is needed is a violent appropriation that preserves and overcomes; in other words, what is needed is a reading into our traditions, those that are constitutive of our historical identity and those that, while framing our present and our future, reject or marginalize us. In the Mexican challenge to philosophy we read the possibility of challenging such narratives, and such traditions, but especially those that aim, through fear, coercion, or promises of reward, to strip us of all traces of difference and particularity. For Latino philosophers, these challenges will be the content of our philosophy. After all, to paraphrase Karl Jaspers from the chapter epigraph, *Latino philosophy exists wherever and whenever Latino/as are aware of their existence.*

References

Alcoff, L. M. (2006) *Visible Identities: Race, Gender, and the Self*, Oxford: Oxford University Press.
Berndston, A. (1953) "Teaching Latin American Philosophy," *The Americas* 9 (3): 263–271.
Brimelow, P. (1995) *Alien Nation: Common Sense about America's Immigration Disaster*, New York: HarperPerennial.
Buchanan, P. J. (2007) *State of Emergency: The Third World Invasion and Conquest of America*, New York: St. Martin's Griffin.
Chavez, L. R. (2008) *The Latino Threat Narrative: Constructing Immigrants, Citizens, and the Nation*, Stanford: Stanford University Press.
Corlett, J. A. (1999) "Latino Identity," *Public Affairs Quarterly* 13 (3): 273–295.
Gracia, J. J. E. (2000) *Hispanic/Latino Identity: A Philosophical Perspective*, Malden, MA: Blackwell.
Huntington, S. P. (2005) *Who Are We? The Challenges to America's National Identity*, New York: Simon & Schuster.
Hurtado, G. (2006) *El Hiperión*, Mexico City: Universidad Nacional Autónoma de México.
Hurtado, G. (2007) *El Búho y la serpiente: Ensayos sobre la filosofía en México en el siglo xx*, Mexico City: Universidad Nacional Autónoma de México.
Jackson, M. S. (2011) "Priming the Sleeping Giant: The Dynamics of Latino Political Identity and Vote Choice," *Political Psychology* 32 (4): 691–716.
Jaspers, K. (1963) *Philosophy and World: Selected Essays*, E. B. Ashton (trans.), Washington, DC: Regenery Gateway.
Mendoza, J. J. (2009) "Introduction to the Ethics of Illegality," *Oregon Review of International Law* 11 (1): 123–128.
Michael, C. D. (2014) *Octavio Paz en su siglo*, Mexico City: Aguilar.
Portilla, J. (1952) "La crisis espiritual de los Estados Unidos," *Cuadernos Americanos* 65 (5): 69–86.
Ramos, S. (1982) *El perfil del hombre y la cultura en México* (10th ed.), Mexico City: Espusa-Calpe Mexicana.
Reyes, A. (1950) *The Position of America and Other Essays*, H. de Onis (trans.), New York: Alfred A. Knopf.
Sanchez, C. A. (2011) "Philosophy and the Post-Immigrant Fear," *Philosophy in the Contemporary World* 18 (1): 31–42.
Sanchez, C. A. (2012) *The Suspension of Seriousness: On the Phenomenology of Jorge Portilla*, Albany: State University of New York Press.
Sánchez, C. A. (2016) *Contingency and Commitment: Mexican Existentialism and the Place of Philosophy*, Albany, NY: SUNY Press.
Schuck, P. (1989) "Membership in the Liberal Polity: The Devaluation of American Citizenship," *Georgetown Immigration Law Journal* 3: 1–18.
Schutte, O. (2004) "Negotiating Latina Identities," in J. J. E. Gracia and E. Millán-Zaibert (eds.), *Latin American Philosophy for the Twenty-First Century: The Human Condition, Values, and the Search for Identity*, 337–354, Amherst, NY: Prometheus.
Uranga, E. (1952) *Análisis del ser del mexicano*, Mexico City: Porrua y Obregon.
Uranga, E. (2013) "Análisis del ser del mexicano," in G. Hurtado (ed.), *Análisis del ser del mexicano y otros escritos sobre la filosofía de lo mexicano, (1949–1952)*, Mexico City: Bonilla Artigas Editores.

Villegas, A. (1979) *La filosofía de lo mexicano*, Mexico City: Universidad Nacional Autónoma de México.
Zea, L. (1952) *La filosofía como compromiso y otros ensayos*, Mexico City: Fondo de Cultura Económica.

Notes

1 I am thinking here of those influences that shape the nativist consciousness and, in turn, the very idea of "American," exemplified in the work of Huntington (2005), Buchanan (2007), and Brimelow (1995), among others.
2 One readily acknowledged example of such legislation is Arizona's Senate Bill 1070 of 2010.
3 I have made this argument elsewhere (Sanchez 2011).
4 Stories of this struggle abound. I refer the reader to Mendoza (2009) and Sanchez (2011).

Reading Questions

1. How does Sánchez characterize the position of latinidad in the U.S.? Do you agree with his characterization? Why or why not?
2. What is the "threat narrative" that Sánchez discusses?
3. According to Sánchez, why is Latinx or Mexican philosophy worth studying, doing, or pursuing?
4. The Roman playwright Terence once said, "I am human. Nothing human is alien to me." Does this view conflict with Sánchez's view? Why or why not?
5. Sánchez holds that Latinxs need to be reflective about their otherness to the idea of the US, and that Latinxs need to redescribe their role as citizens and intellectuals, lest they be disempowered by a narrative that marginalizes and oppresses them, that was not constructed for them. Do you agree or disagree? Why? Can you think of potential counterexamples to his view about this?

34 Implicit Bias and Latinxs in Philosophy

Alex Madva

Can research on implicit bias shed light on issues related to teaching Latinxs in philosophy? Yes, with caveats. In particular, no one will be surprised to learn that implicit bias against (and among) Latinxs and Latin Americans is severely understudied. While Latinxs make up the largest minority group in the United States, recent estimates suggest that there is more than *six times* as much research on stereotyping and prejudice against African-Americans as there is against Latinxs (see e.g. Dovidio et al. 2010; Guillermo and Correll 2016: 265). I speculate about some causes and remedies for this disparity below, but my primary aims in this essay are different. First, I attempt to stitch together the general literature regarding anti-Latinx bias with the general literature regarding bias in education in order to convey some of the basic challenges that bias likely poses to Latinx students. Second, I consider whether Latin American philosophy might itself serve a bias-reducing function. Specifically, I sketch—in tentative and promissory terms—how the traditional "problem" of group identity explored in Latinx and Latin American thought might function as part of the "solution" to the stereotypes and prejudices that have helped to sustain an exclusionary atmosphere in Anglo-American philosophy. Given the dearth of literature on the situation of Latinxs in philosophy, my claims here will build on findings about the situations of minorities in education more broadly.

Anti-Latinx Bias: What Do We Know and Why Don't We Know More?

The limited existing research tends to suggest that Latinxs face many of the same prejudices as African-Americans in criminal justice, education, healthcare, and so on. The well-known "shooter bias" exhibited against blacks also exists, to some extent, against Latinos: in a video game setting, police officers are quicker to shoot Latinos than whites and Asians (Sadler et al. 2012). Mock jurors are more likely to think a criminal defendant is guilty and aggressive if he is Latino than if he is white (Bodenhausen and Lichtenstein 1987). Bias against Latino defendants is even more pronounced when they are undocumented immigrants—although white participants (in this case, undergraduates in Southern California) tend to deny that the defendant's immigration status has affected their judgment (Minero and Espinoza 2015).[1] The pervasive tendency for individuals to disavow prejudice on an explicit level led researchers in the 1980s and '90s to develop more indirect measures, which could detect attitudes that individuals were unwilling or unable to self-report. On the most popular indirect measure, the Implicit Association Test (IAT), undergraduates have more difficulty associating Hispanic names (like "Juanita" and "Miguel") than non-Hispanic names ("Nicole" and "Robert") with words related to intelligence ("brainy") (Weyant 2005). And while very few clinical doctors openly admit to

DOI: 10.4324/9781003385417-49

being prejudiced against Latinxs, one Denver-based study found that roughly two-thirds of participating clinicians demonstrated anti-Latino bias on the IAT (Blair 2013). Clinicians' implicit biases, in turn, predict the quality of their interactions with patients, their treatment decisions, and patients' health outcomes (Hall et al. 2015). However, the overwhelming majority of studies tying implicit (and explicit) bias to "real-world" outcomes has focused on anti-black bias, so the extent to which this research can illuminate the ongoing discrimination faced by Latinxs remains unknown. Many of the relevant impediments to doing better research are structural, for example, the lack of sufficient funding for in-depth, longitudinal, field-based research, and the underrepresentation of Latinxs in the sciences (Crisp and Nora 2006/2012).

I suspect that the "black/white binary"—the tendency to implicitly model all forms of ethnic, racial, and cultural discrimination on the attitudes and actions of white Americans toward African Americans—also plays a role in stifling more wide-ranging and innovative research on biases against and among Latinxs (for further discussion see Dovidio et al. 2010). Researchers who investigate biases against Latinxs at all have tended to design experiments specifically to test whether antiLatinx biases are similar to known anti-black biases. That is, researchers hypothesize similarity and then—lo and behold!—tend to find it. After a handful of studies uncovering similarities were published, I suspect a tendency emerged to assume that knowledge about anti-black bias could generally be transferred over, *mutatis mutandis*, to anti-Latinx bias.

This is clearly a mistake. Excessive focus on white-against-black bias has obscured the diverse and distinctive challenges faced by Latinxs (and by members of other disadvantaged or stigmatized groups), and this seems to be as true in implicit bias research as it is in other domains. One obvious difference between anti-black and anti-Latinx biases revolves around associations with immigration. Latinxs are more likely than African Americans to be immigrants or children of immigrants, to have close family and friendship ties to immigrants, to maintain relationships across borders, and so on. They are, accordingly, more likely to be *assumed* to be immigrants, to be "exoticized," and to be perceived as unable or unwilling to adopt dominant American (white) norms. (Antiimmigrant biases toward Latinxs will also be importantly different from anti-immigrant biases toward Asian and European immigrants [Lee and Fiske 2006; Cottrell et al. 2010]).

As an illustration of this fact, many people continue to underestimate the profound effects that anti-Latino bias *per se* can have, for example, on immigration policy and political discourse. Consider how pundits have attempted to downplay the role of anti-Latino (and anti-Muslim) prejudice *per se* in explaining the current popularity of Donald Trump (Frank 2016). Many attribute the popularity of Trump's anti-immigrant messages to economic factors, as if Trump is "channeling" preexisting economic anxiety into bigotry. It may also be, however, that Trump is channeling preexisting bigotry into economic anxiety, much as he once channeled racism into nativism by questioning Obama's citizenship (Yglesias 2015; Roberts 2015). One study found that support for broadly restrictionist U.S. immigration policy was *not* predicted by individuals' partisan affiliations or economic circumstances (having a low-skilled job, being anxious about one's financial status, or living in high-unemployment areas) (Shin et al. 2015). Instead, general opposition to immigration seemed to stem primarily from anti-Latinx biases, such as endorsements of stigmatizing stereotypes, denials that Latinx immigrants have contributed to society, and preferences not to live near Latinxs or have Latinx in-laws. Such findings make salient the extent to which anti-Latinx prejudice is a self-standing problem, not merely an offshoot of anxiety about immigrants taking jobs and suppressing wages.

In fact, xenophobia and hostility to immigration are also common in the Latinx community. Texas undergraduates of Mexican descent tend to agree that "illegal immigration" is a "growing problem" that contributes to "the decline of society."[2] Researchers speculate that these individuals may "resent the ongoing tide of illegal entry to the country and view illegal immigration as undermining the legitimacy of those who have gained citizenship and upward mobility" (San Miguel et al. 2011: 104). In this vein, numerous studies demonstrate *intragroup* biases among Hispanic individuals. These biases seem to occur primarily along two dimensions: country of origin and skin color. Related to the former, foreign-born Latinx youth often report experiencing discrimination from U.S.-born Latinxs (Córdova and Cervantes 2010).[3] Related to the latter, Hispanic undergraduates in both Seattle, Washington, and Santiago, Chile, implicitly favored "Blancos" over "Morenos" (Uhlmann et al. 2002). This implicit "colorism" was found even among self-identified Morenos, although to a somewhat lesser extent than among Blancos.[4] Skin-tone preferences tend to be considered more socially acceptable in Chile, and participants there were more likely to explicitly acknowledge a preference for light skin. Participants in Seattle, however, tended to report no skin-tone preferences (see also March and Graham 2015), again demonstrating how these indirect measures can tap into preferences that participants are unwilling to acknowledge openly—perhaps because such preferences are inconsistent with their reflective egalitarian commitments, and perhaps because they simply don't want to *appear* non-egalitarian. These forms of implicit colorism likely have political ramifications. Light-skinned Latinxs tend to perceive more "commonality" with whites than with other minority groups (Wilkinson and Earle 2013).[5] Intragroup bias and discrimination is particularly disheartening because it suppresses the kind of group solidarity necessary for mobilizing collective political action (Sanchez and Espinosa 2016).

Such findings serve as reminders that Latinxs are an incredibly diverse group in terms of race, ethnicity, nationality, language, religion, history, and familial and cultural traditions, values, and styles. Anti-Latinx biases will surely vary depending on these more particular aspects of social identity and context. It is extremely likely, for example, that non-Hispanics share Hispanics' implicit skin-tone preferences, and an IAT using photos of Hispanic faces may reveal significantly different biases depending on the extent to which the faces tend to have stereotypically Eurocentric, Afrocentric, or indigenous features, or stereotypically masculine versus feminine features (Johnson et al. 2012). Existing measures of anti-Latinx bias, which tend to use names and faces, can be complemented with measures using other signifiers of Latinx identities—such as accent, clothing, and food—in order to uncover the diversity and distinctiveness of anti-Latinx biases. For example, undergraduates (in this case, in Western Pennsylvania) tend to perceive speakers with Spanish accents as less competent and knowledgeable, especially when the speaker is a woman or the listener is a man (Nelson et al. 2016). I would also predict that anti-Latinx biases will take on different shapes depending on occupation and social role. The stereotypes of Hispanic maids, pool boys, drug dealers, farmhands, guerilla fighters, abuelitas, etc., each occupy distinctive positions in the American collective imagination, and the sorts of discriminatory treatment individuals will experience in particular contexts could vary tremendously depending on whether they are perceived to resemble one or another of these stereotypes.

The natures and varieties of anti-Latinx biases remain an open question. In fact, I believe that Latin American and Latinx academic thought and philosophy could provide a rich resource for directing scientists' attention toward the particularities of Latinx experiences of prejudice and discrimination. I return to this point below, but consider this another call for greater cross-talk between the humanities and social sciences. I also feel compelled to note that, while more research on these topics is needed, a further problem is that the research that *is* being done is not sufficiently well-known or publicized. One need only scroll through recent issues of the *Hispanic Journal of Behavioral Sciences* to find a plethora of valuable research on issues related to bias, as well as education and mentoring. Yet a gap persists between these findings and our ears. We need better, more consistent mechanisms for broadcasting ongoing empirical developments. Perhaps the APA could devote a blog or podcast to discussing exciting new research, stressing its relevance to philosophy and philosophers.

What are the implications of research on anti-Latinx bias for philosophy? Just as many pundits may underestimate the full effects that anti-Latinx biases *per se* can play in politics, philosophers may underestimate the role that biases, perhaps of a subtle and unintentional nature, can play in the marginalization of Latin American philosophy, and the exclusion and alienation of Latinx philosophy students. Contrast two narratives we might tell about these exclusions.[6] The first might seem, on an individual level at least, relatively innocuous: a given philosopher was not exposed to Latin American philosophy in his education, and as a result does not seriously engage with it in his professional career. Stories like this insinuate that the marginalization of Latin American philosophy is first and foremost a structural problem. If only Latin American philosophy were taught more widely and regularly, then more people would be exposed to it, recognize its value, pursue it further, and so on. Moreover, such a change would surely attract more Latinxs to philosophy.

But consider a different narrative: a given philosopher (call him Tobias) does not introduce himself to Latin American philosophy because, well, he prefers not to, and his preference is caused, in part, by implicit biases that Hispanics are not "brainy" and have not made valuable contributions to society. (Tobias thinks that success in philosophy depends much more on having an innately penetrating intellect than it does on hard work or acquired skills (Leslie et al. 2015).) Tobias' biases make it the case that when he *does* encounter Latin American philosophy and philosophers, he is unimpressed. For example, he finds that philosophy professors and students with Spanish accents somehow don't sound as incisive and knowledgeable as those with French, German, or Oxbridge accents. (He may be relatively unaware of the impact of these biases on his judgments, or he may be aware but unwilling to acknowledge it—to others or to himself.) Tobias is, moreover, inevitably able to confabulate alternative reasons, which ostensibly have nothing to do with anti-Latino bias, to justify his impressions and preferences (Uhlmann and Cohen 2005). In light of all this, Tobias thinks that it is not a priority to add Latin American philosophy to his department's curriculum, to hire Latinx faculty, and so on. A few of his colleagues share these views, and when they discuss these issues in formal or informal settings, they form an echo chamber of mutual validation (a "shared reality" [Echterhoff et al. 2009]). Thereafter, the confidence exuded by Tobias and his likeminded colleagues about these matters helps to persuade those colleagues who had been undecided or lacked strong opinions, and together they form a bloc in the department just large enough to sway decisions about which areas to hire in, which courses to add to the curriculum, and so on. I hope this second narrative illustrates in microcosm how bias can play a significant role, independently from structural factors, in the continued marginalization and exclusion of Latinx and Latin American philosophy and philosophers. Of course, bias is operative in classrooms as well as faculty meetings. I turn next to research on bias in pedagogical contexts.

Implicit Biases in Education

Although research in the United States is dominated by the black/white paradigm, there is a substantial—and quickly expanding—body of research on ethnic and anti-immigrant biases in Europe, especially in the Netherlands and Germany. This constitutes some of the most suggestive research for thinking about biases toward Latinx and Latin American students. European social scientists have investigated teachers' explicit and implicit prejudices and stereotypes related to students' socioeconomic status (SES), gender, and Arab-Muslim identity.

One landmark study found that Dutch teachers explicitly reported unprejudiced attitudes toward Arab-Muslim students but harbored implicit biases (van den Bergh et al. 2010). Teachers' implicit biases predicted their expectations of student success as well as the ethnic achievement gap between Dutch-origin and ethnic minority students (largely of Turkish or Moroccan descent). That is, the ethnic achievement gap was larger in classrooms with more implicitly biased teachers. (This research group found the same pattern of results regarding teachers' explicit egalitarianism, implicit bias, and the achievement of students with dyslexia [Hornstra 2010].) Another study, set in Midwestern communities that have recently seen an influx of Muslim and Christian immigrants from the Arab world, found that teachers with anti-Arab implicit biases were less likely to foster interethnic respect among their students or to explore proactive strategies to help students work through interethnic conflict (Kumar et al. 2015: 533).

At first glance, these correlational studies do not settle whether ethnic minority students do worse in school because their teachers implicitly dislike them, or whether teachers implicitly dislike them because of how they behave. However, subsequent research has revealed numerous ways in which teacher bias negatively affects students. One study in an urban Texas district found that teachers' biased perceptions of their students (specifically, the gap between how motivated students perceived themselves to be and how motivated their teachers believed they were) significantly affected students' final grades in math and English, even when controlling for standardized measures of ability (Harvey et al. 2015).[7] The effects of teacher bias are especially pronounced for low-income African-American and Latinx students. Such findings are all the more troubling because Latinx students already tend to have less confidence in their ability to succeed in math (Stevens et al. 2004). Teachers' biases likely influence how they interact with students and grade their work, and, in turn, how students come to think of themselves.

In one impressive demonstration of the causal effects of implicit bias on teaching performance, white undergraduates were tasked with giving lessons to other students, who were either white or black (Jacoby-Senghor et al. 2016). Among these "instructors," those who were more implicitly biased were more visibly anxious while teaching black learners and gave poorer lessons. In fact, even non-black learners who subsequently watched videos of their lessons did significantly worse on tests measuring how well they had absorbed the material.

Cumulatively, the research shows that teacher bias has pernicious effects on student performance and well-being across a variety of academic subjects. There is no reason to suppose philosophy is an exception from these trends. Let us return to the example of Professor Tobias from the preceding section: we are now poised to peek further into the workings of his implicit biases toward his Latinx students. It is not just that Tobias thinks these students sound less brainy and knowledgeable when they speak in class or office hours. He also underestimates the time and effort they invest on reading and writing assignments. These false perceptions, in turn, lead him to grade them unfairly. He is, for example, more likely to notice and penalize the grammatical mistakes in their writing than in the writing of U.S.-born white students (Reeves 2014). But the harmful effects of Tobias' biases are not limited to discounting Latinx students' contributions to class discussion or grading them inaccurately. His discomfort around them leads him to give poorer lessons. They actually learn less. And they internalize the biases he projects onto them, becoming less motivated, less identified with school, and more anxious in test-taking situations.

Debiasing Strategies

Thus far, I have drawn on general patterns of research to sketch the complex, self-perpetuating situation of bias against Latinxs, and especially against Latinx philosophy students. But what can we do to combat anti-Latinx bias in educational settings, and specifically in philosophy? I first mention a few general strategies that teachers can employ to reduce their own biases and to help buffer students against the effects of bias. I then consider whether Latin American philosophy might itself serve a bias-reducing function.

Research has uncovered a variety of effective "debiasing" strategies that each of us as individuals can pursue.[8] One is to identify the contexts in which we suspect that we'll be biased, and form concrete if-then plans (or "implementation intentions") for how to act in those contexts (see e.g. Mendoza et al. 2010). For example, form plans such as, "If a Latina student raises her hand, then I will call on her!" and "If a Latina student makes a contribution to class discussion, then I will refer back to her point later!" In general, when interacting with students from diverse social backgrounds, consider taking an "approach-oriented" mindset, in which you have an opportunity to engage with and learn from someone else, rather than an "avoidance-oriented" mindset, in which you are concerned about what not to say and how to avoid appearing prejudiced (Murphy et al. 2011). Research also suggests that a common strategy is mistaken: don't try to compensate for your biases simply by being especially warm and friendly; it is often more important to members of disadvantaged groups that they feel *respected* rather than liked (Bergsieker et al. 2010). To better convey respect and understanding for the student as an individual, actively imagine yourself in the student's position (Galinsky and Moskowitz 2000: 708), and look for the student's "individuating" features, interests, and traits. One simple strategy to facilitate taking a student's perspective and homing in on individuating features is to focus on the student's eyes (Kawakami 2014: 1), which are a rich source of emotional cues. Implicit biases lead us to make less eye contact with outgroup than ingroup members, and this attentional difference partly underlies the awkwardness and communicative difficulties of intergroup interactions. Eye gaze can, in most contexts, be adjusted with minimal thought and effort, and, after a little practice, improved eye contact in intergroup situations may become a relatively effortless habit. (Form the plan: "When students speak to me, I will look them in the eye!")

Although these represent a few of the many strategies teachers can employ to be less biased, their cumulative impact will be difficult to assess. For one thing, Latinx students may still experience discrimination outside of the classroom and internalize negative views about their group from mass media. These experiences can lead to stereotype threat, which occurs when being reminded of stereotypes about one's social identity (for example, by telling Latina undergraduates that they are about to take a "genuine test" of their intellectual "abilities and limitations" [Gonzales et al. 2002]) induces anxiety and harms performance. Here, however, there is another set of strategies that, I believe, will be of use to philosophers. Although teachers may not be able to prevent their students from internalizing stereotypes in the first place, a number of strategies have emerged to counter stereotype threat, and, more broadly, to buffer students against discrimination and other obstacles to psychological well-being and academic success. One example is values affirmation. This is a simple but incredibly powerful 15-minute exercise wherein students identify, and write in an open-ended way about, the values most important to them.[9] This intervention has been found to reduce the achievement gap between white, black, and Hispanic middle schoolers (with the beneficial effects on minority student achievement persisting for at least three years) (Sherman et al. 2013), and to reduce the achievement gap between men and women in college physics (Miyake et al. 2010). This intervention has not yet been tested in academic philosophy, but it is such a low-cost intervention that I nevertheless recommend philosophy departments include this exercise, e.g., on the first day of all introductory courses. (Your very own department could do a virtually costless controlled study comparing classes that get this intervention to those that don't.)

Another strategy for reducing stereotype threat is to emphasize that tests and papers are not measures of innate or fixed abilities, but rather are merely indices of students' gradual progress toward the mastery of learnable skills (Stout and Dasgupta 2013). One way to bring home the message that philosophy—and undergraduate life in general—consists in learnable skills is to bring senior philosophy majors to discuss their personal experiences adapting to college life and learning how to do philosophy. One study found that this sort of intervention (not specifically focused on philosophy majors) was especially helpful for students who were the first generation in their family to go to college. In their first month at college, these students spoke for one hour with a diverse panel of upper-division students, who emphasized "that students' different backgrounds can shape the college experience in both positive and negative ways and that students need to utilize strategies for success that take their different backgrounds into account" (Stephens et al. 2014). This intervention led first-generation students to feel less stressed and better prepared, to make more use of school resources, and to earn significantly higher GPAs through their first year (reducing the achievement gap between first- and continuing-generation students by 63 percent).

The "Problem" of *Mestizaje* as Part of the "Solution" to Bias

I conclude by considering the possible role that Latin American philosophy might play in addressing some of the challenges discussed above. Explaining what I have in mind requires first bringing into view the benefits and limitations of what is perhaps the most intensively studied intervention for reducing intergroup bias and inequality: social integration (Anderson 2010). Meta-analyses suggest that integrating schools reduces racial and ethnic achievement gaps ("bringing up" minority students without "bringing down" whites) (see e.g. Mickelson and Bottia 2009), and that positive intergroup contact reduces bias, often by creating a shared sense of identity across groups (Pettigrew and Tropp 2006). Integration is likely beneficial for reducing both inter- and intra-group biases. For example, emphasizing a shared pan-ethnic Latinx identity may reduce implicit colorism among Latinxs (Uhlmann et al. 2002).

However, a significant body of research has revealed that successful instances of intergroup contact incur unforeseen costs (for a review, see Dixon et al. 2012). The virtue of contact—that it breaks down "us" vs. "them" group differences and leads individuals to think of themselves as members of a larger, shared group—is also its vice. As disadvantaged-group members come to think of themselves as sharing a superordinate identity with advantaged-group members, they simultaneously become less likely to recognize social injustice as a serious problem, and they come to expect—often mistakenly—to receive fair treatment from advantaged-group members. These "ironic" effects of intergroup contact suggest that prejudice reduction—where this is conceived solely in terms of finding common ground and forging a shared identity across group lines—undermines disadvantaged-group members' motivation to fight collectively for social justice. The counterproductive effects of intergroup contact have led some theorists and activists to conclude that, so long as substantive intergroup inequalities persist, prejudice reduction is a misbegotten aim (Dixon et al. 2012). They think we should instead animate certain forms of intergroup conflict in order to spark effective collective action.

Rather than abandoning prejudice reduction altogether, however, another tradition of research suggests that leading models of prejudice reduction have been oversimplified. Prejudice-reduction advocacy has been focused too narrowly on eliminating intergroup distinctions and building a common identity, even as decades of research show that there is another way. This other way is disarmingly straightforward: emphasize commonality *and* difference. There is obviously no *logical inconsistency* in thinking of oneself, e.g., as *both* an American *and also* a Latina. Research suggests that there need be no *psychological inconsistency* in this either (Dovidio 2016). Often, disadvantaged-group members prefer to think of themselves in terms of a "dual identity," e.g., as adopting a shared identity with all residents of the United States, or with all members of their university, while simultaneously maintaining a distinctive subgroup identity, whether it is constituted by a set of idiosyncratic interests, or by broader ethnic or cultural inheritances. In a range of intergroup interactions, discussing dual identity—emphasizing common ground without dismissing difference—brings many of the benefits of positive contact, without incurring its most pernicious costs. Maintaining a sense of oneself as a member of distinctive subgroups prevents one from conflating the advancement of intergroup harmony with the achievement of intergroup equality.

But what, exactly, does it mean to "discuss" dual identity in intergroup contexts? Much of the empirical literature leaves the content of these conversations underspecified, but my sense is that they risk slipping into what Edward Said called "a lazy . . . feel-good multiculturalism" (Said 2004: 50). Is there a more rigorous, challenging, or nuanced way of thinking through dual identity? It is in this context that I propose that Latin American and Latinx philosophy has much to offer, for example, in the wide-ranging and diverse traditions of thought surrounding *mestizaje*.[10] I can think of no intellectual traditions better suited to examining and debating the complexity of social identity than those embodied in thinkers from Bolívar to Vasconcelos to Anzaldúa to Lugones and Alcoff.

Although *mestizaje* has at times been rhetorically invoked to stress pan-ethnic Latin-American homogeneity and common cause, many theorists go to lengths to emphasize precisely the opposite: the heterogeneity, tension, and contestation inherent in mestiza/o identities. In a similar way, the empirical research doesn't suggest that individuals must settle on some conclusive, definitive interpretation of ingroup, outgroup, or subgroup social identities. To the contrary, several studies find that emphasizing the internal heterogeneity of groups is more effective for reducing explicit and implicit bias than is portraying groups in a homogeneous and unequivocally positive light (Brauer et al. 2012).

Perhaps, then, the longstanding practical and theoretical "problem" of characterizing Latinx and Latin American group identity can figure as one part of the "solution" to the downsides of integration. While the danger of positive intergroup contact is that it leads us to form misleadingly simplified and unified conceptions of our social identity—conceptions that sap our motivation to struggle for social change—Latin American and Latinx thinkers have long been oriented toward constructing more complex and contextualized conceptions of social identity, often with an eye toward inspiring political activism.

But what are the real prospects of Latin American philosophy serving a bias-reducing function? One immediate challenge is that advantaged-group members (e.g., white undergraduates) tend to prefer to focus exclusively on commonality and shared superordinate identities (Dovidio et al. 2010). They are often reluctant to acknowledge and openly explore intergroup differences. There is, in these contexts, a genuine risk of white backlash and hostility. Based on my own (very, very) limited experience, however, I find that the history of thought surrounding *mestizaje* can actually serve as an exciting point of entry for thinking more generally about social identity, and for confronting the challenge—faced by individuals from virtually all walks of life—of making sense of one's self *qua* inheritor of diverse traditions and inhabitor of multiple identities. To take a low-stakes example, while white undergraduates may be uncomfortable, resentful, or even jealous of the code-switching they observe among their African American or Latinx peers, it doesn't take much to get them to realize that they engage in rampant code-switching as well. For example, they speak differently with their friends than with their grandparents, they communicate differently on social media than in the classroom, and so on. Appreciating the pervasiveness of their own code-switching may reduce white students' perception that minority code-switching is somehow especially exclusionary or problematic. Code-switching is a ubiquitous feature of contemporary linguistic life; it is one clear manifestation of how we all take up and move between a variety of social roles and identities.[11]

What is the nature of the "self" who inherits, navigates, and actively reinterprets these multiple social identities? How can we embrace our disparate multiple roles and traditions when they seem to conflict with each other? Latin American thought has long engaged such questions. When I frame Latin American philosophy as an especially well-developed tradition of grappling with problems that, at a certain level of generality, are faced by nearly everyone, non-Hispanic students seem at least a little more open to exploring it. As Alcoff explains, "In certain respects the philosophical issue at stake is the same whether the object is mixed race, mixed ethnicity, or mixed culture: all have been devalued as incoherent, diluted, and thus weak" (Alcoff 2005: 265). Of course, this way of framing *mestizaje* introduces the danger of the colonizer "appropriating" or "assimilating" the identities and experiences of the colonized. But my suggestion that thinking about *mestizaje* can be a springboard—even for students who do not identify as mestiza/o—into thinking either more generally or more idiosyncratically about social identity is not meant to imply that, deep down, all human beings are really mestizos. In fact, acknowledging the risk of appropriation itself needs to be part of the class discussion.

Another potential challenge for the idea that philosophical reflection on *mestizaje* might accrue substantial social-psychological benefits is that emphasizing dual identity can sometimes be a source of stress instead of strength. Under another guise, "bicultural stress"—navigating the felt expectation to live up to two distinct cultural ideals—can lead to significant mental health challenges for Latinxs (Romero et al. 2007). One worry, then, might be that what I am identifying as the "solution" in this context is in fact the "problem" in other contexts. Indeed, when it comes to navigating social identity and prejudice, there is no ready-made, context-general solution. How to approach these issues is a context-sensitive matter. In some cases, an individual suffering from bicultural stress might benefit from cultivating a more "mainstream" superordinate identity (Basáñez et al. 2013). That said, researchers make a crucial distinction between two ways of responding to bicultural stress: "active" vs. "avoidance" coping (Basáñez et al. 2014). Mental-health setbacks tend to be concentrated among "avoidance copers," who respond to tensions among their multiple identities by not thinking about it (e.g., by distracting themselves with TV). Active copers have a more "problem-solving" orientation, and are more open to proactive strategies for talking and thinking through these experienced conflicts of identity. Seen in this light, then, rather than being a genuine problem for my proposal, research on coping with bicultural stress might point toward much the same conclusion. Specifically, engaging seriously with the Latin American philosophy of group identity might itself constitute an avenue for active coping among Latinx youth. In this way, philosophically oriented reflection on *mestizaje* might function in some contexts as an instrument for prejudice reduction and in others as a form of therapy.[12]

References

Alcoff, L. M. (2005) *Visible Identities: Race, Gender, and the Self*, Oxford: Oxford University Press.
Anderson, E. (2010) *The Imperative of Integration*, Princeton: Princeton University Press.
Basáñez, T., et al. (2013) "Perceived Discrimination as a Risk Factor for Depressive Symptoms and Substance Use Among Hispanic Adolescents in Los Angeles," *Ethnicity and Health* 18 (3): 244–261.
Basáñez, T., et al. (2014) "Perceptions of Intragroup Rejection and Coping Strategies: Malleable Factors Affecting Hispanic Adolescents' Emotional and Academic Outcomes," *Journal of Youth and Adolescence* 43 (8): 1266–1280.
Bergsieker., H. B., Shelton, J. N., and Richeson, J. A. (2010) "To Be Liked Versus Respected: Divergent Goals in Interracial Interactions," *Journal of Personality and Social Psychology* 99 (2): 248–264.
Blair, I. V., et al. (2013) "Clinicians' Implicit Ethnic/Racial Bias and Perceptions of Care Among Black and Latino Patients," *The Annals of Family Medicine* 11 (1): 43–52.
Bodenhausen, G. V., and Lichtenstein, M. (1987) "Social Stereotypes and Information-Processing Strategies: The Impact of Task Complexity," *Journal of Personality and Social Psychology* 52 (5): 871–880.
Brauer, M., et al. (2012) "Describing a Group in Positive Terms Reduces Prejudice Less Effectively Than Describing It in Positive and Negative Terms," *Journal of Experimental Social Psychology* 48 (3): 757–761.
Córdova, D., and Cervantes, R. C. (2010) "Intergroup and Within-Group Perceived Discrimination Among U.S.-born and Foreign-born Latino Youth," *Hispanic Journal of Behavioral Sciences* 32 (2): 259–274.
Cottrell, C. A., Richards, D. A. R., and Nichols, A. L. (2010) "Predicting Policy Attitudes from General Prejudice versus Specific Intergroup Emotions," *Journal of Experimental Social Psychology* 46 (2): 247–254.
Crenshaw, K. (1991) "Mapping the Margins: Intersectionality, Identity Politics, and Violence Against Women of Color," *Stanford Law Review*, 1241–1299.
Crisp, G., and Nora, A. (2006/2012) "Overview of Hispanics in Science, Mathematics, Engineering, and Technology (STEM): K–16 Representation, Preparation, and Participation," *Hispanic Association of Colleges and Universities*.
Dixon, J., et al. (2012) "Beyond Prejudice: Are Negative Evaluations the Problem and Is Getting Us to Like One Another More the Solution?" *Behavioral and Brain Sciences* 35 (6): 411–425.
Dovidio, J. F., et al. (2010) "Understanding Bias Toward Latinos: Discrimination, Dimensions of Difference, and Experience of Exclusion," *Journal of Social Issues* 66 (1): 59–78.
Dovidio, J. F., et al. (2016) "Included but Invisible? Subtle Bias, Common Identity, and the Darker Side of 'We'," *Social Issues and Policy Review* 10 (1): 6–46.
Du Bois, W. E. B. (2007) *The Souls of Black Folk*, Oxford: Oxford University Press.
Echterhoff, G. E., Higgins, T., and Levine, J. M. (2009) "Shared Reality Experiencing Commonality with Others' Inner States about the World," *Perspectives on Psychological Science* 4 (5): 496–521.
Frank, T. (2016) "Millions of Ordinary Americans Support Donald Trump. Here's Why," *The Guardian*, March 7, http://www.theguardian.com/commentisfree/2016/mar/07/donaldtrump-why-americans-support.
Galinsky, A. D., and Moskowitz, G. B. (2000) "Perspective-Taking: Decreasing Stereotype Expression, Stereotype Accessibility, and In-group Favoritism," *Journal of Personality and Social Psychology* 78 (4): 708.
Garza, C. F., and Gasquoine, P. G. (2013) "Implicit Race/Ethnic Prejudice in Mexican Americans," *Hispanic Journal of Behavioral Sciences* 35 (1): 121–133.
Gonzales, P., Blanton, H., and Williams, K. J. (2002) "The Effects of Stereotype Threat and Double-minority Status on the Test Performance of Latino Women," *Personality and Social Psychology Bulletin* 28 (5): 659–70.

Guillermo, S., and Correll, J. (2016) "Attentional Biases Toward Latinos," *Hispanic Journal of Behavioral Sciences* 38 (2): 264–278.

Hall, W. J., et al. (2015) "Implicit Racial/Ethnic Bias Among Health Care Professionals and Its Influence on Health Care Outcomes: A Systematic Review," *American Journal of Public Health* 105 (12): e60–e76.

Harvey, K. E. Suizzo, M.-A., and Moran Jackson, K. (2015) "Predicting the Grades of Low-Income-Ethnic-Minority Students from Teacher-Student Discrepancies in Reported Motivation," *The Journal of Experimental Education* 1–19.

Haslanger, S. (2015) "Social Structure, Narrative, and Explanation," *Canadian Journal of Philosophy* 45 (1): 1–15.

Hornstra, L., et al. (2010) "Teacher Attitudes Toward Dyslexia: Effects on Teacher Expectations and the Academic Achievement of Students with Dyslexia," *Journal of Learning Disabilities* 43 (6): 515–529.

Jacoby-Senghor, D., Sinclair, S., and Shelton, J. N. (2016) "A Lesson in Bias: The Relationship between Implicit Racial Bias and Performance in Pedagogical Contexts," *Journal of Experimental Social Psychology* 63: 50–55.

Johnson, K. L., Freeman, J. B., and Pauker, K. (2012) "Race Is Gendered: How Covarying Phenotypes and Stereotypes Bias Sex Categorization," *Journal of Personality and Social Psychology* 102 (1): 116–131.

Kawakami, K., et al. (2014) "An Eye for the I: Preferential Attention to the Eyes of Ingroup Members," *Journal of Personality and Social Psychology* 107 (1): 1.

Kumar, R., Karabenick, S. A., and Burgoon, J. N. (2015) "Teachers' Implicit Attitudes, Explicit Beliefs, and the Mediating Role of Respect and Cultural Responsibility on Mastery and Performance-focused Instructional Practices," *Journal of Educational Psychology* 107 (2): 533.

Lee, T. L., and Fiske, S. T. (2006) "Not an Outgroup, Not Yet an Ingroup: Immigrants in the Stereotype Content Model," *International Journal of Intercultural Relations* 30 (6): 751–68.

Leslie, S.-J., et al. (2015) "Expectations of Brilliance Underlie Gender Distributions Across Academic Disciplines," *Science* 347 (6219): 262–265.

Madva, A. (2016) "Virtue, Social Knowledge, and Implicit Bias," in J. Saul and M. Brownstein (eds.), *Implicit Bias and Philosophy, Volume 1: Metaphysics and Epistemology*, Oxford: Oxford University Press.

Madva, A. (2017) "Biased Against Debiasing: On the Role of (Institutionally Sponsored) Self-Transformation in the Struggle against Prejudice," https://alexmadva.com/sites/default/files/Madva%20-%20Biased%20Against%20Debiasing%202017%20final.pdf

March, D. S., and Graham, R. (2015) "Exploring Implicit Ingroup and Outgroup Bias Toward Hispanics," *Group Processes and Intergroup Relations* 18 (1): 89–103.

Mendoza, S. A., Gollwitzer, P. M., and Amodio, D. M. (2010) "Reducing the Expression of Implicit Stereotypes: Reflexive Control Through Implementation Intentions," *Personality and Social Psychology Bulletin* 36 (4): 512–523.

Mickelson, R. A., and Bottia, M. (2009) "Integrated Education and Mathematics Outcomes: A Synthesis of Social Science Research," *North Carolina Law Review* 88: 993–1090.

Minero, L. P., and Espinoza, R. K. E. (2015) "The Influence of Defendant Immigration Status, Country of Origin, and Ethnicity on Juror Decisions: An Aversive Racism Explanation for Juror Bias," *Hispanic Journal of Behavioral Sciences* 38 (1): 55–74.

Miyake, A., et al. (2010) "Reducing the Gender Achievement Gap in College Science: A Classroom Study of Values Affirmation," *Science* 330 (6008): 1234–1237.

Murphy, M. C., Richeson, J. A., and Molden, D. C. (2011) "Leveraging Motivational Mindsets to Foster Positive Interracial Interactions," *Social and Personality Psychology Compass* 5 (2): 118–131.

Nelson, L. R., Signorella, M. L., and Botti, K. G. (2016) "Accent, Gender, and Perceived Competence," *Hispanic Journal of Behavioral Sciences* 38 (2): 166–185.

Pettigrew, T. F., and Tropp, L. R. (2006) "A Meta-analytic Test of Intergroup Contact Theory," *Journal of Personality and Social Psychology* 90 (5): 751–783.

Plaut, V. C., et al. (2011) "'What About Me?' Perceptions of Exclusion and Whites' Reactions to Multiculturalism," *Journal of Personality and Social Psychology* 101 (2): 337–353.

Reeves, A. N. (2014) "Written in Black and White: Exploring Confirmation Bias in Racialized Perceptions of Writing Skills," *Nextions Yellow Paper Series*, April.

Roberts, D. (2015) "Are Trump Supporters Driven by Economic Anxiety or Racial Resentment? Yes," *Vox*, December 30, www.vox.com/2015/12/30/10690360/racism-economic-anxiety-trump.
Romero, A. J., et al. (2007) "Adolescent Bicultural Stress and Its Impact on Mental Well-being Among Latinos, Asian Americans, and European Americans," *Journal of Community Psychology* 35 (4): 519–534.
Sadler, M., et al. (2012) "The World is Not Black and White: Racial Bias in the Decision to Shoot in a Multiethnic Context," *Journal of Social Issues* 68 (2): 286–313.
Said, E. (2004) *Humanism and Democratic Criticism*, New York: Columbia University Press.
San Miguel, C., et al. (2011) "Xenophobia Among Hispanic College Students and Implications for the Criminal Justice System," *Journal of Contemporary Criminal Justice* 27 (1): 95–109.
Sanchez, G. R., and Espinosa, P. (2016) "Does the Race of the Discrimination Agent in Latinos' Discrimination Experiences Influence Latino Group Identity?" *Sociology of Race and Ethnicity*, https://doi.org/10.1177/2332649215624237.
Sherman, D. K., et al. (2013) "Deflecting the Trajectory and Changing the Narrative: How Self-affirmation Affects Academic Performance and Motivation Under Identity Threat," *Journal of Personality and Social Psychology* 104 (4): 591–618.
Shin, H., Leal, D. L., and Ellison, C. G. (2015) "Sources of Support for Immigration Restriction Economics, Politics, or Anti-Latino Bias?" *Hispanic Journal of Behavioral Sciences* 37 (4): 459–481.
Stephens, N. M., Hamedani, M. G., and Destin, M. (2014) "Closing the Social-class Achievement Gap: A Difference-education Intervention Improves First-generation Students' Academic Performance and All Students' College Transition," *Psychological Science* 25 (4): 943–953.
Stevens, T., et al. (2004) "Role of Mathematics Self-efficacy and Motivation in Mathematics Performance Across Ethnicity," *The Journal of Educational Research* 97 (4): 208–222.
Stout, J. G., and Dasgupta, N. (2013) "Mastering One's Destiny: Mastery Goals Promote Challenge and Success Despite Social Identity Threat," *Personality and Social Psychology Bulletin* 39 (6): 748–762.
Telles, E. (ed.) (2014) *Pigmentocracies: Ethnicity, Race, and Color in Latin America*, UNC Press Books.
Timmermans, A. C., Kuyper, H., and Werf, G. (2015) "Accurate, Inaccurate, or Biased Teacher Expectations: Do Dutch Teachers Differ in Their Expectations at the End of Primary Education?" *British Journal of Educational Psychology* 85 (4): 459–478.
Uhlmann, E., et al. (2002) "Subgroup Prejudice Based on Skin Color Among Hispanics in the United States and Latin America," *Social Cognition* 20 (3): 198–226.
Uhlmann, E. L., and Cohen, G. L. (2005) "Constructed Criteria Redefining Merit to Justify Discrimination," *Psychological Science* 16 (6): 474–480.
van den Bergh, L., et al. (2010) "The Implicit Prejudiced Attitudes of Teachers Relations to Teacher Expectations and the Ethnic Achievement Gap," *American Educational Research Journal* 47 (2): 497–527.
Weyant, J. M. (2005) "Implicit Stereotyping of Hispanics: Development and Validity of a Hispanic Version of the Implicit Association Test," *Hispanic Journal of Behavioral Sciences* 27 (3): 355–363.
Wilkinson, B. C., and Earle, E. (2013) "Taking a New Perspective to Latino Racial Attitudes Examining the Impact of Skin Tone on Latino Perceptions of Commonality with Whites and Blacks," *American Politics Research* 41 (5): 783–818.
Yglesias, M. (2015) "President Obama Has a Theory about Why People Support Donald Trump. But He's Wrong," *Vox*, December 22, www.vox.com/2015/12/22/10636538/obama-trump-theory.
Yogeeswaran, K., and Dasgupta, N. (2014) "The Devil Is in the Details: Abstract Versus Concrete Construals of Multiculturalism Differentially Impact Intergroup Relations," *Journal of Personality and Social Psychology* 106 (5): 772–789.

Notes

1 Note that most participants in this and other studies are college students. This is usually considered to be a limitation, but in the context of a special issue on the educational experiences of Latinxs, the specificity of the research participants strikes me as something of a virtue.
2 This tendency is stronger among men, and, strikingly, it is especially strong among individuals with very positive attitudes toward Mexico. See San Miguel et al. (2011: 100).
3 This was a qualitative, focus-group study, and it would be invaluable to follow it up with quantitative and experimental-interventional work. See e.g. Basáñez et al. (2014).

4 For a similar pattern of results (explicit egalitarianism and implicit ingroup bias) among Texas undergraduates, see Garza and Gasquoine (2013).
5 On the broader social importance of skin color, see Telles (2014)
6 On the role of narrative for understanding injustice, see e.g. Haslanger (2015).
7 Another study found that, considered in the aggregate, Dutch teachers tended to have accurate expectations of their minority students' performance, but that these overall average trends concealed substantial variability *between* specific teachers, such that many held very negatively biased and many held very favorably biased expectations of their ethnic minority students. See Timmermans, Kuyper and Werf (2015).
8 I say more about such strategies in (2016) and "Biased Against Debiasing: On the Role of (Institutionally Sponsored) Self-Transformation in the Struggle Against Prejudice" (ms).
9 A ready-made version of a values affirmation handout can be downloaded here: https://www2.humboldt.edu/diversity/sites/default/files/Paselk_values_affirmation_activity_1.pdf.
10 In lieu of *mestizaje*, one might also speak here of "hyphenation," "hybridity," or other terms denoting mixed, complex identities. I focus in what follows on *mestizaje* partly for ease of presentation, but also because it is a historically fraught, contested, mercurial notion. It is *because* it has meant different things to different people across times and places, and because very many Latinxs and Latin Americans do *not* identify as mestiza/o, that it can play the role I'm interested in here. Also, I would not suggest that Latin American thought is the *only* tradition to engage with the complexity of social identity. From African-American thought, for example, consider Du Bois' notion of "double-consciousness," or Kimberlé Crenshaw's notion of "intersectionality." See Du Bois (2007) and Crenshaw (1991).
11 For empirical research on strategies to mitigate white anxiety and backlash in discussions of diversity and multiculturalism, see e.g. Plaut et al. (2011) and Yogeeswaran and Dasgupta (2014).
12 I am indebted to Caroline Arruda for insightful and constructive feedback on prior drafts of this essay. [This essay was originally published with the title "Implicit Bias and Latina/os in Philosophy," but the terminology in the title and throughout has been updated for this volume to reflect the author's current preferences.—Eds.]

Reading Questions

1. What is "implicit bias"? How is it studied, according to the text?
2. How does implicit bias specifically affect Latinx communities in domains such as education, healthcare, and criminal justice, according to the text?
3. Discuss how "shooter bias" manifests in experimental settings, and the real-world implications of this research.
4. How do teachers' implicit biases affect Latinx students' academic performance? Provide specific examples from the text.
5. Why is there significantly less research on anti-Latinx bias when compared to similar research related to African Americans, according to Madva? What are the consequences of this disparity?
6. What are some effective debiasing strategies that Madva suggests for educators to reduce their implicit biases? How might these strategies be applied in the context of teaching philosophy?
7. What are some ways that teaching Latin American philosophy can help to counteract harmful classroom dynamics, according to Madva? Discuss the concept of mestizaje and the different ways that learning about it might be relevant to Latinx students and non-Latinx students.

35 Notes on Decolonizing Philosophy
Against Epistemic Extractivism and Toward the Abolition of the Canon

Nelson Maldonado-Torres

There has been a proliferation of writings on the decolonization of various areas of knowledge in the last decade.[1] One reads about decolonizing anthropology, psychology, political science, critical theory, and, of course, philosophy, among other fields and disciplines. While these discussions open up spaces for the circulation of ideas that are grounded on decolonial movements, it is nonetheless the case that many of the recent publications are mainly academic in a narrow sense and that perhaps too many of the scholars who pursue these topics have little connection with the movements that are mainly responsible for keeping the discourse of decolonization urgent and relevant.[2] One notices the usual pattern of taking social movements as objects of research more than as producers of knowledge. In critical theory and philosophy, including some work often cited as liberationist or decolonial, this takes the form of theoretical, cognitive, or epistemic extractivism: social movements and their intellectual creations are taken as zones for intellectual excavation and as springboards for theoretical and philosophical reflection that remains caught within the liberal order of knowledge production in academia.[3]

It is an essential part of the modern academic and liberal order of knowledge production that epistemic extractivism—not only in Philosophy, but throughout the liberal arts and sciences—becomes dominant and that a few authors are made to appear as a vanguard of sorts, or as part of a proto-canon that unsurprisingly includes figures whose problematic translations and elaborations of movement-based knowledges undermine the very movements with which their work is often identified. From then on, the limited and compromised reflection and theoretical elaboration of decolonial themes takes the place of actual engagement with producers of knowledge at the forefront of decolonial movements. Extractivism is combined with a new kind of scholasticism, leading to the formation of a cadre of experts on decolonization and decoloniality: from senior scholars to assistant professors and soon to be assistant professors, who in turn help to produce an entire industry of publication about—a largely detached and purely academic conceptualization of—decoloniality. Since the modes of knowledge production in the modern Western and liberal academy were imposed, reproduced, and imported globally—they were part of the civilizing mission of the West and belong to the apparatus of the modern nation-state—epistemic extractivism takes place in the "north" as well as in the "south." As a result, geopolitical location alone is not a sufficient condition of possibility for delinking from this system of knowledge production. Racial or gender designation or identity are not a sufficient condition, either.

In some cases, engagements with decolonization in scholarly debates go beyond publications and help promote calls for institutional change—in degree granting departments and programs, professional organizations, and journals, for instance. However, these efforts tend to be met by what Houria Bouteldja refers to as the "white immune system," among

DOI: 10.4324/9781003385417-50

which she counts Western humanism as a centerpiece (Bouteldja 2017: 43).[4] Today, the "white immune system" is most active and present in universities in the uncritical reproduction of the white academic field, including calls for multiculturalism and mistranslations of Black Lives Matter and other such movements in terms of diversity, equity, and inclusion (Maldonado-Torres 2020a). Diversity and inclusion has become the most recent dominant expression of modern/colonial humanism, perhaps its liberal and neoliberal face in the contexts of racial formations that include formulaic rejections of vulgar racism and even certain celebrations of racial difference; an industry seeking to protect corporate and liberal institutions by monopolizing the terms of legitimate calls for transformation and change.

It is only thanks to student movements that defy the liberal grammars of knowledge production and their allies that a few places have been able to break through the monopoly of diversity and inclusion with explicit calls for decolonization. This is particularly the case in South Africa where there was a powerful movement for "free and decolonised education"—Rhodes Must Fall and Fees Must Fall (RMF/FMF)—that shook the nation in 2015 and 2016. The ripple effects from the settler colony of Azania were felt in one former imperial metropolis, leading to calls for Rhodes to fall at Oxford University in the United Kingdom as well.

Surely, the white immune system has many ways of protecting the white academic field beyond seeking to limit the terms of debate about institutional change to matters of diversity and inclusion. This is one reason why pursuing the decolonization of the university or the decolonization of disciplines within the university today is a difficult and risky endeavor, as Naomi Snow, a philosophy student at King's College London (KCL) recently put it in the opening to a panel on "Decolonising Philosophy" at KCL. Snow, whose work is greatly inspired by the Rhodes Must Fall movement, considers that:

> What has become clear throughout the course of my project is that decolonisation is no easy task. It is a very risky endeavor. On the one hand there is the risk of the call being reduced to a box-ticking approach. Within neoliberal universities there is the risk that decolonisation becomes a performative exercise whereby the core structures that have upheld systems of coloniality remain vastly unchanged.

On the other hand, there is the risk that calls for decolonisation will not be sufficiently strategic or practical to be incorporated into the mechanics of the university. There has indeed been a fine line to walk between the practical and the radical.[5]

Snow's formulation captures the drama of calls for decolonization of the university, and of philosophy in particular, as well. South African student activists and their close supporters, among which I count myself, would probably agree with this general assessment concerning the difficulty and the risks in having liberal institutions consider the question of their own decolonization.[6]

In the United States perhaps the principal generator of claims for decolonizing the university so far has been the Third World Liberation Front, which emerged in 1968 and led to the formation of Ethnic Studies, the family of trans-disciplinary studies that includes what today is called Latinx Studies, among other crucially important fields.[7] Since its inception, Ethnic Studies has been confronting the severity of the white immune system, and there is much to learn about the difficulty and risk of calls for decolonization in liberal and academic institutions by examining its history carefully. Anyone with a serious pretension of advancing decolonization in any area of the academy today should seriously consider the promise and the challenge to create the equivalent of what the Third World Liberation

Front referred to as Third World College.[8] The existence of a College of Ethnic Studies at San Francisco State University, which emerged out of the Third World Strike, has long defied the idea that it is impossible to approach knowledge production outside the largely nineteenth-century Eurocentric institutional formations of the humanities and the sciences. The ongoing struggle for Ethnic Studies in California and the recent call for "the creation of visionary institutional spaces, such as centers, institutes, schools, and new divisions" by a group of Black and Indigenous faculty as well as faculty of color at Rutgers University, New Brunswick (USA) helps to considerably expand and challenge the narrow realm of the possible within liberal academic frameworks (Ethnic Studies Now Coalition n.d.; Akinlabi et al. n.d.).

I would like to contribute to national and international calls for decolonizing the university and decolonizing philosophy, more specifically, from my perspective as someone who has spent most of his career teaching and writing theory and philosophy within Ethnic Studies units. There is no doubt that part of my interest in advocating for decolonizing philosophy comes from my own grounding in the history and efforts of the Third World Liberation Front, but another part of it comes from my exposure to philosophy in Puerto Rico, a contemporary colony of the United States, followed by my work in Africana Studies and Africana Philosophy.[9] If, rephrasing Paul Ricoeur's sentence in *The Symbolism of Evil* (1986), one could say that colonialism and coloniality—two very concrete and complex forms of evil; that is, not only symbolic—give rise to thought, how are we to expect philosophers in a territory facing a long history and contemporary reality of colonization and coloniality not to want to engage in the question of decolonizing philosophy—and do so against the coloniality of philosophical education, the humanities, and the liberal arts and sciences in the island and elsewhere? It may be easier for some to ignore or set aside colonization as a problem and a concept while working in academic institutions in the US, but not for contemporary colonial subjects or others whose thinking has been marked by the questions raised by the anticolonial and antiracist movements all across the world.[10]

It was in the colonial territory of Puerto Rico that I was first introduced to philosophy as an activity and to Philosophy as an academic discipline. We should not confuse one with the other: while philosophy—with lower letter p, or, in the context of this reflection, philosophy conceived as an activity and an attitude—could be characterized as a rigorous formulation and exploration of fundamental questions, the discipline of Philosophy—with capital letter P—not only tends to confuse rigor with disciplining, but also significantly narrows the definition and the scope of fundamental questions.[11]

In a colonial context, Philosophy, the academic discipline, serves the interests of colonization when it fails to consider the ways in which colonization raises fundamental questions, which is often paired with the apparent impossibility to consider the colonized as a questioner.[12] Approaching the colonized as questioner is different from seeking to include them in the discipline of Philosophy. Given that many of those who have questioned colonization most profoundly have done so outside of academia, it is rather about the possibility of finding philosophy outside Philosophy, which can only raise questions to and about Philosophy itself. In a colonial context, Philosophy tends to delegitimize the philosophical interrogation of colonialism while simultaneously seeking to colonize philosophy itself.

If Philosophy plays an active role in the colonization of philosophy, decolonizing philosophy can be understood as a way of countering the colonization of philosophy by Philosophy and as a form of reintroducing philosophy into Philosophy. This is not to mean that we should delimit the decolonization of philosophy to decolonizing the discipline of

Philosophy. When limited in such a way, the so-called decolonization remains within a limited and problematic framework that reproduces, rather than challenges, coloniality.

One could conclude, for instance, that decolonizing philosophy is about adding more authors into the canon of Philosophy, or about adding more classes focused on non-European or non-Western thinkers into the specialization in Philosophy. Decolonizing philosophy is not a matter of multiculturalism or of diversity and inclusion. Paying attention to the culture of the colonized without addressing colonialism is as problematic as incorporating texts written by colonized subjects to the canon without seriously addressing the ways in which the discipline of Philosophy, its scope, and its pedagogy reproduce coloniality. That is why while practices of hegemonic multiculturalism, diversity, and inclusion—the new woke white man's and woman's burden, as well as the new marker of liberal and neoliberal benevolence—seek to appear as progressive—when, in truth, they seek to accommodate the interests, perspectives, and rights of (principally white) individuals within a liberal legal order and to counter robust appeals to justice and reparations, not to speak of decolonization—they easily collapse into the categories of the offensive and the obscene. There is no apparent harm done in a colonial and racial world when the offense and the obscenity are only seen and felt by minoritized sectors, especially if they are colonial and racial subjects, and not even all of them. How else could coloniality continue for so long?

So how should one then approach the project of decolonizing philosophy? I'd like to submit two basic ideas: first, that decolonizing philosophy should be less about decolonizing the discipline of Philosophy, an activity that still leaves the academic discipline at the center and therefore always remains oriented and limited by it, and more about the rigorous pursuit of the fundamental questions that emerge in the historical and still unfinished struggle for decolonization. I am proposing a shift from decolonizing Philosophy, the discipline, to producing a philosophy—an activity and attitude that explores fundamental questions—that advances decolonization. Second, I submit that the struggle for decolonization is an intergenerational and collective project, as well as one that bridges spaces and temporalities in the process of creating another world. Let me explore these two proposals.

1. Decolonizing Philosophy as a Counter-Catastrophic Task

The main idea that I would like to explore here is that decolonizing Philosophy is less about decolonizing a particularly academic field than about generating a philosophy that is itself decolonizing or a philosophy that is decolonial. Without generating a decolonial philosophy, any effort to decolonize Philosophy—the discipline—is bound to remain caught in the coloniality of modern Western scholarly research and scholarly production. Decolonial philosophy, or maybe even better put, decolonial philosophical thinking, does not abandon but rather reclaims the material taught by Philosophy—the discipline—to assess it and in the process critically revise it, reject it, and/or transform it. Too much has been left out of the corpus of academic Philosophy for decolonial philosophizing to be restricted to it or oriented by it. Decolonial philosophical thinking demands the abolition of the canon, which does not mean the rejection of every idea found in existing canonical texts, but rather, a fundamental reorientation of the ways of conceiving knowledge production and creation—one that cannot take place without active involvement in decolonial struggles and without generative relations with knowledge creators and explorers embedded in those struggles.

Since decolonization is an ongoing movement, decolonial philosophical thinking is to be anchored, not in a discipline, but in a movement or movements: the movements of and for decolonization. From the perspective of decolonial philosophical thinking, movements for decolonization are not simply social manifestations of various forms of resistance against the catastrophe of modernity/coloniality, which includes the presence and afterlives of Indigenous genocide, conquest, colonization, and racial slavery in the contemporary world. Rather decolonial movements, looked at philosophically, are movements that seek to restore the conditions of possibility for love and understanding in our world. Likewise, philosophy, looked at decolonially, cannot possibly seek to affirm the "love of wisdom" without committing itself to counter the catastrophe that makes love and wisdom an exception to a colonial rule in the world. Decolonial philosophical thinking can therefore be understood as a counter-catastrophic practice that seeks to restore the ample conditions of possibility for love and wisdom to flourish in our world. Decolonial philosophical thinking does this in part by identifying, engaging, critically assessing, and building from the fundamental questions that are posed by decolonial movements. Decolonizing philosophy is rooted in questions that emerge in movement and in movements.

2. Decolonial Philosophical Thinking as a Collective and Intergenerational Project

If love and understanding are eminently intersubjective activities, this should mean that philosophy is too.[13] If so, this would indicate that decolonial philosophical thinking has a point of departure in the struggles for love and for understanding that emerge in the midst of the catastrophe of modernity/coloniality. This view has various consequences. For example, it means that decolonizing the curriculum of Philosophy—the discipline—cannot be done without decolonizing the multiple other areas in the academy that can potentially offer insight into these struggles for love and understanding in an antiblack, anti-Indigenous, and colonial world. The classroom has to be decolonized too: it should no longer be in the service of the occupation of land and the erasure of questions that emerge from the ground of decolonial struggle, but be opened to contact and engagement with decolonial struggles outside the university.

If decolonial philosophical thinking is to be nurtured in academic settings, it has to include an effort not only to critically revise and expand the reading materials, but also to decolonize the classroom and the very conception of education and research. The decolonial classroom cannot end in the physical walls of a room or the library, as important as these could be. The decolonial classroom extends to the streets and to spaces led by community and activist organizations that also counter catastrophe by making love and understanding an increasing possibility for those whom Fanon called the condemned of the earth.

Decolonial philosophical thinking cannot emerge without this form of learning, as many crucial lessons for decolonial thinking are much better formulated by community and activist organizations than by academics. In fact, the symbolic value of academic work often depends on and advances a schism with other forms of knowledge production, just as it reproduces the ethos of modern/colonial scholarly work. Instead of starting with the discipline, or taking the academy as the point of departure, we should start from who we are and where we are: not merely as individuals, but as part of networks of oppression and emancipation; and not so much to assert our individual importance in the world or the uniqueness of our individual or regional perspective, but first and foremost to practice solidarity, understood as "the enactment of the social debts we owe each other" (Strike MoMA n.d.). These are "acknowledgement of debts owed: from top to bottom and horizontally too, between and within groups, communities, and movements" as a transition to a post-extractivist decolonial world—also a post-MoMA's world, in the terms of the "Strike MoMA" document cited here. In this approach, solidarity is a quintessential task in the effort to restore and expand love, understanding, and intersubjective reason, and therefore philosophy in the world. By participating with others in decolonial struggles and by learning from our ancestors' ways of thinking and acting, we can seek to become worthy of saying some of these things and be heard.[14]

References

Akinlabi, A. et al. (n.d.) "Letter from Black and Indigenous Faculty and Faculty of Color who Specialize in the Study of Race at Rutgers, New Brunswick," https://sites.google.com/view/rutgers-blm-bipoc-lettter/home.

Bouteldja, H. (2017) *Whites, Jews, and Us: Toward a Politics of Revolutionary Love*, Cambridge, MA: MIT Press.

Boyce Davies, C., et al. (eds.) (2003) *Decolonizing the Academy: African Diaspora Studies*, Trenton, NJ: Africa World Press.

Césaire, A. (2000) *Discourse on Colonialism*, J. Pinkham (trans.), New York: Monthly Review Press.

Copeland, H., Foster, H., Joselit, D., and Lee, P. M. (2020) "A Questionnaire on Decolonization," *October* 174: 73–78.

Ethnic Studies Now Coalition. (n.d.) www.ethnicstudiesnow.com.

Fanon, F. (2008) *Black Skin, White Masks*, R. Wilcox (trans.), New York: Grove Press.

Gordon, L. (2019) "Decolonizing Philosophy," *The Southern Journal of Philosophy* 57 (S1): 16–36.

Grosfoguel, R. (2019) "Epistemic Extractivism: A Dialogue with Alberto Acosta, Leanne Betasamosoke Simpson, and Silvia Rivera Cusicanqui," in B. de Sousa Santos and M. P. Meneses (eds.), *Knowledges Born in Struggle: Constructing the Epistemologies of the Global South*, 203–218, New York: Routledge.

Jorge, A. S. (2018) *Nada es igual: bocetos del país que nos acontece*, Toa Alta: Editora Educación Emergente.

Jorge, A. S. (2020) *Convidar*, Toa Alta: Editora Educación Emergente.

Jorge, A. S., and Quintero Rivera, M. (eds.). (2019) *Antología del pensamiento crítico puertorriqueño*, Buenos Aires: CLACSO.

Klein, N. (2012) "Dancing the World into Being: A Conversation with Idle-No-More's Leanne Simpson," *Yes Magazine*, March 5.

Lebrón, P. (2020) *Filosofía del cimarronaje*, Toa Baja: Editora Educación Emergente.

Maldonado-Torres, N. (2016) "Outline of Ten Theses on Coloniality and Decoloniality," *Frantz Fanon Foundation*, October 26, http://fondation-frantzfanon.com/outline-of-ten-theses-on-coloniality-and-decoloniality.

Maldonado-Torres, N. (2017) "Foreword," in C. Chinguno et al. (eds.), *Rioting and Writing: Diaries of the Wits Fallists*, Johannesburg: University of Witwatersrand Press.

Maldonado-Torres, N. (2020a) "Interrogating Systemic Racism and the White Academic Field," *Frantz Fanon Foundation*, June 16, https://fondation-frantzfanon.com/interrogating-systemic-racism-and-the-white-academic-field.

Maldonado-Torres, N. (2020b) "Hashtag Lessons from the US and South Africa about Racism and Antiblackness," *Mail & Guardian*, June 29, https://mg.co.za/opinion/2020-06-29-hashtag-lessons-from-the-us-and-south-africa-about-racism-and-antiblackness.

Maldonado-Torres, N. (forthcoming) "What Is Decolonial Critique?" *Graduate Faculty Philosophy Journal*.

Maldonado-Torres, N., et al. (2018) "Decolonising Philosophy," in G, Bhambra, D. Gebrail and K. Nisancioglu (eds.), *Decolonising the University*, 64–90, London: Pluto Press.

Ricoeur, P. (1986) *The Symbolism of Evil*, E. Buchanan (trans.), Boston: Beacon Press.

"Strike MoMA," (2021) *YouTube, 2:15:05*, June 3, www.youtube.com/watch?v=a4HNvsf8XEs&t=1s.

"Strike MoMA," (n.d.) www.strikemoma.org.

Zambrana, R. (2021) *Colonial Debts: The Case of Puerto Rico*, Durham, NC: Duke University Press.

Notes

1 The first draft of this essay was presented at the "Decolonising Philosophy" panel discussion organized by philosophy students at King's College London on May 10, 2021. I thank philosophy student Naomi Snow as well as the student groups Decolonise KCL and KCL Minorities and Philosophy for the invitation and for making the event possible. I also thank the Strike MoMA! working group of the International Imagination of Anti-National and Anti-Imperialist Feelings (IIAAF) for providing a space to explore the linkages between extractivism and coloniality.

2 I also comment on this phenomenon in my response to Copeland et al. (2020). For a critical engagement with the coloniality of critical theory see Maldonado-Torres (forthcoming).

3 I turned my attention to epistemic extractivism and the abolition of the canon in the context of discussions about extractivism and abolition as part of Strike MoMA!, some of which is documented on video. See the conversation among Kency Cornejo, Saudi García, Macarena Gómez-Barris, Nelson Maldonado-Torres, and Mónica Ramón Ríos, facilitated by Nitasha Dhillon and Shellyne Rodríguez (2021). Strike MoMA! is an initiative led by the Strike MoMA Working Group of the International Imagination of Anti-National and Anti-Imperialist Feelings (IIAAF) and supporters (see www.strikemoma.org). I approach epistemic extractivism as a normative practice in the modern research university, which means that, most likely, everyone who has gone through the university has practiced it or become complicit with it in one form or another. Epistemic extractivism is the order of the day in doctoral seminars, academic reading groups, professional organizations, etc., even in spaces that engage colonization, racism, sexism, and homophobia critically. To be sure, this does not mean that epistemic extractivism needs to be condoned. It is necessary to identify it, criticize its operations, and, most importantly, engage in non- and post-extractivist practices of knowledge creation. Other approaches to epistemic extractivism include Klein (2012) and Grosfoguel (2019).

4 Bouteldja analyzes the "white immune system" as a political-ideological apparatus, but her reference to humanism suggests that it is also an epistemic-academic one. This is how I approach the concept here. This is part of a conversation with Bouteldja's work that I have pursued elsewhere. See Maldonado-Torres (2020a).

5 Snow's opening comments to "Decolonising Philosophy: Panel Discussion," Zoom online panel on May 10, 2021. Thanks to Snow for facilitating her opening comments in writing.

6 I have been visiting South Africa and collaborating with South African academics for about seven years, and I happened to be in South Africa for three months during one of the most intense periods of activity for Rhodes Must Fall and Fees Must Fall. In 2017, I wrote the "Foreword" to the student-led publication *Rioting and Writing: Diaries of the Wits Fallists* (2017). My "Outline of Ten Theses on Coloniality and Decoloniality" (2016) is also heavily marked by my time in South Africa during the Rhodes Must Fall and Fees Must Fall activities. See also Maldonado-Torres (2020b).

7 Decolonizing the university has been one of the persistent themes in ethnic studies scholarship. Consider publications such as Boyce Davies et al. (2003) and the conference that commemorated the 40th anniversary of the birth of Ethnic Studies at the University of California, Berkeley, "Decolonizing the University: Fulfilling the Dream of the Third World College" (2010).

8 Among other sources, see the special issue of the fiftieth anniversary of the founding of Ethnic Studies in the *Ethnic Studies Review* 42 (2) (2019).

9 I have written about my experience as a philosophy student in Puerto Rico and about doing philosophy in Ethnic Studies in "Thinking at the Limits of Philosophy and Doing Philosophy" as "a name for the basic coordinates of human subjectivity: the modality of intersubjective love and understanding."

10 The most recent work of Rocio Zambrana (2021) is an example of this. Also of crucial importance are works in Puerto Rico by Anayra Santory Jorge, whose publications, classes, as well as her initiatives while chair of the Department of Philosophy at the University of Puerto Rico, Río Piedras, played an important role motivating and supporting a new generation of philosophy students with interests in decolonization and who are now in the process of completing their PhDs. This includes Pedro Lebrón, author of the recently published *Filosofía del cimarronaje* (2020). From Anayra Santory Jorge, see, among others: *Nada es igual: bocetos del país que nos acontece* (2018), *Convidar* (2020) and the co-edited anthology *Antología del pensamiento crítico puertorriqueño* (2019). Another important author and teacher in Puerto Rico whose work in the history

of Caribbean and Puerto Rican philosophy has animated interest in the philosophical exploration of questions and themes that are prevalent in the island-archipelago and the Caribbean is the Colombian-born Carlos Rojas Osorio, winner of the 2005 Frantz Fanon Lifetime Achievement Award by the Caribbean Philosophical Association.

11 I have developed related ideas about the meaning of philosophy in Maldonado-Torres, "Outline of Ten Theses on Coloniality and Decoloniality," as well as in the co-authored chapter "Decolonising Philosophy." See Maldonado-Torres et al. (2018) and Gordon (2019).

12 As evinced in the "Outline of Ten Theses," the works of Frantz Fanon and Aimé Césaire's *Discourse on Colonialism* have been crucial in the formulation of this view of philosophy and its operations and mutations in colonial settings. See Césaire (2000).

13 I am building here from a view of philosophy presented in Maldonado-Torres, "Outline of Ten Theses on Coloniality and Decoloniality," where I write: "That is, while philosophy is traditionally conceived as the love of wisdom, for Fanon, or rather through Fanon, we can conceive of philosophy as the intersubjective modality of love and understanding. Philosophy is therefore not simply a particular form of questioning or production of knowledge that characterizes the work of some people called philosophers. Rather, philosophy can be conceived as a name for the basic coordinates of human subjectivity: the modality of intersubjective love and understanding."

14 This last sentence is to be read along with Fanon's initial lines in the introduction of *Black Skin, White Masks*: "Don't expect to see any explosion today. It's too early . . . or too late. I'm not the bearer of absolute truths. No fundamental inspiration has flashed across my mind. I honestly think, however, it's time some things were said. Things I'm going to say, not shout. I've long given up shouting. A long time ago." See Frantz Fanon, *Black Skin, White Masks*, trans. Richard Wilcox (2008: xi).

Reading Questions

1. What is coloniality and how is it related to colonization, according to the text? What is the idea of decolonization?
2. What is the (neo-)liberal order, according to Maldonado-Torres, and why is it objectionable?
3. How does Maldonado-Torres describe "epistemic extractivism"? Discuss how does epistemic extractivism is said to be related to the colonial extraction of natural resources.
4. What's the difference between Philosophy and philosophy, in Maldonado-Torres' terms?
5. What does Maldonado-Torres mean by "the canon" and why does he want to abolish it? What do you think about this idea, and why?
6. Discuss the issues Maldonado-Torres raises about the detachment of academic work from social movements. How does this detachment impact the decolonial discourse?
7. What does Maldonado-Torres mean by "the white immune system?" How could we decide if such a thing exists or not?
8. Why does Maldonado-Torres critique the concepts of multiculturalism, diversity, and inclusion in the context of decolonization efforts? How might the humanities in higher education function to undermine transformative political change?
9. Discuss this textbook from the perspective of Maldonado-Torres' theory. If you were designing your own philosophy textbook, how would you approach it, and why?

Index

abnegation 185, 187–188
Abt, Theodore 499, 510
accidentality: accidents and 237–238; aversion and 239–240; biculturality and 244, 247–248; concept of 172, 238; contingency and 236–237; culture and 236–237; dignity and 239–240; double-consciousness and 244–245; experiences of moving to new place and 235; introversion and 239–240; misalignments and 235, 238; nihilism and 243, 246; other accounts of 244–248; overview 172, 235–236; psychology of 238–240; subordination and 243; substance and 237–238; subversive substitution and 244–246; theoretical insights 249; transplanted substantiality and 244, 246–247; ungroundedness and 238; unwillingness and 239–240; Uranga's account and 241–244, 248–249; value creation and 243
accidents 237
achievement gap 172, 229–230
Ackerman, Bruce 473
"active" coping 544–545
activism 299, 373, 414–417, 467, 474, 500, 526, 533–534, 543
Adamic, Louis 416
Addams, J. 416
affective injustice 358–359
affirmative action 19, 79, 212, 288, 396
Afghanistan 464
African Americans 16, 20, 22–25, 70, 77, 160, 400, 462, 520, 536–537; *see also* black identity/blackness
Afro-Caribbean identity 52
Afro-Cuban Santería 331–332
Afro-Latin identity: Caribbean philosophy and 67–70; "Discourse of Memory" and 60–61; identity markers and 68–69; Latinx philosophy and 67–70; overview 10, 59; political thought and 69–70; subjectivity and 68; U.S. discourse about 61–67
agency 285–287, 375–377

Alarcón, Norma 315
Alcoff, Linda Martin 12, 171, 400, 422, 433–439, 527, 544
Alhambra Decree 148
Ali, Ben 284
Allen, Anita 22
Allen, Paula Gunn 265, 267–270, 273
alphabets of survival 315–319
Amazonia 101
ambiguity 64, 125–126
ambivalence and autonomy 200–202, 210
American Civil Liberties Union (ACLU) 481
American Community Survey (2016) 350
Americanization model 423–424
American Philosophical Association 382, 521
amnesia, historical 381–382
"anchor babies" 462, 482; *see also* birthright citizenship
Anderson, Chris 163
Anderson, Elizabeth 448
anglicisms (*pochismos*) 343–344
Anglo Americans 117, 202, 214n8
Anglo-Protestant culture 464, 466–467
Anglo Saxons 53
Anishinabe people 116–120, 155
anti-immigrant arguments 180–181
anti-Latinx bias in philosophy: "active" vs "avoidance" coping and 544–545; debiasing strategies and 541–542; education and 539–541; immigration policy and 537; measures of 538; *mestizaje* and 542–545; nature of 538–539; overview 494, 536; research on 536–539; varieties of 538–539
Anzaldúa, Gloria: ambiguity and, tolerance for 125–126; autohistoria and 315–316; crossroads and 126–127; cultural collision/stress and 125, 298, 518, 520–521; divided loyalties and 129–130; gendered nature of U.S. immigration policy and 485; language/communication and 339–340, 360, 383; Latinx philosophy and 94; macho concept and 128; mestizaje and 124–134, 155–156, 158, 171–68, 202–205, 208, 214n9,

256, 368; mestiza way and 127; "new consciousness" and 94, 124–134; rejection and 131; return to home and 131–134; social dislocation and 94; support among mestizas and 128–129; undocumented Latinx and 452; visibility of mestizas and 130
apartheid 430–431
Appiah, Anthony 23, 81
Arellano, J. E. 510
Aristotle 469
arrogant perception 185–186
artistic freedom 177
artists, Latinx 177
Arvin, M. 151
Asian Americans 138
assimilation 4, 17, 93, 120, 171, 174, 180, 182, 195, 222, 246, 304–305, 322, 330, 340, 360, 411, 425
"asylum ban" 485
Atencio, Tomás 493, 520
Athenian Enlightenment 468
Atlantic race 95–96
Atwater, Lee 426
Augustine 470
August Twenty-Ninth Movement 22
authentic belonging 297
autohistoria 315–316
autonomy: achievement of 212; ambivalence and 200–202, 210; concept of 199, 213n2; education 229; emancipatory acts of 211–212; endorsements and 204–210, 215n19; mestizaje 199–200, 202–210, 212, 215n22; mestizaje consciousness and 199–200, 202–210; overview 172, 199–200; procedural 200–201, 204, 209; relational 199–202; socialization/social relationships and 199–200; wholeheartedness and 200–201, 203, 205, 209–211, 214n4
aversion and psychological syndrome of accidentality 239–240
"avoidance" coping 544–545
Aztecs 148, 519
Aztlán concept 142

Baldwin, James 182
Barbalet, J. M. 400
Barceló, Axel 13
Barvosa, Edwina 172, 299–300
Beauvoir, Simone de 373
Bell, Derrick 180
belonging concept 295–301
Bennett, William 181
berdache (third gender) 269, 273
Bermudez, Alenka 319
Berry, Wendell 510
Bettcher, T. M. 81–82
Bhabha, Homi 368

Bianchi, Enzo 510
biculturality 172, 244, 247–248
bicultural stress, reacting to 544–545
Biden, Joseph 428, 432, 485
Bidwell, Kristina Fagan 152–153, 163–164
Bill of Rights 461, 474
Binational Migration Institute 482
birthright citizenship: "anchor babies" and 462, 482; background information 460–463; constitutionalization of 463, 474; evolution of citizenship and 468–474; Huntington's view 463–468; *jus sanguinis* principle and 382, 463, 474, 476n7; *jus soli* principle and 394, 463, 473–474, 476n7; "Latino Threat" narrative and 394, 414, 463–468; overview 394; unfinished revolution and 474; white nativism and 464, 467–468; *see also* citizenship; U.S. citizenship
Black Codes 472
black identity/blackness: African American theorists and 26–27; counteridentification from 322, 334n2; disidentification from 322, 334n1; in Latin America 20; Marxism and 63–64; politics and 62; skin color and 65–66, 71n6; in U.S. 22, 61–67
Black Lives Matter Movement 550
black/white or nonwhite binary 136, 315–316, 520, 537
Blake, Michael 449
Böckenförde, Ernst-Wolfgang 461
Bolívar, Simón 16, 178, 383–384
Borges 20
Bouazizi, Mohamed 284
Bourgois, Philippe 80
Bouteldja, Houria 549–550
Brazil 27
Brendston, Arthur 529–530
Buber, Martin 279
Buchanan, P. J. 527
Bulgarian identity 112–113
Bureau of Indian Affairs 117, 162
Burke, Edmund 466–467
Burt, Stephanie 73
Bush, George H. W. 427
Butler, Judith 176

Calhoun, Cheshire 224
Callan, Eamonn 227
Camp Grant Indian massacre (1871) 139
capitalism 64, 138, 258, 261–262, 265, 267, 269–270, 323–324, 330, 382–383, 425, 425–426, 505
Carens, Joseph 445, 456–457
Caribbean philosophy 60, 67–70, 323
Carillo Rowe, Aimee 296, 301
Carnap, R. 384
Carranza, Elihu 520

Carter, Prudence 221
Casanova, José 468
caste 93, 109, 112–121
Central American Latinos 402–403
Césaire, Aimé 63
Chavez, Cesar: cultural transmission and 413–414; democracy and 409–411; impact of 284; *juntos pero no revueltos* principle and 412–413; as labor leader 407–409; *La Causa* and 409, 414, 416; "Latino Threat" narrative and 414; legacy of, democratic 416–417; melting pot model and 411; Mexican-American philosophy and 519–520; Mexican identity and 347; Mexican immigration and 407–408, 414; multiculturalism and 394; overview 393–394; protégés of 416; radical democratic tradition and 411–413; undocumented Latinx and 407–409; U.S. citizenship and 407; U.S. immigration policy and 409
Chavez, Juana Estrada 414
Chavez, Leo R. 414, 462, 527–528
Che Guevara 17
Cherokees/Cherokee Nation 113, 116, 118, 139, 268
Chicano Civil Rights Movement 519–520
Chicano identity 18, 21, 111–112, 121, 139–142, 315, 502
Chicano indigeneity 139–142
Chicano Movement in northern New Mexico: background information 495–498; collection of data on family origin and 5; cyber age and 493, 507–511; el oro del barrio and 493, 495, 498–501, 504–507; future and 504–506; ideas of 415; La Academia de la Nueva Raza and 501–504, 508, 513n12; la resolana and 498–501, 507–510; la vida buena y sana concept and 507, 511; learning society and 507–510, 514n20; *manito* cultural enclave and 496, 513n1; overview 493; Penitente society and 100, 514n21; personal account of 495–498; rise of 500; storytelling and 499, 508; term Chicano and 502; traditional knowledge and 510–511
Chicano Spanish language 342–344
Chicano studies 136, 138–143
Christianity 49, 106, 111–112, 147, 237, 267, 289–290, 464
Churchill, Winston 121, 180
Cicero 468–469
citizenship: Aristotle and 469; Augustine and 470; birthright 394; Cicero and 468–469; civil rights and 397; cultural 400; democracy and 393, 395–396; development of 396–397; Diderot and 471; evolution of 468–474; Fourteenth Amendment and 462–463, 471–474, 476n6; ideal 397; overview 7, 393–394; political rights and 397–398; Riesenberg's view 468–469; second-class access to 322, 335n3; social movements and 398–400; social rights and 397–398; *see also* birthright citizenship; U.S. citizenship
civil rights 138, 330, 397–398; *see also specific movement*
Civil Rights Act (1866) 472–474
Civil Rights Act (1964) 350, 474
Civil Rights Movement in U.S. 3, 67, 175, 182, 284, 288, 398, 414, 426
Clark, Ramsey 408
Cleisthenes's reforms 468–469
Clinton, Bill 39, 427
Clinton, Hillary 431–432
Code, L. 177; Obama and 216
code-switching, cultural: achievement gap and 229–230; appeal of 227; compartmentalized 224–225; conception of the good and 218–219; definition of 216; education and 218–220, 227–230; equal opportunity and 217–218; integration and 221–223; language/communication and 544; liberal egalitarianism and 218–219; mobility and 229–230; non-cognitive skills and 216–221, 232n3; overview 172, 216–217; as pretense 223–224; research interest in 216; as strategy 217, 220–228, 544; as subsumption 225–228, 230
Colegio Cesar Chavez 415–416
Collins, Patricia Hill 271
colonial cosmovision 325
colonialism/colonization: class/race and 65; European 119; gender system and 258; healing from 73; liberation from 121–122; mestizaje and 114–118, 121–122; myths of mestizaje and 151; philosophy and 551; race and 65; racism and 138; Spanish 97–101; *see also* settler colonialism
coloniality 255–257, 261, 263–264, 269, 323–324
coloniality of power 67, 255, 258, 260–264
Columbus, Christopher 47, 148
Common Bundle view of Latinx identity 437–438
common-sense accounts 75–76
communication *see* language/communication
compound poverty 360
Comte, Auguste 386
conception of the good 218–219
concubinage 270
consensual heteronomy 356–359
constitutional patriotism 404, 405n2
contingency 236–237, 533
conversions, religious 147–148
Corlett, J. A. 527–528
corridos 346

Cortés, Hernán 150, 344
Cortés Maisonave, Almudena 481, 483
Cortés, Martín 50
cosmic race 45, 94, 124, 429
Cosmic Race, The (Vasconcelos) 3, 93, 95–107, 178
Coulter, Ann 428
counteridentification of blackness 322, 334n2
Cree Tribe 163
Crenshaw, Kimberle 262
Crimes Act (1790) 460
Critical Indigenous Studies 154–155
Critical Latinx Indigeneities 159–160
cross-cultural challenges 7, 171–172; *see also specific type*
cross-cultural communication 371–372
Crummell, Alexander 36
Cuban Americans 24, 39, 432, 437–438
Cubans 24, 402
Cudd, Ann 446–448
cultural alterity: concept of alterity and 365; culturally different other and 298, 369–372; dominant cultures and 366; imaginary-symbolic order and, restructuring 375–377; incommensurability of 367–368, 372–373, 378n4; language/communication and 340, 365–377; model for understanding 366–367; otherness and 365–366, 369–374; overview 340, 365–367; postcolonial feminism and 366–367, 374–375, 377–378n2, 378n11; speaking positions and, disparity of 367–368; translatability and, lack of cultural 371, 378n8; values and 372, 378n9; women as Other and 372–374
cultural citizenship 400
cultural code-switching *see* code-switching, cultural
cultural collision/stress 125, 298, 518, 520–521
"cultural congruent education" 227–228
cultural pluralism 415
culture 236–237, 369; *see also* cultural alterity
curdling-separation 197–198n1
Curiel, Gonzalo 462
cyber age 493, 507–511

Das Gupta, Monisha 483
David, Pedro 509
Davidson, Leland 407, 413
Davila, Arlene 19
debiasing strategies 541–542
de Certeau, Michel 256, 281, 296, 301–303
Declaration of the Rights of Man and Citizen (1789) 471
decolonial feminist *movidas*: background information 322–323; coloniality and 323–324; counteridentification of blackness from 322, 334n2; critique of gender and, developing 329–330; deploying gender as is and, problem with 327–329; disidentification from blackness 322, 334n1; feminism and 323–324, 328, 331–332, 335–336n14; futures and, reimagining 324, 330–332; historicizing gender and 324–326, 329; ingredients to disrupt coloniality of gender and 324, 335n8; new practices and 324, 330–332; orientations to disrupt coloniality of gender and 324, 335n9; overview 256–257, 323; power dynamics and mapping 324, 326–327, 329; wages of gender and 326–327, 329; well-being and, call for collective 332
decoloniality 277–278, 540
decolonizing philosophy 494, 549–554
deconstructive resistance to theory 73
Deferred Action for Childhood Arrivals (DACA) program 456, 462
de Gobineau, A. 429
de las Casas, Bartolomé 382–383
de la Vega el Inca, Garcilaso 113–114
del Castillo, Richard Griswold 408
DeMan, Paul 73
democracy: Chavez (Cesar) and 409–411; Churchill's view of 180; citizenship and 393, 395–396; foundations of U.S. 409–411; globalization and 395–396; Latinx immigrants and intercultural 413–416; melting pot model and 411; radical tradition 411–413; tenet of U.S. 395
deracialization 26, 29n3, 474
Derrida, Jacques 383–384
Dewey, J. 227–228, 413, 415
Dickens, Charles 295
Diderot, D. 470–471
dignity and psychological syndrome of accidentality 239–240
dilution theory 153
"Discourse of Memory" 60–61
discrimination 16, 18–19, 26, 41–42, 69, 75, 180–181, 264, 351, 398, 431, 521, 537–538, 541; *see also* anti-Latinx bias in philosophy; racism
disempowerment 177, 260, 420, 430, 528
disenfranchisement 61, 82, 162–164, 268, 399, 404, 431, 461–462, 469, 473–474, 529–530
disidentification from blackness and 322, 334n1
disintegration of Latinx racial category thesis: demographic trends and 420–421, 423, 439–440; dog-whistle politics and 421, 425–429, 430–432, 438; double-play of whiteness objection and 438–439; elasticity objection and 436–438; eliminativism objection and 434–436; in-between race groups and 425, 439–440; Latinx identity and whiteness and 433–439; overview 394,

421–422; pessimistic view of 429–433; whiteness in U.S. and 421–425, 432–433
disjunctive temporality 368
disremembering (*una desmemoria*) 317
dissidence of dissent 466–467
distorted identity model 422, 435–436
diversity 2, 15, 18–20, 27, 201–204, 207, 280, 367, 515, 520, 550, 552
dog-whistle politics 421, 425–429, 430–432, 438
Dolezal, Rachel 82
double bind 480
double-consciousness 172, 244–245
"Dreamers" 456
Dred Scott decision (1857) 472–473
Dred Scott v. Sandford (1857) 422
Du Bois, W. E. B. 36–37, 172, 244–245, 298, 411, 493, 515, 520–521
Dukakis, Michael 427
Duncan, Quince 60–61, 68–69
Dussel, Enrique 12
Duvisac, Sara 481

education: achievement gap and 172, 229–230; anti-Latinx bias in philosophy and 539–541; autonomy 229; code-switching and 218–220, 227–230; cultural congruent 227–228; SAT identification for Puerto Ricans and 15
egalitarianism 265–266, 267–269, 448
eliminativism 31–33, 36, 39, 42, 75–76, 89n1, 159–160, 434–436
Eliseo, Tio 504–507
Elk v. Wilkins (1884) 422
Ellul, Jacques 500
El Morro fortress painting 34
El Movimiento de Mjueres de Cuscatlán 314
el oro del barrio 493, 495, 498–501, 504–507
emotion work 358
empowerment 68, 84, 298, 300, 311, 314, 323, 326, 331, 395, 397–398, 404, 461, 528, 533–534
endorsements 204–210, 215n19
England 111
epistemic extractivism 549
Espiritu, Yen Le 272
essentialism 23–23, 26–27, 31–33, 36–37, 39, 42, 76, 249, 527
Essentialism vs. Eliminativism Dilemma 32–33, 42
Estrada, Gabriel 158–159
Estupiñán Bass, Nelson 60–61
ethnic art 177
ethnic identity 11, 14–16, 25, 360, 517; *see also specific type*
ethnicity: concept of 24; European 26; mestizaje and 112–114; Omi and Winant's view of 63;

paradigm 21–23; race versus 63, 424; social identity and 41–42; Wallerstein's view of 63
ethnorace 28
ethnos 517–518
Eurocentrism 261–262, 383–384
European ethnicities 26
European philosophy 255, 380
E-verify system 453
exclusion, social 76, 78, 102, 138, 147, 161, 178, 180–181, 205–206, 259, 266, 272, 316, 373, 380–382, 385, 395–396, 399, 404, 413, 539
existentialism 33, 236, 516, 520, 529
extractivism 494, 549, 555n3

fairness 287–288, 293n17; *see also* justice
Falcón, Sylvanna 481
Familial-Historical View of Latinx identity 12, 36–40, 42
family separation immigration policy 462, 478–479, 483
Fanon, Frantz 64, 179, 553
Far East history and Hispanic identity 46–48
Far North of the South history and Hispanic identity 50–52
Far South of the North history and Hispanic identity 50–52
Far West history and Hispanic identity 48–50
Faulstich Orellana, Marjorie 352–353, 355, 363n7
Federal Criminal Code (1790) 460
Fees Must Fall Movement 550
feminism: decolonial feminist *movidas* and 323–324, 328, 331–332, 335–336n14; gendered nature of U.S. immigration policy and 479–480, 489n2; imaginary-symbolic order and, restructuring 375–377; incommensurability and 368; Latina 314–315; Latinx 486; pluralistic 185; postcolonial 366–367, 374–375, 377–378n2, 379n11; Third World 259; twentieth-century, development of 270; Western 373–374, 378–379n10; white-dominated 174, 258, 270–271
Fernández Retamar, Roberto 381–383, 386
feudalism 435–436
fifth race 95, 99–102, 106–107, 124
First Amendment 411
Fletcher, George P. 472–473
Foner, Eric 474
Forbes, Jack D. 93
Fordham, Signithia 221
Fourteenth Amendment 394, 398, 422, 462–463, 471–474, 476n6
Frankfurt, Harry 200–201, 209, 211
Franklin, Benjamin 423, 433
free coloreds 117

freedom 69, 244, 285–287, 310–311, 326–327, 332, 397, 415, 471–473, 525; *see also* liberty
Freire, Paulo 277, 508
Freyre, Gilberto 151
Friedman, Marilyn 199, 212
Frondizi, Risieri 516
Frye, Marilyn 78, 185–188, 190, 351, 359, 480
Fusco, Coco 177

Gabaccia, Donna 424
Gadamer, Hans-Georg 194–195
Gallegos, Lori 340, 479
García Canclini, Néstor 45, 368, 378n6
Garcia, Richard 408
Garífuna peoples 160–161
Gaspar de Alba, Alica 150
Gates, Henry Louis Jr. 474
gender-based violence 481
gendered nature of U.S. immigration policy: Anzaldúa and 485; detention centers and 481, 489n4; feminism and 479–480, 489n2; immigration justice and 480; incidents illustrating 478; Latinx philosophy and 485–487; meaning of analyzing 479–480; oppression of women and 483–487; overview 394–395, 478–479; pregnancy and 481; women and 480–483
gender system *see* decolonial feminist *movidas*; hetersexualism/gender system
genealogical materialist analysis 64
genealogical materialist analysis of race 64
Generalism vs. Particularism Dilemma 32, 42
Georas, C. S. 23–25
German immigrants 423, 439
German philosophy 384
Gilbert, Elizabeth 73
Gilroy, Paul 26–28, 386
Gingrich, Newt 181
Gitlin, Todd 16, 174–175
Glazer, Trip 357
globalization 395–396
global periphery flow 255
Goldberg, David Theo 28, 61–62
Goldwater, Barry 426
Gomez-Pena, Guillermo 174
Gomez-Quiñones, Juan 518
Gonzalez de Allen, Gertrude 12
González, Lélia 151
González, M. 139
Gooding-Williams, R. 26–28
Gordon, Lewis 26, 62, 64
Gore, Al 427
Gould, Carol 410
Gracia, Jorge J. E. 12, 19, 21, 25, 35, 453–454, 517, 526–529
Grant, Madison 423, 429–430, 433
Great Society programs 24

Greek philosophy 380
Greenberg, Julie 264–265
Grimmonds, Marguerite 445, 456
Grosfoguel, Ramón 23–25, 420, 430–431
group identity 176
Grupo Hiperión see Hyperion
Guadalupe Hidalgo Treaty (1848) 141, 399, 517–518
Guatemalans 403
Guidotti-Hernandez, N. 139
Gulf Wars 465–466
Gupta, Anil 75
Gutierrez, Jose 466
gynecratic egalitarianism 265, 267–269

Habermas, J. 398, 404
habitable categories: common-sense accounts 75–76; discourse on 74; overlapping of 84–85; overview 12–13, 72; performative accounts 75, 80–85; reconciling 85–86; role of 72–74; socio-historical accounts 75, 77–80, 83; subjectivization of 73, 75; what-makes question and 74; whether questions and 74; which questions and 74
Haney López, Ian 425
Haywood, Harry 176
Heidegger, Martin 384, 509, 514n24
Henry, Paget 60
hermeneutics 255–257
hermeneutic violence 312–315, 320n4, 321n5
Hernandez v. Texas (1954) 438, 518
Hernandez, X. 81–83, 85
heterogeneity 21
heteronomy, consensual 356–359
heterosexualism/gender system: *berdache* (third gender) and 269, 273; binary sex system and 264–265; colonial 269–274; coloniality and 261, 263–264, 269; coloniality of power and 255, 258, 260–264; concubinage and 270; dark side of 273, 275n18, 324–326; gender categories and 324–325; gynecratic egalitarianism and 265, 267–269; historical perspective 269–273; historizing 258; homosexuality and 269; intersectionality and 258–259, 262–265; light side of 273, 275n18, 324–326, 328; modern 273; nongendered egalitarianism 265–267; overview 255, 258–260; Quijano and 255, 258–267, 269–270, 273; sexual purity and 272; slave women and 271; sodomy and 269
Heyman, Josiah 451–452, 454
Hierro, Graciela 311, 314, 320n2
Higgins, Peter 447
Hispanic identity: Afro-Caribbean history and 52; background information 45–46; as "Border Land" between many "Worlds"

48; concept of 45–46; Far East ("Mother's" Side) history and 46–48; Far North of the South ("Brother/Sister" Side) history and 50–52; Far South of the North history and 52–54; Far West ("Father's" Side) history and 48–50; generic category of 21; historical perspective 5–6; overview 12, 46; usage of term 347, 348n1, 348n3, 400–401, 405n1
historical amnesia 381–382
Hoagland, Sarah 298
Hochschild, Arlie 358
Hokowhitu, Brendan 154–155
Holmes, Seth 453
hometactics (home concept): belonging concept and 295–301; concept of 300–307; deployment of 303–304; hooks's idea of 295; location concept and 295–301; nurturing spaces and 296–297, 308n3; overview 256, 295–296; practices 301–307; selfhood and, multiplicitous 295–300, 304; self-mapping and 295, 307n1; tactics and 256, 296, 301–303; will to belong and 297, 308n4
homogeneity 14–15, 21, 178, 189, 401
homosexuality 208–209, 269
honesty 287
Hooker, Juliet 161
hooks, bell 295, 375
Horswell, Michael 269
HOVENSA oil refinery 65, 71n4
Huizinga, Johan 194–195
humanism 470, 550
humanity, categories of 262
human subjectivity 286–287
Huntington, Samuel P. 463–468
Hurtado, Guillermo 531
hybridity, racial 45, 178, 368, 520
Hyperion 527–528, 531–532

Ibero-American race 102
identity politics 16–17, 68, 174–181; *see also* Latinx identity politics
identity scheme 204, 214n13
Illegal Immigration Reform and Immigration Responsibility Act (1996) 482
Immigrant Worker Freedom rides 416
immigration: anti-Latinx bias and 537; arguments against 180–181; Deferred Action for Childhood Arrivals program 456, 462; "Dreamers" 456; family separation policy and 462, 478–479, 483; German 423; ICE and 462; Irish 423–424; justice 443, 445, 455, 457, 479–480, 487; law of 1965 and 18; melting pot model/narrative and 411, 423–425; Mendoza's views 443–444; Mexican 407–408, 414; Operation Wetback and 462; overview 7, 393–394; quotas 18; U.S. policy 409, 462, 478–479, 483–485;

Welsh 453–454; women 394, 480–483; xenophobia and 538; *see also* gendered nature of U.S. immigration policy; *specific law/policy*; undocumented Latinx
Immigration and Custom Enforcement (ICE) 462
Immigration Reform and Control Act (1986) 482
impartiality 287–288, 293n17
imperialism *see* colonialism/colonization
Implicit Association Test (IAT) 536–537, 538
impoverished people 278–279, 284–291, 360
in-between race groups 425, 439–440
inclusion 53, 137, 164, 268, 287, 328, 376, 386, 398–399, 407, 413, 424, 433–434, 550, 552
incommensurability of cultural alterity 367–368, 372–373, 378n4
"Indian giver" 152
Indian identity 21
indigeneity: activism and 415; Chicano 139–142; community knowledge-based views of 153; critical Indigenous studies and 154–155; Critical Latinx 155–164; identity 4–5; Latinx philosophy and 94; legal framework around identity 5; mestizaje and 155–164; overview 93–94; Quebec settlers and 82; race-based views of 153; settler colonialism and 136–139, 143; *see also specific group*
"*indios*" 113–114, 118, 120, 139, 148–149, 155, 502
individualism 62, 206, 366, 464, 507
injustice *see specific type*
integration 112–114, 200, 221–223
interculturalism 45, 49, 313, 367, 394, 413–416, 522
interpreter's dilemma: background information 350; concept of 351–355; emotion work and 358; examples of 350, 353–354; heteronomy and, consensual 356–359; injustice and, affective 358–359; moral burden and 351, 356–361; moral injuries and 356; objection to, initial 355–356; occurrences of 350; oppression and 351, 360–361; overview 340, 351–352; power dynamics and 355; reasons for 350–351; research on 352–353, 355, 363n2; self-sacrifice and 354–355
intersectionality 32, 258–259, 262–263, 354–355
intersexuality 264–265
introversion and psychological syndrome of accidentality 239–240
Inuit Tapiriit Kanatami 164
Irish identity 25–26
Irish immigrants 423–424

Iroquois 268
Isasi-Díaz, Ada María 256

Jackson, Jesse 22–24
Jamaicans 24
Jameson, Frederic 385
Jaramillo, Luis 502–503
Jaspers, Karl 534
Jefferson, Thomas 473
Jenkins, K. 82
Jesuits 51
Jewish identity 25–26, 37, 39
Jim Crow segregation 426, 461, 474
Johnson, Andrew 472
Johnson, Lyndon 24
Johnson Reagon, Bernice 295–297
jus sanguinis see nationality
jus soli see birthright citizenship
justice: assumption of 175; government and 41; immigration 443–445, 455–457, 479–480, 487; *jus soli* and 463; racial 330, 427, 430, 433–436; redistributive 79; social 83, 175, 199, 313–315, 396, 409, 415–416, 543; *see also specific movement*
Justice for Janitors campaign 416

Kallen, H. 412–413
Kant, Immanuel 384
Kaplan, C. 295
Kaplan, Gregory 147
Khader, Serene 353
Khatibi, Abdelkebir 68
K'iche women 316–317
King, Martin Luther 69
Klor de Alva, Jorge 22–23
Know-Nothing Party 422–423, 433
Kristeva, J. 366
Kymlicka, W. 80

La Academia de la Nueva Raza 501–504, 508, 513n12
Labrador Métis 163–164
La Causa (farmworker struggle) 409, 414, 416
Lafferty, John 394, 483
La Hermandad Mexicana Nacional 408
language brokers 352, 363n3; *see also* interpreter's dilemma
language/communication: anglicisms (*pochismos*) 343–344; Anzaldúa and 339–348, 360, 383; assimilation 304–305, 340; attitudes about 340, 350–361; barriers to non-English speakers 350–351; Chicano Spanish 342–344; code-switching and 544; cross-cultural 371–372; cultural alterity and 340, 365–377; heathen and 24; Mexican literature and 345; native 314; *nosotras* and 342, 346–347; oppression and 339–348; overview 7; *Pachuco* 343; research on 352–353, 355, 363n7; silence and, tradition of 341–343; social identity and 360; Spanglish 343; Tex-Mex 343; as weapon 344–345; *see also* language and U.S. philosophy
language and U.S. philosophy: cosmopolitanism and, striving for 385–386; exclusionary practice and 380; historical amnesia and 381–382; "mendacious cultural autobiography" and 380, 387–388n1; overspecialization and 386–387; overview 340; silence of Spanish language tradition and, correcting 380–381; Spain as non-European concept and 382–385
Lareau, A. 228
la resolana 498–501, 507–510
Latina experience in U.S.: abnegation and 187–188; arrogant perception and 185–186; culture and 369; dominant differences and 189; ease in a "world" and 192–194; identification and 186–192; love and 186–192; nondominant differences and 189; overview 171–172, 185; phenomenology of 525–527; playfulness and 185–186, 194–196; separatism and 187–189, 197–198n1; servitude and 185, 187–188; sexism and 482, 486–487; "world"-traveling and 185, 190–194, 196–197
Latina identity 6, 322
Latin America 19–20, 178–180, 382–385
Latin American philosophy 323, 382–383
Latino Heritage Month 20
"Latino Threat" narrative 394, 414, 463–468, 528
Latins 96, 100
Latinx artists 177
Latinx feminism 486
Latinx identity: Anglo American view of 173; categories of 4, 401–403; characteristics of, statistical 403; *Common Bundle* view of 437–438; debates over 14; dilemmas of 31–33; Essentialism vs. Eliminativism Dilemma and 32–33, 42; ethnorace concept and 28; Familial-Historical View of 12, 36–40, 42; Generalism vs. Particularism Dilemma and 32, 42; as historical marker 40; historical perspective 5–6; homosexuality and 208–209; issues 11, 31; language and, fraught relationship with 339; marketing and 17, 19; as "Other" 171; overview 6–7; pan 17, 19, 174; participation in U.S. dialogue and 174, 182; preferences in 6, 12; as racial versus ethnic category 11, 14–16, 25; resistance and 527–528; skin color and 22–23; terminology 4–5; in U.S. 12, 17, 19–20, 27; usage of term 400–401, 405n1;

as U.S. Census category 6, 22–23; visibility of 173–174; whiteness and 433–439
Latinx identity politics: lessons from Latin America 178–180; Nuestra America concept and 180–183; overview 171; particularism versus universalism and 174–180; U.S. discourses 180
Latinx philosophy: adaptation of 257; Afro-Latin identity and 67–70; anti-Latinx bias in 494, 536–545; Anzaldúa's work and 94; characterizations 1–2; contingency and 533; contributions of 493; *Cosmic Race, The* and 3, 93, 95–107; gendered nature of U.S. immigration policy and 485–487; genesis point for contemporary 3; historical perspective 3; indigeneity and 94; issues in 3; language/communication and 340, 380–387; mestizaje and 93; questions surrounding 532; studying, reasons for 2; terminology 1
la vida buena y sana concept 507, 511
learning society 507–510, 514n20
Lee, Erika 423
Leon de Portilla, Miguel 519
Lerner, Gabriel 466
Levinson, Meira 221, 226, 228
liberal egalitarianism 218–219
liberalism 176, 218–220, 227, 311
liberation 80, 121–122, 125, 178, 256, 259, 277–278, 280, 283–284, 286–287, 311, 314, 323, 330, 366, 521
liberty 97, 101, 103, 310–311, 423, 461, 471; *see also* freedom
location and hometactics 295–301
lo cotidiano (the quotidian) 256, 278–284, 289
Lopez, A. 427
Lorde, Audra 189
Los Alamos 497, 499, 513n3
Lowery, Malinda Maynor 161–162
Lugones, María 79–80, 171–172, 202–204, 208–210, 224, 255, 298–300, 302–303, 324–326, 485–487
Lumbee Tribe 161–162
Luna, Jennie 158–159

MacPherson, C. B. 397
Madva, Alex 494
Maldonado-Torres, Nelson 494
Malintzin/Marina/Malinche 150–151
marginalization, social 46, 75, 77, 80, 84, 94, 177, 209, 238, 278, 280, 288, 297, 306, 314–316, 322, 351, 360–361, 393, 404, 443, 447, 526, 529, 531, 533–534, 539
Mariátegui, José Carlos 178
Marshall, T. H. 396–397
Martí, José 17, 35, 381, 385
Martinez, Elizabeth "Betita" 520
Martinez, Jacqueline M. 521

Martínez, María Elena 147–149
Marxism 63–64
Mato, Daniel 19
matriarchy 265, 268, 330
Mayas 150, 269
McClintock, Anne 272
McIntosh, Peggy 434
melting pot model/narrative 411, 423–425
Méndez, Xhercis 256–257
Mendieta, Ana 295
Mendieta, Eduardo 393–394
Mendoza, José Jorge 394, 443–444, 453–454, 479
merit 195, 287–288
Meso-American communities 314
mestizaje ("mixedness"): ambiguity of 125–126; Anishinabe peoples and 116–120; anti-Latinx bias in philosophy and 542–545; Anzaldúa's view 94, 124–134, 155–156, 158, 171, 202–205, 208, 214n9, 256, 368; autonomy 199–200, 202–210, 212, 215n22; caste and 109, 113–118; categories of 109–112; characteristics of 109–110; colonialism and 114–118, 121–122; concept 109, 114; consciousness 199–200, 202–210, 256, 300, 486; as cop out 120–121; *Cosmic Race, The* and 93, 95–107; current discourses 155–164; definition 93, 109; endorsements and 204–210; ethnicity and 112–114; indigeneity and 155–164; inferiority of, belief in 105–106; integration and 112–114; issue of 146; Latinx philosophy and 93; liberation from colonization and 121–122; Mexican identity and 78–79; Miranda's perspective 156–158, 163; myths of origin of 149–155; nationalism 162; "new consciousness" and 94, 124–134, 158, 171; as outcast 112–114; overview 7, 93–94, 146; pre-conquest and colonial discourses 147–149; skin color and 117; terms for 109; value of 146
mestizo see mestizaje ("mixedness") 7, 93
metaphilosophy 7, 493–494
Métis 109, 115–116, 152–153, 155; *see also* mestizaje ("mixedness")
Métis National Council (MNC) 163
Mexican American philosophy in U.S.: background information 515; canon 515, 519; Chavez (Cesar) and 519–520; contributions of 520–522; Du Bois and 515, 520–521; features of 518–520; overview 493, 515; possibility of 515–518
Mexican Americans 19, 347, 462, 517–518
Mexican border music 346
Mexican historiography 152
Mexican identity 25, 38, 78–79, 81–82, 111–112, 121, 141–142, 241–244, 346–347, 401–402

566 Index

Mexican immigration 407–408, 414
Mexican literature 345–346
Mexican movies 346–346
Mexican philosophy and Latinx life: Hyperion Group and 527, 531–532; Latinx consciousness and, toward liberatory 530–532; Latinx as "Other" and 526–530; model of 532–534; overview 494; phenomenology of Latinx experience 525–527; questions asked of 532–534; self-empowerment and 533–534; value of 526, 532–534
Mexico 98, 429, 465
Meyers, Diana 210
Mignolo, Walter 68
Migrant Protection Protocols 484
migrant women 394
Miles, T. 138
Millán Brusslan, Elizabeth 439, 439
Miller, David 361
Mills, Charles 64, 80, 522
Minh-ha, Trinh 373
Miranda, Deborah A. 156–158, 163
misalignments 235, 238
Mize, Ronald 416
modernity 49–50, 53, 55n1, 61, 66, 162, 260, 262, 265, 267, 270, 273, 369, 373, 376, 378n6, 382, 388n2, 553
Mohanty, Chandra 295–296
Mohanty, S. 177
Mohawks 154
Mollar, Michel 470
Moody-Adams, Michelle 27
Moors 269
Moraga, Cherie 521
moral subjectivity 285–287
Morrill, A. 151
Morton, Jennifer M. 172
mother-centered people 265, 269, 330
mother identity 79–80
movidas see decolonial feminist *movidas*
Moya, P. M. L. 299
Moynihan Report (1965) 330
mujerista thought/theology: concept of 277; decolonial thought and 277–278; fairness and 287–288, 293n17; goals of 277; honesty and 287; impartiality and 287–288, 293n17; Latina's thinking and 277–278; liberation and 277–278; *lo cotidiano* and 278–284, 289; merit and 288; oppression and 278–279; option for oppressed and 284–288; overview 256, 278; partiality and 287–288; self-determination and 285–287; theological considerations and 289–291
multiculturalism 25, 69, 137–138, 160, 175–176, 181, 218, 229, 394, 416, 520, 543, 550, 552

multiplicitous selfhood 295–300, 304
multitemporal heterogeneity 368
Mumford, Lewis 500, 505
music, Mexican border 346

NAFTA 402, 465
Nahuas 269
nationalism 96, 138, 152, 156, 158, 162, 179, 404, 423–424, 440, 468
nationalist state 410
nationality 41–42
Native American identity 5, 79, 117, 141–142; see also specific tribe
Native American Tribes 265, 267–270; see also specific tribe
Native Amerindians 314
Nativism 180, 182, 402, 422, 434, 464, 467–468, 537
Naturalization Act 422
Navarette, Ruben Jr. 407–408
neo-apartheid approach 420–421, 431
neoliberalism 311–312
neonativism 408
Neurath, Otto 317
"new consciousness" 68, 94, 124–134
New Deal coalition 426–427
"New" Democrats 427
New Mexico 115; see also Chicano Movement in northern New Mexico
Ng'Weno, Bettina 162
Nicaraguans 403
Nietzsche, Friedrich 297, 317
nihilism 243–244, 246
Nixon, Richard 401, 408, 426–427
non-cognitive skills 216–221, 232n3
nongendered egalitarianism 265–267
nonidentity problem 79
normative culture/norms 236–237
nosotras 342, 346–347
Nuccetelli, Susana 519
Nuestra America concept 180–183
Nuevomejicano communities 298, 300
NunatuKavut 163–164
Nuñez-Mchiri, Guillermina 451–452
Nuremberg Trial of Nazi criminals 461
nurturing spaces 296–297, 308n3

Obama, Barack 216, 427, 429, 456
Oboler, Suzanne 18
Office of Refugee Resettlement (ORR) 482
Ogbu, John 221
Omi, Michael 17, 63
one-drop rule approach to racial classification 429
Operation Wetback 462
oppression: causes of 278; colluding with 189, 196; double bind and 480; gender 483–487;

interlocking 198n1; intermeshing 198n1; interpreter's dilemma and 351, 360–361; language/communication and 339–348; *mujerista* thought/theology and 278–279; options for 284–288; race and 64–67; resistance and 80, 189; social groups and 448–449, 454, 458n5; socio-historical accounts and 80; undocumented Latinx and 448–449, 454, 458n5; "world"-traveling and 185, 189
oppressive power relations: alphabets of survival and 315–319; hermeneutic violence and 312–315, 320n4, 321n5; options 284–288; overview 256, 311–312; third critical space and 315, 318–319
Optata people 113
Oquendo, Angel R. 15, 21
Orosco, José-Antonio 393–394, 423–424, 493
Ortega, Mariana 256
Ortega y Gasset 511
overspecialization 386–387
Oyewùmí, Oyéronké 265–266, 270–271, 273, 329

Pachuco 343
pan-Latinx identity 17, 19, 174
Pappas, Gregory 439
Parks, Rosa 284
Parsons, K. P. 77–78
partiality 287–288
particularism 174–180
Pascua Yaqui tribe 5
"passing" 12, 25, 437
patriarchy 258–260, 265, 267–268, 329–330, 435
Paz, Octavio 45, 50, 150, 166n2
Peller, Gary 175
Pena Delgado, G. 416
Penitente society 508, 514n21
Pereda, Carlos 516
performative accounts 75, 80–85
Perry, Helen 484
personal freedom 285–287
personal identity 214n12
Petrini, Carlo 510
phenomenology 255–257, 509, 514n24, 525–527
Phillips, Kevin 426
Phillips, Steve 428, 431
philosophy: canon 340, 380–381, 385–387, 552; colonial context of 551; cosmopolitanism/internationalism for 385–386; decolonizing 494, 549–554; formal training in 3; ghettoization of 382–384; historical perspective 380; liberation 521; self-criticism and 384; transformation in 494, 549–554; *see also specific type*
pícaros 498, 513n6

Pico della Mirandola 470
Pirenne, Henri 470
Pita, B. 138–139
Pitts, Andrea J. 94, 316
Pizarro, Francisco 48
Plato 468–469
Playfulness 185–186, 194–196
Plessy vs. Ferguson (1896) 69, 474
pluralism 25, 89n4, 298, 300, 385, 411, 415–416
"Pocahontas perplex" 151
polis 176, 468
political rights 397–398
politics of location 296, 307–308n2
Polt, John 93
Portes, A. 403
Portilla, Jorge 516, 525, 527, 530
postcolonial feminism 366–367, 374–375, 377–378n2, 379n11
postmodernism 174, 177
poverty 278–279, 284–291, 360
Powell, Lorein 68
power dynamics, mapping 324, 326–327, 329; *see also* oppressive power relations
praxis learning 508
preferential option 285, 290
Principal of Cultural Group Flourishing 412, 417
Principle of Cultural Contribution 413–414
progressive politics 425–426
Puerto Rican philosophy 518, 551
Puerto Ricans 15, 19, 22, 25, 65–66, 401–402, 518
Pulido, Laura 94

Quechua people 20–21, 42, 120
Quijano, Aníbal 255, 258–267, 269–270, 273

race 59, 63–67, 70, 424; *see also specific type*
race projects, national 429
racial identity/category 11, 14–16, 20, 23–28, 59, 64, 360; *see also* disintegration of Latinx racial category
racialization 15, 21–22, 24, 26–27, 61–67, 148, 177, 262, 270, 332, 395, 399, 468
racial justice 330, 427, 430, 433–436
racism 19, 138, 185, 187, 201, 310, 399, 482
Ramos, Samuel 179, 516
Rawls, J. 218–219
Reagan, Ronald 427
Reconstruction Amendments 471
Reconstruction period 474
Redemption period 474
redistributive justice 79
Red River Métis 116, 163
Reed-Sandoval, Amy 394, 462, 479, 482–483
relational autonomy 199–202

relational egalitarianism 448
relational powers, mapping 324, 326–327, 329
Remain in Mexico Policy 484–485
Renaissance period 470
Rendon, Armando 520
Rey, Alberto 34
Rhodes Must Fall Movement 550
Richard, Nelly 315, 317, 375
Ricoeur, Paul 551
Riel, Louis 163
Riesenberg, Peter 468–469
rights of man 175
Rodó, José Enrique 386–387
Rodriguez, Richard 181
Roediger, David 425, 433
Roman Empire/society 103, 105
Romero, Mary 453
Roosevelt, Franklin 426–427
Rosaldo, Renato 400
Ross, John 117
Rousseff, Dilma 314
Ruíz, Elena Flores 256
Rumbaut, R. G. 403
Russians 111

Saenz, José María "Chema" 501
Said, Edward 543
Salazar Bondy, Augusto 516–517
Saldaña-Portillo, María Josefina 151–152, 159–161, 166n4
Salinas, Maria 482
Sánchez, Carlos Alberto 479, 494, 520
Sanchez, Miguel 456–457
Sánchez, R. 138–139
Santana, Alejandro 518–519
Saranillo, D. 138
Sarmiento, Domingo F. 69
Sarr, Felwine 73
Sartre, Jean-Paul 33
Saxons 96–97, 100
Schapiro, Tamar 243
Schlesinger, Arthur 16
Schmitt, Carl 50
Schutte, Ofelia 18, 340, 528
Scofield, Gregory 153
Scotland 111, 115
Second Gulf War 464
segregation 69, 162, 206, 222, 228, 360, 426, 461, 474; *see also* separatism/separation
Segura, Maestro Andrés 503–504
Seidel, Michael 295
self-criticism 384
self-determination 176, 286
self-empowerment 533–534
selfhood, multiplicitous 295–300, 304
self-identification 41
self-mapping 295, 307n1

Semple, Jesse B. 180
separatism/separation 129–130, 187–189, 197–198n1, 200, 259, 262; *see also* segregation
Sequoyah 118
servitude 185, 187–188
settler colonialism: Asian American studies and 138; Aztlán concept and 142; black studies and 138; Chicano studies and 136, 138–143; concept of 136; decolonization and 142; geography and 136; indigeneity and 136–139, 143; Metis and 152–153; nonwhite others and 136–139; overview 94, 136–137; as structure 151, 166n3
sexism 201, 310, 482, 486–487
sexualization 395
Sharma, N. 138
Shaw, Randy 408
Shelby County v. Holder 431
Sherman, Nancy 356
Shklar, Judith 399
Sigal, Pete 269
silence, tradition of 341–343
Silva, Grant 439, 479
Simpson, Audra 153–154
slavery 271, 399, 472–474
Smith, Ray Gwyn 341
Snow, Naomi 550
social constructive theories 77
social dislocation 94
social fragmentation 189
social groups/grouphead 444, 446–449, 454, 458n5
social identity: attachments to 16; attitude about 16–17; categories 12–13; context of 17–21; diversity of 202–206, 214–215n16; enduring of 35–36; entails of 36; ethnicity and 41–42; ethnicity paradigm and 21–23; function of 33–34; internalization of 346; language/communication and 360; nationality and 41–42; normative culture and 236–237; number and kind of 31–33; overview 6–7, 11–13; personal identities versus 214n12; problems raised by 31; questions about, four basic 33–36; questions surrounding 11; racial realities and 24–28; relationship between various 31–32, 41–42; rising of 34–35; *see also specific type*
social institutions 447–448, 497
sociality 62, 71n2, 286–287
social justice 83, 175, 199, 313–315, 396, 409, 415–416, 543
social movements and citizenship 398–400; *see also specific type*
social rights 397–398
Society for Mexican American Philosophy (SMAP) 522

socio-economic gap 217–218
socio-historical accounts 75, 77–80, 83
Socrates 498
sodomy 269
soft skills *see* non-cognitive skills
solidarity 16–17, 24, 34, 45, 48, 142, 157, 164, 259–260, 277, 286, 376, 386, 412, 414, 438–439, 497, 507, 516, 538, 553–554
Sophists 498
Sosa, Lionel 466
South Africa 430–431
South American Latinos 402–403
Southern Strategy 426
Spain 110–111, 114–118, 382–385
Spanglish 343, 466
Spaniards in New World 97–101
Spanish philosophy 382
specialization 386, 515, 519–521, 552
Spivak, Gayatri 375
split-separation 197–198n1
splitting *see* separatism/separation
Srinivasan, Amia 358
Stoler, Ann Laura 182–183
Stoljar, N. 77–78
storytelling 499, 508
subjectivity, moral 285–287
subjectivization 73, 75
substance and accidentality 237–238
subversive substitution 244–246
suffrage 398, 431, 472
Sullivan, Irene 481
Sumner, Charles 473
systemic violence 484

tactics 256, 296, 301–303
Talavera, Victor 451–452
Tanner Lectures 399
technology and *el oro del barrio* 506–507
Teilhard de Chardin, Pierre 503
Tex-Mex language 343
Tex-Mex music 346
Theobald, Robert 500, 505
third critical space 315, 318–319
third gender (*berdache*) 269, 273
Third World College 550–551
Third World Liberation Front 550–551
Thurmond, Strom 426
Tietjens Meyers, D. 177, 201
Toffler, Alvin 504
Tohono O'odham Nation 5
Toro, Luis Angel 23
Townsend, Camilla 148
translation 363n1; *see also* interpreter's dilemma
transplanted substantiality 244, 246–247
treason 460–461
Treaty of Guadalupe Hidalgo (1848) 141, 399, 517–518

Trump, Donald 427–428, 431–432, 442n7, 462–464, 467–468, 481, 537
Truth, Sojourner 331
Tuck, E. 138, 151

undocumented labor 410
undocumented Latinx: Anzaldúa's and 452; cases, hypothetical 445–446, 449–451; Chavez (Cesar) and 407–409; El Paso (Texas) raids 451; E-verify system and 453; immigration justice and 443, 445, 455, 457; legally 443–446, 457; Mendoza's view 394, 443–444, 453–454; numbers of 465; objections to new vision for immigrant rights and 455–457; oppression and 448–449, 454, 458n5; overview 394, 444–445; socially 444–446, 448–454, 457, 462; status of 445–446; working conditions and 453
ungroundedness 238
United Farm workers Union 409
United States vs. Brignoni-Ponce (1975) 453
Unite the Right Rally (2017) 467
Universal Declaration of Human Rights 463
universalism 174–180, 182, 516
unwillingness and psychological syndrome of accidentality 239–240
Uranga, Emilio 241–244, 248–249, 527, 533
Ureña, Henríquez 381
U.S.: Afro-Latin identity and 61–67; betrayal of citizens and 460–462; Black Codes in 472; black identity in 22, 61–67; blue-collar industrial worker in 506; Civil Rights Movement in 3, 67, 175, 182, 284, 288, 398, 414, 426; demographic trends and political landscape in 420–421, 423; discrimination in 181; identity discourses in 180; immigration policy 409, 462, 478–479, 483–485; imperial politics of 403–404; Jim Crow segregation in 426; Latinx identity in 12; Latinx population in 420; Mexico and 465; middle class in 506; multiculturalism in 175, 181; progressive politics in 425–426; race relations in 59, 70; racialization in 15, 61–67; Southern Strategy in 426; treason against 460–461; welfare state in, birth of 495; white identity/whiteness in 421–425, 432–433; *see also* gendered nature of U.S. immigration policy; language and U.S. philosophy; Latina experience in U.S.; *specific agencies/laws*; U.S. citizenship
U.S. Census Bureau 5–6, 22–23, 350, 396
U.S. citizenship: challenges to 395–396; challenge to 404; Chavez (Cesar) and 407; constitutional patriotism and 404, 405n2; development of citizenship and 396–397; documentation for 407; for Latinos 173, 400–404; "Latino Threat" narrative

and 394; overview 393; racism and 399; Trumpism and 462–463
Üstübdağ, Nazan 79
U.S. Virgin Islands 64–67, 71n7

value creation 243
van der Straet, Jan 272
Van Dresser, Peter 510
Vargas, Manuel 172, 521–522
Vasconcelos, José 3, 45, 93, 124, 146, 151, 156, 178–179, 429
Velásquez, Ernesto Rosen 437
Vigil, Diego 502
Villalobos Moreno, Tito 501
violence 312–315, 320n4, 321n5, 481, 484
Vizenor, Gerald 155
voting rights 398, 431, 472
Voting Rights Act (1965) 431

Wallace, George 426
Wallerstein, Immanuel 63
Walzer, Michael 410, 466, 474
Welsh immigrants 453–454
West, Cornel 64
Western civilization 195
Western values 181
white identity/whiteness: attitude about 16; distorted identity model 422, 435–436; double-play of 438–439; elasticity and 436–438; eliminativism and 434–436; Latinx identity and 433–439; nativism 464, 467–468; "passing" as 12, 25, 437; politics and 62; as racial identity 421; in U.S. 421–425, 432–433; whiteness-as-domination model 422, 435–436
white nativism 464, 467–468

whiteness-as-domination model 422, 435–436
white privilege 434
white supremacy 434–436
wholeheartedness 200–201, 203, 205, 209–211, 214n4
will to belong 297, 308n4
Williams, Patricia 26
Winant, Howard 17, 63
Wittgenstein, Ludwig 519, 529
Wolf, Allison B. 394
Womack, Craig 153
Woman Suffrage Movement 398
women: of color 185, 189, 259, 310–311, 322–323, 335n5; immigration and 394, 480–483; K'iche 316–317; mother-centered people and 269; mother identity and 79–80; as "Other" 372–374; slave 271; voting rights and 398; *see also* decolonial feminist *movidas*; feminism
Women's Refugee Commission (WRC) 484
"world"-traveling 185, 190–194, 196–197, 202, 256
Wright, C. 138

xenophobia 156, 402, 422–425, 433, 437, 538

Yancy, George 434
Yang, W. 138
Yoruba deities 368
Yoruba people 265–266, 271
Young, Iris Marion 78, 446, 480, 484

Zack, Naomi 23
Zapata Olivella, Manuel 60–61, 69
Zea, Leopoldo 516, 527, 533
zozobra 244, 494, 525

Made in the USA
Middletown, DE
24 August 2025